ORGANIC PSYCHIATRY

ORGANIC PSYCHIATRY
The Psychological Consequences of
Cerebral Disorder

William Alwyn Lishman
MD, DSc, FRCP, FRCPsych, DPM

Professor of Neuropsychiatry,
Institute of Psychiatry, London;
Consultant Psychiatrist,
The Bethlem Royal and
Maudsley Hospitals, London

SECOND EDITION

OXFORD

BLACKWELL SCIENTIFIC PUBLICATIONS

LONDON EDINBURGH BOSTON

MELBOURNE PARIS BERLIN VIENNA

Second edition © 1987 by
William Alwyn Lishman
First edition © 1978 by
Blackwell Scientific Publications
Editorial offices:
Osney Mead, Oxford OX2 0EL
25 John Street, London WC1N 2BL
23 Ainslie Place, Edinburgh EH3 6AJ
3 Cambridge Center, Suite 208, Cambridge
    Massachusetts 02142, USA
54 University Street, Carlton
    Victoria 3053, Australia

First published 1978
Reprinted 1980
Second edition 1987
Reprinted 1987, 1988, 1989, 1990

Photoset by Dublin University Press and
Enset (Photosetting)
Midsomer Norton, Bath, Avon
Printed and bound
in Great Britain by
Butler & Tanner Ltd
Frome and London

DISTRIBUTORS

Marston Book Services Ltd
PO Box 87
Oxford OX2 0DT
(*Orders:* Tel. (0865) 791155
          Fax. (0865) 791927
          Telex. 837515)

USA
Year Book Medical Publishers
200 North LaSalle Street
Chicago, Illinois 60601
(*Orders:* Tel. (312) 726–9733)

Canada
The C. V. Mosby Company
5240 Finch Avenue East
Scarborough, Ontario
(*Orders:* Tel. (416) 298–1588)

Australia
Blackwell Scientific Publications
(Australia) Pty Ltd
54 University Street
Carlton, Victoria 3053
(*Orders:* Tel. (03) 347–0300)

British Library
Cataloguing in Publication Data

Lishman, William Alwyn
    Organic psychiatry: the psychological
    consequences of cerebral disorder.—2nd ed.
    1. Mental illness—Physiological aspects
    I. Title
    616.89′07   RC455.4.B5

    ISBN 0–632–01235–8
    ISBN 0–632–01496–2 Pbk

Contents

Foreword to the First Edition

Since medicine began there has been the belief that there are two main categories of mental disorder, those due to natural or medical causes and those due to supernatural or 'moral' causes. Throughout history either the one or the other gained the greater recognition and attention. Medicine had little responsibility for the mentally ill throughout many centuries, and apart from the belief among medieval physicians in the Greek notions of the humoral pathology of mental disorder, the prepotence of moral or supernatural causes was accepted by most educated persons. The great advances in physical and biological science during the last century led to the recognition of man's place in nature as a biological entity. The development of medicine and particularly pathology led in Europe to the intensive study of the mentally ill from the point of view of the natural sciences. This phase in the development of organic psychiatry was limited by the concept of different forms of degeneration in the brain which was associated with the emergence of neuropathology, and by the absence of any knowledge or techniques for other types of enquiry. By the turn of the century it was overtaken by the immense influence of psychoanalysis which directed attention once again, particularly in Europe and in USA, to the 'moral' and psychological causes of mental disorder. Mental disorder was seen not so much as a disturbance of man's place in nature, but as a disorder of man as an individual. Psychopathology became for many a disorder of intrapsychic or interpersonal relationships.

It is only in the present century that psychiatry has begun to break free from the constraints of philosophy. The essential nature of the relationships between mental events and physical events in the nervous system remains as much as ever an unresolved mystery, but the amount of knowledge relevant to our understanding has increased vastly in the last few decades. This applies not only to the cerebral mechanisms upon which such fundamental functions as consciousness, memory, emotion, attention and learning are dependent but also to the ways in which pathological processes can alter them. The application of techniques of investigation based upon discoveries in the neurosciences and psychology has made this possible. This too has been paralleled by greater precision in the recognition and description of the clinical phenomena of organic cerebral disease. The tools of clinical diagnosis and investigation have been refined and extended.

Many emphasise that the approach to every patient should remain a holistic one. Above all his essential individuality as a person in all respects is our concern. It is necessary to investigate the patient's psychic reality and experience and the bearing this has on his disorder. It is also necessary to investigate the psychosocial environment and culture within which the patient lives and works. But it is equally necessary to examine the patient as a biological organism and in this the psychiatrist needs the knowledge and skills of modern medicine. If this is not understood and accepted there is no reason why psychiatrists should be medically trained. It is very difficult, and indeed impossible, to think about all three avenues to understanding and explanation at the same time, but they are not mutually exclusive, and they are equally important. The psychiatrist's capacity to know, after the initial interview, to which area he should in the main direct his attention is dependent upon his clinical experience and training, his skill in examination, but above all upon his detailed knowledge of the clinical phenomena which mental disorder presents, and their significance.

The author of this book sets out to examine and to describe in detail the psychological phenomena associated with the various organic disorders of the nervous system, and the psychological consequences of those numerous extracerebral diseases, toxic, metabolic and endocrine, which affect the brain indirectly. He describes how the clinician can go about identifying them; his extended treatment of this neglected field of clinical enquiry is more complete than any hitherto available. He has provided a textbook in which the clinical manifestations of various pathological processes affecting the brain are examined in the light of knowledge derived from the applications of the neurosciences and psychology, and has critically evaluated the evidence. The task has been a major one, for knowledge in the various fields has greatly increased in the last few decades, as the selected references, more than 2,000 in number, show. The book is therefore a comprehensive text from the point of view of the clinician of the state of knowledge or organic psychiatry at the present time.

In the first part of the book, four chapters are concerned with the principles underlying our understanding of the relation between specific psychological deficits and brain function, methods of clinical assessment and differential diagnosis. In the second part of the book a series of chapters describe the clinical, psychiatric and psychological consequences of the different pathological processes. A final chapter summarises what is known from this point of view of numerous neurological disorders of diverse pathogenesis.

The appearance of this work at the present time comes to fill a much required need. There is no comparable book in the English-speaking world. The importance of organic psychiatry, if it was ever in doubt, has been emphasised by the movement of psychiatry into the general medical scene, and by the large numbers of physically ill patients presenting with disorder of behaviour for whom the psychiatrist's help is now sought. The work will no doubt become standard reading not only for postgraduate students of psychiatry and neurology, but also for neuropsychologists and for specialists engaged in continuing education and across a wide spectrum of medical specialties. Above all it provides a reference source book which will prove invaluable for clinicians and medical scientists alike whose enquiries direct them to some aspect of this large clinical field.

Institute of Psychiatry   DENIS HILL
University of London

Preface to the First Edition

The impetus for writing a book on organic psychiatry has come largely from clinical practice and teaching. Both reveal the lack of focused knowledge concerning the overlapping territories between psychiatry and neurology—a gap manifested in the paucity of textbook literature on the subject. Clearly, as with any borderland zone, there has been a risk of relative neglect as each separate discipline has proceeded on its specialised way, leaving, perhaps inevitably, an uneasy interface between.

Neurology deals directly with the apparatus of mind by investigating malfunction of the brain. Yet paradoxically it has often paid scant attention to mental disorder itself. Psychiatry on its part deals essentially with mental disorder, yet has had little in relative terms to do with the hardware upon which mind depends. The rich complexity of human behaviour, and the multitude of factors which can shape and distort it, have clearly demanded a multifaceted growth of clinical psychiatry; the subject had profited from psychodynamic, psychosocial and pharmacological approaches to mental disorder, but with the expert neurologist waiting in the wings the factor of brain malfunction has sometimes tended to be eclipsed. Sir Denis Hill, in his Foreword to the book, has touched on the dilemma and set it in much wider historical perspective.

It has therefore seemed worthwhile to attempt a comprehensive review of the cognitive, behavioural and emotional consequences of cerebral disorder, and the problems in this area which are encountered in clinical practice. The task proved greater than at first envisaged. In the first place neurology and psychiatry with their attendant disciplines have both proceeded apace, sometimes drawing closer together and sometimes further apart in their different approaches to disease. The literature on their common ground has correspondingly flourished, but in a scattered manner. Secondly it soon became obvious that a text devoted to psychiatric disorders associated with structural brain disease would be unduly restrictive, and that certain metabolic, toxic and other systemic disorders must also be considered if brain malfunction was to be the central theme.

Others could have argued for the inclusion of a good deal more than is here presented. Very little will be found on mental subnormality or child psychiatry since such fields are beyond the author's competence. And the temptation to speculate in detail on possible 'cerebral' contributions to the major functional psychoses has been resisted. Boundaries have in general been drawn short of hypothetical situations, and the work is mainly confined to disorders of cerebral function which are indubitable and well-established.

Within the selected field coverage of different topics will no doubt be found inequitable. An avowed preoccupation with focal cerebral disorder, and the light which disease has thrown on regional brain function, will be apparent to the reader. But other considerations have also been at work. Some very rare disease processes are given considerable attention when their psychiatric components can on occasion be important or when important lessons have been learned from them. Similarly the selection of case reports will sometimes illustrate rare conditions or phenomena, if case presentation seems much better than lengthy description for communicating the essence of the matter. In the sections on treatment, physical approaches will often be described in more detail than psychotherapeutic or social interventions, without any necessary assumption that these have less important parts to play in overall management of the patient. Thus in many respects the emphases in the book must be construed, not as reflecting the absolute importance of a topic, but rather the particular slant indicated in a work devoted to organic aspects of psychiatry. Finally if scant attention seems to have been paid to purely psychological reactions to physical disorder this in no sense implies that such aspects are less intriguing or practically important. Matters of space and time, and the patience of the reader, have dictated that lines must be drawn, however arbitrarily and painfully.

Acknowledgements for the help of others are traditionally given, but the list would be long indeed if I were to pay tribute to all the teachers, colleagues and students who have fostered my interest and guided my thinking on the subjects dealt with herein. I will list instead those who have been directly concerned with the book and have often spent generous hours in detailed discussion and the reading of drafts. The late Sir Aubrey Lewis took a keen and encouraging interest in the earlier stages of the work. Sir Denis Hill has given both detailed criticism and constant helpful support. I am greatly indebted to him for generously providing a Foreword to the book. Special thanks must go to Dr Richard Pratt for reading large parts of the manuscript and allowing me to draw on his exceptional knowledge of the literature. Those who have criticised individual sections and chapters include Professor Frank Benson, Professor Robert Cawley, Dr Elaine Drewe, Dr Griffith Edwards, Professor George Fenton, Dr John Gunn, Dr Derek Hockaday, Dr Raymond Levy, Professor David Marsden, Dr David Parkes, Dr Felix Post and Dr Sabina Strich. Others who have helped in innumerable ways include Dr Christopher Colbourn, Mrs Isobel Colbourn, Dr John Cutting, Dr May Monro, Dr Maria Ron and Dr Brian Toone. Miss Helen Marshall put at my disposal her unrivalled expertise in guiding me to the rich store of information in the Institute of Psychiatry library. To all of these kind friends and colleagues I am very deeply grateful.

Finally I must record my gratitude to the two people who have been most intimately concerned of all. Mrs Dorothy Wiltshire has not only collaborated on an arduous task, but has positively welcomed the burden and done much to sustain my enthusiasm. Her expert secretarial skills and untiring patience have, in effect, made the venture possible. My wife, Marjorie, deserves the warmest thanks of all—meticulous help with the manuscripts and with problems of the English language have been but a tiny part; over several years she has paved the way, deflected obstacles and taken over numerous burdens in an ever-helpful manner which is most affectionately acknowledged.

June 1977   ALWYN LISHMAN

Preface to the Second Edition

This new edition has entailed a considerable amount of rewriting, particularly in the clinical sections, and the addition of material which had been overlooked before. Meanwhile, pruning has been attempted to ensure that the book remains reasonable in size.

The preparation for the updating has been a rewarding exercise, involving new reading in the psychiatric, neurological, neuropsychological and medical literature. The necessary library research was facilitated by the award of a six month Visiting Fellowship at Green College, Oxford, and I am much indebted to Sir Richard Doll and the Fellows of the College for their generous hospitality. It was a special delight to work once more in the Radcliffe Science Library division of the Bodleian Library, where my first clinical papers were written some twenty-five years ago.

The most remarkable advances since the first edition have come from developments in brain imaging. Such is the present pace of progress in the imaging field that no doubt the information contained herein will soon appear as rudimentary as that of the previous edition. Progress with dementia, particularly in the neurochemical aspects, is also a welcome sign, betokening a new courage to tackle the fundamentals of a long-neglected problem. New information concerning the brain damage associated with alcoholism has been a personal interest in recent years, accounting for the emphasis placed on the topic in several places. The movement disorders, with their special fascination and lessons for both psychiatrists and neurologists have now earned a chapter of their own. Altogether, to my surprise, almost as many new references were consulted for this new edition as appeared in the first, and over a thousand of them have been incorporated.

I have sometimes been questioned about the title 'Organic Psychiatry' and this perhaps deserves a word of explanation. Some might have preferred 'Biological Psychiatry' or 'Neuropsychiatry' to define the area of specialised interest. Biological Psychiatry would, I think, be inappropriate. It represents, not a circumscribed clinical field, but rather a particular approach to the understanding of mental illness generally; it is concerned with mechanisms and pathophysiologies of a biological nature which can be sought out and studied in relation to virtually all forms of psychiatric disorder—organic conditions certainly, but also the major psychoses, the personality disorders and the neuroses. Biological psychiatry has many achievements but this book does not seek to encompass them.

The appeal of Neuropsychiatry as a title is more difficult to dispel. Neuropsychiatry defines a territory within the corpus of mental disorder, *viz* that which can be demonstrated to owe its origins to brain malfunction of clearly identifiable nature. (Research in biological psychiatry seems, incidentally, to be bent on extending this territory.) The term might therefore have seemed admirable for delineating the areas surveyed in this book. The decision not to use it came from two main considerations. First, neuropsychiatry is often regarded as the interface between neurology and psychiatry, which indeed it is, clinical neurology constituting by far the most relevant discipline additional to psychiatry itself. But my aim was to broaden the scope somewhat further by considering endocrine, toxic and metabolic disorders as well. These may also operate to disturb brain function, but they are the concern of general medicine rather than of neurology *per se*.

The second consideration has historical and conceptual roots though it emerges as immensely important in clinical practice. The term neuropsychiatry has sometimes earned for itself pejorative connotations. It has been regarded as narrow in approach and eschewing the rich diversity of psychiatric progress. At the worst it has been seen as the provenance of amateurs in both neurology and psychiatry, an imperfect chimera poorly endowed with the fruits of either discipline. This could scarcely be further from my conception of what neuropsychiatry entails. The study and treatment of those psychiatric disorders deriving from brain malfunction must capitalise on all that psychiatry has to offer. There are psychodynamic, social and cultural aspects of neuropsychiatry to be considered; exploration of conflict must take its place alongside the physical examination in differential diagnosis, psychotherapy alongside pharmacotherapy in treatment. To circumscribe a particularly complex and multi-dimensional segment of mental disorder, then to discard much that we have learned from psychiatry generally would be absurd. Neuropsychiatric practice requires a widening, not a narrowing of psychiatric skills and interests.

Altogether it seemed a neat side-stepping of several pitfalls to choose a title not widely employed before—Organic Psychiatry—though no doubt this still raises problems of its own.

Among those friends and colleagues thanked in the previous preface I have lost the two who perhaps did most to sustain early efforts with the book—Sir Denis Hill and Dr Richard Pratt. Their passing has been an immense blow to psychiatry and to medicine generally. For help with this second edition I must especially thank Dr Maria Ron, also Dr Peter Fenwick, Dr Simon Fleminger, Dr Robin Jacobson, Dr Eileen Joyce, Dr Michael Kopelman, and Dr Brian Toone. Dr Maria Wyke has kept me in touch with the fascination of neuropsychology. It must also be appropriate to thank those patients from whom I have learned continually. The appearance, regularly over the horizon, of students with new talents and ideas has perhaps done most of all to help keep me abreast of progress.

Mrs Patsy Mott deserves my warmest gratitude for her untiring and expert secretarial skills. By ensuring the smooth running of day-to-day affairs she has made time available for the work to go ahead. The typing of drafts and extensive work with the bibliography and proof-reading have proceeded steadily despite the demands of other activities. As with the first edition I have been singularly fortunate to have had such enthusiastic and meticulous secretarial help. In this connection I must record my gratitude to Mrs Dorothy Wiltshire once again, who gave further invaluable help in her retirement.

Finally my wife Marjorie, and children Victoria and William, have played an enthusiastic part in the preparation of this book—checking of the manuscript and cross-referencing in particular. Victoria gave willing and extensive help in the library. More than this they have provided the domestic background against which to mix long hours of work with diversion, sustenance and affection. I thank them for their forebearance. The generosity of a lively family has made the appearance of this new edition possible.

June 1985   ALWYN LISHMAN

SECTION 1
PRINCIPLES

Chapter 1. Cardinal Psychological Features of Cerebral Disorder

In most psychiatric illnesses the clinical picture is profoundly coloured and sometimes decisively shaped by factors specific to the individual and his environment. Hence the notorious difficulty in identifying separate disease processes in psychiatry. This is compounded still further by the lack of collateral evidence by way of tissue pathology where most mental disorders are concerned. Organic psychiatric illnesses escape in some degree from both of these constraints. The psychological disturbances which result from brain pathology often share common ground which cuts across differences in background, personality and social situation. They are related to pathological processes within the brain, or acting on the brain, which can often be identified by the techniques of medical investigation. In these respects organic psychiatry draws closer to the rest of medicine, and should at least in theory be amenable to a similar approach in leading towards useful clinico-pathological correlations.

In large measure this is so. However, psychological symptoms are hard to identify objectively and can rarely be measured accurately. Difficulties of assessment increase abruptly as we ascend from basic motor and sensory processes to mental phenomena, and especially when we move from simple cognitive impairments to changes in emotion, personality and other complex aspects of behaviour. Moreover when symptoms characteristic of the neuroses or major psychoses emerge in the brain-damaged person it is necessary to consider the possibility that he may have been specially predisposed to their development. Ultimately, indeed, we are often forced back again to the problems of the main body of psychiatry, since the more complex effects of cerebral disorder can be properly assessed only when the whole individual is viewed in the context of his personal history and environment. The situation is therefore a good deal more complex than in most other branches of medicine, and the opportunities for relating abnormalities of behaviour to precise aspects of cerebral pathology are limited in several important respects.

Fortunately for the diagnostic process, organic psychiatric disorders tend to have certain features in common which usually allow them to be distinguished from non-organic mental illnesses. Different varieties of pathological change are often associated with similar forms of functional impairment. Bonhoeffer (1909, 1910) deserves the credit for recognising this and discarding the Kraepelinian view that each noxious agent affecting the brain evokes a specific psychiatric picture. Impairment of consciousness, for example, may result from a number of toxic processes acting on the brain or from raised intracranial pressure; dementia may result from anoxia, from trauma or from primary degenerative disease. It is therefore possible to extract important symptoms and syndromes which indicate the possibility of cerebral disorder whatever the basic pathology and despite the colouring lent by pathoplastic features. Such symptoms form the cornerstone of diagnosis in organic psychiatry and it is essential to recognise their earliest and most minor manifestations. Many disease processes affecting the brain will come to attention with psychological symptoms alone and well before the appearance of definite neurological signs, and it is often by the correct appreciation of these common forms of reaction that a mistaken diagnosis of functional psychiatric disorder will be avoided.

Other forms of presentation may indeed occur with change of personality, affective disturbance, neurotic symptoms or even pictures indicative of the functional psychoses. The clinician must remain aware that occasionally a mental illness presenting purely as a functional psychiatric disorder may be related to the early stages of cerebral disease. Such cases are relatively rare, however, and as the condition progresses organic mental symptoms will usually appear.

Nosology and the Use of Terms

The present chapter will describe the cardinal psychological symptoms and signs of cerebral disorder*. The principal accent will be on the shared forms of reaction common to most individuals and to different pathological processes, though features particular to individuals will also be briefly described where appropriate.

The recognition of common forms of reaction has led to the widespread use of all-embracing terms. A main division into acute and chronic forms of reaction is customary. In addition a number of syndromes have been delineated, such as clouding of consciousness, delirium and dementia. These terms are clinically useful for purposes of broad classification, and for shorthand description of groups of clinical phenomena. They are not, however, diagnoses in themselves, and must be appreciated as interim judgements which await clarification by further observation and investigation of the patient.

Unfortunate tendencies have developed in the use of some of these terms. Some are used to refer interchangeably to symptoms, syndromes or to disease entities; others have had restrictions placed upon them by virtue of aetiological or prognostic considerations. 'Dementia', for example, may refer to a syndrome in which failing intellect is prominent, or to a number of specific disease entities. In addition it has acquired implications for irreversibility of the process. 'Confusion' may refer to a lack of clarity in thinking, or be used as in 'acute confusional state' to indicate a broad nosological category of disorders. The term 'toxic confusional state' is similarly widely used but can properly be applied only when toxic influences on the brain have been established.

'*Acute organic reaction*' and '*chronic organic reaction*' are the terms best used for the first major division of organic psychiatric illnesses, each functioning as no more than a pointer to a class of problems, and serving only as starting points for further enquiries into aetiology. These terms carry implications for abruptness and onset and to some extent for the constellation of symptoms which are most in evidence. Each may show features not seen in the other, and requiring specific approaches for their identification. The terms also carry implications for likely duration, but not directly for ultimate prognosis. It is more usual for acute than for chronic organic reactions to recover, but the prognosis in each case will depend upon the precise aetiology at

---

* The distinction between symptoms and signs which is customary in general medicine is often difficult to make where psychological phenomena are concerned. To avoid repetition, 'symptoms' will often be used alone when both the patient's complaints and the psychological abnormalities detected by the examiner are being considered together.

work. A separate category of 'subacute organic reactions' is sometimes demarcated, and merely implies less sudden onset than the acute disorders, somewhat longer continuation, and an admixture of clinical symptoms characteristic of acute and chronic reactions. It must be accepted however that both acute and chronic reactions will vary in the degree of their acuteness or chronicity, and that in some cases the former will, with time, prove to merge into the latter.

'*Confusion*' refers to symptoms and signs which indicate that the patient is unable to think with his customary clarity and coherence. It is seen in both organic and non-organic mental disturbances, and the term is useful merely as a shorthand clinical description of an important aspect of such mental states. In acute organic reactions confusion is due largely to impairment of consciousness. In chronic organic reactions it betrays the disruption of thought processes due to structural brain damage. In the functional psychoses confusion of thinking may be much in evidence without any identifiable brain pathology whatever, similarly when powerful emotions from any cause interfere with the efficient ordering of cognitive processes.

It is unfortunate therefore that 'confusion' has sometimes been made the hallmark of organic mental states and incorporated into terms denoting categories of organic mental disorder. Victor and Adams (1962) for example, recognise three syndromes within the class of 'confusional state', depending on the associated increase or decrease of psychomotor activity or the presence of associated degenerative brain disease ('delirium', 'primary mental confusion' and 'beclouded dementia'). Such classifications are cumbersome and of uncertain clinical usefulness. It would seem preferable to restrict the use of the term confusion to denote phenomena as defined above, and to avoid its use in nosological classifications.

'*Clouding of Consciousness*' denotes the mildest stage of impairment of consciousness, which is detectable clinically, on the continuum from full alertness and awareness to coma. As such it is manifest as slight impairment of thinking, attending, perceiving, and remembering, in other words as mild global impairment of cognitive processes in association with reduced awareness of the environment. The patient will frequently, though not always, appear to be drowsy. As Lipowski (1967) points out, clouding of consciousness is not exactly synonymous with reduced wakefulness. The one is a stage on the way to coma, the other on the way to sleep which is very different (p. 6). In clouding of consciousness the patient's awareness of himself and his surroundings is impaired, but his activity may vary from drowsiness and lethargy on the one hand to increased excitability on the other.

Unfortunately the term has sometimes been endowed with broader meaning. Jaspers (1963) distinguished between torpor and clouding, only the former representing a stage on the continuum from full alertness to unconsciousness. Clouding in this view has additionally the hall-marks of fragmentation of psychic experience and florid subjective events in the form of fantasies, vivid affects and hallucinations. In such a conception 'clouding of consciousness' embraces additional phenomena and describes a complete mental state rather than one definable component. It would seem preferable to restrict its use in the manner described above.

'*Delirium*'. Many meanings and definitions have been given to this term sometimes embracing all varieties of acute organic reaction, sometimes referring to the degree of overt disturbance, and sometimes confining its use to clinical pictures with certain specific features. Special characteristics have included wakefulness with ability to respond verbally, increased psychomotor activity, pronounced disturbance of affect, defective reality testing, or the appearance of productive symptoms in the form of illusions and hallucinations. Delirium tremens is often taken as a prototype for delirium, and contrasted with the 'simple confusion' of subdued cognitive impairment in other illnesses.

In the DSM III classification in use in the USA 'delirium' is broadly synonymous with 'acute organic reaction', and includes all varieties of the latter (American Psychiatric Association, 1980; Lipowski, 1980a). In the UK the term is usually reserved for patients whose acute cerebral disorder has resulted in some degree of disturbed or disruptive behaviour, i.e. to describe *a syndrome of impairment of consciousness which is accompanied by intrusive abnormalities derived from the fields of perception and affect.* Thus consciousness is not merely quantitatively reduced, but also qualitatively changed. Typically the patient becomes preoccupied with his own inner world which is distorted by illusions, hallucinations and delusions, and by powerful affective changes derived therefrom or more directly from dysfunction of specific brain systems. Though conscious awareness of external events is impaired, arousal is high enabling these productive symptoms to occur, and accordingly psychomotor activity is usually increased in the form of restless and excited behaviour. Delirium commonly fluctuates in intensity and content and manifests a continuously changing clinical picture. As a syndrome it is common among acute organic reactions, but is not specifically tied to any one ultimate cause.

'*Twilight States*'. Among Bonhoeffer's 'forms of exogenous reaction' due to pathogenic factors acting on the brain, twilight states and delirium were separately demarcated along with hallucinosis, epileptiform excitement and amentia. The last three terms have mostly been discarded in this context, but 'twilight state' continues to be used. The essential features appear to include abrupt onset and ending, variable duration from hours to weeks, and the interruption of quiet periods of behaviour by unexpected and sometimes violent acts or outbursts of rage or fear. Thereafter clinical descriptions are often divergent. Consciousness is sometimes said to be severely impaired, with profound slowness of reaction and monotonous stereotyped movements, while others stress relatively normal outward behaviour between episodes of disturbance. Other descriptions include dreamlike 'oneiroid' states, vivid hallucinations and delusional ideas which dictate powerful affective disturbance. Clearly, therefore, the term is used to cover a variety of syndromes and can now have little useful meaning. It is, moreover, widely employed to describe hysterical manifestations in addition to acute organic reactions. In the organic field current practice appears increasingly to be to restrict its use to a type of psychomotor seizure as considered on p. 222.

'*Coma*' represents the extreme of a graded continuum of impairment of consciousness, at the opposite pole of the spectrum from full alertness and awareness of the environment. The patient is incapable of sensing or responding adequately to external stimuli or inner needs, shows little or no spontaneous movement apart from respiration, and no evidence whatever of mental activity.

Coma is itself a graded phenomenon. At its deepest there is no reaction to stimuli of any intensity, and corneal, pupillary, pharyngeal, tendon and plantar reflexes are absent. Respiration is slow and sometimes periodic (Cheyne-Stokes respiration) and cardiovascular regulating processes may show signs of failure. Lighter degrees of coma ('semi-coma') allow partial response to stimulation, though this is incomplete, mostly non-purposive, and usually consists of ineffectual movements or rubbing and scratching of the stimulated area. Bladder distension may call forth groaning or ill-coordinated motor stirring but the patient is still incontinent. Tendon reflexes may or may not be obtainable, and the plantars may be either flexor or extensor. The Glasgow Coma Scale which has proved its usefulness for the grading of depth of coma is described on p. 140.

Coma needs to be distinguished from deep sleep and from stupor. In deep sleep and in coma the pictures may be closely similar on superficial observation. But the sleeper can be roused again to normal consciousness by the efforts of the examiner. He may wake spontaneously to unaccustomed stimuli, or in response to inner sensations such as hunger or bladder distension. In sleep there is sporadic continuing mental activity in the form of dreams which leave traces in memory. Coma is more difficult to demarcate from stupor which is described below. The distinguishing features usually accepted are that in coma the eyes remain shut even in response to strong arousal stimuli, do not resist passive opening, and do not appear to be watchful or follow moving objects; movements in response to stimulation are never purposeful, and there is no subsequent recall of events or inner fantasies from the time in question.

'*Stupor*' is an exceedingly difficult term to define, principally because it has been used widely in neurological and psychiatric practice to refer to conditions with markedly different causation. Sometimes it is used loosely and wrongly to refer to an intermediate stage on the continuum of impairment of consciousness which leads ultimately to coma; sometimes to refer to a syndrome characteristic of lesions in the neighbourhood of the diencephalon and upper brain stem ('akinetic mutism'); and sometimes to clinical states superficially similar to this but due to reversible functional psychiatric illness.

Stupor is thus a term without definite nosological status, but valuable when properly used in referring, in essence, to a clinical syndrome of akinesis and mutism but with evidence of relative preservation of conscious awareness. It would appear that with the exception of 'akinetic mutism' due to brain damage, stupor may be a non-specific general reaction of the central nervous system, with some individuals presumably predisposed towards its development. In some cases at least stupor appears to be experienced as a volitional act, sometimes delusionally motivated.

There is a profound lack of responsiveness, and evidence of impairment, or at least putative or apparent impairment, of consciousness. Speech and spontaneous movement are absent or reduced to a minimum, and the patient is inaccessible to the great majority of external stimuli. Unlike coma and semicoma, however, the patient may at first sight appear to be conscious, since the eyes may be open and seem to be watchful. The patient may direct his gaze towards the examiner and the eyes may follow moving visual stimuli in a manner which appears to be purposeful rather than random. When the eyes are shut they may resist passive opening. Relative preservation of consciousness is also betrayed by the response to stimulation—strong painful stimuli may induce blinking or purposeful co-ordinated efforts to dislodge the noxious agent. Moreover in some cases there is subsequent recall of events or delusional phantasies occurring in the stuporose state.

Typically spontaneous movements are absent, but there may be tremors, coarse twitching or, in light stupor, restless stereotyped motor activity. The latter may seem to occur in response to hallucinatory experiences, or to display special meaning in stupors due to psychotic illness. Here also the resting posture may be awkward or bizarre, or it may be meaningful in the context of the patient's delusions. Reflexes are usually entirely normal. Complete mutism is the rule, but again there may sometimes be partially coherent muttering, or arousal may be possible to the extent of brief stereotyped exclamations. In light stupor there may be no sphincter disturbance, and even feeding may be possible with coaxing. Simple responses to commands may then be obtained, though these are slow, inaccurate and often ill-co-ordinated. The least severe examples may merge indefinably with severe psychomotor retardation in psychotic depression, or with severe blocking of thought and volition in catatonic schizophrenia. The causes of stupor and their differential diagnosis are considered on p. 130.

'*Dementia*' is used in two contexts which must be clearly distinguished; first to label a group of specific disease entities, namely the 'presenile and senile dementias', and secondly to refer to a clinical syndrome which can have many other causes.

The specific diseases for which the term is used are considered in Chapter 10. They are characterised by progressive and widespread brain degeneration with, at the moment, a hopeless prognosis. When denoting a syndrome, however, the term may validly be used more widely, and is best defined quite simply as *an acquired global impairment of intellect, memory and personality, but without impairment of consciousness*. As such it is almost always of long duration, usually progressive, and often irreversible, but these features are not included as part of the definition.

The syndrome therefore consists of a constellation of symptoms which suggest chronic and widespread brain dysfunction. Global impairment of intellect is the central and essential feature, manifest as difficulty with memory, attention, thinking and comprehension. Other mental functions are usually affected concurrently, and changes of mood, personality and social behaviour may sometimes be the outstanding or even presenting features. Nevertheless 'dementia' should not be used to describe such changes unless intellectual deterioration can be identified or predicted with certainty.

Historically the term has acquired implications for inevitable decline and irreversibility. This remains true for the disease entities of dementia, but not for all the settings in which the syndrome may appear. The dementia accompanying general paresis can be arrested, and that due to head injury or normal pressure hydrocephalus may improve with time or treatment. Thus when matters of prognosis are kept out of the definition the term can be used whatever the cause of the syndrome and whatever future discoveries may bring.

It is also important that the syndrome be defined in terms of global impairment of *functions,* and not in terms of diffuse cerebral damage. Brain damage may not exist at all in readily definable form, as in the dementia which accompanies myxoedema. Moreover focal brain damage can sometimes lead to global impairment of intellect, memory and personality in addition to regional defects. Frontal lobe tumours are notorious in this regard, and can produce a picture of dementia indistinguishable at first sight from other causes. In such cases it remains logical to use the term to describe the clinical picture which presents for attention, even though diffuse affection of brain tissue is not the immediate cause. Indeed some forms of dementia are best regarded as the end result of multiple focal pathologies which coalesce and combine to impair functions globally, as in arteriosclerotic dementia. It is essential, therefore, to avoid defining the syndrome in terms of a pathology which has yet to be displayed.

The term is thus reserved for the description of a group of clinical symptoms, while all considerations of prognosis and aetiology are excluded from the definition. This has a certain practical importance, in that once the syndrome has been identified it must always dictate a search for ultimate causes. These may be focal or diffuse, within or without the brain, and may have possibilities for treatment.

'Organic Personality Change'. Brain damage often results in changes of temperament, or changed patterns of reaction to events and to other people. As a result behavioural tendencies which have previously been enduring characteristics of the individual are found to be altered. Areas typically affected include the control of emotions and impulses and as-

pects of motivation and social judgement (Lipowski, 1980a). Such 'change of personality' is usually prominent in dementia, as already described, and is then seen along with cognitive defects. But sometimes brain damage may operate more directly by disruption of regional cerebral systems upon which the synthesis of the personality depends. This situation is compatible with excellent preservation of intellect to formal testing, yet the personality change is nonetheless organic in origin. Thus when disturbance of cognitive processes cannot be identified, the term 'organic personality change' is preferable to 'dementia'. Most examples occur with strictly focal brain damage, the best known being with lesions of the frontal lobes of the brain.

'Chronic Amnesic Syndrome'. Disorder of memory, especially for recent events, is an integral part of dementia, but can also exist without global impairment of intellect. Such memory disturbance may emerge as the sole defect, as after bilateral hippocampal lesions, or more commonly may stand out as the obtrusive defect while other cognitive processes are but little affected. Such a syndrome may ensue on an acute organic reaction which clears to reveal a relatively isolated defect of memory, as when Wernicke's encephalopathy leads on to Korsakoff's psychosis.

The term 'chronic amnesic syndrome' usefully describes the essential features of disorder in all such cases, and emphasises the distinction from dementia. It may be defined as an organic impairment of memory out of all proportion to other cognitive changes. A focal rather than a diffuse brain pathology can be confidently predicted as described on pp. 25 to 27.

'Organic Hallucinosis' refers to a syndrome of recurrent or persistent hallucinations, occurring in a setting of full preservation of consciousness and awareness of the environment yet attributable to organic factors. The patient is not disorientated and proves capable of thinking with normal clarity throughout. The hallucinations occur mostly in the auditory or visual modalities but any sensory channel can be affected. Insight into the unreal nature of the phenomena may vary markedly in degree, but any delusions that occur are secondary to the hallucinatory experiences. Such a syndrome may be occasioned by circumscribed brain lesions, strategically placed to irritate cortical or subcortical areas, but is more commonly seen as a result of toxic processes. The hallucinations occurring during the early phase of alcohol withdrawal (p. 512) or after lysergic acid diethylamide (p. 528) are typical examples.

In the DSM III classification of mental disorders it has been proposed that further organic syndromes should be recognised, to take account of those patients who show predominantly non-cognitive psychopathological features in the presence of brain malfunction (American Psychiatric Association, 1980; Lipowski, 1980b). The *'organic affective syndrome'* shows abnormalities of mood, either depression or mania, that are judged to be the direct consequence of a cerebral disorder rather than a reflection of the subjective meaning of an event or situation for the person. Before applying such a label it is necessary to establish the provoking organic cause, normally with a definable temporal relationship to the development of the affective disorder. Examples would include the depression frequently seen with Cushing's disease and other endocrinopathies, or that induced by rauwolfia alkaloids.

The *'organic delusional syndrome'* encompasses paranoid and schizophrenia-like disorders which are judged in the individual case to be the direct result of a specific organic factor. Certain psychoses seen with epilepsy fall within this category, also the acute paranoid psychoses following amphetamine intoxication. The delusions which form the core feature of the syndrome may be accompanied by hallucinations, thought disorder or other schizophrenic manifestations, but impairment of consciousness is absent. Any substantial impairment of intellect must also be absent. Here again it is necessary to have evidence of an association with an organic cause known to be liable to produce such psychopathological manifestations; the designation cannot be based on the descriptive clinical picture alone.

Generalised Versus Focal Cerebral Disorder

A great number of organic psychiatric disorders are due to widespread disturbance of brain function. This may be the result of diffuse disease processes within the brain, as in certain degenerative diseases, or of systemic disturbances, for example those leading to anoxia which impair brain function indirectly. Moreover, well localised brain lesions may declare themselves only when secondary diffuse effects supervene, as with raised intracranial pressure in association with cerebral tumour. The majority of acute and chronic organic reactions therefore reflect widespread disorder of cerebral activity and contain symptoms of defective function in many spheres.

It has become customary to talk of 'generalised cerebral disorder' and to distinguish this from the effects of strictly focal pathology. It must, however, be appreciated that both generalised and focal disturbances of brain function represent theoretical extremes which are rarely if ever encountered in practice. It is most unlikely that intrinsic brain disease is ever uniformly distributed throughout the brain, and some degree of focal emphasis can usually be discerned with careful observation. Extrinsic factors which impair brain function are likewise selective in their effects, sparing some neural systems while disrupting others. Impairment of consciousness, for example, represents interference with brain stem alerting functions while cardiovascular and respiratory functions proceed with little alteration. Similarly disruption of cortical and subcortical functions very rarely occurs to an equivalent extent.

Strictly focal disorder, on the other hand, is also very rare except when purposely produced by surgical procedures. In naturally occurring disease we merely see a focal emphasis of pathology, which in greater or less degree is complicated by the additional effects of damage elsewhere.

Nevertheless it is of great importance in practical clinical terms to preserve the distinction between clinical pictures which result from widely disseminated or from relatively circumscribed brain dysfunction. The distinction is essential in the formulation of likely causes and thence in deciding on the lines which investigation must follow. Each, in practice, contains different symptoms of fundamental importance.

The plan in the present chapter will be first to describe in broad terms the characteristic clinical pictures seen in 'generalised' acute and chronic reactions, and then to summarise the salient features seen with focal damage or focal emphasis of pathology in specific brain regions. The focal significance of certain symptoms and symptom complexes will be dealt with in more detail in Chapter 2.

The Clinical Picture in Acute Organic Reactions

ACUTE BRAIN SYNDROME; ACUTE CONFUSIONAL STATE; ACUTE ORGANIC PSYCHOSIS; ACUTE PSYCHO-ORGANIC SYNDROME

The acute organic reactions are called forth by a great number of different pathological processes affecting the brain, including trauma, cerebral anoxia, epilepsy, metabolic derangements such as uraemia, or the toxic effects of drugs or alcohol. A list of causes is presented in the table on p. 129. The onset is always fairly abrupt, though when slight in degree the disorder may not declare itself in an obvious fashion from the outset. The majority of acute organic reactions are reversible when the underlying pathology can be remedied, but some may progress directly to a chronic organic syndrome, as when an acute post-traumatic psychosis clears to reveal dementia or when Wernicke's encephalopathy results in an enduring amnesic syndrome.

The clinical pictures which result are essentially due to disruption of normal brain function, by virtue of biochemical, electrical or mechanical disturbances. The symptomatology follows a surprisingly constant pattern despite these various causes. To some extent there are specific features depending on rate of development, the intensity and perhaps the nature of the noxious agent, but this variability is small in relative terms. The personality and background of the patient will also colour the picture, especially in minor affections and particularly where matters such as intensity of emotional disturbance or content of delusional thinking are concerned. The main emphasis in what follows, however, will be on shared and common forms of reaction.

Impairment of Consciousness

Impairment of consciousness is the primary change in acute organic reactions, and in some degree is universal. It therefore holds a fundamentally important place in the detection of acute disturbances of brain function and in the assessment of their severity. Other features such as disordered psychomotor activity, perception, and emotion, may be more striking but are less constantly found, and are also more variable in their manifestations.

Impairment of consciousness ranges on a single continuum from barely perceptible dulling of awareness to profound coma. Characteristically the impairment fluctuates when mild in degree, often worsening at night with fatigue and with decreased environmental stimulation. The fluctuations and the appearance of lucid intervals are observations of great clinical importance in the differential diagnosis of organic from non-organic psychiatric disorders, also in distinguishing acute from chronic organic reactions. Daytime visits may find the patient at his best, and it is thus essential to pay attention to reports of changed behaviour as nightfall approaches.

Considerable difficulties can surround the conception of levels of consciousness in patients with acute organic reactions, partly because of problems inherent in the use of certain terms and partly because of the expectation that impaired consciousness must necessarily be accompanied by decreased responsiveness to stimuli. In fact surprising instances may be seen. In most conditions impairment of consciousness is accompanied by diminished arousal and alertness which become clinically apparent at some stage of the disorder. But in others, as in delirium tremens, the patient may be hyper-aroused and hyper-alert. Arousal and alertness, in this context, refer to the readiness with which the patient responds to environmental stimuli, 'arousal' being best used to describe the physiological state of the organism and 'alertness' to describe the observational data from which this state is inferred.

Preserved alertness is not, however, the sole yardstick by which preservation of normal consciousness is assessed. To be useful alertness must be coupled with an ability to select discriminatingly between those stimuli which are important and meaningful and those which are not. Moreover the relevant stimuli must gain access to conscious awareness where they can be related to past experience and present needs. For these purposes alertness must be accompanied by a *capacity to attend*. When consciousness is impaired certain qualities of attention will invariably be found to be defective — qualities referred to as *phasic, modulated, selective* or *directed attention*.

They involve the capacity not merely to allow a stimulus to elicit a response, but to mobilise, focus, sustain and shift attention in a fluid and changing manner according to the needs of the moment. Whether the patient is hypo- or hyper-alert it will often soon become apparent that such mechanisms are at fault. Failure to be selective can result in indiscriminate, often excessive, responses to stimuli with the result that the patient is *distractible;* failure to mobilise and sustain attention is seen in *impaired concentration;* inability to shift attention can lead to *perseveration*. The examiner's difficulty in engaging with the patient may owe much to all of these factors. A more pervasive change may also occur, whereby internal percepts, thoughts and images come to hold attention more readily than percepts from the environment, allowing them to become elaborated in an unrestrained manner. This would appear to be important in the genesis of the vivid affects, fantasies and hallucinations of 'delirium', as described on p. 514.

A true appreciation of the patient's level of consciousness must therefore include assessment, not only of his alertness and responsivity, but also of his capacity to attend in a discriminating manner to what is going on around him.

A minor degree of impairment of consciousness may present merely with complaints of vague malaise and feelings of uncertainty. It may escape detection at the time, and be revealed only in retrospect by the amnesic gap left for the period in question. Other sensitive indicators are minor difficulties in judging the passage of time, in focusing attention as described just above, or in thinking coherently. The latter again may initially be more apparent subjectively than to external observation. Sometimes there may be neglect of appearance and of needs, or an episode of incontinence may be an early sign. The sleep-wakefulness cycle is almost universally disturbed in some degree, with various combinations of insomnia, vivid dreams and dream-like mentation (Lipowski, 1980a). The diurnal rhythm of activity is sometimes clearly disordered, with a tendency to somnolence by day and excitability at night.

With more severe degrees of impairment the patient is observed to be slow in responding, loses the thread in conversation, and attention to outside events is hard to arouse and sustain. Responses to requests may betray inadequate understanding or lack of volition to carry them out. Later still the patient is clearly drowsy, sleeps excessively, and if rousable shows only a torpid and muddled awareness.

Psychomotor Behaviour

Motor behaviour usually diminishes progressively as impairment of consciousness increases. When left to himself the patient shows little spontaneous activity and habitual acts such as eating are carried out in an automatic manner. His capacity for purposive action is diminished. When pressed to engage in activities the patient is slow, hesitant and often perseverative. He responds to external stimuli apathetically if at all, though highly charged subjective events such as hallucinatory experiences may still call forth abrupt and even excessive reactions. Speech is slow and sparse, answers stereotyped or incoherent, and difficult questions are usually ignored. There is often slurring, perseveration, or dysphasic difficulties. In severe cases there may be no more than incoherent muttering.

While the above is the rule with most acute affections of the brain, some show the reverse with restless hyperactivity and noisy disturbing behaviour. Delirium tremens and the deliria which accompany certain systemic infections are the well-known examples. Not surprisingly these florid cases figure disproportionately highly in most published accounts of acute organic reactions. Psychomotor activity is greatly increased with an excessive tendency to startle reactions. Typically the overactivity consists of repetitive, purposeless behaviour, such as ceaseless groping or picking movements. Behaviour may be dictated by hallucinations and delusions, the patient turning for example to engage in imaginary conversation, or ransacking the bedclothes for objects thought to be hidden there. More rarely he

may perform complex stereotyped movements, re-enacting the driving of a car or miming his usual work ('occupational delirium'). Sometimes there is dangerously belligerent combative behaviour, or sudden frantic efforts to escape. When purposive, the activities are usually misdirected, inappropriate or bizarre, and voluntary movements are often jerky and uneven. The overactivity is often accompanied by excitement with noisy shouting, laughing or crying. There may be pressure of speech with repeated stereotyped exclamations or incoherent flight of ideas. Most of the behaviour is obviously dictated by the patient's own internal world, and alertness to external stimuli is seen to be impaired. Not uncommonly the clinical picture shows rapid changes from phases of overactivity to periods of apathy and aspontaneity.

Thinking

Thought processes show characteristic changes when consciousness is impaired. In the early stages there is subjective slowing, with difficulty in focusing thoughts or in formulating complex ideas. Ready mental fatigue may be obvious in the course of examination. Later on reasoning becomes less clear and coherent, logic is impaired, and thinking more concrete and literal. The organisation of thought is weakened, with fewer associations and less integration between past and present experience. Even when speeded by excitement and high arousal the thought content is seen to be stereotyped, banal, and impoverished. Trains of thought become isolated and chaotic, showing in speech as fragmentation and incoherence.

An important change is in the relative importance of the internal and external worlds, and in decreasing ability to preserve the distinction between the two. As a result perceptions and thoughts become inextricably interwoven with one another (defective 'reality testing'). Comprehension of outside events is impaired, with inability to embrace the elements of experience and relate them meaningfully to one another (impaired 'grasp'). The patient may be unaware of the most obvious features of his immediate-situation, whether he is standing or lying, whether indoors or in the street. At the same time increased meaning and significance are attached to subjective experiences, ideas or false perceptions, which come to dominate the content of consciousness. Bizarre thoughts and fantasies intrude into awareness and are passively accepted, and false significance is attached to external cues. Illusions and hallucinations are readily incorporated, and vivid dream material may be carried over into waking life.

Ideas of reference and delusion formation may be prominent features, depending almost certainly to some extent on qualities in the premorbid personality. Delusions of persecution are especially common, and may well up suddenly with conviction. Usually they betray their organic origin in being poorly elaborated, vague, transient and shallow, and are not retold with any consistency. When consciousness is relatively clear, however, the delusions may be more coherently organised and systematised, producing a picture more closely resembling schizophrenia. In rare cases delusions may even persist when the patient has recovered from the acute illness, along with an obstinate belief in the reality of the hallucinatory experiences which occurred.

Insight is typically lost early, but may vary from time to time along with fluctuations in the level of consciousness. Sometimes even in moderately severe affections the patient may be briefly roused to self awareness and to a better appreciation of reality.

Memory

With impairment of consciousness there is disturbance of registration, retention and recall. Registration of current experience is hampered by defects in attention, perception and comprehension. Accordingly the immediate memory span for digits or similar material is found to be reduced. Defective retention leads to difficulty with new learning which is a sensitive clinical indicator in mild stages of disorder. Recent memories prove to be faulty while long-term memories are reasonably intact, though with moderate impairment of consciousness both are ultimately found to suffer.

An early change is defective appreciation of the flow of time, and the jumbling of time sequences especially for recent events. This quickly leads to disorientation in time, which is sometimes regarded as the hallmark of acute organic reactions. Disorientation may however be transient in the early stages, and a normally orientated patient may sometimes prove later to be amnesic for all that passed during the interview in which he was examined.

Disorientation for place and later still for person may follow with worsening of perceptual and cognitive disorganisation. Patterson and Zangwill (1944) have drawn attention to the interesting way in which patients may maintain two incompatible attitudes towards their orientation without seeming aware of the inconsistency. This can emerge strikingly where orientation for place is concerned, the patient saying quite correctly, for example, that he is in hospital in one town, yet interpreting his surroundings and behaving in every other way as though he were at home in another part of the country ('reduplicative paramnesia'). Such correct and incorrect orientations may exist side by side in a vacillating and unrelated manner, or be reconciled by shallow rationalizations. The patient may insist that the two places are the same, or contiguous with each other, or confabulate a recent journey between the two.

False memories and confabulation may occasionally be much in evidence, and misidentifications, including pseudo-recognition, may be facilitated by the perceptual abnormalities described below.

On recovery there is typically a dense amnesic gap for the period of the acute illness, though where fluctuation has been marked islands of memory may remain. Sometimes sensory impressions, and especially vivid hallucinations, may stand out clearly and be remembered in great detail when all else is forgotten, attesting again to the greater importance of subjective experience than of external reality in severe stages of the disorder.

Perception

Quite commonly it is the more florid perceptual abnormalities which draw attention to the presence of an acute organic reaction in a patient suffering from some physical disease. However it must be stressed that these are not essential features in every case, and the diagnosis should be made by seeking out the subtle defects of thinking, memory and attention which betray impairment of consciousness.

Early on the patient may be aware that accurate perception requires unusual effort, particularly where vision is concerned. Sometimes, by contrast, perceptions may appear subjectively to be hyper acute. Disturbance of vision may lead to micropsia, macropsia or distortions of shape and position. Disordered auditory perception may hinder clear communication. There may be distortions of weight and size, or bizarre disorders of the body image in which body parts feel shrunken, enlarged, misplaced, or even disconnected. The whole body may feel to be tilted or floating. Disordered perceptiong of internal bodily sensations are liable to elaboration in the context of disorganised and illogical thinking, leading sometimes to bizarre complaints. Genuine physical symptoms such as vertigo, headache, weakness, and paraesthesia are likewise often reported in distorted fashion

Depersonalisation and derealisation are common, though usually poorly and incompletely expressed. Dissolution of the perceptual boundaries between inner psychic experience and the environment, and between the self and others, may have issue in terrifying feelings of imminent dissolution or loss of bodily and personal integrity.

Perceptual abnormalities readily lead on to misinterpretations and illusions which are usually fleeting and changeable. The visual modality is affected more often than any other. Difficulty with visual recognition combines with faulty thinking and memory to lead to false recognition and faulty orientation in place. The unfamiliar tends to be mistaken for the familiar, or may be interpreted as hostile and persecutory. Thus the patient may misidentify a nurse as a relative, or a doctor as a close friend or enemy. The hospital ward may be mistaken for home or for prison. Personally meaningful fantasies may be projected, as when a table top is misperceived as a coffin. Chance noises may similarly be misinterpreted, and often in a manner which contributes towards delusion formation. The latter in turn reinforces the direction which misinterpretations may take, and the whole is often further reinforced by disordered affects of fear and suspicion.

Hallucinations are also commonest in the visual modality, though tactile and auditory hallucinations occur as well. They are probably derived partly from failure to distinguish inner images from outer percepts, and partly from vivid dreams and hypnagogic phenomena which are carried over into the waking state as consciousness waxes and wanes. Simple visual hallucinations consist of flashes of light, geometrical patterns, or colours. More complex continuing phenomena, sometimes kaleidoscopic in nature, may occur, or there may be fully-formed hallucinations of scenes, people and animals. These may be endowed with movement or with colour, and a bizarre fantastic quality is not uncommon. The hallucinated material may be grossly distorted, as for example with Lilliputian hallucinations where objects and people appear to be minute in size. The reality of the phenomena is fully accepted by the patient who may participate and react accordingly, usually with fear and alarm but sometimes with interest or even amusement.

Hallucinations appear to be particularly characteristic of the acute organic reactions occasioned by certain pathological processes. Delirium tremens remains the classical example with extremely florid and productive hallucinations as described on p. 514. Certain toxic agents such as LSD are also notorious for the wealth of formed and unformed hallucinations which they produce. Animals are said to feature particularly frequently in the hallucinations of delirium tremens, though adequate comparative studies do not appear to have been made. Similarly, visual hallucinations of 'nets' were said to characterise the organic reactions seen in bromide intoxication when this was common.

Emotion

In early stages mild depression, anxiety and irritability may be expected, though typically the affect is rather shallow. With deeper impairment, and further impoverishment of mental processes, apathy usually becomes the striking feature, and the whole course of the illness may pass with indifference and emotional withdrawal. More lively affects are seen in those patients who show increased psychomotor activity when affective disturbance may become intense. Anxiety and fear are especially common, increasing sometimes to terror and panic with tachycardia, flushing and tremor. A state of wondering perplexity forms a common background to other affective states. Depression is frequent, elation or anger less so. The development of paranoid attitudes may show in marked hostility and suspicion. The affective reactions are often fleeting and change abruptly with changing delusional ideas and misperceptions. Sudden displays of primitive and highly charged emotion, again mostly of fear, are often called forth by hallucinatory experiences.

In part the affect is likely to be determined by the stress of the physical illness, and in part by a vague awareness of cognitive impairments. The individual's personality structure may contribute in considerable measure, some patients being pre-disposed to react by apathetic withdrawal and others by projection of fantasied dangers onto the environment. The extent of the influence of such matters has not been determined, nor indeed to what degree different aetiological conditions may shape the picture by virtue of their specific actions on the brain. There are strong clinical impressions that delirium tremens tends to be accompanied by intense fear, hepatic encephalopathy by euphoria or depression, and uraemia by apathy, but reliable and systematic observations are not available for true comparisons.

Other Features

Especially in the milder stages of disorder the definitive organic features may be less in evidence than features which depend on individual traits and characteristics. Psychological reactions to early cognitive impairment, or to the stress of the underlying physical disease, may dominate the picture and emerge in the form of neurotic symptoms. Similarly, vulnerable aspects of the patient's personality may be exaggerated, with the appearance of depressive, hypochondriacal, or phobic features. Histrionic and importunate behaviour may sometimes be much in evidence. Hysterical conversion symptoms, usually transient but sometimes persistent, may similarly lead to mistakes in diagnosis. Paranoid developments occur frequently, and can become the overriding feature at an early stage in susceptible individuals. A distinct schizophrenic colouring to the total clinical picture is likewise not uncommon. With progression of cognitive disorganisation the true situation readily becomes apparent, but mild self-limiting acute organic reactions can occasionally be misdiagnosed as functional psychiatric illness.

The Clinical Picture in Chronic Organic Reactions

CHRONIC BRAIN SYNDROME, CHRONIC CONFUSIONAL STATE, CHRONIC ORGANIC PSYCHOSIS, CHRONIC PSYCHO-ORGANIC SYNDROME, 'DEMENTIA'

Chronic, like acute organic reactions, may result from many different pathological processes, yet the clinical picture shows a large measure of similarity from one disease entity to another. A distinctive time course may lend a characteristic slant to the evolution of symptoms, or a focal emphasis in pathology produce special patterns of impairment, but the purpose in what follows is to describe the general clinical picture and to emphasise the shared and common forms of reaction which occur.

The majority of chronic organic reactions are due to diffuse and widespread affections of the brain, hence the similarity in the clinical pictures which result. Some, however, may owe their origins to focal pathology as already discussed, so careful examination for signs of localising value must always be undertaken. The principal causes are listed in the table on p. 129. Most of the illnesses concerned are slowly progressive with increasing disablement, but static pictures may be seen as with arrested general paresis, or gradual improvement may occur over long periods of time as after head injury. In a small but extremely important group therapeutic

intervention can decisively reverse the process, for example with myxoedema or normal pressure hydrocephalus, or when a frontal meningioma is discovered to be the cause.

Mode of Presentation

Before discussing the clinical picture in detail the common ways in which chronic organic reactions present for attention may be briefly outlined.

Some follow upon acute episodes such as trauma or anoxia, and are then revealed in full when the patient recovers consciousness, or else emerge by a process of transition from an acute organic reaction. The great majority, however, develop insidiously from the start.

The commonest mode of onset is with evidence of impairment of memory or more general disorganisation of intellect. Failures of memory are usually noted earlier by relatives and workmates than by the patient himself. They show in missed appointments, apparent unawareness of recent happenings, a tendency to mix up times or to lose things. More general cognitive failure emerges in slipshod work and loss of overall efficiency. The patient may be noticed to think and speak less coherently than usual, to fail with money, or to fail to grasp essentials.

Change in personality as the first manifestation is much less common, but when it occurs the patient is especially likely to come before the psychiatrist. Here intellectual deficits are absent in the early stages, or pass unnoticed in consequence of curtailment of activities and the use of props and evasions. Deterioration of manners may be the earliest sign, or diminished awareness of the needs and feelings of others. Some social blunder may disclose the illness, such as an episode of stealing or disinhibited sexual behaviour out of character for the individual. Sometimes the earliest change is merely the aggravation of long-standing personality traits such as depression, suspiciousness or selfishness. Neurotic traits may be elaborated with the production of obsessional, hysterical or hypochondriacal symptoms. More rarely still the illness may present with the picture of a functional psychotic illness of depressive, paranoid or schizophrenic type in especially predisposed individuals. It is then only by careful examination that the intellectual deterioration is revealed.

Whatever the form of presentation the illness may declare itself abruptly even though its evolution has been insidious. Some episode of acute mental disturbance may bring the disease to attention. Or understanding relatives may have adjusted to the slow decline until some dramatic instance forces their attention to the true situation. Not infrequently a tenuous adjustment is concealed until new demands must suddenly be met, for example on the death of a partner or a move to a new environment. Admission to hospital may be the step which reveals the disorder, and only careful retrospective enquiry may then establish that the onset has been gradual. Intercurrent illness may bring the situation to light by pushing the patient below the threshold at which the brain was previously coping; especially infection, anoxia or post-operative metabolic derangements.

General Behaviour

Although impairment of intellectual ability is the hall-mark of chronic organic reactions this may be manifest only indirectly by way of behavioural change. Typical early signs are loss of interest and initiative, inability to perform up to the usual standard, or minor episodes of muddle and confusion. Episodes of bizarrely inappropriate behaviour may occur, as when the housewife unloads her shopping in the oven, prepares a meal at a quite inappropriate time, or when a man appears at work in a state of disarray. As described just above, some cases present with changes exclusively in the field of social behaviour, well before impairment of cognitive processes is overt.

In progressive disorders the same division is seen, some aspects of behaviour reflecting the intellectual disorganisation, and some the change in emotional control and social awareness. Intellectual impairment shows as incapacity for decisive action, loss of application to the task in hand, and inability to persist in a consistent course of conduct. Despite full alertness and the preservation of normal levels of consciousness the patient fatigues readily on mental effort. He responds appropriately to stimuli within his limited range of comprehension, and is capable of directed attention as the need arises, but powers of concentration are impaired. Goldstein (1939, 1942) has stressed the various behavioural changes which reflect the attempts of the personality to cope with such defects. There is often restlessness, with purposeless overactivity. Typically this occurs within a progressively diminishing sphere of interests and activities ('shrinkage of the milieu'), with rigid adherence to routines and stereotyped organisation of behaviour ('organic over-orderliness'). In this manner the patient may be enabled to cope for a while. When taxed beyond his ability, however, he may become evasive and sullen, or react abruptly with an explosion of primitive affect such as anger, anxiety or tears ('catastrophic reaction'). Social interaction is often marked by lack of concern or even callousness towards others, stubborn egocentricity, or withdrawal from social contact ('self-exclusion').

In the later stages hygiene and personal appearance are neglected and ritualistic hoarding may develop. Food is eaten sloppily, habits become uncouth, and there is bland indifference to urinary or faecal incontinence. In contrast to all of this, however, some patients may preserve their social competence until surprisingly late in the course of the disease.

Eventually behaviour becomes futile and aimless, often with stereotypies and mannerisms. Impoverishment of thought is reflected in total lack of purposive activity, and physical deterioration follows with increasing weakness and emaciation.

Thinking

Thinking is impaired both qualitatively and quantitatively. It becomes slow and laboured, with reduced powers of concentration and ready mental fatigue. The content of thought is impoverished with fewer associations, inability to produce new ideas, and a tendency to dwell on set topics and memories from the past. Themes are banal and stereotyped, and perseveration is usually marked. The ability to reason logically and to manipulate concepts is impaired, likewise the ability to keep in mind various aspects of a situation simultaneously. Specific skills such as calculation are usually impaired from an early stage.

Intellectual flexibility is lost, with difficulty in shifting from one frame of reference to another. The lack of effective counter-ideas leads the patient to become tied to immediate situations which arise, so that he is readily distracted by accidental impressions and events and becomes 'stimulus bound' to them. Such difficulties are compounded by inability to extract the essentials and discard the redundant aspects of a situation or experience ('disturbance of figure-ground relationships'). Abstract ideas present especial difficulty and concepts tend to be given their most literal interpretation ('concretisation').

Judgement is impaired early as a result of these various changes. The patient's insight into his defects is characteristically poor and sometimes there is little awareness of illness at all. False ideas readily gain ground and paranoid ideation is particularly common. Ideas of reference may partly reflect an exaggeration of premorbid tendencies, likewise the specific form which delusions may take. Characteristically the delusions are poorly systematised and evanescent, though occasionally they become entrenched and unshakable. As Roth and Myers (1969) point out they may be delusions in the technical sense, in that the beliefs are held in the face of evidence of their falsehood, but this is largely because the evidence fails to be understood, not because it is rejected. Delusional themes are often crude and bizarre, typically of being robbed, poisoned, threatened or deprived. Delusions of influence and other frankly schizophrenic phenomena may appear, perhaps by virtue of special premorbid vulnerability in this regard.

In the later stages thinking appears to be entirely restricted to circumscribed reiterative themes, and becomes grossly fragmented, incoherent, and disorganised.

Speech

The disturbances in thinking are mirrored in speech. The most characteristic disturbance is poverty of speech with excessive employment of clichés and set phrases. The pool of vocabulary available for use is greatly reduced, and there is lack of speech initiative. Sentences are often simple, incomplete, and poorly constructed, with perseveration in the form of stereotyped utterances and echolalia.

Paraphasic errors, and nominal dysphasia, are not uncommon. Barker and Lawson (1968) suggest that diffculty in word finding is a general feature in dementia if proper care is taken to test with words of low frequency of usage. Stengel (1964) has described special characteristics of nominal dysphasia in patients with diffuse brain lesions. There may be little evidence of disability until the patient is pressed to name an object, whereupon he may show little awareness of his errors or insist that he is right. This complacency is in contrast to the situation in nominal dysphasia due to focal brain lesions. Sometimes the patient may improvise boldly to produce new words, showing the effects of perseveration and 'clang' associations. Stengel also describes 'lowering of the speech conscience', in which words are used as fancy dictates, all being part of the general disregard of language as a code of communication. Concretisation shows in the excessive use of words which refer to the self, and the tendency for external stimuli to influence the words which are chosen—'the situation and the self tend to intrude excessively into the process of naming'.

Ultimately speech becomes grossly disorganised and fragmented, and used exclusively in the service of bodily needs. The patient may become mute or capable only of a restricted range of semi-coherent ejaculations.

Memory

Memory disturbance is frequently the earliest sign of an ingravescent chronic organic reaction, and at first may be intermittent. Allison (1962) makes the important point that with diffuse as opposed to focal cerebral lesions the onset of memory disturbance can rarely be dated with accuracy because it has been of such gradual evolution. The onset may be marked by minor forgetfulness and 'absent mindedness', or by more definite episodes in which new impressions fail to register and striking lapses of memory occur. Loss of topographical memory is often seen, with the patient losing his way when wandering from home. Disorientation in time is a frequent early sign, disorientation for place and person much later in development.

The memory defect is typically global, affecting all categories of material and remote as well as recent events, as described on pp. 30 to 31. Failure at new learning is usually the most conspicuous sign, but there is rarely the sharp demarcation between remote and recent memory which characterises the purer amnesic syndromes. Recall is affected as well as registration and retention, as shown by increased success with prompting and better performance at recognition than at free recall. Memory for names is sometimes particularly affected. Temporal sequences are early disorganised, with faulty appreciation of the flow of time, and mislocation of past events. Berlyne (1972) found that over a third of an unselected group of demented patients showed unequivocal confabulation, sometimes representing a true memory displaced in time, but sometimes consisting of more sustained and elaborate productions.

Characteristically the patient's awareness of his memory diffculties is lacking, or there may even be an apparently motivated desire to hide the defects with facile excuses and shallow confabulations. In the early stages the patient may sometimes show surprising ingenuity in covering up his failures, and compensate by means of a rigid daily routine and the use of a note book. Ultimately, however, memory for current events may become completely void, and the patient can produce only a few jumbled recollections from the past.

Emotion

Emotional changes form an integral part of the clinical picture in chronic organic reactions and deterioration of emotion and intellect frequently pursue a parallel course.

Early emotional changes probably reflect the struggle to cope with incipient intellectual defects, and are coloured by premorbid personality characteristics. Anxiety is common, likewise depression with agitation and hypochondriacal features. Serious suicidal attempts may occur at this stage. Irritability leads to querulous morose behaviour, and sometimes to outbursts of anger and hostility. Perplexity and suspicion are other common early developments, leading on to paranoid beliefs and attitudes.

Further deterioration produces emotional changes of a distinctive organic type. Affective blunting and shallowness may progress to states of apathy or empty euphoria. Emotions may take on a childlike aspect, with petulant importunate behaviour and short-lived excessive responses to trivial annoyances and disappointments. Thus the death of a spouse may leave the patient unmoved, yet interference with some simple routine may provoke violent and spiteful anger.

Emotional control may show a characteristic threshold effect in which there is little response to mild stimulation but thereafter an excessive and prolonged disturbance. Emotional lability may be extreme, with episodes of pathological laughing and crying for little or no cause. The 'catastrophic reaction' may be observed when the patient is taxed beyond his ability to cope, as mentioned on p. 14.

The ultimate picture in progressive disease represents a combination of these various emotional changes, but characterised above all by increasing emptiness of affect, shallowness, dullness, and lack of emotional response.

Other Features

The impact of chronic diffuse brain disease is not entirely unaffected by features specific to the individual. As already mentioned neurotic manifestations may be conspicuous in mild stages of disorder. Hysterical conversion symptoms and obsessional disorders may figure prominently, the former perhaps by virtue of increased suggestibility and the latter as a mode of coping with reduced resources.

A predisposition towards affective or schizophrenic psychosis may lend a distinctive colouring to the clinical picture and lead to mistaken diagnosis in the early stages. Hallucinations may occur in visual, auditory and tactile modalities, and are typically paranoid in content. With progressive disease all such manifestations are usually ultimately engulfed in the general pattern of progressive intellectual and social decline.

The Clinical Picture in Focal Cerebral Disorder

Strictly focal brain damage can be responsible for both acute and chronic organic reactions. Symptoms and signs of localizing significance may then be much in evidence, and must be kept in mind in the clinical assessment of all patients who show organic psychiatric illnesses.

Epileptic phenomena, and especially those of temporal lobe epilepsy, are clear examples of acute psychological disturbances due to focal brain dysfunction, also some of the disturbances seen after small acute cerebrovascular accidents. Wernicke's encephalopathy is another classical example, with its own distinctive chronic end-state in the chronic amnesic syndrome. For obvious reasons, however, focal brain disorder has been most comprehensively studied in slowly progressive or static lesions of long duration, which allow the focal components to be disentangled from any generalised defects which coexist.

In Chapter 2 the complex problems of the focal significance of psychological symptoms will be dealt with in detail. Here, those which emerge with fair consistency after lesions of different parts of the brain will be described in summary form. Neurological defects are in general more reliable than psychological symptoms in pointing to the site of focal pathology, and these too will be included. The content of focal epileptic seizures, as discussed on pp. 215 to 218, provides additional information which must also be taken into account.

In general all focal signs and symptoms serve only to indicate the site of likely pathology, and are of relatively little value in suggesting the nature of the lesion.

Frontal Lobe

Frontal lesions may confer distinctive changes of disposition and temperament subsumed under the term 'change of personality'. Most characteristic is disinhibition, with expansive over-familiarity, tactlessness, overtalkativeness, childish excitement ('moria') or prankish joking and punning ('Witzelsucht'). Social and ethical control may be diminished, with lack of concern for the future and for the consequence of actions. Sexual indiscretions and petty misdemeanours may occur, or gross errors of judgement with regard to financial and interpersonal matters. Sometimes there is marked indifference, even callous unconcern for the feelings of others, equally lack of anxiety and insight on the part of the patient into his own condition. Elevation of mood is often seen, mainly as an empty and fatuous euphoria rather than as a true elation which communicates itself to the observer. In other cases the principal changes are lack of initiative, aspontaneity, and profound slowing of psychomotor activity, particularly with frontal lobe tumours. This may progress to a state of extreme aspontaneity which can amount virtually to stupor.

Concentration, attention and ability to carry out planned activity are impaired by these changes, but performance on tests of formal intelligence is often surprisingly well preserved once the patient's cooperation has been secured. Even with sharply circumscribed frontal lesions, however, the overall picture may at first sight strongly resemble a generalised dementing process. The hazards of misdiagnosis are increased by the 'silent' nature of frontal lobe lesions, which can allow them to grow large before declaring themselves with neurological signs.

When frontal lesions encroach upon the motor cortex or deep projections there will be contralateral spastic paresis, usually seen earliest in the face and more obvious on voluntary movement than emotional expression. Paresis may be extremely slight, and show only as slowness of repeated movements or falling away of the outstretched arm. A grasp reflex may be the only definite sign. Firmer evidence may be found in hyperactive tendon reflexes and a positive Babinski response. Characteristic decomposition of gait may be seen, with trunk ataxia or awkward postures.

Lesions affecting the orbital part of the frontal lobes may be associated with the 'forced utilisation' of objects presented to the patient, as described on p. 90. This appears to be an extension of the more commonly observed forced grasping. Posterior lesions of the dominant lobe may produce a primary motor dysphasia, a motor agraphia, or an apraxia of the face and tongue. Ipsilateral optic atrophy or anosmia may result from orbital lesions of the lobe, the latter being commonly overlooked in clinical examination. Sphincteric incontinence may occur surprisingly early in view of the reasonable preservation of intellect, and is a valuable added indication.

Parietal Lobes

Parietal lobe lesions are associated with a rather bewildering variety of complex cognitive disturbances, including defects of language and number sense, defective appreciation of external space, and disorders of the body image. Where some are concerned it is uncertain how far the lesions of the parietal lobe are alone responsible, or how far adjacent lesions in the temporal and occipital lobes contribute to the total picture. These matters are dealt with in Chapter 2, but the following is presented as a brief clinical guide.

Lesions of either parietal lobe may result in visuospatial difficulties and topographical disorientation. Visuospatial difficulties are most readily revealed by asking the patient to copy simple drawings or construct patterns from coloured blocks or matchsticks ('visuospatial agnosia', 'constructional dyspraxia'). Defective performance is seen more commonly with lesions of the non-dominant than dominant lobe but may occur with either. Difficulty in locating objects in space, or in describing the relationships between different objects by vision alone, may also be observed. Topographical disorientation is revealed by difficulty in learning or remembering the way about, with the result that the patient mislocates his bed in the ward, fails to find the bathroom, or loses himself even in familiar surroundings.

Dominant parietal lobe lesions are associated with various forms of dysphasia, primary motor dysphasia being most in evidence with anterior lesions and primary sensory dysphasia with posterior lesions. The latter may include alexia in association with agraphia. Motor apraxia similarly accompanies dominant parietal lobe lesions, and usually affects the limbs of both sides of the body. Various components of Gerstmann's syndrome may be seen, namely finger agnosia, dyscalculia, right-left disorientation and agraphia. The syndrome is rarely seen in its entirety, and individual components often occur along with other parietal lobe symptoms. Bilateral tactile agnosia is occasionally seen, and various forms of visual agnosia when the lesion lies posteriorly in the parieto-occipital region.

Non-dominant parietal lobe lesions may produce disturbed appreciation of the body image and of external space, particularly involving the contralateral side. The left limbs may fail to be recognised, or may be disowned by the patient. If paralysed or hemi-anaesthetic the disability may be ignored or refuted ('anosognosia'), a part of the body may be felt to be absent ('hemisomatognosia'), or in rare cases there may be phantom reduplication of body parts. Neglect of the left half of external space may show in the omission of left-sided details when drawings are copied, or in the crowding of writing into the right-hand part of the paper. Left-hand turnings may be overlooked when finding the way about. 'Dressing dyspraxia' consists of difficulty in inserting limbs into garments or putting garments over the head. In addition to visuospatial agnosia there may be a marked defect of the recognition of faces ('prosopagnosia') when the lesion is posterior and involves the occipital lobe.

Neurological signs indicative of a parietal lobe lesion include cortical sensory loss and the phenomena of extinction and inattention. Cortical sensory loss consists not of analgesia but of a more complex impairment of sensation and difficulty with discrimination; objects cannot be identified by palpation ('astereognosis'), figures written on the hand cannot be named ('agraphaesthesia'), two point discrimination is impaired, and the localisation of sensory stimuli is inaccurate. Sensory extinction is shown when two parts of the body are lightly touched simultaneously and that on the side contralateral to the lesion is not perceived. Visual inattention may be demonstrated by asking the patient to point to moving objects in both half fields of vision; when two objects move simultaneously that in the contralateral half field is ignored.

Sensory defects are often accompanied by evidence of mild hemiparesis in the limbs contralateral to the lesion. Deep lesions affecting the optic radiation produce a contralateral homonymous hemianopia, usually more fully developed in the lower than the upper quadrants.

Temporal Lobes

Lesions restricted to the poles of the temporal lobes can be entirely asymptomatic. More commonly, however, temporal lobe lesions are associated with considerable disturbance of intellectual functioning, the dominant more so than the non-dominant.

Dominant temporal lesions may produce language difficulties alone. This is typically a severe sensory dysphasia resulting sometimes in jargon productions. More posterior lesions on the dominant side may also impair visual aspects of language in the form of alexia and agraphia. Parietal lobe symptomatology may then also appear in the form of motor apraxia, constructional apraxia, and aspects of the Gerstmann syndrome.

Non-dominant temporal lobe lesions may show a paucity of symptoms and signs. Sometimes, however, visuospatial difficulties may be much in evidence, also prosopagnosia and hemisomatognosia.

Bilateral lesions of the medial temporal lobe structures can produce amnesic syndromes of great severity and virtually uncontaminated by other intellectual disturbances (p. 26). Unilateral temporal lobe lesions may produce a more restricted disturbance of memory for certain classes of material along with related perceptual defects, but this is rarely a spontaneous complaint and is usually revealed only by special testing. Lesions on the dominant side impair the learning and retention of verbal material even in the absence of overt dysphasia. Non-dominant lesions impair the learning and retention of non-verbal patterned stimuli, such as music, or faces and drawings to which a name cannot be attached.

Personality disturbances identical with those accompanying frontal lesions may occur, but will more commonly be associated with intellectual and neurological defects. Chronic temporal lobe lesions are notorious for their association with severe disturbance of personality, and particularly with emotional instability and aggressive misconduct. Similarly lesions of the temporal lobe appear to carry an increased risk of psychotic disturbances akin to schizophrenia (p. 75). Depersonalisation may be prominent, also disturbance of sexual function. Epileptic phenomena are common with temporal lobe lesions, and are important for localisation since their form is characteristic (p. 216).

The most reliable neurological sign of deep temporal lobe lesions is a contralateral homonymous upper quadrantic visual field defect, caused by interruption of the visual radiation in the central white matter. This sign alone may occasionally betray the presence of a temporal lobe lesion in a dementing process which has been attributed to diffuse brain damage. Deep lesions may likewise result in a mild contralateral hemiparesis or sensory loss due to encroachment upon fibres in the corona radiata. Equilibrium and hearing are not impaired, even by extensive unilateral lesions of the temporal neocortex.

Occipital Lobes

Occipital lobe lesions lack well-established focal symptomatology other than in the field of vision.

Complex disturbances of visual recognition characterise lesions of the parastriate areas. Agnosia for written or printed material ('alexia without agraphia'), colour agnosia, and the rare 'visual object agnosia' are characteristic of dominant occipital or occipito-temporal lesions. In 'simultanagnosia' the individual elements of a scene or picture can be perceived but meaning cannot be derived from the whole. Visuospatial agnosia occurs more commonly from non-dominant than from dominant occipito-parietal lesions. Prosopagnosia is rather characteristic of non-dominant lesions, likewise metamorphopsia in which the appearance of objects is distorted. Complex visual hallucinations are said to occur more commonly from non-dominant than dominant occipital lesions.

Lesions of the striate cortex produce homonymous defects in the opposite half-field of vision. Extensive bilateral lesions may produce cortical blindness, distinguished from peripheral blindness by the normal appearance of the optic fundi and the preservation of pupillary light reflexes.

The Corpus Callosum

Expanding corpus callosum lesions typically extend laterally into adjacent parts of the hemispheres, producing a picture of severe and rapid intellectual deterioration along with changes specific to the lobes involved. Anterior tumours produce marked frontal lobe disturbance, often with extreme psychomotor retardation and aspontaneity. Dysphasia, apraxia and asymmetrical pyramidal signs are common along with other evidence of parietal lobe disorder. Involvement of the diencephalic structures leads to somnolence, stupor and akinesis. Bizarre postural motor abnormalities may strongly resemble the pictures seen in catatonia. Disruption of communication between the two hemispheres may result in lack of access of the non-dominant hemisphere to the speech mechanisms in the dominant hemisphere; there will then be left-sided apraxia to verbal commands, with agraphia and astereognosis in the left hand (Geschwind and Kaplan, 1962). Lesions restricted to the posterior part, in association with lesions of the left occipital lobe, may result in dyslexia (without agraphia) for similar reasons (Geschwind, 1962).

The Diencephalon and Brain Stem

The most characteristic symptoms of lesions in the deep midline structures of the brain are amnesia of the Korsakoff type and hypersomnia. These may stand out against a background of progressive intellectual deterioration or present initially as the sole disturbance. Amnesia, which is strikingly more marked for recent than remote events, and sometimes accompanied by confabulation, is characteristic of lesions in the neighbourhood of the third ventricle, aqueduct, and posterior hypothalamus. Somnolence and hypersomnia suggest a lesion of the posterior diencephalon and upper mid-brain. It may fluctuate in intensity, or occur in brief attacks suggestive of narcolepsy. Sometimes it may progress to states of profound stupor or coma. 'Akinetic mutism' ('coma vigil') is a characteristic syndrome in which the patient lies immobile and mute, though the eyes may be open and follow moving objects (p. 197).

Generalised intellectual deterioration may occur by virtue of raised intracranial pressure consequent upon obstruction of cerebrospinal fluid circulation. Some focal lesions may, however, produce rapidly progressive dementia without such generalised disturbance, particularly those which originate within the thalamus. Features closely akin to those seen with frontal lesions may occur with diencephalic and brain stem lesions—disinhibition, indifference, carelessness and fatuous euphoria. Insight into the changes is said to be better preserved than with the equivalent pictures produced by frontal lobe lesions. Swings of mood and sudden outbursts of violent emotion are also held to be characteristic. Bilateral lesions within the upper brain stem and diencephalon, seen for example with pseudobulbar palsy, are associated with extreme emotional lability and 'emotional incontinence'. The patient laughs or cries excessively in response to trivial stimuli, yet if questioned he denies experiencing the degree of emotion he displays, and may well be distressed at his inability to control the response.

Focal neurological signs may be surprisingly absent in the early stages of progressive diencephalic lesions. Raised intracranial pressure with headache and papilloedema are found with the great majority of obstructive lesions, though even here mental symptoms may be severe before this develops. Visual field defects will betray lesions such as craniopharyngiomas which grow upwards from the sella turcica and compress the optic chiasma. However, the patient who has considerable intellectual loss may make no spontaneous complaint of the visual field disturbance, and testing can sometimes be impossible.

Disturbance of hypothalamic function may result in polydypsia, polyuria, obesity or elevation of temperature. Amenorrhoea or impotence may occur in the adult, delayed or precocious sexual development in the child. Involvement of the pituitary gland will result in a wide variety of endocrine changes, which may however be overlooked for a time when psychiatric disturbance is prominent.

Thalamic lesions cause the sensory disturbances characteristic of parietal lobe lesions, with in addition hypalgesia or analgesia to painful stimuli. Brainstem lesions cause characteristic cranial nerve palsies, along with evidence of dense long-tract motor and sensory disturbances.

Chapter 2. Symptoms and Syndromes with Regional Affiliations

Certain psychological manifestations deserve particular attention because they are sometimes found in association with relatively circumscribed brain lesions. In every case they can also be seen with disease processes which involve the brain diffusely or disturb its functions widely, so that their presence is not by any means a certain indication of a single localised lesion. Nevertheless when they emerge as isolated defects, or stand out prominently against a background of mild impairment of other cerebral functions, they command especial care in the search for focal pathology.

What we ask of psychological symptoms as guides to focal pathology must be considerably less than we expect of neurological signs. The latter will often point with fair precision to the site of the lesion, but psychological symptoms can often tell us little more than that the pathology is unlikely to be diffuse. The careful analysis of dysphasia or of visual perceptual defects may take us some way towards assessing the site of the lesion, but even here we must usually be content with rather broad indications of the areas of brain which fail to function. Thus with rare exceptions there remains uncertainty about the 'regional' as opposed to the 'focal' implications of most of the syndromes considered in this chapter. Some of them will be found to owe their origin, in different patients, to focal lesions in a variety of sites.

The majority of focal psychological symptoms represent defects of cognitive functioning. Less can be said with certainty about the focal significance of emotional, motivational, or 'personality' abnormalities. 'Psychotic' symptoms have in particular eluded ties to focal brain pathology despite some extensive investigations, and here other determinants are known to be very much more important. Nevertheless certain non-cognitive disorders and even perhaps some psychotic manifestations do show interesting regional affiliations, and these will also be briefly reviewed.

Strictly focal brain damage or dysfunction is rare, except when produced purposely by operations on the brain. In naturally occurring disease we see merely a focal *emphasis* in pathology, with effects which are then compounded by the effects of damage elsewhere. Focal head injury, for example, is usually accompanied by brain damage remote from the site of principal destruction; epileptic disturbances which originate focally disrupt other cerebral systems more or less widely; and circumscribed tumours produce distant effects by distortion of brain tissue, vascular complications or raised intracranial pressure. It is not surprising therefore that knowledge of regional cerebral disorder has been slow to accumulate and raises many areas of controversy. Evidence from work with animals has given important and sometimes essential leads, but even so has obvious limitations. It has also sometimes produced results which have appeared directly to undermine the supposition that discrete lesions can produce discrete defects of function. Thus both laboratory work and clinical observation have taken part in determining the swings of the pendulum between holistic and atomistic theories of brain function which have characterised progress during the past 100 years.

Historical Development

Holistic views of brain function fitted well with early humoral theories of the mind and appeared to be upheld by the early experiments of Flourens (1824) in the first part of the 19th century. It was shown that piecemeal removal of the pigeon's cerebral hemispheres produced a decline in many abilities, so that by the time they were blind the birds were also unable to learn. In the 20th century the influential work of Lashley (1929) again led to an holistic orientation, this time specifically in relation to the acquisition of new knowledge. In tests of maze learning in rats it was shown that the size but not the location of the lesion was related to impairment of learning. Lashley's law of mass action expressed the view that learning ability is determined by the total mass of normally functioning cortex, and his law of equipotentiality that no part could be considered prepotent in this regard. In the clinical field Goldstein (1939) was the most determined antagonist of mosaic theories of brain function, claiming that clinical reporting often highlighted the rare and exceptional in pointing to focal functions, and that the techniques of clinical examination had led to spurious findings where many clinico-pathological correlations are concerned.

Radically opposite views have meanwhile flourished alongside these opinions. Strict localisationist views gained impetus in the early 19th century from the widespread credibility accorded to Gall. Though a leading neuroanatomist, he propounded the doctrines of phrenology, which ultimately reached the fantastic lengths of claiming cerebral centres for such functions as 'hope', 'patriotism' and 'attraction to wine'. The reaction and counter-reaction to such excesses has perhaps continued to influence the building of theories where definitive information is lacking. As recently as 1937, Kleist was still attempting elaborate diagrams which partitioned functions such as 'skills', 'efficiency of thought', and 'personal and social ego' to discrete parts of the cerebral cortex.

Focal representation of function has of course been firmly established for basic sensory and motor functions. Early notable observations were those of Hughlings Jackson (1869) who saw that motor seizures developed on the side opposite the cerebral lesion, and Fritsch and Hitzig (1870) who showed that discrete motor movements followed discrete stimulation of the cortex. Knowledge of the cerebral representation of such 'lower level' functions is now extensive, though even here it is important to realise the immense complexities and intricacies which have been found to be involved.

The symbolic functions of language were also recognised at an early stage to depend on circumscribed regions of the brain. Dax (1836) and Broca (1861) noted that articulated speech was disturbed by left posterior frontal pathology, and shortly thereafter Wernicke (1874) found disturbance of comprehension of speech with a left superior temporal lesion. Since this time there has been a steady though far from smooth accumulation of evidence concerning the cerebral representation of language and of other symbolic 'gnostic' functions. Unfortunately much of this initially depended upon uncritical compilations of case material, and at the turn of the century the 'diagram makers' were frequently in confusion. Hughlings Jackson's theory of *levels* of functional organisation within the nervous system, and the issue of symptoms by a process of dissolution of such levels, received little attention at the time. Progress

even now remains bedevilled by the complexities of the issues involved in analysing impairment of higher cognitive functions, quite apart from the difficulty of finding suitable case material on which detailed pathological observations can be made.

Luria (1964) has set forth some of the problems in the way of clearer understanding, and the fallacies which have led to error both in the hands of over-localisers and the hands of those who hold an over-holistic view. His arguments have such general significance that they will be dealt with in some detail. Luria points out that even so elementary a process as the knee jerk has in fact a complex structure which can be affected by lesions at many points in a chain. Even simple visual recognition requires eye movements to investigate the object, the registration of its most informative signs, and the participation of language to relate it to a certain class. More complex mental functions will have a correspondingly more complex structure, involving many functional systems and many hierarchically arranged localisations within the nervous system. Destruction of any one of many links may impair performance, and it is therefore not surprising that the symptoms of defect may follow from lesions at very different points in the brain. Observations which remain restricted to the level of gross functional defects will therefore tend towards holistic views of brain function. But careful qualitative analysis of the nature of the defects may still allow localisation, because the particular way in which the function is disturbed will depend upon which particular link is broken. The accomplishment of writing, for example, may be disturbed in a number of ways and by several factors, with a net result superficially the same but in fact with a variety of underlying disturbances of function. Agraphia may prove to be due to defective acoustic analysis of speech, in which case consonants close to each other in sound will be especially confused and copying of a clear visual image of well known words will be relatively preserved (left temporal lesion); or the patient may handle separate sounds well but easily lose the correct ordering of sequences (pre-motor lesion); or the essential difficulties may lie in the visuospatial analysis of letters and the motor act of writing (parieto-occipital lesion). Here then the detailed analysis of the symptom may still allow disturbance of a complex mental function to be used in local diagnosis.

A related task is to search for common factors in a series of seemingly disparate symptoms, since a single functional defect may have issue in many forms. A left parietal lesion may disturb orientation in space and numerical schemes together, which at first sight appear to be very different functions. But Luria suggests that detailed analysis shows a common factor in that both represent disturbance of the organisation of elements into simultaneous spatially oriented schemes.

All such analyses are of course harder because strictly focal damage is rarely seen, and usually the lesion touches on several zones and damages several overlapping systems together. Moreover the plasticity of organisation is such that the structure of a psychological function may vary with the particular mental task involved; for example the recall of one series may utilise a mnemonic logical path, and the recall of another a path based on visual images.

Finally Luria underlines Hughlings Jackson's important warning that a clear distinction must always be maintained between the localisation of the pathology accounting for symptoms, and the localisation of the functions whose disturbance the symptoms represent. The undisturbed function may emanate from the central nervous system in a much more complex manner and may have a completely different organisation.

In the field of new learning, Lashley's views of mass action and equipotentiality in rats have had to be decisively modified for man. Whilst the cortex as a whole is undoubtedly involved in learning and in the storage of information, lesions in different parts do not have equivalent effects. Left temporal lesions impair verbal learning, and right temporal lesions non-verbal learning to a special extent. And highly discrete lesions in the hypothalamic-diencephalic region, or damage restricted to the hippocampal zones, may virtually abolish new learning in any modality. Thus we now have clear evidence that the proper organisation of memory functions involves to some considerable degree discrete systems within the brain.

The search for focal defects has also been extended into matters other than cognitive function. In animals focal brain lesions can lead to dramatic changes of temperament—rage reactions or placidity—depending on the site of the lesion. In the split-brain monkey Downer (1962) has shown that the emotional disposition can vary according to the hemisphere which processes information; visual information fed to an amygdalectomised hemisphere elicits a mild response, whereas in the same animal information fed to the intact hemisphere meets with the animal's usual ferocity. Papez (1937) has proposed that the limbic system constitutes an essential mechanism for the elaboration of emotional experience and emotional expression, and MacLean (1955) has reviewed the evidence suggesting that this applies to man as well as to lower animals.

With special parts of the brain involved in cognitive functions and emotional regulation, what of higher functions still such as 'personality' and social behaviour? Certainly in monkeys interesting results can follow focal extirpations of brain tissue. Removal of the temporal lobes leads not only to placidity, but also to strong oral tendencies in examining available objects, tendencies to attend and react to every visual stimulus, and an increase in sexual behaviour (Klüver and Bucy, 1939). The human counterpart of such a syndrome has been reported in certain patients (Pilleri, 1966; Marlowe et al., 1975; Lilly et al., 1983). Cingulectomy in monkeys leads to inquisitiveness, loss of shyness for man, and loss of 'social conscience' in interaction with other monkeys (Ward, 1948; Glees et al., 1950). In man the hope for further discoveries has been spurred on by the observation of frontal lobe deficits which can clearly involve profound disturbance of aspects of personality and social behaviour. The temporal lobe has also frequently come under suspicion, especially in view of the personality disturbances which may accompany epilepsy arising within the temporal lobes (p. 231).

However, systematic attempts to investigate the relationship between location of brain damage and such matters as personality or social behaviour have so far given disappointing results. In view of the foregoing discussion this should perhaps not be surprising, since the complexity of structure of such higher order functions must indeed be immense. Chapman and Wolff (1959) for example carried out an exceedingly thorough survey of the life patterns and behaviour of patients in whom circumscribed cortical excisions had been performed. Four categories of 'highest integrative function' were measured by detailed interview and rating procedures. They comprised: the capacity to express needs, appetites and drives, such as ability to express affect, to interact with the environment and to engage in purposive activity; the mechanisms for goal achievement, including learning, memory and the categorisation of information; the capacity to initiate, organise and maintain appropriate adaptive reactions, as evidenced by the deployment of psychological defence mechanisms such as projection and denial; and the capacity to maintain organisation during stress and to recover promptly from its effects. For a given amount of tissue loss, impairment was less in those who premorbidly had shown a high order of adaptive versatility, but as the amount of tissue loss increased this individual variation was seen to a diminishing extent. Overall the degree of impairment in such functions was directly related to the mass of cerebral cortex which had been lost, but was entirely without regard to side or site.

Chapman and Wolff concluded that where highest level integrative functions were concerned, impairment due to brain damage is likely to be related to the total number of neurones lost but not to the area from which the loss occurs. Other evidence indicated that it was immaterial whether the loss was aggregated in one place or distributed diffusely throughout the hemispheres. The verdict therefore remains 'unproven'. It remains possible that with less ambitious design, and a closer focusing on predetermined areas of 'higher function', some focal effects may yet emerge to supplement what we already know about the frontal lobes.

Finally the most ambitious development is to carry the debate into the field of mental pathologies, such as affective disorders and schizophrenia. Focal biochemical pathology is suspected in some depressive illnesses (Bourne et al., 1968; Pare et al., 1969), and schizophrenia appears to show a special relationship with temporal lobe disturbance. This last development is discussed at the end of the present chapter.

Disorder of Memory

Memory disorder is a symptom of the utmost importance in psychiatric practice, in that it is often the decisive clinical feature which indicates the presence of underlying cerebral disease. It is, in fact, one of the most sensitive indicators of brain damage or dysfunction, regardless of the ultimate pathology.

Organic amnesias can be divided into two broad categories, which are not mutually exclusive—those due to focal and those due to diffuse cerebral disorder. In the former amnesic defects can result from lesions in highly discrete parts of the brain and stand out against the relative preservation of other cognitive functions. In the latter, amnesic defects form an integral part of acute or chronic generalised organic reactions but may nonetheless be for some time the most intrusive psychological symptom. It is possible that memory disorder in these two categories depends on different fundamental disturbances of the memory mechanisms of the brain, and this may to some extent be reflected in the detailed nature of the amnesic defects which are produced. In both, moreover, the form of memory loss is different from that seen in amnesias of psychogenic origin where

brain damage does not exist. Two aspects of memory disorder will therefore be considered below—first the cerebral systems which appear to be mainly involved, and then the psychological structure of common amnesic states.

CEREBRAL SYSTEMS INVOLVED IN MEMORY

The relationship between disorder of memory and cerebral pathology has repaid detailed study, and clinico-pathological correlations have here reached firmer ground than where most other psychological symptoms are concerned. This has been largely because many aspects of memory are amenable to objective measurement by simple testing procedures, and can often be studied in lower animals as well as in man himself. These are both features that are rarely encountered in symptoms and syndromes of key importance in psychiatry.

What we have learned in the clinical field, however, still leaves unanswered the more fundamental question of the mechanisms of memory storage itself. The various possibilities which have been considered must all remain highly speculative and unsatisfactory. Physiological theories which postulate changes in electrical activity of neurones and their interconnections serve to explain very short term storage, but for the establishment of durable memories there must be ability to withstand profound derangement of electrical activity as in anaesthesia, hypothermia or convulsions. Connectionist theories, which propose anatomical changes in synaptic relationships between cells, fail to explain why focal extirpation of brain tissue does not produce loss of detailed memory for particular past events (while paradoxically punctate stimulation of the brain may sometimes evoke specific recall of past experiences (Penfield, 1968)). The development of biochemical theories, which suggest changes in the synthesis of neurotransmitters, brain proteins or RNA as the basis for the encoding of memories, may perhaps ultimately offer more hope for an explanation if taken in conjunction with earlier theories (Richter, 1966; Russell, 1968; Squire and Schlapfer, 1981). The problems of coding for storage are, however, only less baffling than the possible mechanisms of recall, which can allow near-instantaneous retrieval of the required information from the past.

The two main regions of the brain which have emerged as specially significant in relation to amnesia are the hypothalamic-diencephalic region and the hippocampal apparatus. Damage to either of these relatively circumscribed areas can selectively impair the capacity to form durable records of experience. It is associated also with a variable retrograde gap for memories laid down before the damage occurred, whilst beyond this the great body of remote memories remains substantially intact. Thus although these are the sites where the smallest lesions can have the most devastating effect they do not represent the 'repositories' or storehouses of memories. They appear rather to be concerned with adding to the store and perhaps with retrieval from the store as will be considered further below. The whereabouts as well as the mechanism of memory storage remains unknown. Phylogenetic considerations point to the participation of the cerebral cortex in the storage of past experience, but no one part of it can be singled out as pre-eminent in this function.

Besides these parts of the brain, other neural systems must be implicated in the processes of remembering. We preserve in memory mainly those things towards which attention is directed, and the alerting mechanisms of the brain must therefore be involved. The emotional connotations of material can also influence its recall (Lishman, 1972, 1974; Master et al., 1983), and here the emotional apparatus of the brain must play a part. Other complex variables normally affect the detailed content of what is available for future recall, such as interest in the material perceived, its relevance, importance, and consistency with existing frames of reference for the subject (Bartlett, 1932; Edwards, 1942). These complexities can be carried even further by consideration of the highly individual determinants of specific amnesias as revealed by psychoanalytic study. Clearly therefore the clinico-pathological correlations outlined below reveal but a small part of the total mechanisms involved in remembering. They perhaps reveal something of the mechanisms which determine the distinction between memory for remote and recent events, but very little indeed about the neural basis which underlies other more complex features. Fortunately our appraisal of amnesia as a symptom in cerebral disease depends principally on the temporal sequence by which memories are impaired, and very little on higher order distinctions.

The Hypothalamic-Diencephalic System

Lesions in the posterior hypothalamus and nearby midline structures were the first to be firmly linked with amnesia. They constitute the principal pathological basis of Korsakoff's psychosis, and involve areas around the third ventricle, the periaqueductal grey matter, the upper brain stem, certain thalamic nuclei, and the posterior hypothalamus. The mamillary bodies along with the terminal portions of the fornices are nearly always affected, and certain publications reviewed by Brierley (1966) have suggested that damage confined almost exclusively to the mamillary bodies can account for the Korsakoff memory defect. Victor (1964), however, in a particularly careful study has suggested that lesions in the medial dorsal nuclei of the thalamus are of more critical importance and may in fact be crucial for the development of amnesic symptoms in Korsakoff's psychosis. The importance of the thalamus has been reinforced by the remarkable example of patient 'NA', who became severely amnesic after a stab wound from a miniature fencing foil; CT scans showed damage apparently restricted to the left dorsal thalamus, in a region corresponding to the dorsomedial nucleus (Squire and Moore, 1979). Debate continues, nonetheless, over the relative importance of the mamillary bodies and the thalamic nuclei in Korsakoff patients, or indeed whether both must be involved together (Mair et al., 1979).

The common cause for lesions in this situation is thiamine deficiency, the amnesic difficulties developing as a sequel to Wernicke's encephalopathy (p. 490). Chronic alcoholism is the usual prelude to the vitamin deficiency, but other established causes include carcinoma of the stomach, pregnancy, severe malnutrition, or persistent vomiting from any cause.

Some authorities reserve the term 'Korsakoff's psychosis' for cases with such an aetiology, while others employ it more widely to include the similar amnesic states which may follow other forms of damage to the same brain regions. Tumours in the neighbourhood of the hypothalamus and third ventricle may produce a closely similar picture (p. 195). Subarachnoid haemorrhage may occasionally be followed by a pronounced amnesic syndrome, due to local haemorrhage or organisation of the clot in the basal regions of the brain (p. 334). In the severe stages of tuberculous meningitis a picture closely similar to Korsakoff's psychosis may be witnessed over many weeks (p. 309). With recovery normal memory function gradually returns, leaving only an amnesic gap for the acute phase of the illness and a retrograde amnesia for a variable period before it (Williams and Smith, 1954). The characteristic pathology of tuberculous meningitis in the amnesic phase is an inflammatory process with organisation of exudate, largely limited to the anterior basal cisterns of the brain and involving the mamillary region and the floor of the third ventricle. There is evidence to suggest that these regions have escaped the main impact of the infective process in those few cases where memory difficulties do not appear.

The Hippocampal System

Long after the description of Korsakoff's pyschosis, the opportunity arose to study an amnesic syndrome closely similar in phenomenology to that of Korsakoff's defect, but which surprisingly stems from lesions in quite different parts of the brain. This results from bilateral lesions of the hippocampus and hippocampal gyrus, which lie on the inferomedial margins of the temporal lobes. That such regions should be closely implicated in amnesia is all the more remarkable in that the hippocampal zones are usually free from damage in the typical case of Korsakoff's psychosis. The responsible lesions can be demarcated with some precision because the syndrome was first fully recognised after surgical extirpation of brain tissue for the relief of psychotic illness and epilepsy (Scoville, 1954; Scoville and Milner, 1957).

Lesions of the temporal neocortex are without effect on memory, similarly damage restricted to the uncus and amygdaloid region of the archipallium. It is essential that the lesions should extend far enough posteriorly to damage portions of the hippocampus and hippocampal gyrus, and the extent of their removal then appears to be roughly proportional to the severity of the memory disorder (Milner, 1966). It is also fairly certain that bilateral lesions are required before global amnesia will appear and persist. When amnesic symptoms have followed unilateral temporal lobe resection there has usually been evidence that the remaining hippocampal zone was already defective. Thus in occasional patients global amnesia has followed unilateral temporal lobectomy, but only when bilateral temporal lobe damage has been suspected. Serafetinides and Falconer (1962a) found that mild subjective forgetfulness sometimes followed unilateral right lobectomy, but in all such cases there was evidence of a post-operative spike discharging focus at the opposite temporal lobe, indicating dysfunction if not a lesion there.

These clear examples produced by circumscribed surgical lesions almost certainly reveal the mechanism responsible for other naturally occurring amnesic states. Cerebrovascular accidents may sometimes be followed by the acute onset of similar amnesic difficulties, as in the patient described by Victor et al. (1961) who suffered occlusion of each posterior cerebral artery in turn, and at autopsy was found to have lesions in the inferomedial portions of each temporal lobe. Two years intervened between the two strokes and it was only after the second episode that the amnesic syndrome appeared. Glees and Griffith (1952) recorded a patient with sudden onset of dementia in whom amnesic symptoms figured very prominently, and who at autopsy showed cystic degeneration, consistent with old infarction, in the medial temporal lobe structures. The enduring memory difficulties which follow some cases of encephalitis (Rose and Symonds, 1960) may also depend upon pathology in this distribution, since encephalitis due to the herpes simplex virus is known to have a predilection for the 'limbic lobe' which includes the hippocampus and the hippocampal gyrus (Fields and Blattner, 1958; Brierley et al., 1960). Evidence from epilepsy similarly points to the importance of the hippocampal areas for memory, since these are the regions implicated in psychomotor seizures where amnesia constitutes an essential feature of the attacks.

Other Clinico-Pathological Correlations

It is tempting to see a unitary mechanism for memory functions in the two brain regions described above. However, the fornix bundles, which provide the main connection between the hippocampi and the hypothalamic structures, can be cut bilaterally without disturbing memory (Dott, 1938; Cairns and Mosberg, 1951), and the occasional case in which amnesia has followed (Sweet et al., 1959) cannot be exonerated from damage elsewhere.

With regard to the neocortex, difficulty with memory appears to be related to size rather than locus of cortical lesions (McFie and Piercy, 1952; Chapman and Wolff, 1959), but it is difficult to obtain firm evidence because damage needs to be widespread before generalised memory impairment results. The accompanying intellectual disturbance then hampers careful analysis of the memory disorder.

The frontal lobes have sometimes been highlighted where memory functions are concerned. Operations on the frontal lobes rarely produce enduring memory disorders, though in the early post-operative period there may be a striking defect of retention of current experience together with patchy retrograde amnesia (Klein, 1952; Kral and Durost, 1953). Whitty and Lewin (1960) have described a transient memory disorder involving especially the temporal sequence of events following limited ablations of the

e frontal
amnesic
rs of the
écaen and
ecorded by
etrical areas
, strategically
res from the
ain. However,
has remained
something ...

Special parts of t... to be related to memory for special types of ex... ence as displayed in verbal, visuospatial or motor learning, though it remains uncertain how far defects in such individual functions should be regarded as failures of memory rather than defects in perception or in the categorisation of ideas. A temporal lobe (hippocampal) lesion in the hemisphere dominant for speech impairs the learning and retention of verbal material, resulting for example in forgetfulness for names, for material read in newspapers or material heard in lectures. Conversely, patients with non-dominant temporal lobe lesions are impaired in the memorising of matters which cannot be categorised in words, such as tunes, faces, and meaningless drawings (Milner, 1966). Iversen (1977) reviews the considerable body of experimental data now available on such distinctions between left and right hemisphere lesions. These specific disorders are, however, relatively trivial, often requiring special testing for their detection, and do not affect the recall of events.

Some forms of dysphasia, apraxia or agnosia can be regarded as 'limited amnesias' consequent upon focal cortical damage, but as their manifestations are so specific they are best considered quite separately from amnesia.

THE CLINICAL PICTURE IN AMNESIA

The detailed structure of amnesic states has been most comprehensively studied in patients who are relatively free from other intellectual impairments, namely in patients with focal lesions in the hypothalamic-diencephalic or hippocampal systems. This has provided important clinical guides which help in distinguishing them from amnesia due to diffuse brain damage and from psychogenic ammesia. In clinical practice a complex admixture of causes will sometimes be seen, but first the classical pictures may be outlined.

For purposes of clinical description a somewhat arbitrary division is made into 'immediate', 'recent' and 'remote' memory. The *immediate memory span* (or 'ultra-short-term-memory') is reflected in the reproduction of material such as brief digit sequences which fall within the span of attention. It appears to represent the functioning of short-term storage mechanisms, which need not, even in normal circumstances, lead on to an enduring record. Clinically it provides evidence that registration is intact. *Recent memory* is reflected in ability to acquire and retain new knowledge ('current memorising', 'new learning') and requires a process of consolidation in addition to registration. Clinically it is assessed by noting ability to learn or retain material over short spans of time, usually by testing ability to repeat simple information after several minutes have elapsed. *Remote memory* is reflected in ability to recall information which has happened at a considerable distance in time, and certainly before the onset of the memory difficulties. It therefore represents a process of retrieval of material which has been held in long-term storage.

In everyday clinical practice it is convenient to employ the terms 'immediate', 'recent' and 'remote' as outlined just above. Unfortunately, however, considerable confusion can arise over some of the terms used in referring to memory mechanisms, and particularly when attempting to translate the experimental literature to clinical practice. 'Short-term memory', for example, is often used by psychologists as synonymous with immediate memory and often in medical practice as broadly congruent with recent memory.

An important division is recognised between short- and long-term memory mechanisms (STM and LTM respectively) both in animal and human experimental work. STM is also referred to as 'primary memory' and LTM as 'secondary memory'. Each has certain characteristics not shared by the other. Primary memory (STM) has a strictly limited capacity, being able to hold only a small number of unrelated items of information at a time. Decay from it is rapid when rehearsal is prevented. This is the aspect of memory tested by the digit span. The material held in primary memory is retained in a form closely tied to the qualities of the initial percepts (timbre, visual detail, precise verbal content, etc.); it is non-selective, and material can be reproduced from it without comprehension of the meaning. Subsequent entries to the system displace what is already there. Primary memory thus acts as a short-term back-up to perceptual experience, giving time for directive and selective attention to focus on what is meaningful and valuable for transfer into secondary memory.

Secondary memory (LTM) has very different properties. Material held in secondary memory is encoded mainly in semantic terms, i.e. in the form of meaningful concepts, and the primary qualities of the percepts involved become obscured. The result is a far more durable record. There is no known limit to the amount that can be stored. Secondary memory thus embraces both the recent and the remote memory of the usual clinical terminology.

Studies carried out both in normal subjects and in patients with amnesia have in general upheld these broad divisions, though complex interrelationships clearly exist between the two memory storage systems. Valuable reviews of more recent experimental work in the area are to be found in Baddeley (1976, 1984), Piercy (1977) and Cermak (1982).

Other terms in vogue include 'working memory', 'episodic memory' and 'semantic memory'. Working memory (Baddeley, 1976; Hitch, 1984) is an elaboration of primary memory as described above. It emphasises the role of short-term storage processes in other tasks such as problem-solving and comprehension, and recognises the existence of different subsystems dealing with temporary storage of specialised forms of material. The episodic-semantic distinction was introduced by Tulving (1972) and can have relevance in describing the detailed content of losses from the long-term memory store. Episodic memory refers to memory for specific, personally experienced events, usually in the form of temporally dated episodes; semantic memory is less personally oriented and deals essentially with stored knowledge of the world—words, labels, principles and the use of concepts.

Amnesia Due to Diencephalic and Hippocampal Lesions

There are many important respects in which the memory defects are closely similar, whether produced by lesions in the hypothalamic-diencephalic system or in the hippocampal regions. Thus perception is unimpaired, the immediate memory span is well preserved, and beyond a variable retrograde gap remote memories are substantially intact. The principal defect with both types of cerebral lesion emerges in the field of recent memory (current memorising) so that current events become less available for future recall. More recent detailed studies have served to qualify the view that all amnesic syndromes are identical, as described on p. 35, but in broad outline they can be described together as follows:

The preservation of the immediate memory span is a point of great importance clinically. Performance on a test of digit span is usually normal, and therefore will fail to reveal the existence even of a severe amnesic syndrome. The cases with bilateral temporal lobe resection, in whom good ability to cooperate is well preserved, have shown that in the absence of distraction such brief information can be retained for several minutes by dint of constant verbal rehearsal. Forgetting occurs, however, as soon as new activity demands a shift away from the task in hand. Moreover the learning of a list which slightly exceeds the normal digit span is markedly impaired, revealing the essential difficulty in getting new material into longer term store (Drachman and Arbit, 1966).

Recent memory is thus defective, and disorientation at least in time is almost universal. New learning is impaired, and that which is learned is forgotten more quickly than normal. Current memorising may in the most extreme cases be reduced to nil, so that as time goes by there is a continuing and extending anterograde amnesia. If recovery subsequently occurs, a dense and permanent gap will be left for the period of the illness. In less severe examples the problem shows as uncertainty about events which occurred minutes, days or weeks before, some being vaguely recalled and others having made no lasting impression at all. The retelling of simple stories is marked by gross omissions, incorrect juxtapositions and condensations of material. More careful testing shows that the problem affects all types of material, both verbal and non-verbal, such as word associations, drawings, and numbers, though the learning of new motor skills is relatively preserved.

It seems clear also that these defects of memory are to a large extent independent of the significance of the material involved. In mild cases it is sometimes found that memory for personal matters is better preserved than impersonal, and concrete matters better than abstract. Events of high emotional significance may sometimes appear to be remembered especially well. But within this framework there will usually be exceptions and surprising instances. Victor (1964), in a group of alcoholic Korsakoff patients, was unable to discern any factors which governed what was remembered and what was forgotten. A patient might fail to retain news of a bereavement which shocked him profoundly at the time, yet retain other matters of no significance whatever. The most severe case following bilateral hippocampal resection described by Milner (1966), 'H.M.', showed a failure of retention which cut across all factors of vividness or emotional significance: '. . . His initial emotional reaction may be intense, but it will be short-lived, since the incident provoking it will soon be forgotten. Thus, when informed of the death of his uncle, of whom he was very fond, he became extremely upset, but then appeared to forget the whole matter and from time to time thereafter would ask when his uncle was coming to visit them; each time, on hearing anew of his uncle's death, he would show the same intense dismay, with no sign of habituation'.

The *retrograde amnesia* often covers a period of months or years before the onset of the illness. This is usually dense for events just prior to the onset, but may be incomplete and patchy where the parts most distant in time are concerned. Time sense is characteristically disordered within the retrograde gap, with jumbling of the sequential ordering of those events which are recalled. In patients with Korsakoff's psychosis of alcoholic origin the retrograde amnesia is often of particularly long duration, extending even over several decades but showing a clear-cut temporal gradient. In discrete amnesic syndromes of other aetiologies the difficulties with recall seem rarely to exceed 2–4 years. The careful experimental studies which have addressed such issues are described on p. 34. Over the course of time many retrograde amnesias may shrink considerably, especially those seen after temporal lobe resection or when the pathology resolves as in tuberculous meningitis.

Disturbances of time sense and of the ordering of events is an outstanding characteristic, particularly in Korsakoff's psychosis. The patient may allocate some recent remembered event to the distant past, or bring up a past event as a recent happening. He may condense long periods of time or telescope repeated happenings into one. This affects recent memory and the period of the retrograde gap particularly, but may often be observed for more remote happenings as well. Talland (1965) suggests that the problem is due not to loss of appreciation of the flow of time, but rather to 'contextual isolation'; that is to say, events within the memory store appear to lose relationship with the totality of experience which surrounds them and in which they would normally be framed sequentially.

Remote memory, for matters beyond the retrograde gap, is much better preserved. Certainly long-established skills such as speaking, writing and calculation are unaffected. In the most severe amnesias after temporal lobe resection, remote events are often reported to be perfectly preserved, though in Korsakoff's psychosis the distinction is less clearcut and remote memories are often found to be somewhat impaired when opportunities arise to check them in detail. It is, of course very difficult to assess the competence of remote memory in any comprehensive way as discussed on p. 84.

Confabulation can be a striking feature in amnesias due to lesions of the hypothalamic-diencephalic structures, but does not seem to occur in those which follow bilateral hippocampal destruction. Traditionally it seems to have been greatly overstressed. When present it is commoner in the early stages than in the chronic phases of the disease, but it is certainly not universal (Victor *et al.*, 1971). It may appear as an evanescent phenomenon, or in rare cases it may last for many years.

Typically the patient gives a reasonably coherent but entirely false account of some recent event or experience, usually in relation to his own activities and often in response to suggestion by the examiner. Berlyne (1972), who provides a useful review of the subject, defines confabulation as 'a falsification of memory occurring in clear consciousness in association with an organically derived amnesia'. He upholds Bonhoeffer's early distinction between two varieties. The common 'momentary type' is brief in content, has reference to the recent past, and has to be provoked. The content can often be traced to a true memory which has become displaced in time or context. Much rarer is the 'fantastic type' in which a sustained and grandiose theme is elaborated, usually describing far-fetched adventures and experiences which clearly could not have taken place at any time. This form tends to occur spontaneously even without a provoking stimulus, and the content is often related to wish-fulfilment and the seeking of prestige.

There is probably not a unitary mechanism underlying the appearance of confabulation. It occurs in a setting of amnesic difficulties, but the memory disorder itself is not the complete explanation since it does not occur after bilateral hippocampal damage. Often, as already stated, it appears to represent fragments of genuine past experience which are dislocated in time. As Barbizet (1963) points out the patient who is unable to retain new material will tend to live on his stock of old memories, and will react to a new situation with what he has available. Sometimes confabulation may represent the residue of abnormal and confused experiences, including misidentifications and misinterpretations which occurred in the delirium of the initial Wernicke's encephalopathy. Thus it commonly sets in as clouding of consciousness is receding and persists thereafter while insight into the unreal nature of the delirious experiences is lacking. Others have sought to explain it in terms of unawareness or even motivated denial of the memory disorder, though this is likely to have only limited application. In many well-established and persistent cases a strong iatrogenic component can often be discerned, and the symptoms may then reflect in considerable measure the patient's suggestibility and desire to please.

Interesting evidence has also come forward to link confabulation to the presence of frontal lobe dysfunction in certain instances, particularly confabulation of the expansive or 'fantastic' type. Stuss *et al.* (1978) reported 5 patients in whom frontal deficits, superadded to their memory problems, appeared to account for their persistent and extraordinary confabulation. Kapur and Coughlan (1980) were able to chart the change from fantastic to momentary confabulations in a patient with left frontal damage following subarachonoid haemorrhage, and to show that this change was paralleled by improvement in performance on frontal lobe tests. It seems possible, therefore, that a special combination of deficits may be the essential prerequisite for the more elaborate and striking instances of confabulation in association with memory disorder.

Other cognitive functions are relatively well preserved, and the above amnesic defects are out of all proportion to other disturbances of intellect or behaviour. In particular the patients are alert, responsive to their environments, and without any evidence of clouding of consciousness. The amnesic states following temporal lobe resection are in all respects astonishingly pure, with no evidence of other cognitive defects and with good preservation of insight into the memory difficulties. Where pre-morbid personality has been sound there is no disturbance of social behaviour, of motivation or of emotional control.

In Korsakoff's psychosis, however, the situation is less straightforward. Other cognitive functions are usually found to be disordered when carefully examined (Talland, 1965; Zangwill, 1966; Victor *et al.*, 1971). There is often difficulty in sustaining mental activity, coupled with inflexibility of set and reduced capacity to shift attention from one task or train of thought to another. Thinking is usually stereotyped, perseverative and facile, with inadequacy of concept formation and defective ability to categorise. Butters and Cermak (1980) review the visuoperceptual impairments which are almost universally revealed when sought out by special tests, for example the digit symbol substitution test, hidden figures tasks, or tests requiring the sorting and discrimination of complex visual stimuli. All of these deficiencies are nonetheless grossly overshadowed by the prominence of the memory disorder. It is this disproportion between memory deficits and other cognitive deficits which is the hallmark of the condition.

Even superficial acquaintance with Korsakoff patients also reveals certain marked disturbances of personality. There is often a pronounced degree of apathy and loss of initiative, a bland or even fatuous disposition, and a tendency towards self neglect. Left to himself the patient occupies himself poorly, makes few demands or enquiries from those around, and obeys instructions in a passive and indifferent manner. A virtual disinterest in alcohol may represent a particularly striking change. Lack of insight is also almost universal; few Korsakoff patients appreciate that they are ill, and in those who do the gravity of their defects is minimised or explained away by facile rationalisations.

Thus while surgical resection of the medial temporal lobe structures produces clear evidence of circumscribed memory disorder, the neuropathological picture seen in Korsakoff's psychosis must account for a good deal more than the memory defects alone. In the latter the admixture of motivational and attitudinal defects probably accounts for the somewhat capricious nature of the memory disorder and leads to difficulties in attempts to analyse it with the same degree of precision.

Amnesia In Diffuse Cerebral Disorder

When associated with diffuse cerebral disorder, amnesia lacks the definitive structure described above. In addition it is often submerged among more widespread impairments of intellectual function, which make precise analysis of the memory defects extremely difficult if not impossible. In acute organic reactions some of the memory difficulties can be traced directly to impairment of consciousness and to the problems with attention and perception which result. In chronic organic reactions amnesia often represents no more than the earliest manifestation to come to light of general cognitive failure, in the sense that memory difficulties tend to be more readily spotted than other aspects of intellectual loss.

The general picture of the memory difficulties in acute organic reactions has been discussed on p. 11 and in chronic organic reactions on pp. 15 to 16. Certain distinctive features may, however, be summarised here for comparison with the picture in focal amnesic states.

The amnesic defects of diffuse brain disease are commonly global, affecting both recent and remote events to an obvious degree. Only rarely is there a clear-cut disturbance of recent memory along with a retrograde gap beyond which remote events are found to be well preserved.

Recent events may be the most obviously affected,

but in part at least this may be due to lack of interest and involvement in current experiences. Remote memories may appear to be relatively intact, but often prove in fact to be banal, stereotyped, and lacking in detail. On structured tests Wilson *et al.* (1981) were unable to demonstrate relative preservation of very remote memories in a group of patients with dementia. To a marked extent performance may be variable from one occasion to another, and capricious in that some events are easily recalled while others, apparently equally trivial or unimportant, are not. Indeed much of the difficulty can often be seen to lie in failure to sustain attention and concentration on the general task of directed recall.

It is on evidence such as this that the memory disorder in dementia is thought to reflect the diffuse pathology which exists throughout the cortex and elsewhere. Thus defects are attributed to losses within the memory store, and to disruption of the mechanisms of association and of access to the store which must follow upon reduction of interconnections between one cortical region and another. It is also clear that primary as well as secondary memory functions (p. 27) are implicated in dementia. The immediate memory span is impaired (Miller, 1973; Kaszniak *et al.*, 1979), unlike the situation in patients with circumscribed amnesic syndromes, and losses occur more rapidly from the primary memory store (Corkin, 1982; Kopelman, 1985a). It is interesting, however, that once material is acquired into secondary memory, forgetting rates have emerged as essentially normal (Corkin *et al.*, 1984; Kopelman, 1985a). Kopelman (1985b) reviews the evidence that depletion within the cholinergic system in dementia (p. 382) can account only partially for the memory disorder encountered in such patients.

However it would be premature to conclude that diffuse brain damage is always the complete explanation for the amnesic symptoms in dementing illnesses. In Alzheimer's disease there may be a relative intensity of pathological change in the hippocampal regions and mamillary bodies, and perhaps particularly when memory defects have been severe (Brierley, 1961; Corsellis, 1970). Conversely in Pick's disease the pathological process may spare in large degree the hippocampal regions, and here striking memory defects are rarely an early manifestation. It is therefore probable that when amnesia is pronounced in relation to other disabilities, the pathological changes may have progressed especially far in the cerebral systems which are particularly concerned with memory functions.

The common memory defects of old age may likewise depend in part on generalised and in part on focal degenerative changes. The pathological changes characteristic of ageing occur so frequently and so diffusely that clinico-pathological correlations are again hard to obtain, but sometimes the hippocampal regions have proved to be particularly affected (Gellerstedt, 1933). Busse (1962) has reported a relatively high incidence of electroencephalographic abnormalities in the region of the temporal lobes in elderly people, and more markedly so when learning ability is clearly deficient.

Similar uncertainty surrounds the pathogenesis of the amnesic phenomena which accompany closed head injury, as discussed on p. 136.

Psychogenic Amnesia

Psychogenic amnesia is commonly either dense and global, or alternatively restricted to certain circumscribed themes. When global it may involve the blotting out of long periods of past life, or even loss of personal identity, in a manner which is inconsistent with the general preservation of intellect. Amnesias of this severity do not occur in organic states unless at the same time there is abundant evidence of disturbance of consciousness or of severe disruption of cognitive functions generally. Inconsistencies in the account may also be noted. The subject with hysterical amnesia, for example, may insist that certain events could not have occurred during the period covered by the amnesic gap, while at the same time he is in no position to refute the proposition. More restricted psychogenic amnesias will usually be found to centre on a related constellation of events, or circumscribed areas such as the patient's work or marriage. Repeated episodes of psychogenic amnesia will frequently betray stereotyped themes or settings as with the patient described on p. 358.

Psychogenic amnesia is suspected when from the outset profound difficulty with recall of past events is coupled with normal ability to retain new information, or alternatively when there is total inability to retain information even for the few seconds required for the immediate memory span. A delayed curve of forgetting, which during the course of some days or weeks leads to complete extinction of important and significant material, is likewise sometimes seen in psychogenic but not in organic amnesias.

Special difficulties, of course, arise when psychogenic and organic aspects of memory loss occur together. Psychogenic factors may sometimes be obtrusive in amnesias which are clearly due primarily to brain damage, or an organic memory defect may come to be selectively reinforced or perpetuated on a psychogenic basis. Such difficulties are well illustrated by the celebrated dispute, reviewed by Zangwill (1967), which surrounded the Grünthal-Störring case for more than thirty years.

Memory Disorder in the Functional Psychoses

While it is traditionally held that memory disorder is the hallmark of organic brain damage there are indications that memory may sometimes be defective in the so-called 'functional' psychoses. At an anecdotal level it is not infrequently noted that patients lack detailed knowledge of key features of their abnormal beliefs and experiences on recovery from schizophrenia or severe affective disorder. Depression, moreover, has been shown to have a marked effect upon the selective processes normally operative in memory, leading to readier recall and more accurate recognition of unpleasant compared to pleasant material (Lloyd and Lishman, 1975; Dunbar and Lishman, 1984). Among normal subjects such selectivity operates in the reverse direction.

However detailed exploration of overall memory efficiency has rarely been undertaken in patients with functional psychiatric disorder. Cutting's (1979) findings are therefore of considerable potential interest. Groups of patients with acute schizophrenia, chronic schizophrenia and depressive illness were compared with normal subjects and patients with organic brain disease. Verbal learning and pattern recognition memory were separately assessed. The most prominent finding was that chronic schizophrenics were impaired on both types of task compared to normals, being often comparable in performance to patients with confusional states, dementia or Korsakoff's psychosis. The depressives were also impaired on both tasks but to a less marked degree. Acute schizophrenics were impaired on verbal memory alone. The differing patterns of results from one group to another, and details of the mode of patient selection, made it unlikely that coincidental brain damage or motivational factors could be the complete explanation. The possible effects of medication were harder to discount. Nevertheless such observations dictate caution in placing too great a reliance on tests of memory as a means of distinguishing between patients with functional and organic psychosyndromes. The situation in schizophrenia is fully discussed by Cutting (1985), including the possibility that there may be subtle but important difficulties over the employment of normal memory strategies.

Consolidation Defect, Encoding Deficit, or Failure of Inhibition?

The amnesic syndrome was for many years regarded as reflecting a failure of consolidation of new experience. Thus while the immediate memory span is normal, and old memories may remain substantially intact, current experience cannot gain proper access to the long-term store.

Evidence has, however, come forward to challenge this straightforward view, despite the appeal that it holds on first acquaintance. Careful testing has shown that the anterograde defects in amnesic patients are not so absolute as their behaviour in daily life or on conventional tests of learning would suggest. Milner (1966), for example, found that one patient showed a normal learning curve for a task of mirror drawing, even though on each test occasion he was completely unaware that he had done the task before. Tests of motor and other skills have also revealed learning and retention over considerable periods of time (Corkin, 1968; Starr and Phillips, 1970; Cohen and Squire, 1980). In terms of verbal memory a simple consolidation hypothesis is hard pressed to explain why some forms of cueing can improve performance, or why patients can achieve better results on recognition tests than when tested by free recall.

Butters and co-workers have stressed the role of *deficient encoding of information* in leading to the poor performance of amnesic subjects (Cermak and Butters, 1972; Butters and Cermak, 1980). This, it seems, may account in considerable degree for their failure to store material adequately. Thus Korsakoff patients have been found to rely unduly on simple acoustic encoding of the information they receive, rather than analysing it more deeply in terms of semantic meaning. Experiments have shown in addition that they use inappropriate strategies for the rehearsal and 'chunking' of information, all rendering it more susceptible to interference and rapid decay. When specifically instructed to attend to semantic features of the words presented, for example when forced to analyse them in terms of categories, attributes or meaning, the Korsakoff patient is found to achieve a somewhat improved performance on memory tasks.

Other approaches have emphasised difficulties at the level of retrieval, occasioned perhaps by failure to inhibit the intrusion of irrelevant material. This *'retrieval-interference' theory* holds that amnesics encode and store with reasonable efficiency, though the items in memory are poorly insulated from one another; in consequence they are in constant competition when retrieval is attempted. Support for such a mechanism came from experiments using the 'technique of partial information' (Warrington and Weiskrantz, 1968, 1970; Warrington, 1971):

A technique was elaborated for testing learning and retention by the presentation of graded clues. A word or picture may, for example, be prepared in several forms, ranging from a very indistinct image through progressively clearer forms until the word or picture emerges with full clarity. When such a graded series is presented to the subject, the point at which recognition occurs can be established; on subsequent presentations of the same material recognition occurs earlier in the course of the series if learning has occurred. With this technique it was shown that severely amnesic subjects, both with hippocampal damage and with Korsakoff defects, displayed learning and retention over considerable periods of time, when such was not the case with conventional test material. Moreover there was evidence that it was in the processes of retrieval that the technique of partial information allowed the amnesic subject to demonstrate that learning had occurred. Thus conventional tasks of rote learning could also emerge as unimpaired when recall was tested by this special means.

This evidence suggests that the amnesic patient is continuing to store information, but in such a manner that the usual processes of retrieval cannot demonstrate that this is so. Stored material is perhaps not inhibited or dissipated in the normal manner, and as a result intrudes disruptively into the processes of recall. Such a view would be consistent with other anomalous findings in amnesic patients, such as the tendency in verbal learning experiments for items learned in one list to re-occur as intrusion errors in subsequent lists ('proactive interference'). Retrieval by the technique of partial information could thus produce superior results because it restricts the choice of possible responses available to the subject, and helps him to eliminate incorrect false-positive responses. In essence, far from storing too little, the amnesic patient may store or retrieve too much.

This fascinating suggestion has come under criticism, as reviewed by Piercy (1977) and Butters and Cermak (1980). Warrington and Weiskrantz (1978) have themselves reported experiments which necessitate a re-casting of the theory in considerable degree. In particular it now seems difficult to uphold response competition as accounting directly for the amnesic patients' retrieval difficulties. And it can be shown that partial information techniques enhance recall in normal as well as in amnesic subjects, so the demonstration may be of a general effect, not of a special problem arising with amnesia (Woods and Piercy, 1974). Furthermore, it is difficult to account for the temporal gradient seen in retrograde amnesias on such a basis. The observations of Warrington and Weizkrantz have, nonetheless, emphasised yet another aspect of the memory apparatus which must be taken into account. The naïve view of a consolidation defect alone obviously requires extensive qualification.

It has emerged, indeed, that any theory concerning the underlying deficits in amnesia can only provide a partial explanation of the phenomena encountered. Some observations emphasise the encoding aspect, some the storage difficulties, and others the problems with retrieval processes. All these stages, however, are highly interactive and interdependent, one upon the other. It is clear that they are not neatly separable in normal memory, so it would be unreasonable to expect to pin-point the source of the difficulties in amnesic patients with great precision.

The Long Retrograde Amnesia

The short retrograde amnesia (RA) of several minutes' duration, such as commonly occurs after head injury, can be plausibly explained on the view that new learning requires a period of consolidation for stable long-term memory to be established. It is very difficult, in contrast, to provide an explanation for the very long RA's which may extend for months or years prior to the onset of an amnesic syndrome.

If regarded as a failure of the mechanisms of retrieval, this can in no sense be a general defect of the recall apparatus. RA's are often patchy, and in any case the patient continues to retrieve well for events prior to the retrograde defect. Furthermore, recovered cases of tuberculous meningitis or head injury may be left with long RA's when current memorising ability has again returned to normal, so that here retrieval can be observed to operate well on both sides of the retrograde gap.

An explanation in terms of loss of retention for events within the retrograde gap is equally unsatisfactory. To explain very long RA's on this basis it would be necessary to suppose that full consolidation takes months or even years before the memory trace becomes resistant to extinction. Moreover, RA's may sometimes shrink with the passage of time, showing that the memory trace must have been intact all along.

It is probably a fault in principle to try to partition the blame too rigidly between primary faults in recall or in consolidation. Symonds (1966) put forward a novel hypothesis which may help towards resolving the dilemma of the long RA. He suggested that certain amnesic syndromes should be viewed in terms of excess, or acceleration, of the natural process of forgetting. This might normally be opposed by an activating system situated mainly in the hippocampal system. When the operation of the activating system ceases from any cause decay will prevail, affecting most severely the memory units most recently established, and progressively less those which have existed, perhaps with structural modification within the central nervous system, over a period of time. Decay, or forgetting, is thus seen as a graded process: some of the more recent memories will decay to zero potential and will then be included in the dense RA which persists, even in those cases where current memorising ability is again restored; beyond this will be a zone in which memory units have decayed to a non-functional level but can gradually recover their function if activation is restored. On such a basis the long retrograde amnesia which ultimately shrinks becomes more readily explainable.

An alternative escape from the dilemma is to discount the long RA as an artefact of clinical examination. It is hard to assess the preservation, or loss, of memories for personal events far back in time, and most impressions of long, temporally graded RAs are based on anecdotal or unsystematic observations. Sanders and Warrington (1971), in a pioneering experiment, appeared to obtain support for the view that retrograde memory difficulties extended over virtually the whole of past experience, and affected all time periods equivalently. Using a standardised questionnaire concerning distant public events, and a recognition test of well-known public figures, they found that recall ability was steadily lowered in amnesic subjects for periods of up to 40 years. No clear onset to the retrograde gap could be discerned. More recent studies, however, have reinstated the temporal gradient and shown that the retrograde amnesia in circumscribed amnesic syndromes is truly a time-linked phenomenon:

Albert et al. (1979) developed tests concerning previous public events and recognition tests of famous faces. Patients with Korsakoff's psychosis showed retrograde memory deficits extending over several decades, but with clear-cut temporal gradients and relative preservation for the remote past. More events and pictures, for example, were recognised from the 1930s and 1940s than from the 1960s. An expecially interesting feature was the inclusion in the tests of pictures of well-known individuals both early and late in their careers, for example of Marlon Brando from the 1950s and the 1970s; whereas normal subjects were more accurate at identifying the later pictures, Korsakoff patients showed precisely the reverse.

Squire and Slater (1975) produced a test based on titles of television programmes which had been broadcast for one season or less and were equivalently matched for public exposure. These showed that the transient RA following electroconvulsive therapy was limited to several years, with normal performance beyond such a gap. Other tests derived from the procedures of Albert et al. confirmed temporal gradients in Korsakoff patients also (Cohen and Squire, 1981; Squire and Cohen, 1982).

Meudell et al. (1980) used voices of famous people recorded over the past 50 years. Again this demonstrated poor recognition extending over several decades in Korsakoff subjects, but with relative preservation of memories for the more remote past.

These carefully conducted and controlled studies show, therefore, that the RAs, however long, do tend to spare memories dating from childhood or early adulthood. Moreover they have emphasised that the RA in patients with alcoholic Korsakoff's psychosis is remarkably severe and extensive, in contrast to that seen with other amnesic syndromes. In Squire's studies, for example, Korsakoff patients showed deficits extending over several decades, whereas patients tested very shortly after electroconvulsive therapy showed gaps limited to 4 years or less (Cohen and Squire, 1981; Squire and Cohen, 1982). Milner's patient 'HM' who had suffered hippocampal resection, and Squire's patient 'NA' who had sustained a focal lesion in the thalamus, also showed retrograde gaps of no more than a few years or months duration. Butters and Albert (1982) discuss the possibility that the very extensive RAs in alcoholic Korsakoff patients may derive, in part at least, from their poor acquisition of material into long-term memory throughout their alcoholic careers. The anterograde memory difficulties of the typical alcoholic will have led to tenuous storage of material even before the Korsakoff's psychosis supervenes; and the progressive increase in severity of such difficulties over the years might account for the temporally graded nature of the retrograde amnesia once

Korsakoff's psychosis is established. Squire and Cohen (1982) stress the possible role of cognitive deficits, over and above problems specifically related to memory, which may stand to compromise the Korsakoff patient's performance on tests of remote memory; a relatively brief retrograde gap, in line with that of other amnesics, may thereby come to appear to be very greatly extended.

Finally it is noteworthy that the temporal gradient characteristic of the RA in patients with amnesic syndromes is not evident in patients with dementia. When the remote memory tests of Albert *et al.* were applied to patients with presumed Alzheimer's disease, uniformly poor performance was observed for items throughout the whole 40 year span of the tests (Wilson *et al.*, 1981). There was no discernible trend towards relative preservation of memories from the earliest decades. A similarly 'flat' curve has been observed in patients with Huntington's chorea (Albert *et al.*, 1981). Thus it would seem that with diffuse cerebral pathology retrieval is equivalently impaired for all parts of past experience. Other ways in which the memory disorder seen with diffuse brain dysfunction differs from that of the classical amnesic syndrome have already been discussed (p. 30).

Amnesic Syndrome or Syndromes?

It is commonly assumed that amnesic syndromes of varying aetiology are fundamentally similar. The alcoholic Korsakoff syndrome may have superadded deficits, in subtle aspects of cognitive function and personality, as mentioned on p. 30, and the retrograde amnesia in such cases tends to be exceptionally long, as described above. Nevertheless the 'core' structure of the amnesic deficits themselves has been viewed as identical whatever the causative process.

This assumption has recently begun to be challenged in certain respects. There is now some evidence, for example, that the amnesias seen with hippocampal and diencephalic pathology may not be entirely congruous.

A first pointer in this direction was provided by Lhermitte and Signoret (1972), who compared 3 post-encephalitic patients (with presumed hippocampal damage) with a group of Korsakoff patients. The former performed at a lower level on a test of memory for spatial position, whereas the latter were worse on tests of temporal sequence. This was interpreted as indicating that the post-encephalitic patients had a more profound failure of retention, whereas the Korsakoffs were more impaired with regard to the organisation of material and with recall.

Firmer evidence has come from studies of speed of forgetting. Huppert and Piercy (1978, 1979) designed an ingenious method for examining forgetting rates over long time spans after ensuring that material had been learned to a constant criterion. A large number of pictures were exposed to the subjects, then recognition rates tested at 10 min., 1 day and 7 days. By 'titrating' the time of initial exposure, recognition performance at the 10 min. interval was brought to a constant level in different groups. By this technique it was possible to show that forgetting over the subsequent week was indistinguishable between Korsakoff patients and normal controls; in other words, provided the Korsakoff patients had been given enough time to analyse the stimuli thoroughly they were able to display normal recognition memory over an extended period of time. Milner's patient 'HM', by contrast, showed abnormally rapid forgetting when tested similarly. His amnesic syndrome had resulted from bilateral hippocampal resection.

Squire (1981) has reinforced this distinction by applying the technique to Korsakoff patients, to patient 'NA' who had sustained focal damage to the thalamus, and to patients tested shortly after electroconvulsive therapy. The diencephalic amnesics (Korsakoff patients and 'NA') showed normal rates of forgetting, whereas the ECT patients forgot at an accelerated rate. The amnesia following ECT is presumed to derive from dysfunction in the medial temporal regions.

Taken together these studies provide support for the view that the underlying amnesic difficulties may be qualitatively different, depending on the brain regions affected. The normal rate of forgetting in patients with diencephalic lesions suggests that their deficit must lie at the stage of registration or encoding, or in acquiring information into the long-term store. Rapid forgetting in patients with hippocampal damage implies a deficit in the consolidation occurring after initial learning has been achieved.

Other rather complex distinctions have also begun to emerge on tests of pro-active interference, and on tests which examine rates of forgetting from the primary memory store. These are reviewed by Butters and Cermak (1980) and Squire (1982). When taken in conjunction with differences between groups in the duration of retrograde amnesia (see above), the unitary character of the amnesic syndrome can now be seen to be under question. Further detailed studies may be expected to clarify the situation further.

Possible Mechanisms in Psychogenic Amnesia

Traditionally a rather rigid distinction is maintained between psychogenic and organic disturbances of memory, with indeed quite separate systems of explanation for the one and the other. This may be convenient in the present state of knowledge, but is perhaps a somewhat artificial dichotomy. It may fairly be presumed that a pathophysiology of some kind accompanies psychogenic amnesia, just as there must be a physiological basis for the influence of emotional and motivational factors on the normal processes of remembering and forgetting.

It may be asked whether the study of organic amnesic states and their neuropathology leads us any nearer to understanding the physiological basis of these more complex phenomena. Certainly the neurological structures important in committing new experience to memory turn out to be strategically situated for allowing an integration between affective and cognitive aspects of experience. The hippocampal system forms part of the neural substrate proposed by Papez (1937) for the experiencing and expression of emotion; and the mamillary bodies, as Kral (1959) points out, lie at the intersection of Papez's emotional circuit and the reticular formation upon which arousal depends. Here is a possible mechanism to account for the emotional determinants of what is committed to memory and what is not. In states of profound emotional disturbance, perhaps also in dissociative fugue states, it is possible that the total apparatus fails to function harmoniously, so that a durable memory trace cannot be established in the usual way. A simple explanation will not, however, suffice, and very often it appears that in psychogenic amnesias the principal fault lies with mechanisms for subsequent voluntary recall. Thus, behaviour during dissociative states often indicates that memorising, at least in the short term, must still be taking place, and much may later be accessible to recall under hypnosis or drug abreaction.

It is possible, furthermore, that certain cases of psychogenic amnesia may depend, at least in part, on failure in the initial processing of experience, rather than on a process of forgetting or repression (Kopelman, 1985b). Thus Taylor and Kopelman (1984) found that inability to recall a criminal offence was frequent when this had been committed in a state of very high emotional arousal, in the context of florid psychotic delusions, or under heavy alcoholic intoxication. All such factors would be liable to impair normal registration of what was happening at the time.

The mechanisms which may underlie psychogenic disturbances of *recall* receive little clarification from the study of organic memory defects. Organically determined retrograde amnesia is to a large extent time-related and tends to cover all experiences, whether significant emotionally or not. Psychogenic amnesia, on the other hand, may cover a circumscribed period in the distant past, and classically affects a system of related ideas or experiences. However, certain observations by Zangwill (1961) on the shrinkage of RAs after head injury are very interesting. Careful anamnesis in such cases sometimes shows that vulnerability during the retrograde gap is not wholly a function of recency, but that what is disturbed above all is the temporal coherence of the memory train. Shrinkage later occurs by the emergence in sporadic fashion of islands of memory, at first without firm context, which are later amplified and linked by rearousal of associative links. Zangwill suggests that this is not so very dissimilar from what is seen in psychogenic amnesia. Here again there is functional isolation of memory systems, with failures of associative linkage. The comparison is, however, no more than suggestive, and in general our understanding of the mechanisms of recall is too fragmentary to allow more detailed speculation where psychogenic disturbances are concerned.

Disorder of Language Functions

Disturbance of language function is an important source of evidence of focal brain disorder, and indeed historically provided the chief impetus for attempts at correlating focal psychological deficits with regional brain pathology. Dysphasic symptoms probably remain more useful clinically than any other cognitive defect in indicating the approximate site of brain pathology. Yet despite 100 years of careful enquiry and observation the analysis of dysphasia remains a controversial area, and beyond certain broad limits its relationship to regional cerebral disorder remains in many respects uncertain. This should not be surprising in view of the complex interrelationships that exist between different aspects of language processes, and the intimate way in which language must enter into many other cognitive functions. The parts of the brain concerned with language are multiple and extensive, and necessarily diffused over a considerable area so that auditory, visual and motor mechanisms can be subserved. Consequently cerebral lesions which produce dysphasia can lead to many varieties of defect, and at the same time to other defects which render the appraisal of clinico-pathological correlations difficult. It is moreover likely that individual variation is considerable where the anatomical substrate for language is concerned.

CEREBRAL DOMINANCE FOR LANGUAGE

The earliest anatomical observation to gain universal acceptance was that dysphasia was overwhelmingly more common after lesions of the left hemisphere than the right. Later right hemisphere lesions were reported to produce dysphasia in left-handed subjects, and the general rule was accepted that the hemisphere contralateral to handedness governed speech. This has been upheld in large measure where right-handed subjects are concerned; Piercy (1964) reviews the evidence that the incidence of dysphasia in right-handed subjects is 67% when the lesion is in the left hemisphere and only 1% when the lesion is right-sided. But it is now known from large unselected series of patients with brain lesions that left-handers also suffer dysphasia more often from left than from right hemisphere lesions, in fact in a ratio of approximately 2:1. Bilateral speech representation appears to be more common in left-handers than right-handers though remaining rare in both.

The most direct confirmation of these relationships has come from observing the transient effect on speech of injecting sodium amytal into the carotid arteries of the left and right sides separately by the Wada technique (Wada and Rasmussen, 1960). Sodium amytal, 150–200 mg as a 10% solution is rapidly injected into the common carotid artery. This results in a contralateral flaccid paralysis lasting for several minutes during which the preservation or disruption of language functions can be briefly assessed. Milner et al. (1964) reported 119 consecutive patients examined under such conditions. Among the right-handers 90% were found to have left hemisphere speech, 10% to have right hemisphere speech, and in none was there bilateral representation. Among left-handers and ambidextrous patients (without early brain damage) 64% had left hemisphere speech, 20% right hemisphere speech, and 16% had bilateral speech representation.

An alternative method for assessing language laterality involves the use of dichotic listening. Verbal information in the form of groups of spoken digits or monosyllabic words is fed through earphones to the two ears, but in such a way that different information arrives at each ear simultaneously. The subject must report whatever he hears, and is found to report more accurately and comprehensively from the ear contralateral to the hemisphere subserving language. The results are less clear-cut than with the Wada technique, but dichotic listening has the advantage that it can readily be applied to a non-selected sample of subjects, including those in whom there is no reason to suspect that brain damage might exist. Satz et al. (1967) used this method to explore the relationship between left and right-handedness and the hemisphere subserving speech in 123 healthy volunteers. First it was shown that the situation in left-handed subjects becomes more complicated the more carefully left-handedness is evaluated. Handedness in fact proves to be a relative term, many 'left-handed' subjects showing a division of hand preferences and skills for different operations between the right and left hands. Thus a significant proportion of subjects who are left-handed in the ordinary sense of the term prove to prefer the right hand for certain tasks, and sometimes even for a greater number of activities than the left. With objective tests of manual dexterity Satz et al. found that almost half showed better performance with the right hand than the left. On a composite score derived from all such evidence 17% of left-handed subjects emerged in the end with strong right hand superiority, 22% as ambidextrous, and only 61% could be judged as strongly left-handed in practice. All of this was in contrast to right-handed subjects who showed more consistency across preferences and tasks, 97% being confirmed in right hand superiority. Interesting findings emerged when a dichotic listening technique was used to assess the hemisphere subserving language in these subjects. The self-reported right-handers showed strong evidence of left hemisphere dominance for language; so also did the 17% of left-handers who had proved to have right-handed superiority and the 22% who were ambidextrous. The 61% who were truly strongly left-handed were divided approximately equally, half showing left hemisphere dominance and half right hemisphere dominance. In a similar though smaller study Lishman and McMeekan (1977) found evidence of a progressively decreasing incidence of left hemisphere dominance for language in right-handed, mixed-handed and left-handed individuals (100, 67 and 60% respectively). Moreover, among strong left-handers a family history of sinistrality appeared to be another significant variable; the ear difference scores on dichotic testing were then smaller, indicating reduced lateralization or bilateral representation of language in such individuals.

Electroconvulsive therapy has also been used as a means of determining language laterality, again in subjects who are free from any evidence of cerebral disease (Pratt and Warrington, 1972; Warrington and Pratt, 1973, 1981). By testing for dysphasia shortly after unilateral ECT to each side of the head, in patients undergoing treatment for depressive illness, it was shown that right hemisphere speech existed in only 1 of 55 right-handed subjects and in about 25% of 24 left-handed subjects.

Some two-thirds of normal adults are strongly right-handed and approximately 90% use the right hand for writing (Subirana, 1969; Annett, 1970). For this there appear to be strong genetic determinants. Even so, environmental pressures seem to be capable of altering the genetically-determined preference, likewise damage to the upper limb or to the brain in childhood. The age of 10–12 years is generally accepted as the upper limit beyond which brain damage will not alter handedness and beyond which the second hemisphere will not develop language skills by way of compensation. But that shifts in cerebral dominance do occur in relation to early left hemisphere damage is strongly upheld by Milner et al.'s (1964) results of intracarotid amytal injection already mentioned above. Where left-handedness or ambidexterity was accompanied by a history of early left hemisphere damage there was, in contrast to all other groups, a large percentage of cases with language representation in the right hemisphere (22% left hemisphere speech, 67% right hemisphere speech, 11% bilateral speech representation).

Anatomical evidence has now come forward to complement the frequency with which language is represented in the left hemisphere. Yakovlev and Rakic (1966) reported that in foetal and newborn brains the cortico-spinal tract from the left hemisphere usually begins to decussate higher in the medulla than that coming from the right, and the cortico-spinal tract is usually larger on the right side of the cord than the left. Right hand preference therefore probably develops on the basis of the increased motor innervation available to the right side of the body. More directly Geschwind and Levitsky (1968), examining one hundred adult human brains at postmortem, have reported marked differences between the two hemispheres in the size of the planum temporale which lies on the superior surface of the temporal lobe immediately behind Heschl's gyrus. This is the region which contains the auditory association cortex, and represents the classical Wernicke's area

known to be important for language. This area was found to be larger on the left in 65 brains, larger on the right in 11, and equal on left and right in 24. These findings have been confirmed by others, as reviewed by Le May and Geschwind (1978).

Further interesting evidence has come from neuroradiological studies which have been able to display a number of differences between right- and left-handers. Le May, for example, has shown that in right-handers the occipital lobe is usually wider on the left than the right, whereas the frontal lobe is wider on the right than the left; these asymmetries are less striking in left-handers who, moreover, quite commonly show a reversal of the normal situation (Le May, 1976, 1977; Galaburda et al., 1978). Such differences are readily detectable on the CT scan, also differences in the degree of forward or backward extension of the left and right hemispheres of the brain. The configuration of the lateral ventricles is likewise revealing, with a tendency for the occipital horns to be longer on the left in right-handers but less regularly so in left-handers (McRae et al., 1968). Arteriography has given indications of further differences, for example in the relative levels of the posterior ends of the Sylvian fissures and of the disposition of the transverse sinuses (Le May and Geschwind, 1978).

New evidence with regard to cerebral dominance for language has also come from observations after section of the corpus callosum for the relief of intractable epilepsy (Sperry, 1966; Sperry and Gazzaniga, 1967; Gazzaniga and Sperry, 1967). As a result of the operation the two hemispheres are virtually isolated from each other and information can be fed tachistoscopically to either hemisphere alone by brief exposures in the opposite half-field of vision. When a picture of an object is exposed to the dominant hemisphere it can be named promptly or recorded in writing; but similar exposures to the nondominant hemisphere meet with no such response. If pressed to answer after information has been fed to the non-dominant hemisphere, the patient may deny seeing anything, or alternatively the speaking hemisphere may resort to pure guesswork and produce a random response. Nonetheless the patient can select the appropriate matching object, by means of palpation with the left hand, from among a group of objects concealed behind a screen, indicating that the non-dominant hemisphere has correctly perceived the picture despite the patient's inability to name it. In a similar way an object concealed from view can be named when palpated by the right hand but not when palpated by the left hand. The non-dominant hemisphere is therefore mute as would have been expected.

In some of these patients however, it seems certain that while language cannot be expressed, limited comprehension of language can take place in the non-dominant hemisphere. The left hand can correctly select or point to an object which corresponds to a name exposed briefly to the non-dominant hemisphere alone. That the dominant hemisphere can have played no part is shown by the failure of the right hand to perform accurately in this situation; moreover the subject cannot name the matching object if this has been selected by the left hand but remains concealed from view. Auditory comprehension can be demonstrated by flashing a picture to the non-dominant hemisphere then asking the patient to signal when the matching word is read aloud to him; this he can do by signalling with the left hand but not with the right. Alternatively a word can be spoken out loud, and the patient asked to signal when the corresponding printed word is exposed visually to the non-dominant hemisphere. In such experiments it appears that even short phrases can be comprehended, the word 'clock' being selected in response to the spoken phrase 'used to tell time'. Ingenious research techniques have allowed considerable further exploration of the receptive language capacities of the non-dominant hemisphere, as described by Zaidel (1977, 1978).

It is not known how far these fascinating results have general application. It is possible that the patients reported to date have been unusual in the extent to which language was already represented bilaterally within the brain, and definite conclusions on the issue still cannot be drawn.

Some exceedingly rare observations have been made on patients after total surgical removal of the dominant hemisphere. One such patient was investigated by Smith (1966a) after left hemispherectomy for recurrence of a glioblastoma. The patient had previously been strongly right-handed. In the immediate post-operative period there was, as expected, a severe sensory and motor dysphasia along with the right hemiplegia and hemianopia. Even then, however, he could follow some simple commands, indicating some preservation of comprehension of speech. He could also utter emotional expletives such as 'Goddamit' with good articulation, at a time when single words could not be repeated and when there was no ability at all to communicate in propositional speech. Suddenly in the tenth post-operative week he asked his nurse 'What does "B.M." mean?' in response to her en-

quiry about his bowel movements. Thereafter the occasional use of fragments of propositional speech increased, along with ability to repeat progressively longer sentences on command, though most of the time the patient remained incapable of speaking voluntarily. Comprehension of speech, by contrast, appeared to reach approximately normal levels at one year post-operatively before the tumour recurred (Smith, 1972). Of particular interest in view of the evidence linking musical functions with the minor hemisphere (p. 56), was the patient's eventual ability to sing familiar songs and hymns, with little hesitation and few errors of articulation, even though speaking remained very severely impaired. A remarkably similar post-operative course has now been documented in a second patient (Burklund and Smith, 1977). Other scattered examples in the literature are reviewed by Searleman (1977).

The rarity of such cases again makes it difficult to estimate how far the results may have been due to an unusual degree of bilaterality of language already present before operation, or how far new capacities to organise language were developed in the non-dominant hemisphere.

Finally, there is now considerable evidence that the affective components of language, including prosody and emotional gesturing, are the special prerogative of the right hemisphere (Ross and Mesulam, 1979; Ross, 1981). Thus patients with right hemisphere strokes may lose the ability to express emotion by voice or gesture, or to perceive the affective colouring in the speech or gestures of others, while formal propositional aspects of language remain intact. Ross (1981) suggests, indeed, that the functional organisation of the affective components of language in the right hemisphere may closely mirror that of propositional language in the left, and has produced evidence of a similar range of 'aprosodic' subsyndromes to that encountered among the dysphasias ('motor aprosodia', 'sensory aprosodia', etc.).

SPEECH FUNCTIONS WITHIN THE DOMINANT HEMISPHERE

We have little direct knowledge about the physiological mechanisms which underlie language functions in the healthy intact brain. Since language is unique to man there is no paradigm which can be studied in animals, and evidence has had to accumulate slowly from the study of the damaged human brain. Inferences about normal from abnormal function are notoriously dangerous, and not surprisingly numerous theories abound on psychological, physiological and anatomical levels. Many of the most eminent neurologists have struggled to provide a functional conception of language organisation, against which to arrive at a rational classification of the dysphasias. But even recent authorities can offer little more than speculations which serve to guide future enquiry. It is, however, useful to have a framework against which to view the phenomena of dysphasia, and the theoretical background will therefore be briefly reviewed before the clinical data are considered.

The detailed history of past endeavours was outlined by Brain (1965). Early and primitive localisationist views postulated 'speech centres' for speaking, reading, and writing, which contained the repositories for word images and could be disturbed either directly by lesions or by damage to various connecting pathways. Such views became discredited by more careful neuropathology and by more detailed clinical appraisal of the range of defects shown by dysphasic patients. The need was seen for a more dynamic explanation in terms of impairment of symbolic functions as a whole. Freud was one of the first to attack the 'diagram makers' and propose a more holistic view of the functions of the speech territory in the dominant hemisphere. Head further developed the dynamic concepts of Hughlings Jackson and proposed a classification of dysphasia which depended primarily on symptoms of defect rather than locus of lesion.

In recent years linguists and psychologists have joined increasingly in the debate and have produced objective evidence to countermand or support the impressions of clinicians. A concise review which incorporates the psycholinguistic contribution is provided by Wyke (1971), and a more extended discussion by Lesser and Reich (1982). The psycholinguistic classification of the dyslexias is discussed by Newcombe and Marshall (1981). Psychologists have used batteries of tests and factor analysis of the results to refine major categories of disorder. From this and other evidence Piercy (1964) was led to conclude: 'The language areas of the brain are not mutually undifferentiated, nor can they be envisaged as a collection of discrete centres. Rather one discerns gradients of specialisation in the neural sub-strata of language; gradients which are steeper in some areas and for some functions than others, and perhaps steepest for verbal articulation and for reading'.

Two major contributions attempt to reach beyond the objective evidence and present a partial theory of language function from which the phenomena of dysphasia can be derived. The first, by Brain, is largely psychological and physiological in emphasis, the second, by Geschwind is slanted towards an anatomical explanation. Both start with 'naming' as the essential function upon which language comes to be built.

Brain (1965) suggested that the physiological basis for the recognition of words must rest with the acquisition of 'schemas', which operate as enduring physiological standards of comparison but do not enter consciousness. The development of naming during childhood implies increasing accuracy in the recognition and abstraction of the precise elements of the concept for which the name stands; furthermore the elements which constitute 'the name' must come to be recognised without conscious effort despite variations in the pitch, speed and intonation with which the name is pronounced. Simple 'phoneme-schemas' must be built into 'word-schemas' at a higher level of organisation, since the second phoneme of a word may influence the recognition accorded to the first. Word-schemas are linked to the physiological bases of perception and thought connected with that which the word symbolises, and so enable the word to be endowed with meaning. At the same time 'word-meaning-schemas' must be capable of modification when the grammar or syntax of the sentence containing the word is altered. At a higher level of organisation still there must therefore be 'sentence-schemas'. Similarly on the efferent side there must be schemas for the motor production of speech. And to serve the purposes of reading and writing there must be visual and graphic schemas superimposed upon the fundamental schemas of speech. This complex physiological organisation may be damaged in whole or in part; to the extent that each type of schema is organised anatomically in relative isolation from others it may be possible to move towards an explanation of some of the varieties of dysphasia.

Thus word schemas are regarded in Brain's formulation as the basic element both in the comprehension and expression of words, and their disorganisation will result in defective understanding and expression in both spoken and written modalities. Word-meaning-schemas, when disorganised, may leave words freely available but their power to evoke or express meaning will be impaired. Disorganisation of sentence-schemas will impair meaning derived from syntactical relationships while leaving the meaning of individual words relatively intact.

Pure word-deafness may be regarded as a disorder restricted to auditory phoneme-schemas, pure word-dumbness as a disorder of motor phoneme-schemas. Disturbances of higher order schemas are more difficult to illustrate from clinical material, since all appear to depend on a comparatively limited area of the temporal and parietal lobes in the dominant hemisphere. However, word-schemas appear to be principally disturbed in 'central' dysphasias, in which both comprehension and expression are impaired, and word-meaning-schemas in nominal dysphasia. The predominantly motor dysphasias may represent a breakdown in the relationship between the word-schemas and the motor-schemas for the production of articulated speech. In pure alexia the perception of words fails to arouse the visual word-schemas which serve to evoke their meaning, whereas in agraphia the graphic-schemas fail to arouse the motor-schemas organised in relation to the parts of the motor cortex which control the hand in writing.

This suggested organisation, while necessarily at a theoretical level, serves to emphasise the complexities inherent in conceptualising the anatomophysiological basis for language functions. It has the virtue of attempting to bring together a psychological and a physiological interpretation of the processes which underlie speech, and of insisting on a dynamic approach towards the understanding of dysphasic disturbances. In clinical practice, however, it clearly suffers from attempting to impose a philosophical theory upon the facts, instead of allowing observed phenomena to generate the explanatory theory.

Geschwind (1967) provided a model based upon the learning and arousal of associative links. He pointed out that the distinctive element in human language, which is not present in animal communication, derives from man's ability to form higher-order associations between one sensory stimulus and another. In sub-human primates the principal outflow from sensory association areas is to the limbic system, enabling the animal to learn which stimuli have importance with regard to drives for food, sex or aggression; interconnections between the sensory association regions for different sensory modalities are meagre by comparison. The impressive advance in the human brain lies in the expansion of the zone in the region of the angular gyrus at the junction of the temporal, parietal and occipital lobes, which is an area strategically situated with respect to the association cortices for hearing, touch and vision. This may constitute the neural substrate which allows the human being readily to form linkages between two or more 'non-limbic' stimuli, and achieve the higher-order associations which underly the acquisition of language skills. It is noteworthy that inputs to this part of the brain are almost exclusively from other cortical regions, and furthermore that it is one of the last brain regions to myelinate during development.

In Geschwind's model for naming, an object which is seen stimulates the visual association cortex, and thereafter connections via the angular gyrus arouse associations with regard to the 'heard name' in the auditory association cortex of the first temporal convolution (Wernicke's area). This in turn is transmitted via the arcuate fasciculus to the motor association cortex in the posterior part of the frontal lobe (Broca's area), where the 'rules' are contained for turning the output from Wernicke's area into the motor acts of speech. At each way-station there is not only transmission of the 'message', but certain operations are carried out on it so that coding is reorganised in distinctive ways. The two crucial processes therefore consist first of comprehension, then of repetition by which we learn to reproduce the auditory stimulus. Each has a different anatomical location. Thus the type of disturbance of speech produced by circumscribed lesions will change as we move from one region to another.

A lesion in Wernicke's area will impair verbal comprehension. Comprehension is developmentally a process by which we learn to associate the auditory stimulus of a word with a visual or other sensory stimulus. A lesion here will prevent the incoming auditory signals from being classified into patterns as a prelude to recognition, and from being conveyed elsewhere in the brain to arouse such meaningful associations. Reading will likewise be impaired since this is learned by the child in association with the spoken language, the essence of which has already been mastered; when visual language can no longer excite auditory associations it will fail to be comprehended. Writing will also be impaired because the first step in writing consists of the reverse act of arousing visual associations from the auditory forms of the word. Speaking is impaired because this depends first upon the arousal of auditory associations which are then transmuted into motor speech by Broca's area. Since Broca's area remains intact, however, it may 'run on' to some extent autonomously and produce a fluent flow of faulty speech; overlearning has occurred there for many of the sequences of language, and when deprived of the control of higher functional levels the output of speech may even be excessive while faulty.

Lesions of the arcuate fasciculus also allow a fluent dysphasia, since Broca's area remains intact, and comprehension is relatively preserved because Wernicke's area is intact. But the speech is abnormal and repetition markedly defective, because Broca's area normally 'repeats' the messages which arrive from the temporal lobe.

Lesions in Broca's area itself leave comprehension relatively well preserved because Wernicke's area remains intact. The output of speech is sparse, laboured and with poor articulation, because the rules for translating the message into motor speech are damaged.

Geschwind's scheme does not attempt to explain how meaning can be derived from the relationships between words in their syntactical context. It adheres remarkably closely, though with more persuasive evidence, to the essential theory put forward by Wernicke in 1874.

Dysphasia and Other Aspects of Intelligence

Opinion has differed about the extent to which dysphasia can be regarded merely as 'loss of a linguistic tool' while the rest of intellect remains intact. Language is of course an integral part of conceptual thinking and of problem solving in many areas; but it may be that some dysphasic patients retain in large degree the automatic and subconscious use of words in thinking processes. The question of the relative preservation of internal speech is very hard to assess. Quite apart from this, however, it is likely that the cerebral structures subserving language also subserve other functions, so that lesions will almost always impair more than language alone. Some aspects of dysphasia can be seen as reflecting the general difficulties of brain-injured patients as stressed by Goldstein (1936): a difficulty in differentiating 'figure from background' may contribute to inability to pronounce a word in isolation while it can still be produced as part of a series, or general difficulties in categorisation may contribute to problems in naming objects. Impairment of the ordered perception of space or time may worsen the dysphasic difficulties, since a proper conception of such matters is essential for symbolic thought.

Psychological testing has helped to some extent to clarify the subject, and is discussed by Piercy (1964), Newcombe (1969) and Zangwill (1969). Dysphasic patients are certainly impaired on language intelligence tests to a greater degree than brain-injured patients without dysphasia. Performance is also inferior on certain non-verbal tests when compared to normals, and sometimes even when compared to non-dysphasic brain-injured subjects. In particular Weinstein et al. (1955) have reported difficulty with a test of conditional reactions to combinations of visual shapes and backgrounds, and Teuber and Weinstein (1956) with a test of perceiving hidden figures. In both of these it is hard to blame any hypothetical difficulty with internal speech or impaired comprehension of instructions. The often difficult question of assessing legal competency in dysphasic patients is discussed by Benson (1976, 1979).

Subcortical Dysphasia

The possibility that subcortical pathology might contribute to, or even be responsible for, certain dysphasic syndromes has a considerable history. Renewed attention has been directed to the issue now that CT scanning is capable of revealing discrete subcortical infarcts, and certain syndromes such as 'thalamic' and 'striatal' dysphasia have been proposed. Benson (1979) reviews the still uncertain status of such syndromes, and the difficulty in deciding whether the language disturbance reflects the direct effects of the subcortical lesion or derives from distant effects produced elsewhere in the brain.

The picture usually described is of mutism following an acute intracerebral haemorrhage, followed by hypophonia and slow, amelodic output. This may evolve to a combination of severely paraphasic speech with relatively well preserved capacity for repetition, which appears to be the characteristic pattern. The subcortical structures involved are virtually always situated in the hemisphere dominant for language.

Thalamic dysphasia begins with mutism but generally changes to a fluent, paraphasic, jargon output. Difficulty with naming is often dramatically severe, but comprehension and repetition are comparatively well preserved. In most cases the language disorder is transient, showing improvement over the course of weeks or months. The puzzling feature is the rarity of such a development among the considerable number of persons who develop thalamic lesions.

Striatal dysphasia appears to derive chiefly from lesions of the putamen and internal capsular area. The patients reported by Damasio et al. (1982a) had prominent involvement of the anterior limb of the capsule and also the head of the caudate nucleus. Speech remains sparse, non-fluent, dysarthric and paraphasic, though again comprehension and repetition are usually good. The ability to name is better preserved than with thalamic dysphasia. Naeser et al. (1982) have pointed to subdivisions within the syndrome according to the precise site of the lesion and its extension into neighbouring territories.

CLINICAL SYNDROMES OF LANGUAGE IMPAIRMENT

For purposes of clinical evaluation it is useful to consider a broad division into defective understanding of speech or written material, and defective production of speech or writing. However, the great majority of patients with language disturbance show a complicated mixture of defects. This was well illustrated by Brown and Simonson's (1957) review of one hundred dysphasic patients who were examined without reference to conventional categories and simply scored in terms of disorder of speaking, listening, reading and writing. Only nine had a defect limited to one function and this was always slight in degree. Sixteen had defects in two components, 14 in three, and the remaining 61 had defects in all components of language. Many of the patients with disordered appreciation of spoken speech had severe impairment of all four components and appeared most commonly to represent the cases of 'global dysphasia'.

The syndromes considered below represent no more than approximations which may be regarded as clinically useful. The first four syndromes, pure word-deafness, word-blindness, word-dumbness and pure agraphia, though all rare, are outlined first because they represent the purest forms of defect. All are produced by lesions near the areas of association cortex for vision, hearing or motor skills. Lesions in such locations will more commonly be sufficiently extensive to produce widespread dysphasic difficulties, resulting for example in combinations of primary motor dysphasia with pure word-dumbness. The next three syndromes, 'primary sensory dysphasia', 'primary motor dysphasia', and 'nominal dysphasia', represent the more commonly occurring clinical pictures and show defects in more than one component of language. The terms 'sensory' and 'motor' are used as a guide to the *source* of primary breakdown of language function, since this has implications for site of pathology. The terms must not be taken to indicate the *nature* of functional impairment, for of course primary sensory dysphasia has itself a marked defect in motor expression. Finally certain other clinical syndromes are briefly outlined.

Table 1 on p. 90 summarises the rather bewildering array of disturbances of function found in these different syndromes. For an extended presentation and discussion of the various disorders Benson (1979) should be consulted. At least partial support for the principal subvarieties and their anatomical localisation has come from recent CT scan studies (Naeser and Hayward, 1978), though many authorities still argue against the neatness with which language disturbance can be subdivided (Smith, 1978). The syndromes outlined below are clearly to a considerable extent abstractions from a very complex whole.

Pure Word-deafness (subcortical auditory dysphasia)

The patient can speak fluently and virtually without error, and similarly can write normally. He can also read and comprehend what he reads. The defect is restricted to the understanding of spoken speech, even though other aspects of hearing are intact. In fact the patient hears words as sounds but fails to recognise these sounds as words. Hemphill and Stengel's (1940) patient said: 'Voice comes but no words. I can hear, sounds come, but words don't separate. There is no trouble at all with the sound. Sounds come. I can hear, but I cannot understand it'. As a result the patient cannot repeat words spoken to him, and cannot write to dictation.

Such a defect can equally be regarded as an agnosia for spoken words. It is extremely rare, but there is general agreement that the lesion is in the dominant temporal lobe, closely adjacent to the primary receptive area for hearing—Heschl's gyrus of the first temporal convolution. Geschwind suggests that it is caused by interruption of the auditory pathway to the dominant temporal lobe together with a lesion of the corpus callosum. The patient can still hear because the auditory pathway to the non-dominant cortex is intact, but incoming auditory information cannot gain access to the speech receiving mechanisms of the dominant lobe. The disorder is rare because a lesion in this situation will usually extend far enough to the surface to damage the speech receiving mechanisms themselves, resulting in the more widespread disabilities of a primary sensory dysphasia.

Pure Word-blindness (alexia without agraphia, agnosic alexia, subcortical visual aphasia, occipital alexia)

The patient can speak normally and has no difficulty with comprehension of the spoken word. His difficulties with language are entirely restricted to his understanding of what he reads. In the most severe examples even letters cannot be comprehended, while in less severe cases occasional words are understood. The patient can still describe or copy letters even though he cannot recognise them, showing that the defect is not due to loss of the visual images of the letters. Some patients manage better with written script than printed material, presumably because they can more readily reproduce the letters in imagination with the right hand and thereby obtain kinaesthetic cues. Occasionally figures continue to be recognised when letters are not, perhaps again via kinaesthetic cues derived from early associations between counting and manual activities.

The patient can write spontaneously and to dictation, though subsequently he cannot read what he has written. The writing is usually entirely normal, though it may contain minor errors of reduplication or misalignment of letters. He may be able to copy written material slowly and laboriously.

An invariable accompaniment is a right homonymous hemianopia. Colours cannot be named, even though colour perception can be shown to be intact by sorting tests. Here it is probably significant that colour naming represents a purely visual-verbal association process and cannot derive support from other cues.

Essentially word-blindness is a failure to recognise the language values of the visual patterns which make up letters and words, and there is no disturbance of the symbolic function of the words themselves. This is confirmed by the fact that the patient can spell out loud and recognise words that are spelled out loud. The lesion is of the left visual cortex together with the splenium of the corpus callosum; thus visual input is possible only to the right hemisphere, and cannot gain access to the language systems of the left. The situation is therefore analogous to that of the lesion causing pure word-deafness. Pure word-blindness is commoner, however, because the lesion does not so readily impinge on the language areas themselves. The usual cause is occlusion of the left posterior cerebral artery.

Pure Word-dumbness (apraxic anarthria, subcortical motor dysphasia, aphemia)

The patient can comprehend both spoken speech and written material without difficulty, and shows this by his ability to respond to complex commands. He can express himself normally in writing, which also serves to demonstrate that inner speech is perfectly preserved. The defect is restricted to the production of spoken speech, which is marked by slurring and dysarthria. The patient cannot speak normally at will, cannot repeat words heard, and cannot read aloud. In severe cases he may be totally unable to articulate. Yet for other purposes the muscles of the tongue and lips function without impairment.

The condition may thus be regarded as an apraxia restricted to the movements required for speech. The exact site of pathology is uncertain, but the lesion is probably beneath the region of the insula, interrupting the pathway from the cortical centres responsible for motor schemas for words to the motor systems used in articulated speech. It is extremely rare because the lesion usually also involves the former at the same time, resulting in a primary motor dysphasia.

Pure Agraphia (agraphia without alexia)

Agraphia may accompany almost any form of generalised dysphasia, or be a component of generalised apraxia. As an isolated defect, however, it may be seen as the graphic equivalent of pure word-dumbness. Comprehension of written and spoken material is normal, and the patient's own speech is unimpaired. However he is unable to write either spontaneously or to dictation, though he may fare rather better at the copying of written material.

Brain (1965) points out that writing is a considerably more complex process than articulated speech, since after the processes leading up to speech there must then be evocation of visual graphic schemas in the posterior parts of the brain, and of motor schemas in close relation to the motor cortex. The lesion in pure motor agraphia is thought to interrupt the pathway from the left angular gyrus to the hand area of the left motor cortex, and to lie usually in the second frontal gyrus anterior to the hand area, or sometimes in the parietal lobe.

Primary Sensory Dysphasia (receptive dysphasia, Wernicke's dysphasia)

The primary deficit here is in the comprehension of spoken speech. There is defective appreciation of the meaning of words, and in particular of meaning conveyed by grammatical relations. The patient has corresponding difficulty in repeating what is said to him and in responding to commands. In less severe examples the difficulty in responding to commands can be observed to increase with the complexity of instructions, though interestingly enough quite complex 'whole-body' commands can prove to be surprisingly well performed (Benson and Geschwind, 1971). Other aspects of hearing are intact, as with pure word-deafness, but unlike the latter there are also impairments of spontaneous speech, writing, and reading. These added difficulties are attributable to the fact that the cortical mechanisms for analysing incoming speech are directly implicated by the lesion, not merely cut off from input as in pure word-deafness.

Thus ability to speak is also impaired, presumably because auditory associations or schemas must first be aroused before the efferent speech mechanisms can produce speech in a normal manner. Words are used wrongly, paraphasic errors and neologisms are frequent, and sentences tend to be poorly constructed with errors of grammar and syntax. However the faulty speech is produced fluently and without effort. Normal rhythm and inflexion are preserved and there are no articulatory defects. The speech may even be excessive in flow or under pressure, perhaps because the effector mechanisms 'run on' to a large degree autonomously when freed from the control of higher functional levels.

A patient reported by Brain (1965) responded as follows: When asked 'Do you have headaches?' he replied 'No. I've been fort in that way. I haven't been headache troubled not for a long time'. When shown a picture of an elephant he was unable to name it, but pointed to the mouth and said 'That's his sound, he is making his sound—seems to have got his voice opened there'. When shown a picture of a penguin he said 'A kind of little ver (bird)—machinery—a kind of animal do for making a sound'. When shown a tape measure he called it 'A kind of machinery', and when immediately afterwards shown a bunch of keys and asked to name it he said 'Indication of measurement of piece of apparatus or intimating the cost of apparatus in various forms'.

Perseverative errors are obvious in the above example, in that the speech is contaminated by words which the patient has once used but then cannot easily discard. The patient is usually unaware of his mistakes and makes no attempt to correct them. Unlike the patient with nominal dysphasia (see below) he is often unable to recognise the correct name for an object when this is told to him.

Reading and writing are also impaired since these are presumably also dependent on the cortical areas involved in comprehending spoken speech (and developmentally they are learned in association with spoken language). Single words may be read aloud correctly, but reading out of sentences becomes jumbled and contaminated by paraphasic errors. Written instructions, even if correctly read, may not be carried out, indicating that the patient has failed to understand what he has read. Generally the degrees of disability in understanding spoken and written language parallel each other closely. The disturbances of writing also closely mirror those of spoken speech, except that a copious fluent flow is much less common in writing than in speaking.

The lesion is in the auditory association cortex of the first temporal convolution of the dominant hemisphere (Wernicke's area), presumably preventing the re-coding of auditory messages for recognition, and debarring the arousal of auditory associations as a necessary step for reading, writing and the production of spoken speech. According to Brain's conception outlined above, the complex deficit is due to impaired utilisation of word-schemas, which constitute the physiological link between the various neural processes connecting the sensory stimuli of words to their meaning.

Primary Motor Dysphasia (cortical motor dysphasia, expressive dysphasia, Broca's dysphasia)

The primary defect is on the effector side of speech, thus concerning the mechanisms by which words are chosen and articulated and sentences constructed. Unlike pure word-dumbness, however, writing is affected in parallel with speaking, and while comprehension is relatively intact there may be difficulty in carrying out complex instructions. This may be on account of apraxia, or because the instructions require complex internal verbalisation for their efficient execution.

Speech is characteristically sparse, slow and hesitant, with marked disturbances of rhythm, inflexion and articulation, unlike the fluent expressive defects of primary sensory dysphasia. Moreover the patient is clearly under stress while trying to speak. Word finding provides obvious difficulty, wrong words are often chosen, and the words which are chosen are often mispronounced. Marked perseveration is common. However, the patient usually recognises his mistakes, attempts to correct them and becomes impatient about them. Moreover he can select the correct word when this is offered to him. He often tries to compensate for his speech defects by means of pantomime and gesture, all again in contrast to the patient with primary sensory dysphasia.

The phrase length is short, and the style may be abbreviated and 'telegraphic' with omissions of words, but the speech that does emerge is meaningful. Ability to repeat what the examiner says to him may be an improvement on what the patient can produce spontaneously, but nevertheless is always profoundly impaired. In the most severe examples the patient may have only one or two words at his command, or there may be stereotyped repetition of some word or phrase ('recurring utterance'). Total loss of ability to speak is not seen however, and the occasional speech sound can usually be discerned.

Among these marked expressive difficulties it may be noted that the automatic repetition of serials, such as numbers or days of the week, is relatively well preserved, even though they are not well articulated. Also in severe cases emotional ejaculations may be surprisingly intact when voluntary utterance is reduced to the minimum. Sometimes an object exposed to view can be named when the same name cannot be found in spontaneous speech. Similarly an habitual situation may call forth a word such as 'good-bye' when the patient is quite unable to produce it on request.

Comprehension of written, like spoken instructions may be relatively intact, and the patient may be well aware of the meaning of a word which he reads even though he cannot pronounce it aloud. Reading out loud shows a halting, jerky flow, with slurring and occasional mispronunciations. Disturbances of writing are closely similar to those of speaking. In contrast to spontaneous writing, however, the patient may be well able to copy written material.

The lesion is in the posterior two-thirds of the third frontal convolution, i.e. the pars triangularis and operculum of the premotor cortex, the classical Broca's area. Sometimes this extends also on to the lower part of the precentral convolution.

Nominal Dysphasia (amnesic aphasia, anomic aphasia)

Though this is one of the commonest forms of aphasia it is the least understood in terms of pathophysiology. The principal difficulty lies in evoking names at will. This may vary from total inability to name any object on confrontation to a mild disorder demonstrable only where uncommon words are concerned. Rochford and Williams (1962, 1965) have shown that there is a close parallel between the difficulty presented by a name and the frequency with which the word appears in language. The patient can describe the object and give its use, even when the name eludes him, and like the patient with primary motor dysphasia can usually recognise the correct name when this is offered him. He can often use the same word without difficulty a moment later in spontaneous connected speech.

Conversational speech is fluent, with no difficulty in articulation and little or no paraphasic interference, but circumlocutions are used and word-finding pauses may be evident. 'Empty words' such as *thing* or *these* may be frequently employed, and there is a notable lack of substantive words. Otherwise the grammatical structure of sentences is usually well preserved. The patient can repeat fluently what is said to him, and he usually performs relatively well on well-learned serials such as numbers or days of the week.

Comprehension is relatively well preserved in most instances, but internal speech is often affected so there may be difficulty in understanding or executing some oral or written commands.

It is not generally agreed whether nominal dysphasia represents a distinct form of defect. Some view it merely as a mild form of primary sensory dysphasia, since with expanding lesions one may merge progressively into the other. Brain considers the essential fault to lie in the use of words in their capacity as symbols, resulting from a break in the link between word-schemas and meaning-schemas. Geschwind views it as the consequence of difficulty in evoking intermodal associations, which normally allow the auditory associations of a word to be found from some of its other attributes. This explains the good preservation of grammatical structure, since grammar develops entirely within the auditory system and does not, like naming, depend on intermodal associations.

This is the type of dysphasia which in mild degree has most often been attributed to diffuse rather than focal brain damage. Certainly it may occur with diffuse brain dysfunction due to toxic or degenerative conditions. However it may also be found with focal brain lesions, perhaps particularly (though not exclusively) with dominant temporo-parietal lesions in the neighbourhood of the angular gyrus. Acalculia and other components of Gerstmann's syndrome often occur as associated defects.

Conduction Dysphasia (central dysphasia, syntactical dysphasia)

Under the above headings many authorities separate a further category of dysphasia, while others regard it merely as a further variant of primary sensory dysphasia. Essentially conduction dysphasia consists of a grave disturbance of language function in which speech and writing are impaired in the manner described above for primary sensory dysphasia, but in which comprehension of spoken and written material is none the less relatively well preserved as shown for example by simple yes/no responses. Repetition of speech is very severely impaired. Errors of grammar and syntax are a marked feature in cases designated 'syntactical dysphasia'.

According to Geschwind it results from a lesion which spares both Wernicke's and Broca's areas but disrupts the major connections between them. Thus Wernicke's area can function relatively well to analyse incoming information, though it can no longer act to guide the patient's own productions. There are contending views about the site of the responsible lesion (see Benson, 1979). One view, which accounts for the essential features of the disorder, blames a lesion of the arcuate fasciculus as it passes from the temporal to the frontal lobe by way of the parietal lobe. The more the lesion comes to implicate Wernicke's area itself the more will comprehension be impairment of the immediate memory span for auditory verbal material which was directly related to

The repetition defect in conduction dysphasia has come under closer scrutiny as a result of the work by Warrington and Shallice (1969) and Warrington *et al.* (1971), who consider that in a sub-group of these patients there is a highly specific impairment of immediate verbal memory. Three patients have been reported who showed a marked repetition defect for verbal material presented in the auditory modality. This appeared on analysis to be a selective impairment of the immediate memory span for auditory verbal material which was directly related to the 'memory' load of the task. There was much less difficulty when comparable material was presented visually. Moreover auditory verbal learning and verbal long-term memory were relatively intact, indicating that material could nonetheless gain access to the long-term memory store.

The Syndromes of the Isolated Speech Area

Under this title Goldstein (1948) and Geschwind *et al.* (1968) describe further variants of dysphasia, which though rare demand an alternative explanation in terms of the mechanism of defect. Comprehension is profoundly disturbed, but in contrast to primary sensory dysphasia the patient can easily repeat what is said to him, and the ability to learn new verbal material is retained. Spontaneous speech is moreover slow and laboured and lacks the fluency of primary sensory dysphasia. It is postulated that both Wernicke's and Broca's areas, and the connections between them, remain intact, but the whole system is cut off from other parts of the cortex. It

is the lack of these widespread connections which leads to impaired comprehension and defects of propositional speech.

Though in pure form the syndrome is extremely rare two variants are well recognised. '*Transcortical motor dysphasia*' differs in that the patient can comprehend spoken speech, and is ascribed to a lesion anterior and/or superior to Broca's area. '*Transcortical sensory dysphasia*' differs in that the fluency of output is preserved, and here the lesion is usually large and involves either the parietal or temporal border zone areas.

Alexia with Agraphia (visual asymbolia, parieto-temporal alexia)

The patient is unable to read as with pure word-blindness, but in addition he is unable to write. However the execution and comprehension of spoken speech are substantially unimpaired.

The difficulty in reading is similar to that described for pure word-blindness. The difficulty in writing varies from complete inability to form letters to preservation of partial attempts at writing words. Copying is better than spontaneous writing, which is the converse of the situation in pure word-blindness. Moreover the patient cannot understand words that are spelled out loud, revealing that he is truly illiterate unlike the patient with pure word-blindness.

The condition may rarely be the predominant symptom from the outset, but more usually is found as the residual disturbance when a more global dysphasia clears up. It is usually accompanied by some degree of nominal dysphasia, dyscalculia, spatial disorganisation or visual object agnosia.

The defect results from disturbance of those parts of the brain which deal with the visual symbolic components of language, in Brain's terminology with 'visual word-schemas'. The lesion is in the angular gyrus and adjacent supramarginal gyrus of the dominant parietal lobe.

Jargon Aphasia

Jargon aphasia is the term used when speech is produced freely, volubly and clearly, but with such semantic jumble and misuse of words that meaning cannot be discerned. Typically there are phonetic distortions, neologisms, words put together in meaningless sequence, and sequences which are entirely irrelevant. The intonation and rhythm of formal speech are nevertheless preserved. Jargon aphasia is conventionally regarded as representing a severe example of primary sensory dysphasia, perhaps with superadded difficulties due to pure word deafness, or perhaps with a marked degree of generalised intellectual impairment. Kertesz and Benson (1970) have reported typical severe neologistic jargon in cases both of Wernicke's dysphasia and conduction dysphasia. Weinstein *et al.* (1966) were led to conclude quite differently that jargon aphasia represents dysphasia in conjunction with anosognosia, rather than a distinctive pattern of breakdown in the intrinsic speech structure. In their patients receptive difficulties were rarely severe, and the distinctive accompanying feature was disturbance of consciousness sufficient to produce confabulation, disorientation, and reduplicative delusions. In conformity with their observations on anosognosia generally (p. 62) the jargon often appeared selectively when the patient was questioned about his disabilities, and more coherent speech was produced in relation to neutral topics. The pathological basis was a lesion of the dominant hemisphere along with additional brain damage elsewhere, and all patients had bilateral cerebral involvement. However in favour of the conventional view that jargon represents a primary receptive defect, with failure to monitor speech productions, is the finding that patients who display it are not disturbed in the normal fashion when made to listen to delayed auditory feed-back of their own speech productions.

Psychiatric Disturbance and Dysphasia

Benson and Geschwind (1971) and Benson (1973, 1976) summarise the common forms of reaction which may be seen in dysphasic patients. These differ considerably in the different forms of language defect.

In primary motor dysphasia (Broca's dysphasia) frustration and depression are frequently seen, or more rarely the 'catastrophic reaction' in which tension and embarrassment culminate in a sudden outburst of weeping or anger with the patient's realisation of his failings. Indeed the absence of distress among such patients is usually indicative of widespread cerebral damage and consequent impairment of general intellectual ability. Both frustration and depression are considered to indicate a more favourable prognosis for recovery with therapy, representing as they do an awareness of the speech difficulties. On the other hand, angry negativism with hostile responses and refusal to participate in treatment can sometimes emerge and seriously complicate rehabilitation.

By contrast the patient with primary sensory dysphasia (Wernicke's dysphasia) typically shows a lack of interest in, or even unawareness of his language problems. Such patients often act as though they believe their own speech to be normal and as though they feel that people around them fail to speak normally. Agitation, and sometimes severe paranoid reactions may ensue, with suspicions that others are talking about them, plotting against them, or deliberately using unintelligible jargon to prevent them from understanding. Outbursts of impulsive, aggressive behaviour may be seen. In Benson's experience almost every patient who had needed custodial care during recovery from dysphasia had suffered a paranoid reaction secondary to severe comprehension disability.

From the diagnostic point of view the disordered language productions of certain schizophrenic patients, and the phenomena of dysphasia due to brain damage, need to be very carefully distinguished from each other. This can only be done by careful attention to the *form* of language output and by comprehensive tests of language function. The 'word salad' of the chronically deteriorated schizophrenic may sometimes closely resemble dysphasic speech; conversely some cases of dysphasia are mistakenly diagnosed as psychotic for long periods of time, especially the patient with primary sensory dysphasia who produces a wealth of paraphasic neologisms. The neurological examination is often totally negative in such patients, their output is vague and apparently 'confused', and they may react negatively or not at all to the examiner's speech in a manner suggestive of psychosis. Any *sudden* onset of speech disorder must therefore always dictate caution, even in the established chronic schizophrenic patient.

Gerson *et al.* (1977) have analysed tape-recorded interviews with groups of posterior aphasic and schizophrenic patients in order to determine the features most useful in making the clinical distinction. Paraphasic substitutions of incorrect words, and perseverative responses at some point in the interview, were common among the dysphasics but absent among the schizophrenics. The length of verbal responses to open-ended questions was considerably shorter among the dysphasics, and these did not show the bizarre reiterative themes frequently encountered among the schizophrenics. The dysphasic patients showed at least some awareness of their language difficulties, and used gestures or pauses to enlist the examiner's aid, whereas the schizophrenic patients were impervious to the adequacy or otherwise of their communication. Vagueness of response arose from word-finding difficulties in the dysphasic patients but was apparently attributable to shifts of attention in the schizophrenics. The 'circumlocution' of dysphasia could thus often be contrasted with the 'circumstantiality' of schizophrenic speech.

It is only on rare occasions that difficulty arises in distinguishing between psychogenic and organic disturbances of language function. The most common hysterical speech disorder consists of complete aphonia or mutism; or if sounds are produced there are usually no recognisable words at all. A very rare example of dyslexia and dysgraphia of psychogenic origin has been described by Master and Lishman (1984).

Apraxia and Related Executive Disorders

Apraxia is notoriously difficult to define. In essence it refers to an inability to carry out purposive voluntary movements, or movement complexes, when this cannot be accounted for in terms of paresis, incoordination, sensory loss or involuntary movements. The patient cannot at will set the movement in train or guide a series of consecutive movements in their correct spatial and temporal sequence, even though the same muscles can be used and analogous movements performed in other contexts.

The essential nature of apraxic disturbances is incompletely understood. Dysphasia is an accompanying defect in the great majority of cases and deficient comprehension of commands may sometimes play a part. Agnosia for an object may hinder the patient from carrying out purposive movements appropriate to its use, while agnosia for spatial relationships will similarly interfere with the copying of a movement by imitation. Over and above such complications however, one must in many cases postulate some higher order difficulty with aspects of cerebral organisation which have a specific bearing on motor functions.

The difficulties for any explanatory system include the observation that movements which cannot be performed to command can sometimes be performed in imitation of the examiner, or a movement which cannot be initiated is performed a moment later when the patient's attention is not directed towards it. Sometimes simple discrete movements are affected, and sometimes complex coordinated sequences as in the lighting of a candle or the use of

a tool. Frequently performance is much better in the actual presence of the tool than when the patient is asked to demonstrate its use in imagination. Finally, and to a surprising extent, whole body movements to command are often found to be perfectly preserved, while limb and facial movements are defective. Simple hierarchies of difficulty do not provide an explanation for these anomalies, and systems which attempt to classify the pictures meet with many exceptions. The precise details of the test situation can obviously have a considerable influence on the assumptions which are drawn.

Brain (1965) suggests that purposive movements are organised by 'schemas' which may or may not enter consciousness depending on the context of the movement. The more practised the act, and the more automatic it has become, the more it will be carried out without conscious awareness and conscious volition. Apraxia may be regarded as the result of disorganisation of such schemas, and taking place at various levels of complexity. At the highest level will be found disturbance where the schemas are involved in the formulation of the idea of a movement, and at the lowest where the schema consists of a motor pattern which regulates the selection of the appropriate muscles.

Geschwind (1965) puts forward a simpler model which views the apraxias as failures of connection between certain cortical regions. Lesions which disrupt connections between the auditory association cortex and motor association cortex of the dominant hemisphere will result in inability to carry out motor commands with the limbs of either side of the body, since this depends on impulses carried forward to the left motor cortex and thence across the corpus callosum to equivalent regions on the right. A lesion of the left motor cortex itself will produce a right hemiplegia together with apraxia limited to the left arm, since the origin of the transcallosal pathway has been destroyed. The dysphasia accompanying both of these lesions is of a type which leaves comprehension perfectly adequate for the understanding of the commands. Lesions of the corpus callosum itself result in apraxia to command without dysphasia, and limited to the left limbs, since the motor cortex of the right hemisphere is now isolated from the speech mechanisms of the left. When imitation of movements is also disrupted this is presumed to depend on loss of essential connections between the visual and the motor association cortices. Geschwind makes the further interesting point that the patient's own explanations for his defects are often quite inadequate, because he cannot introspect in the usual way and produce verbal reports about the failures of right hemisphere function.

Ajuriaguerra and Tissot (1969) review these and other theories of apraxia and find them to be inadequate. They present instead a view of apraxia derived from the developmental psychology of Piaget, and closely linked to the processes involved in the mastery of space. The child begins with understanding the space involved in the manipulation of objects, then proceeds to master space centred on his body, and finally external and 'objective' space. This process is intimately bound with extensions outwards of the developing body schema. Experience in manipulating objects leads to progressive dissociation of the concept of time from that of space, and finally the spatial schema of 'action' becomes conceivable independently of time. Disintegration of this process may result variably in different classical syndromes, *viz.* disordered appreciation of spatial relationships (constructional apraxia), disturbance of body gestures, disturbance of spatial and temporal relationships in movement, or inability to utilise tools and objects. The forms of apraxia may thus depend upon the type of space in which the movements are realised, whether external space, space centred on the body, or the 'concrete space of manipulation'.

The relationship of apraxia to intellectual impairment must also be considered. Apraxia is perhaps more often seen with diffuse than with strictly focal brain lesions, so that other intellectual processes are frequently also impaired. With focal lesions, however, other cognitive processes may prove to be largely intact, even though at first sight the severely apraxic patient is often misdiagnosed as demented. Nonetheless such patients are severely handicapped in many tasks requiring the demonstration of intelligence, and it is likely that schemas for purposive movement are so interwoven in cognitive processes that their disruption is bound to have an adverse effect.

The chief varieties of apraxia which are recognised in clinical practice are outlined below.

Limb-kinetic Apraxia

The skill and delicacy of movements is disturbed, both for complex and simple actions. The difficulty which the patient experiences is a function of the muscular complexity rather than the psychomotor complexity involved. It may be confined to particular muscle groups, and even to certain fingers of a hand. This form has characteristics intermediate between paresis and apraxia and is therefore often excluded from the apraxias proper. It results from a relatively small lesion of the contralateral premotor cortex.

Also of frontal origin is the 'magnetic syndrome', in which a grasp reflex is coupled with an irrepressible tendency to follow objects with the hands when they are touched or when they enter the field of vision. This fixation interferes with the execution of other movements, since the hand adheres to the paper when the patient wishes to write, or the foot to the ground when he wishes to walk. Once the foot is lifted a complete step follows immediately. The 'utilisation behaviour' which may also accompany a frontal lesion is described on p. 91

Ideomotor Apraxia

This may be regarded as a disturbance of voluntary movement at a fairly low level of motor organisation, or alternatively as a disturbance in the use of space centred on the body. The patient can often formulate to himself the idea of the movement which he wishes to perform, but finds that he cannot execute it. Thus the voluntary impulse does not evoke the appropriate organisation of the movement in space and time. For example the patient cannot raise his hand or wave it to command, even though the instructions are understood. In some cases he can copy equivalent movements, but this too may fail. Yet essentially the same movements can be performed automatically as in signalling goodbye, or in the course of other activities to which his attention is not directed. In general the greater the volitional nature of the act, and the less it has become automatic, the more it is disrupted.

The disorder is usually bilateral, and most commonly involves the upper limbs. Unilateral apraxia almost always involves the left upper limb, and is then typically seen with right hemiplegia and aphasia. In facial apraxia the patient cannot smile or produce tongue movements to order, and this too may be bilateral or unilateral. In trunk apraxia the patient cannot organise at will the movements required for sitting or lying. This however is relatively rare and whole body movements are usually well preserved in the other forms.

There is general agreement that lesions of the dominant left hemisphere are much commoner than non-dominant lesions in apraxia (Piercy, 1964). The parietal lobe has been chiefly incriminated though attention has also been drawn to lesions of the temporal lobe (Ajuriaguerra and Tissot, 1969). With apraxia of the face and tongue the lesion is usually placed at the base of the precentral motor cortex. In cases of left unilateral apraxia, a lesion of the corpus callosum or of its lateral extension into the left motor association cortex is likely to be responsible.

Ideational Apraxia

The patient is unable to carry out co-ordinated sequences of actions, such as taking a match from a box and striking it, or to perform the complex movements involved in using such tools as a comb or a pair of scissors. Ideomotor apraxia may coexist, or the patient may by contrast be capable of straightforward imitation of simple movements. Sometimes performance is clearly better when the tool is held by the patient than when he attempts to demonstrate the action in the abstract. Variability may be seen from one task to another and on different occasions.

In ideational apraxia the concepts of the required movements appear to be disturbed, together with the planning of the act to be accomplished. This may represent a disturbance of the 'schemas' at a high level of their organisation, while lower levels remain comparatively intact. The conception of the movements as a whole can be seen to be faulty, with disruption of the relationships between their spatial and temporal components. It may be regarded as a 'programming' apraxia, whereas ideomotor apraxia is a more basic executory defect. Others, however, discount such a distinction based on functional levels, and base it rather on the nature of the task. In ideomotor apraxia the essential disorder lies in the formation of gestures in space, while tools are used normally. In ideational apraxia the problem lies not with the complexity of the task but in the requirement that tools should be used to a purpose; it is thus an 'agnosia of utilisation'. Still others doubt the validity of any distinction between the two forms when patients are investigated with due attention to detail, and view ideational apraxia merely as a more severe form of ideomotor apraxia.

Ideational apraxia is always bilateral. If based on circumscribed pathology the lesion usually involves the dominant hemisphere, and again usually the parietal or temporal lobes. It is in fact mostly seen with bilateral or diffuse brain lesions, and is usually accompanied by severe dysphasia or considerable generalised dementia.

Apraxia for Dressing

The patient has obvious difficulty in putting on clothes. He cannot relate the spatial form of garments to that of his body, puts the jacket on back to front or the arm into the wrong sleeve. Buttons and laces present particular difficulty and are often left undone.

Clinically the concept of dressing apraxia is useful in drawing attention to a dramatic symptom when more refined tests of apraxia and agnosia have yet to be performed. It is improbable, however, that it represents a distinct form of apraxia, and the symptoms probably depend on a variety of defects which differ from case to case. There is often a mixture of apraxia and agnosia, the latter with visuospatial components. In many cases, right-left disorientation, unilateral inattention, neglect of the left limbs and other disturbances of the body image are likely to contribute. Generalised cognitive impairment can also often be detected.

The disorder is seen more commonly with right sided or bilateral lesions than with left sided lesions. The parieto-occipital regions are usually involved.

Constructional Apraxia

Constructional apraxia is identified when the spatial disposition of actions is altered without any apraxia for individual movements. It thus becomes apparent in tasks which involve the use, and more particularly the representation, of space, for example the construction or copying of patterns under visual control. It is obvious that such disorders will have a profound effect on many conventional tests of non-verbal intelligence, and this is how they sometimes come to light. Raven's matrices and Kohs' block test will be particularly affected along with the assembly items of the Wechsler performance scale.

The defect is obviously not purely motor, but involves perceptual functions as well. This is usually immediately apparent in the patient's satisfaction with a grossly imperfect copy of presented test material. For many authorities constructional apraxia is broadly synonymous with visuospatial agnosia, and this form of defect is therefore further considered on p. 54.

Other Forms of Executive Defect

Executive defects of smaller degree, and not amounting to formal apraxias, have been investigated by Wyke (1968). Detailed measurements were made of motor skills which required timing and precision of movement in patients with a variety of focal brain lesions. Patients with right hemisphere lesions showed unilateral defects of the opposite hand only, whereas patients with left hemisphere lesions showed bilateral defects, albeit more severe in the contralateral limb. These interesting findings support the view that left hemisphere lesions result in some higher order executive defect which cannot be explained in terms of paresis or incoordination alone.

The Agnosias and Related Defects of Perception

The term 'agnosia' was introduced by Freud (1891) although the condition had been described much earlier than this. It may be defined as 'an impaired recognition of an object which is sensorially presented while at the same time the impairment cannot be reduced to sensory defects, mental deterioration, disorders of consciousness and attention, or to a non-familiarity with the object' (Frederiks, 1969). It implies therefore a disorder of perceptual recognition which takes place at a higher level than the processing of primary sensory information. Even though the sensory processes are themselves unimpaired there is inability to interpret sensory information, to recognise its significance and endow it with meaning on the basis of past experience. This essential distinction between the perception of sensory impressions and the further step of their associative recognition was made early on by Lissauer (1890) and by Liepmann (1908). Clinically the situation is identified when there is failure of recognition which cannot be attributed to a primary sensory defect or to generalised intellectual impairment. A patient may, for example, fail to recognise an object by sight and be unable to name it, demonstrate its use or relate it to a matching picture, even though vision is intact for other purposes. Nevertheless the same object is readily recognised by means of touch, showing that he is suffering from a modality-specific defect of higher cerebral function, and not from aphasia or apraxia. The several types of agnosia related to vision have received most attention, but agnosias are also described in relation to hearing and to touch.

Brain (1965) points out that the underlying disorder of function must have something in common with both aphasia and apraxia, since a patient can only demonstrate that he recognises an object by using speech or action; in effect agnosia represents an isolated aphasia and apraxia related to a particular object when it is perceived through a particular sensory channel. During development an object is presented to more than one sense and thereby comes to be perceived as an entity. Thereafter perception via one channel alone is able to evoke a large number of sensorimotor experiences in relation to the object, and moreover to allow its identification whether seen from one aspect or another, or even when represented in two-dimensional form. Brain therefore postulates physiological sensory 'schemas' which represent the bases of patterns common to manifold presentations, and which allow recognition. Separate schemas for vision, touch and hearing must be to some extent anatomically distinct, since we do not lose recognition through all sensory channels by any focal brain lesion but only in dementia due to diffuse brain disease. Equally this means that the actual process of recognition to which the schema gives access is a function of the brain as a whole.

The whole concept of agnosia has, however, come under increasingly critical discussion. Lesions producing so restricted a form of defect are rare (with the exception of visuospatial agnosia), and examples reported in the literature are often open to argument. A formidable amount of controversy has surrounded such questions as the independence of agnosic defects from subtle aspects of primary sensory defects, and the rarity of cases without some degree of dementia has made such questions hard to resolve. Geschwind (1965) has suggested that most agnosias are in fact no more than modality-specific defects resulting from the isolation of the primary sensory cortex from the areas subserving language. Benson and Greenberg (1969) point out, in the case of the visual agnosias, that the number of suggested mechanisms very nearly equals the number of recorded cases. This confusion is often paralleled by conflicting claims about the site of responsible pathology. For detailed discussion of these points Frederiks' (1969) comprehensive review should be consulted.

Neuropsychology has therefore come to concern itself less with the search for examples of pure agnosic defects and arguments over their significance, but to concentrate instead on an operational analysis, in large numbers of subjects, of the correlations between site of lesion and the form of the deficits that follow. Such deficits may be absolute or relative in degree, sometimes involving simple perceptual processes and sometimes implicating other higher mental mechanisms. Their precise nature is amenable to dissection by means of standardised examination techniques, and ultimately this is likely to be more fruitful in leading to a coherent understanding of cerebral organisation.

In the sections which follow the classical agnosic syndromes will be described, and also the more common forms of related perceptual defect.

VISUAL AGNOSIAS AND VISUAL PERCEPTUAL DEFECTS

Visual Object Agnosia

In visual object agnosia an object cannot be named by sight but is readily identified by other means such as touch or hearing. There is equally failure to select a matching picture from a group, or to indicate the appropriate use of the object. Sometimes the patient may describe a use appropriate to an incorrect recognition. The difficulty may vary from day to day, and sometimes an object may be recognised from other cues in its familiar surroundings but not elsewhere. Usually the difficulty is restricted to small objects, but in severe examples it may extend to larger objects, with consequent difficulty in finding the way about. Commonly faces continue to be recognised while other objects are not. In most reported examples there has also been difficulty in describing objects from memory and in drawing them (i.e. loss of visual images for objects), difficulty with colour recognition, dyslexia and dysgraphia.

Bay (1953, 1965) and others have been sceptical of gnostic activity generally, and have suggested that visual forms of agnosia are attributable to impaired primary perception combined in most cases with general mental impairment. Attention is drawn not only to the visual field defects which are commonly present, but also to other subtle defects of primary visual perception in the intact parts of the field. Ettlinger (1956), however, has argued against such an interpretation, and points out the frequency of patients with severe sensory disorders compared to the rarity of agnosia. Nevertheless, very few satisfactory cases of visual object agnosia have been reported. One of the most convincing is that of Hécaen and Ajuriaguerra (1956b) which followed left occipital lobectomy. In all others the occipital lobe has proved to be the site of the lesion, usually the left but occasionally the right. The lesions are frequently extensive and bilateral, and the defect may sometimes emerge only after an initial period of cortical blindness.

Prosopagnosia

Agnosia for faces has been described as a distinct and separate defect, which may or may not be combined with visual object agnosia and is certainly much commoner than the latter (Hécaen and Angelergues, 1962). In extreme form the patient cannot recognise his own face in a mirror. The defect has been reported to be commoner with right than with left hemisphere lesions but in most cases there is probably bilateral involvement (Meadows, 1974). Damasio et al. (1982b) strongly support the latter in their analysis of post mortem and CT scan data; bilateral lesions of the central visual system, situated specifically in the medial occipitotemporal regions, proved to be crucial for the development of prosopagnosia.

Warrington and James (1967a), studying defects of facial recognition, have indicated a distinction between impaired recognition of previously well-known faces, which depends on long-term storage of visual information, and impaired recognition of a previously unknown face from immediate memory. The former appears to be associated more with right temporal lesions, and the latter with right parietal lesions. Damasio et al. (1982b) argue that the primary factor in the appearance of prosopagnosia may be the requirement to evoke the specific context of a given visual stimulus. They suggest, indeed, that the defect in prosopagnosia may not be specific to human faces, but may be prone to emerge in relation to any visual stimulus provided that its 'ambiguity' is sufficiently high and that its recognition depends on recalling the specific context in which it has previously been perceived.

Agnosia for Colours

The patient is unable to name colours or to recognise named colours in the absence of any impairment of colour sense. Thus he can still sort coloured objects into categories, match them, and arrange them in series. The difficulty is usually seen as part of a visual object agnosia, and in association with alexia and right homonymous hemianopia. The distinction from straightforward colour naming defects is obviously difficult, but can sometimes be upheld, especially when colour recognition is defective in one half field of vision only.

Clear cut examples are again rare, and this form of agnosia is one of the most disputed. Dominant occipital lobe lesions are usually responsible.

Simultanagnosia

Classically the patient fails to recognise the meaning of a complex picture while details are correctly appreciated. This is not due to difficulty in forming meaningful concepts, however, since with auditory information there is prompt understanding. Moreover if plenty of time is given, or every individual feature of the picture pointed out, the patient ultimately comprehends the meaning. In a similar way, words cannot be read except by spelling out individual letters. The key problem appears to be with the perception of more than a limited number of units or configurations at a time. Thus tachistoscopic studies have shown that such patients have normal thresholds for the perception of single shapes and letters, but greatly elevated thresholds when more than one stimulus is presented at a time (Kinsbourne and Warrington, 1962a, 1963). Luria *et al.* (1963) have described an impairment of the eye movements involved in visual scanning in simultanagnosia, but probably as a secondary effect resulting from restriction of visual attention. Posterior lesions of the dominant lobe have been implicated in patients who display the complete syndrome.

Visuospatial Defects

The abstract conception of space is derived from the spatial relations which are observed to exist between objects. As Brain (1965) points out this must be learned primarily in relation to the position of our own bodies, with compensation for the apparent movement of objects when it is our own eyes or body which move. After cerebral lesions a number of defects of visuospatial perception may be demonstrated. It has proved difficult, however, to reach agreement about their classification and the precise nature of the defects involved, since many tests require at the same time perception, construction and even visual memory. It remains, for example, uncertain whether failure to reproduce simple models and drawings depends on dyspraxic difficulties or failure of visuospatial analysis, likewise how far inability to draw from memory may further depend on defective visual imagery. Classical visuospatial agnosia is indeed widely regarded as broadly synonymous with constructional apraxia as will be discussed below. Nevertheless certain syndromes of localising value can be recognised as follows:

Visuospatial Agnosia is identified by failure on tasks which demand explicit analysis of the spatial properties of a visual display. This is most readily tested by asking the patient to reproduce simple constructional tasks under visual control—the copying of drawings or the construction of patterns with bricks or sticks. The Block Design and Object Assembly subtests of the Wechsler Adult Intelligence Scale will most readily indicate minor degrees of such a defect.

Usually the patient has no difficulty in finding his way about, though an itinerary on a map cannot be indicated and towns cannot be correctly located. In the most severe examples a loss of topographical memory (p. 55) may be present as well. An interesting fact, often noted, is that patients with marked visuospatial defects rarely make specific complaints about them. Thus visuospatial agnosia easily eludes routine examination and special tests are needed for its detection.

Visuospatial agnosia results from lesions in the parietal lobe, and appears to be considerably more common and severe with lesions of the right lobe than the left. Piercy (1964), De Renzi and Faglioni (1967) and Warrington (1970) discuss this evidence, also the indications that the defects may be qualitatively different when produced by left or right sided lesions. The former appear to depend more on executive difficulties and the latter on perceptual components in the task. Thus drawings made by patients with left parietal lesions tend to be coherent but simplified versions of the model, with omission of details but with relative preservation of spatial relationships. Performance is notably improved when the patient is provided with a model to copy. Frequent associated defects are aphasia, apraxia, or components of the Gerstmann syndrome such as right-left disorientation. Patients with right parietal lesions produce more elaborate drawings, but made hastily and without care, and the result is typically scattered and fragmented. Disorientation on the page is marked, the left side of the page is relatively neglected, and the drawings are often asymmetrical and show gross disorganisation of spatial relationships. The presence of a model is of little extra help. Some therefore prefer to retain the term constructional apraxia when the disorder results from dominant hemisphere lesions, and visuospatial agnosia when due to non-dominant lesions, though the distinctions between the two are by no means universally acknowledged.

Strong evidence has come from studies of patients after section of the corpus callosum to uphold the greater importance of the non-dominant hemisphere in tasks demanding visuospatial analysis. After the operation, which effectively disconnects the hemispheres from each other, patients show better ability to copy geometrical figures with the left hand than the right, even though the right hand had been superior before the commissure section. The ability to assemble complex object puzzles, or to reconstruct from a model standard geometrical patterns of the Kohs' block design test, are also better performed with the left hand than the right (Bogen and Gazzaniga, 1965).

Visual Disorientation. A further defect of visuospatial ability consists of defective ability to localise objects in space by vision alone. As a result the patient cannot point accurately to an object, or estimate its distance. It can occur in either half-field of vision alone, contralateral to the side of a lesion, or in the whole visual field with bilateral lesions. When involving the whole field of vision the patient has difficulty in finding his way around objects, or in learning the topography of a room.

Visual disorientation is usually seen in conjunction with impairment on more complex visuospatial tasks, and the lesions are situated posteriorly within the hemispheres. Warrington and James (1967b) suggest that there may be areas within the occipital lobes which contribute to the absolute localisation in space of a single object, whereas the integration of several spatial stimuli necessary for the appreciation of spatial relations between two or more objects is impaired by unilateral lesions within the right parietal area. De Renzi *et al.* (1971) have reported a test of spatial judgement which appears to demonstrate complete dominance for the post-Rolandic region of the right hemisphere. This involves the moving of a hinged rod into the same position as a model, and patients with right posterior lesions were found to perform much worse than patients with lesions in any other location. This applied whether visual or tactile forms of the test were used. De Renzi *et al.* suggest that the test measures spatial perception at a very basic and simple level, thus accounting for the more complete right-hemisphere dominance than is found with more complex tasks such as the copying of drawings.

Visual Neglect. Unilateral visual neglect (or unilateral spatial agnosia), may be seen in spontaneous drawings, copies, description of pictures, or use of paper when writing. It may also lead the patient to fail to take turnings to the left and consequently he may lose his way on familiar routes. This is an agnosia for space as such, not merely an agnosia for spatial relations between visual objects. It may be seen in many degrees of severity. It is well confirmed that neglect of the left half of space is very much more common than right, and depends upon a right parietal lesion.

Loss of Topographical Memory. Patients with visual object agnosia or visuospatial agnosia may some-

times still be able to visualise familiar scenes or describe familiar routes. Loss of topographical memory may, however, occur, and again in conjunction with lesions in the parietal lobes. Semmes *et al.* (1955) have shown that on tasks of following routes from maps, patients with parietal lesions do worse than patients with lesions elsewhere. Neither parietal lobe has emerged as especially important in this regard. The difficulties occurred irrespective of whether visual or tactile maps were employed, suggesting a defect of appreciation of extrapersonal space which was not modality specific. Hécaen (1962) studied the clinical evidence of loss of topographical memory for a previously familiar environment, and found that in most cases the parietal lesions were bilateral, but with more of the unilateral cases involving the right than the left hemisphere.

Ratcliff and Newcombe (1973) have produced especially interesting findings from a study of men with penetrating missile wounds of the brain. Two tests were employed — a visually guided stylus maze task, and a locomotor map-reading task in which the subject was required to trace out a designated route on foot. These were designed to tap visuospatial agnosia and topographical disorientation respectively. Patients with lesions in the posterior part of the right hemisphere were significantly worse than those with left posterior lesions on the maze-learning test, but a significant deficit on the map-reading test emerged only in those with bilateral posterior lesions. A clear dissociation between the two tasks could sometimes be observed. Ratcliff and Newcombe were led to conclude that while the right hemisphere has a special role in the perception of space, it does not bear an exclusive responsibility for the maintenance of spatial orientation. Bilateral lesions appear to be necessary before route finding is impaired, perhaps because this involves a constant reorientation to stimuli as the subject moves around and alters his frames of reference. Further experiments on the topic are described by De Renzi (1982), along with a detailed discussion of the various deficits which may contribute to topographical disorientation.

Other Visual Perceptual Defects

Other disorders of visual perception and of visuospatial analysis, which fall short of complete agnosia by any definition, have also proved to show interesting associations with the site of brain pathology. In particular they are more frequent and more marked with right hemisphere lesions than left.

Patients with right temporal lesions have been shown to do worse than other groups with focal brain damage on tasks of rapid visual identification, picture comprehension, and picture arrangement. These deficits are reflected for example in their scores on the Picture Completion and Picture Arrangement subtests of the Wechsler Adult Intelligence Scale, or on the McGill Picture Anomalies test in which the patient is required to identify incongruous features in a series of sketchily drawn pictures (Milner, 1958; Ettlinger, 1960; McFie, 1960). Right temporal lobectomy has been found to lead to greater difficulty than left in the learning and recall of material such as nonsense figures which are not susceptible to verbal mediation (Kimura, 1963). Warrington and James (1967c) have similarly found that patients with right hemisphere lesions are specially impaired on the recognition of incomplete drawings, but in this a parietal rather than a temporal lesion was found to be crucial, suggesting that difficulties with spatial perception may have made a decisive contribution.

Nevertheless it does appear from these various findings that the non-dominant hemisphere plays some special part in the processing of visual sensory data, and is to a considerable extent specialised in visual matters in a manner which complements the dominant hemisphere's specialisation for speech. Within the non-dominant hemisphere it is probable that the temporal lobe is especially important for pattern recognition, and more posterior regions in the parietal lobe for the appreciation of spatial relationships. Such a distinction was in general upheld by Newcombe's (1969) analysis of the long-term effects of missile wounds of the brain.

AUDITORY AGNOSIA AND AUDITORY PERCEPTUAL DEFECTS

In auditory agnosia hearing is unimpaired, as tested by pure tone thresholds, but the patient fails to recognise or distinguish the sounds which he hears. Thus in his everyday life he may give the appearance of being 'deaf'. Typically the onset is with severe dysphasia, which then clears substantially to leave the auditory problem in evidence. The patient is unable to recognise speech, as in pure word-deafness (p. 43), but in addition cannot recognise non-speech sounds such as the pouring of water, crumpling of paper or jingling of keys. Usually there is also failure to recognise musical sounds. These three defects— word-deafness, auditory agnosia, and 'sensory

amusia'—can occur together with varying degrees of severity.

The disorder is extremely rare and few convincing examples have been reported. Vignolo (1969) provides an excellent review, both of the phenomena observed and of their relationships to dysphasia. Most examples have been associated with bilateral lesions of the posterior parts of the temporal lobes.

Less complete difficulty with the processing of auditory information may be demonstrated in some patients with brain lesions. Vignolo (1969) has shown that patients with right hemisphere lesions fail relatively on tests of discriminating meaningless sounds, whereas patients with left-sided lesions have greater diffculty in identifying sounds to which meaning can be attached. This indicates that the auditory receiving areas of the two hemispheres are to some extent specialised, that of the right being specifically concerned with grasping the acoustic structure of the auditory input (i.e. subtle perceptual discrimination), and that of the left with endowing the input with meaning by virtue of semantic associative links (i.e. semantic decoding). Double dissociation was demonstrated in the patients with right and left hemisphere lesions between these two aspects of the 'understanding' of the auditory inputs. Thus where non-verbal sounds are concerned it appears likely that there are two types of 'agnosia' depending on the hemisphere involved; the left hemisphere defect is essentially one of semantic identification of the perceived sound and is closely linked with dysphasic defects, whereas the right hemisphere defect is qualitatively different and essentially of a perceptual discriminative nature.

With regard to music, the right temporal lobe appears to be more important than the left. Right temporal lobectomy has been found to impair performance on tests of musical aptitude, whereas left temporal lobectomy does not (Kimura, 1961; Milner, 1962). Shankweiler (1966) played extracts of familiar songs to patients who had had temporal lobectomies, and found that the left lesion group had greater difficulty in recalling the titles or words, whereas the right lesion group had greater difficulty in reproducing or recognising the melody. Dichotic listening tasks, in which different information is fed simultaneously into the two ears, have supported these findings in normal subjects; words fed to the right ear (and proceeding thence by crossed pathways predominantly to the left hemisphere) are reported better than words fed to the left ear, whereas with fragments of melodies the situation is reversed (Kimura, 1961, 1964). Moreover, when dichotic tests are given to lobectomised patients it is found that left temporal lobectomy produces a more severe decrement in the contralateral ear where words are concerned, and right temporal lobectomy for the recognition of musical passages (Shankweiler, 1966).

Gordon and Bogen (1974) have also reported interesting effects when patients are asked to sing familiar songs during the course of unilateral intracarotid amytal injections. When the left hemisphere is sedated with the drug the words of the song are severely affected while the melody continues well; by contrast when the right hemisphere is sedated the words remain relatively intact whereas pitch and melodic line are severely disrupted.

Clinically it has often been reported that musical ability may be selectively impaired after right hemisphere lesions, and conversely that musical ability may be preserved after left hemisphere lesions despite severe aphasia. This evidence is reviewed by Bogen (1969).

It seems clear, therefore, that the right hemisphere is superior to the left for the perception and mediation of 'structured' musical passages, i.e. of sounds built up into tuneful, melodic and harmonious combinations (Wyke, 1977). However more detailed experimental analysis of the components of musical perception — pitch, timbre, discrimination and rhythm — have often given conflicting results, suggesting that neither hemisphere alone is unequivocally specialised for all aspects of musical cognition. Interesting differences have also sometimes emerged between musically naïve and musically experienced subjects, perhaps illustrating the effects of learning processes on cerebral organisation. Wyke (1977) reviews the studies proceeding in these areas.

TACTILE PERCEPTUAL DEFECTS

In tactile agnosia the patient is unable to recognise an object by touch, even though the sensory functions of the hand being tested are normal. The same object is immediately recognised by other means, for example by touching it with the opposite hand or by vision.

It is not certain that the condition is distinguishable from the 'astereognosis' of cortical sensory loss, in which there is equally failure of tactile recognition. Some, however, claim that in tactile agnosia the patient can still distinguish the size, shape and texture of the objects even though the object cannot be recognised, whereas in astereognosis there is impaired appreciation of these sensory elements as well.

Commonly tactile agnosia is restricted to one hand, and results from a lesion in the opposite parietal lobe. The supramarginal gyrus has been especially incriminated. Bilateral tactile agnosia is said to follow damage in this region in the dominant hemisphere, and it is possible that in such cases callosal fibres to the opposite lobe have also been implicated in the lesion.

The 'Gerstmann Syndrome'

The concept of a 'Gerstmann syndrome' resulting from dominant parietal lobe lesions has become firmly entrenched in the neurological and psychological literature. It consists of finger agnosia, right-left disorientation, dyscalculia and dysgraphia. As such it remains a useful venue for the discussion of these disorders and provides a useful group of simple clinical tests when one is looking for subtle signs of a lesion in the dominant hemisphere. The essential clustering together of the defects has, however, been seriously questioned, and it is now clear that they do not constitute a 'syndrome' in the accepted sense of the word.

It is well known that the four components are not always found together, one or more being often absent when the others can be demonstrated clearly. Similarly one or more components can occur along with other disorders of cognitive function—dysphasia, dyslexia, constructional apraxia, visual disorientation, or generalised intellectual impairment. Benton (1961) examined the intercorrelations on tests of the four Gerstmann symptoms and of three other functions related to the parietal lobes (constructional ability, reading, and visual memory) in a large unselected series of brain-damaged subjects, and found that the correlations of the Gerstmann abilities with each other was no higher than with the three abilities not included in the syndrome. In a separate analysis of patients with damage restricted to the left parietal lobe the Gerstmann defects again failed to cluster together. Heimburger *et al.* (1964) in a similar study found that as the number of Gerstmann components increased the lesions tended to be larger in size. When all four defects did appear together they were usually accompanied by severe impairment of many other functions.

Moreover it has not been possible to establish a common fundamental disturbance underlying each of the four defects, which can indeed result individually from more than one kind of functional loss. For example, finger agnosia and right-left disorientation may be due to limited forms of body image disturbance or result from comprehension defects, dyscalculia may exist in many forms as described below, and dysgraphia may represent a disturbance of language function or result primarily from dyspraxia. It has been suggested, however, that if the concept were re-examined, taking into account a more restricted definition of each of the elements, the status of the syndrome might be further clarified (Warrington, 1970).

Dysgraphia has already been dealt with briefly on pp. 44 and 47, and the remaining three components are considered below.

Finger Agnosia

Finger agnosia is shown by loss of ability to recognise, name, identify, indicate or select individual fingers, either on the patient's own body or on that of another person. Traditionally the patient is asked to point to named fingers or to name an individual finger, but the presence of dysphasia may confound this simple procedure. Kinsbourne and Warrington (1962b) advocate a test in which two fingers are simultaneously touched by the examiner and the patient is asked to state the number of fingers between the ones touched, first in practice sessions with the eyes open and then with the eyes closed.

The disorder appears bilaterally. The patient does not report it spontaneously, and thus like constructional apraxia it is a defect usually only revealed by specific testing. A lesion in the left parieto-occipital area appears to be critical for its appearance, but it is possible that it can occur very occasionally with right hemisphere lesions. The angular gyrus and the second occipital convolution have been especially incriminated.

Gerstmann (1958) himself suggested that finger agnosia may represent a minimal form of whole body autotopagnosia, in other words a defect of recognition of the body or appreciation of the interrelations of body parts (see p. 63). He suggested that complete autotopagnosia is very rarely seen because lesions which are sufficient to produce it also produce concomitant defects which obscure the picture, whereas in the restricted form of finger agnosia it can be recognised as a clear-cut entity. Kinsbourne and Warrington (1964) view it instead as a difficulty in classifying fingers in terms of their relative positions, and see this as part of an underlying disorder in processing information in terms of a spatio-temporal sequence. Thus they found a particular type of spelling error in association with finger agnosia, namely errors relating to the ordering of the

letters in a word. Frederiks (1969) considers the defect to be polymorphous in origin, though usually closely bound to nominal dysphasia as the fundamental disturbance of function. He points out that no other part of the body is verbally differentiated to so great a degree as the hand, and also that despite its extensive cerebral representation we habitually disregard the hand when in use. Thus the physiological representation of the hand is in many ways different from that of other body parts, which may account, whatever the exact pathogenesis, for the special vulnerability which emerges in finger agnosia.

Right-Left Disorientation

This defect shows as inability to carry out instructions which involve an appreciation of right and left. The patient fails to point on command to objects on his right and his left, to indicate parts of his body on the right and the left, or to perform more complex instructions in which these directions form an integral part of the task. It undoubtedly can reflect several complex disorders of function. Gerstmann (1958) suggested that like finger agnosia it represented a restricted form of body image disturbance. Benton (1959) on the other hand stresses that language is likely to be intrinsically concerned with many forms of the disorder. Sauget et al. (1971) have investigated the relationship between sensory dysphasia and various forms of disturbance including right-left disorientation and finger agnosia, using both verbal and non-verbal tests. They conclude that these disturbances are closely linked to impairment of language comprehension, but that in addition impairment of somatosensory functions is necessary for their appearance.

Right-left disorientation can itself be accepted as a sign of left hemisphere dysfunction, but is of little value for more precise localisation within the hemisphere.

Dyscalculia

Dyscalculia is a disorder of the capacity for calculation in persons who have hitherto shown no disturbance of their arithmetical faculties. The complex problems in this field are reviewed by Grewel (1969), who points out that a detailed analysis of the nature of the calculation defect is necessary if the symptom is to have any localising value since there are many possible sources of failure. Arithmetical functions can be disturbed to an important extent independently of language functions and general intelligence, but pure cases of this nature are very rare. Secondary dyscalculia can result from disturbed spatial ability, defects of short-term memory, perseveration, or simple impairment of concentration.

Primary dyscalculia may be due to loss of ability to appreciate or manipulate numbers as symbols, or failure to combine them syntactically to produce a meaningful digit notation. Alternatively comprehension of the nature of arithmetical operations such as addition or multiplication may be lost while notation and mechanical aspects are unimpaired.

Dyscalculia has been found in one form or another with lesions of the frontal, temporal, parietal and occipital lobes of the brain, but the parietal lobes have been most frequently involved and the left lobe more often than the right. In this connection Hécaen (1969) describes three forms which can be distinguished symptomatically. Dyscalculia in the restricted sense of inability to perform arithmetical sums, and dyscalculia due to alexia, are both commoner with left-sided lesions than right, whereas dyscalculia due to incapacity for spatial organisation in numerical operations is commoner with right-sided lesions than left. Warrington (1970) concludes that in general, when a patient is unable to do simple mechanical additions and subtractions, without sufficient dementia or dysphasia to explain it, a focal lesion may be suspected in the left parietal cortex.

Disorders of the Body Image

The body image, or 'body schema' may be regarded as a subjective model of the body against which changes in its posture, in the disposition of its parts, and in its soundness or integrity can be appreciated. As such the body image is not static, but changes constantly under the influence of internal and external sensory impressions. Moreover it invariably includes important unconscious as well as conscious components, so cannot be viewed as a mere picture in the mind. Normally it exists on the fringe of awareness, but aspects can be brought into consciousness when subjective attention is focused upon them.

The body image is thus an abstract conception, acquired during development and compounded of physiological and psychological elements. Schilder (1935) has extended the concept and in particular has stressed that data from a wide range of sources must be incorporated into any notion of the body image, including aspects of personality, emotion and social interaction. For him the postural model proposed by Head (1920) represents only a low level of body image organisation, whilst higher levels are built out of instinctual needs and personal interactions.

Clearly therefore the body image occupies a central place among the problems of brain-mind relationships, and not unnaturally its disorders must often be considered in relation to both cerebral pathology and individual psychopathology. Disorders of the body image are implicit in a wide range of puzzling and often bizarre clinical states, around which a good deal of controversy exists. Some disturbances represent the influence of structural or physiological changes in the brain, as seen for example in the presence of cerebral disease or in the effects of drugs such as cannabis or LSD. Other disturbances may accompany severe sensory deprivation or functional psychiatric illnesses such as neurosis or schizophrenia, and then may appear to be mainly psychogenic in origin. In some particularly puzzling disorders, such as anosognosia, it is probably necessary to invoke both organic and psychogenic factors in an attempt at a complete explanation. The concept of body image disturbance is thus involved in many different areas of study. Frederiks (1969) suggests that we must strive at least to keep clear whether we use it in a neurological or a psychopathological sense. In the former the aim is to find data which can contribute to topographical diagnosis of brain disease, whereas in the latter the interest is in relationships which are psychologically understandable.

The body image disturbances which follow brain lesions are themselves very incompletely understood. Sometimes they have been regarded as based on primary perceptual disturbances of kinaesthetic or proprioceptive inflow and sometimes as purely agnosic defects. At least a partial contribution may result from deficits in language comprehension, spatial analysis, or ability to analyse a whole in terms of its parts, as will be discussed in connection with individual disturbances below. In some manifestations of body image disturbance hallucinatory experiences appear also to be directly involved. Precise analysis is often hampered by some degree of impairment of consciousness or generalised intellectual loss which frequently accompany the more severe disorders.

Here the body image disorders most closely tied to brain pathology will be considered first and in most detail, then those encountered in non-organic psychiatric illness will be briefly reviewed. It must be appreciated, however, that the dividing line where pathogenesis is concerned is sometimes far from clear cut.

Body image disturbances associated with brain lesions can be broadly divided into those affecting half of the body only, and those which involve bilateral disturbances. Unilateral body image disturbances are commoner with right hemisphere lesions than left, and the left side of the body is therefore most often affected. They include unilateral inattention, neglect, feelings and beliefs that the left limbs are missing (hemisomatognosia), and lack of awareness or denial of disability (anosognosia). Bilateral body image disturbances are commoner with left cerebral lesions than right. They are usually restricted to finger agnosia (p. 58) or right-left disorientation (p. 58), but very occasionally there is difficulty in naming or pointing to any body part (autotopagnosia). Complex illusions of bodily transformation or displacement are less closely tied to lesions in known locations and more intricately involved with non-organic psychopathology.

Unilateral Unawareness and Neglect

This represents perhaps the best known and most frequently encountered change in the body image. For reasons incompletely understood the disorder affects the left limbs in the great majority of cases, and appears to derive particularly from lesions in the neighbourhood of the supramarginal and angular gyri of the right parietal lobe. A spectrum of disturbances is seen, ranging from inattention and unawareness to neglect.

The range and interrelationships of these phenomena are excellently described by Critchley (1953). A minor degree of inattention to the left limbs may require special techniques of examination to reveal it, such as double simultaneous stimulation of both sides of the body together. In unawareness the disorder is more obtrusive, the patient failing to utilise the left hand in bimanual activities, or ignoring the left foot when putting on his slippers. When attention is specifically drawn to the left limbs, however, they are used with normal efficiency, or if a degree of paresis exists the patient admits his difficulties. It is as though the limbs of this side were 'occupying a lower level in a hierarchy of personal awareness' (Critchley, 1953).

The disorder may progress no further than this, or may develop into more elaborate symptoms of neglect. The limbs may be actively neglected in washing or dressing, one half of the face may be left unshaven, or the hair uncombed. This is more likely in the presence of confusion or other impairment of intellect. Sometimes unawareness or neglect foreshadow the development of a hemiparesis, and when this is present the more florid features of anosognosia may be added (p. 61).

Such disorders are seen more commonly after acute brain lesions, and particularly after cerebrovascular accidents. The degree of unawareness or neglect appears to be related to the abruptness of the lesion, the clarity of consciousness, and whether or not motor weakness is present. Usually these are transient phenomena, and changeable from time to time during clinical examination, but occasionally the disability persists in some form as an enduring defect.

While a special association has been noted with parietal, and especially right parietal lesions, typical syndromes of neglect have been reported following damage in other locations. Damasio et al. (1980) reported 5 examples of contralateral inattention and neglect, coupled with limb akinesia, after lesions in the frontal lobes or basal ganglia. Surprisingly the frontal lesions were in the left hemisphere, leading to neglect on the right side of the body. Damasio et al. suggest that the various structures involved may belong to an anatomically interconnected system subserving selective attention. Right thalamic infarcts have also been noted to lead to contralateral neglect of hemiparetic or akinetic limbs, along with anosognosia, marked emotional flattening and visuospatial difficulties (Watson and Heilman, 1979; Watson et al., 1981).

Hemisomatognosia (hemidepersonalisation)

In this much rarer phenomenon the patient feels as though the limbs on one side are missing, sometimes episodically but sometimes as a continuous subjective state. It may feature as part of an aura in a focal epileptic attack. Like unilateral neglect it affects the left limbs much more commonly than the right, and can occur either with or without hemiparesis. It is frequently accompanied by unilateral spatial agnosia.

The disorder is accompanied by various degrees of loss of insight. The limbs may feel absent though the patient knows this is not so, or he may say they are absent but can be corrected in his belief, or he may have a fixed delusion that they are absent which cannot be corrected. When consciousness is clear the patient usually retains insight into the illusory nature of the condition, even though it may feel to be very vivid, and can reassure himself as to the presence of the limbs by feeling or looking at them.

In the presence of confusion, however, he may proclaim that the limbs are missing, look for them under the bed, or accuse others of taking them away.

Anosognosia

Anosognosia implies lack of awareness of *disease,* and is most commonly shown for left hemiplegic limbs. It may occur along with unilateral neglect, hemisomatognosia, or with the illusions of transformation and displacement which are considered below.

In mildest form the patient merely shows a lack of normal concern for his disability, attaching little importance to it and not grasping its implications. Or when confronted by the disability and obliged to admit it, he shows an inappropriately flat or facetious reaction ('anosodiaphoria'). In true anosognosia, however, the patient appears to be completely unaware of the hemiplegia, makes no complaints about it, and ignores the inconvenience it causes.

Commonly anosognosia is merely a transient state in the early days after acute hemiplegia has developed, and recedes along with the initial clouding of consciousness. It may, however, persist and become more floridly developed with obstinate denial or bizarre elaboration on a delusional basis. When attention is firmly drawn to the defect, the patient makes some shallow rationalisation for not performing the task, perhaps explaining that he has been ill recently or that he is too tired. In more bizarre cases he insists that the paralysed limbs do not belong to him or attributes them to some neighbouring person ('somatoparaphrenia'). He may claim that the limbs are some mechanical object, or talk to them and fondle them as though they had an existence of their own ('personification'). Feelings of anger or hatred may be expressed towards them ('misoplegia').

A woman of 39 with left hemiplegia, hemianaesthesia and hemianopia, was garrulous and confused. She denied she was paralysed and insisted that her left arm and leg belonged to her daughter Ann, who she said had been sharing her bed for the past week. When the patient's wedding ring was pointed out to her she said that Ann had borrowed it to wear. The patient was encouraged to talk to Ann and to tell her to move her arm—she then became confused and talked vaguely about Ann being asleep and not to be disturbed. When asked to indicate her own left limbs she turned her head and searched in a bemused way over her left shoulder.

The left arm of a patient with a right parietal lesion kept wandering about in the blind homonymous half field of vision. When the patient wrote, the left hand would wander across and butt in and rest on the right hand. Not recognising this as his own he would exclaim: 'Let go my hand!' He would swear at it in exasperation: 'You bloody bastard! It's lost its soul, this bloody thing. It follows me around and gets in the way when I read'.

(Critchley, 1964).

Such highly colourful reactions are rare, and it is doubtful whether they occur in the absence of clouding of consciousness or generalised dementia. They can usually be understood most readily in terms of psychogenic elaboration of some partially perceived defect, sometimes illustrating in unusually clear form the common psychological mechanisms of defence.

Anosognosia is also used as a generic term for imperception of disease processes and defects other than hemiplegia. Here again it may range in degree from lack of concern and attention, to explicit verbal denial, and again it is often uncertain how far the disturbance is an intrinsic function of cerebral disorder or how far it reflects superadded psychogenic mechanisms. It is perhaps most commonly seen in relation to dysphasic symptoms, classically with primary sensory dysphasia when the patient seems not to appreciate his mistakes. Unawareness or denial of amnesic defects is common as part of Korsakoff's psychosis. Blindness, especially when due to lesions of the optic radiations or striate cortices may be denied, the patient attempting to behave as though he can see and describing purely imaginary visual experiences when tested ('Anton's syndrome'). Deafness due to cerebral lesions may more rarely be denied. Unawareness of painful stimuli ('pain asymbolia') is another incompletely understood example, in which the patient may perceive a painful stimulus but fails to recognise it as unpleasant, so that little or no defensive reaction is produced. This has been regarded as a failure to integrate the awareness of pain with awareness of the body image, or alternatively as a gross denial in the psychogenic sense of painful experience.

Anosognosia for hemiplegia has been more closely studied than these other forms of the disorder. Nevertheless the mechanisms involved remain unclear and are the subject of controversy. In the majority of cases there are sensory as well as motor deficits in the limbs concerned, but the condition is not explainable in terms of perceptual deficit alone, since occasionally hemiplegia is denied while the patient remains fully aware of the existence of the limbs. Frederiks (1969) puts forward the interesting suggestion that sometimes kinaesthetic hallucinations of movement may occur in the paralysed limbs, explaining at least those cases where verbal denial of paralysis is the main feature rather than neglect. The role of general intellectual disturbance is also disputed. Some claim that anosognosia can occur in the presence of strictly focal brain damage and when the patient is mentally clear, while others deny its localising significance and find it only with evidence of some degree of clouding of consciousness. Still others emphasise the psychogenic component, and see anosognosia essentially as a motivated desire to repress the unpleasant facts of a disability. Such primitive defensive behaviour may admittedly be brought to the fore by the presence of cerebral disease.

Weinstein and Kahn (1950, 1955), in a large population of brain-injured patients, stress this last point of view. In addition to denial of the defects already mentioned they noted denial of incontinence and impotence, and patients totally confined to bed might occasionally insist that they had recently returned from a walk. Some degree of mental confusion was always present in their patients when specially sought out, though often it was of a subtle nature. Moreover when the signs of anosognosia disappeared, intravenous sodium amytal could cause them to return by lowering the level of consciousness. Generalised brain damage appeared to be the cause in the great majority of cases.

Weinstein and Cole (1963) continued these observations in a later study restricted to anosognosia for hemiplegia. Half of their patients showed explicit verbal denial of paralysis while the others showed neglect. Those with denial disclaimed other aspects of the illness such as vomiting, incontinence or recent craniotomy, and all showed either disorientation for time and place, reduplicative delusions, other delusions and confabulations, or paraphasic misnaming. Frequently some degree of awareness of the defect was betrayed, and medication or operation was accepted without demur. Those with neglect alone showed less evidence of mental confusion but some degree could still be detected in every case. Mood changes were more striking in this second group, with depression, euphoria or paranoid developments.

Common mental mechanisms for defence against anxiety could be seen to operate. The premorbid personalities of the patients had often shown strong perfectionistic traits, tendencies to deny illness, and to view health as important for their self-esteem. Where verbal anosognosia was concerned this often appeared to be an artefact of the interview situation, and the attitudes of observers and of the patient's

relatives were important in determining the degree and duration of the denial.

Such observations have led some authorities to argue against the implication of focal brain damage in anosognosia, or indeed against any special relationship to body image disorder. However there remains the rather obstinate fact that anosognosia, like uncomplicated unilateral neglect, has usually been found to be very much commoner for the left than the right side of the body. Moreover the lesion, when focal, appears to implicate the parieto-occipital region rather than the pre-rolandic cortex or lower levels of motor organisation. Those upholding strict localisation point even to the supramarginal and angular gyri of the parietal lobe. Hence it is often suggested that anosognosia represents a special example of focal derangement of the body schema, dependent on subtle defects of sensory experience and higher order defects of conceptualisation. In this view any concurrent diffuse cerebral disorder acts only to actualise the defect or allow its elaboration by lowering the patient's overall grasp and alertness.

Ullman et al. (1960) in an unusually clear review, attempted a synthesis of both physiological and psychodynamic factors in leading to anosognosia. In the more florid examples of denial they suggest that the patient's initial subjective experiences have come to mesh and synchronise with his defensive mechanisms. Thus, for example, his first experience may be of an arm without feeling lying across his chest. This is not experienced as his own, and the feeling of separateness may be heightened when spontaneous movements are noted in it as on yawning. The initial fright and puzzlement can then be immediately relieved by disowning the limb or even identifying it as belonging to someone else. Early 'potential' anosognosic responses could be identified in a high proportion of patients with hemiplegia ('I didn't feel like I had an arm'; 'It seemed like something attached to me that wasn't mine'), but this did not progress to further elaboration in the absence of diffuse brain damage with accompanying mental changes. With a shift to concrete modes of thinking, however, and when the total social context could not be grasped, the patient might begin to utilise cues in a selective fashion to support and substantiate delusional beliefs.

The elaboration of explicit verbal denial could thus reflect the operation of various sets of factors. It could sometimes be primarily related to motivational factors embedded in the personality as Weinstein and Kahn suggest, but in others one might be witnessing a degree of functional loss great enough to prevent the patient from making the necessary compensatory judgements. Social and interpersonal aspects of the immediate situation could then be closely implicated, in addition to the role of brain damage itself.

The rarity of anosognosia and related defects in the right limbs is by any system very hard to explain. It has been suggested that since the left limbs are normally subordinate to the right, cerebral lesions merely exaggerate this tendency, or alternatively that with lesions of the dominant hemisphere intellectual defects and dysphasia readily swamp these more subtle manifestations. Others have escaped the dilemma by proposing that the non-dominant hemisphere is prepotent where the body image is concerned, or at least that it contains some specific centre for the recognition of unilateral inequalities. More complex formulations include the suggestion that the dominant hemisphere is principally concerned with the body image proper, but the non-dominant with the adequate recording of bodily alteration or disablement upon the body schema (Gerstmann, 1958). Cutting's (1978a) recent study renders many of these arguments unnecessary, in that a high incidence of anosognosia and associated 'anosognosic phenomena' was detectable in patients with right as well as with left hemiplegia:

Cutting took care to interview patients within a few days of onset of the hemiplegia, and to divide the right hemiplegics into those who were adequately testable (i.e. free from dysphasia) and those who were not. Fifty-eight per cent of the left hemiplegics showed explicit verbal denial in this early stage, and another 29% showed phenomena such as minimising the defect, adopting unusual attitudes to the limbs, or feeling that the limbs did not belong. Of the testable right hemiplegics 14% showed explicit denial and 41% showed the related phenomena. Clear examples of non-belonging and of 'misoplegia' could be detected among the latter. If the presumption were made that the dysphasic right hemiplegics might also harbour unusual attitudes to their disability, then the incidence of anosognosia from left and right brain lesions might not be very dissimilar. Some findings, nevertheless, lent support to the idea that different factors might be responsible in each hemisphere; left hemiplegics, for instance, could develop anosognosia or the related phenomena in the absence of disorientation or impairment of memory, whereas virtually all right hemiplegics with abnormal attitudes had obvious cognitive impairment.

Autotopagnosia

Autotopagnosia refers to inability to recognise, name or point on command to various parts of the body both on the right and on the left. The defect may apply to other people's bodies as well as to the subject's own, yet other external objects are dealt with normally.

Autotopagnosia in any extensive sense is extremely rare. However restricted forms are seen in conjunction with many other types of body image disorder, in that a tendency may occur to misidentify certain body parts. Such a defect confined to one body half is seen in patients with unilateral neglect or anosognosia. Finger agnosia (p. 58) is sometimes regarded as a minimal degree of whole body autotopagnosia, and to represent the only clear-cut example which cannot be better explained in terms of other defects.

Most examples which implicate the body bilaterally are explainable in terms of apraxia, agnosia, dysphasia or disorder of spatial perception. De Renzi and Scotti (1970) describe a case which perhaps illustrates essential mechanisms of another type. The patient, who had a tumour of the left parietal lobe, failed to point to body parts, but by contrast could promptly name all parts pointed to by the examiner. He could also correctly monitor the accuracy or otherwise of another person's pointing. The same dissociation between pointing himself and naming could be seen for parts of objects other than the human body, for example for parts of a bicycle. The defect thus appeared to be a part of a more general disturbance of failure to analyse a whole into parts, in other words a difficulty in conjuring up clear mental images of how individual parts were related to one another and to the whole. The patient's errors were noted to be concentrated on body parts which lacked definite boundaries, such as the wrists, cheeks, ankles and chin.

Autotopagnosia is usually seen in conjunction with diffuse bilateral lesions of the brain. Lesions of the left hemisphere alone can produce it, but must be extensive and must involve the parieto-occipital region (Hécaen, 1962).

Illusions of Transformation
Displacement or Reduplication

A great variety of body image disturbances may be loosely grouped together under this heading. They are relatively uncommon, and little is understood about the mechanisms underlying their appearance except that both physiogenic and psychogenic factors can be responsible. They are seen in many clinical settings. Some of the less dramatic, such as feelings of heaviness or enlargement of a limb, may occur in healthy subjects in states of extreme exhaustion, sensory deprivation, or in the course of falling asleep. Others, like feelings of distortion or free-floating of the body, occur with generalised cerebral disorder as in delirium or under the influence of LSD. Many unilateral examples are seen with focal brain disturbance, particularly as part of an epileptic aura, and some of the most bizarre instances, including autoscopy, can occur in the course of migrainous attacks. A further group appear in association with static lesions, particularly those which have led to left hemiplegia and anosognosia, but here again the phenomena are usually short-lived even if recurrent. Psychiatric illness without evidence of brain damage also contributes to such disorders as discussed in the section which follows.

This group therefore depends sometimes on neuropathological and some times on psychopathological mechanisms, and probably often on an inextricable mixture of the two. Strictly focal brain damage can sometimes be incriminated in the more basic examples, but in the more elaborate such an origin remains hypothetical.

Macrosomatognosia and microsomatognosia consist of feelings of abnormal largeness or smallness of parts, half, or even the whole of the body. Most commonly a single limb or a hand is affected alone. It may be accompanied by sensations of heaviness, distortion or displacement of the part concerned, or features such as these may constitute the sole abnormality. Feelings of swelling, elongation, shortening or twisting may be experienced, rather than a change which preserves the normal proportions of the part. Rarely the experience may be of physical separation of the part from the rest of the body. The following examples are reported by Lukianowicz (1967):

An epileptic girl sometimes had a somatic sensory aura during which she felt that '. . . my whole body grows very rapidly almost to the point of bursting. After a few seconds it collapses, like a deflated balloon, and then I lose consciousness and have a turn'.

A lorry driver discovered to have epilepsy had attacks 'when everything seems to run away from me, and then I get the feeling in my eyes that they tear out of their sockets, and rush out from the cabin, till they touch the people and the houses and the lampposts along the road. . . . Then everything rushes towards me again and my eyeballs hurry back into their sockets. At other times I might feel that my hands and arms grow long very rapidly, till they seem to reach miles ahead. A moment later they begin to shrink until they come back to their normal size. I may have such a feeling several times in a minute or two'.

A woman with migraine complained: 'Before the headache I see coloured zig-zag stripes appearing always from the left side. After a while I begin to feel that my head shrinks until it becomes not bigger than a small orange. At that time it always occurs to me that my head must look like the small dried up heads of the head-hunters in Borneo, which I had once seen on T.V. This sensation lasts about one minute and then my head at once comes back to its normal size. This feeling of my head shrinking and expanding goes on for some time, until I get my usual splitting headache'.

An epileptic girl had attacks ushered in by the feeling of spinning round on her own axis: 'This speed is so terrific that my body can't stand its centrifugal force: at first my head falls to pieces, and then the rest of my body, its parts flying apart like sparks. In a second or two my whole body falls apart, disintegrates, ceases to exist, is reduced to a formless splash on the spot where I was standing just a minute ago. And then I lose consciousness and fall down'.

The patient almost always retains insight into the alien nature of the experiences, describing the abnormality in 'as if' terms. A truly delusional or hallucinatory experience is rare in the absence of marked impairment of consciousness or psychotic illness. It is of course hard to discern, in cases such as those just quoted, how far the abnormal experience is due to primary disturbance of the body schema, or how far it represents an imaginative building-up of simple kinaesthetic and vestibular sensory changes. Derangements of either right or left hemisphere function may lead to such phenomena, and when a focal lesion is responsible the parieto-temporo-occipital region is said to be usually involved.

Reduplicative phenomena usually involve the limbs, and most often the hand or fingers alone. Such phantoms are usually transient, appearing with darkness and drowsiness. Many cases occur with anosognosia for left hemiplegia, and may lead to illusions of movement in the paralysed limbs. Insight is again usually preserved in large degree, and when the patient looks at the actual limbs the phantom promptly disappears. Occasional cases are reported however in which enduring phantoms prove an embarrassment and inconvenience, and the patient feels obliged to make the real limb coincide in position with the phantom. More dramatic instances of reduplication may involve the whole body image, as in the following case:

A student with migraine had severe splitting headache 'and after a while I suddenly would have the feeling that I have two bodies and two heads. It is like this: for a second or two I sort of "lose" myself and then it's there: I feel all doubled, I have two heads, two right hands and two left hands, I have four legs instead of two. Often I wonder how I am going to walk and to move about. I feel like a centipede, but her movements are perfectly synchronised and co-ordinated, while I feel awkward, like a dismembered doll or a rubber toy. I don't know which of my two right hands or legs to use—the "real" one, or so to say, the "imaginary" one. After a while I become confused and again "lose" myself. And then it is all over: my headache at once disappears and I feel my old "single" self again'.

(Lukianowicz, 1967).

Weinstein *et al.* (1954) have reported a few patients with reduplicative phenomena all with cerebral lesions of rapid onset and producing some degree of generalised confusion. One patient with a left hemiplegia claimed to have an extra left hand, one with a left hemiparesis and a fracture of the right leg stated that he had four legs, and one with a severe head injury who had previously had an eye removed claimed to have several eyes. Another patient with a cerebellar astrocytoma and meningitis said that he had three heads and four bodies, one of each with him and the remainder upstairs in a closet. In all four cases the reduplications were accompanied by other forms of reduplication for time, place or person. The 'body image' disturbance therefore appeared to be but one manifestation of a general pattern of reduplicative delusions. As in the case of anosognosia these authors viewed the reduplication of body parts as symbolic mechanisms to express some personal motivation, particularly denial of illness.

In autoscopy (the Doppelgänger phenomenon) there is 'a complex psychosensorial hallucinatory perception of one's own body image projected into external visual space' (Lukianowicz, 1958). Usually the image is in front of the patient at a certain distance, mostly fleetingly but very occasionally lasting for days at a time. It may be transparent, or coloured and definite, or show expressive movements. It may consist of the whole or a part only of the body, but the face is always included. Cases have been described in which the image occurs to one side of the mid-line in a hemianopic field of vision. The experience may be extremely realistic but is almost always recognised by the subject to be a pathological event. The emotional reaction may be of anxiety or quiet surprise, depending on the patient's mental state.

Usually the experience is visual, as the name implies, but sometimes the body image is experienced as projected into outside space by senses other than vision:-

A draughtsman of 34 reported: 'Often during an attack of migraine, or towards the end of it, I feel as if my head would split into two parts, right in the middle. Then a miniature image of myself emerges from the fissure. It rapidly expands to the size of my real body, and then for a moment I have two separate bodies. They are both "me" or "I". They are about one foot apart, the "new" body being always on the right side. It seems that I could touch him, i.e. "the other me". Yet, I have never seen him with my eyes, though I feel his presence very intensely. He mostly appears towards the end of a splitting headache and soon after he emerges from my head the headache ceases. Then this 'other me' also disappears'.

(Lukianowicz, 1967).

This striking phenomenon may occur episodically with epilepsy or migraine, in delirium, or with a variety of other cerebral diseases. The cerebral pathology is usually diffuse, and no focal origin has been established. Classical examples occur sporadically in the course of depressive or schizophrenic psychoses, though an organic pathology is the more common cause. Lukianowicz (1958) distinguishes between a symptomatic and an idiopathic form, the latter perhaps explainable on a psychodynamic basis in terms of wish-fulfilment or narcissism together with a situation of stress. A highly developed visual memory sense with strong eidetic imagery has also been proposed. Others see autoscopy as essentially a disturbance of the body schema, with separation of the visual components of the body image from the other components, and projection of this into external visual space. Whatever the precise mechanism, Frederiks (1969) makes the important practical point that autoscopy can very occasionally be the first manifestation of cerebral disease and always warrants a careful neurological examination.

The phantom limb which occurs after amputation or peripheral lesions of the nervous system has a basis quite distinct from the supernumerary phantom that occurs with cerebral disease. It is nonetheless in some ways the most decisive proof of the existence of the body schema. Phantom limbs are seen most commonly after amputation, but similar phenomena may follow severe nerve plexus lesions, or lesions of the brain stem and thalamus. Equivalent phantom phenomena have also been reported after removal of the breast, the genitalia or the eye.

Frederiks (1969) provides a comprehensive review, and distinguishes between the perception of the missing limb itself, including its spatial characteristics, and the perception of phantom limb sensations such as paraesthesiae, heaviness, cold, cramp and pain. If the phantom is to develop it usually does so immediately after the operation, persisting sometimes for several months and sometimes for the rest of life. It has a markedly realistic character, can usually be 'moved' at will, and may assume a relaxed or a cramped position. In the course of time it may appear only sporadically, or it may gradually telescope, the distal portion ultimately approaching the stump and disappearing into it.

Pain in the phantom limb can be distressing and intractable. It is typically paroxysmal, burning or shooting in character, sometimes occurring alone and sometimes with paraesthesiae. As with other phantom limb sensations the pain may be markedly affected by influences such as a change in the weather, use of a prosthesis, use of the contralateral limb, pain elsewhere in the body, or firm efforts at mental concentration. Morganstern (1964) has shown the efficacy of frequently repeating a task of sensory distraction in diminishing awareness of the phantom and lessening pain. The current emotional state may likewise have a profound effect, depression contributing to such an extent that electro-convulsive therapy has sometimes been found to abolish phantom limb pain. Stengel (1965) mentions a man whose phantom limb pain was markedly increased whenever he watched scenes of violence on television.

A psychogenic component thus undoubtedly exists, and has been interpreted in terms of loss of bodily integrity and reaction to disablement. Psychotherapy and hypnosis have accordingly sometimes met with success in treatment. However a physiological component is also indicated by the efficacy, short-lived though it may be, of surgical procedures. Relief may follow the excision of a stump neuroma, chordotomy, or lesions in the thalamic radiation or sensory cortex. Both peripheral and central nervous mechanisms thus appear to contribute to its genesis, in addition to psychological factors in certain cases. It has been suggested that unpatterned somaesthetic sensory input acts in some way to stimulate and sensitise the central structures involved with the body image for the missing part.

Body Image Disturbances in
Functional Psychiatric Illness

The majority of the body image disturbances so far considered have been associated with cerebral pathology or pathophysiology. With some forms, how-

ever, psychogenic mechanisms have also had to be taken into account, and seem to be strongly implicated for example with anosognosia, phantom limb phenomena and some of the more bizarre illusions of transformation and reduplication.

It is therefore interesting to view the range of body image disturbances that may accompany psychiatric illnesses devoid of known brain pathology. It is, of course, often hard to clarify the phenomenology when other mental disturbances are present as well. Many examples appear on close acquaintance not to represent true disturbance of the body schema, but rather to be based primarily on pathological changes in bodily experience. In neuroses, for example, minor bodily sensations may become exaggerated by anxiety or hypochondriacal concern, and in psychoses kinaesthetic hallucinations may become the subject of delusional elaboration. The area has rarely been examined systematically, and Lukianowicz's (1967) survey provides a valuable set of observations.

Among 200 consecutive admissions to a mental hospital, 31 patients complained spontaneously of unusual sensations and experiences in various parts of their bodies, and a further 21 answered affirmatively when questioned about such phenomena. Excluding the patients with epilepsy or migraine, 38 patients (19% of the total) were considered to show some body image disturbance, 23 in the presence of schizophrenia, 12 with depressive illness and 3 with anxiety neurosis. In the latter the disturbances were manifest only in the drowsy hypnagogic state.

Experiences of depersonalisation were not included in the survey. The remainder were classified entirely on phenomenological grounds in order to avoid the aetiological implications of the terms which are usually employed. Experience of change of shape was the commonest abnormality, followed by change of position in space, reduplication or splitting, change of size and change of mass. The schizophrenic patients contained some excess who experienced changes of shape, and the depressed patients change of mass.

Disturbances of the shape of the body image took many forms. In schizophrenic patients there were examples of feelings of change of shape to that of another animal, the hands feeling shrunken like crab's claws or the whole body feeling as though transformed into a dog. Such changes appeared to be based essentially on misinterpreted bodily sensations, combined often with hallucinations of the sense of smell. Insight into the unreality of the experiences was commonly retained, though sometimes incompletely expressed. In some cases complex sensory experiences appeared to underlie feelings that the body was changing into that of the opposite sex, likewise in some examples of transformation into Christ or other figures. Care was taken to distinguish as far as possible between mechanisms such as these, in which there was a discernible relationship to corresponding bodily sensations and hallucinations, and the more usual situation in which a delusional belief in a new identity or sex was purely ideational.

Feelings of change of position in space included levitation, floating and falling, sometimes as hypnagogic phenomena but sometimes occurring in the full waking state. In epileptic patients equivalent sensations were sometimes observed as a kinaesthetic aura preceding an epileptic attack.

Feelings of reduplication and splitting occurred in schizophrenia and in depression:

A schizophrenic student had the feeling of 'two bodies, one outside the other, only a bit larger than my actual body. I feel that the "inner" body is the real one, and the "outer" is more like something artificial, a sort of shell over a hermit crab although it has the shape and the appearance of my "real" body'.

A woman when depressed had the feeling 'as if my body was split into two halves, like a stem of a tree struck by lightning. They both feel a few inches apart and there is nothing between them, but a black, empty hole; black and empty and dead'.

Again in epileptic patients such experiences could herald an attack. Experiences of autoscopic doubling were also seen in patients with schizophrenia and depression.

Feelings of additional body parts occurred in several bizarre forms, sometimes inviting a psychodynamic formulation which would see them as symbolically representing displaced sexual organs:

A man whose potency was dwindling as a result of spinal injury developed recurrent depressive episodes. In one there were visual and haptic hallucinations of spurs and horns growing from his ankles, in another of a ball sticking out of his thigh, and in another of big screws growing from his abdomen and thighs. He retained insight into their unreal nature, and electroconvulsive therapy was effective in banishing the phenomena along with the depression.

Change of size sometimes affected the whole body, and sometimes parts only, such as the ears, nose or limbs. Again displaced sexual symbolism sometimes provided the most ready explanation, though anal-ogous examples occurring in the course of epileptic and migrainous attacks may have rested primarily on disturbed cortical function. Lilliputian experiences were rare in comparison to feelings of enlargement, but one depressed woman had distressing hypnagogic experiences in which she felt her body shrink rapidly to the size of her little finger.

Changes in mass were usually manifest as feelings of emptiness and hollowness of body parts, particularly of the head. They were confined to patients with depressive illness or neurotic disorder, and often came close to nihilistic delusions. The following case illustrates the possible distinction:

A man with anxiety neurosis described a recurrent hypnopompic experience as follows: 'Just after I wake up, but before I move, I have a terrifying feeling that my whole body consists of skin with nothing inside, like an empty blown up balloon, or an empty shell, only pretending to be a human body. It is a very frightening feeling, which lasts only a few seconds and disappears immediately when I move any part of my body'.

In general these various disturbances in psychiatric patients seemed to be an integral part of their mental illnesses, along with the more common hallucinations and related psychotic symptoms. Misinterpretation of normal bodily sensations, or of hallucinations, appeared to be mainly responsible, rather than changes originating in the body schema itself. The initial sensations seemed often to be complex, mainly of visceral, kinaesthetic or labyrinthine origin, and then to become secondarily elaborated in terms of change in shape, position, size or mass. In schizophrenic patients the end result was frequently bizarre, in keeping with their tendencies towards bodily preoccupation, weakening of ego functions and autistic modes of thinking. In depressive illness the body image disturbances were often consonant with hypochondriacal and nihilistic developments. Successful treatment of the psychiatric illness invariably resulted in resolution of the body image disturbances.

Non-Cognitive Disturbances and Regional Brain Dysfunction

The forms of disability discussed above have all been more or less closely tied to cognitive or perceptual deficits, even though these have sometimes been of a rather subtle nature. There remain, however, certain abnormalities of emotion, behaviour and 'personality' which appear to be related to regional brain dysfunction yet do not necessarily have cognitive disturbance at the core. These are clearly of special interest to the psychiatrist. Certain examples will be selected for discussion.

The 'frontal lobe syndrome' will be considered first because it has been most comprehensively studied. Aggressive behaviour will then be examined in relation to focal brain disturbances. Finally the evidence linking schizophrenia-like illnesses to regional brain dysfunction will be outlined.

With all of these examples the task of elucidating the nature of the ties between clinical symptoms and brain pathology has been considerable. Abnormalities of emotion and personality cannot be assessed with anything like the precision that is usually possible for cognitive defects. It has already been seen how much uncertainty surrounds our understanding of such measurable disorders as memory impairment, and such testable defects as dysphasia or apraxia. With the body image disturbances there was an uncertain admixture of physiogenic and psychogenic mechanisms to be considered. Such problems are greatly multiplied in any analysis of disordered emotion or abnormalities of personality and social behaviour. A large element of subjectivity is involved in attempts at classifying or quantifying the phenomena concerned, and in trying to separate the abnormal from what must be judged as normal variation; the abnormalities are more variable from one situation to another than are cognitive defects and more protean in their manifestations; and their determinants will include factors which have nothing to do with damage to the brain—matters of genetic constitution, interpersonal relationships and current environmental circumstances. It is inherently likely, moreover, that the 'higher order' the function concerned the more complex will be the interplay between the different cerebral systems subserving it.

Despite such difficulties important leads have been obtained, and interesting clinicopathological correlations have emerged in the examples discussed below.

FRONTAL LOBE SYNDROME

Certain clinical features appear to emerge with especial frequency after damage to the frontal lobes. They are not unique to frontal lobe pathology, but are seen more regularly and perhaps more strikingly than after damage to other cerebral regions. A good deal of debate has surrounded this issue, likewise the question of the range of symptoms to be included and the mechanisms by which they come about. Detailed reviews are provided by Teuber (1964), Blumer and Benson (1975) and Hécaen and Albert (1975)

Clinical Picture

In the typical case the personality of the patient is more profoundly and obviously affected than his cognitive functions. The striking changes in well-marked examples are in the areas of volitional and psychomotor activity, habitual mood, and social awareness and behaviour.

Lack of initiative and spontaneity is usually coupled with a general diminution of motor activity. Responses are sluggish, tasks neglected and left unfinished, and new initiatives rarely undertaken. In consequence the capacity to function independently in daily life can be profoundly affected. Yet when vigorously urged the patient may function quite well. He may achieve virtually normal performance in situations where the examiner provides the impetus, and thus show little or no difficulty over formal tests of intelligence. What is most impaired is the propensity to initiate new behaviour spontaneously. How far this represents a true loss of interest, or an apparent loss due to impaired volition is often hard to discern. Occasional patients tend to be restless and hyperactive rather than sluggish, but again are likely to display a lack of purposive goal-directed behaviour.

The mood is often mildly euphoric and out of keeping with the patient's situation. Rather empty high spirits may be accompanied by a boisterous over-familiarity of manner. Such changes are rarely sustained, however, and when left to himself the patient becomes inert and apathetic. Outbursts of irritability are also common and a child-like petulance may be seen. True depression is rare though the picture of asthenia and inertia may mimic it closely. The euphoria is sometimes elaborated into a tendency to joke or pun, to make facetious remarks or indulge in childish pranks ('Witzelsücht'). Very occasionally it extends to a state of excitement approaching hypomania ('moria').

Serious changes are observed in social awareness and behaviour. Typically the patient is less concerned with the consequences of his acts than formerly. Loss of 'finer feelings' and social graces form part of a general coarsening of the personality. In interpersonal relationships there is a lack of the normal adult tact and restraints, and a diminished appreciation of the impact of his behaviour upon others. Disinhibition is sometimes apparent in the sexual sphere with lewd remarks, promiscuity, or the emergence of perverse tendencies.

Judgement may be markedly impaired in the conduct of affairs. The patient shows little concern with his personal future, and fails to plan ahead or carry through ideas. Inability to forejudge the consequences of actions can lead to foolish or irresponsible behaviour. Social and ethical controls may be weakened and have issue in antisocial conduct.

Psychometry, as already stressed, may show little by way of impairment on formal tests of intellectual ability, even when behaviour is markedly abnormal. Special test procedures, however, may show loss of abstracting ability and incapacity to shift between different frames of reference as discussed below. Inattention may also be marked, and memory may appear to be faulty. The latter, in particular, can be very hard to evaluate; it may sometimes seem that failures over recall represent a lack of initiative in memory rather than a true forgetting of material, in that given time and encouragement the answers are ultimately forthcoming.

Such changes are seen in varying degree, sometimes merely as a blunting of a previously sophisticated personality, but sometimes as a radical change of personality which is grossly disabling. The patient himself usually has little insight into the changes that have occurred. The component symptoms may be seen in different combinations, but with sufficient similarity from one patient to another to convey a definitive stamp to the picture.

The evidence concerning the 'frontal lobe syndrome' has come from studies of patients with various forms of brain pathology. That derived from head injured patients is described in Chapter 5 (p.152) and observations on patients with frontal lobe tumours in Chapter 6 (p. 190). Evidence has also accumulated from studies of patients after surgical excisions of frontal lobe lesions (Rylander, 1939, 1943) and of patients exposed to early extensive frontal leucotomies (Partridge, 1950; Tow, 1955; Greenblatt and Solomon, 1958). The consensus of evidence suggests that lesions of the convex lateral surface are especially prone to produce aspontaneity and slowing, while lesions of the orbital undersurface are liable to have adverse effects on personality and social behaviour. Bifrontal lesions are especially hazardous in this regard.

Possible Mechanisms

A number of intriguing suggestions have been put forward in attempts at explaining why such symptoms should arise. Detailed neuropsychological studies have produced a wealth of information both in animals and man, but it remains difficult to draw these strands together to form a satisfactory theory.

This is scarcely surprising in view of the elusive nature of frontal lobe function in the intact brain.

What is particularly interesting is the manner in which detailed analysis of failure on problem-solving and perceptual tasks has allowed tentative explanatory hypotheses to be put forward. The obvious deficits in man are in matters of personality and social behaviour rather than in cognitive and perceptual processes, yet experiments dealing with these more basic functions have sometimes seemed to illuminate the behavioural deficits observed.

Pribram *et al.* (1964) trace the development of experimental work on primates from the classical studies of Jacobsen onwards. Jacobsen (1935) showed that monkeys with frontal lobe lesions were selectively impaired on a delayed choice reaction task, in which they had to select which of two cups contained a food reward after witnessing the baiting of the cups some time before. Subsequent experiments have shown that this is not simply due to failure of memory or spatial perception, but rather to disturbance of complex aspects of the monkey's attention and response at the time of baiting one or other cup. Further work has shown that monkeys with frontal lesions have severe difficulty in learning to reverse a discrimination problem, despite normal ability to master the problem initially. Similar difficulty is seen in shifting back and forth between other related problems due to perseverative interference from previous responses. Yet paradoxically they also are unduly ready to select novel cues when new cues are progressively introduced into the experimental situation. The perseveration of set is thus combined with an enhancement of the normal monkey tendency to be attracted to what is novel in the environment. In other words they show unusual difficulty in overcoming a preferred mode of response, whether spontaneous or experimentally induced, and despite a lack of reward for errors. They cannot suppress whatever response naturally prevails in a given situation, and they appear to be less affected than normal animals by the immediate consequences of their actions. Even in monkeys, therefore, detailed analysis of problem-solving behaviour turns out to reveal complex abnormalities of motivation and behavioural control.

Milner (1963, 1964) has examined performance on certain psychometric tests which are particularly susceptible to frontal lobe damage in man. Again careful analysis of sources of failure has produced interesting results. On the Wisconsin Card Sorting Test (described in Chapter 3, p. 104), patients with frontal lesions show difficulty in shifting from one mode of response to another, which reveals itself as a strong perseverative tendency. In particular they fail to abandon a particular sorting strategy after being repeatedly told that it is wrong. This appears not to be due to lack of motivation, since the patients often work carefully and are manifestly distressed by their poor performance. They also seem capable of grasping the principle of the test in prior discussion. Yet they may continue to sort erroneously while themselves saying 'right' or 'wrong' as they place the cards. Thus the essential deficit emerges as persistence of inappropriate sets in the face of mounting errors, coupled perhaps with inability to modify behaviour in accordance with verbal signals. The failure to suppress an on-going reaction tendency, despite growing proof of its inadequacy, recalls the concept of disinhibition so often invoked to account for the behavioural changes observed clinically.

Similarly on a stylus maze test Milner (1964) reports a special type of frontal deficit—the patients fail to heed instructions, break rules and make repetitive errors much more than other groups. They seem unable to restrain themselves from impulsive mistakes which impair their learning curves. Milner points out that these tests, and others, demonstrate that patients with frontal lesions cannot maintain a constant shifting of response to meet changing environmental demands. Normal behaviour depends on simultaneous functioning of many complex 'sets', any one of which can become prepotent when appropriate signals arise from the environment. Frontal lobe damage appears to disturb this modulating function, which may explain the co-existence in such patients of inadequate social behaviour and lack of initiative in many everyday situations, despite good achievement on standard tests of intelligence.

Teuber's (1964) contribution is more far-reaching. He and co-workers have shown specific frontal deficits on several tasks which at first sight seem unrelated. Patients with frontal lesions are able to set a vertical mid-line correctly under normal conditions, but not when their bodies are tilted to one or other side. They fail in visual searching tasks and in certain aspects of the perception of reversible figures. And they have special difficulty over orienting-tasks in relation to their own bodies when asked to transpose from front to back view. Teuber proffers a unitary interpretation in terms of a defect of 'corollary discharges' which allow the subject to predict, and thereby prepare for, incoming sensory stimuli. Such a defect would stand to impair the proper maintenance of the perceived upright during changes of posture, and the proper direction of voluntary gaze; it could alter the facility of 'assumptive shifts' of the viewer's position on inspecting ambiguous figures, or the required reversals of standpoint when dealing with mirror images of the body.

Arguing further Teuber points out that 'will' involves anticipation of the future course of events coupled with an awareness of the role of the self in bringing these events about. The patient with frontal lobe pathology is not altogether devoid of capacity to anticipate a course of events, but lacks the ability to picture himself as a potential agent in relation to those events. From such changes could follow lack of initiative, fixity of set, oscillation of action, and impulsiveness. Thus the seemingly lower-level sensorimotor defects revealed in the experiments might well be the conditions that give rise, in more severe forms of frontal lobe dysfunction, to pervasive changes of behaviour.

Finally Luria's conclusions are not so very dissimilar to the above, involving as they do a consideration of feed-back processes and self-regulating systems in the control of behaviour (Luria and Homskaya, 1964; Luria, 1966; Luria et al., 1966). Luria points out that the organism not only reacts to stimuli, but can anticipate future events and prepare for them by constructing appropriate series of actions. In man such programmes become enormously complex as a result of social development, and are formed with the assistance of language which achieves an important role in the regulation of behaviour. During on-going activity there are not only 'action plans', but also a complex process of matching effects achieved against the initial intentions. Frontal lobe damage has a disruptive effect on the programming of complicated activities and on this 'psychological control of action'. Behaviour in consequence loses its selective character and easily falls under the influence of outside associations.

Using a simple bulb-pressing task Luria and Homskaya (1964) showed that patients with large frontal lesions were unable to translate verbal instructions accurately into motor behaviour. The instructions were understood and remembered but appeared to have lost their signalling function. With less severe frontal lesions similar deficits could be shown on more complex bulb-pressing tasks—when told to press twice for a single stimulus and once for a double, for example, behaviour soon gave way to a simple mirroring of the properties of the stimuli. The disturbed verbal regulation of function was shown in that errors persisted even when the patient was asked to repeat the instructions every time the signal appeared, and despite his running commentary which showed he knew what was required.

Disordered programming and feed-back control have also been shown in the domain of complex perceptual processes, especially those requiring a preliminary planned approach (Luria *et al.*, 1966). Eye movements were monitored while patients with frontal lesions were invited to study a picture and answer questions about it. The eye movements were found to be disorganised and random, with failure to concentrate on important and significant details. Instead of singling out and correlating the most informative features, the patients would perceive a single detail and come up with an immediate impulsive idea of what the picture represented. Moreover eye movement records showed a stereotyped form of scanning no matter what question was asked about the picture, in sharp contrast to the situation in normal subjects. Thus patients with frontal damage lack the organised visual scanning needed to seek out cues relevant to solving a task, to compare them, and to match them with several hypotheses.

Both experiments reveal disturbed regulation of activity and disordered feed-back and correction of errors. In everyday life such deficits would stand to impair many aspects of behaviour. Disordered regulation of activity, i.e. the loss of the controlling function of intentions upon behaviour, may underlie the apathy and aspontaneity of patients with frontal lesions and their lack of goal-oriented behaviour. Impaired feedback may account for their lack of critical attitudes towards the results of their own behaviour, their failure to modify it, and their satisfaction with actions regardless of whether or not they are effective.

DISORDERED CONTROL OF AGGRESSION

The emotional disturbances classically associated with brain damage include emotional lability and loss of control of emotional expression. In the former the prevailing mood shifts rapidly on little provocation and is ill-sustained. In the latter, which in severe form is termed 'emotional incontinence', there are outbursts of crying or laughing in response to minimal stimuli and sometimes with little or no affective change subjectively.

Increasingly, however, attention has been focused on the specific question of impaired control of aggressive behaviour and its possible cerebral correlates. In extreme form this may be manifest as outbursts of uncontrollable violence. In some instances such disturbance is clearly attributable to focal cerebral pathology—in relation to epilepsy, certain cerebral tumours and other forms of brain disease. But the argument has been extended to suggest that in some habitually aggressive individuals, not showing overt signs of cerebral disorder, there may be abnormalities of the neural apparatus subserving aggressive responses. Attention has been directed particularly at possible dysfunction of the 'limbic brain', and especially of the amygdaloid nuclei within the temporal lobes.

In seeking correlates between aggressive behaviour and brain pathology one is handicapped by the difficulty of defining in what circumstances and to what degree aggression must be displayed before it is regarded as 'abnormal'. A great variety of motivations may enter in, and many aspects of aggression are biologically valuable in man as in other animals. Its determinants include environmental, social, cultural and intrapsychic factors, which will often emerge as crucial in individual instances. But there are groups of persons who are subject to recurring and harmful outbursts of aggressive behaviour, sometimes on little or no provocation, and certain aggressive offenders whose episodes remain inexplicable in terms of personality, social adjustment and the situation at the time (Gibbens, 1969). Here it would seem that there may be important cerebral determinants of this pattern of behaviour—an abnormal triggering of aggressive responses based in disturbed cerebral functioning.

Neural Substrate for Aggressive Responses

A neural substrate for the elaboration and display of aggression has been amply demonstrated both in animals and man. A large literature exists to show that in animals aggressive behaviour can be facilitated, decreased or abolished by cerebral lesions, mostly situated in or near the limbic system and hypothalamus. Bard (1928), for example, showed the importance of the caudal half of the hypothalamus for the elaboration of 'sham rage' in decorticate cats, and Klüver and Bucy (1939) demonstrated an abnormal absence of anger and fear after bitemporal lesions in monkeys. Downer (1962) showed elegantly how removal of the amygdaloid nucleus from a single temporal lobe would, after section of the cerebral commissures, allow the monkey to display normally aggressive behaviour when stimuli were fed to the sound hemisphere but unnatural tameness when fed to the lesioned side.

Delgado's work has been particularly impressive in illustrating the need to take into account both intracerebral mechanisms and social-environmental factors in the understanding of aggressive behaviour in animals (Delgado, 1969). Radio-stimulation via implanted electrodes in the amygdala, hypothalamus, septum and reticular formation, allowed discrete areas of the brain to be stimulated while monkeys and chimpanzees were free-ranging and interacting with their fellows. Certain areas when stimulated produced a threatening display or social conflict, but this depended on the hierarchical position of the animal in the group; such responses could be observed when a submissive monkey was at hand as a target, but were inhibited in the presence of a dominant animal. Moreover elicited behaviour which might be interpreted as aggressive by the experimenter was apparently not always perceived as such by the other animals in the colony.

In different species of animals similar brain regions have emerged repeatedly as important in connection with 'aggressive' behaviour. Nonetheless considerable interspecies differences exist, and applicability of the results to man is a far from straightforward matter. Observations in man are necessarily limited in scope, and rely principally on indirect methods of study in a variety of pathological situations.

Clinical Evidence

Some of the principal evidence has come from studies of patients with epilepsy. This is set out in Chapter 7, where the question of a special association between temporal lobe epilepsy and aggressive behaviour is discussed (p. 231 *et seq.*). A high proportion of patients with temporal lobe epilepsy appear to show explosive aggressive tendencies, not only in relation to attacks but as an enduring trait of their personalities. Temporal lobectomy carried out for the relief of epilepsy may be followed by pronounced improvement in the control of such disorder (p. 235). The lesions in these patients commonly consist of sclerosis in the limbic structures on the medial aspects of the temporal lobes.

Patients with cerebral tumours have occasionally been observed to show abnormal outbursts of rage and destructive behaviour. Poeck (1969) reviews the literature, showing the frequent involvement in such cases of the hypothalamus, septal regions, and medial temporal structures including the hippocampus and amygdaloid nucleus. Some patients have described their condition as a feeling of rage building up in spite of themselves, others as waiting tensely for the first opportunity to release their accumulated

aggression. Poeck stresses, however, that the relation between symptoms and lesions is by no means strict and constant. Important additional factors derive from the premorbid emotional make up, and the presence or absence of diffuse brain damage.

A patient reported by Sweet *et al.* (1969) showed in very striking fashion the possible relationship between a circumscribed tumour and the wildly aggressive behaviour that ultimately ensued. It also illustrates the complex nature of 'aggressive' behaviour in man, and the hazards of attempting a simplistic formulation of the nature of the link between such behaviour and cerebral pathology:

In August 1966 a young man murdered his mother and wife in their apartments, then ascended the University of Texas tower, stepped on to the parapet and killed by gunfire 14 people, wounding 24 others. In his personal diaries he had recorded over several months that something peculiar was happening to him, which he did not understand but which he was noting down in the hope that its mention would help others to do so. Five months before the mass murder he had consulted a psychiatrist, stating early in the interview that sometimes he became so mad he could 'go up to the top of that University tower and start shooting at people'. Autopsy disclosed a glioblastoma multiforme; the damage to the brain from the gunshot wounds which terminated his barrage led to uncertainty about the precise location of the walnut-sized tumour, but it was considered to be probably in the medial part of one of the temporal lobes.

Other examples of an association between lowered threshold for aggression and brain pathology include patients who become seriously disturbed as a result of birth trauma, head injury and intracerebral infections. However in such situations clinico-pathological correlations are rarely exact enough to allow firm conclusions to be drawn about the role of circumscribed as opposed to diffuse brain damage. The question of impaired control of aggression after head injury is discussed in Chapter 5 (p. 160) and of antisocial conduct after encephalitis lethargica in Chapter 8 (p. 294).

Opportunities for assessing the effects of stimulating discrete brain structures in man have occasionally seemed to produce direct evidence for the role of limbic structures in elaborating emotional responses, including short-lived feelings of rage. Heath *et al.* (1955) stimulated the amygdaloid nucleus via implanted electrodes in a chronic schizophrenic patient, resulting in a sudden rage response when the current reached a certain intensity. She was perfectly aware of her feelings and was able to discuss them objectively between stimulations. The result was unstable, however, and later stimulation of the same point produced feelings of fear in place of rage. Delgado *et al.* (1968) found that stimulation of the amygdala and hippocampus in patients with temporal lobe epilepsy produced a variety of effects including pleasant sensations, elation, deep thoughtful concentration, relaxation and colour visions. However in one patient with post-encephalitic brain damage and epilepsy, stimulation of the right amygdala led to episodes of assaultive behaviour reminiscent of her spontaneous outbursts of anger. Seven seconds after stimulation she interrupted her activities, threw herself against the wall in a fit of rage, then paced around the room for several minutes before resuming her normal behaviour. During the elicited rage no seizure activity was evident on depth recording. The observation proved to be of crucial importance for selecting the appropriate site for a destructive lesion within the temporal lobe.

Psychosurgery for Aggression

It thus seems fair to conclude that pathological derangements affecting the limbic areas, and perhaps especially the amygdaloid nuclei, are capable of leading to abnormal tendencies towards aggressive behaviour in man. The conclusion has led to attempts at modifying such behaviour by a variety of psychosurgical procedures. Unilateral temporal lobectomy meets with success in patients with temporal lobe epilepsy, as already described, but bilateral operations are contra-indicated by the severe memory deficits that follow. Turner (1969, 1972), however, has reported success with bilateral division of tracts within the temporal lobes and with posterior cingulectomy, mostly in patients with temporal lobe epilepsy but also in some abnormally aggressive patients who have never had seizures.

Considerable attention has also been directed at stereotactic operations on the amygdaloid nuclei in patients with temporal lobe epilepsy and violent behaviour (Hitchcock *et al.*, 1972; Mark et al., 1972). The results are reported as often markedly successful, and without disabling side effects. Narabayashi, the pioneer of such operations, has performed amygdalectomies on one or both sides in a large population of patients, some with epilepsy and some with 'severe behaviour disorders and hyperexcitability' (Narabayashi *et al.*, 1963; Narabayashi and Uno, 1966). Nearly all were mentally subnormal. Of 60 patients aged 5–35, 51 were said to show marked reduction in emotional excitability and 'normalisa-

tion of social behaviour'. The improvements were described in terms of increased obedience, calmness, a diminution of labile mood, and a decreased tendency to attack persons and destroy objects. Of 40 patients followed 3–6 years later, 27 continued to show a satisfactory outcome, though older patients who had been markedly aggressive fared less well than younger patients who had shown hyperactive behaviour, poor concentration and 'unsteady moods'.

It is hard in these reports to discern how specific were the effects on aggressive behaviour, and how far the improvements may have been related to improved control of epilepsy. Sweet *et al.* (1969) review the discrepant results obtained by different workers. In a patient of their own they found that stimulation of the medial part of the amygdala led to feelings of imminent loss of control, whereas stimulation just four millimetres lateral to the same point produced feelings of relaxation. The variable results of operation may thus be attributable to the fact that the amygdala is a relatively large complex of nuclei with many different functions.

Other reports have shown improvement in aggressive psychotic patients after amygdalectomy and basofrontal tractotomy (Vaernet and Madsen, 1970), and in aggressive epileptic children and young adults after surgical lesions in the posteromedial hypothalamus (Sano *et al.*, 1966, 1972). All such operations, needless to say, have become the focus of considerable social controversy, especially so when applied to minors and to persons held in custody on account of offences.

The Habitually Aggressive Offender

It remains to consider the situation in individuals who show persistently aggressive behaviour yet are without overt evidence of brain pathology. These are the persons traditionally labelled as 'aggressive psychopaths'. Their outbursts of violence are usually merely a part of wide-ranging personality and social maladjustments. They are notoriously resistant to efforts at therapeutic intervention, yet many seem to outgrow their aggressive propensities in middle years. It is obviously a matter of importance to seek to clarify whether in some such persons there are definable abnormalities of the neural apparatus subserving aggressive responses, and to what degree such abnormalities are inherited or acquired.

A high proportion of persons with disturbed personalities are known to have abnormal EEGs, especially those who show aggressive antisocial behaviour. The evidence is discussed in Chapter 3 (p. 110). Such EEG abnormalities involve the temporal lobes particularly, are often of a type suggesting cerebral immaturity, and tend to decrease with age in parallel with improvements in behaviour. Hill (1944) found that the abnormal rhythms in predominantly aggressive psychopaths were often bilateral, synchronous, and post-central in location, suggesting dysfunction in subcortical centres or the deep temporal grey matter.

An important study by Williams (1969) reinforced the importance of earlier findings. In a review of EEGs carried out on 333 men convicted of violent crimes he divided the population into two groups— 206 who had a history of habitual aggression or explosive rage, and 127 who had committed an isolated act of aggression. In the first group the aggression appeared to be largely endogenous and personality related, and in the second to be provoked by unusually stressful environmental factors. Sixty five per cent of the habitually aggressive offenders had abnormal EEGs compared with only 24% of the remainder. Eighty per cent of both groups showed dysrhythmias known to be associated with temporal lobe dysfunction.

When persons with disabilities suggesting structural brain damage were excluded (i.e. those who were mentally backward, with epilepsy, or with a history of major head injury) 57% of the remaining habitual aggressives showed EEG abnormalities, whereas the figure for solitary aggressives had fallen to 12% (which was equivalent to the general population). It thus seemed reasonable to conclude that in the former the EEG abnormalities were directly related to the disturbed behaviour, and were not attributable to otherwise unrelated structural brain disease. Williams considered the disturbed behaviour and the EEG findings in the habitually aggressive men to be 'constitutional' in origin and to reflect a disturbance of cerebral physiology. They appeared to derive from dysfunction of diencephalic and limbic mechanisms, as judged by the features and distribution of the EEG abnormalities. A study by Krynicki (1978) in repetitively assaultative adolescents, though based on very small numbers, has produced essentially similar findings.

The question has been argued further by certain workers who elaborate the concept of a syndrome of 'episodic dyscontrol' (Mark and Ervin, 1970; Bach-y-Rita *et al.*, 1971; Maletzky, 1973). The suggestion is that after excluding patients who have demonstrable epilepsy, brain damage or psychotic illness as a basis for their aggressive acts, (also those

pursuing a motivated career of premeditated crime for gain), one is left with a large number of persons who are victims of their disturbed cerebral physiology. The essence of the claim is that violent behaviour can, in effect, be the only overt symptom of brain disorder.

The great majority of such persons are male, from seriously disturbed family backgrounds, and with a history of repeated outbursts of violent behaviour dating back to adolescence or even childhood. Provocation for such outbursts has often been minimal. Evidence of minor neurological dysfunction is not uncommon, and there is a high incidence of abnormal EEGs, often involving the temporal lobes and sometimes quasi-epileptic in nature. Many have symptoms reminiscent of epileptic phenomena, even when not suffering from seizures; in particular the outbursts may be preceded or followed by features akin to those seen with temporal lobe epilepsy. The clinical picture is further described in Chapter 7 (p. 262).

The implication is that such persons have functional abnormalities of the neural systems subserving aggressive responses, which set the threshold for the elicitation of outbursts at an unusually low level. There is then a complex interaction between such brain dysfunction, social disorganisation, and dynamically significant psychopathological experiences in the individual concerned.

Such a 'syndrome' appears to stand at the borderland between what is conventionally regarded as psychopathic personality, and what with slightly more definite clinical evidence might be included as temporal lobe epilepsy. Clear definition of the syndrome, and estimates of its frequency, are rendered difficult by the elusive nature of the ancillary evidence of cerebral dysfunction, and the ever-present confounding evidence of social and interpersonal stresses in the group. It will be an important task to refine such a conception further, and to attempt to separate those patients with abnormally aggressive propensities dependent on cerebral dysfunction from those without such a basis. A further task will be to explore the origins and nature of the cerebral dysfunction— whether it is inherited or acquired, whether acquired by processes of learning and conditioning, and to what extent it may represent delayed maturation of normal processes of control.

Schizophrenia

The problems of defining schizophrenia, and of separating off a central group of 'nuclear', or 'idiopathic' schizophrenias from their surrounding territories, are immense. Nevertheless a considerable body of evidence is now available to suggest that illnesses virtually indistinguishable from, if not identical with, schizophrenia on phenomenological grounds may sometimes be associated with brain lesions. The subject has been comprehensively reviewed in detailed analyses of the literature by Davison and Bagley (1969) and Davison (1983).

There are clearly great difficulties in resolving the nosological problems inherent in such an exercise, and particularly when dealing with data reported by others. Moreover having identified a reasonably acceptable group of cases the further problem must be faced of how far any association with brain damage is fortuitous, or due to the unmasking of genetic propensities to the disorder, or more directly related by way of a causal influence of the brain lesion upon the development of the mental illness. These questions too have been tackled by Davison and Bagley and their conclusions are presented at many points in the chapters that follow.

Association with Regional Brain Pathology

The conclusion which emerges repeatedly is that brain lesions, particularly lesions of the temporal lobes and diencephalon, do appear to carry a small but definite hazard of increasing the likelihood that a schizophrenia-like illness will develop. This hazard appears to exceed what would be expected in view of the known genetic propensities in the populations concerned. Thus, at least where certain forms of brain lesions are concerned, there would seem to be a causal link of some nature between the disturbance of cerebral function engendered and the appearance of the psychosis. The nature of such a link is very uncertain, but if the observations are accepted as valid a pathophysiology of some sort must be postulated.

Such conclusions have emerged only slowly, and not without many contradictions of evidence. It remains to be seen how far they can be applied to the central core of 'nuclear' schizophrenias as opposed to the surrounding circle of 'schizophrenia-like' psychoses. Davison and Bagley stress, however, that these illnesses have a range of symptoms similar to the general run of psychoses diagnosed as schizophrenia; phenomenologically, at least at a given point in time, they appear in the main to be indistinguishable from schizophrenias occurring in the absence of detectable organic brain disease. It also remains uncertain to what extent the association may apply

to hebephrenic, catatonic and paranoid varieties. The current impression is that paranoid forms of schizophrenia are especially liable to develop in association with cerebral disorder; some may therefore prefer to retain the term 'paranoid-hallucinatory states in clear consciousness' when referring to such illnesses, rather than accepting the suggestion that schizophrenia *per se* can arise in such a way.

Irrespective of such nosological refinements, the striking fact appears to be that psychotic illnesses with the major features of schizophrenia, and certainly resembling the generality of schizophrenias very closely, may co-exist with cerebral lesions and may be generated in some fashion by such lesions. The acute and chronic organic reactions described in Chapter 1 are by no means the exclusive hallmarks of mental disorder occasioned by cerebral dysfunction. The corollary implication is that, while in the vast majority of schizophrenias no cerebral pathology will be displayed, in some there may be identifiable lesions which warrant careful appraisal.

The evidence has come from studies of diverse forms of cerebral pathology— head injuries, tumours, infections, epilepsy etc. And a further point of note is that lesions of the limbic system, or more accurately of the temporal lobes and diencephalon, have been repeatedly highlighted as important in this regard. This special incrimination of regional pathology tends to discount the notion that the psychoses have merely been precipitated in predisposed persons; on the contrary it rather strongly suggests some special, though undetermined, pathophysiology at work. The evidence concerning head injuries is described in Chapter 5, that concerning cerebral tumours in Chapter 6 (p. 193) and that in the field of epilepsy in Chapter 7 (p. 244). While far from satisfactory or entirely conclusive, for the reasons discussed above, the sum total of evidence begins to look impressive.

What bearing this rare group of organically derived schizophrenias may have on the aetiology of schizophrenia generally is very uncertain. Evidence has occasionally been adduced, however, of limbic system dysfunction in cases of schizophrenia occurring in the absence of frank brain pathology. Torrey and Peterson (1974) discuss electrophysiological, pharmacological and other evidence on the matter, all of which remains circumstantial.

It is also necessary to recognise that abnormalities of other parts of the brain have been incriminated in schizophrenia when special techniques of examination have been employed. Ingvar and Franzen (1974), for example, have shown a distinctive pattern of regional cerebral blood flow in older chronic schizophrenic patients; the overall mean blood flow remains normal, but that to the frontal lobes is relatively diminished in a manner not so far found in other disease states. Lowered uptake of glucose has also been demonstrated in the frontal regions in recent PET-scan studies (p. 124; Buchsbaum *et al.,* 1982).

Clinical evidence, meanwhile, has also pointed to disease of the basal ganglia as having a special relationship with schizophrenia-like illnesses, for example in Huntington's chorea (p. 397), Wilson's disease (p. 565), and the rare syndrome of idiopathic calcification of the basal ganglia (p. 646). Bowman and Lewis (1980) have reinforced this association in their analysis of the site of major pathology in a large variety of cerebral disorders liable to show aspects of schizophrenic symptomatology.

Finally neuropathological studies have once again recommended in relation to schizophrenia after a period of disillusionment occasioned by earlier conflicting reports. Weinberger *et al.* (1983) provide a concise review of the more recent findings. Attention is now focused particularly on basal brain structures in view of the importance accorded to them by modern neuropharmacological developments. Fisman (1975) has claimed 'glial knots' and perivascular infiltration in the brain stem, consistent with an encephalitic process, though there is some doubt whether this is specific for schizophrenia (Hankoff and Peress, 1981). Stevens (1982), in an exceptionally thorough investigation, has found evidence of increased fibrillary gliosis affecting the periventricular structures of the diencephalon, the periaqueductal region of the midbrain and the basal forebrain. The hypothalamus, midbrain tegmentum and substantia innominata were most affected, with appearances suggestive of previous low-grade inflammation. Certain CT scan studies lend support to the possibility of pathological changes in such a location (Dewan *et al.,* 1983).

These varied approaches to a 'focal' neuropathology in schizophrenia still obviously lack cohesion. Many indeed await proper confirmation. Their possible relationship to the cerebral atrophy revealed in CT scan studies in a proportion of schizophrenic patients (p. 121) remains to be determined.

Hemispheric Differences

A separate but perhaps complementary strand to the picture concerns findings which suggest that the hemisphere dominant for language may bear a special relationship to schizophrenia. As described in Chapter 7 (p. 247) there is evidence that among psychotic temporal lobe epileptics the schizophrenia-like psychoses which arise tend to be associated with foci in the left hemisphere. Flor-Henry (1969) deserves credit as the first to point out this special association between schizophrenia and the left temporal lobe. In Davison and Bagley's (1969) material there was a significant association between left hemisphere lesions and the development of features such as primary delusions and catatonic symptoms. It seems possible, therefore, that the hemispheres are in some respects unequal to one another in their potential for giving rise to schizophrenia-like illnesses when damaged.

Furthermore in schizophrenic patients without obvious brain lesions there have been numerous observations suggesting that left (dominant) hemisphere functions may be disturbed. This evidence comes from a multitude of sources and is not always easy to evaluate and interpret. For a comprehensive review of cerebral laterality in relation to schizophrenia and other forms of psychopathology Flor-Henry (1983) should be consulted. Two impressive compilations of research papers are to be found in Gruzelier and Flor-Henry (1979) and Flor-Henry and Gruzelier (1983). Brief reviews are presented by Wexler (1980), Marin and Tucker (1981), Gruzelier (1981), Merrin (1981) and Lishman (1983a). The issues involved are often complex and, as might be expected, different avenues of study are not always in agreement with one another.

The implication of dominant lobe dysfunction in schizophrenia comes from findings of unusual distributions of patterns of handedness (Taylor *et al.,* (1980), asymmetrical development of skin conductance responses in a manner that could reflect deficits in the left temporo-limbic system (Gruzelier 1973; Gruzelier and Venables, 1974), and patterns of functioning on dichotic listening and tachistoscopic tests (Colbourn and Lishman, 1979; Gruzelier, 1979; Connolly *et al.,* 1983). Psychometric data can also be marshalled in support of left hemisphere dysfunction (Flor-Henry and Yeudall, 1979; Taylor *et al.,* 1981; Flor-Henry *et al.,* 1983), likewise EEG data (Abrams and Taylor, 1979, 1980) and data from visual and auditory evoked responses (Buchsbaum *et al.,* 1979; Shagass *et al.,* 1979, 1983). In many of these respects depressive illness can be shown to be associated, on similar evidence, with dysfunction of the other side of the brain (Kronfol *et al.,* 1978; Yozawitz *et al.,* 1979; Von Knorring, 1983).

Recently a neurochemical indication of left hemisphere abnormality in schizophrenia has been added to the other strands of evidence; at autopsy a specific increase in dopamine has been detected in the amygdala of the left cerebral hemisphere in schizophrenic patients — specific in that there is no corresponding asymmetry of noradrenaline in the amygdalae, nor of dopamine in the caudate nuclei (Reynolds, 1983).

A further set of observations has suggested a disturbance, not only of left brain function, but of functional interrelationships between the two hemispheres in schizophrenia. Rosenthal and Bigelow (1972), for example, found an increase in the size of the corpus collosum at autopsy in chronic schizophrenics. Green (1978) and Carr (1980) have shown impairment of transfer of information from one hand to another in schizophrenics, and Dimond et al. (1980) found impairments in pointing with one hand to areas touched lightly on the other. All of this combines to suggest inefficient transfer across channels of communication from one hemisphere to another.

Other interesting observations have been reported by Green and associates (Green and Kotenko, 1980; Green et al., 1983). In normal subjects the monaural comprehension of short prose passages can be shown to be equivalent whether the input is to the left or right ear; however simultaneous input to the two ears yields slightly improved scores. Schizophrenics, by contrast, tend to perform better through one ear than the other, the right usually being superior. And, rather strikingly, binaural inputs yield poorer scores than monaural input to the better of the two ears. The suggested explanation is that the right-left monaural differences reflect abnormal callosal transfer; and the impairment in binaural scores may likewise result from abnormal callosal function preventing the smooth processing and integration of information when this is fed simultaneously to the two hemispheres of the brain. Abnormal information transfer across the corpus callosum may in effect lead to competition between the hemispheres, with consequent impairment of comprehension.

It is tempting to speculate that certain schizophrenic symptoms could conceivably arise on such a basis. Thought disorder, for example, might be the product, at least in part, of inefficient callosal transfer and complex interactions between rival systems in the two cerebral hemispheres.

Thus in addition to a role for focal brain pathology in relation to schizophrenia, it appears that dominance relationships between the hemispheres, and certain aspects of interhemispheric collaboration, may have a bearing on the disorder. In the present state of knowledge many of these findings must be regarded as provisional; they nevertheless emerge as impressive in their totality. They must be set alongside totally dissimilar avenues of research into genetic, biochemical and psycho-developmental approaches to unravelling so complex and mysterious a disorder as schizophrenia.

Chapter 3. Clinical Assessment

The assessment of patients with organic psychiatric disorder follows the time honoured principles of clinical practice generally. It is sometimes a time-consuming process, requiring a good deal of patience and persistence. A careful history is essential, the mental state must be systematically examined, and a thorough physical examination will be required as well. The picture will then often remain incomplete without evaluation by a clinical psychologist and the undertaking of certain ancillary investigations. A period of observation in hospital can do much to clarify the situation when the diagnosis is unclear, and may prove more valuable than a great number of visits to the out-patient clinic. In many cases, therefore, the initial contact with the patient will merely serve to establish the major probabilities in diagnosis and allow more detailed planning for further enquiries.

No attempt will be made in the present chapter to outline a comprehensive schema for psychiatric history taking or examination. This is dealt with in text books of general psychiatry and summarised in the publication by the Departmental Teaching Committee of the Institute of Psychiatry (Notes on Eliciting and Recording Clinical Information, 1973). The purpose here will be to focus on those aspects of clinical enquiry which assume particular importance when one suspects an organic disease process in the genesis of the patient's mental symptoms. The value of certain psychometric tests and other investigatory procedures will also be discussed.

History Taking

Where the great majority of organic psychiatric illnesses are concerned the stage is clearly set by the history, certainly when the relatives have been consulted. Or if the history is equivocal, certain features on examination usually soon indicate that there is likely to be an organic basis for the disturbance. The main task thereafter is to refine the diagnosis by seeking to determine the nature of the pathological process. It is only in a minority of patients, albeit a vitally important group, that the presentation may be misleading—in the very early case or in cases with an abundance of 'functional' psychiatric features.

Time spent in obtaining a detailed history is almost always rewarded, and may yield more important leads to the correct diagnosis than a host of investigations. Certainly it will indicate what investigations, if any, need to be pursued. Moreover the patient's account and his behaviour during interview will provide a wealth of information about his mental state and the intactness or otherwise of his cognitive functions.

His own account will usually need to be supplemented by information from others. Statements derived from the patient alone frequently prove misleading, both with regard to the gravity of the symptoms and the time course of their evolution. This is clearly so when the patient is confused or suffering from obvious memory impairment, but can be equally important in other situations. The changes occasioned by brain damage can be hard for the patient to evaluate subjectively, even when insight is largely retained. Certainly, when asked to judge whether memory or other difficulties are worsening or improving, he will often seize on some recent instance which may have more to do with chance and circumstance than with the course of his clinical condition. In many cases there will be genuine loss of insight, and sometimes a desire to conceal from himself and from others that intellectual functions are failing. Sometimes, too, the early changes will be of a type more obvious to outsiders than to the patient himself—changes in mood, enthusiasms, habitual activities and attitudes. Such matters obviously require the detailed testimony of someone who has known the patient intimately throughout the evolution of the disorder.

Abnormalities are likely to include such matters as disordered behaviour, and disturbances of mood, memory and subjective experience. Physical symptoms will also often figure prominently. The full range of all complaints and apparent defects of functioning must be carefully explored, with readiness to search beneath the immediately presenting picture. Physical symptoms may have come to serve as the focus of attention for the patient and his relatives, and the true extent of mental abnormalities may only be revealed by specific enquiry. On the other hand the physical components should not be lightly brushed aside; in particular complaints of headache, malaise or generalised weakness must not be underestimated. When there is a problem of differential diagnosis between functional and organic mental illness it will be necessary to preserve a delicate balance in the enquiries until information begins to tip the balance in one direction or the other.

Particular attention must always be paid to the mode of onset of the disorder, the duration of symptoms and the way they have progressed. Where developments have been insidious the onset is often dated very imprecisely, even by relatives, with some striking incident serving as a screen for much that went before. Systematic enquiry about the level of functioning prior to the alleged onset can then be useful—behaviour on a previous holiday or at Christmas time for example—and serve to remind informants of the earlier evidence of disorder.

Enquiry should always be made about fluctuations in behaviour or changes which have been observed from one situation to another. Nocturnal worsening is an important indicator of minor degrees of clouding of consciousness. Behaviour which is relatively intact in the restricted field of domestic activities may be dramatically changed when new experiences need to be encompassed. Episodic abnormal behaviour of sudden onset and ending will raise the suspicion of an epileptic component.

Other salient features which deserve specific enquiry are outlined in Chapter 4 where differential diagnosis is discussed. These include not only features among the presenting symptoms but also antecedent conditions such as head injury, alcoholism or drug abuse. Any recent physical illness must be noted, or medications recently prescribed, or conditions predisposing to anoxia such as cardiac failure, respiratory inadequacy or the recent administration of an anaesthetic. Any history of dysphasia, paresis, fits or other transitory neurological disturbances must be ascertained.

It is perhaps worth emphasising that the formal psychiatric history remains important even when the presenting complaints have a markedly organic flavour. Where the question arises of a differential diagnosis between functional and organic mental illness, all parts of the standard psychiatric enquiry will need to be completed. Previous reactions to stress, and symptoms observed during previous episodes of ill-health, may help to clarify the significance of the present clinical features. Of course when there is abundant evidence of a cerebral pathological process some parts of the formal psychiatric history will be redundant. But there is still a need to know about premorbid patterns of functioning, special vulnerabilities, and details of the patient's social and family setting. Such information may throw light upon the content of the illness and on special factors which will need to be borne in mind in management. Knowledge of the level achieved in education and at work can similarly be valuable in assessing present evidence of intellectual decline.

Physical Examination

The more one suspects an organic basis for the patient's mental condition the more important will be the physical examination. Often it is the latter which yields decisive information about the precise aetiology and the treatment required. In practice the dichotomy between the physical and the mental examination often tends to melt away, with each providing essential leads to the other. This is particularly evident in the examination of higher mental functions where the neurological examination overlaps in large measure with the detailed assessment of cognitive status.

Special attention will usually need to be devoted to the neurological system, but other systems can sometimes be just as crucially important. Johnson (1968) found that among 250 consecutive admissions to a psychiatric hospital 12% had some physical illness which was an important aetiological factor in the presenting mental disorder. The majority were diagnosable by routine physical examination and had been missed prior to admission. Among his examples were cases of myxoedema, neurosyphilis, cerebral anoxia due to cardiac failure, chest infections, anaemia, liver failure, carcinoma and cerebral arteriosclerosis. In addition many other physical disorders were discovered which did not contribute directly to the presenting clinical picture. Among 534 elderly patients admitted to psychiatric receiving wards Simon and Cahan (1963) found that 13% had an acute and reversible physical cause for their symptoms, and another 30% had an acute component added to their senile or arteriosclerotic dementia. Cardiac failure, malnutrition and recent cerebrovascular accidents made up most of the latter group. In Chapter 4 some of the principal physical signs which must be sought out with care are described (pp. 128 and 131).

It is important, especially in the neurological examination, to interpret abnormal findings in relation to all the clinical features. Among the elderly in particular, isolated neurological abnormalities can often be without significance (Critchley, 1931; Prakash and Stern, 1973). Absent vibration sense, mild tremors, sluggish and irregular pupils, isolated abnormalities of tendon reflexes or a doubtfully positive plantar response may lack diagnostic significance, or be related to minor pathology without relevance to the present problem. On the other hand, when viewed against the total picture these can occasionally be just the features which lead eventually to the true diagnosis.

Gross neurological abnormalities will rarely be encountered in patients with diffuse cerebral impairment, but certain less striking features should be carefully observed. Some of these are not very widely appreciated, and can be important in raising suspicion of a degenerative brain process. Lack of manual precision, motor impersistence, and perseveration of motor acts may emerge clearly in the course of neurological testing. A clumsy graceless walk or minor unsteadiness may betray cerebral pathology, even in the absence of definite pyramidal, extrapyramidal or cerebellar signs (Allison, 1962). This may be striking once attention has been directed towards it. In patients suspected of cerebral vascular disease special attention should be paid to swallowing, speech, and the jaw jerk as indicators of early pseudobulbar palsy. A wide-based gait has been stressed as an early indicator of normal pressure hydrocephalus (p. 640). Minor parkinsonian features, such as a stooping posture or lack of associated arm movements on walking, may also be noticed in diffuse cerebral atrophy.

Paulson (1971) describes certain reflex abnormalities which can occasionally precede definite evidence of intellectual impairment in cortical disease processes. Reflex grasping movements of the hand may occur on stroking the palm, or sucking reflex movements of the mouth on touching the lips. Both are linked especially to frontal lobe disease. The 'palmo-mental reflex' consists of unilateral contraction of the muscles of the chin producing a wince-like movement when the thenar eminence of the ipsilateral hand is stroked briskly. The 'corneo-mandibular reflex' consists of a movement of the opposite side of the chin in addition to blinking when a cotton-tip is applied to the cornea. The 'glabella-tap reflex' is elicited by repeated tapping of the forehead above the root of the nose—this produces blinking in response to each tap which fails to habituate rapidly as it does in normal persons. Keshavan

et al. (1979) illustrate the limitations of such reflexes as an aid to diagnosis; the palmo-mental reflex, for example, was found to be positive in as high a proportion of patients with affective disorder or schizophrenia as in patients with organic brain disorder.

The Mental State

The evaluation of the mental state provides the cross-sectional view which supplements the longitudinal view of the illness derived from the history. It can also add decisive information of its own. It is essential to realise that key features such as memory impairment may have to be sought after diligently if they are to be properly displayed.

There are obviously certain aspects of the mental state which are of especial importance in organic psychiatric disease, and these will be described in some detail below. In particular the correct evaluation of cognitive functions is often central to the identification of cerebral pathology. However too early or exclusive a preoccupation with the assessment of cognitive functions can be hazardous, and stands to leave much valuable information uncharted. Short cuts should not be taken, and the aim must always be towards a systematic and comprehensive examination with full attention to the usual range of mental phenomena. Often, for example, it is uncertain how much of the picture may be explained on the basis of functional rather than organic mental disturbance, and such a differentiation requires a careful assessment of all aspects of the mental state. And even when cerebral pathology is abundantly obvious it is still necessary to be thoroughly aware of the patient's affective state, the nature of his interpersonal reactions and the detailed content of his subjective experiences. The emphasis below on certain aspects alone should therefore not be taken to imply that other areas are necessarily of subsidiary importance.

The mental state observed at interview must be evaluated against background information from the family and others who have observed the patient in real-life situations. The interview has its own importance in allowing a systematic exploration of relevant areas of function, but is necessarily restricted in scope and in many ways an artificial situation. It is for this reason that admission to hospital for a period of observation often adds greatly to the assessment. Nurses' reports of behaviour in the ward, interactions with others, and variability from time to time throughout the day can yield crucial information. Occupational therapy can provide the most realistic setting of all when it comes to observing the detailed nature of the patient's difficulties over everyday tasks.

Appearance and General Behaviour

Certain features obvious at a glance can raise suspicion of an organic basis for mental symptoms. Any evidence of physical ill-health should be noted—pallor, loss of weight, or indications of physical weakness. The facies can be tremendously important. A certain laxness of the muscles of the lower face and lack of emotional play about the features will suggest a cerebral degenerative process in the absence of marked depression of mood. Movements may be slow, sparse or tremulous. The appearance may be in excess of normal age, or standards of self-care and general tidiness may be lowered. A lapse of standards which cannot readily be explained on the basis of severe emotional disturbance can be a sensitive and early pointer to cerebral pathology.

Features which should be noted in the course of conversation include slowness or hesitancy of response, perseverative tendencies, and defective uptake or grasp. This is the time to note whether the patient is alert and responsive or dull and apathetic, whether he is friendly and cooperative or distant and truculent. The adequacy with which attention can be held, diverted or shifted from one activity to another may be seen to be abnormal. Impulsiveness, disinhibition, or blunted sensitivity to social interaction are other important features which may emerge during the interview, and the patient may be noted to tire unusually quickly with mental effort.

Behaviour in the ward can be still more revealing. The patient may prove to be largely indifferent to events and out of contact with his surroundings, sometimes with variability from one part of the day to another. Impaired awareness of the environment may be manifest in a puzzled expression, aimless wandering, restlessness or repetitive stereotyped behaviour. His responses to various requirements and situations may reveal defects not previously suspected. He may lose his way, misidentify people, or betray serious lapses of memory. His interactions with others may reveal paranoid tendencies, or he may be observed to react to hallucinatory experiences not previously disclosed. His level of competence over dressing, undressing and matters of hygiene can be assessed. Disordered feeding habits can occasionally reveal the inroads of dementia in a patient with an otherwise well preserved social

manner. Any episode of incontinence will of course be noted, along with the patient's reaction towards it.

Mood

A variety of abnormalities of mood may occur with organic cerebral dysfunction, depending partly on the nature of the cerebral pathology and partly on the premorbid personality. Some forms of reaction are particularly common and immediately raise suspicion.

Clouding of consciousness is often accompanied by an inappropriate placidity and lack of concern, coupled with some degree of disinhibition. The florid hostile or fearful moods of delirium are also characteristic, often rapidly changeable from one moment to another and sometimes with expansive or elated phases. In early dementia a quiet wondering perplexity is often the predominant mood, or emotional lability in which signs of distress resolve as abruptly as they appear.

An empty shallow quality to the emotional display should always raise suspicion of organic cerebral disease, likewise apathy in which there is little discernible emotion, and euphoria in which a mild elevation of mood goes unbacked by a true sense of happy elation. Emotional blunting and flattening are other characteristic signs. These classical forms are not invariable, however. Some patients with organic brain damage show heightened and sustained anxiety, or marked depressive reactions.

Characteristic emotional reactions may emerge when the patient is faced with problems which tax his ability. He may over-react in an anxious aggressive manner, or alternatively become quiet, sullen and withdrawn. Goldstein (1942) described the catastrophic reaction ('katastrophenreaktion') which can be observed in such circumstances, occasionally without warning but usually heralded by increasing anxiety and tension. The patient looks dazed and starts to fumble. Whereas a moment before he was calm and amiable he now shows an intense affective response, varying from irritability and temper to outbursts of crying and despair. Autonomic disturbance is seen in the form of flushing, sweating or trembling. He may become evasive where further questions are concerned, or show a sudden aimless restlessness.

Talk and Content of Thought

The patient's talk, both spontaneously and in

response to questions, provides a wealth of important clues. Discursive tendencies may be noted, with his mind wandering frequently off the point, or minor incoherence, or perseverative and paraphasic errors. Perseveration in particular is a sign of the greatest importance. The formal examination for dysphasic disturbances is considered below (p. 86 *et seq.*)

There may be pressure of talk which serves as a screen to cover defects. The patient may employ denials or evasions when pressed for details about his history, or try to explain away his failures with facile rationalisations. It can be very important to push gently beneath a well-preserved social façade in order to determine the true extent of the inroads made by cerebral pathology.

Observation of the content of talk is the chief means of access to the patient's thought processes. A surprising poverty of thought may be revealed, or preoccupation with restricted and reiterative themes. Associations may be found to be impoverished and reasoning power impaired.

Time should be spent in attempts to get as complete a picture as possible of any pathological ideas, experiences or attitudes which may be present. Paranoid tendencies are common in the presence of intellectual deterioration and ideas of reference may be marked. Delusional ideas may be stamped with certain characteristic features as already described on p. 11 and pp. 14–15.

Perceptual distortion, illusions and hallucinations must be noted. In organic psychiatric disorders these occur chiefly in the visual modality; they tend to be commoner when sensory cues diminish towards nightfall, and may be fleeting and changeable. Feelings of familiarity or unfamiliarity may be intrusive, with depersonalisation, derealisation or déjà vu. Body image disorders will merit careful exploration and assessment.

The patient's attitude to his illness should always be ascertained. He may fail to recognise that he is unwell, deny any disability, or take a surprisingly lighthearted view of his case. At the same time he may prove to be fully compliant over examination or admission to hospital. His own explanations for his symptoms should be determined. This alone can give important indications about his capacity for making realistic judgements.

ASSESSMENT OF THE COGNITIVE STATE

The cognitive state examination can be crucial for producing evidence of an organic component in a mental illness. The number of tests and procedures available for assessing cognitive functions is rather bewildering, and it is therefore helpful to acquire a standard routine. This also has value in building up the clinician's experience of the different tests and the meaning to be put on failure in various situations. He will then be in a position to formulate subjective judgements in cases where the evidence is not clearcut; such judgements in turn are essential when deciding whether more detailed investigations should be undertaken.

Most of the brief shorthand tests employed by the psychiatrist lack adequate standardisation and validation. Indeed when their value has been tested they have often, taken individually, proved to be remarkably inefficient in distinguishing between organic and functional psychiatric illness (Shapiro *et al.*, 1956; Hinton and Withers, 1971). Many prove to be closely related to educational level and general intelligence, some are markedly affected by increasing age and others by emotional disturbance. Some of the more detailed psychometric procedures elaborated by psychologists are clearly superior for the task of identifying organic psychiatric disorder, but are too cumbersome for use in every patient.

Nevertheless the routine tests available to the clinician have a definite value of their own. They have the important virtue of throwing a very wide net and touching upon a number of facets of cognitive function in a reasonably concise manner. In the course of administering them the examiner also picks up numerous indirect clues; the patient's behaviour during attempts at the tests, and the nature of his approach, provide important information in themselves. Thus when taken in conjunction with observations gleaned during interview there is a substantial chance that cerebral impairment will come to be suspected when it exists. Such suspicions can then be followed up by more decisive means.

The fact that patients with non-organic psychiatric conditions may sometimes show impaired performance on the tests is paradoxically of use as well. It is important, for example, to gauge how severely concentration is impaired in a patient suffering from depression, to observe how little impact outside events have made in a patient with severe and sustained anxiety. The routine use of the tests in every patient is therefore seldom a waste of time.

The important matter is to recognise the limitations of the tests, and to have a clear strategy for knowing how far to press the cognitive status examination in a given situation. A brief examination is described below for use in every psychiatric patient, and then a more detailed battery for use when organic cerebral disease is definitely suspected.

ROUTINE COGNITIVE STATE
EXAMINATION*

Orientation

Orientation for time is assessed by asking the patient to name the day of the week, date, month and year. Minor degrees of temporal disorientation may be identified by asking the patient to estimate the time of day, or to estimate how much time has elapsed since the interview was begun. Orientation for place is assessed by asking the patient to name his present whereabouts and to give the address. Orientation for person is tested simply by asking the patient his name.

Common sense must obviously be used in administering these simple questions. It will usually have become apparent in the course of history taking if the patient is correctly oriented for place and person and these questions can therefore often be omitted. Orientation for time is worth testing in all patients, however, since this is commonly the first to suffer in the course of mild impairment of consciousness or intellectual impairment.

Attention and Concentration

Marked difficulties with attention and concentration will usually have become apparent in the course of history taking and examination. When so it is important to *record qualitative observations in full*.

Note deficiencies in the way in which attention is *aroused* or *sustained*, whether the patient is readily *distracted* by extraneous or internal stimuli, and whether *attention fluctuates* from one moment to another. There may be difficulty in *shifting attention* from one topic or frame of reference to another, or attention may be *diffuse* so that it cannot be directed to a particular purpose. Note impairment of ability to *concentrate upon a coherent line of thought or reasoning*, or undue readiness with which powers of concentration become *fatigued*.

Brief tests which can be used to record attention and concentration include asking the patient to give the days of the week or months of the year in reverse order; recording and timing his efforts to subtract serial 7s from 100; asking him to perform other simple tests of mental arithmetic appropriate to his level of intelligence.

The ability to repeat digits forwards and backwards

---

provides another useful yardstick ('digit span'). The digits must be delivered in an even tone and at a rate of one per second if accurate comparisons are to be made. A start will usually be made with two or more digits forwards, increasing by one each time until the patient's limit is reached.

Memory

The ability to register, retain and retrieve information should be assessed by two or three simple tests. The patient's capacity for current memorising (new learning) has the most important clinical implications and warrants close attention.

Test ability to repeat a sentence immediately after a single hearing. The sentence should be appropriate to the patient's intellectual level as in the following examples from the Stanford–Binet series. Year 13:—'The aeroplane made a careful landing in the space which had been prepared for it'. Average adult:—'The red-headed woodpeckers made a terrible fuss as they tried to drive the young away from the nest'. Superior adult:—'At the end of the week the newspaper published a complete account of the experiences of the great explorer'.

If suspicion of impairment has arisen test the number of repetitions necessary for the accurate reproduction of one of Babcock's (1930) sentences:—'One thing a nation must have to become rich and great is a large secure supply of wood'. Or 'The clouds hung low in the valley and the wind howled among the trees as the men went on through the rain'. Or 'As the great red sun came over the hills the Indians broke camp and prepared for another hard day's work'. Three repetitions of one of these sentences should allow word perfect reproduction in a patient of average intelligence.

Ask the patient to listen carefully while you tell him a name and address, then ask for its immediate reproduction. Record his answer verbatim, and repeat if necessary when the first response is unsatisfactory. Test retrieval 3–5 minutes later after interposing other cognitive tests, and again record the answer verbatim.

A technique similar to that of Irving *et al.* (1970) (p. 102) may be useful with patients of limited ability or when it is hard to ensure cooperation, as follows. The patient is told he will be given the name of a flower and asked to repeat it ('The flower is — a daffodil — please repeat daffodil'), then a colour ('The colour is — blue — please repeat blue'), then a town ('The town is — Brighton'), etc. The list may continue with makes of car, days of week, etc., until some six or ten items have been given according to the patient's ability. Recall is tested 3–25 minutes later, first without prompting then if necessary after giving each category name. This provides the opportunity for testing free recall and cued recall separately, and will sometimes demonstrate good learning ability

---

* Much of the material in the sections which follow up to p. 92 has previously appeared in condensed form in the publication produced by the Departmental Teaching Committee of the Institute of Psychiatry ('Notes on Eliciting and Recording Clinical Information', 1973) published by Oxford University Press.

when other techniques have failed. Perseveration is sometimes clearly displayed on the test, likewise confabulatory tendencies.

Other aspects of memory assessment are necessarily largely subjective. Discrepancies may already have emerged between the patient's account of his illness and that given by informants. *Pay special attention to memory for recent happenings and in particular for the temporal sequence of recent events.* The circumstances surrounding his admission to hospital and happenings in the ward thereafter should be briefly reviewed, since these are matters about which the examiner will have independent knowledge.

Retrieval from the remote past is more difficult to evaluate, but an attempt should be made to judge the adequacy of the patient's account of his earlier life, and to examine this for evidence of gaps or inconsistencies. Care must be taken in doubtful cases to frame questions in such a way that memory for the past its truly tested. Williams (1968) points out that many of the questions which patients are asked about their earlier life can be answered in very general terms. Thus the question 'How old were you when you started school?' can produce an easy habitual response and secure a correct reply, whereas 'Can you describe your first day at school?' requires the mobilisation of actual memories.

Record any *selective impairments of memory* which become apparent in the interview for *special incidents, periods, or themes* in the patient's life. *Retrograde and anterograde amnesia* must be specified in detail in relation to head injury or epileptic phenomena. Describe any evidence of *confabulation* or *false memories. Note the patient's attitude to any memory difficulties which he displays.*

General Information

A brief estimate should be made of the patient's knowledge of current events, and of his ability to handle material from his long-term memory store ('utilisation of old knowledge').

Ask about recent items of interest in the news, political, sporting or otherwise, in accordance with the patient's known interests and activities. Ask him to name key personalities, again in conformity with his expected interests and abilities—members of the Royal Family, Prime Ministers, members of the cabinet, or well-known television performers. (Clearly such questions will only need to be pursued when reason has emerged to doubt the patient's competence.)

Ask him the dates of the first and second world wars, and test his knowledge of capitals and countries. In the face of poor responses pursue his general knowledge further by asking for names of cities in England, rivers, etc.

If reason has emerged to suspect a disturbance of abstract thinking ask him to explain the difference between concepts such as 'child' and 'dwarf', 'poverty' and 'misery', 'river' and 'canal', 'lie' and 'mistake', and test his ability to give the meaning behind well-known proverbs.

Intelligence

The patient's educational and occupational history, taken in conjunction with his own interests and activities, should allow a rough estimate to be made of the expected level of intelligence. *Any aspects of performance during testing which are at variance with this should be carefully noted.* Patients in hospital can usually be asked to complete the Mill Hill Vocabulary Test and Raven's Progressive Matrices (p. 97) and these may provide further evidence to uphold a suspicion of deterioration.

The above battery of tests can often be abbreviated when responses are clear and accurate from the start. It is important, however, to gain a clear understanding of the patient's capacities under each of these headings whatever form the presenting illness may take. Much will have been learned about the patient's grasp and efficiency, and about his reactions and approach to problems. Covert organic disorders may be revealed, and obvious cerebral impairment will have been charted in a preliminary and valuable way.

The headings employed are not, of course, mutually exclusive. Orientation for time and place is closely bound up with current memorising ability and with clarity and coherence of thought. The tests of orientation as described above are nevertheless very useful, and have repeatedly emerged as among the most discriminating features in the mental state examination for distinguishing between organic and functional psychiatric disorders (Shapiro *et al.*, 1956; Hinton and Withers, 1971). Sometimes they have even been found to compare favourably for this purpose with more elaborate and time consuming psychometric procedures (Irving *et al.*, 1970).

Attention is not a clearly defined concept, and overlaps with functions described as alertness, awareness and responsiveness (Klein and Mayer-Gross, 1957). It is nonetheless widely accepted as a clinically useful concept, with particular relevance to general mental acuity and the state of consciousness. Concentration is a similarly imprecise term, referring to capacity for focusing and sustaining mental activity on the task in hand. Both stand to be markedly affected by preoccupations or abnormalities of mood, and can therefore be disturbed in functional psychiatric illness. Equally, however, they can give important indications of clouding of consciousness or general intellectual impairment.

It will be noted that simple tests of arithmetical functions form an integral part of the tests for attention and concentration, and this in itself can be valuable in revealing any marked defect in numerical ability. The digit repetition test is included in this section, rather than in the assessment of memory, since it is well established that the immediate memory span is usually normal in amnesic subjects (Zangwill, 1946; Milner, 1966).

The assessment of memory is of the utmost importance, since memory failure is a particularly sensitive indicator of cerebral dysfunction. It is here that the most decisive evidence of an organic component in the illness will often be obtained. Fortunately for clinical practice the aspect of memory that is most amenable to careful testing is also the aspect most vulnerable to cerebral dysfunction, namely the capacity for acquiring and retaining new information.

The section on general information extends the possibility of exploring memory difficulties, and at the same time brings added information against which to judge the likelihood of generalised intellectual impairment.

EXTENDED COGNITIVE STATE EXAMINATION

The examination described above is probably adequate for routine psychiatric practice. The abnormalities which emerge will need to be evaluated against the total picture presented by the patient—sometimes they will raise the suspicion of organic cerebral disorder, but quite often they will be attributable to factors such as low intelligence, emotional disturbance or psychotic thought disorder. More latitude will be allowed when there is abundant evidence on which to base a primary diagnosis of functional mental illness. However truly suspicious findings will indicate the need for more thoroughgoing examination.

The problem is different in certain special clinical situations. When, for example, there is doubt from the beginning about the differential diagnosis between organic and non-organic psychiatric disor-

der the approach must be more extensive, and cognitive functions must be examined with greater thoroughness. Equally if a patient presents with symptoms which immediately raise the possibility of cerebral dysfunction there must be a more comprehensive and systematic exploration. In particular the search must embrace the possibilities of circumscribed defects of higher mental function due to focal brain pathology.

Some points of caution must be observed before embarking on the extended cognitive state examination. In the first place the examination can be lengthy and fatigue may produce misleading results; the procedures should not be hurried, and several brief sessions are usually preferable to a single comprehensive examination. Secondly the examiner must remain sensitive to the patient's reactions to failure. A given test must sometimes be set aside for a while in the interests of sustaining morale and cooperation; tests which are pressed too firmly may provoke 'catastrophic reactions' or bewilder the patient to the point where useful information is no longer obtained. Thirdly the tests must always be adapted to the patient's intelligence and educational level, and to his particular difficulties. Finally it is essential to remain aware that one disability may have repercussions upon performance at other tasks. Defective comprehension, for example, will cloud the issue when it comes to testing for dyspraxia. Due allowance will need to be made for this in the selection of the tests, the order of their administration, and the assessment of results.

Consequently it is helpful to have a simple routine at the outset which allows key areas of function to be assessed in a somewhat abbreviated fashion, before proceeding to detailed and lengthier parts of the examination:

First take careful note of the patient's *level of cooperation*. His willingness and ability to apply himself to the test procedures will be fundamental to the amount of reliable information which can be obtained.

Make a preliminary assessment of his *level of conscious awareness*. This must have an early priority since performance on all other tests may be affected by minor degrees of clouding of consciousness.

Next assess *language functions*. Much of what follows later will depend upon the accuracy of verbal communication. In addition to noting his verbal ability during conversation and history taking, ask him to name a series of objects and to perform a series of simple commands.

Memory functions, if not already tested, should be briefly examined as already described.

Visuospatial ability should always be screened because non-verbal deficits of this nature may otherwise remain concealed. Ask the patient to copy simple designs such as those illustrated on p. 89.

Test the integrity of *volitional movements* and at the same time of *right-left orientation* by asking the patient to point to various parts of his body. Ask him for example to 'Touch your left ear with your left hand', 'Touch your left knee with your right hand' etcetera.

This overture to the detailed examination will often save a good deal of time and avoid confusion later. It will serve to chart important areas of disability and go some way towards exonerating others. The significance of the patient's failures during later more detailed testing will then be more readily appreciated.

Thereafter individual areas of cognitive function must be systematically explored, with the aim of covering each of the sections described below. Some areas will need to be explored in detail and others merely in an abbreviated fashion. The areas which require most careful assessment in the particular patient will by now be apparent—attention will have been directed towards them by the history, the neurological examination, and the cognitive deficits already displayed.

Level of Conscious Awareness

Impairment of consciousness is obvious when there is frank drowsiness or somnolence during examination. It is with the minor degrees that difficulties are encountered. There are no pathognomonic signs or tests for minor impairment of consciousness, and its detection is largely a matter for subjective clinical judgement based on a variety of clues:

Record any obvious impairment in the form of drowsiness or diminished awareness of the environment. Note fluctuations during examination, and question relatives or nursing staff about changes which occur from time to time during the day. Impairment may only become obvious towards nightfall or when the patient is fatigued.

Minor impairment will be suspected when the patient is dull, inert and uncertain in behaviour even though he is not drowsy, or when responses to external events are diminished and made in a relatively undiscriminating way. There may be a vagueness and hesitancy about his manner of speaking. Once the examiner is suspicious about a reduction of the level of consciousness it can be helpful to repeat questions concerning dates and names of places concerned with the patient's illness, with the object of determining whether consistent answers are given. Tests of orientation, attention, concentration and memory may be found to be poorly performed, often with variability from one occasion to another. Judgement of the passage of time will often be markedly inaccurate. Attention will

be ill-sustained and ill-focused, and he will tend to lose the thread in conversation. Subjective events and stimuli will tend to occupy his attention at the expense of external happenings. Lucid intervals may emerge from time to time and form a marked contrast to the general tenor of his behaviour. Even when seemingly alert it may be discovered that he has failed to register on-going experiences, including those of the interview itself.

Simple procedures may be employed in order to assess the patient's capacity for sustained attention or 'vigilance' over a period of time. The patient may be asked, for example, to raise his hand whenever an 'A' is spoken, and a series of letters are then delivered in an even tone and at a constant rate. A more difficult version will consist in raising the hand whenever any vowel is spoken, or whenever two vowels succeed one another. A written form of the test can easily be achieved by asking the patient to cancel all letters of a designated type on a printed sheet or in a passage of prose material.

If somnolent, can the patient be roused to full or only partial awareness? If his attention cannot be sustained does he drift back towards sleep or does his attention wander onto other topics? When consciousness is severely impaired describe the nature of the stimulus required to evoke a response (for example conversation, firm commands, commands following arousal by shaking, painful stimuli) and the character of the response produced (for example a correct verbal reply or motor act, an incorrect and muddled response, failure to respond to commands but accurate localisation of a painful stimulus, ill-coordinated and ineffectual motor movements). The Glasgow Coma Scale (p. 142) will prove of value for monitoring progress in patients with seriously impaired consciousness.

Evidence for 'delirium', 'stupor' or 'coma' should be specified in detail.

Language Functions

Language functions are conveniently examined under the six headings described below. Thorough examination of dysphasic disturbances can take a considerable time, but in the non-dysphasic subject screening need take only a few minutes.

At the onset it is important to *note whether the patient is predominantly right- or left-handed,* otherwise this important item of information may come to be overlooked.

Motor Aspects of Speech

Note the quality of spontaneous speech and that in reply to questions. Minor expressive speech defects may only emerge when the patient is pressed to engage in conversation, to describe his work, his house, or some event in his life.

Is there any disturbance of articulation (dysarthria)? When slight dysarthria is suspected test ability to pronounce a phrase such as 'West Register Street'.

Is there slowness or hesitancy with speech production and is the output sparse? Or conversely is the output excessive with a definite pressure of speech (logorrhoea)?

Does he use wrong words, words which are nearly but not exactly correct, or words that do not exist? *Paraphasic errors* may be defined as 'substitutions within language' (Benson and Geschwind, 1971) and exist in several forms; they may involve the substitution of one correct word for another, the distortion of one syllable within a word, or the production of a group of sounds with no specific meaning (neologisms).

Note whether words are omitted and sentences abbreviated (telegram style). Are there inaccuracies of grammatical construction (paragrammatisms)? Is the normal rhythm and inflexion of speech disturbed (dysprosody)? Is speech totally disorganised and incomprehensible (jargon aphasia)?

Observe for perseverative errors of speech in the form of repetition of phrases just spoken (echolalia), of single words (pallilalia) or of a terminal syllable (logoclonia).

When defects are found test whether automatic speech or the naming of serials is better preserved than conversational speech—ask him to repeat a well-known nursery rhyme or prayer, to count to twenty, or to give the days of the week. Are emotional utterances or ejaculations preserved when formal speech is defective?

From the phenomenological point of view Benson and Geschwind (1971) recommend a basic division into *fluent and non-fluent forms of dysphasic speech,* the former characterising posterior lesions and the latter anterior lesions. Fluent dysphasias in general show clear articulation, the words are produced without effort, output is normal or excessive, paraphasic errors are frequent, phrase length is not curtailed, and normal rhythm and inflexion are preserved. Non-fluent dysphasias show poor articulation, the speech is produced with obvious difficulty, output is sparse but nonetheless the content is meaningful when this can be discerned, phrase length is reduced to one or two words, and the rhythm and inflexion are disturbed.

Comprehension of Speech

The understanding of speech must be separately assessed, whether or not production is defective. Even when the patient is mute or his utterances totally incomprehensible it is still necessary to determine whether he can understand what is said to him.

Can he point correctly on command to objects around him? Can he carry out simple orders on request, for example pick up an object, show his tongue? Failure can be misleading since it may be due to dyspraxia; thus if commands are not carried out test whether he can signal his response to simple 'yes-no' questions.

Can he respond to more complex instructions, for example walk over to the door and come back again, or take his spectacles from his pocket and put them on the table. Can he follow a series of commands sequentially,

for example go to the window, tap it twice, turn around, then come back again.

Marie's Three Paper Test is widely employed for the rapid assessment of mild comprehension defects. Three pieces of paper of different sizes are put before the patient. He is told to take the biggest one and hand it to the examiner, take the smallest and throw it to the ground, and take the middle sized one and put it in his pocket.

The understanding of prepositional and syntactic aspects of speech can be a sensitive indicator of minor comprehension difficulties. It is readily tested by providing the patient with three objects such as a book, pen and coin, then issuing increasingly complex instructions as follows: 'Put the coin on the book; put the coin and the pen under the book; tap the book and then the coin with the pen; put the book between the pen and the coin; place the book over the coin then put the pen inside it', etc.

If comprehension of spoken speech is defective, test whether understanding of written words and instructions is better preserved. *Test whether other hearing functions are intact,* for example the startle response to sudden noise. Test for *auditory agnosia* by noting whether he can recognise non-verbal noises—clapping hands, snapping fingers, jingling money—or copy the production of such sounds when they are made outside the field of vision.

Repetition of Speech

Can the patient repeat digits, words, short phrases, or long sentences exactly as you give them? Successful repetition involves both motor and sensory parts of the speech apparatus and also the connections between the two. Failure in repetition may occur despite adequate spontaneous articulation and good comprehension. Paraphasic errors often emerge most clearly in the testing of repetition.

Word Finding

Does the patient have difficulty in finding words during conversation, or use circumlocutions? Test specifically for nominal dysphasia by asking him to name both common and uncommon objects (for example the parts of a wrist watch, and other objects in the room). Include an examination of his ability to name colours.

Nominal dysphasia may be the only language disturbance in patients with cerebral damage and must therefore always be tested with care. Newcombe *et al.* (1965) have shown that the ease of word finding is inversely related to the frequency of occurrence of the name-word in the language, and that the detection of slight nominal dysphasia requires testing with objects whose names occur at a frequency of less than 1 per 100,000 words. The latter include words such as 'buckle', 'pointer' or 'dial', but not 'watch' or 'strap'; 'lapel' or 'knuckle', but not 'button' or 'finger'; 'radiator' or 'linoleum', but not 'picture' or 'carpet' (Thorndike and Lorge, 1944).

Reading

Present the patient with the written names of objects in the room, and ask him to point to them. If this is performed correctly present him with written instructions to perform specific actions.

Test his ability to read aloud, and determine whether he understands what he has read. If he fails to read aloud it is still necessary to assess whether he has read, since some dysphasics comprehend well even though they fail to read aloud.

Writing

Test ability to write spontaneously and to dictation. Examine written productions for substitutions, perseverations, spelling errors and letter reversals. Is copying better preserved than writing to dictation? Is spelling out loud better preserved than spelling on paper? Is the writing of habitual material (signature, address) relatively intact? Are numbers written more accurately than words or letters?

The main syndromes of language impairment can be distinguished by the pattern of breakdown in the above examination. Table 1 summarises performance on the different tests of language function in relation to the syndromes of dysphasia described in Chapter 2.

Verbal Fluency

Verbal fluency may be separately assessed, even in patients who show no other form of language disturbance, since fluency is characteristically impaired in patients with frontal lesions (Benton, 1968; Perret, 1974; Lezak, 1976). A simple technique is to ask the patient to give as many words as he can think of beginning with a certain letter of the alphabet, for example one minute for words beginning with F, then one minute for A and one minute for S. The number of words accomplished will often be strikingly low even though there is no evidence of dysphasia. This accords with the marked impoverishment of spontaneous narrative speech which may emerge with frontal lesions. The effect is more pronounced with left frontal lesions than right. Corresponding deficits can also be demonstrated on a 'design fluency test', similarly susceptible to frontal lesions but in this case more affected by right frontal lesions than left (Jones-Gotman and Milner, 1977).

Number Functions

Test the patient's ability to perform simple arithmetical operations—addition, subtraction, multiplication, division—in relation to his educational and occupational background. Assess his ability to handle money correctly.

Can he count objects, and make a rough estimate of the number of matches laid before him? Can he give the average size and weight of a man? Can he estimate the size of various objects in the room?

Test his ability to read and write numbers of two and more digits.

Memory Functions

Full examination of memory functions will always be required along the lines already set out on p. 83. Special attention should be directed at recent memory and new learning ability.

A convenient and sensitive method for supplementing the examination of new learning ability consists of testing the patient's capacity for learning supra-span lists of digits (Drachman and Arbit, 1966; Warrington, 1970). The normal digit span is first determined (as on p. 83), then ability to extend the list by one or two items is assessed by repeated presentations. Amnesic subjects can perform adequately on the straightforward digit-span test, but show a dramatic breakdown in performance as soon as this is exceeded.

Simple paired-associate learning may also be tested, using for example the pairs described by Isaacs and Walkey (1964) as outlined on p. 102.

Non-verbal memory should be tested in addition to verbal memory by asking the patient to reproduce simple geometrical figures (as on p. 89) after an interval of five minutes.

Visuospatial and Constructional Difficulties

Patients with visuospatial agnosia may have no complaints to direct attention towards it. It is always important, therefore, to include tests which betray such difficulties when a cerebral lesion is suspected.

Test the patient's ability to judge the relation between objects in space—to estimate distances, to say which of two objects is nearer to him, and which is larger. Can he with eyes closed indicate the spatial order of objects in the room around him?

Visuospatial agnosia is often associated with constructional dyspraxia and the distinction between the two defects is usually far from clear-cut. Constructional dyspraxia is tested as follows:

Test ability to connect two dots by a straight line, and to find the middle of a straight line and of a circle. Test his ability to draw simple figures such as a square, circle and triangle. Ask him to copy a series of line drawings of increasing complexity such as those whown below:—

The test may be made more difficult by removing the model and asking the patient to draw the figure from immediate memory.

Ask him to draw a house, a bicycle, a clock face and set the hands, and to indicate the principal towns on a rough map of England. Note particularly whether he shows neglect of one half of visual space, or crowds material into one part of the paper.

Test ability to construct simple figures when presented with sticks or matches. Can he construct a triangle, a square, or copy more complex designs?

Can he assemble a simple jig-saw puzzle, or reassemble a piece of paper which has been cut into several fragments?

If available test his ability to reproduce patterns with Kohs' blocks.

The copying of a range of geometrical figures has the virtue of being graded in difficulty and of providing a permanent record. Most normal subjects will succeed in copying at least the first four of the figures illustrated above. Free drawing of a house or bicycle has the advantage of being more natural and also more difficult. It often reveals more subtle forms of defect, but can be hard to interpret since normal individuals vary considerably in drawing skill. Sometimes highly characteristic defects may emerge, as when windows are placed in the roof or outside the main body of the building. The drawing of a clock is particularly useful in showing how accurately the figures can be spaced around the dial, or for revealing unilateral neglect of space by the omission of figures from one half of the dial. The use of sticks and other materials for constructional tasks gives the opportunity to observe the patient's capacity to improve his performance and to alter mistakes.

Other Agnosic Disturbances

Other forms of agnosia are very rare. Before concluding that agnosia is present it is essential to try to ensure that defective performance is not due to impairment of primary perception (such as impaired visual acuity, field defects, or deafness).

Can the patient describe what he sees and identify objects and persons? Ask him to name a particular object in a group exposed to view, to describe its use, or if dysphasic to indicate its use *(visual object agnosia)*. If he fails, test whether he can identify the object by other senses such as touch. Ask him to name the colours of objects, to indicate their colour on a chart, to group objects according to their colour *(colour agnosia)*. Ask him to describe a meaningful situation in a picture shown to him *(simultanagnosia)*. Is his recognition of faces defective *(prosopagnosia)*? Ask him to point out a named person known to him among a group or to name photographs of relatives or of well-known public figures.

Auditory agnosia will already have been assessed (see under comprehension of speech, p. 87).

Tactile agnosia is tested by asking the patient to identify objects by touch with the eyes closed. Each hand must be tested separately. Care must be taken that other sensory information (such as the rattle of money) does not give the necessary clue. Ask him to name the objects, and to describe their shape, texture and use. In the event of failure test whether the objects can then be identified by vision. If dysphasic his responses must be assessed by testing selection from a group of objects exposed to view.

Dyspraxia and Related Disturbances

Before diagnosing dyspraxia make sure that the patient's difficulties cannot be adequately explained on the basis of muscular weakness, incoordination or profound sensory disturbance. Many dyspraxic patients are also dysphasic, so care must be taken to check whether instructions are understood. To prove dyspraxia it is necessary to show that a movement not made under one set of conditions (e.g. on command) can be performed under others (e.g. spontaneously), or that movements of equal or greater complexity can be made under other circumstances. It is also necessary to exclude simple unwillingness to cooperate. Because of the complexities of this area of dysfunction it is advisable in all cases to make a careful note of what the patient does, how he does it and what he fails to do (Critchley, 1953).

Test the patient's ability to carry out purposeful movements to command, such as holding out the arms, crossing legs, showing teeth, screwing up eyes, nodding head. Test each hand separately for making a fist, opposition of thumb and little finger, pronation and supination.

Test expressive and make-believe movements such as knocking at a door, waving goodbye.

Test ability to imitate postures of the hand and arm demonstrated by the examiner, and to adopt with one limb the posture imposed on the other.

TABLE 1. Performance on tests of language function in different varieties of dysphasia (derived from Benson and Geschwind, 1971)

	Spontaneous speech	Compre-hension	Repetition	Naming	Reading	Writing
Pure Word Deafness	F	—	—	+	+	+ (not to dictation)
Pure Word Blindness (Alexia without Agraphia)	F	+	+	+	—	+
Pure Word Dumbness	NF	+	—	±	+	+
Pure Agraphia (Agraphia without Alexia)	F	+	+	+	+	—
Primary Sensory (Wernicke's) Dysphasia	F	—	—	±	—	—
Primary Motor (Broca's) Dysphasia	NF	+	—	±	Aloud — Compr ±	—
Nominal Dysphasia	F	+	+	—	±	±
Conduction Dysphasia	F	+	—	±	Aloud — Compr +	—
Isolation Syndrome	NF	—	+	—	—	—
Transcortical Motor Dysphasia	NF	+	+/—	—	Aloud — Compr +	
Transcortical Sensory Dysphasia	F	—	+	—	—	—
Alexia with Agraphia (Visual Asymbolia)	F	+	+	+	—	—

F = fluent speech productions   NF = non-fluent speech productions   Compr = comprehension

Test the patient's ability to carry out complex coord-inated sequences of movements, such as taking a match from a box and striking it, winding a watch, cutting with scissors, folding a piece of paper and putting it in an envelope.

Does the patient show undue difficulty with dressing and undressing, get muddled when inserting limbs into clothing, or try to put garments on the wrong way round ('dressing dyspraxia')?

When a frontal lesion is suspected it can be useful to carry out further tests which reflect *the dynamic organisation of the motor act* (Luria, 1966). The most suitable tests are those which require the subject to perform a simple series of movements whose compo-nents follow in a connected alternating sequence. These are particularly disturbed by premotor frontal lesions:

Reciprocal coordination of the hands is tested by asking the patient to place both hands before him, one with the fist clenched and the other with the fingers extended. He is then asked to simultaneously change the position of both hands, stretching the first and clenching the other. The smoothness and speed of the alternating actions is observed; he may break the task down and perform each movement separately, or perform similar movements with both hands so that reciprocal coordination is lost.

Alternating tapping is tested by asking the patient to alternately tap twice with the right hand and once with the left hand in an on-going alternating sequence.

A single limb may be tested by asking the patient alternately to make a fist and a ring with the fingers of the hand.

Alternating written sequences may be tested by asking the patient to draw a design composed of two alternating components, for example: x o x o x o x o x o, or in cursive script: u n u n u n u n u n.

An alternating choice task has similarly been shown to be sensitive to frontal lesions (Stevenson, 1967). A simple version consists of asking the patient to predict in which of the examiner's hands a coin is hidden, when this is alternated R L R L R L, or R R L L R R L L.

An interesting form of motor behaviour has been described by Lhermitte (1983) in patients with frontal lesions ('utilisation behaviour') and is tested as follows: Everyday objects are presented visually or tactually to the patient, without speaking, and his response observed. In the presence of a frontal lesion, particularly involving the orbital parts of the lobe, the patient may seem compelled to grasp and use them. When presented with a paper and pen, for example, the patient takes the pen and writes; when given spectacles he puts them on; when a jug of water and a glass are advanced towards him he pours the water and drinks it. Once started the patient may continue using objects presented to him in this manner, persisting even after being told that this is not required.

Tests of *verbal fluency* will also often be employed when a frontal lesion is suspected, as described on p. 88.

Topographical Sense and Right-Left Orientation

Does the patient find his way easily about the ward when he would be expected to do so (topographical disorientation)? Does he confuse his bed with other people's? Can he describe the relations between parts of the ward or of his own house? Can he describe the route from home to hospital? If necessary test his ability to follow a simple route in the ward or hospital.

Can he point on command to objects around him on the right and on the left? Ask him to move on command right and left parts of the body, to point to individual parts on the right and on the left side of his own body, and of the examiner sitting opposite him. Can he perform complex instructions like 'touch your right ear with your left hand', 'pick up the left hand coin with your left hand and place it in my right hand'.

Body Image Disturbances

Body image disturbances will often be revealed by the patient's behaviour or his own subjective complaints, but sometimes special tests or questions will be required to elicit them. Asking the patient to make a rough drawing of a man will sometimes give the first indication of body image disorder (Cohn, 1960).

Test for *finger agnosia*. Ask the patient to move on command or point to individual fingers—his own and the examiner's. Kinsbourne and Warrington (1962b) describe various tests which have proved to be more sensitive indices of finger agnosia than the conventional tests. In one such, two of the patient's fingers are touched simultaneously and he is asked to state how many fingers lie between them.

Test for disturbance of identification of other body parts (*autotopagnosia*). Ask the patient to move on command and name various parts of his body, to point to them and to parts of the examiner's body.

Note any evidence of *unilateral unawareness or neglect* of the body. When present this will usually involve the left side. Does he utilize the left hand normally in bimanual activities? Is the left side of the body relatively neglected in washing, combing, dressing? When attention is drawn to such defects does he recognise them and correct them?

Determine whether he has unusual subjective sensations or beliefs about the limbs of one half of the body. Do they feel to be absent or changed, either intermittently or continuously (*hemisomatognosia*)?

Does he ignore or show lack of concern about an injured or functionally defective part of the body, for example a left hemiparesis or hemianopic field defect (*anosognosia*)? He may verbally deny the defect or deny ownership of the affected body part.

Other General Indications of Organic Cerebral Disorder

Note the ability of the patient to *sustain attention* during the above test procedures. Did he *fatigue unduly easily*? Was he able to *shift attention* readily from one task to another? Did he show *perseveration* in the use of words, in simple motor acts, or in response to commands? Test carefully for *difficulties with abstract thinking* (p. 84) if these are suspected. Note and describe any evidence of *lability of mood* or *euphoria*. Were emotional responses *exaggerated, flattened or lacking*? When confronted with a task beyond his ability did he show evidence of a *catastrophic reaction* (p. 81)? Did he show *impulsiveness, disinhibition,* or *over-familiarity* at any point during the testing? Did he *appreciate his failings* and show *appropriate concern*? Did he use *evasions* or *excuses* to cover up his defects?

EXAMINATION OF THE MUTE OF APPARENTLY INACCESSIBLE PATIENT

States of mutism, 'stupor', and apparent inaccessibility may be due to organic brain disease, or functional psychiatric disorders such as depression, catatonic schizophrenia, or conversion hysteria. In all cases it is necessary to carry out a *detailed neurological examination* and to assess the apparent *level of conscious awareness* as outlined on p. 86 before considering other aspects of the problem.

The differential diagnosis of stupor is considered on p. 131 *et seq*. In addition to the intracerebral causes it is essential to bear in mind the possibilities of physical illness such as uraemia, hypoglycaemia or myxoedema, and to examine for physical complications of stupor such as hypotension or retention of urine. It is also important to remember that in stupors due to functional psychiatric illness the patient's comprehension of remarks made in his presence may be good despite appearances to the contrary.

Stupor, Semi-coma and Hypersomnia

The definitions of these terms are not sufficiently precise to be used as the sole description of the phenomena they comprise. The following features should therefore be described separately:

To what extent does the patient dress, feed himself or cooperate with feeding, attend to matters of hygiene and elimination?

Are the eyes open or shut? If open, are they apparently watchful and do they follow moving objects? If shut, do they open in response to stimulation, and is there resistance to passive opening?

Assess his response to graded stimulation as outlined on p. 86). When aroused does he become briefly alert and verbally responsive?

Is the physical posture comfortable, constrained, awkward, bizarre, or in any way indicative of possible delusional beliefs? Does the patient resume a previous posture if moved or when placed in an awkward or uncomfortable position? If so are movements meaningful? Do acts display special meaning, for example on a possible delusional basis or in response to possible hallucinatory experiences?

Is the facial expression constant or varying, alert or vacant, blank or meaningful? Is it secretive, withdrawn, indicative of sadness, hopelessness or ecstasy; does it betray attention to hallucinatory experiences?

Is there any physical or emotional reaction to what is said or done to the patient, or within his hearing? Does he show an emotional response when sensitive subjects are discussed? Does he show signs of irritation or annoyance when moved against his wishes?

Examine the state of the musculature. Is it relaxed or rigid? Is rigidity increased by passive movements? Examine for negativism, flexibilitas cerea, automatic obedience, echopraxia. Note evidence of resistiveness, irritability or defensive movements during examination.

In the neurological examination pay special attention to evidence of raised intracranial pressure or of diencephalic or upper brain stem disturbance: thus examine for papilloedema, observe equality and reactivity of pupils, note quality of respiration, look for evidence of long tract deficit in the limbs, and test for conjugate reflex eye movements on passive head rotation.

After recovery examine for memory of events occurring during the abnormal phase, and for fantasies or other subjective experiences occurring at the time.

Mutism

'Mutism' is a condition in which the person does not speak and makes no attempt at spoken communication despite preservation of an adequate level of consciousness. It may sometimes be the only abnormality in otherwise normal behaviour.

Is it elective, confined to some situations, or in relation to some persons but not others? Is the patient himself disturbed by it as shown by gesticulations or evidence of distress? Does he attempt to communicate by signs? When offered paper and pen does he communicate in writing?

Distinguish mutism from severe motor dysphasia, dysarthria, aphonia, poverty of speech, or severe psychomotor retardation: Is partial vocalisation preserved, are emotional ejaculations possible, can simple 'yes-no' answers be given? Test separately for ability to articulate (to whisper or make the lip movements of speech) and ability to phonate (to produce coarse vocalisations or to hum). Can he cough? Does he speak very occasionally and briefly on restricted themes? Does he reply or signal responses to some questions but only after a long delay?

A careful history from informants may sometimes enable distinctions to be made more readily than from examination alone.

Psychometric Assessment

The clinical value of psychological testing in the field

of organic psychiatry has been much debated. Over-enthusiastic claims have sometimes followed the introduction of new tests and procedures for the identification of cerebral dysfunction, and have had to be tempered later in the light of experience. But even when the claims themselves have been modest the psychiatrist has often misunderstood the situation, and has expected a degree of exactitude from psychometric testing that is unrealistic. The experience of the present author has been that the collaboration of the clinical psychologist is extremely helpful, both in diagnosis and in other areas of patient management, provided a jointly balanced view is taken of the situation. In the diagnosis of brain damage the psychiatrist's and the psychologist's approach are both in their own ways fallible, but each may usefully supplement the other. In very general terms it may be said that psychological tests tend to over-diagnose organicity while the psychiatric examination is prone to under-diagnose it, so that a combination of the two approaches will often give the most discriminating assessment.

The limitations of psychometric tests must be appreciated. There appears to be no single test that will differentiate brain damaged patients from others without some degree of overlap, and even the most skilful selection of groups of tests will occasionally produce misleading results. Accordingly test results should only be interpreted in conjunction with all other sources of information relevant to the issue in question. The worst service to psychometry, and to the patient, is likely to come from attempts to rely on test scores viewed in isolation. Similar disappointment would be expected to follow if any clinical diagnostic procedure were singled out and given unique importance. It is essential therefore to retain a 'general clinical impression' as a back-up to the detailed findings.

Advantages

As diagnostic instruments psychological tests have certain definite advantages over the ordinary procedures of clinical assessment. The tests can be given in strictly standardised form, and the results are usually scored numerically. Hence they can be validated on large groups of patients, so that norms can be established and the extent of individual variation gauged with some precision. In these respects they represent a marked advance on the psychiatrist's assessment of the mental state. With their aid one can talk meaningfully in terms of *probabilities* where the presence or absence of brain damage is

concerned, and the level of probability is often crucial in deciding what action to pursue. Similarly the measures can be repeated on more than one occasion, permitting accurate comparisons over an interval of time. This can be invaluable when equivocal findings have emerged on first consultation; after establishing a base line the patient's progress can be charted with some accuracy, and any evidence of decline will be highlighted.

Psychological testing has another advantage in that it can concentrate in detail on an individual area of functioning which has come under suspicion. Minor degrees of memory impairment or verbal disability, for example, can be pursued with much more thoroughness by psychometric tests than in the clinical interview. The structure of such defects can also be explored in greater detail. It is here that the psychologist must sometimes be prepared to sacrifice the rigid standardisation of his approach in order to follow the leads which emerge. Piercy (1959) has argued cogently that some kinds of evidence are better assessed by an experienced human observer than by a standardised procedure; the nature of the failure can be important, and this is not always obvious from the score alone. In other words the very advantages of the standardised approach must not be allowed to become an unduly restrictive influence or valuable information will sometimes be lost.

Limitations

Some fundamental difficulties concerning tests for brain damage are discussed by Yates (1954, 1966), Smith (1962) and Herbert (1964). Modern tests represent a distinct advance on their forerunners, but certain in-built difficulties remain.

Typically a test is standardised on groups of subjects known to be suffering from brain damage, and groups in whom this is known to be absent by independent criteria. A highly satisfactory level of discrimination is frequently achieved, and the test is then further validated on a separate population. It is important to remember, however, that the efficiency of the test has still emerged only where clear-cut cases are concerned. In clinical use the test will often be applied to borderline problems in which other evidence of brain damage is equivocal, and here it will not yet have established its credentials. The indications which it gives about the presence or absence of brain damage must still be viewed with caution, and may be no more valid than the clinical evidence which led to the patient being referred for testing. This is why expectations must not be unrealistic. The difficulty in establishing the sensitivity of the test in equivocal cases lies in the problem of obtaining a final arbiter of brain damage. Follow-up of disputed cases can help by displaying the *predictive* value of the test but such studies have not been carried out extensively.

A separate problem arises from the fact that all tests require a certain level of attention and co-operation. Consequently they are vulnerable to emotional disturbance and other influences which have nothing to do with brain damage. Tests which distinguish well between brain damaged and healthy subjects may therefore give misleading results when applied to psychiatric patients. Depression for example, may disrupt performance on sensitive tests of memory, and schizophrenic thought disorder may lead to poor performance on tests of abstract thinking. Thus any test which is to be usefully employed for differential diagnosis between organic and functional psychiatric illness must first be administered to patients suffering from a wide range of mental disorders. It is at this point that many excellent tests fail to uphold their promise. They may nonetheless still be useful when functional mental illness is clearly not a complicating factor.

Common misconceptions have also concerned the nature of brain damage itself, and the constancy of its relationship to the behavioural deficits which follow. Tests have sometimes relied heavily on a unitary theory of cerebral dysfunction, and many of those put forward as global indicators of 'brain damage' pay little regard to what is known of regional cerebral organisation. The aim has often been to identify a fundamental disturbance of function which would emerge in every case, no matter what the extent, location or nature of the responsible brain damage. But brain damage can lead to a variety of behavioural deficits, and no one defect or set of defects can be expected to emerge in all brain-injured individuals. Thus tests which sample a restricted aspect of cognitive activity may fail to identify cerebral lesions which are sufficiently circumscribed to leave that particular function intact. Purely verbal tests, for example, may fail to detect visuospatial difficulties resulting from a restricted lesion of the nondominant hemisphere. Even with diffuse brain damage the behavioural effects which follow may vary at different levels of functional disorganisation, so that tests which tap one hierarchical level of behaviour may fail entirely to tap another. Many of the differences between one validation study and another would appear to arise from difficulties of this type. The greater the number of functions sampled by the test the greater will be its usefulness as a general screening device, though a price will then usually be paid in that it will be less sensitive at detecting minor degrees of dysfunction in restricted areas of cognitive activity.

In some circumstances the identification of patterns of impairment on different tests can be of more value than indicators of brain damage generally. McFie (1960) pointed out that psychologists had been rather slow to proceed from neurological knowledge and examine whether disturbances of higher cortical function, as revealed by tests, could be used as a guide to local cerebral injury. His own survey of cases from the National Hospital gave indications that this was a fruitful line of enquiry. Left parietal lesions, for example, were associated with special difficulty with arithmetic, digit span and sentence learning, right parietal lesions with picture arrangement and memory for designs. On tests of learning and retention the impairment depended to a considerable extent on the nature of the material to be learned—verbal material was mainly affected by left-sided lesions (especially left temporal) and visual material by right-sided lesions (particularly right parietal). When the material to be retained was neither verbal nor visual, as in the estimation of the passage of time, the impairments appeared to have general rather than focal associations. Such regional associations have since been explored further, as outlined by De Renzi and Faglioni (1965) and as described at many points in Chapter 2. Their importance in the present context is to stress that psychometric testing can occasionally be useful in viewing the patient's performance, not so much in terms of deviation from statistical normality, as in terms of conformity with a recognised syndrome of cognitive defect (Piercy, 1959). In such an exercise the identification of brain damage will depend much less on carefully validated norms, but will closely follow the strategies of clinical enquiry generally.

Applications

From the foregoing it will be clear that the questions asked of the psychologist must be realistic, and should reflect some knowledge both of the limitations and special advantages of the psychometric procedures available. It will usually be helpful to discuss the patient fully beforehand in order to focus on the problems to be solved. Requests that the psychologist should 'exclude the possibility of brain damage' or 'localise the lesion' will not yield unequivocal answers, but to ask for his collaboration in assessing the *likelihood* of brain damage, focal or diffuse, may bring valuable evidence to add to that already available.

A faint suspicion of early dementia may be greatly sharpened by failure on sensitive tests of learning ability, even when the physician's examination has yielded doubtful results. In the absence of depression or other emotional disturbance such findings may be crucial in indicating that further investigations should be pursued. Minimal dysphasia or perceptual difficulties may likewise be exposed. Conversely, excellent performance on a reasonably wide range of cognitive tests can be greatly reassuring. And even when test results are less than clearcut in one direction or another an important baseline will have been achieved for reference later on. In a similar manner psychometry may help in the differentiation of focal and diffuse brain damage by quantifying the various aspects of cognitive impairment which the patient shows.

Apart from diagnosis, psychometry can also be valuable where rehabilitation is concerned. Areas of relatively intact function can be identified, and problems highlighted on which re-education should be concentrated. Progress can be monitored with a fair degree of accuracy, enabling ultimate goals to be discerned.

In the sections which follow some of the available tests are briefly described. Some provide essentially qualitative information while others yield numerical scores. Some rely on profiles of comparison between different functional capacities, or help to demonstrate the fall from estimated levels of premorbid intelligence (e.g. Wechsler Adult Intelligence Scale). Others concentrate on certain areas alone which are considered to be especially sensitive to brain damage. Chief among such functions are abstraction or concept formation (Goldstein-Sheerer Tests), perceptual functions and especially those concerning spatial relationships (Bender-Gestalt Test, Minnesota Percepto-Diagnostic Test), and memory as reflected in capacity for new learning (Modified Word Learning Test, Paired Associate Learning Tests). Some tests combine an examination of both perceptual and memory functions (Graham Kendall Memory for Designs Test), while others attempt a systematic exploration of several aspects of memory (Wechsler Memory Scale). A further interesting group assess vigilance over a period of time in monitoring external cues (Continuous Performance Test, Continuous Choice Reaction Test).

Certain tests will also be described which are of value in the identification of focal cerebral disorder, such as the Wisconsin Card Sorting Test for frontal lobe damage, and the Token Test for receptive language disturbance. Brief mention is made of certain aptitude tests, often initially designed for healthy individuals, but also useful as a guide to the rehabilitation and resettlement of brain-damaged patients. Questionnaires and rating scales which have been employed with severely brain-damaged subjects are also discussed.

The tests themselves vary widely in the extent to which they have been validated and the adequacy with which norms have been established. This is not the place to attempt a thorough review of their respective credentials, but rather to give an outline of their aims and procedures.

Wechsler Adult Intelligence Scale (WAIS)

The WAIS is an extensively standardised instrument for the measurement of intelligence, providing separate scores for 'verbal' and 'performance' abilities. Possible deterioration from estimated or established premorbid levels can be assessed, and this alone can yield important information about the possibilities of brain damage. Qualitative interpretation of different sub-test scores provides leads for further enquiry by indicating areas of special cognitive difficulty.

Eleven sub-tests are involved:

Verbal sub-tests

(1) Information: 29 questions covering a wide variety of information which adults have presumably had an opportunity of acquiring in our culture.

(2) Comprehension: 14 items in which the subject must explain what should be done in certain circumstances, the meaning of proverbs etc. This aims at measuring practical judgement and commonsense.

(3) Arithmetic: 14 problems resembling those of elementary school arithmetic.

(4) Similarities: 13 items in which the subject must say in what way two things are alike.

(5) Digit Span: lists of 3-10 digits to be reproduced forwards and 2-8 digits to be reproduced backwards.

(6) Vocabulary: 40 words of which the subject must give the meaning.

Performance sub-tests

(1) Digit symbol: the subject must follow a simple code in matching symbols to digits, as quickly as he can.

(2) Picture completion: the subject is shown a number of pictures with parts missing and must identify what is lacking.

(3) Block Design: this is similar to the Kohs' Block Test. The subject must reproduce designs with red and white blocks.

(4) Picture Arrangement: sets of cards must be arranged in a proper sequence so as to tell a story.

(5) Object Assembly: objects must be assembled from their parts.

The raw score on each sub-test is transmuted into a standard score (scaled score), which represents the individual's distance from the mean in terms of the distribution for that particular sub-test. By this procedure all sub-test scores are expressed in units which can be compared one with another.

In addition to yielding an intelligence quotient, various diagnostic uses have been proposed for the WAIS as reviewed by Anastasi (1968). Wechsler himself proposed such functions for the test (Wechsler, 1958), including its use for the identification of brain damage. Others have carried these possibilities further. All such procedures involve comparisons between the individual's performance on different sub-tests. Some measure the amount of overall scatter, others seek to identify patterns characteristic of different illness processes, while others involve the computation of 'indices of deterioration'. All have come under criticism, and have generally proved inferior to other psychometric tests for brain damage.

At the simplest level brain damage may be reflected in discrepancies between the verbal and performance IQs. The functions measured by the performance sub-tests usually prove to be more vulnerable than those measured by verbal sub-tests, though this is by no means invariable. Damage which is restricted to the dominant hemisphere may, for example, severely impair ability on the comprehension, arithmetic and vocabulary sub-tests of the verbal scale, while leaving performance abilities relatively intact. Moreover significant discrepancies emerge in some normal subjects and in some patients suffering from functional mental illness.

Deterioration indices involve comparisons between other contrasting groups of sub-tests. 'Hold tests' are identified which are found to be relatively impervious to the effects of brain damage, whereas 'Don't Hold tests' show early decline. The former include sub-tests which reflect the use of old knowledge (such as vocabulary, information, and picture completion), whereas the latter require speed or the perception of new relations in verbal or spatial content (digit symbol, digit span, similarities, block design). Several such indices have been elaborated,

but are open to the objection that they fail to allow for the diversity of the effects of brain damage of different types and locations. In practice they have sometimes shown a close correlation with severity of diffuse cerebral degeneration (McFie, 1960; Gonen, 1970), but equally they have often proved disappointing in the differentiation of brain damaged patients from those with functional psychiatric disorders (Watson, 1965; Bolton et al., 1966; Bersoff, 1970).

The application of the WAIS as a diagnostic instrument has been widely criticised on theoretical grounds, in that the reliability of sub-tests taken individually is not high enough to allow a confident interpretation of any but the largest differences. Scatter can result not only from pathological processes, but from differences in educational, occupational and cultural factors. Nevertheless qualitative interpretation of sub-test scores may still on occasion provide useful clinical information, yielding important pointers for verification by more specialised and intensive testing.

National Adult Reading Test (NART)

A simple technique for yielding an approximate estimate of general intelligence consists in administering a series of words to be read aloud (Nelson, 1982). Nelson and McKenna (1975) introduced this rapid method using words from the Schonell Graded Word Reading Test, and Nelson and O'Connell (1978) then modified it by drawing up a list of words spelled in an irregular manner. The level of word reading ability achieved by an adult has been shown to correlate highly with intelligence, and being a well practiced and overlearned skill it proves to be relatively resistant to influences which impair other aspects of cognitive function.

It is this last aspect which makes the test especially useful. The authors have shown that even in patients with dementia the ability to read words declines little if at all, at least in the patients used in the samples they examined. Thus groups of subjects without brain disorder gave results closely comparable to patients with cerebral atrophy, even though in the latter the WAIS IQ had deteriorated considerably. It was possible to show that estimates of premorbid intelligence derived from the NART were more stable even than those derived from the vocabulary subtest of the WAIS.

In this respect the words of irregular spelling used in the NART have proved more suitable for estimating previous intelligence than the words of the

Schonell Test. Since their spelling does not conform to rules (e.g. 'ache', 'bouquet', 'naïve', 'sidereal') they depend for correct pronunciation on long familiarity and cannot be pronounced by guesses based on their literal structure. Moreover the words available in the list extend the ceiling of the test further than is possible with the Schonell test, allowing estimation of IQs in the bright normal and superior range.

After administering the NART, regression equations are used to obtain an estimate of 'minimum premorbid intelligence', and discrepancies between this and current WAIS IQ can then be observed.

Raven's Progressive Matrices

Raven (1958a, 1960) developed a test of non-verbal intelligence which requires the perception of relations among abstract items. Both coloured and non-coloured forms are available.

The test consists of a series of printed designs from each of which a part has been removed. The subject must choose the missing portion from among a series of alternatives in a manner which tests his ability at discrimination, analogy, permutation and alternation of patterns, and other logical relationships. Factor analysis has shown the test to be heavily loaded with a factor common to most intelligence tests, but to be influenced also by spatial aptitude, inductive reasoning, perceptual accuracy and other factors (Anastasi, 1968).

The test is widely used as a rapid device for estimating the Performance IQ, often in association with the Mill Hill Vocabulary Test which provides a similar rapid estimate of verbal ability (Raven, 1958b). Surprisingly for an intelligence test it has sometimes compared well with other psychometric tests for differentiating between psychiatric patients with and without diffuse brain damage (Kendrick and Post, 1967; Irving et al., 1970). The coloured form of the test has been especially commended in this regard. Some authors have found it to be more affected by right-sided lesions than left (Piercy and Smyth, 1962), whereas others have found it to be equally impaired by damage to either hemisphere (Costa and Vaughan, 1962; De Renzi and Faglioni, 1965).

Goldstein-Sheerer Tests

A large number of tests aim at displaying the subject's capacity for abstract thinking and catego-

risation, on the basis that such functions are particularly sensitive to brain damage. Tests in this group investigate ability to abstract common properties of objects, to grasp essential qualities, to break up a whole into parts, and to shift from one aspect of a situation to another. A typical example is the group of tests developed by Goldstein and Sheerer (1941):

Goldstein-Sheerer Cube Test. This consists of a set of blocks with the sides painted different colours. The blocks must be assembled to match designs printed on cards. Essentially this is an adaptation of the Kohs' Block Test.

Gelb-Goldstein Colour Sorting Test. Woollen skeins of different colours and shades are presented to the subject. He must select all those that go with samples shown to him. Either colour or brightness may serve as the basis for classification.

Gelb-Goldstein-Weigl-Sheerer Object Sorting Test. A large number of miscellaneous objects are presented—eating utensils, tools, candle, matches, pipe, etc. The subject must pick out the articles belonging with one selected by the examiner, or he is asked to place all the articles into groups of his own choice. Alternatively he may be asked to state the basis for the examiner's placing of objects into groups before him (according to colour, form, use, etc.).

Weigl-Goldstein-Sheerer Colour Form Sorting Test. The subject is presented with four circles, four squares and four triangles, each shape occurring in four different colours. The task is to sort them according to one common property, and then according to another.

Goldstein-Sheerer Stick Test. A number of sticks of different lengths are presented to the subject and he is asked to copy simple geometrical designs with them. He is later asked to reproduce the same figures from memory.

Unfortunately this type of test relies heavily on qualitative observations, being concerned with the methods employed by the subject as well as with the end-point achieved. In consequence it is difficult to evolve objective methods for scoring or standardisation. Many aspects of performance are highly correlated with the subject's general level of intelligence, and the types of defect seen with brain damage may also emerge in schizophrenic patients. In consequence the tests have tended to lose favour and give way to more objective and better validated procedures.

Bender-Gestalt Test (Bender Visual Motor Gestalt Test)

Bender (1938, 1946) produced what is primarily a

copying test, independent of memory and learning ability, though it can be varied to test reproduction from memory after a lapse of time if required.

Nine simple designs are presented to the subject, one at a time, and he is asked to copy them. The type and frequency of errors are noted, and serve as the basis for identifying neurotic, psychotic and brain-damaged subjects. Interpretation relies to a large extent on subjective intuitive procedures, but attempts have been made to standardise it for certain purposes.

It is widely used as a rapid screening test, but the overlap between groups reduces its value when applied to the individual subject. Nevertheless its efficiency at detecting brain damage has sometimes received surprisingly strong support when compared with other long-established psychometric tests (Shapiro *et al.*, 1956; Brilliant and Gynther, 1963).

Minnesota Percepto-Diagnostic Test

Fuller and Laird (1963) and Fuller (1967) have presented another copying test for the rapid identification of brain damage in adults and children.

The subject is asked to copy six designs with the originals before him. The reproduced designs are scored simply in terms of the degree of rotation from the original, which is considerably increased in brain-damaged subjects. Rotations are also produced by emotionally disturbed subjects but to a less degree. Age, intelligence and education do not materially affect performance.
  The test depends upon the instability of perceptual processes in brain-damaged subjects, who have difficulty in correcting for ambiguities in figure-ground relationships. The subject reproduces his perceived distortions which on this test are rotations from the correct vertical axis. The designs were selected from a larger sample in the Bender-Gestalt Test in order to optimise this effect.

  The test has been carefully standardised on groups of subjects with diffuse brain damage, functional mental illness, and normal subjects, and shown to distinguish between groups at a high level of reliability. The scoring system allowed correct identification of 82 per cent of organic subjects, 80 per cent of the functionally mentally ill, and 90 per cent of the normals. Uyeno (1963) confirmed a similar level of differentiation between organic and psychotic patients.

Benton Visual Retention Test

Benton (1955, 1963) has produced another test which requires the reproduction of a series of geometrical figures.

The essential difference from the Bender-Gestalt Test is that the subject must draw the design from memory after the card has been exposed for ten seconds and then removed. Performance therefore requires a combination of spatial perception, short-term retention and recall, and visuo-constructive abilities. The test can be varied by giving shorter exposures, or by imposing delays before reproduction is required. Copying of the designs while the card is in front of the subject allows separation of memory difficulties from perceptual difficulties. Performance is scored in terms of the number of cards correctly reproduced and the number of errors made.

  Performance correlates highly with intelligence and chronological age, but normative data are available to make allowance for this. Additional qualitative information may be derived from inspection of the type of errors made—omissions, distortions, perseverations, rotations, misplacements and errors of size. The value of the test in differentiating brain-damaged and non-brain-damaged groups has often been upheld, though some degree of overlap occurs and many conditions other than brain damage can affect performance (Anastasi, 1968).

Graham Kendall Memory for Designs Test

Graham and Kendall's (1960) test again involves the copying of a series of simple geometrical figures from immediate memory, after exposure to the subject for five seconds at a time. In evolving the test a specific effort was made, not to measure some function of theoretical significance, but rather to crystallise in the scoring system the differences in response which served to distinguish defined groups of patients. Raw scores in terms of the number and kind of errors can be transmuted into scores which control for the effects of age and intellectual development as reflected in the patient's vocabulary level.

  The test has been extensively validated. Poor performance has been found to indicate a high probability of brain damage, though good performance does not necessarily indicate an intact brain. Patients with damage to the left and right sides of the brain are equally affected. The test has been commended in comparison with others (Yates, 1966), and the ease of its administration adds considerably to its popularity. Unfortunately patients with chronic functional psychoses show a good deal of overlap with brain-damaged subjects, and healthy elderly subjects have sometimes also been found to score within the brain-damaged range. A significant correlation has also emerged between performance on the test and estimates of premorbid intelligence (Turland and Steinhard, 1969).

Trail Making Test

The Trail Making Test consists of 25 circles distributed over a sheet of paper. In the first part the circles are numbered, and the subject must draw a line connecting them in numerical sequence as quickly as possible. In the second part the circles contain both numbers and letters and the subject must alternate between numbers and letters as he proceeds in ascending sequence. The score is the time taken over the task. Errors must be corrected and are thus incorporated in the time scores.

Performance on the test requires spatial analysis, motor control, ability to shift attention between alternatives, alertness, concentration, and number and letter sense. In consequence it is likely to be affected by brain damage in many different locations.

Reitan (1958) has demonstrated excellent differentiation with the test between brain-damaged and non-brain-damaged subjects, with a relatively small amount of misclassification. However the effects of functional mental illness do not appear to have been extensively examined.

Perceptual Maze Test

Elithorn (1955) has introduced a maze test consisting of dots superimposed at certain points on a lattice-like background of paths and tracks. The task is for the subject to find the pathway from the bottom to the top of each maze which passes through the greatest number of dots, but without deviating from the paths and without backtracking at any stage. Performance is timed, and successively more complex mazes are administered.

The test has been found to be sensitive to small focal cerebral lesions (Elithorn, 1955). Benton *et al.* (1963) showed that it discriminated well between brain-damaged patients and controls, and was more impaired by right-sided lesions than left. On present evidence it compares well with many other instruments for the detection of cerebral dysfunction but further validation is required (Meier, 1972; Yates, 1972).

Halstead-Reitan Battery

One of the most ambitious and comprehensive attempts in the field of psychological testing for brain damage has been Reitan's extension of Halstead's original battery of tests. Reitan (1966) and Russell *et al.* (1970) describe the evolution of the battery and the on-going attempts to explore its diagnostic usefulness. The aim has been not only to detect brain damage, but to indicate whether this is likely to be focal or diffuse, lateralised to the right or left hemisphere, and whether acute and progressive or relatively static. So far, however, the battery has been used mainly for comparison between different categories of brain-damaged patients, or between brain-damaged subjects and healthy controls, and there is little information about its discriminating power where functional psychiatric illness is concerned. Some of the principal tests incorporated in the battery are as follows:

Halstead's Category Test consists of groups of pictures displayed on a screen, in response to which the subject must press one of four levers. The lever required at each exposure is determined by certain unifying concepts among the group of pictures, and the subject must discover the rules by repeated trial and error. It is thus a relatively complex concept formation test which requires the subject to note similarities and differences, to set up hypotheses, and to test and modify them.

The Critical Flicker Frequency Test measures the speed of flicker required before repeated brief exposures of light become fused.

The Tactual Performance Test requires the subject to fit blocks into their spaces on a board while blindfolded and later to draw the board from memory. It requires tactile form discrimination, manual dexterity and coordination, and the visualisation of spatial configurations.

The Rhythm Test requires the subject to differentiate between several pairs of rhythmic beats, assessing alertness, ability for sustained attention, and ability to perceive differing rhythmic sequences.

The Speech Sounds Perception Test consists of a series of tape-recorded nonsense words which the subject must identify by selection from printed alternatives.

The Finger Tapping Test is a simple measure of motor speed.

The Time Sense Test requires the subject to observe the time taken for a hand to rotate around a dial, then after several practice trials to estimate the time from memory.

The Halstead-Wepman Aphasia Screening Test contains items for testing ability to name objects, spell, identify single numbers and letters, read, write, calculate, name body parts, and distinguish right from left.

The Trail Making Test already described on p. 99 is added as a further part of the battery.

Other Tests include detailed assessments of the accuracy of sensory perception on each side of the body, and tests of finger recognition, graphaesthesia and stereognosis.

Face Hand Test

This is not strictly speaking a psychometric test, but rather an extension of one part of the neurological examination. It has, however, proved of value in distinguishing between organic and functional psychiatric disorder, and appears to compare well in this regard with many more complex procedures (Irving *et al.*, 1970).

Fink *et al.* (1952) showed that when light touch stimuli are applied simultaneously to the cheek and the hand, patients with brain damage often report only one of the stimuli, or when reporting both may mislocate one of them to another part of the body. Errors are apparent on both sides of the body, in contrast to the well-known phenomenon of contralateral extinction with parietal lobe disease. Moreover the mistakes usually concern the more peripheral stimulus, i.e. it is the stimulus to the hand which is usually extinguished or misplaced.

Patients with a variety of forms of diffuse brain damage have been compared with normal subjects and with patients suffering from schizophrenia, depression and severe anxiety (Green and Fink, 1954). Normal subjects could make initial errors, but as the stimuli were repeated the errors disappeared, so that by the tenth trial nearly all subjects correctly perceived both stimuli and thenceforward continued to perform correctly. A similar result was obtained with patients suffering from functional psychiatric illnesses. By contrast 90% of the brain-damaged subjects persisted with errors of extinction or displacement as long as testing was continued. Healthy children between the ages of 3 and 6 behaved like the brain-damaged patients.

Fink *et al.* (1952) consider that such changes form a consistent part of the 'organic mental syndrome', and conclude that the persistence of errors in an adult strongly suggests the presence of organic brain damage. Kahn *et al.* (1960) have given further evidence of the validity of the test by applying it to a large population of aged persons. The test requires little time and therefore finds a place as a useful screening test, though its sensitivity is unlikely to be high enough to aid materially in uncertain cases.

Walton Black Modified Word Learning Test

This test was specifically designed by Walton and Black (1957) to help with the problem of differentiating patients with organic brain disease from patients with functional mental illness. In large measure it upheld its early promise and has emerged as one of the most reliable tests for use in such a situation.

The test is based on the principle that successive opportunities to learn should help to distinguish between the functionally and the organically mentally ill. Depressed patients, for example, are often found to do badly on a task which requires intensive intellectual effort and may give a spuriously low performance if only one attempt is allowed. But when urged to repeat their efforts they rise in performance whereas brain-damaged patients usually fail to improve.

The test consists of administering a vocabulary test of ascending difficulty (the Terman Merrill Test) until the subject fails to give the meanings of ten consecutive words. He is then told their meanings and immediately tested for these ten words again. This procedure is repeated until the subject can give correct definitions for any six of the ten. At each repetition the precise wording of the definitions given to the subject is changed in order to avoid simple rote learning and to ensure that their meanings are genuinely appreciated. The fact that the test is based on failures in the initial vocabulary test, rather than an arbitrary selection of unknown words, ensures that the subject is only required to learn at a level consistent with his own intellectual ability.

The initial validation study showed excellent differentiation of patients with diffuse cortical damage from normals and from the functionally mentally ill. Further cross-validation studies were satisfactory, and predictive value was demonstrated when checked against the eventual clinical diagnosis (Walton and Black, 1959; Walton *et al.*, 1959; Walton and Mather, 1961). On the scoring system devised for the test, the lower the score the worse the performance. No normal, neurotic or functionally psychotic patient achieved a score of less than 6, yet 85% of patients with general cortical damage scored 5 or below.

Patients of low intelligence have, however, occasionally been found to give 'false organic' scores, and patients with strictly focal brain damage may fail to be detected. Orme *et al.* (1964) cast some doubt upon the test by showing a considerable degree of misclassification with non-organic patients and in particular with schizophrenics. Bolton *et al.*

(1967) found that no normal subjects were misclassified, and that approximately three-quarters of elderly patients with affective disorder, schizophrenia and diffuse brain damage were correctly identified. In part the misclassifications of the depressed and schizophrenic patients were due to falsely organic scores being found in the less intelligent patients.

Thus while the high degree of success found in early studies has not been entirely upheld, the results remain good. Certainly when the problem is the identification of early suspected dementia in a patient of reasonable intelligence, the test can be of considerable help in refining the probabilities derived from clinical examination

Synonym Learning Test

A modification of the preceding test was proposed by Kendrick et al. (1965) for use particularly with elderly depressed subjects when the question of dementia has arisen. The Walton Black test was found to be difficult to administer to geriatric patients, and its tendency to misclassify patients with low intelligence was seen as a limiting factor.

Ten words unfamiliar to the subject are identified as before (in this case from the Mill Hill Test), and learning is assessed by repeated administration. Exactly the same definitions are used for each presentation, however, and a modified scoring system allows more variance to be obtained from the test.

No overlap was found between normal and brain-damaged subjects, but 16 per cent of depressed elderly patients were still found to obtain scores in the brain-damaged range. The misclassifications tended to occur with a particular type of elderly depressed patient, namely in those with low intelligence, severe affective disturbance accompanied by a delusional system, complaints of perplexity and confusion, and poor knowledge of recent general events (Kendrick and Post, 1967). Such transient difficulties in the course of a depressive illness were not found to foreshadow the development of dementia at a later date, but appeared to be due to a temporary lowering of arousal (Hemsi et al., 1968).

Kendrick (1967) later indicated that the combination of the Synonym Learning Test with a simple test designed to measure the speed of copying digits ('Digit Copying Test') could distinguish even more effectively between elderly demented patients, and elderly depressed patients who give a semblance of

being demented.

Object Learning Test

Kendrick et al. (1979) have more recently described an Object Learning Test which proves more acceptable and less stressful to elderly patients than the Synonym Learning Test. This is again used in conjunction with the Digit Copying Test for aiding the distinction between depressed and demented elderly persons. The new 'battery' can be administered in approximately ten minutes, and its reliability and validity have been examined on large samples of patients and controls.

Four cards are divided into twenty-five equal sections within which there are drawings of familiar objects (for example a comb, a teapot, etc.). The first card contains ten items, the second fifteen, the third twenty and the fourth twenty-five. Six of the items are repeated across all four cards and are always in the same position. Some items form a category across the cards. The cards are exposed to the subject for a standard length of time, and the score represents the total number of correct items recalled.

Paired Associate Learning Tests

Paired associate learning involves the mastery of the appropriate response when the first member of a pair of words is presented. Inglis (1959) elaborated such a test, designed to be sensitive to memory impairment in the elderly and as independent as possible of the patient's general level of intellectual functioning:

Three simple paired associates must be learned by repeated auditory presentation. In one form of the test, for example, the pairs are 'cabbage-pen', 'knife-chimney', and 'sponge-trumpet'. The examiner reads the list after telling the subject to remember the pairs which go together. The stimulus words are then given alone in random order, and repeated with appropriate corrections for errors until the subject gets three consecutive correct responses on every one of the three different stimulus words. Any given stimulus word is dropped out as soon as its own criterion is reached. The score is the sum of the times the stimulus words must be presented before the total criterion is reached.

The test has proved to be a sensitive indicator of memory disorder in the elderly and to be independent of the patient's verbal intelligence. It is useful for measuring impairment in the acquisition phase of memory, but again abnormally high scores may be obtained in severely depressed and perplexed elderly subjects without evidence of brain damage (Post, 1965). The test has been shown to correlate highly with the Modified Word Learning Test and the Synonym Learning Test (Bolton *et al.*, 1967, Kendrick *et al.*, 1965).

Isaacs and Walkey (1964) have prepared a simpler and shorter form which is less fatiguing and can be administered along with the clinical interview:

Three easy paired-associates are given, and tested three times only in random order ('knife-fork', 'East-West', 'hand-foot'). The procedure is then repeated with three rather harder associates ('cup-plate', 'cat-milk', 'gold-lead'), and the result is simply scored in terms of the number of errors from 0 to 18. Normal scores were judged to be in the range of 0 to 2, moderate impairment 3 to 9, and severe impairment 10 to 18.

The range of functions covered includes attention, registration, short-term recall, and to some extent verbal learning. Motivational factors are clearly involved as well. Priest *et al.* (1969) found significant differences between organic and functional patients with Isaacs and Walkey's test, but many misclassifications occurred as would be expected from such an abbreviated procedure. It may be useful as a screening device, however, provided its limitations are known.

Irving *et al.* (1970) have assessed a similar simplified test in which the appropriate response must be learned for each of twelve items. For example in response to 'colour' the subject must learn 'purple', for 'country'—'Portugal', for 'flower'—'daisy' and so on. A series of trials are given if necessary, and the number of correct responses charted. This was found to discriminate as efficiently as several more complicated procedures when a battery of tests were administered to depressed and demented patients.

Rey-Osterrieth Test

This involves the copying of a single geometrical figure of complex design, then testing reproduction from memory some time later (Rey, 1941; Osterrieth, 1944).

The figure is too complex to be adequately verbalised, hence the test is of visual, non-verbal memory. The subject is first asked to copy the design as accurately as he can with the original before him. Forty minutes later and without previous warning he is asked to draw the figure again, but this time from memory. The initial copying reflects any drawing disability or disorder of spatial perception, but the recall score reflects in addition any visual memory impairment.

The test usefully complements others which measure verbal memory functions. Patients with temporal lobe damage in the hemisphere dominant for speech show no impairment with the Rey-Osterrieth Test, in contrast to their difficulties with verbal memory tests. Right temporal lobectomy, however, leads to a slight but significant defect on copying the figure, and a pronounced and disproportionate impairment when tested for delayed recall (Teuber *et al.*, 1968; Teuber and Milner, 1968: Milner, 1969). Patients with parietal lobe lesions appear to show relatively stable retention despite having difficulty in copying the figure initially.

Recognition Memory Tests

Warrington (1974, 1984) has described a simple technique for separately assessing verbal and non-verbal memory by means of an easily administered recognition memory task. A recognition paradigm is used in preference to free recall, since recognition tasks appear to be less vulnerable to anxiety and depression. Moreover identical procedures can be followed for the verbal and non-verbal material, allowing direct comparisons between the two.

The material consists of fifty high frequency words, each printed on a card, and fifty photographs of unknown faces. The words are presented to the subject at 3-second intervals, and he is asked to respond 'yes' or 'no' each time according to whether he judges the word to be pleasant or not pleasant. This strategy is adopted to ensure attention to the words. Recognition is tested immediately the presentation is complete by showing pairs of words, one of which is new and one of which has already been shown. A choice must be made each time between the two items.

The fifty photographs of faces are then shown at 3-second intervals, again with the requirement that the subject decides at each presentation whether the face is pleasant or unpleasant. Recognition is again tested as soon as presentation is complete, by a similar forced-choice technique.

Wechsler Memory Scale

This consts of seven sub-tests which aim at measuring several different aspects of memory function by rapid standardised procedures (Wechsler, 1945; Wechsler and Stone, 1945). The total raw score can be transmuted into a 'Memory Quotient' which makes allowance for the effects of age and can be compared directly with the subject's intelligence quotient. The severity of memory impairment can thus be viewed in relation to intellectual ability generally.

The first sub-test consists of six simple questions concerning *personal and current information*, such as 'How old are you?', 'Who is the president of the USA?'. This is included to reveal the severe disturbances of memory which may appear in dementing illnesses.

The second test includes five simple questions concerning *immediate orientation* such as naming the year and the month.

The third is a test of '*mental control*' aimed at detecting minor brain damage which might not emerge in tests of simple rote memory. The subject is required to count backwards from 20 to 1, to repeat the alphabet, and to count in threes. His performance is timed.

The fourth is a test of '*logical memory*', in which the subject must recall logical material presented in a short passage of two to three sentences. This is scored in terms of the number of items which are reproduced correctly.

The fifth estimates the *digit span* forwards and backwards.

The sixth is a test of *visual reproduction,* in which the subject must draw from immediate memory simple geometrical figures which have been exposed to view for ten seconds.

The seventh tests *paired-associate learning* for 10 sets of words.

The Wechsler Memory Scale is widely used in helping to detect minor degrees of diffuse brain damage, and in clarifying the extent to which memory functions are impaired out of proportion to other cognitive functions. Re-testing may be carried out after an interval of time using an alternative form of the test.

Williams' Memory Scale

Williams' (1968) battery of memory tests has certain advantages over the Wechsler Memory Scale. The latter is scored in terms of overall performance, and an accurate assessment cannot be made of the relative breakdown in different aspects of the memory process. Moreover it does not include a measure of retention over a period of time. Williams' scale aims at remedying these defects and provides a profile of disturbance where several different aspects of memory function are concerned. The scale consists of five sub-sections:

Immediate recall is tested by measuring the digit span forwards and backwards, with carefully standardised instructions for administration and scoring.

Non-verbal learning is tested with the Rey-Davis peg boards. These consist of four boards, three inches square, each containing eight loose pegs and one fixed peg. The subject must discover by trial and error which peg is fixed in each of the boards, then retention is tested by pointing. The procedure is repeated until all four boards are learned, then the boards are rotated through ninety degrees and the test repeated.

Word learning is assessed by a procedure rather similar to the Modified Word Learning Test (p. 100), except that the same words are employed for every subject irrespective of his vocabulary level, and the definitions are given in exactly the same form throughout the test.

Delayed recall is measured by showing nine pictures of common objects and asking the subject to name them. Seven to ten minutes later he is asked to recall the objects. If he cannot do so spontaneously he is given standard clues or prompts, and if recall is still not forthcoming he is asked to pick out the pictures by recognition from a group. The score is represented by the amount of reinforcement needed to reach the given criterion of recall.

Memory for past personal events is assessed by questions which aim at sampling events from specified periods of earlier life—early childhood, middle youth, twenty-first birthday, etc. For obvious reasons standardisation is difficult, and this section is chiefly used as a time filler during the interval for the test of delayed recall.

Williams' Memory Scale is available in three parallel forms. When given to psychiatric patients, those with organic mental syndromes showed defects on delayed recall out of proportion to the other sub-tests (Williams, 1968). White *et al.* (1969) have reported further detailed observations on the reliability, validity and independence of the various sub-tests when administered to patients in whom the question of brain damage had arisen.

Vigilance Tests

A different approach, less frequently employed in the investigation of brain-damaged patients, attempts to measure the subject's capacity for continuous monitoring of stimuli over relatively long periods of time. Such 'vigilance tests' come closer than most other procedures to measuring ability for sustained attention and concentration. They would therefore appear to have special advantages for detecting intermittent spells of confusion or clouding of consciousness.

Typically the subject is required to react rapidly in response to signals which arrive in a preset random manner. Efficient performance requires the prolonged maintenance of a high level of attention and the rapid activation of perceptual and motor mechanisms. De Renzi and Faglioni (1965) point out that the cerebral mechanisms involved in performing such tests are represented diffusely and bilaterally, and performance is likely to be less affected by the specific consequences of a local lesion than with most other psychological tests. The tasks are elementary so should be understood by the patient with dysphasic difficulties, and the required motor responses do not involve any special motor capacity. Their disadvantages are that special apparatus is required, and that performance is likely to be disturbed by a multitude of factors of a non-organic nature. The influence of functional psychiatric disturbance on the tests has so far received little systematic investigation. In routine clinical practice the simpler procedures outlined on p. 86 will often suffice for obtaining an estimate of sustained attention.

The simple estimation of *reaction times* has often shown good differentiation between brain-damaged subjects and controls (Blackburn and Benton 1955; Benton and Joynt 1959). De Renzi and Faglioni (1965) showed that measures of the reaction time to visual stimuli were more efficient than an intelligence test (Raven's Matrices) in discriminating between normal subjects and patients with focal cerebral lesions. Benton *et al.* (1959) however, found that reaction times were also significantly slowed in schizophrenic patients.

Rosvold *et al.* (1956) explored the value of a '*Continuous Performance Test*' in which letters were exposed by a revolving drum at one-second intervals for periods of up to ten minutes. The subject was required to press a button whenever the letter 'x' appeared, or in a more difficult version whenever an 'x' was preceded by an 'a'. Brain-damaged adults and children were significantly poorer at the test than normal controls, and differences increased considerably when the more difficult task was employed.

McDonald and Burns (1964) described a test in which the subject was required to monitor a dial for long periods of time and press a key whenever the pointer deviated beyond a certain mark. Brain-damaged subjects were again inferior to controls. Low rates of presentation of the critical signals produced an especially poor response.

The '*Continuous Choice Reaction Test*' used by De Renzi and Faglioni (1965) involved a screen on which various combinations of circles or squares in black or white could be briefly illuminated. The combinations were made to follow one another in irregular sequence, a new combination appearing every 1·5 seconds. The task was to press a button every time the combination 'black circle–white square' appeared, all other combinations being ignored. The score was the sum of the subject's errors and omissions. The test was superior to Raven's Matrices in distinguishing between normal subjects and patients with focal brain damage. Performance was equally impaired by right and left hemisphere lesions in non-dysphasic patients, but was especially impaired in the presence of dysphasia, presumably because internal verbalisation was utilised during performance of the task.

Wisconsin Card Sorting Test

This is a complex sorting test which has proved to be particularly sensitive to frontal lobe damage (Milner, 1963, 1964, 1969). It accordingly has considerable importance, since frontal lesions may often be difficult to detect by ordinary psychometric tests.

The material consists of 64 cards, each containing from 1 to 4 geometrical figures. The latter consist of any one of 4 shapes (triangles, stars, crosses and circles) in any one of 4 colours. Four stimulus cards are set out before the subject who must sort the remainder beneath them. His task is to discover by trial and error whether he is required to sort according to colour, form or number, the clue being the examiner's remark of 'right' or 'wrong' after each response is made. In administering the test the subject is required to sort first of all to colour, all other responses being called wrong, then when he has achieved ten consecutive correct responses to colour the required sorting principle shifts *without warning* to form. Later it shifts to number, then back again to colour, and so on. The test thus combines the requirement for shifting frames of reference with a need for empirical discovery of categories. A total score can be obtained, also scores for perseverative and non-perseverative types of error.

Nelson (1976) has reported a simplified and improved version of the test ('*Modified Wisconsin Card Sorting Test*') in which those cards which share more than one attribute with a stimulus card have been eliminated. Possible ambiguities for the patient are thereby reduced and the time of administration considerably shortened. The total number of cards to be sorted in the modified test is reduced from sixty-four to twenty-four.

Milner (1963) obtained clear evidence that impairment was closely related to lesions of the frontal lobes of either hemisphere, with no comparable effects from lesions in other areas of the brain. The impairment was chiefly with lesions of the dorsolateral convexities of the frontal lobe, rather than with inferior and orbital lesions. Moreover the errors in the frontal patients were chiefly of the perseverative type. These results were obtained in patients with focal cortical excisions for epilepsy. They have been broadly confirmed by Drewe (1974) in a heterogeneous group of brain-damaged patients. Certain qualitative differences were found between the nature of the errors with left and right frontal lesions, and the former produced the greater overall impairment.

The precise nature of the defects revealed by the test is uncertain. Motivational defects or primary disturbances of abstract thinking may contribute to failure, but do not appear adequate as a complete explanation. By analogy with observations on monkeys with frontal lesions it seems that there may be especial difficulty in overcoming a preferred mode of response, so that the immediate consequences of actions have less influence in modifying on-going behaviour. Luria and Homskaya (1964) have stressed impairment in the verbal regulation of behaviour after frontal lobe lesions, and this may also contribute to failure on the test.

McGill Picture Anomalies Test

This simple perceptual test was introduced by Hebb and Morton (1943), and has been shown by Milner (1958) to be particularly sensitive to right temporal lobe damage. It may sometimes be useful in confirming suspected dysfunction in this part of the brain.

The subject is confronted with a series of sketchily drawn cartoon-like pictures, and must point out the incongruous feature in each. (In one, for example, a picture is shown hanging on the wall of a monkey's cage.) Patients with right temporal lobe lesions seem to find these pictures confusing, and often tend to focus their attention on quite irrelevant details. By contrast their behaviour when confronted with clearly drawn pictures may be perfectly intact, with correct identification of anomalies when sufficient time is given.

The Token Test

De Renzi and Vignolo (1962) have introduced a test which is especially sensitive to minor degrees of impairment of language comprehension. This can be of considerable value, since routine examination often fails to reveal slight receptive language disorder. A patient with dysphasia may seem to have difficulties which are limited to verbal expression alone, and it can then be difficult to explore the more subtle aspects of language comprehension without taxing other cognitive functions as well.

The test uses a number of simple 'tokens' which are manipulated by the subject. He is given a series of oral commands expressed in progressively more complex messages, in response to which he must perform simple manual tasks such as picking up, moving, or touching the

tokens. The tokens used are of two different shapes (circles and rectangles), two different sizes and five different colours. It is first necessary to ensure that the subject appreciates the meaning of circle and rectangle and that his colour recognition is intact.

In the first part of the test the large circles and rectangles are displayed and the patient is asked to pick up each in turn by telling him to 'pick up the yellow rectangle', 'pick up the white circle' etc. Subsequent parts proceed in graded stages by introducing the small as well as the large tokens, by asking the subject to pick up two at a time, and by introducing more complex instructions which involve new grammatical elements. In the final part of the test prepositions, conjunctions and adverbs are introduced so as to radically change the meaning of the action which the subject is required to perform. Thus: 'put the red circle on the green rectangle', 'touch the blue circle with the red rectangle', 'pick up all the rectangles except the yellow one', 'put the red circle between the yellow rectangle and the green rectangle', 'after picking up the green rectangle touch the white circle' etc.

The test therefore consists of messages which are elementary conceptually and short and easy to memorise, but which make two kinds of demand on the subject's comprehension—the token must be identified by three independent features, and the subject must grasp the semantic complications which are later introduced. Defects often become obvious only in the later stages of the test, and can then emerge clearly even among dysphasics who have shown no evidence of difficulty with comprehension during normal conversation.

Boller and Vignolo (1966) found that the test was not only more impaired in aphasic than non-aphasic patients, but among non-aphasics it was significantly more impaired by left-sided brain damage than right. The 'latent sensory aphasia' identified in this way was independent of non-language impairments as measured by Raven's Progressive Matrices, and was therefore not merely a consequence of impaired general intelligence. The test was shown to be more sensitive for the detection of mild comprehension defects than 'Marie's Three Paper Test' which has been widely employed for this purpose (p. 87).

Benton (1967) has described a more extensive battery of tests for the detailed investigation of language function, which incorporates the Token Test as one of many components. Other parts assess visual and tactile naming, sentence repetition, sentence construction, word fluency, and several aspects of reading and writing. Profiles of language dysfunction can be drawn up, and help to identify areas of relative difficulty and to assess progress during recovery.

Aptitude Tests

Tests are available for providing information concerning ability and aptitude for different kinds of task. These have mostly been introduced for educational and vocational guidance and have accordingly been standardised on healthy subjects. Nevertheless they sometimes find a useful place in the management of brain-damaged subjects. During rehabilitation they may indicate which functions require most attention, and when it comes to resettlement at work they can be valuable in indicating which forms of employment may be particularly suitable or unsuitable.

The *Differential Aptitude Test* yields scores on verbal reasoning, numerical ability, abstract reasoning, clerical speed and accuracy, mechanical reasoning, spatial relations, spelling and grammar. The *Primary Mental Abilities Test* produces similar scores on a more restricted range of functions. The *General Aptitude Test Battery* includes in addition scores for motor coordination, finger dexterity and manual dexterity, which may of course be crucial factors in the resettlement of a brain-damaged patient. Details are provided by Anastasi (1968).

Dementia Questionnaires and Rating Scales

A number of questionnaires are available for making a very approximate assessment of functions which tend to be impaired by diffuse brain damage. These are not psychometric tests in the ordinary sense, but merely questionnaires filled in by doctors, nurses or relatives who have observed the patient closely. They often include questions relevant to social and emotional functioning in addition to observations about the patient's cognitive status.

Standardisation is at best very approximate, but the questionnaires can give useful information in certain settings. Some have especial value in quantifying the degree of impairment when patients are too severely incapacitated to yield scores on formal psychometric tests. Others are useful for research purposes in allowing the separation of groups according to overall severity of disability. In clinical practice they can serve as a very approximate screening device, or they can be repeated after an interval of time to gauge the rate of the patient's decline or improvement.

The '*Gresham Ward Questionnaire*' for use with elderly patients has been described by Post (1965):

Different sections contain questions relevant to orientation in time and place, memory for past personal events, memory for recent personal events, general information, and topographical orientation within the ward, each being scored separately. Uneven performance, or a total score of less than 35 points, should serve as a basis for more intensive enquiry about the possibility of brain damage.

Blessed *et al.* (1968) used a standard '*dementia scale*' in their study of the relationship between impairments of function and severity of neuropathological changes in the brains of old people (p. 376):

The questionnaire is administered to a close relative or friend, who must answer the questions on the basis of the patient's level of performance during the preceding six months. One group of questions contains items concerning competence in personal, domestic and social activities, such as ability to perform household tasks, to cope with small sums of money, to find the way in familiar surroundings and to recall recent outings and visits. The next group concerns changes of habits, such as impairment of eating, dressing and sphincter control. The third is relevant to change in personality, interest and drive, such as increased rigidity, egocentricity, coarsening of affect, impaired emotional control, or the abandonment of habitual interests.

An '*Information-Memory-Concentration-Test*' was also introduced by Blessed *et al.* (1968), after finding that many demented subjects could not complete more formal psychometric procedures. The test contains simple questions and tests which can usually be attempted even by very demented subjects, thus yielding numerical scores across all grades of severity:

Information is tested by questions about name, age, time, date, place and recognition of persons. Memory is assessed by questions about past personal events and certain non-personal matters, and by testing five-minute recall of a name and address. Concentration is tested by asking the patient to count forwards and backwards from 20, and to give the months in reverse order.

The '*Mini-Mental State Examination*' (MMSE) was elaborated by Folstein *et al.* (1975) as a simplified form of the routine cognitive status examination. It has the virtue of brevity, taking only 5–10 minutes to administer, yet test-retest reliability is high and it has been shown to discriminate well between patients with dementia and delirium (Anthony *et al.*, 1982).

The first section covers orientation, memory and attention. Memory is tested by noting the number of trials required to learn three object names, then testing recall later. Attention is assessed by the serial subtraction of 7s or by spelling a word backwards. The second section tests ability to name common objects, follow verbal and written commands, write a sentence spontaneously and copy a simple figure. The total score obtainable is 30, scores of less than 24 usually being indicative of cognitive impairment.

The *'Geriatric Mental State Schedule'* (GMS) is not simply a questionnaire but a standardised, semi-structured interview for examining and recording the patient's mental state. It takes 30–40 minutes. to administer and covers the period of a month prior to examination (Copeland *et al.*, 1976).

Items are drawn from the 8th edition of the Present State Examination (Wing *et al.*, 1967) and the Present State Schedule (Spitzer *et al.*, 1964) with extra sections dealing with disorientation and other cognitive abnormalities. The patient is required, for example, to spell his names, learn and recall the name of the interviewer, give his own age and date of birth, the present day and year, etc., and to recognise common objects and their functions. The cognitive sections are interspersed with less stressful questions of a more general nature. Most ratings are on a 5 point scale, with each point carefully defined. The examiner is allowed to cross-examine the patient with additional questions if he is not clear how an item should be rated.

The GMS allows classification of elderly patients by symptom profile and can demonstrate changes in the profile over time. Good reliability between raters has been shown both for individual items and for diagnoses made on the basis of the schedule (Copeland *et al.*, 1976). In a correlational procedure twenty-one factors were produced, including three dealing with cognitive impairment ('impaired memory', 'cortical dysfunction' and 'disorientation') and others concerned with depression, anxiety, somatic concerns, etc. The ability of these factors to discriminate between patients with functional and organic disorders of the elderly has been demonstrated (Gurland *et al.*, 1976).

The related *Comprehensive Assessment and Referral Evaluation Schedule* (CARE, Gurland *et al.*, 1977) contains psychiatric components largely derived from the GMS along with questions covering medical disorders, social functioning and capacity to undertake activities of daily living. Henderson *et al.* (1983) have combined parts of both instruments to produce an interview for use in community surveys.

The *'Crichton Geriatric Behaviour Rating Scale'* is a group nursing assessment applied retrospectively on impressions gained during the preceding week (Robinson, 1961, 1977). The ten items involved convey a vignette of behaviour and functional capacities which can be drawn up rapidly and with reasonable reliability.

The areas covered have been selected specifically for use with brain-damaged elderly patients: Mobility, Orientation, Communication, Cooperation, Restlessness, Dressing, Feeding, Continence, Sleep and Mood. Each is rated on a 5 point scale, 1 representing normality and 5 severe failure on the function concerned. Points on the scale are verbally described and the level most appropriate to the patient must be checked. In scoring Communication, for example, the scale is as follows: Always clear and retains information (1); can indicate needs, can understand verbal directions, can deal with simple information (2); understands simple verbal and non-verbal information but does not indicate needs (3); cannot understand simple verbal or non-verbal information but retains some expressive ability (4); no effective contact (5).

The *'Clifton Assessment Schedule'* is a brief assessment procedure for use with psychogeriatric patients. Twelve items are scored by nurses covering aspects of information, orientation and such mental abilities as counting, reading, writing and repeating the alphabet. The Gibson Spiral Maze is used in addition as a brief test of psychomotor performance. Scores derived from the schedule have been shown to have good predictive validity in terms of outcome at follow-up, and in the distinction between functional and organic psychiatric disorders in the elderly (Pattie and Gilleard, 1975, 1976, 1978).

The *'Stockton Geriatric Rating Scale'* was introduced by Meer and Baker (1966) as a thirty-three item scale for assessing both physical disability and behaviour in elderly patients. It has been modified for British use and shortened to eighteen items by Gilleard and Pattie (1977). Each item is rated by nurses on a simple 3 point scale and summated to yield four sub-scores: Physical Disability, Apathy, Communication Difficulties, and Social Disturbance. Their validity in terms of outcome and diagnostic groupings has been examined as for the Clifton Assessment Schedule (Pattie and Gilleard, 1975, 1978).

The *'Performance Test of Activities of Daily Living'* (PADL) is a simple and rapidly administered test for assessing capacity for self care. It is unaffected by lack of insight and has the special advantage of requiring the mininum of verbal communication. The patient is required to demonstrate his ability to perform sixteen tasks which are essential for functional independence, such as drinking, dressing, etc. He is then assigned to a category of 'independent', 'moderately independent' or 'dependent' according to the proportion of tasks correctly performed. Kuriansky *et al.* (1976) have shown that the results obtained agree closely with an informant's assessment of the patient's self-care capacity, but not with the patient's own assessment. An objective test of this nature is thus preferable to a questionnaire administered to the patient himself. The test has been shown to discriminate well between elderly patients with organic and non-organic disorders and to correlate well with short-term outcome of hospitalisation.

The *'Vineland Social Maturity Scale'* (Doll, 1947) has been mainly used for studies in child development and mental retardation, but can also be useful in providing a measure of social functioning in brain-damaged adults. Repeat administration after an interval of time can reveal gains or losses in the social field, usefully supplementing measures of intellectual ability.

The scale consists of 117 items which sample various aspects of social ability—capacity for self-care, social independence in personal activities, and social responsibility. The items are scored by interviewing someone closely acquainted with the patient. The chief categories of function measured by the scale are as follows:

'Self-help general' (for example 'cares for self at toilet', 'tells time to quarter hour'); 'Self-help eating' (for example 'drinks from cup or glass unaided', 'uses table knife for spreading'); 'Self-help dressing' ('dresses self except for tying', 'bathes self assisted', 'bathes self unaided'); 'Self direction' ('makes minor purchases', 'uses money providently'); 'Occupation' ('uses tools or utensils', 'does simple creative work'); 'Communication' ('prints simple words', 'makes telephone calls', 'follows current events'); 'Locomotion' ('goes about neighbourhood unattended', 'goes about home freely', 'goes to distant places alone'); and 'Socialisation' ('plays simple table games', 'assumes responsibilities beyond own needs', 'shares community responsibility').

Ancillary Investigations

Further investigations will often be required when an organic basis is suspected for psychiatric disorder. Certain routine tests should ideally be performed on all psychiatric in-patients, including estimation of haemoglobin, erythrocyte sedimentation rate, serological tests for syphilis, chest X-ray and routine urine examination. The patient's temperature should always be taken, sometimes with four-hourly record-

ing if minor rises are suspected. These serve as screening tests for coincidental as well as causally related physical disorders. Other investigations will be indicated on the basis of the history and clinical examination when specific disorders are suspected. An important principle is that investigations should always be planned to give the maximum of required information with the minimum of inconvenience to the patient. Investigations which are without discomfort or risk will obviously be more readily undertaken than those which carry the possibility of pain or complications. Skull X-ray, EEG and CT scanning, for example, will sometimes be performed even when the level or suspicion of organic involvement is low, whereas lumbar puncture or contrast radiography will be reserved until very specific and important questions need to be answered.

Some indication of the relative use made of different investigatory procedures is provided by Macfie (1972) who reviewed the diagnostic practices on a number of general psychiatric units at the Maudsley Hospital. Among 136 consecutive new admissions the investigations shown in Table 2 were carried out.

It can be seen that the yield of abnormal results was low where many of the commoner investigations were concerned, but these were procedures which caused little discomfort to the patient. Some investigations such as serum protein bound iodine, B_{12} and folate, and estimation of urinary porphyrins gave uniformly negative results, yet were each undertaken in approximately 10% of the patients. Here a very low level of suspicion clearly dictated the investigations because of the importance of detecting abnormalities when they exist. Lumbar puncture, by contrast, was used with considerable discrimination and yielded a high proportion of abnormal findings.

The requests for EEG may be contrasted in the table with requests for psychological investigation for brain damage. EEGs were requested three times as often as psychological tests yet the yield of abnormal results was very much lower. Here it would seem that common practice has been to use the EEG in a less discriminating manner, perhaps even as a screening test, whereas psychometry was undertaken only after full consultation between psychiatrist and psychologist.

This study was, of course, carried out before the introduction of CT scanning. The yield of abnormal CT scan results in psychiatric patients from various series is described by Roberts and Lishman (1984).

Examination of the blood will usually include estimation of haemoglobin, erythrocyte sedimentation rate and white blood count and differential. In the presence of anaemia full haematological studies

TABLE 2. Ancillary investigations among 136 consecutive psychiatric inpatients (after Macfie, 1972)

	% Patients examined	% Abnormal of those examined
Routine haematology	89	7
Serological tests for syphilis	75	1
Chest X-ray	75	12
Electroencephalogram	42	14
Serum electrolytes	33	9
Skull X-ray	29	5
Drugs in urine	24	3
Serum proteins and liver function tests	18	28
Serum protein bound iodine	14	nil
Psychological tests for brain damage	13	65
Serum B_{12}	11	nil
Urinary porphyrins	9	nil
Serum folate	7	nil
Lumbar puncture	7	20

will be needed. Serological tests for syphilis remain extremely important. The serum B_{12} and folate will sometimes be estimated even in the absence of anaemia (pp. 503 and 506). Biochemical investigations may include estimation of urea and electrolytes (including on occasion calcium and phosphorus), serum proteins, liver function tests and blood sugar studies. The serum T_3 and T_4 may give indications of thyroid disorder. The blood barbiturate, alcohol or other drug levels may need to be investigated. Very occasionally LE cells or antinuclear antibodies will be searched for.

Examination of the urine will include routine tests for sugar, albumin and specific gravity, and sometimes microscopy and culture. Examination for drugs, especially barbiturates and amphetamines will sometimes be indicated, and more rarely for porphyrins, catecholamines or steroids. Very occasionally a search will be made for heavy metals in the urine or the blood.

Chest X-ray is important for the evaluation of cardiac and pulmonary status, and in particular for the detection of carcinoma of the lung or tuberculosis. Electrocardiography may provide evidence of dysrhythmia, cardiac ischaemia or recent coronary thrombosis, and can occasionally provide evidence of serum potassium abnormalities.

The indications for these and other investigations are detailed in the relevant chapters later in the book.

Certain other investigations of particular relevance to cerebral dysfunction will be discussed in detail below.

ELECTROENCEPHALOGRAPHY

The electroencephalogram has the important advantage over many other procedures that it is safe and without discomfort to the patient. It is accordingly used extensively when organic psychiatric disorders are suspected. It remains, furthermore, the major non-invasive means of determining the physiological or functional state of the brain, as opposed to its anatomical configuration. Certain marked limitations in its diagnostic usefulness must, however, be borne in mind.

Characteristics

EEG rhythms are conventionally classified into four components according to their frequencies—delta rhythms at less than 4 Hz, theta at 4–7 Hz, alpha at 8–13 Hz, and beta in excess of 13 Hz (Terminology Committee, Storm van Leeuwen et al., 1966). The normal EEG has a well developed alpha rhythm, maximal in the occipital and parietal regions, which attenuates on opening the eyes and reappears when they are closed again. It similarly attenuates when the patient engages in mental activity such as simple mental arithmetic. The average voltage of the alpha rhytm is 30–50 µV with spindle-shaped modulations. Small amounts of other rhythms are allowable provided the alpha activity is well developed. Beta activity is seen mainly in the precentral regions, and low voltage theta becomes more obvious with relaxation and drowsiness. Delta activity is normally seen only in very young children and during sleep.

Abnormal EEG elements which can be important in diagnosis include the following:

'Spikes' are high peaked discharges which rise and fall abruptly and stand out above the general amplitude of the other waves. 'Sharp waves' rise steeply then fall more slowly, and may occupy the alpha, theta or delta range. Composite elements may consist of spikes alternating with delta waves ('spike and wave' or 'wave and spike' discharges), or slow waves preceded by several spikes ('poly-spike and wave'). Wave and spike discharges occurring at a rhythm of 3 Hz constitute the classical EEG feature of petit mal epilepsy; those faster and slower than this may be referred to as 'wave and spike variants'. Abnormal rhythms and other elements can be generalised, unilateral or focal, and may be described as synchronous or asynchronous depending on the coincidence of their appearance in different leads.

Various activating procedures may be used to clarify marginal abnormalities, or to bring out those which are concealed in the resting record. Hyperventilation is used to increase the excitability of cortical cells, probably mainly as a result of hypocapnic constriction of cerebral vessels leading to cerebral hypoxia (Meyer and Gotoh, 1960). Epileptic foci and other disturbances may emerge more clearly. Photic stimulation consists of repetitive light flashes of varying frequency. Within certain ranges of flash frequency (especially 8–15 Hz) the occipital alpha rhythm adjusts itself to the flash rate (occipital 'driving'), and paroxysmal abnormalities may emerge in the form of high-voltage complex elements spreading to the frontal and temporal regions. Seizure patterns may emerge, and a generalised seizure may even be provoked. Sleep may be induced by oral quinalbarbitone or pentobarbitone if it does not occur naturally. This can be useful in activating the spike or sharp wave discharges of epilepsy, especially those arising within the temporal lobes. Thiopentone may be given intravenously, and typically induces beta activity, often in the form of discrete runs or spindles. The induced beta activity is commonly less well developed at the electrodes over the site of damage in the affected temporal lobe. Other drugs which may occasionally be employed for the activation of seizure patterns are chlorpromazine or injections of metrazole or megimide (bemigride). The latter drugs must be reserved for use under highly skilled supervision in specialised centres, since fits are liable to be provoked.

In addition to the normal electrode placements over the scalp, sphenoidal electrodes inserted deeply below the zygomatic arch can be valuable for locating discharges from the antero-inferior portions of the temporal lobes. Sphenoidal lead recording is chiefly used when assessing the suitability of epileptic patients for temporal lobectomy. For other special purposes there may be much to be gained from depth electrode studies, or by recording directly from the exposed cortex at operation ('electrocorticography'). These procedures can obviously be undertaken only in special centres.

Limitations

In many ways the EEG has failed to satisfy early expectations as a diagnostic aid for reasons which are discussed by Kiloh *et al.* (1981). Accordingly it must only be interpreted with its limitations clearly in mind.

In the first place the EEG can be normal in patients with obvious cerebral dysfunction, certainly if reliance is put upon a single recording. It is probably true to say that a normal EEG never excludes any clinical condition, but can merely serve to diminish the probability of its existence. Conversely a certain proportion of healthy individuals will show abnormal EEGs. The EEG is particularly sensitive to such physiological variables as level of awareness, acid/base equilibrium and blood sugar level. Such physiological changes in the record are indistinguishable from those associated with many pathological states, and can readily be misinterpreted as evidence of disease.

Again, with rare exceptions the patterns obtained have little diagnostic specificity, and the EEG should only be used as an additional source of information to add to the evidence of the history and clinical examination. It can be a valuable aid in localisation but is of little help in pathological diagnosis. Even with regard to localisation it is known that a focal lesion can occasionally be associated with disturbance some distance away, or alternatively give rise to generalised EEG abnormalities. For these reasons the most useful help will be obtained from the investigation when the person interpreting the record is fully acquainted with all relevant clinical information about the patient's illness.

There can be added difficulties in psychiatric patients, in that mental disorders of apparently nonorganic origin are known to be associated with an increased incidence of abnormalities in the EEG. This can sometimes cloud the issue when it comes to the differential diagnosis between functional and organic psychiatric conditions. The large and often confusing literature on the subject has been reviewed by Ellingson (1954), Hill (1963a) and Fenton (1974). Whereas perhaps 10–15% of normal subjects show some abnormality on the EEG this figure has often been somewhat higher among patients with neurotic disorders. The abnormalities in such patients commonly lie just outside the normal range, with some excess of generalised theta or beta rhythms of rather low amplitude. Patients with manic depressive disorder have been reported to show marginally abnormal records in up to 20% of cases, though again the finding is far from consistently upheld. Schizophrenia is sometimes associated with more definite abnormalities, in perhaps a quarter of cases (Abenson, 1970). Catatonic schizophrenia shows abnormal records more commonly than other varieties. No particular pattern is characteristic, but

Hill (1957a) has reported epileptiform activity in a high proportion of schizophrenic patients, usually of low amplitude. This may consist of grouped spikes, fast spikes and waves or paroxysmal slow waves with the spike components minimally in evidence. In catatonic stupor normal rhythms tend to be replaced by low amplitude slow activity, sometimes extending to the delta range. These changes are not constant however, failing to appear altogether in some patients, and sometimes varying from one attack to another in the same patient.

In patients with disorders of behaviour and personality the incidence of abnormalities is perhaps highest of all. Hill and Watterson (1942) found that 48% of patients diagnosed as psychopathic had abnormal EEGs compared to 15% of controls, and among aggressive psychopaths the proportion rose to 65%. A 70% incidence of EEG abnormalities in prisoners convicted of apparently motiveless murders has been observed (Stafford-Clark and Taylor, 1949; Okasha et al., 1975). The majority of the abnormalities in patients with personality disorder appear to reflect cerebral immaturity, and are of a type which would be accepted as normal in a very much younger age group. Hill (1952) listed the abnormalities as bilateral rhythmic theta activity in central and temporal regions, alpha variants, and posterior temporal slow wave foci which were usually episodic. Personality disorder with antisocial conduct was especially liable to be associated with focal abnormality in the temporal lobes and particularly the posterior temporal areas. Sometimes the so-called immaturity may be the result of past cerebral insults, even of birth injury, but it would appear that the great majority are merely associated with delayed maturation. Thus the abnormalities tend to decrease with age, and this may be accompanied by a parallel improvement in behaviour.

Another difficulty with psychiatric patients can be the result of treatments currently or recently given. Many of the widely prescribed drugs affect the EEG, and in some individuals to a marked extent. Fenton (1974) and Kiloh et al. (1981) review the main changes that occur. Barbiturates, chloral and other sedatives increase fast activity and sometimes produce a small amount of diffuse theta or even delta activity. Most sedatives also tend to aggravate epileptic discharges. Anti-convulsants other than barbiturates, on the other hand, have little effect on the EEG. Chlorpromazine in low dosage may disturb alpha activity, with the occasional appearance of slow frequencies. In high dosage it may produce generalised delta waves or hypersynchron-

ous high voltage discharges. Chlorpromazine also potentiates epileptic discharges. Similar changes are produced by other phenothiazines, butyrophenones, tricyclic antidepressants and lithium. Chlordiazepoxide and diazepam are usually associated with increased fast activity.

Electroconvulsive therapy can render the EEG hard to interpret for a time. Each fit is followed by generalised theta and delta activity which becomes more persistent as successive treatments are given. After 3 or 4 treatments spaced at intervals of 2 to 3 days the abnormal rhythms may persist in the intervals between, often with frontal preponderance. As the course of treatment proceeds the disturbance becomes more widespread and of higher voltage, and alpha activity may disappear. Individual patients differ in the severity of these effects and in the time taken for return to normality. Shagass (1965) reports that most patients have regained a normal pattern 1 to 3 months after the termination of a course of 6 to 12 treatments given thrice weekly.

Uses

This brief description of some of the difficulties surrounding the interpretation of the EEG is necessary before discussing situations where it can serve a useful purpose. In general terms suspicions of abnormality of brain structure or function are confirmed by the EEG in 60% of cases (Kugler, 1964); hence it can bring added information in any psychiatric patient when the question of an organic basis for the illness has arisen. In diagnostically obscure cases one can look for clues which may indicate the need for further special investigation. A single focus of abnormally fast or slow activity will always suggest the presence of a cerebral lesion and must be followed up further, likewise gross asymmetries of normal or abnormal activity between the hemispheres. The EEG also plays a part in the differentiation between organic and functional illness, though caution must be observed. A normal record will be of little help in the distinction, but it will certainly be less easy to maintain a diagnosis of purely psychogenic disturbance in the presence of a grossly abnormal record.

The disturbances seen in *epileptic subjects* are considered in detail in Chapter 7. Characteristic epileptic discharges consist of spikes, sharp waves, or wave and spike complexes. When recurrent these are very strong evidence indeed in favour of an epileptic process. In generalised (primary subcortical) epilepsy wave and spike complexes may consist of runs of classical three per second spike and wave, but in the presence of grand mal attacks they are commonly somewhat faster or consist of variants with polyspike and wave. Other abnormalities common in epileptics, but without the same degree of specificity, include paroxysms of symmetrical delta activity, bursts of theta, or a diffuse excess of delta and theta. Epilepsy which originates within the cortex shows a spike and sharp wave focus, or local spike discharges either singly or in groups. These often betray the point of origin of the seizures, though sometimes they are transmitted widely to other areas. Temporal lobe epilepsy often shows spike discharges over the temporal region, but occasionally the record can be normal until sleep is induced and sphenoidal electrodes employed.

The principal value of the EEG in epilepsy is to distinguish patients with a discharging cortical focus from those with primary subcortical epilepsy. In patients without an aura to their grand mal attacks there may be no other means of making the distinction. The EEG can often localise the cortical lesion, and indicate whether it is circumscribed in extent, unilateral or bilateral. This becomes very important when deciding how far to explore the responsible pathology, and when the question of surgery for the relief of epilepsy is likely to arise.

On the broader question of the diagnosis of epilepsy the EEG can be useful but is not an infallible guide. Epileptiform discharges are found in occasional normal persons, in many degenerative brain disorders, and in some patients with psychosis or personality disorder. Conversely approximately 30% of patients with epilepsy have normal EEGs between attacks. In exceptional cases the record can remain normal even during an attack, as in some cases of Jacksonian and psychomotor epilepsy when the foci are so discrete, and of such low voltage, that they fail to reach the surface electrodes. The recognition of the epileptic nature of a group of symptoms must therefore remain primarily a clinical task, but one which obtains firm confirmation from the EEG in the great majority of cases. Where the clinical features are dubious this confirmation can have a decisive influence on the diagnosis and future management. Classical spike and wave discharges, for example, may resolve doubts when an adequate witnessed account of attacks is not forthcoming. And in temporal lobe epilepsy the EEG can sometimes point directly to the diagnosis in patients who have hitherto been considered to suffer from 'hysteria', anxiety attacks, or short-lived functional psychotic reactions.

Space occupying lesions are revealed by the EEG in a high proportion of cases, and sometimes the EEG may give the first indication of a lesion in an otherwise puzzling picture. A focal delta wave focus will constitute strong presumptive evidence of a cerebral tumour, especially when combined with the other features outlined in Chapter 6 (p. 202). Alternatively it may give the first indication of a developing cerebral abscess when this arises as a complication of a generalised infection. A subdural haematoma in the elderly sometimes presents with a psychiatric picture, and the EEG can sometimes be the factor which alerts one to the diagnosis. Typically there is diminished amplitude or suppression of cerebral rhythms over the affected hemisphere, and some irregular slow activity on the affected side, though the contralateral hemisphere may be affected as well (p. 356).

Positive findings are therefore of value, but negative findings must not be interpreted as excluding possible pathology. In approximately 20% of tumours a normal record may be obtained, particularly with slow-growing varieties which carry the best prognosis. The EEG may fail to reveal evidence of a subdural haematoma in a similar proportion of cases. One must also beware of the occasional cases with well-defined but utterly misleading foci, even sometimes locating the tumour or haematoma to the wrong side of the head. Short of this the EEG will often prove of value in indicating the next step to be taken in investigation when neurological signs are insufficient in themselves for lateralisation.

With *cerebral infarctions* the EEG can be of help in gauging prognosis. Patients with miminal changes during the acute episode can in general be expected to make a good recovery, also patients in whom the EEG changes resolve steadily from an early date. An EEG which becomes normal while neurological defects persist, however, will suggest that little further clinical improvement can be expected.

After *head injury* the EEG may again sometimes help in gauging prognosis (p. 141), or in pointing to an organic component in disturbances which have seemed to be purely psychogenic in origin. EEG changes may occasionally foreshadow the development of post-traumatic epilepsy, but unfortunately the inter-seizure record remains normal in a high proportion of patients even when fits have already become established.

In *encephalitis* the EEG, together with examination of the cerebrospinal fluid, can be a valuable means of following progress. Indeed as Kugler (1964) points out there are few other ways of doing so while the patient remains unconscious. Abnormalities consist of diffuse irregular slow waves and scattered sharp waves, with slowing or reduction in alpha activity. Seizure patterns are not uncommon in the acute stage. There may be a warning of complications and of permanent brain damage when slow waves persist. The appearance of new spikes or spike and wave complexes raises the possibility that secondary epilepsy will develop. In subacute sclerosing panencephalitis the EEG changes described on (p. 306) have high diagnostic value.

In *metabolic disorders* the EEG is a sensitive indicator of cerebral insufficiency, and can reflect worsening or improvement of the clinical condition with a fair degree of accuracy. The changes lack specificity for the metabolic disorder in question, being for example similar in hypoglycaemia, anoxia, hypokalaemia, carbon dioxide retention or vitamin B_{12} deficiency. Nevertheless they can provide important information in patients who present with indefinite organic features in the mental state. They may help to confirm the organic basis for paranoid syndromes or disturbances of behaviour in patients who are only minimally confused. Or when organic features are well developed the EEG may help in the sometimes difficult distinction between reversible causes and progressive brain pathology. Obrecht *et al.* (1979) have demonstrated the value of the EEG in patients with acute confusional states in general hospital practice, in particular in helping to distinguish metabolic and other systemic disorders from intracranial pathologies.

The earliest changes are slowing of the alpha rhythm along with diminution of voltage. Later there is progressive slowing and disorganisation with runs of theta which come to replace all other activity. Finally in metabolic coma regular high voltage delta activity appears, sometimes bilaterally synchronous and sometimes more random in distribution. In deep coma, when the patient is quite unresponsive, the amplitude of the EEG diminishes and ultimately the record becomes flat and featureless.

Engel and Romano (1959) have re-emphasised earlier findings about the importance of the EEG in the diagnosis of delirium and in the detection of minor degrees of impairment of consciousness. A close correlation has been demonstrated between the degree of slowing of the EEG, and the degree of disturbance of consciousness as reflected in impairment of functions such as awareness, attention, memory and comprehension (Romano and Engel, 1944). Moreover when the effects of hypoxia, hypoglycaemia and alcohol were observed in the same individuals, an equivalent degree of cognitive disturbance was obtained for comparable degrees of slowing of the EEG, even though more personal aspects of behaviour, affect and thought content might be very different (Engel *et al.*, 1945). With very mild affections, when cognitive difficulty can be hard to detect on clinical examination, the EEG has already begun to slow. This can be shown by serial recordings, and can occasionally be useful in the retrospective diagnosis of minimal degrees of clouding of consciousness. The absolute frequency of the dominant rhythm is less important than the degree of slowing. Thus 8–9 Hz may be abnormal if it has replaced alpha of a higher frequency. This explains why patients with clouding of consciousness can have an apparently normal EEG. When slowing has reached 5–6 Hz the characteristic disruption of activity on eye-opening no longer occurs, representing the physiological correlate of the reduced impact of perceptions derived from the environment. Fluctuations in the severity of delirium, as reflected in outward behaviour, prove not to be related to changes in the underlying metabolic disturbance as reflected in the EEG, but to be more closely tied to psychological and environmental factors.

How widely Engel and Romano's findings may be applied to all causes of delirium is unknown. Kiloh *et al.* (1981) suggest that there is very often a direct relationship between level of consciousness and degree of EEG abnormality but not invariably so. Delirium tremens is an obvious exception, in that during profound delirium the EEG may be normal or show low to moderate voltage fast activity rather than slowing of rhythms.

Finally in addition to providing evidence of the depth of impairment of consciousness the EEG can be of some diagnostic help in comatose patients. Comas due to metabolic disturbance will show diffuse high voltage delta activity as described above, whereas in barbiturate overdosage there will be augmented amplitude and an increase in fast frequencies. Space occupying lesions may be indicated by focal abnormalities, or epileptic activity may be revealed.

In *the presenile and senile dementias* the degree of EEG abnormality appears to be more closely related to the rate of progression of the disorder than to the degree of intellectual impairment at a given point in time. The changes are described along with the individual diseases in Chapter 10. Briefly, in senile dementia of the Alzheimer type the commonest abnormality is accentuation of the normal EEG changes with ageing, and may therefore be difficult to diagnose with confidence. Alpha activity is slowed in frequency and reduced in quantity, and diffuse theta or delta rhythms may appear. The vascular dementias show a similar picture, though often with focal features where local cerebral infarctions have occurred. Presenile Alzheimer's disease is associated with a particularly high incidence of abnormalities. Alpha activity tends to disappear, and is replaced with irregular theta upon which runs of delta activity may be superimposed. Pronounced flattening of the record will raise the possibility of Huntington's chorea, whereas repetitive spike discharges or characteristic triphasic sharp wave complexes may be indicative of Creutzfeldt–Jakob disease.

In all of these conditions the EEG abnormalities may fail to develop in a significant proportion of mild to moderate cases, and even advanced dementia can occasionally exist alongside a normal EEG. Moreover, with few exceptions, the changes that occur lack specificity for the illnesses in question. This reduces the clinical usefulness of the investigation, and reliance must obviously be placed on more definitive measures such as the CT scan. Nevertheless an EEG can be helpful in early and uncertain cases of dementia. A normal EEG in such circumstances will make Alzheimer's disease unlikely, but will not exclude other varieties. The EEG may also help in the distinction between diffuse and focal lesions.

Finally in elderly patients the EEG may aid in the differentiation between depressive pseudodementia and degenerative brain disease. A normal EEG in a patient who has been diagnosed as suffering from Alzheimer's disease or vascular dementia, and who shows features of depression, will at least suggest that the diagnosis should be re-scrutinised with care (Kiloh *et al.*, 1981).

LUMBAR PUNCTURE

Examination of the cerebrospinal fluid can give valuable information in many clinical situations. It is usually a safe procedure but should never be undertaken lightly. The principal hazard is in patients with raised intracranial pressure and particularly when an intracranial tumour is present. The abrupt reduction of pressure due to withdrawal of fluid can bring about tentorial herniation or a medullary pressure cone with fatal results. Even when the needle is quickly removed there may be continued leakage from the puncture hole in the dura mater so that complications can follow some time later. Lumbar puncture is therefore strictly contra-

indicated in the presence of papilloedema or when there are symptoms suggestive of raised intracranial pressure, except under skilled supervision and when neurosurgical help is immediately to hand.

In the absence of raised intracranial pressure the risk attached to lumbar puncture is small. Conversely the risk of withholding it can be high. In psychiatric practice it will sometimes be indicated in patients who show disturbance of consciousness or unexplained change of behaviour, even in the absence of definite neurological signs. It can be a dangerous mistake to postpone the investigation on account of the severity of illness or uncooperative behaviour, though it will often be wise to delay in such circumstances until a CT scan and a neurological opinion have been obtained.

Walton (1982) reviews the information to be obtained from lumbar puncture. The pressure is raised in the presence of tumour, haematoma, abscess or cerebral oedema. A moderate rise is seen in patients with severe arterial hypertension. The pressure may also be raised in certain rare disorders such as lead poisoning or hypoparathyroidism.

A pleocytosis implies inflammatory changes in the meninges, either primary as in meningitis, or secondary to cerebral infection as in encephalitis or cerebral abscess. Polymorphonuclear leucocytes predominate with pyogenic infections, and may number many thousands per cubic millimetre rendering the fluid turbid. Virus encephalitis shows mainly lymphocytes, though with some varieties there may be polymorphs in the early stages. The number of cells is normally rather low. When present the pleocytosis can be an essential observation for confirming the diagnosis. A moderate cellular reaction can similarly be important in the diagnosis of cerebral abscess, usually with 20–200 cells, most of which are polymorphs. In untreated general paresis 5–50 lymphocytes are usual, and as described on pp. 287–8 the monitoring of the cellular content of the cerebrospinal fluid is essential for judging the adequacy of treatment and for the early detection of relapse. A slight pleocytosis, nearly always of lymphocytes, may be present in other conditions including primary and secondary cerebral tumours, cerebral infarctions or multiple sclerosis.

Blood is found in the cerebrospinal fluid after subarachnoid haemorrhage or when a primary intracerebral haemorrhage has extended to the subarachnoid space. Xanthochromia may persist as a yellow discolouration for several weeks thereafter. Xanthochromia in the absence of frank blood is also sometimes found with subdural haematomas.

An increased protein content is common to many conditions and can be difficult to interpret. The protein rises with meningitic infections and this can persist for some time after the pleocytosis has resolved. A moderate increase to 1·0 g/l or a little more may occur with encephalitis, cerebral abscess, cerebral infarction, neurosyphilis, cerebral tumours and multiple sclerosis. Similar levels can be seen with cervical spondylosis or with myxoedema. In the latter situation it can be particularly misleading. With certain tumours such as meningiomas or acoustic neuromas the level is often considerably higher. Very high levels of up to 10 g/l without an accompanying cellular reaction is characteristic of the polyneuropathy of the Guillain-Barré syndrome, also of spinal blockage from any cause.

The globulin fraction is raised in relation to the albumin in many inflammatory conditions. The gamma globulins are abnormally high, with a selective increase in the IgG fraction in the majority of cases of multiple sclerosis. The colloidal gold (Lange) curve, which probably reflects selective changes in the protein content of the fluid, can give additional information. The 'paretic' first zone curve is characteristic of general paresis (e.g. 5544322110), the 'luetic' early mid-zone curve is seen with tabes dorsalis (0123322100), and the 'meningitic' late midzone curve with meningtis of various kinds (0001223210). These changes can also be helpful with some other conditions, for example a paretic curve with multiple sclerosis and subacute sclerosing panencephalitis.

The sugar content of the fluid is greatly lowered or abolished in pyogenic meningitis. A moderate fall is found in tuberculous meningitis and can be a valuable pointer in differentiating this from the various forms of aseptic meningitis due to viral infection. The chloride content is also low in tuberculous meningitis.

Examination of films and culture of the fluid are important for determining the responsible organism when infection is present. Virological studies can be useful, but usually only in retrospect since a considerable time is required before the results become available. Examination of films may also reveal neoplastic cells, especially in carcinomatosis and the medulloblastomas of childhood. Serological tests for syphilis are important since sometimes they are negative in the serum in active cases of general paresis.

Thus in many situations examination of the cerebrospinal fluid gives important information which contributes to the diagnosis. In some conditions such as encephalitis, general paresis and cerebral abscess it may be crucial in alerting one to the diagnosis. A normal cerebrospinal fluid does not, however, mean that a pathological process within the central nervous system can be excluded. The degenerative processes responsible for the presenile and senile dementias do not as a rule show changes, and a completely normal fluid may be found in occasional cases of encephalitis. Moreover many pathological processes responsible for enduring brain damage and neuropsychiatric disturbance will have subsided by the time the patient is examined, and will have left a normal fluid in their wake.

RADIOGRAPHY OF THE SKULL

Skull X-ray may reveal a number of conditions relevant to psychiatric disorder though the principal indication is usually suspicion of a cerebral tumour. Over the vault there may be erosion or bony overgrowth due to a meningioma, or abnormal vascular markings indicative of a tumour or angioma. Osteolytic bone lesions may give the first indication of carcinomatosis or multiple myeloma. General thickening or 'woolliness' may indicate Paget's disease.

The next main focus of interest is in the sella turcica. Decalcification or erosion of the posterior clinoid processes is an important indication of raised intracranial pressure, or the fossa may be enlarged due to a pituitary or suprasellar lesion.

Intracranial calcification provides other clues. The pineal is calcified in approximately 50% of adults and may display shifts of the midline structures. The choroid plexuses and the falx cerebri may occasionally be calcified as well. Calcification within the body of a tumour can be of direct localising value, similarly calcification within the walls of a large cerebral aneurysm. Other rare conditions include calcification within the basal ganglia in hypoparathyroidism, calcification within the nodules in tuberose sclerosis or in the cysts of cysticercosis.

Unsuspected skull fractures may be revealed, and special views may show erosion of the internal auditory meatus due to an acoustic neuroma.

The value of skull X-ray in psychiatric practice has been indicated by the surveys of Kraft et al. (1963, 1965) and Rubin and Rubin (1966). Kraft et al. (1965) found abnormalities in 2·5% of patients when a chronic psychiatric population was screened routinely. Rubin and Rubin (1966) found relevant positive findings in 3% of a younger and more acutely ill psychiatric population, even though all cerebral tumours had been excluded by careful pre-admission screening. Routine skull radiography is, of course, rarely practicable on any widespread scale. In the interests of economy of time, Bull and Zilkha (1968) suggest that in the absence of physical signs a single lateral film will often serve the purposes for which full projections are commonly requested.

ECHOENCEPHALOGRAPHY (ultrasound)

Echoencephalography is used as a simple screening test for detecting displacement of midline structures within the skull. It is a rapid procedure, entirely without discomfort or risk to the patient. When necessary it can be carried out at outpatient consultation, though considerable expertise is needed in order to achieve reliable results.

A beam of ultrasound is passed transversely through the skull, and some of the waves are reflected back when they meet surfaces with different physical properties. They are then transduced into electrical energy so that the resulting impulses can be displayed to view. Midline displacements are readily detected, and more recent techniques display ventricular shifts as well.

Unfortunately the incidence of false negative and false positive results is too high to allow reliance on the echoencephalogram alone, and when shifts are demonstrated no guidance is given to the nature of the responsible pathology. It is therefore very rarely undertaken when facilities for CT scanning are available. In their absence it can form a useful preliminary to decisions regarding contrast radiography, particularly in patients with very indefinite signs and symptoms or in those too severely ill to be submitted to more hazardous procedures.

RADIOISOTOPE SCAN
(radionuclide scan, gamma-encephalography)

Radioisotope scanning has proved to be a valuable technique for the investigation of cerebral tumours and some cerebral infarctions. It is entirely safe and causes negligible discomfort to the patient. Moreover in some instances the appearances and location of the scan lesion can be used in conjunction with the clinical history to allow an aetiological diagnosis to be made with a high degree of probability. Use of the technique has declined very markedly since the introduction of CT scanning, though it still finds an important place where access to the latter is limited.

An isotope preparation such as technetium-99 is injected intravenously in a dose according to body weight. This is picked up by vascular tissue, especially neovascular tissue, and the gamma radiation may be detected by a 'scan' of the skull with radioactive counting equipment. Remarkably precise localisation can be achieved. The exact mechanism of localisation of the tracer substance within the lesion remains unknown but is probably related to changes in the blood-brain barrier. Readings are usually taken 15–30 minutes after injection or at 2–4 hours when a tumour is suspected. Rapid readings may be taken immediately after injection in suspected cerebrovascular disease.

The clinical usefulness of the procedure is reviewed by Heck et al. (1971). Its chief value is in the detection of cerebral tumours. Diagnostic accuracy is high for vascular tumours though with others it may fail. Lesions which are cystic or necrotic in the centre, such as astrocytomas or abscesses, may show a characteristic 'doughnut' sign. In general, however, resolution is poor in comparison to CT scanning, and a tumour is unlikely to be revealed if a CT scan has already given negative results. An advantage over angiography is that multiple tumours, as with metastases, are usually readily detected.

Cerebral infarctions are revealed if the timing is correct. The conversion of a normal scan to abnormal in the distribution of one of the major cerebral vessels within a few days of a suspected cerebrovascular accident allows the diagnosis to be made with a high degree of confidence. The usual sequence of changes is an initially negative result which then becomes positive within 2–7 days indicating the area of brain tissue involved. A later negative phase is followed after some weeks by positive results again as vascularisation occurs in the area of the infarct. A distinction cannot always be made from a tumour on a single examination, but repetition of the study can be a valuable aid to the differentiation.

A subdural haematoma may show as a crescent shaped defect over the hemisphere. Here the results can be very helpful towards the diagnosis, particularly in haematomas which have become isodense with brain tissue on the CT scan (p. 356).

RISA CISTERNOGRAPHY (Isotope Encephalography)

Risa cisternography provides a means of obtaining a dynamic picture of the cerebrospinal fluid circulation. It found its main clinical application in conjunction with air encephalography in the investigation of patients with communicating hydroceph-alus, but since the advent of CT scanning its usefulness has declined. When it is thought neces-sary to visualise the morphology and the dynamics of the CSF circulation it is now generally preferable to employ an intrathecal injection of metrizamide in conjunction with a CT scan (Isherwood, 1983).

In performing a risa scan, serum albumin labelled with [131]I ('RISA') is injected intrathecally by lumbar puncture in a dose of 100 μCi, and serial scintillation scans of the head are made at time intervals ranging from 2 hours to several days. In normal subjects the radioactivity appears in the basal cisterns within 1–3 hours, and by 24 hours is well disseminated over the hemispheres and along the superior longitudinal sinus with little remaining at the base of the brain. Activity fades rapidly after 48 hours, and at no stage does the scan show activity within the ventricular system.

Distinctive findings were demonstrated in patients with normal pressure hydrocephalus (Bannister *et al.*, 1967; Patten and Benson, 1968; Bannister, 1970; Benson *et al.*, 1970). The dilated ventricles show early filling, and come to contain a high concentra-tion of RISA which persists throughout the series. Moreover the radioactive material fails to circulate over the hemispheres and does not appear in the saggital area. A delay may be seen with degenerative diseases such as primary presenile dementia, but within 48 hours these ultimately show adequate saggital activity. They may also show areas of increased activity over the cortex where the cerebro-spinal fluid has pooled in widened sulci. When little or no radioactivity has appeared in the saggital area after 48–72 hours, normal pressure hydrocephalus is strongly suggested.

The procedure is safe, with little or no discomfort to the patient afterwards. It was accordingly sometimes employed before air encephalography in the investigation of patients suspected of normal pressure hydrocephalus, though air studies were still required for definitive confirmation. Each investi-gation usefully complemented the other, the risa cisternogram being probably the more reliable indicator of the patency or otherwise of the cortical subarachnoid spaces, while the air encephalogram was most conclusive in displaying gross ventricular enlargement. CT scanning and techniques for continuous intracranial pressure monitoring have now, however, emerged as the favoured diagnostic procedures when hydrocephalus requires investi-gation (p. 640).

CEREBRAL ANGIOGRAPHY

Cerebral angiography consists of taking X-ray films in rapid succession after an injection of contrast medium into the cerebral circulation. Injection of the common carotid artery displays the internal carotid and its area of supply by way of the anterior and middle cerebral arteries, and sometimes the posterior cerebral arteries also. Vertebral arteriog-raphy is rather more hazardous, but can be used to outline the vertebral, basilar and posterior cerebral arteries.

Angiography is in the main without serious risk, but can be dangerous in the presence of cerebro-vascular disease or severe hypertension. The injected vessel may go into spasm, or a clot may be dislodged leading to cerebral infarction; or damage to the wall may be slow to heal and form a focus for thrombosis later. For this reason arteriography by means of a catheter inserted into the femoral or radial artery is often preferred to direct puncture. On the other hand angiography is safer than air encephalography when the intracranial pressure is raised.

Vascular lesions are usually clearly demonstrated, including intracranial aneurysms, arteriovenous malformations, or stenosis or obstruction of the internal carotid arteries. A subdural haematoma may show as an avascular area beneath the vault of the skull in the anteroposterior view. Space occupying lesions of the cerebral hemispheres are often well localised, including tumours, abscesses or haema-tomas. The nature of the tumour may be indicated by its degree of vascularity, and meningiomas often produce a characteristic 'blush' in the venous phase of the angiogram. Supply of the capillary circulation of the tumour by a meningeal artery may be clearly visualised. Vertebral arteriography may help in the diagnosis of tumours of the posterior fossa, and is of value in patients suspected of having vascular abnormalities of the hind-brain circulation.

Angiography carries small but definite hazards, so has now been supplanted by CT scanning as a screening procedure for tumour. It is still required, however, for the demonstration of most aneurysms and angiomas, and is still sometimes employed to confirm that a tumour is a meningioma. The precise delineation of vascular anomalies and occlusive vascular disease seem likely to remain essential roles for the procedure.

AIR ENCEPHALOGRAPHY (Pneumoencephalography)

Before CT scanning became available air encephalography was a technique of great importance for visualising intracranial pathology. It was the only means available for demonstrating cortical atrophy or yielding reasonable estimates of ventricular size. Space occupying lesions were shown by displacements of the ventricular system. In virtually all respects, however, it has now been superseded by CT scanning, which is a great deal safer and without discomfort for the patient. A place still remains for it in a small minority of patients, chiefly for visualising small basal tumours near the optic or auditory nerves or in the brain stem, and for clarifying obstructions in the aqueductal region. Such regions tend to be relatively inaccessible on the CT scan. It also retains a place in the investigation of patients with temporal lobe epilepsy, being superior to the scan in demonstrating the temporal horns of the lateral ventricles. With progressive improvements in CT scan technique, however, and especially with the advent of nuclear magnetic resonance (p. 123), it seems likely that even these indications may one day be eclipsed. A knowledge of the uses of air encephalography nevertheless remains important, particularly since in many parts of the world the new imaging techniques are not available.

Lumbar air encephalography involves the introduction of air into the subarachnoid space by lumbar puncture, and allowing it to ascend to outline the ventricular system and basal cisterns of the brain. Earlier techniques which utilised large quantities of air have given way to more refined procedures which employ no more than 20–40 cm^3, but nonetheless considerable discomfort usually results. Headache can be severe, and may persist for 48 hours or longer, with nausea and meningeal irritation.

The decision to perform air encephalography therefore always requires the most careful consideration of the benefits which might result. In addition to discomfort there is a considerable element of risk in certain situations. When the intracranial pressure is raised the alteration of cerebral hydrodynamics following the introduction of air may lead to the development of tentorial herniation or a medullary pressure cone, and patients with degenerative brain disease may be worsened at least temporarily after the procedure. These limitations are especially unfortunate since the information obtained by air studies can be valuable where several disease processes are concerned.

A chief indication is to explore the possibility of cerebral atrophy due to degenerative or other brain diseases. Ventricular dilatation is shown more clearly by air studies than by angiography or risa cisternography. Cortical atrophy may also be revealed by pooling of air in dilated sulci over the convexity of the brain or around the cerebellar hemispheres. Air encephalography can thus bring important confirmatory evidence in patients suffering from presenile dementia, and may be indicated in borderline cases to add to the other evidence available. The difficult question of the significance of cerebral atrophy in certain situations, and particularly in psychiatric patients, is discussed further on p. 120.

In normal pressure hydrocephalus the findings on air encephalography may be virtually diagnostic, showing massive symmetrical dilation of the lateral ventricles but complete absence of air over the cortical surface. Risa cisternography may already have given strong indications of the disorder, but the air encephalographic findings are the more decisive.

Space occupying lesions are revealed by shift of the midline structures and local deformities of the ventricular system. The relative value of air studies or angiography in individual cases requires careful and expert judgement in the absence of facilities for CT scanning. The radioisotope scan to some extent diminishes the need for both air encephalography and angiography but may fail with avascular neoplasms and with those which are still rather small.

This said, air encephalography should never be carried out when the intracranial pressure is known to be raised, and when a tumour is suspected it should be withheld unless full neurosurgical facilities are to hand. Ventriculography will often be considered a safer procedure, the air being injected directly into a lateral ventricle via a burr-hole in the skull. This also allows contrast material to be inserted in order to outline the caudal parts of the ventricular system within the posterior fossa.

Local abnormalities of the ventricular system may have diagnostic importance in several other conditions. After head injury and after cerebral infarction there may be unilateral ventricular enlargement, or local distortions which persist and increase with time. Severe intracranial infections may leave similar residua. The main cause appears to be contraction of scar tissue which has formed in the damaged areas.

Finally evidence of arrested development and of a variety of malformations may be revealed, including porencephalic cysts, cerebral aplasia, aqueduct atresia, agenesis of the corpus callosum and the Arnold–Chiari malformation.

COMPUTERISED AXIAL TOMOGRAPHY
('CT Scan', 'EMI Scan')

Computerised axial tomography probably represents the most significant advance in the use of X-rays for diagnosis since their discovery, and has quickly established itself as invaluable in the diagnosis of cerebral disorder. Very significantly, wherever facilities for CT scanning have been established, the requirements for other neuroradiological procedures have dropped abruptly. In particular it has come to replace the air encephalogram except in a tiny minority of cases.

Descriptions of the technique and early reports of its value in clinical practice are provided by Hounsfield (1973), Ambrose (1973, 1974), Gawler, Du Boulay et al. (1974), Paxton and Ambrose (1974) and Kazner et al. (1975). It is essentially a procedure in which X-ray transmission readings are taken through the head at a multitude of angles by means of a narrow collimated beam of X-rays; from these data, absorption values of the material contained within the head are calculated by computer, and presented as a series of pictures of transverse slices of the cranial contents. The system is approximately one hundred times more sensitive than conventional X-ray systems, yet exposes the patient to no greater radiation dosage than a standard series of ordinary skull X-rays. There is no need for anaesthesia or any form of invasive procedure, rendering it entirely safe for patients who might be unfit for contrast neuroradiology.

Gawler, Bull et al. (1975) describe the findings in the normal brain and the range of structures identified. The ventricular system is clearly shown along with certain of the basal cisterns. The cortical sulci are often detectable, and readily so when enlarged. Within the cerebral substance variations in soft tissues of nearly similar density may be displayed; thus the thalami and heads of the caudate nuclei are generally identifiable as discrete structures, also the internal capsule and optic radiations. The cortical grey matter mantle is visible over the surface of the cerebral hemispheres. Progressive refinements incorporated into the more recent scan machines have considerably increased the amount of detail displayed.

In investigating cerebral pathology the scan may show displacements of normal intracranial contents, but in addition many focal pathological processes produce changes in density which enable lesions to be displayed directly. Space occupying lesions are readily shown, including tumours, abscesses and haematomas. Local cerebral oedema is demonstrated as by no other procedure, and an infarction is revealed as a region of low absorption values as early as 8 hours after the stroke.

The nature as well as the location of a tumour can often be demonstrated — whether benign or malignant, solid or cystic — as well as the degree to which surrounding oedema infiltrates brain tissue. A diffuse increase in absorption density is seen with meningiomas, colloid cysts, and pituitary adenomas, whereas gliomas and metastases may be hyper- or hypo-dense. A special advantage is the capacity to distinguish tumours from infarctions at an early stage, and in cases where angiography might well have been contraindicated. Intravenous injections of sodium iothalamate (Conray) can be used in doubtful cases to enhance the contrast between the tumour and surrounding brain tissue. A high level of efficiency in diagnosis has been found, though certain tumours near the base of the skull can be difficult to visualise (Kendall, 1980). Scanning after the introduction of intrathecal metrizamide can greatly improve the detection of small brain stem, suprasellar and cerebellopontine tumours.

In the management of strokes the differentiation between infarction and haemorrhage is relatively simple. The location, size and direction of propagation of intracerebral haematomas can be defined. After head injuries it is possible to distinguish acute extradural, subdural and intracerebral haematomas, and to differentiate these from contusion with local oedema. Coup and contre coup lesions may be revealed. In the acute stage of injury scanning can be invaluable in demonstrating intracranial haematomas before the patient's deterioration makes them obvious to the surgeon.

Cerebral atrophy shows as enlargement of the ventricles, broadening of the Sylvian and interhemispheric fissures, and widening of the cerebral sulci, much as after air encephalography. Enlarged sulci are best seen from a very high slice near the vertex. Computerised axial tomography is without the hazards of air contrast studies and is now regarded as the intracranial investigation of choice in the dementias (British Medical Journal, 1975). Fox et al. (1975) have shown its value in patients with senile dementia. Gawler et al (1975, 1976) have found it to be as accurate as conventional neuroradiological methods for revealing cerebral atrophy or hydrocephalus. Metrizamide studies can add important information in the investigation of communicating hydrocephalus.

Areas of relative translucency may be revealed in

the cerebral white matter in demyelinating disorders such as multiple sclerosis (p. 592) and Schilder's disease (p. 599). White matter changes may also point to the Binswanger variant of cerebral arteriosclerosis in certain demented patients (p. 390). A more recent development, still largely confined to research, involves the direct estimation of brain absorption density values as a guide to more subtle changes in brain parenchymatous structure in, for example, patients with dementia (see below). Some of the potentials which CT scanning has opened up for research into psychiatric disorders are briefly indicated on p. 121 et seq.

The Significance of Cerebral Atrophy

Sometimes the air encephalogram or CT scan shows changes which are hard to interpret, particularly where cerebral atrophy is concerned. It is often easier to assess distortion by a space occupying lesion than to decide on the significance of minor ventricular enlargement. Sometimes, moreover, the ventricles may prove to be enlarged or the sulci prominent in patients who show no evidence of cerebral disorder. Such examples raise obvious diagnostic difficulties, and remind us that we must take into account a range of normal variation where radiographic appearances are concerned.

Attempts were made to establish criteria of normality on the air encephalogram, but for obvious reasons it was impossible to study unselected groups of healthy individuals. Indications were obtained that the ventricles increase in size with age, at least over the age of 60, though even this was far from clearly established (Willanger et al., 1968). CT scanning has allowed more reliable assessments to be made. It is now clear that ventricular size increases with age even in healthy persons, and particularly so in the later decades of life (Barron et al., 1976; Haug, 1977; Gyldensted, 1977; Jacobs et al., 1978). Barron et al. (1976), for example, examined 135 normal volunteers by CT scan, demonstrating a gradual increase from the first to the sixth decades followed by a dramatic increase from the age of 70 onwards. The range encountered in ventricular size also became wider among the elderly subjects.

With regard to dementia there is usually an obvious association with radiological evidence of atrophy, though this is not absolute in every case. Younger demented patients are more likely to show decisively abnormal findings, in comparison with their peers, whereas in the elderly there may be considerable overlap with healthy persons of equivalent age.

Gosling (1955) reviewed the air encephalograms of a large group of patients suspected of dementia, mostly in the presenile age range, and found that 85% showed cerebral atrophy. Among those who did not, the features indicative of dementia had usually been slight and follow-up often showed a lack of progression. During the same period, and in the same department, 19% of air studies on non-demented patients had shown atrophy, sometimes with an obvious cause but in 11% without. Many of the latter patients were suffering from epilepsy of late onset. The features particularly associated with dementia were cortical sulci wider than 0.5 cm, air trapped in the insular regions, and enlargement of the lateral ventricles most marked in the trigone area.

Among elderly demented patients CT scan studies have shown greater sulcal and ventricular size than in age-matched healthy controls, though the overlap tends to be considerable (Jacoby and Levy, 1980a; Gado et al., 1982). Jacoby and Levy found on discriminant function analysis that CT scan measurements produced a correct prediction in 83% of elderly subjects, cortical atrophy being a rather better discriminator than ventricular size. Interestingly, however, patients over the age of 80 were significantly less likely to have large ventricles than those a decade or so younger, perhaps reflecting the more benign course of dementia in the very elderly. Hubbard and Anderson (1981) were able to show by detailed autopsy measurements that the ventricles were of normal size for age in approximately 40% of patients with senile dementia.

The severity of cognitive impairment in dementia has proved to be closely related to the degree of cerebral atrophy, both in air encephalographic and CT scan studies, and in the elderly as well as the middle-aged (Kiev et al., 1962; Willanger et al., 1968 Roberts and Caird, 1976; De Leon et al., 1979; Jacoby and Levy 1980a). Most agree that the relationship with cognitive impairment is closer for ventricular enlargement than for widening of the sulci. There are indications, too, that the progression of cognitive deterioration on follow-up is paralleled by further ventricular enlargement (Naguib and Levy, 1982b).

Interest in the CT scan in dementia has also centred on the absorption density to X-rays in various brain regions. White matter absorption density appears to decrease gradually with age among healthy volunteers (Zatz et al., 1982), but in both presenile and senile Alzheimer's disease further reductions are seen (Naeser *et al.*, 1980; Bondareff *et al.*, 1981a). As mentioned on p. 374, there is some evidence that decreased absorption density in the parietal region may be associated with shorter survival. How far measurements such as these may prove of value in refining diagnostic accuracy in dementia remains to be determined.

In general, therefore, clinical evidence of dementia is accompanied by the radiological appearances of atrophy, and this tends to be more severe the more deteriorated the patient. In occasional early cases, however, no abnormality will emerge, and in the elderly it may be hard to judge the significance of the findings. It is extremely important, as stressed on p. 419, that X-ray appearances should only be interpreted in conjunction with the total clinical picture, and that the diagnosis of a dementing illness should not be allowed to hinge on radiographic findings alone.

This point obtains a special importance in that indications of cerebral atrophy are found in a considerable number of persons without dementia. Among institutionalised epileptic patients, for example, Larsby and Lindgren (1940) found abnormalities on air encephalography in over two-thirds of cases. CT scan studies have shown abnormalities in a high percentage of epileptics (see p. 256), focal or generalised atrophy being by far the commonest finding. Alcoholic subjects are similarly prone to show a high incidence of cortical shrinkage and ventricular dilation, sometimes quite marked in degree and not necessarily accompanied by obvious cognitive change. The findings in this area are discussed in some detail on pp. 519–20. Finally, chronic psychiatric illness of many varieties has been found, when investigated, to be associated with a considerable incidence of radiographic changes as described immediately below.

Haug (1962) carried out a large air encephalographic survey on 278 long-stay patients in a mental hospital, and reported 'definite cerebral atrophy' in 60% of patients. This usually consisted of ventricular enlargement, but cortical atrophy was shown in many where filling over the cortical surface had been achieved. Among patients with organic mental disorders abnormalities were found in 72%, in those with schizophrenia 61%, and in those with other 'functional' illnesses 49%. The latter consisted of a variety of paranoid, affective and neurotic illnesses, all of which had been long-lasting and rather resistant to treatment. Haug suggested that earlier brain damage may have contributed to the genesis of these illnesses by lowering resistance to stress. Among the

patients with organic mental syndromes the atrophy was usually diffuse, whereas half of the non-organic group showed purely focal abnormalities, often of a single temporal horn. The majority appeared to be non-progressive on follow-up, but mortality was increased in patients with abnormal air encephalograms.

Hunter *et al.* (1968b) attempted a similar study in patients who had been continuously in hospital for more than 40 years. Twenty-seven patients were examined, all previously diagnosed as schizophrenic. More than half showed abnormal air encephalograms, usually with unilateral ventricular enlargement. The suggestion again was that some underlying condition, of uncertain nature, may have caused structural damage as reflected both in the air encephalogram and in the patient's mental illness.

The findings in schizophrenia were the subject of several air encephalographic studies, notably Huber's (1957) investigation of 190 patients. Those with the more severe defects in social competence showed the most marked changes on air encephalography. Broadening of the third ventricle went step by step with the severity of personality deterioration when the effects of age were controlled, and frontal atrophy was associated with illnesses of long duration. In a prolonged follow-up of many of these patients it emerged that ventricular enlargement was associated with a poor outcome (Huber *et al.*, 1975). Many similar indications of atrophy in chronic schizophrenia are scattered through the air encephalographic literature as reviewed by Storey (1966). Negative reports emerged as well (Peltonen, 1962; Storey, 1966) and much of the evidence tended to be contradictory. The availability of CT scanning has, however, brought more clarity to the picture.

Starting with a small study by Johnstone *et al.* (1976, 1978) several CT scan surveys have been carried out on carefully diagnosed schizophrenic patients, the non-invasive nature of the scan permitting relatively unselected groups to be examined (for example Weinberger *et al.*, 1979a, 1979b; Nasrallah *et al.*, 1982a; Andreasen *et al.*, 1982). Comparison with age-matched controls has repeatedly shown mild but definite ventricular enlargement in a considerable proportion, this varying up to 60% from one study to another. Cortical atrophy has also been detected, though less commonly, and atrophy of the vermis of the cerebellum can be shown in perhaps 20% of cases (Weinberger *et al.*, 1979c; Lippmann *et al.*, 1982). The implications of such findings have been the subject of several reviews (Weinberger *et al.*, 1983; Pearlson *et al.*, 1983;

Lishman, 1983a; Reveley, 1985). The CT changes show a number of associations — with severity of cognitive change, preponderence of 'negative' symptoms, poor response to neuroleptics and poor premorbid adjustment — but appear in the main to be unrelated to duration of illness or length of hospitalisation. They have been detected in patients quite soon after onset of the schizophrenic disorder (Weinberger et al., 1982), and there are indications that they are commoner in patients who lack a family history of major psychiatric illness (Reveley et al., 1984). The sum total of evidence therefore suggests that the atrophy antedates the development of the schizophrenic illness, but may be a significant factor in helping to determine it and shape its manifestations. Adverse influences operating very early in life are perhaps chiefly to be held responsible. On present evidence there is little to support a causative role for neuroleptic medication in leading to the changes, or to suggest that a specific pathological process is at work.

Not dissimilar findings have begun to emerge in some patients with affective disorder, where ventricular enlargement and cerebellar vermis atrophy have also been reported (Pearlson and Veroff, 1981; Lippmann et al., 1982). Both patients with mania and patients with major depressive illness have sometimes shown significantly larger ventricles than controls (Nasrallah et al., 1982b; Scott et al., 1983). Elderly patients with first-onset depression have been found to have larger ventricles than age-matched healthy volunteers (Jacoby and Levy, 1980b), and there are indications that this is predictive of increased mortality at follow-up (Jacoby et al., 1981).

CT scan studies are thus increasing our appreciation that a minor degree of cerebral disorder may play a part in contributing to a considerable range of mental illness. The degree of cerebral change encountered on CT scanning will only rarely lead to difficulties with diagnosis, but on occasion it will be sufficient to call for detailed re-evaluation of the patient's illness. The cortical shrinkage and ventricular dilatation accompanying severe alcohol abuse will quite often be perplexing when the drinking history is unknown, likewise the appearances of atrophy that may accompany steroid administration (Bentson et al., 1978; Lagenstein et al., 1979). The latter appears to be largely reversible on discontinuation of the steroids. Minor reversible changes have also been reported in patients with anorexia nervosa (Heinz et al., 1977; Enzmann and Lane, 1977).

Studies dating from the air encephalographic era have confirmed that unexpected cerebral atrophy need not imply progressive cerebral disorder or necessarily impair response to treatment for the associated psychiatric condition. Eitinger (1959) followed 46 psychiatric patients with cerebral atrophy of unknown origin and found that 11 improved in social functioning over the years that followed. He concluded that it must often represent a static condition, perhaps dating from early life, thus altering the patient's reaction pattern and increasing his vulnerability to psychological trauma. The important conclusion was that the discovery of atrophy should not lead to therapeutic pessimism, and that treatment should be given in the normal manner for the psychiatric symptoms present.

Mann (1972, 1973) followed a consecutive group of 49 patients from the Maudsley Hospital who showed significant generalised atrophy, with both ventricular dilation and widening of sulci over the cortex. Some were suffering from obvious dementia but others had presented with functional psychiatric syndromes. Follow-up 5–10 years later allowed 16 survivors to be traced and 15 were available for re-examination. The majority of those who had died had shown clear evidence of dementia prior to death, but among the survivors there was no suggestion of progressive organic disease. Most were still under outpatient psychiatric supervision, but half were leading an active social life and many of them were working. Others were functioning at a reduced social level which appeared to be static, with a good deal of depression or anxiety and sometimes with complaints of subjective memory impairment. Seven had originally presented with depression, 6 with epilepsy, 2 with paranoid states and 1 with suspected dementia, but in all there had been sufficient clinical indication of brain damage at the time to warrant air encephalography. Detailed comparisons of the radiographic finding in those who had demented and those who had not, surprisingly showed no difference in the amount of air over the cortical surface. Significant differences emerged, however, in ventricular measurements which were increased in those who deteriorated later.

CT scan studies obviously stand to clarify this situation further. The readiness with which large samples of patients can be examined without risk of discomfort, and the facility with which the scan can be repeated after an interval of time, should allow us to gain increasing understanding of the significance of cerebral atrophy in various psychiatric settings.

NUCLEAR MAGNETIC RESONANCE ('NMR Scan' 'MRI Scan')

Nuclear magnetic reasonance is a still more recent technique used for non-invasive imaging of the brain. It is clearly a method which complements, and could ultimately come to compete with, CT scanning as a neurodiagnostic procedure, though limited availibility and the high costs involved restrict its present application. Unlike CT scanning it involves no X-irradiation, but makes use of the magnetic properties of nuclei and their capacity to be excited by radiofrequency pulses. Reviews of the procedure and its clinical applications are to be found in Moore and Holland (1980), Doyle *et al.* (1981), Bydder and Steiner (1982), Young *et al.* (1982), Anderson (1982) and Henderson (1983).

At present all medical NMR imaging utilises the hydrogen nuclei of the tissues. In essence these are made to 'resonate' in response to rapidly changing magnetic fields around them, and the signals they emit are then processed to yield a visual image based on their distribution and physico-chemical state.

The patient is placed in a static magnetic field which produces a net alignment of the magnetic moments of the hydrogen nuclei in the tissues. Under such circumstances the nuclei 'precess' in a circular course about this axis, much as a spinning top will wobble. Brief bursts of radio-frequency pulses, applied at the appropriate frequency from a surrounding coil, augment the precession, and when the excitation pulse ends the nuclei return to their lower energy state. The electrical signals emitted from the tissues in the course of these energy changes can be detected and analysed by computer to reveal the distribution of the hydrogen nuclei involved. Techniques are used to 'scan' the tissues systematically, yielding visual images much as in the CT scan.

A variety of scanning 'sequences' can be selected according to the fundamental parameters chiefly utilised in image reconstruction. 'Repeated free induction decay' (RFID) produces images that reflect changes in proton density; 'inversion-recovery' (IR) and 'spin-echo' (SE) sequences are strongly dependent on variations in 'spin-lattice relaxation time' (T1) and 'spin-spin relaxation time' (T2) respectively. These different scanning sequences are each suited to different purposes in visual imaging.

An outstanding feature of NMR is the high level of soft tissue contrast obtained by scanning in the IR sequence. Grey and white matter are strongly differentiated, yielding fine anatomical detail. The cortical grey matter is shown clearly and the thalami and basal ganglia are demarcated from the surrounding white matter and ventricular system. Saggital scans show the corpus callosum, the columns of the fornix and the brain stem. In the posterior fossa the substantia nigra and the middle cerebral peduncles can be discerned. Cerebral and cerebellar atrophy are of course well displayed. IR sequences also show infarcts, and can reveal plaques of multiple sclerosis in a manner superior to CT scanning (p. 592). Spin-echo (SE) sequences, by contrast, produce little grey-white differentiation, but have proved to be a sensitive indicator of pathological change (Bailes *et al.*, 1982). Infarctions, haemorrhages and tumours are well displayed, likewise tissue changes in cerebral oedema and encephalitis. Repeated free induction decay (RFID) is of less value in routine diagnosis but has the special advantage of revealing blood flow and thus outlining major vessels.

NMR scanning holds promise of several advantages over computerised axial tomography. Improved detection of small demyelinating lesions is coupled with excellent visualisation of the posterior fossa and pituitary regions, since there is little or no bone artifact to intrude on the images obtained. The various scanning sequences available give versatility of choice; and the slices to be viewed are readily switched from transverse to coronal or saggital planes without disturbing or moving the patient. The images produced, moreover, reflect the physiological state of the tissues as well as giving anatomical information. It is here that NMR scanning may find the most valuable applications of all.

For visual scanning the strong natural resonance of the hydrogen nuclei has been principally used to date. Hydrogen nuclei are abundant in tissues, and the distribution of water and other small hydrogen-rich molecules (e.g. lipids) are known to be altered in many disease states. But the technique is open to the study of other elements as well by the proper choice of frequency in the resonating coil. Phosphorus (^{31}P) scanning, for example, yields strong NMR signals from a number of compounds, and the frequency of resonance is qualified by the compound it is in (Pykett, 1982; Shulman, 1983; Bottomley *et al.*, 1983). Since phosphorus is a major constituent of molecules such as adenosine triphosphate and phosphocreatine, which mediate energy transfer in the cell, NMR spectroscopy can give close indications of the metabolic status and health of tissues. Similarly glucose labelled with carbon–13 can be administered; appropriate NMR spectra are then used to follow steps along the glycolytic pathway, to give information about triglyceride levels and glycogen deposition and mobilisation. The use of NMR to study metabolic processes in this manner requires more powerful magnetic fields and remains at present a research technique.

No hazards have emerged to date from NMR. Budinger (1981) reviews the evidence concerning safe levels for the static and changing magnetic fields, the principal risk being induced heating in large metal objects such as skull prostheses. There is a theoretical risk of producing cardiac fibrillation or cerebral dysrhythmia from the currents induced by the rapid field changes, and on this account persons with heart disease, epilepsy or pregnancy must be excluded in volunteer procedures.

POSITRON EMISSION TOMOGRAPHY
('PET Scan', 'ECAT Scan')

Positron emission tomography represents the most complex and ambitious method of brain imaging to date. It is restricted to special centres, since a cyclotron must be close at hand for the manufacture of the short-lived isotopes involved. In essence the PET scan produces a cross-sectional image of brain radioactivity after the injection of a suitably labelled compound, yielding information about the site and rate of dynamic processes such as cerebral blood flow and metabolism. The great virtue of the technique is the promise it holds for revealing aspects of regional brain metabolism which would not otherwise be accessible to study.

The principles involved are outlined by Oldendorf (1980). Compounds labelled with short-lived isotopes, for example fluorine-18, oxygen-15, nitrogen-13 or carbon-11, are injected or inhaled and allowed to reach a steady state in the tissues. The excess of protons over neutrons in such isotopes confers instability, leading to the emission of positrons (positively charged electrons). With the discharge of a positron one of the protons in the nucleus becomes a neutron and stability is achieved again.

An emitted positron has a range of only a few millimetres in the tissues before it encounters an ordinary electron and the two then annihilate each other. Their mass is converted into two gamma rays, which originate simultaneously and propagate in almost precisely opposite directions. This allows their point of origin to be determined by suitably placed detectors, and this point of origin will be very close to the point where the positron was released. Hence paired detectors arranged around the head can be used to compute the distribution of the isotope with a fair degree of accuracy. Algorithms similar to those used in CT scanning can yield a visual image of its location within the brain. With appropriate calibration the absolute tissue concentrations of the labelled tracers can be determined. And by using a stereotaxic head holder it is possible, when required, to collect both CT and PET scan data, allowing accurate integration of structural and functional information.

The isotopes mostly used to date are oxygen-15 and fluorine-18. Oxygen-15 is inhaled and the arterial blood sampled, to yield quantitative measurements of regional cerebral blood flow and regional cerebral oxygen utilisation (Frackowiak et al., 1980). By such a technique Frackowiak et al. (1981) have demonstrated lowered blood flow and oxygen utilisation in both grey and white matter in demented patients compared with age-matched controls, the degree of lowering showing a significant relationship to the severity of the dementia. In patients with primary degenerative dementia (presumed Alzheimer's disease) the reductions were most marked in parietal and temporal regions in the earlier stages, with profound frontal losses appearing in the severely demented group.

Fluorine-18 is incorporated into 2-deoxy-D-glucose (^{18}FDG) which is injected to measure local glucose metabolic rates (Phelps et al., 1979). The compound enters the brain as though it were glucose, but cannot be degraded and remains trapped within the cells for several hours. Estimates of regional glucose utilisation can therefore be made by repeated venous sampling in conjunction with the scan. Using such a technique it has been possible to demonstrate severely impaired cerebral glucose utilisation in Alzheimer's disease in proportion to the severity of dementia, maximal in the frontal and parietal areas but also evident in the subcortical nuclear masses (Benson, 1982a; Benson et al., 1982). Other areas, such as the calcarine cortex and the motor and sensory strips are relatively spared, in keeping with the lack of visual impairment or focal neurological signs in the disorder. Patients with multi-infarct dementia also show global reductions in cerebral glucose utilisation, but unlike the situation in Alzheimer's disease the areas of hypometabolism tend to be focal and asymmetrical (Benson et al., 1983).

In Huntington's chorea marked hypometabolism has been shown in the caudate and putamen, appearing early and preceeding obvious tissue loss (Kuhl et al., 1982). By contrast, values were normal in other brain regions despite the presence of severe disability and CT scan evidence of atrophy. Caudate hypometabolism was also observed in occasional subjects at risk of Huntington's chorea, even though they were asymptomatic. Relative preservation of cortical metabolic rates has also been reported in normal pressure hydrocephalus and Wilson's disease (Benson et al., 1982). A patient with Creutzfeldt–Jakob disease showed a totally different picture, with mottled areas of hypo- and hypermetabolism scattered throughout cortical and subcortical regions.

These examples illustrate the potentials of the technique. Intriguing observations have also been made in small groups of patients with 'functional' psychiatric disorder, for example in schizophrenia where frontal metabolism has appeared to be depressed and readings have been found to be lower over the central grey matter of the left but not the right side of the brain (Buchsbaum *et al.*, 1982).

Special promise attaches to further possibilities of examining the brain in the resting state and during responses to defined tasks. Other molecules can be labelled, such as aminoacids, fatty acids, sugars and drugs, similarly compounds with high affinity for specific receptor sites. A considerable variety of active metabolic processes should thus become accessible to study, including protein synthesis and the correlates of response to drugs. Accurate mapping of receptor sites could yield particularly valuable information.

Chapter 4. Differential Diagnosis

The correct appraisal of patients with organic psychiatric disorders is a test both of psychiatric and general medical skills. The detailed differential diagnosis of individual conditions will be considered in the appropriate sections elsewhere, but here certain general principles will be outlined.

Of first importance is the ability to distinguish between 'organic' and 'functional' psychiatric illness, in other words to recognise when organic brain disorder is the root cause of the presenting clinical picture. The nature of the cerebral disorder must then be determined by a process of enquiry which proceeds logically in accordance with reasonable expectations. A distinction between acute and chronic organic reactions is often helpful in deciding on probabilities, likewise the distinction between diffuse or focal cerebral disorder. Thereafter the range of possible causes remains wide, and will also be briefly discussed below.

Differentiation from Non-organic Conditions

There can be little difficulty in deciding on an organic aetiology when impairment of consciousness or of cognitive processes is marked, when there are epileptic fits, or when psychiatric symptoms are accompanied by obvious neurological symptoms and signs. But this is not always the case. Some organic disorders can present with hallucinations, affective change or schizophrenia-like symptomatology and lack clear organic accompaniments throughout their course. Others unfold very gradually, with indefinite organic features and with symptomatology suggestive of virtually any form of functional psychiatric illness. Special predisposition to neurotic forms of reaction, or to psychotic illness, may confer distinctive features which for some time obscure the true situation.

The converse is also true, since patients with functional illness may show features which raise the possibility of organic cerebral disturbance when this does not exist. For example, disorientation and minor impairment of consciousness may be detected at the onset of acute schizophrenia, also sometimes in mania and agitated depression, yet without evidence of brain damage either at the time or subsequently. Similarly, cognitive impairment, including marked difficulty with recent memory, may accompany purely affective disorders particularly in later life, as discussed on p. 410. Features resembling delirium, including characteristic disturbances of thought processes and even hallucinations, can follow psychological stress, as in sensory deprivation (Zuckerman, 1964) or sleep deprivation (Morris and Singer, 1966).

The line of demarcation between functional and organic psychiatric disorders is therefore not hard and fast. It remains valid and useful in practice for the great majority of cases, but in a substantial number there can be continuing uncertainty. The margin for error is reduced when special investigations are undertaken, but even so is not removed completely. The electroencephalogram can yield equivocal results. Psychometric testing can occasionally be misleading. Radiographic procedures may reveal cerebral atrophy of uncertain significance. Clinical examination therefore remains of the first importance, and is in any case the chief guideline which determines whether or not special investigations should be undertaken.

Neurotic disorder may be simulated in the early stages of organic cerebral disease by virtue of diffuse complaints of anxiety, depression, irritability and insomnia. The patient may himself complain of forgetfulness and difficulty in concentration, but these tend to be discounted because of the multitude of other vague somatic symptoms. Phobic and obsessional symptomatology is not uncommon at the onset of organic brain disorder, and may remain a prominent feature for some considerable time. It is axiomatic to be wary of neurotic developments beginning only in middle life and when the previous mental constitution was good, also to seek for clear evidence of adequate immediate causes for their appearance.

Sometimes the clue may lie in the patient's attitude towards his symptoms. The organic patient will often tend to play down his defects so that a graver picture is obtained from relatives than from the patient himself. The neurotic patient, by contrast, presses home his symptoms and actively seeks a remedy for them. The patient's evasiveness may raise suspicion, or when pressed he may display abrupt 'catastrophic' reactions of distress or anger. Typically also the organic patient's symptomatology lacks the richness and diversity seen in purely neurotic disorders.

Hysterical forms of reaction may also be simulated. Acute organic reactions tend to fluctuate with periods of lucidity, and symptoms may thus be fleeting. A shallow affective quality and a tendency to make light of symptoms may suggest the 'belle indifference' of hysteria. In mild delirium the cardinal feature of impaired consciousness may sometimes be hard to determine, and behaviour may be seemingly motivated for display. Thus it may be necessary to watch closely for signs of perseveration, slight dysarthria and other minimal features which betray the organic basis of the disorder.

Episodes of bizarre behaviour in hypoglycaemic attacks, or of paralysis in porphyria, provide well-known diagnostic hazards in which hysteria comes to be suspected. Similar difficulty is sometimes found with periods of long-continued abnormal behaviour following encephalitis. Frank conversion symptoms may, of course, occur with chronic brain disease and be mistaken for the primary disorder. It is not known how far these reflect in some way the direct effects of cerebral damage, or how far they merely represent a psychogenic response to the patient's partial awareness of his defects. Again it is axiomatic to view with grave suspicion hysterical symptoms which make their first appearance only in middle life. The problem of the differential diagnosis of hysterical pseudodementia is discussed on page 407.

Schizophrenic symptoms in association with cerebral disease can readily be misleading. A preponderance of visual over auditory hallucinations should always raise suspicion of organic cerebral disorder, similarly an empty or shallow affective colouring to delusional beliefs and passivity phenomena. Delusions in both acute and chronic organic reactions may take any form which is seen in schizophrenia, but paranoid delusions are by far the most common. Certain qualities of the delusions strongly suggest an organic basis, namely those which are vague, poorly systematised, incoherent, fleeting and changeable, or restricted and stereotyped in content. Nevertheless schizophrenic illnesses which are typical in every respect occasionally prove ultimately to be founded on organic cerebral disease.

Depressive symptoms can also give rise to difficulty. Ordinary affective disorder can be associated with marked slowness of thinking, difficulty with concentration and uncertainty of memory. There may be considerable doubt about the correct evaluation of such features, and psychometric testing may give equivocal results. The difficulties are of course increased when electroconvulsive therapy has already been given.

Features which may help in distinguishing primary depressive illness from organic psychiatric disorder include the careful appraisal of the setting in which disturbances of concentration and memory occur. In depressive illness it can often be observed that lack of interest or excessive anxiety prevent the focusing of attention on the matter in hand, rather than any pervasive difficulty with the organisation of thought and memory. Preoccupation with morbid thoughts may be seen to operate similarly. Typically the patient with uncomplicated depression is able to give a more coherent account of his discomforts and a more accurate chronology of his illness than would be possible in the presence of organic cerebral disease.

These important problems of differential diagnosis are considered more fully in the section on depressive pseudodementia (p. 410).

Differentiation Between Acute and Chronic Organic Reactions

In practice this distinction is most directly made from the history of the mode of onset of the disorder. A short history and firm knowledge of an acute onset virtually excludes a chronic organic reaction. Onset in association with a physical illness rather strongly suggests an acute organic reaction. But when such leads are lacking close attention to phenomenology may be necessary.

Acute organic reactions are characterised by impairment of consciousness in some degree, as revealed by careful observation of the patient's alertness, wakefulness, and ability to focus and sustain attention. In chronic organic reactions, by contrast, the patient is fully in touch, and attempts to co-operate despite cognitive difficulties. Fluctuation from time to time is also an observation of importance in pointing to acute disorders. There is often nocturnal worsening, or a picture which changes rapidly from one occasion to another. When stimulated he may become lucid for a while, and one can then determine that the intellect is basically intact.

Moreover during lucid periods he may demonstrate adequate recall of events immediately preceding the development of the illness, confirming that until very recently mental functioning had been intact.

Acute rather than chronic cerebral disorder is suggested when there are severe perceptual disturbances and distortions, with prominent illusions and hallucinations in the visual modality. Defective appreciation of reality may lead to rich and intrusive fantasies, in contrast to the emptiness and impoverishment of thought characteristic of chronic organic reactions. Similarly when there is florid behaviour disturbance this will be seen to be dictated by disturbed thought processes of a more sophisticated kind in acute than in chronic cerebral disorder. Roth and Myers (1969) describe this difference well: 'Psychic life in clouding is full, sometimes extravagantly so, but distorted : the patient lives in a private world of shifting experiences richly supplied with detail from the resources of a brain which is essentially intact. . . . His statements about his experiences and misconstrued orientations are positive and sometimes detailed. In dementia, by contrast, the patient lives in the actual world but does so deficiently. His disorientation results from ignorance, and when asked about his experiences, he is likely querulously to dismiss the question as unimportant, or proffer feeble inventions or readily accept suggestions, however absurd.'

The affective state of the patient may also help with the distinction. In acute organic reactions the emotional disturbances are typically of a positive kind—fear or terror, perplexity and agitation— whereas the demented patient may be flat, apathetic and emotionally unresponsive (Roth, 1981). Emotional rapport can usually be established in patients showing clouding of consciousness but tends to be poor in dementia.

This said, however, it must be recognised that in practice the differentiation between acute and chronic organic reactions can sometimes be very difficult. Despite careful observation the distinction may come to be revealed only by the time course which is followed. For example, a prolonged subacute delirious state due to anoxia, uraemia or hepatic disorder can simulate dementia very closely. Or the patient may be admitted to hospital without a history to point to the acute and recent onset of such disorders. Perhaps most difficulty is encountered with elderly patients who show post-operative disturbances, due to metabolic derangements or anoxia, and in whom the mental state was incompletely evaluated beforehand. The electroencephalogram may provide some guidance in such examples (p. 113).

Acute disturbance of cerebral function may, of course, give way gradually to irreversible structural pathology with a corresponding admixture of features appropriate to both. The two may also coexist when a chronic dementing process is complicated by superadded anoxia, metabolic upset, or some other concurrent disease, or when fresh progressions occur in arteriosclerotic dementia. Not uncommonly it is such a transient phase of acute disorder which first draws attention to chronic brain disease which has hitherto gone unrecognised.

Differentiation Between Diffuse and Focal Lesions

Symptoms and signs of localising significance must be carefully sought out in all organic psychiatric disorders, and when discovered they must never be ignored. Local disturbances do, of course, occur with progressive cortical destruction before it is sufficiently extensive to give rise to dementia; well-known examples are a circumscribed amnesic syndrome in the early stages of Alzheimer's disease, or a frontal lobe syndrome in Pick's disease. Evidence of focal brain damage may also emerge later in the course of these disorders when the pathological changes become especially advanced in certain regions of the brain. Signs of focal damage must therefore be carefully assessed in relation to the clinical picture as a whole, but will usually dictate that further investigations should be undertaken. The important problem is to distinguish the essentially focal lesion from diffuse brain damage, because a remediable cause may then come to light.

Neurological signs are of first importance in this connection. Every attempt must be made to exclude the possibility of raised intracranial pressure, and to examine for cranial nerve palsies, visual field defects or unilateral motor and sensory disturbances. Physical signs in the presenile and senile dementias are rarely strictly unilateral or even markedly asymmetrical, and dense motor and sensory disturbances are strongly suggestive of cerebral tumour, cerebrovascular disease or cerebral syphilis. Unilateral anosmia or optic atrophy are important signs which may betray a frontal tumour. Finally the neurological examination should always be supplemented by careful enquiry and observation for epileptic disturbances of focal origin.

Psychological symptoms of possible localising value include amnesia out of proportion to other cognitive defects, dysphasia, somnolence, and the several aspects of parietal lobe symptomatology which have been discussed. It is necessary to beware especially of an amnesic syndrome which masquerades as generalised dementia. The relative preservation of other cognitive functions must be carefully assessed, and due attention paid to any marked discrepancy between memory for remote and recent events or the presence of a circumscribed retrograde gap. Although the patient with Korsakoff psychosis is anergic and apathetic, he shows a better backing of intellect in general conversation than the patient with dementia. In the latter it often proves difficult to determine the relative contributions of impaired memory and impairment of other cognitive functions to the total disability.

Mild dysphasia due to focal cerebral disease may also be mistaken for early dementia, when the patient's account is hesitant and incoherent, or when he is anxious and depressed as a result of his disability. Careful observation usually shows, however, that behaviour not involving language remains substantially intact. Dysphasic difficulties, and especially nominal dysphasia, may be seen with diffuse cerebral disorder, but then insight into the defect is less likely to be well preserved. Indeed the demented patient is often oblivious of or unconcerned by his disability, and complacent in the face of errors rather than distressed and struggling. The greatest difficulty in differentiation is therefore likely to arise with primary sensory or conduction dysphasia (pp. 44 and 46). A clinical point which is said to be helpful in the distinction is that dysphasic patients with focal lesions have as much difficulty in naming objects from sight as in recalling names from memory, whereas patients with diffuse brain disease perform better when the object can be seen or handled.

Agnosic and apraxic defects, disturbances of the body image and of spatial orientation, likewise raise suspicion of focal cerebral disorder when severe and out of all proportion to other cognitive difficulties. Such defects are, however, relatively common in acute organic reactions when consciousness is impaired to a significant extent, and when chronic diffuse brain disease has progressed beyond the early stages.

Special investigatory procedures, as outlined in Chapter 3 are, of course, the most reliable arbiters in the distinction between focal and diffuse brain damage, and will often need to be undertaken before a firm differential diagnosis is achieved.

The Causes of Acute and Chronic Organic Reactions
The specific cause in the majority of cases will readily become apparent in the course of history taking and examination. In many it is self-evident from the outset. Sometimes, however, the cause may be elusive and it is then essential to consider systematically a wide range of possibilities. These are shown in Tables 3 and 4 on p. 130.

It is helpful in approaching a given case to consider, first the possible causes arising within the central nervous system itself, then the derangements of cerebral function consequent upon disorders in other systems of the body. This division is reflected approximately in the ordering of causes in Tables 3 and 4. Even some of the very rare conditions are remediable, and enquiry must therefore be extensive when the solution is not soon forthcoming.

The antecedent history will give important clues, and it is essential that a relative or close acquaintance should be seen. The time and mode of onset must always be carefully established. The presenile and senile dementias usually begin insidiously and their history commonly extends over several months, whereas remediable illnesses often have an abrupt and relatively recent onset. Careful enquiry should always be made for a history of head injury, fits, alcoholism, drug abuse, recent illness or anaesthesia. Even in the absence of known head injury the possibility of subdural haematoma should be kept in mind, since this may follow trivial injury in arteriosclerotic subjects or be forgotten in alcoholics. It may be followed by a latent interval, and be accompanied by minimal neurological signs. A known epileptic tendency may suggest that the present disturbance is an unusually prolonged psychomotor seizure or post-ictal state. Fits of recent onset may indicate a space occupying lesion, or some acute cerebrovascular accident or injury which has left a residual focus of brain damage. A history of alcoholism or drug abuse may be long concealed in some cases, even on occasion by relatives as well as by the patient. Suspicion may only be raised by indirect evidence from the patient's attitudes to enquiry or unwillingness for hospitalisation. A history of repeated episodes over a considerable period of time may strongly suggest that drug abuse is responsible.

Apart from self-administered drugs it is always important to enquire about medication recently prescribed. This may have contributed by way of toxic effects, idiosyncratic reactions, or the lowering of blood pressure. Diuretics given injudiciously or without proper supervision may have led to electrolyte depletion. If the patient is a known diabetic, enquiry must be made about previous hypoglycaemic reactions, the current dose of insulin, and

TABLE 3. Causes of acute organic reactions

1. *Degenerative*	Presenile or senile dementias complicated by infection, anoxia, etc.
2. *Space Occupying Lesions*	Cerebral tumour, subdural haematoma, cerebral abscess.
3. *Trauma*	'Acute post-traumatic psychosis'.
4. *Infection*	Encephalitis, meningitis, subacute meningovascular syphilis. Exanthemata, streptococcal infection, septicaemia, pneumonia, influenza, typhoid, typhus, cerebral malaria, trypanosomiasis, rheumatic chorea.
5. *Vascular*	Acute cerebral thrombosis or embolism, episode in arteriosclerotic dementia, transient cerebral ischaemic attack, subarachnoid haemorrhage, hypertensive encephalopathy, systemic lupus erythematosus.
6. *Epileptic*	Psychomotor seizures, petit mal status, post-ictal states.
7. *Metabolic*	Uraemia, liver disorder, electrolyte disturbances, alkalosis, acidosis, hypercapnia, remote effects of carcinoma, porphyria.
8. *Endocrine*	Hyperthyroid crises, myxoedema, Addisonian crises, hypopituitrism, hypo- and hyperparathyroidism, diabetic pre-coma, hypoglycaemia.
9. *Toxic*	Alcohol—Wernicke's encephalopathy, delirium tremens Drugs—barbiturates and other sedatives (including withdrawal), salicylate intoxication, cannabis, LSD, prescribed medications (antiparkinsonian drugs, scopolamine, tricyclic and MAOI antidepressants, etc.) Others—lead, arsenic, organic mercury compounds, carbon disulphide.
10. *Anoxia*	Bronchopneumonia, congestive cardiac failure, cardiac dysrhythmias, silent coronary infarction, silent bleeding, carbon monoxide poisoning, post-anaesthetic.
11. *Vitamin Lack*	Thiamine (Wernicke's encephalopathy), nicotinic acid (pellagra, acute nicotinic acid deficiency encephalopathy), B_{12} and folic acid deficiency.

adherence to any diet that has been prescribed.

A history of recent illness and operation should be noted, also the quality of recovery from anaesthesia if this has been recently given. In considering anoxia it may on occasion be necessary to enquire specifically for a history of coal gas poisoning in the recent past. A family history of illness such as Huntington's chorea will be noted. A history of previous transient episodes of dysphasia, paralysis, or other neurological defect will be suggestive of cerebral arteriosclerosis.

In patients with acute organic reactions it is important still to enquire for an antecedent history of failing memory or intellect over some period of

TABLE 4. Causes of chronic organic reactions

1. *Degenerative*	Senile and presenile Alzheimer's disease, arteriosclerotic dementia, Pick's, Huntington's, Creutsfeldt-Jakob, normal pressure hydrocephalus, multiple sclerosis, Parkinson's disease, Schilder's, Wilson's, progressive supranuclear palsy, progressive multifocal leucoencephalopathy, progressive myoclonic epilepsy.
2. *Space Occupying Lesions*	Cerebral tumour, subdural haematoma.
3. *Trauma*	Post-traumatic dementia.
4. *Infection*	General paresis, chronic meningo-vascular syphilis, sub-acute and chronic encephalitis.
5. *Vascular*	Cerebral vascular disease, 'état lacunaire'.
6. *Epileptic*	'Epileptic dementia'.
7. *Metabolic*	Uraemia, liver disorder, remote effects of carcinoma.
8. *Endocrine*	Myxoedema, Addison's disease, hypopituitarism, hypo- and hyperparathyroidism, hypoglycaemia.
9. *Toxic*	'Alcoholic dementia' and Korsakoff psychosis, chronic barbiturate intoxication, manganese, carbon disulphide.
10. *Anoxia*	Anaemia, congestive cardiac failure, chronic pulmonary disease, post anaesthetic, post carbon-monoxide poisoning, post-cardiac arrest.
11. *Vitamin Lack*	Lack of thiamine, nicotinic acid, B_{12}, folic acid.

time, since an incipient chronic dementia may be being aggravated by intercurrent disease. The adequacy of diet should be assessed in elderly patients, especially when living alone, or in patients of low intelligence and low economic means. Vitamin depletion is, indeed, not excluded in patients suffering from one of the primary presenile or senile dementing illnesses, and may be aggravating the degree of disability. Finally in the more immediate history, specific enquiry should always be made for headache, vomiting, or visual disturbance indicative of raised intracranial pressure, and in elderly patients for breathlessness, ankle swelling or sub-sternal pain which may indicate recent cardiac decompensation.

On examination one must pay attention to any appearance of physical ill-health which may betoken metabolic disorder, carcinoma or an infective process. The general appearance of the patient may indicate anaemia, either hypochromic or pernicious, or an endocrine disorder such as myxoedema which is otherwise easily missed. Dehydration suggests uraemia or diabetic pre-coma. Muscular twitching suggests uraemia, electrolyte disturbance or hypoglycaemia. There may be skin lesions diagnostic of exanthemata or indicative of vitamin deficiency. It may be necessary to search closely, by four-hourly temperature recording, for evidence of low-grade intermittent pyrexia indicating, for example, encephalitis or cerebral abscess. Finally, very careful general observation may sometimes reveal the choreiform movements diagnostic of early Huntington's chorea.

Examination of the central nervous system must pay scrupulous attention to the optic fundi for signs of raised intracranial pressure, to abnormalities of pupil size or reactions indicative of syphilis, or nystagmus which may suggest drug intoxication. Transient disorders of external ocular movement may be the essential sign for confirming a diagnosis of Wernicke's encephalopathy. Evidence of focal neurological defects in motor or sensory systems (including unsuspected visual field defects) will suggest a space occupying lesion or cerebrovascular disease. Neck stiffness may indicate subarachnoid haemorrhage or meningitis, and evidence of recent ear infection will raise the possibility of cerebral abscess.

Signs of arteriosclerosis should be noted both at the periphery and in the optic fundi. The patency of the carotid arteries should be tested by palpation and auscultation in the neck. Hypertension must be assessed, likewise evidence of cardiac failure, heart block or recent coronary infarction. Respiratory

infection or inadequacy must also be noted as possible causes of cerebral anoxia. Even in the absence of hepatic or splenic enlargement it may be necessary to examine for liver flap, spider naevi, or foetor hepaticus. Prostatic enlargement should be investigated as a possible cause of renal embarrassment. Carcinoma with secondary cerebral deposits, or secondary 'remote' effects upon the central nervous system, may need to be excluded by palpation of breasts, neck, axillae, and rectal and vaginal examinations. Chest X-ray will be obligatory for exclusion of carcinoma of the lung.

Particular features in the mental state will only rarely help in the differential diagnosis of causes. The ceaseless over-activity of delirium tremens may sometimes be virtually diagnostic of this disorder, when coupled with evidence of marked autonomic disturbance and vivid visual and tactile hallucinations. In general hallucinations appear to be commoner in acute organic reactions due to drugs or metabolic derangements than after trauma or anoxia. The myxoedematous patient is typically dull, sluggish and underactive, likewise the patient with uraemia who will probably also be somnolent. Episodes of euphoria and foolish jocularity may suggest hepatic disorder, while expansiveness is still sometimes seen with general paresis.

Investigations in every case should include haematology, ESR, serological tests for syphilis, urine examination and chest X-ray, no matter what may appear to be the cause. The EEG should also be carried out as a routine whenever this is feasible. Skull X-ray may be required and a CT scan will often be undertaken. It may be necessary to proceed with estimation of blood urea, serum electrolytes and proteins, liver function tests, serum thyroxine, estimation of blood sugar and further tests for hypoglycaemia, serum B_{12} and folate, or urinary examination for drugs or evidence of porphyria. An ECG may be indicated if a silent coronary infarction or Stokes-Adams attacks are suspected. Lumbar puncture will sometimes be required when the diagnosis remains in doubt, and in particular to confirm suspicions of intracerebral infection. Further investigations such as a radioisotope scan, angiography or even air encephalography will sometimes be indicated, though CT scanning has greatly reduced the need for these.

The Causes of Stupor

Finally mention may be made of the differential diagnosis of stupor. The causes of stupor may be

TABLE 5. Causes of stupor (from Joyston-Bechal, 1966)

All causes		Organic causes	
Schizophrenia		Presenile or senile dementia	7
Depressive illness	25	'Confusional state'	4
Organic disease	20	Cerebral tumour or cyst	3
Neurosis and hysteria	10	Neurosyphilis	3
Uncertain	14	Post-encephalitic disturbance	2
	—	Post-epileptic	1
Total	100		—
		Total	20

organic or non-organic, and the differential diagnosis must embrace schizophrenia, depression and hysteria in addition to organic brain dysfunction.

Joyston-Bechal (1966) examined the records of one hundred cases of stupor diagnosed at the Bethlem Royal and Maudsley Hospitals in order to obtain an indication of the frequency of different causes. The results are shown in Table 5.

In this setting organic causes are seen to have been relatively uncommon. The essential features of the stupor were closely similar in the organic and non-organic cases, but in the majority a firm diagnosis could ultimately be made. The 14 cases where the cause remained uncertain had, however, led to great diagnostic difficulty. Sometimes the true situation was unclear at the time of the patient's presentation, but was revealed in retrospect when the stupor had resolved.

Knowledge of the antecedent psychiatric history is often invaluable in suggesting the cause, and a careful neurological examination is always essential with special attention to signs which may indicate a diencephalic or upper brain stem lesion (p. 92). Stupors due to functional psychiatric illness are more likely to show some partial preservation of ability to help with feeding or eliminative functions, though this is by no means invariable. The facial expression and posture is also more likely to be meaningful or show some emotional reaction to what is said or done. On recovery, patients with functional stupors often prove to have retained awareness of what transpired during the episode, whereas in organic stupor the level of awareness as well as the level of responsiveness is usually grossly diminished.

Schizophrenic stupor is essentially a catatonic phenomenon, and is usually seen along with other catatonic features such as negativism, echopraxia, posturing or flexibilitas cerea. The patient's position is often fixed and bizarre, and may have symbolic meaning in connection with his delusions. When disturbed the special posture is often resumed. The facial expression may be secretive, withdrawn, or meaningful, and may betray attention to hallucinatory experiences. Some schizophrenic stupors appear to represent withdrawal into a world of delusional fantasies, whereas in others it seems that nothing at all is experienced by the patient. The latter may represent a prolongation in severe form of schizophrenic blocking of thought and of willed action.

Depressive stupor may occasionally be just as profound as the above, and the differentiation can be difficult if the antecedent psychiatric history is unknown. Usually it can be seen to develop out of severe psychomotor retardation, which increases until there is universal motor inhibition. The posture and expression are sometimes indicative of sadness and hopelessness, and silent tears may be shed. Sometimes however the expression is totally apathetic and vacant. Conscious awareness is usually fully retained and the patient can later relate most of what was said and done to him.

Manic stupor is much less common. The expression is of elation or ecstasy, and the patient later reports that his mind was filled with teeming ideas to such an extent that he was unable to react to anything around him.

Hysterical and psychogenic stupors usually occur in a situation of stress, and manifest superficial motives can often be discerned. Signs of conversion hysteria are commonly in evidence. The condition is more likely than others to wax and wane, and there may be a marked emotional reaction when sensitive subjects are discussed. Completely passive dependence on others for feeding and toilet functions is rare, and the patient may show signs of irritability and annoyance when moved against his wishes.

Organic stupor has many causes, the most urgent of which is raised intracranial pressure producing a medullary or midbrain pressure cone. Focal pathologies in the region of the posterior diencephalon or upper midbrain include tumours (especially craniopharyngiomas), infarctions, meningitis (especially tuberculous meningitis), neurosyphilis, and formerly encephalitis lethargica. Senile or presenile dementias may lead to stupor late in their course. Epileptic equivalents may take this form, or alternatively stupor may follow briefly in the wake of an epileptic seizure.

When a brain lesion is responsible for stupor the site will commonly lie in the upper brain stem or mesencephalon. Sometimes, however, stupor is due to involvement of the anteromedial frontal lobes and adjacent septal area (Segarra, 1970). With stupors of brain stem origin the patient tends to be apathetic and somnolent most of the time and will frequently show pareses of external occular movement. Patients with frontal stupor are more likely to appear alert, ready to be roused, and with seeming vigilant gaze ('hyperpathic akinetic mutism').

Extracerebral causes which must be considered include a number of the conditions listed in Table 3. Pictures typical of stupor may occasionally be seen with uraemia, hypoglycaemia or liver disorder, or post-operatively with electrolyte disturbance or water intoxication. Endocrine disorders include myxoedema, Cushing's disease, Addison's disease, hypopituitarism and hyperparathyroidism. Stupor may also be seen with severe alcoholic intoxication, barbiturate intoxication, nicotinic acid deficiency encephalopathy, or terminally with certain infections such as typhus fever. It is important to remember that stupor can occasionally emerge as an adverse reaction to psychotropic medication; in Johnson's (1982) series of 25 cases, two were due to intoxication with lithium and one to excessive medication with flupenthixol.

Fortunately, with the great majority of organic causes, there will be evidence of neurological dysfunction or systemic disturbance. In equivocal cases the electroencephalogram will often be helpful in deciding between a functional or an organic aetiology. When psychogenic causes are suspected, an interview under sodium amytal may confirm the situation, while in schizophrenic and depressive stupors the response to electroconvulsive therapy can be dramatic.

In Joyston-Bechal's (1966) series almost half of the cases resolved within a week, and only one-fifth lasted more than a month. The 6 patients who remained in stupor for more than 6 months were all severely brain damaged.

Part 2
SPECIFIC DISORDERS

Chapter 5. Head Injury

The size of the problem presented by head injuries to medical services and to the economy of the country generally is immense. In the UK some 100,000 patients with head injuries are admitted to hospital yearly, and as many again are estimated to receive out-patient care for minor injuries (Lewin, 1966). Between 1955 and 1963 there was a 50% increase, mostly due to road traffic accidents (*British Medical Journal*, 1968a), and this trend is probably still continuing. Moreover, more than half of the hospital admissions are of persons under the age of 20 (Field, 1976). London (1967) calculated that head injuries produced 1,000 severely disabled people every year, of whom approximately half would never work again. Lewin (1968) estimated that 1,200 people per year were so handicapped that they would have to work at a simpler level or require special care. In the USA the problem is worse. In 1967 three-quarters of a million people suffered head injuries, of whom 18,000 died, 13,000 sustained permanent disability, and 7,000 temporary disabilities. The cost to the community was estimated at two billion dollars (Irving, 1969). The toll taken among the young is particularly disturbing.

Early mortality has been considerably improved as a result of advances in the management of the early acute stages. The chronic sequelae remain, however, as a serious challenge to medical care and communal resources, and this can only be reflected very approximately in statistics. Quite apart from the physical sequelae, the psychiatric consequences and their social repercussions may be judged to be significant in upwards of a quarter of patients who survive. Precise figures are hard to obtain because it is clear that many patients, even with severe incapacities, do not present themselves for continuing medical attention. But what is virtually certain is that the mental sequelae outstrip the physical as a cause of difficulty with rehabilitation, hardship at work, and social incapacity generally, and in terms of the strain thrown on the families to whom the head-injured patients return.

Fahy *et al.*'s (1967) follow-up of a small group of very severe civilian head injuries illustrates vividly the amount of disturbance enduring 6 years later. Only 5 of 22 patients were free from psychiatric sequelae, and psychiatric disturbance was a prominent cause of incapacity for work. Problems in the home included affective outbursts, chronic irritability, epileptiform and hallucinatory episodes and paranoid developments, in addition to impairment of intellectual processes. Yet only 2 of the patients had been referred for psychiatric advice during the follow-up period. It appears, therefore, that the psychiatrist sees only a small proportion of the problem.

The greater part of the present chapter will be devoted to the long-term mental sequelae of head injury, since this is the sphere in which the psychiatrist is most frequently engaged. The acute phases are primarily the province of the casualty officer, neurologist or neurosurgeon. Nevertheless the psychiatrist must also have a proper understanding of acute effects, since these have important bearings on the correct evaluation of the mechanisms which underlie the longer-term disturbances.

The Pathology and Pathophysiology of Head Injury

The pathological changes following head injury have been carefully documented, and provide important guides for the clinician. Such investigations have illuminated some of the principal mechanisms by which clinical symptoms follow head injury, and indicate in general terms what sort of pathology may be expected to follow from different types of trauma. This information must be taken into account when considering matters of prognosis, or when marshalling evidence for the relationship likely to obtain between the injury and symptoms which persist long afterwards.

Unfortunately there must remain a margin of conjecture, particularly in milder injuries where opportunities for pathological study are rare. Yet these are the changes about which we need most understanding for routine clinical practice. In particular we lack a satisfactory experimental paradigm in animals, where the margin is extremely narrow between the blow which barely concusses and the blow which kills the animal outright. The more recent development of pathophysiological studies during life is therefore to be welcomed, and may ultimately help to answer some of the outstanding questions.

Pathology of Concussion

Most elusive of all has been firm evidence concerning the basis for the brief loss of consciousness which follows all but the mildest blow to the head. Cerebral ischaemia was at first thought to be the cause, either from temporary paralysis of the vasomotor regulating centres, or from arrest of the cerebral circulation due to the abrupt rise of intracranial pressure at the moment of injury.

Support for the ischaemic hypothesis has been slight, however, and direct traumatic paresis of nervous functions has been proposed instead. But the most notable advance has come from the conception of rotational sheer stresses within the brain. Denny-Brown and Russell (1941) showed that in anaesthetised animals uncomplicated concussion, as observed by loss of brain stem reflexes, could be produced only if the head was free to move when struck, that is when forces of acceleration or deceleration acted upon the brain within the cranium. Holbourn (1943) experimented with gelatin models of the brain, and Pudenz and Shelden (1946) directly observed the brains of monkeys after replacing their skull caps with transparent material; swirling movements of brain tissue could be witnessed after acceleration injury, both at the point of impact and elsewhere. This, then, may explain why concussion is common when the head is in motion at the time of injury, but relatively rare in static crushing injuries (Russell and Schiller, 1949).

An additional problem is whether concussion depends on diffuse or focal damage to brain tissue. Swirling movements within the rigid skull stand to produce diffuse effects throughout the brain, yet the cardinal symptoms of concussion point to a major involvement of brain stem centres. In addition to loss of consciousness there is respiratory arrest, generalised vasoconstriction, loss of corneal reflexes and paralysis of deglutition. Histological studies can provide only indirect evidence on this issue, especially since mild examples may represent functional change without structural alteration. Chromatolysis and loss of neurones have been shown in the brain stem of animals, in proportion to the strength of the blows inflicted (Windle et al., 1944; Groat and Simmons, 1950). Friede (1961) has confirmed such findings, but proposes that they are secondary to damage in the upper cervical region, and suggests that bending and stretching of the neck may be the basic mechanism for producing concussion. Brain stem damage has also been implicated in penetrating injuries, where a 'plunger effect' of the brain stem within the foramen magnum has been shown even after missile wounds confined to the anterior fossa of the skull (Webster and Gurdjian, 1943). Nevertheless the possibility cannot be excluded that equivalent cell damage may also exist throughout the cortex and play a contributory role in the genesis of concussion.

Biochemical and electrical evidence concerning the basis of concussion is outlined on p. 140.

Pathology of Amnesia

The pathological basis for the amnesic defects which accompany concussion is equally uncertain. These too may depend on focal or diffuse brain changes, and there is insufficient evidence to decide between the two.

The fact that current registration and retrograde recall are affected together would suggest that the special neural mechanisms in the hippocampus or diencephalon have been temporarily put out of action. The temporal lobes are tightly encased within a bony framework, and the medial temporal lobe structures may accordingly be liable to disproportionate damage when the brain is set in sudden motion. However the length of post-traumatic amnesia is very intimately associated with measures of the overall severity of brain damage in closed head injuries, and it is widely assumed that this at least depends on diffuse rather than focal disturbance of cerebral function. Moreover, substantial amnesia is much less common in crushing injuries or penetrating injuries where shearing stresses are unlikely to occur throughout the brain. It has even been suggested that amnesia after head injury might be due to widespread disturbances of the macromolecular pattern of proteins and lipoproteins within the nerve cells themselves (Dixon, 1962).

It is probable that both diffuse and focal effects contribute in different degree from one case to another. The hippocampal or diencephalic mechanisms may be especially affected in cases with long and persistent retrograde amnesias, whereas a generalised effect on the brain may produce the more common situation in which the retrograde amnesia is brief (and compatible with the time required for registration) no matter how long the post-traumatic amnesia. Certainly in the occasional patient who is left with permanent memory difficulties, but without gross disturbance of other intellectual functions, it is reasonable to assume that focal damage has been caused to the parts of the brain especially concerned with memorising.

General Pathology of Head Injury

The more severe injuries which come to operative exploration or post-mortem examination show a variety of pathological changes. Some are the result of direct physical damage to the brain parenchyma, and some the result of complicating factors such as vascular disturbances, cerebral oedema and anoxia. In penetrating injuries infection brings added changes.

Direct physical damage will vary in important respects according to the type of trauma inflicted. Closed head injury is by far the commonest form in civilian practice, and here important factors are the direction of the blow, its force and velocity, and whether or not the head was free to move at impact. Contusion and laceration tend to be marked at the site of impact, at the opposite pole ('contre coup') and at the poles of the hemispheres generally. When the head is at rest at the time of injury, as in assault, the lesion will be maximal at the site of impact, but when in motion, as in falls or traffic accidents, the contre coup effect is likely to be the most pronounced (Bloomquist and Courville, 1947; Löken, 1959). Contre coup effects are often particularly marked in the temporal and orbital regions. Such lesions lead to loss of neurones locally, and ultimately to areas of subcortical demyelination.

Acceleration injuries, as in the impact of a car with the head, or deceleration injuries, as when the motorcyclist hits a wall after flying through the air, cause swirling movements throughout the brain as already described. The resulting rotational and linear stresses tear and damage nerve fibres throughout the brain. First reported in patients dying after very severe brain injuries, there is now little doubt that a distinctive diffuse pathology can result from such a mechanism in mild closed injuries as well (Strich, 1956, 1969; Teasdale and Mendelow, 1984). Widespread interruption and degeneration of nerve fibres can be detected, with breakdown and resorption of myelin and the formation of retraction balls. The changes are mainly confined to the central white matter of the hemispheres, the corpus callosum, and the long tracts in the brain stem. The distribution of lesions is often asymmetrical. A striking aspect is that severely affected tracts of fibres may be seen near normal areas, with a sharp boundary between the two, suggesting selective sparing or involvement by virtue of fibre tract direction. Such pathology can exist with only moderate cerebral atrophy, and only very limited dilatation of the ventricles. Recent studies by Adams *et al.* (1977) have emphasised that diffuse white matter damage of this nature can occur from the moment of injury, and is probably the most important single factor governing outcome in closed head injuries. In patients remaining in a 'persistent vegetative state' until death (p. 157) this was the typical finding, rather than any special accent of pathology on the brain stem.

Vascular lesions include scattered punctate haemorrhages throughout the brain, along with infarcts large and small. Sometimes the whole or part of the territory of a major cerebral artery may become necrotic. Such vascular lesions probably result from a combination of factors—reduced cerebral blood flow immediately after the injury, hypotension, embolism, pre-existing atheroma, rise of intracranial pressure sufficient to occlude the arteries, and spasm of vessels due to mechanical strain at the junction of brain and vessel (Strich, 1969; Graham and Adams, 1971).

Extensive bleeding may occur into the subarachnoid space, with the appearance of blood in the cerebrospinal fluid. Subdural haematomas may collect and become organised over the cerebral hemispheres. Blood collecting in the basal cisterns or over the surface of the brain may later lead to organised adhesions which obstruct the flow of cerebrospinal fluid and lead to hydrocephalus. Bleeding into the brain tissue itself may result in an intracerebral haematoma.

Cerebral oedema may develop in the acute stages and further complicate the picture. It is especially liable to occur in the region of contusions, lacerations, infarcts and haematomas. The raised intracranial pressure which results can have serious consequences in terms of herniation of brain tissue through the tentorium and under the falx cerebri. If severe such 'coning' may be fatal. Less severe cases can be followed by focal necrosis and haemorrhage in the medial temporal lobe structures and brain stem.

Cerebral anoxia accounts for other pathological findings, such as cortical necrosis in the depths of the cortical sulci, lesions in Ammon's horn and the basal ganglia, and disappearance of Purkinje cells from the cerebellum. Cases studied early after injury show widespread chromatolysis in neurones both in the brain stem and throughout the cortex. The anoxia will derive not only from cerebral oedema and other local changes, but also from hypotension, blood loss, disturbances of regulation of the cerebral circulation, and ventilatory insufficiency in the acute stages. The importance of early metabolic derangements in leading to brain damage has also come increasingly to be recognised.

Resolution of these different acute changes will be followed by variable gliosis and cerebral atrophy, often with considerable distortion of brain tissue, cyst formation, enlargement of the ventricles, or the formation of ventricular diverticula. Where prolonged coma has followed injury a special emphasis of pathology may be expected in the central part of the upper brain stem, chiefly as a result of the mechanical and vascular sequelae of raised intracranial pressure (Jellinger and Seitelberger, 1969).

In open head injuries the skull and dural coverings are perforated. Laceration of brain tissue is marked at the site of impact but contre-coup is slight or even totally absent. This is probably explained by the limited and direct effect of the trauma which expends its energy locally, together with the resilience of fractured bones which act as a buffer to prevent the propagation of the force (Löken, 1959). Extensive local laceration may lead to large cystic cavities and ventricular dilatations. Haemorrhage may occur locally, and infection is an ever-present risk. Small fractures in the neighbourhood of the nasal sinuses may easily be missed, and pave the way for meningitis or local abscess formation.

Any inflammatory process provokes a connective tissue reaction from the vascular adventitia, and results in a fibro-glial scar in which infection may linger. This tends to be adherent to the dura, and ultimately retracts with distortion and traction on the brain. Such a lesion brings special hazards for the later development of epilepsy.

Biochemical and Physiological Changes

In addition to the structural changes following head injury, alterations occur in the biochemical, circulatory and electrical mechanisms of the brain, and will play a part in the determination of the clinical picture.

Free acetylcholine, normally absent from the cerebrospinal fluid, appears in relatively large quantities after injury and may persist for days or even weeks. The amount roughly parallels the degree of unconsciousness and the severity of the EEG changes, and with clinical improvement the level gradually falls. The acetylcholine is probably released from neural membranes as a direct result of the trauma or the massive neuronal discharge at the time of impact. It has been suggested that this may constitute a biochemical basis for concussion, and even for some cases of prolonged coma after head injury, by the blocking of neural transmission in the reticular formation (Ward, 1966).

Cerebrospinal fluid lactate is also raised immediately after injury, produced no doubt from anoxic damage to brain tissue. The level is approximately related to prognosis for recovery (Kurze *et al.*, 1966). Marked changes in brain lipids have also been demonstrated after experimental brain compression, and may underlie disturbances of neuronal metabolic function after injury (Ishii, 1966). Other lines of investigation have stressed changes in vascular permeability and the blood-brain barrier, and the shift in fluids and electrolytes which may follow (Tower, 1966).

The rate of cerebral circulation after head injury also shows interesting alterations and is probably important in the development of delayed or 'secondary' brain changes. Overgaard and Tweed (1974) demonstrated wide variability in resting cerebral blood flow after severe head injuries. Commonly, normal or low flow rates in the first 24 hours were succeeded by relative hyperaemia ('luxury perfusion') which persisted into the second or third week and then subsided. Either ischaemia or hyperaemia in the acute stage appeared to be related to a poor clinical outcome. Distinct regional changes in cerebral blood flow, either ischaemic or hyperperfusion in type, were also observed, chiefly in relation to focal lesions such as haematomas or lacerations.

The Electroencephalogram after Head Injury

Neurophysiological studies (reviewed by Ward, 1966) have emphasised the importance of disturbance of brain stem structures in concussion. Experimental concussion in monkeys produces surprisingly little effect on cortical EEG rhythms, but far more disturbance in the medial reticular formation. Evoked potential studies similarly show the preponderance of brain stem over cortical dysfunction.

Bickford and Klass (1966) review the general EEG changes seen after head injury. One of the most sensitive changes is local suppression of alpha rhythm in the region of a localised blow or in the contre coup area. This can occur with trivial injuries and can be helpful in indicating unsuspected damage, especially in a region which is clinically 'silent'. With greater severity the suppression may extend bilaterally and occasional slow waves appear. With severe injury delta waves at 1–3 Hz appear and may persist for several weeks or months. During recovery there is a gradual trend towards increase of frequency and normality over the weeks and months that follow. The development and persistence of spike discharges indicate that gliosis has occurred.

The EEG can be helpful in the differential diagnosis of the unconscious patient, chiefly by pointing to causes other than head injury which might be missed. Fast activity may suggest barbiturate overdosage, marked localised delta will point to a tumour or other primary intracerebral lesion, and spike and wave bursts will indicate an epileptic process. In the diagnosis of complications of head injury the EEG can also provide important leads. A delta focus of increasing magnitude after open head injury suggests the development of a cerebral abscess. With a subdural haematoma there may be increasing slow activity over one hemisphere, or the development of unilateral alpha wave suppression.

With regard to prognosis less can be said with certainty. The degree of overall abnormality of the EEG is not a firm guide to prognosis, and must always be taken in conjunction with other clinical data. Serial recordings may be helpful, however, especially in revealing the organic component in cases where psychogenic mechanisms have been thought to be entirely responsible for the clinical picture. Sometimes the early return of the EEG to normal, while neurological defects remain prominent, will indicate that the major part of recovery has already taken place so that enduring handicap is likely. Where the later development of epilepsy is concerned, the EEG is not a reliable guide, and some 50 per cent of patients who develop post-traumatic epilepsy have a normal or only minimally abnormal EEG. Jennett (1975) found no consistent correlation between EEG abnormalities during the first year after injury and the development of late epilepsy. However the appearance of focal discharges which spread and intensify can be taken as a strong indication that pathology is developing which will ultimately lead to the appearance of seizures.

The Acute Effects of Head Injury

The most constant of the acute effects of head injury is impairment of consciousness, ranging from momentary dazing to prolonged coma. This is usually succeeded during recovery by a variable period of confusion, and the whole episode proves later to be surrounded by characteristic amnesic defects. These three features form the cardinal symptoms of the early effects of head injury. They provide important information about the severity of brain damage that is likely to have occurred, and must therefore be taken carefully into account when assessing prognosis. In addition, of course, there may be added effects due to damage to specific parts of the brain, and as a result of the various complications outlined above.

IMPAIRMENT OF CONSCIOUSNESS

A good deal of sterile debate has surrounded the definition of 'concussion'. That given by Caveness and Walker (1966) is reproduced here: '. . . a clinical syndrome characterised by immediate and transient impairment of neural function, such as alteration of consciousness, disturbances of vision, equilibrium, etcetera, due to mechanical forces'.

The important point is that impairment of consciousness, however transient, follows all but the mildest blow in closed head injuries, and especially when the head is free to move at impact. After penetrating head injuries it is considerably less common, also in static crushing injuries as already discussed. In occasional cases there may be no detectable impairment of consciousness, but merely transient dizziness or blurring of vision; or there may be no outward sign of impairment of consciousness to onlookers, yet the patient is without recollection of the injury, showing that at least the memorising functions of the brain were out of action for a time.

In the typical case loss of consciousness is complete. The patient falls to the ground, displays no response to stimuli, and for a moment shows arrest of respiration, profound fall of blood pressure, pallor, dilated pupils, loss of corneal reflexes and paralysis of deglutition. Mass contraction of the limbs may be followed by flaccid paralysis and loss of tendon reflexes. With recovery shallow sighing respiration is resumed and the circulatory state gradually returns to normal. Consciousness is resumed at a variable interval depending on the severity of injury. Usually this is followed by a period of confusion, drowsiness and headache, and sometimes by vomiting and dizziness. The duration of complete unconsciousness is often overestimated by the patient, because of the confusion which follows and the post-traumatic amnesia which may greatly outlast the resumption of outwardly normal behaviour. Conversely the patient may sometimes underestimate the period of unconsciousness, or in rare cases deny any knowledge of it.

Periods of unconsciousness lasting several hours are compatible with uneventful and complete recovery. The longer its duration however, and the deeper the level of coma, the more probable it is that permanent brain damage will have been sustained. It is no longer fashionable on clinical grounds to attempt to distinguish between simple concussion, contusion and laceration of the brain, but prolonged unconsciousness is more likely to be accompanied by evidence of brain damage on neurological examination, by evidence of raised intracranial pressure, and by the presence of blood in the cerebrospinal fluid. It is also more likely to be followed by a considerable period of post-traumatic confusion and by both physical and mental long-term sequelae.

In severe cases unconsciousness may persist for weeks or even months, and here permanent after-effects are to be expected. Lewin (1959) has assessed the quality of recovery in 102 patients who had remained unconscious for over a month. Thirty-nine died, 15 were left very severely disabled, 29 made partial recoveries and 19 were ultimately well enough to return to their former work. If a good recovery was to be made then some improvement was usually seen within the first month after injury—not necessarily return of consciousness but certainly increased responsiveness to pain or diminution of spasticity.

The 'Glasgow Coma Scale' (Teasdale and Jennett, 1974) is now in routine use in many countries, in units caring for acutely head-injured patients. It has proved to be of considerable predictive value in pointing to long-term outcome, in terms of both survival and ultimate levels of disability (Jennett *et al.*, 1975, 1977). The patient's clinical state is charted regularly on a number of graded parameters: motor responsiveness (no response, extensor response to pain, flexor response, localising response, obeying commands), verbal performance (nil, without recognisable words, no sustained exchange possible, confused conversation, oriented for person, place and time), and eye opening (nil, in response to pain, in response to speech, spontaneously). Numerical scores are summated for the best responses obtained under each category at a defined point in time. In this way useful predictions can be made, often within 24 hours of injury and more certainly within the first week.

The prolonged post-traumatic coma may be profound from the outset, or may deepen rapidly in the early stages due to intracerebral or subarachnoid bleeding. Decerebrate rigidity is common, with tonic fits, stertorous breathing, tachycardia and hyperpyrexia. Anoxia is a special hazard, resulting from obstruction of the airways or damage to the respiratory and vasomotor centres in the brain stem. Ominous signs of brain stem compression include muscular flaccidity, failing respiration, falling blood pressure and fixed dilated pupils. Skilled nursing and watchful medical supervision are therefore essential, with readiness to operate for extradural, subdural and intracerebral haematomas. Artificial aids to sustain respiration may be required for considerable periods of time, and electrolyte imbalance or anaemia due to blood loss may need correction.

ACUTE POST-TRAUMATIC PSYCHOSIS
(Post-traumatic acute organic reaction;
post-traumatic confusional state)

As unconsciousness recedes the patient passes through a phase of disorientation and impaired cognitive ability before the ultimate level of recovery is attained. This stage shows much variation, depending on the severity of the injury and its complications, and coloured also by aspects of the pre-traumatic personality and present surroundings. The term 'acute post-traumatic psychosis' thus covers a wide range of different clinical pictures.

After momentary concussion a return to normal may be expected within a few minutes. After unconsciousness lasting several hours the ensuing disturbance may last for some days or weeks. In the most severe injuries, where permanent disablement is to follow, the phase of acute confusion may last for many months and ultimately shade imperceptibly into the picture of post-traumatic dementia. Thus in general there exists a fairly close relationship between severity of injury and the duration of disorientation, which may be used in the early stages as an approximate guide to prognosis (Moore and Ruesch, 1944). Exceptions are seen, however, since the severity of the acute traumatic psychosis also often depends on complicating factors such as anoxia, electrolyte disturbance, systemic infection or severe blood loss which need not lead to enduring brain damage. The disturbance is usually more prolonged and severe in the elderly, the arteriosclerotic and the alcoholic.

The form which the disturbance takes is also variable, ranging from apathetic withdrawal, through restless irritability, to pictures of florid 'post-traumatic delirium'. The determinants of the clinical picture will include not only the nature of the brain damage and complicating factors, but also the pre-traumatic personality of the patient. Insecure subjects may react by marked depression, extraverted subjects by boisterous noisy disturbance, and others by petulant and childish behaviour. Hysterical or paranoid traits may be released, and sometimes a schizophrenic colouring is much in evidence.

In many cases outward behaviour is little disturbed beyond obvious lethargy and failure of cognitive function. A mood of perplexity is common, and there may be initial restlessness and irritability. Thereafter progress usually follows a torpid apathetic course until consciousness is fully regained. On the other hand, some patients pass through an excitable and overactive phase with florid disturbance of behaviour which can be long continued and pose serious problems of management. Sometimes this is clearly attributable to the abnormal experiences and delusional misinterpretations of a post-traumatic delirium, but sometimes it proves to foreshadow enduring changes of temperament and behaviour occasioned by the injury. The patient may be abusive, aggressive and markedly uncooperative. Very occasionally serious crimes of violence are committed at the height of such disturbance, and afterwards the patient has no knowledge of their occurrence.

In this stage there is always some degree of residual impairment of consciousness and failure to retain new information. Accordingly the period of the acute traumatic psychosis comes to be incorporated within the post-traumatic amnesic gap. Impairment of consciousness is usually clinically obvious, though occasionally the patient may seem to be fully alert and capable of a high degree of motivated behaviour. The subsequent amnesic gap is then important evidence that the brain was still in an abnormal state at the time.

Disorientation for time and place, and sometimes even for personal identity, is marked at first. Later during recovery a bizarre state of double orientation may be maintained as described on p. 11. Confabulation is sometimes much in evidence. Cognitive dysfunction is also shown in difficulty with simple mental tests, and obvious inability to concentrate or sustain mental effort.

Misinterpretation of surroundings and misidentification of people are common. Sometimes these are confessed only upon recovery. There may be suspicious disbelief of the role and purpose of those around, such that nurses and other patients are thought to be spies or gaolers. More openly expressed delusions are often part of an acute delirium, originating in sensory falsifications and poverty of grasp. They are usually highly charged with emotion, changeable and unsystematised, and paranoid in content.

Very occasionally the circumstances of the injury are recalled in a confused and muddled manner, and become woven into a delusional system. This can have important medico-legal repercussions. Russell (1935) reports a patient who had a motor-cycle accident and subsequently ascribed his injuries to an attack by the dog which had caused it. He later elaborated this by maintaining that the dog's owner had attacked him directly. In this case the delusions were short-lived and cleared as the post-traumatic confusion receded. A similar case was cited in which a doctor motored home a boy who had fallen off his cycle and was later accused by the boy of having run him down.

Weston and Whitlock (1971) describe another fascinating example in which delusions apparently stemmed from a vivid hallucinatory experience occurring as part of the early post-traumatic delirium. The patient related an episode in which he believed he saw his parents being shot by Chinese communists. Thereafter when his family visited him he believed them to be impostors who had assumed their exact appearance in order to trick him ('Capgras' syndrome'). The profound memory disturbance from which the patient was suffering at the time had prevented him from realising that the head injury had occurred, or from reintegrating his vivid fantasy into normal daily experience. Denial and confabulation were then used in order to structure the otherwise inexplicable circumstance of his family being once more around him.

With resolution of the acute post-traumatic psychosis the patient may recover completely or be left with defects of intellect or change of temperament. These may yet improve slowly over time or remain as permanent sequelae.

AMNESIC DEFECTS SURROUNDING INJURY

On recovery of consciousness, and whether or not an acute post-traumatic psychosis has followed, events often fail to be recorded in memory for a period of time. The injury is therefore followed by a post-traumatic amnesic gap. In addition, events immediately preceding the injury are sometimes no longer available for recall so that a retrograde amnesic gap exists as well. The correct evaluation of these amnesic phenomena is of considerable clinical importance, particularly in relation to prognosis.

Post-Traumatic Amnesia (PTA)

The length of the PTA may be defined as *the time from the moment of injury to the time of resumption of normal continuous memory*. It therefore ends at the time from which the patient can later give a clear and consecutive account of what was happening around him. It includes any period of unconsciousness or overt confusion, and often in addition a further period thereafter during which outward behaviour has appeared to return to normal.

Characteristically the termination is abrupt, except in those very severe injuries where enduring memory difficulties or dementia are to supervene. The amnesic phase may have lasted from several minutes to several weeks, yet finally ends sharply with the return of normal continuous memory. It is for this reason that the majority of patients can retrospectively give a firm end-point to their PTA, usually though not inevitably with some highlighted experience of a pleasurable, painful or surprising nature. In some cases brief islands of memory at first emerge, vaguely recalled and jumbled with regard to temporal sequence, before the continuity of memory is restored, but this is exceptional.

Behaviour during the post-traumatic gap may vary from apparent normality to obvious difficulty with memory and mental confusion. Some degree of temporal disorientation is almost always in evidence if opportunities arise to test for it with care. The general tenor of behaviour may, however, be surprisingly intact so that observers are easily misled into thinking that full recovery has occurred. Even questions designed to test short-term memory may in some cases be answered adequately, since memory functions may have recovered sufficiently for this but not yet sufficiently to lay down a permanent record. It is thus only in retrospect that the true duration of the post-traumatic gap can be determined with certainty. Commonly the patient appears to be unaware himself of the abnormality of memory functions at the time, and gives superficial explanations or confabulations for the defects which are discovered.

False memories, which at first sight are convincing enough, have sometimes been found to centre on a previous injury:

A despatch rider was concussed in a motor cycle accident. Following a period of complete unconsciousness he was confused and drowsy for 2–3 days, and after treatment at a local hospital was transferred to a special head injury unit ten days later. When seen at that time he gave details of the accident, including its locale and the incident leading up to it, and recounted his journey from the first hospital. He gave his name and army number correctly, but persistently underestimated his age by two years. At clinical examination he appeared to be rational and fully orientated. It finally transpired, however, that he was giving details of an accident he had had before joining the army some two years previously, and that the description of his journey to the second hospital was also a false reminiscence. His final PTA was assessed as 12 days. It involved the period of false reminiscence and the first two days of his stay in the second hospital.

(Whitty and Zangwill, 1966)

In the majority of cases, as already indicated, the purely dysmnesic phase follows upon the clearing of overt signs of confusion and impairment of consciousness, but occasional cases are seen in which it follows immediately upon the injury and is the sole defect. The classical example is that of the schoolboy struck during a game of football but not rendered unconscious. He may then continue to play, but later proves to have no recollection of the part of the game which immediately followed the injury ('post-traumatic automatism'). Similar examples are sometimes seen in boxers. Usually performance is noted to be substandard during the continuation of activity.

Occasionally, but rarely, the dysmnesic period is delayed by a few moments after the blow. Some brief isolated experiences are recalled immediately after the injury, usually in an inaccurate and confused way, and thereafter the dense amnesic period begins:

A boy of 18 skidded in a car and hit a telegraph pole, sustaining a fractured skull and broken leg. He clearly recalled switching off the engine and forcing open the jammed car door, both of which were subsequently corroborated. Thereafter he could recall nothing until he came round in hospital some 48 hours later.

(Whitty and Zangwill, 1966)

A more delayed onset to the amnesic phase may of course be seen when complications such as extra-dural haemorrhage lead to a second period of unconsciousness after full recovery has been attained; here events may subsequently be recalled from the lucid interval preceding the haemorrhage, and this may be of several hours duration.

Retrograde Amnesia (RA)

The duration of the RA is measured as *the time between the moment of injury and the last clear memory from before the injury which the patient can recall*. The patient can often indicate with fair precision the last event which he can clearly recollect. In road accidents the journey is typically recalled up to a certain point, and this then allows an estimate to be made of the extent of the retrograde gap.

The retrograde amnesia is usually dense, including events of high emotional significance and, of course, involving details of the accident itself. Usually the RA is much shorter than the PTA, though in rare exceptions the reverse is seen. Indeed the great majority of RAs are surprisingly uniform in extent, occupying only a few seconds or up to a minute in time, which may be regarded as the period required for the processes of consolidation of the original perceptions. Longer retrograde gaps are generally seen only with the more severe injuries, but these may be of many days or weeks duration. Conversely, cases of mild injury are seen in which no RA occurs whatever, and full details of the injury can be recalled up to the moment of loss of consciousness.

The organic basis for the very long RA has come under suspicion, and certainly those which follow mild head injury have often proved to be psychogenic in origin. Here the emotional shock of the accident is principally to be blamed. Nevertheless long RAs may be seen with other forms of organic brain damage, and experienced observers have agreed that after severe head injury a long RA may sometimes be directly attributable to organic factors. Symonds (1962a), for example, has reported a permanent RA of one year for which there was no indication that other than organic factors were at work. Russell and Nathan (1946) investigated the effect of thiopentone narcosis on the duration of amnesias, and found a reduction in only 12 of 40 cases investigated. The reductions were mostly trivial in amount, and did not include material likely to have been repressed by psychogenic mechanisms. Moreover the recovered material always bordered the fringes of the amnesic gap, suggesting again that it was substantially organic in origin.

With long RAs it is usual to find that the amnesia is most dense for events shortly preceding the injury, with only patchy loss for the more remote periods. Dislocation from correct temporal sequence is also characteristic for those events which are recalled from within the retrograde gap.

The RA as determined shortly after injury may prove to be misleading. At first it may be very long, then shrink in the days or weeks that follow as normal orientation is regained. The final estimate should therefore not be made until the patient has emerged from the period of the PTA and the fullest possible recovery of cerebral function has occurred. The shrinkage of the RA is itself a phenomenon of some interest, as described on pp. 29 and 34.

Amnesia in Relation to Severity of Injury

The importance of the duration of amnesia as a guide to the severity of injury and prognosis for recovery was first clearly shown by Russell (1932). This has now become a well-attested part of clinical practice, hence the importance of striving to record in every case the precise details of the retrograde and post-traumatic gaps.

The PTA has proved to be more valid and useful than the RA in this regard. In general the RA tends to increase in length with the PTA (Russell and Nathan, 1946), but since the great majority of RAs are extremely brief they are less valuable as a guide to severity. The PTA shows all gradations of length and is highly variable from case to case, thus allowing it to be used as an index of severity. It also emerges as more valid for this purpose than the duration of unconsciousness or overt confusion, probably because the latter depend more closely on secondary complications. The PTA is, moreover, a permanent index of severity, and available to the clinician who enquires long after the injury.

Viewed first in the most general terms, the duration of the PTA in closed head injuries is related to the time which is likely to elapse before the patient returns to work (Symonds and Russell, 1943; Steadman and Graham, 1970). Within broad limits it may be predicted that a patient with a PTA of less than an hour will usually return to work within a month, with a PTA of less than a day within two months, and with a PTA of less than a week within four months. PTAs exceeding a week will often be followed by invalidism extending over the greater part of a year.

More specifically the duration of PTA shows close correlations with objective evidence of damage to brain tissue, as reflected in neurological residua such as motor disorder, dysphasia or anosmia, or enduring defects of memory and calculation (Russell and Smith, 1961; Smith, 1961). Psychiatric disablement likewise shows an important relationship to the duration of PTA, particularly where organic mental disabilities such as intellectual impairment, euphoria, disinhibition or aspects of the 'frontal lobe syndrome' are concerned (Lishman, 1968). In Steadman and Graham's (1970) series the mean duration of PTA was significantly increased in patients who showed post-traumatic change of personality.

An important, though not over-riding qualification to the above, concerns the situation in open as opposed to closed head injuries. In penetrating injuries, particularly those due to high velocity missiles, there is a tendency for the PTA to be very short or even absent in up to 50% of cases (Russell, 1951). Similarly in crushing injuries, where the brain is not subject to the forces of acceleration, loss of consciousness is relatively rare (Russell and Schiller, 1949). Nevertheless Table 6 shows that even among penetrating head injuries a close relationship exists between the length of PTA and the amount of psychiatric disability or intellectual impairment as assessed in general terms one to five years later.

The Chronic Sequelae of Head Injury

With recovery from the acute stages, a mild head injury is quite compatible with return to full efficiency, both physically and mentally. This important fact is not always appreciated by the patient and his relatives for whom the very term 'concussion' can have ominous overtones. Nevertheless head injury does account for a great deal of chronic disability. Common physical defects include cranial nerve lesions such as anosmia, oculomotor pareses, visual field defects, and motor disorders resulting from cortical or brain stem lesions. Peripheral sensory defects are seen less frequently. In penetrating injuries, or after complications due to intracranial bleeding, such focal neurological defects will be more common. They are fully described in textbooks of neurology and neurosurgery and will not be dealt with further here.

Only the mental sequelae will be considered in detail. These are extremely important in clinical practice, and furthermore provide valuable material for academic study—both in demonstrating the complex interplay of many factors in the genesis of psychiatric disorder, and in increasing our understanding of the cerebral basis of behaviour.

The clinical importance of the mental aftermaths cannot be overstressed. Observers are uniformly agreed that problems such as cognitive incapacity or change of personality far outstrip the physical sequelae as obstacles in rehabilitation and as a source of long-term disability (Field, 1976; Bond, 1976). Decline in employment is more likely to be associated with mental than physical factors (Roberts, 1976), likewise the strain imposed on families and those responsible for care (Thomsen, 1974; McKinlay et al., 1981).

The range of mental sequelae is very great and embraces most that can be found in psychiatric symptomatology. It is therefore most unlikely that all will share a common aetiology, even though all will have appeared to take origin from a common event, namely the blow to the head. At one extreme we have enduring defects of cognitive function which can confidently be ascribed to the brain damage sustained. At the other extreme there are certain groups of symptoms—phobias, anxiety states, and depression—which sometimes follow the most trivial injuries and commonly occur in a setting of environmental and interpersonal difficulties consequent upon the injury. These often differ little if at all from the general run of functional neurotic reactions, and appear to owe little to the brain damage which may have been sustained. In between there exists a range of phenomena in which the relative contribution of organic and psychogenic factors can be particularly hard to disentangle, such as enduring difficulty with concentration, persistent headache, undue irritability and other subtle changes of temperament. Schizophrenic and affective psychoses may also follow head injury, and have likewise been the subject of controversy concerning the aetiological mechanisms involved.

TABLE 6. Duration of post-traumatic amnesia in relation to psychiatric disability and generalised intellectual impairment (from Lishman, 1968). (Figures in italics represent percentages calculated on the equivalent totals shown at the bottom of each column)

Length of Post-Traumatic Amnesia	Psychiatric Disability						Intellectual Impairment					
	Nil		Mild		Severe		Nil		Mild		Severe	
(a) < 1 hour	62	*67*	226	*52*	41	*28*	116	*65*	208	*45*	5	*16*
(b) < 7 days	17	*18*	83	*19*	31	*22*	32	*18*	95	*21*	4	*12*
(c) > 7 days	14	*15*	124	*29*	72	*50*	31	*17*	156	*34*	23	*72*
Total cases	93		433		144		179		459		32	

TABLE 7. Aetiological factors in psychiatric disturbance after head injury

Mental Constitution
Premorbid Personality
Emotional Impact of Injury
Emotional Repercussions of Injury
Environmental Factors
Compensation and Litigation
Response to Intellectual Impairments
The Development of Epilepsy
Amount of Brain Damage Incurred
Location of Brain Damage Incurred

Thus it has steadily become apparent that over and above any obvious brain damage there are a multitude of factors, constitutional and environmental, which can decisively shape the psychiatric picture in the individual. Such a situation is, of course, common in psychiatric illness, and head-injured patients illustrate particularly well the complex interplay of many contributory factors rebounding each upon the other. Confronted with an individual case the clinician must nevertheless try to decide which are the causal factors presently operating, and the relative weights to be given to each, before he can hope to tackle the problem effectively or make a reasoned estimate at prognosis. It will therefore be useful first to review the range of aetiological factors which may contribute to post-traumatic psychiatric disability before describing the common clinical pictures which result.

AETIOLOGY OF PSYCHIATRIC DISABILITY AFTER HEAD INJURY

The aetiological factors shown in Table 7 have all been demonstrated to operate significantly in contributing to the mental after-effects of head injury. The case in which any one of them operates alone will be rare, and in particular we cannot expect a firm dichotomy between physiogenic and psychogenic causes. Most often the two will be found to operate inextricably together. However each aetiological factor will first be considered individually since this is the process which clinical enquiry must follow in seeking to clarify the determinants of disability in an individual case.

Some factors, such as the influence of environmental difficulties, have been readily shown to exert a powerful effect; others, including the effects of brain damage itself have been more difficult to demonstrate, certainly where symptoms other than cognitive deficits are concerned. But it is important to avoid the fallacy of concluding that where aetiol-

ogical factors are easy to demonstrate they are necessarily most potent in action. In particular it is difficult to demonstrate minor degrees of brain damage during life, and one must therefore be wary in dismissing the physiogenic contribution. On the other hand we must not cling to the possibility that 'subclinical' brain damage is responsible in the face of overwhelming evidence that psychogenesis leads the field.

In the discussion which follows it is equally important to remember that even very large series of head-injured patients are liable to special selection by virtue of the settings in which they are studied and the populations from which they are drawn. Most civilian series consist predominantly of closed head injuries due to road traffic accidents, whereas soldiers wounded in combat suffer mainly from penetrating missile wounds. Series derived from acute sources will differ substantially from patients referred later for special treatment in rehabilitation units. Patients seen solely in connection with claims for compensation will be different again. All such factors may strongly bias interpretations concerning causal factors.

Mental Constitution

Reliable assessments of premorbid mental constitution are hard to make and it is therefore not surprising that different studies have placed different emphasis on its importance. Among soldiers invalided after head injury, a family or personal history of mental disorder has been found to increase the likelihood of chronic incapacity (Symonds and Russell, 1943). A history of character deviations, feeble-mindedness and psychosis in near relatives has likewise emerged as important in both soldiers and civilians (Hillbom, 1960; Kozol, 1945; Adler, 1945).

Several studies have directly assessed the importance of constitutional factors by comparing head-injured patients with non-head-injured neurotics. Lewis (1942) studying soldiers in an army neurosis centre found a remarkable degree of similarity in constitutional background between the two, and concluded that the 'long-lasting relatively intractable post-concussional syndrome is apt to occur in much the same person as develops a psychiatric syndrome anyway'. Ruesch and Bowman (1945) showed that head-injured patients, with neurotic symptoms but who lacked obvious signs of brain damage, resembled non-head-injured neurotics very closely, both in the range and diffuseness of their complaints and in profiles from the Minnesota Multiphasic Personality Inventory. In particular it appeared that the longer the disability persisted the less likely was it to be the expression of brain damage.

An alternative approach has been to compare head-injured twins with their non-head-injured controls. Dencker (1958, 1960) collected 37 monozygotic pairs and 81 dizygotic pairs in which only one of the twins had been injured. The head-injured twins were inferior to their controls on a variety of tests of intellectual function, though the defects were usually subtle and unobtrusive in everyday life. No significant differences were found where emotional and other psychiatric symptoms were concerned, nor in rates of admission to mental hospitals in the years that followed injury. The monozygotic pairs were more concordant than the dizygotic where certain post-traumatic symptoms were concerned—headache, dizziness, impaired memory, sensitivity to noise and decreased alcohol tolerance—suggesting that these at least were founded in genetic constitution rather than in any brain damage that had occurred. Several patients were found to have undergone a 'change of personality' since the injury, with increased tension, fatiguability or lessened ability to work, but where monozygotic partners were available for comparison these proved to be closely similar for the traits concerned. Among the dizygotic pairs the 'new' personality traits were often found to have caused divergence from the partner before the head injury occurred.

Dencker's investigation was carried out with scrupulous attention to detail and underlines the misleading impression which can be obtained from a cursory psychiatric history; constitutional factors emerged as crucial in many areas of disability which would otherwise have been readily ascribed to the head injury itself. It is important to note, however, that the patients were examined on average ten years after injury, by which time many of the more specific consequences had probably become submerged. It seems therefore to be long-continued psychiatric disability which relies most heavily on constitutional factors as opposed to the specific consequences of brain damage.

Slater's (1943) classical study of 2000 neurotic soldiers also showed the importance of constitutional factors, but here a contribution due to brain damage also emerged. In this investigation acute conditions were under scrutiny. A quantitative relationship was demonstrated between the degree of stress antedating breakdown and the degree of constitutional vulnerability in the soldiers concerned. But it was clearly shown that soldiers who had sustained brain damage scored lower than average on most items of constitutional vulnerability, just as did the soldiers who had undergone maximal military stress before breakdown. Head injury, in effect, appeared to contribute something additional to disturb the overall balance which could be discerned between stress and predisposition in the genesis of neurotic symptoms. A similar conclusion emerged from Guttmann's (1946) investigation of service patients.

The development of psychotic illness after head injury appears to rely heavily on constitutional predisposition, and it is only recently that more specific factors related to brain damage have come under serious suspicion. This is considered in some detail on p. 164.

Finally under the heading of constitution it is important to note that many aspects of post-traumatic disability, and especially intellectual impairments, increase with increased age at time of injury. This is probably attributable to the rising incidence of complicating factors such as cerebral arteriosclerosis, the diminishing reserve of neurones, and the general loss of resilience and adaptability among older persons. Mortality also rises sharply. In Kerr et al.'s (1971) series of civilian head injuries a steady rise in mortality occurred after the age of 50, which appeared not to be due to more severe injuries in the older age groups but to be attributable to age-related factors such as complications or pre-existing disease. The result was a 5-fold increase in mortality in the over 50s compared to the under 50s. In Heiskanen and Sipponen's (1970) group of severe brain injuries less than 30% of the survivors aged 50 or over were able to return to their former work, whereas more than 70% of those under 20 were able to do so. Russell (1932) found that memory difficulties increased regularly with age and were three times as common among patients over 40 as in younger patients. Adler (1945) found that nervous symptoms, mainly anxieties and fears, were more frequent as age at time of injury advanced, and attributed this to the increased problems of occupational and financial adjustment which had to be faced by older people.

Premorbid Personality

Head injury is liable to accentuate special vulnerabilities of personality, and to call upon personality resources during the often difficult stages of convalescence. Thus it is not surprising that in general terms more psychiatric disability is likely to follow when premorbid traits of instability or inadequacy have been in evidence (Adler, 1945). Further than this, however, it has proved difficult to specify in detail what special vagaries of personality are important. Classification into personality types such as psychopathic or neurotic does not add much additional information (Kozol, 1945, 1946), though studies with the Minnesota Multiphasic Personality Inventory have indicated that high scores on the hysterical, depressive, and hypochondriacal scales are associated with the long persistence of neurotic complaints (Walker and Erculei, 1969). In general, however, analysis of individual personality traits allows only broad generalisations to be made:

'The patient who was altrocentric rather than egocentric, social minded and endowed with a high sense of responsibility was most likely to escape substantial sequelae, despite the fact that such a person might be heavily endowed with neurotic traits' (Kozol, 1946). '. . . people who pity themselves instead of making attempts at more rational and active behaviour in conditions of stress do so also after head injuries and consequently are prone to meet with later difficulties in the course of rehabilitation' (Gruvstad et al., 1958). Such generalisations are of course of little help in assessing the individual case.

It is likely that specific personality features will to some extent influence the form that post-traumatic disability takes. Patients with neurotic tendencies have been shown to be especially liable to fatigue, insomnia, headache and dizziness (Kozol, 1946). It has also been suggested that when disinhibition occurs after frontal lesions it tends to involve those aspects of personality where previously inhibition had been especially marked (Jarvie, 1954). Such evidence is however highly impressionistic and hampered by lack of opportunity for objective assessments before the injury occurred. Details of personality structure will of course also contribute to the way in which the psychogenic factors, discussed immediately below, come to shape the pattern of disability after head injury.

Emotional Impact of Injury

The purely emotional shock engendered by the injury can be an important determinant of the psychiatric disturbances that follow. Certain individuals will be particularly susceptible in this way, and early reactions will be coloured more than those which persist long afterwards. Sometimes however the circumstances of the accident may recur vividly in dreams, set up states of chronic anxiety, or become the focus for obsessional rumination or conversion hysteria. Psychiatric illness may be precipitated in predisposed individuals.

Neurotic disabilities and the so-called post-traumatic syndrome (p. 168) appear to be related especially closely to emotional shock. These are found more commonly when emotional reactions have been marked immediately after injury (Brenner et al., 1944), or when the injury has occurred in an emotionally loaded setting (Guttmann, 1946). A striking finding is that neurotic disabilities have sometimes proved to be most frequent after minor injuries, and sometimes to be particularly common when there has been no post-traumatic amnesia to obliterate the memory of the accident and its immediate consequences (Denny-Brown, 1945; Miller 1961).

The head holds an especially important place in the body image, and is widely regarded as the seat of the soul or of sanity. The lay attitude to 'concussion' is one of unusual alarm, and unconsciousness and confusion are always deeply impressive symptoms. There may be lurking fears of insanity which are hard to quell, or an inner conviction that one can never be quite the same again. Psychoanalysts have stressed the part which barely conscious factors may play, and have described the trauma situation in terms of a threat to the patient's integrity and a blow to his ego-security (Ferenczi et al., 1921).

Emotional Repercussions of Injury

The emotional repercussions of an accident may sometimes stir up more than was at first sight supposed. Time spent in detailed enquiry here can sometimes be rewarding, especially in intractable neurotic states or long-continued affective reactions. Such enquiry is particularly indicated when psychiatric disability is disproportionate to the likely severity of the brain damage incurred, or when it outstrips expectations derived from knowledge of previous mental stability.

A man aged 48 was coshed on the way to bank his firm's takings and rendered briefly unconscious. For twelve months thereafter he showed enduring symptoms of anxiety and depression despite full physical and intellectual recovery. His ability to function at work appeared to be unaccountably impaired. It ultimately emerged that after a series of unusually frustrating setbacks he had come to be employed in a humble capacity by his successful younger brother who ran a flourishing business. Years of suppressed resentment and hostile feelings were now focused on the injury, and the full significance to him of being attacked while banking the firm's profits immediately became apparent.

A woman of 45 was disabled for many months by a number of neurotic complaints after surviving intact from a car crash. The head injury had been mild but her vision had been threatened for a time. Her persistent neurotic reaction was surprising in view of her excellent previous mental health and stability. She eventually confessed to a long-standing secret liaison with the husband of a friend, in whose company the accident had occurred. She had made a fervent resolve to end the relationship by way of atonement if her sight should be spared, and this she was now striving to do. Here the injury served as a focus for long-standing conflict and guilt, in addition to providing on-going emotional distress of a deeply disturbing kind.

(Lishman, 1973)

In both of these examples the true nature of the conflict underlying the neurotic symptoms needed to be revealed before treatment could begin to be effective.

Environmental Factors

Environmental difficulties which are encountered during convalescence and thereafter must always be carefully evaluated, along with the general social setting of the patient. In practice such aspects are extremely important since environmental problems are not infrequently remediable.

Careful convalescent management and a healthy home environment have been found to be factors of great prognostic importance (Aita, 1948). In the less severe injuries these features become of correspondingly greater significance in determining the degree of disability. Threats to family or personal security and occupational difficulties frequently assume crucial importance, especially if physical or intellectual deficits require a new adaptation on the part of the patient. Fear of returning to a dangerous occupation which has been the setting of the accident can have a powerful influence in determining prolonged invalidism. An unstable domestic background is often found to impede progress, or conversely the patient may be held back by the attention and over-solicitude of his family.

It is necessary to consider not only the new problems accruing from the injury, but also environmental and interpersonal difficulties which may have been long present. Sometimes prolonged disability turns out to be motivated by problems which have antedated the head injury, and the latter then serves as a tangible focus on which they can be blamed (Ruesch and Bowman, 1945). Sometimes frustra-

tions which have previously been tolerated are now released in full force. Patients who have long feared economic disaster may focus their anxiety on the reality of the injury; others may be seen to utilise it as an escape from some unbearable situation. With the injury in the forefront of his mind the patient now has a reason around which to crystallise his discomforts—to become outspokenly irritable with a nagging wife or to find his uncongenial work exhausting. Detailed exploration of the life situation antedating as well as following the injury is therefore often indicated. The patient, of course, is usually less than fully aware of the psychological origin of the symptoms which he is displaying.

Compensation and Litigation

The important medico-legal aspects of head injury are dealt with on pp. 176 to 181. Here it will suffice to note that impending litigation can strongly motivate the aggravation and prolongation of disability. Especially after industrial accidents powerful social influences are often brought to bear on the patient and lead him to hope for financial reward. Advice is received from many sources, and tempting examples of other similar cases are often much discussed.

That the compensation issue, like other conflicts, should operate at many levels of consciousness should be no cause for surprise. In some, probably rare cases, there will be entirely conscious simulation for gain, but in the great majority the compensation issue colours the picture in more subtle ways. Once the possibility of compensation is raised the patient finds himself in complex legal dealings; there are frustrations due to delay, anxieties due to conflicting advice, and often capital outlay. In effect the injured person is invited to complain and, having done so, finds he must complain repeatedly, often over years, to a number of specialists (Cole, 1970). Repeated questioning from lawyers and doctors not only focuses the patient's attention on early symptoms which perhaps were due to recede, but in addition reinforces the prospect of their continuance or of worse to come. Nor is it surprising that conflict over compensation should dictate neurotic forms of disability; it is in the nature of conflict, both conscious and subconscious, to provoke subjective forms of disability which lack external and objective cues to keep it in proportion.

Where patients have been selected to optimise the chance of revealing the compensation issue, as in series seen especially for the courts, it is sometimes found to outweigh all other factors in the prolongation of disability. But just how common or important it may be in the generality of head-injured patients is hard to determine, because we lack fully comprehensive investigations of parallel series of cases in which compensation is and is not a possible consequence. Miller (1961, 1966a) estimated that the compensation issue contributes to disability in one-quarter to one-third of all patients when the accident has fulfilled two criteria—when someone else is at fault in the patient's view, and when payment of financial compensation is at least a possibility. In reviewing two hundred patients seen for medicolegal assessment after head injury he found that gross psychoneurotic complaints or the post-concussional syndrome were the outstanding disabilities in more than a third. Patients of low social status, unskilled or semi-skilled, were particularly affected, and men were implicated twice as often as women. Neurotic disability was twice as common after industrial as after road traffic accidents, and employees of large organisations or nationalised concerns were affected more commonly than those of small intimate firms. The alarming nature of the accident was not clearly related to neurotic disability in this group, and the actual severity of the injury to the head was inversely related to such developments. Additional evidence of the importance of litigation has been deduced from the fact that post-concussional symptoms are rare after injuries at sport or in the home where compensation is not payable (Miller, 1969).

With regard to outcome it is clear that prolonged legal negotiations often aggravate the situation. It is also sometimes reported that disability continues until the compensation issue is settled, then clears abruptly whether or not financial reward has accrued. These oft-quoted instances show the tenacity with which the compensation motive can sometimes operate. Even so, improvement on settlement need not imply that the patient has been 'manufacturing' his symptoms—genuine uncertainty and worry have been decisively removed (Merskey and Woodforde, 1972).

Examples of abrupt resolution on settlement are, in fact, much rarer than is commonly supposed. Steadman and Graham (1970) found that patients whose claims were rejected took a long time to recover or return to work, and 'neurotic resentment' seemed a possible explanation for this. Kelly and Smith (1981) traced 43 of 100 patients to determine the long-term outcome of the post-traumatic syndrome when the compensation issue was at stake; of twenty-six who had failed to return to work by the settlement date, only 1 was at work 18 months later, yet all but 4 had considered the settlement adequate.

Response to Intellectual Impairments

Intellectual impairment after head injury is important not only for its direct effects, but also for the role that subtle impairments may play in dictating emotional and behavioural changes. Goldstein (1942, 1952) has made an important contribution here in stressing how the various psychological results of brain injury can have repercussions one upon another.

After brain injury some symptoms are the direct result of loss of brain tissue, while others represent the necessary modification of related functions consequent upon this. Furthermore, in Goldstein's view, a large number of symptoms and alterations of behaviour are in no direct sense a result of damage to a part of the brain, but must be viewed holistically as 'the expression of the struggle of the changed organism to cope with the (primary) defect and to meet the demands of the milieu with which it is no longer equipped to deal'. Some symptoms reflect the struggle, and some the tendency to build up substitute performances. In this way Goldstein saw the origin of such symptoms as anxiety, restlessness, over-orderliness, social withdrawal and the catastrophic reaction (pp. 14 and 81).

The disabilities which Goldstein thought to be fundamental lay chiefly within the intellectual sphere. These are often of a subtle nature and not obvious until special testing is carried out. He emphasised disturbances in conceptual thinking, such as difficulty with abstract as opposed to concrete matters, and difficulty in singling out important features from the general background of perceptions. Such disturbances have found ample confirmation in the hands of subsequent workers. In the twin studies of Dencker (pp. 148 and 157) these were the outstanding post-traumatic defects which distinguished the injured twin from his partner.

Goldstein perhaps overstated his case in contending that so large a spectrum of secondary disabilities followed only in the wake of intellectual disturbance, but he drew attention to possibilities which were previously neglected. Goldstein's point of view is implicit in Hillbom's (1960) explanation for the special frequency of severe neuroses after mild head injuries, namely that 'contradictions with the environment originate more easily when invalidity is not easily visible and the requirement is too high'. Also in Guttmann's (1946) suggestion that attempted denial of mild intellectual impairment is often the basis for neurotic reactions after head injury. It is therefore essential when considering psychiatric disturbance after head injury to explore in detail for minor intellectual deficits. Clinical impressions must be adequately backed by psychometric testing.

The Development of Epilepsy

Post-traumatic epilepsy is known to develop in about 5% of closed head injuries and in over 30% when the dura mater has been penetrated. The general question of post-traumatic epilepsy is considered on p. 213.

The development of seizures represents a serious aftermath of head injury, and is regarded by Jennett (1962) as next in frequency to organic psychological deficits as the cause of enduring occupational difficulty. It certainly stands to aggravate the psychiatric disability ensuing on the injury. First there is the psychogenic and socially disruptive effect of the epilepsy which increases self-concern, hinders rehabilitation, and brings special problems in re-adaptation to daily life. The fits may make their appearance when the patient is on the point of regaining confidence, and represent an added hurdle to be overcome. In addition the physiological disturbance which the epilepsy represents may add to the effects of brain damage already present. After closed head injury temporal lobe epilepsy is the commonest form (Jennett, 1962), and this is just the type most frequently incriminated in leading to psychological disturbance.

Lishman (1968) found that epilepsy occurred during the ensuing five years in 45% of patients with penetrating injuries, and there was a highly significant relationship between its development and the degree of overall psychiatric disability. Epilepsy of early rather than late onset was chiefly responsible for the association, and that developing during the first year after injury was especially closely related to psychiatric disability. The relationship remained significant after controlling for the differing amounts of brain damage sustained among the epileptic and non-epileptic patients.

The Amount of Brain Damage Incurred

The main difficulty in estimating the contribution of brain damage to different forms of post-traumatic psychiatric disability lies in the problem of detecting minor degrees while the patient is alive. The available techniques of radiography, electroencephalography and psychometry cannot be expected always to reflect small amounts of neuronal loss or focal brain dysfunction. And when positive findings emerge it can be difficult to assess their causal relationship to different aspects of the clinical picture. Intellectual impairment after head injury is readily attributed to brain damage, but there is a less clear answer where emotional and behavioural disorders are concerned. Some common somatic symptoms, such as headache and dizziness, have sometimes been attributed to brain damage and sometimes not.

The divergences of opinion in the literature are very striking. Mapother (1937) was led to include psychasthenia among the organic consequences of head injury. This was defined as 'the persistence of ultimate incapacity for employment by mental disabilities which are not gross or obvious'. Similarly many clinicians have been impressed with the stereotyped nature of post-traumatic headache and associated nervous symptoms, and have urged that these too must have some constant basis in minor neuronal damage, perhaps even at the subcellular level. Doubt has now been cast on such clinical impressions, and has grown with a more sensitive appreciation of the role of psychogenic factors of the type outlined above.

A direct search for evidence of brain damage has often produced conflicting results. Cortical atrophy has been found on air-encephalography among patients with symptoms previously thought to be psychogenic, even when consciousness had not been lost at the time of injury (Friedman, 1932; Falk and Silfverskiöld, 1954). Conversely, electroencephalographic changes have shown poor correlations with the incidence of psychiatric symptoms (Adler, 1945). In particular they have failed to reveal a clear distinction between post-traumatic headache and other forms of headache (Silfverskiöld, 1952).

An alternative approach has been to examine the nature and severity of post-traumatic symptoms against clinical indices known to reflect severity of brain damage, such as length of coma, length of post-traumatic amnesia, and other clinical features seen shortly after injury. Personality change has been found to be commoner after the more severe injuries, also the average severity of overall psychiatric disability (Kremer, 1943; Aita, 1948; Steadman and Graham, 1970). In Walker and Jablon's (1959) large series the severity of injury appeared to bear some relation to many aspects of psychiatric disorder—

impaired judgement, mentation, memory, alterations of personality, and even the post-traumatic syndrome. Norrman and Svahn (1961) however, in injuries studied more than two years later, found that severity correlated only with impairment of intellectual functions and very little, if at all, with emotional instability or post-traumatic headache and dizziness.

Lishman's (1968) investigation of 670 soldiers with penetrating injuries used objective measures from X-ray data and surgeons' operating notes, to allow a direct estimation of the extent of brain tissue destruction. This material was chosen to optimise the chance of obtaining reliable measures of brain damage and of demonstrating their relationship to symptoms. All cases had been followed up irrespective of the development of mental sequelae, and thus served as their own controls when the clinical picture one to five years later was reviewed. A wide spectrum of psychiatric disabilities was investigated, including intellectual, affective and behavioural changes, also persistent somatic complaints for which no physical basis could be discovered. From this a global measure of psychiatric disability was obtained and graded according to severity.

It was readily shown that simple measures of the amount of brain damage incurred were related to the amount of psychiatric disorder encountered one to five years later. A close and regular relationship was found, for example, between the depth of penetration of brain tissue at initial wounding and severity of ensuing psychiatric disability, and this relationship was broadly maintained when control was made for effects due solely to intellectual impairment. In a similar manner post-traumatic amnesia was used as an index of diffuse as opposed to focal brain damage, and again regular correlations were seen with the severity of eventual psychiatric disability (Table 6, p. 146). Statistical analyses of the data strongly upheld the significance of these results.

Analysis of individual symptoms and symptom groups allowed some estimate to be made of those components of psychiatric disability which were particularly closely tied to the indices of brain damage. These included generalised intellectual impairment and dysphasia, as might be expected, but also apathy, euphoria, and behavioural disorders such as disinhibition, facile or childish behaviour, and lack of judgement and lack of consideration for others. Among symptoms which had apparently contributed little if at all to the relationships with brain damage were difficulty in concentration, depression, anxiety, irritability, and somatic complaints such as headache, dizziness, fatigue and sensitivity to noise. Difficulty with memory occupied an intermediate position suggesting a more variable aetiology—some patients suffering principally from organic lesions of the memory apparatus and some from psychogenic elaboration of minimal defects.

Brain damage thus emerged as undeniably important in contributing to the long-term psychiatric sequelae of head injury, and appeared to be operative where several different types of disability were concerned. Nevertheless the correlations between brain damage and psychiatric disability, while highly significant in the statistical sense, were relatively small (the correlation coefficients being in the region of 0.25). In other words brain damage could be shown to contribute little more than one-fifteenth part of the total causation of psychiatric disability in the material, and other unmeasured aetiological factors had also clearly been at work.

The Location of Brain Damage

The question of how far psychiatric disability depends on the *location* of damage within the brain has been extensively studied. Here the difficulties inherent in attempting to measure brain damage during life are further increased by the problem of estimating its location with the necessary degree of accuracy.

Efforts in this direction have formed a substantial part of the general endeavour to seek correlations between disturbed mental function and regional brain disorder. Head injury material is in some ways particularly suitable for such investigation. Seen in the stationary state, post-traumatic brain lesions are in the main non-progressive and uncomplicated by changes in intracranial pressure. The principal disadvantage is the uncertainty which often exists about the site of focal pathology, particularly in closed head injuries where the region of the blow or even of skull fracture cannot be taken as an accurate guide to the site of maximal injury. Moreover focal deficits are often overlaid by the generalised effects of brain damage. Penetrating injuries are more suitable for analysis than closed head injuries in these regards, and have been studied in more detail, though even here it must be recognised that covert damage may exist where it is unsuspected.

Certainly focal syndromes of cognitive defect may result from head injury, and it is likely that several aspects of emotional and behavioural disorder may similarly depend on focal rather than generalised pathology. Dysphasia remains the prime example in the cognitive sphere, and frontal lobe symptoms in the behavioural sphere. Both may stand out against the background effects of generalised brain damage which coexists.

After each world war extensive series of head-injured patients were investigated from this point of view. Unfortunately many early studies suffered from bias in sampling and relied rather heavily on impressionistic statements. Moreover earlier work was often interpreted in terms of an outmoded psychopathology, and the quest for a unifying theme or a 'fundamental disturbance of function' produced concepts which were vague, hard to confirm, and hard to translate into the language of another psychiatric school (for example 'Antriebstörung'—disturbance of vital force or drive, and 'Hirnleistungsschwäche'—general weakness of brain capacity or performance). As a consequence the valuable clinical material of early studies is nowadays hard to assess and hard to compare with more recent investigations.

The frontal lobes were soon the site of special interest, and Phelps' (1898) investigation has historical importance. In a series of head-injured patients he investigated the site of laceration of the brain at autopsy and compared this with the presence or absence of mental abnormalities immediately before death. Opportunities for observation were limited since most cases died within a few days of injury, but among 225 autopsies mental change had existed in only 4 cases where lacerations had spared the left frontal lobe. Furthermore among 28 cases with frontal lobe laceration abnormalities had been noted only when the left lobe was damaged. Phelps concluded that there 'seems to be a general law of relationship between a very limited region of the brain and the manifestation of the higher psychical phenomena'. This was supported by his analysis of 110 pistol shot wounds of the brain culled from the English and American literature of the period.

Some of the first detailed reports from war-injured patients were produced by Röper (1917) and Forster (1919) and Feuchtwanger (1923). Feuchtwanger compared 200 frontal gunshot wounds with 200 cases where bullets had penetrated other parts of the skull. The outstanding changes in the frontal group included euphoria, facetiousness, irritability, apathy, and defects of attention. There was often an incapacity for planning ahead, tactlessness, and moral defects. Where intellect was disturbed this seemed usually to be secondary to disorders of emotion and volition. Much of this of course has since been well substantiated from observation of leucotomised patients.

Kleist (1934) in a similar study added loss of initiative, aspontaneity of motor activity, lack of ideation and mutism as characteristic of frontal injuries. The special psychiatric hazard of bifrontal injuries was noted (Heygster, 1949), also the liability of frontal lesions to produce changes of character which led to criminality (Lindenberg, 1951; Mutschler, 1956).

Differences have been described between wounds of the convex lateral surface and wounds of the orbital parts of the lobe, the former producing mainly intellectual and motor changes while the latter had more serious effects on the personality (Kleist, 1934; Walch, 1956; Faust, 1955, 1960). Walch found that with convexity lesions the disturbance was mainly lack of drive (Antriebstörung) or disinhibition, though many patients showed no psychic changes whatever. By contrast, few among the patients with orbital lesions were without striking psychological symptoms, and a high proportion showed changes in 'the more highly developed qualities of personality'. Faust similarly stressed the lack of productive thinking, indifference, and incapacity for decisions with convexity lesions. Patients with orbital lesions often failed to show defects on formal intelligence testing, but were prone to develop radical personality changes. They failed to maintain satisfactory human relationships, lacked perseverance, were sometimes demanding, disinhibited, interfering and aggressive. The sexual life was often marked by increased libido and potency, coupled with disregard for the partner. Criminality was especially marked in the orbital group and often took the form of sexual offences.

Injury to the basal parts of the brain has also attracted special attention. Kretschmer (1949, 1956) described a 'basal syndrome' which has found wide support in the German literature. This results from lesions of the midbrain, hypothalamus and orbital frontal cortex. There is marked sluggishness and apathy along with fluctuations of mood and sudden outbursts of irritability, typically coupled with disturbance of fundamental drives and instincts—appetite, thirst and sleep rhythm—and varied sexual pathologies. Hoheisel and Walch (1952) have described five patients with marked bipolar fluctuations of mood persisting for a long time after head injury; one such case had a shell splinter in the hypothalamus, and the other four showed clinical signs which indicated diencephalic injury.

In contrast to the above, remarkably little has been written of distinctive psychiatric pictures after injury to other parts of the brain. Teuber (1959, 1962) and co-workers have investigated cognitive and perceptual defects in a large series of penetrating injuries with regional brain damage. Patients with left parieto-temporal lesions showed significant losses on the AGCT test of general intelligence when pre- and post-traumatic scores were compared. No such losses were found after lesions elsewhere. The differences persisted after excluding patients with dysphasia, and the left parieto-temporal cases also showed maximal impairment on a non-verbal task (a visual conditional reaction). The evidence, therefore, suggests that lesions of this region of the brain may be especially associated with intellectual deficits, and to a considerable extent independently of language loss.

Temporal lobe injuries appear to show a special frequency of personality disorder, both in their own right and by virtue of the temporal lobe epilepsy which may accompany them (Ajuriaguerra and Hécaen, 1960). Hillbom (1951, 1960) also noted a preponderance of atypical psychoses after temporal lobe injury, and especially schizophreniform psychoses.

Hillbom's (1960) important investigation surveyed a large number of wartime head injuries, of which 415 were randomly selected for special study. Amongst unilateral wounds the left were associated with more psychiatric disturbance than the right, particularly where dementias and psychoses were concerned. Bilateral and midline wounds appeared to cause a great excess of dementias. Frontal injuries were associated with a significant excess of psychiatric disturbance, especially changes of character, and especially when disordered behaviour was prominent. By contrast, parietal, occipital, and cerebellar lesions were relatively free from gross psychiatric disturbance.

The study described on p. 153 (Lishman, 1968) paid special attention to the site of known brain damage in a sub-sample of 345 cases of penetrating head injury. Left hemisphere lesions again proved to be more closely associated with overall psychiatric disability than right. Temporal lobe wounds had led to significantly more psychiatric disability than frontal, parietal or occipital lobe wounds, and this was very largely due to injuries of the *left* temporal lobe.

Some neurological defects appearing immediately after injury were also used as a guide to the location of cerebral damage, and showed special associations with psychiatric disability. In effect damage to different 'functional systems' within the brain could be shown to carry special hazards for psychiatric disability, in addition to damage to specific anatomical areas. Thus sensorimotor defects originating within the left hemisphere, but not those originating within the right hemisphere, were associated with a significant excess of psychiatric disability. Similarly, visual field defects were closely associated with psychiatric disability when they originated in the left parietal or temporal lobes, but not when caused by occipital lobe lesions.

The number of cases available did not allow confident conclusions to be drawn about special regional associations for different types of psychiatric disability. However intellectual disorders were found more commonly after left hemisphere damage, while affective disorders, behavioural disorders and somatic complaints were more frequent after right hemisphere damage (Table 8). Intellectual disorders were especially associated with damage to the parietal and temporal lobes, and were in fact less frequent after damage to the frontal lobe than after damage to other parts of the brain. Affective disorders, behavioural disorders, and somatic complaints were more frequent after frontal lobe damage than after damage elsewhere. All component symptoms among the group of behavioural disorders showed this special frontal association. Sexual disturbances were seen only after frontal wounds, and with one exception this was also true of criminal behaviour. The 'frontal lobe syndrome' (recorded for patients who showed euphoria, lack of judgement, facile or childish behaviour or disinhibition) was especially common after frontal wounds, but nine of the 32 examples were found after wounds which did not apparently involve the frontal lobes at all.

It has therefore steadily become apparent that psychiatric disability after head injury may vary according to the location of damage within the brain. Taken together the various studies quoted above provide considerable support for the broad generalisation that lesions in some areas provide a greater psychiatric hazard than others, and that this involves emotional and behavioural disturbances as well as cognitive defects.

Categories of Post-Traumatic Psychiatric Disorder

The many different forms of post-traumatic psychiatric disablement cannot be rigidly classified, and complex admixtures of symptoms are frequently seen. For example changes of temperament may occur along with intellectual impairment, or paranoid developments may arise in association with neurotic disability. Quite often however, specific features or a combination of related features are outstanding, or even seen in relative isolation. For this reason in what follows the four main categories of psychiatric disturbance will be examined separately—cognitive impairment, change of personality, psychosis and neurosis. The problem of the so-called 'post-traumatic syndrome' will be dealt with separately because of the special difficulties surrounding its nosological status.

The relative frequency of these changes may be gauged from the analysis of two large series of patients in which these broad divisions have been observed. Hillbom's (1960) follow-up of 3552 wartime injuries, of which 1505 were penetrating, showed cognitive impairment in 2%, changes of character in 18%, psychoses in 8% and severe neuroses in 11%. Ota's (1969) large series of 1168 closed head injuries among Japanese civilians showed cognitive impairment in 3%, changes of character in 6%, psychoses in 5% and neuroses in 22%. The differences between the two reflect matters of definition, selection, and type of injury, but both agree in finding that changes of character and neurotic manifestations are the most common, and enduring cognitive defects the least common among psychiatric sequelae. The frequency of the post-traumatic syndrome is difficult to judge because of the many different ways in which the syndrome is defined (p. 168), though often this is reported to rank as the commonest after-effect of all.

Under each heading below the clinical pictures will be described along with comments on the aetiology, course and differential diagnosis.

COGNITIVE IMPAIRMENT AFTER HEAD INJURY

Cognitive impairment is, of course, the direct result of the damage to brain tissue which has occurred. Minor injuries are compatible with full intellectual recovery, even when indubitable loss of consciousness has occurred, in the sense that the patient feels himself to be unimpaired and psychometric tests

TABLE 8. Symptoms and symptom groups seen 1–5 years after penetrating injury in relation to location of brain damage (from Lishman, 1968)
(*indicates strong evidence of special association)

	Number of Cases N = 345	Hemisphere		Lobe(s) (R, L, or both)			
		Left	Right	Frontal	Parietal	Temporal	Occipital
Any Intellectual Disorder	117	★			★	★	? ★
General intellectual impairment	32	★				★	? ★
Dysphasia	24	★			★	★	
Impairment of memory	50	★			★		★
Difficulty in concentration	87		★				★
Any Affective Disorder	113		★	★			
Depression	58		★	★	★		
Anxiety	40						★
Irritability	72	★		★	★		
Aggression	10				★		
Apathy	35	★					
Euphoria	10				★		
Any Behavioural Disorder	40		★	★			
Crime or misdemeanours	5			★			
Sexual disturbance	8			★			
Lack of judgement, etc.	20			★			
Facile or childish	17	★		★			
Disinhibition	13			★			
Somatic complaints	71		★	★			
Headache or dizziness	62			★			
Fatigue	16					★	
Sensitivity to noise	24			★			
'Frontal lobe syndrome'	32		★	★			

reveal no deficits in performance. It is arguable nevertheless that subtle changes too minor to be detected may still exist.

More severe head injuries are likely to be followed by persisting cognitive impairment of a degree proportional to the amount of brain damage incurred. In closed head injuries a post-traumatic amnesia of 24 hours may be taken as a very approximate clinical guide; below this complete intellectual recovery may be expected in a fair proportion of cases, but with durations in excess of 24 hours the patient will be fortunate to escape without some intellectual impairment. With penetrating injuries due to missiles or with depressed skull fractures, however, the length of post-traumatic amnesia is a somewhat less reliable guide. Concussion and amnesia may then be brief or absent, yet focal cognitive defects can be severe especially if haemorrhage or infection have occurred. Any such complicating factors must be taken carefully into account in assessing the prognosis. With increasing age the chance of intellectual impairment is increased (p. 148), and, in general, damage to the dominant hemisphere will produce more severe effects on intellectual function than damage to the non-dominant hemisphere (Teuber, 1959, 1962; Piercy, 1964).

Generalised Intellectual Impairment

After closed head injury the impairment of intellect is usually global, affecting a wide range of cognitive functions together. Marked post-traumatic dementia is usually accompanied by hemiparesis, quadriparesis or other striking neurological disablement. In the most severe cases the patient remains mute and immobile on recovery from coma, persisting thus until death supervenes, usually within a year. This is the 'persistent vegetative state' which represents the most severe form of disability compatible with survival (Jennett and Plum, 1972; Jennett and Bond, 1975). The sleep–waking cycle is preserved, indicating that the patient is no longer comatose, but all mental function appears to be lost. The eyes may be open and blink to menace or follow moving objects, but they are not attentive. Liquids placed in the mouth may be swallowed. Beyond this, however, responsiveness is usually limited to primitive postural and reflex movements of the limbs. Such a condition represents essentially a state of wakefulness without awareness. The similarity to akinetic mutism (p. 199) is obvious, though in the latter the potential for responding may be at a considerably higher level. The responsible lesions may lie in the cortex, subcortex or brain stem, diffuse white matter damage being universal at autopsy.

Short of this the patient is profoundly slow and apathetic, frequently with incontinence and gross dysarthria. All intellectual processes are severely affected and even recognition of relatives may be long delayed. Further recovery often brings evidence of emotional lability, with episodes of uncontrolled weeping or laughing, or more rarely with outbursts of poorly coordinated aggressive behaviour. The 'catastrophic reaction' may be called forth when the patient is confronted with a task beyond his ability— sudden flushing, restless overactivity, and either explosive anger or weeping.

Slow improvement over many months or sometimes years may be expected in all but the most severe examples. The final level of incapacity remains characterised by mental slowing, sluggishness of response, impairment of memory and blunting of affect. Apathy or empty euphoria may remain as persistent features. Loss of libido is the rule, and paranoid developments are not uncommon. In the purely cognitive sphere logical and abstract thinking will be most markedly affected as in other forms of dementia.

All gradations are seen between such pictures of established post-traumatic dementia and minimal degrees of intellectual impairment which may come to light only when the patient returns to work. It is the slight degrees of impairment which present most difficulty for clinical evaluation. Complaints of forgetfulness and difficulty with concentration can be particularly hard to assess, especially when persisting after minor injuries or occurring along with features suggestive of neurotic disturbance. Both may represent organic changes of slight degree, but both are also met with frequently in non-organic psychiatric disorders. After head injury they may therefore sometimes represent a purely psychogenic disturbance consequent upon depression, preoccupation or anxiety. Careful psychometric examination will often, but not invariably, resolve the dilemma; follow-up over time and close attention to other concomitant symptoms will sometimes be necessary to clarify the picture. With regard to psychometry, tests should explore the subtler aspects of cognitive function in addition to the orthodox tests of memory and intelligence; Dencker and Löfving (1958) made careful psychometric comparisons between head-injured twins and their identical uninjured partners, and found that while the groups were almost identical in general intelligence and capacity for new learning, the probands were significantly inferior in ability for abstraction (sorting tests), tests of figure-ground discrimination, and ability to shift frames of reference. More recent studies have focused on deficits in selective attention, speed of information processing and receptivity, as reviewed by van Zomeren et al. (1984); problems in such areas appear to be common and may contribute to the genesis of quasi-neurotic symptomatology.

Focal Cognitive Impairment

A focal emphasis of brain pathology may result in focal psychological defects, which either stand out against a background of general intellectual impairment or on occasion appear in highly circumscribed form. Strictly focal defects are more likely after penetrating injuries than closed head injuries, but nonetheless the search for focal emphasis in disorder must always be thoroughly pursued. A dysphasic or an amnesic syndrome can readily come to be mistaken for global dementia. And areas of relatively intact cognitive function must always be demarcated so that they can be used to the full in rehabilitation.

Newcombe (1983) and Brooks (1984a) provide valuable reviews of the range of deficits encountered and the problems involved in charting and quantifying them by psychometric tests. Disorders of memory, language and visuospatial competence will often require appraisal. Deficits in sustained attention and mental speed may emerge when carefully sought out and will sometimes prove most handicapping of all.

Selective impairment of memory may persist despite excellent restitution of other intellectual functions. This may be sufficiently marked to constitute a 'post-traumatic Korsakoff syndrome', and presumably depends upon circumscribed damage to structures in the diencephalon or medial temporal lobe structures.

Dominant hemisphere damage is associated with language difficulties, manifested variously as difficulty with comprehension, speech production, reading, writing or spelling. Short of overt dysphasia, subtle impairments of verbal function may be revealed by special testing—deficits in verbal fluency, verbal learning, or verbal retention. Arithmetical functions may also be specifically impaired. Dyspraxic difficulties rarely persist in relative isolation, but again characterise dominant hemisphere lesions.

Non-dominant hemisphere damage tends to be associated with special difficulties with visual and spatial functions, including visuo-spatial agnosic defects and disturbances of topographical orientation. Disturbances of body image, dressing dyspraxia and anosognosia may be marked in the early stages, but rarely persist in the absence of gross generalised impairment of cognitive function.

It is unfortunately true that when focal deficits are very marked and persistent, the likelihood of impairment in other areas of intellectual function is also increased, but this is not invariably so. Newcombe (1969), studying men with focal injuries due to high velocity missiles, was able to demonstrate highly selective impairments in language, visual perception and spatial orientation persisting twenty years after injury, yet without any evidence whatever of generalised intellectual deterioration.

Recovery of Intellectual Function

A surprising finding is the relative rarity of profound enduring dementia even after injuries of considerable severity. It is known that some patients, possibly those with severe brain stem injuries, show little improvement over time, also that many partially demented patients survive precariously in their own homes and escape medical attention (Fahy et al., 1967). Nevertheless the fact remains that others improve slowly to an extent that would probably not have been predicted. Certainly experience teaches that in all but the most extreme cases a firm prognosis should not be attempted until two or three years have elapsed from the time of injury.

Several studies have attempted to chart the pattern and speed of recovery in patients followed prospectively. All agree that the major gains are usually made during the first post-injury year, the most substantial improvement occurring in the first 6 months. During subsequent years continuing improvement can certainly be encountered, but much of this can be seen as adaptation and adjustment to the deficits which persist.

The Glasgow workers (Bond and Brooks, 1976; Jennett et al., 1977, 1981) have used broad categories of social outcome rather than focusing on cognitive defects alone; patients are classified in terms of remaining dependent on daily support, being able to travel and work in sheltered environments, or resuming normal life even in the face of minor continuing deficits. Only a minority of patients followed after severe head injury proved to change from one major grade of social outcome to another after the first post-injury year, though further gains insufficient for reclassification could clearly continue after that period.

Detailed psychometric testing has shown that different components of cognitive function tend to plateau at different periods. Thus Mandleberg and Brooks (1975) found that scores on verbal subtests of the WAIS tended to approach those of a non-injured control group after a year, whereas recovery on performance subtests continued for about 3 years. The slower restitution on performance items no doubt depends on their complex nature, requiring a synthesis of numerous capacities such as perception, attention, learning and psychomotor speed. The recovery of memory functions has been investigated similarly (Brooks, 1976; Parker and Serrats, 1976), again with indications that most of the improvement takes place during the first year.

Surprising examples of apparent long-continued cognitive improvement can, however, be seen. This was underlined by Miller and Stern's (1965) follow-up of 92 patients injured on average 11 years earlier. Despite the severity of the initial injuries, with a mean PTA of 13 days, only 10 patients showed persistent cognitive impairment and of these only 5 were unemployed. Half had escaped any loss of occupational status. Of 38 in whom an initial report, made on average 3 years after the injury, had expressed serious doubts whether they would ever work again, 28 were employed and 16 without loss of status. Spastic paresis likewise showed an unexpected degree of recovery, persisting in only 4 out of 25 cases.

These observations obtain support from clinical experience and call for some attempt at explanation. They are a challenge to any simple concept that the appearances of dementia are always due solely to the extent of brain pathology. It would seem unlikely that long-continued improvement over a number of years could be due to those aspects of brain pathology which are reversible. The time course is more in keeping with the re-education of intact brain tissue to take over new functions, and such capacities in the adult brain may be greater than is generally recognised. But an additional explanation is perhaps that a part of the dementia seen in the early phase of recovery is more apparent than real, and that from the outset there has in fact been less brain damage than one was led to infer from the total clinical picture. Two situations may have been responsible for this; first that the patient was suffering from coincident affective disorder, and secondly that motivational defects have been a particularly marked feature and have then slowly yielded to the process of rehabilitation.

Affective disorder may easily be missed in the early months of convalescence when the patient is already slowed, anergic and withdrawn. It is important to remember that the typical patient with severe dementia after gross brain injury shows a bland, even euphoric disposition, in spite of his disabilities; a complicating depressive reaction is therefore to be suspected if the patient remains agitated or profoundly apathetic, or if anorexic or sleeping badly. Antidepressant medication may sometimes produce dramatic improvement, and electroconvulsive therapy is not absolutely contraindicated.

With regard to motivational defects, these may lead to spuriously low performance on tests of intellectual capacity, and the general sluggishness of the patient may increase the clinical impression of the severity of dementia. It is therefore perhaps in the areas of motivation and drive that we should sometimes seek an explanation for the progressive improvement over very long periods of time which may occasionally occur. Little is known about the neural basis of motivation, but it is not beyond possibility that motivational defects are themselves based in cerebral pathology, at least in the early post-traumatic phase. Later in recovery, psychological processes of readjustment and adaptation will play back powerfully to improve motivation, and personality resources are likely to contribute increasingly. Certainly psychological means are necessary to combat the motivational defect, and it is for this reason that graded and stimulating programmes of rehabilitation can often meet with conspicuous success when instituted early and pursued with constant encouragement.

Complicating Factors

In rather rare instances a degree of persistent dementia may be seen which is out of keeping with the severity of the injury that has occurred. This should raise the possibility of subdural haematoma, of normal pressure hydrocephalus, or of a coincident presenile or senile dementing illness.

The possibility of subdural haematoma (p. 355) is a particular hazard in the arteriosclerotic and the elderly, and should be especially suspected when the degree of intellectual impairment appears to fluctuate from time to time. Normal pressure hydrocephalus (p. 639) is a rare but important complication which must also be considered, especially when intellectual failure sets in or worsens some time after the injury. The patient reported by Christie Brown (1975), in whom profound mental impairment persisted for 1-2 years after injury then spontaneously and progressively resolved, would appear from the evidence to represent a rare example of normal pressure hydrocephalus which underwent spontaneous resolution.

The rare cases of post-traumatic dementia in which subsequent histological examination of the brain reveals changes typical of a primary presenile dementia have been discussed by Corsellis and Brierley (1959) and Strich (1969). Here it remains possible that trauma has precipitated or at least accelerated the degenerative process, but for this there is no proof. In the great majority of instances it would seem more likely that the patient was already suffering from a dementing illness to which attention has been drawn by the injury. Roberts (1976, 1979) focused particular attention on the question of late dementia in his follow-up of 291 survivors from very severe injuries. Careful enquiry 10–25 years later yielded evidence of worsening in 31 patients, and in 10 the possibility was raised of a progressive dementia. On taking all associated factors into account, however, such as age, alcoholism, epilepsy and hydrocephalus, there was little to support the notion that a single head injury could set in train a progressive dementing process. Some patients may have had Alzheimer's disease unrelated to the injury, but a more general explanation seemed to lie with the natural processes of ageing affecting a brain already depleted of its functional reserves. The situation with regard to repeated mild head injuries, as received in boxing, is rather different, as described on p. 173.

CHANGE OF PERSONALITY AFTER HEAD INJURY

'Change of personality' implies an alteration in the patient's habitual attitudes and patterns of behaviour, so that his reactions to events and to people are different. This may occur as a persistent sequel of head injury and is undoubtedly one of the most distressing after-effects for the families of the victims. The patient may be aware of the change in himself, though quite often he is completely oblivious of it. Sometimes the alterations are gross and obvious, or sometimes detectable only to those who knew him well beforehand.

Alexander (1982a) points out that head injury is particularly prone to damage the neocortical portions of the limbic system — the fronto-polar, orbito-frontal and anterior temporal regions; few other pathologies routinely damage such areas in a symmetrical fashion while largely sparing the rest of the neocortex. This may explain why behavioural

problems are often greatly out of proportion to the severity of neurological defects, and why profound changes in behaviour, affect and emotion can occur even when there is little by way of long-term cognitive impairment.

The term is used to cover a wide variety of disturbances which can be hard to evaluate and hard to classify with precision. Accordingly this area of post-traumatic change is particularly difficult to interpret. Different aspects tend to be singled out for discussion by different observers. Sometimes the changes are determined by brain damage, sometimes by complex psychogenic factors, and sometimes by a combination of the two together. Aspects of the pre-traumatic personality or current situational difficulties will usually be found to colour the picture, but where brain damage is insubstantial these will often be found to be the decisive elements. Many such changes represent an intensification of personality traits which were present all along. But sometimes, as with frontal lobe damage, there will be elements of change which are new and broadly similar in all individuals affected.

A broad division may be made into personality changes consequent upon brain damage and those in which it appears to play little or no part.

Personality Change with Brain Damage

Here the personality change will often be but one aspect of the global dementia which follows injury, and cognitive defects of some degree will be in evidence. Or with minor degrees of intellectual loss the change may be understandable in terms of the patient's reaction to awareness of impairment. In other cases, however, circumscribed brain damage may operate more directly by disruption of cerebral systems upon which the synthesis of the personality depends. The latter situation is compatible with excellent preservation of intellect to formal testing, yet the personality change is nonetheless 'organic' in origin.

The changes which accompany intellectual impairment may be no more than a loss of refinement or lessened vitality of behaviour, sometimes seen only as transient disturbances which gradually recede over the months that follow. Even so these may combine with adverse circumstances in marriage or at work to set in train severe problems for the patient and his family. Minor degrees of cognitive impairment may also call forth anxiety and depression, especially when the previous personality has been marked by traits of insecurity or feelings of personal inadequacy. Much will depend on the demands made by the environment, and on the handling which the patient receives during the early post-traumatic phase.

With more severe dementia there will be slowing, impairment of motivation, loss of libido and withdrawal of interest in surrounding events and people. Emotional changes include blunting, instability, apathy or euphoria. Irritability and explosive anger occur in some cases and paranoid developments in others. A passive and childish dependence may develop, with petulant behaviour and marked egocentricity. In very severe examples the essential individuality of the person may be to a large extent obscured.

Frontal lobe lesions remain the best known example of the effects of regional cerebral damage on personality. These have already been described on pp. 68 to 69. Centrally there are changes which it is difficult to quantify or demonstrate objectively—lack of foresight, tact and concern, inability to plan ahead or judge the consequences of actions, and a facile euphoric disposition. This may lead to antisocial conduct and conflict with the law. Disinhibition is often marked, emerging in social interactions and in some cases in sexual behaviour. Amorous advances may be made from soon after recovery, conversation is interlarded with sexual innuendos, perverse sexual tendencies may emerge, or interest come to be focused on pornographic material. The patient typically has little insight into the changes which occur.

The alterations are seen in varying degree, sometimes representing little more than coarsening of a previously sophisticated personality or sometimes appearing with gross and disabling severity. Different components of the picture may be prominent, depending perhaps on attributes of the previous personality and on the precise location of damage within the brain. As indicated on p. 154 bilateral frontal lesions, particularly of the orbital parts of the lobes, appear to lead to the most severe examples, often with markedly irresponsible and antisocial conduct. While not entirely the prerogative of frontal lesions they are seen more commonly with frontal damage than with damage restricted to other parts of the brain.

In Roberts' (1976, 1979) survey of the long-term outcome of severe head injuries, the commonest pattern of personality change had a distinctly frontal character. This he termed 'fronto-limbic dementia' — a combination of disabling euphoria, disinhibition or anergia, associated in the majority of cases with intense irritability. Outbursts of ungovernable rage had in some cases led to commitment to institutions. Marked examples were seen only after very severe injuries. Memory was usually also very defective. Less commonly the frontal personality change was present without undue irritability. Occasional patients indeed could be said to have shown *improvement* in personality, in that they were now less prone to worry and were more outgoing and sociable.

A point of great clinical importance is that frontal lobe personality change can occur without evidence of impairment on formal tests of cognitive ability, though of course the two may also be seen together.

A 34-year-old man was referred for psychiatric rehabilitation seven years after head injury. A fall at work had resulted in fractures of the frontal bones of the skull and these had opened up pathways of infection from the frontal sinuses to the brain. Despite careful neurosurgical care over the ensuing years extensive chronic abscess formation had caused much brain destruction in both frontal lobes. Prior to the accident he had been a stable thoughtful man, happily married and interested in his family. Now he was talkative, restless and grossly disinhibited. His wife had divorced him on account of his preoccupation with pornographic material and his irresponsibility generally. Twelve thousand pounds awarded to him by way of compensation had been spent within a few months, partly on extravagant presents for relatives and acquaintances, and partly on the reckless purchase of a business which soon went bankrupt. He showed no concern or insight into his disabilities, and made jocular comments about the troubles which had befallen him. Full psychometric testing showed a level of intelligence within the average range and consistent with his previous education and work record. No memory or learning deficits could be detected.

(Lishman, 1973)

A 24-year-old guardsman shot himself through both frontal lobes while playing 'Russian roulette'. He was in coma for ten days, and mute, incontinent and profoundly anergic for many months thereafter. When seen three years later he was permanently hospitalised and appeared to have reached a plateau where improvement was concerned. Apart from dysarthria there were no neurological abnormalities. He was polite and friendly, and on first acquaintance there was little abnormal to detect. Conversation revealed a rather fatuous and off-hand manner with some degree of euphoria, but he was reasonably well-informed about current events. In his daily life, however, he was profoundly lacking in initiative and needed supervision to care for his appearance. When left to his own devices he preferred to lie in bed for most of the day. He was inclined to indulge in childish pranks, and to buy pin-up magazines and talk of women though libido was totally lacking. He was extremely easily led into mischief and had twice been convicted for breaking and entering while on leave from hospital. The only change he recognised in himself was that nothing worried him any more. He showed no remorse about the recent conviction and no concern about his future. When asked about the game of 'Russian roulette' he replied that it had been 'a bit silly, I suppose'. Psychological testing showed intelligence in the average to superior range with no disturbance of memory. But perseverative tendencies were marked and there was considerable difficulty in shifting attention from one task to another.

The picture just described has obtained recognition on account of the uniformity of the changes seen from case to case. Frontal lobe personality change bears a definitive stamp which in large measure cuts across differences in circumstances and differences in premorbid personality. Little is known in comparison about specific personality changes which may follow circumscribed lesions of other parts of the brain, though such may yet remain to be discovered. The characteristic picture claimed for *hypothalamic and basal brain injuries* has already been outlined (p. 154). *Temporal lobe injury* might also be expected to confer distinctive features, by analogy with what is known of personality disturbance in temporal lobe epilepsy, though these have not yet been defined in any detail.

The symptom of reduced control over aggression deserves special consideration. This is seen with sufficient frequency after head injury, and often enough in relative isolation, to suggest that it may sometimes be founded in focal cerebral pathology. Typically the patient is subject, under minor provocation, to sudden explosions of violent behaviour which sometimes bring him repeatedly before the courts. Hooper *et al.* (1945) described 12 such cases. They stressed that the condition was very different from the more common symptom of post-traumatic irritability, especially in its explosive quality. It could, moreover, occur without evidence of irritability between attacks. In general the problem was found to follow severe head injury, though in a few cases the blow had been quite mild.

These cases do not form a homogeneous group. Sometimes the outbursts of aggression may merely represent an exaggeration of personality traits which were previously well in evidence. Careful enquiry may show, indeed, that aggressive outbursts have characterised the individual from childhood and adolescence onwards, and that the head injury is merely being blamed for a pre-existing condition; a recent interpersonal crisis, or impending court action for violent behaviour may have led to the patient

presenting his complaint at this particular point in time (Lishman, 1978).

Other habitually aggressive persons may, however, show true worsening. The more severe the injury, the more likely it will be that brain damage is responsible. Frontal lobe damage may be particularly significant on account of its disinhibiting effects on the personality. One must remain alert, nonetheless, to the possibility that current life stresses or affective disorder are the factors principally operating to aggravate the situation. Paranoid developments may be important, including conspicuous jealousy within the marital context.

Alcohol will often prove to be a highly significant factor. The consumption may have increased since the injury, or brain damage may have conferred sensitivity to the intake of normal amounts. The so-called 'pathological intoxication' or 'mania à potu' has been ascribed to head injury, as discussed on p. 509.

In other cases no such associated conditions will be found. The explosive diathesis will have emerged as a new and disturbing feature, out of character for the individual and relevant directly to the injury. Occasionally it may represent an epileptic phenomenon. Short of this, EEG studies may reveal focal temporal lobe disturbance, and on theoretical grounds suspicion falls heavily on brain damage implicating the periamygdaloid region within the temporal lobes. Sweet *et al.* (1969) have discussed the evidence linking violent behaviour with diverse forms of pathology within the medial temporal lobe structures.

Clearly every case must be carefully assessed on its merits. The setting of the outbursts, their character and concomitants, the degree of provocation, and the persons against whom aggression is habitually displayed, may all provide essential clues for the origins of the disorder. Sometimes psychogenic factors may emerge in the end as playing the most important part:

A man of 21 had shown repeated episodes of markedly aggressive behaviour, chiefly directed towards the police, since a road traffic accident two and a half years earlier. These had led to repeated convictions and several brief periods of imprisonment. He had previously been a police cadet and there was ample evidence that his conduct prior to the injury had been entirely satisfactory. Detailed investigations failed to show any evidence of brain damage; full EEG studies revealed no abnormality, psychological testing indicated good intelligence without evidence of intellectual impairment, and prolonged fasting showed no evidence of hypoglycaemia. The injury itself had been mild, without neurological sequelae and with a post-traumatic amnesia of only twenty minutes.

The great majority of aggressive outbursts occurred after excessive drinking, and when the patient felt that he had been provoked in some degree. Excessive drinking had set in during a phase of severe depression following loss of a friend in the accident, and continued as the patient became progressively embittered and disgruntled at his failure to find a new career. He now found himself in a vicious circle as a result of repeated convictions, and much of his aggressive behaviour could be seen as bravado in attempts to regain his self-esteem. His hatred of the police force was overt, and he felt their rejection keenly. When drunk, encounters with the police led immediately to the release of explosive outbursts of violence.

Personality Change Without Brain Damage

Changes of temperament less likely to be based on brain pathology include fluctuating depression, morbid anxiety, obsessional traits, and persistent irritability. All are common, and frequently come to be included under the title of personality change. Often they represent an intensification of previous personality traits, and will have emerged on other occasions under different conditions of stress. They may emerge as responses to physical defects or minor cognitive impairments, certainly in the early stages of convalesence, but when persistent they can more commonly be traced to purely psychogenic stresses consequent upon the injury. They are, in fact, often more accurately to be regarded as neurotic reactions than as changes of personality.

It must be allowed, however, that the stress of a head injury and its attendant disruptions may sometimes have profound effects on patterns of life adaptation. A head injury can be a major life event, with profound sequelae in terms of career, marriage and lifestyle, and in certain persons even minor injuries may be invested with great significance. Individuals who are narcissistic, insecure, or who prize their bodily integrity and activity, may develop far-reaching changes in habitual attitudes and behaviour. Those who must cope with physical incapacity or disfigurement will be especially likely to do so.

Here, as so often with the psychological consequences of head injury, the time course has to be taken into account — the longer the changes persist in the absence of evidence of organic defect, the more confidently can they be ascribed to psychogenic rather than physiogenic mechanisms.

PSYCHOSES AFTER HEAD INJURY

The acute post-traumatic psychoses of organic origin have already been described (p. 142). Psychotic episodes may develop later in association with post-traumatic epilepsy, and here also an organic basis can be discerned. The problem is more complex when schizophrenic, paranoid or affective psychoses develop in a patient whose head has been injured. The causal role of the injury may then be far from clear, especially if some considerable time has elapsed between the trauma and the onset of the illness. Frequently the patient or his relatives will seize upon the injury in retrospect as an acceptable and understandable cause, and the issue may become a matter of medico-legal importance.

Various possibilities exist. Organic brain disturbance may itself contribute directly to such developments; or it may act merely as a precipitant in someone already predisposed; or cerebral damage may create a proneness to psychotic disorder by altering the subjects' patterns of reaction to stresses and difficulties. Alternatively organic factors may be unimportant in themselves: the injury or its psychological repercussions may have acted as a non-specific stress to precipitate the psychosis, or psychogenic causes may lie in the changes wrought in the patient's life or the special difficulties he has to face. Finally, of course, the possibility of simple coincidence must also be considered.

These matters have not been disentangled to a satisfactory extent. Large numbers of cases are hard to assemble, and comparisons between different series raise special difficulties, not least with regard to diagnostic criteria. In general the longer the lapse of time between the injury and the onset of the psychosis, the more likely will it be that the relationship is coincidental. But even with a lapse of many years it can be very difficult to discount the injury entirely as a contributory factor, especially if there is clear evidence of persisting brain damage with symptoms derived therefrom in the interim. Both organic disturbances and psychological aftermaths can sometimes be expected to operate over long periods of time in contributing to psychotic developments, *vide* the the long interval characteristically observed between the onset of epilepsy and the onset of the schizophrenia-like psychoses related to it (p. 246).

Nevertheless the generally accepted view is that a constitutional predisposition to the psychosis is a major factor in most cases of schizophrenia or affective psychosis following head injury. Early observations such as those of Tennent (1937) showed that evidence of special vulnerability could usually be found, even in cases where the psychotic illness followed directly on the head injury and became manifest as soon as the acute confusional stage subsided. In five such cases of schizophrenia Tennent found that all had shown evidence of schizoid traits in the premorbid personality, and the illnesses followed the course of ordinary schizophrenia. Among four depressive psychoses three had been treated previously for similar affective disorder. The injuries, therefore, appeared to have made manifest at a particular point in time what would in all probability have followed other stressful situations in that particular person. Since then, however, other studies have combined to suggest more specific factors at work, at least where schizophrenia is concerned.

Schizophrenia After Head Injury

All forms of schizophrenia have been reported after head injury—hebephrenic, paranoid and catatonic. Cases indistinguishable from the naturally occurring disorder may be seen, also certain variants and atypical forms. Davison and Bagley (1969) review the extensive literature on the subject. Paranoid forms are reported to be especially common, also schizophrenia-like hallucinoses in which affect is preserved and thought disorder is not intrusive. Definite information appears to be lacking about the course of schizophrenia following head injury (Davison and Bagley, 1969). Gradual progression to a state of organic defect has been reported, and factors of adverse prognostic significance have included a latent interval before the onset of the illness, but such matters are far from well established.

Achté et al. (1967, 1969) have produced one of the most comprehensive studies of psychotic illness after head injury by following 3552 Finnish soldiers from World War II for 22-26 years. During this period 92 patients (2.6%) developed psychoses resembling schizophrenia, which is well above the incidence to be expected in the general population. However only 0.84% developed 'primary or malignant' schizophrenia, the remainder being schizophreniform or borderline states. These findings are strikingly similar to the earlier survey of Feuchtwanger and Mayer-Gross (1938), who found no excess of 'process' schizophrenia in brain-injured subjects when compared to the general population, but a considerable excess of schizophrenia-like

states. Clearly these somewhat tantalising results reflect the difficulties encountered in achieving precise diagnostic criteria for schizophrenia.

Achté et al. found that patients with mild injuries developed schizophrenia more frequently than those with severe injuries, and suggested that factors independent of the injury generally played a decisive role. Detailed analysis of the location of brain damage failed to highlight any region as having special importance. Other investigations, however, have produced rather different findings, suggesting that brain damage may be important in itself, and especially damage to the temporal lobes.

Shapiro (1939) for example, reported 21 patients in whom schizophrenia had followed within a few hours to three months after injury. Ten showed no enduring evidence of injury to the brain but all had shown evidence of a constitutional predisposition to schizophrenia; eleven did show evidence of brain damage, and in this group only 2 had positive family histories and 7 had had well-integrated premorbid personalities. Thus in the former group the trauma appeared to have precipitated a latent tendency towards schizophrenia, whereas in the latter brain injury would seem to have played a more direct role in the formation of the clinical picture. Hillbom (1951) further supported an organic contribution by noting that 17 of his 20 patients with schizophrenia-like symptoms after head injury had sustained damage to the temporal lobes of the brain. Finally Davison and Bagley (1969) have made an extensive and detailed review of evidence from many sources, including a re-analysis of data from several of the largest and most comprehensively reported series of patients in the literature. Their conclusions, which cannot be bettered to date, are that the incidence of schizophrenia-like psychoses after head injury is certainly greater than chance expectation, and that the trauma may often be of direct aetiological significance rather than merely a precipitating factor. The total evidence of genetic or personality predisposition was found to be less than in the naturally occurring disease, the early onset of the psychosis was related to severity of diffuse brain injury, and a possible special association with temporal lobe damage was upheld.

Paranoid Psychoses

Paranoid developments may be the cause of much distress and disturbance after head injury. They not uncommonly colour the picture of post-traumatic dementia, or emerge as one facet of personality disturbance. Ideas of persecution or of marital infidelity often figure prominently. Frank paranoid psychoses occurring independently of schizophrenia were seen in 77 patients (2·1%) in Achté et al.'s (1967) series, and represented the second largest group of psychotic developments. The onset of the psychosis was often long-delayed and typically occurred in middle age. No relationship was shown to severity of injury, and no particular site of brain damage could be especially incriminated. Evidence of premorbid instability and early deprivation was particularly common, and the development of the psychosis appeared often to be related to serious difficulties in life and to marital conflicts. Conspicuous jealousy was manifest in half of the cases. Almost a quarter were impotent and this proportion was significantly higher than in the series as a whole.

Affective Psychoses

Affective psychoses may emerge in all degrees of severity, both in the presence and in the absence of objective signs of brain injury. Marked examples may be seen after minimal trauma. Here the idea of precipitation in the predisposed person remains substantially unchallenged, and there has been little to suggest an additional organic aetiology.

Symonds (1937) described two cases of depressive psychosis in which the symptoms developed before the patient had recovered from the acute post-traumatic confusion. He suggested that as the patient could not appreciate the effects of the injury at the time, this was evidence in favour of the view that the illness was the direct result of organic brain disturbance. The argument, however, is difficult to uphold: a variety of non-specific stresses may precipitate affective disorder in the predisposed person, even when the brain is not directly damaged, and the patient need not necessarily be aware of a responsible cause. Hoheisel and Walch (1952) have suggested that hypothalamic damage may play a part, reporting five patients with lasting bipolar manic-depressive illnesses after injuries implicating this part of the brain. But organic features were also present in the mental state, and the pictures differed from typical manic-depressive psychosis in that the fluctuations of mood were rapid, lasting only hours or days. More suggestive was the case reported by Parker (1957), in which marked swings of mood developed within two and a half months of a severe closed head injury and continued over the next ten years with repeated attacks of depression and hypomania. There was no previous history or family history of such disorder, but strong psychogenic factors were in evidence in that the patient's wife deserted him soon after the injury.

Depressive psychosis is very much more common after injury than hypomania. Achté et al. (1967) found 47 cases of affective disorder (1·3% of their series) which could confidently be described as 'psychotic'. Only 3 were typically manic-depressive, the rest showing depressive illnesses without manic phases. No relationship could be discerned with severity of injury or with brain damage in any particular location.

Other Psychoses

Other forms of psychosis considered by Achté et al. (1967) included epileptic psychoses, episodes of delirium, and rarer forms such as hysterical psychoses, hypochondriacal psychoses, and hallucinoses. The epileptic psychoses consisted of confusional states associated with seizures, and were the next most frequent after schizophrenic and paranoid psychoses. States of delirium were due to abuse of alcohol or drugs. 'Hysterical' (or reactive psychogenic) psychoses were diagnosed when the disorder, though undoubtedly psychotic, could be seen as a reaction to difficulties, and were characterised by demonstrative behaviour and hysterical conversion symptoms. Hypochondriacal psychoses and simple hallucinoses were very rare.

Suicide after Head Injury

Death by suicide is very considerably increased among head-injured patients, accounting for up to 14% of all deaths (Vauhkonen, 1959; Achté and Anttinen, 1963). In Vauhkonen's series of 3,700 soldiers injured in World War II, no less than 1 per cent had committed suicide by 1957. In many there had been financial difficulties or family disputes arising from the disability, or the patient had been depressed on account of inability to adjust to new forms of work. The lesions were commonly in the frontal and temporal lobes of the brain. Achté and Anttinen (1963) found a tendency for the frequency of suicide to increase with the length of time elapsed since injury, reaching a maximum after 15–19 years. In the majority of cases the injuries had been severe, but the predominance of frontal or temporal lesions could not be confirmed. Most of the patients had had marital problems or other difficulties in personal relationships, and excessive drinking had often helped to make these worse. Over half had been psychotic at some stage in the past, and it seemed that a change of character had taken place in over 40%. Hillbom (1960) found that change of character made the largest single contribution to the suicides in his series, occurring in approximately a third. In Achté *et al.*'s (1967) series 41% of suicides had taken place during a depressive psychosis.

NEUROTIC DISABILITY AFTER HEAD INJURY

The post-traumatic neuroses represent the commonest of the psychiatric sequelae of head injury, in some series outnumbering all other forms of disability together (Ota, 1969). Included here are a number of emotional disorders—depression less in degree than in affective psychosis, and states of tension and anxiety, often with phobic symptomatology; neurasthenic reactions with fatigue, irritability and sensitivity to noise; cases of conversion hysteria and of obsessional neurosis; and most common of all, a variety of somatic complaints including headaches and dizziness, which may be the subject of anxious introspection and hypochondriacal concern.

The above may be found in any and every combination, and patients will sometimes show different components from one time to another. Sometimes they occur as mild and transient disturbances during convalescence, but sometimes as severe and persistent disabilities which can present formidable therapeutic problems. They can also provide protracted difficulty with diagnosis:

A 50-year-old man was referred for assessment 6 years after an injury which had occurred when his lorry was involved in an accident. He had not been rendered unconscious at the time, and indeed the likelihood of trauma to the head had been very slight indeed. He had, however, been exposed to severe emotional shock. During the early months after the accident he had been extremely depressed and lacking in confidence, afraid to meet people and afraid to leave the house. He had attended regularly at a psychiatric day centre and was found to be grossly slowed and lacking in initiative or spontaneity. Psychological testing at this time had shown intelligence within the average range but certain memory tests raised the possibility of organic brain damage.

During the second year after injury he continued to be severely disabled with depression, insomnia and inability to concentrate. His wife described episodes at night in which he would wet the bed, wander from the house, or wake in fear claiming that spiders, frogs and snakes were biting him in bed. He was able to wash and dress himself but his wife had to shave him. She was noted to be excessively overprotective and to smother him with affection.

At a medical interview in connection with a claim for compensation it was reported that he appeared to be largely unaware of his surroundings, and that it was virtually impossible to get coherent statements from him. The clinical impression at this time was of 'a fairly rapidly dementing process'.

During the third and fourth years after injury he continued to deteriorate, becoming increasingly retarded and vague, with incoherent speech and flattened affect, although the florid nocturnal features were no longer in evidence. He was unemployable at the day centre and unable to take part in group activities. The diagnosis remained that of 'a steadily progressive cerebral degenerative process of uncertain cause'.

When examined five years after injury it was reported that he could not answer simple questions regarding his name, age or address. He exhibited a gross tremor of the hands, however, and his general demeanour now suggested an element of psychogenic elaboration.

Six years after injury he was referred anew for full evaluation, and for the first time was hospitalised at a considerable distance from his home. At first he was hesitant, anxious, and incoherent in speech, and the general picture strongly suggested an organic dementing process. Gradually, however, he improved with encouragement, and was observed at times to perform efficiently and well in occupational therapy. At times he would converse normally, display full orientation and reasonable memory for the events of the past 6 years. During his wife's visits, however, he was observed to relapse into his earlier vague manner, to become childishly dependent, and to express irrational fears about being abandoned or subjected to unnecessary operations.

By the end of his 4 weeks' stay in hospital it was obvious that he was capable of functioning at a normal level of intelligence, and comprehensive investigations, including full psychometric testing, failed to reveal any evidence of brain damage. He remained somewhat tense but there was no evidence of depression. He expressed a desire to return to work, and appeared quite genuine in his statement that he wished to have nothing further to do with proceedings for compensation. He viewed the previous 6 years as 'blown out of all proportion' and 'being caught up in a network of problems'. Unfortunately his wife insisted on removing him from hospital before definitive steps could be taken to secure his return to work.

In this case the appearance of severe and progressive dementia proved ultimately to be due to a severe neurotic reaction in response to the psychological trauma of the accident. This had then become intensified and prolonged by the pathological degree of dependence which he had formed in relation to his wife. There was abundant evidence that his wife had colluded and reinforced this aspect of the situation, and in many ways the compensation motive appeared to be more active where his wife was concerned than with the patient himself.

(Lishman, 1973)

Clearly these are the areas in which psychogenic factors come into their own, and can often be seen to operate exclusively. Severe neurosis is chiefly found in subjects prone to neurotic reactions generally, and post-traumatic neurotics, when compared to non-organic neurotics, have shown much the same range of complaints and a similar degree of vulnerability as judged by family and personal history (p. 147).

The important question arises, however, whether subtle aspects of brain damage may sometimes operate in addition as further contributory factors. Such matters are hard to disentangle and require comparisons among large numbers of subjects. Slater's (1943) study of soldiers subject to breakdown in war has already been described (p. 148), and appeared to indicate that organic factors did play some part. But Slater was dealing essentially with acute neurotic breakdowns. In psychiatric practice it is chiefly the long-lasting post-traumatic neuroses which present for attention, and here in the great majority there is little to suggest that organic factors continue over the years to play a part. There is, for example, a conspicuous lack of relationship between severity of injury and severity of enduring neurotic disability, and neurotic symptoms are rare in the presence of marked intellectual or neurological disabilities. It would appear, indeed, that when the consequences of injury are not immediately obvious to external view, the patient with neurotic potential is more than ever liable to manifest subjective forms of complaint. Thus in general it seems fair to conclude with Ruesch and Bowman (1945) that the longer neurotic symptoms persist, the less likely are they to be the expression of brain damage.

Depression in this context shows the features conventionally regarded as characteristic of 'neurotic depression'. Anorexia, insomnia and early morning waking are rarely marked. The depression often fluctuates in severity, and may be responsive to change of activity and surroundings. Sometimes it proves to be no more than a readiness to be cast down by the troubles of daily life, and sometimes it is more accurately described as a state of gloomy and morose preoccupation.

Complaints of difficulty with concentration, lack of normal interest and minor forgetfulness may be marked, and will, of course, require careful investigation to exclude the co-existence of minor intellectual deficits. Paranoid features may sometimes be prominent. Hypochondriasis may be intrusive, with overconcern about real or imagined disabilities. Headache often fluctuates with the prevailing mood.

Anxiety may co-exist with depression or stand alone. Persistent states of anxiety and tension tend to be seen after accidents of an especially frightening nature. The patient may dwell on the circumstances of the injury or relive it in terrifying dreams. Phobic states also may be directly derived from the circumstances of the injury—fear of heights or of traffic, or fear to leave home and venture abroad.

Among long-term survivors of severe head injury Roberts (1979) found two characteristic patterns of disability dominated by anxiety, and rarely associated with more than minimal evidence of brain damage. 'Dysmnesic inadequacy' appeared as a neurotic response to memory or other less obvious cognitive defects; 'phobic imbalance' had emerged in response to various forms of vestibular damage. The anxiety was commonly manifest as reluctance to leave the home and could remain severely disabling over the course of several years. An example of the latter syndrome was as follows:

A man of 30 was seen 18 months after a head injury occasioned by a falling ladder. He had been only briefly concussed, but immediately afterwards became dizzy and vomited several times. Thereafter he experienced vertigo and nausea on sudden head movement, persisting on occasion one month later. During this time he became acutely phobic of enclosed spaces and travelling and gave in his notice at work.

The dizziness subsided but the phobias persisted and intensified. He began drinking heavily and quarrelled with his wife, who left him. Detailed examination showed no evidence of brain damage, and it was strongly argued by the defendants that his present neurotic condition owed much to alcohol and little, if anything, to the injury. The genuineness of the phobias themselves was called into question.

Examination, however, revealed two striking signs. On tilting him backwards to a horizontal position with the head to one side he developed bursts of nystagmus, indicative of labyrinthine damage. And on persuading him to enter the hospital lift he developed obvious signs of autonomic distress, with the pulse rate rising from 84 to 120 per minute. Subsequent neuro-otological examination showed that the right labyrinth was completely non-functioning. Crucial evidence was thus available to demonstrate labyrinthine damage accruing from the injury, and to confirm the genuine nature of his phobias.

(Lishman, 1978)

A neurasthenic reaction may incapacitate the patient for months or even years after injury. The patient complains that he is always tired, feels weak and is lacking in energy. Fatigue, both mental and physical, is readily precipitated by effort and there is marked curtailment of activity. A great deal of hypochondriacal concern typically comes to centre around such disability.

Irritability is among the most common of the emotional consequences of injury. The patient is more short-tempered than usual, more inclined to be snappy and stricter in matters of discipline. All grades are seen, extending to the serious loss of control of aggression already considered on p. 162. It can therefore be difficult to decide how far this symptom represents an affective disturbance on a neurotic basis, or alternatively a personality change due to organic brain damage. Among patients with severe irritability persisting more than a year after injury Lishman (1968) found little evidence to suggest that brain damage was an important factor in the group as a whole. Moreover it showed strong associations with other non-organic symptoms such as depression, anxiety and post-traumatic headache.

Hysterical symptoms have figured prominently in some series of head-injured patients, perhaps especially those admitted to army neurosis centres during times of war (Anderson, 1942). The usual range of dissociative states may occur—fits, fugues, amnesias, Ganser states, motor paralyses, anaesthesias, and disturbances of speech, sight or hearing. The onset is usually soon after the injury, though later developments may occur in association with depression or when complex neurotic states emerge in relation to compensation issues.

Whitlock (1967a) compared 56 patients admitted to psychiatric units with hysterical conversion symptoms, with a group of controls matched for age and sex but suffering from depressive or anxiety states. Almost two-thirds of the patients with hysterical disorders had suffered significant preceding or coexisting brain disorder, compared to only 5% of the controls. Head injury had preceded the onset of hysterical phenomena within six months in 21% of the hysterical patients but in none of the controls. It would seem therefore that head injury may be a more frequent antecedent of the clinical picture of hysteria than is commonly supposed.

Obsessive-compulsive symptoms may emerge in susceptible individuals, usually as a colouring to pictures of depression or anxiety. Typically the patient is tense and ruminative, focusing his doubt, indecision and compulsive preoccupation on the injured head (Anderson, 1942). Frank obsessional neuroses are rarely mentioned in the literature, with the exception of Hillbom (1960) who reported 14 examples among 415 cases (3.4%). Several also had depersonalisation symptoms, and epilepsy occurred

in almost two-thirds which was three times the incidence in the material generally. Unlike the more common neuroses, Hillbom found that compulsive disorders tended to occur after reasonably severe rather than mild injuries. They appeared to be associated with lesions which had caused a noticeable but not very severe disability; in other words just those circumstances where the patient was still able to struggle against his disability in attempts to preserve his former standing.

More recently McKeon *et al.* (1984) have reported 4 patients with severe obsessive-compulsive disorders following directly on head injuries of moderate severity. Three were from a consecutive series of 25 patients suffering from obsessive-compulsive neurosis, the fourth from a pair of monozygotic twins discordant for the disorder. The prompt onset of symptoms, usually within 24 hours of injury, and the absence of premorbid obsessional traits in all but one case suggested that the brain trauma may have contributed directly to the neurosis by some physiogenic mechanism rather than acting as a nonspecific stress.

Headache and dizziness are considered in detail immediately below.

THE 'POST-TRAUMATIC SYNDROME' ('post-concussional syndrome')

The so-called 'post-traumatic syndrome' is the area around which most controversy has existed. The term is unsatisfactory, chiefly because it has come to be used in a somewhat capricious way. The syndrome is rarely clearly defined and different authors include different symptoms under the heading. Central to most definitions are headache and dizziness, but to these may be added fatigue, intolerance of noise, irritability, emotional instability, insomnia, difficulty with memory, difficulty with concentration or simply 'mental symptoms'. Minor degrees of overt intellectual impairment or of change in personality have sometimes also been included, which complicates the picture further. It is not surprising that the concept lacks clarity, and that its aetiology has remained in doubt. Lewis (1942) referred to it as 'that common dubious psychopathic condition—the bugbear of the clear-minded doctor and lawyer'.

Headache and dizziness are two of the most common post-traumatic symptoms in this category. Their correct evaluation is of the utmost importance, since both can be due to organic causes of a nature easily overlooked and which may continue to operate for long periods of time. Yet both can on other occasions represent purely psychogenic disability.

Jones (1974), in a follow-up of 3,500 patients discharged from emergency room practice after slight head injuries, illustrated the natural history of such complaints. Forty-two per cent of the patients became asymptomatic within three weeks of injury, another 57% continuing with headache, dizziness or both for at least 2 months. These too had become asymptomatic by the 1 year follow-up. Of the remaining 1% (36 patients), 30 were still symptomatic at 1 year and had continued to seek medical advice. Twenty of these had been hospitalised for re-examination but nothing abnormal was discovered. Four patients had developed haematomas or hydrocephalus, and 2 had died from non-related causes.

Persistent headache must raise the possibility of subdural haematoma (p. 355) and demands full and careful neurological examination supplemented at least by electroencephalography. It may derive from pathology in the upper cervical spine, especially after whiplash injuries. Focal areas of tenderness in the occipital muscles or in relation to healed scalp laceration must be carefully sought out. Abnormal vasospastic responses of the arteries of the scalp, or tension headache due to muscle contraction must also be considered. Meningeal adhesions have been proposed as a possible organic cause in some cases (Penfield and Norcross, 1936) but this is now considered unlikely. Friedman (1969) reviews the numerous theories about the pathogenesis of chronic post-traumatic headache, and concludes that there is no specific type. He suggests that it may mimic almost any form of chronic recurring headache, which supports the idea that no single mechanism is responsible.

Commonly, however, and particularly when headache has persisted for many months after injury, no demonstrable physical basis will be discovered. Headache which is diffuse, vaguely described, and unremitting throughout the day, immediately raises the possibility of a psychogenic basis. The lack of clear precipitants which cause it to worsen, and resistance to analgesics, also bias the diagnosis in this direction. Frequently post-traumatic headache is found along with other components of neurotic disability, and may be noted to fluctuate in severity along with tension or depression.

Walker and Erculei (1969) analysed the features of post-traumatic headache seen in men 14–17 years after injury. The onset and termination of episodes was usually gradual, the headache was commonly bilateral and referred to frontal regions. Precipitants in order of frequency included noise, nervousness, work, eye strain, and lack of sleep. Aggravating factors in order of frequency were noise, movement, light, coughing or sneezing, and breathing. The descriptions used by the patients were of dull ache, throbbing, pressure, sharp pain or scalp soreness. Headaches were occasionally coupled with nausea and visual disturbances, but then it was hard to know if the headache was of the post-traumatic variety or ordinary migraine.

Dizziness must likewise be carefully distinguished from true vertigo, and in borderline cases careful testing of labyrinthine and vestibular function will be necessary by caloric and other tests, including where possible electronystagmography. Toglia (1969) has shown the value of comprehensive tests of vestibular function in doubtful cases. Harrison (1956) has stressed the frequency after head injury of positional nystagmus of the benign paroxysmal type when this is properly investigated. Seventeen of 108 post-traumatic subjects, most of whom complained of dizziness, showed characteristic nystagmus after rotation of the head to right or left, then hyperextension of the neck so that the head is almost upside down and to one side. Most of these patients however reported a true rotational component to their dizziness, and they were seen very early within two weeks of injury. Care must also be taken to exclude orthostatic hypotension which may lead to feelings of syncope.

Dizziness which persists for many months will, like headache, often be found to have no demonstrable physical basis. Careful enquiry often shows that it is no more than uncertainty of balance, light headedness, or subjective unsteadiness of gait. It is frequently associated with psychogenic headache and likewise with other neurotic complaints. The syndrome of 'phobic imbalance' which may be traceable to early vestibular damage but then persists as a disabling neurosis, is described on p. 167.

When easily demonstrable causes cannot be found we are left again uncertain how much is physiogenic and how much is psychogenic in the post-traumatic syndrome. Much undoubtedly depends on whether the symptoms are under observation early or late after injury. The very frequency of such symptoms in the early stages of convalescence, and their stereotyped occurrence along with sensitivity to noise or alcohol, has often led experienced observers to conclude that they must be founded on some subtle aspect of disturbed cerebral function.

There is now some objective support for a physiogenic basis to the post-traumatic syndrome during the early weeks or months after injury. Thus Taylor and Bell (1966) obtained indications of prolongation of the mean cerebral circulation time in patients suffering from post-concussional symptoms (here including headache, dizziness, poor effort tolerance, difficulty in concentration, nervous irritability, and poverty of memory) when compared with controls. Recovery of normal cerebral circulation times was sometimes found to coincide with resolution of the symptoms. It is noteworthy, however, that the majority of Taylor and Bell's subjects were tested between 1 and 2 months after injury. Similarly studies of brain stem auditory evoked responses have shown significant delays in patients with post-traumatic dizziness, headache and difficulty in concentration, even when the injury had been very mild and led to little more than momentary dazing or stunning (Rowe and Carlsen, 1980; Noseworthy et al., 1981; Montgomery et al., 1984).

Gronwall and Wrightson (1974) employed a serial addition task to examine the rate of information processing in patients following concussion, comparing those who showed post-concussional symptoms (headache, fatigue, irritability and poor concentration) with those without. The task was to listen to digits presented continuously at a standard rate, and to add each digit to the one immediately preceding it. Testing was carried out repeatedly over the course of several weeks. The patients with post-concussional symptoms showed diminished accuracy on the task, and took longer than the others to achieve scores in the normal range; moreover, symptoms could often be observed to recede in step as the patients' scores improved. Gronwall and Wrightson concluded that the test was revealing an identifiable cognitive component, not otherwise apparent, and contributing towards the early post-traumatic syndrome. Such difficulties with information processing could underlie complaints of difficulty with concentration, induce fatigue, and bring on headache and irritability.

Rutherford et al. (1977), in an important study of 145 patients with minor head injuries, assessed the prevalence of symptoms at 6 weeks after injury, the great majority consisting of headache, anxiety, insomnia and dizziness. The symptom rate was significantly elevated when there had been diplopia, anosmia or other abnormalities on neurological examination during the first 24 hours after injury. Concurrently, however, it was possible to show that non-organic factors were also influential even at this early stage; the symptom rate was significantly higher in those who blamed employers or large impersonal organisations for their accidents than in those who blamed themselves. Keshavan et al. (1981), in a similar study, were able to show that premorbid 'neuroticism' scores were strongly related to the prevalence of subjective symptomatology even shortly after injury.

It appears, therefore, that at a relatively early stage an organic component can be discerned in the genesis of these common symptoms. Often it will release them in particularly susceptible persons. But persistence over many months or years may rest upon quite another basis, with brain dysfunction playing little or no part whatever. At 3–6 months after injury, Kay et al. (1971) found that psychosocial factors such as marital status, social class, type of accident and previous mental stability distinguished patients with post-concussional symptoms (headache, dizziness, depression, anxiety, irritability, lack of concentration and fatigue) from those without. No measure of severity of injury did so. Interestingly, however, as in Rutherford's study, disturbances of vision and anosmia persisting after the acute stages were significantly commoner in the group with post-concussional symptoms.

Lidvall et al. (1974) observed that early and late pictures could be discerned when patients were followed prospectively over the course of several months. Headache and dizziness predominated early on, but thereafter the symptomatology became more polymorphous. Anxiety formed the nucleus for the varied later complaints, seemingly principally related to emotional shock or strain dating from the time of the accident. Apprehension that early headache and dizziness might be of serious portent appeared also to dictate the later symptoms.

When persisting beyond a year, the evidence becomes overwhelming that such *long lasting* 'post-concussional symptoms' rest principally on psychogenic mechanisms. The component symptoms lack demonstrable relationship to extent or severity of brain damage (Norrman and Svahn, 1961; Lishman, 1968), show close concordance between injured and non-injured twin pairs (Dencker, 1958, 1960) and figure with great frequency among litigants for compensation (Miller, 1961). They may indeed sometimes set in only after a considerable latent interval following injury, and sometimes the fully-fledged syndrome follows an injury in which there has been no physical trauma to the head but merely severe emotional shock (Walshe, 1958). Finally such symptoms are remarkably rare, as long-continued and disabling features, in the presence of marked intellectual impairment or neurological disability.

Thus it may be concluded that the 'post-traumatic syndrome' has a complex aetiology in which numerous factors may come to play a part. While often initially founded in physiogenic disturbance, it readily thereafter becomes prolonged, and nonetheless disabling, by virtue of a complicated interplay of psychogenic factors.

HEAD INJURY IN CHILDHOOD

The after-effects of head injury in children differ from those in adults in certain important respects, and the reasons are to be sought in several different factors. On the one hand the neural apparatus as a whole appears to be more resilient to damage in childhood. Yet conversely certain functions are particularly vulnerable when they are damaged during the course of their development. The social setting of the child is also different to the adult's and will have important influences—the compensation motive is likely to be absent, whereas the cognitive and emotional aftermaths of injury are likely to hamper school work and call forth interactions with the parents which may have important influences.

There is general agreement that the overall incidence of sequelae is lower in children than adults (Black et al., 1969). On a purely physical plane this can be partly attributed to the greater pliability of the skull and intracranial structures in childhood. The pressure effects of the blow will be better absorbed, vessels less readily ruptured, and transient rises of intracranial pressure more easily accommodated. The powers of restitution and compensation also seem to be greater in the young nervous system; Teuber and Rudel (1962) review the evidence which indicates that animals are less disabled from brain lesions sustained early in life than in maturity, at least where elementary sensorimotor functions are concerned. Thus severe head injury in childhood may be followed initially by grave neurological defects, but these quite often regress rapidly with treatment, and marked early psychiatric symptoms can sometimes be observed to resolve remarkably well (Hjern and Nylander, 1962).

Valid comparisons between groups of child and adult patients are, however, difficult. In particular it is hard to use the usual criteria of severity of injury when comparing cases. The length of post-traumatic amnesia cannot be measured accurately in young children, and it cannot be regarded as certain that this carries the same implications for severity in children as in adults. Duration of unconsciousness or disorientation are also often hard to assess— immediately after the injury the child is often apathetic, fretful and morose, and this may later clear abruptly, suggesting that the emotional disturbance alone has been the principal manifestation of impairment of consciousness (Guttmann and Horder, 1943).

The form which residual disturbances take is also rather different in children as described below. Cognitive disturbances will be profoundly influenced by the stage of development which has been reached. And whilst in adults somatic symptoms such as headache and dizziness are the most frequent and long-lasting effects, these are rarely disabling in children. Instead certain serious disorders of behaviour may be much in evidence, and tend to take distinctive forms.

Cognitive defects have different implications compared to adults, since the child is in the process of developing his mental skills. He stands not only to lose what has already been acquired, but also to prejudice his chances of future intellectual growth.

In practice profound intellectual disablement appears to be distinctly rare as a result of head injuries sustained other than at birth. This is probably because injuries of the necessary severity are not often compatible with survival. However, occasional examples of severe dementia do occur in children, usually in association with spasticity and other gross neurological defects.

More commonly the child is observed to be set back only temporarily, and to make this good in the months that follow. Recently acquired abilities to walk or talk may be lost, or school work is found to be impaired for a time in relation to his fellows. For a while he may appear to be more backward than is truly the case, as a result of ill-sustained attention, sluggishness, or ready mental fatigue. While they persist, however, such factors can hamper education to a serious degree. The behavioural changes outlined below are sometimes even more disruptive of progress at school, leading to persistent underachievement even when no intellectual loss can be identified.

Chadwick et al. (1981) have reported one of the few prospective studies of the cognitive sequelae of head injury in school-age children. A group of 29 children with 'mild' injuries (post-traumatic amnesia less than 7 days) and 31 with 'severe' injuries (PTA more than 7 days) were followed with repeat testing for up to $2\frac{1}{4}$ years. Twenty-eight non-head-injured children served as controls. There was no convincing evidence of intellectual impairment, even transient in nature, when the PTA had been less than 24 hours. Deficits were common, however, when the PTA had exceeded three weeks and in some cases could still be detected at the final follow-up examination. Transient impairments, resolving completely, seemed to characterise those in the intermediate PTA range. In general visuospatial and visuomotor skills tended to be more severely affected than verbal skills. Substantial recoveries in intellectual function could be charted during the follow-up period; improvement was most rapid during the early months, but further clear gains were observed for a year and sometimes continued into the second post-injury year as well. A definitely adverse effect upon school performance was observed only in children with the most severe injuries, where the PTA had exceeded 3 weeks in duration.

Klonoff *et al.* (1977), in a 5 year prospective study of a large cohort of head-injured children, were able to demonstrate the long time-scale of the improvements that could occur. Serial testing, carried out along with matched non-injured controls, showed that recovery sometimes extended over the whole 5 year period, with significant gains still occurring between the fourth and fifth year follow-up examinations.

The precise effects of childhood injury on intellectual function are incompletely understood. Teuber and Rudel (1962) illustrated the complex relationships which may obtain between brain injury in childhood and performance on different types of task. Performance on one of the perceptual tasks which they examined was lowered by injury at any age, another revealed the effects only up to the age of eleven but no abnormality could be detected thereafter, whereas a third revealed no impairment in young children but from eleven onwards the deficits became increasingly apparent. Clearly the dynamics of cerebral organisation change during the course of development, so that functions which are crucial at one stage can later be supplemented by others, or defects which at first remain latent may later be revealed. In this connection Russell (1959) suggested that damage to the frontal lobes may be particularly harmful in very early life, and described occasional cases where such a lesion had apparently led to severe mental retardation as the child matured. He postulated that the frontal lobes might play a special part in mental development during the early years, but lose this function once adulthood is attained.

Among focal defects dysphasia has been most closely investigated. A change in cerebral dominance is possible after unilateral brain injury in early life, and this plasticity appears to persist in some degree in later childhood (p. 38). A particular feature of childhood dysphasia is often the quantitative reduction of spoken and written language, extending even to gesture activities (Alajouanine and Lhermitte, 1965). Spontaneous speech is sparse, and the child must be strongly encouraged to get him to reply to questions. Loss of acquired language is sometimes less striking than subsequent slowing of speech maturation, especially in very young children who are still in the process of learning to talk. Comprehension difficulties may only become obvious when the child must sustain attention for long periods as at school, or difficulties in learning to read or spell may later emerge even when spoken speech has made a good recovery. Thus even though the prognosis is better than in adults, Alajouanine and Lhermitte found that continuing difficulties were still to be found in a large proportion of children.

Behaviour disturbances are repeatedly stressed as the commonest and most disruptive of the sequelae of head injury in children (Dillon and Leopold, 1961; Black *et al.*, 1969). Commonly they consist of restless overactivity ('hyperkinesis'), impulsive disobedience at home and at school, and explosive outbursts of anger and irritability. Marked delinquency may appear by way of stealing, cruelty and destructiveness. Black *et al.* (1969) followed up an unselected cohort of 105 children injured between the ages of 2 and 14 years and showed the incidence of such changes. At one year after injury approximately 20% of the children showed behaviour disorders which had not been present before. The most disruptive effects on adjustment were produced by hyperkinesis (present in 32% and appearing as a new phenomenon in 15%) and problems with anger control (present in 20% and a new development in 13%). Both represented a very definite increase in incidence compared to the pre-traumatic state. Problems of discipline such as lying, stealing or destructiveness were a major problem in 10%, and excessive lethargy or passivity had persisted since the accident in 8%. Sleep disturbances and problems with appetite were also occasionally observed. Hyperkinesis was commoner in younger than older children, and behaviour disturbance generally was more frequent in boys than girls.

Brown *et al.*'s (1981) careful prospective study of 50 school-age children demonstrated clearly that the development of new behavioural disorder was related to severity of injury. The group with post-traumatic amnesias of less than 1 week showed a raised level of *pre*-accident psychiatric disturbance compared to controls, but no increase following injury. By contrast approximately half of those with PTAs exceeding 1 week developed new behavioural disorders, this being commoner the more severe the injury. In general there was little that was specific about the forms of psychiatric disturbance encountered in this study, the sole exception being a tendency to disinhibition and socially inappropriate behaviour reminiscent of the adult frontal lobe syndrome. Hyperkinesis in particular did not emerge in this sample as strongly related to brain damage.

Both organic and non-organic factors can be discerned in the development of post-injury behavioural disturbances and it can be difficult to apportion the blame. The combination of restless hyperactivity, impulsiveness and resistance to discipline is reminiscent of that seen after encephalitis lethargica (p. 296) and has often been regarded as a distinctive result of brain damage in childhood (Strecker and Ebaugh, 1924; Blau, 1936). The child appears to be dominated by instinctual and emotional impulses, as though he has lost the inhibiting and restraining influences normally acquired during development. As with post-encephalitic children, and unlike delinquents generally, these children are said to know that what they do is wrong, and to realise that they lack the ability to control their misbehaviour. They have a proper sense of right and wrong, acquired before the accident, but cannot act on it when confronted by the actual demands of daily living (Blau, 1936). In these respects an organic origin is strongly suggested.

There is evidence, however, that other factors contribute as well. Brown *et al.* (1981) were able to demonstrate the influence of the child's pre-accident behaviour, his cognitive level and his psychosocial circumstances in leading to behaviour disorder, in addition to the effects of brain damage. Harrington and Letemendia (1958) compared a group of head-injured children attending a child guidance clinic with a group who were not under psychiatric care. The latter, as expected, showed less psychiatric disorder, but proved to have had the more severe injuries. In general terms the pre-traumatic personality and family setting of the child emerged as more important for the psychiatric outcome than the nature and severity of the injury. A favourable outcome was possible even after severe injuries provided the child had previously been well adjusted; and the families of children who presented with chronic behaviour disturbance showed a high incidence of emotional and psychiatric disorder among immediate relatives. The authors were further led to challenge the specificity of the pictures so often described after head injury. The range of disturbances in their material was similar to that encountered in non-organic child psychiatry generally, with aggression, tics, tension habits and hyperactive behaviour heading the list.

Clearly, as with head injuries in adults, the environment of the child and his premorbid constitution will have important effects, particularly where later progress is concerned. But it would seem unwise to discount the organic contribution entirely. The observations already outlined imply a definite organic stamp in the more severe examples, and in Black *et al.*'s (1969) series the incidence of new behavioural disorder was identical in the groups with and without evidence of pre-morbid behavioural difficulties.

Whatever its origin, post-traumatic behaviour disturbance can have serious consequences in terms of school achievement, which may be markedly impaired despite a good preservation of intellect to formal testing. In the most severe examples schooling is completely disrupted, and prolonged in-patient care is sometimes required. Prognosis is variable but is generally regarded as poor. However minor degrees of disturbance are sometimes tolerated for several years before psychiatric help is sought, and the apparent worsening may then merely be due to the manifestations becoming more marked as the child's behavioural repertoire expands. Sometimes self-control is gradually re-established as the child matures, and hyperkinesis appears usually to wane as the child grows older.

Neurotic disturbances are by contrast rare in head-injured children. Nightmares, tension habits and hysterical features are said to be uncommon as enduring features unless the child has shown obvious maladjustment beforehand. Headache may be present in the early post-traumatic phase, but is rarely prolonged and usually has negligible effects on the child's adjustment. It becomes more pronounced and frequent as age at time of injury increases, and in older children may approach the adult pattern with psychological and social features which account for its continuation (Guttmann and Horder, 1943; Black *et al.*, 1969). Dizziness is likewise very rare after injuries early in life.

HEAD INJURIES DUE TO BOXING

The question of 'chronic traumatic encephalopathy'

in boxers is of special interest, because here serious sequelae appear to follow repeated mild head injuries, each in itself leading to no more than brief concussion. The mechanisms underlying such a cumulative effect are unknown. It is interesting, however, that Gronwall and Wrightson (1975) have been able to show that even a single concussion renders the brain slower to recover from a subsequent episode. Using a sensitive psychological test procedure (p. 170) they demonstrated that rates of information processing were slower after a second mild head injury than after a single injury of equivalent severity, despite a mean of $4\frac{1}{2}$ years between the two. The time taken to recover to normal levels of functioning was also significantly delayed.

The whole subject has been a matter of dispute for many years. The picture of 'punch-drunkenness' in retired boxers is widely recognised, but the supporters of boxing have sought to explain it on the grounds of coincidentally occurring neurological disease, or have attributed it to alcoholism rather than to the patient's boxing career. Several series of cases have combined to suggest a syndrome with highly characteristic features, but have been open to criticism on the grounds of special selection (Martland, 1928; Critchley, 1957; Spillane, 1962; Mawdsley and Ferguson, 1963). Roberts' (1969) extensive survey, described below, was therefore particularly important in establishing the syndrome as a valid entity, and in providing clear indications that the boxing career had been responsible.

In its fully developed form the syndrome consists of cerebellar, pyramidal and extrapyramidal features, along with a varying degree of intellectual deterioration. This unusual combination of neurological features provides a characteristic picture, and suggests that a distinctive pathological process is responsible. Severe examples date mostly from boxing careers pursued before the Second World War when medical control over boxing was less rigorous than at present. Fair-ground booth boxing appears to have been especially hazardous. However there are indications, especially from recent CT scan studies, that present safeguards are still inadequate to prevent brain injury, as will be discussed below. Kaste *et al.* (1982) suggest, indeed, that modern medical control creates a dangerous illusion of safety.

Neurological Features

In mild examples there is dysarthria, facial immobility and poverty and slowness of movement. Unsteadiness of gait may not be present, but evidence of asymmetrical pyramidal lesions is common from an early stage. At its most severe there is disabling ataxia, disequilibrium, a festinant gait, tremor of the hands and head, and spasticity or rigidity of the limbs. All grades of cerebellar, pyramidal and extrapyramidal disorder may be seen between these extremes. The disabilities usually set in towards the end of the boxing career while the patient is still relatively young. Sometimes the onset is acute and can be traced to a series of particularly hard fights, thereafter dictating retirement.

Roberts (1969) carefully sought out and traced a random sample of professional boxers who had held a professional licence for at least three years between 1929 and 1955. Of the 250 boxers chosen for study, 224 were available for examination. Thirty-seven (17% of the total) showed evidence of the characteristic syndrome, while 11 more had other neurological lesions which could not be attributed to boxing. Approximately one-third of the 37 were judged to be affected severely enough to be recognisable by a layman as 'punch drunk'. The clinical picture, while varying in degree, was remarkably constant from one case to another, and appeared distinct from other common neurological diseases. Moreover the prevalence of the syndrome increased with increasing exposure to boxing as judged from the history, again strongly upholding a causal relationship. A number of other isolated symptoms such as vertigo and impairment of vision also increased with the length of exposure, but epilepsy occurred no more frequently than in the general population.

Progression of the disablement has been described as characteristic, but Roberts found that the majority of cases remained static once boxing was discontinued. Occasionally the condition had become more obvious with advancing age, but it was hard to distinguish this from the changes associated with ageing generally. However undoubted progression was seen in four cases, three with extrapyramidal disturbance and one with cerebellar symptoms and dementia, at an age and with a rapidity that was clearly independent of ageing. In a few cases there had been undoubted improvement after retirement from the ring.

Psychiatric Features

Almost half of Roberts' 37 cases showed intellectual and personality changes indicative of dementia in addition to their neurological disablement. This occurred in all degrees of severity. Nine had severe memory impairment, often in conjunction with apathy, irritability or marked disinhibition. In 5 others thinking was profoundly slowed. Two were demented to a degree which required permanent hospitalisation. In the series as a whole subjective difficulty with memory increased in proportion to the length of the boxing career.

The incidence of personality change was hard to assess, but the boxers' wives often described irritability, progressive apathy, and liability to outbursts of temper. Severe paranoid illness appeared to be common, particularly in subjects who showed intellectual deterioration.

Johnson (1969) paid special attention to the psychiatric features in 17 ex-boxers with chronic traumatic encephalopathy. The neurological features had usually appeared before the psychological manifestations, and each could then follow an independent course. Four main areas of psychiatric disturbance were apparent:

A chronic amnesic state was present in 11 patients, chiefly affecting recent memory and without any tendency to confabulate. Progression was uncommon, and apart from social embarrassment the memory defect caused little concern. *Progressive dementia* with disorganisation of intellect and personality occurred in 3 cases, and paralleled progressive neurological disablement in 2. *Morbid jealousy* had led to the primary psychiatric referral in 5 cases, with persistent accusations and sometimes frank delusions concerning the wives' infidelity. All showed evidence of brain damage, and some degree of impotence appeared to be an important determining factor. *Rage reactions,* with uncontrolled outbursts of anger and violence, were prominent in 3 patients. All had shown impulsive aggressive behaviour as a life-long trait, and the worsening after boxing was attributed by the patients to decreased alcohol tolerance. In addition 5 had shown evidence of psychotic illness; one a chronic paranoid state associated with organic memory disturbance, 2 with transient paranoid-hallucinatory states, one with endogenous depression, and one with acute catatonic schizophrenia which developed after a fight and was followed by gradual intellectual and social deterioration.

Recent Investigations

Certain recent studies have concentrated on 'modern era' boxers who have fought under present medical controls. The consensus of these studies is that brain damage is still prone to occur, even in comparatively young boxers who are pursuing successful careers. Cerebral atrophy, as revealed on the CT scan, has been found to antedate overt signs of brain damage; moreover it shows a significant association with the number of bouts fought, rather than with the number of knock-outs sustained, suggesting a cumulative effect of multiple subconcussive blows to the head (Casson *et al.*, 1982, 1984; Ross *et al.*, 1983). It is unfortunate, however, that control observations have not been employed in the studies to date, which detracts from the impact they might otherwise make.

Casson *et al.* (1982) found mild to moderate cerebral atrophy on the CT scan in 5 of 10 active professional boxers aged 20–31. None of the 5 showed mental or neurological abnormalities. Atrophy was detected in 3 of 6 professionals and 1 of 8 amateurs by Kaste *et al.* (1982), the mean age of the group being 31. Ross *et al.* (1983) examined 40 ex-boxers, finding a significant relationship between the number of bouts fought and both ventricular enlargement and EEG changes. The presence of CT abnormalities was associated with more frequent neurological symptoms and signs.

Casson *et al.*'s more recent study focused on boxers with no known medical, neurological or psychiatric illness, and without histories of drug or alcohol abuse (Casson *et al.*, 1984). All 18 had been active since the Second World War, and 15 since 1960 only. Ages ranged from 18 to 60. Eight were found to have atrophy on the CT scan, 3 also showing a cavum septum pellucidum. Seven of 13 had abnormal electroencephalograms. Neuropsychological testing revealed deficits in several areas of functioning, performance being particularly poor on tests of short-term memory. Neuropsychological impairment, like cerebral atrophy, showed a significant relationship to the number of bouts fought, and was significantly more common in those with CT or EEG abnormalities. Three of the older subjects had a clinically obvious organic mental syndrome manifested by disorientation, confusion and memory loss.

These results, while uncontrolled, clearly give cause for concern, as expressed by a recent report from the British Medical Association (Report of the Board of Science and Education Working Party, 1984).

Pathology

Cerebral atrophy is commonly revealed on air encephalography or CT scanning, with dilation of the ventricles, sulcal shrinkage, and sometimes obvious cerebellar atrophy. A characteristic finding is perforation of the septum pellucidum ('cavum septum pellucidum') which is rarely seen in other conditions. It is thought to be a direct result of rupture of the walls of the septum consequent upon recurrent abrupt rises of intracerebral pressure.

The electroencephalogram may be abnormal with flattening of the record, diminution of alpha rhythm, or diffuse slow waves. However Roberts (1969) found no reliable differences between his boxers and a healthy control group, nor within his sample in relation to the clinical condition or the degree of exposure. Single EEG records are therefore of little use in establishing or refuting a diagnosis of traumatic encephalopathy, and cannot be used to detect early changes which might indicate that retirement is advisable.

At autopsy cerebral atrophy is often obvious to the naked eye, and ragged holes may be seen in the septum pellucidum. The detailed neuropathological findings have been clarified by the thorough study of Corsellis et al. (1973). Microscopically there is extensive loss of neurones in the cerebral cortex, and neurofibrillary degeneration of a type similar to that seen in Alzheimer's disease or senile dementia but without accompanying senile plaques. The cerebral damage and degeneration is concentrated on the septal regions, on the medial temporal grey matter, and on certain neurones along the cerebellar and nigral pathways.

Johnson (1969) suggests that the clinical features are probably related to damage to two main areas of the brain—the upper brain stem and the hippocampal-limbic system, accounting for the fact that the neurological and psychiatric features may progress independently of each other. Dysarthria, ataxia, parkinsonism and pyramidal disorder are consistent with a lesion in the midbrain, and neuropathological studies have demonstrated gliosis in this area. The lesion probably derives from the repeated rotational stresses to which the brain stem is subjected in the blows of boxing. The memory difficulties probably depend on hippocampal or mamillo-thalamic lesions. Corsellis et al. (1973) ascribe them to the intense neurofibrillary changes which may be seen in the hippocampi and related parts of the limbic grey matter, and perhaps also to the atrophic state of the fornix bundles which are often displaced by the septal damage. Johnson suggests that impotence may also be due to lesions within the limbic system or in the neighbourhood of the third ventricle. With regard to the accentuation of rage reactions, this may depend on limbic lesions, or even directly on structural changes in the septal area.

In the occasional cases of severe and progressive dementia it is hard to discount the possibility of coincident Alzheimer's disease. In cases coming to necropsy a picture typical of this condition has been reported. It remains possible, of course, that repeated head trauma may precipitate the disease, though for this there is no evidence. It has also been suggested that repeated mechanical agitation of the brain may induce disturbances of the gel-sol equilibrium within the brain, or produce an auto-immune response from damaged cells, but direct support for such theories is lacking.

Medico-Legal Considerations

In peace-time the great majority of head injuries result either from road traffic accidents or accidents at work, and therefore frequently become an issue before the courts. Motor insurance covers road traffic accidents, and personal accident insurance covers many accidents which occur in other settings. Legal problems may involve the proof of prime responsibility or of negligence, though industrial injuries which come within the terms of the Industrial Injuries Act (1948) are subject to compensation whether negligence can be shown or not. The armed services have their own machinery for compensation through Boards set up by the Department of Health and Social Security (formerly by the Ministry of Pensions and National Insurance).

The system now operative in New Zealand has attracted considerable interest, in that injured persons have no need to take legal action. An Accident Compensation Corporation exists as a statutory body, with responsibility for compensation, rehabilitation and accident prevention, being funded from a levy on all employers and from vehicle licence fees (Smith, 1982a, 1982b). In such a system there is no requirement to prove that anyone was at fault; problems can hinge, nonetheless, on defining what may properly be deemed an 'accident'.

Whatever the setting of the accident a medical report usually comes to form an important part of the proceedings, and few neurologists or psychiatrists are in practice for long without being required to furnish such evidence. In complicated or disputed cases attendance at court may be obligatory.

Facilities for legal aid allow patients of modest means to obtain legal representation after satisfying a panel of lawyers that their claim has a reasonable chance of success. In industrial accidents the patient will normally consult his trade union where applicable, and the union's lawyers will act on his behalf. Formerly it was usual for solicitors to call in chosen medical experts to intercede on the patient's behalf and to argue his case in return for a special fee, but present practice is increasingly to contact the consultant under whose care the patient has always been treated.

The defendant in the case, usually an insurance company, will often wish to seek an independent opinion and may call upon doctors specially retained for such a function. In many instances the doctors from the two sides meet and agree on a report for the court, but this is not always the happy solution. It is then that clashes of medical opinion may arise and legal proceedings become burdensome and prolonged. Nevertheless in the interests of justice to all parties the situation must be accepted, and a proper skill in the presentation of evidence must be acquired.

The court will need to make its decision on three main aspects of the situation where the medical evidence is concerned: first on the nature and degree of disablement which has followed the injury; secondly on the likely duration and future course of such disablement, and the impact it will make on the quality of the patient's life; third, and fundamental to all the rest, the causative relation between the disability and the injury which preceded it. All three can in some circumstances be the subject of uncertainty and open to argument.

Nature and Degree of Disablement

The nature of the disablement and its severity are decided from clinical examination, supplemented wherever possible by objective test procedures. With many areas, however, it is necessary to depend largely on the patient's own account, that of his friends and relatives and sometimes that of his employers. Evidence from observation in hospital or rehabilitation units is invaluable, since the other sources can hardly be expected to be free from bias once litigation is under way.

All too often it is necessary to accept unsubstantiated evidence and to make a reasoned interpretation of its reliability. Evidence of altered disposition or of emotional instability, for example, must often be derived from accounts of behaviour furnished by others. The situation can be particularly difficult when subjective complaints form the main burden of the patient's disability, as with persistent headache, dizziness, fatigue or inability to concentrate.

The impression made at interview, and equally that made before the court, can be misleading in both directions. The patient with intellectual impairment or frontal lobe damage may cheerfully disclaim any symptoms whatever, and the likely impact of the injury on his life may be revealed only by skilled examination and psychological testing. Conversely the patient may greatly exaggerate his symptoms, and claim unfitness for work or inability for enjoyment when objective evidence of disability is slight. The circumstances of the clinical interview do not permit a wealth of suspicious cross-questioning and the follow-up of every lead for verification, but the patient's permission for access to important informants should always be sought when there is room for doubt.

A diagnosis of deliberate simulation must be made with extreme caution. The distinction from hysteria will sometimes be difficult if not impossible, though the criteria outlined on p. 410 may help in arriving at a reasonably valid conclusion. Miller and Cartlidge (1972) rather brusquely criticise the unwillingness of doctors to consider simulation, and report a vivid example as follows:

A 30-year-old labourer had sustained a mild head injury without loss of consciousness. During the ensuing months he developed anxiety, depression and stammering, unrelieved by psychotropic drugs, and after a course of ECT he became totally mute. At the time of examination he had not been heard to utter for nearly two years. Numerous referrals had led to a multitude of diagnoses, but eleven psychiatric reports had failed so far to mention the possibility of malingering.

'As can be imagined, examination presented considerable difficulty. The case was well-documented and the patient's wife most informative. His own contribution consisted in grimly nodding his head in affirmation or negation of questions and of written notes passed across the table. This he accomplished fluently and accurately. In this manner he registered complaints of frequent headaches, dizziness on change of posture, forgetfulness, and intermittent severe depression......... From the beginning of this remarkable consultation it was difficult to escape the impression that the patient was malingering. He was tense, evasive, suspicious, and defensive—and his wife's attitude was very similar. The examiner's conviction that the patient was endeavouring to deceive was so strong that he telephoned a colleague and arranged for him to accompany the claimant unobserved on his mainline train back to the Midlands. The patient exchanged his first remarks with his wife as the train drew out of Newcastle station, and by the time his companion left the train at Durham the whole compartment was engaged in uninhibited and cheerful conversation on matters of the day.'

Miller and Cartlidge (1972)

Careful note should be made of the patient's attitude to detailed history taking, and of any striking inconsistencies which emerge. For example the vigour with which he pursues the claim, and the detail with which he recounts events connected with it, may be at variance with his complaints of torpor, failing memory, or difficulty in sustaining concentration. His appearance may belie complaints of insomnia or constant headache. Or the clinical features of the latter may raise suspicion, especially when it is said to be unremitting over very long periods of time and totally unresponsive to analgesics. The medical advice which the patient has sought in the interim, and the regularity with which he has attended and followed the treatment prescribed, may also give important indications of the true extent of his suffering. It is fair and just to tell him on occasion of conflicts in his evidence, and to reassess this further in the light of his response and explanations.

Estimate of Prognosis

The question of prognosis will certainly be considered by the court. Here it is usually possible to do no more than give a reasoned expectation and to be frank about the measure of uncertainty which surrounds it. It could be argued that after head injury of any severity the patient's condition is never likely to reach stability, and that full justice could only be met by a lifetime's follow-up (Miller, 1969). This is indeed the practice for the war-injured, and those who are compensated via the Industrial Injuries Act, where injuries of more than moderate severity are awarded an on-going pension which remains under regular review by the Department of Health and Social Security. In the rest of civil practice however, a compromise must be accepted, since compensation is likely to be paid as a lump sum on the basis of shorter-term assessment together with prediction of the likely future course. Steadman and Graham's (1970) review of a series of civilian head injuries in the UK showed that in one-third the compensation issue was settled within one year, in one-third within two years, and in all by five years. However in particularly complex cases much longer periods can ensue.

Follow-up studies of patients coming before the courts are remarkably few, and opinions expressed by eminent medical men in the literature are not uncommonly at variance with one another. Such a situation is grist to the mill of contending counsel. The frustrating delays which so commonly attend legal proceedings can here sometimes prove to be an indirect advantage, especially when the patient has remained under regular surveillance and when repeated detailed examinations have been carried out. Even severe dementias are known to be compatible with improvement over long periods of time (p. 158), and serial testing may already have indicated the course which is likely to be followed in the present instance. Moreover a truly confident prognosis can sometimes only be given when the patient has returned to work. Examination may have failed to reveal much by way of intellectual loss, yet impaired judgement and irresponsibility may later prove to make him totally unsuitable for his former occupation.

On the other hand, where the compensation motive is suspected to be active it may be felt that until litigation is ended the future course will remain uncertain. If the compensation issue is thought to play a part in determining the prolongation of symptoms this should be clearly stated in the report. If a substantial element of simulation has been confidently detected the likely resolution of disorder after settlement may likewise be predicted. Otherwise it is sometimes better not to venture on too firm a forecast but merely to state the uncertainties which surround the patient's future course. It is the decision of the court which will be operative, and where present medical knowledge is insufficient to help in this decision it must not be allowed to bias it unfairly.

The question of post-traumatic epilepsy should be considered in every case, and when epilepsy has not already occurred the possibility of its future development should be kept in mind. The court should be reminded of the possibility of onset even some years after injury, otherwise final settlement may deprive the patient of adequate compensation for what is later to prove his most substantial handicap. Other possible late effects of head injury—post-traumatic parkinsonism or the precipitation of multiple sclerosis—are too rare and too controversial to warrant mention unless they have already made an appearance.

In all questions of prognosis, and particularly where mental symptoms are concerned, the patient's age, general physical and mental health, and the intelligence which he may bring to bear on adjusting to his disability should be fully considered. His social setting must also be carefully evaluated. A patient of restricted ability or resources is likely to experience greater continuing hardship in response to new disabilities than one who is better endowed. On the other hand the patient who relies on his intellect for pursuing his career may be especially handicapped by even slight disturbance of cognitive function. A professional man, for example, is likely to be more handicapped in his occupation than a labourer when the injury is followed by some degree of loss of verbal fluency. Since the court will strive to make a just award on the basis of the *impairment of the quality of life to be followed,* rather than on the actual severity of individual symptoms, these important background factors will need to be appropriately evaluated and stressed.

Relationship to Injury

With regard to the causative relationship between the injury and the disability that follows, we are liable to find that the further we move away from purely physical disabilities, the more is causation likely to be open to question. Cosmetic and neurological defects can usually be directly blamed upon the injury, but psychiatric sequelae with their multifactorial aetiologies can raise very special problems.

The physician must not always expect to find a strict concordance between what is accepted as causal medically and what is viewed as causal in the legal sense of the term (Spielmeyer, 1969; Zülch, 1969; Trimble, 1981a). The medical definition of causation is based on 'natural' correlations and deduced from knowledge of the interplay of factors, external and internal to the patient, in leading to medical disorder. It embraces all things which have contributed to the result, not only the proximate events but also pre-existing conditions such as special vulnerability in the individual. Its primary concern is with finding some means of treatment. The juridical definition of causation, on the other hand, depends on artificial correlations set up by man through regulations and laws, and modified through accumulated experience as reflected in case law. The interest here is almost wholly absorbed in whether some specified event, in this case an injury, can be shown to have contributed to the result. Consequently the law cannot always be expected to recognise the niceties of the interplay of factors which are propounded in the medical view of the problem.

When predisposing factors have existed it is logical to argue that liability should not be limited, even though these were previously concealed. Arteriosclerotic brain disease, for example, may have led to a more severe deficit from head injury than would have been found with a healthy brain. In just the same way a neurotic constitution, special vulnerabilities of personality, or a genetic loading for psychotic illness may have predisposed the patient to suffer prolonged disability from an injury which in the 'normal' person would not have called forth such a reaction. In general nowadays the courts prove sympathetic to such an argument when there is abundant evidence of special vulnerability which can be presented. On the other hand compensation may not be awarded if the court decides that a similar result could have occurred with a high probability at any time or in other circumstances, no matter how closely associated with the injury it may happen to be. Thus a patient long subject to recurring neurotic disability may receive scant sympathy from the court when injury is seen to lead once more to a situation which has often occurred before. The correctness or otherwise of such views could be the subject of long debate. Again it is the legal decision which carries force, and the duty of the medical referee is to place before the court the sum total of evidence in the individual case.

When complicating factors follow injury the court will similarly need to decide what weight to put upon them. Sometimes the injury will be seen to have set in motion a whole chain of circumstances which contribute towards the psychiatric disability. Thus the break up of a marriage or the loss of a career may be traceable directly to the injury, and may be factors of great importance in prolonging affective disorder or neurotic forms of reaction. The injury itself may have been mild, even when repercussions have been severe.

It is therefore essential for the physician to formulate all aetiological factors which have a clear bearing on the case, in addition to the restricted role of trauma itself. Unfortunately, in the determination of psychiatric sequelae some of the contributory factors will be idiosyncratic to the individual concerned, and it will be more difficult to demonstrate their operation than to display aspects of causation which have universal application.

Finally, when the clinical picture agrees closely with what would have been expected from the severity or location of known brain damage, this concordance should be stressed. For example, egocentricity, irresponsibility, or coarseness of personality will be more readily attributed to head injury when damage has involved the frontal lobes, even if the premorbid personality was poorly integrated beforehand. Similarly the auras of post-traumatic epileptic attacks may conform to the site of penetrating injury, and confirm that a new disorder has been produced even though the patient has experienced epilepsy before.

THE COURT REPORT

A first essential in undertaking examinations for the courts is to obtain the patient's written permission for access to any additional sources of information, and his consent for the report to be sent to the solicitors who request it. Adequate time should be devoted to the interview and examination, or to a series of examinations if these are indicated. Full notes must be kept of all the information obtained since medical documents may be called before the court.

Time should be spent in obtaining *the fullest possible information about details of the injury itself,* from which to judge the likely severity and distribution of brain damage. The duration of unconsciousness, confusion, retrograde amnesia and post-traumatic amnesia should be carefully assessed, along with the extent of early neurological defects. Complications such as skull fracture, raised intracranial pressure, blood in the cerebrospinal fluid, haematomas, or intracranial infection should be noted, also early episodes of fainting or other transient disorders which may prove to be the prelude to post-traumatic epilepsy. Due regard must also be paid to features of the initial injury which may specially predispose to epilepsy developing later (p. 213).

Any deficiency in investigations which come to light should be remedied. Skull X-ray, electroencephalography and careful psychometric testing are the minimum of investigations which should be to hand. The last two should be repeated if a considerable time has elapsed since they were previously carried out. It is rarely possible to compare the results of psychological testing with results obtained before the injury occurred, but valuable interpretations can often be made when results are judged against previous educational and occupational attainments. The results of psychological testing should not be given unbacked by the general clinical impression of severity of impairment, since dementia may be manifest in behaviour and personality deterioration as well as in cognitive dysfunction. When there are substantial cognitive deficits, or when the question of impairment is in serious doubt, CT scanning may help by displaying the extent of brain damage.

The report should embody the date and place of examination and specify the length of contact with the patient and his illness. Additional sources of information which have contributed to the material in the report should be listed—reports from informants and other hospitals, and results of special investigations performed. The patient's symptoms and all objective evidence of defects should be described in detail, and only thereafter should any tentative opinion be expressed about the reliability or otherwise with which the patient's complaints can be taken to represent the true state of his disability. In other words, full descriptive evidence should always be presented before matters of interpretation.

The question of prognosis should be handled with caution, and expressed in probabilities rather than certainties. Writing in 1938 about the problem of dementia Lewis said: 'The subtleties of modern psychiatric classification and prognosis are unfamiliar, and perhaps unwelcome, to the legal mind; clearcut diseases, simple labels, and firm statements are likely to obtain readier hearing'. This is probably less true today than formerly, but nevertheless the temptation to oversimplify the situation must be avoided. Whatever guidance can be given regarding the future course of events should be spelled out in full, remembering that it is the reflection of disability on the quality of future life, rather than the symptoms and defects themselves, that will be of most interest to the courts. In this the problems peculiar to the case in question—matters of age, intelligence, general health and social setting—will need to be described.

Finally the formulation of aetiology will embrace the likely role of trauma in relation to the individual picture presented by the patient, together with such constitutional and other antecedent circumstances which may have conferred special vulnerability. Where causal chains of circumstances have followed in the wake of injury and added to the disability, these should also be clearly and simply explained. Full supporting data must always be given to help define the contribution due to injury and that due to other additional factors. Evaluations which merely state opinions or conclusions do not help the lawyers to present the case or to argue it in a satisfactory manner.

The report should be as concise as possible and should avoid technical jargon, or where this is inevitable simple explanation may need to be included. It is sometimes necessary to bear in mind that the patient may himself have access to the report, though this should not be allowed to dictate any alteration in material content. Finally, it is perhaps worth mentioning that in the interests of justice it behoves the doctor to re-read his report with scrupulous attention to the overall impression which it makes. His evidence will have a powerful influence, even though the final decision regarding compensation will be made by others. It is all too easy for the doctor to identify with the patient's wish for compensation, especially when this is to be forthcoming from a large impersonal body, or when the patient is already well-known to him. Conversely, when the patient has been importunate, dilatory or already a disappointing therapeutic subject, a careful re-reading of the report may indicate that the writer has come to be unfairly biased against him.

Treatment

The treatment of the acute stages and early complications of head injury will not be dealt with here, since this is rarely the province of the psychiatrist. However, with commencing recovery the proper psychological management of the patient becomes of great importance, and can probably do much to reduce prolonged and disabling sequelae.

Early Management

Rehabilitation should be planned and supervised with care from the early stages of recovery. Fortunately the majority of patients with mild injuries make satisfactory progress without a great deal of specialised attention, but every effort should be made to identify those who are specially at risk, by virtue of premorbid instability or environmental difficulties, before confidence is lost and invalidism established.

The initial convalescent period is usually undertaken in hospital, and ideally in an atmosphere as free from stress as possible. Demands upon the intellect should at first be at a minimum since ready mental fatigue is likely to be evident. Physical activities, on the other hand, are beneficial, provided certain limits are imposed, and the value of early mobilisation has come to be generally recognised (Lewin, 1966, 1968). Graduated exercises and games help to restore the patient's physical self-confidence, and morale is improved by opportunities for social interaction. Simple advice should be given to avoid sudden bending or stooping if headache and dizziness are intrusive. At a later stage the patient should be encouraged to seek fresh air and avoid oppressive surroundings.

Usually little is needed by way of psychotherapy in any formal sense, but the value of the doctor-patient relationship should not be overlooked. It is essential that the patient should know that a full assessment has been made of any possible damage to his brain, and feel confident that the advice he is given is soundly based. Time devoted to sympathetic exploration of his anxieties is always well spent, and fears should not be lightly brushed aside however unfounded they may seem. The patient is often in a highly suggestible state, and lurking fears can easily take root. Explanation should be given about residual symptoms at an early date—fatigue, mental slowing, headache, dizziness—but difficulties not already present must not be implanted in the patient's mind.

An appropriate period of time away from work will need to be advised, after taking into account the severity of the injury, its complications, and the patient's personality and the stresses of the work to which he will return. Too early a return is liable to provoke a second wave of anxieties, if headache remains troublesome or powers of concentration are still deficient; conversely a long period of enforced idleness can itself engender morbid preoccupation and pave the way for neurotic developments. The general practitioner who is well acquainted with the patient is often well placed to know what suits his temperament best. Patients of striving and conscientious disposition must sometimes be held back from premature attempts, while others may need considerable encouragement to try.

More detailed and specialised care is required by patients who have sustained substantial brain damage with neurological sequelae and intellectual impairment, also by patients with minor injuries where psychiatric complications have become pronounced. The treatment programme will then need careful planning and must often be pursued over a long period of time.

From what has gone before it will be apparent that the first step must always be the systematic evaluation of residual disabilities and assessment of the causes operating in the individual case. In general it is less important to place the patient in a firm diagnostic category than to aim at a comprehensive understanding of his individual problems, personality and environment. Treatment will often need to follow a many-sided approach involving medical and ancillary workers from several different disciplines. The key question of the patient's motivation will almost always require attention, with special efforts to maintain it or augment it.

Neurological Sequelae

The main areas which require evaluation are locomotion, upper extremity function and impairment of communication. Visual acuity and visual field defects must also be assessed. Hemiparesis requires physiotherapy when more than mild and transient, similarly paraparesis or ataxia of gait. Occupational therapy has a special place in restoring useful function to the upper limb, and speech therapy in helping the resolution of dysphasia or dysarthria. When treatment is undertaken in hospital or in rehabilitation units the nursing staff can be taught to contribute usefully in these areas, likewise the relatives when patients are treated on an outpatient basis.

Intellectual Impairments

The rehabilitation of cognitive functions presents a special therapeutic challenge, and is a field where further research is badly needed (Newcombe *et al.*, 1980). Full psychometric assessment is always a first essential, and serves both to highlight areas of defect and areas of preserved function on which to capitalise. Memory functions are of crucial importance and must be comprehensively evaluated from the outset. Verbal ability, comprehension, visuo-spatial ability, manual dexterity, and capacity for sustained attention also require careful assessment.

Some general principles which should underlie the planning of the therapeutic programme can be stated. First the confidence, and where possible the full cooperation of the patient must be secured. The relatives also must be kept informed of aims, progress and necessary limitations. Second, an optimistic and positive approach is required in order to instil enthusiasm, with ready allowance for fatigue and tolerance of shortcomings. The personalities of the therapists can therefore be of great importance. Third, the programme must be graded, with goals at any stage which are realisable, rational and acceptable to the patient (Jousse *et al.*, 1969). Self-esteem is bolstered by the setting of tasks which can be mastered, however simple these may need to be at first. Success then serves as a catalyst which encourages and maintains endeavour. The tasks must also be suited to the patient's needs and inclinations. Simple repetitive craft work has a place only with the most severely disabled, or when planned specifically as remedial exercises for the restoration of manual skills. Assembly or packing work is more realistic for the factory worker, or domestic activities

for the housewife. Simple clerical tasks find a special place in those better oriented towards mental than physical occupations. Finally, throughout the course of rehabilitation careful attention must be paid to basic matters such as the maintenance of optimal physical health. It is vital to detect depression, and to make due allowance for matters of personality change as well as intellectual impairment.

Zangwill (1947) has stressed the emphasis that should be placed on *re-education, compensation* and *substitution* in rehabilitation. Re-education involves a direct attempt to retrain the patient in skills and accomplishments which have been impaired. For intellectual deficits, simple exercises of an ordinary scholastic kind are often of definite benefit and prove to be surprisingly well accepted. However, compensatory functions must be systematically trained if improvement of a primary function is not noted over time, since the rehabilitation aim must be to train and augment remaining functions rather than to exercise destroyed faculties (Gerstenbrand, 1969). Compensation may take place spontaneously, but can often be helped further. Obvious examples are the use of props to memory, or compensatory methods of expression in severe motor dysphasia. Again the speeding of recovery through such means can have a powerful effect on the patient's morale and thus influence progress in other spheres. Substitution is required when a function is damaged irreparably, and a new method of approach must then be acquired to replace it. Zangwill describes a patient who lost all ability to recognise printed symbols, until he was taught to rapidly trace the form of the letters with his forefinger. Lip-reading for the deaf is another obvious example, or methods of seeking to alleviate the difficulties of dyscalculia (*vide* Slade and Russell, 1971).

Newcombe (1983) reviews the various strategies now being developed to assist with cognitive retraining. An important requirement is to separate primary defects, attributable directly to brain injury, from the coping mechanisms adopted by the patient. The latter may be successful and deserving to be encouraged, or in some cases may be counterproductive. In the retraining of memory it can be valuable to teach the use of visual imagery, verbal coding or other systems of mnemonics (Patten, 1972; Lewisohn *et al.*, 1977; Glasgow *et al.*, 1977). Systematic re-training on attentional tasks appears to hold special promise.

Future hope may lie in the development of teaching machines, by which, for example, memory training might be allowed to proceed at the pace best suited to the individual. Or machined instructions could allow skilled tasks to be broken down to simpler components, enabling more comprehensive retraining than is at present possible (Lewin, 1970). Other possible developments of this nature have been outlined by Gedye (1968), but do not appear to have been exploited on a widespread scale.

Personality Change and Behavioural Disorder

Personality changes following brain damage are notoriously difficult to modify. There is relatively little that can be done by way of specific treatment, though much may be achieved by broader lines of management.

A period spent in hospital or a rehabilitation unit is often valuable for assessing the full extent of the patient's difficulties and limitations, and may help towards the elimination of socially disruptive behaviour.

Psychotherapy at a relatively superficial level can be of considerable benefit if a working relationship can be established. It should aim at helping the patient to achieve some insight when this is lacking, at least into the more disturbing aspects of his behaviour. Thereby a useful measure of control may be achieved in such matters as disinhibition, impulsiveness or emotional outbursts. The problems likely to arise from his altered disposition should be discussed, and methods sought to circumvent them.

A recent development is the application of behavioural modification techniques to brain-injured persons, with the aim of reducing disruptive behaviour and encouraging more constructive involvement in the rehabilitation process. Such methods have so far been tried mainly with severely injured persons, usually in special units, but could perhaps find wider application. Hollon (1973) reported success with a form of operant therapy in a rehabilitation unit, whereby co-operative self-helping behaviour was systematically rewarded, while belligerent or manipulative behaviour was ignored. By such means particularly disruptive patients could become accessible to therapy when this had not been possible before.

Wood and Eames (1981) and Wood (1984) have described their extensive experience with behaviour modification in St. Andrew's Hospital, Northampton. They point out that maladaptive patterns of behaviour have often been acquired by a process of learning, then become positively reinforced by the attention they evoke. Programmes are devised to control such matters as temper outbursts or antisocial behaviour, while at the same time shaping and encouraging more constructive responses. A token economy régime is fundamental in the treatment, being carefully adapted to the circumstances of each individual patient. Tokens are earned or forfeited in relation to key aspects of the day's behaviour, then exchanged for privileges within the unit. Imposed periods of social isolation ('time out') may also be required, or abrupt 'on the spot' withdrawal of staff attention, all against a background of positive reinforcement when things are going well. More intensive conditioning sessions may further help in the elimination of particularly resistant matters such as repetitive spitting, striking, or stereotyped nonsensical utterances. In favourable cases such programmes can apparently meet with considerable success, bringing the patient closer into contact and allowing further adaptive behaviours to be progressively encouraged.

Short of such decisive intervention much may still be required by way of clinical surveillance. When irresponsibility is a marked feature close supervision may be needed over matters of finance, and the patient's family must be brought fully into the picture. Indeed post-traumatic personality change is often the area in which the relatives most require advice, explanation and support. On-going contact with a social worker can prove invaluable in helping to avoid domestic, financial and occupational crises. Placement in work requires careful choice, sometimes with full discussion with the employer.

Tranquillising drugs such as diazepam may help with tension and anxiety, and antidepressants should be tried if an element of depression is thought to colour the picture. The author has observed benefit from chlorpromazine in a patient with frontal lobe damage where euphoria and disinhibited prankish behaviour were disturbing in degree. There may also be a place, under carefully supervised conditions, for a cautious trial of stimulating agents such as methylphenidate (Ritalin) or amphetamine in patients whose sluggishness and anergia derive from hypothalamic damage. Anticonvulsants are of doubtful value in preventing outbursts of aggression unless these are clearly related to epileptic activity, though phenytoin or other agents may warrant a trial in certain cases (p. 265).

Psychotic Illness

Functional psychoses after head injury require, in general, the same psychiatric management as the equivalent illnesses which occur in other settings. Schizophrenia and affective disorder may need appropriate medication along with attention to psychosocial aspects of the patients' situation. Electroconvulsive therapy is not contraindicated when other measures have failed, and can occasionally be dramatically effective in cases of severe depression or prolonged stupor following head injury (Silverman, 1964).

Neurotic Sequelae

Neurotic complications call for particularly careful evaluation especially when long-continued after injury, with readiness to explore the detailed factors operating in the individual case. The total situation of the patient, including his family setting, must be comprehensively reviewed; where litigation is in progress liaison with the lawyers representing the case can be helpful.

Once the possibility of brain damage has been fully assessed, further physical investigations are best kept to a minimum. Repeated questioning about symptoms can also delay the patient's progress, and in cases of litigation it may be advisable to let the lawyers know that this is considered to be the case.

Antidepressant medication and the minor tranquillisers are valuable aids, but the mainstay of treatment lies usually in psychotherapy and in attention to the social problems which exist. Psychotherapy may need to consist of little more than ongoing support, reassurance, and the ventilation of anxieties. But as the patient's confidence is gained more detailed problems may emerge as in the cases outlined on pp. 149–50. Phobic conditions will often respond well to behaviour therapy.

Speedy resolution of litigation is in general to be desired, certainly in cases where brain damage does not play an identifiable part. Return to work should also be secured at the earliest possible opportunity. In very severe and protracted examples removal from the home environment can be valuable in clarifying the issues at stake, either by admission to hospital or to a rehabilitation unit. Indeed severe neurotic sequelae, no less than intellectual impairments, may need the full range of rehabilitation facilities for the restoration of morale and preparation for taking up the normal course of life again.

Post-traumatic Headache

Long-continued and disabling post-traumatic headache can come to pose a difficult therapeutic problem. Frequently a number of simple remedies will have been tried without success, and the headache will be found to be inextricably intertwined with a variety of neurotic complaints. Evaluation and treatment must aim at the broadest possible approach, with full attention to both organic and psychological factors. The range of organic causes which need to be considered has already been outlined on p. 169.

Friedman (1969) provides a useful review of treatment. Short-term psychotherapy can be surprisingly helpful, and must aim at understanding the role the symptoms play in relation to the patient's personality and environment. Anxieties, frustrations, and in particular resentments, must often be ventilated in full.

Non-addictive analgesics have a place, also tranquillisers such as diazepam. The latter is especially indicated when tension headache is the cause. Ergotamine tartrate may be tried when episodic headache is suspected to have a vascular basis. Antidepressants can sometimes produce dramatic results:

A man of 60 was somewhat depressed and tense 2 years after a second mild head injury to the left parietal region. He felt that he was failing at his work, and complained of severe persistent headache and odd indefinable sensations in the left side of the head. After one week on amitriptyline he was surprised to find that the headache and other sensations had abruptly disappeared. The depression yielded more slowly but ultimately he made an excellent recovery.

Physical treatments which will often have been tried include local heat, procaine injections to tender sites and to the upper cervical spine. These have a useful place, but when over-employed they carry the danger of focusing attention exclusively on one aspect of the problem alone.

Post-traumatic Epilepsy

This important complication needs to be managed along the same lines as epilepsy due to other causes as outlined on p. 265 *et seq.* There may be a place, in carefully selected cases, for operative removal of an epileptogenic scar. Prophylactic medication is reserved for those forms of head injury which carry special risk (p. 213).

Rehabilitation Units: Resettlement at Work

From the range of treatments required, and the many special problems encountered, it is clearly advantageous to have centres for the rehabilitation of the more severely disabled patients. This need is widely recognised, but facilities are not equally widely available.

Head-injured patients often present a combination of physical handicap with disturbances of intellect, mood and behaviour. They are therefore liable to fall between the two stools of adequate provision for physical therapy and adequate facilities for psychiatric supervision (Lishman, 1983b). Properly organised rehabilitation units allow a multidisciplinary approach, both in evaluation and in the supervision of treatment, with neurologists, psychiatrists, and specialists in physical medicine and orthopaedics working together. Moreover the patient can receive the prolonged attention of a variety of other skilled personnel whose services can be coordinated—physiotherapists, psychologists, occupational therapists, speech therapists and social workers. Social aspects of rehabilitation are also facilitated when large numbers of patients can be treated together.

Where special units are not available rehabilitation must often be managed on an *ad hoc* basis within the hospital or out-patient department. Industrial rehabilitation units ultimately provide a valuable service, but as structured at present their pace and organisation are often geared too high for head-injured patients at an intermediate stage of recovery.

An essential part of rehabilitation lies in the help and guidance offered when the time comes for preparation for return to work. The ideal of return to the original occupation may have to be changed on account of persistent physical or mental handicaps. In practice the chief hindrances usually prove to be of a psychological kind—inadequacy of memory, weakness of attention, early fatigue, lowered vitality, slowness, or persistent depression (Schmid, 1969). Dresser *et al.* (1973), in a study of Korean war veterans in the USA, showed the importance of *premorbid* mental capacity, as well as severity of injury, in predicting return to work. A period of re-training may be necessary, or entry to a sheltered workshop or day centre, for those who are unable to manage under ordinary working conditions.

Short of this a full assessment must be made to guide the patient and the Disablement Resettlement Officer towards a suitable form of intermediate or final employment. Conditions usually to be avoided include shift work, night work, noisy or oppressive conditions, high frequency vibration, chemical vapours, stooping, working at heights or with moving machinery, and time-pressure work such as on conveyors. The patient's individual circumstances and aptitudes must be borne in mind, and he may require detailed and sympathetic help when compromises are to be made. The patient's family may also need help at this important stage, especially in adjusting to the social and financial implications of a change in occupational status. The social worker who has been involved from early in the process of rehabilitation can make a special contribution here.

Rusk *et al.* (1969) followed the results of rehabilitation from the New York Institute of Rehabilitation Medicine with interesting results. Female patients more often needed to be institutionalised than males, perhaps because a wife can more easily assume the major care of a disabled husband than vice versa. Patients adequately ambulant at discharge maintained their progress, whereas those only partially ambulant frequently regressed. Similar findings emerged with regard to dressing, feeding and toilet care, the principal cause of failure being lack of adequate time to perform the functions unaided, rather than loss of basic skills. Two factors of importance in the patients' continuing welfare proved to be the presence or absence of depression, and the continuity of care after discharge. Those who lived near to the centre, or maintained contact with an interested doctor or social worker, were more likely to maintain or even improve their gains. Conversely isolation from skilled advisers was markedly evident in those who relapsed.

Social Adaptation and Effects Upon the Family

Consideration of the sequelae of head injury is incomplete without mention of the broad effects on the quality of the patient's life and that of his family. Valuable reviews are presented by Oddy (1984) and Brooks (1984b). It is abundantly clear that leisure and social activities are often profoundly disrupted, sometimes in the long-term view, quite apart from consequences in terms of employment and finance. Family relationships can come under considerable strain. In all these respects the mental aftermaths, and particularly changes in personality, can prove more disruptive than purely physical disabilities (Bond, 1975, 1976).

Jennett *et al.* (1981) discuss various aspects of living relevant to 'quality of life'. First are the 'activities of daily living' most related to dependence on others—capacity to feed, dress, move and cope with toilet requirements. Next is the question of mobility beyond the patient's immediate surroundings, which can be as severely hampered by mental as physical handicaps. Social relationships require quite separate assessment, much depending on the patient's capacities for initiative and response. Work and leisure activities, and present satisfaction and future prospects, must also be borne in mind. Finally there is the question of the burden borne by the persons with whom the patient lives.

It was apparent in Thomsen's (1974) follow-up of severely head-injured patients that loss of social contact featured prominently among their problems. Most had lost touch with previous friends, and possibilities for making new acquaintances were few. Intellectual deficits, but even more so changes in personality, created the major problems in daily living. A prospective follow-up by Oddy and Humphrey (1980) reinforced these findings — leisure activities were still impaired 2 years after injury in half of their patients, this rarely being due to physical problems alone. Weddell *et al.* (1980) demonstrated marked changes in the social milieu of young adults followed 2 years later, in terms of changes in work, leisure activities, contact with friends and family life. Working capacity was affected by neurophysical status, memory difficulties and personality problems; it was the last, however, which contributed most to loss of friendships and dependence on the family.

Direct assessment of the relatives of head-injured persons has shown the extent of their burden, and has consistently related this to the mental rather than the physical aftermaths. Oddy *et al.* (1978) interviewed relatives at intervals over a year, finding that scores for depression were related not to severity of injury but to factors reflecting the patient's social adjustment. Two aspects emerged as particularly distressing: first the patient's forgetfulness and disorientation; second his 'verbal expansiveness' which referred to talking too long, too loudly, and with poor logical continuity.

McKinlay *et al.* (1981) in a similar study found that the problems most frequently encountered by the family concerned the patient's slowness, irritability, poor memory and emotional changes. Physical disability was less commonly a problem. Thomsen (1974) stressed the burden of aspontaneity, irritability, restlessness and stubbornness. Emotional lability and outbursts of pathological laughter were especially embarrassing features.

Very strikingly Rosenbaum and Najenson (1976) compared the wives of 10 patients suffering from severe head injury with those of paraplegic controls who had sustained no loss of cognitive function. At one year follow-up the wives of the head-injured patients were significantly more depressed, had experienced greater changes in their lives and suffered greater social restriction.

For reasons such as these the National Head Injuries Association ('Headway') has been established as a voluntary charitable trust, with the aim of providing counselling, support and social activities for patients handicapped in the long-term view and for their families.

Chapter 6. Cerebral Tumours

Cerebral tumours commonly present with symptoms of raised intracranial pressure, focal neurological signs or epileptic fits which lead the patient directly to the neurologist or neurosurgeon. Some, however, develop such evidence only late in the evolution of the tumour, and the earliest manifestations may consist of mental symptoms alone. When mental disturbance is the most prominent feature the patient may come first to the attention of the psychiatrist, and thereby run the risk of delayed or even missed diagnosis.

It is, of course, comparatively rare for the psychiatrist to find a cerebral tumour in a patient with mental disorder. Parry's (1968) finding of 1 per 200 patients admitted to a psychiatric unit is probably higher than average. The reverse, however, is extremely common and many patients with cerebral tumours show pronounced mental symptoms at some time in their course. The frequency has been reported variously from 10 per cent to virtually 100 per cent of cases, depending on the care with which psychological symptoms are sought out and recorded, and the stage of evolution of the tumour at the time the observations are made. Two of the larger series of tumour patients studied personally by the authors, and with psychological symptoms in mind, were those of Keschner *et al.* (1938) and Hécaen and Ajuriaguerra (1956a). Keschner *et al.* reported mental symptoms in 78% of 530 cases, Hécaen and Ajuriaguerra in 52% of 439 cases.

From the clinical point of view, mental symptoms are in general of little use as a guide to the location or the nature of the tumour. Neurological signs are greatly superior in this regard, and radiographic procedures have diminished the importance even of those mental symptoms which might have been of value. Tumour material has also proved disappointing for the study of the cerebral basis of mental phenomena. The lesion is rarely static, with the result that the clinico-pathological correlations which ultimately emerge tend to be imprecise. In addition, it is often hard to disentangle the effects of the lesion itself from remote pressure effects, circulatory disturbances, and the generalised effects of raised intracranial pressure. Nevertheless the psychological effects of cerebral tumours show many features of interest, and can on occasion be of crucial clinical importance.

General Characteristics of Mental Symptoms with Cerebral Tumours

Changes may be seen in any aspect of psychological function, with the result that there is no mental picture entirely specific for cerebral tumour. Sometimes certain areas are affected alone, for example the level of consciousness, aspects of cognitive function, or the affective state, though usually several areas are affected together. The interaction and synthesis of several functions may be disturbed in a manner which emerges as 'change of personality'. Complex psychological symptoms such as hallucinations and delusions may also appear, and the picture can be complicated by paroxysmal disorders consequent upon an epileptogenic focus. Occasionally frank psychotic illnesses are seen, or more frequently neurotic disturbances occasioned by the make-up of the individual.

In very general terms it may be said that slow growing tumours tend to produce changes of personality, and allow premorbid tendencies to manifest themselves; more rapid tumours lead to cognitive defects; whereas the most rapid lead to acute organic reactions with obvious impairment of consciousness (Minski, 1933).

Impairment of Consciousness

Disturbance in the level of consciousness is the most commonly noted psychological change. In minor degree it shows as diminished capacity to attend and concentrate, faulty memory, impaired responsiveness and ready mental fatigue. Characteristically in the early stages the impairment fluctuates in degree, with periods of relative lucidity. These rather subtle changes may be the first manifestation of the lesion, and sometimes provide the sole indication of disease for long periods of time. Later drowsiness and somnolence appear, and as the lesion extends the level of consciousness declines progressively, ending, if untreated, in coma.

While consciousness is impaired memory will prove defective, especially for recent happenings, and disorientation will become apparent. Thinking will be slowed, impoverished and often incoherent. Misinterpretations may occur, and behaviour is often outwardly muddled and bizarre.

Other Cognitive Changes

Even when consciousness is not impaired, intellectual disorganisation is frequently seen with cerebral tumours. The difficulties may be global and present in the form of a mild dementia, with slowed and concrete thinking, impoverished associations, defective judgement and difficulty with memory. Fatiguability of mind and perseveration are often marked. Speech may be slowed and incoherent, even in the absence of dysphasia and even with tumours of the non-dominant hemisphere. Such changes may be steadily progressive, but more characteristically tend to fluctuate in severity from one occasion to another.

Focal cognitive changes are commoner than generalised dementia as befits the focal nature of the lesion. Or a focal emphasis may be detected even when global deterioration is present. A circumscribed amnesic syndrome may appear while other functions remain well preserved, with markedly defective memory for recent events, disorientation, and even confabulation. All varieties of dysphasia may be seen, also apraxia, visuospatial defects, topographical disorientation and components of the Gerstmann syndrome. These will be important pointers to the focal nature of the disorder and may serve as a guide to its location.

Certain cognitive disturbances characteristic of tumours in special locations will be considered further below.

Affective Changes

Affective changes rarely occur in isolation, but frequently accompany other mental manifestations. With intellectual impairment there is often emotional dullness, apathy and aspontaneity; or euphoria may stand in striking contrast to what would be expected in view of the patient's physical defects and disabilities. However, depression and anxiety are also common with cerebral tumours, sometimes as understandable reactions and sometimes pathological in degree. Querulousness and irritability can be prominent features, or emotional lability with marked and evanescent swings of mood. Sustained elation is rarely seen.

Henry (1932) has attempted to outline the usual sequence of mood changes during the evolution of cerebral tumours. He found that irritability and peevishness in the early stages typically gave way to growing anxiety and depression. Suicidal tendencies were estimated to occur in 10% of cases, attempts often being impulsive and made during paroxysms of headache. Up to this point the emotional reactions were largely determined by inherent tendencies in the patient, but thereafter the disease process itself appeared more important, leading to indifference, apathy, euphoria, or emotional lability.

Hallucinations

Hallucinations may occur in any modality, commonly as part of an epileptic disturbance but also without evidence of paroxysmal activity. The nature of the hallucinations will depend on the location of the tumour. Occipital tumours are associated with simple visual hallucinations; temporal lobe tumours with more complex formed visual and auditory hallucinations, also gustatory and olfactory hallucinations; and parietal lobe tumours with localised tactile and kinaesthetic hallucinations. These distinctions are not, however, absolute. Circumscribed frontal lobe tumours may sometimes produce visual, auditory or even gustatory hallucinations, presumably through irritative effects on the neighbouring temporal lobe (Strauss and Keschner, 1935). Medial frontal lesions can also discharge directly to the temporal lobe and produce hallucinations and other phenomena by this means. Subtentorial tumours may be accompanied by visual hallucinations, presumably by pressure effects on the adjacent occipital lobe (Keschner et al., 1937).

Psychotic and Neurotic Phenomena

Any form of psychotic illness may accompany cerebral tumour, either early or late in its evolution. Depressive, schizophrenic, paranoid and hypomanic illnesses have all been reported, usually but not inevitably in association with evidence of organic brain dysfunction. Delusions when they occur may have a characteristic organic colouring, being poorly elaborated, shallow, or fleeting. A wide variety of neurotic manifestations also occur, especially in the early stages, and may likewise be misleading as discussed on p. 205.

Such disorders are obviously more common in those cerebral tumours which come the way of the psychiatrist. Minski's (1933) report of functional psychiatric pictures among patients from the Maudsley Hospital is typical: 25 out of 58 patients with cerebral tumour showed functional mental illness, and in almost half of these physical signs were absent. Fourteen patients displayed severe depression, 7 excitement, and 1 each schizophrenia, an anxiety state, an obsessional disorder and hysteria.

Factors Governing Symptom Formation

The mental disturbances accompanying cerebral tumours have, as is usual with psychiatric symptomatology, several sources of origin. Some of these are common to all patients affected, while others are largely idiosyncratic to the individual.

Raised Intracranial Pressure

Raised intracranial pressure accounts for a good deal of the mental symptomatology. When the pressure is lowered by decompression operations or by infusion of hypertonic solutions, dramatic changes in mental state can follow, with resolution of confusion, drowsiness, apathy or even coma.

Fluctuations in the level of consciousness probably depend principally upon fluctuations in the dynamics of the cerebrospinal fluid circulation. Other symptoms — difficulties with thinking, perception and memory, also emotional dullness and apathy — may often be similarly ascribed to impaired cerebral function consequent upon raised intracranial pressure. The pathophysiology of these effects lies largely with disturbance of the brain stem reticular formation and its rostral projections to the cortex, but raised pressure is also likely to exert effects by direct compression of brain tissue, impeded circulation and impaired CSF flow. After long-continued elevation of pressure there may be extensive parenchymal damage resulting from such factors, and the mental impairments will then remain even after the pressure is lowered.

Focal effects in the region of the tumour may also be aggravated by increased pressure, as seen for example when dysphasic symptoms recede as the pressure is lowered. But much psychiatric symptomatology appears to have little connection with intracranial pressure. Busch (1940) contrasted the overall incidence of psychiatric disturbance and of raised intracranial pressure in a large unselected series of

tumour patients. Temporal lobe tumours showed mental symptoms in 50% of cases, whilst intracranial pressure was raised in only 25%; infratentorial tumours by contrast showed mental symptoms in 10% but raised intracranial pressure in 99%. Similarly the studies of Keschner et al. (1938) and Hécaen and Ajuriaguerra (1956a) have confirmed this distinction in tumours arising above and below the tentorium. Thus even when intracranial pressure is raised, there are likely to be other important factors at work which lead to the appearance of mental symptoms.

The Nature of the Tumour

The nature of the tumour and the rapidity of its growth appear to be important in relation to the incidence and severity of mental symptoms. Keschner et al. (1938) found that tumours which produced no mental symptoms whatsoever were mainly of the slow-growing type. Busch (1940) found that symptoms were more frequent with malignant tumours than benign.

Gliomas have repeatedly been found to produce a higher incidence of mental disturbance than meningiomas. In Hécaen and Ajuriaguerra's (1956a) series, for example, mental disturbances were noted in 61% of gliomas as compared to 43% of meningiomas. Furthermore, within the group of gliomas, rapidity of growth appears to be important. Busch (1940) found, among left-hemisphere tumours, that 25% of astrocytomas had mental symptoms compared to 70% of glioblastomas; the corresponding figures for right-hemisphere tumours were 35% and 80% respectively. It is important, of course, to distinguish these general associations from the relative diagnostic hazards of slow and fast-growing tumours. Rapid growth is associated with more severe mental disturbance, but slow-growing tumours are more liable to present with mental symptoms alone so that they may more easily be missed.

The greater incidence of mental disturbances among malignant as compared to benign cerebral tumours is probably due to the greater incidence of raised intracranial pressure in the former group. Malignant tumours also invade the brain more widely. It is perhaps for the latter reason that metastatic tumours with several deposits scattered throughout the brain have proved to be associated with a higher incidence of mental disturbance than any variety of primary intracerebral tumour (Keschner et al., 1938). The same authors reported an impression that a small amount of destruction on both sides was liable to cause more mental disturbance than a larger amount on one side alone.

The Location of the Tumour

The importance of tumour location in relation to mental symptoms has been much debated. Many observations concerning special regional effects can be offset by negative findings. There are, of course, considerable difficulties in amassing large and unselected series of tumour patients, in a setting which allows for careful appraisal and comparison of psychiatric features. Most tumours are progressive and present changing mental pictures during their evolution. Moreover there may be effects which derive from cerebral involvement at a distance, due to distortions of the brain, displacement of parts through bony and dural openings, or obstruction to free arterial supply and venous drainage. The patient's awareness of his plight, when retained, will profoundly influence his response, and this in turn will depend on many features of his personality and situation. Thus any direct contribution made by the location of the lesion can be hard to disentangle from other factors.

Bleuler (1951), reviewing 600 unselected tumours from the Zurich neurosurgical clinic, suggested that the psycho-pathological picture was, in fact, very uniform. Eighty-three per cent of his patients showed mental symptoms, but there were no significant differences according to the site of the tumour. Only two mental syndromes could be reliably differentiated–clouding of consciousness in the acute stage and a 'chronic amnesic syndrome' in the chronic stage. The latter embraced much more than memory defects alone, including also widespread cognitive disturbances, emotional instability, and impairment of personality.

Bleuler's results, however, run counter to most of the findings in the literature, and special associations between site of tumour and certain aspects of psychiatric disturbance have frequently emerged. This will be discussed further in the sections that follow, but here we may note that focal cognitive defects may appear with parietal tumours, and focal amnesic syndromes with tumours of the diencephalon. Hallucinations also clearly derive from focal lesions of the brain.

It is when we depart from such relatively elementary symptoms that it becomes harder to demonstrate the role of focal cerebral disorder in the pictures that result. Thus disturbances of affect and personality cannot be tied convincingly to tumours in specific parts of the brain, and functional psychotic illness when it emerges appears to be largely determined by other factors. The evidence indicating special characteristics of personality disturbance in association with frontal lobe tumours is outlined on p. 192 and that which seeks to link schizophrenia-like psychoses with temporal lobe tumours is discussed on pp. 194–195. In these areas, however, the evidence which can be derived from tumour material remains rather slender.

Table 9 shows the overall frequency of mental symptoms with tumours in different locations, as reported by Keschner et al. (1938) and Hécaen and Ajuriaguerra (1956a). These are two of the largest series investigated by observers whose primary interest was to evaluate mental symptoms against a constant set of criteria. A fair degree of agreement is seen between the two, even though Hécaen and Ajuriaguerra's criteria for recording symptoms were clearly stricter than those of Keschner et al. Supra-

TABLE 9. Incidence of mental symptoms with cerebral tumours

Location of Tumour	From Keschner et al. (1938) (N.B. excluding paroxysmal disturbances)			From Hécaen and Ajuriaguerra (1956a) (N.B. including paroxysmal disturbances)		
	Number of Cases	% with Mental Symptoms	% with Mental Symptoms 'early'	Number of Cases	% with Mental Symptoms	% Onset with Mental Symptoms
All tumours	530	78	15	439	52	18
All supratentorial	401	87	18	354	56	19
All infratentorial	129	47	5	85	40	12
Frontal	68	85	25	80	68	20
Temporal	56	93	29	75	68	28
Parietal	32	81	19	75	52	16
Occipital	11	82	9	25	52	32

tentorial tumours show a greatly increased incidence of mental disturbances when compared to infratentorial tumours, and this is especially marked when attention is restricted to symptoms appearing at the onset or early in the illness. This finding is particularly noteworthy since raised intracranial pressure was considerably less frequent among the supratentorial than the infratentorial tumours in both series of cases. Frontal and temporal lobe tumours show a somewhat higher incidence of mental disturbance than do tumours in the parietal or occipital lobes. Parry (1968), commenting on Hécaen and Ajuriaguerra's series, points out that the high frequency of cases with mental symptoms at onset in the temporal and occipital groups is entirely due to paroxysmal disturbances; if one considers only the cases with enduring mental symptoms the frontal preponderance is statistically significant, and all other locations come afterwards and are approximately equivalent with one another. However in Keschner *et al.*'s series, where patients with paroxysmal disturbances were excluded, temporal lobe tumours still retain their lead.

Individual Constitution and Response

Finally the individual response to a cerebral tumour must be remembered in seeking an explanation for mental symptoms. The importance of this may easily be eclipsed in the urgency of the clinical situation, and probably emerges less forcibly in most published studies than its true importance would warrant.

In patients with special genetic predisposition to mental disorder the tumour may act as little more than a precipitating factor in the psychiatric disturbance that develops. This is likely to be especially so where neurotic disorders or functional psychoses are concerned. Much emotional and personality disturbance will also be an understandable response to physical impairments such as paralysis, fits or visual symptoms, or to the discomfort of headache or the threat presented by the illness. In all of this the patient's response will be largely shaped by his premorbid personality and will reflect his habitual modes of reaction to stress. It will also be modified to a very considerable extent by the handling the patient receives from medical and nursing personnel.

Such highly individual factors may be expected to modify the psychological effects of a cerebral lesion wherever it is situated. It is not surprising, therefore, that precise evidence about aetiological factors becomes harder to obtain as one deals with the more complex aspects of psychiatric disorder in the presence of cerebral tumour.

Mental Symptoms with Tumours in Different Locations

Despite the complexities outlined above, a large literature has accumulated describing characteristic mental pictures for tumours in different parts of the brain. A good deal is contradictory from one report to another, but certain aspects emerge repeatedly. These deserve emphasis since they can be of diagnostic importance. Much of what follows has been drawn from the detailed monograph by Hécaen and Ajuriaguerra (1956a).

Frontal Lobe Tumours

Frontal lobe tumours are notorious for their liability to present under guises which may lead to a mistaken diagnosis of a primary dementing illness. This is due partly to the paucity of striking neurological signs which accompany frontal lesions, and in part to the frequency with which mental disturbances appear from a very early stage.

Impairment of consciousness and intellectual deterioration were found more frequently with frontal tumours than with tumours in any other location in Hécaen and Ajuriaguerra's own series. Sachs (1950), in a large series of meningiomas, found 8 which presented with dementia before any symptoms indicative of tumour had appeared, and 6 of these were frontal in location. Sometimes dramatically successful results can follow the removal of such a tumour:

A woman of 64 was admitted to hospital in a deteriorated state and unable to give an account of herself. Her husband stated that the illness had begun 2 years previously when she became excessively preoccupied with the ills of her pet dog. For 3 months there had been episodes of trembling all over, worse in the morning, but not associated with any loss of consciousness. She had gradually become forgetful and muddled and had lost all initiative. For 3 weeks she had been confined to bed and was too confused to dress herself. She was doubly incontinent, mainly it appeared because she lacked the initiative to go to the bathroom as she was quite able to get about. There had been no headache, fits or vomiting.

On examination she showed a profound dementia with disorientation in time and place. She lay inert in bed but was not difficult to rouse. There was no dysphasia or apraxia, but she could not cooperate over tests of intelligence. The only neurological signs were a persistent tremor of the outstretched hands and an equivocal left plantar response. The sense of smell was intact.

The EEG showed evidence of a lesion in the left frontotemporal region, and skull X-ray showed erosion of the posterior clinoid processes. At operation a left frontal parasaggital meningioma was removed.

Two months post-operatively her mental state was judged to be entirely normal and she said she felt better than for several years. She recalled little of her pre-operative condition except that she had been distressed over her incontinence.

(Sachs, 1950)

A woman developed grand mal epileptic fits at the age of 40, and at 53 was admitted to mental hospital because she had become apathetic, inert, incontinent and bedridden. She was aggressive when approached and degraded in habits. A skull X-ray was interpreted as showing hyperostosis frontalis interna. After 12 years in hospital she remained severely demented, was somnolent and showed little response to questions. She sat with the tongue protruded to the right, and making purposeless repetitive movements of the right arm and leg. She was anosmic, could only just distinguish between light and dark, and showed a left-sided facial weakness. There was no obvious weakness of the limbs but she could neither stand nor walk.

Investigations revealed a massive bifrontal meningioma, probably attached above the crista galli. After its removal she made a remarkable improvement, regained some degree of spontaneity, speech and sight and was able to get about. She recognised and talked with relatives for the first time in 12 years. She had a dense amnesia for the 15-20 years before the operation and misjudged events and ages accordingly.

(Hunter et al., 1968a)

Tumours of the left frontal lobe appear to be associated with greater cognitive disturbance than tumours of the right. Smith's (1966b) careful analysis of psychometric test results showed greater losses in both verbal and performance abilities with left compared to right frontal tumours, the difference still persisting when aphasic patients were excluded. Bilateral involvement, as with tumours originating in the midline, produce more disturbance than when a single lobe is implicated alone (Strauss and Keschner, 1935).

Generalised dementia is most frequent, but disturbance of memory can occasionally be seen in relative isolation. Hécaen and Ajuriaguerra found that 10 of their 80 cases presented with mental disturbances in which *amnésie de fixation* was prominent. In one case there was a typical Korsakoff psychosis together with confabulation. Often however, the apparent memory failure occurs in a setting of profound apathy and indifference which makes it hard to decide whether the patient is trying to remember or to give the answer, even if he should know it.

Other special characteristics of cognitive disturb-

ance include aspontaneity, slowing and inertia. The slowing of mental and physical activities may be striking, with long periods during which virtually all activity comes to a halt. Speech may be extremely slow and laboured, even when the tumour is in the non-dominant lobe and evidence of dysphasia is lacking. Akinetic states have been described in which the patient is mute and immobile, yet when forcibly roused proves to be normally oriented. In other cases somnolence may be extreme, usually but not invariably in association with raised intracranial pressure.

The disturbances of affect most characteristic of frontal lobe tumours appear to be irritability, depression, euphoria, and apathy. Irritability is repeatedly stressed and may sometimes occur as a presenting symptom. Some of Direkze et al.'s (1971) patients had initially been admitted to psychiatric units on account of depression, which then proved unresponsive to electroconvulsive therapy. Euphoria and apathy generally occur along with intellectual enfeeblement, or in conjunction with other organically determined changes of personality.

Frontal lobe tumours may present with changes of disposition and behaviour, even in the absence of intellectual deficits or neurological signs. This appears to be particularly characteristic of slow-growing meningiomas. In Strauss and Keschner's (1935) series of frontal tumours, for example, change of personality was one of the earliest manifestations in almost a quarter of the cases. Eleven of 25 patients reported by Direkze et al. (1971) presented with subtle personality alterations. A 53-year-old clergyman began outlining rather smutty jokes, a greengrocer was charged on five occasions for speeding, all within 3 weeks, and a pharmacist became forgetful, easily provoked, and asked his wife to play Cowboys and Indians with him. All proved to have frontal astrocytomas.

Irresponsibility, childishness and lack of reserve are the changes stressed most frequently, and can sometimes occur before there is any evidence of intellectual deterioration. A tendency towards facetiousness and indifference to those around may combine to give a particular stamp to the overall clinical picture. Disinhibition sometimes leads to striking social lapses or minor misdemeanours as the first obvious sign of change; sexual excitation and erotic behaviour very occasionally occur.

A man of 58 presented with a 12 month history of extravagance, boastfulness, excessive drinking, marital discord, unrealistic planning and several changes of job. He had previously held a responsible job in a senior position. He showed a happy confident manner and believed he was rich, but was self-neglectful and grossly lacking in insight. The plantar reflexes were up-going and there was left papilloedema with reduced visual acuity. A left olfactory groove meningioma was discovered.

(Avery, 1971)

Frontal lobe tumours are not unique in their capacity to engender such personality changes, and it has even been questioned whether they show them more frequently than tumours elsewhere in the cortex. Keschner *et al.* (1936) found little difference between frontal and temporal lobe tumours in this regard. Most are agreed, however, that bifrontal tumours show such changes with especial frequency and severity. Tumours arising from the small sphenoidal wing, which marks the transition between the frontal and temporal lobes, have also been noted to show a very high frequency of mental changes (David and Askenasy, 1937).

Lack of insight is characteristically marked, and may partly represent a general lack of feed-back from environmental cues. Frequently the patient is completely indifferent about his illness and situation, even when intellect is well-preserved. In a paradoxical fashion denial of illness may coexist with placid compliance and calm acceptance of treatment.

Severe urgency, frequency and incontinence are often present early in the course of a frontal tumour, and can occur in the absence of dementia, indifference or lack of social concern (Andrew and Nathan, 1964). There is impairment of ability to prevent the micturition reflex occurring, and of stopping it once it has begun. A similar disorder of defaecation may develop, though less often and less severely. Contrary to common teaching the patients are usually much upset and embarrassed by their incontinence.

The neurological signs which may betray frontal lesions are outlined on p. 17. In addition hallucinations may derive from the neighbouring temporal lobe (p. 188), and hypothalamic damage due to pressure or distortion may occasionally lead to obesity, stupor or narcoleptic attacks (Hunter *et al.*, 1968a).

Corpus Callosum Tumours

Tumours originating within the corpus callosum are notorious for the severity of the mental disturbances that follow. They are said, moreover, to present with mental symptoms from the outset more frequently than tumours elsewhere. The largest series was reported by Schlesinger (1950), who found mental changes in 92% when the rostrum was involved, in 57% with mid-callosal tumours and in 89% with tumours of the splenium. Selecki (1964) in a small consecutive series confirmed the special frequency of mental symptoms with anterior and posterior tumours when compared with those arising from the middle portion. Anterior tumours in particular tended to lead to rapid mental deterioration before the appearance of neurological signs, headache or other evidence of raised intracranial pressure.

The usual picture is of a rapidly progressive impairment of cognitive functions, beginning with marked memory difficulties. Sometimes there is striking blocking of thought and action which may resemble that seen with catatonic schizophrenia. Alpers (1936) thought that the clinical picture was often sufficiently characteristic for the diagnosis to be made directly:

A man of 64 had a 4-week history of behaving strangely at work, seeming oblivious of questions and unable to focus his attention. At home he would sit in the same place for hours at a time, once wound a clock for 3 hours on end and once lathered his face for 2 hours. On examination there was bilateral spasticity but no papilloedema. He sat staring ahead oblivious of his surroundings, or with his eyes closed picking aimlessly at the bed clothes. Sometimes he lay for long periods tapping his head with his hand. It was hard to make contact with him, and most questions met with no response. He was disoriented, but at times seemed to recognise people. Perseveration was extremely marked. He proved to have a glioblastoma practically confined to the genu of the corpus callosum.

(Alpers, 1936)

Personality change may also be an early feature, similar in all respects to that seen with frontal lobe tumours. Florid psychotic symptoms have also been reported. Elliot (1969), in his comprehensive review, suggests that the combination of delusions and stupor can come to resemble schizophrenia closely.

A large part of the severe mental disturbance is probably due to the tendency for tumours of the corpus callosum to involve adjacent structures. Those of the anterior portion rapidly extend into the frontal lobes bilaterally, and those of the splenium invade the thalamus and midbrain posteriorly. Almost all involve the third ventricle and diencephalon at some stage, which probably accounts for the somnolence, akinesis and stupor which ultimately appear (Selecki, 1964). However the lesion of the corpus callosum is also likely to be important in itself by leading to disturbance of interhemispheric coordination, also the disruption of fibres in the neighbouring cingulum bundle which connects important association areas ipsilaterally (Schlesinger, 1950). Such lesions may account for the frequency of mental changes with corpus callosum tumours even before a rise of intracranial pressure has occurred.

Temporal Lobe Tumours

As noted in Table 9, temporal lobe tumours produce perhaps the highest incidence of mental disturbances. In part this may be ascribed to the paroxysmal phenomena occasioned by temporal lobe epilepsy, though temporal tumours retain their lead over other groups in Keschner *et al.*'s series where disturbances due to epilepsy were excluded.

Apart from features particular to temporal lobe epilepsy, there does not seem to be any form of mental disturbance specific for temporal lobe tumours to the extent of being of localising value. The early onset and rapid progression of dementia has been said to be characteristic, though this impression may be largely due to the marked dysphasic disturbances which accompany tumours on the dominant side. Certainly non-dominant temporal lobe tumours can be clinically silent until they are very large.

With regard to other aspects of the relative effects of dominant and non-dominant tumours, the evidence is hard to evaluate. Bingley (1958) reported one of the largest series of temporal lobe tumours—253 temporal lobe gliomas—and concluded firmly that tumours on the dominant side produced the greater impairment of intellect. This appeared to apply to both verbal and non-verbal functions. Moreover the excess of intellectual disturbance with dominant tumours was even more pronounced when attention was restricted to cases without papilloedema, suggesting that dominant lobe tumours were especially liable to produce mental symptoms before the intracranial pressure had risen. Bingley also found that among the dominant lobe tumours those with dysphasia did not have a higher incidence of mental changes generally than those without dysphasia. These findings, however, do not go unchallenged, and tumour material is in many ways unsatisfactory for exploring the complex inter-relationships between language and non-language impairments after cerebral lesions.

The slowing and aspontaneity of speech and movement seen with frontal lobe tumours has also been frequently reported with temporal lobe tumours. Keschner *et al.* (1936) compared frontal and temporal tumours in this regard and could find no substantial difference between them. Sixty-three per cent of temporal cases showed dullness, apathy, or torpor; some showed no spontaneous speech whatever, yet when roused spoke slowly and deliberately without evidence of dysphasia. Indifference to surroundings may also be seen with temporal as with frontal lobe tumours; memory disturbances may likewise feature prominently, including occasional cases which present with a florid Korsakoff psychosis.

Affective disturbances are common. In Hécaen and Ajuriaguerra's (1956a) series, frontal, fronto-temporal and temporal tumours taken together showed double the frequency of affective changes seen with tumours in other locations. Euphoria is probably as common with temporal as with frontal tumours (Keschner *et al.*, 1936; Schlesinger, 1950), and again occurs mainly in the presence of intellectual impairment. Paroxysms of anxiety or anger have frequently been described, and occasional cases have presented with mania or hypomania. Depression, anxiety and irritability are all common, perhaps particularly with tumours on the dominant side and in association with dysphasia (Keschner *et al.*, 1936). Bingley (1958) found that emotional changes generally were more frequent with dominant than non-dominant tumours, especially where blunting and flattening of affect were concerned.

There does not appear to be a form of personality change which is specific for temporal lobe tumours. A change towards facetiousness, foolish joking and childish behaviour may be indistinguishable from that seen with frontal lesions, and has been reported to be just as common. Strobos (1953) observed marked personality alterations in 7 of 62 patients with temporal lobe tumours, including psychopathic and paranoid trends, hypochondriasis and extreme irritability. Three of these patients were without papilloedema. Most examples seemed to represent a reaction to the disease or to the epileptic attacks which occurred, and to reflect aspects of the premorbid personality. An accentuation of neurotic personality traits has also been stressed, with dramatisation of complaints, unjustified fears and preoccupation with troubles remote from the present situation (Hécaen and Ajuriaguerra, 1956a). Here much may again be a reaction to the disabilities and threats occasioned by the illness.

Occasionally patients with temporal lobe tumours develop psychotic illnesses resembling schizophrenia. This may sometimes be the initial manifestation. Such cases are rare, but have been drawn together in a review of the literature by Davison and Bagley (1969). The location of the tumour in 77 cases of 'schizophrenia' from 42 published reports was compared with two large unselected series of tumours. A significantly higher proportion of temporal lobe tumours and pituitary tumours were present in the schizophrenic group. There was insufficient information to indicate whether such patients had been genetically predisposed to schizophrenia, or whether the temporal lobe pathology might play a more direct aetiological role.

Some isolated clinical examples rather strongly suggest that the temporal lobe pathology may itself be responsible:

A 53-year-old woman was admitted to hospital after attacking her husband with a knife. She had recently been behaving bizarrely, accusing her family of trying to poison her and refusing to eat in self-defence. She believed they were spraying the house with poison gas in an attempt to harm her, and that her son was turning her into a dog. She also complained of severe headache and pains in the chest and stomach. Immediately prior to admission she spent two nights in an alley improperly dressed. Her previous personality had been that of a sociable, quick tempered and outspoken woman.

On examination there were no abnormal neurological signs. Speech was incoherent but she was mostly unresponsive to questioning. She showed bizarre facial mannerisms and sudden unexpected actions from time to time, for example sudden rolling of the eyes or abrupt attempts at undressing. After 3 weeks in hospital she became stuporose and died. A glioblastoma was found in the right temporal lobe.

(Haberland, 1965)

In a case seen personally, a woman of 51 developed florid schizophrenic symptomatology in association with a possible local recurrence of a temporal lobe tumour which had been removed 2 years previously. There was no family history of schizophrenia, and her premorbid personality had shown no schizoid traits.

She had presented originally with a 15-year history of attacks of visual disturbance in the right field of vision, and a one-year history of grand mal epilepsy. A slow-growing astrocytoma of the left temporal lobe was discovered and partially removed. She made an excellent recovery, apart from transient dysphasia in the early post-operative period, but 2 years later became depressed for several weeks after her husband had a stroke. As the depression receded she gradually developed a number of strange ideas—she believed that strangers could read her thoughts and communicate with her, became distressed when she saw the colour red, and felt that words had special significance for her if they contained 'a' as the second letter. With this she developed occasional hallucinations in the right half-field of vision—of an eye, of a man standing in a room or by a car, or of a sepia-coloured scene.

These disturbances increased over several months until she was admitted to hospital. She then showed many of the first rank symptoms of schizophrenia. She believed that her thoughts were read by some radio mechanism, and that others betrayed this by gestures; she believed that her husband could alter the train of her thoughts and cause them to block, and that he had taken over control of the limbs on the left of her body; she felt that other patients were talking about her and looking at her in a special way, and that when she put on her spectacles a neighbouring patient and her doctor could both see more clearly. She also felt strongly attracted to a certain doctor in the ward, but saw an orange light which meant 'no' to her wish to see him alone. She felt that she was caught up in some ill-defined plan involving many people.

Her speech was somewhat circumstantial with loosening of associations, tangential thinking and occasional thought block. However her affect remained warm and her personality intact, and she preserved a certain measure of insight into the abnormal nature of her beliefs and experiences.

Examination revealed a new upper quadrantic visual field defect, a return of her dysphasia, some defect of recent memory and slight dropping away of the outstretched right arm. The EEG also showed an increase in slow activity in the left fronto-temporal region. A local extension of the tumour was suspected but angiography failed to give definite evidence of this.

She was started on chlorpromazine, increased to 100 mg three times a day, and over the next 2 weeks the schizophrenia-like symptoms began to recede. Coincidentally her dysphasia and right arm weakness also began to resolve, and the EEG improved to its base-line state. Within 2 months all psychotic symptoms had disappeared and she had regained full insight. She remained well when followed up 6 months after starting chlorpromazine, apart from occasional grand mal and other minor epileptic attacks and a persistent mild defect of recent memory. Residual dysphasic symptoms were again evident, especially when she was tired.

One year later she was re-admitted with increasing dysphasia and frequent attacks of falling. She developed increasing drowsiness and a right hemiparesis, and died after 3 weeks in hospital. At autopsy recurrence of the tumour was found in the left fronto-temporal region.

In addition to cases which present with schizophrenic symptomatology, the complex hallucinations of temporal lobe tumours may lead to diagnostic confusion. Fifteen of 110 cases reported by Keschner *et al.* (1936) showed hallucinations independently of epileptic phenomena. Visual and auditory hallucinations can be either simple or complex, the latter being particularly liable to lead to a mistaken diagnosis of functional psychotic illness. Visual hallucinations occurring within a hemianopic field of vision are virtually diagnostic of temporal lobe disturbance. Olfactory and gustatory hallucinations may arise from the uncinate region. Characteristically the patient accepts all such hallucinatory experiences as real at the time of their occurrence, but thereafter rapidly regains insight into their abnormal nature, unlike the situation with functional psychotic illness.

Epilepsy occurs in approximately 50% of patients with temporal lobe tumours, which is commoner than with tumours in other locations (Strobos, 1953; Paillas and Tamalet, 1950). In addition to hallucinatory experiences, the epileptic auras may contain a variety of abnormal subjective experiences which lead to diagnostic difficulty—unreality, déjà vu, dreamy states, forced thoughts, overwhelming fears, and other sudden emotional changes (p. 218). Automatisms and other complex psychomotor seizures may occur, though these are probably less common with tumours than with temporal lobe epilepsy arising from other causes (Hécaen and Ajuriaguerra, 1956a; Bingley, 1958).

Parietal Tumours

Tumours of the parietal lobe appear to be distinctly less likely than frontal or temporal lobe tumours to produce psychological changes. Table 10 shows this clearly where several different areas of mental disturbance are concerned. They are also prone to lead to early neurological signs in motor and sensory systems, so that an erroneous diagnosis of primary psychiatric disorder is less likely to be made.

Affective changes occur, and depression in particular has been noted with considerable frequency (Hécaen and Ajuriaguerra, 1956a). Personality disturbances appear to be relatively uncommon. Hallucinatory disturbances consist of tactile or kinaesthetic hallucinations confined to the opposite half of the body, and 'tactile perseveration' as when the patient continues to perceive a contact long after the stimulus has been removed.

The principal psychiatric interest of parietal lobe tumours lies in the complex and fascinating cognitive disturbances which may occur. It is here that care must be taken, since the clinical picture may at first sight be mistaken for dementia or hysteria. Dominant lobe tumours may produce dysphasia, more rarely ideomotor or ideational dyspraxia. Components of the Gerstmann syndrome—finger agnosia, dyscalculia, dysgraphia, and right-left disorientation—may be found in relative isolation or stand out among more generalised cognitive disturbance. Tumours of the non-dominant lobe are associated with disorders of visuospatial perception, dressing

difficulty and topographical disorientation, which again can sometimes occur in relative isolation. Any of these disorders, when accompanied by marked indifference or social withdrawal, may easily lead to an erroneous diagnosis of dementia. However with careful examination it can often be established that other cognitive functions remain intact.

Non-dominant tumours are also liable to be associated with complex disturbances of the body image. Best known are the phenomena of unilateral inattention or neglect, and anosognosia in which the patient appears to be unaware of a left hemiplegia or denies the disability when this is pointed out to him. A range of disturbances is seen, extending even to denial of ownership of the affected limbs, or attribution of the limbs to another person (p. 61 *et seq.*). Though less common with tumours than with other parietal lesions, these elaborate disturbances may at first sight strongly suggest hysteria. Fortunately such a diagnostic error is unlikely to be made after even a cursory neurological examination. Critchley (1964) has stressed other similarities between hysteria and parietal disease: difficulties with communication may make it hard to secure the patient's attention or cooperation, and performance may show marked inconsistencies such that he succeeds in a task which a moment before had appeared to be beyond him.

Finally the epileptic manifestations which accompany parietal lobe tumours, and which may antedate the appearance of neurological signs, sometimes consist of transient disturbances of the body image. These again may be sufficiently bizarre to suggest a functional psychiatric disorder. Examples reported by Hécaen and Ajuriaguerra (1956a) included the spasmodic feeling of someone standing close by, absence or displacement of a part of the body, transformation of a limb into a mechanical object, and the phantom appearance of a third limb.

Occipital Tumours

In the early literature, occipital tumours were sometimes reported to show a particularly high frequency of mental disturbances. This may have been a result of their tendency to produce early and pronounced elevation of intracranial pressure. Allen (1930), for example, stressed the frequency of psychoneurotic manifestations early in the course of forty patients with occipital tumours, and noted pronounced defects of attention and memory in almost a third.

However, detailed comparisons between groups of

TABLE 10. Incidence of forms of mental disturbance with cerebral tumours

| Location of Tumour | From Keschner *et al.* (1938) | | | | | From Hécaen and Ajuriaguerra (1956a) | | |
	Number of Cases	% with Disturbance of Consciousness	% with Change of Intellect	% with Disturbance of Memory and orientation	% with Disturbance of Affect	Number of Cases	% with Intellectual Disturbance	% with Affective and Personality Disturbance
Frontal	68	65	47	50	59	80	60	38
Temporal	56	75	50	57	61	75	43	24
Parietal	32	69	38	25	38	75	35	19
Occipital	11	64	36	45	45	25	24	20
Mesodiencephalic	—	—	—	—	—	61	26	21
All supratentorial	401	69	44	45	54	—	—	—
All infratentorial	129	37	12	8	23	85	22	12

tumours in different parts of the brain have failed to reveal an excess of mental symptoms with occipital tumours (Table 10). Amnesic difficulties and dementia can occasionally be striking, but affective disturbances and personality changes seem to occur with rather less frequency than with tumours elsewhere.

Visual agnosic defects and other features which may be of localising value are outlined on pp. 18–19.

Diencephalic Tumours

Tumours which originate in the deep midline structures of the diencephalon (i.e. the thalamus, hypothalamus, and other structures in the neighbourhood of the third ventricle) are not remarkable for the overall frequency with which they produce mental symptoms, as shown in Table 10. However the disturbances which do occur are often striking and some have important localising significance.

Marked amnesic difficulties are now well established as typical of tumours in the neighbourhood of the third ventricle (Delay *et al.*, 1964). Hécaen and Ajuriaguerra (1956a) regarded this as one of the few psychiatric syndromes of practical importance to the neurosurgeon. The picture is of marked inability to fixate current events, impairment of new learning and distortion of the recent past, while remote memory and other cognitive functions remain substantially intact. Confabulation may be much in evidence. Sprofkin and Sciarra (1952) reported three such cases, in which the clinical picture was that of a Korsakoff syndrome but alcoholism had been excluded. All had tumours limited to the region of the hypothalamus and third ventricle. Previously simple coincidence had been held to account for cases of Korsakoff psychosis with third ventricle

tumours, and a history of alcoholism was said to be usually present.

Williams and Pennybacker (1954) provided further evidence from a systematic study of 180 patients with cerebral tumours, all of whom were given psychological tests for memory function. In 26 impairment of memory was the outstanding cognitive defect, and more than half of these had tumours involving the region of the third ventricle. Four cases had a classical amnesic-confabulatory syndrome, and all four had localised lesions directly involving the floor or walls of the third ventricle. Pursuing the question of localisation further, these authors reviewed 32 cases of craniopharyngioma implicating the diencephalon and third ventricular structures, and compared them with a group of posterior fossa tumours to control for the effects of raised intracranial pressure. The craniopharyngiomas showed a clear excess of cases with characteristic memory defects, especially when the more posterior parts of the hypothalamus and third ventricle had been involved.

One of Williams and Pennybacker's cases illustrates the distinction which can at times be made between the general mental changes of raised intracranial pressure and the specific memory changes related to the focal lesion:

A young man of 22 was found to have a craniopharyngioma involving the floor of the third ventricle. It had interrupted the circulation of the CSF and caused a marked rise of intracranial pressure, giving rise to some local brain stem signs, severe confusion, drowsiness, and intermittent coma. Ventricular tapping relieved these symptoms and he became alert and cooperative. However a marked memory defect for recent events then emerged, with elaborate and detailed confabulation. Part of the tumour was cystic and was directly tapped, thereby reducing local pressure on the hypothalamus. Following this he became fully orientated and his confabulation ceased. As the cyst again filled up the amnesic confabulatory syndrome reappeared. As the CSF circulation was again interrupted and general intracranial tension rose, so drowsiness and mental confusion supervened. These sequences were repeated on several occasions.

A patient reported by Burkle and Lipowski (1978) is also instructive in that memory defects were accompanied by such prominent psychiatric disorder that the organic nature of her troubles was at first overlooked. The lesion, a colloid cyst of the third ventricle, was eventually removed with excellent results:

A woman of 24 complained of increasing depression, sleepiness, loss of interest and energy and recurrent memory lapses. Her depression had been coming on gradually over several months. On examination she was disoriented for the day of the week, showed poor recall of objects, but had no neurological abnormalities. She was apathetic, spoke slowly, and stared impassively. A diagnosis was made of severe depression.

Further examination confirmed marked impairment of judgement and recent memory, and she was considered to be affectively flat rather than depressed. The possibility was raised of hysteria or an organic brain syndrome. Skull X-ray surprisingly showed evidence of raised intracranial pressure, and a CT scan showed dilated lateral ventricles and a spherical mass in the third ventricle. A colloid cyst was removed and she ultimately made a full recovery.
(Burke and Lipowski, 1978)

Steadily progressive dementias with tumours of the diencephalon are usually the result of cortical atrophy consequent upon chronic obstruction to the cerebrospinal fluid circulation. Thus even simple cysts of the third ventricle may present with progressive dementia. Russell and Pennybacker (1961) have shown that craniopharyngiomas, when coming to light only in middle or old age, may present with clinical pictures which are dominated by failing intellect and memory; obvious neurological signs were sometimes absent, so the picture could simulate senile or presenile dementia. Visual symptoms were common but not universal. These tumours are strategically situated to compress the optic chiasma, but the demented patient was sometimes unaware of field defects even when these could be demonstrated. The clue in such diencephalic dementias may lie in marked somnolence, or the other symptoms of hypothalamic disturbance considered below, but these also are not obvious in every case.

Thalamic tumours have been reported to show early and severe dementia which may run a rapid course. Smyth and Stern (1938) reported six such cases. In two, severe dementia coexisted with little evidence of raised intracranial pressure or ventricular dilation, and at post-mortem examination the tumour had not extended widely into the surrounding white matter. The focal lesion may therefore be significant in itself in causing intellectual disturbance, perhaps by virtue of the important connections between medial thalamic structures and the cerebral cortex. Again neurological signs need not be an early feature in thalamic tumours which produce dementia; disturbances of pupillary reflexes were common in Smyth and Stern's cases, but sensory and motor focal signs were sometimes late in appearance or even completely absent.

Somnolence and hypersomnia are frequent with diencephalic tumours. They are symptoms of localising importance, and can alert one to the diencephalic origin of disturbances of memory or intellect. Fulton and Bailey (1929) reviewed the subject extensively, and stressed that it is necessary to distinguish true hypersomnia from the impairment of consciousness that results from raised intracranial pressure. The hypersomnia due to diencephalic lesions is essentially an excess of normal sleep, and when roused the patient awakens normally and fully; patients with torpor due to raised intracranial pressure may similiarly be roused, but usually then display a muddled awareness and obvious intellectual impairment. With some diencephalic lesions there may be a history of transient attacks of hypersomnia for several years during the evolution of the tumour, and well before the intracranial pressure has risen. Very rarely attacks virtually indistinguishable from idiopathic narcolepsy are said to occur, with uncontrollable drowsiness and sometimes also with episodes of weakness of the limbs. These may be provoked by laughter or other sudden emotional reactions.

Such disorders of sleep are due to lesions which impinge upon the hypothalamus, especially in its posterior part, and the contiguous regions of the upper mid-brain. The tumour may originate within the hypothalamus itself, but more commonly compresses it from above as with third ventricular tumours, or from below as with craniopharyngiomas or pituitary tumours. Frequently, but not invariably, the sleep disturbances are accompanied by other evidence of hypothalamic disorder—amenorrhoea, impotence, diabetes insipidus with polydipsia and polyuria, or a voracious appetite. Disturbances of thermoregulation may cause pyrexia and lead to a mistaken diagnosis of an infective process. Tumours affecting the hypothalamus or third ventricular region in childhood, such as craniopharyngiomas or pinealomas, can lead to delayed sexual development, or occasionally to precocious puberty. These varied disturbances may, of course, also occur in the absence of somnolence and provide their own clues to the diencephalic origin of disturbances of memory and intellect.

'Akinetic mutism' is another striking syndrome seen with lesions of the posterior diencephalon or upper mid-brain. It was first clearly described by Cairns et al. (1941) in a patient with an epidermoid cyst of the third ventricle:

The patient sleeps more than normally, but he is easily roused. In the fully developed state he makes no sound and lies inert, except that his eyes regard the observer steadily, or follow the movements of objects, and they may be diverted by sound. Despite his steady gaze, which seems to give promise of speech, the patient is quite mute or he answers only in whispered monosyllables. Oft-repeated commands may be carried out in a feeble, slow and incomplete manner, but usually there are no movements of a voluntary character; no restless movements, struggling, or evidence of negativism. Emotional movement also is almost in abeyance. A painful stimulus produces reflex withdrawal of the limb and, if the stimulus is sustained, slow feeble voluntary movements of the limbs may occur in an attempt to remove the source of stimulation, but usually without tears, noise, or other manifestations of pain or displeasure. The patient swallows readily, but has to be fed. Food seen may be recognised as such, but there is evidently little appreciation of its taste and other characteristics: objects normally chewed or sucked may be swallowed whole. There is total incontinence of urine and faeces.

Fluctuations may occur in the intensity of this state. In its incomplete manifestations the patient may respond at times, though slowly and imperfectly, by speech and voluntary movement. Voluntary movement may be accompanied by a coarse tremor of the limbs. Incontinence persists, and there is little or no trace of spontaneous activity or speech. The onset of the condition is gradual. In certain circumstances there may be slow spontaneous recovery; but if the state is caused by pressure of a tumour it may be followed by coma. The condition is sometimes, though not always, associated with decorticate rigidity.

When caused by a cystic tumour which can be aspirated the syndrome is found to be potentially reversible. A dense amnesic gap is then left for the duration of the episode. The syndrome is thus clearly not due to the general effects of raised intracranial pressure, but attributable to focal disturbance of particular diencephalic mechanisms. It may very occasionally need to be distinguished from depressive stupor or catatonic stupor (pp. 132–3).

Affective disturbances with diencephalic tumours have been much discussed, but mainly in anecdotal form. Marked swings of mood have been described, from severe depression to exuberant gaiety, or defective emotional control leading to sudden outbursts of temper on minor provocation (Alpers, 1940). Reeves and Plum (1969) reported a patient whose dementia was accompanied by outbursts of rage and marked hyperphagia; at autopsy a circumscribed hamartoma was found in the hypothalamus. Transient manic reactions have occasionally been observed during the course of operations on hypothalamic tumours, also in the post-operative phase. Other cases have presented from the outset with psychotic depression of marked degree. In the presence of dementia a euphoric or grandiose colouring has led to mistaken diagnoses of general paresis.

Complex disturbances of personality have also been reported in occasional cases of hypothalamic tumour:

A patient of 39 was found at post-mortem to have a teratoma of the third ventricle which had destroyed the hypothalamus, but without evidence of hydrocephalus or cortical damage. For a year before signs of the tumour developed he had become irritable, hypersensitive, aggressive, unreasonable and stubborn, in contrast to his previous personality. He had shown periods of great excitement, and frequently flew into a rage over trivial matters. Meanwhile his business judgement had become impaired and he had become careless of responsibilities. Ultimately he exhibited severe loss of memory.

(Alpers, 1937)

Other patients are described with features suggestive of frontal lobe disturbance—carelessness, fatuous serenity, disinhibition and lack of concern for those around. Indifference to the gravity of the condition may be striking, with affirmation of well-being and denial of illness.

Pituitary Tumours

Tumours arising from the pituitary gland commonly present with raised intracranial pressure, pituitary dysfunction or visual failure. Other tumours in the region of the sella turcica, such as suprasellar meningiomas and craniopharyngiomas, may show similar symptoms. All, however, may also produce mental changes at an early stage and well before these other features are marked.

With some forms of pituitary tumour the psychiatric picture may in part be attributable to the endocrine disturbances which result, for example when Cushing's disease develops with basophil tumours (p. 436) or acromegaly with acidophil tumours (p. 442). The common prolactin-secreting adenoma may result in marked hypogonadism. It is often hard to apportion the blame between the effects of hormonal changes and the effects of the lesion of the nervous system, but there is general agreement that much of the psychiatric disturbance is due directly to extensions of the tumour beyond the sella turcica. Upward extension occurs in the direction of the third ventricle, and will cause the mental symptoms typical of diencephalic tumours. Forward extension may occur between the frontal lobes, or laterally into the temporal lobe, all of which will contribute to the picture that ensues. Clearly pituitary tumours are prone to involve some of the regions where damage is especially likely to lead to psychiatric disturbance. They are also well situated to cause obstruction to the CSF circulation, with additional effects on the mental state due to raised intracranial pressure.

It is therefore not surprising that the literature on pituitary tumours reports a high incidence of mental changes. Accurate comparison with other groups of tumours is difficult since strictly comparable series are not available, but reviews by White and Cobb (1955) and Jefferson (1955) indicate the range of disturbances seen—hypothalamic disturbances with somnolence, polyuria and obesity, circumscribed amnesic states, deterioration of personality, and epilepsy including the uncinate fits of temporal lobe epilepsy.

Dullness, apathy and passivity appear to be particularly characteristic, with mental slowing out of proportion to changes in intracranial pressure. Lack of concern may be striking, even in face of progressive blindness. Emotional instability is also stressed, with liability to episodes of irritability and sudden rage.

A tendency towards paranoid developments seems to be common, and Davison and Bagley's (1969) data (pp. 194–5) have suggested a particular association between pituitary tumours and schizophrenia.

Apart from the amnesic syndrome and the disturbances of hypothalamic regulatory function, it is difficult to apportion these psychological changes between diencephalic, frontal and temporal lesions. Even so it is vital to pay attention to early mental changes, since they are likely to represent extensions of the tumour beyond the sella turcica which may

later render the tumour inoperable (White and Cobb, 1955).

Sub-tentorial Tumours ('Posterior Fossa Tumours')

Under this heading are included tumours of the cerebellum, cerebellopontine angle and brain stem. As already seen, tumours originating below the tentorium cerebelli have a considerably lower incidence of mental symptoms than those originating above (Table 9, p. 190) despite the fact that raised intracranial pressure is much commoner and tends to occur earlier in the former. This distinction is one of the firmer strands of evidence in favour of the view that tumour location plays a part in determining the severity of mental sequelae.

Table 10 (p. 197) shows that cognitive, affective and personality disturbances are all less frequent with subtentorial tumours when compared to tumours elsewhere. Moreover Keschner et al. (1937) found that the mental disturbances which did occur were usually mild, rarely persistent, and tended to occur late in the disease.

Cognitive disturbances appear to be very closely tied to evidence of raised intracranial pressure. The intellectual impairment is usually global, and amnesic defects or other focal cognitive defects rarely appear in isolation. The impairments usually develop insidiously, and parallel the development of internal hydrocephalus caused by obstruction to the flow of cerebrospinal fluid. Very slow-growing subtentorial tumours sometimes result in profound ventricular dilatation before they present for attention, and by then dementia may be severe.

It is important, however, to allow for exceptional instances. Wilson and Rupp (1946) reported a group of 21 patients with posterior fossa tumours, of whom 5 had initially been admitted to psychiatric units with symptoms of memory disturbance, confusion, retardation of thinking and emotional instability; in these cases evidence of raised intracranial pressure was sometimes absent at the time of their presentation. A patient reported by Whitty (1956) is also instructive in this regard:

A woman of 59 with no previous or family history of mental disorder became increasingly depressed and unable to manage her housework following the unexpected death of her mother. Her family noted marked memory impairment. She would put household utensils and money carefully away and then forget where they were, which upset her greatly. When first examined there were no abnormal physical signs and her symptoms were considered to be a psychological reaction to the death of her mother two months before.

Over the next six months she developed occasional incontinence of urine and some ill-defined difficulty with walking. She was now euphoric and showed much emotional lability. There was a marked memory defect for recent events, some nominal dysphasia and a suggestion of constructional apraxia. Neurological examination showed a fine tremor of the outstretched hands, brisk tendon jerks and a shuffling gait, but no papilloedema or other abnormal signs. The CSF protein was 90 mg./ 100 ml but under normal pressure.

She was considered to have an early organic dementia, but in view of the high CSF protein ventriculograms were carried out when lumbar air encephalograms proved unsatisfactory. A posterior fossa tumour was found, and at operation a haemangioblastoma of the right cerebellar lobe was successfully removed. Over the next three months she improved rapidly and steadily, and on discharge she was sensible, fully orientated and with normal memory to formal testing. She returned to full household duties and social life, and had maintained the improvement when followed up three years later.

Disturbances of affect include euphoria and emotional lability in association with intellectual impairments, and sometimes a marked degree of depression, apprehension or irritability. The latter are probably chiefly reactions to the threat of the disease and the neurological defects which result from cerebellar, brain stem or cranial nerve lesions. Change of personality appears to occur mainly as part of the general dementing process, though sometimes frontal lobe disturbance is prominent as a result of internal hydrocephalus.

The mental symptoms that can emerge with acoustic neuromas have attracted some attention. Shepherd and Wadia (1956) reported 6 examples in which chronic hydrocephalus produced confusion, impaired memory, change of personality, apathy and lack of insight. In 2 the mental changes formed the presenting feature. Woodcock (1967) found mental changes in 7 of 31 cases—personality deterioration, impairment of memory and intellect, confusion, depression, euphoria and psychoneurotic traits—and concluded that these were attributable to vascular disturbances consequent upon brain stem distortion. Psychotic developments have been reported both pre-operatively and post-operatively in a surprising number of cases, chiefly depressive or paranoid delusional psychoses occurring in clear consciousness (Dobrokhotova and Faller, 1969; Scott, 1970).

In children, as opposed to adults, posterior fossa tumours appear to lead rather often to early and pronounced changes of behaviour. In Hécaen and Ajuriaguerra's (1956a) series there were four cases of cerebellar tumour in children which had produced anxiety, withdrawal, deterioration in school work, hyperactivity, insolence and problems of control. Pontine tumours may present similarly in childhood. Cairns (1950) reported three children with astrocytomas of the pons in which the initial symptoms included irritability, fretfulness, cruelty and obstinacy. In two these were sufficiently pronounced to constitute a complete change of character, and in all three they antedated the appearance of headache or the development of physical signs. Cairns suggested that the inhibitory functions of the cortex over lower centres were perhaps less well developed in children, allowing emotional and behavioural disorders to declare themselves more promptly in the presence of a subtentorial lesion.

Visual hallucinations may occur with subtentorial tumours, presumably via pressure effects transmitted through the tentorium to the adjacent occipital cortex. Pictures resembling functional psychotic illness appear to be rare.

The Investigation of Cerebral Tumours

When there are grounds for seriously suspecting the existence of a tumour neurological or neurosurgical help should be obtained without delay. But in doubtful cases certain preliminary investigations may be undertaken by the psychiatrist himself, so a brief survey may not be inappropriate here.

The value of different investigatory procedures is usefully outlined by Sumner (1969). Kendall (1980) reviews the changing situation now that CT scanning is available. A detailed neurological examination is the first essential, and here the importance of false localising signs must be remembered. Oculomotor and other cranial nerve palsies may result from secondary distortion of the brain stem, the stretching of cranial nerves, or compression of the cerebral peduncle against the tentorium. An extensor plantar response may be obtained on the side ipsilateral to the tumour for similar reasons.

Full medical examination and chest X-ray are essential in case the tumour should be a secondary deposit from primary neoplasia elsewhere. The erythrocyte sedimentation rate is more commonly raised in secondary than primary intracerebral tumours. Serological tests for syphilis should be carried out while any uncertainty persists.

Skull X-ray may be expected to outline the pineal gland in approximately 50% of adults and lateral shift may be revealed. Evidence of raised intracranial pressure may be seen in erosion of the dorsum sellae or posterior clinoid processes, or the situation of the tumour may be indicated by bone destruction, new bone formation or enlarged vascular channels in the overlying skull. Sometimes there may be calcification within the tumour itself when this is very slow growing. With many pituitary tumours the pituitary fossa shows expansion, and special views may reveal widening or erosion of the internal auditory meatus with acoustic neuromas.

The electroencephalogram can be a valuable aid, though its usefulness has sometimes been over-estimated. The EEG in cerebral tumours is discussed by Cobb (1963) and Kiloh *et al.* (1981). In approximately 20% of cases a normal record is obtained, so the investigation must not be relied upon to exclude the possibility of a tumour. Occasionally it may point to the lesion when other methods short of contrast radiography or CT scanning fail, being particularly valuable with tumours situated in 'silent' areas such as the frontal regions.

Tumour tissue is itself electrically inactive, and whether changes occur in the EEG will depend on the tumour's location, distance from the convexity, rate of growth and other factors. Malignant tumours produce more abnormalities than benign, and meningiomas may occasionally yield abnormal tracings only several years after the onset of clinical symptoms. A single recording will often fail to distinguish between a tumour and an infarct, though serial recordings can be of value, with worsening indicating the former and improvement the latter.

Focal evidence consists usually of a delta-wave focus, irregular in form and amplitude, often with faster waves in the vicinity. A local alteration in background activity commonly occurs. Local spikes or spike and wave complexes may be seen, especially if the patient has symptomatic epilepsy. Focal theta or delta activity in association with a sharp wave focus increases the likelihood that this is due to a tumour. Diffuse changes may consist of less well developed alpha activity or an increase of slow waves on the side of the tumour. Distant signs may also be produced by transmitted intracranial pressure, mass displacements and cerebral circulatory disturbances; focal evidence of a tumour may therefore sometimes be misleading as to site.

Computerised axial tomography now takes pride of place in the investigation of suspected tumours and is the most accurate single test in the great majority of cases (Kendall, 1980). It can be expected to reveal some abnormality in 98% of patients, failing only with very small tumours, particularly those near the base of the skull or in the posterior fossa. It usually gives firm indications as to site, and the nature of the tumour may also be disclosed. A particularly useful feature is the capacity to distinguish tumours from infarctions in the early stages.

The tumour will often be visualised directly — as an area of increased density with meningiomas, colloid cysts or pituitary adenomas, whereas gliomas and metastases may be either hyper- or hypo-dense. Calcification or bleeding within the tumour mass may be shown. Brain displacements, surrounding oedema, ventricular dilatation and overlying bone changes will give important information in other cases.

Contrast enhancement (by the injection of iothalamate intravenously) is essential before concluding that the examination is negative. Abnormal enhancement shows with vascular tumours and may reveal extravasation within others. Cystic or necrotic areas may be clearly displayed.

The yield remains somewhat lower with posterior fossa tumours, where bone artefacts can obscure the definitive evidence. It is here that nuclear magnetic resonance scanning (p. 123) seems destined to make an important additional contribution. Meanwhile CT scanning after the cautious introduction of metrizamide intrathecally is valuable for demonstrating small tumours in the brain stem, cerebellopontine angle and suprasellar regions.

The echoencephalogram was formerly of value as a non-invasive procedure. It may demonstrate shift of the midline structures in cases where the pineal is not calcified, but provides no information about the nature of the lesion. It has the advantage of occupying only a few minutes of time, though both false positives and false negatives are sometimes seen. At best it is therefore no more than a screening test.

The radioisotope scan (p. 116) is also entirely safe but has considerably lower resolution than the CT scan. Its use is now largely confined to places where access to CT scanning is restricted. It demonstrates vascular tumours such as glioblastomas, many meningiomas and multiple secondary deposits. With the latter it can be valuable in preventing fruitless operative exploration. Failure is more likely with slow-growing avascular tumours such as certain astrocytomas, oligodendrogliomas and pituitary tumours, and with tumours smaller than 2 cm in diameter.

Lumbar puncture is best avoided when a cerebral tumour is suspected, and certainly when there are indications of raised intracranial pressure. Abnormalities in the cerebrospinal fluid are not, moreover, universal. Warning signs of increased pressure include headache and papilloedema, though even the latter is not invariably present. Thus if a cerebral tumour is remotely suspected lumbar puncture must always be deferred until a CT scan and neurological opinion have been obtained.

Lumbar air encephalography should likewise be avoided in any tumour suspect, certainly unless full neurosurgical cover is immediately to hand. CT scanning has now rendered air studies obsolete in this context. Ventriculography is similarly very rarely required.

Angiography is comparatively safe in the presence of raised intracranial pressure. It is unlikely to show a tumour when the CT scan is negative, but is still needed for differentiation from aneurysms and angiomas. It can also be valuable in confirming that a tumour is a meningioma, by revealing the capillary circulation supplied by a meningeal artery. Angiography, however, is no longer acceptable as the primary screening procedure for tumours.

Clearly these different investigations can have a special place, and several carry definite hazards. Expert guidance is therefore essential in deciding upon priorities in the individual patient, especially where facilities for CT scanning are not easily to hand.

Problems of Misdiagnosis

The possibility of the psychiatrist overlooking a cerebral tumour in a patient under his care is small in numerical terms, but nevertheless of great importance. Kraft *et al.* (1963) carried out routine skull X-rays in 1000 new admissions to a psychiatric hospital and found 14 unsuspected tumours, 11 of which were pituitary adenomas. Extending their investigation to 1200 chronic schizophrenic in-patients 3 more cerebral tumours came to light, plus 14 more pituitary adenomas (Kraft *et al.*, 1965). Waggoner and Bagchi (1954) similarly reported cases discovered by EEG, and urged the use of this investigation in all psychiatric in-patients.

Surveys of autopsy material from mental hospitals have given cause for concern. Patton and Sheppard (1956) suggested that the chance of finding a cerebral tumour at autopsy was significantly greater among patients dying in State Mental Hospitals in North America than in non-mental hospitals (3.7% compared to 2.4%). Moreover this difference was particularly great for benign meningiomas, which constituted 33% of the tumours in mental hospitals

but only 14% in non-mental hospitals. Such statistics have been disputed, but obtain support from several quarters. Klotz (1957) could not confirm a higher overall incidence of tumours in mental hospital autopsies, but agreed that meningiomas were about twice as frequent in comparison to other forms of tumour as emerged in neurological practice. Klotz also agreed that approximately half of the tumours had been unsuspected during life.

It is hard to estimate what proportion of such tumours may have been incidental to the presenting mental illness. Certainly the pituitary tumours mentioned above could have been without pathological effects. But Remington and Rubert (1962) reported 34 patients discharged from a psychiatric hospital over a 30-year period with a diagnosis of cerebral tumour, all of whom had been admitted initially with disturbances of behaviour or cognition, but in only 10 of whom the tumour was diagnosed on admission. Where opportunities for careful screening are sparse, such patients may easily remain undiagnosed. Andersson's (1970) findings from the State Mental Hospitals of Denmark are also relevant. A tumour frequency of 3% was found at autopsy and two-thirds had been missed during life; moreover the great majority of these patients had been hospitalised for less than 6 months prior to death, so presumably the tumour had been present at the time of admission. In some, at least, the tumours are likely to have been directly responsible for the symptoms which led to hospitalisation.

The distribution of tumour types is important, since as seen above benign meningiomas appear to be especially common in psychiatric patients. Raskin's (1956) series from the Boston State Hospital is typical—86 tumours were discovered in 2430 consecutive autopsies on mental patients (3.5%), with the distribution of tumour types shown in Table 11. Comparison is made in the table with two large series from neurological units as reported by Sumner (1969). Meningiomas are clearly over-represented and gliomas under-represented among the psychiatric patients. Dumas-Duport (1970), in a detailed survey of the literature, makes the further interesting point that when tumour types are studied in a living psychiatric population the frequencies approach much more closely to that of the general population; it is only when autopsy psychiatric material is studied that the proportion of meningiomas rises and the proportion of gliomas falls so markedly. This is probably because autopsy surveys deal mostly with chronically hospitalised patients, and meningiomas tend to produce chronic pictures

TABLE II. Comparison of tumour types between psychiatric and neurological patients with cerebral tumours

	Psychiatric Patients (from Raskin, 1956)	Neurological Patients (from Sumner, 1969)
Meningiomas	30%	15%
Gliomas	20%	45%
Metastatic Tumours	18%	5%★
Pituitary Tumours	13%	10%
Others	19%	25%

★40% considered more realistic today by Sumner.

of mental disorder and therefore to be missed.

Some of the principal misdiagnoses met with in psychiatric practice include the following:

Presenile or senile dementia is all too readily diagnosed when a patient comes before the psychiatrist with features of organic brain dysfunction. In particular the predilection of meningiomas for the anterior basal parts of the skull often allows them to grow large without clinical findings other than progressive failure of intellect. Hunter *et al.* (1968a) were able to report three patients with frontal meningiomas who had been mentally ill for 3, 25, and 43 years respectively before the correct diagnosis was made, and suggest that every patient with dementia in a long-stay mental hospital should be exposed to the full range of ancillary neurological investigations. Focal neurological signs of great importance may easily be missed owing to the intellectual enfeeblement of the patient; in particular it is difficult to assess visual fields or unilateral anosmia without the patient's full cooperation.

The misdiagnosis of dementia is, of course, a special hazard among the elderly. Deterioration of intellect and personality is readily ascribed to senility, and in addition the subarachnoid space becomes more capacious with increasing age so that symptoms of raised intracranial pressure are especially liable to be late (McMenemy, 1941).

Cerebral arteriosclerosis is likewise among the common misdiagnoses, and in Raskin's (1956) series accounted for all ten of the meningiomas which had been missed during life. Evidence of arteriosclerosis on clinical examination, or a past history of focal cerebrovascular accidents, may lead the examiner to undervalue the significance of focal symptoms and signs even when these exist. In addition some tumours first declare themselves with an episode of infarction, and further investigation may then not be pursued.

Alcoholism may also be misleading. When a clear history of alcohol abuse is obtained, persistent amnesic difficulties will often be ascribed to this, or symptoms of dementia to 'alcoholic deterioration'. Similarly, episodes of confusion in the early stages of a tumour may be mistaken for intoxication. In the following patient the diagnosis was only made because of the patient's request for a CT scan:

A man of 34 was referred because of his concern over impaired concentration and memory. He had been a severe alcoholic until two years previously, but since then had abstained completely. Problems with memory had been marked when drinking and had improved considerably since he stopped, but this improvement had reached a plateau. He was also aware of ready mental fatigue, and was eager to know whether brain damage due to alcoholism had persisted. His only other complaint was of episodes of vertigo and nausea for the past three months, ascribed by his general practitioner to labyrinthitis. Examination showed positional nystagmus but no other neurological signs. There was no evidence of cognitive impairment on examining his mental state.

He was strongly reassured that there was little likelihood of alcohol-induced brain damage, and it was thought that he was presenting now because of neurotic concern about his past alcoholic history. Psychometric testing reinforced this conclusion, showing superior intelligence and intact memory functions.

By way of further reassurance he was offered a CT scan and this he eagerly accepted. A large cystic lesion was revealed in the cerebellum, compressing the fourth ventricle and causing dilatation of the third and lateral ventricles. By the time of the scan examination, one month after presentation, he had developed ataxia of gait and papilloedema was apparent. This had not been present before. At operation a benign cystic astrocytoma was removed and he made an excellent recovery.

Epileptic fits may be misinterpreted as due to idiopathic epilepsy. Approximately 20 per cent of tumours are estimated to present with epilepsy, mostly of a focal nature. In psychiatric practice temporal lobe epilepsy will present a special hazard, since even the epileptic nature of the phenomena may be missed. Malamud (1967) reviewed the case histories of 18 patients coming to autopsy in psychiatric hospitals with tumours of the limbic areas of the brain; all had been diagnosed as suffering from functional psychiatric illnesses, though much of the symptomatology appeared to have been based in temporal lobe epilepsy which had been overlooked.

Functional psychoses, both schizophrenic and affective, can be particularly misleading. Symptoms of psychosis in association with tumours usually occur along with evidence of organic defect, but occasionally exist alone as the presenting clinical picture. It is then only with further progression of the tumour that the true situation is revealed.

As described on pp. 194–5, Davison and Bagley (1969) have collected the evidence where schizophrenia is concerned in several large series of tumour patients. They conclude that the association between cerebral tumour and schizophrenia exceeds chance expectation, though the question of special genetic predisposition could not be resolved. Epilepsy did not seem to be the significant factor linking tumour to psychosis. There was no evidence for a special association with different pathological types of tumour, but a significant association emerged with tumours of the temporal lobe and hypophyseal region. Such conclusions can of course only be tentatively drawn in view of the large number of uncontrolled variables.

The question of affective psychosis is equally hard to evaluate with regard to the aetiological role of the tumour and its location. Depressive symptoms are common but often transient, and only rarely take on the features of a depressive psychosis (Hécaen and Ajuriaguerra, 1956a). Mania is rare, though occasional cases presenting in this way are reported.

Neurotic symptoms can be an early feature and are sometimes severe enough to dominate the picture. Minor degrees of depression, irritability and anxiety are extremely common, representing an exaggeration of premorbid traits and probably often occurring in response to subjective awareness of subtle changes in intellectual function. Occasionally elaborate neurotic developments may emerge, with obsessional, hypochondriacal and hysterical features, before the focal signs of the tumour have declared themselves.

A special source of error is the readiness with which the patient's family, and his physician, are liable to interpret such early symptoms in terms of current stresses in the life situation. Minski (1933) found that 19 of 58 cases of cerebral tumour admitted to the Maudsley Hospital had a clear history of stress antedating admission in the form of recent accidents, bereavements or occupational difficulties. Sometimes the stress may have served to focus attention on early symptoms, or sometimes the patient's attempt to cope with the problem may have unmasked his reduced adaptability.

A man of 37 was referred by a neurologist for psychiatric treatment on account of depression and irritability of recent onset, together with panicky feelings when travelling. He had developed epilepsy 4 years earlier, after a mild head injury, but this remained well controlled by anticonvulsant medication. He also complained of intermittent headache and difficulty in concentrating on his job, but in fact was coping well and had recently been promoted. Neurological examination was entirely normal.

He had always been of an anxious, pedantic disposition and prone to take his responsibilities very seriously. His wife was now expecting the birth of a second child and they were due to face considerable financial difficulties. He was treated with minor tranquillisers and supportive psychotherapy for six months, and showed a measure of improvement. Suddenly, however, he developed a hemianopia and a sixth nerve palsy, and was admitted to hospital in semi-coma. A slow-growing astrocytoma in the non-dominant temporal lobe was discovered.

The principal safeguard in such difficult examples is to be especially cautious in accepting as 'neurotic' someone whose previous adjustment has been good, and in whom precipitating causes seem insufficient. These highly subjective assessments must of course be backed up by careful neurological examination and a readiness to investigate whenever there is room for doubt.

Hysteria is a well-known source of error. Neurological signs of a puzzling or unconvincing nature readily invite this label, especially in patients with a markedly unstable background. Certain symptoms, such as somnolence, may be viewed with suspicion when they are unbacked by physical findings. The patient who has displayed conversion symptoms in the past is especially at risk:

A 'kept woman' was finding it hard to maintain influence over the man who supported her as she grew older. On several occasions she had shown evidence of conversion hysteria, once going blind temporarily when he refused to take her on a customary Spring trip to Florida. Again he declined to take her on this trip, and she became too weak on the left side to care for herself. She was admitted to hospital with the diagnosis of 'major hysteria'. The left plantar response was found to be up-going and the abdominal reflexes were absent on the left. A right temporal lobe glioma was eventually discovered.

(Chambers, 1955)

Factors Contributing to Misdiagnosis

It it useful to look at some of the principal reasons why tumours appear to have been overlooked in psychiatric patients, as listed by workers who have made a retrospective analysis of the situation (McIntyre and McIntyre, 1942; Olin and Weisman, 1964; Hunter *et al.*, 1968a; Dumas-Duport, 1970).

A lack of 'brain tumour consciousness' in the mind

of the examiner is repeatedly stressed. Such a lack is perhaps not surprising in view of the rarity of cerebral tumours even in busy psychiatric practice. But a greater awareness, and readiness to investigate, could undoubtedly reduce the errors that occur.

It is likely that the doctor often allows himself to be influenced by explanations furnished by the patient or his family, and too readily views the early symptoms in terms of current psychosocial stresses. The problem can be seen as part of the general tendency for psychiatrists to underrate physical causes as a possible basis for mental symptoms, at least until the physical disorder becomes obtrusive.

The psychiatrist's preoccupation with the mental picture may further lead him to disregard important details of the history or symptomatology. Olin and Weisman (1964), for example, report a patient whose episodes of severe anxiety, and an offensive manipulative manner, allowed the physician to overlook his clear report of intermittent attacks of an unpleasant taste sensation. Ultimately a temporal lobe tumour was revealed. Again, with psychiatric troubles in the foreground an adequate neurological examination may fail to be performed, or there may be considerable practical difficulties in carrying this out. Not only does the intensity of psychiatric disorder make a primary psychiatric diagnosis more plausible but it also makes the neurological diagnosis more difficult. It may be hard to get an adequate description of symptoms in the mentally disturbed patient, or to secure cooperation for a fully comprehensive neurological examination.

Other sources of error include failure to realise that headache, vomiting and papilloedema may be absent in the early stages of tumours. It is particularly unfortunate that it is the slow-growing and potentially remediable tumours which are apt to be late in declaring themselves by evidence of raised intracranial pressure. False assurance is also sometimes derived from a normal skull X-ray, or normal cerebrospinal fluid pressure at lumbar puncture.

Finally one must contend with the relative lack of specificity in the psychiatric symptomatology of cerebral tumours, and especially with the risk attaching to the term 'organic dementia'. When such a label has been applied it frequently discourages attempts at the further refinement of the diagnosis. Unfortunately in many psychiatric hospitals the situation is aggravated by a lack of facilities readily at hand for suitable investigations.

Chapter 7. Epilepsy

The manifestations of epilepsy include facets of equal importance to the psychiatrist and the neurologist. Some manifestations indeed stand firmly at the junction between the two disciplines. The seizure itself may take the form of the classical motor convulsion or consist instead of complex abnormalities of behaviour and subjective experience. Associated disorders may sometimes include cognitive difficulties, personality disturbances or psychotic illnesses of various types and durations. In all these respects the study of patients with epilepsy has played an important part in advancing our knowledge of brain function and dysfunction, and in indicating something of the pathophysiological basis for certain forms of psychological disorder.

The accent in the present chapter will be on those aspects most relevant to the work of the psychiatrist. It is now clear that the great majority of epileptics suffer little or no mental disturbance, but those who do can present difficult and complicated problems. Psychosocial and organic factors are often inextricably mixed in causation, and the assessment of all the evidence available in the individual patient can be a complex and time-consuming matter.

At a theoretical level epilepsy presents considerable problems of terminology and classification and these must often be met by compromise solutions. Such difficulties become compounded when seeking to explore the psychiatric concomitants of seizures, and many areas remain in which our understanding is remarkably incomplete.

The Varieties of Epilepsy

Brain (1955) defined epilepsy as 'a paroxysmal and transitory disturbance of the functions of the brain which develops suddenly, ceases spontaneously, and exhibits a conspicuous tendency to recurrence'. It may be desirable, however, to bring electrophysiological events into the definition to separate the above from, for example, migraine or syncope. Alter *et al.* (1972) recommend defining an epileptic patient as 'one who has a paroxysmal alteration of intellectual, sensory, motor, autonomic, or affective activity,

TABLE 12. Varieties of epilepsy

1. Generalised epilepsies
   (a) Primary generalised epilepsy (petit mal, grand mal)
   (b) Secondary generalised epilepsy
2. Focal epilepsies ('partial' or 'local' epilepsies)
   (a) With elementary (simple) symptomatology (e.g. motor Jacksonian epilepsy)
   (b) With complex symptomatology (mostly temporal lobe in origin, e.g. with cognitive or affective symptomatology, psychomotor attacks, psychosensory attacks)
3. Unclassifiable and mixed forms

which is time limited (usually under one hour) and presumably associated with neuronal hypersynchronous overactivity'.

Epilepsy may be subdivided according to observed content of attacks, presumed aetiology and pathology, EEG manifestations, or presumed site of origin of the abnormal activity within the brain. No single classification is entirely satisfactory, and attempts at any comprehensive sub-division soon become unwieldy. A broad classification which is useful for clinical purposes is shown in Table 12. It is derived from proposals put forward at a meeting of the International League Against Epilepsy for an international classification of the epilepsies and epileptic seizures (Merlis, 1970; Gastaut, 1970).

Generalised Epilepsies

Generalised epileptic attacks derive from disturbances in subcortical structures, most probably the brain stem reticular formation and the nuclei of the diffuse thalamic projection system, whence discharges spread rapidly to involve all areas of the cortex at virtually the same moment. The resulting seizures are bilaterally symmetrical and consciousness is impaired from the outset. An aura is lacking, and there is no evidence whatever of a local onset. Usually there is no warning at all, though very occasionally the patient may experience ill-defined malaise for a few seconds immediately before the seizure.

The great majority originate directly in subcortical structures ('primary generalised epilepsy', 'primary subcortical epilepsy', 'centrencephalic epilepsy'), though occasional cases have been found to originate elsewhere, principally in the basal frontal cortex, and to spread thereafter immediately to involve the subcortical structures ('secondary generalised epilepsy', 'secondary subcortical epilepsy'). The clinical manifestations are identical and the differentiation is essentially made by electroencephalography.

The generalised epilepsies are divided into two sharply differing forms, petit mal and grand mal, as described below.

Petit mal is seen most commonly in children. In most cases the prognosis is good, attacks gradually ceasing in adolescence, though occasionally they persist into adulthood or give way to grand mal seizures. Petit mal is always of primary subcortical origin. Occasionally both petit mal and grand mal seizures may be seen together, and the prognosis is then less favourable.

Three varieties are distinguished and may occur alone or in combination:

The commonest and most clear-cut form is the '*petit mal absence*'. This is sometimes termed 'pyknolepsy' when, as is usual, it sets in in childhood and clears at adolescence. It is virtually always without evidence of any gross brain lesion. Without warning the patient loses contact with his environment, usually for four or five seconds but occasionally for as long as half a minute. To the onlooker he appears momentarily dazed, stops speaking and becomes immobile. The face is pale, the eyes assume a fixed glazed appearance, and the pupils may be observed to be fixed and dilated. Posture and balance are usually well maintained, though muscular relaxation may allow the head to slump forward. Brief muscular twitches may be seen around the eyes, occasionally extending to brief myoclonic jerks of the limbs. Such movements are always bilateral and symmetrical. Consciousness is typically deeply impaired during the attack, though in rare cases the subject may remain dimly aware of what is happening around him. There are usually no after-effects whatever. The patient may later be aware of the attack as a momentary break in the continuity of events, but quite often does not know it has occurred and continues immediately with the word or activity that was interrupted. While each attack is brief, runs of attacks sometimes occur in rapid succession. The frequency of episodes is commonly five to ten per day, but sometimes hundreds may be noted in the course of a single day. Lennox (1960) suggests that if attacks do not occur daily the diagnosis should be questioned.

The above is now commonly referred to as the 'simple absence'. 'Complex absences' show more protean manifestations, often akin to those seen with temporal lobe epilepsy, yet accompanied by the typical EEG features of petit mal. The duration is likely to be longer, lip-smacking, chewing, mouthing or fumbling movements may occur, and there may be vocalisations. Such cases can present difficulty over clinical differentiation from brief temporal lobe seizures, particularly when the latter are partially controlled by drugs. Close observation of the content of the attacks and the EEG picture usually serve to make the distinction, but sometimes even the latter will yield inconclusive results. In such circumstances one may ultimately be forced to a trial of different medications (Marsden and Reynolds, 1982).

The second variety consists of '*akinetic seizures*'. These primarily involve the mechanisms governing posture, resulting in profound and generalised muscular relaxation so that the patient abruptly slumps in the chair or falls to the ground. Attacks again occur without warning and last for only a few seconds. After effects, other than those due to bruising or emotional shock, do not occur. Such attacks may be seen along with petit mal absences in children which justifies their inclusion as part of the '*petit mal triad*'. Quite often, however, drop attacks of this nature occur in patients with grand mal epilepsy and represent unusually brief and abortive forms of major seizure discharges.

The third form consists of *generalised myoclonic jerks*—sudden shock-like movements lasting for only a fraction of a second and mainly affecting the neck, arms and shoulders. Objects which are held may be dropped or flung violently. If the trunk or legs are affected the patient may be flung off balance. It is uncertain whether consciousness is lost or retained, since the seizures last for so very short a time. Single myoclonic jerks of this nature are frequently seen in subjects suffering from petit mal absences or akinetic seizures, hence their inclusion as part of the petit mal triad. Myoclonic jerks may, however, also be seen as an occasional manifestation in normal persons when falling asleep, or in association with grand mal epilepsy or several serious brain diseases. They are characteristic of subacute encephalitis, the cerebral lipoidoses and Creutzfeldt-Jakob disease. The rare progressive myoclonic epilepsy of Unverricht consists of increasingly frequent myoclonic jerks in association with progressive dementia. It is due to an autosomal recessive gene.

The three forms of petit mal are unified by the fact that a single patient may display different members of the triad on different occasions, by their improvement with certain medications which do not help grand mal, and by the EEG pattern.

The EEG picture is striking and very characteristic. During attacks the record is suddenly interrupted by bilaterally synchronous spike and wave complexes of high amplitude, occurring at approximately three per second and seen synchronously (simultaneously) throughout all scalp leads. Petit mal absences show the closest association with, and the most classical manifestations of, three per second wave and spike discharges. Akinetic seizures usually show slower two per second wave and spike formations, and myoclonic jerks may sometimes be accompanied by a single wave and spike complex, by multiple spikes or by 'polyspike and wave'.

The interseizure record may display brief bursts of similar activity unaccompanied by overt attacks, or symmetrical spike and wave variants without the strict three per second regularity. These subclinical manifestations are usually less well organised and of lower amplitude than in the actual attack, but are always widespread, bilaterally synchronous and more or less symmetrical. Their incidence is considerably increased by overbreathing. The runs are unaccompanied by obvious clinical phenomena, but Tizard and Margerison (1964) have shown that during wave and spike discharges there is slowing of response times and an increase in errors on simple psychological tests.

Grand mal seizures of subcortical origin occur without immediate warning and consciousness is lost abruptly. Thus there is no preceding aura. Some subjects, however, may be aware that a fit is imminent on account of ill-defined prodromata which build up for hours or days, such as malaise, tension, nausea or headache. In subjects liable to myoclonic jerks these may increase in frequency for some hours before the grand mal attack. The seizure consists of tonic and clonic phases which involve all parts of the body symmetrically and from the same moment. The fit is usually followed by a deep sleep which may then be succeeded by nausea, vomiting and headache. If sleep does not occur a period of confusion is usually seen before full consciousness is regained. During this period the patient is disoriented, often restless, rambling and incoherent, and sometimes unaware of his personal identity. On recovery there is total amnesia for the content of the attack, and frequently for a period of several seconds extending in a retrograde direction.

The EEG pattern during the attack is characteristic. For a few seconds before the fit there is a crescendo of low voltage fast activity. With the tonic phase this gives way to a generalised synchronous discharge of high amplitude spikes at eight to twelve per second. After some 15-30 seconds the spikes become grouped and separated by slow waves as the clonic phase begins. When the fit is over low amplitude delta waves predominate throughout the record, often as slow as one per second and without focal preponderance. Thereafter the record gradually resumes its usual appearance, though the slow activity sometimes persists for several hours. After status epilepticus random diffuse slow activity can persist for several days.

In approximately 20–30% of cases the interseizure EEG is normal on a single routine record (Kiloh *et al.*, 1981). forty per cent show non-specific abnormalities in the form of paroxysms of symmetrical delta, bursts of theta, or a diffuse excess of slow rhythms. The remainder show *formes frustes* of seizure discharges with wave and spike or polyspike and wave complexes. As with petit mal these are always widespread and more or less symmetrical. Patients with grand mal alone can show paroxysms of three per second wave and spike, but faster variants at three and a half to four and a half per second are more typical.

Focal Epilepsies

In focal epilepsy the seizure discharge begins in some part of the cortex. This always implies the presence of a localised brain lesion, even though techniques presently available may fail to reveal its nature. Focal symptoms in the form of an aura therefore usher in the seizure, the precise symptomatology depending on the area of the brain in which the discharge originates and the direction of its subsequent spread. The main varieties of aura and their significance for localisation are discussed on p. 217 *et seq.*

All varieties of focal epilepsy are liable to lead on to a generalised convulsion, but this is not an invariable sequel. Some attacks may consist of no more than the focal manifestations of the epileptic process. They may be very brief indeed, consisting only of the opening phases of the aura. Such 'minor' attacks are more common when the patient is already on medication. Even extended attacks may fail to generalise to the rest of the brain, in which case the seizure consists only of the focal disturbance while consciousness is wholly or partially retained. In Jacksonian epilepsy, for example, the motor 'march' may sometimes spread along a limb and then recede, while the subject retains full awareness throughout. The grand mal convulsions which do occur are often asymmetrical in distribution, and may be followed by longer lasting focal functional defects such as dysphasia or transient weakness of the affected limb ('Todd's paralysis').

Sometimes, and particularly in temporal lobe epilepsy, the focal discharge spreads to the limbic system rather than to the centrencephalic system, and remains confined there throughout the attack. In such cases consciousness is profoundly impaired during the seizure, yet complex behaviour can still be carried out ('psychomotor attack'). Whether or not a grand mal convulsion eventually ensues will depend upon the degree of generalisation of the seizure discharge, i.e. whether there is ultimate involvement of subcortical structures.

The precise classification and the terminology used for the focal epilepsies have been the subject of considerable debate, as outlined by Parsonage (1982). The terms 'focal' and 'partial' are in general used interchangeably. Thereafter such epilepsies may be classified according to their predominant type of seizure—simple, complex, psychomotor, etc. When cognitive, perceptual or emotional disturbances figure prominently (thought disturbance, déjà vu, hallucinations, fear, etc.) the attacks may be referred to as 'psychic seizures', though this term is now being replaced by 'complex partial seizures' (see below).

Elementary (simple) partial seizures will often lack impairment of consciousness, as in the Jacksonian motor attacks mentioned above. By contrast those with complex symptoms ('complex partial seizures') will tend to arise in areas of higher cerebral organisation and will be very likely to show impairment of consciousness. In some classifications the preservation or impairment of consciousness is used as the primary criterion for separating simple from complex partial seizures, though this is not universally accepted. The great majority, though not all, complex partial seizures will be temporal lobe in origin.

During attacks of focal epilepsy the EEG may show a variety of abnormal electrical discharges. There may be rhythmic spikes, sharp waves, spikes and slow waves, or rhythmical runs of theta and delta. The abnormal activity may remain strictly localised, or spread widely over one or both hemispheres. In occasional cases the record may remain normal during an attack, as in some cases of Jacksonian epilepsy when the focus is very discrete and of insufficient voltage to reach the surface electrodes. Once the attack has ceased normal rhythms may return at once, or after a period of random low voltage slow activity.

During temporal lobe automatisms bilaterally synchronous theta or delta discharges are usually seen, most marked in the fronto-temporal regions and sometimes interspersed with slow waves or spikes. Other pictures may occur, however, such as generalised fast activity, 'normalisation' of the record with disappearance of interictal discharges, or no change whatever. (The EEG during automatisms and other psychomotor attacks is discussed further on p. 226). After the attack focal slow activity may persist in the affected temporal lobe for hours or days.

In the interseizure record the commonest evidence of a cortical epileptogenic lesion is a spike and sharp wave focus. Alternatively there may be local spikes, singly or in groups, spikes and slow waves, or paroxysmal theta or delta. The underlying lesion may produce electrical disturbance itself, usually in the form of focal slow waves. The abnormal discharges commonly betray the point of origin of the attacks though sometimes they are transmitted widely to other areas. There may even be a 'mirror' focus over the homologous area of the contralateral hemisphere. Such distant foci can be seriously misleading, but it is usual for them to be less consistent than the primary focus from one recording to another.

The interictal record in temporal lobe epilepsy typically shows spikes or sharp waves at the temporal electrodes, but the record can be normal until sleep activation is employed. Sphenoidal electrodes may be needed to detect discharges originating in the medial temporal lobe structures. Light thiopentone anaesthesia is also useful for inducing beta activity, which may be less well developed at the electrodes over the site of damage in the affected temporal lobe.

Unclassifiable and Mixed Forms of Epilepsy

In some patients the most careful investigation will fail to clarify the source of origin of attacks, or alternatively there may be diffuse and scattered lesions leading to multiple foci both in cortical and subcortical structures. Some of the more severe and intractable cases of epilepsy fall into this latter category. Clinical manifestations may include a mixture of focal fits, grand mal, myoclonic and psychomotor attacks. There are likely to be abnormal neurological findings. Progressive dementia may sometimes occur.

In patients with mixed forms of epilepsy the EEG is more continuously abnormal than in other groups. It can occasionally be difficult to find normal stretches of record. Multiple independent foci may be seen, with groups of spikes, sharp waves, or spike and slow waves. Slow waves may be widespread over the hemispheres and often irregular in form.

Other Special Forms of Epilepsy

Other forms of epilepsy which occur more rarely but

can produce puzzling clinical pictures may be mentioned briefly.

'*Reflex epilepsy*' is the term used for attacks which are liable to occur in response to some specific precipitating stimulus. Detailed reviews of the many varieties are provided by Daube (1965), Merlis (1974) and Fenwick (1981a). In some patients fits result from sensory stimulation of discrete regions of the body. Music is the precipitating stimulus in '*musicogenic epilepsy*', sometimes music with special emotional significance for the patient (Critchley, 1937; Shaw and Hill, 1947; Daly and Barry, 1957). In 'television epilepsy' the photic stimulation from the flickering of the television screen is the precipitant (Pallis and Louis, 1961; Mawdsley, 1961; Jeavons and Harding, 1970). An interesting variety, also due to photic stimulation, has been reported in children who pass the hand repeatedly in front of the eyes while staring at the sky, or jump up and down in front of venetian blinds, and perhaps derive satisfaction from the minor seizures that result (Robertson, 1954; Sherwood, 1962). Other patients have been reported with attacks precipitated by reading (Bickford *et al.*, 1956; Critchley *et al.*, 1959), or by sudden voluntary movement of the limbs (Lishman *et al.*, 1962; Whitty *et al.*, 1964).

The chief importance of reflex epilepsy for the psychiatrist is that attacks may easily be suspected of being psychogenic in origin until their reflex epileptic basis is recognised. The existence of such clear-cut examples is also a reminder of the importance of searching for possible precipitating factors in other epileptic patients as discussed on p. 216.

'*Tonic seizures*' consist of sustained spasm, usually affecting the whole musculature but often asymmetrically so that slow twisting writhing movements are produced. Groping and grasping of a limb may occur. There is no clonic phase, the attacks are usually brief and after-effects are slight. The bizarre nature of the attacks may again suggest a purely psychogenic disorder. Such seizures have been thought to originate in the basal ganglia, and have been variously termed extrapyramidal, striatal or subcortical epilepsy (Lennox, 1960). 'Tonic postural fits' represent a more severe variety, with sustained rigidity of the antigravity muscles resulting in opisthotonos, extension of the neck and legs, and flexion of the arms as in decerebrate rigidity. Such attacks have been presumed to have a focal origin in the lower mid-brain or upper pons. They may sometimes be seen with cerebellar tumours by virtue of pressure effects on the neighbouring brain stem ('cerebellar fits'). It is likely that many examples are in fact not epilepsy at all but represent transient attacks of decerebrate rigidity.

'*Gelastic epilepsy*' is a term occasionally used for seizures preceded or accompanied by uncontrollable laughter. A child, for example, may suddenly bend his head and giggle for no apparent reason. Such attacks may be regarded as a curious habit, and not recognised as epileptic in origin for a considerable time until more definitive features appear. It is probable that the laughter is often evoked by the emotional content of a brief temporal lobe aura. Roubicek (1946) reviews the literature concerning such seizures and reports three cases of his own, with the laughter sometimes occurring as part of an aura and sometimes in the course of a psychomotor automatism.

'*Diencephalic*' or '*autonomic*' epilepsy is a variety in which marked autonomic symptoms predominate during attacks. Such phenomena are common as part of any generalised epileptic seizure but are sometimes said to occur in relative isolation. It is uncertain, however, whether the condition warrants recognition as a separate entity. Fox *et al.* (1973) reported a patient whose attacks consisted of episodic flushing and sweating, lasting 10–20 minutes, followed by feeling cold and shivering. Slight confusion could sometimes ensue. The rectal temperature fell during attacks and was recorded as low as 34°C. In other cases seizures may take the form of a sudden desire to urinate, to defaecate, sensations of heat or cold, flushing, hyperpnoea, difficulty with breathing, salivation, lachrymation or abnormal gastric sensations. It may be hard to distinguish such symptoms from those of an anxiety state, though the sudden onset and ending and the regular stereotyped nature of the attacks may give the clue. It is likely that most examples of epilepsy falling within this category derive not from mid-line subcortical structures but from the medial temporal lobe.

'*Hypsarrhythmia*' is the term used to describe a characteristic EEG record seen in some infants and very young children suffering from widespread cerebral disorder, most commonly in the first year of life. It is not a specific clinical condition but may result from a wide variety of pathological processes. The EEG shows almost continuous abnormal activity, with irregularly occurring spikes and slow waves of high amplitude in all leads. Clinical manifestations include frequently occurring major and minor seizures of many types along with massive myoclonic jerks. 'Salaam attacks', consisting of bowing movements of the head and trunk, are a common but not a constant clinical manifestation. Arrest or regression of mental development often occurs. ACTH or steroids have proved to be of value in treatment, at least for a time, but the prognosis depends essentially on that of the underlying cerebral condition. Mental deficiency of some degree is often a permanent sequel even when the fits are brought under control.

Prevalence and Aetiology

General practice surveys have indicated that in England and Wales some 4–6 persons per 1000 are currently suffering from epilepsy, and that approximately 5% of the population will have a fit of some sort during their lifetime (Pond *et al.*, 1960; College of General Practitioners Report, 1960). The overall incidence is about the same in males and females. Age of onset shows the highest rate in the first year of life, a considerably lower incidence during childhood and adolescence, and a lower level still during adulthood. In Pond *et al.*'s (1960) survey almost a quarter of cases had begun before the age of 5, another quarter during schooldays (5–14), one tenth during adolescence (15–19), and the remaining 40% after 20. Of the different types of epilepsy the great majority appearing in the first twenty years of life are generalised grand mal attacks, while after this age the proportion of focal epilepsies rapidly increases.

With regard to aetiology epilepsy must be viewed as a symptom and not as a disease in itself. A great variety of causes may underlie the occurrence of the fits and need to be carefully investigated. When this is done, however, a considerable proportion of cases remains in which no cause is discernible, either during life or on eventual histological examination of the brain. It is therefore necessary to make a first division into epilepsy of unknown aetiology and epilepsy of known aetiology. The latter is often referred to as 'secondary' or 'symptomatic' epilepsy.

Epilepsy of Unknown Aetiology

This simply represents those cases in which no evidence can be found in the history or on examination for an adequate underlying cause. The older term 'idiopathic' epilepsy has fallen into disfavour, because it carries the implication that the group represents a distinct clinical entity and this is far from clearly established. Other terms are 'crypto-genic' epilepsy, suggesting that some brain lesion is responsible but evades detection, or 'functional' or 'metabolic' epilepsy suggesting that the fits result

from disordered metabolism or other fault of cerebral function rather than any structural abnormality. For obvious reasons all of these terms can be misleading, and the group is most accurately termed 'epilepsy of unknown aetiology'.

The proportion of such cases has been remarkably constant in different surveys, representing approximately two-thirds of cases in several large populations (Alstrom, 1950; Juul-Jensen, 1964; Gudmundsson, 1966). The proportion was somewhat higher (75%) in Pond *et al.*'s (1960) survey, but here there was no first-hand opportunity for investigating causes. Alstrom (1950) found that the sexes were equally represented among the epilepsies of unknown aetiology, but males were twice as frequent as females in the remainder, chiefly due to the excess of males with post-traumatic epilepsy.

The great majority of epilepsies of unknown aetiology are generalised from the start, being either petit mal or grand mal without warning. Indeed the classical petit mal absence proves virtually always to be without demonstrable cause. A focal component to the seizures will strongly indicate that some form of structural brain lesion is present, but of course this will not invariably be demonstrated. In a small proportion of cases with focal seizures no cause will be found even at autopsy, and here it must be presumed that the 'idiopathic discharge' simply happens to arise in some particular area other than the usual midline structures. In most epilepsies of unknown aetiology no neurological abnormality will be found between attacks. The incidence of psychiatric disabilities is also lower than in other groups; Alstrom (1950) found mental disturbance in 21% of cases of unknown aetiology, in 37% where a probable cause could be discerned, and in 58% where the epilepsy was clearly secondary to a structural lesion.

The exact mechanism of the electrical abnormality responsible for the seizures is unknown, but appears to be based in biochemical changes in the neurones. An hereditary basis almost certainly plays some part as discussed on p. 215 and a family history is found more commonly than for epilepsies secondary to known brain lesions.

Epilepsy Due to Birth Injury or Congenital Malformations

Complications of pregnancy and delivery may damage the brain and lead to epilepsy. Most often the seizures will be declared in infancy or date from very early in childhood. Anoxia is an important cause of damage, likewise direct trauma leading to cerebral haemorrhage. In the early neonatal period similar brain damage may result from cardiorespiratory disorders, infections or metabolic disturbances. A large proportion of children with spasticity, infantile hemiplegia or severe mental defect will accordingly suffer from seizures. Covert brain injury without such gross defects is likely to account for fits in many more.

Congenital disorders and developmental defects may likewise be found in epilepsies of very early onset. The causes are legion, including porencephaly, microgyria, other malformations of the cortex, tuberous sclerosis, and arteriovenous malformations (Sturge-Weber and Lindau's diseases).

Post-traumatic Epilepsy

Head injury is a common cause of secondary epilepsy in young adults. The underlying pathology may be a small cicatrix due to organisation of a circumscribed and superficial haemorrhage, or a more extensive glial reaction with focal atrophy and distortion of brain tissue demonstrable on air encephalography.

The development of post-traumatic epilepsy can be profoundly disabling and has important medicolegal implications. Guidance towards the likelihood of its appearance in the individual case is therefore important. Jennett (1975) has shown that the overall incidence after closed head injury is 5% after excluding cases with fits only in the first week after injury. More than half of the cases have their first fit within one year of injury, and three-quarters within 3 years; this means, however, that the risk of developing post-traumatic epilepsy is by no means over when the third year has gone by. Indeed almost one-fifth made their first appearance only 4 years after injury; and these late onset fits were more likely to occur frequently and less likely to remit. Temporal lobe epilepsy amounted to almost 20% in Jennett's (1975) series, again underlining the seriousness of this possible complication.

Certain features can be identified which substantially increase the risk (Lewin, 1970; Jennett, 1975). About 1% of patients are likely to develop epilepsy when there has been no fit within 1 week after injury, and when there has been no haematoma or depressed skull fracture. Irrespective of the severity of injury, a fit occurring within the first week raises the incidence to 25%. The occurrence of a depressed skull fracture raises the incidence to 15%, and an intracranial haematoma to 31%. A depressed fracture associated with a post-traumatic amnesia in excess of 24 hours leads to an incidence of 32%. If in addition these features are associated with a fit within the first week the incidence is 57%.

There is reason to regard fits which develop within the first week after injury rather differently from those which develop in subsequent weeks or later. Thus Jennett (1969, 1975) has shown that the prognosis is better, with a lessened tendency for the epilepsy to persist (even though as described above, subsequent epilepsy is still much commoner than in those who do not have such an early fit). Fits within the first week are commonly focal motor attacks, in contrast to epilepsies which develop later, but temporal lobe seizures are rare.

Penetrating injuries carry a much higher incidence of post-traumatic epilepsy, reported in from 30 to 50% (Russell and Whitty, 1952; Walker and Jablon, 1961). In Russell and Whitty's series the highest incidence was from wounds in the central regions of the brain (parietal 65%, motor and pre-motor cortex 55%), with a diminished incidence towards the poles (pre-frontal 39%, temporal 38%, occipital 38%).

Caveness et al. (1979), reviewing studies from World Wars I and II and the Korean and Vietnam wars, show that the incidence of post-traumatic epilepsy has remained substantially the same despite marked improvements in the management of acute head injuries. With regard to prognosis, experience from the Korean campaign showed that approximately half of the patients with seizures had ceased to have them within 5–10 years, and that in half of the remainder (here 8%) the fits proved to be intractable.

Post-infective Epilepsy

Infections of the brain and its meningeal coverings may lead to fits in the acute stage, or produce scarring which becomes the source of seizures some considerable time later. Encephalitis is more likely to be followed by epilepsy than meningitis, likewise cerebral abscess or venous sinus thrombosis. The incidence of epilepsy due to covert brain involvement during the course of mumps, whooping cough and other infectious diseases of childhood is impossible to determine. Neurosyphilis must not be overlooked as a cause of late-onset epilepsy. Parasitic cysts within the brain are an important cause of fits in certain parts of the world (p. 314).

The common 'febrile convulsions' of childhood are distinct from the above. Any systemic infection may be responsible, presumably by virtue of a lowered threshold for seizures induced by the effect of toxins or pyrexia on the brain. A genetic predisposition is found to be operative, siblings of affected children being also more likely to respond to pyrexia with convulsions, but nonetheless the predisposition appears to fade rapidly after the age of three or four and the great majority of cases do not develop persistent epilepsy. Febrile convulsions nevertheless warrant careful management. When severe they may be responsible for the genesis of the anoxic brain lesions which underlie temporal lobe epilepsy in later years (p. 215).

Epilepsy due to Cerebrovascular Disease

Cerebral arteriosclerosis and episodes of hypertensive encephalopathy are important causes of epilepsy in later adult life. A cerebral embolus is more likely to lead to a fit than a thrombosis or haemorrhage, but any cerebral infarct may leave behind a focal source for epileptic seizures. Sometimes the acute cerebrovascular episode may have gone undiagnosed at the time.

Epilepsy due to Cerebral Tumour

A space occupying lesion may first declare itself by fits and must be given special consideration in late-onset epilepsy. Tumours in the so-called silent regions of the brain naturally present a special hazard in this regard. It is estimated that in approximately 20% of cerebral tumours a fit will be the first sign (Sumner, 1969). Both primary and secondary tumours can be responsible. Nevertheless the risk of overlooking such a lesion is sometimes over-emphasised, since even with late-onset epilepsy a tumour is relatively rare—3 examples were discovered by Serafetinides and Dominian (1963) among 51 patients whose first fit occurred after the age of 25.

Epilepsy due to Degenerative Disorders

Epilepsy may be caused by demyelinating and degenerative disorders both in childhood and later life. In childhood the lipoidoses or tuberous sclerosis may be responsible. In adult life multiple sclerosis or one of the presenile or senile dementias may be complicated in this fashion.

Epilepsy due to Drugs and Toxins

Alcohol and drug withdrawal are important causes of seizures as described in Chapter 13. The abuse of barbiturates can easily be overlooked as a cause of epilepsy beginning only in adult life. The administration of certain drugs such as amphetamines, ergot alkaloids or steroids may provoke seizures, also certain psychotropic medications such as phenothiazines or tricyclic antidepressants (Toone and Fenton, 1977). Intoxication with substances such as lead, or the chlorinated hydrocarbons found in insecticides, may be responsible.

Metabolic Causes

In infancy seizures may be associated with specific metabolic disorders such as galactosaemia or pyridoxine deficiency. Uraemia or hypocalcaemia may be responsible at any age. Electrolyte disturbances are important, particularly in eclampsia and perhaps in occasional seizures which occur premenstrually. Hypoglycaemia due to islet cell tumours of the pancreas may very occasionally emerge as the cause for seemingly idiopathic epilepsies of later onset. Porphyria may declare itself similarly.

The relative likelihood of these various aetiological factors will vary according to the nature of the population studied. Gudmundsson's (1966) survey of 987 epileptic patients in Iceland, most of whom were examined personally, showed that of those with an identifiable cause 38% were attributable to birth injuries, 23% to head injuries, 14% to encephalitis or meningitis, 10% to cerebrovascular lesions, and 2% to cerebral tumours. The absence of examples associated with alcoholism, drug abuse or metabolic disorders was doubtless because such patients would not be included in a survey of persons with established epilepsy.

The relative incidence of causes will also differ according to the age group studied. Juul-Jensen's (1964) large Danish series showed clearly that the proportion of cases attributable to cerebrovascular lesions rose steadily with age, from 9% among the patients as a whole to 70% among those over 50. Cerebral tumours rose similarly from 4% to 15% when the epilepsy began only after 50.

The Aetiology of Temporal Lobe Epilepsy

A good deal of interest has centred on the pathological substrate of temporal lobe epilepsy, since this may be examined in resected brain tissue obtained at temporal lobectomy. A variety of lesions are found—scars, infarcts, small benign tumours of developmental origin ('hamartomas'), or 'mesial temporal lobe sclerosis'. The latter is by far the commonest lesion found at operation, occurring in some 50% of cases, and appears to be the commonest single finding in any epileptic patient who dies a natural death (Falconer and Taylor, 1968). The pathogenesis of mesial temporal lobe sclerosis is thus a subject of considerable importance.

The sclerosis consists of dense glial infiltration of Ammon's horn and adjacent structures such as the amygdala and uncus in the medial part of the temporal lobe. It is usually unilateral. The associated epilepsy commonly sets in during the first decade of life, is frequently severe, and responds particularly well to surgical resection of the lesion. Initially it was thought to result from birth injury, either through generalised hypoxia or as a result of herniation and compression of the posterior cerebral arteries against the tentorial opening. Careful studies, however, suggest that this is not so (Ounsted et al., 1966; Falconer and Taylor, 1968; Falconer, 1974). Neither high birth weight nor prematurity predispose to temporal lobe epilepsy, and the incidence of birth injury in patients with medial temporal lobe sclerosis is no higher than in other groups with temporal lobe epilepsy.

What is especially common is a history of severe febrile convulsions, often with status epilepticus, occurring in early life. It is suggested that the anoxia resulting from such episodes, if sufficiently prolonged at this vulnerable period, may cause irreversible damage to the medial temporal lobe structures and result in due course in the sclerotic epileptogenic lesion. A similar lesion can be produced experimentally in adolescent baboons by inducing serial epileptic attacks or status epilepticus, and as in man the resulting lesion is usually unilateral (Meldrum et al., 1973, 1974).

In the absence of febrile convulsions, other severe infections in early childhood or other causes of anoxia may perhaps have operated in a similar manner to produce the pathological changes. Birth injury may indeed have sometimes contributed to the lesion—not directly as formerly thought, but by setting up some other epileptogenic focus which eventually leads, by way of anoxic episodes during severe seizures, to the mesial temporal lobe sclerosis.

The Genetics of Epilepsy

Genetic aspects of epilepsy have been extensively studied but have met with a good deal of difficulty. An hereditary contribution has usually emerged in large-scale studies but the evidence has been variable and hard to interpret. Clear-cut patterns have

seldom been found. As Alstrom (1950) emphasised this should not be surprising since the epilepsies are clearly a heterogeneous group of disorders. No satisfactory genetic hypothesis could be expected to fit the facts when the epileptic symptom may result from so many different forms of cerebral disorder. The underlying disease may sometimes be inherited, or sometimes determined by non-genetic factors such as injury or infection.

Moreover the capacity to have an epileptic attack is apparently universal in the population provided precipitating circumstances are sufficient, and a substantial proportion of the normal population shows epileptiform discharges on the EEG. It is possible, therefore, that there may be separate genetic mechanisms governing such matters as the aptitude for convulsions ('convulsive threshold'), even though the subject has not experienced a seizure, and the specific epileptic predisposition which may not be paralleled by definite lowering of threshold (Radermecker and Dumon, 1969).

Pratt (1967) and Slater and Cowie (1971) provide detailed reviews of the evidence drawn from many sources. Twin studies have shown much greater concordance for epilepsy among monozygotic than dizygotic twin pairs, especially when attention is restricted to epilepsies without identifiable cause. Large-scale family studies have also tended to support a genetic factor. Conrad's surveys from German hospitals and institutions in the 1930s showed, for example, that when epileptic patients were classified into those showing 'idiopathic', 'intermediate' and 'symptomatic' clinical types, the incidence of epilepsy in their children was 6·0, 2·7 and 1·6 respectively (Slater and Cowie, 1971). These, however, were severely handicapped propositi. Alstrom's (1950) survey of patients attending a neurological clinic revealed occasional family concentrations, but overall the morbidity risk among relatives was little more than might have been expected in the general population.

More recent family investigations have shown that family concentrations are more marked with certain types of epilepsy, namely in those with 'idiopathic' epilepsy, with febrile convulsions, in those below the age of 12, and those with non-focal EEG abnormalities (Pratt, 1967). Metrakos and Metrakos (1960, 1961) have produced evidence that a definite genetic component exists in children whose seizures, whether petit mal or grand mal, are backed by a 'centrencephalic' type of EEG record (typical three per second wave and spike discharges which are paroxysmal and bilaterally synchronous). They concluded that this was the expression of a single autosomal gene whose penetrance varied with age, rising rapidly to near complete penetrance between $4\frac{1}{2}$ and $16\frac{1}{2}$ and declining gradually thereafter. Matthes (1969) concentrated attention on petit mal absences in children, and suggested that these were genetically distinct from other petit mal manifestations. Matthes' evidence seemed to favour a recessive mode of inheritance. Other groups discussed by Slater and Cowie (1971) which have shown marked family concentrations include epilepsy accompanied by focal temporal lobe spike abnormalities, and certain forms of focal epilepsy which tend to disappear at puberty.

It seems, therefore, that there may be a number of major genes in circulation whose most obvious effect is to produce a clinically recognisable form of epilepsy. These, however, must still be regarded as unusual, even when attention is restricted to rather special varieties of epilepsy. For many of the remainder Slater and Cowie (1971) conclude that we can be reasonably certain that polygenic inheritance plays a considerable role.

The important point for genetic counselling is that the chance of an epileptic patient having an epileptic child appears to be not very greatly increased providing the partner is unaffected. Hill (1963b) recommends that as a prelude to any advice with regard to procreation, a full personal and family history should be obtained from both partners of the marriage with special reference to the occurrence of epilepsy in both families, also comprehensive EEG examinations of both partners. 'If the partner's EEG is normal and the family history negative, and the patient's epilepsy clearly of acquired origin (focal cortical EEG), the chances that a child of the marriage will be epileptic are probably not more than 1 in 40. The risk of epileptic progeny increases from this, depending on the evidence that the patient's epilepsy is dependent upon a genetic factor (e.g. family history positive, EEG showing subcortical three per second spike and wave discharges) to the opposed extreme position in which both partners are epileptic and both show this type of seizure discharge in their EEGs'.

Aggravating and Precipitating Factors in Epilepsy

Whatever the underlying cause of the seizures, certain factors may operate to facilitate attacks. Some are largely idiosyncratic to the individual concerned, as seen in extreme degree in reflex epilepsy (p. 211). Some may be responsible for a single attack in an otherwise unaffected person whose threshold for an epileptic seizure merely happens to be relatively low.

Lowering of physical health from any cause may increase the chance of attacks. Sleep deprivation or extreme fatigue are sometimes found to be important. Starvation or even mild degrees of hypoglycaemia can be responsible for attacks in some patients, similarly transient states of anoxia. In women attacks sometimes increase in the premenstrual phase, probably by virtue of shifts in water and electrolyte balance. Drugs which increase the likelihood of attacks have already been mentioned (p. 214).

Frequently noted precipitants include emotional disturbances, startle, shock or surprise (Daube, 1965). Interpersonal stresses and tensions are widely recognised to increase the frequency and severity of attacks; accordingly the emotional stability of the patient may be a factor of considerable importance in securing optimal control. Servit et al. (1963) made an analysis of activating situations in 895 epileptics, and found that more than a third had an increase of seizures in relation to factors in the external environment. Conflict situations were reported to aggravate seizures in 23%, and mental or physical activity in 6%. Eighteen per cent of the patients claimed that their first seizure had followed immediately upon an emotional trauma, mostly an episode of alarm or an experience of horror or fear.

Stevens (1959), in an interesting experiment, found that an emotionally stressful interview could have a markedly adverse effect on the stability of EEG patterns in a large proportion of epileptics, but was without effect in normal controls. More specifically Barker and Wolf (1947) indicated the highly individual triggering which could occur in relation to certain conflict situations. They presented a detailed psychological study of a patient whose epileptic attacks appeared to be related to occasions when his anger broke through customary inhibitory restraints. When interviewed under sodium amytal he expressed mounting rage against his mother, culminating in a fit with coincident epileptic discharges on the EEG.

Fenwick (1981a) distinguishes between 'evoked' and 'psychogenic' seizures, the former depending upon a specific external precipitant and corresponding to 'reflex epilepsy', as discussed on p. 211. Psychogenic seizures, in the correct sense of the term, are generated by an act of will or by the mind *without* any external stimulus. He estimates that evoked seizures probably account for 5–6 % of all cases of epilepsy, whereas the psychogenic variety may be three times as common. Some patients, for example, find that an act of attention, a particular emotion, or some mental function such as thinking or calculating increases the likelihood of seizures. A direct act of will may be involved, such as making the mind blank, attending closely to a particular point in the visual field, or concentrating on an emotion of sadness. In such cases the particular mental function which serves as a precipitant may not always be vouchsafed readily.

By contrast some patients find that they can arrest or abort a seizure after it has begun by some form of mental or bodily activity. Symonds (1959) recorded such a situation in 53 of 1000 cases seen consecutively. Twenty-five stated that they could cut short attacks by some kind of mental effort, usually described as 'pulling themselves together' or making an 'effort of concentration'. Eight patients volunteered that a deliberate switch of mental attention could be successful, for example away from the contents of the aura. Twelve could arrest focal seizures by local stimulation of some part of the body. Such inhibitory manoeuvres may be discovered spontaneously by the patient. Failing this, it may be possible to direct his attention towards them and to utilise the process in therapy, as discussed on p. 272.

The Auras of Epilepsy

The auras which precede focal epileptic attacks are of great clinical importance. They represent the initial focal onset of the attack, and in conjunction with the EEG findings can give essential information about the site of origin of the epileptic disturbance within the brain. Moreover, auras may sometimes arise without further progression to the fully developed seizure, especially early in the evolution of a lesion or when the epilepsy is partially controlled by drugs. They will then produce irregularly recurrent symptoms whose significance may easily be overlooked or misinterpreted.

The detailed content of auras can range from simple discrete sensations to complex abnormalities of ideation and emotion as described below. The pattern shows a fair degree of specificity for the brain region in which the epileptic discharge originates, and in a given patient is usually constant from one attack to another. The symptoms appear abruptly, and in the majority of cases are experienced passively as foreign intrusions on the stream of awareness. They probably rarely occupy more than a few seconds or perhaps a minute, though subjectively

the time course may seem much longer (Pond, 1957). With recovery of consciousness the aura is usually recalled but not invariably so. At the time the patient may have indicated his aura by a frightened look, an exclamation, or by moving to safety, yet afterwards can remember nothing of it. Or he may distinctly recall having had some warning by way of a definite sensation or experience which now cannot be described.

'Auras' must be distinguished from 'prodromata'. The latter do not appear abruptly, but build up slowly for hours or days before the attacks occur. Prodromata are commoner in children than adults, and probably commoner in temporal lobe epilepsy than other forms. Typically they consist of psychological manifestations—mounting irritability, apprehension, sullenness, apathy or periods of mental dullness. Rarely the patient may have a feeling of well-being and show increased energy during the prodromal period. Changes in appetite may occur, or autonomic changes such as pallor, flushing or dyspepsia. Such prodromata are incompletely understood and lack the clinical siginificance of the well-defined aura. Nevertheless they may be of value in occasional patients in warning that attacks are to be expected.

Frontal Seizures

Seizures originating within the frontal lobes sometimes begin without an aura, and therefore resemble primary generalised grand mal attacks until the EEG betrays their focal origin. Seizures originating in the more posterior parts of the frontal lobe may begin with an 'adversive aura', in which the head and eyes turn away from the side of origin of the discharge. Those originating in the pre-rolandic cortex may begin with a classical Jacksonian motor 'march', consisting of involuntary rhythmic clonic movements commencing in some part of the opposite limb or side of the face or tongue, and spreading thence to involve contiguous regions until the major convulsion results. Dysphasia may feature as part of such an aura when the attack originates in the hemisphere dominant for speech. The Jacksonian seizure may die away without progressing to generalised convulsions, and in this case consciousness may be fully retained throughout. The term 'Jacksonian epilepsy' is sometimes restricted to attacks of this particular type.

Seizures beginning in the orbital parts of the frontal lobe are distinct from the above, in that the discharges may occasionally come to implicate the limbic system wth the production of auras indistinguishable from those of temporal lobe epilepsy (see below). In particular, posterior frontal foci may be associated with 'intrusion' or 'crowding' of thoughts as in temporal lobe seizures (Penfield and Erickson, 1941).

Parietal Seizures

Parietal lobe seizures may commence with a 'sensory Jacksonian march' consisting of paraesthesiae, numbness, tingling, or feelings of heat and cold, which begin focally and spread to contiguous areas of the body as the sensory cortex becomes progressively involved. Seizures beginning more posteriorly may lead to pronounced disorders of the body image. A limb or even half of the entire body may appear to be heavier, larger, smaller, missing, or separated from the rest of the body. The limb may feel to be displaced, extended or contracted into the body, even though the patient can see for himself that it is normal. Very occasionally a phantom limb may be felt to be present. Some of the bizarre forms which such auras can take are illustrated in the examples described in Chapter 2 (p. 64).

Medial Surface Seizures

Seizures arising from the medial surface and superior border of the hemisphere show several interesting features (Kennedy, 1959). Involvement of the supplementary motor area, just anterior to the Rolandic fissure, may produce tonic postural movements, chiefly raising of the contralateral arm and turning of the head towards the arm. Epigastric sensations indistinguishable from those of temporal lobe epilepsy may occur, also speech arrest and confusion. More posterior lesions are associated with paraesthesiae in the contralateral foot and leg, rectal sensations, and sometimes genital sensations including feelings of orgasm. Erickson (1945) reported a woman who for sixteen years had suffered attacks of feelng 'hot all over' as if she were having coitus, associated with a marked increase of libido. Although the feeling in the genitalia was a pleasurable sensation, resembling ordinary intercourse, it was limited to the contralateral side of the vagina. Nevertheless she had twice been hospitalised with a diagnosis of nymphomania. Later the sensory experience was followed by Jacksonian seizures and finally by progressive paraplegia. A haemangioma was ultimately removed from the upper end of the right Rolandic sulcus on the medial surface of the

hemisphere, with prompt cessation of the sexual disturbance.

Occipital Seizures

These commence with visual disturbances, well localised within the opposite half-field of vision. A scotoma or hemianopic field defect may occur, or more commonly simple visual hallucinations consisting of flashes of light, colours, zig-zags, or radiating spectra. Complex formed hallucinations with meaningful content do not occur.

Temporal Lobe Seizures

Temporal lobe seizures produce the most varied and complex auras of all. They are of great importance to the psychiatrist since they often contain elements which may raise a suspicion of functional mental disorder. This is particularly likely when the auras arise repeatedly without an ensuing motor convulsion. Isolated auras with prominent psychological content such as hallucinations, depersonalisation, or other subjective experiences are sometimes referred to as 'psychic seizures'.

A variety of *autonomic effects and visceral sensations* figure prominently in temporal lobe auras. The 'epigastric aura' is perhaps the most common, consisting of ill-defined sensations rising from the epigastrium upwards towards the throat, typically described as churning in the stomach, fear in the stomach, or even pain (Falconer and Taylor, 1970). Also frequent are inexplicable odd feelings in the head. Other autonomic effects include salivation, borborygmi, flushing, pallor, tachycardia, praecordial pain, cough and apnoea. Subjective dizziness is common, or true vertigo accompanied by tinnitus and changes in auditory perception.

Altered perceptual experiences include both distortions of real perceptions and spontaneous hallucinations. Sounds may seem suddenly remote or intensely loud, objects may seem larger or smaller, nearer or further away. The evaluation attached to percepts may change, so that objects, sounds or events suddenly acquire a peculiar vivid significance. Alternatively the subject may feel remote from the environment and out of meaningful contact with things around him. Feelings of derealisation and depersonalisation may be marked. The essential quality of recognition may change, with strong feelings of familiarity or unfamiliarity which lead to *déjà vu* and *jamais vu*. Stimulation studies carried out on the temporal lobes exposed at operation have suggested that visual hallucinations, interpretive illusions (such as objects seeming nearer or further away) and illusions of familiarity derive more commonly from the right temporal lobe than the left (Mullan and Penfield, 1959; Penfield and Perot, 1963).

Visual hallucinations may consist of the simple elements described for occipital seizures, but also complex formed hallucinations of scenes, faces, or visions of past experiences. 'Lilliputian hallucinations', in which hallucinated visual material appears very small, must be distinguished from 'micropsia' in which actual objects look to be smaller than normal. Auditory hallucinations stemming from the region of the superior lateral temporal gyrus may also be simple or complex—ringing and buzzing, or organised experiences of music or voices.

Hallucinations of taste and smell derive from the medial temporal lobe structures, particularly the uncinate region, and are of great significance for the diagnosis of temporal lobe epilepsy. They may be accompanied by a characteristic smacking or pursing of the lips, or chewing, tasting and swallowing movements. Olfactory and gustatory sensations may occur alone, or in conjunction with a peculiar alteration of consciousness composed of depersonalisation, déjà vu and dream-like reminiscence—the classical 'dreamy state' or 'uncinate crisis' of earlier writers.

Cognitive abnormalities include disturbances of speech, thought and memory. Transient dysphasia may occur, or sudden ejaculations, or a press of incorrect and inappropriate speech. Dysphasia as part of an aura indicates a left temporal lobe focus, whereas speech automatisms (recurrent, irrelevant or emotionally toned utterances) are strongly related to a right temporal lobe focus (Serafetinides and Falconer, 1963).

The purely subjective disorders of thinking and memory constitute some of the most striking manifestations of temporal lobe auras. The patient may become abruptly aware of difficulty in thinking coherently, of mixing things up, or of great confusion and turmoil in his mind. There may be a compulsion to think on certain restricted topics such as eternity, suicide or death ('forced thinking'). Or there may be intrusion of thoughts or of stereotyped words or phrases against the subject's will ('evocation of thoughts'). A sudden cessation in the stream of thought may occur and later be described in a manner indistinguishable from schizophrenic 'blocking'.

Disturbances of memory range from sudden difficulty with recall to compulsive reminiscence on topics, scenes or events from the past. Many of the phenomena of *déjà vu* or *jamais vu* should perhaps be interpreted as distortions of the memory process. In the rare 'panoramic memory' the patient feels that whole episodes from his past life are lived through again in a brief period of time as complex organised experiences. Indeed distortion of time sense is often an integral part of the experience of the aura, time appearing to rush by precipitately, or alternatively to stand quite still. Amidst all of these experiences the patient usually retains a hold on reality to some degree, so that subsequently he can relate that he was aware of himself experiencing the abnormal phenomena.

Finally strong *affective experiences* frequently appear in temporal lobe auras. The most common are fear and anxiety, which well up suddenly without provocation. Other unpleasant affects include depression, guilt and anger, all of which may reach extreme degree. Pleasurable affects of joy, elation or ecstasy occur more rarely, though Cirignotta *et al.* (1980) have documented a patient with a well-marked ecstatic content to the attacks (so-called 'Dostoevsky epilepsy'). Williams (1956) showed that fear was experienced when the epileptic discharge involved the anterior half of either temporal lobe and occurred in 70% of patients with foci in this region. Depression was associated with lesions anywhere in the temporal part of the brain. Non-specific pleasant and unpleasant affects were mainly associated with posterior temporal lesions.

These affective experiences must be accepted as an intrinsic part of the attack, and not merely a reaction to other aspects of the aura (Daly, 1958). Thus the affect aroused is usually stereotyped and crude, and lacks the subtlety of normal emotions. It tends to be constant both in quality and in time of occurrence during the attack, though it may sometimes change sequentially over time in a given patient. The emotional content of the aura may nevertheless colour hallucinatory experiences, or occasionally have issue in disturbed behaviour.

These manifold aspects of the auras can occur in any and every combination. There is often a characteristic 'march', passing for example from an initial epigastric sensation to gustatory hallucinations to forced thinking, or from intense déjà vu to an overwhelming sense of fear. Sometimes various aspects of the aura appear to occur simultaneously, or the content is so rich and strange that the patient lacks the vocabulary to describe his experiences. Many are extremely bizarre, particularly those which involve disturbance of appreciation of reality and of the self. Williams (1966) points out that the temporal lobes perform the function of integrating sensations of all kinds, and in addition probably contain the neural substrates for emotion itself: 'It is the integration of the whole of exteroceptive and proprioceptive sensations with emotions and moods which culminates in the ultimate sense of 'I am', so that it is not at all surprising that disintegration of this organisation, with retention of sensation, leads to so many of the bizarre disturbances of self which disturb the patient with temporal lobe epilepsy'.

The precise content of the auras may sometimes change with the passage of time, and scrutiny of the patient's notes may reveal well-documented phenomena earlier in the illness of which the patient now has no recollection. This tendency can sometimes increase the risk of the patient being regarded as suffering from a psychogenic disorder.

Special interest attaches to the possible psychopathological significance of some temporal lobe auras. The perceptual–ideational content may prove to be related to an early traumatic situation which is perhaps only partially if at all accessible to recall in the normal state. But when activated by the epileptic process the claim of the material to occupy the field of consciousness becomes irresistible and overwhelming:

A man of 39 had fits from the age of 10. The aura consisted of nausea, raising a hand above the face, and saying 'Don't hit me Dad, please don't hit me'. The patient described a visual scene of his father threatening him with a poker. An informant stated that the father had actually struck the patient with a poker just before the first fit.
(Hill and Mitchell, 1953)

A patient's aura consisted of vertigo, a bell ringing, and the subjective compulsion to think of 'number two' before losing consciousness. The patient had been faecally incontinent until the age of 6, and had at that time called faeces 'number two'.   (Hill and Mitchell, 1953)

A patient had her first epileptic attack in an anxious situation after living in a desolate war environment. The aura consisted of a scene of a city in ruins accompanied by strong déjà vu. Even many years later it was possible to provoke a characteristic dysrhythmia in the EEG by inviting the visual evocation of the symbolic scene of the city in ruins.   (Krapf, 1957)

Hill and Mitchell (1953) discuss the gradations which may be seen in such auras, between the complete re-enactment of organised experience from the past as in the first example, to more abbreviated

forms in which merely a word or two, or a simple forced thought, intrude into consciousness. These may be devoid of meaning to the patient, yet, as in the second example, have a possible relation to emotionally significant past events. Hill and Mitchell found cases in which the ideational content of the aura had changed over time from complete memories to the more abbreviated and hidden forms. These then resembled 'screen memories', and had apparently undergone the psychological processes of repression, condensation or symbol formation. In some cases the process had gone still further: the patient merely experienced strong déjà vu and felt that some important memory was about to be recalled but lost consciousness before it arrived. Or he might later say that an important memory was recalled just before the fit but was now forgotten again.

The mechanisms underlying these changes over time are unknown. They may rest on physiological mechanisms, whereby the neuronal circuits responsible for the activation into awareness of the content of the aura become destroyed or bypassed, or on psychological mechanisms of defence by which the significant event is barred increasingly from access to consciousness. The two, of course, may in the last analysis be synonymous.

'Psychomotor Seizures'

The term psychomotor seizure is used here to refer to a number of epileptic manifestations which may replace the fit proper as the ictal manifestation of the epilepsy. The clinical phenomena involved range from periods of disturbed motor behaviour, sometimes of a complex and semi-purposeful nature, to periods of abnormal subjective experience of varying duration. All have in common an abrupt onset and a more or less abrupt termination, and all are accompanied by alteration of the electrical activity of the brain throughout the time they are taking place. In essence, therefore, these are *the complex behavioural and experiential manifestations of on-going epileptic discharge*.

They are frequently preceded by aural manifestations of the type which usher in more conventional motor seizures. They may displace the grand mal convulsion entirely and constitute the sole manifestation of the seizure, or give way later to grand mal which then terminates the episode. When of long duration they may occasionally be interrupted by one or more convulsions which punctuate their course.

A bewildering number of names are used for such episodes—'epileptic equivalents', 'psychomotor attacks', 'psychic variants', 'automatisms,' 'fugues' and 'twilight states'. Such terms have often been used without clear definition, or even interchangeably, which has led to very considerable confusion in the literature. 'Epileptic equivalent' has had long usage as a generic term but cannot be commended; these attacks are not the 'equivalents' of epilepsy in any exact sense of the word. 'Psychomotor seizure' comes nearer to indicating the content of the attacks. Its chief disadvantage is that 'psychomotor epilepsy' is sometimes regarded as synonymous with 'temporal lobe epilepsy', namely as referring to seizures arising within the anatomical boundaries of the temporal lobes. Psychomotor seizures certainly have a special association with epilepsy originating in the medial temporal lobe structures, but this association is by no means exclusive. It is now accepted that some 20% of psychomotor seizures derive from lesions elsewhere in the brain, and will fail to show a temporal lobe focus on repeated EEG examination, while 20% of patients with temporal lobe epilepsy suffer from grand mal seizures alone (Stevens, 1966).

An additional complication is that clinically similar but physiologically distinct phenomena may ensue upon a grand mal convulsion. They are then not manifestations of the ictus itself, but of the disturbance of cerebral activity which follows upon the ictus. The close similarity of content between psychomotor seizures and some of these post-ictal disorders is discussed on p. 225.

In what follows an attempt will be made to describe the various psychomotor manifestations under headings which reach some measure of agreement in the literature, while recognising that the distinctions between them are often far from clear-cut and that a good deal of overlap must be expected to occur.

Epileptic Automatisms

An epileptic automatism may be defined as 'a state of clouding of consciousness which occurs during or immediately after a seizure, and during which the individual retains control of posture and muscle tone but performs simple or complex movements and actions without being aware of what is happening' (Fenton, 1972). It is accompanied by continuous electrical disturbance in the EEG.

Commonly an ictal automatism is preceded by aural manifestations, usually those typical of temporal lobe epilepsy. Eighty per cent of Feindel and Penfield's (1954) patients had warnings of their attacks, chiefly in the form of epigastric sensations, confusion or difficulty with memory, feelings of strangeness or unreality, lightness or dizziness in the head, or masticatory movements with salivation. Occasionally, though not very frequently, the automatism terminates with a grand mal convulsion. The majority of patients with automatisms also suffer from other forms of seizure, especially grand mal attacks, though occasionally they occur as the sole manifestation of the epilepsy.

The great majority are brief, lasting from a few seconds to several minutes, though occasional examples have lasted for up to an hour. Knox (1968) found that 80% occupied less than five minutes, and another 12% less than fifteen minutes. The detailed patterns of behaviour are variable, sometimes even in the same individual on different occasions. The subject may merely continue with what he was doing, a dazed expression and sudden inaccessibility being the only indications of the seizure. Or there may be no more than some regular stereotyped manoeuvre such as pulling at the clothes, passing a hand over the face, or fumbling with objects near at hand. Brief automatisms can in fact pass unnoticed by onlookers. In more extended attacks the patient performs a whole sequence of related actions—walking about the room, searching in drawers, moving objects, or attempting to remove his clothing. The actions tend to be repetitive, fumbling and clumsy, but are sometimes reasonably well-coordinated. The apparent purposiveness behind the movements also varies considerably. Intentions are usually poorly conceived and executed, but are sometimes successfully carried through even though inappropriate to the situation.

The following examples described by Lennox (1960) are typical:

A woman abruptly ceased her conversation, assumed a strained worried expression and walked away. Led into an adjoining room, she walked quickly from place to place saying 'I must get my coat'. After five minutes she consented to sit down and converse, asking what she should do about her affairs, but seemingly not satisfied with the answers because her questions would be repeated again and again. She had no recollection of this seizure or of the postictal conversation nor, in fact, of anything until after she awoke the next day.

While in a physician's office a patient suddenly stopped talking and stared into space. He slumped in his chair for a brief moment, then sat up and began to rub his abdomen with both hands. A flashlight was shone into his eyes and he turned away. He began to rummage about the desk as if looking for something. When questioned as to what he wanted he said 'I wanna, I wanna'. At this point he took a cigarette from his packet, lit it, and started to smoke. He then got up from his chair, walked out of the office and wandered down the hall opening all the doors and saying 'I want a toilet'. Next, he walked down the hall but could not be distracted by any outside contact. He then lay on the bed and appeared to regain contact gradually.

A policeman directing traffic walked to a waiting car, opened the door, opened and examined the contents of the woman driver's handbag, then returned the bag and went back to his post. The woman reported the occurrence and the policeman denied knowledge of it. Subsequent seizures were predominantly convulsive.

Environmental cues may to some extent determine the detailed patterns of behaviour, accounting perhaps for the variations seen from one attack to another in the individual patient (Forster and Liske, 1963). Patterns of cognitive function in train at the time no doubt also help to shape behaviour. Thus the content may be in accord with the current environment, as in patients who continue with on-going behaviour during the attack—performing household tasks, or even continuing to drive and obeying regulations with subsequent dense amnesia for what has transpired. Sometimes, however, behaviour is in direct opposition with environmental cues. One patient, for example, developed an attack while playing the organ for a carol service—he interrupted the carol to render jazz music for three minutes, thereafter returning to the exact bar of the hymn when the seizure was over (Forster and Liske, 1963).

To the onlooker the subject is clearly out of touch with his surroundings in the great majority of automatisms. Typically he looks somewhat dazed and vacant, and often anxious and tense. When spoken to there may be no response, or he may mumble incoherently or answer quite irrelevantly. Attempts at distraction are likely to be resisted, and interference may meet with opposition amounting on rare occasions to combative behaviour. Only very rarely are patients reported in whom judgement and awareness were seemingly maintained during attacks. Hughlings Jackson (1889) recorded the case of a physician who apparently persisted with reasonably competent behaviour during some of his automatisms—in one he continued to write a prescription though the details of dosage were incorrect, and in another he correctly diagnosed a case of pneumonia during an episode for which he was afterwards completely amnesic. Such examples are

exceptional and should perhaps be accepted with reserve. It is now widely agreed that behaviour is unlikely ever to be entirely normal, or conversation rational, while the attack is in progress (Jasper, 1964; Fenton, 1972). Even when complex coordinated activities are maintained these are usually inappropriate in some respects to the immediate situation, and judgement will be seen to have been impaired.

Subjectively the essential and constant feature noted by the patient himself is amnesia for the period of the automatism, and sometimes for a period after its termination as well. The amnesia is usually total, though a vague and muddled awareness of some parts may very occasionally be retained. Failure to lay down a durable record of experience is often clinically important in allowing automatisms to be recognised even in retrospect.

The commonest source of origin of automatisms is epilepsy arising within the medial temporal lobe structures. This evidence comes from the study of traumatic epilepsy after brain wounds of known location, from the EEG, and especially from the study of responses to stimulation of the brain at neurosurgical exploration. Feindel and Penfield (1954) found that 78 of 155 patients undergoing temporal lobectomies for epilepsy had a history of automatisms at one time or another. Such attacks were usually accompanied by spontaneous epileptic discharges in the medial and inferior temporal regions, contemporaneous with the duration of the seizure; in such cases electrical stimulation within a fairly discrete region around the amygdaloid nucleus and deep in the uncus could reproduce the automatism. In a very much smaller group automatisms were found to depend on discharges originating in the frontal grey matter and spreading thence to involve subcortical structures. Falconer and Taylor (1970) also report that ictal automatisms can occur with focal pathology of the inferior frontal region or cingulate cortex. Little is known about the propagation of seizure discharges in such cases, but presumably the cortical focus causes secondary activation of the periamygdaloid hippocampal structures.

Petit Mal Status

A type of automatism similar to the above, but rather longer-lasting, has been found to depend essentially on runs of three per second spike and wave discharges in the EEG. The discharges may sometimes be discontinuous, but the periods of normality which separate them are too brief for the resumption of complete awareness. It is essentially the EEG pattern which distinguishes this variety of automatism from those initiated from within the temporal lobes (Lennox, 1960).

The features of the disorder are summarised by Fenton (1978) and Toone (1981). In most cases the patient will already have experienced typical episodes of petit mal, or more rarely grand mal, though occasionally petit mal status appears without a prior history of epilepsy. It occurs before the age of 20 in three-quarters of cases but can appear for the first time in middle age. With late onset cases there will frequently be some underlying toxic or metabolic disturbance which serves as a precipitant.

The episodes usually start and stop abruptly, occasionally finishing with sleep or a grand mal convulsion. They may last from several minutes to several hours or even days, during which the subject is markedly confused, uncoordinated, slowed and perseverative. The degree of clouding of consciousness varies: at its slightest there is simply slowing of ideation and expression, but more commonly there is marked disorientation, impaired grasp and automatic behaviour. The patient may be virtually stuporose, remaining motionless and apathetic, but if partially aroused is usually capable of limited voluntary action and may sometimes even respond to simple commands. Fluttering of the eyelids and myoclonus of the arms and face are common. Sometimes environmental stimulation will interrupt the condition, both in its clinical and EEG manifestations (Landolt, 1958). Subsequently there is complete amnesia for the episode, or only a blurred and fragmentary memory.

Niedermeyer and Khalifeh (1965) reported similar examples, but preferred the term 'spike and wave stupor' since regular three per second spike and wave discharges were seen less commonly than atypical spike-wave complexes, slow spike-wave variants and intermingled multiple spikes. In some of their cases the level of awareness was not markedly lowered, and relatively light arousing stimuli could immediately block the paroxysmal activity.

Abnormal mental states other than clouding are very uncommon, but psychotic pictures have been reported in late onset cases with paranoid delusional ideation, thought blocking, and visual and auditory hallucinations (Toone, 1981). Presentation as a depressive psychosis in middle age has been described. Schwartz and Scott (1971) reported an important group of four cases presenting *de novo* with acute confusion in middle age, in whom the provisional diagnoses had included subdural haem-

atoma, acute psychosis and acute confusional state. Without an EEG the correct diagnosis would almost certainly have been missed. When the acute episode was over 3 of the 4 patients had no further attacks and required no further treatment.

The course of petit mal status is essentially benign. Episodes can usually be successfully terminated with intravenous diazepam.

Psychomotor Status

Psychomotor status has been much less commonly reported than the above, perhaps surprisingly in view of the frequency of temporal lobe epilepsy. In part this may be due to the difficulty in recognising it on clinical or EEG grounds and of differentiating it from petit mal status (Toone, 1981).

The episodes last for hours or days, and can be ushered in or terminated by a grand mal seizure. The patient is confused, withdrawn and retarded, sometimes with continuous movements of the hands, lip-smacking and picking at the clothes. Recurrent automatisms can be interspersed with long periods when the patient is withdrawn but able to respond to simple stimulation. Hallucinations may figure prominently during the course of attacks.

The EEG shows unifocal, predominantly medial temporal lobe discharges, spreading bilaterally to involve the prefrontal and lateral temporal regions at times of unresponsiveness. Periods of relatively normal EEG may be interspersed between such episodes. Markand *et al.* (1978) report a typical example with EEG recording during two attacks. Intravenous diazepam promptly terminated both the abnormal behaviour and the ictal discharges on the EEG.

Fugues

Epileptic fugues are much less common than automatisms and their physiological basis is less completely understood. They consist of longer-lasting disturbances of behaviour associated with a tendency to wander away. The distinction between automatisms and fugues can thus be partly a matter of degree; consciousness is said to be less severely impaired in fugues and the abnormal behaviour more complex, extended and integrated.

A confident differentiation between epileptic fugues and those which rest on an hysterical or depressive basis (p. 263) is often difficult, since detailed observation, including EEG recording, has rarely been possible during the occurrence of the abnormal state. Some experienced observers are even inclined to doubt whether epileptic fugues constitute a valid clinical entity, and view all examples as essentially psychogenic in origin. Organic and psychogenic factors may often, of course, be inextricably mixed, with epileptic clouding helping to release abnormal traits in the personality. Thus in some cases an initial brief automatism may become greatly prolonged thereafter as an episode of hysterical dissociation.

In general the longer-lasting the fugue the more wary one will be of accepting a basis in cerebral dysrhythmia alone. Considerable doubt also surrounds the 'orderly' fugue in which purposive extended behaviour is carried through, and especially when antisocial acts have been performed. A history of grand mal epilepsy or of typical brief automatisms will certainly bias the diagnosis towards an epileptic aetiology, also EEG findings which are strongly indicative of seizures arising within the temporal lobes.

Epileptic fugues are described as lasting for many hours or even days. The patient may wander far from home, and later recover spontaneously in a strange setting not knowing how he has got there. Or he may be discovered while still in the abnormal state, appearing vague, perplexed and incoherent. These are among the patients who are picked up by the police not knowing their personal identity. The patient may have walked long distances, made purchases, or, travelled by public transport. A limited amount of conversation may sometimes have taken place, though none of this is subsequently remembered. During most periods when the subject is under obsevation, however, his behaviour is clearly abnormal. Actions are usually seen to be erratic and he may appear to be drowsy or intoxicated. His appearance is often untidy and his demeanour absent-minded. Money will usually have been spent carelessly, and the wanderings will rarely have had any clear aim or purpose. Upon recovery amnesia is typically complete for all events which have occurred while the fugue was in progress.

A man of 48 set out for his work in Oxford at the normal time one morning and remembered nothing more until he found himself on the sea-front at Bournemouth. This was some 10 hours later. He had apparently travelled by train, changing twice, and had eaten a meal and paid for it normally. During this period he had lost his hat and coat. The patient was known to have had occasional grand mal epilepsy. Further investigation showed that he had an epileptic focus in the left temporal region. His wife recalled

previous episodes of brief confused behaviour of which he himself had been unaware.

(Whitty and Lishman, 1966)

Epileptic fugues lasting for several weeks have occasionally been reported as in the case described by Spratling (1902) where a travelling salesman undertook his normal circuit of work, recording events in his diary including convulsive seizures from which he was known to suffer. The total period covered was 28 days, for all of which there was no recollection afterwards. The purely epileptic nature of such a case must however remain very doubtful.

As with automatisms the epileptic focus will usually be sited in the inferomedial temporal lobe structures. Fugues and automatisms will quite often be found to occur at different times in the same individual.

Twilight States

The term 'twilight state' has been applied to many forms of abnormal episode in epileptic subjects, ranging from automatisms and fugues, as described above, to brief discrete periods of functional psychotic disorder. Sometimes it has been used as a generic term for all episodes short of grand mal convulsions in which the level of consciousness is temporarily reduced. Its most useful application in connection with epilepsy, however, would seem to be to separate off those episodes which are distinguished by the occurrence of abnormal subjective experience, rather than by objective motor manifestations.

Twilight states of this nature commonly last from one to several hours, though sometimes they may be prolonged for a week or more. Consciousness is always impaired but this varies greatly in degree from one example to another. It may show only as dream-like absent-minded behaviour, or some slowness of reaction and muddling of comprehension, while at the other extreme there may be complete unawareness of the environment with lack of all response to external stimuli. Pyschomotor retardation is commonly profound throughout the attack, with marked perseveration in speech and action.

The outstanding phenomena are in the realms of affective and perceptual experience. Abnormal affective states figure prominently in most attacks—panic, terror, anger or ecstasy being the most frequent. Affective storms of great intensity occasionally break up the otherwise passive and apathetic picture which is observed externally. Hallucinations may occupy a large part of the twilight attack, and often contribute directly to the patient's reactions of fear or ecstasy. They are usually visual and typically vivid and highly coloured, perhaps involving whole complex scenes which unfold before the mind's eye. Delusions may be extensively elaborated. A paranoid colouring is often marked and may have issue in the behaviour displayed.

The patient often sits quietly throughout the attack and only tells of his experiences afterwards, or he may show spells of sudden overactivity including aggressive and destructive behaviour. There is sometimes great irritability and sensitivity to minor stimuli, and attempts at interference can precipitate outbursts of primitive rage.

Twilight states usually run their course and end spontaneously, but are said to terminate with a grand mal convulsion rather more commonly than automatisms. Indeed electroconvulsive therapy can meet with considerable success in terminating twilight states of long duration. Memory for the content of the attack is usually incomplete and fragmentary, though sometimes a remarkably detailed account can be given. In particular a vivid recollection of the hallucinations may be retained. What the patient tells of his experiences can frequently be supplemented by what has been inferred from observation of his expression and reactions at the time.

It is clear that a great variety of abnormal mental states are subsumed under the heading of twilight states, even when the term is restricted in the manner described. Some appear to be characterised by cognitive, some by affective, and some by complex 'psychotic' experiences. The precise classification of these varied manifestations and their electrophysiological correlates must await further clarification. All are accompanied by profound disturbance of the electrical activity of the brain, and again the source of origin of the epilepsy is most commonly within the medial temporal lobe structures.

POST-ICTAL DISORDERS

Post-ictal disorders are conveniently considered immediately after psychomotor seizures, since some of their manifestations are similar or indeed indistinguishable if the preceding convulsion has gone unrecognised. The majority of grand mal convulsions are followed by a period of sleep or by transient malaise, headache and nausea. Sometimes, however, post-ictal manifestations are more complex and a period of disturbed behaviour ensues directly upon recovery from the fit itself.

The recovery of full consciousness may lag behind the resumption of motor activity, resulting in an episode of *post-ictal automatic behaviour*. Particularly in temporal lobe epilepsy the actual epileptic attack may be brief and trivial in comparison to the post-ictal automatism which follows. The majority of such episodes are brief, lasting no more than a minute or two, but post-ictal automatisms are rather more likely than ictal automatisms to be prolonged, and more likely to involve complex behaviour which may be semi-purposive in nature.

The patient is usually very obviously confused and his movements clumsy and incoordinated, but the acts committed vary in the degree to which they are organised in proportion to the depth of disturbance of consciousness. Pond (1957) points out that psychogenic factors may on occasion play a considerable part in determining behaviour, since emotionally charged impulses are more likely to gain control while the higher-level functions are impaired. Agitation and irritability are sometimes prominent features, and paranoid thought content may be much in evidence. In a small minority of patients, usually those with gross brain damage, dangerously aggressive behaviour may occur. This is the 'epileptic furore' in which the subject becomes wildly overactive for several minutes after the fit, and may indulge in seriously destructive behaviour including physical attacks on people. In all post-ictal automatisms complete amnesia for what transpires is the rule.

Post-ictal 'twilight states' often last considerably longer, sometimes for several hours or even days. As with the ictal twilight states already described they are characterised by psychomotor retardation, vivid hallucinations, and marked abnormalities of affective experience. In the patients reported by Landolt (1958) post-ictal twilight states were often accompanied by marked resistance and restlessness, and violent reactions could sometimes be released by even light touch stimuli.

Other post-ictal disturbances take the form of paranoid-hallucinatory states closely akin to schizophrenia, but with clouding of consciousness and a tendency to subside over several days. These are considered further on p. 245.

Interrelations Between Automatisms, Twilight States and Post-ictal Disturbances

From the descriptions already given it will be obvious that psychomotor attacks and post-ictal disturbances embrace a wide variety of clinical phenomena which are hard to classify with precision. All share an intimate relationship with disturbances of the electrical rhythms of the brain, but our understanding of such relationships awaits clarification in many important respects. A step in this direction was reported by Dongier (1959) who presented a synthesis of the experience of several contributors to a colloquium in Marseilles on 'acute psychotic episodes' in epileptics.

Five hundred and thirty-six episodes were considered in 516 epileptics. The several series of patients included were often highly selected, so even with this large material the findings may not have wholly general application. The episodes were classified purely on their symptomatic content, and viewed in relation to the type of epilepsy from which the patient was suffering, the timing of the episodes in relation to overt seizures, and the EEG disturbances observed during the course of the abnormal behaviour. Twenty-five per cent of the episodes were preceded by seizures, 10% ended in seizures, and in the remainder the relationship was questionable or lacking entirely.

Those episodes which were characterised mainly by confusion and disturbance of consciousness showed two types of EEG abnormality during attacks—either continuous bisynchronous spike and wave discharges, or diffuse delta dysrhythmia. The former clearly corresponded to the 'petit mal status' type of automatism, were commoner in children than adults, and showed exclusively simple confusion without marked affective change, agitation or delusions. Most were brief, and none lasted for more than a few hours. They rarely either began or ended with a grand mal convulsion. The confusional states accompanied by diffuse delta dysrhythmia often followed a grand mal convulsion, and thus corresponded mainly to post-ictal automatisms. These were also mostly brief and similarly showed impairment of consciousness as the main feature, but here agitated behaviour was more often in evidence. Dongier suggested that agitation and aggression may more readily appear in post-ictal states because the impairment of consciousness is less profound than during episodes of petit mal status.

In this material confusional episodes were commoner among generalised than focal epilepsies, but this may have been because examples of petit mal status were over-represented. When confusion was accompanied by marked agitation or visual hallucinations, however, focal epilepsy originating in the temporal lobes was much commoner than other forms of epilepsy. Aggressive behaviour was also somewhat more common in the temporal lobe epilepsies than in other groups. It was suggested that in post-ictal confusional states associated with temporal lobe epilepsy the aggression might be due to exclusion of cortical function by virtue of the diffuse delta dysrhythmia, which then permitted emotionally charged impulses originating within the temporal lobes to be directly expressed in behaviour.

In general the episodes seen in conjunction with temporal lobe epilepsy stood in considerable contrast to those seen with the generalised epilepsies. The accent tended to be less on impairment of consciousness and a great deal more on affective changes, delusions and schizophreniform disturbances. These episodes were sometimes long, even days or weeks in duration, and often occurred without relation to grand mal convulsions. Some no doubt corresponded to 'twilight states' as described above, and others to the transient psychotic developments discussed on p. 251. The EEG in such episodes often showed reinforcement of the focal temporal lobe discharges, but sometimes no change from the inter-ictal state and sometimes disappearance of all abnormal rhythms ('normalisation'). Thus the majority of episodes in the temporal lobe group were best conceived as pre-ictal or sub-ictal, with their manifestations representing the direct on-going effects of focal disturbance of brain function. Ultimately, in some cases, the prolonged increase in focal or peri-focal excitation might exceed the threshold for generalisation to the rest of the brain, accounting for the occasional cases in which the episode terminated with a grand mal convulsion.

Dongier's review stressed, however, that a good deal of overlap occurred between the varieties of epilepsy, the type of episode produced, and to a less extent the nature of the accompanying electrical disturbance in the brain. The neurophysiological mechanisms hypothesised for the genesis of these complex disturbances must therefore be regarded as no more than provisional approximations.

Psychiatric Disability among Persons with Epilepsy

It is difficult to form an accurate estimate of the frequency of psychiatric disturbances among persons with epilepsy. The general problem is compounded when attempts are made to compare the frequency of disabilities in patients with different types of epilepsy, and here a special controversy has centred over the question of temporal lobe epilepsy. Yet these are matters of both practical and theoretical importance—for the proper planning of services and for the understanding which might follow concerning brain-behaviour relationships.

Surveys have often produced conflicting results, largely because most are based on highly selected populations of epileptics. Clearly, patients coming before a psychiatrist, or requiring institutional care, will have a higher frequency of psychiatric and social problems than epileptics in general. Equally, patients under surveillance in neurological clinics will be unrepresentative of epileptics as a whole. Thus the College of General Practitioners Report (1960) indicated that hospital consultants probably saw no more than 75% of the epileptics in the community.

Perhaps the most accurate estimates are to be found in general practice surveys, or better still in surveys of the general population, though again these will miss the relatively small group of patients who are institutionalised. The College of General Practitioners (1960) collected information about 1209 chronic epileptics from 67 practices in England and Wales, and found that 17% had significant social problems. Eight per cent of those of employable age were out of work or incapable of work because of their epilepsy, and a further 12% were capable only of restricted employment. Pond and Bidwell (1960) made a more detailed survey of 245 cases from 14 practices in South-East England, and found that 10% were unemployable, most on account of mental defect and the remainder because of marked behaviour disturbance. No case was found in which the fits alone were adequate to account for unemployability. Altogether, however, over 50% of the men had experienced serious job difficulties, being presently downgraded or having had long periods out of work in the past. The difficulties in retaining satisfactory employment were principally due to the occurrence of fits, and next most frequently to behaviour disorder. Job difficulties were markedly more frequent in patients with psychiatric symptoms.

Other data demonstrated the hardships imposed by epilepsy (Pond *et al.*, 1960). Compared to the normal population there was an excess of single over married persons, and social class as measured by occupation, was much reduced. These differences were especially marked in the younger age groups, and particularly among the males.

With regard to psychiatric disability Pond and Bidwell (1960) found that 29% showed conspicuous mental problems and this was felt to be an under-estimate. The figure rose to over 50% among patients with temporal lobe epilepsy. At the time of the survey 7% of the total had already had psychiatric inpatient care, which was twice the rate to be expected in the general population. The special hazards of temporal lobe epilepsy were again indicated—the proportion of patients with temporal lobe epilepsy who had already been in mental hospitals was three times that of the total epileptic population.

The commonest problem throughout was neurotic disability and this appeared to be reactive to environmental difficulties. Some 15% of the patients were affected in this way, which may not be substantially higher than in the population as a whole. Rather less common were those psychiatric disturbances—intellectual defects and personality disorders—which could be more directly attributed to the epileptic process itself or to associated brain damage.

Graham and Rutter's (1968) survey dealt with school children between the ages of 5 and 14 on the Isle of Wight, and showed a very high prevalence of psychiatric disturbance. The entire population of children on the island was screened and 85 cases of epilepsy were discovered (7·2 per thousand). Twenty-nine per cent of those with epilepsy, but no other evidence of a brain lesion ('uncomplicated epilepsy'), showed some psychiatric disorder; when in addition to epilepsy there was other independent evidence of brain damage the figure rose to 58%. Children with temporal lobe epilepsy showed significantly more disturbance than children with other types. These figures could be compared with the prevalence of psychiatric disorder among the rest of the school children of the island which emerged at 6·8%.

The type of psychiatric disorder shown by the children with 'uncomplicated epilepsy' was closely similar to that seen in other disturbed children—mainly neurotic disorders or anti-social conduct. Teachers' ratings showed that they were more restless and fidgety and more inclined to fight than the generality of schoolchildren, but again these characteristics applied to disturbed children even in the absence of epilepsy.

In a careful analysis of causes it was shown that lowered intelligence was unlikely to be a factor. The uncomplicated epileptic group showed a normal distribution of intelligence, likewise the sub-group with temporal lobe epilepsy. The handicap alone was unlikely to be responsible, since less than 12% of children with other chronic handicaps (asthma, heart disease, diabetes) showed psychiatric disorder, and in any case many of the children with epilepsy were little handicapped by it. Widespread community prejudice against epilepsy was thought to be an adverse factor in the epileptic child's development, though many of the sample had nocturnal seizures only and psychiatric disability was not especially frequent in children whose teachers knew of their condition.

Thus by exclusion it seemed that an important factor was probably the dysfunction occurring specifically within the brain. In addition the influence of parental handling appeared to be important; an adverse family background, measured in terms of the mother's emotional stability, was significantly more common among the epileptic children with psychiatric disability than in those without.

Thus, while in the majority of persons epilepsy is compatible with normal mental health, psychiatric disturbance is far from uncommon and greatly outstrips that found in the general population. That it is found from a very early age and is accompanied by a good deal of chronic social handicap, underlines the importance with which it must be viewed. The genesis of such disability is clearly a complex matter, partly psychological, partly social, and partly pathophysiological in origin. In the sections which follow an attempt will be made to explore in further detail the forms which psychiatric disability may take, its aetiology, and its association with different varieties of epilepsy.

COGNITIVE FUNCTION AND EPILEPSY

The earlier gloomy view that epileptic patients were characterised by low intelligence has been corrected over the years. Vislie and Henriksen (1958) review numerous studies which show that while intellectual impairment is common in institutionalised epileptics, the range of intelligence is almost normal when outpatient populations are studied. In the Isle of Wight survey, described above, the epileptic children without other evidence of brain damage showed a normal distribution of intelligence. Similarly, twin studies have indicated that epilepsy rarely lowers the genetic endowment for intelligence unless there is additional evidence of a gross brain lesion (Lennox, 1960). In general therefore there is little reason to fear that epilepsy, in the absence of overt brain damage, will lead to a sustained lowering of cognitive ability.

Nevertheless a proportion of epileptics show obvious impairment of intellect, and in rare cases even progressive intellectual deterioration. The factors which contribute to such difficulties are incompletely understood. They are likely to include the effects of hereditary endowment and psychoso-

cial influences as with intelligence generally; also the effects of brain damage, the effects of the epileptic process itself, and the effects of anti-convulsant drugs. Both Lennox (1960) and Pond (1961) agreed in the relative ordering of importance with which these various factors might affect intelligence— hereditary endowment was placed first and foremost along with the effects of associated brain damage, psychosocial factors and the seizures themselves occupied an intermediate place, and the effects of anti-convulsant drugs were placed last of all. More recent studies have served to incriminate drugs to a considerably greater extent, as described below.

Psychosocial effects. Environmental influences during childhood doubtless affect the degree to which the epileptic child can achieve his intellectual potential. Parental attitudes and the child's own reaction to his epilepsy may have a profound effect, determining his stability, his receptivity, and the degree to which he will be exposed to normal formative influences. Schooling may be unnecessarily disrupted, and the normal processes of play are sometimes needlessly curtailed. A vicious circle is likely to develop in which emotional disturbance, consequent upon poor attainment, leads to further difficulties with education. The high level of psychiatric disability noted by Graham and Rutter (1968) was particularly marked in children of low intelligence and when reading was severely retarded in relation to the child's potential.

Effects of brain damage. It is widely agreed that the brain damage responsible for the fits is chiefly to be blamed when intelligence is substantially reduced. Thus simple petit mal absences, in which there is no evidence of structural brain damage, are very rarely associated with lowered intelligence, even when attacks are very frequent indeed (Metrakos and Metrakos, 1960). Conversely severe mental retardation is almost invariably accompanied by evidence of severe and extensive cerebral lesions.

The location of the cerebral damage is a factor of importance. Patients with grand mal tend to have lower intelligence than patients with petit mal, but when grand mal and pyschomotor seizures occur together intelligence is lowest of all (Vislie and Henriksen, 1958). Thus temporal lobe epilepsy appears to carry the greatest hazard for impaired intellectual function, and almost certainly by virtue of the location of brain damage responsible for the seizures. In Ounsted et al.'s (1966) series of children with temporal lobe epilepsy, retardation was restricted to those who had suffered acute cerebral insults in the form of perinatal damage, head injury or infection, or who had experienced status epilepticus at an early age. In the remainder there was no evidence whatever of intellectual loss.

Stores (1978) has carried out a series of careful studies on epileptic children attending ordinary schools. Children with generalised epilepsy were matched with those showing temporal lobe discharges, and compared with non-epileptic children in the same school class. Reading attainment (when viewed against age and IQ) was significantly impaired among the temporal lobe epileptics, but only in those who showed foci in the left temporal lobe. Children with generalised epilepsy, or right temporal lobe epilepsy, performed as well as their controls. When subdivided according to sex it was only the boys who showed retarded reading skills, girls appearing unaffected irrespective of type of epilepsy. On ratings and measures of inattentiveness the epileptic boys again fared worse than the girls, likewise on ratings of behaviour disorder and hyperactivity. Sex effects, in addition to location of brain paroxysmal activity, thus appeared to be operative in determining the relationship between epilepsy and disturbed performance at school.

Among adults, subtle forms of cognitive defect have been discerned when patients with temporal lobe epilepsy are compared with patients suffering from generalised grand mal, even after controlling for full scale intelligence. Quadfasel and Pruyser (1955) showed a high frequency of defects on tests of verbal ability and on efficiency of retention and recall. Many temporal lobe patients were aware of their difficulties in verbal usage, though the deficits were not constant or gross enough to be labelled as dysphasia. Guerrant et al. (1962) similarly found that temporal lobe epileptics had an especially high incidence of psychological impairments indicative of brain damage—memory difficulties, slowed speech, and impaired concentration and attention.

Detailed comparisons of patients with lateralised foci have shown that the patterns of deficit may vary with the side of the lesion. Even prior to lobectomy, patients with epileptogenic foci in the dominant temporal lobe tend to be impaired on verbal as compared to non-verbal tasks, and patients with foci in the non-dominant lobe show the reverse (Milner, 1958, 1962; Dennerll, 1964). Similar differential effects on memory and learning tasks have been demonstrated in children with temporal lobe epilepsy (Feido and Mirsky, 1969), and will clearly have implications for processes of education. These special problems in temporal lobe epilepsy may partly be due to the location of the fixed brain

damage in the temporal lobes, and partly be attributable to on-going subclinical epileptic disturbances as discussed below.

Effects of seizures and abnormal electrical activity. The seizures themselves can provide an educational handicap by disruption of schooling and lessening of concentration when attacks are frequent. In addition, however, it is possible that intelligence may sometimes be adversely affected by the pathological and pathophysiological disturbances occasioned by seizures, or by interictal subclinical discharges.

Grand mal seizures may contribute to further brain damage as a result of cerebral anoxia, particularly if prolonged and particularly when status epilepticus occurs. It is possible that this is a particular hazard in childhood, and may account for Taylor and Falconer's (1968) finding that patients with temporal lobe epilepsy showed lower intelligence the earlier the onset of epilepsy. Here however it is difficult to sort out the social from the organic contributions to the problem.

Secondly, epileptic activity may intensify the extent to which existing brain damage interferes with cerebral function, particularly when frequent attacks and their associated electrical storms disrupt the activity of normal parts of the brain (Pond, 1961). In addition to the overt disturbance which is manifest as seizures one must take account of the continuing 'sub-clinical' disturbance of electrical activity which persists during inter-ictal periods. Chaudhry and Pond (1961) found that the adequacy of control of attacks was a significant factor distinguishing between a group of 'deteriorating' epileptic children and a group of non-deteriorating brain-damaged epileptic controls. And such deterioration could occasionally be reversed when attacks came under control once more, either spontaneously or as a result of removal of epileptogenic brain tissue (Pond, 1961). Certainly in animals it has been shown that discharging lesions in the amygdaloid region can have a profoundly disturbing effect on learning, and with marked improvement after excision of the discharging lesion (Morrell et al., 1956).

Several experimental observations have directly demonstrated the short-lived effects of seizures on ongoing intellectual activity. Jus and Jus (1962) carried out tests of continuous registration while recording the EEG in patients subject to frequent petit mal. During petit mal lapses or myoclonic jerks there was lack of registration of material as expected, but also a variable retrograde amnesia, usually 4–15 seconds in length for events preceding the seizure. The amnesic period was greater when the subject was passively listening to the observer than when actively involved in the task. Ounsted *et al.* (1963) showed similar deficits during episodes of spike-wave discharge induced by stroboscopic stimulation. Goode *et al.* (1970) employed a pursuit-rotor task, requiring continuing vigilance over eye–hand coordination, while recording the EEG in patients with petit mal. A strong relationship was observed between the incidence of errors in performance and the presence of spike-wave bursts lasting for more than 3 seconds at a time. Hutt *et al.* (1977) showed impairments in reaction time on a continuous choice response task. Such observations suggest that generalised spike-wave activity functions as 'neural noise', thereby reducing the child's information processing capacity.

Tizard and Margerison (1964) studied adults subject to frequent bursts of generalised synchronous wave-spike discharges, and demonstrated that cognitive efficiency was lowered during runs of EEG abnormality even though no overt clinical seizures occurred. Tasks were performed more slowly and inaccurately during periods of discharge than between them; even discharges lasting as little as half to one and a half seconds were accompanied by significantly slower response times.

Finally direct comparisons have been made between children with temporal lobe epilepsy and children with generalised centrencephalic epilepsy on various tasks of memory and sustained attention (Lansdell and Mirsky, 1964; Feido and Mirsky, 1969). The centrencephalic children were without the focal deficits of memory and learning which characterised the temporal lobe children, but performed more poorly when selective attention was required over a period of time. Some indications were obtained that this was not solely due to subclinical attacks of petit mal, since poor performance could be observed in the absence of concurrent EEG abnormality. The task of sustained attention was thus possibly revealing some permanent disturbance of central subcortical structures. Such deficits, which would otherwise be likely to pass unnoticed, would stand to have a considerably adverse effect on the natural processes of learning.

Effects of anticonvulsant drugs. High dosage of drugs can undoubtedly impair concentration and lead to sluggishness of intellectual processes. Folic acid deficiency due to anticonvulsants may also have an adverse effect on mental function, as discussed in Chapter 12 (p. 506). Trimble *et al.* (1980) showed that epileptic children in a hospital school who experienced a fall in IQ had significantly lower

serum folates than the remainder. With well conducted régimes, however, it has generally been held that drug effects are rarely important as a cause of lowered cognitive performance, and careful studies in children and in adults seemed initially to support this conclusion (Loveland *et al.*, 1957; Chaudhry and Pond, 1961).

More recently, however, the question has come under critical review, and it seems indubitable that the chronic administration of anticonvulsants has been underestimated as a cause of impairment (Trimble and Reynolds, 1976, 1984). There are indications, moreover, that intellectual impairment may sometimes occur even when conventional signs of toxicity are absent. Reynolds and Travers (1974) surveyed 57 patients taking phenobarbitone and phenytoin, and showed that the serum levels of each drug were considerably higher in patients with certain mental symptoms than in those without. Psychomotor slowing and intellectual deterioration both appeared to be related to high serum levels of the drugs, even after excluding patients with clear clinical evidence of drug toxicity.

Psychometric investigations have underlined such effects. Guey *et al.* (1967) tested 25 children before and after adding ethosuximide to their régimes, and observed a negative influence on intellectual efficiency. Slowing, perseveration and memory troubles emerged, particularly in the older (adolescent) child. Tchicaloff and Gaillard (1970) examined 20 patients of normal intelligence who were taking varied doses of phenobarbitone and phenytoin, and found significant correlations between the dosages employed and impaired performance on certain tests. Phenobarbitone was associated with impairment on the object assembly and comprehension sub-tests of the WAIS, and phenytoin with impaired digit repetition. The cumulative effects of the two medications given together were revealed on certain tests of visuo-spatial ability which had failed to show a correlation with the dose of either drug alone.

In careful prospective studies, Thompson and Trimble (1982, 1983) have explored the effects of alterations of dosage or reduction of polypharmacy on psychometric performance, testing control groups in parallel in whom there had been no drug change. Significant improvements could be charted on measures of concentration, memory and motor speed, when serum levels were reduced or the number of drugs diminished. An important finding was that several months sometimes had to elapse before the beneficial effects of the change became evident. A change to carbamazepine led to particularly clear improvements and these were more quickly apparent.

Over and above any such general effects it is important to be alert to idiosyncratic reactions in certain individuals and to adjust their medication accordingly. Phenobarbitone is perhaps most often responsible for adverse reactions where cognitive function is concerned. Hutt *et al.* (1968) have demonstrated that in therapeutic dosage it sometimes affected the patient's capacity for sustained attention very considerably. Rosen (1968) also reported decreased intellectual performance attributable to phenytoin in therapeutic dosage, as a rare but important idiosyncratic reaction; 20 epileptic patients were found in whom IQ and school or work performance rose markedly after stopping the drug, even though there had been no obvious signs of sedation or lethargy beforehand. Stores (1981) describes more recent evidence of problems with learning and behaviour in children attributable to phenobarbitone or phenytoin.

Conversely the administration of anticonvulsants can sometimes dramatically improve intellectual function when fits are brought under control. Smith *et al.* (1968) showed in a double-blind study that ethosuximide given to children with educational problems and epileptiform discharges in the EEG could selectively improve performance on a wide range of psychometric tests.

'Epileptic Dementia'

Most large series of epileptic patients include a small proportion who undergo a decline in intellectual ability, with progressive impairment of memory, concentration and judgement. This may set in after many years of functioning at a reasonably adequate level. Usually it is coupled with severe personality deterioration, and sometimes with marked behaviour disorder in the form of impulsivity, irritability and outbursts of rage. Air encephalography may demonstrate diffuse cerebral atrophy (Vislie and Henriksen, 1958). Such cases appear to be commoner when the epilepsy is secondary to a known brain lesion, and when the epilepsy has been severe and of long duration. Temporal lobe epilepsy seems to be the most frequent variety.

As a group these conditions have attracted remarkably little attention and the responsible factors are far from clear. Betts (1982) suggests that the concept of epileptic dementia requires critical examination, and that it is still uncertain whether epilepsy itself can be responsible for a progressive dementing process; apart from children who sustain severe brain damage as a result of prolonged febrile status, it would seem unlikely that even repeated fits can lead directly to fixed cognitive impairment.

The aetiology in those patients who appear to dement probably differs from one case to another. A progressive cerebral pathology may sometimes be present, such as a tumor or degenerative process; it will therefore always be important to search anew for an underlying cause which may be responsible at one and the same time for the fits and the intellectual decline (Williams, 1963). In later years it is quite likely that epileptics with substantial brain damage may dement earlier than the general population, since their neuronal reserves are reduced even though the brain damage underlying the epilepsy remains static. In all cases the anticonvulsant régime will need careful reappraisal, including the estimation of serum levels, since the patient may be displaying unsuspected toxic effects or abnormal metabolic responses to certain drug combinations (p. 265).

Sometimes the dementia will be found to be more apparent than real, representing mainly a neurotic withdrawal or the effects of institutionalisation (Pond, 1957). In others it may represent the chronic end-state of a schizophrenia-like psychosis (p. 248), a depressive disorder, or progressive worsening of personality traits which have long been present.

PERSONALITY AND EPILEPSY

Among the prejudices which have surrounded epilepsy and coloured public attitudes towards it, is the old established idea that the sufferer is in some fundamental way changed by the disorder. Guerrant *et al.* (1962) have summarised the changing views on the personality of epileptics, starting with the previous century when 'deterioration' was thought to be the rule and a consequence of the seizures. Early in the present century personality changes were still regarded as common, but ascribed to an hereditary 'degenerative stigma' of which the epilepsy was one manifestation and certain personality attributes another. Gradually, however, the idea of a specific epileptic personality has come to be rejected, and most epileptics are now recognised as substantially normal in this regard. When personality problems are present they can take many forms and can be ascribed to a variety of factors including brain damage, uncontrolled seizures and psychosocial influences. The most recent debate centres on the possibility that temporal lobe epilepsy carries special hazards where personality function is concerned, and this will be further discussed below.

The older concept of an 'epileptic personality' is now seen as an artefact derived from close observation and selective reporting of patients long confined to an institutional life. The epileptic was said to be untrustworthy, sly, and disruptive in the community. He was prone to curry favour, but beneath his subservience lay resentment and strong paranoid feelings. He was liable to sudden explosions of affect, sometimes with dangerously aggressive behaviour as a result. In general he tended to be egocentric, importunate, irritable, and needed tactful handling. Religiosity of an obtrusive and sentimental kind was particularly common. He was ponderous, slow and perseverative, and his thinking tended to be stereotyped and concrete. In both thought and emotions he was described as 'adhesive', 'sticky' or 'viscous'.

In the above some traits can be discerned which were probably a direct result of 'institutional neurosis', and others which are characteristic of patients with substantial brain damage from any cause. The widespread use of bromides at toxic levels no doubt added a further contribution. It is also worth noting at this stage that the majority of patients in mental hospitals, from whom the above picture was largely derived, were likely to be suffering from temporal lobe epilepsy rather than other forms (Liddell, 1953; Margerison and Liddell, 1961).

It is now clear from the community surveys already mentioned that only a small proportion of patients with epilepsy suffer from personality difficulties of any great degree. It seems equally clear that those that occur do not conform to any broad pattern which is distinctive for epilepsy generally. Certain traits may characterise certain types of epilepsy, but even this is still a matter for controversy. What is certain is the seriousness in terms of social adjustment and overall prognosis of those personality problems which do occur. They markedly interfere with ability to hold employment, as shown by surveys in general practice and in neurological and psychiatric clinics (Pond and Bidwell, 1960; Gordon and Russell, 1958; Kennedy and Seccombe, 1959). The emotional disturbances they engender can render the control of fits difficult and they are themselves very hard to remedy. Personality difficulties are therefore an extremely important aspect of epilepsy, and their origins and associations deserve careful study.

Association with Varieties of Epilepsy

It is commonly held that personality disturbance is more frequent with epilepsy of known than unknown aetiology (Alstrom, 1950), commoner in grand mal than petit mal, and commonest of all in temporal lobe epilepsy (Gudmundsson, 1966). Such assertions are found repeatedly in the literature, but rest principally on clinical impressions, or on comparisons between groups of cases which are small and specially selected. Satisfactory surveys are hard to find, and contradictory results have frequently emerged.

Disturbance of personality appears to be rarely obtrusive with petit mal. Pond (1952a) reviewed 150 epileptic children seen at the Maudsley Hospital and described those with petit mal as generally passive and 'nice mannered'. They had been referred for treatment on account of neurotic symptoms rather than disorders of conduct. By contrast the brain-injured epileptic children in the same population were often aggressive, explosive and unpredictable, and suffered from many varieties of grand mal and focal epilepsy but never from petit mal alone. Children with temporal lobe epilepsy showed behaviour disturbance to the most marked degree.

Nuffield (1961) pursued the question in detail by analysing neurotic symptoms (fears, timidity, nightmares) and manifestations of aggression (temper tantrums, violence, cruelty) in 233 Maudsley epileptic children. Classification both by fit pattern and EEG showed highly significant differences between those with petit mal and those with temporal lobe epilepsy. The petit mal child showed more neurotic symptoms and less aggression than other groups, and the temporal lobe epileptic child a great deal more aggression and less neurotic disorder. These differences demarcated the two groups clearly from a neutral sample of cases with non-temporal cortical foci.

Such contrasting personality patterns in children may, however, depend partly or even wholly on their different home backgrounds. Pond had already noted that the petit mal child usually came from a gentle but anxious family, whereas the brain-injured child often had a family history of instability and emotional disturbance. The differences therefore, while marked, cannot be definitely attributed to the type of epilepsy suffered and its electrophysiological correlates.

The important symptom of hyperkinesis has also shown certain relationships to the type of epilepsy suffered in childhood. Ounsted (1955) found that petit mal children were not liable to the disorder, whereas all other forms of generalised and focal seizures were represented in his material. Most if not all of the children with hyperkinesis had considerable brain damage, and half had intelligence quotients below 70. Boys were affected much more commonly than girls. The special vulnerability of epileptic boys also emerged in Stores' (1978) investigations of school-age children referred to on p. 229. On ratings of conduct disorder, overactivity, inattentiveness and social isolation boys fared particularly badly, those with left temporal lobe epilepsy being the worst affected of all.

In adult life the patient with temporal lobe epilepsy is singled out repeatedly as being especially prone to personality disturbance. Gibbs (1951) reported the prevalence of psychiatric disturbance in 275 patients with restricted seizure discharges on electroencephalography; 'severe personality disorder' was found considerably more frequently with temporal lobe discharges than with discharges elsewhere—it occurred in 32% of cases with anterior temporal foci, 13% with mid-temporal foci, 10% with occipital foci and 5% with frontal foci. Hill (1953) estimated that some 50% of patients with temporal lobe epilepsy showed severe personality disorder, and Gibbs and Gibbs (1964) estimated that 44–58% had moderate to severe psychopathology compared to less than 10% of patients with other types of seizure. Left temporal lobe foci possibly carry a greater hazard than right. Lindsay et al.'s (1979a) follow-up of temporal lobe epileptic children into adult life showed that only 12% of left focus children achieved full independence, compared with 43% of those with foci on the other side.

Aggressiveness of an explosive and immature kind is regarded as especially characteristic of patients with temporal lobe epilepsy, occurring as a predominant symptom in about a third of the patients who present for temporal lobectomy (Falconer and Taylor, 1970). Outbursts are described as typically sudden, extreme, inexplicable and without remorse (Serafetinides, 1965; Taylor, 1969a). Sherwin (1980) found quite strong evidence that aggression was more commonly associated with left temporal lobe epilepsy than right, both in terms of side of EEG focus and side of temporal horn dilatation on air encephalography.

Herrington (1969) has reviewed other personality characteristics seen in temporal lobe epileptics— impulsiveness which can lead to antisocial conduct, sensitive suspiciousness, frankly paranoid attitudes, moodiness, anxiety, depression, and hysterical manifestations. The 'ixophrenic syndrome' of slowness, perseveration and 'viscosity' of thought has been said to be particularly common.

Unfortunately there is a lack of well controlled studies to support or refute these strong clinical impressions. Pond and Bidwell's (1960) community survey found an increased incidence of psychiatric disturbance among temporal lobe epileptics compared to patients with other forms of seizure, and this often consisted essentially of personality disorder. But the numbers were too small and the personality assessments too approximate to allow definite and detailed conclusions to be drawn. Similar criticisms apply to several studies which have sought to refute the special frequency of personality disorder in temporal lobe epileptics (Small et al., 1962, 1966; Stevens, 1966). Guerrant et al.'s (1962) study involved especially careful comparisons between matched groups of patients with temporal lobe epilepsy and generalised grand mal epilepsy, but the numbers involved were again relatively small (32 and 26 patients respectively). The total psychiatric disturbance was similar in both, but the predominant forms differed—the temporal lobe epileptics had a higher incidence of organic brain symptoms, and the grand mal group a higher incidence of personality disorder.

Reynolds (1983) emphasises the numerous confounding variables that are often at work in contributing to psychopathology in epilepsy, probably accounting in large measure for this continuing controversy. It could be relevant, for example, that temporal lobe seizures are often hard to control, especially when associated with brain damage, so that the patients experience more frequent attacks, take more drugs, and suffer more psychosocial stresses than patients with generalised epilepsy. The association between temporal lobe epilepsy and aggression may similarly depend on factors which are not always readily apparent (Kligman and Goldberg, 1975; Fenton, 1981). In addition to matters of special selection in the groups reported to date, socioeconomic factors have rarely been given due consideration: clusters of adverse environmental factors such as poor parenting, neglect, and impaired general health, may have themselves conspired to produce the seeming correlations with irritability and violent behaviour.

There is, of course, abundant evidence from animal experimental work to support the notion that disturbance within the limbic system should be paticularly closely associated with aggressive behaviour (Ursin, 1960). Stimulation in the region of the amygdaloid nucleus in human subjects has also been shown to lead to rage reactions (Heath *et al.*, 1955; Delgado *et al.*, 1968).

Treffert (1963) showed that EEG disturbance within the temporal lobes, whether or not it was associated with clear evidence of epilepsy, was closely associated with aggressive behaviour in psychiatric patients. Patients with clinically obvious temporal lobe epilepsy, and patients with temporal lobe spiking on the EEG but without temporal lobe epilepsy, were carefully matched with a variety of controls. The temporal lobe patients, with and without fits, were remarkably like one another in terms of presenting behaviour and in the historical evolution of the disorder. Aggressive behaviour, including episodic rage, assault, and impulsive acting out, had led to their admission more often than in the control subjects.

Further indirect evidence to support the association of temporal lobe epilepsy with aggression comes from the marked improvement in personality which may follow temporal lobectomy as discussed below (p. 237).

Thus in the present state of knowledge we can only conclude that there is a good deal of presumptive evidence for a special relationship between temporal lobe epilepsy and personality disorder, but that as yet this lacks a firm scientific foundation. Any simplistic view about the mechanisms underlying such an assocation is almost certain to be erroneous, since multiple determinants will usually be at work.

The 'temporal lobe syndrome'. A recent approach to the problem has sought to side-step the question of categories of personality or psychiatric disorder, and to concentrate instead on defining clusters of behavioural traits in epileptic patients. In this manner a 'syndrome' characteristic of the interictal behaviour of temporal lobe epileptic patients has been proposed. The concept, however, has not proved to be without difficulties.

Bear and Fedio (1977) selected a number of traits previously highlighted in the literature as being characteristic of patients with temporal lobe foci. Dewhurst and Beard (1970), for example, had noted a tendency towards mystical experiences and sudden religious conversions in a number of patients who were psychotic ('religiosity'). Waxman and Geschwind (1974, 1975) had reported a group who showed unusually detailed and copious writings, of a degree out of proportion to their educational background ('hypergraphia'). These often centred on moral, philosophical or religious issues ('hypermoralism'). The deepened emotionality, the hyposexuality, and the excessive tendency to adhere to each thought and action ('viscosity') could be viewed in certain respects as the converse of features noted in the Klüver-Bucy syndrome (p. 23) following extirpations of the temporal lobes. These, along with a number of other traits (elation, anger, aggression, guilt, obsessionality, circumstantiality, sense of personal significance, dependence, humourlessness and paranoia), were incorporated in a detailed questionnaire filled in by temporal lobe epileptics and also by observers who knew them well. Fifteen patients with right temporal lobe foci and 12 with left were compared with normal controls and with patients with neuromuscular disorders.

The great majority of the chosen traits differentiated the epileptic patients from the controls to a significant extent. Particularly striking differences were seen with humourlessness, circumstantiality, dependence, sense of personal destiny, and preoccupation with philosophical concerns. A possible unifying mechanism behind the cluster seemed to centre on enhanced affective associations to previously neutral stimuli, events or concepts; by this means even the smallest acts might come to be endowed with emotional importance, and affective colouration would tend to encourage a mystically religious outlook on the world.

The profiles of traits tended to differ according to the hemisphere primarily involved. Patients with right temporal foci showed an excess of overt emotional traits (deepened emotionality, sadness, hypermoralism), whereas those with left temporal foci showed ruminative intellectual tendencies (religiosity, philosophical interests, humourlessness, sense of personal destiny). Each hemisphere thus appeared to have responded to the enhanced affective colouration of experience in a manner reflecting its own particular style.

Further studies, however, have thrown doubt upon many of these associations, in particular detracting from their unique association with temporal lobe disorder. Bear and Fedio's initial study failed to include patients with other forms of epilepsy, nor did it control for the presence or absence of psychiatric disorder. Hermann and Riel (1981) compared patients with temporal lobe epilepsy and patients with primary generalised epilepsy, and found that only four of the traits differentiated them significantly (sense of personal destiny, philosophical interests, dependence and paranoia). Mungas (1982) found that no trait discriminated between patients with temporal lobe epilepsy and patients with psychiatric disorder; indeed when tested on a separate group of patients a large proportion of the variance in the trait scores seemed attributable to the presence or absence of psychiatric illness. Master *et al.* (1984), in a thorough, recent study compared patients with temporal lobe epilepsy, other forms of epilepsy, psychiatric disorder and normal volunteers. The results again underlined the prominent effect of psychiatric disturbance. Temporal lobe epilepsy made no discernible contribution of its own, and no differences in trait scores were observed between patients with right or left temporal lobe foci.

Sensky *et al.* (1984), after excluding patients with a history of psychiatric illness, found that religious beliefs and practices were similar in patients with temporal lobe epilepsy and generalised epilepsy, and corresponded to norms for the general population. No special association could be discerned between mystical experiences and temporal lobe attacks.

Thus the temporal lobe syndrome as first proposed does not appear to hold up or have general application. In effect it meets with the same doubts as did earlier concepts of distinctive personality categories. However the possibility remains that a *subgroup* of patients with temporal lobe epilepsy may display significant clusterings of some components of the syndrome, perhaps especially in the presence of psychiatric disorder. The search for clearly definable traits, and their detailed associations, still has much to commend it. Considerable interest still attaches, moreover, to phenomena such as hypergraphia. This continues to be reported, and may be particularly common in patients with right-sided epileptic foci (Roberts *et al.*, 1982).

Aetiology of Personality Disorders in Epilepsy

When epileptic patients show personality disorder a multifactorial aetiology must usually be recognised. The interplay of factors will often be complex, especially when the epilepsy has dated from the formative period of life. As in the section on cognitive function it will be convenient to consider separately the contributions of psychosocial influences, the effects of brain damage, the effects of the epileptic process itself, and the effects of anticonvulsant drugs.

Psychosocial effects. Psychosocial contributions will often be evident. The epileptic child reacts keenly to his emotional background, and behaviour disturbance in epileptic children is closely tied to adverse factors in the family environment (Grunberg and Pond, 1957; Graham and Rutter, 1968). Thus far, as with any child, the early environment may contribute to enduring problems of personality.

But in addition, the epileptic child is liable to be the object of anxious concern and over-protection, to excite parental anxiety, or to become the focus of conflict between the parents. He will almost certainly be treated differently from his siblings. Others may be encouraged to protect him and make allowances for him, and many play activities may be debarred. His own reaction to the fits themselves may contribute to fundamental aspects of self-evaluation. Feelings of isolation and estrangement are likely to result, and the foundations may be laid for attitudes of dependency, egocentricity, hypochondriasis, or general inadequacy in the personality.

At adolescence further problems must be faced in relation to sexual identity and choice of career. In adult life frustrations must be tolerated in many spheres, particularly in work and in the attitudes of others to the disorder. Taylor and Falconer (1968) showed that in temporal lobe epileptics the frequency of fits affected social adjustment, mainly in those situations where the patient had to relate to others outside the family; thus work and non-family relationships were adversely associated with fit frequency, family relationships less so.

Williams (1963) has vividly described the problems which the epileptic patient has to face in adult life:

'To have epilepsy is to be different from one's fellows as the result of a persistent, intangible, and recalcitrant disorder which even in the most enlightened society carries with it the stigma of the unusual. The epileptic nearly always feels different from his contemporaries; the more intelligent and enlightened he is, and the more understanding and enlightened his contemporaries, the bigger the problem he has to face, for it is greater trauma to have to be consciously treated as normal than to be naturally accepted as different. This hurtful dilemma, in all its degrees ranging from sententious and embarrassing over-understanding to miserable restriction and loneliness, pervades his life at home, at school, at work, and sometimes into marriage. . . .

. . . At work the adult pattern of the problem asserts itself first with limitation of choice of vocation, secondly with lowering of levels and ambition either through limitations of choice or through acquired disturbance of attitude. A career having been started there is often insecurity of tenure, limitation of activities, and the faulty attitudes of ill-informed equals or defensive and self-protective seniors, including the insurance companies responsible for his future security.

In marriage the mate's attitude is usually ideal, which is one reason why the marriage took place, and one's impression is that marriage to an epileptic is usually a secure one. Nevertheless, the epileptic subject now has the attitude of two families and a new circle of friends to contend with. He may be less privileged than they in his work, is less secure, and for the first time begins to feel guilty rather than bitter about his afflictions. . . .

. . . There are as many causes for disorders of feeling and behaviour in the epileptic subject whether brain damaged or not as in the ordinary population, but his stresses are more continuous, usually more intense, and many are peculiar to him.'

Caveness *et al.* (1969) demonstrated the steady improvement in social attitudes to epilepsy in the USA during the previous 20 years by repeated Gallup-poll analyses. Nevertheless in 1969, 9% of the population still answered that they would object to their children associating in school or at play with persons who had seizures, and 12% still thought that epileptics should not be employed. In the UK attitudes were less favourable than in the USA, the respective figures being 15% and 23% (Burden, 1969). The epileptic patient is clearly obliged to face strong social prejudices which only slowly yield to more enlightened attitudes. It is easy to see how traits of sensitivity, insecurity or suspiciousness may become implanted or enhanced. Progressive social failure may then result in a vicious circle, with increasing aggravation of vulnerable areas of personality.

If the patient carries the added burden of low intelligence, poor genetic background, or poor social status the impact of adverse psychosocial factors will stand to be increased. Taylor and Falconer (1968) were able to demonstrate that broad measures of social adjustment were related to such features—being significantly worse in the presence of low intelligence, a family history of mental illness and difficulties with schooling. The effect of intelligence was particularly marked. When epilepsy had been of early onset social adjustment was poorer, and psychopathic traits were more likely to be evident.

Effects of brain damage. Many of the personality problems seen in epilepsy are similar to those seen with brain damage due to any cause. There is probably nothing specific to epilepsy about mental slowing, ponderousness and perseveration, nor in the 'stickiness' or 'viscosity' of thoughts and emotions which has been labelled the 'ixophrenic syndrome'. Irritability, impulsiveness and emotional lability are similarly the hallmarks of many forms of brain damage. The majority of abnormal personality attributes which cannot be attributed to psychosocial causes are therefore likely to be due to the brain damage of which the epilepsy is but one manifestation.

This probably accounts for the rarity of behaviour disorder or personality problems with petit mal, even when attacks are very frequent. The high incidence of psychiatric disturbance in epilepsy secondary to known brain damage will also rest on such a basis, and the special associations claimed between temporal lobe epilepsy and personality disorder is likely to be due to the strategic location of the underlying brain damage in the limbic system of the brain.

Effects of seizures and abnormal electrical activity. In addition to the effects of structural brain pathology, a further contribution to personality disorder may come from the disorganisation of cerebral functioning occasioned by epileptic discharges. Pathophysiological effects due to abnormal electrical activity may spread widely in neural systems beyond the area of the structural lesion. Moreover it is abundantly clear that in addition to overt attacks, a good deal of background subclinical discharge may continue in the inter-ictal periods. Electrocorticography at operation has shown that prolonged and widespread discharges can often be recorded without any accompanying clinical phenomena (Pampiglione and Falconer, 1960). The question arises how far these special aspects of the epileptogenic lesion may affect personality functioning, over and above the effects due to any structural brain damage which is present.

A particularly intriguing suggestion has concerned the possible pathophysiology underlying certain behavioural changes in patients with temporal lobe epilepsy, occasioned by the frequent spike discharges arising within the limbic structures (Waxman and Geschwind, 1975; Bear and Fedio, 1977; Bear, 1979; Geschwind, 1979). It is proposed that such discharges lead in time to a 'hyperconnection' between neocortical and limbic systems ('sensory-limbic hyperconnection') with far-reaching effects on the patient's behaviour and experience. Such an alteration of limbic reactivity to environmental stimuli, it is suggested, could result in the suffusion of experience with affective colouration and a deepening of the patient's emotional life. The features considered to derive from this—religiosity, mystical and philosophical tendencies, and an enhanced sense of personal significance—are discussed in some detail on p. 234.

In more general support one may note that some patients show increasing disturbance of behaviour for hours or days prior to a fit, with moodiness, tension or irritability which are relieved when the convulsion occurs. Conversely some habitually disturbed patients show a marked improvement in temperament after a fit, becoming calmer and easier to manage for some time afterwards. Here one may hypothesise the gradual build up of sub-clinical discharges, or the post-ictal diminution of such discharges, to account for the behavioural changes seen.

Brady (1964) studied these phenomena in a group of hospitalised epileptic patients, most of whom were suffering from marked personality disturbance. Fit frequency was recorded each month, along with a check-list to monitor disturbed behaviour. Among patients with temporal lobe epilepsy both varied in the same direction, disturbed behaviour increasing when seizures were frequent. Among non-temporal lobe epileptics the converse tended to occur, disturbance of behaviour being significantly less common when fit frequency was elevated. Thus among the temporal lobe epileptics it could be argued that the disturbed behaviour and the seizures were both manifestations of a common pathophysiological disturbance, which waxed and waned over considerable periods of time. In the non-temporal lobe epileptics the disturbed behaviour and the seizures appeared to be alternative manifestations, representing different facets of the pathophysiological background. Brady stressed, however, that explanations on a physiological basis might yet be faulty. The relationships between fits and behaviour could also be mediated by psychological or social mechanisms, especially in a hospitalised population where fits would call forth both positive and negative reactions from other patients and staff.

Direct recording of electrophysiological disturbance within the brain would obviously be necessary to clarify the situation. It is interesting, therefore, that Ervin *et al.* (1969) noted electrophysiological correlates of aggression by depth recording from the limbic system in patients. Aggressive behaviour could be elicited by stimulation of appropriately placed electrodes, occurring independently of traditional seizures. The stimulation was followed by focal electrophysiological changes which preceded the disturbed behaviour. Such focal discharges, usually in the amygdaloid region, could also be seen to occur in reponse to appropriate environmental stimuli as a prelude to the alterations in behaviour.

It is a common observation that difficult traits in the personality may improve when fit frequency is reduced by appropriate medication. Evidence has also accumulated to suggest that when epileptogenic brain tissue is removed at operation personality disorder may improve dramatically along with abolition of the seizures. Wilson (1970) reported such effects in a high proportion of children undergoing hemispherectomy for intractable epilepsy associated with infantile hemiplegia—behaviour disorder could sometimes improve remarkably, with abolition of violent rages, explosive tantrums, hyperactivity, and stubborn negativism.

The effects of temporal lobectomy on personality have attracted especial attention. Between a half and two-thirds of disturbed temporal lobe epileptics are reported to show significant improvement in psychiatric status post-operatively (Hill *et al.*, 1957; James, 1960; Taylor and Falconer, 1968). In part this may depend on the psychological effect of improved fit control, since the most marked benefits follow when fits are greatly reduced (Jensen and Larsen, 1979a). The latter is not, however, always essential, and the improvement is often striking enough to suggest that removal of the discharging focus has had a more direct effect.

Most striking is the reduction in aggressiveness in patients who have previously shown aggressive personality disorders with liability to unpredictable explosive outbursts. After operation tolerance of frustration is increased, irritability subsides, and there is no longer the constant risk of provoking displays of anger. In this group improvement has proved to be very closely related to fit control. It has been particularly gratifying in patients with mesial temporal lobe sclerosis (Falconer, 1973).

A high proportion have shown depressive episodes during the first year or two after operation despite the excellent result in other respects. Such episodes are frequently severe, with retardation and delusion formation, but respond well to ECT and tend not to recur after the first eighteen months. It has been suggested that the substitution of depression for aggression is physiologically based, a new equilibrium being required between aggression which is turned outwards and that which is turned inwards upon the self (James, 1960). Alternative explanations have, however, been put forward in psychodynamic terms (Ferguson and Rayport, 1965; Horowitz *et al.*, 1970). The depression may reflect the need for psychological readjustments—learning to live without the help of an accustomed handicap, or being suddenly 'burdened' with normality. When seizures are abolished the family may begin to express their negative feelings more openly, and become more critical of behaviour previously excused. In effect the patient now has to establish his identity as a person without conspicuous disability.

Improvement in sexual adjustment is a second area in which gratifying results have been reported after temporal lobectomy. Increased drive and potency, and replacement of perverse tendencies by normal libidinal interest have been observed. In Taylor's (1969b) series of 100 consecutive cases, of whom two-thirds had had significant sexual difficulties, almost a quarter showed improved adjustment after surgery. This is further considered on p. 238.

Thirdly, Hill *et al.* (1957) reported increased warmth in social relationships after temporal lobectomy. This could be striking from the early months onwards, with lessened egotism, more friendliness and concern for the feelings of others, and a more 'extroverted' attitude towards life.

Such changes after surgery strongly suggest that the previously discharging lesion may have exerted a continuing effect on certain aspects of personality functioning. They also add to the evidence discussed on p. 233 that special personality attributes may be connected with this particular type of epilepsy. The fact that in some cases personality improvement can follow resection, not of diffuse but of highly discrete focal lesions within the temporal lobe, underlines the importance of regional cerebral damage in contributing to personality difficulties.

Effects of anti-convulsant drugs. Finally it remains to consider the effect which anticonvulsant medication may have on personality functioning. Improved control of fits by medication is often followed by improved emotional stability, but the converse can also be seen. Sometimes as fits are reduced disturbances of behaviour increase. Very occasionally, in very disturbed patients, a balance must be struck between the control of fits and control of behaviour, but such cases are relatively rare. The dilemma can usually be resolved by the addition of psychotropic drugs to the anticonvulsant régime.

Over and above the effects of fit control, it is important to know whether anticonvulsant drugs can have an aggravating or beneficial effect on personality attributes. The situation is unclear and has rarely been tested by controlled comparisons. Reynolds and Travers (1974) have produced evidence that several aspects of mental disturbance, including personality change, may be related to increased serum levels of phenobarbitone or phenytoin, even while these remain within the therapeutic range. It is still uncertain, however, how common such effects may be in clinical practice. Trimble and Reynolds (1984) review anecdotal reports of depression as a side effect of phenobarbitone and phenytoin, personality change following primidone, and hysterical reactions seen with phenytoin. Conversely drugs such as carbamazepine or diazepam are reported to have beneficial effects on behaviour, as discussed in the section on treatment, though here it is far from clear whether their action is by way of a direct psychotropic effect or improved control of seizures.

In certain situations drugs are widely recognised to have adverse effects. In children sedative and stimulating drugs can have a paradoxical action (Pond, 1961); phenobarbitone may make epileptic children restless and irritable, whereas amphetamines can improve behaviour disorder and reduce hyperkinesis (Ounsted, 1955). Phenobarbitone may also increase the irritability of adult patients with temporal lobe epilepsy, and a change to an alternative anticonvulsant may then have a markedly beneficial effect. This may in part underlie the reputation which newer drugs come to acquire for helping the personality difficulties of patients with temporal lobe epilepsy.

The observations of Reynolds (1967a) and others on the disturbances of folate metabolism which may be associated with anti-convulsant medication are also relevant. Disturbances of mood and behaviour, in addition to intellectual retardation, have sometimes appeared to be due to the lowering of folate levels and to improve when this is remedied. However the situation is complex and to some extent controversial as discussed in Chapter 12 (p. 506).

Sexual Disorder in Epilepsy

Sexual disorder appears to have attracted little attention in epileptic patients until relatively recently. Several reports, however, now stress the frequency of sexual disturbance in patients with temporal lobe epilepsy. Hyposexuality has emerged as the commonest abnormality, with perversions of sexual interest and outlet occurring in a much smaller number.

Gastaut and Collomb (1954) were the first to draw attention to hyposexuality after specific enquiry in 36 patients with temporal lobe epilepsy. More than two-thirds showed marked diminution or absence of interest, appetite or sexual activity. Other forms of focal and generalised epilepsy appeared to be unassociated with such problems. There was often a remarkable lack of sexual curiosity, fantasies or erotic dreams, yet little to suggest inhibition since the patients talked easily and without reserve about such matters. Indeed they appeared to be quite indifferent about the subject.

Gastaut and Collomb's patients were resident in a mental hospital and none were living in a normal environment. Hierons and Saunders (1966), however, reported impotence in 15 patients with temporal lobe lesions, all of whom were living at home. Twelve were suffering from temporal lobe epileptic attacks. In contrast to Gastaut and Collomb's patients libido appeared to be normal, and in 4 patients the impotence improved when the epilepsy was brought under control with drugs.

Taylor (1969b) found poor sexual adjustment in two-thirds of 100 consecutive cases referred for temporal lobectomy. The commonest problem was again lack of sexual drive and a bland denial of interest in sex. Masturbation was rare, and marital problems were attributable to lack of interest in sex rather than actual impotence. Blumer (1970) found hyposexuality in 29 of 50 patients with temporal lobe epilepsy, and observed improvement in a third of those who underwent temporal lobectomy, especially when seizures were substantially relieved.

Shukla *et al.* (1979) have upheld the special association between temporal lobe epilepsy and hyposexuality in a controlled study. Seventy patients with temporal lobe epilepsy were compared with 70 patients with generalised epilepsy attending the same clinic in India. The groups were similar in age, duration of illness, seizure frequency and marital history. By detailed interviews it was established that 41% of the male temporal lobe epileptics were hyposexual, compared to 8% of the males with generalised epilepsy. The corresponding figures for females were 38% and 5% respectively. On restricting attention to patients over the age of 15 and where adequate information was available these differences were accentuated, reaching statistically significant levels. Among the males the disorder was manifest as a global lack of interest, failure of erections and nocturnal emissions, and absence of fantasies or dreams of a sexual nature. The females remained totally passive in sexual relations and failed to reach orgasm. When the temporal lobe epilepsy had set in during childhood the patients had commonly failed to develop any interest in sexual matters; when it was of late onset there had been a decline in interest and activity. The lack of concern evidenced by the patients, and their failure to make complaints, probably accounted for the problem having attracted so little attention in the past.

Lindsay et al.'s (1979b) follow-up into adult life of 100 children with temporal lobe epilepsy showed the striking importance of time of remission of seizures where sexual maturing was concerned. Of those men who were marriageable 17 had married and 24 were unmarried, the two groups being comparable in terms of age, intelligence, and frequency and severity of seizures. The distinguishing factor was whether or not their seizures had remitted before the age of 12. Twelve of the 15 early remitters had married, compared to only 5 of the 26 non-remitters, a statistically significant difference. Furthermore at least 14 of the 24 single men showed no interest in sexual matters and only one of these had been an early remitter. It thus appeared that continuing epileptic disruption of temporo-limbic functions during the normal period of sexual maturing often resulted in a lack of interest in sex; conversely remission before puberty allowed relatively normal sexual development.

Male hormone metabolism also appears to be often disturbed in epileptic patients. Following a report by Christiansen et al. (1975) of reduced androgen excretion in male epileptics, Toone et al. (1983, 1984) have carried out hormonal studies in several groups of patients. Free testosterone levels were found to be significantly reduced in a mixed group of male epileptics resident in the David Lewis Centre, in male epileptics attending an outpatient clinic, and in those recruited from general practice. Lutenising hormone, follicle stimulating hormone

and sex hormone binding globulin were by contrast significantly raised. When the resident patients were divided into low and high sex drive categories on a number of measures, the free testosterone levels were shown to be significantly lower in the former than the latter. The hormonal abnormalities seemed likely to be the product of metabolic changes consequent upon anticonvulsant medication. Thus in addition to impaired maturation of sexual interest, male hyposexuality may also derive in part from hormonal derangements.

Hypersexuality, by contrast, appears to be rare. Taylor (1969b) and Shukla et al. (1979) each found only one example, but Blumer (1970) found seven who showed distinct episodes of increased sexual drive. This occurred post-ictally, but in one patient accompanied the actual seizures. Two hyposexual patients showed it as a transient post-operative reversal, severe in degree. One patient experienced increased desire when the seizures were controlled by medication.

Fifteen per cent of Taylor's (1969b) patients showed perverse tendencies in the form of masochism or exhibitionism. None showed transvestism or fetishism though several other reports have drawn attention to examples. Kolarsky et al.'s (1967) patients showed a wide range of sexual deviations—sadomasochism, exhibitionism and fetishism—the disorders ofter appearing to be associated with temporal lobe damage dating from very early in life.

The relationship of abnormal sexual activity to the epileptic process has sometimes emerged as very close indeed:

Hunter et al. (1963) reported a patient with transvestism and fetishism of 30 years duration and temporal lobe attacks for 10 years. The abnormal sexual impulses diminished as the epilepsy was controlled by drugs and were later abolished completely by temporal lobectomy. The onset of the perversion 20 years before the epilepsy was considered to be compatible with the natural history of the temporal lobe gliosis found at operation.

Of particular interest are cases in which transvestism has appeared in association with temporal lobe epilepsy well after the attainment of a normal adult sexual orientation:

Davies and Morganstern (1960) reported a patient of 36 who had developed grand mal epilepsy twelve years previously This proved to be due to cerebral cysticercosis. For seven years the auras to attacks had included features typical of temporal lobe epilepsy, and for some 3 years had consisted of epigastric and jaw sensations. The epigastric auras were followed by an episodic desire to transvest. Initially this was exclusively in relation to the epigastric and jaw sensations, but for 2 years the desire to transvest had increased and become independent of any epileptic phenomena.

Mitchell *et al.* (1954) reported a striking example of fetishism in association with temporal lobe epilepsy which deserves to be described in detail:

A man of 38 had enjoyed what he described as 'thought satisfaction' for as long as he could remember when looking at a safety-pin. This was highly pleasurable to him but even as a child he felt that it was an odd and potentially embarrassing habit. Between the ages of 8 and 11 the 'thought satisfaction' began to be followed by a blank period, but since the phenomenon was kept secret no such attacks were observed until after his marriage.

Attacks were first accidentally observed by his wife when he was 23. She reported that he would stare at a pin for a minute, then become glassy-eyed, make a humming noise and sucking movements of the lips. This was followed by a 2 minute period in which he would be immobile and unresponsive. Just before some of his attacks his right pupil would dilate. By 31 the period of immobility was regularly succeeded by a brief motor automatism in which he would mark time and later march backwards while his right hand plucked at his left sleeve. Brief post-ictal confusion was evident during which he occasionally dressed himself in his wife's clothing.

Such seizures occurred only after staring at a safety-pin or after fantasies of doing so. A 'bright shiny' whole pin was essential and often several of them were more effective than one. Two or three attacks occurred every 7–10 days. The desire to look at a pin arose mostly during sexual stimulation or in anxiety provoking situations. During sexual intercourse or masturbation he occasionally had a seizure if he thought about the fetish. He had become increasingly impotent during the past five years. There had been three episodes of florid but short-lived paranoid psychosis in the past twelve months.

A left-sided temporal lobe focus was found on EEG. This was exacerbated by exhibiting pins, followed after some thirty seconds by a clinical seizure. Air encephalography showed focal dilatation of the left temporal horn. At operation the left temporal lobe was resected, and showed slight atrophy and gliosis but no other abnormality.

Post-operatively there were no further fits, and at follow-up 16 months later he reported that he had had no further desire to look at a safety-pin. He had become as potent as in early marriage. The EEG was now normal, and the exhibition of a safety-pin did not affect it.

The mechanisms which may underlie the association of such abnormal sexual behaviour with temporal lobe epilepsy are far from clear. Epstein (1961) suggested that the limbic system may subserve mechanisms concerned with such functions as imitation, identification and sexual arousal; dysfunction within this neural system may prevent the proper subordination and integration of such features during sexual development, so that the 'symbol and sign' aspects of sex are allowed to become dominant. This may then have issue in fetishism or transvestism, in both of which sign and symbol serve not only as stimulus but also as object of consummation. Hunter *et al.* (1963) suggested that rather than a direct pathophysiological link the disorders may arise by purely psychological means. Sexual ideas may occur as an integral part of dreamy states or déjà vu experiences, and by repeatedly reviving memories of childhood scenes and fantasies may keep alive early autistic forms of sexual activity. Neither theory, however, would explain the onset in adult life of transvestism in Davies and Morganstern's (1960) patient after many years of apparently normal sexual behaviour.

Such theories are of course no more than speculation. It remains possible that in the great majority of cases there is no direct causal link with the temporal lobe dysfunction, but that the disturbed sexuality is merely the outcome of distorted relationships during vulnerable phases of development, and the limitations imposed on opportunities for experimentation and choice.

Occasional cases have been reported in which sexual activity accompanies or follows temporal lobe epileptic discharges. Freemon and Nevis (1969) described a woman of 32 who experienced auras of genital sexual stimulation followed by automatisms of sexual statements and actions, sometimes proceeding thereafter to grand mal convulsions. Currier *et al.* (1971) reported a woman with temporal lobe epilepsy who carried out the activities of sexual intercourse in the course of psychomotor attacks, and another who masturbated briefly during an attack while an EEG examination was in progress. Both had chronically frustrating marital situations, and were regarded as showing unconscious release or lack of inhibition in relation to post-ictal confusion. Activation of temporal lobe 'sexual connections' within the limbic system or hypothalamus may have taken place during the preceding seizure.

Other less colourful disturbances of sexual function may also occur, and again appear to be reported mainly in temporal lobe epilepsy. In Taylor's (1969b) series one woman claimed that her fits always followed the excitement of sexual intercourse. Two men reported that they could only have intercourse mechanically and unemotionally lest fits should be precipitated. Another woman only experienced desire post-ictally. Hunter *et al.* (1963) mention a woman with temporal lobe epilepsy whose frigidity was threatening her marriage. When her husband approached her she experienced such strong déjà vu that she could not sustain interest in present reality. It emerged that she had in fact experienced an incestuous assault in her teens. Finally, Hooshmand and Brawley (1969) report 2 patients initially thought to be exhibitionists when they had undressed in public during the course of a temporal lobe automatism. One of them had never been known to have a grand mal seizure.

Crime and Epilepsy

Early writers such as Lombroso (1911) came to view epilepsy and criminality as intimately related. Though not all epileptics were criminals, most criminals were thought to have an 'epileptoid' constitution. 'If fully developed epileptic fits are often lacking in the born criminal, this is because they remain latent, and only show themselves later under the influence of the causes assigned (anger, alcoholism), which bring them to the surface.' Violent crimes such as murder, arson, rape and theft were thought to be particularly characteristic of epileptic subjects. Maudsley (1873, 1906) emphasised that epilepsy should always be considered in aggressive crimes, and felt that crimes committed suddenly and in a 'blind fury' were often due to some form of epileptic process.

These views were decisively altered when careful surveys were carried out. Alstrom (1950) found no excess of criminal records compared to the population generally in 897 epileptics attending a Swedish clinic, provided they were not mentally affected. Those with psychiatric complications did show a significant excess, though even so the figure was not strikingly high (12% compared to 5%). Major aggression was not observed in the sample, and the acts of violence which had occurred were usually trivial and closely connected with abuse of alcohol. Juul-Jensen's (1964) large Danish survey of 1020 adult epileptics substantially confirmed these findings. Both surveys, however, were largely confined to patients attending hospitals and clinics, and many epileptics in institutions and in the community were doubtless omitted. Gudmundsson's (1966) attempt to survey all epileptics resident in Iceland (987 patients) produced rather different results—the male epileptics had been convicted three times as often as the male population generally.

Gunn approached the problem by an extensive survey of the prevalence of epilepsy among the prison and borstal populations of England and Wales (Gunn, 1969; Gunn and Fenton, 1971). At a conservative estimate 7–8 prisoners per 1000 were found to be suffering from epilepsy, which is considerably higher than the prevalence of epilepsy in the general population. Young prisoners in particular were much more likely to be suffering from epilepsy than persons of a similar age in the community. It seems, therefore, that epileptics do have a higher probability of being committed to prison than other members of the population.

A representative sample of epileptic prisoners was then examined to see whether the types of crime committed differed from those of matched controls (Gunn and Bonn, 1971). The great majority had been convicted for non-violent larceny, as with prisoners generally. There was no suggestion that epileptics were more prone to any particular form of offence, and no support for the view that they were especially liable to crimes of violence.

The number of homicides committed was too small for testing an earlier suggestion that there may be some special relationship between epilepsy and murder. Thus Stafford-Clark and Taylor (1949) reported a remarkable association between EEG abnormality and type of crime among 64 prisoners facing charges of murder. Where the killing had been incidental to some other crime or in self defence 9% of EEGs were abnormal; where there was a clear motive for killing 25% were abnormal; where the crime was apparently motiveless 73% were abnormal; and among those found unfit to plead or guilty but insane 86% were abnormal. Hill and Pond (1952) extended this series to 105 murderers and reinforced the findings; accidental murderers appeared to have no greater incidence of EEG abnormality than the general population, clearly motivated murderers were intermediate, and motiveless murderers had an extremely high proportion of abnormal EEGs. Eighteen of the 105 subjects had definite evidence of epilepsy, which was more than thirty times the incidence of epilepsy in the population generally. Even allowing for matters of special selection, in that referral for EEG meant that epilepsy or brain disease had already been suspected, Hill and Pond (1952) concluded that there was undoubtedly some relationship between murder and epilepsy.

The question arises whether murder, or lesser crimes of violence, often occur during seizures or post-ictal 'automatisms'. Most now agree that although this can occur it must be very rare indeed. Hill and Pond (1952), for example, could not find a case in their material where they were satisfied that a seizure had preceded the murder. Gunn and Fenton (1971), in a survey of 158 prisoners with epilepsy, found 5 who had fits just after committing a crime, 4 who had fits just before committing a crime, and 4 others in whom a possible association with automatism could be considered. However, when the detailed evidence was reviewed none showed convincing evidence of 'automatic' criminal behaviour. Subsequently, however, further evidence came forward to suggest that one of these prisoners probably killed his wife in the course of an epileptic attack or its immediate sequelae (Gunn, 1978). Moreover among 32 epileptics committed to Broadmoor hospital, Gunn and Fenton (1971) found 2 who had probably committed their crimes during a post-ictal confusional state as in the following example:

A 32-year-old patient in Broadmoor had developed convulsions at the age of 18. Two and a half years later he had a generalised convulsion early in the morning while getting ready for work. On recovery 20 minutes later his speech was slurred and his eyes seemed 'vacant'. He violently attacked an elderly man who lived in the house, striking him with a spade and kicking him. (The man died as a result of severe head injuries 6 days later). He then attacked his girl friend and the victim's wife, smashed some panes of glass, and cycled aimlessly away with blood on his arms. One and a half miles from the house he fell off the cycle, and on admission to hospital was mentally confused and amnesic for all events following the seizure.

In Broadmoor he continued to have major seizures every 1–2 years without aura. Each was followed by confusion for up to an hour during which he would appear perplexed and frightened, and if restrained in any way he would become dangerously aggressive. His behaviour at all other times was impeccable. The EEG showed spike and wave discharges of subcortical origin, but no evidence of a focal lesion.

Dangerous behaviour during ictal automatisms is also occasionally reported. The patient may continue with an act in progress at the time and do harm by virtue of a confused state of mind. A patient mentioned by Macdonald (1969) was filling a kettle with a view to placing it on the fire when her seizure commenced, and placed her baby on the fire instead. Such situations are, however, exceedingly rare, and acts of violence have emerged as distinctly unusual in reviews of patients subject to automatisms (Knox, 1968). Roth's (1968) conclusion would therefore seem to be valid—that in so far as there is any increased risk of violent or antisocial conduct among epileptics, it is unlikely to arise from the attacks themselves but rather from the psychiatric complications of the epilepsy.

It can be important in medico-legal work to have guidelines for assessing the probability that a crime may have been committed during an episode of ictal or post-ictal confusion. Walker (1961), Knox (1968) and Fenton (1972) have discussed a series of criteria which may be applied:

First of all the patient should have a past history of unequivocal epileptic attacks. In the majority of cases it is likely that a history of grand mal attacks or other partial epileptic attacks will be elicited, as well as the alleged automatic behaviour. A story of vague perceptual disturbances, such as déjà vu sensations or feelings of depersonalisation, should not be accepted as indicating temporal lobe epilepsy in the absence of other distinctive features, since these are frequently experienced by neurotic patients and can sometimes be elicited on enquiry from perfectly healthy people. There need not necessarily be a previous history of automatism as such, though clearly when this is elicited it will strengthen the confidence with which the present example is so diagnosed. The diagnosis must always be made on clinical grounds, for epilepsy can occur in the presence of a normal EEG, and conversely abnormal records may be obtained in patients who have never had a clinical attack. Nevertheless an EEG compatible with the type of clinical disorder presumed to be present will constitute important additional evidence.

With regard to the circumstances of the crime itself, this will always have been sudden, obvious motives will be lacking, and there should be no evidence of planning or premeditation. The crime will appear to be senseless, there will typically have been little or no attempt at concealment and often no attempt at escape. The abnormal behaviour will usually have been of short duration, lasting minutes rather than hours, and will never have been entirely appropriate to the circumstances. Witnesses may have noted evidence of impairment of awareness, for example inappropriate actions or gestures, stereotyped movements, unresponsiveness or irrelevant replies to questions, aimless wandering around, or a dazed and vacant expression. These features may not, however, be readily apparent to the untrained eye. Amnesia for the crime is the rule, but there should be no continuing anterograde amnesia for events following the resumption of conscious awareness. The more these several criteria are not fulfilled, the more will an epileptic basis for the act be regarded with suspicion.

NEUROSIS AND EPILEPSY

The more florid types of psychiatric disturbance in epilepsy are greatly outnumbered by neurotic forms of reaction. In Pond and Bidwell's (1960) general practice survey half of the epileptic patients with psychological difficulties were suffering from neurosis, making up some 15% of the total. It is difficult to know whether this represents an increased prevalence over the population generally. Nevertheless those epileptics who are subject to neurotic disturbance warrant close attention, since emotional stability is likely to be an important factor in contributing to adequacy of fit control. States of heightened anxiety, in particular, may come to be self-reinforcing in leading to an increase of seizures.

The form which the neurotic disability takes has little that is distinctive for epilepsy. Pond (1957) concluded that the characteristics of the neurotic reaction depended principally on patterns of premorbid personality and family relationships, as with neurosis generally, and owed little to the epileptic phenomena themselves. The epileptic has, of course, more than his share of psychosocial difficulties to account for such developments.

States of depression and anxiety are the most frequent and can usually be related to current environmental difficulties. Many epileptic patients pass through a painful period of adjustment when first given the diagnosis; others react adversely to the social and personal problems occasioned by the disorder (Betts, 1981). Surveys of epileptics attending neurological clinics have repeatedly highlighted the frequency of depressive mood and anxiety symptoms, even among patients unknown to psychiatric agencies (Standage and Fenton, 1975; Currie et al., 1971; Kogeorgos et al., 1982). The relationships between affective disorder and epilepsy are discussed in more detail on p. 252.

Hysterical forms of reaction can often be traced to stresses operating on the vulnerable personality. These occur chiefly in patients of low intelligence or with marked personality disorder, but this is not always so. Sometimes the association between hysterical symptoms and epilepsy may be determined, in part at least, by organic brain dysfunction as implied by Slater and Roth (1969)—'It is probably true that, as with many chronic organic conditions, the long persistence of an epilepsy can encourage the changes on which a hysterical alteration of personality, and an enhanced susceptibility to hysterical symptoms, can arise'. There has been some suggestion that 'hysteria', as measured by the CCEI self-rating questionnaire, may be more prominent among generalised as compared to focal epilepsies (Kogeorgos et al., 1982), but as yet there is no firm evidence to link hysterical symptoms with specific forms of epilepsy or with any particular locus of cerebral disorder. The important matter of the differential diagnosis between hysterical and epileptic seizures is discussed on p. 259.

Obsessive-compulsive disorders do not appear to be unusually common among epileptics. Phobic states sometimes come to centre around the dread of having an attack, and it is perhaps surprising that this is not encountered more frequently. Occasionally agoraphobia develops to an incapacitating degree, sometimes immediately after a fit which has occurred in a particularly dangerous situation. Pinto (1972) has described the successful treatment of a case by behaviour therapy, with parallel improvement in seizure frequency.

An unusual case of agoraphobia, which also illustrates pitfalls in the diagnosis of epilepsy was as follows:

A woman of 34 had attended an epileptic clinic for many years on account of nocturnal attacks. These commenced at the age of 8, but increased greatly in severity at the age of 23 when she first presented at the clinic. They had shown temporary responses to various medications but were still occurring several times per week on phenobarbitone, epanutin and mysoline.

For several years there had been a progressive restriction of activities and increasing dependence on her husband. Two years previously she had been knocked down by a car when crossing the road, and since then had been unable to leave the house on her own. She complained of many strange symptoms—a feeling of unsteadiness, of walking on air, of internal shaking and of being dragged down from behind. On this account she was referred for psychiatric opinion.

She was clearly terrified of her 'epilepsy' and it was the dread of a day-time attack that prevented her from going out on her own. She described a striking family history; her father had had attacks during childhood and adolescence, two cousins had had epilepsy, one of whom had died in bed as a result, and her brother, three years her junior, had had nocturnal fits and had died in bed at the age of 20. At inquest his death was attributed to smothering during an epileptic fit.

Her own attacks were exclusively nocturnal. She was woken with abdominal cramps followed by a shooting pain passing from the right cheek to the left temple. She did not lose consciousness but felt an uncontrollable urge to bury her head in the pillow, and was obliged to struggle against this for up to ten minutes. There had been no tongue biting or incontinence. Her husband confirmed that he would find her groaning, flushed, staring and anxious, attempting to talk and sometimes crying 'Hold me!'. She was stiff but there was no twitching or jerking. He had never seen her turn her face into the pillow. He had known of her attacks and of the family history since marrying her eight years previously but the subject of epilepsy was taboo within the family.

The attacks were clearly most unusual for epilepsy and the EEG showed only mild and non-specific abnormalities. After much persuasion she allowed her father and his sister to be interviewed in order to clarify the family history.

It transpired that she had kept all knowledge of her own attacks from her father and her aunt in view of the tragedy which had befallen her brother. Her father was vague about his own youthful attacks, but his sister said that they had been diagnosed as hysterical in nature. Of the cousins with epilepsy, one had merely been examined by EEG after an episode of fainting, and the other had had no history of epilepsy but had died in bed from a brain haemorrhage following a cycle accident. It was only the patient's brother who had truly suffered from epilepsy, and he indeed died from smothering as the patient described. It also emerged that the father's mother had achieved notoriety in the national press in 1907 when her doctor had prescribed strychnine in mistake for some stomach medicine; she had died in convulsions, witnessed by her children including the patient's father when he was five years old.

It was decided that in all probability the patient's attacks were psychogenic in origin as possibly her father's had been in his youth. She appeared, indeed, to represent the second generation of psychogenic attacks, deriving perhaps from the incident in 1907. Her fear of epilepsy was clearly intense and had led her to misinterpret and distort the family history. This fear was greatly aggravated by her brother's death, and it was shortly after this, when the patient was 23, that she had first presented herself at the epileptic clinic.

She was admitted to hospital for withdrawal of anti-convulsants after full explanation that no evidence for epilepsy could be found. Withdrawal was accomplished over several weeks, though the period was stormy with intense anxiety and many obviously psychogenic nocturnal attacks. Gradually, however, the attacks subsided, along with her daytime odd sensations. After 2 months she had recovered her confidence in going out alone, and the following year she obtained employment as a travelling saleswoman. She felt better than for many years previously and accepted that she did not suffer from epilepsy. When followed up eighteen months later there were still occasional disturbances at night, presumed to be hypnagogic in origin, but these no longer occasioned her much concern.

Another unusual patient was for a long time suspected of a psychogenic disorder, but in this case her complex phobias proved to be accompanied by post-ictal electrophysiological disturbance within the brain. The patient has already been briefly reported by Marks (1969):

A woman of 51 developed attacks suggestive of temporal lobe epilepsy from the age of 29. Prior to this she had seemed a stable and healthy person, surviving the loss of her husband and bringing up her daughter alone. Every 1–2 months she experienced brief attacks of feeling light-headed together with numbness bilaterally in the face. These were sometimes accompanied by a strange smell or taste, or incontinence of a few drops of urine, but she did not lose consciousness. For several days after each attack she felt depressed and generally unwell. The EEG showed no definite abnormalities.

At 38 she remarried and encountered great domestic disharmony. Her attacks increased to runs of 3 or 4 at a time, and she began to show marked hysterical features. There were three episodes of blindness lasting several minutes, and an episode of loss of speech for an hour. She made several suicidal gestures, and often collapsed motionless to the floor after rows with her husband. The epileptic basis of her previous seizures began to be questioned and EEGs continued to show no abnormalities.

In 1958, at the age of 41 she had two of her usual seizures in quick succession, and was in her usual post-ictal phase of feeling 'washed out' and nervous when a furious row developed with her husband. He became violent towards her and she sought refuge by locking herself in a room. From this point onwards the post-ictal phase of all attacks became characterised by intense and unreasonable fears of men and of the dark. The invariable pattern was now for attacks to be followed by a period of 7–10 days during which these phobias were incapacitating, while in the interim they did not trouble her at all. Two years later she separated from her husband and resumed work as a telephonist, but the pattern of attacks continued unaltered.

The extent of the phobias was remarkable. Her fear of the dark made it essential to keep the light on all night, and she would take a bucket into her room since she was unable to go to the lavatory downstairs. Her fear of men made it difficult or impossible to travel to work lest a man should come close in the street or on public transport. The phobias always ran a characteristic course, setting in 12–24 hours after the seizure, remaining at their peak for several days, then gradually waning over 3 or 4 days thereafter.

In 1966 Dr R. T. C. Pratt obtained an opportunity to perform an EEG shortly after an attack and while the phobias were present. A marked abnormality, consisting of theta and delta waves together with some sharp elements, was seen in the right fronto-temporal region. Sphenoidal leads confirmed focal sharp waves in the right anterior temporal region. After another attack the findings were confirmed and followed by repeat examinations; the right temporal abnormalities were marked immediately after the fit, and waned over 10 days as the phobias subsided.

The seizures changed somewhat in character at about this time, though she was an unreliable witness and gave different descriptions at different times. In place of the olfactory warning she noted a feeling as of water trickling over her back, epigastric sensations, and mild confusion of thought. In some attacks she would slump in her chair and pick at her left cheek, and occasionally she lost consciousness and frothed at the mouth. After some attacks she claimed total amnesia for the events of several days preceding the seizure. The only constant and invariable feature continued to be the post-ictal phobias.

During 1968–9 she was admitted to the Maudsley Hospital on several occasions following attacks, and the focal right temporal disturbance on the EEG was repeatedly confirmed during phobic periods. In addition Dr Isaac Marks was able to obtain physiological confirmation of the post-ictal phobias—fantasies of the phobic situations led to marked physiological fear responses on the polygraph, whereas fantasies of neutral situations produced no such response. In between attacks, fantasies of the phobic situations were without effect. Physiological measures thus confirmed that selective phobic anxiety was present post-ictally but absent inter-ictally.

It therefore emerged that the patient suffered from genuine and disabling phobias, uniquely during a ten day period following each of her temporal lobe seizures, and accompanied by contemporaneous electrical disturbance within the right temporal lobe of the brain. The apparent onset of the phobic disorder in 1958, dating from an emotionally traumatic experience shortly after a seizure, was a striking feature in the history. It would appear that she may have been unusually vulnerable to the acquisition of a new 'neurotic' pattern of disability during the period immediately following her attacks, perhaps by virtue of temporal lobe dysfunction occurring at such times.

PSYCHOSES AND EPILEPSY

The proper understanding and classification of the epileptic psychoses is beset with difficulties. A bewildering variety of pictures may be encountered, ranging from transient self-limiting episodes to chronic illnesses which persist for many years. Some are immediately related to the fits themselves, or to identifiable alterations in the electrical activity of the brain, while others appear to arise independently of any seizure manifestations. The clinical content is similarly variable, some disturbances being dominated by organic features in the mental state, while others show affective or schizophreniform symptomatology with no evidence of clouding of consciousness. The well known difficulty of detecting minor degrees of clouding adds to the problems of understanding and classifying such phenomena.

The epileptic psychoses are of great theoretical interest for obvious reasons. They provide an unusual opportunity for exploring relationships between cerebral dysfunction and mental disorder, both of organic and 'functional' types. It is unfortunate, therefore, that the literature concerning the forms they may take and their electrophysiological associations has often been far from clear. The selection of patients for report is open to many influences, terminology is often confused, and phenomenology inadequately described. Efforts have been made to reach some workable conclusions (Landolt, 1958; Lorentz de Haas and Magnus, 1958; Dongier, 1959) but none is entirely satisfactory. Our present state of knowledge is therefore likely to prove no more than an approximation to the true state of affairs.

A simple division may be made into psychoses in which confusion and impairment of consciousness are the outstanding features while affective or schizophreniform elements are absent or unintrusive; psychoses which contain an admixture of 'organic' and 'functional' manifestations; and psychoses which occur in a setting of clear consciousness and take a form characteristic of the functional psychoses, either schizophrenic or affective.

As might be expected the first and most decisively organic group shows the most regular and definite relationship with the cerebral dysrhythmias of epilepsy. Indeed such episodes prove almost universally to reflect either ictal or post-ictal disturbances of cerebral function. As such they are transient phenomena, lasting for minutes, hours or occasionally days but rarely longer. The great majority of these disturbances represent ictal automatisms, petit mal status or post-ictal confusional states, as already described in the sections on psychomotor attacks and post-ictal disorders (p. 220 *et seq.* and p. 225).

The intermediate group, showing both impairment of consciousness and functional psychotic features, tends likewise to be tied to ongoing electrical disturbances within the brain, though perhaps less commonly in direct apposition to seizures. Temporal lobe epilepsy appears to be particularly associated with such manifestations (see discussion on p. 226). A common picture is the combination of marked confusion, visual and auditory hallucinations, paranoid delusions, and depression sometimes amounting to stupor. The impairment of consciousness may be obvious at the time, or revealed only subsequently by evidence of patchy or complete amnesia for the episode. Such disorders may be many days or weeks in duration, but again are almost always self-limiting. Pond (1957) has drawn attention to similar paranoid-hallucinatory pictures which may follow directly on grand mal convulsions, and at first sight closely resemble schizophrenia. The differentiation from schizophrenia depends on the presence of clouding of consciousness and their relatively brief duration of two to three weeks at most. They may sometimes respond to anticonvulsants, or be more directly curtailed by electroconvulsive therapy. Clearly some of the psychoses within this intermediate group overlap with 'psychomotor seizures' and especially with the 'twilight states' as described on pp. 223 and 224.

The psychotic illnesses which occur in clear consciousness may occur either as transient self-limiting episodes, or alternatively, as chronic and severely disabling illnesses. They may be affective, schizoaffective or schizophrenic in form. It is this group, and particularly the schizophrenia-like psychoses within it, which has been clarified in several respects in recent years and which accordingly warrants more extended discussion.

Schizophrenia and Epilepsy

The study of the relationship between schizophrenia and epilepsy has had a curious history reviewed, for example, by Davison and Bagley (1969), Flor-Henry (1969) and Wolf and Trimble (1985). The relationship has been extensively investigated from two different points of view—the occurrence of epileptic manifestations in schizophrenic patients, and the development of schizophrenia in established epileptics.

With regard to the former, Hill (1948, 1957a) illustrated the unusual incidence of epileptic wave forms in the EEGs of schizophrenics. These were found in up to 25% of young acute cases and particularly in catatonic schizophrenia. Typical paroxysmal phenomena with three per second spike and wave activity may be seen. Among such patients convulsions were sometimes observed during the course of insulin coma therapy, or occurred spontaneously shortly after recovery. Variations could sometimes be demonstrated in the photo-metrazol threshold during periods of catatonic stupor, or in the ease of provoking spike and wave discharges by induced hypoglycaemia.

With regard to the incidence of schizophrenia in known epileptics, directly contradictory conclusions arose from different investigations in the past. Thus some suggested an affinity between the two disorders, such that they occurred together in the same patient more often than chance expectation. Others, however, found quite the reverse, with a lowered incidence of schizophrenia in epileptics. The idea of a fundamental antagonism between the two disorders was strengthened by reports of patients in whom epileptic and schizophrenic manifestations appeared to alternate, periods of psychosis developing when seizures were in abeyance and periods of sanity accompanying the return of convulsions.

The latter viewpoint led to Meduna's introduction of convulsive therapy for the management of schizophrenia in 1937.

Recently the situation has become clearer. It now appears that chronic paranoid-hallucinatory psychoses closely similar to schizophrenia, and phenomenologically often indistinguishable from it, do occur more often than chance expectation in epileptic patients, and show a particularly close relationship to epilepsy arising within the temporal lobes. The work of Slater, Beard and Glithero (1963), described below, has been of central importance in arriving at this conclusion. It furthermore seems probable that a distinct sub-group of schizophrenia-like psychoses may warrant separate recognition from the above; in these the psychotic episodes are transient and self-limiting, often setting in when fits are diminishing in frequency and tending to subside when fits return. These are discussed further on p. 251.

Thus both the 'affinity' and the 'antagonism' hypotheses appear to have had their roots in valid clinical observations, but of different groups of patients. A given series of patients will sometimes have contained a preponderance of one type of schizophrenia-like psychosis, sometimes of the other, accounting for the divergent views expressed in the literature. It is also likely that the distinctions are not absolute, but that a variety of intermediate forms occur.

Chronic Schizophrenia-like Psychoses

The occurrence of chronic paranoid-hallucinatory states in patients with temporal lobe epilepsy was reported by Hill (1953, 1957b) and Pond (1957). These were described as resembling schizophrenia very closely indeed. Delusions were often systematised and coupled with ideas of influence and auditory hallucinations. Frank thought disorder could appear, with neologisms, condensed words and inconsequential sentences. In contrast to ordinary schizophrenia, however, the affect tended to remain warm and appropriate, and typical hebephrenic deterioration was not seen. In the patients described by Hill and Pond the psychoses tended to begin at a time when fit frequency was declining, either spontaneously or as a result of medication.

Slater *et al.* (1963) tackled the problem by systematically collecting patients who had unequivocal evidence of epilepsy and who had subsequently developed an illness diagnosed as schizophrenia. Sixty-nine patients, 36 male and 33 female, were collected from the Maudsley Hospital and the National Hospital, Queen Square over a ten year period. Care was taken to include only those in whom there was abundant clinical evidence for the diagnosis of schizophrenia, and in whom the psychosis had persisted for several weeks or months. Cases were excluded where psychotic symptoms had been confined to episodes in which alteration of consciousness could have played some part.

The clinical features were as follows. The mean age of onset was 30, after a mean duration of epilepsy of 14 years. The range extended, however, from 12 to 59, and the duration of epilepsy prior to onset from several months to 48 years. In the great majority (80 per cent) the onset had been insidious with the gradual development of delusions as the first manifestation. In a smaller proportion there was an acute or subacute onset which then passed on to a more lasting psychosis. Sometimes there had been a number of acute episodes, perhaps in association with confusional states, before the chronic condition supervened. In the series as a whole there was no clear relationship between onset and alteration of fit frequency, but in a small number there was a suggestion of diminishing frequency before the psychosis appeared.

The following case from Slater *et al.* (1963) is typical:

The patient had had epilepsy since the age of 10. At 38, when he was having one major attack a month, he began to complain of depression. He told the psychiatrist he did not know whether he was coming or going. Someone had told him he was being a 'Billy Muggins'. For 6 months he had had the idea he was being followed; people had followed him around who looked like foreigners. At a tea bar the man who served him had said 'thank you very much, your Majesty'; and he was only a plain mister—as far as he knew. These vague ideas in course of time became systematised into the delusion that he was a scion of a noble family and could expect a vast sum from a will. He became auditorily hallucinated and heard voices in his head which said 'Duke of York', 'Duke of Cambridge' (the names of pubs in his neighbourhood), 'Duke of Salisbury' and 'Squire'. The voices knew everything he had done, and they must have recordings of his entire life. There was a pick-up in his body, 'a pin in my body to pick up the nerve vibrations', which transmitted thoughts from the brain, and also made the brain receive.

Sometimes the psychosis became manifest as a gradual change of personality as in the following example:

The patient had had screaming attacks as a little girl, and grand mal attacks without aura or focal signs since 13. Her attacks practically ceased at the age of 32. From this time on there was a progressive personality change. From being normally affectionate and active, she became unaffectionate, sulky and aggressive and lost all her interests. When admitted to hospital at the age of 38 she was becoming more and more difficult, refusing her food and her tablets, and refusing to get out of bed or to wash herself. In hospital she showed thought blocking, incongruities of thought and affect, grimacing and fragmentary delusional ideas. The state persisted even when the possibility of drug intoxication, which had first been considered, had been eliminated. She was then found to be also auditorily hallucinated.

The established psychoses were in the main chronic paranoid illnesses typical of paranoid schizophrenia. A small number, some 10%, showed the picture of hebephrenic schizophrenia. Delusions occurred in almost every case, frequently of a religious or mystical nature. Some clearly took origin from primary delusional experiences, others apparently arose from feelings of depersonalisation or derealisation. Passivity feelings of being controlled or influenced were prominent, and were more closely connected with systematised ideas of persecution. Bizarre features characteristic of schizophrenia often entered into these delusions—rays, electronic wires, magnetic powers, thought reading and hypnosis. Special powers were often claimed, special significance attached to commonplace events, and happenings fell into a special pattern.

Hallucinations were chiefly in the auditory modality (46% of cases), though visual, somatic, olfactory and gustatory hallucinations occurred as well. Persecutory voices were particularly common, commenting on the patient's actions, repeating his thoughts, discussing him in the third person, or telling him what to do. Visual hallucinations (16% of cases) were often complex and full of meaning, and often of a mystical nature. Almost always they were accompanied by auditory hallucinations as well.

Almost half of the patients showed thought disorder of schizophrenic type, with answering beside the point, neologisms, thought blocking, and occasional incoherence amounting to word salad. Several patients felt that their thoughts were read or interrupted, or that thoughts could be put into their minds. Manneristic behaviour was sometimes observed, and impaired volition or initiative could be marked. Gross catatonic phenomena were rare, but occasional patients showed negativism of the classical type, statuesque postures, sudden impulsive acts, or repetitive stereotyped movements.

The commonest emotional disturbances were irritability, aggressiveness and short-lived severe depression. Exaltation or ecstasy were usually associated with some semi-mystical experience. Occasional patients described intense fear, bewilderment or loneliness. Flatness of affect was shown, at least at times, by rather less than half of the patients, and some showed silly or inappropriate emotional responses.

In summary, therefore, all of the cardinal symptoms of schizophrenia were exhibited at some time or another by this large group of patients. Slater et al. (1963) stressed that it would not be possible to diagnose them, on psychological symptomatology alone, as suffering from anything other than a schizophrenic psychosis. They noted, however, that the combination of symptoms shown by individual patients differed slightly from the usual schizophrenic patterns. Thus catatonic phenomena of gross degree were rare, and loss of affective response did not occur so early or become so marked as in the usual run of schizophrenias. By and large the patients were friendlier, more cooperative and less suspicious towards hospital staff. Moreover at the time of observation a very high proportion (80%) showed what Slater et al. (1963) interpreted as 'organic' personality changes in addition to their schizophrenia-like symptoms—lack of spontaneity, dullness and retardation, concrete and circumstantial thinking, and impairments of memory.

Slater et al.'s observations concerning phenomenology rested essentially on clinical judgements. More recent studies have attempted direct control comparisons between smaller groups of epileptic and non-epileptic psychotic patients, in an attempt to define the clinical symptomatology more precisely. Toone et al. (1982b), in a retrospective review using the Syndrome Check List, confirmed that catatonic syndromes were less common in epileptic schizophrenics than in their non-epileptic counterparts. Paranoid delusions and delusions of reference were significantly more common. Affective flattening and grandiose and religious delusions did not, however, differentiate the groups. Perez et al. (1985) used the Present State Examination to identify 'nuclear schizophrenias', and compared 11 temporal lobe epileptics with non-epileptic controls. The profiles of symptoms proved to be virtually identical in the two groups. Intelligence quotients were in the main within the normal range, and there was little to suggest impairments of an organic nature.

The course in Slater et al.'s series was usually a tendency to chronicity once the psychosis had been declared. This was the course followed by almost half of the patients. When the onset had been acute the prognosis was better, sometimes with improvement even to the point of recovery. Those with an episodic onset sometimes pursued a fluctuating course thereafter. Follow-up at a mean interval of 8 years from the onset of the psychosis showed that a third had achieved remission, and a further third had improved with regard to psychotic manifestations. The epilepsy had also tended to become less troublesome with time. Many patients, however, showed psycho-organic sequelae in the form of perseveration, dullness, retardation or impairment of memory, half being substantially handicapped on account of such defects. It seemed that the chronic schizophrenia-like illness had often merely been one phase in the total course of the illness, with later development towards a picture more characteristic of organic cerebral disorder.

This last point has not been confirmed in other series to date. Toone et al. (1982b) found evidence of organic deterioration in only 6 of a mixed group of 68 psychotic epileptics. Perez et al. (1985) found that most patients with a clear diagnosis of temporal lobe epilepsy and schizophrenia showed little to indicate deterioration of intellect; indeed they comment that most patients within this category seem to avoid institutionalisation and to live reasonably well within the community, perhaps by virtue of preserved affect and family relationships.

The epilepsy from which Slater et al.'s 69 patients suffered was most frequently temporal lobe in origin. Two-thirds had clinical evidence, and rather more had EEG evidence of such a focus. The few patients with centrencephalic epilepsy (7 in number) showed predominantly hebephrenic rather than paranoid-hallucinatory pictures, and their age of onset was considerably earlier than the average. Chance association may well have been operative in this small subgroup. Perez et al. (1985) found that when the Present State Examination was used to define 'nuclear schizophrenia' this was entirely confined to the temporal lobe epileptics in their series.

A high proportion of Slater et al.'s patients appeared to have a lesional basis for their epilepsy, in that some definable cause could be detected in the history—birth injury, middle ear infection or encephalitis. Kristensen and Sindrup (1978a) have confirmed this impression in a controlled study. Ninety-six temporal lobe epileptics with paranoid-hallucinatory psychoses were matched with non-psychotic patients with the same type of epilepsy, age of onset and present age. The former contained a greater proportion with histories indicative of brain damage as a basis for their epilepsy, also a significantly greater number of left-handers which may similarly have reflected brain insult. Slater *et al.* found that air encephalography demonstrated cerebral atrophy in two-thirds of cases; Toone *et al.* (1982a), however, found that CT scan abnormalities were no more frequent in epileptics with schizophrenia than in those with other psychoses or psychiatric disorders, the incidence being approximately 50% in all subgroups.

An additional curious finding is that where patients with schizophrenia-like psychoses have come to temporal lobectomy, mesial temporal lobe sclerosis has been distinctly less common than in temporal lobe epileptics generally, and small cryptic tumours ('hamartomas') have been particularly common (Taylor, 1972; Falconer, 1973). Taylor (1975) compared 47 patients whose resected specimens showed 'alien tissue' (small tumours, hamartomas and focal dysplasia) with 41 showing mesial sclerosis; 23% of the former but only 5% of the latter had been psychotic. A marked effect of left-handedness was also seen in Taylor's material, 7 of the 13 psychotic patients being left-handed compared with only 11 of the 75 non-psychotic patients. In the alien tissue group females, and particularly left-handed females, were especially likely to have developed a schizophrenia-like psychosis. The significance to be attached to these observations remains unknown, but they combine to suggest that the development of psychosis in temporal lobe epilepsy is more than a random matter. The indications of a special association with left-sided temporal lobe foci, discussed below, is further evidence in this regard.

The idea of a special association with temporal lobe epilepsy has been criticised by Small *et al.* (1966) and Stevens (1966). It is not known for example, how large a proportion of non-psychotic epileptic patients of equivalent age would show discharges arising within the temporal lobes. The matter will be hard to resolve decisively until further large series of psychotic and non-psychotic epileptics can be accumulated, in a manner which avoids special selection and permits careful categorisation of both the psychoses and the epilepsy. Meanwhile arguments can be marshalled to uphold the special association, which was supported by Davison and Bagley (1969) in their careful review.

Moreover Flor-Henry (1969) has produced further evidence in favour of special regional associations, by demonstrating that among psychotic temporal lobe epileptics the schizophrenias were strongly associated with foci in the dominant rather than the non-dominant lobe. This important finding has been both confirmed (Gregoriadis *et al.*, 1971; Taylor, 1975; Lindsay *et al.*, 1979c; Sherwin, 1981; Perez *et al.*, 1985) and refuted (Kristensen and Sindrup, 1978b; Jensen and Larsen, 1979b), though the balance of evidence clearly supports Flor-Henry's initial observation. Perez *et al.* (1985) present a summation of reports from the literature, concerning 180 patients with schizophrenia-like psychoses and temporal lobe epilepsy, yielding a total of 62% with left, 15% with right, and 23% with bilateral foci. They point out that the link with left-sided foci has emerged most consistently when Schneiderian criteria have been employed in the diagnosis of the schizophrenia.

The mechanisms behind the association of epilepsy and chronic schizophrenia-like psychoses have been considered in some detail (Pond, 1962; Symonds, 1962b; Slater *et al.*, 1963; Davison and Bagley, 1969; Flor-Henry, 1969). Chance association may be operative, or precipitation in individuals already predisposed to schizophrenia. Or there may be more direct links of a psychological or physiological nature.

A merely chance association appears to be unlikely. Statistical reasoning from the known frequencies of epilepsy and of schizophrenia in the general population makes it improbable that 69 examples could have been collected by Slater *et al.* (1963) from two hospitals over a relatively short period of time. Moreover the 'schizophrenia' was mainly of a particular type (paranoid), and the epilepsy of a particular type (temporal lobe epilepsy), whereas chance association should have led to a more normal representation of all varieties. And the psychoses had some features unusual for schizophrenia, such as relatively good preservation of affective response. The special associations with alien tissue lesions and with left-sided foci, as discussed above, also argue for more than a chance association.

Precipitation in individuals predisposed to schizophrenia similarly appears unlikely. A family history of schizophrenia was very rare in first-degree relatives in Slater *et al.*'s material, occurring no more often than in the general population and certainly less often than in ordinary schizophrenia. Nor did the premorbid personalities of the patients contain an undue incidence of schizoid traits. Both of these points were confirmed by Flor-Henry (1969). In a direct comparison between epileptic and non-epileptic schizophrenics, Toone *et al.* (1982b) again found that abnormal premorbid personality had been less common in the epileptics.

Thus one is led to infer more direct aetiological links between the epilepsy (or its attendant brain dysfunction) and the psychosis. The latter may be viewed as a 'symptomatic schizophrenia' analogous to that emerging with other brain lesions (p. 75) or with amphetamine abuse. Taking a more conservative view some have argued that the psychoses observed are not, strictly speaking, schizophrenias at all, but are more properly to be regarded as epileptic psychoses of a special kind ('paranoid-hallucinatory psychoses'). Though taking on the appearances of schizophrenia, and resembling it very closely indeed, they differ markedly from 'endogenous' examples of the disease in their associations. To some extent the argument is tautologous; but whatever the precise nosological position may be the pathogenesis of such disorders is clearly a matter of considerable interest.

The aetiological link with the epilepsy could be via the seizures themselves, or alternatively by way of the basic disorder of cerebral functioning which manifests itself as epilepsy. In favour of the view that the fits themselves might be responsible is the finding that they have usually been occurring for many years before the psychosis supervenes, also that they tend to be of a special clinical type. Temporal lobe seizures commonly involve much abnormal experience, often of a compelling and disquieting kind—sudden affects of fear, anxiety or ecstasy unconnected with external reality, or abnormal perceptual experiences in the form of hallucinations, déjà vu or derealisation. Symonds (1962b) suggests that there is hardly one of the characteristic symptoms of schizophrenia, of a positive kind, which may not be experienced at some time or another in the auras of temporal lobe epilepsy. The psychotic patients in Slater et al.'s series had often experienced such aural symptoms, and a number explained them in a delusional way; the symptoms in fact came to enter into the content of the delusional psychoses. Epileptic twilight states may also contain material of a mystical or religious nature which is later recollected, and some patients remain convinced of the reality of such experiences. Years of attacks of clouding of consciousness may accordingly lead to a confusion between reality on the one hand and autistic thinking and experience on the other. Thus Pond (1962) advanced the view that there may sometimes be a causal relationship of a psychological kind between the fits and the psychosis, the latter depending essentially on abnormal emotional experiences, physically caused, which then become integrated into the totality of psychic life as a psychodynamic process.

There are difficulties, however, in accepting such a mechanism as a general explanation. Slater et al. (1963) were unable to find evidence that the frequency or severity of attacks was related to the development of psychosis. More decisively, Flor-Henry (1969) compared psychotic and non-psychotic temporal lobe epileptics and found that the former had had significantly fewer seizures than the latter, in particular fewer seizures of a psychomotor or psychosensory character. Kristensen and Sindrup (1978a), in a similar comparison, showed that psychotic patients experienced fewer 'psychical' seizures involving disturbance of interpretive functions such as derealisation or hallucinations. Furthermore a psychological explanation might be plausible for the derivation of delusional symptoms, but it would be hard to account for thought disorder or volitional disturbance on such a basis.

A physiogenic formulation of the link was put forward by Symonds (1962b). In this view, both the epilepsy and the psychosis are manifestations of the same basic disorder of cerebral function within the temporal lobes, the epilepsy being an earlier and intermittent manifestation, and the psychosis a later product. Symonds commented that in other situations temporal lobe pathology rarely led to persistent psychological disorder resembling schizophrenia; the postulated abnormality might therefore consist not so much of the static lesion responsible for the epilepsy, but rather of the disordered electrophysiological activity which spreads within the temporo-limbic system. At peaks of such disorder seizures are likely to occur, but the background disturbance may persist continuously between with far-reaching effects on psychic function. In effect Symonds suggested that 'the temporal lobe includes within its boundaries circuits concerned with the physiological basis of the psychological disorder we call schizophrenia . . . it is not the loss of neurones in the temporal lobe that is responsible for the psychosis, but the disorderly activity of those that remain'.

A pathogenesis of this nature is supported by several observations. Thus in Slater et al.'s material a high correlation was observed between the ages of onset of epilepsy and of psychosis, suggesting an underlying process with autonomous developmental tendencies, liable to produce fits at one stage and psychosis at another. The finding of a lesional basis for the epilepsy in a high proportion of cases lends further support. Slater et al. suggested that it might be cells in the process of dying which contribute largely to the psychosis, rather than cells which are dead, as indicated by the eventual tendency for the psychosis to subside and its occasional progression to a syndrome of organic defect.

Further support for a physiogenic link comes from the increasing evidence that site of focus may be significant in relation to liability to psychosis. The indications of a preponderance of left-sided foci have already been discussed (p. 249), this association emerging most clearly when the psychoses resemble classical schizophrenia closely. Kristensen and Sindrup (1978a, 1978b) have emphasised dysfunction deep within the temporal lobes as an important aetiological factor, as revealed by spike foci in the medio-basal temporal regions on sphenoidal recordings. The interesting suggestion has been made that a process akin to 'kindling' (p. 512) might be involved, with progressive and spreading changes occurring within the limbic system as a result of repeated interictal discharges continuing over the years (Livingston, 1977). This could be relevant to the long time interval commonly observed between the onset of the epilepsy and of the psychosis.

The relative claims of psychological and physiological explanations remain unresolved in what is clearly a complex pathogenesis. In the meantime the essential conclusions put forward by Slater et al. in 1963 should perhaps be allowed to stand—that there is an 'aetiological relationship between the epilepsy, or a pathological process causing epilepsy, and the psychosis . . . . The evidence is however ambiguous in value and insufficient to let us decide on the nature of the relationship, whether the epileptic fits themselves tend to cause the psychosis, or whether the cause of the epilepsy tends to cause the psychosis . . . . Our final conclusion then must be a somewhat inconclusive one. Both the modes of explanation suggested by Pond and by Symonds have evidence in their favour and seem likely to account for at least a part of the observations. Our own tendency is to think the physiogenic causation of the psychosis the more important factor . . .'.

Transient Schizophrenia-like Episodes

In addition to the chronic psychoses described above, certain transient self-limiting schizophrenia-like episodes may also arise in epileptic patients. It is possible that these may rest on a different pathophysiological basis, and that they should be viewed as a distinct subgroup (Davison and Bagley, 1969). It remains to be determined, however, how far such distinctions are valid: overlap may occur, with transitional forms and several sub-varieties

The justification for regarding transient episodes as physiologically distinct lies largely with the work of Landolt, who has drawn attention to the phenomenon of 'forced normalisation' of the EEG during certain epileptic disturbances. In reporting 107 examples of 'epileptic twilight states and psychotic episodes', he included 47 patients in whom the EEG showed reduction of paroxysmal foci or other epileptic activity during the episode, with subsequent reappearance of the abnormal electrical activity when the psychosis subsided (Landolt, 1958). Usually the EEG abnormalities were absent altogether while the psychotic manifestations were in evidence. The clinical features witnessed in such episodes were polymorphous, but some examples apparently showed pictures virtually indistinguishable from schizophrenia.

The patients were often restless, noisy and overactive, though some remained composed and seemed only slightly tense. Hallucinations and delusions were prominent. Orientation was normal, or when abnormal this appeared to be due to autistic preoccupation rather than impairment of consciousness. Most remained entirely lucid and with normal clarity of thought processes, though with little awareness of the morbid change within themselves. Some episodes were followed by amnesia, but with others there was normal recollection of the content. They lasted usually for several days or weeks, and fits remained in abeyance throughout the psychotic period. The onset had often followed the institution of anticonvulsant treatment, and cautious discontinuation of medication could frequently be seen to have a beneficial effect. Sometimes the psychotic episode was terminated by an induced fit (electroconvulsive therapy). The majority of patients had focal temporal lobe epilepsy, but similar pictures could also be observed with other focal seizures or with generalised epilepsy.

Landolt reviewed evidence from other series which supported his observations, and sought to extend his thesis into schizophrenias occurring in non-epileptics. Thus among 42 schizophrenics, spontaneous relapses were often accompanied by normalisation of the EEG, by way of reduction of generalised or focal dysrhythmias which had existed in non-psychotic phases. Remissions of schizophrenia were similarly associated with a return of abnormal rhythms.

Davison and Bagley (1969) refer to other examples of schizophrenia-like psychoses in epileptics which may reflect a process analogous to this—episodes arising shortly after starting a new anticonvulsant drug and subsiding when this is discontinued. Dongier (1959) found an association between paranoid episodes and normalisation of temporal lobe discharges. Others, however, have failed to confirm such findings. Glaser *et al.* (1963) could rarely discern distinct time relationships between EEG changes and psychotic developments, and when present there was usually an increase rather than a decrease in paroxysmal activity.

The possibility that some schizophrenia-like psychoses may bear an antithetical relationship to fit frequency and EEG disturbance could have important implications for treatment. And as discussed on p. 246 the existence of this class of disturbance might stand to reconcile the conflicting views about the affinity or antagonism existing between epilepsy and schizophrenia. Certainly it may explain some of the divergent findings in the literature concerning fit frequency prior to the onset of schizophenia-like psychoses; Pond (1957) and Kristensen and Sindrup (1978a) specifically mention diminished fit frequency in relation to such developments, whereas in Slater *et al.*'s (1963) large series no clear associations of this nature were observed. Here it may have been significant that the great majority of Slater's cases did not pursue an episodic course.

Reynolds (1967b, 1968) has discussed the possibility that there may be a biochemical contribution to the aetiology of schizophrenia-like psychoses in epileptics. Disturbance of folate or B_{12} metabolism was proposed as playing a part in precipitating such disorders, and it is perhaps in the type of psychosis just discussed that this warrants most careful further exploration.

Affective Disorder

Affective disorder, and particularly affective psychoses, have been less comprehensively studied in epileptic patients than the schizophrenia-like psychoses discussed above. Disturbance of affect is common in epileptics, but chiefly takes the form of neurotic disorder with fluctuating depression and anxiety. Others show periodic 'dysphoria', in the form of episodes of irritability and aggressiveness which contrasts with a basic pattern of good mental stability (Lorentz de Haas and Magnus, 1958). These disturbances, when severe, can be difficult to distinguish from frank affective psychoses so that the incidence of the latter is hard to determine accurately. Pond (1957) further suggests that many short-lived depressive or hypomanic episodes are labelled as manic-depressive when in fact they represent post-ictal confusional states or automatisms

with only minor disturbance of consciousness.

Nevertheless clear-cut examples of affective psychosis do occur, depressive episodes being commoner than mania or hypomania. Among 72 epileptic patients admitted to psychiatric hospitals Betts (1974) found that almost a third were suffering primarily from depressive illnesses, 12 being endogenous in type and 10 being reactive in nature. Moreover a significant relationship was observed between decline in fit frequency prior to admission and the onset of endogenous depression.

Apart from the possible relationship to declining fit frequency, few special associations or unique characteristics have been described for affective disorder. Betts (1981) reports a clinical impression that the onset and remission of depression both tend to be sudden in epileptic patients, also that the mood disorder may fluctuate quite markedly while present. Serafetinides and Falconer (1962b) suggested that paranoid features were often found in association with psychotic depression, sometimes with an alternation between the paranoid and affective manifestations. As yet, however, firm evidence for such distinctive features has not been forthcoming.

Robertson has provided a detailed account of 66 patients referred to hospital with diagnoses of both epilepsy and depression (Robertson, 1983, 1985; Robertson and Trimble, 1983). The depression was judged to be endogenous in type in 40%, and 13 of the 66 were 'psychotic' as defined by the presence of mood-congruent hallucinations or delusions. Characteristics of the depression included high scores on anxiety, neuroticism, hostility and feelings of depersonalisation as reflected in questionnaire responses, and there was a suggestion that the duration of epilepsy correlated with the severity of the depression. More than half of the patients had a family history of psychiatric illness, mainly depressive in nature. Patients receiving phenobarbitone were significantly more depressed than the remainder, while those receiving carbamazepine were less so. The serum and red cell folate levels were significantly lower than in a control population. No clear relationship emerged, however, between depression and age of onset of epilepsy, seizure type or frequency, or site of focus on the EEG. The overall results thus combined to suggest that the depression was not directly interlinked with epileptic variables themselves, but was more likely to be the outcome of multiple factors operating in genetically predisposed individuals.

Toone *et al.* (1982b), in a retrospective survey, similarly found little support for a special relationship between affective psychoses and epilepsy. Nineteen patients who had received the combined diagnoses were compared with non-epileptic manic-depressive controls. The epileptic depressives often lacked convincing psychotic features, and objective scoring procedures (Catego diagnosis derived from the Syndrome Check List) indicated that half had probably been improperly labelled. Electroconvulsive therapy and lithium had rarely been prescribed, and only 3 of the 19 epileptics had shown bipolarity. In this material the conjunction of affective psychosis and epilepsy was therefore judged to represent no more than a chance association.

In clinical practice affective and schizo-affective psychoses appear to be considerably more common than purely schizophrenic disorders (G. W. Fenton, personal communication). This seems rarely to be reflected in published reports, perhaps because many affective episodes are fleeting and relatively mild in degree. In Dongier's large series of transient psychotic episodes 30% showed change of affect as the predominant feature, compared to 56% with predominant change of consciousness and 10% with schizophrenia-like features. Depressive episodes were more closely related to temporal lobe epilepsy than to other varieties. Among patients who come to temporal lobectomy affective psychoses have again been rather commoner than schizophrenia-like psychoses, though here the selection of cases may have contributed to the result (James, 1960; Serafetinides and Falconer, 1962b). Hypomanic and manic psychoses rarely appear to be reported in epileptic patients. Wolf (1982) reviews the cases in the literature and reports 6 additional patients, 5 of them suffering from temporal lobe epilepsy.

Flor-Henry (1969) presented a detailed comparison between affective and other forms of psychosis in a series of 50 patients with temporal lobe epilepsy. These comprised all cases admitted to the Maudsley Hospital over a fifteen year period with a combined diagnosis of temporal lobe epilepsy and psychosis. Nine were diagnosed as manic-depressive, on the basis of elation or depression which exhibited periodicity and left the personality intact between phases: 11 were schizoaffective, showing features of both schizophrenia and affective disturbance; 21 were schizophrenia-like psychoses; and 9 showed an organic picture dominated by disorientation and clouding of consciousness. The manic-depressive and schizoaffective psychoses lasted on average several months, compared to several years for the schizophrenia-like psychoses and several weeks for the confusional psychoses. The patients with affective psychoses showed more stable previous personalities and better marital and occupational adjustment than the other groups. The manic-depressive patients tended to have less frequent seizures than the others, and the fits that occurred were usually grand mal rather than psychomotor in type. Manic-depressive and schizoaffective patients showed a lower incidence of structural brain damage than those with schizophrenic or confusional psychoses.

A potentially interesting finding in Flor-Henry's series was that the manic-depressive patients showed a preponderance of foci in the right temporal lobe, whereas the schizophrenia-like and confusional groups had an excess of left temporal lobe involvement. There was a suggestion that the schizoaffective group might be transitional in this regard. However, while the association between schizophrenia-like psychoses and left-sided foci has received substantial confirmation (p. 249), affective psychoses have emerged in other series as independent of laterality (Robertson, 1983, 1985; Perez et al., 1985). Gregoriadis et al. (1971) seem to be alone in also finding predominantly right-sided pathology among psychotic epileptics with affective symptomatology.

Suicide and Epilepsy

Several studies have indicated that the suicide rate is almost certainly higher among epileptics than in the general population. Prudhomme (1941) gathered data on an estimated 75,000 epileptic patients by contacting numerous physicians and institutions in the USA. Sixty-seven deaths had occurred by suicide, which was considered greatly in excess of expectation. At one colony in New York it was estimated that the incidence was twice that of the general population, or five times greater when the figures were corrected for age.

Henriksen et al. (1970) produced a more definitive study from Denmark. A representative sample of all adult epileptics discharged from four neurological clinics was traced, and the cause of death ascertained from death certificates. One hundred and sixty-four deaths had occurred among 2,763 patients, which was $2\frac{1}{2}$ to 3 times the number to be expected. The overall mortality was higher among the mentally abnormal than the mentally normal epileptics. After excluding patients with other diseases likely to have reduced life expectancy, 20% of the deaths were due to suicide, representing three times the number which could have been predicted.

More recently White et al. (1979) have produced

further striking figures. Some 2,000 patients admitted to the Chalfont Centre for Epilepsy between 1931 and 1971 were followed up to the end of 1977, and their mortality rates compared with expected values from English life tables. Of 425 deaths 21 were due to suicide, compared to an expected value of less than 4. Reviewing this and other studies in the literature Barraclough (1981) concludes that the risk of suicide is increased approximately 5-fold among epileptic patients; moreover four investigations relevant to temporal lobe epilepsy concur in showing the highest risk of all, with suicide occurring at some 25 times expectation.

Suicide attempts, as opposed to successful suicide, also appear to be especially common. Delay *et al.* (1957) found that almost a third of a large series of epileptics, either hospitalised for treatment or detained on criminal charges, had made suicide attempts. There had been multiple attempts in more than half of the cases. Gunn (1973), comparing epileptic prisoners with matched controls from the prison population, found a higher frequency of suicide attempts in the previous history, and a higher incidence of suicidal feelings at interview.

In studies of patients presenting with self-poisoning or self-injury, Mackay (1979) in Glasgow and Hawton *et al.* (1980) in Oxford both found that epileptic patients were over-represented some 5–7-fold when viewed against the prevalence of epilepsy in the community. Both observed, moreover, that repeated attempts were more common than in non-epileptic patients. Mackay found that two-thirds of the epileptics used their current anti-epileptic medication in the suicide attempts, phenobarbitone being involved in 55% of cases compared to only 2% of matched non-epileptic patients. In Hawton *et al.*'s series the attempted suicide rate was twice as high in epileptic men as in women, perhaps reflecting the special psychosocial handicaps imposed by epilepsy in men.

Investigation and Differential Diagnosis of Epilepsy

In the majority of cases a carefully taken history leaves little doubt about the epileptic nature of attacks, especially when an adequate account is available from witnesses. Enquiry must always be made into the circumstances of attacks, the details of their commencement, the subjective sensations felt by the patient, and the disturbed behaviour witnessed by others. Seizures of petit mal or grand mal type are usually readily identified, though more difficulty is likely to be encountered with psychomotor attacks. In the presence of undoubted epilepsy the aims must be to reach conclusions concerning the type of epilepsy and its focus of origin within the brain, and to elucidate possible causes for the seizures. This will almost always require the undertaking of certain ancillary investigations as described below.

It is only in a minority of patients that diagnostic difficulties arise, but it may then be necessary to embrace a wide range of possibilities other than epilepsy itself. Indeed Slater and Roth (1969) suggest that the differential diagnosis of epilepsy can be one of the most complex problems in medicine. Problems of diagnosis are likely to be particularly great among patients who come before the psychiatrist, since very often they will have been referred to him because the attacks are of an unusual type, or because a disturbed mental state has raised the question of a psychogenic component to the seizures. Here again ancillary investigations may be indispensable, but as in many other areas of psychiatry the cornerstone for differential diagnosis will usually rest on a full and detailed history, coupled with careful clinical examination and close observation of behaviour. Observation may need to be prolonged and on an in-patient basis, especially when differentiation is required from hysteria, psychopathy, or other forms of functional psychiatric disorder.

INVESTIGATION OF KNOWN EPILEPTIC ATTACKS

It must be re-emphasised that epilepsy is to be regarded as a symptom and not as a disease entity on its own. Consequently every effort must be made to determine the underlying cause. In some patients this will remain elusive, but in others a structural or biochemical basis may be revealed. Obviously the extent to which investigations are pursued in the individual will depend on the likelihood in the mind of the physician that a responsible pathology is to be discovered. Increased age at the time of the first attack will increase the chance that a cerebral lesion may be responsible. Associated symptoms such as headache, or associated neurological signs or evidence of systemic disturbance, will similarly dictate more rigorous investigation.

Another important factor in guiding the extent of investigation is the type of epileptic attack that occurs. In cases of pure petit mal it will rarely be necessary to pursue a search for structural pathology; with grand mal one will need to be more cautious, and most careful of all with focal attacks. In making these distinctions the information provided by the EEG can be invaluable when viewed in conjunction with evidence from other sources.

The type of epilepsy from which the patient suffers also has implications for treatment (p. 265 *et seq.*). Particular care must be taken to distinguish between petit mal attacks and brief automatisms of temporal lobe origin, since each will stand to respond to different anti-convulsant medication.

Falconer and Taylor (1970) particularly stress the importance of recognising temporal lobe attacks in children. If diagnosed as petit mal, ethosuximide would be ineffective, and if diagnosed as grand mal and treated with phenobarbitone the associated behavioural abnormalities could be worsened. Here the history and observation of attacks may sometimes be the sole basis for the correct diagnosis, since the EEG may show little to support the temporal lobe origin until many years later. Young children will often fail to verbalise their auras, but may produce giveaway signs such as clutching the abdomen and flexing the hips in pain (epigastric aura), flying to their mother (fear), or show obvious borborigmi, drooling, pallor or flushing.

Some patients who suffer from generalised convulsions will prove to have a focal discharge limited to one temporal lobe, raising the possibility of surgical treatment. Conversely the EEG may reveal multiple foci of origin, effectively precluding surgery even though medication has achieved only poor control.

In searching for the cause of the epilepsy *the clinical history* will usually be of first importance. Genetic factors may be obvious from the family history. Enquiry must be made for known difficulties surrounding the patient's birth, a history of febrile convulsions in childhood or illnesses suggestive of encephalitis. Any history of head injury must be carefully evaluated with regard to severity and timing in relation to the onset of the epilepsy. Enquiry must always be made for headache or other possible indications of cerebral tumour. Abuse of alcohol or drugs will sometimes be suspected. In older patients a history of even minor cerebral infarction may be relevant, or indications may be obtained of cerebral degenerative disease.

In *the clinical examination* attention will be directed primarily towards the central nervous system, with a search for focal neurological signs or indications of raised intracranial pressure. Slight inequalities in the size of limbs or hands may provide the clue to brain damage dating from early life. General medical assessment is essential, particularly when metabolic disease is suspected. In older patients the possibility of secondary cerebral malig-

nancy must be borne in mind.

Investigations will usually include the routines of blood count, erythrocyte sedimentation rate, serological tests for syphilis, urine examination and chest X-ray. The possibilities of hypoglycaemia, uraemia, hypocalcaemia and drug abuse may occasionally require appropriate exploration. In all cases a skull X-ray and EEG will normally be performed. A CT scan will commonly be carried out where facilities are readily available, and will be specially indicated in certain situations as described below. Prolonged EEG recording by telemetry or ambulatory monitoring can give valuable information in specially selected patients (p. 256).

The skull X-ray may show displacement of the pineal or calcification within a glial hamartoma or angioma. In temporal lobe epilepsy it may be of lateralising value, showing a slightly smaller middle cranial fossa on the affected side when the lesion dates from early life.

The electroencephalogram is often indispensable for determining the type of epilepsy and its source of origin within the brain. Its value can be paramount in the following situations (Parsonage, 1973)—when seizures are habitually generalised and there is no indication of their site of origin; when they have no lateralising features as in many temporal lobe attacks; if there is more than one source of seizure discharge; and when the clinical description of the seizures does not permit accurate or reliable localisation. It can be of practical value in management, as mentioned above, in distinguishing petit mal from brief temporal lobe seizures. In addition the EEG may show abnormalities of background activity which indicate something of the underlying cause. A structural lesion such as a tumour will be suspected when there is a local decrease in background activity or a delta wave focus, and metabolic derangements may be indicated by slowing of the dominant rhythm or generalised disorganisation with runs of theta activity.

These should be regarded as the principal uses of the EEG in epilepsy. It may also help towards deciding whether or not epilepsy is present, but as discussed in Chapter 3 (p. 112) its value here is limited in certain important ways. A normal EEG can never be accepted as excluding epilepsy or a causative lesion, and the recognition of epilepsy remains essentially a clinical matter whatever the EEG may or may not show.

Clinical studies have not supported the common assumption that records obtained while the patient is on anticonvulsants are less liable to disclose epileptic activity (Marsan and Zivin, 1970). It is therefore not necessary routinely to discontinue medication prior to the recording, although in cases where the EEG is normal and the diagnosis still in doubt it may sometimes be reasonable to reduce or gradually stop anticonvulsants before repeating the examination (Gibberd, 1973). Activating techniques can be of considerable value, light sleep for example revealing a temporal lobe focus when the waking EEG has been within normal limits. Sphenoidal recordings may be indicated for more precise localisation of discharges originating in the medial temporal lobe structures, and asymmetry of barbiturate induced fast activity may be further used as a guide to lateralisation. More complex explorations such as metrazol activation or even electrocorticography may be required if surgical treatment is envisaged.

EEG telemetry has established itself as especially useful in the investigation of bizarre or unusual attacks, enabling a more reliable differentiation between epileptic and non-epileptic seizures (Binnie *et al.*, 1981; Fenwick, 1981b; Cull *et al.*, 1982). In patients with refractory epilepsy it can yield more precise information about seizure type, thus permitting improved pharmacological control (Sutula *et al.*, 1981). Other advantages are in increasing the detection rate of inter-ictal seizure discharges, in locating a possible focus, in monitoring the effects of anticonvulsant treatment, or in identifying possible factors which trigger attacks.

A variety of systems are in use, predominantly in special centres. For recordings over the course of some hours or even days the patient occupies a special room or suite of rooms, the EEG being transmitted to the recording apparatus by a light flexible cable or radio-transmission. The former is less prone to artefacts. Closed-circuit television or video monitoring of the patient's behaviour allows any change or ictus to be viewed in relation to the accompanying EEG pattern by split-screen display. The patient or the observer can be equipped with a button to allow storage of epochs of special significance.

Even when artefacts obscure the EEG during the course of an actual seizure, review of the record may reveal spiking immediately preceding it or slowing or asymmetry of the record as an aftermath. Conversely, the presence of well marked alpha rhythm in an apparently unconscious patient following a substantial seizure will strongly suggest that this was an hysterical or simulated attack. Overnight studies, using an infra-red camera, may clarify the distinction between nocturnal seizures, nightmares and night terrors.

For more prolonged recordings in the patient's home or in special situations a portable cassette recorder can be used. The EEG and other physiological parameters can thus be monitored while the patient is fully ambulant and engaged in normal activities. An event marker is used by the patient to draw attention to periods of special significance. Such a system lacks the advantage of simultaneous video monitoring and the number of channels is limited, but it has proved useful in searching for epileptic activity over prolonged periods of time and from one situation to another. With petit mal, particularly, it may allow precise monitoring of the effects of different treatment régimes.

The CT scan has proved invaluable in the detection of structural cerebral abnormalities in patients with epilepsy. It is obviously indicated whenever a space-occupying lesion is remotely suspected, and should ideally be carried out in all patients when there is clinical or EEG evidence of a focal onset to the attacks. Beyond this, where access to scanning is limited, patients will be selected when the epilepsy has begun only in late adolescence or adult life, or when patients are being considered for surgery (Fenton, 1983).

Surveys have demonstrated the yield and range of abnormalities likely to be encountered in various groups of patients (Gastaut, 1976; Gastaut and Gastaut, 1976). Those with primary generalised epilepsy, whether grand mal or petit mal, show the lowest incidence of changes at some 10% or less; primary and secondary generalised grand mal seizures considered together show abnormalities in 39–63% of cases from one series to another; and patients with focal (partial) seizures show the highest incidence of all, often in excess of 60%. Altogether abnormalities may be expected in approximately a third to a half of any large series of epileptic patients.

Rather more than half of the abnormal findings will be atrophic changes, and some 10% space occupying lesions. In Gastaut and Gastaut's (1976) series the incidence of tumours rose from 11% overall, to 16% when the epilepsy had begun after the age of 20, to 23% in partial epilepsies with complex symptomatology, and to 49% in partial epilepsies with elementary symptomatology. In 80% of cases the tumours had previously been unsuspected, and 11% had been missed on skull X-ray. Bauer *et al.* (1980) confined attention to focal epilepsies after excluding patients with known space occupying lesions or progressive neurological disease; 5% were found to have slow-growing tumours and some 50% other lesions, mainly the residue of perinatal, post-traumatic or post-infectious brain damage. The correspondence between CT and EEG evidence of focal disorder was in general high but by no means exclusive, an important number of EEG foci lacking a CT scan counterpart and vice versa.

The CT scan and the EEG thus complement each other in the investigation of epilepsy. The former may reveal the location and often the nature of associated cerebral lesions, whereas the latter remains the only technique for demonstrating the epileptic character of the disorder. Since the advent of CT scanning other investigative procedures have receded greatly in importance. If no abnormality is shown on plain skull X-ray or CT scan it is unlikely that further radiological studies will reveal significant findings in patients with well controlled epilepsy and no other symptoms (Kendall, 1982). *Angiography* may nevertheless be indicated in special situations, as when a vascular malformation is suspected. *Air encephalography* also retains importance in the investigation of patients with temporal lobe epilepsy who are being considered for surgery (Polkey, 1982); the dilatation of the temporal horn of the lateral ventricle on the side affected by mesial temporal sclerosis may otherwise easily be missed on all but the latest generation of CT scanners. *Lumbar puncture* is rarely employed in the investigation of epilepsy, but may occasionally be helpful in excluding conditions such as encephalitis or neurosyphilis.

Psychometry is often helpful as a further guide to localisation, and in particular for confirming the laterality of a temporal lobe focus. Assessment of the patient's intellectual capabilities will help in judging possibilities for employment or rehabilitation, and serve as a general guide to management. Establishing a reliable base-line of intellectual performance will be particularly important in any patient who is suspected of gradual intellectual decline.

The investigations described above may need to be repeated from time to time when the initial evaluation has given negative results. The need to re-open enquiry will be indicated particularly when seizures increase in frequency or severity at a later stage, or if signs of intellectual or personality deterioration set in.

Finally, *serum prolactin estimations* will often prove of value when uncertainty surrounds the genuinely epileptic nature of attacks. After generalised tonic-clonic seizures the serum prolactin rises sharply to a peak at 20 minutes, returning to baseline levels after approximately one hour. No such effect was observed in a group of hysterical seizure patients with major attacks who had previously been diagnosed as having epilepsy (Trimble, 1978). With partial seizures the rise in less pronounced, particularly in the case of simple partial seizures where the estimation is unlikely to be of value.

Dana-Haeri *et al.* (1983) recommend taking blood for prolactin estimation 20 minutes after an attack, then again at one hour to check that baseline levels had been within the normal range (100–360 mU/l). After generalised tonic-clonic seizures they observed a rise to more than 1000 mU/l at 20 minutes in 60% of patients, and to more than 500 mU/l in 96%. Rises in excess of 500 mU/l after supposedly complex partial seizures can be regarded as highly suggestive that the attack was epileptic. The phenomenon is probably related to abnormal electrical activity within the parts of the central nervous system that regulate anterior pituitary hormone release; equivalent rises are seen in non-epileptic patients following electroconvulsive therapy carried out with full muscular relaxation under anaesthesia.

DIAGNOSTIC POSSIBILITIES OTHER THAN EPILEPSY

A number of conditions which lead to intermittent disturbance of cerebral function may be mistaken for epilepsy—for example syncope, hypoglycaemia, transient cerebral ischaemia, and occasionally migraine. Various psychiatric disorders can also resemble certain epileptic manifestations, and vice versa. Here hysteria takes pride of place, but diagnostic difficulties can also be encountered with anxiety attacks, certain schizophrenic manifestations, and other short-lived acute organic reactions. Special problems may surround the diagnosis of epileptic automatisms, in particular their distinction from outbursts of violence in patients of unstable personality. These and related matters are discussed in some detail below.

Paroxysmal Disorders of Cerebral Function Resembling Epilepsy

The classical *vasovagal attack* or *syncope* is usually readily distinguished from epilepsy by its setting. The subject is typically standing or has just risen to his feet when fainting occurs. In some instances an acutely upsetting experience may be the precipitant, or pain or an injection. The onset tends to be more gradual than with epilepsy, with a feeling of faintness, dizziness or darkening of vision leading directly into loss of consciousness. Unconsciousness is accompanied by pallor, a slow pulse and general flaccidity. When cerebral hypoperfusion is prolonged, there may be stiffening or twitching movements which are hard to distinguish from seizures, but they lack the typical tonic-clonic sequence (Riley, 1982). Incontinence or tongue biting are very rare indeed. Recovery is prompt after a minute or two, whereas after a fit there may be sleep or gradual recovery through a phase of confusion. Memory is intact up to the point where consciousness was lost, whereas an epileptic fit may be followed by a brief period of retrograde amnesia.

Diagnostic difficulty is more likely to be encountered with so-called 'micturition syncope', in which the patient gets out of bed to void urine, faints due to postural hypotension, and is then incontinent due to fullness of the bladder. Very occasionally, moreover, the cerebral ischaemia responsible for syncope may trigger a true convulsive attack.

EEG studies have discounted any pathophysiological relationship between syncope and epilepsy (Gastaut and Fischer-Williams, 1957). The loss of consciousness in syncope is accompanied by slow activity in the EEG, or in longer attacks by a period of electrical silence which resolves when consciousness is regained. Thus while in epilepsy the cortex is functionally active, in syncope it is electrically silent. On recovery there is none of the generalised slow activity in the EEG that may persist for several hours after resolution of a grand mal attack.

Hyperventilation (p. 479), common in states of anxiety or stress, can actually precipitate a seizure. Short of this the induced tetany may cause spasms or shaking in the extremities, and this can be sudden in onset resembling an epileptic attack. Focal paraesthesias, dizziness and feelings of unreality may likewise mimic seizures. Riley (1982) suggests that syncope and hyperventilation are probably the most common episodic disorders of consciousness to be confused with epilepsy. Differentiation can on occasion only be made by witnessing or provoking a characteristic attack.

Stokes-Adams attacks may lead to repeated episodes of unconsciousness, with or without convulsions. These can be hard to diagnose because the change in cardiac rhythm may be abrupt and transient. Usually, however, the electrocardiogram will reveal conduction defects or abnormal rhythms even between attacks. Schott *et al.* (1977) have reported 10 patients referred to hospital as possible cases of idiopathic epilepsy whose symptoms appeared to derive largely from various cardiac

arrhythmias. Many were relatively young, and the arrhythmias were sometimes only apparent after prolonged ECG monitoring. *Aortic stenosis* may similarly lead to sudden episodes of unconsciousness.

Hypoglycaemic attacks can simulate epilepsy closely. The periods of confused and abnormal behaviour are easily mistaken for epileptic automatisms. Characteristic features of faintness, sweating, palpitations, tremor or dizziness should immediately raise suspicion. Occasionally true petit mal, grand mal or focal seizures may be provoked.

Transient cerebral ischaemic attacks, when brief, can produce symptoms very similar to focal epilepsy (Gibberd, 1973). Attacks may start suddenly, develop, and then regress over a period of several minutes or sometimes hours. Usually, however, motor symptoms are of a positive kind in epilepsy, whereas in transient cerebral ischaemia paralysis is the rule. Considerable uncertainty may arise when motor weakness persists after a focal epileptic attack (Todd's paralysis). Usually this lasts for only a few hours; when persisting longer it is likely to have resulted from cerebral ischaemia or a localised structural lesion.

Migraine leads to positive symptoms as in epilepsy, usually in the form of visual disturbance of a highly characteristic kind. Other sensory phenomena may, however, be encountered and lead to a suspicion of epilepsy. The associated headache usually allows a distinction, but in some attacks this may be lacking. Syncopal manifestations may occasionally occur. Even so the history will usually be decisive in revealing typical migraine at other times. Special difficulty can be encountered in the rare migrainous attacks associated with amnesia, lasting sometimes for several hours then clearing gradually (Moersch, 1924; Nielsen, 1958). These can arise during attacks of visual disturbance and headache, or as a variant of classical attacks (p. 350). Brief automatisms are also said to occur in certain migrainous attacks (p. 351).

Paroxysmal choreoathetosis is a rare condition, sometimes familial, which appears to incorporate features both of convulsive disorder and extrapyramidal dyskinesia. Opinion is divided over whether it should be regarded as a form of reflex epilepsy (Lishman *et al.*, 1962; Lishman and Whitty, 1965; Stevens, 1966) or whether it is essentially a disorder of the extrapyramidal motor system (Rosen, 1964). Kertesz (1967) and Alexander (1982b) have drawn together the literature on this interesting condition.

Short paroxysms of tonic posturing or choreiform

and athetoid movements are provoked by sudden movement, as when the patient rises quickly from a chair or abruptly accelerates his pace while walking or running. Attacks last no more than a minute or two and may be unilateral or generalised, involving the limbs, trunk and face. Sudden startle or surprise may often induce the paroxysms. In a subgroup similar attacks occur spontaneously, then tending to be more prolonged and less frequent. A vague sensory aura, or a feeling of tightness in the limb of origin, may precede attacks. Many episodes are commonly aborted by slackening the pace or standing still. Awareness of the environment is generally fully retained throughout.

In most examples the condition has set in in childhood or adolescence, affecting males predominantly and proving to be a significant social embarrassment. Gradual amelioration is usually seen as the patient gets older. A good response to anticonvulsants, particularly to phenytoin, has been observed in the majority of cases described, even though the EEG may show little by way of paroxysmal features.

Hyperekplexia ('startle disease') is another rare condition, often familial, though sporadic cases are also reported. Andermann *et al.* (1980) describe three examples and review accounts of the disorder. In essence it represents a greatly exaggerated response to startle, even to minor stimuli, to the extent that the patient loses his balance and falls.

There is no associated loss of consciousness but self-injury is common. The patient freezes as he falls, with the arms held stiffly at the sides, and thus cannot protect himself. The minor form shows the startle response alone. In the major form there are a number of associated features: hyper-reflexia, repetitive jerking of the limbs, chiefly at night, and a peculiar insecure gait. In addition the major form often carries a history of generalised hypertonia in infancy, in response to handling or awakening, which gradually recedes during the first year of life. From the time of learning to walk the child then tends to fall on account of momentary periods of generalised muscular stiffness in response to noise or startle.

The course thereafter is variable, some patients gradually improving while others tend to worsen. The drug of choice in treatment appears to be clonazepam, which can greatly reduce the falling attacks and jerking though the startle response does not return to normal.

The EEG between attacks is essentially normal, but a distinctive response is seen to startle. An initial spike is recorded from the centro-parieto-occipital regions, followed by a brief train of slow waves, then desynchronised background activity lasting for 2–3 seconds.

Many cases are liable to be diagnosed as epileptic when first encountered, others as suffering from states of heightened anxiety. However there is little to suggest an epileptic basis for the condition. The essential pathophysiology would seem to lie with a disorder of motor control, perhaps by way of impaired maturation of higher inhibitory centres over lower motor mechanisms.

Epilepsy versus Hysteria

Hysterical manifestations that take the form of major convulsions appear to be less common nowadays than formerly. Problems of differentiation between the two disorders centre more often on episodes of simple loss of consciousness, or episodes of disturbed behaviour followed by amnesia. A major difficulty in clinical assessment is that hysteria and epilepsy do not preclude each other; there will sometimes be an admixture of the two, with hysterical disturbances appearing against a background of cerebral disease. In consequence it is important to follow very carefully any patient whose attacks do not appear at first sight to have an organic basis.

It is estimated, indeed, that some 5% of genuinely epileptic patients are also liable to develop pseudo-seizures at some point in their course (Scott, 1982a). Occasionally it will appear that improved control of the epilepsy by medication provokes the appearance of classical hysterical seizures, the balance reverting again once the drugs are decreased (Trimble, 1982). This paradoxical effect may reflect the patient's need to maintain his dependence on the family, or alternatively a liability to hysterical symptoms may have been exacerbated by some degree of intoxication with the anticonvulsant drugs.

It is unlikely, moreover, that in the last analysis the distinction between epileptic and hysterical episodes is always absolute. Physiogenic or psychogenic influences will be seen to operate exclusively in a large proportion of cases, but in some the two will be inextricably combined.

Krapf (1957) has traced the recent history of our conceptions in this area. In the 1920s the differentiation between epilepsy and hysteria seemed to offer no difficulty. Epilepsy was the term for attacks which had an elementary or strictly 'neurological' character, and hysteria the term for attacks which contained elaborate and psychologically meaningful symptomatology. Even at that time some problem cases were noted, but the basic notion persisted that epilepsy and hysteria were different diseases between which no transition could exist. In part this attitude was born out of opposition to Charcot's concept of 'hystero-epilepsy'.

The EEG, however, failed to corroborate so firm a distinction, and correlations between type of attack and abnormalities of record were soon found to be imperfect. The recognition of psychomotor seizures did still more to dispel so clear-cut a view. Seizures clearly related to neuronal discharges were found to go far beyond what could clinically be considered as elementary and 'epileptic'. Pronounced instability of personality was found to characterise some patients with clearly organic seizures, and the role of psychologically disturbing situations in provoking epileptic attacks became recognised increasingly.

Krapf suggested that all 'epileptiform' seizures should be regarded as the outcome of an interplay between stress and predisposition, in which both of these factors were of a multifactorial nature. The predisposition could lie in pathophysiology of the brain, or in psychological maturity, or in a combination of the two together. The nature of the seizures themselves might then be determined by the level of 'physiogenic or psychogenic regression' which prevailed in different cases.

Such a view can be useful in the understanding of borderline cases, though one would hesitate to follow Krapf further in seeing a fundamental parallel between the genesis of psychological and physiological immaturity, and in interpreting epileptiform dysrhythmias as sometimes reflecting functional immaturity of the brain.

The features which lead one to suspect hysteria, or at least a psychogenic component in a motor convulsion, are as follows. The hysterical fit usually fails to conform to any recognised type of epilepsy, and may be bizarre in pattern or variable from one occasion to another. A typical tonic-clonic phase will normally be absent and movements will often have an organised pattern. An element of display may be noted, with movements obviously expressive in nature. Convulsions may increase if restraint is imposed.

Cyanosis or pallor accompany most epileptic attacks but are rarely seen with hysterical seizures. Reflexes are unaltered during or immediately after the attack, whereas in grand mal convulsions upgoing plantars and wide fixed pupils may be observed for a time. The loss or preservation of corneal reflexes is rather less clear cut as a differentiating sign. Incontinence and self-injury are rare, though exceptions are occasionally seen. Severe self-injury may indeed be skilfully avoided. Tongue biting is uncommon in hysterical seizures, but the inner mouth or lips may be abraded. Henry and Woodruff (1978) have described a positive sign which they regard as strongly indicative of feigned or hysterical unconsciousness: when the patient is turned from one side to another the eyes deviate each time towards the ground, in a manner not seen with organic coma.

The presence or absence of diminished awareness during the attack can be difficult to determine. Moreover some epileptic attacks, especially those of focal cortical origin, are compatible with preservation of consciousness throughout their course. Nevertheless the demonstation of retained awareness of the environment while bilateral whole body convulsions are in progress will strongly suggest that the attack was not epileptic in origin. A marked emotional display when the attack is over is suggestive but by no means conclusive of hysteria. Precipitation by shock, surprise or distress must also be interpreted with caution, since such factors may trigger epileptic attacks in susceptible individuals. Moreover over-breathing, ensuing on mental distress, may ultimately precipitate a genuine epileptic fit.

The taking of a detailed history can often be informative. Painstaking appraisal of the total situation must always be attempted, with evaluation of current stresses and premorbid modes of functioning. Roy (1979) identified several factors which were significantly more common in patients with hysterical seizures than in epileptic controls: a past history or family history of psychiatric disorder, a history of attempted suicide, and the presence of sexual maladjustment or of a current affective disorder. The mode of evolution of the attacks must also be considered. Sudden loss of control in an established epileptic, for example, may indicate the development of non-epileptic seizures, particularly when anticonvulsant levels have remained stable and recent stresses can be identified (Trimble, 1983). When a history of obvious pseudoseizures is of long duration it can be important to obtain full details of the earliest attacks, since these may represent the genuine epilepsy upon which pseudoseizures have come to be superimposed. When repeated episodes occur their habitual setting can be of value in diagnosis: hysterical attacks almost invariably take place where they can be witnessed, particularly in the home and in the presence of the family.

Admission to hospital is indicated when uncertainty persists, though sometimes even close observation by skilled personnel can fail to resolve the issue. Estimation of serum prolactin levels shortly after attacks can give important and sometimes decisive information as described on p. 257. The

EEG can also prove invaluable. The interseizure record may give a lead, in that it would be rare for this to show no abnormalities in a patient experiencing several epileptic attacks per day. The converse, however, can be misleading, since many patients with pseudoseizures will also be liable to genuine attacks and will then show epileptiform abnormalities in the EEG. A record taken during or shortly after an attack provides the firmest evidence of all (Scott, 1982a, b). Consistent absence of seizure discharges, or of the slow activity that commonly succeeds a grand mal fit, will strongly suggest a non-organic seizure. Epilepsy will be indicated by spiking and other discharges which are seen to commence locally and spread widely, or in the post-ictal period by flattening of background elements and localised or generalised slow activity persisting for many minutes or even hours. Rare examples exist, nonetheless, in which definite epileptic seizures, particularly partial seizures, are witnessed by the clinician without EEG concomitants. Where facilities exist for prolonged EEG monitoring (p. 256) the chances of clarifying the diagnosis will be considerably increased.

The mistake of interpreting epilepsy as hysteria is probably much commoner than the converse situation. Special difficulty is likely to be encountered with temporal lobe epilepsy, where attacks may be bizarre in character and accompanied by pronounced emotional disturbance. The EEG may fail to reveal abnormalities until activating techniques are employed. Psychomotor attacks which are unaccompanied by grand mal convulsions are especially liable to be mistaken for functional disturbances, and particularly when consciousness is not very obviously altered. Abnormalities of behaviour are more likely to be epileptic in origin when they are sudden in onset, short-lived, irregularly recurrent, and out of character for the individual concerned (Falconer and Taylor, 1970). The problems of diagnosis raised by automatisms and fugues are further considered below.

Epilepsy Versus Other Psychiatric Disorders

Epilepsy may not only be associated with a wide range of neurotic and psychotic manifestations but can also be mistaken for them. These difficulties in diagnosis again centre principally on temporal lobe epilepsy.

Episodic attacks of anxiety may be difficult to distinguish from temporal lobe epilepsy, especially when panic wells up suddenly accompanied by marked depersonalisation. Harper and Roth (1962) illustrated this clearly in their comparison between 30 patients with temporal lobe epilepsy and 30 patients suffering from the 'phobic anxiety depersonalisation syndrome'. In both conditions there were episodic bouts of fear, depersonalisation, déjà vu and distortions of perception. In rare cases the neurotic patients also reported hallucinations. Occasionally they had fainted at the height of their attacks, even voiding urine if the bladder was full. Disturbance of conscious awareness was sometimes observed at the peaks of emotional disturbance.

Important differences lay in the tendency for severe psychiatric symptoms to persist between episodes in the anxious patients, and for their attacks to have more clear-cut emotional precipitation. Attacks began abruptly in both groups, but tended to end gradually in the neurotics and abruptly in temporal lobe epilepsy. There was often a characteristic 'march' in the evolution of symptoms in the epileptics, and complete loss of consciousness typically dominated the clinical picture. Episodic disturbances of speech and automatic behaviour were also largely confined to the epileptics. Other differences, of more value in distinguishing groups than individuals, lay in the greater neurotic background of the anxious patients, with more prominent traits of immaturity or over-dependence in the personality. The patients with temporal lobe epilepsy frequently had a history of some disease leading to cerebral damage, and they alone had abnormalities of a specifically epileptic nature in the EEG.

Occasionally the true diagnosis could remain in doubt even after detailed clinical enquiry and a period of observation. The majority of such patients were considered by Harper and Roth to suffer from neurotic disturbance. They suggested that only specifically epileptic abnormalities in the EEG should be allowed to decide the issue in favour of epilepsy when the problem could not be resolved by other means.

Schizophrenia and temporal lobe epilepsy may sometimes be confused with one another. Karagulla and Robertson (1955) drew attention to several psychic phenomena which may be seen both in schizophrenia and in the auras of temporal lobe epilepsy—the evocation of thoughts, either indefinite or formulated and including thoughts which entered the mind unbidden, the hearing of voices both within and without the head, and visual hallucinations. To these may be added thought block, perceptual distortions of space, time and the body image, sudden experiences of unreality and perplexity, and the autochthonous welling up of emotions such as dread, anxiety and ecstasy.

It may therefore happen, when grand mal is absent or infrequent, that such auras will be interpreted as evidence of schizophrenia. Special difficulties are likely to be encountered in patients with markedly schizoid personalities who experience complex auras including hallucinations and thought disorders (Pond, 1957). The clue will usually lie in the episodic nature of attacks in temporal lobe epilepsy, and in the evidence of impairment of consciousness at the time. Epileptic hallucinations are typically fleeting, and sometimes tantalisingly difficult if not impossible to recall. Those of schizophrenia are usually longer-lasting, can be described in more detail, and are less stereotyped and restricted in content. Schizophrenic disorders of thought and affect also persist in between such episodes. Post-ictal confusion may similarly be mistaken for schizophrenia when hallucinations and paranoid ideas are prominent.

Conversely epilepsy may be suspected in patients with typical schizophrenic illnesses who are discovered to have temporal lobe spiking on the EEG (Treffert, 1963), or when a grand mal convulsion is precipitated in a schizophrenic patient on phenothiazine medication. Catatonic schizophrenics are especially liable to show epileptic phenomena during relapses, either in the EEG or in the form of myoclonic jerks or grand mal convulsions. When such illnesses have been of relatively short duration it may be questioned whether the psychotic episode has been in fact a prolonged psychomotor attack or 'twilight state'. Usually the dullness and retardation of the epileptic twilight state is distinctive, and the hallucinations are more massive, complex and chiefly in the visual sphere. Short recurrences of abnormal experience are also usual in twilight states, with intervening lucid periods during which no gross abnormality or loss of affect can be detected (Slater and Roth, 1969).

Episodic visual hallucinations may occasionally raise the suspicion of an epileptic disorder, for example in the so-called 'Charles Bonnet syndrome' of the elderly. Here extremely vivid and well-formed visual hallucinations occur with great profusion, sometimes episodically and compellingly. Typically they are experienced in clear consciousness, and insight is either retained or very quickly attained into the unreal nature of the phenomena. In these respects the similarity to formed visual hallucinations of epileptic auras can sometimes be striking.

The Charles Bonnet syndrome is reviewed by Damas-Mora *et al.* (1982) and Berrios and Brook (1982). It appears to represent a heterogeneous collection of patients and the usefulness of the eponym is doubtful. Defining characteristics have included the occurrence of visual hallucinations in the elderly, the preservation of intellectual competence, the absence of impairment of consciousness and the preservation of insight. Peripheral ocular pathology may be present or absent. The quality of the hallucinations is commonly vivid, elaborate and well organised, persisting for seconds or hours at a time. The scenes may change continously, and richness of themes is the rule—trees, flowers, buildings or persons appear in considerable array. The patient sometimes greets such phenomena with surprise, curiosity or delight. They may disappear or persist when the eyes are closed. The cause is unknown and other psychiatric disorder is commonly absent.

Finally epileptic disturbances may sometimes be diagnosed as *acute organic reactions due to some other cause*. On rare occasions ictal twilight states or postictal disturbances can last for a week or more, and a history of epilepsy may not be forthcoming. The abruptness of onset of the condition is usually the feature which suggests an epileptic basis. Petit mal status may similarly be misleading until the highly characteristic disturbance in the EEG is discovered.

Differential Diagnosis of Automatisms

Epileptic automatisms can raise special diagnostic problems, particularly when, as is commonly the case, they are unaccompanied by a grand mal convulsion. In the majority of cases the diagnosis rests primarily on clinical assessment of the pattern of behaviour manifest during attacks, so eye-witness accounts should be obtained whenever possible. Particular enquiry should be made about the occurrence of other types of epileptic seizure, either in the past or present. Where the possibility of hysteria has arisen it is essential to be conversant with the patient's current life situation, personality and previous history, and to corroborate this from someone who knows him well. In working towards the correct diagnosis full medical evaluation will usually be required, together with careful EEG and other investigations.

Possible misdiagnoses in this area are discussed by Fenton (1972). The episode may be attributed to *intoxication with alcohol or drugs*. Or the subsequent amnesia may be attributed to *hysteria* or *simulation*, especially when the personality is abnormal or antisocial behaviour has occurred. In the converse direction epileptic automatism may be diagnosed in mistake for attacks of *hypoglycaemia,* due to an islet cell tumour or overdosage with insulin in diabetic subjects. Clouding of consciousness due to other conditions such as *encephalitis* or *cerebral ischaemia* may need to be excluded. Automatic behaviour can occasionally occur with cerebral degenerative conditions such as *Alzheimer's disease.* However episodes of confusion due to toxic, metabolic, infective or structural causes are usually more prolonged, lasting days or weeks, and are not necessarily recurrent events.

Very occasionally the posturing and stereotyped movements seen in brief episodes of *catatonic schizophrenia* may be mistaken for epileptic automatisms. Episodes of *transient global amnesia* (p. 357) can resemble automatisms in being of sudden onset, lasting a few minutes then recovering spontaneously, and in sometimes being recurrent. However the patient's 'confusion' is restricted to difficulties with memory—during the amnesic episode he usually acts quite normally, movements are perfectly coordinated, and he responds to questions appropriately apart from his obvious memory defects. There is no clouding of consciousness and the personality remains intact.

Ictal automatisms confined to sleep may be confused with *somnambulism* (p. 631). However sleep-walking episodes are usually of longer duration, the behaviour is better integrated, and the sleep walker may mumble or answer monosyllabically if spoken to. During epileptic automatisms the patient is completely inaccessible, and stereotyped automatic behaviour is more likely to be prominent. Pedley and Guilleminault (1977) have described an interesting group of 6 patients who presented with unusual sleep-walking episodes but in whom the balance of evidence favoured an atypical form of epilepsy. Attacks commonly occurred in the early morning hours, were characterised by screaming, unintelligible vocalisations and complex automatisms, and in several the EEGs showed epileptiform abnormalities. Treatment with phenytoin or carbamazepine led to cessation of the abnormal behaviour. A striking example was as follows:

A previously healthy 18-year-old man began having episodes lasting 2–10 minutes between 2 and 6 a.m. He would jump suddenly from the bed, climb onto a chair, and begin leaping from one piece of furniture to another. The movements were violent, and occasionally punctuated by screaming or hitting his head against the wall. Each episode characteristically ended by his diving onto the bed where he would grab semi-purposefully at his sleeping partner then fall deeply asleep. If awakened a few minutes later he was amnesic for what had transpired. During the episode he was unresponsive to questions, admonitions or stimuli. At other times he would sit up, shout, then stare for 30–40 seconds before falling back asleep; or mumble incoherently and appear frightened. Initially attacks occurred once every 6 months, but 2 years later they were happening five nights out of seven. An active epileptic focus was present in the right temporal region, and phenytoin abolished the disorder within 2 weeks.

(Pedley and Guilleminault, 1977)

Hysterical dissociation with amnesia is a particularly common source of uncertainty. This, however, usually occurs at a time of crisis in the patient's life, and the behaviour will often be purposeful and directed at removing him from a situation of stress. The features typical of hysterical amnesia (p. 31) may be evident when the patient presents for attention. Moreover the amnesic gap may last for hours, days or weeks, in contrast to the brief duration of most automatisms. The behaviour displayed during the episode itself will usually reveal little firm evidence of loss of awareness of the environment.

Longer-lasting epileptic fugue states, in which the patient wanders away, may raise similar problems of diagnosis. An hysterical basis is strongly suggested in fugues which have lasted for several days or more, when there is no clear history of conventional epileptic attacks, and when the patient has been observed during the course of the episode to show well-integrated behaviour. At the end of the fugue the hysterical patient is usually well preserved—has eaten and cared for himself quite normally—whereas in the case suggesting epilepsy he is often dirty, dishevelled and neglected. In hysterical fugues, personal emotional factors will usually be found to be operative. Sometimes the patient may return to some place which has special meaning for him, as in the example described on p. 360, whereas in epileptic fugues he will have wandered quite aimlessly.

Stengel (1941, 1943a), however, emphasised the areas of overlap which occur between fugue states of hysterical and epileptic origin, and concluded that there was little fundamental difference between them. His survey also showed the importance of a depressive component in the great majority of fugues, whether or not epileptic tendencies were present. Often a suicidal impulse appeared to have been transformed into an impulse to wander. Clearly the possibility of an affective disorder needs to be carefully borne in mind in the management of such patients.

Simulation rather than hysterical dissociation may sometimes be suspected. Amnesia may occasionally be feigned by the patient to protect himself from the legal consequences of an act, or in attempts to maintain self-esteem. Detailed investigation of the circumstances surrounding the behaviour concerned will usually reveal discrepancies and inconsistencies in the patient's story. The criteria which may usefully be applied in assessing whether or not an epileptic automatism was likely to be in progress when a crime was committed are discussed on p. 241.

Aggressive outbursts in patients with unstable personalities can raise the possibility of epileptic automatism, especially when the disturbed behaviour is of an impulsive and paroxysmal nature. The distinction can on occasion be difficult; a high proportion of patients with aggressive personality disorders show temporal lobe abnormalities on the EEG, and problems in the control of aggression are found in a number of patients with epilepsy. Yet the distinction has important implications for treatment, and can be crucial in medico-legal proceedings.

Clinical assessment of the details of the attacks is of first importance. Epileptic automatisms usually begin abruptly, whereas in simple outbursts of aggression there is often a gradual build-up of anger and tension before the peak of disturbance is reached. Automatisms also usually end abruptly, with spontaneous resumption of the patient's normal personality. The abnormal behaviour during automatisms is typically purposeless and unmotivated, whereas aggression is directed against specific targets in most outbursts of anger. Motor coordination in automatism will often be faulty, and the patient's expression may clearly reveal that consciousness is clouded. Subsequent amnesia cannot, however, always be taken as firm evidence of epilepsy, since memory can be blurred during phases of intense emotion, and an element of dissociation may have occurred at the peak of an outburst of anger.

The circumstances in which attacks occur must be taken into account— outbursts which are *regularly* precipitated by external circumstances are most unlikely to represent epileptic automatisms. Careful enquiry into the patient's life situation may reveal specific stresses which dictate his behaviour. Sometimes the aggressive tendencies will have extended far back into childhood or adolescence, but occasionally they will have appeared only recently in relation to definable marital or other difficulties. In some patients the personality may prove to be inhibited rather than habitually aggressive, with difficulty in the expression of feelings until a threshold of provocation or frustration has been exceeded.

The existence of specific epileptic abnormalities in the EEG, and the appearance of epileptic fits in intimate relationship to outbursts, will of course bias the diagnosis towards epilepsy. In recurrent cases, where the diagnosis remains in doubt, a trial of anticonvulsant medication is usually indicated and may help to resolve the dilemma.

In occasional cases, however, assessment of all the available information will leave one undecided whether organic or psychogenic factors are mainly to be blamed. This is well illustrated by the *syndrome of episodic dyscontrol* (p. 74) which has been elaborated in recent years (Mark and Ervin, 1970; Bachy-Rita *et al.*, 1971; Maletzky, 1973). The term is used for patients characterised by uncontrollable storms of aggression, sometimes on minimal or no provocation and sometimes associated with phenomena of a quasi-epileptic nature.

Maletzky (1973) in a study of 22 such patients has suggested that 'episodic dyscontrol' may represent a fairly distinct clinical entity. Patients were excluded from consideration if their outbursts had occurred in the context of pathological intoxication, acute drug reactions, or schizophrenia, or if they showed evidence of undoubted temporal lobe epilepsy. All were men in their 20s or 30s from the lower socio-economic groups, and with a history of episodes of violence increasing in frequency and severity from adolescence onwards. Sometimes isolated episodes could be traced back to childhood. Two-thirds had seriously injured their victims at some time or another, and five had committed homicide. The outbursts were usually provoked but the stimuli were typically minimal. The frequency varied from one episode per day to several per year, the average being one per week. In most cases the anger had habitually been directed against a close family member. There was a high incidence of a history of violence among the male relatives of patients, and also of epilepsy. The patients' personal situations were mostly chaotic, with frequent histories of divorce, arrest and repeated dismissal from work.

Attacks were similar to epilepsy in a number of ways. There were often auras preceding attacks in the form of hyperacusis, visual illusions, numbness of the extremities or nausea. Headache and drowsiness often followed the outbursts. More than half of the patients had episodes of altered consciousness without associated aggression, usually in the form of brief staring spells. Some claimed amnesia for the attacks or even for a period just preceding them. Extreme remorse was prominent, and the majority viewed the episodes as foreign and distasteful. Many showed mild recent memory impairments, or 'soft' neurological signs in the form of minor ataxia, incoordination or some degree of left-right uncertainty. Fourteen had abnormal EEGs, six with temporal lobe spiking and the remainder with non-specific abnormalities which, however, always involved the temporal lobe.

Liability to attacks was notably worsened by alcohol and sometimes also by attempts at treatment with chlordiazepoxide. In an uncontrolled trial phenytoin was found to have a markedly beneficial effect—19 of the 22 patients achieved a good response, with approximately 75% reduction in the frequency and severity of attacks. Usually this was evident within the first two weeks of treatment. Other reports have indicated possible benefit from lithium (Sheard, 1971; Tupin et al., 1973) or propanolol (Williams et al., 1982).

In such patients it can clearly be difficult to decide how far epileptic or non-epileptic factors are operative. Maletzky suggests that it is reasonable to assume that in the majority there are functional abnormalities of the limbic (or amygdaloid) regions of the brain. Such abnormalities may set the threshold for episodes of uncontrollable anger at an unusually low level. Nevertheless the problem appears to become less disabling with age, since it is rare to encounter similar examples in older patients.

The Treatment of Epilepsy

The management of patients with epilepsy requires appropriate investigation as already discussed, with diagnosis of type of attack and definition of the cause as far as possible. Anticonvulsant drugs then form the mainstay of treatment and are accordingly given pride of place below. Drug treatment, however, is but one part of the care required by the majority of epileptics—psychological and social aspects warrant attention to some degree in virtually every patient who is subject to recurring attacks. In those who come before the psychiatrist these aspects can be of overriding importance, and are often decisive in determining the level of overall success achieved.

ANTICONVULSANT DRUGS

Many drugs are available, some of which have stood the test of time. Other more recent acquisitions can prove efficacious but may have serious side effects which limit their usefulness. The field is large and has been the subject of several reviews (Reynolds, 1978a, 1981; Richens, 1982; Fenton, 1983). Reynolds (1982) outlines the special considerations which may govern the drugs of choice in patients with psychological disorder.

Whenever possible drugs should be used singly or at most in small-sized combinations. The temptation to add several drugs in sequence must be resisted; unfavourable interactions can lead to disturbances in drug metabolism, either increasing the serum concentrations to toxic levels or lowering them so that seizure control is impaired The feasibility of monotherapy for a high proportion of patients, and the benefits which result when polypharmacy is carefully rationalised to one or two drugs, have been amply demonstrated (Shorvon and Reynolds, 1979; Reynolds and Shorvon, 1982). A start should be made with drugs which are well established for the type of epilepsy in question, and in general once started a drug should not be discarded until it has been increased to tolerance.

Nevertheless several drugs may need to be tried in rotation in difficult cases. Sometimes the administration of two or even three together will be indicated in order to obtain their additive effects, but this must only be tried when the first drugs have been used to full efficiency. The various classes of drugs are known to act by different mechanisms— probably none have a significant effect in suppressing the focus itself, but some appear to block the spread of the seizure discharge by suppressing post-tetanic potentiation, and others may modify the levels of neurotransmitters or affect ionic transport within the brain (Calne, 1973; Reynolds, 1978b).

The aim is complete abolition of seizures, but this must not be at the expense of side effects which handicap the patient. It is better to tolerate occasional fits than to leave the patient permanently drowsy or muddled. Sometimes complete control may lead to severe disturbances of mood, with recurring tension states or even the appearance of epileptic psychoses. Thus drug treatment is a highly individual matter which needs to be carefully adjusted to the patient's particular needs and responses.

The monitoring of therapy by estimation of blood levels has shown its value, since the relationship between the dose ingested and the plasma levels obtained can vary considerably from one patient to another. With some drugs, moreover, the difference between therapeutic and toxic levels is narrow, and when several drugs are used together there can be complex interactions (Richens, 1982). Serum monitoring is of especial importance in any patient whose seizures are poorly controlled, when toxic reactions are suspected, during pregnancy, or in the presence of hepatic or renal disease which can markedly affect blood levels. Ranges can now be defined within which most patients will be expected to obtain substantial benefit, and above which toxic effects are likely to be encountered: phenytoin 10–20 μ/ml (40–80 μmol/l); phenobarbitone 15–40 μg/ml (65–170 μmol/l); carbamazepine 4–10 μg/ml (17–42 μmol/l); sodium valproate 50–100 μg/ml (350–700 μmol/l); ethosuximide 40–100 μg/ml (285–700 μmol/l). Primidone is monitored in terms of its major metabolite, phenobarbitone. These ranges may not be required by all patients, but they should always be achieved on a single drug before contemplating the addition of a second.

When difficulties of control arise it will often be necessary to look beyond the details of medication. Before automatically increasing the dose one must be alert to psychological conflicts or emotional disturbances which may have temporarily aggravated the situation and which obviously require first attention. It is also important to bear in mind that deteriorating seizure control may sometimes indicate the need for reduction rather than increase of medication, since toxic levels, particularly of phenytoin or phenobarbitone, can increase seizures.

The indications for stopping therapy are 3 years of freedom from attacks on treatment (Fenton, 1983). Even then the presence of marked epileptiform activity on the EEG may make relapse so likely that withdrawal is contraindicated. Cessation will also be deferred if having a seizure stands to imperil the patient's well-being, for example if loss of a driving licence on account of a fit will threaten the patient's livelihood.

Special problems arise with pregnancy in that almost all surveys show a 2- to 3-fold increase in the incidence of congenital abnormalities among babies born to epileptic women (Current Problems, 1983). Nevertheless withdrawal of anticonvulsants is not generally advisable, since foetal hypoxia during maternal fits may be at least as damaging as the drugs themselves; and the relationship of congenital abnormalities to the drugs has not been firmly proven, nor the chief offender identified. Anticonvulsant medication should be reviewed at the outset of pregnancy and reduced to the simplest effective régime, along with careful serum monitoring. The present consensus of opinion is that carbamazepine may be the safest anticonvulsant in this situation.

Choice of Drugs

The drug of first choice is determined by the type of seizures and EEG findings. Within a given category of epilepsy there is often little to choose in terms of anticonvulsant effect, and liability to side effects will be the important consideration.

Generalised tonic-clonic seizures respond best to phenytoin or carbamazepine, which seem to be largely equivalent in efficacy. Experience increasingly favours the latter on account of its fewer side effects. In resistant cases both may be needed together. If control is not achieved one may need to add sodium valproate, or to resort to phenobarbitone or primidone which are considerably more sedative. There is no good evidence that clonazepam is superior to these well established medications for this type of epilepsy.

Partial seizures tend to respond to the same drugs as generalised grand mal but may need to be taken in higher dosage towards the top of the therapeutic range. Temporal lobe epilepsy can be particularly difficult to control. Carbamazepine is consequently now regarded as the drug of choice for this form of epilepsy, since it can be given in high dosage with less risk of confusion or sedation. It may also have psychotropic properties as discussed below.

For petit mal absences ethosuximide has until recently been the drug of choice, but sodium valproate is probably equally effective. The latter has the advantage of also helping any grand mal seizures which may be present in addition. Atypical absences and myoclonic seizures can be hard to control, and here the newer drugs sodium valproate and clonazepam have proved particularly helpful. Sodium valproate is preferable because clonazepam is often markedly sedative. A combination of the two should be avoided since this can lead to stupor.

Most of these drugs will be given twice per day to ensure stable serum levels, though phenobarbitone, primidone and phenytoin can be given once per day, at night. Sodium valproate may need to be given three times per day on account of its short half life.

While the above represents a consensus of opinion concerning drugs of first choice, individual differences in response exist. Other drugs must therefore be tried when the first gives incomplete control, and sometimes the additional drugs mentioned below will prove their worth.

Carbamazepine (Tegretol) was formerly principally employed in the treatment of trigeminal neuralgia. However it has now established itself as a highly effective anticonvulsant for use with grand mal and partial seizures, though not with petit mal. In general it emerges as equivalent to phenytoin and phenobarbitone in anti-epileptic potency, but may be preferred to these on account of its lack of sedation and side effects. As mentioned above it is now widely regarded as the drug of choice for temporal lobe epilepsy, particularly in the presence of complex symptoms or psychomotor seizures.

Carbamazepine almost certainly has less adverse effects on cognitive functioning than phenobarbitone, phenytoin or primidone. This makes it particularly useful in patients who are already impaired. In both children and adults striking improvements in alertness and personality have been noted on changing to the drug (Bower, 1978; Reynolds, 1982). Thompson *et al.* (1980), in studies on normal volunteers, showed that while phenytoin produced a dose-related impairment in cognitive processes, this was insignificant with carbamazepine. Indeed there was a tendency for the subjects to rate themselves as more active, less tired and less depressed while taking the drug. Dodrill and Troupin (1977) compared epileptic patients on monotherapy with phenytoin or carbamazepine in a cross-over study, and showed fewer errors on tasks requiring attention and problem-solving with the latter.

Several reports have raised the further possibility that carbamazepine may have a positive psychotropic influence in improving mood and behaviour, though it remains uncertain whether this is a primary effect or the result of withdrawal of more sedative medications. Dalby (1971) described the improvements in psychiatric status which could be seen among patients with temporal lobe epilepsy. The most marked effect emerged in patients with phasic psychiatric disturbances, especially phasic depression, though benefit was also observed in patients with emotional instability and 'hysterical elaboration'. These psychotropic effects were largely related to improved control of seizures, but were also attributed to the disappearance of the debilitating side effects caused by previous medication. Sillanpää (1981) reviews other studies in which a psychotropic effect is emphasised. It could be relevant that carbamazepine has a tricyclic structure similar to that of imipramine, and is the only tricyclic anticonvulsant in clinical use.

The starting dose is 100 mg twice daily, increased when necessary up to 1800 mg per day. Serious side effects are rare. If the dose is increased too rapidly the patient may experience drowsiness, nausea and unsteadiness of gait, though these disappear with time. Diplopia and blurring of vision may also occur. A rash develops in some 4 per cent of cases. In chronic use agranulocytosis and aplastic anaemia have very occasionally been encountered.

Phenytoin sodium (Epanutin, Dilantin) vies with carbamazepine as the drug of first choice in grand mal. Some use it first for all forms of seizure other than petit mal. Its highly effective anti-epileptic properties are, however, combined with disadvantages in terms of long-term side effects.

The margin between therapeutic and toxic levels is rather low and the therapeutic level varies from patient to patient. The plasma level is also markedly affected by interaction with other drugs, including phenothiazines and antidepressants. Serum monitoring is therefore especially important when using phenytoin, particularly when control of seizures is poor or if toxic symptoms have appeared. The pharmacokinetics are moreover distinctive in that phenytoin undergoes 'saturable metabolism'. This means that as the dosage increases the plasma levels can rise to a greater degree than would be expected. Increases in dosage should therefore not exceed 25 mg when the therapeutic range is approached.

The chief toxic effects are ataxia, with dysarthria, nystagmus and incoordination. Such symptoms may set in abruptly and to such an extent that a cerebellar lesion is suspected, either early in treatment or after many years on the drug. The syndrome almost invariably subsides rapidly on withdrawal, though the development of permanent cerebellar deficits appears to be a rare possibility (Reynolds, 1975). Diplopia, blurring of vision and headache may occur, or occasionally confusional states. After prolonged use acne and gum hypertrophy are common, and hirsutism may be a distressing side effect in females. The general coarsening of facial features which may ultimately emerge was strikingly demonstrated by Falconer and Davidson (1973) in comparisons of twins. Hypocalcaemia, with rickets or osteomalacia, may develop.

Experience has shown that even in the absence of overt toxic symptoms phenytoin can have subtle effects on concentration, memory and psychomotor performance. This 'subacute encephalopathy' can easily pass unnoticed as a cause of mental deterioration, especially since serum levels are not always elevated beyond the therapeutic range (Reynolds, 1981, 1982). Brain damaged and retarded patients appear to be especially susceptible. Another hazard in psychiatric practice is toxicity from the combination of lithium with phenytoin; serum lithium levels may become unreliable when the drugs are given together.

The dosage of phenytoin is 100 mg twice per day, up to 600 mg per day in adults. A combined tablet containing 50 mg phenobarbitone with 100 mg phenytoin is available ('Garoin'); while combined medications are in general undesirable this may simplify treatment for patients who are unreliable or of limited intelligence.

Phenobarbitone (Gardenal, Luminal) held sway in the treatment of epilepsy for many decades after its introduction in 1912, but has gradually yielded pride of place to the above medications. It has a wide margin of safety, is cheap in relation to other anticonvulsants, and serious side effects other than sedation are rare. Unfortunately, however, it is now apparent that it produces an unacceptable degree of cognitive impairment in many patients.

It is probably equal in anticonvulsant effect to carbamazepine or phenytoin for generalised grand mal, also for focal motor and sensory seizures. It is often less satisfactory in temporal lobe epilepsy, and may indeed aggravate attacks or lead to an increase in aggressive behaviour. Young children can react paradoxically to phenobarbitone, becoming restless, hyperactive and with worsened behaviour.

The chief drawback of phenobarbitone in routine practice is a tendency to produce over-sedation. Occasional patients are particularly sensitive in this respect, developing mental dullness, drowsiness and lethargy. Impotence, blurred vision, headache and muscular incoordination may also be troublesome. Depression can become severe and should be watched for carefully. Phenobarbitone also shares with phenytoin and primidone the liability to disturb folate metabolism, with the possible psychological effects discussed in Chapter 12 (p. 506). *Methyl phenobarbitone* (Prominal) was introduced in attempts to overcome the sedative actions of phenobarbitone but has proved to be less effective as an anticonvulsant.

The dose of phenobarbitone is 30 mg at night, increased usually to no more than 120 mg per day on account of sedation.

Primidone (Mysoline) may be tried when the above drugs have proved ineffective. It is often used in place of phenobarbitone while phenytoin is continued, though it remains uncertain whether this combination is superior. There is little point in using phenobarbitone and primidone together, since the latter is largely metabolised to phenobarbitone in the liver. In the past primidone was regarded as the drug of choice for temporal lobe epilepsy, although there has been no controlled evidence to support this opinion.

The chief side effect is sedation with drowsiness, dizziness and confusion, but this usually soon subsides. Slowing of mental performance may, however, persist. Ataxia and dysarthria may occur, or less commonly nausea, anorexia and skin rashes.

It is important to start primidone gradually, in a dose of 125 mg each night, because of initial intolerance. Up to 1500 mg per day may ultimately be required.

Sulthiame (Ospolot) is of relatively little value as a primary anti-epileptic agent, but can occasionally be useful as an adjunct to other medication in the treatment of generalised grand mal and focal seizures. Its success probably largely depends on inhibiting the metabolism of phenytoin, phenobarbitone or primidone given concurrently, thereby raising their blood levels. It is now less used than formerly.

Sulthiame enjoyed a vogue in the treatment of temporal lobe epilepsy, also for ameliorating disturbed behaviour. Improvements in conduct, social adjustment and emotional stability were occasionally reported, particularly among mentally handicapped epileptics (Liu, 1966), and even among such patients who did not suffer from epilepsy (Moffatt *et al.*, 1970).

Toxic symptoms may appear at high dosage— headache, drowsiness, paraesthesiae, weight loss, and hyperpnoea. Phenytoin intoxication can be induced. It must therefore be used cautiously in relatively low dosage, 200 mg twice per day up to 600 mg per day.

Beclamide (Nydrane), another weak anticonvulsant, may similarly have beneficial effects on the behaviour of mentally handicapped patients. Side effects appear to be uncommon.

Diazepam (Valium) has a potent initial anticonvulsant effect, coupled with low toxicity, which makes it extremely effective in status epilepticus. It has proved less impressive in the treatment of chronic epilepsy, however, because tolerance develops and the anti-convulsant effect declines. Nevertheless it may be given as an adjunct to other anticonvulsants, and here its action as a tranquillising agent may be its principal value. Among hospitalised epileptic patients it has sometimes been shown to have a favourable effect on seizure frequency and to control excitement, hostility and possibly paranoia (Lehmann and Ban, 1968; Goddard and Lokare, 1970).

Clobazam (Frisium), another benzodiazepine, possesses strong anticonvulsant properties, but adaptation to its effects has similarly been found. Dellaportas *et al.* (1984), however, have reported sustained benefit in a group of patients with poorly controlled generalised and partial seizures when the drug was added to existing régimes. This was maintained over a 6 month trial period. The chief side effect is tiredness.

Ethosuximide (Zarontin) has been regarded as the drug of first choice in patients with petit mal seizures alone, though sodium valproate now appears to be equally effective. It has a marked and almost specific effect on simple absences accompanied by characteristic 3 per second wave and spike discharges, but is unlikely to be of use in other forms of epilepsy. For the control of complex absences it usually needs to be combined with sodium valproate.

Ethosuximide has few side effects. The chief problems that arise are gastric disturbances and nausea, also dizziness, headache and drowsiness. It may occasionally precipitate a grand mal convulsion but this appears to be rare. In adults brief psychotic episodes have sometimes been reported, with visual and auditory hallucinations, depression, and slight impairment of consciousness (Fischer *et al.*, 1965). The adult dose is 250 mg twice daily, up to 1500 mg per day.

Sodium valproate (Epilim) has proved to be particularly useful in the treatment of petit mal. It has a wide spectrum of action, controlling grand mal in addition, though probably not as effectively as carbamazepine or phenytoin. This, however, commends its use when both petit mal and grand mal occur together. It is of limited value in the treatment of partial seizures.

Sodium valproate is regarded as equal, if not superior to ethosuximide in the treatment of simple absences. Complex absences and myoclonic seizures also stand to be controlled and it is of special value with the latter. The mode of action of sodium valproate appears to be different from that of most other anti-epileptics in that it increases the level of gamma aminobutyric acid (GABA) in the brain.

Side effects are in general slight, though weight gain and drowsiness may occur. The combination of sodium valproate and phenobarbitone is particularly liable to lead to additive sedative effects. Temporary gastrointestinal irritation and nausea can develop at the start. Liver disorder has proved to be a rare complication, and liver function should be monitored during the first few months of therapy and at intervals thereafter. Platelet disturbance is indicated by the appearance of bruising or petechiae. A 'valproate encephalopathy' has occasionally been reported, with profound impairment of cognitive processes leading to semi-stuporose states and dystonic posturing. This is reversible on withdrawal of the drug.

Treatment should be started with 200 mg twice daily, increasing up to 2000–3000 mg per day. In adults the short half-life of sodium valproate may lead to large fluctuations in blood levels, requiring it to be given three times per day.

Clonazepam (Rivotril), a benzodiazepine, was initially reported to be successful against a wide variety of seizures (Lund and Trolle, 1973; Mikkelsen and Birket-Smith, 1973). However its chief value has proved to lie with myoclonic seizures as an alternative to sodium valproate. The two should not be given together.

The main drawback of clonazepam is its sedative effect in therapeutic doses. A tendency to aggravate behaviour disorder has also been reported. Tolerance gradually develops to the drowsiness induced, but adaptation to the anticonvulsant effect may occur along with this. In children it is usually too sedative for use, but in the myoclonic epilepsies of infancy and adulthood it can be given as a single dose at night. Sometimes this sedative effect is of value with other types of seizure when anxiety levels are high. Clonazepam is also important as an alternative to diazepam for the treatment of status epilepticus *vide infra*.

The dosage in routine treatment is 0.5–1.0 mg, gradually increasing to a maximum of 10 mg per day.

Nitrazepam (Mogadon) can also be of value in the myoclonic epilepsies of infancy, childhood and adolescence, when necessary combined with sodium valproate.

Troxidone (Tridione) was formerly extensively used for petit mal, but its popularity has declined in favour of newer medications. It can aggravate concurrent grand mal seizures and have serious toxic effects on the bone marrow or kidney. Regular blood counts are essential while patients are on treatment. Skin rashes may occur, or photophobia and 'glare' due to the increased time required for adaptation to changes in illumination. The dose is 300 mg twice a day, to a maximum of 1200 mg in adults. The related drug *paramethadione* (Paradione) is rather less toxic than troxidone but also less potent.

Dextroamphetamine sulphate (Dexedrine), 5–10 mg mane, occasionally produces good results in children with petit mal, also in epileptic children who show hyperkinesis or other behaviour disorders. *Acetazolamide* (Diamox) can sometimes produce improvement but its usefulness is limited by the rapid development of tolerance.

Status Epilepticus

Status epilepticus is a grave medical emergency in which speed of control is of the utmost importance.

Cerebral anoxia may lead to permanent physical or mental handicaps, and there is a significant mortality with long-continued attacks.

An adequate airway must be ensured from the outset and oxygen administered where possible. Blood should ideally be withdrawn at an early stage to measure serum anticonvulsant levels, since non-compliance with medication is a common precipitating cause. Intravenous diazepam is regarded as the treatment of choice when veins are readily accessible—5–20 mg injected not more quickly than 5 mg per minute. This should be followed immediately by 250 mg of phenytoin intravenously (at a rate not exceeding 50 mg per minute), or 10 ml of paraldehyde intramuscularly, to prevent recurrence. Although unpleasant, paraldehyde remains an effective drug. When intravenous diazepam is not available the latter drugs may be used alone, or phenobarbitone 200–300 mg intramuscularly. Clonazepam (Rivotril) has also been shown to be extremely effective, sometimes succeeding even when intravenous diazepam has failed (Gastaut *et al.*, 1971; Kruse and Blankenhorn, 1973). The dose is 1 mg by slow intravenous infusion.

If these measures do not suffice an intravenous drip is likely to be required. Diazepam, 100 mg in a litre of normal saline or isotonic dextrose-saline, was formerly recommended, administered at a rate of about 1 mg/minute (Parsonage and Norris, 1967). However when large doses have been infused coma may persist for several days after the status has been controlled. An intravenous infusion of a 0.8% solution of chlormethiazole may be more satisfactory, having the advantage of short duration of action and therefore better moment to moment control (Richens, 1982). Care must be taken to watch for overhydration, respiratory depression or hypotension. If status continues intubation may be necessary, with curarisation, positive pressure respiration, and continuous monitoring of abnormal electrical activity in the EEG. This may very occasionally be required for several days along with the administration of anticonvulsants and chlormethiazole.

When status has been controlled it is important to assess the factors which have led to it. The anticonvulsant régime may need reappraisal, infection may be present, or a progressive cerebral lesion may require investigation.

Petit mal status (p. 222) is a benign self-limiting disorder, but when necessary can usually be abruptly terminated by a small amount of intravenous diazepam.

PSYCHOLOGICAL AND SOCIAL ASPECTS OF MANAGEMENT

As already emphasised drug treatment is rarely the sole aspect of management that needs to be considered. A liability to seizures, at unpredictable intervals and often with serious or embarrassing consequences, is bound to be a deeply unsettling disability. Social repercussions may add profoundly to the patient's difficulties of adjustment, particularly in the fields of education, employment and personal relationships. Time must therefore be devoted to understanding the patient and his current situation in some detail if he is to receive the optimum help with his handicap.

Ongoing surveillance will always be required, with periodic reviews even when things are going well. Much can be achieved by sympathetic and concerned support over long periods of time, with discussion of difficulties as they arise. The doctor-patient relationship is of particular importance and must sometimes be fostered with more than the average degree of skill. Some patients seek to ignore their epilepsy and are careless about medication; others become markedly frustrated by the problems they encounter, develop paranoid attitudes, or seek fresh consultations and frequent changes of doctor. Thus a good deal of tolerance and understanding may be required if continuity of care is to be achieved. Patients who are handicapped by low intelligence or difficulties of personality will pose special problems in this regard, and will, of course, be particularly common among those who come before the psychiatrist.

The nature of the disorder should be explained frankly and realistically to the patient and his relatives. Any necessary limitation of activites must be discussed, and the need for regular medication emphasised. Where the patient appears to be unreliable, medication may need to be entrusted to a parent or spouse. Exploration of attitudes to the disorder will often prove helpful, particularly in correcting misconceptions and prejudices which can otherwise become deeply ingrained. Young patients must be helped to regard themselves in as normal a light as possible. Parents should be encouraged to allow every possible freedom, to use normal discipline, and to integrate the child into ordinary family life if social and emotional growth is to be fostered.

Beyond this, psychotherapy at any intensive level is rarely indicated. It may indeed be harmful, with aggravation of seizures if too much anxiety is engendered. The occasional patient, however, will repay a more detailed approach, particularly when passing through vulnerable periods of development such as adolescence, or when special emotional or interpersonal difficulties need to be resolved. Claims have occasionally been made for the efficacy of analytically oriented psychotherapy as a direct aid to the alleviation of seizures, by revealing their dynamic origin and symbolic significance (Sperling, 1953), but here the credentials of psychotherapy are not impressive.

Obviously some restrictions on the patient's life will be necessary as long as a liability to seizures persists. Those that are indicated are dictated largely by commonsense. Climbing or cycling should be forbidden in children. Swimming should be undertaken only in company. Other athletic pursuits are usually to be encouraged. With regard to employment the patient must not be in a position to injure himself or others if a seizure should occur. Thus working at heights or in proximity to fire will be unsuitable, likewise driving or work involving dangerous machinery. Certain professional activities are best avoided if it is considered that even an occasional attack could have seriously adverse consequences.

With regard to driving, a person who has had epileptic seizures will not be issued with a driving licence unless the licensing authority is satisfied that he is unlikely to be a source of danger to the public. New regulations came into force in the United Kingdom in 1970 which allow a more fair and realistic approach than formerly. Before the issue of a licence the patient must have been free from any epileptic attacks in the daytime or in waking hours for a minimum of three years. No mention is made in the regulations of whether or not he is taking anticonvulsants, and there is thus no incentive to try going without medication in order to qualify more surely for a licence. In effect these newer regulations recognise the existence of the fully controlled epileptic, and of the epileptic who consistently has attacks only while sleeping. It is important, of course, that if medication is subsequently withdrawn the patient should cease to drive for a period of at least twelve months, during which it can be ensured that seizures remain in abeyance.

Fitness for marriage or procreation are among the more emotionally loaded social problems which the epileptic must face. If advice is requested this can only be given on an individual basis. Psychological fitness for marriage or parenthood will often be a more important deciding factor than the occasional fit that occurs, yet the latter may have weighed unduly in the patient's mind. Qualities in the spouse will need to be considered, and the degree of the patient's disablement in economic terms. The advice which can be offered on the question of heredity is discussed on p. 215.

Valuable assistance can be given in the epileptic clinic by a social worker experienced in the problems encountered by epileptics. Most patients tend to be confronted with difficulties in making an adequate social adjustment, and must face considerable rejection from time to time. Counselling of relatives can often usefully be extended to school teachers, employers and wardens of hostels. The patient may be put in touch with fellow sufferers through branches of the British Epilepsy Association, which also provide advice and information on a wide range of social and employment problems.

A hard core of patients will require very considerable help on account of refractory epilepsy, personality difficulties and severe social problems. A multidisciplinary team can then be essential for proper guidance, with collaboration among physicians, social workers, occupational therapists, nurses and employment officers. Dennerll (1970), Barnes and Krasnoff (1973) and Rodin (1982) discuss the principles of rehabilitation involved. A period away from home will often help where deteriorating family relationships are concerned, and a stay in hospital or a rehabilitation centre can provide new support by way of a disciplined yet sympathetic environment. Employment problems typically loom large in such patients, and a comprehensive evaluation may be required of the patient's assets and liabilities, motivation for work, and social competence in interpersonal relationships. Fortunately it is only a small minority of patients who defeat all efforts at rehabilitation and prove ultimately to require long-term institutional care.

OTHER ASPECTS OF TREATMENT

Certain relatively simple matters deserve attention, particularly in patients who have shown a disappointing response to medication. Daily life should be as well ordered as possible, with regular sleep, regular meals, and the avoidance of sudden changes in routine. Prolonged physical exertion should be discouraged, also sudden excitement or situations predisposing to tension or emotional stress. Alcohol intake should be strictly controlled. Careful consideration of factors such as these may indicate why seizures have occurred on some occasions but not on others. Sometimes highly specific precipitants will be discovered as already discussed (p. 216).

Conditioning and Deconditioning

A rather neglected aspect of treatment concerns the conditioned inhibition or arrest of seizures. This may occasionally prove possible as in the interesting example reported by Efron (1957):

The patient had a complex aura to her seizures, beginning with depersonalisation then leading on to forced thinking, olfactory hallucinations, auditory hallucinations and adversive head movements preceding the grand mal climax. The march of the aura, and thereby the grand mal convulsion, was found to be averted by the application of a strong unpleasant odour at a sufficiently early point in the development of the aura. This was assumed to be due to the activation of a widespread inhibitory system by the unpleasant olfactory stimulus. Later it was shown that repeated couplings of the odour with a visual stimulus (a silver bracelet) allowed the latter alone to become effective in terminating attacks. By looking at the bracelet the patient could inhibit impending attacks. In other words it had become a conditioned stimulus. Later, merely thinking intensely about the bracelet could arrest the seizures without the necessity of looking at it—a second order conditioning situation had been achieved.

Systematic deconditioning may also be effective when a specific precipitating situation can be identified. Forster and colleagues reported success with a number of types of sensory-evoked seizures (Forster et al., 1965; Forster, 1969). In patients with photosensitive seizures repeated stroboscopic stimulation was employed, at first in a brightly lit room so that the stroboscope was barely perceptible, then gradually proceeding to stimulation in darkness. Or a start could be made with monocular presentations, or presentations outside the flash frequency to which the patient was sensitive. Pattern-provoked epilepsies were deconditioned by starting with presentations in dim light or out of focus, then gradually moving to clear presentation of the noxious patterns. Somatosensory seizures were treated by tapping outside the sensitive area of the body then moving into it; or starting with very light taps and gradually increasing their intensity. In startle epilepsies the provoking stimulus was delivered with gradually increasing intensity, starting well below the level which evoked a seizure.

An interesting example of deconditioning to musicogenic epilepsy involved a patient in whom psychomotor attacks were provoked by a particular piece of music when presented in an orchestrated version but not when rendered on the piano or organ (Forster et al., 1965). The availability of many commercial variants allowed decon-

ditioning to be achieved by proceeding carefully along a gradient from innocuous to noxious forms of the music; generalisation was ultimately achieved, extending to other noxious music not directly implicated in the deconditioning process. In other cases a simpler method was employed, utilising the refractory period after a seizure—the music was continuously replayed during the ictal and post-ictal period until it lost its ability to provoke dysrhythmia.

Adams (1976) provides a useful review of other methods employed to decondition patients to special precipitants in reflex epilepsy. In startle epilepsy to sound, for example, ambient background noise can be progressively decreased while the patient is trained to relax. For reading-induced seizures the patient may be trained in competing responses, such as tapping the knee whenever selected letters occur in the text. With all such deconditioning procedures the beneficial outcome often tends to be temporary, and reinforcement may be necessary on a day-to-day basis. Sometimes a 'second signal system' can be elaborated, for instance by coupling auditory clicks with flashes of light during the process of deconditioning photosensitive patients, thereby enabling the clicks to acquire protective properties.

Powell (1981) discusses the range of psychological manoeuvres which may warrant a trial even in patients whose seizures do not have an obvious external precipitant. Sometimes it may be possible to identify emotional triggers to the fits, and desensitise the patient to these by frequent rehearsal or systematic desensitisation; or to train the patient in relaxation while he imagines situations in which fits are likely to occur. Operant management techniques may involve the withdrawal of positive reinforcement, by ignoring seizures or shifting attention away from them, coupled even with noxious stimulation immediately after a fit. Positive reinforcement for non-seizure periods can be conducted by way of a token régime, as employed by Lavender (1981) in children in a residential hospital school. The patients were first helped to develop methods for interrupting their seizures, then rewarded systematically to motivate their use. Success from such methods will obviously stand to be greater in patients with self-induced seizures or hysterical seizures.

A controversial area, of still unproved value, concerns biofeedback training to augment specific EEG rhythms. This is based on the premise that epileptiform discharges are incompatible with certain frequency bands in the EEG. The studies carried out with such methods are reviewed by Fischer-Williams et al. (1981), Fenwick (1981a) and

Kogeorgos and Scott (1981). It has proved possible, for example, to train patients to enhance their occipital alpha rhythm, to suppress low frequency activity in the neighbourhood of a focus, or to augment low voltage fast activity. Training in the augmentation of the 12–14 Hz 'sensorimotor rhythm' (SMR) has attracted considerable interest. Reports of success have not, however, been uniformly upheld, and powerful placebo effects are often likely to be at work. The biofeedback setting is conducive to relaxation which may be beneficial in itself. Further careful studies may be expected to define the true value of such approaches.

Treatment of Psychiatric Complications

Where patients show the various complications of epilepsy already outlined, every effort must be made in the first place to reduce seizures to a minimum. There will often be a corresponding improvement in personality disorder, emotional instability or intellectual deterioration. Unfortunately, however, this is not always so. Some patients may show an antithetical relationship between frequency of seizures and mental disturbance; moodiness and irritability may increase when seizures are few in number and improve when fits occur, or psychotic episodes may make an appearance shortly after seizures are brought under strict control (pp. 236 and 251). In such patients an uneasy compromise may need to be established, in which occasional seizures are tolerated for the sake of improved overall adjustment.

An important step in any patient showing psychiatric disorder is to review the anti-epileptic medication currently being given. Subtle toxic effects may otherwise readily escape detection. The benefits observed when polypharmacy is reduced, and those sometimes strikingly achieved when patients are transferred to carbamazepine, are outlined on pp. 230 and 265.

The management of personality problems proceeds along the lines applicable to personality disorders generally. Supportive psychotherapy and intensive social work help may need to be combined with appropriate psychotropic medication. Phenothiazines and butyrophenones can be a considerable aid in patients who are markedly aggressive or paranoid, but must be used with caution on account of their liability to increase seizures. Anticonvulsant medication may need to be adjusted accordingly. Benzodiazepines may be indicated for tension or apprehension, though care must be taken that irritability and aggression are not worsened coincidentally.

Problems can be encountered in the treatment of depression in that most antidepressants, both tricyclics and monoamine oxidase inhibitors, lower the seizure threshold. Drugs particularly incriminated in this regard include imipramine, amitriptyline and mianserin. Nomifensine is an exception though this has now been withdrawn in the UK on account of toxic effects. In a double-blind comparison Robertson (1985) showed that nomifensine was significantly more effective than amitriptyline in relieving depression in epileptic patients. The same trial demonstrated, however, that response to a placebo was common in the early phases of treatment, so it may be worth withholding antidepressants for a while when the depression is not severe. The rationalisation of polypharmacy can usefully be undertaken in the interim, perhaps with the substitution of carbamazepine for other anticonvulsants.

Medication will play an important part in the management of many epileptic psychoses. For transient psychotic states occurring in close relationship to seizures it may be possible to avoid major tranquillisers, with their risk of aggravating seizures, and to sedate the patient with benzodiazepines or chlormethiazole instead (Trimble, 1981b). Stronger neuroleptics will usually be required, however, for inter-ictal psychoses with schizophrenic or paranoid features. Of the phenothiazines, thioridazine is perhaps the least liable to provoke seizures, and the butyrophenones may be safer still. Pimozide is possibly even safer in this respect. Close monitoring of serum anticonvulsant levels will always be indicated once such treatment is commenced. When dealing with a first episode of psychotic illness, the antipsychotic drugs will warrant withdrawal once the symptoms are controlled and the mental state is stable. Relapse will then indicate the need for maintenance therapy, but the possibilities of spontaneous remission must still be kept in mind—attempts to withdraw medication should in principle be deferred rather than abandoned altogether (Toone, 1981). In addition, chronically disabled patients with a schizophrenia-like psychosis will require management as for schizophrenia generally, with every effort at rehabilitation towards life within the community.

The majority of acute organic psychoses resolve spontaneously, either with or without a convulsion occurring. Prolonged twilight states and post-ictal disorders are best treated conservatively initially, or at least as long as the patient is no danger to himself or others. Hospitalisation will obviously be indicated for long-continued episodes, and nursing observation must be close. Anticonvulsants are rarely effective in terminating such episodes, but treatment as for status epilepticus may occasionally be required if the patient becomes dangerously overactive. Electroconvulsive therapy can bring an abrupt resolution and should not be long withheld if the patient is in danger of becoming exhausted. ECT is said to be particularly effective in episodes accompanied by marked abnormalities of mood or florid delusions and hallucinations (Slater and Roth, 1969). The presence of confusion and clouding of consciousness is no contraindication, provided the epileptic basis of the disorder is well established and other intracranial causes have been excluded.

Here it may be noted that electroconvulsive therapy has very occasionally found a place in the management of epileptic patients who show no psychotic phenomena. It is an old observation that a major convulsion may resolve a phase of mood or behaviour disturbance in epileptic subjects, and a case can sometimes be made for trying the effect of a single induced convulsion in such a situation.

ECT has also been used as a temporary protection against spontaneous fits. Kalinowsky and Kennedy (1943) showed that after ECT the threshold for convulsions was temporarily raised, and in two patients with regularly recurring seizures they were able to avert spontaneous attacks for several months by the judicious use of ECT. With modern anticonvulsant medication, however, there will rarely be occasion to attempt such a therapeutic approach.

Surgical Treatment

Surgery has a restricted but valuable place in the management of epilepsy. Two main approaches have been developed—the excision of damaged cortex responsible for focal seizures, and the interruption of tracts which propagate seizure discharges to other parts of the brain. Unfortunately the number of patients who stand to benefit is relatively small, since few parts of the brain can be resected or transected with impunity. Even then, surgery can usually be considered only in patients whose seizures are seriously disabling and have proved recalcitrant to other measures. Further prerequisites are that there should be either an electrically discrete epileptogenic area or a localised structural lesion as the cause of the epilepsy (Polkey, 1981b).

Within this group, however, the degree of success can be highly gratifying. Williams (1968) estimated that in the best hands, and after proper selection of material, between one-half to two-thirds of patients undergoing surgery would be rendered fit free. These results may of course reflect not only the direct effects of surgery but also, in part at least, the psychological benefit of the intensive rehabilitation which is usually an integral part of the treatment.

The specialised nature of the work means that surgical approaches to epilepsy are restricted to a few special centres. Polkey (1981a, 1982) outlines the different techniques available. Local ablations must embrace not only the obvious focus of seizure discharge (usually after confirmation by electrocorticography), but also sufficient of the surrounding brain tissue to ensure that other potential epileptogenic neurones have been removed. The work of Penfield and his colleagues in Montreal was the classical example in this field as reviewed by Rasmussen (1969). Unilateral temporal lobe excisions are the most common operation, but anterior frontal or cingular excisions are also performed. More rarely occipital lobectomy may be indicated, or in children removal of an entire damaged cerebral hemisphere. Severance of tracts may involve frontal or temporal lobotomy, either unilaterally or bilaterally. Division of the corpus callosum has occasionally been undertaken. Stereotactic procedures have been aimed at a variety of targets—the internal capsule, pallidum, thalamic nuclei, fields of Forel, amygdala, fornix and hypothalamus, sometimes singly and sometimes in combination (Polkey, 1981a).

Temporal lobectomy for the relief of temporal lobe epilepsy has been extensively investigated in England by Murray Falconer and co-workers. Their series of over 200 patients is particularly valuable by virtue of the attention given to psychological and social aspects of outcome in addition to benefits in seizure control. Falconer's operation involves removal of a single block of tissue incorporating the anterior six centimetres or so of the affected temporal lobe, including the medial temporal structures such as the amygdala, the anterior part of the hippocampus, and the uncus (Falconer, 1969).

Patients are selected for the operation only when the epilepsy is drug resistant and disabling, and when evidence points firmly to a focal origin restricted to one temporal lobe. The EEG must show a spike discharging focus consistently within the temporal lobe; preferably it should be strictly unilateral, but if spiking is bilateral operation may be undertaken if it is at least four times greater on the side to be resected. Sphenoidal lead recordings and intravenous barbiturate activation are employed to further refine the evidence of a unilateral focal lesion.

Skull X-ray may help by showing a smaller middle cranial fossa on the affected side, and further radiographic procedures may reveal inequalities in the size of the temporal horns indicative of mesial temporal lobe sclerosis. Psychometric testing often contributes further to the total information. The better the concordance between these various indices of localisation the more readily will surgery be undertaken. An intravenous sodium amytal test by means of the Wada technique (p. 37) is a valuable check on speech laterality, and helps to ensure that the opposite temporal lobe is healthy before the damaged lobe is resected (Milner, 1966). In general, operations are more readily undertaken on the side non-dominant for speech. Polkey (1982) provides a detailed review of current practices in the selection of patients for operation, and of additional evidence derived from the CT scan which can influence the decision.

Clear evidence of multiple independent foci precludes operation, similarly firm evidence of marked cerebral atrophy. The only psychiatric contraindication is mental subnormality (IQ below 70).

The results have been summarised by Falconer (1969) and Falconer and Taylor (1970). Some 40% of patients are rendered completely fit free on 2 to 10 year follow-up. Another 20% have no more than one or two seizures a year, and a further 20% have their seizures reduced by half. Less than 20% remain unimproved. A more recent review of outcome on all published cases in the literature, numbering some 2,000 operations, shows that two-thirds of patients become either free or almost free of seizures (Jensen, 1976); in a smaller group of 831 patients 42% were rendered completely seizure free, and a further 22% had seizures at less than a quarter of the preoperative rate. The operative mortality was 0.5%. Anticonvulsant medication can usually be withdrawn in successful cases.

Where the epilepsy is relieved or lessened social adaptation is often markedly improved, with reduction of behaviour and personality problems (Taylor and Falconer, 1968; Falconer, 1973). It must be emphasised, however, that such disturbances are not the prime reason for operation, and do not stand to improve with surgery if the epilepsy is already well controlled. The particular benefit which may be seen in patients with aggressive personality disorders has already been discussed (p. 237), likewise improvement in psychosexual adjustment (p. 237). Inadequate or hysterical traits are not benefited and may contraindicate operation (Hill, 1958). Patients with

psychotic disorders appear to be variable in response (Serafetinides and Falconer, 1962b; Falconer, 1973). Episodic organic psychoses can be expected to cease when the epilepsy is controlled by operation, though chronic schizophrenia-like psychoses often persist and may even worsen (Polkey, 1982). Depressive psychoses, and those with paranoid symptomatology, show an unpredictable response. Jensen and Larsen (1979a, 1979b) found that surgery had no discernible effect on psychoses that were present preoperatively, and concluded that the presence of such disorder was not useful as a criterion either for or against operation. Of 74 patients followed up 1–10 years later, 11 had had a schizophrenia-like or schizoaffective psychosis before operation and 9 others developed during the follow-up period; in six of these nine cases the operation had been successful in terms of abolishing the seizures.

The mortality and morbidity from unilateral temporal lobectomy are low. Upper quadrantic visual field defects are almost always produced but usually pass unnoticed by the patient. Material-specific memory deficits can usually be displayed on psychometric testing—for verbal material after dominant lobectomy and for non-verbal material after non-dominant lobectomy—but these are rarely sufficiently severe to intrude in daily life. Such deficits may possibly improve with time though this has not been an invariable finding (Blakemore, 1969); certain data indicate that paired associate learning tends gradually to recover in patients after left temporal lobectomy, after a stationary period of three years or so, with the result that verbal memory has returned virtually to the preoperative level by the fifth post-operative year (Blakemore and Falconer, 1967).

Temporal lobotomy is by comparison a relatively minor procedure, involving the division of tracts within the temporal lobe but without removal of tissue. Unlike lobectomy it can be carried out bilaterally without risk of producing a severe amnesic syndrome, when epileptogenic foci implicate both temporal lobes independently. Turner (1969) has reviewed his experience of such operations in patients with bilateral foci, intractable major psychomotor attacks and outbursts of uncontrollable rage. The tissues lying above the anterior parts of both temporal horns, one centimetre from the tip, are severed. Outbursts of rage are said to be uniformly improved, and seizures have been abolished in 65% of cases.

Unilateral lobotomy, if unsuccessful, can be followed by lobectomy, or lobotomy on one side may be safely combined with lobectomy on the other. To some extent the operations can be tailored to the needs of the individual patient. Lesions just behind the uncus in the floor of the temporal horn may need to be added for the complete abolition of minor attacks. Lower quadrant prefrontal lobotomy may be indicated when the medial frontal bases are the seat of epileptogenic discharges and when symptoms of depression or tension are prominent. Turner recommended posterior cingulectomy for patients with severe interictal tension and paranoid outbursts. Various combinations of these operations have occasionally been carried out.

Hemispherectomy involves the removal of all cortex and white matter lateral to the basal ganglia. So radical an operation can only be justified in occasional patients, but has met with strikingly beneficial results in carefully selected cases (Wilson, 1970, 1973). The ideal candidate is a child or young adult with severe infantile hemiplegia, disabling and drug-resistant seizures and unmanageable behaviour disorder; but at the same time he should be educable, of stable domestic background, and with potential for social rehabilitation. There must, of course, be neuroradiological evidence that only one cerebral hemisphere is implicated in the underlying disease process.

Of the patients followed up by Wilson the epilepsy was completely or substantially relieved in 80%, and behaviour disorder in the form of explosive rage, negativism and hyperactivity was abolished or greatly improved in even more. Early surgical morbidity and mortality were low, but over one-third developed serious long-term sequelae due to chronic subdural bleeding leading to obstructive hydrocephalus of the remaining hemisphere. This drastically restricts the readiness with which the operation can be recommended.

Section of the corpus callosum was introduced as a means of preventing the spread of ictal discharges from one hemisphere to the other, and thereby the recruitment of abnormal discharges which culminates in the major seizure (Van Wagenen and Herren, 1940). The operation was revived by Bogen and Vogel (1962) and considerable success was claimed for its efficacy in certain patients. After section of the corpus callosum and other midline commissures, patients are apparently remarkably free from subjective psychological difficulties, despite the fact that appropriate testing procedures show that each hemisphere now processes information largely independently of the other (p. 38–39). The post-operative psychological studies carried out on these patients have clarified our understanding of many aspects of brain organisation and function, particularly with regard to cerebral dominance for language and visuospatial functions (Gazzaniga *et al.*, 1965; Sperry and Gazzaniga, 1967; Bogen, 1969). Some of the neurological and psychiatric implications of the findings have been summarised by Lishman (1969, 1971). It seems unlikely, however, that the operation will come to occupy a permanent place among techniques for the management of epilepsy.

Anterior cerebellar stimulation was introduced by Cooper and associates for the contol of intractable seizures (Cooper, 1973). Chronic in-dwelling electrodes are applied to the anterior part of the upper surface of the cerebellum, and activated by means of an electronic device implanted in the subcutaneous tissues of the chest wall. Preliminary results were encouraging in certain patients whose epilepsy had not responded to orthodox forms of treatment. More recent experience, however, reviewed by Upton (1982), casts doubt upon the efficacy of the procedure. In a double-blind trial Wright *et al.* (1984) found no evidence that reduction in seizures could be attributed to the stimulation, even though many patients felt that they had benefited. At present, therefore, the procedure does not find wide acceptance.

Chapter 8. Intracranial Infections

Intracranial infections rarely have to be considered in the differential diagnosis of psychiatric patients, with the important exception of cerebral syphilis. They are usually the province of the neurologist or the general physician, except when it comes to the management of enduring mental sequelae.

The present chapter will not attempt to be comprehensive, but will draw attention to those aspects of infective processes where psychiatric features can be marked. Cerebral syphilis will be dealt with in some detail, also certain encephalitic illnesses in which diagnostic confusion can arise. More space will be devoted to encephalitis lethargica than its present-day incidence warrants, because of the important lessons which were learned for psychiatry during earlier outbreaks of the disease. Meningitis, cerebral abscess and other nervous system infections will be dealt with very briefly.

Syphilis of the Central Nervous System

Syphilitic infections of the nervous system have shown a tremendous decrease during the present century in England, and particularly since the introduction of penicillin. During 1936–9 there were 1629 deaths registered as due to general paresis or tabes, but by 1966–9 these had fallen to 224 (Wilkinson, 1972). The occasional reports of a seeming increase of general paresis in the late 1950s were probably artefactual, and perhaps attributable to the increasing establishment of psychiatric units in general hospitals.

Primary syphilitic infections had already shown a gradual decline from the time of the first world war onwards. A new peak arose during the second world war but this too subsided rapidly in the years that followed. A recent small increase in primary syphilis in the 1960s has been variously attributed to immigration or to increased promiscuity among the young (Jefferiss, 1962). The important point, however, is that there has been no firm evidence of an increase in late syphilitic manifestations as an aftermath of the peak of new infections in world war two, and adequate treatment in the early stages has

clearly proved to prevent the development of late sequelae (Laird, 1962). Early misgivings that the widespread use of penicillin for treating other conditions would often mask early syphilis also appear to have been unfounded. It was feared that patients harbouring a syphilitic infection might often receive unwitting and inadequate treatment, so that late manifestations would ultimately increase again, but sufficient time has now elapsed to make it seem unlikely that this occurs on any substantial scale. What does seem to have occurred is that partial but incomplete suppression of infection can lead to neurosyphilis appearing later in atypical and attenuated forms with consequent difficulty in diagnosis in many instances. This important problem is discussed on p. 284.

It can still be said that syphilis represents the most important infection of the nervous system which is encountered in psychiatric practice. Paradoxically the success of treatment brings its own particular risks, since as the disease becomes increasingly rare it runs the hazard of being more often overlooked. The psychiatrist must continue to bear it constantly in mind, to check regularly with serological tests, and look carefully for cardinal signs in the pupillary reactions and tendon reflexes. The 'classical presentation' of general paresis is nowadays rare, and syphilis of the central nervous system can present with virtually any form of psychiatric complaint.

Traditionally the effects of syphilis are divided into four stages: the primary stage with the appearance of the local lesion at the site of inoculation; the secondary stage with early generalised lesions, chiefly manifest as a variety of skin rashes which appear within 4–8 weeks; the tertiary stage with the appearance of late destructive lesions such as gummata, gummatous ulcers, glossitis and bone changes; and the quaternary stage of parenchymatous changes in the central nervous system leading to tabes dorsalis and general paresis. These divisions are empirical, and with the exception of the last not easily applied to the spectrum of changes which occur in the central nervous system. Meningovascular syphilis can appear in the secondary or tertiary stages; and even with primary infections the nervous system is sometimes involved without overt signs of disorder ('early asymptomatic neurosyphilis').

Walton (1977) suggests that of every 12 patients with neurosyphilis approximately 5 have general paresis, 4 meningovascular syphilis and 3 tabes dorsalis. General paresis is by far the most important in psychiatric practice. Meningovascular syphilis will also be described because it often presents in a misleading fashion, and tabes dorsalis will be outlined because its distinctive features are sometimes seen in conjunction with general paresis. Other affections which fall principally on the spinal cord—myelitis, cervical pachymeningitis and syphilitic amyotrophy—will not be dealt with here.

EARLY ASYMPTOMATIC NEUROSYPHILIS

This term is used for cases with abnormalities in the cerebrospinal fluid but no symptoms or signs of central nervous system disorder. The cells or protein may be raised, the pressure increased, or the CSF immunological tests give a positive result. Such findings emerge in approximately 10% of cases of primary syphilis and 30% of cases of secondary syphilis when the cerebrospinal fluid is examined routinely (Hahn and Clark, 1946a).

Thus it appears that a meningeal reaction can set in very early in a surprising number of cases and without producing overt disorder. When adequate treatment is given the disturbance dies out within a year or two and proves to have been benign. In some cases the prognosis is favourable even when treatment has been inadequate (Hahn and Clark, 1946b), though in others the changes probably have implications for the later development of quaternary neurosyphilis. It remains uncertain whether tissue immunity is the protective factor, or whether a neurotropic strain of spirochaete is responsible for those cases which progress to general paresis.

Slater and Roth (1969) raise the possibility that so-called 'syphilitic neurasthenia' may depend upon such early invasion of the central nervous system. Sometimes from shortly after infection the patient complains of headache, malaise, vague bodily discomfort and difficulty with concentration, but it is hard to judge how far this reflects organic affection of the brain or merely the psychogenic reaction to the disease and the anxieties aroused by exposure.

ACUTE SYPHILITIC MENINGITIS

In rare cases infection of the nervous system may be overwhelming with the production of an acute meningitis. This usually develops within the first 2 years, and can even accompany the secondary rash within a month or two of the primary infection. The illness is indistinguishable from other forms of acute meningitis until specific tests are performed.

There is a pyrexia of 102–103°F with headache, delirium, neck stiffness and somnolence. Lumbar puncture reveals fluid under pressure, containing upwards of 1000 cells per millilitre of which a considerable proportion may be polymorphs. The WR and similar tests may be negative in the cerebrospinal fluid but are invariably positive in the blood. With prompt treatment there is usually good recovery, though some permanent intellectual impairment may result.

SUB-ACUTE AND CHRONIC MENINGOVASCULAR SYPHILIS

A variety of clinical pictures are subsumed under this heading and are most easily understood in terms of the underlying pathology. The disorders usually declare themselves within 1–5 years of the primary infection, though the range may extend from the first few months to thirty years or more.

Pathology

Changes affect both the meninges and the cerebral vasculature, sometimes with the accent predominantly upon the one or the other. In the meninges there is a diffuse inflammatory process with thickening, areas of necrosis, and the formation of exudate which may become gelatinous and adherent ('gummatous leptomeningitis'). Changes are often most in evidence at the base of the brain, resulting in cranial nerve lesions or hydrocephalus due to obstruction of the flow of cerebrospinal fluid. Less commonly they are localized over the convexity, or extend to envelop the whole of a hemisphere in a thickened sheath. Similar changes may extend along the perivascular channels, with the formation of localised gummata within the brain or in relation to the overlying bones of the skull.

Vascular pathology forms an integral part of the reaction in the meninges but can also involve the cerebral vessels directly. The vessels at the base of the brain are chiefly affected, first the small and then the larger branches of the circle of Willis. There is both a periarteritis and an endarteritis, the latter producing great hypertrophy of the intimal layer and leading to thrombosis. Around affected vessels there is fibroblastic proliferation and necrosis, again sometimes proceeding to scattered gummata. The large isolated gumma leading to tumour-like symptoms is extremely rare.

Clinical Picture

Subacute forms of meningitis may progress rapidly once they are declared, though chronic forms are often insidious and intermittent with periods of several months between exacerbations of disease. Hence the delay which may be encountered in diagnosis.

Early generalised symptoms consist of intermittent headache, lethargy and malaise. The patient is usually slow and forgetful, with difficulty in concentration and faulty judgement. Emotional instability and irritability are common. Mental deterioration may progress to definite evidence of dementia, sometimes with fleeting delusions or episodes of excited overactivity. Alternatively there may be periods of clouding of consciousness or florid delirium separated by intervals of relative normality. Sometimes the patient retains insight into his early intellectual impairments, and may be misdiagnosed as neurotic on account of the anxiety he displays. The vague quality of the complaints, and the fleeting nature of the early disabilities, can lead to the organic nature of the disturbance being overlooked for some considerable time.

The focal evidence of basal meningitis consists chiefly of cranial nerve disturbances. Paresis of external ocular movements and abnormalities of pupil size and reaction are common, but the fully developed Argyll-Robertson pupil (p. 283) is rarely seen. Papilloedema, optic atrophy, and visual field defects from chiasmatic lesions also occur. Hypothalamic involvement may produce polyuria, obesity and somnolence. Convexity meningitis can result in focal fits, aphasia or hemiparesis. Headache is often sharply localised and the overlying skull may be tender.

When vascular pathology is predominant there may be premonitory symptoms of headache, transient paresis or muscle twitching. Minor arterial occlusions lead to recurrent episodes of transient neurological disorder—hemiparesis, hemianopia, aphasia or amnesia—while occlusion of major vessels can result in a massive stroke with enduring disability. The picture of 'pseudobulbar palsy' may develop with bilateral spasticity and striking emotional lability.

The cerebrospinal fluid shows a moderate cellular reaction with up to 200 cells per millilitre, mostly mononuclear leucocytes, and a moderate increase of protein. The pressure is usually normal. Serological tests are usually positive in the blood but may be negative in the cerebrospinal fluid.

With adequate treatment the prognosis is generally good provided extensive cerebral infarction has not occurred. Sometimes the patient is left with fits, hydrocephalus, or permanent intellectual impairment.

TABES DORSALIS

Tabes dorsalis is seen in conjunction with approximately 20% of cases of general paresis. Its highly characteristic signs and symptoms may therefore alert the psychiatrist to the latter disease.

Onset is usually 8–12 years after primary infection, though a range of 3 to 20 years is seen. Males are affected much more frequently than females with a peak age of onset in the fifth decade (Orban, 1957). The essential pathology consists of degeneration of the ascending fibres from the dorsal root ganglia, resulting in atrophy of the dorsal roots and shrinkage and demyelination in the posterior columns of the cord.

Characteristic symptoms include pain, paraesthesiae and a marked disturbance of gait. These usually develop insidiously. The lightning pains of tabes are extraordinarily severe, typically stabbing in nature and sharply localised in the legs. Attacks last only a few seconds at a time. Burning and tearing pains may also occur, or girdle pains of neuritic distribution around the trunk. Paraesthesiae are also most common in the legs and feet; the skin may be hyperaesthetic to touch, or the patient may feel he is walking on cotton wool.

The ataxia is sensory in origin and due to loss of proprioceptive sensibility. The patient walks with a wide base or a typical 'high stepping gait', and finds more difficulty in the dark when visual control is reduced. Romberg's test is positive from an early stage.

'Tabetic crises' are another classical feature, consisting of episodic pain in the viscera. The gastric crisis is most common, with attacks of epigastric pain and vomiting lasting for hours or days. Laryngeal crises consist of dyspnoea, cough and stridor, rectal crises of tenesmus, and vesical crises of pain in the bladder and penis. Other manifestations are impotence and sphincter disturbances.

On examination sensory changes are found earliest in the legs. Loss of postural sense and vibration sense are marked, and compression of the Achilles tendon may fail to produce pain. Other characteristic sites of sensory loss, involving both touch and pain, are the side of the nose, the ulnar aspect of the arms, patchy loss over the trunk and the dorsum of the feet. The musculature is hypotonic and the tendon reflexes diminished or absent. Loss of the ankle jerks is a particularly common finding.

The pupils are abnormal in 90% of cases. Usually they are contracted and irregular, or one may be contracted while the other is dilated. The iris is often pale or atrophic. Reflex contraction to light is often lost while that to accommodation is retained, though the complete Argyll-Robertson pupil (p. 283) tends to be a late development. Ptosis and optic atrophy are frequently seen.

Painless disorganisation of joints may result in gross deformity ('Charcot's joints'), most frequently at the knee or the hip. Perforating ulcers and other trophic skin changes may appear.

The cerebrospinal fluid is usually under increased pressure, with a moderate number of mononuclear cells and a slightly raised protein. The Lange colloidal gold curve is 'luetic' with increased precipitation in the middle zone. The VDRL reaction may be negative in both the blood and the cerebrospinal fluid in 20% of cases, but the treponema immobilisation test is positive in the fluid in 60% and almost invariably positive in the blood (Walton, 1977).

Without treatment the disease is slowly progressive. General paresis may appear after a lapse of many years, or even without this long-standing cases may develop psychotic illnesses of a paranoid or depressive nature (Wilson, 1940).

General Paresis

('Dementia Paralytica', 'General Paralysis of the Insane', 'G.P.I.')

Hare (1959) has traced the fascinating history of this disease. It was first clearly described in the early nineteenth century by physicians working in the mental hospitals of Paris, though there are disputed contenders for rather earlier reports. Certainly it appears to have assumed epidemic proportions in France soon after the Napoleonic wars, and thereafter the spread by venereal infection can be traced along the trade routes of Europe and to the New World. Hare adduces detailed evidence to suggest that general paresis may have arisen as a new disease by mutation of the syphilitic spirochaete. He argues that so striking a disease would be unlikely to have

escaped description earlier. The slow spread of a new mutant would also explain the curious time lapse before its recognition in other countries, even by careful observers who had studied cases earlier in Paris, and the fact that on its first appearance in a new country the ratio of male to female patients was characteristically high then fell gradually to the customary value of 2 or 4 to 1. The more recent decline in the prevalence of the disease, which cannot entirely be attributed to therapeutic intervention, also provides evidence in support of Hare's point of view.

The disease occupies a unique place in several respects in the history of psychiatry. The final proof of its aetiology was an important landmark, likewise the discovery of its response to treatment. A relationship between syphilis and insanity had long been recognised, but there was much controversy before a syphilitic aetiology became accepted for general paresis. Hereditary taint, alcohol consumption, mental strain, and even sexual excess were all championed as causes by various authorities despite the increasing epidemiological evidence that syphilis was responsible. The development of the Wassermann test in 1906 did not end the disputes, which persisted until Noguchi and Moore (1913) finally demonstrated the Treponema pallidum in the brain itself. Thus a clear aetiology was eventually established for a mental disorder which was then extremely common. Some few years later the same disease proved to be the first major mental illness to respond to medical treatment, and ultimately earned the Nobel prize for Wagner-Jauregg in 1927.

PATHOLOGY

General paresis is the only syphilitic disease in which spirochaetes can be demonstrated in the tissues of the brain, and the lesions are thought to be the direct result of their action there.

Macroscopically the dura mater is thickened and opaque, and chronic subdural haemorrhage may contribute to the formation of a thick membrane over the brain ('pachymeningitis haemorrhagica'). The pia mater is firmly adherent to the underlying cortex. The brain itself is small and atrophied with widening of cerebral sulci and dilatation of the ventricles.

Microscopically there are inflammatory lesions throughout the cortex, consisting of dense perivascular collections of lymphocytes and plasma cells and attributable to the irritation produced by the spirochaetes. Equally prominent are degenerative changes, with cortical thinning and outfall of neurones, especially in the frontal and parietal regions. Typically the cortex is so disorganised that the normal laminar cytoarchitecture is no longer recognisable. In the neurones which remain all degrees of degeneration may be seen. Neuroglial proliferation is marked, forming a dense feltwork below the meninges and beneath the ventricular walls, the latter giving a 'frosted' granular appearance to the naked eye. Enlarged microglial cells ('rod cells') are characteristically arranged in rows, and stain with Prussian blue to show iron-containing pigments in their cytoplasm. This reaction is held to be pathognomonic for general paresis.

The spinal cord may show secondary degeneration of the pyramidal tracts, or a combination of paretic and tabetic pathology with degeneration of the posterior columns.

CLINICAL PICTURE

In essence general paresis is a dementing process of insidious onset, but often coloured at first by other features which tend to obscure the intellectual impairment. Changes in affect or personality are frequently the presenting feature, and may be marked in degree before cognitive deficits are declared; alternatively the dementing process may be concealed until some sudden unexpected lapse of conduct brings the true situation abruptly to light. Thereafter the progress of the disorder is marked by certain characteristic features and by neurological disabilities which give the disease its name.

It is usual to describe several forms of general paresis according to salient features in the mental state. This remains useful in serving to underline the varied manifestations of the disease, although as indicated below the frequency of the different varieties appears to have changed considerably during the present century and many atypical forms are seen. Moreover, as described on p. 284, present-day neurosyphilis commonly appears in markedly atypical and attenuated forms.

The disease affects males approximately three times as commonly as females. The peak age of onset is between 30 and 50, but a wide latitude on either side is seen. Congenital general paresis may declare itself in early childhood, and cases are also found in extreme old age. The time from infection is difficult to establish by systematic enquiry, but is usually quoted as from 5 to 25 years with an average of 10 to 15 years.

Presenting Features

In retrospect it is often discovered that the patient has experienced minor ill-defined symptoms such as headache, insomnia and lethargy for several months before more definite manifestations appear. Frequently the relatives report an insidious change of temperament—moodiness, apathy, outbursts of temper, or lessened emotional control with ready tears or laughter. Other common early changes may suggest frontal lobe involvement by way of coarsening of behaviour, egocentricity, and general loss of refinement in the personality. A carefully taken history will often reveal that such disturbances were well in evidence before the first signs of intellectual impairment became overt.

Episodic forgetfulness is usually the first cognitive change, followed by defective concentration, reduction of interests, and mental and physical slowing in the manner typical of a dementing process. Difficulty with calculation is stressed as an early feature, also disturbances of speech and writing. Insight is impaired from an early stage.

In approximately 50% of patients the presentation is abrupt, with some striking incident which first brings the patient to medical attention (Dewhurst, 1969). It is then found that the dementing process has been concealed for some months, or the change of temperament has been attributed to some other cause. Sometimes it is a lapse of social conduct which reveals the true state of affairs—law-breaking, an outburst of violence or an episode of indecent exposure. Foolish, eccentric or reckless behaviour may be the opening sign:

In one case the first whim was the purchase of a quantity of old silver for which payment could not be made; another patient rose in his stall at the theatre and threw sovereigns at a comedienne on the stage; a third ordered 700 hymn books for a hospital ward of 16 beds, and a ton of guano for the ward plants. Another wrote to the War Office demanding three Victoria crosses which he considered he had won in fighting some 10 years before. At the outbreak of hostilities in August 1914, an incipient paralytic sent telegrams to all the crowned heads and rulers, proffering his services as peacemaker.

(Wilson, 1940)

Alternatively some organic feature may be abruptly declared, such as an episode of amnesia, an epileptic fit, or an acute delirious episode. In Dewhurst's (1969) series 5 out of 91 cases presented with attempted suicide.

Increasingly patients now seek medical attention on their own initiative and at an earlier stage of the disorder than formerly (Fröshaug and Ytrehus, 1956). In a considerable proportion, therefore, there may be little in the patient's outward behaviour to indicate the inroads of dementia, and formal evaluation of the cognitive state is more than ever essential if early cases are to be detected (Hahn *et al.*, 1959).

Grandiose or Expansive Form

This was apparently by far the most frequent type of general paresis when the condition was first described, and it has tended to remain the prototype of the disorder in medical teaching. But there is evidence that it had already become less common in Europe during the latter half of the nineteenth century and perhaps somewhat later in England (Hare, 1959). Nowadays it is comparatively rare. In large series of cases from England, America and Norway it has represented only 10, 18 and 7% of cases respectively (Dewhurst, 1969; Hahn *et al.*, 1959; Fröshaug and Ytrehus, 1956). How far the change over time has depended on alterations in the host or in the infecting organism is unknown, but cultural factors almost certainly play some part. In some countries the proportion apparently continues to be high: from India Varma (1952) reported grandiose delusions in 58% of patients, and in Peking Liu (1960) found an expansive or manic picture in 72%. Dewhurst (1969) suggests that grandiose delusions may formerly have been especially frequent in patients from the higher social groups which are now decreasingly represented among Western patients with general paresis.

Florid examples are certainly impressive, which may lead to their being highlighted in reports of the disease. The hallmark is the patient's bombastic and expansive demeanour, with delusions of power, wealth or social position. The patient boasts of fantastic riches, exploits in battle, or tells of his athletic and sexual prowess. He may believe he is some eminent person from the past or present, yet at the same time accepts his stay in hospital without complaint.

The mood is euphoric, good humoured and frequently condescending. Typically the patient enjoys an audience for his display. His recital may be amusing but his jocularity is rarely infectious. Usually the underlying dementia imparts a shallowness and a naïve quality to the prevailing affect. If his beliefs are questioned or his wishes thwarted, the mood may readily turn to petulance or anger.

In some cases there may be extreme irritability with outbursts of violent behaviour, but this is rare.

With arrest of the disease the clinical picture can remain remarkably static over many years. Formerly the delusions tended to die out with progression of the disease, and expansiveness gave way to apathy, lethargy and indifference.

Simple Dementing Form

This appears over time to have gradually replaced the grandiose form and is now a great deal more common. It represented 20% in Dewhurst's series, 60% in Hahn *et al.*'s series and 48% in Fröshaug and Ytrehus' series.

The usual symptoms of generalised dementia are in evidence, with impairment of memory, slowed and laboured thinking and early loss of insight. All intellectual processes become progressively disorganised in the manner outlined on pp. 14 to 16. Progress may be punctuated by transient episodes of impairment of consciousness during which behaviour becomes even more confused. The affect is shallow; a mild and benign euphoria is common, though many patients are dull and apathetic from the start. As with other dementing illnesses the patient may develop fleeting and ill-systematised delusions, mostly of a persecutory nature. Generally, however, such patients are quiet, lethargic and amenable throughout the course of the disease.

Depressive Form

This important variety appears also to have increased considerably at the expense of the grandiose form. It was increasingly reported towards the turn of the century, and emerged as the commonest variety at 27% in Dewhurst's (1969) series.

The patient presents with classical symptoms of a depressive illness. If dementia is already well advanced it may be noted that the affect is somewhat shallow, and that the patient is more readily lifted from his gloom than in primary affective disorders. Sometimes, however, no such distinction can be made. The patient is slowed, silent and suicidally inclined. Delusions are of a typically melancholic kind; nihilistic and hypochondriacal delusions may be grotesque in degree, though again the mood may be noted to be disproportionately shallow.

Taboparetic Form

In perhaps 20% of patients the pictures of general

paresis and tabes dorsalis are combined. Along with dementia the classical tabetic symptoms and signs (p. 279) are observed. The mental symptoms are then often rather mild. True Argyll-Robertson pupils and optic atrophy are seen more commonly in this variety than with general paresis alone.

Other Forms

Other forms of the disorder are much less common. There may occasionally be a picture of true *manic elation* accompanied by flight of ideas, or a presentation with *schizophrenic features* which mask the true diagnosis. Paranoid delusions are then common, together with ideas of influence, passivity phenomena, and auditory hallucinations of an abusing or threatening nature *('paranoid' or 'paraphrenic' form)*. In the *'neurasthenic form'* the outstanding features are weakness, fatigue, irritability and complaints of general ill-health. Presentation with an *acute organic reaction* represents an active and rapidly progressive form of the disease. Very occasionally this follows a fulminating course with fever, fits, and a picture simulating encephalitis. Cases have been reported which for some time preserve the appearance of *Korsakoff's psychosis* (Wilson, 1940). An epileptic or apoplectic presentation occurred in 15% of Fröshaug and Ytrehus' (1956) series. In *Lissauer's type* the patient presents with hemiparesis, aphasia or other evidence of focal brain disease as a result of massive localized brain destruction. The common presentation nowadays, with a markedly attenuated picture, is outlined on p. 284.

Juvenile General Paresis

This has always been extremely rare and is now hardly ever seen. Infection is transmitted via the placenta and the disease is declared in childhood or adolescence. The usual age of onset is between 6 and 21 years. Onset in childhood leads to backwardness at school and results in symptoms of mental deficiency. Epileptic fits are common. Onset in adolescence leads usually to the simple dementing type of general paresis. The same neurological and cerebrospinal fluid abnormalities are seen as in the adult form of the disease.

ABNORMALITIES ON EXAMINATION

By the time attention has been drawn to the illness the patient frequently shows evidence of poor physical health. In the mental state there will usually be evidence of some degree of dementia if proper attention is paid to the assessment of recent memory and other cognitive functions. This may, however, require considerable persistence in the face of facile excuses and evasive behaviour.

A complete neurological examination is essential, since confirmatory signs may be found even in the absence of definite organic features in the mental state. In the very early stages neurological examination may be negative, but in most series this has been so in less than 10 per cent of cases. Pupillary abnormalities, tremor and dysarthria head the list of abnormal findings.

The pupils show abnormalities in about two-thirds of cases, and with progression of the disease this becomes one of the most constant physical abnormalities. A variety of changes is seen—inequality, irregularity and sluggishness of reactions. The full syndrome of the Argyll-Robertson pupil may be present but not so commonly—a small pupil, irregular in outline and with atrophy of the iris, which reacts normally to convergence but not at all to light, and does not dilate fully under the influence of a mydriatic. Optic atrophy may be in evidence even when the patient has no complaint of visual impairment.

Tremor is one of the commonest early signs, occurring in about two-thirds of patients when first seen. It is typically coarse and irregular, involving the face and hands particularly. Close attention may be required to detect it in the lips and the facial musculature around the mouth, often increased when the patient is given difficult tasks of verbal articulation. The facies may be characteristic when the typical tremor is associated with a dull and mask-like expression. Tremor of the hands and fingers contributes to the clumsiness which is seen on manual tasks. The tongue may be involved and show characteristic back and forth jerking movements when protruded.

Dysarthria occurred in 80% of Storm-Mathisen's (1969) cases. It is partly due to the tremor of the lips and tongue. Speech becomes slurred, hesitant, jerky, irregular and ultimately incoherent. Tremor may appear in the voice, which is also feeble and lacking in intonation. Dysphasic difficulties may also be found.

Reflex abnormalities are seen in approximately 50% of cases at the time of presentation. The knee jerks and ankle jerks are usually exaggerated, with clonus and spasticity in the lower limbs. With progression of the disease the plantar responses become extensor, and there is increasing weakness of the limbs leading eventually to severe spastic paralysis. By contrast tendon reflexes may be absent when tabes dorsalis is combined with general paresis.

Ataxia is seen in the clumsy incoordinated movements of the hands, and in the characteristic slouching, unsteady gait. In taboparesis it becomes a marked feature, with Rombergism and the classical high-stepping gait.

Further Progress

In the absence of treatment the dementia increases steadily along with marked physical deterioration. Periods of arrest or even complete remission were occasionally seen, but usually only for a few weeks or months at a time. Incontinence of urine often appears early, at first due to lack of attention. Delusions gradually fade away with the other more florid mental features, and the patient typically becomes quiet, incoherent and apathetic. The characteristic picture in the later stages was of a childish gentle personality, seldom aggressive, and with much of the dementia concealed beneath good-tempered polite behaviour (Storm-Mathisen, 1969). Spastic paralysis and ataxia increased until the patient was enfeebled and confined to bed. Epileptic attacks, both grand mal and psychomotor, occurred in approximately half of cases, and the progression of neurological disabilities was often speeded by the appearance of 'congestive attacks'. These consist of sudden episodes of loss of consciousness, hemiplegia, monoplegia, aphasia or hemianopia, lasting a few days or weeks at a time but eventually leaving enduring deficits in their wake. The mechanism responsible remains uncertain, but a vascular basis is probable.

Before the introduction of malaria therapy, death usually occurred within 4 to 5 years of presentation, many patients dying as a result of inactive confinement to bed, other intercurrent disease, or status epilepticus. The uniformly disastrous prognosis has, of course, been dramatically altered by present methods of treatment as described below.

Atypical Present-day Forms of Neurosyphilis

In addition to the risk of overlooking the disease on account of its rarity, we nowadays face the additional problem that neurosyphilis can occur in atypical or attenuated forms. This may be due in large measure to unwitting partial suppression of the infection in the earlier stages by antibiotics given for other purposes.

Thus while fully developed examples of general paresis and tabes dorsalis have become rare, modified forms of neurosyphilis with atypical presentations and relatively minor symptomatology are increasingly encountered (*British Medical Journal*, 1978). In Hooshmand *et al.*'s (1972) series of 241 patients in the USA, almost half presented with unrelated symptoms, the diagnosis being made by routine investigation after suspicion had been aroused by neurological or ocular findings. In a quarter the presentation was with focal or generalised seizures. Twelve per cent presented with declining vision or other ophthalmological features, and 11% with confusion following a cerebrovascular accident. Only 5% had the full clinical picture of general paresis. Three-quarters, however, showed abnormal neurological signs, particularly absent tendon reflexes at the ankles, loss of posterior column sensation in the legs, or pupillary changes. Uveitis and choroidoretinitis were common. Joyce-Clark and Molteno (1978) report similar experience from South Africa.

In such atypical cases little may appear to be pathognomonic, either in the clinical picture or on cerebrospinal fluid (CSF) examination. Hooshmand *et al.*'s (1972) criteria for the diagnosis of neurosyphilis are therefore important. They recommend a firm diagnosis when the blood FTA-ABS test (see below) is positive and there are ocular or neurological findings suggestive of neurosyphilis; when the FTA-ABS test is positive in both blood and CSF and the CSF contains over five leucocytes per millilitre in the absence of bacterial or viral meningitis; or when the blood and CSF FTA-ABS are positive in the presence of progressive neurological symptoms not otherwise explained. In the last category there must also be either a transient leucocytosis in the CSF after administering penicillin, or the patient must improve clinically on penicillin. A positive FTA-ABS result in the blood and CSF as the sole abnormal finding may not necessarily imply active neurosyphilis, since this can have persisted as a serological finding after adequate antibiotic treatment.

INVESTIGATIONS

Serological tests such as the Wassermann reaction (WR) or Venereal Disease Research Laboratory test (VDRL) are positive in the blood in 90% or more of untreated cases of general paresis, but this figure may be considerably lower if penicillin has been given for some other infection or if a previous course of treatment has been carried out. A false positive WR may be obtained in certain diseases, notably leprosy, disseminated lupus erythematosus, thyroiditis, haemolytic anaemia and some cases of rheumatoid arthritis. The WR may also be positive for a while after some virus infections, after vaccination, during pregnancy, and in an appreciable proportion of drug addicts. The cardiolipin WR uses a purer antigen and gives fewer false positives in these situations. The Kahn test and its modern derivative, the VDRL, parallel the WR in these respects. The Reiter Protein Complement Fixation Test (RPCF) operates on spirochaetal material from non-pathogenic treponemes, and is therefore negative in the above diseases but may be positive in other spirochaetal infections such as yaws.

Positive results from the WR or VDRL, along with a positive RPCF test, means that the possibility of syphilitic infection is high. More certainty will be given in marginal cases by modern procedures such as the TPI, TPHA or FTA. The *Treponema* immobilisation test (TPI) is reasonably specific to *T. pallidum,* but is technically difficult to perform. The *Treponema pallidum* haemagglutination test (TPHA) uses an indirect haemagglutination technique, yielding a high degree of specificity and lending itself to automated methods. The development of the Fluorescent Treponemal Antibody test (FTA) has marked an important advance, particularly in the form of an absorption test (FTA-ABS). This is in general very reliable, though false positives occasionally occur with sera containing antinuclear or rheumatoid factor. The FTA-ABS is fortunately almost invariably positive, both in CSF and blood, in the modified forms of neurosyphilis encountered in present day practice (Oates, 1979).

The possibility of negative results with certain serological tests in the blood means that the CSF must be examined in every case when the presence of general paresis is even remotely suspected. Serological tests are positive in the CSF in almost every untreated case, the pressure is often raised, there is a moderate lymphocytosis of five to fifty cells per millilitre, and the protein is also usually elevated (50–100 mg/ml). The globulin ratio is greatly increased, and Lange's colloidal gold curve typically shows the 'paretic' form with maximum change in the first five tubes (e.g. 5544322110). There is in general little correlation between the initial CSF cell or protein levels and the severity of the clinical picture. A CSF without raised cells or protein may be seen if there has been previous treatment.

The electroencephalogram is abnormal in the great majority of patients, with an excess of theta and slower wave activity.

DIFFERENTIAL DIAGNOSIS

General paresis and other forms of neurosyphilis are so variable in presentation that serological tests should be carried out on the blood in all patients admitted to psychiatric units. In the out-patient clinic there must similarly be a readiness to do such tests. At the very minimum the pupil reactions and tendon reflexes should be examined at every new consultation. However, clinical examination without serology is not always enough to avoid mistakes in diagnosis; this was clearly illustrated by Steel (1960) in cases seen in a psychiatric observation ward and by Joffe *et al.* (1968) in cases seen in a neurological clinic. The present-day frequency of attenuated forms and atypical presentations makes the application of routine serology very much more important.

A history of change of personality, impaired emotional control and intellectual decline will immediately suggest general paresis, and the presence of tremor, dysarthria, pupillary or reflex abnormalities will almost suffice to confirm the diagnosis. But such well established cases are nowadays rare at the time of initial presentation. In Dewhurst's (1969) series only 24 out of 95 cases were diagnosed as neurosyphilis from the outset. The most common initial diagnosis was of a depressive illness (28 patients), and others had been diagnosed as dementia (13 patients), confusional states (8 patients), schizophrenia (6 patients), hypomania (6 patients) and epilepsy (3 patients).

General paresis must obviously be considered in all patients who present with organic impairment of intellect, and no patient should be diagnosed as suffering from a primary senile or presenile dementia until syphilis has been firmly excluded. Among older arteriopathic patients mistakes are particularly likely to be made, since tremor and dysarthria are then not entirely unexpected. Pupillary abnormalities are, however, rarely seen in cerebral arterio-sclerosis or other dementing illnesses.

Affective psychoses appear to have been closely simulated in many of Dewhurst's patients. On occasion the clinical picture may also be typical of schizophrenia, to the extent that the cerebrospinal fluid findings come as a surprise (Fröshaug and Ytrehus, 1956). Where routine serological testing is not possible the principal safeguard must lie in careful and systematic examination of the nervous system, and due attention to any organic mental impairments which emerge.

There is a special risk of overlooking the diagnosis in alcoholic patients. Emotional instability or expansiveness may be attributed to alcoholic deterioration, likewise social lapses, facile behaviour, tremulousness and dysarthria.

General paresis may be confused with cerebral tumour when headache is marked and the personality attributes of frontal lobe damage conspicuous. An anterior basal meningioma may mimic the disease closely when compression of the optic pathways leads to pupillary changes and optic atrophy.

General paresis must also be borne in mind in the differential diagnosis of epilepsy of late onset, and in all acute organic reactions when other causes are not immediately obvious.

Finally it is necessary to distinguish general paresis from other neurosyphilitic diseases, in particular chronic meningovascular syphilis and asymptomatic neurosyphilis. In chronic meningovascular syphilis the prognosis is much better than in general paresis, though the cerebrospinal fluid may show similar changes including a paretic Lange curve. Meningovascular syphilis tends to occur earlier than general paresis, shows a more acute development, and fluctuations in its course are usually marked. Insight is generally better preserved, the personality less deteriorated, and focal neurological lesions somewhat more common. Some patients with asymptomatic neurosyphilis will tend to be diagnosed as having general paresis when in reality the problem is of coincidental cerebral arteriosclerosis, chronic alcoholism, mental retardation or functional psychotic illness. This group will, however, be small, and antisyphilitic treatment will still be indicated in full.

TREATMENT

Adequate treatment of syphilis in the primary stage prevents the development of general paresis later. Similarly energetic treatment must be pursued, essentially as for general paresis, in those cases of 'asymptomatic neurosyphilis' where lumbar puncture reveals abnormalities in the cerebrospinal fluid before any clinical signs or symptoms of nervous involvement have become apparent. For this reason routine lumbar puncture is often advocated in every case of primary syphilis, and yearly examination of the cerebrospinal fluid in those who show abnormalities in the early stages.

Penicillin Therapy

For the treatment of established general paresis penicillin alone is generally agreed to be adequate, and can eliminate syphilitic infection in the brain in the great majority if not all cases. Benzylpenicillin G is the preparation of choice and must be given by intramuscular injection; as procaine penicillin G it can be given by daily injections. Benzathine penicillin, given as a single injection per week, will not however suffice. This régime appears to be effective for the treatment of primary syphilis in patients who are likely to be uncooperative over daily attendance, but there is now evidence that it yields inadequate cerebrospinal fluid levels for the treatment of neurosyphilis (Mohr *et al.*, 1976; Tramont, 1976).

The minimum effective dose is not known with certainty, but in Hahn *et al.*'s (1959) series a total of 6,000,000 units appeared to be sufficient. This would represent 600,000 units of procaine penicillin intramuscularly each day for 10 consecutive days. Catterall (1977) advises such a course continuing for 3 weeks. Others recommend one mega-unit per day for this period of time (Hooshmand *et al.*, 1972). There is no need to give penicillin intrathecally.

The first course of treatment should be carried out in hospital because of the danger of a 'Herxheimer reaction' which is liable to occur in 5–10% of cases within the first few days of treatment. To prevent its occurrence many give prednisone orally, 5 mg every 6 hours, on the day before and on the first 2 days of treatment. The Herxheimer reaction may consist merely of fever, or there may be an exacerbation of symptoms and signs, sometimes with epileptic fits. Its likelihood is unrelated to the severity of the illness, but it is commoner when an active inflammatory process is present as indicated by a high cell count in the cerebrospinal fluid. With proper clinical management of the crisis little harm is done. In fact patients developing Herxheimer reactions are generally found to respond well to treatment, no doubt because they have been treated while the disease is still active.

Whenever a Herxheimer reaction occurs, penicillin should be stopped immediately and prednisone 5 mg t.d.s. commenced orally. Penicillin is recommenced when the exacerbation has died down, and prednisone should continue to cover the first three days of resumed treatment. When fits have occurred, anticonvulsant medication will be required before penicillin is recommenced.

Penicillin sensitivity represents another hazard. In mild cases this can usually be overcome by beginning with graded doses, and by coincident administration of prednisone or antihistamines. In severe cases it may be necessary to substitute oxytetracycline, 2 g daily for 12 to 15 days, or erythromycin 2 g daily for 20 days (Gilroy and Meyer, 1969), though the long-term adequacy of such treatment is not yet known. In such cases the course should be repeated twice, at monthly intervals. Fortunately spirochaetal resistance to penicillin does not appear to have developed; all early syphilis continues to respond completely (Jefferiss, 1962) and it is therefore most unlikely that other antibiotics will confer extra benefit in seemingly resistant cases of general paresis.

Pyrexia Therapy

Towards the end of the last century observation had suggested that intercurrent pyrexia could influence the course of the disease favourably and sometimes dramatically. This led to the trial of various procedures for inducing pyrexia artificially—tuberculin injections, typhoid vaccines, infection with malaria, and radiant heat—which came to be employed very widely before the advent of penicillin. Malaria therapy enjoyed a special vogue after its introduction by Wagner-Jauregg in 1917, and was used throughout the world in units specially equipped for the purpose. The patient was infected with benign tertian malaria through the bite of an infected mosquito, and 6 to 12 rigors were allowed before termination with quinine sulphate or mepacrine. The technique is described in detail by Sim (1968).

It is extremely doubtful if any additional benefit is conferred by combining artificial pyrexias with penicillin. In Hahn et al.'s (1959) survey of 1086 cases some 40% had been treated with pyrexias in addition to penicillin. In general this was found to confer no extra benefit either in mild or severe cases, though with severe institutionalised patients there was some suggestion of decreased mortality and a slightly improved chance of rehabilitation when fever had been employed. They concluded that the possible additive effects of fever therapy did not justify its use in any significant number of patients.

Other Drug Treatment

Arsenic, bismuth, iodides and mercurials are now no longer used in general paresis. Formerly potassium iodide and mercuric chloride were given by mouth along with penicillin, with the aim of helping the absorption of gummatous material in the brain, but the benefit has not been proven and the practice has gradually ceased.

Neuroleptic drugs are indicated for the control of excitement, agitation, or florid delusions or hallucinations as in any other psychotic illness, similarly antidepressant drugs for severe depressive symptoms. Anticonvulsants are required for the symptomatic treatment of epilepsy. It must be borne in mind that a small proportion of cases may represent a coincidence between asymptomatic neurosyphilis and some independent psychotic illness, and the latter will then warrant full psychiatric management in its own right.

Electroconvulsive Therapy

There is some evidence to contra-indicate the use of electroconvulsive therapy in general paresis, particularly in the presence of an active disease process as mirrored in the cerebrospinal fluid. Sudden worsening with focal signs of neurological defect has been reported to follow electroconvulsive therapy in such cases, and Dewhurst (1969) provides figures which at least suggest the possibility of an impaired overall prognosis.

Other Treatment

The complete care of the patient must include attention to all aspects of the disturbed behaviour shown, including its social repercussions. The need for hospitalisation and its duration must be carefully judged. The patient's readiness to return to work must be viewed in relation to the nature of the responsibilities involved, the deficits remaining, and the abnormalities of behaviour which persist when anti-syphilitic treatment is completed. Planned rehabilitation will need to be undertaken with patients who are left with substantial impairments, in the knowledge that continued slow improvement can sometimes take place for up to two years after treatment, and even in patients who have shown little immediate benefit.

From the outset it is necessary to make every possible effort to test the blood serology of the patient's spouse and children. This can require much tact and is usually best arranged through the patient's general practitioner.

Follow-up and Re-treatment

The cerebrospinal fluid should be re-examined two months after penicillin treatment is completed. If abnormalities in cells or protein persist a second course should be given immediately. Failure to show clinical improvement does not automatically warrant re-treatment if the cerebrospinal fluid has shown an entirely satisfactory response. In this situation the essential step is a re-evaluation of the diagnosis, since syphilitic infection may have been coincidental with other disease.

Thereafter lumbar puncture should be repeated at 6 months, 12 months, then yearly for the next 5 years at least. The first sign of relapse is seen in the cell count of the cerebrospinal fluid, and if this rises above five cells per millilitre at any follow-up examination re-treatment is strongly indicated. A persistently elevated protein or paretic Lange curve is not of the same significance, and can usually be disregarded if cell counts remain low and there is no clinical evidence of progression. The Wassermann reaction and associated serological tests may remain positive in the blood and the cerebrospinal fluid for several years after resolution of all active infection. Rising titres in the blood serology should cause concern, however, and may point to continuing activity or reinfection. This will always indicate the need for re-examination of the CSF at any point during the follow-up period.

The patient must similarly remain under regular clinical observation for evidence of relapse during the five post-treatment years. Clinical evidence of progression of the disease will always raise the possibility of the need for retreatment, especially when the initial response was good. Routine re-treatment, however, confers no additional benefit.

In summary, re-treatment is indicated when cell counts in excess of 5 cells per millilitre persist or reappear in the cerebrospinal fluid, or when temporary clinical improvement is followed by evidence of progression of the disease; also of course, if it cannot be firmly established that a minimum course of 6,000,000 units of penicillin was given in the first place. Re-treatment is not indicated by the absence of initial clinical improvement provided the cerebrospinal fluid response is satisfactory, nor by persistent abnormalities in the protein or serology of the fluid.

OUTCOME OF TREATMENT

The outcome which can be expected has been comprehensively described by Hahn *et al.* (1959) from a multi-centre follow-up study of 1086 patients in the USA. Their general conclusion is of the utmost importance, namely that success depends essentially on early diagnosis and the prompt administration of a fully adequate course of treatment.

Eighty per cent of mild or early cases obtained a clinical remission and proved capable of resuming work. In this group there were hardly any deaths from paresis. The prognosis for ability to work and live in the community was directly proportional to the duration of decreased work capacity at the time of treatment. However, even severely affected institutionalised patients were still capable of considerable benefit, and stood a 1 in 3 chance of improving sufficiently for rehabilitation and ultimate return to work.

The overall clinical severity of the illness was of prognostic importance, but little difference was found with different types of illness. Depressive forms tended to fare rather better and paranoid forms rather worse than the simple dementing or grandiose varieties, though these differences were not marked. Certain symptoms were associated with a poor overall prognosis, including incontinence, inability to dress, and neglect of personal hygiene. In patients over 60 remission or improvement became much less frequent, probably because of their high incidence of cerebrovascular changes.

Interesting correlations were found in relation to the cerebrospinal fluid abnormalities at the time of treatment. The more active the fluid in terms of cell count, the greater was the chance of a good clinical response to treatment; at the same time, however, the chance of clinical progression was then also increased in certain cases. This apparent paradox is explained by the fact that pleocytosis in the cerebrospinal fluid reflects an active and labile process, whereas an inactive fluid indicates a relatively static pathology. The latter is less susceptible to treatment but also less likely to result in clinical progression. Persistent borderline cerebrospinal fluid cell counts at follow-up were associated with poor clinical outcome, but persistently elevated protein levels were not.

The quality of recovery extended to a wide range of organic mental symptoms and florid psychotic phenomena. At 5 year follow-up the following symptoms and signs had resolved completely in over half of the patients who showed them: disorientation, convulsions, tremors, incontinence, euphoria and depression. In over a quarter there was resolution of impaired memory, judgement, insight, speech, calculation, delusions and hallucinations. Clearly there is considerable leeway for restoration of function in favourable cases, though in chronic patients with long-established disease one can realistically hope merely to halt progression of the disease.

The overall death rate 10 years after treatment

was 31%, 9% being attributable to general paresis and a further 22% to other causes. Altogether this was almost four times the death rate to be expected for nonsyphilitic patients of a similar age.

Encephalitis

An encephalitic process can occasionally arise in pyogenic infections such as septicaemia, or develop by direct extension of the inflammatory reaction in diseases such as cerebral abscess or meningitis. But in the more restricted sense to be dealt with here, encephalitis refers to a primary disease in which inflammation of the brain is caused by viral agents. Meningoencephalitis is the more appropriate term when a marked element of meningeal irritation exists as well.

Virological studies have gone some way towards isolating and demonstrating the responsible organisms, especially in large epidemics, but a very large number of cases remain in which a viral aetiology is merely presumed to operate on account of the general features of the illness. This applies particularly to sporadic cases where opportunities for extensive virological investigations are not often available, but is also true of some large epidemics, notably the epidemics of encephalitis lethargica in which a specific agent was never conclusively demonstrated.

In some cases of known viral infection it is uncertain whether the virus actually gains access to the central nervous system, or whether the central nervous changes represent an auto-immune or hypersensitivity reaction to the presence of viral infection elsewhere in the body. The latter is thought to be the principal mechanism in many of the forms of encephalitis which follow upon childhood infectious diseases.

A recent development is the increasing evidence that viruses and virus-like agents play some part in sub-acute and chronic degenerative diseases of the brain. These are the so-called chronic, latent or slow viruses, which are now under suspicion in sub-acute sclerosing panencephalitis (p. 305), Creutzfeldt-Jakob disease (p. 400), progressive multifocal leucoencephalopathy (p. 646), and kuru (p. 645).

A comprehensive classification of encephalitis is difficult but Table 13 delineates the main categories for discussion.

Kennard and Swash (1981) illustrate the principal varieties encountered in the UK, by a retrospective review of 60 patients with encephalitis admitted to the London Hospital. Of the 12 where the causative virus was proven this was herpes simplex in 6, infectious mononucleosis in 3, mumps in 2 and influenza in one. In 29 with similar features to the above no specific virus could be incriminated. Of the 19 post-infectious cases, 15 followed upon upper respiratory tract infections or influenza-like illnesses, 3 followed acute exanthemata, and one vaccination against smallpox.

The clinical picture in most forms of acute encephalitis is of a rapidly developing illness with headache, considerable prostration, and features of central nervous system involvement. Vomiting, irritability and photophobia are common. Some degree of neck stiffness is often detectable, and papilloedema may develop due to cerebral oedema. Pyrexia is variable, but may be low-grade and easily overlooked.

TABLE 13. Varieties of encephalitis (after Robbins, 1958)

Epidemic Virus Infections of the Central Nervous System
Arthropod borne
—Eastern Equine, Western Equine, St. Louis
—Japanese B
—Murray Valley
—Russian Spring-Summer
—Louping Ill.
Entero viruses
—Poliomyelitis
—Coxsackie group
—Echo group
Encephalitis lethargica

Sporadic Virus Infections of the Central Nervous System
Herpes simplex
Mumps
Infectious mononucleosis
Herpes zoster
Infectious hepatitis
Rabies

Post-Infectious Encephalitis
Following upper respiratory tract infections
Influenza
Post-vaccination
Measles
Rubella
Chickenpox
Scarlet fever
Atypical pneumonia

Sub-acute and Chronic Encephalitis

The dominant feature of cerebral involvement is disturbance of consciousness, ranging from mild somnolence to coma. Delirium figures prominently in some varieties. Epileptic fits are common, especially in children, and can be the opening feature of the illness. Focal neurological signs vary greatly according to the site of major impact of the inflammatory process, and are sometimes remarkably slight or even totally absent. Among the most common are pupillary changes, ocular palsies, nystagmus, ataxia, or affection of the long tracts with alteration of tendon reflexes, upgoing plantar responses and pareses of the limbs. Symptoms of temporal lobe involvement such as dysphasia strongly suggest herpes simplex infection. Sometimes the spinal cord is involved with retention of urine or paraparesis.

Special interest attaches to the occasional cases which present with psychiatric disorder. This was recognised in the early epidemics of encephalitis lethargica (p. 293) and examples still occur with other varieties. Sometimes impairment of consciousness and neurological signs are entirely absent at the time of presentation, as in the three patients reported by Misra and Hay (1971) who were admitted to a psychiatric unit with a provisional diagnosis of schizophrenia. Virological studies were apparently not performed:

A boy of 18 was admitted with a 2 day history of odd behaviour. He was excited, overactive and aggressive, with thought disorder and catatonic features. Two days after admission one plantar response was equivocal, and 2 days later both plantars were extensor and the left abdominal reflexes diminished. Lumbar puncture revealed no abnormality. He became pyrexial and developed subacute delirium. The electroencephalogram showed a reduction of alpha rhythm and generalised slow activity. He was treated with corticotrophin. Subsequently he developed post-encephalitic parkinsonism.

A woman of 45 was admitted with a 3 week history of depression and irritability and a 2 week history of paranoid delusions. On examination she admitted to thought withdrawal and auditory hallucinations. Three days after admission she became pyrexial and an extensor plantar response was elicited. Lumbar puncture was normal but the electroencephalogram showed a general excess of symmetrical fast activity. She developed auricular fibrillation and congestive heart failure. She was treated for encephalitis and myocarditis and eventually made a complete recovery.

(Misra and Hay, 1971)

Wilson (1976) presents further striking cases of this nature, showing abrupt onset of psychological disturbance and little by way of neurological dysfunction in the early stages. Crow (1978) reviews other scattered examples which illustrate the potential overlap with schizophrenia. The majority probably represent cases of herpes simplex encephalitis (p. 299).

The course can vary greatly from one patient to another, and from time to time in a single patient no matter what the causative organism. Profound coma may improve dramatically after some days or weeks, or unexpected relapse may follow steady recovery. When the acute phase is over there is generally a long period of physical and mental recuperation which may continue for several months. Occasionally the acute phase is succeeded by a prolonged phase of disturbed behaviour which may outlast all evidence of active infection and closely simulate a psychogenic reaction.

There may be no residua, or these may vary from trivial neurological signs to profound brain damage. Organic personality change may occur. Young children are especially at risk, and the contribution of encephalitis to childhood behaviour disturbance has probably been underestimated. Greenbaum and Lurie (1948) described 78 children referred on account of personality difficulties or behaviour disorder attributable to previous encephalitis, representing almost 3% of their total patients. Boys showed post-encephalitic changes much more often than girls, and the psychiatric sequelae were worse the younger the patient at the time of the attack. Characteristically there was lack of inhibition, restlessness, impulsiveness and extreme distractability; intellect was often well preserved, but the prognosis was poor in terms of social adjustment.

Further aspects of the clinical picture and after-effects will be described as the varieties of encephalitis are dealt with in turn.

ARTHROPOD-BORNE ENCEPHALITIS

This group contains illnesses broadly similar to one another. They occur in epidemics in different parts of the world and are transmitted to man by the bite of an infected insect, chiefly the mosquito, though in some cases tics and mites have been suspected. In the USA the main varieties are Eastern and Western encephalitis and St. Louis encephalitis, distinguished mainly by their geographical locations. Louping ill is the only member of the group which is seen in England and this is very rare. It is derived from sheep via sheep tics. Japanese B encephalitis became well known to the Western world by affecting troops in the Far East during the Second World War.

Recurrent epidemics are a feature of all the diseases listed, often with a seasonal incidence in the warm summer months, and varying somewhat in virulence from one epidemic to another. In some epidemics overt disease is rare in comparison to the number of abortive cases who are found to harbour the viruses without showing signs of illness. This naturally leads to considerable difficulty in reaching a satisfactory laboratory confirmation of the disease when sporadic cases arise, though rising titres of antibodies on repeat examination may help.

Pathological changes are similar in the different varieties. There is diffuse rather than focal cerebral involvement, affecting the grey matter particularly. Microscopy shows infiltration of lymphocytes and polymorphs, congregated especially around the blood vessels, ('perivascular cuffing'), scattered small focal haemorrhages, necrosis of neurones, and areas of neuroglial proliferation. Various forms of inclusion body may be found in the neurones and neuroglia. Demyelination is rarely seen, in contrast to the post-infectious encephalitides (Casals, 1958).

The clinical picture is similarly uniform, though varying in intensity and prognosis according to the virulence of the epidemic. There is usually a predilection with regard to age, the very young and the old being especially affected. The onset is with fever, headache and gastrointestinal disturbance, often with signs of meningeal irritation. Fits are common, likewise progression to coma or semi-coma, but marked delirium is rarely a feature (Drachman and Adams, 1962). Focal signs include cranial nerve palsies, especially of the oculomotor nerve, and paresis in the limbs of upper motor neurone type. Eastern equine encephalitis is among the most severe, with early onset of profound neurological deficits and death in approximately 70% of cases (Feemster, 1957).

The blood usually shows a polymorphonuclear leucocytosis. The cerebrospinal fluid shows some increase of pressure, a moderate rise of protein, and 200–1000 cells of which polymorphs predominate early and mononuclears late. The cerebrospinal fluid sugar is normal. Serological tests may allow the identification of the causative organism by neutralization or complement fixation tests (Robbins, 1958).

The incidence of enduring sequelae is related to the length of coma in the acute stage and to the age at which infection occurs. Follow-up of a large Californian series showed residual defects in some 50% of infants under one year and in 20% of adults, the former being much the more severe and including mental deficiency, spastic paralysis, athetosis and fits (Finley, 1958). Among adults, transient depression and exhaustion are common during convalescence but serious organic residua are rare. Occasionally some degree of dementia or personality change becomes apparent in the year that follows, and a very small number show ataxia, dysarthria or hemiparesis. Post-encephalitic parkinsonism is very rare indeed. Subjective complaints are much more frequent—depression, irritability, insomnia and nervousness—and can persist for a year or two in a manner which simulates neurosis. These may be accompanied by forgetfulness, difficulty in concentration, tremors or ataxia which suggest a basis in minor cerebral damage. Zeifert et al. (1962) found that the electroencephalographic findings on follow-up were often at variance with the objective evidence of neurological damage, and abnormal recordings proved to correlate more closely with emotional disturbances than with motor or intellectual defects.

ENTERO-VIRUS ENCEPHALITIS

The entero-viruses are more prone to produce the picture of aseptic meningitis than encephalitis (p. 309). The poliomyelitis virus is distinguished by its effects on the spinal cord and the accompanying encephalitis is usually very slight in degree, but the related Coxsackie and Echo viruses can occasionally produce definite encephalitic manifestations.

Outbreaks are commonest in summer and autumn. The Coxsackie and Echo illnesses usually run a benign course, accompanied by other systemic symptoms characteristic of the virus concerned—maculopapular rashes, muscular pains, or pleurodynia. The changes in the cerebrospinal fluid resemble those of poliomyelitis, with a moderate elevation of protein, normal sugar, and 50–100 cells (polymorphs early and mononuclears later). The virus may be isolated from the stools, but is of more significance if found in the cerebrospinal fluid. A rise in serum antibodies may be demonstrated during the course of the disease by neutralisation or complement fixation tests, though many asymptomatic infections evoke the same response. Serological testing is also made difficult on account of the large number of antigenically distinct viruses in this group.

Children affected before one year of age may occasionally be left with neurological impairment and seizures (Sells et al., 1975). Otherwise serious sequelae are uncommon with Coxsackie and Echo virus infections. Muscular weakness may be marked and persist for some time during convalescence, but true paralysis is rare. Poser *et al.* (1969) have reported the occasional development of post encephalitic parkinsonism after such infections, but this is usually a transient and mild disability unlike that following encephalitis lethargica (p. 295).

ENCEPHALITIS LETHARGICA
('Epidemic Encephalitis')

An earlier generation of neurologists and psychiatrists was much concerned with this disease on account of the devastating epidemics of 1918 to 1920 and the chronic sequelae that occurred. From the 1930s onwards it largely disappeared, at least in its original form, though champions exist for the view that variants still occur sporadically and often go unrecognised (p. 297). Strangely no causative organism was isolated despite extensive researches, and laboratory proof has never been available to uphold the diagnosis in disputed cases.

Whether or not the disease may be relegated to history, it remains an exceptionally important disorder. The thousands of cases available for observation displayed a wealth of psychopathological phenomena which could be clearly ascribed to pathological changes in the brain. This had an important influence on psychiatric thinking at a time when psychodynamic explanations for mental pathology were gaining perhaps too much ground. Certainly it focused attention on the relation between mental symptoms and brain structure in a way which few affections of the nervous system had done before. The sequelae of the disease demonstrated that an organic basis could sometimes exist for 'functional' disturbances, including tics, psychotic developments, far-reaching disturbances of personality, and particularly compulsions and other profound disturbances of will. Hendrick (1928) reviews the attempts which were made by psychiatrists of every school to capitalise on the lessons to be learned from encephalitis lethargica for understanding the neuroses and psychoses, and von Economo (1929) wrote: '. . . just as we find it hard today to follow up the trend of thought of our scientific predecessors for whom bacteriology and the lore of brain-localization did not exist, future generations will hardly be able to appreciate our pre-encephalitic neurological and psychiatric conceptions, particularly with regard to so-called functional disturbances'. There is, of course, a danger that these important lessons will be forgotten with the passage of time. The clinical features of the disease will therefore be described in some detail.

Encephalitis lethargica was first reported by von Economo in 1917, after a small local epidemic had led to numerous patients being seen in the Vienna Psychiatric Clinic with a strange variety of symptoms that did not fit into any known diagnostic category. The shared features were slight influenza-like prodromata followed by a variety of nervous manifestations, marked lethargy, disturbance of sleep and disturbance of ocular movement. At autopsy the picture of microscopic foci of inflammation, particularly in the grey matter of the midbrain and basal ganglia, was sufficiently constant to suggest a common cause despite the variety of neurological and psychiatric phenomena which occurred. Complete recognition followed in the great pandemic which started in London in 1918 and spread throughout Europe during the next two years, approximately coincident with the influenza pandemic of that time. The polymorphic forms of the disease continued to be a striking feature, fresh epidemics often running close to type and differing from those nearby both in the acute phases and in the incidence of sequelae.

There was a seasonal pattern, most epidemics beginning in early winter. The peak incidence was in early adult life from age 15–45, though no age group was spared. At one time a toxic agent was suspected, but the general pattern combined to suggest an airborne infective agent, gaining access via the nasopharynx and transferred by carriers or those in the pre-symptomatic stages of infection. The agent was shown to be filter-passable and the disease was transmissible to monkeys by injection of brain tissue from infected patients, but the virus itself continued to elude attempts at isolation. It was a matter of controversy whether the coincident influenza epidemics had predisposed the host to react abnormally to some relatively innocuous organism, and some evidence suggested that the herpes virus might itself be responsible. These questions were not decisively settled, but the great majority of epidemiological evidence suggested that an independent virus was responsible.

In retrospect it appeared that this was not entirely a new disease, and similar widespread epidemics could be traced in history. In England a second peak occurred in 1924, but thereafter there was a striking fall off of new cases throughout the 1930s, though sporadic cases continued to be seen and small local epidemics appeared from time to time.

The following description is largely taken from von Economo's (1929) classical account.

Acute Clinical Picture

A prodromal stage lasting several days consisted of malaise, mild pharyngitis, headache, lassitude and low pyrexia, all symptoms being slight and resembling the prodomata of influenza. A great variety of decisive nervous symptoms then appeared, depending on the localisation of the virus within the central nervous system. The polymorphic forms of the disease were much documented at the time, varying somewhat between epidemics and to a rather less extent in different patients during the same epidemic. Often there was change from day to day in a given patient.

The 'basic' form, and that most usual in sporadic cases, was the *somnolent-ophthalmoplegic variety*. Somnolence developed after the prodromal phase, with slight signs of meningeal irritation. Initially there was merely a tendency to drowsiness from which the patient could easily be roused, sometimes with evidence of confusion or mild delirium but rarely with marked motor unrest. If recovery did not occur at this stage it progressed further to more or less permanent sleep for weeks or sometimes months, often deepening to coma. On recovery disturbances of sleep function might persist for many months during convalescence.

Paresis of cranial nerves set in early, especially of the 3rd and 6th, with ptosis, paralysis of ocular movements, and less commonly pupillary abnormalities or nystagmus. Such signs were usually persistent, but sometimes fugitive and fleeting. Facial palsy or bulbar palsy occasionally developed. In the limbs isolated pareses and reflex abnormalities were seen, with spasticity, hypotonia or ataxia. An admixture of other phenomena appeared in some cases—parkinsonism, chorea, athetosis, and catatonic phenomena. Rarely there were fits, transient aphasias, or cerebellar symptoms.

In other cases the picture was dominated after the prodromal stage by signs of motor unrest. This was the *hyperkinetic form,* with myoclonic twitches, severe jerking chorea, wild jactitations and anxious excited behaviour. Sometimes compulsive tic-like movements, torticollis and torsion spasm appeared. Oculomotor signs and epileptic fits were common. Delirium could be marked with constant urgent unrest by day and might, sometimes closely resembling delirium tremens with anxiety amounting to terror in response to vivid hallucinations. Typically the acute disturbance lasted a few days only, but insomnia or reversal of sleep rhythm then usually persisted for weeks or months after recovery. Other cases passed on to the typical somnolent-ophthalmoplegic form or to the parkinsonian form.

The *parkinsonian form* was characterised by rigidity and akinesis from the outset. Movements were remarkably slowed and sparse, the patient lying still for hours at a time or responding with profound psychomotor retardation. Speech, like motor movements, was greatly delayed, yet the patient could be shown to be mentally intact despite a superficial appearance of gross dementia. The limbs showed increased tone of extrapyramidal type and often a coarse tremor. The gait was festinant, and salivation occurred as in paralysis agitans. Catatonic phenomena could be seen, including classical flexibilitas cerea. Along with these features somnolence, sleep inversion and oculomotor signs might be in evidence. Many progressed thereafter to the chronic parkinsonian phase of the disease.

The *psychotic forms* were rare, but presented with acute psychiatric disturbance as the initial feature. Here mistakes in diagnosis frequently occurred until neurological signs declared themselves. The usual picture was of an acute organic reaction, but stupor, depression, hypomania and catatonia were also reported. Sometimes impulsive and bizarre behaviour was the sole manifestation for several days, accompanied by bewildered and fearful affect. Or mental conflicts were brought to the fore, adding a psychogenic colouring to the presenting symptoms. Several examples were reported by Sands (1928):

A woman of 28 developed a sore throat lasting for a week. A few days later she became excited, rambling and impulsive and was diagnosed as suffering from manic-depressive psychosis. No neurological abnormalities were found. She became extremely fearful, asking whether she was about to die or if something terrible was going to happen to her family. She spoke irrelevantly and was very tense. The pupils were later found to be irregular with sluggish reactions, and the tendon reflexes were diminished. In the following week she developed choreiform and athetoid movements and a left facial weakness. She died a few days later after a period of disorientation, high pyrexia and noisy disturbed behaviour.

A woman of 32 suddenly became restless and noisy, sang and screamed, and claimed to be the daughter of Christ and impregnated by him. She lay in bed in a strained attitude, and was markedly deluded and uncooperative. The pupils were widely dilated and reacted sluggishly to light, and the tendon reflexes were diminished. She continued in a state of excitement for three days then became drowsy, with diplopia and irregularity of the pupils. Three weeks later she recovered completely.

A woman of 30 developed headache for two days then

became excitable, restless and uncooperative. She was admitted to hospital with a diagnosis of manic-depressive psychosis. She proved to be deluded and occasionally hallucinated, and claimed at times to be a physician or a great singer. Her temperature was found to be 102°F, and the cerebrospinal fluid was under increased pressure with six cells per milliletre. Many weeks later she developed ocular palsies and other neurological signs typical of encephalitis lethargica.

It was disputed whether some cases might run their course as a psychotic illness alone without somatic symptoms at any stage. This could neither be proved nor disproved owing to the lack of specific tests for the disease. But in 1924 the Board of Control reported that many patients had been admitted to mental hospitals with diagnoses of non-specific confusional, delusional and hallucinatory states, yet in later years proved to show the classical sequelae of encephalitis lethargica (*Lancet*, 1966a). The psychiatric literature abounded with case reports, and arguments centred on whether the cases had been missed because the neurological signs had been mild and fleeting, or whether the disease could present as a 'cerebral' form without localised manifestations.

Other forms presented with acute bulbar palsy, or monosymptomatically with intense chorea, persistent hiccough or neuritis. Abortive types were common in most epidemics, with symptoms capable of arousing suspicion during the epidemic but easily overlooked at other times. There might be little more than headache and sleeplessness, with perhaps diplopia as the suggestive feature. Hysterical symptoms or mild confusion might be all that was noted in the mental state.

During the acute phase there was usually rapid debility and loss of weight. Fever might accompany the prodromal phase or persist throughout, while other cases ran their whole course without pyrexia at any stage. A moderate leucocytosis was often present but was not invariable. Examination of the cerebrospinal fluid was not in any way decisive, though most cases showed some abnormalities—moderate increase in pressure, 5–20 lymphocytes, a slight rise in protein, or a weakly luetic Lange curve. In other well-marked cases, however, the fluid was entirely normal. Many abortive cases developed only the prodromata, while others recovered early after definitive symptoms and signs had appeared. Some ran a fulminating course with death after a few days or weeks. Usually, however, the acute disturbances lasted for several weeks, with some months more before ocular palsies, lethargy and sleep disturbances resolved.

A protracted convalescence was not uncommon, with repeated relapses and fresh exacerbations. Convalescence also brought prolonged asthenic states, incapacitating depressive illnesses and a variety of sleep disturbances—insomnia, sleep reversal, and narcoleptic phenomena.

Upon recovery focal neurological abnormalities might persist. Paralysis of external ocular movements or of isolated eye muscles were frequently permanent, also pupillary abnormalities, difficulty with accommodation and inability to converge the eyes. Hemiparesis, aphasia, or other focal cerebral symptoms might remain, likewise chorea, tics, torticollis, torsion spasm or epilepsy. Hypothalamic damage was seen in adiposity, menstrual disturbance, impotence, or precocious puberty. The outstanding sequelae, however, were parkinsonism and changes of personality as considered below.

Altogether in clinically well-marked acute cases, some 40% ended fatally, 40% were left with residual defect, and 20% recovered completely. Approximately half of those with residual defects were permanently disabled from working, mostly on account of progressive parkinsonian symptoms (von Economo, 1929).

Chronic Sequelae

The most seriously disabling sequelae consisted of parkinsonian developments, change of personality, and mental defect. Severe psychiatric illnesses were also seen. The incidence of each varied in different epidemics, but a definite relationship emerged with regard to the age at which the acute infection had occurred. Adults tended to develop parkinsonism, children personality disturbances, and infants were left with mental defect. Generalised dementia did not appear to occur when the mature brain had been affected.

Parkinsonism sometimes developed gradually out of the acute stage, or could set in unexpectedly after full recovery. In the interval the patient may have shown persistent symptoms such as headache, irritability and sleep disturbance but this was by no means invariable. Indeed as time went by it became apparent that sequelae could develop after many months or years of completely normal health. By contrast personality change and mental defect were usually evident immediately after the acute infection.

Sometimes typical sequelae were seen without any clear history of acute disturbance, perhaps because the latter had been exceptionally mild, or perhaps because the causative agent could produce chronic disturbance from the outset. Certainly the severity of sequelae was unrelated to the severity of the original attack. Interestingly the brain pathology accompanying chronic sequelae usually showed new foci of disease as well as the residua of the acute attack, even when a latent interval had occurred, suggesting that the inflammatory process had once again become reactivated.

Post-encephalitic Parkinsonism

This was the most common sequel and could develop even when parkinsonian symptoms had been absent during the acute phase. Its development was usually insidious, with weakness and slowing of movements or the gradual development of a stiff and unnatural posture. The ensuing picture closely resembled other forms of parkinsonism, with mask-like face, stooping posture, festinant gait and excessive salivation. Tremor was less common than in paralysis agitans; the typical pill-rolling tremor was rarely seen, but coarser tremor and violent shaking of the limbs occasionally occurred.

Paucity of movement was sometimes a striking sign even in the absence of paresis or marked rigidity. It appeared that in large degree this represented a *primary disturbance of willed movement,* such that the patient was unable to supply the volitional impulse in spite of a wish to perform. There might be much difficulty in passing from rest to activity, the patient remaining for minutes on end in a state of trance-like immobility. Or a movement once started might freeze half-way, as when raising a spoon to the mouth. Later typical rigidity developed, with extrapyramidal increase of tone which was obvious on examination. Characteristically the akinesis and the rigidity could vary markedly, improving at some stage during the day, or allowing some activities while preventing others which required exactly the same musculature. Speech became slurred, jerky and monotonous, and writing was often strikingly small and cramped (micrographia).

Other distinctive features were *repetitive motor phenomena* in the form of tics, blepharospasm, torticollis, spells of sighing and yawning, or complex respiratory spasms. Complicated motor stereotypy developed in advanced cases, for example stamping of the feet accompanied by writhing movements of the head and neck. Speech might show marked repetitive phenomena—of a phrase ('echolalia), word ('pallilalia') or syllable ('logoclonia').

A compulsive element was often very prominent indeed, and emerged in speech and thought as well as in motor behaviour. A repeated phrase or question might accompany the motor movements, or the latter might be 'subjectivated' in a characteristic fashion; the patient would state 'I have got to move my hand that way' rather than 'I have a twitch in my hand' as would be the case with ordinary tics. Compulsive thoughts and urges also appeared independently of the motor phenomena, with the patient ruminating endlessly on restricted themes or being driven to complex rituals. Compulsive urges sometimes led to trouble with the law, for example with repeated episodes of indecent exposure. Claude *et al.* (1927) reported patients with compulsions to tear their clothes, pull out teeth, tie themselves with bonds and to strangle cats; he stressed the abrupt appearance of the obsessions, their fixity and stereotypy over time, and the patient's clear awareness of the absurdity of the acts.

It is of considerable theoretical interest that motor and psychological features of compulsion should so regularly have occurred together and in intimate association. Schilder (1938) considered that the compulsive phenomena could often be directly traced to motor sources. The encephalitic process liberated motor impulses, with a tendency towards impulsive actions of a sadistic nature, and when checked these led in turn to the compulsions. He believed that in ordinary obsessional neurosis a similar impulse disturbance on an organic basis might sometimes be at work, and estimated that a third of obsessional neurotics at that time showed slight organic signs similar to those found in chronic encephalitis lethargica.

Oculogyric crises were another characteristic feature, again often intimately associated with compulsive phenomena. For a few minutes, or rarely hours, the eyes would deviate upwards or to the side, perhaps with contortions of the head, neck and extremities. Flushing and other autonomic disturbances were common accompaniments. At the onset the patient might be beset by some compulsive thought, or enact some complex compulsive ritual. The crisis was sometimes accompanied by a fugue-like mental state, with inability to speak and lack of response to commands, or by marked affective disturbance—surges of depression, anxiety or fear, ideas of reference or feelings of persecution. Schwab *et al.* (1951) mention a patient whose episodes of paranoia were localised to one side of her body during oculogyric crises—she felt that everything and everybody on her left were hostile and unfriendly, whereas the environinent on her right was normal. When the attack was over her thinking returned to normal.

Suggestibility was sometimes found to be an important factor, oculogyric attacks being provoked by talking about them or terminating in response to a sharp command. Attacks could also be precipitated by annoyance, shock, or grief, and could be contagious in a ward of patients similarly affected. Thus again we see the complex admixture of motor and psychological phenomena which characterised the disease.

The typical mental state in post-encephalitic parkinsonism was of marked slowing ('bradyphrenia') and lack of the normal fluidity of thought, though otherwise with good preservation of mental clarity. Depression was common, in the early stages at least, and suicide was frequent. Torpor, irritability and disinclination for activity usually accompanied the compulsive elements of the disease ('psychasthenia'). Later, apathy became the striking emotional feature, with marked difficulty in arousing an affective reaction and little evidence of subjective distress. As the parkinsonian features progressed the patients showed increasing emotional impoverishment, egocentric restriction, and peevish hypochondriasis, no doubt aggravated by the institutionalised lives which many were obliged to lead.

The parkinsonism itself usually advanced steadily, sometimes with intermittent progressions, but occasionally came to a halt with fixed residual defect. The combination of physical and mental disabilities inevitably meant that a large number of victims were permanently incapacitated for work, and such patients came to form a substantial proportion of the chronic mental hospital population. Sacks (1973) has provided a striking account of the remarkable motor and behavioural abnormalities encountered in a group of very long-term institutionalised survivors in the USA, and of the effects of attempted treatment with levodopa (see p. 561).

Post-encephalitic Personality Change

Children and young adolescents were mostly the victims of this serious development but adults were not completely immune. It was estimated that approximately a third of patients below the age of 16 developed some form of mental change after encephalitis lethargica. Frequently it was accompanied by other sequelae such as parkinsonism, sleep disturbance, obesity or other evidence of hypothalamic damage.

The common change was in the direction of overactivity and impulsive antisocial behaviour, as though the child now had lessened control over his instinctual drives. He became excited and restless, alert for mischief and prone to quarrel, with inability to settle at school or remain occupied at any task for long. He was talkative, importunate and disinhibited, often indulging in dangerous pranks, stealing or sexual misbehaviour. Emotional lability was marked, with cheerful affectionate behaviour one moment and outbursts of anger and malicious spite the next. Moral and social senses were undermined, so that he became destructive, abusive, and hard to control. There was usually no primary intellectual defect, though as time went by education suffered severely or became impossible. Frequently the child appeared to be aware of the change in himself, to apologise repeatedly, yet immediately afterwards be compelled to err again. The general picture could be seen as a primary excess of 'impetus' (in contrast to the akinesis of parkinsonian developments in adults), resulting from the brain damage which had occurred at a time when personality development was in the process of gaining control over the basic impulsive drives.

The subsequent course was often unfavourable, with worsening over the years leading eventually to the need for institutionalisation. Fairweather's (1947) account of post-encephalitic patients admitted to Rampton State Institution for patients of violent and dangerous propensities gives a vivid illustration of the pictures which could ensue, with repeated serious aggression, sexual perversions, self-mutilation and impulsivity. Some of the most severe behaviour disorders in Fairweather's group were found in the small group of patients with a definite history of encephalitis lethargica but without parkinsonism or other gross physical residua.

At puberty improvement occurred in perhaps a third of cases. In later years some 50% developed parkinsonian changes, with ultimate benefit where the behaviour disorder was concerned (Slater and Roth, 1969).

Post-encephalitic Psychoses

A variety of psychotic illnesses supervened in other patients upon recovery from the acute stages. Depression and hypomania were relatively common, also paranoid-hallucinatory states and a variety of illnesses resembling schizophrenia. Severe hypochondriasis of 'psychotic' severity was often reported.

Hall (1929) described 18 patients from among 113

cases of encephalitis lethargica, mostly with manic-depressive psychoses or schizophrenia. They differed from the usual functional psychoses in that delusions were more transient and variable, and even relatively mild depression was accompanied by profound retardation and immobility. Fairweather (1947) noted that 25% of men and 12% of women admitted to Rampton after encephalitis lethargica were deluded, mainly in paranoid fashion, and that almost twice as many showed 'schizoid emotional imbalance'.

Davison and Bagley (1969) review the evidence concerning schizophrenia. Paranoid-hallucinatory psychoses were estimated to occur in 15–30% of post-encephalitics, and psychoses indistinguishable from paraphrenia or dementia praecox in 10% of those admitted to mental hospitals. All reported patients were selected for psychiatric disorder so the true frequency is unknown, but clearly such developments were not uncommon. Hebephrenic forms of schizophrenia occurred, but paranoid types appeared to predominate. Catatonic motor symptoms were seen, sometimes even independently of psychotic mental phenomena. Some claimed that the illnesses were indistinguishable from other schizophrenias, but others noted better preservation of rapport and lack of personality deterioration. A resemblance to epileptic psychoses was sometimes stressed, in that affect was 'sticky' or 'viscous'. Davison and Bagley's analysis of 40 cases from the literature revealed only one with a schizoid premorbid personality and two with family histories of schizophrenia, discounting the view that there was usually a predisposition towards the disorder. They concluded that parkinsonism was commonly associated with schizophrenic psychoses when these appeared.

Pathology of Encephalitis Lethargica

In patients dying in the acute stage little macroscopic change was seen other than softening and hyperaemia of brain tissue, and perhaps scattered 'flea-bite' punctate haemorrhages. Microscopically, tiny foci of non-purulent 'inflammation' were seen throughout the brain, usually confined almost exclusively to grey matter and with a marked preponderance in the mid-brain, diencephalon and basal ganglia. The distribution of lesions was extremely variable from case to case. Vessels were found to be engorged, sometimes with perivascular collars of chronic inflammatory cells. Toxic-degenerative changes occurred in neurones, with patchy outfall

of cells. Glial overgrowth was seldom marked.

With recovery glial proliferation occurred in damaged areas, and the remaining neurones were often filled with fatty material. The latter was regarded as typical of the chronic disease. Scattered particles of calcification were seen in vessel walls and in the brain parenchyma, and small acidophil inclusions were found in neurones.

In the chronic stages old scarred foci were often seen in conjunction with newly-active lesions, suggesting that the inflammatory process had persisted during the latent interval and then become reactivated. Degeneration and disappearance of the pigmented cells of the substantia nigra was also a striking feature of the chronic stage. Neurofibrillary tangles were prominent in the nerve cells, not only of the pigmented nuclei of the brain stem but often scattered throughout the cortex and subcortical nuclear masses as well.

The exact pathological basis for the mental developments—compulsions, personality changes, etc., could not be determined because the lesions were so very widespread.

Present-day Encephalitis Lethargica

It would be a matter of some importance if sporadic cases of the disease were still continuing to occur. There would be a substantial chance that the diagnosis would be overlooked, especially with mild affections, yet the sequelae might still dictate considerable psychiatric disability. The problem is difficult to resolve. The laboratory findings were variable even when the disease was common, and specific confirmatory tests were not achieved. During life the diagnosis must therefore rest on the clinical features alone yet these were always variable; and von Economo (1929) himself predicted that future examples would probably produce different pictures again.

Many authorities doubt whether new acute cases occur, and consider that the disease disappeared completely before the onset of the Second World War. Leigh (1946), however, reported two possible cases during an influenza epidemic, and thought that one if not both might be regarded as classical examples of the acute disease. Espir and Spalding (1956) reported three further examples, all with acute illnesses, two merging into parkinsonism and the third developing it some years after recovery:

A police cadet of 16 developed frontal headache and later that afternoon was found unconscious in bed. An hour later he regained consciousness but was confused and talked nonsense. In the evening he lost consciousness again and was admitted to the Radcliffe Infirmary at Oxford.

On examination he responded to painful stimulation but did not speak. There was a pyrexia of 100°F, some nasal discharge and slight conjunctival injection. Hiccups occurred intermittently, and myoclonic twitching was observed around the mouth and in the limbs. The pupils were unresponsive to light and the right eye was deviated laterally. All limbs were flaccid with normal tendon reflexes but with bilateral extensor plantar responses.

The CSF was under a pressure of 240 mm but showed normal constituents. The white blood count was normal. The electroencephalogram showed a generalised disturbance but no focal abnormalities.

The fever subsided next day but the level of consciousness fluctuated over the next three weeks. There were almost continuous involuntary movements of chewing, swallowing, yawning, writhing of the limbs and rubbing of the nose. He was occasionally incontinent of urine. The pupils became unequally dilated, and both reacted briskly but transitorily to light. Conjugate movements of the eyes were defective in vertical directions, and slight left facial weakness appeared.

Thereafter he slowly recovered and was discharged 2 months after the onset. By that time he was up and about but almost completely mute and apt to have crying spells. Within the next few weeks he was speaking normally and he returned to work a month or two later.

During the next 18 months he complained of undue sleepiness by day and was treated with dexamphetamine sulphate. In other respects he seemed to have recovered completely, and worked full-time as an apprentice toolmaker.

Subsequently, however, he committed a series of crimes, mainly of a violent and unpremeditated nature and with little attempt at concealment. Previously he had been of exemplary character. The legal proceedings which followed brought him under medical supervision some four years after the initial illness. He then described episodes lasting 15–20 minutes during which his eyes involuntarily turned upwards and to the right in a manner strongly suggestive of oculogyric crises. There was occasional titubation of the head, his facial expression was stiff, and there was slight cogwheel rigidity of the upper limbs.

Espir and Spalding support their diagnosis of encephalitis lethargica by pointing out that such a picture is rarely produced by the many known types of present-day viral encephalitis. Ophthalmoplegia is rare with other varieties, and parkinsonism a distinctly uncommon complication. Most other forms occur in summer, whereas encephalitis lethargica was seen mostly in the winter months as in their own examples. The prolonged sleep disturbance during convalescence was also typical.

Rail *et al.* (1981) review eight further examples occurring during the past two decades, some presenting with prominent psychiatric features. Pathological examination of the brain in two patients showed extensive loss of neurones from the substantia nigra and locus caeruleus, along with widespread neurofibrillary changes elsewhere in the brain stem, dentate nuclei and corpus striatum. They stress that the diagnosis still rests essentially on the clinical features, and suggest that the following criteria be applied: an encephalitic illness, parkinsonism developing acutely or after a delay of months or years, alteration in the sleep cycle, oculogyric crises which are not drug induced, ocular or pupillary changes, respiratory disturbances, involuntary movements, corticospinal tract signs, and mental abnormalities. While these appear to represent the specific features of encephalitis lethargica, it is clear that not all will be present in every case.

The debate concerning present-day examples was extended by Hunter and Jones (1966), who argued that sporadic cases may be appearing in mild or attenuated form and with clinical pictures increasingly dominated by psychiatric manifestations. Consequently the neurological signs on which the diagnosis depends could readily be overshadowed. They reported six possible cases seen in a 3-month period in a mental hospital. All had presented with psychiatric syndromes, and all had initially been seen at general hospitals where diagnoses of hypomania, depression and anxiety neurosis had been applied:

Two were admitted in a state of excitement and confusion, two after overdoses of sleeping pills, one in a catatonic state and one at his own request on account of feeling ill and 'nervous'. Most had a history of progressive personality change over the course of several months with irritability, emotionality, perplexed-paranoid developments, and impaired memory and concentration. They complained of malaise, headache, lethargy, hypersomnia, insomnia, giddiness, blurred and double vision, and altered taste and smell. All had worsened in the week or two before admission, with increasing agitation and depression, paranoid and bizarre bodily delusions, and nocturnal excitement and hallucinosis.

On examination all showed some degree of mental confusion, three had mild pyrexia, and all had some ocular abnormality—dilated or unequal pupils, absent accommodation reflexes, ptosis, nystagmus, or weakness of upward, downward or conjugate gaze. A variety of other neurological signs were present, often fluctuating from day to day. Four showed loss of associated arm movements on walking, indicative of early parkinsonism, and several showed tremor, sialorrhoea and typical vasomotor disturbances.

The authors suggested that the combination of cerebral, hypothalamic and mid-brain involvement was strongly reminiscent of encephalitis lethargica, likewise the symptoms of lethargy, sleep disorder and visual disturbance, the rapid fluctuation of symptoms, the fugitive signs, and the relapsing course.

It is extremely difficult to evaluate these examples, but Hunter and Jones made an important point in urging that encephalitic antecedents should more often be considered in the differential diagnosis of psychiatric patients. Hunter et al. (1969) pursued the question further by examining the cerebrospinal fluid in 256 patients admitted to a psychiatric unit. More than a quarter showed abnormalities, as defined by a total protein in excess of 60 mg/ml or a gamma globulin exceeding 10% of the total protein. More importantly, in a group subjected to serial lumbar punctures the cerebrospinal fluid showed a return to normality more often when the clinical condition improved than when it did not. The abnormal findings emerged in patients with affective, schizophrenic and paranoid syndromes. Among the younger patients there was sometimes evidence of extrapyramidal disturbances or skin eruptions, and here at least the authors concluded that an encephalitic type of illness might have been responsible.

Finally it is worth considering whether encephalitic processes may have contributed to the prevalence of 'catatonia' in earlier psychiatric practice. Mahendra (1981) reviews the decline of 'catatonic schizophrenia' over the past 40 years, and suggests that many examples in the earlier literature may have owed much to a viral, and possibly an encephalitic, origin. Present-day catatonia, when it occurs, may be seen in association with an impressive range of physical conditions, ranging from brain lesions and infections to toxic and metabolic disorders (Gelenberg, 1976). In the absence of clearly organic determinants it appears now to be associated with affective disorder very much more commonly than with schizophrenia (Abrams and Taylor, 1976).

Herpes Simplex Encephalitis

Herpes simplex is now regarded as one of the commonest single causes of severe sporadic encephalitis. It has been incriminated in up to 20% of cases in Britain and this may be an underestimate (Grist, 1967). The disease is severe with a high mortality, and shows certain special features including marked psychological disturbance both in the acute phase and as a major sequel.

The subject was controversial for many years, since herpes simplex infection is very widely distributed with antibodies detectable in 80–90% of adults. It was also known that the virus could occasionally be cultured from random samples of cerebrospinal fluid. But the evidence that it truly caused encephalitis came from the finding of Cowdry type A inclusion bodies in the brains of affected persons, identical with those seen in cutaneous and visceral forms of the disease. Smith et al. (1941) were finally able to show a convincing association with acute encephalitis by isolating the virus from the brain of a case which showed this specific pathological feature.

More recently it has come to be recognised that herpes simplex is responsible not only for cases of ordinary acute encephalitis, but also for many of the cases of 'acute inclusion body', 'acute necrotising' and 'haemorrhagic' encephalitis which had formerly been regarded as distinct entities (Drachman and Adams, 1962). In acute necrotising encephalitis the characteristic inclusion bodies can sometimes be demonstrated in biopsy material from the brain, and the virus has been obtained on culture; inclusion bodies are not invariable, however, so the situation is not definite in all cases.

Pathology

Changes characteristic of other forms of encephalitis are seen—perivascular infiltration of lymphocytes and histiocytes in the cortex and adjacent white matter, proliferation of microglia and the formation of glial nodules. The cerebral cortex is mainly affected in adults, with less involvement of subcortical structures. A distinctive feature is the severity of the process. In areas of maximal involvement there is necrosis with softening, haemorrhage, and loss of all nervous and glial elements. Such lesions tend to be asymmetrical between the hemispheres, and involve the medial temporal and orbital regions especially. They can be seen both grossly and microscopically. Cowdry type A inclusion bodies are often detected in the neurones, astrocytes and oligodendrocytes, in the form of large eosinophilic intranuclear masses surrounded by a clear halo and displacing the nucleolus to the periphery (Drachman and Adams, 1962; Kibrick and Gooding, 1965).

Clinical Features

The disease affects all age groups, occurring sporadically without seasonal incidence. It may be either a primary infection or a recrudescence of an established infection. Only a small proportion of patients give a history of recurrent herpes labialis (Leider *et al.*, 1965; Gostling, 1967).

Typically there is rapid onset with a severe illness in the acute stage. Pyrexia may be up to 103°F, fits are frequent in all age groups, meningeal irritation is common, and drowsiness or global confusion are prominent. Focal neurological signs include reflex asymmetry, up-going plantar responses, cortical sensory loss, and cogwheel rigidity in the limbs.

Sometimes the clinical picture can at first be misleading. In five of six cases reported by Drachman and Adams (1962) psychological symptoms were the most striking initial feature. At first these patients appeared only mildly unwell and it was aberrations of behaviour which called attention to the seriousness of the illness. One patient packed a case a week in advance of a short journey, one dressed by night to go to an imagined funeral, one failed to recognise his wife, and another slept till four o'clock in the afternoon then suddenly rushed from the house without explanation.

Once the illness is declared a delirious phase is often prominent before the patient sinks into coma. Hallucinations can resemble those of delirium tremens in being vivid and colourful, and in provoking a marked emotional reaction. On recovery from coma behaviour disturbance may again be marked, with a phase of restless hyperactivity.

The prominence of psychiatric disturbance no doubt owes much to the characteristic accent of pathology on the temporal lobes and orbital structures. This may bring added focal symptoms such as anosmia, olfactory and gustatory hallucinations, or marked memory disturbance out of proportion to the impairment of intellect. Sometimes an area of focal necrosis becomes swollen to such a degree that the illness presents with features indicative of an acute intracranial mass, usually in the temporal lobe. This may be revealed by CT scan or angiography and lead to referral as a case of brain tumour or abscess (Adams and Jennett, 1967; Potter, 1969). Biopsy then reveals the changes characteristic of acute necrotising encephalitis.

Much more rarely cases present with aseptic meningitis and run a benign course (Leider *et al.*, 1965; Olson *et al.*, 1967). Very occasionally there may be recurrent episodes of organic psychosis, as in the interesting patient reported by Shearer and Finch (1964): a 9-year-old boy had seventeen episodes in a 3 year period, lasting a little over a week at a time, and consisting of fever, headache, drowsiness, disorientation and grossly irrational behaviour. Each episode was accompanied by electroencephalographic abnormalities and an outbreak of herpes labialis.

Investigations

In the typical encephalitic illnesses the pressure is raised at lumbar puncture with an increase of protein and cells (up to 500 cells per ml, mostly mononuclear). In Olson *et al.*'s (1967) series, however, 4 out of 36 cases showed normal cerebrospinal fluid. The electroencephalogram is usually abnormal with diffuse slow waves which may be more marked over one hemisphere than the other. Foci of spikes and sharp waves may be seen in the temporal regions (Kugler, 1964). The CT scan can aid materially in diagnosis and in excluding an abscess or tumour (Claviera *et al.*, 1976; Kaufman *et al.*, 1979). Characteristic low density areas may be demonstrated in one or both temporal lobes and often extending elsewhere. A 4-fold rise of complement fixation or neutralising antibodies during convalescence is usually accepted as evidence of active herpes infection, or a titre in excess of 160 (Gostling, 1967). Brain biopsy may reveal the type A inclusion bodies characteristic of the disease, but a negative result is not conclusive since an extensive search may be necessary to find them even at autopsy. The virus may be recovered from the cerebrospinal fluid, but definitive proof requires its isolation from the brain.

Differential Diagnosis

The disease is not infrequently puzzling. In addition to cases which present as possible tumours or abscesses other conditions can be simulated. When pyrexia is low and neurological signs markedly asymmetrical, the picture may suggest subdural haematoma or head injury. Acute and fulminating examples may resemble meningitis. The prominence of mental confusion with vivid hallucinations may lead to a diagnosis of delirium tremens, or an acute onset with drowsiness, confabulation and fits may suggest Wernicke's encephalopathy. The residual end-state can closely resemble Korsakoff's psychosis or raise the possibility of general paresis.

Treatment and Outcome

Attempts have been made to treat the illness with idoxuridine (5-iodo-2-deoxyuridine) which interferes with the replication of the virus. Illis and Merry

(1972) review the evidence for its efficacy and conclude that it does reduce mortality and diminish neurological sequelae. Side effects can be dangerous, however, and Juel-Jensen (1973) suggests that the evidence of benefit is questionable. Cytarabine or adenine arabinoside may hold some promise if given early, but a recent controlled trial has shown the most decisive benefit of all from acyclovir (Sköldenberg *et al.*, 1984). ACTH and steroids can also have an important place in treatment. Decompression of the brain is a useful adjunct in appropriate cases.

The outcome is fatal in approximately 70% of patients (Illis and Merry, 1972). Among survivors perhaps half recover completely and the remainder are left with sequelae which can be severe. Mental deficiency may ensue in young children, or severe dementia in adults. Dysphasia, fits, motor defects, personality change and severe amnesic states have also been described (Oxbury and MacCallum, 1973). Hierons *et al.* (1978) present a detailed picture of the long-term disability observed in 10 patients following presumed herpes encephalitis. All showed extensive necrotising encephalitis in the temporal lobes and limbic structures at autopsy. The pictures ranged from relatively pure amnesic syndromes to severe dementia, accompanied often by bizarre behaviours reminiscent of the Klüver Bucy syndrome. Several showed strong oral tendencies, sucking fingers and blankets, chewing clothes and putting objects into the mouth. Excessive appetite and indiscriminate eating were sometimes observed. Restless hyperactivity was common, with intermittent bouts of aggressive and destructive behaviour alternating with periods of apathy and depression. All but one of the patients had needed prolonged hospitalisation until death.

The patients reported by Rose and Symonds (1960), in whom encephalitis was followed by a Korsakoff-like syndrome, were probably examples of herpes simplex encephalitis. The defects of memory were out of all proportion to other intellectual deficits, which in some cases were virtually non-existent. Remote memory was relatively preserved but retention of new information was grossly impaired. A striking feature was a period of retrograde amnesia for months or even years before the illness. Such a condition would be consistent with the characteristic accent of herpes simplex encephalitis on the medial temporal lobe structures.

Herpes Simplex Infection in Relation to Other Psychiatric Conditions

It is not known how commonly herpes simplex may invade the brain without producing overt encephalitis, and leave enduring disability of less degree. Fry (1972) reviews the characteristics of the virus which suggest that it could be a pathogen of importance in psychiatric disorder—it is widely distributed in the population, has the ability to remain latent, can pass from cell to cell without release into the extracellular fluid, and certainly in overt cases of encephalitis it shows a predilection for those areas of the brain, such as the temporal lobes, which are important in relation to personality and emotional stability. Accordingly some interesting preliminary investigations have been conducted.

Cleobury *et al.* (1971) found a significantly higher percentage of neutralising antibodies to herpes simplex type 1 in a group of thirteen aggressive psychopaths, when compared to non-aggressive psychiatric patients or normal controls. This appeared to represent a specific rather than a general abnormality of antibody response, since the titres to herpes type 2 and other viruses were within the normal range. The authors suggested that a herpes virus infection in childhood, unapparent or at least unrecognised at the time, may have damaged the temporal lobes and affected the development of personality.

Rimon and Halonen (1969) and Halonen *et al.* (1974) investigated complement fixation and neutralizing antibody titres for herpes simplex in psychiatric patients, and found that evidence of infection was significantly commoner than among controls, particularly so among psychotic depressives. They point out that dysfunction of monoamine metabolism has been demonstrated in the brains of animals infected intracerebrally with herpes simplex, and that depressive illness is possibly associated with a deficiency of brain monoamines in man (Shaw *et al.*, 1967). Lycke *et al.* (1974) have also demonstrated an increased prevalence of infection with the herpes group of viruses (herpes simplex and cytomegalovirus) in patients with depressive psychoses when compared to other diagnostic groups and healthy controls. Thus it could be that a latent herpes infection may operate to inhibit the synthesis of biogenic amines in man, and that perhaps in cases of psychotic depression the latent infection has extended into the central nervous system itself. These suggestions deserve closer investigation in other series of patients.

Type B Herpes Simplex Encephalitis

The monkey form of herpes simplex produces an

almost invariably fatal disease in man, and is a hazard to workers in animal laboratories. It is transmitted by the bite of an infected monkey. A vesicle is produced at the site of entry, and along with encephalitis of severe degree there is often an ascending paraplegia. Widespread necrotic lesions are found in other organs as well as the brain.

OTHER SPORADIC VIRAL ENCEPHALITIDES

In a great number of cases of sporadic encephalitis the cause is never identified, and the yield even with extensive virological studies remains rather low. The following known varieties are all relatively infrequent.

Mumps Encephalitis

It appears that the mumps virus affects the nervous system more commonly than was previously supposed, even in the absence of parotitis or other typical evidence of the disease. This is probably the only common childhood infectious disease in which the virus itself can invade the central nervous system. The usual picture is an aseptic meningitis (p. 309), though an encephalitic illness is occasionally seen. When it occurs there is usually some degree of coincident meningitis and sometimes myelitis.

Symptoms appear some 2–10 days after the onset of parotitis, but can precede it or occur without any overt evidence of mumps elsewhere in the body. Meningeal symptoms are usually prominent with headache, vomiting, fever, neck stiffness and irritability. Drowsiness and delirium occur, sometimes with cranial nerve palsies, ataxia or pareses in the limbs. Fits are uncommon. In the acute myelitic form there is profound paresis and sensory changes in the limbs. The varied psychiatric and neurological pictures which may be seen are reviewed by Keddie (1965).

The cerebrospinal fluid shows a moderate pleocytosis, usually of mononuclears from the outset. Serological tests are useful if a rise in titre of complement fixation or haemagglutination inhibition antibodies can be demonstrated during convalescence. Permanent sequelae are common enough to suggest that the prognosis should be guarded (Lees, 1970; Johnstone *et al.*, 1972).

Infectious Mononucleosis

The neurological complications of infectious mononucleosis occasionally include an encephalitic picture. This may be due to direct viral invasion of the nervous system, but sometimes it appears to represent an allergic encephalomyelitis similar to that following the acute exanthemata (p. 304). A benign lymphocytic meningitis (p. 309) can also occur.

Headache and meningism are frequently encountered in glandular fever, suggesting that minor involvement of the nervous system may be not uncommon (Gautier-Smith, 1965). Diffuse electroencephalographic abnormalities have been reported in up to 30 per cent of cases. Frank neurological complications are, however, rare. Gautier-Smith (1965) and Boughton (1970) have described patients with acute confusion progressing to stupor or coma, usually setting in abruptly within 5 to 9 days of the illness. Other cases present with seizures, or focal cerebral disturbances such as hemiplegia. Syndromes of brain stem, cerebellar or cord dysfunction may also be seen. The cerebrospinal fluid shows a moderate rise of cells and protein. Complete recovery appears to be the rule.

Of considerable interest are patients who develop acute psychiatric disturbances in clear consciousness in the course of glandular fever. Raymond and Williams (1948) described a patient who became acutely psychotic within a few days of onset, settling over 3 weeks as the illness improved. Klaber and Lacey (1968) reported five of seventy-six cases presenting with severe psychiatric disorder during the course of an epidemic, only subsequently being diagnosed as suffering from glandular fever. Two showed pictures of acute schizophrenia and three acute depression. Here it seems likely that the patients were responding to the non-specific stress of the physical illness rather than to direct nervous system involvement.

A depressive aftermath has also been widely recognised (Crow, 1978) though this does not appear to have been studied systematically. A recent investigation by Hamblin *et al.* (1983) could be relevant in pointing to immunological dysfunction. Seventeen patients complaining of lethargy and inability to get back to work for a year or more after the illness were compared with a group making a full recovery. The ratio of T-helper to T-suppressor cells in the blood was significantly lower in the former than the latter, and lower than in controls who had not had the disease. Two patients were followed for several months, and the ratios rose as their complaints resolved. It is conceivable that long-lasting immunological abnormalities of this nature could serve in large measure to precipitate and maintain depression during the convalescent period.

Herpes Zoster Encephalitis

Some degree of meningeal reaction is common in herpes zoster, with elevation of the protein and an excess of mononuclears in the cerebrospinal fluid. Features of meningitis are observed very occasionally and encephalitis more rarely still. Hall (1963) has reported a clear example of encephalitis following ophthalmic zoster and resulting in a chronic amnesic syndrome.

Infectious Hepatitis

Encephalitic or meningitic complications may accompany infectious hepatitis, sometimes antedating the onset of jaundice. Headache, photophobia, neck stiffness and pyrexia progress to typical severe encephalitic manifestations. The condition must be distinguished from the encephalitis occasionally seen with leptospirosis (Weil's disease).

Rabies

Rabies is transmitted by infected animal saliva from dogs, bats or wolves. There is a long and variable incubation period, commonly 1–2 months but with a wide latitude extending sometimes up to a year. The onset is then sudden, with a pyrexial illness, excitement, hydrophobia, and violent muscular spasms involving the oesophagus and respiratory muscles. Crises are characterised by intense fury or profound terror, and in the intervals between the mind is clear. An ascending paralysis may occur. Death occurs during paroxysms, or in coma if the patient survives sufficiently long.

Rabies must be distinguished from tetanus, and from hysteria when a patient has been bitten by a supposedly rabid dog. In hysteria true pharyngeal spasm does not occur, and the mental disturbance is amenable to sedatives and suggestion.

INFLUENZA ENCEPHALITIS

It appears that the influenza virus itself may be responsible for occasional cases of encephalitis. Small groups of cases have been reported during influenza outbreaks in many parts of the world, including the large epidemic of 'Asian' influenza which affected the British Isles in 1957–8 (Dubowitz, 1958; McConkey and Daws, 1958).

A variety of pictures is seen, some setting in at the height of the upper respiratory tract infection, others beginning towards the end of the attack, and others following some days later after a brief afebrile episode. The usual picture is of headache, vomiting, delirium and coma, with transient reflex abnormalities or weakness of the limbs. The cerebrospinal fluid may be normal or show a slight pleocytosis. The electroencephalogram is often diffusely abnormal. The illness usually resolves after several days, and excellent recovery is said to be the rule.

In other varieties the patient shows no more than a period of mental confusion and headache, accompanied by electroencephalographic abnormalities and succeeded by complete amnesia for the episode (Bental, 1958). Cases have been reported from Barbados with an unusual hallucinatory syndrome in which bizarre smells were experienced (Lloyd-Still, 1958). Other forms include spinal and radicular syndromes, transverse myelopathy, and ascending motor and sensory disturbances of Guillain–Barré type (Flewett and Hoult, 1958; Wells, 1971a).

The nature of the causal relationship between these illnesses and the influenza virus remains uncertain. They are rare, even during extensive epidemics, and the possibility of coincident infection with another sporadic virus is hard to exclude completely. Dunbar et al. (1958) estimated that their cases represented only 1 in 10,000 of the persons affected by the influenza epidemic in the area. Other possibilities are the activation of some associated neurotropic virus, or the occasional development by mutation of a neurotropic strain of influenza virus. Kapila et al. (1958) were able to isolate influenza A virus from the brain substance of one fatal case, but such reports are very few indeed. Examples which occur at the height of an attack may sometimes be merely attributable to the cerebral anoxia and metabolic derangements consequent upon pneumonia. However the evidence increasingly favours the view that the great majority represent an autoimmune or hypersensitivity response on the part of the brain, similar to that which occurs after other infective illnesses (p. 304), and precipitated by the presence of virus in the body but not necessarily within the brain (*British Medical Journal*, 1971). The pathology in fatal cases often supports this view by showing perivascular demyelination similar to that of post-infectious encephalitis generally.

The broader question arises of the relationship between influenza and other psychiatric disturbances which follow it. Depression appears to be common and may sometimes be unusually refractory to treatment; this has been ascribed to invasion of the brain by the influenza virus but there is no direct evidence to support the view (*British Medical Journal*, 1971). Hysterical reactions may also be seen, and are usually ascribed to the non-specific stress of the illness and the physically weakening effects of its aftermath.

Steinberg *et al.* (1972) re-opened this question by presenting a case which suggested a more direct pathophysiological relationship between the infection and a manic psychosis which followed:

The illness, in a woman of 21, began with a typical attack of influenza. After a brief remission she again became febrile, with headache, sore throat and an unproductive cough. She complained of paraesthesiae in the limbs, and experienced a transient episode of blindness lasting for less than a minute. Over the next two weeks a typical manic illness developed, with evidence of confusion and disorientation during the first few days. The affective disturbance gradually subsided with treatment over the next few months.

Antibody titres to influenza A were abnormally high at the onset of the psychosis, and showed an unusually slow decline in comparison with other influenza patients while the manic illness was resolving.

Despite normal findings in the cerebrospinal fluid and electroencephalogram the authors postulated that a mild attack of influenza encephalitis had probably occurred, producing minimal brain damage which acted as an intervening factor and contributed to the subsequent affective disorder.

The evidence is clearly tenuous, but combined virological and psychiatric studies on a larger number of patients might illuminate the relationship further as Steinberg *et al.* suggest.

OTHER POST-INFECTIOUS ENCEPHALITIDES

The forms of encephalitis which occasionally follow the acute exanthemata account for a large proportion of the cases seen in childhood. The chief causes are measles, rubella, chickenpox and scarlet fever, though similar developments may be seen after virus pneumonias and infectious mononucleosis (Robbins, 1958). In Kennard and Swash's (1981) series the predominant antecedent was an upper respiratory tract infection of influenzal type. All share a common pathology and possibly a common pathogenesis. Closely similar illnesses may follow vaccination against smallpox, injections of serum, the administration of drugs such as streptomycin, P.A.S. or arsphenamine, or sometimes they arise for no apparent reason at all (Lees, 1970). The brain may be involved alone, or there may be more widespread affection throughout the neuraxis with brain stem or cord involvement. In such cases the term 'acute disseminated encephalomyelitis' is usually employed.

The pathological changes differ from those of the virus infections already described in certain definite respects, though some degree of overlap can be seen. The brain and cord show congestion, often with petechial haemorrhages. But the most striking changes are seen in the white matter, with discrete areas of acute perivenous demyelination. This is accompanied by round-cell perivascular infiltration and neuroglial proliferation. There is no evidence of a direct attack upon the nerve cells themselves, and the cortical neurones are characteristically spared completely.

The exact pathogeneis in unknown. There is little to suggest direct invasion of the central nervous system by the viruses concerned, and the uniformity of the pathological picture has suggested that some other latent agent may have been activated. However, an allergic or autoimmune mechanism is now generally held to be the cause. The picture resembles that of experimental allergic encephalomyelitis, produced in animals by injection of brain tissue together with certain adjuvants, and a response may be seen to treatment with ACTH or steroids.

The clinical picture consists of headache, drowsiness, photophobia and irritability, setting in some 3–14 days after the onset of the specific illness but with a wide latitude of timing. There is commonly an interval of normal health between the acute viral illness and the encephalopathic development. Convulsions are common, and meningism is often prominent. Cranial nerve palsies may appear, or myoclonic and choreiform movements. Loss of abdominal reflexes and extensor plantar responses are usual findings. The brain stem may be principally involved with vertigo, vomiting, nystagmus and dysarthria, or in myelitic forms there may be paraparesis with retention of urine. The form which follows chickenpox is said to be distinguished by ataxia.

The cerebrospinal fluid may be normal, but is often under increased pressure with a mild lymphocytic pleocytosis and a moderate elevation of protein. When infectious mononucleosis is the cause a high protein and the absence of cells are characteristic. For further details of the pictures seen with different infections textbooks of neurology should be consulted.

If the patient does not succumb during the first

week or two a remarkably complete recovery may be seen. The mortality is much higher in infants than in older children or adults, and appears to be highest in post-vaccinal cases at 30–50% (Walton, 1977). In some survivors there may be devastating neurological sequelae with hemiparesis, paraparesis, epilepsy and impairment of intellect. In children behaviour disorders similar to those that follow encephalitis lethargica may occur (Neal, 1942).

SUBACUTE AND CHRONIC ENCEPHALITIS

(Dawson's Subacute Inclusion Body Encephalitis; Van Bogaert's Subacute Sclerosing Leucoencephalitis; Subacute Sclerosing Panencephalitis)

For many years certain rather rare diseases have been suspected on pathological grounds to represent the effects of subacute infection within the brain. These have now come under closer scrutiny with regard to possible viral determinants, the measles virus being particularly incriminated as described below. They commonly present with features of dementia, and it is here that problems of differential diagnosis usually arise. Sometimes, however, the possibility of a functional psychiatric illness is raised initially.

Until a short time ago such illnesses were regarded as uniformly fatal, with a progressive course lasting several weeks or months, but occasional cases have now been reported with arrest or even improvement over long periods of time. The likelihood that mild and relatively benign examples may occur has accordingly brought new interest to the subject.

Cases were first described by Dawson in 1933 ('subacute inclusion body encephalitis'), by van Bogaert in 1945 ('subacute sclerosing leucoencephalitis') and by Brain *et al.* in 1943 and 1948. These now appear to be essentially variants of the same disease process (Adams, 1976). Dawson's cases occurred in infants and young children, and derived their name from the intranuclear inclusions which were seen in affected neurones. Van Bogaert's cases occurred in children and young adults but showed more evident sclerotic lesions in the white matter. However it is now generally accepted that a sharp line of demarcation cannot be drawn; great variation occurs in the incidence of pathological changes in grey or white matter, and inclusion bodies have been reported in van Bogaert's as well as in Dawson's varieties of the disease. 'Subacute sclerosing panencephalitis' ('SSPE') is the term now generally used to refer to these diseases.

Pathology

Adams (1976) describes the typical pathological picture. The brain may be normal macroscopically, or firm and shrunken with areas of focal necrosis. Microscopy shows evidence of subacute inflammation, usually in both the grey and the white matter. There is perivascular infiltration with lymphocytes and plasma cells, and proliferaton of astrocytes and microglia. Slight meningeal infiltration may also occur. In the grey matter neuronal degeneration is seen, often with characteristic intranuclear inclusions, and in the white matter areas of demyelination with fibrous gliosis. Considerable variation is met with from case to case, but the more rapidly progressive cases are more prone to show intranuclear inclusions and the more chronic cases greater demyelination and sclerosis of white matter.

The typical 'type A' intranuclear inclusions are strongly acidophilic homogeneous bodies with a sharp outline, separated from the nuclear membrane by a clear halo. They are the feature which originally suggested a viral aetiology, and are probably identical with those which occur in herpes simplex encephalitis (p. 299). In severely degenerated cells the inclusions may fill the nucleus so that the surrounding cytoplasm is reduced to a vestige. Sometimes they are found in the cytoplasm itself, or in glial cells as well as neurones. Such changes may be focal in distribution, affecting particularly the parieto-occipital and temporal lobes, or the hippocampus and subcortical nuclei. Inclusions have also been reported in the brain stem nuclei, especially the nuclei pontis, and in rare cases in the cells of the spinal cord. In some entirely typical cases they may be very hard to detect; a negative result from biopsy material must therefore be interpreted with caution since inclusion bodies can be found in the same case at autopsy very shortly afterwards (Kennedy, 1968).

Evidence has accumulated to suggest that a paramyxovirus may be responsible, similar to or identical with the measles virus (Connolly *et al.*, 1967; Legg, 1967; Horta-Barbosa *et al.*, 1969). Electronmicroscopy has indicated particles indistinguishable from paramyxovirus budding from cytoplasmic inclusions, very high measles antibody titres are found in the serum and cerebrospinal fluid, and specific immunofluorescence with measles antibody has been demonstrated in brain biopsy material. All of this evidence is somewhat indirect, but Horta-Barbosa *et al.* (1969) have also reported isolation of measles virus from brain cell tissue cultures derived from two patients with the disease.

It is open to conjecture whether the disease represents reactivation of latent measles infection, reinfection with a neurotropic strain of measles virus, or some more complicated mechanism involving an abnormal immunological response to the protracted presence of measles virus in cerebral tissue.

Clinical Features

The great majority of cases occur in children or adolescents, though occasional examples have been reported in middle age (Brierley *et al.*, 1960; Himmelhoch *et al.*, 1970) and are probably to be regarded as variants of the disease.

Classical examples present with insidious deterioration of intellect, such that the child begins to fail at school, becomes forgetful and inattentive, slowed and slovenly. Other early symptoms are nocturnal delirium with hallucinations, marked lethargy, and difficult uncontrollable behaviour. The prodromal manifestations may occasionally occur alone for a period of several months, but neurological abnormalities generally develop early. Characteristically the patient develops marked involuntary movements, including myoclonic jerks of the face, fingers and limbs, athetosis, or rapid torsion spasms of the trunk which lead to sudden stumbles and falls. Myoclonia may be regularly periodic, occurring at fixed intervals of 5–10 seconds for hours or days at a time. The limbs develop bilateral extrapyramidal rigidity or progressive spasticity. Epileptic fits are common, and aphasia, apraxia or akinetic mutism may appear. A low-grade pyrexia may accompany the prodromal or later stages of the disorder, but this is not invariable.

Atypical presentations may sometimes raise the possibility of non-organic psychiatric illness in the early stages. Koehler and Jakumeit (1976), for example, reported a woman of 20 who presented with an apparently hysterical blindness and gave Ganser responses of a classical nature. She showed a profound lack of initiative and spent much of the time asleep. Within a week of admission, however, the true disease was declared.

The electroencephalogram often shows highly characteristic features, though many variants occur. Typically there are high voltage slow wave complexes, synchronous in all leads, and occurring at fixed intervals of 5–10 seconds along with the involuntary jerks. They may also appear in the absence of motor abnormalities, and can sometimes be focal in the frontal or occipital regions. The cerebrospinal fluid may show a slight increase of cells, but the total protein is often normal. A feature of diagnostic importance is that the majority of cases show a raised immunoglobulin G in the cerebrospinal fluid and a paretic curve on Lange's colloidal gold test. The complement fixation titres for measles are high in the serum and the cerebrospinal fluid.

The first descriptions stressed that the disease had a hopeless prognosis, with rapidly progressive dementia over 6 weeks to 6 months and death after a period of coma and decerebrate rigidity. Cases are now reported, however, with temporary arrest for months or even years in the middle stage of the disorder, and a very few have been described with partial recovery. Of Kennedy's (1968) 5 cases in children, 2 achieved remission and one returned to school after regaining much coherent speech and a diminution of myoclonic jerks. Resnick *et al.* (1968) followed a patient for 5 years who showed considerable sustained improvement despite the continued elevation of measles antibody in serum and cerebrospinal fluid. Cobb and Morgan-Hughes (1968) mention other scattered examples in the literature and suggest that the following patient may have had the disease in a mild form:

A 21-year-old chemistry student was admitted with a 5 month history of falling attacks, momentary blank spells and recent difficulty with concentration. Neurological examination was normal apart from brisk reflexes, the electroencephalogram showed persistent slow waves in the left occipito-temporal region, and the cerebrospinal fluid showed a paretic Lange curve. He was readmitted 8 months later with impairment of memory and difficulty with reading, writing and calculation, which had come on over the preceding 2 months. He showed a severe global dementia with loss of recent memory, disorientation in time, agraphia, acalculia and profound constructional apraxia. The Wechsler Adult Intelligence Scale showed a verbal IQ of 79 and a performance IQ of less than 35. Affect was flattened and inappropriate. Neurological examination was still negative, but the electroencephalogram showed bilateral recurrent monophasic and biphasic slow wave complexes. A ventriculogram was normal, but right frontal biopsy showed changes consistent with subacute encephalitis of the Dawson or van Bogaert type. Inclusion bodies were not seen.

He was treated with prednisone in addition to anticonvulsants and slowly improved. By the following year he was working, though he had been dismissed from several jobs on account of general slowness and difficulty with reading and writing. Seven years later he was working as a gardener and had recently married. He was still mildly dysgraphic, with reading difficulties and profound constructional apraxia, but he was oriented in time and place and able to do simple calculations. Psychological testing showed a verbal IQ of 82 and a performance IQ of 40.

Risk *et al.* (1978) estimate that improvement can be expected in about 5% of cases, even after severe illnesses. Relapse may subsequently occur, however, after remissions lasting for several years. Their experience with 118 patients showed substantial long-term improvement in 6. Two of these were still improving 4–5 years later, 2 were stable 4–6 years later, and 2 relapsed after 8 and 11 years respectively. Remittent cases tended to have shown milder variants of the disease and to have been somewhat older than usual at onset. Whether or not the disease will prove always to be fatal in the long-term view cannot yet be judged.

Progressive Rubella Panencephalitis

A variant of subacute sclerosing panencephalitis has now been described in which the rubella rather than the measles virus appears to be responsible (Townsend *et al.*, 1975, 1976; Weil *et al.*, 1975). This sets in, usually duing the second decade, in children who have been affected by rubella *in utero*. Mental and motor deterioration develop as with subacute sclerosing panencephalitis, and the pathological changes in the brain are similar. The serum and cerebrospinal fluid show elevated titres of antibodies to the rubella virus and normal titres to measles. The rubella virus has been isolated from the brain in such cases.

Other Varieties of Subacute Encephalitis

Himmelhoch *et al.* (1970) reported an interesting group of 8 cases, mostly in adults, some apparently representing variants of subacute sclerosing panencephalitis. Symptoms characteristic of functional psychiatric disorder were prominent in all, and 7 had originally been diagnosed as suffering from depression, schizophrenia or hysteria.

In some the onset was acute, with sudden withdrawal and seclusiveness following a period of coryza, malaise and headache. Retardation was prominent, and a psychogenic reaction was usually diagnosed at this stage. The patients then quickly developed disorientation and visual hallucinations and showed intellectual deterioration. In others the development was more protracted, with irritability, depression, phobias and ruminations over a period of several months. They then became mute and retarded and showed progressive intellectual impairment.

The bizarreness of behaviour had strongly biased the initial diagnoses, and neurological signs had often been ignored even when they were noted. Evidence of mild confusion, disorientation or visual hallucinations had sometimes been disregarded, changes of sleep and appetite had been ascribed to depression, and fugue-like states to catatonia or hysteria.

Characteristically there were rapid fluctuations, with impaired awareness and disorientation one day followed by complete lucidity the next. Periods of aggressiveness and sexual provocativeness were often followed by profuse apology, and the patients seemed bewildered by their behaviour. Bizarre behaviour became increasingly frequent as time went on. It was markedly unresponsive to pharmacotherapy. Hallucinations were mainly visual but occurred in other modalities, and clear-cut paranoid delusions were common. At times an isolated episode was hard to distinguish from schizophrenia.

There were no consistently helpful laboratory findings, but all patients showed abnormal electroencephalographic changes at some point in the disease. Some died within several weeks or months, some ran a protracted course with remissions, but three recovered to premorbid levels of intellectual functioning:

A housewife of 38 became deluded after a period of fever, coryza and headache. She was committed to hospital with a diagnosis of paranoid schizophrenia. She alternated between a delusional state, when she was boisterous, abusive and combative, and periods of complete lucidity. Neurological examination revealed nothing abnormal, and her behaviour was unresponsive to phenothiazines or electroconvulsive therapy. Her later course was stormy, with grand mal seizures and periods of coma. She required tracheostomy and intragastric feeding. Lumbar puncture and air encephalography revealed no abnormalities, and the EEG showed episodic synchronous high voltage slow waves alternating with periods of relative electrical suppression. Biopsy of the right temporal lobe showed the features of encephalitis but no inclusion bodies were found.

Over the next 3 months the patient made a partial recovery, but 6 months later she still had severe impairment of memory, with disorientation for time and place and occasional nocturnal seizures. Five years later her memory deficit had cleared markedly, but the seizures continued and she had developed progressive paraplegia. The measles antibody titre remained elevated in the serum.

A 35-year-old woman graduate with a stable previous history become abruptly combative, confused and 'animalistic'. The electroencephalogram was diffusely slowed, and the cerebrospinal fluid showed a mild pleocytosis. She became unkempt, cachectic, and totally uncommunicative, and showed aggressive and sexually provocative behaviour. She was incontinent of urine and faeces and required tube feeding. Even so she had intermittent periods of complete lucidity.

One month later she began to improve, with lessening of memory deficit and improvement of intellectual functions. At the same time, however, her behaviour became increasingly difficult to control. She refused to attend group meetings, with biting, kicking or pulling up her dress when she was urged to attend. With her family she behaved rather better and ultimately she was discharged. Two further admissions were required in the next few months on account of disturbed behaviour, but thereafter she unexpectedly began to improve. At first she had to carry a note book to help with her memory, but after 18 months this became unnecessary. After 2 years she had recovered completely and continued to function normally.

(Himmelhoch *et al.*, 1970)

Himmelhoch *et al.* suggest that the marked behavioural disturbance in their cases was probably due to an accent of the pathological process on the temporal lobes and limbic structures. Since 3 out of 8 recovered they suggest that other examples of subacute encephalitis may be commoner than is realised, especially when the process is mild and the patient is referred for psychiatric treatment on account of disturbed behaviour. The measles antibody titre might give helpful information in suspected cases.

Brierley *et al.* (1960) reported another group of 3 cases, all with onset in the fifties and all of whom were diagnostic problems during life. One had been regarded as having presenile dementia, but in the others a low-grade pyrexia early in the illness had raised the possibility of a viral encephalitis. One presented as a severe depressive illness coloured by bizarre behaviour and later developed minor epileptic attacks, another began with depression following a respiratory infection, and the third began with pains in the shoulders and arms then progressed to tiredness and depression over the course of several weeks. All developed progressive dementia and died in coma several months thereafter. Myoclonic jerks and other motor features characteristic of subacute sclerosing panencephalitis were not seen, but at postmortem all showed severe encephalitic changes concentrated to a notable degree on the medial temporal lobe structures. Inclusion bodies were not present.

Corsellis (1969a) notes that one of these cases suffered from bronchial carcinoma, though a causal connection was not suspected at the time. He adds three further cases of bronchial carcinoma with similar pathological changes in the limbic areas, all of whom had shown marked abnormalities of affect and striking disturbance of memory during life. Whether the process should be regarded as inflammatory or degenerative in these latter cases remains uncertain. The problem is discussed further in Chapter 15, pp. 637–8.

Differential Diagnosis

Subacute encephalitis clearly gives rise to diagnostic confusion during life. It is a rare condition, so that the clinician is unlikely to see more than the very occasional case. Many examples are likely to be missed completely, especially when post-mortem examination is lacking or on the rare occasions when spontaneous recovery occurs.

Difficulties with diagnosis are especially likely to arise in the prodromal period. In children the picture may suggest behaviour disorder or autism, and in adults functional psychiatric disorder may be simulated as described above. Careful attention must be directed towards minor neurological abnormalities, sudden involuntary jerks, evidence of nocturnal delirium or intermittent low-grade pyrexia.

Presenile dementia is probably the commonest misdiagnosis in the later stages in adults. Disseminated sclerosis may be suggested by the combination of early neurological disability with a paretic Lange curve and negative reactions for syphilis in the cerebrospinal fluid. Herpes simplex encephalitis can show identical inclusion bodies in biopsy material, but the course is acute, and progressive dementia and myoclonic jerking are not seen.

Classical examples of subacute sclerosing panencephalitis usually declare themselves eventually when involuntary movements and typical electroencephalographic features appear. It now seems, however, that these developments are not inevitable. A paretic Lange curve in the cerebrospinal fluid should alert one to the possibility of the disorder, and a greatly elevated titre of measles antibody may be discovered in the serum and the cerebrospinal fluid. Brain biopsy can be crucial in demonstrating characteristic changes, though intranuclear inclusions will frequently be missed. Such investigations are often worth pursuing in view of the possibilities of treatment with corticotrophin or steroids.

Meningitis

Meningeal infection is less liable to lead to diagnostic problems than encephalitis. In most varieties pyrexia and neck stiffness are soon in evidence, headache is marked, and lumbar puncture rapidly confirms the diagnosis. Tuberculous meningitis is the important exception, sometimes presenting with insidious and ill-defined mental changes as described below. Enduring sequelae are also less common after meningitis than encephalitis provided full and effective treatment has been instituted early.

Three varieties will be discussed—pyogenic meningitis, aseptic meningitis and tuberculous meningitis.

Pyogenic Meningitis

The principal organisms responsible are the meningococcus, pneumococcus, streptococcus, staphylococcus, *Haemophilus influenzae* and *Escherichia coli*. Among adults the meningococcus accounts for about three-quarters of cases and the pneumococcus for most of the remainder (Grinker and Sahs, 1966).

Headache is usually the presenting feature, with pyrexia and rapidly increasing evidence of general ill-health. Vomiting, photophobia and irritability are common from an early stage. Fits are frequent in children but rare in adults. Mental disturbance takes the form of an acute organic reaction, with drowsiness extending to coma and sometimes hallucinations, excitement and other features of delirium. Neck stiffness and a positive Kernig's sign are important confirmatory features. Pupillary abnormalities and oculomotor palsies are common, slight incoordination or tremor may appear in the limbs, and the tendon reflexes are sluggish. The plantar reflexes are sometimes up-going.

The cerebrospinal fluid is under increased pressure and often cloudy or frankly purulent. Polymorphonuclear cells may number thousands per millilitre, the protein is raised, and Lange's colloidal gold curve is 'meningitic' with a peak in the mid-zone or to the right. The chloride content is slightly reduced and the sugar content greatly diminished or even abolished. The causative organisms may be cultured or demonstrated on films.

Formerly the mortality rate was high and neurological complications were seen in a large proportion of survivors—hydrocephalus, spastic paralysis, mental defect, blindness, deafness and epilepsy. Pneumococcal meningitis carried an especially poor prognosis. Change of personality was also reported in children with moroseness, irritability, or moral deterioration similar to that seen after encephalitis lethargica (Pai, 1945). Nowadays, however, complete recovery is the rule, provided diagnosis has been promptly made and the causative organism has not proved resistant to antibiotics. Meningococcal meningitis in particular proves to be a benign infection in the great majority of cases, despite the severity of the illness which may be seen in the acute stage.

Nevertheless Berg (1962) found that meningitis still accounted for 22 of 800 consecutive admissions of idiot and imbecile children to the Fountain Hospital between 1949 and 1960 (2.8%). Half of these had had tuberculous meningitis and half purulent meningitis. All had received antibiotics and up to date management of the acute illness, but in many the diagnosis had been delayed. Altogether meningitis was second only to mongolism as an identifiable cause of severe mental defect, exceeding in frequency such syndromes as rhesus incompatibility and phenylketonuria.

In adults mild but prolonged depression is common during convalescence, no doubt partly as a reaction to the threat of the illness. A period of fatigue and inefficiency may precede full recovery, and loss of libido may last for several months. Pai (1945) investigated 51 adults after meningococcal meningitis, all of whom were seen in a neuropsychiatric unit. Sulphonamides had been used in the treatment of some but not all cases. Psychogenic reactions outnumbered syndromes of organic defect. Sixteen patients showed intellectual deterioration or organic change of personality, and these were the ones who had had severe meningitis with marked delirium. In the other 35 psychogenic factors seemed to predominate. Disorders of gait and hysterical paresis had often set in after complete recovery and could be related to external stress. Depression was almost universal. Evidence of premorbid instability could often be discerned, but not in every case. Four patients had developed obsessional disorders for the first time. Other symptoms such as headache, blackouts and temporary loss of memory were occasionally hard to apportion to psychogenic or physiogenic causes.

Aseptic Meningitis (Acute Benign Lymphocytic Meningitis)

Aseptic meningitis is mainly due to viral infection. The Echo viruses are most frequently incriminated, or the mumps virus even in the absence of obvious parotitis (Grist, 1967). Other viruses include the Coxsackie group, the virus of acute lymphocytic choriomeningitis, infectious mononucleosis, pre-paralytic poliomyelitis, and psittacosis. Investigation of the precise cause is often inconclusive. Non-viral causes must also be considered, including the early stages of tuberculous meningtis, brain abscess, cerebral syphilis, leptospirosis and incompletely treated pyogenic meningitis (Lambert, 1972).

Cases occur in small epidemics and also arise sporadically. Epidemics are commoner in the summer and autumn when the circulation of enteroviruses among the population reaches a peak. The onset is abrupt with symptoms similar to those of pyogenic meningitis, but most illnesses are mild, running a course of 2–10 days then subsiding spontaneously. General malaise may persist for several weeks thereafter. Occasionally the meningitic symptoms and the cerebrospinal fluid abnormalities persist much longer and tuberculous meningitis may then be diagnosed in error.

The cerebrospinal fluid is under increased pressure and contains 50–1000 cells per millilitre of which most are lymphocytes. The protein is elevated but the chloride and sugar content are usually normal.

Enduring sequelae are distinctly rare, except for the paralysis which follows poliomyelitis and some infections with the Coxsackie type A7 virus. Minor temporary debilities, on the other hand, are fairly common during convalescence. Muller *et al.* (1958) carried out a long-term follow-up of a large group of cases of aseptic meningitis and 'meningoencephalitis of unknown cause', and compared them with controls from the normal population. No major differences could be found with regard to mental symptoms, occupation, school performance or social adjustment. Out of 238 patients only 4 were definitely mentally disordered with impaired capacity for work, 2 had epilepsy, 2 had tonic pupils and 2 had endocrine disorder.

Tuberculous Meningitis

This more than any other form of meningitis is liable to lead to diagnostic error. The onset is insidious, pyrexia is low-grade and often considerably delayed, and neck stiffness can be very slight. Mental symptoms figure prominently from the outset, and evidence of an acute organic reaction can precede overt signs of meningeal infection.

The cerebral pathology is characteristic. A yellowish gelatinous exudate forms mainly at the base of the brain in the anterior basal cisterns and extending along the lateral sulci. Miliary tubercles are visible on the leptomeninges and along the principal cerebral arteries. Microscopically the inflammatory

reaction can be seen to involve the floor of the third ventricle but is usually nowhere pronounced. The neurones show degenerative changes and old caseous foci can often be found in the substance of the brain. Arteritis is prominent in large and small vessels at the base of the brain, and areas of infarction may occur. The basal exudate is often organised and adherent, obstructing the flow of cerebrospinal fluid and leading to internal hydrocephalus.

A prodromal phase of vague ill-health is usual, lasting for two to three weeks or longer. Anorexia is marked, but headache may be transient or even absent at this stage. Mental changes form an integral part of the picture, typically apathy, irritability and insidious change of personality. As long ago as 1868 Trousseau stressed that 'sadness setting in unaccountably is a premonitory sign of great value in a child'. Williams and Smith (1954) found that the earliest mental changes in their cases were often so gradual that they were imperceptible except to those who knew the patient well beforehand. A change towards clouded awareness was usually the first definite sign, the patient lying quietly and without apprehension. In one case the presenting symptom was of subjective impairment of memory.

As the disease progresses headache intensifies and low-grade pyrexia develops. Focal signs appear in the form of ptosis, oculomotor palsies, coarse tremor of the limbs and reflex abnormalities. Hemiplegia or other gross neurological defects may occur. Papilloedema is a late development, but choroidal tubercles are seen in the retina in up to 20% of cases (Walton, 1977). These are rounded or oval yellow patches, approximately half the size of the optic disc.

The cerebrospinal fluid is under increased pressure, with up to 500 cells, mostly lymphocytes. The protein is moderately increased to 100 mg/ml with a meningitic Lange curve, the sugar is reduced below 50, and the chloride much reduced to 500 mg/ml or below. The diagnosis is confirmed when tubercle bacilli can be identified or cultured from the fluid, but this is not achieved in every case. The CT scan may show hydrocephalus, focal infarcts and exudate in basal brain cisterns (Rovira *et al.*, 1980).

The mental abnormalities increase with drowsiness, confusion, disorientation, and inability to sustain a rational conversation. Characteristically the patient sleeps when alone but becomes disturbed when roused, in contrast to the perpetual 'silent struggling delirium' of purulent meningitis. Occasionally the patient is hallucinated and wildly delirious. The terror may resemble that of delirium tremens, or Wernicke's encephalopathy may be simulated when the onset is abrupt and oculomotor palsies are present. Formerly typhoid was often suggested by the combination of headache, fever and delirium.

Without treatment progressive internal hydrocephalus develops, coma supervenes and the patient dies in a state of decerebrate rigidity. Nowadays, however, the 'confusional' stage evolves during treatment to an 'amnesic' stage which may last for many weeks. Williams and Smith (1954) have described the picture in detail. It is remarkably constant in kind though varying in degree, consisting essentially of a disproportionate disturbance of memory in relation to other cognitive defects. The patient may appear reasonably alert, and copes fairly well with intellectual problems, but proves to have a grave defect in retaining new information for more than a few minutes. Confabulation may be much in evidence, and memory for temporal sequences is severely disorganised. Memory is hazy for the events of the illness and those preceding it for several weeks or months, but beyond this is usually intact. This stage was sufficiently characteristic to betray a diagnostic error in one of their cases:

A man with a recent extension of known pulmonary tuberculosis complained of headache, became irrational and aggressive, and later had a fit. The cerebrospinal fluid showed a pleocytosis with raised protein and reduced sugar. He developed a slight dysarthria but no other focal signs.

Tuberculous meningitis was diagnosed and treatment started. In spite of this he deteriorated, became euphoric and fatuous, and showed gross intellectual deterioration. He remained normally oriented, however, and memory functions were well preserved. The diagnosis was reconsidered, the Wassermann reaction was found to be positive in the blood and cerebrospinal fluid, and he proved to be suffering from general paresis.

(Williams and Smith, 1954)

Throughout the amnesic phase the patient is usually euphoric and shows little concern about his memory difficulties. Some, however, are withdrawn, negativistic, paranoid or acutely depressed.

During recovery, memory continues to lag behind improvement in other intellectual faculties. Retention of current events improves gradually, or occasionally returns with dramatic suddenness. The period of retrograde amnesia meanwhile steadily contracts towards the time of onset of the illness.

With cure of the infection, as judged by the return of the cerebrospinal fluid to normal, there is usually a complete restitution of normal memory functions,

though a persistent amnesic gap remains for the period of overt confusion and disorientation. Williams and Smith followed 19 cases for periods of up to 4 years; none showed measurable defects of intellect, personality or memorising ability, although four complained of subjective forgetfulness for minor day to day events. Three others complained of slight defects of concentration or were said by their relatives to show a lessened sense of responsibility. All, however, had amnesia for the early weeks or months of the illness, even those who had seemed alert and rational throughout. Six had a persistent retrograde amnesia, sometimes extending for periods of months or years prior to the illness, with haziness for details, some complete gaps, and inability to organise past events into correct temporal sequence:

A young man of 22 developed severe tuberculous meningitis. He had a long and difficult illness requiring some nine months of treatment. Three years later he was doing well in clerical work and had recently been promoted. His memorizing of current experience was normal. However, he still had a substantial retrograde amnesia for events some 6 months before the clinical onset of his illness, and had entirely lost some specific skills such as typing acquired during this period. The amnesia extended also to the first 4 months of the illness itself.

With present-day management a full physical and mental recovery can usually be secured when diagnosis has been prompt. Williams and Smith (1954) found that the majority of patients returned gradually to their former efficiency. Headache or neurotic developments were conspicuous by their absence. However when neurological complications have been grave at the height of the illness there may be residual hemiparesis, paraparesis, epilepsy or intellectual impairment in association with hydrocephalus. Blindness or visual defects may result from optic atrophy, and deafness occurs in a minority. Hypothalamic damage occasionally leads to diabetes insipidus, disturbance of sleep rhythm, or precocious puberty in children.

Lorber (1961) followed the long-term results in 100 children who survived the acute illness. A large variety of sequelae were seen but the number of children seriously affected was surprisingly small. Seventy-seven had made a complete recovery, including some with very severe neurological abnormalities during the active phase of the illness. Twenty-three showed defects in the form of paresis, fits, deafness or blindness, sometimes with gratifying improvement over time. Fits persisted in only 8 children despite their frequency in the acute stages. Six of the 23 were profoundly mentally retarded; all of these had been under two years of age and severely affected when first seen, and all had major neurological sequelae. In the remainder there was no evidence that intellect had been impaired. Among children of normal intellect there were 6 with disorders of character and behaviour, 4 in association with a physical handicap and 2 without apparent relation to the meningitis.

Details of treatment are fully described by Parsons (1979).

Cerebral Abscess

Cerebral abscesses can present with remarkably few definite signs and symptoms. Headache may be slight and intermittent, papilloedema is often late, focal cerebral signs can be minimal, and pyrexia tends to be absent in the chronic stage. It is essential, therefore, to consider the diagnosis when change of temperament or mild confusion is accompanied by evidence of ill health for which no immediate cause is obvious. In a large series of metastatic brain abscesses Gates et al. (1950) found that psychiatric symptoms were present from the start in almost a quarter of cases, and were exceeded in frequency only by headache.

Cerebral abscess is rarely seen without a focus of infection elsewhere, though this may be well concealed. Important sources near the brain include infection of the middle ear and mastoid cells, and extension from the frontal and sphenoidal sinuses. Head injury may convey infection by direct penetration, or open up pathways from the sinuses or ear when the base of the skull is fractured. The principal extracranial source is chronic suppurative disease of the lungs and pleura—bronchiectasis, lung abscess and empyema. Less commonly the abscess results from a general pyaemic infection caused by pelvic or abdominal suppuration, osteomyelitis, boils, cellulitis, or subacute bacterial endocarditis. Paradoxical embolism of infected material may occur via septal defects in patients with congenital heart disease. With extracranial sources the abscesses are often multiple.

The organisms chiefly responsible are the streptococcus, staphylococcus, pneumococcus or E. coli. The developing abscess arises from an area of suppurating encephalitis which becomes progressively walled off from the surrounding brain by a fibrous and glial reaction. Inflammation of the overlying meninges varies in severity with the activity of the lesion. The abscess may grow large with distortion and compression of surrounding brain structures, but intracranial pressure may be little disturbed because the process is so gradual.

Classical symptoms are headache, vomiting and mild delirum, but these may sometimes be submerged in the symptoms of the predisposing infection. Alternatively the abscess may remain quiescent at the time of the original infection, and a latent interval of many months may follow before symptoms are declared. In the interim the patient shows evidence of chronic ill-health—intermittent headache, malaise, loss of appetite and weight, constipation, occasional chills, depression and irritability. Ultimately more definite signs appear, sometimes closely simulating cerebral tumour. Headache intensifies and may be paroxysmal, evidence of toxaemia increases, fits may occur and focal neurological signs are declared.

The common temporal lobe abscess is usually derived from middle ear infection. Motor signs are often very slight, and careful testing of the visual fields may be needed to display the quadrantic hemianopia. Dysphasic symptoms may be detected with abscesses of the dominant lobe. The alternative route from the middle ear is to the cerebellum. Signs can again be slight, with nystagmus, hypotonia and incoordination of the ipsilateral limbs, or cranial nerve pareses from involvement of the nearby brain stem. Frontal lobe abscesses arise from sinus infection or frontal fracture, and may lack all focal signs apart from unilateral anosmia. Concentration and memory may be markedly impaired and personality change much in evidence. In all such cases signs of raised intracranial pressure can be slight or absent, even with very large abscesses, and papilloedema may be late. In Gates et al.'s (1950) series papilloedema was present in less than one-third of patients.

Some degree of aseptic meningitis may produce obvious neck stiffness on examination. Examination of the cerebrospinal fluid is valuable for diagnosis but can be hazardous. The pressure is often raised and the protein elevated. The cells are mostly lymphocytes and rarely exceed 100/ml so long as the abscess remains walled off. The sugar and chloride are normal, and organisms are not obtained. With the advent of the CT scan lumbar puncture can usually be avoided. The abscess is revealed after scan enhancement and has a characteristic appearance—the capsule shows as a ring-shaped area of increased density surrounded by cerebral oedema. Exploratory puncture may be necessary for final diagnosis and to determine the causative organism. A polymorphonuclear leucocytosis is usual in the blood. The electroencephalogram shows changes broadly similar to those of tumour.

Even with modern management a mortality of up to 40% is still liable to be encountered (Legg, 1979). Some degree of permanent disability may be expected in another 40%. The long-term incidence of epilepsy is high, developing in some 70% of cases and sometimes with a latent interval of years before the fits appear. Anticonvulsants should therefore be prescribed routinely for at least 5 years.

Other Infective Processes

Acute organic reactions may accompany many systemic infections, especially at the extremes of life. An obvious example is the delirium sometimes seen with the acute exanthemata of childhood, likewise the impairment of consciousness or delirium which occur with pneumonia in the elderly. Slater and Roth (1969) discuss the various causes which may be operative. Cerebral anoxia often appears to be responsible, or the influence of toxic substances derived from the infecting micro-organisms. More complex metabolic disturbances must sometimes be postulated, or the accumulation of toxic intermediate products. Fever itself may play a direct part.

In the infections considered below, however, there is more definite evidence of cerebral involvement by the disease process itself. The conditions will be dealt with briefly, and text-books of general medicine should be consulted for further details.

Typhus Fever

Of the several varieties of typhus, that due to Rickettsia prowazeki is the most common. Epidemics are intimately associated with famines and wars and the infection is transmitted by the body louse. Mental and neurological manifestations are usually prominent, and there is abundant evidence that the causative organism invades the nervous system directly. The rickettsiae invade the endothelial cells of small blood vessels, producing foci of thrombosis and necrosis in various organs including the brain. Characteristic 'typhus nodules' consist of perivascular accumulations of glial, endothelial and phagocytic cells.

Symptoms consist of pyrexia, delirum, malaise, severe headache, cough and generalised aching. A characteristic rash appears on the fifth day of fever. More definite nervous system manifestations appear towards the end of the febrile period and are of serious import. Headache becomes continuous and

periods of delirium alternate with stupor or coma. Focal signs appear in the form of hemiplegia, ataxia, bulbar dysfunction, deafness or optic neuritis. Meningeal irritation is common and the cerebrospinal fluid shows a lymphocytosis and increased globulin. Among survivors evidence of cerebral damage frequently persists.

Trypanosomiasis ('Sleeping Sickness')

The South African forms of trypanosomiasis are due to the protozoa Trypanosoma gambiense and T. rhodesiense. They are transmitted by the bite of the tsetse fly. An initial febrile stage consists of bouts of pyrexia, asthenia, adenitis, rashes and hepatosplenomegaly. This merges into the sleeping sickness stage which is essentially a chronic meningoencephalitis with the organisms appearing in the cerebrospinal fluid. The patient develops tremors, fits, incoordination or hemiplegia. Mental disturbances are prominent with somnolence, apathy and eventually coma. Death usually occurs within a year if the disease is untreated.

Cerebral Malaria

Delirium may be marked at the peaks of fever in any variety of malaria, but sometimes there is more acute and dramatic evidence of cerebral involvement. This is most common with infections due to Plasmodium falciparum ('malignant tertian malaria'). In fatal cases the brain is seen to be congested and oedematous, with numerous areas of haemorrhage and softening around vessels.

The cerebral capillaries are filled with parasites in various stages of development. The cerebral symptoms usually appear in the second or third week of the illness, but they can sometimes be the initial manifestation. They can be cataclysmic in onset. Severe delirium is accompanied by bursting headache and high pyrexia. The patient is often combative and excitable before coma supervenes. Fits can be the presenting feature and focal signs are common—hemiplegia, dysphasia, hemianopia or cerebellar ataxia. Retinal haemorrhages and papilloedema may occur.

The picture can simulate encephalitis, meningitis, cerebral tumour, epilepsy, cerebrovascular lesions, or a variety of acute psychiatric disorders (Boshes, 1947). Mistakes are particularly likely to be made in the rare cases when the patient is afebrile. Nadeem and Younis (1977) also stress clouding of consciousness may be absent initially. Of 39 patients admitted to a Sudanese psychiatric hospital with mental illness precipitated by physical disease, 17 proved to have malaria. Half of these showed psychiatric disturbances in clear consciousness. Thus where malaria is endemic it must be borne in mind in all patients with psychoses of acute onset, whether or not organic features are evident in the mental state.

Rapid treatment is vital, so examination of blood smears must not be delayed in possible cases. Care must be taken to enquire about countries in which the patient may have lived or travelled whenever an acute organic reaction occurs without obvious cause.

Cerebral Cysticercosis

The cysticercus stage of the tapeworm may occur in man, usually that of *Taenia solium*. Common sites include the skeletal muscles and the brain. Obrador (1948) has described the clinical picture in Mexico where the infestation is extremely common.

Multiple cysts are usually present within the brain, and the main damage appears to occur when the larvae begin to die. There is then an intense inflammatory reaction in an attempt to wall off the irritating process. The circulation of the cerebrospinal fluid is often obstructed.

The usual presentation is with focal fits, or symptoms of raised intracranial pressure which simulate cerebral tumour. Localising signs are relatively uncommon. In advanced cases the picture may be mistaken for presenile dementia or cerebral syphilis.

The cerebrospinal fluid shows 15–100 cells of which a large proportion may be eosinophils, an increase in protein, and a positive reaction to the complement fixation test for cysticercosis. Calcification of the cysts may be seen on X-ray, both within the skull and in the skeletal muscles.

Benign Myalgic Encephalomyelitis
('Royal Free Disease')

This puzzling disorder usually appears in small epidemics. Features emphasised by Walton (1977) include its liability to occur in institutions, a selective incidence in females, the severity of symptoms in relation to the slightness of signs, and the absence of any evidence as to its cause.

The symptoms have tended to vary considerably in different outbreaks. The onset is usually with intense malaise, lassitude and dizziness, sometimes with sore throat, headache or gastrointestinal disturbance. Pyrexia is slight or absent. Generalised pains occur in the limbs and back, and there is often slight neck stiffness and some degree of lymphadenopathy.

Many cases recover after a few days without involvement of the nervous system, but others develop a variety of neurological symptoms. Flaccid weakness of the limbs is common, with a characteristic intermittency of the muscular contraction on effort. Muscle pain and tenderness may be marked, with paraesthesiae, hyperaesthesia and analgesia of irregular distribution. Cranial nerve palsies have very occasionally been reported. Psychological symptoms are usually prominent, especially severe depression or emotional lability, and an hysterical component may be grafted onto the neurological picture. Typically the symptoms show considerable variation from day to day.

Objective neurological findings are distinctly rare (*British Medical Journal*, 1970a). The tendon reflexes are usually normal, or only slightly increased or decreased, and sensory changes may be difficult to confirm by neurological examination. The blood picture shows no specific changes, and the erythrocyte sedimentation rate is mostly normal. The cerebrospinal fluid is under normal pressure and shows normal constituents.

The great majority of patients recover completely and major persistent disability is rare. Occasional cases have shown continued weakness of the limbs, and in a minority rehabilitation can be long and tedious with marked fatigue, generalised aches and pains, and repeated relapses over the succeeding months (The Medical Staff of the Royal Free Hospital, 1957). Functional disturbances sometimes remain prominent, particularly in those who have spent many weeks or months in hospital.

Kendell (1967) surveyed the widespread psychiatric disturbances observed during and after various epidemics. He described 2 patients in detail who showed long-lasting and severe changes of mood and behaviour as an aftermath. One developed temporal lobe epilepsy and had recurrent bouts of depression for 8 years thereafter, with histrionic attention-seeking behaviour and numerous suicide attempts. The other had similar recurrent depressions and frequent self-destructive outbursts, still present 5 years after the illness. Damage was postulated to have occurred in neural mechanisms underlying the control of mood and behaviour to account for such severe and prolonged disturbances.

The disease is widely believed to represent the effects of a viral infection with involvement of the central nervous system. However McEvedy and

Beard (1970a, 1970b, 1973) re-examined the credentials of the disease and argued against a physical aetiology. In an analysis of data from the 1955 outbreak at the Royal Free Hospital they pointed out that the initial manifestations consisted entirely of subjective complaints—headache, malaise, dizziness, back pain and depression. Moreover these were remarkably similar to those seen in an epidemic of overbreathing among a group of schoolgirls. Cases with pharyngitis may have been due to the coincident outbreak of streptococcal sore throat in the hospital at the time. Pyrexia exceeding 100°F occurred in only 4·5% of cases and the ESR was over 20 in only 1·5%. The sensory changes were mostly of glove and stocking type, and the motor weaknesses were unbacked by reflex changes.

Had an encephalitic process been responsible it was remarkable that prolonged disturbance of consciousness was never seen, that there was no mortality, and that changes were uniformly absent in the cerebrospinal fluid when over 300 persons were affected. McEvedy and Beard concluded instead that a case could be made out for regarding the symptoms as 'the subjective complaints of a frightened and hysterical population'. Covert and intermittent overbreathing may have been responsible for dizziness, paraesthesiae and minor tetanic spasms. The sensory and motor findings appeared to fit such an hypothesis so closely that an organic theory would be tenable only if other evidence could be brought forward to support it.

They reinforced their conclusion by a review of fifteen recorded outbreaks of the disease (McEvedy and Beard, 1970b). The attack rate was always high in females compared to males, and relatively closed communities appeared to be especially susceptible. Eight of the outbreaks occurred among hospital nurses, and sometimes there had been a *bona fide* epidemic of poliomyelitis in the community at the time. In retrospect several of the outbreaks seemed essentially to be psychosocial phenomena, caused either by mass hysteria or altered 'medical perception' of the community. Thus medical attention had come to be concentrated on examination of the central nervous system, and cases had probably often been included when they were not immediately diagnosable as some other condition.

This challenging and interesting view has provoked a good deal of controversy (*British Medical Journal*, 1970b; Ramsay, 1973). The situation is unresolved, but clearly future epidemics will need to be carefully scrutinised with McEvedy and Beard's hypothesis in mind.

Acquired Immune Deficiency Syndrome ('AIDS')

AIDS seems destined to increase in the UK as has happened in the USA in recent years. The first case in England was reported in 1981; by February 1985, 132 patients had developed the disorder. Central nervous system involvement is relatively common.

The cause is a virus — Human T-cell Lymphotropic Virus type III (HTLV-III, commonly abbreviated to Human Immunodeficiency Virus, 'HIV'). This may lead to no more than a pyrexial illness with lymphadenopathy, but in a minority of individuals it produces the full syndrome of AIDS. The incubation period before the disease is declared varies from many months to several years. Promiscuous homosexual men constitute the major risk group, followed by intravenous drug abusers. Haemophiliacs, Haitians and persons with Central African connections are also at special risk.

The spectrum of the disease is summarised in guidelines issued by the Department of Health and Social Security (1985). It consists of multiple severe infections and certain neoplastic disorders, all reflecting an underlying cellular immune deficiency. *Pneumocystis carinii* pneumonia and Kaposi's sarcoma of the skin are the commonest forms of presentation. The mortality to date has been extremely high.

Widespread alarm within populations at risk has led to a high incidence of psychiatric disorder, even among persons not already affected. The social upheavals and repercussions are vividly described by Deuchar (1984). Many patients may therefore present to the psychiatrist with no more than a fear of the disease, and in the absence of a fully reliable diagnostic test the anxiety can at times be prolonged (Miller *et al.*, 1985). Special problems are encountered in that the earliest symptoms of central nervous involvement are frequently non-specific, consisting of lethargy, depression and social withdrawal. More definite signs consist of personality change, memory disorder, confusion, headaches, fits, ataxia or focal neurological signs.

Snider *et al.* (1983) have reviewed the neurological complications among patients affected in the USA. Fifty examples were described from among a total of 160 patients, the nervous system involvement often appearing early in otherwise asymptomatic individuals. Infective processes included a severe subacute encephalitis, toxoplasma brain abscesses, progressive multifocal leucoencephalopathy, cryptococcal meningitis and *Candida albicans* infections. Tumours consisted of lymphomas originating within the brain, or invading the meninges leading to cranial nerve neuropathies. Vascular complications were infarctions and cerebral haemorrhages, sometimes in the setting of thrombocytopaenia. Other patients showed focal brain lesions of an uncertain nature, self-limiting aseptic meningitis, or peripheral neuropathy. Levy *et al.* (1985) have extended these observations in a larger material.

The commonest picture in Snider *et al.*'s and Levy *et al.*'s series was subacute encephalitis, characterised in the early stages by malaise, loss of interests and subtle cognitive changes. Marked psychomotor retardation often gave the impression of depressive illness. Progression over weeks or months then led to profound dementia, the CT scan showing cerebral atrophy and periventricular white matter lucencies. Opportunistic infection with cytomegalovirus is probably often responsible, but recent evidence points to direct infection of brain cells with HIV virus as a major cause (Department of Health and Social Security, 1985).

Treatment is possible for several aspects of the CNS involvement, particularly for toxoplasmosis, herpes simplex infection and cerebral lymphomas. The early diagnosis of cerebral toxoplasmosis is especially important and is facilitated by an agglutination test (McCabe *et al.*, 1983). Suspicion of AIDS must always lead to urgent referral to a consultant physician or clinic dealing with genitourinary medicine or sexually transmitted diseases. Special precautions must be taken over the collection and handling of blood samples and other investigations.

Rheumatic Fever and Rheumatic Chorea

The relationship between these two diseases is incompletely understood, but chorea has sometimes been regarded as a form of 'rheumatic encephalitis' (Lees, 1970). The two may occur together, or chorea may be seen in the absence of joint, skin or heart manifestations. Fatal cases, however, almost always show evidence of rheumatic carditis.

The literature concerning the possible cerebral effects of the diseases is similarly inconclusive. Both rheumatic fever and chorea may occasionally be associated with psychotic illnesses, and behaviour disorder is recognised as extremely common in rheumatic chorea in children. Lewis (1956) pointed out that chorea exemplifies the interplay of hereditary, psychic and structural factors in the production of symptoms; it is more prone to occur in families with nervous disorder, the motor abnormalities can appear and disappear under emotional influences, and after-effects such as tics often seem to be conditioned by the original choreic disturbances of neuromuscular function.

Part of the problem in understanding the genesis of the mental abnormalities lies in the uncertainty which surrounds the cerebral pathology in rheumatic disease. Bruetsch (1940) described 'rheumatic' changes in the cerebral vessels, similar to those seen in the myocardium and elsewhere. Chronic cerebral endarteritis was found with secondary parenchymal damage, also glial nodules in the cortex and white matter, and connective tissue scars derived from proliferated blood vessels. The pathology in rheumatic chorea is incompletely documented, but a wide variety of inflammatory or degenerative changes have been described (Grinker and Sahs, 1966). Walton (1977) describes oedema and congestion, degeneration of neurones, very occasional perivascular infiltration and sometimes a neuroglial reaction. Such changes are said to be most marked in the corpus striatum, substantia nigra and subthalamic nucleus, but affect the cortex in some degree as well. Investigations during life do not greatly help to illuminate the cerebral pathological process—the cerebrospinal fluid is usually entirely normal and the electroencephalogram occasionally shows non-specific abnormalities.

Krauss (1946) described how experience of encephalitis lethargica led observers to turn attention to the sequelae of other infectious 'encephalopathies', chorea being one of the first to be examined. His own investigation of 24 patients showed that hyperkinesis in some degree was almost universal, in the form of restlessness, fidgetiness and inability to sit still. Compulsive utterances might appear, or localised tics such as blinking, stammering or shrugging. Many such features would almost certainly have been regarded as 'hysterical' prior to encephalitis lethargica. Neurasthenic symptoms were common in the form of headache, insomnia, fatigue and diminished perseverance. The patients often lacked vitality or colour in the personality. Intellect was rarely affected, but peculiarities of temperament were frequently marked—patients became sensitive, suspicious and seclusive while retaining awareness of the changes in themselves. Altogether Krauss concluded that these alterations formed a closely knit and sharply defined complex of post-choreic symptoms, though often not grossly obvious to superficial view.

Guttmann (1936) similarly stressed the persistence of personality disturbances and emotional instability after the acute effects of chorea had subsided. But against the implication of a specific cerebral pathology to account for these changes, he reported an equally strong impression that a particular type of person was prone to the disease. Constitutional factors seemed to be important, with a high incidence of mental and nervous disease among the relatives of patients. A 'choreopathic personality' had been described as typical of those who were susceptible to chorea. Thus the problem was conceived at the same time as a premorbid tendency and a post-illness defect, with obvious difficulty in establishing the correct aetiological relationships.

Bender (1942) found that rheumatic chorea was by far the most common form of 'encephalopathy' among child psychiatric referrals to the Bellevue Hospital. Many were sent because they were thought to have primary behaviour disorders, the chorea being either overlooked or considered coincidental. Such children were restless, irritable, emotionally unstable, inattentive and awkward in motility. They often displayed the classical 'naughty child syndrome'. They were unresponsive to discipline or psychotherapy, yet could improve spontaneously as the rheumatic process went on to recovery. Some children showed more bizarre disturbances with vague hallucinations, fears and panicky episodes. The abnormalities of motility occasionally had catatonic as well as choreiform features and the picture could closely resemble schizophrenia. Lewis and Minski (1935) similarly noted that in the more severe cases delusional trends could accompany the fleeting phases of anger or terror.

Still more severe manifestations can appear in the rare cases of rheumatic chorea in young adults, typified by 'chorea gravidarum' in pregnant women. The disease may be fatal in adults, and psychotic features are much more common. Delirium may occur, with hallucinations, delusions of persecution, persistent insomnia and much excitement ('maniacal chorea'). Lewis and Minski (1935) discussed the possibility that the mental symptoms might originate at least in part in the focal cerebral pathology of the disease. One of their patients, a nurse of 18, showed a grave choreic illness accompanied by disorientation, clouding of consciousness, auditory hallucinations, and many misinterpretations and ideas of reference which gradually improved over several months. She was mostly depressed but at times in a state of terror. For two days at the height of the illness she showed a right-sided flaccid paralysis, but the cerebrospinal fluid was entirely normal.

The following is another example in which electroencephalographic evidence pointed clearly to an organic basis for the protracted and puzzling mental illness:

A woman of 36 was seen when her son was referred to hospital on account of truanting from school and delinquent behaviour. She showed a severely abnormal personality, with high anxiety, numerous panic attacks, and bizarre beliefs of a quasi-psychotic nature. In her own previous history she had been hospitalised for over a year at the age of 17 with a diagnosis of 'rheumatic encephalitis associated with hysterical and schizophrenic features'.

She had been a delicate and imaginative child, extremely able at school but with a disturbed home background. At 10 she had suffered rheumatic fever. For some months prior to admission she had been depressed and listless with considerable loss of weight. Gradually she had become restless, with nervous tics of the hands and feet which were diagnosed first as hysterical and later as rheumatic chorea.

On admission there were numerous tic-like movements of the limbs, shrugging of the shoulders and occasional myoclonic-like jerks. No other abnormalities were discovered on physical examination. Her mood was labile, with tears one moment and cheerfulness the next. She eventually revealed a delusional belief that she had an evil thing inside her which accounted for her sister's death two years before she herself was born. She was hallucinated, seeing animals and seeing everything blue from time to time. She insisted that she could feel an insect crawling around inside her skull.

The choreiform movements settled after several weeks, but her subsequent course in hospital was stormy, with unpredictable and impulsive behaviour, marked seclusiveness, and difficulty in making any therapeutic contact. Habitually she carried a teddy-bear and a copy of Shelley to which she attributed magical qualities. From time to time she absconded from hospital or cut her left arm with glass or razor blades.

The electroencephalogram showed marked abnormalities, with frequent high voltage spikes and persistent evidence of a discharging focus in the right frontal region. After 6 months in hospital this improved progressively along with improvement in her behaviour and mental state. On follow-up during the next few years she remained manipulative and disturbed at home from time to time, and occasional choreiform movements appeared when under stress. The electroencephalogram still showed evidence of residual brain damage three years after the onset of the illness. When seen at the age of 36, however, the electroencephalogram was entirely normal.

Finally the affinities between acute rheumatic diseases and schizophrenia have attracted a good deal of attention. It has often been noted that schizophrenia is unusually common in the family histories of choreics (Guttmann, 1936; Krauss, 1946). Guttmann (1936) found in addition that a history of chorea was twice as common in patients with schizophrenia as in patients with manic-depressive psychosis. Krauss (1957) reported 20 patients with schizophrenia-like psychoses following various forms of brain insult, and found that 6 had had rheumatic fever with cerebral involvement. None had a demonstrable hereditary predisposition to schizophrenia. Further evidence comes from Bruetsch (1940). He found that a small group of schizophrenics showed progressive obliterating cerebral endarteritis at autopsy, together with evidence of chronic rheumatic heart disease, even though none had had a recent attack of rheumatic fever. He suggested that, as with valvular lesions, the rheumatic process might remain mildly active in the cerebral vessels throughout the patient's life, with intermittent progressions provoking episodes of psychotic behaviour. Among one hundred consecutive autopsies on schizophrenic patients, rheumatic valvular disease of the heart was discovered in 9%, always in association with possible rheumatic changes in the brain, and this was considered greatly to exceed the incidence in hospital autopsies generally. Unfortunately controlled investigations do not appear to have been carried out to explore the situation further. Fessel and Solomon (1960) have raised the possibility that some of Breutsch's cases may have been examples of systemic lupus erythematosus with psychosis, rather than rheumatic fever with cerebral involvement.

The 'Schizophrenia Virus'

A surprising development in schizophrenia research has involved the possible incrimination of a virus-like agent affecting the central nervous system in certain cases. The preliminary observations on the issue require replication but the evidence to date is intriguing.

Tyrrell et al. (1979) and Crow et al. (1979) discovered that the cerebrospinal fluid from certain schizophrenic patients exerted a cytopathic effect on fibroblast tissue cultures, similar in nature to that induced by viruses. The effect was shown in approximately one-third of 47 patients with acute schizophrenia, including those with entirely typical illnesses. No clinical features distinguished those patients who were positive for the effect from those who failed to show it. The responsible agent has not been identified, however, nor has it been propagated satisfactorily. Similar effects on tissue cultures were obtained by cerebrospinal fluid from 8 of 11 patients with chronic neurological diseases, mostly multiple sclerosis or Huntington's chorea, but were seen with only one of 25 patients with non-neurological disease.

Crow et al. postulate that the viral effects may be localised to systems of the brain concerned with higher mental functions, thus having issue in mental disorder without accompanying neurological features. Certainly schizophrenia-like pictures are not uncommon in the course of encephalitis due to established viruses, as discussed on p. 290. Such a thesis is reflected in Hunter et al.'s (1969) findings presented on p. 299.

Crow (1983a) further suggests that the putative virus may set in train the neurochemical disturbances underlying schizophrenia, acting in this way to make the patient's genetic predisposition overt. In those patients who proceed to a 'schizophrenic defect state' the virus may have spread especially widely within the brain. Other indirect evidence can be quoted in support of an infective aetiology, for example the seasonal incidence of birth and presentations, and certain family data that cannot be explained on a genetic basis alone (Crow, 1983b). Concordance has been found to be higher for schizochphrenia between same sex than different sex dizygotic twins and siblings, and higher in same sex dizygotic twins than in same sex sibs, all suggesting that physical proximity, and thereby infection, may bring additional hazards to genetically predisposed persons.

In a more recent formulation Crow (1984) hypothesises a retrovirus, gaining access to the genetic complement and contributing also in part to the vertical transmission of the disorder. Further epidemiological and family information, and evidence from cerebral dominance studies, are marshalled in support. Until the putative agent or agents have been more clearly established and identified, it will be hard to advance the argument further.

Chapter 9. Cerebrovascular Disorders

Diseases of the vascular system contribute greatly to the sum total of psychiatric disability, chiefly in the elderly population and mainly as a result of stroke. Cerebrovascular accidents will therefore be considered first, with emphasis on their psychiatric sequelae and the problems encountered in rehabilitation. Hypertension and migraine illustrate in an important fashion the possible role of emotional factors in organic disease and will also be dealt with here.

The syndrome of 'transient global amnesia' almost certainly rests on a cerebrovascular basis and, like subdural haematoma, may occasionally lead to mistakes in psychiatric diagnosis. Finally certain diseases of rather obscure aetiology, such as systemic lupus erythematosus and related collagen disorders will be described. The psychiatric components of such illnesses have gained increasing recognition and appear to be attributable in part to involvement of the cerebral vasculature.

Cerebrovascular Accidents

Cerebrovascular accidents are the third commonest cause of death after heart disease and cancer in the Western world. In Great Britain they emerge as the most frequent cause of severe disability in the community (Harris *et al.,* 1971). From a population of 250,000 (the basis for a district general hospital) it is estimated that some 500 strokes will occur per annum, of which 250 will need a lot of help and about 150 will be added to the accumulating number needing continued care (Hurwitz and Adams, 1972). The burden to the community, and to health and rehabilitation services is clearly enormous. Moreover approximately a quarter of victims are affected under 65 years of age and thus disabled during the productive years of their lives.

The principal causes—atherosclerosis and hypertension—slowly yield to greater understanding, though opportunities for taking preventive action remain limited to certain categories of patient. Factors susceptible to modification among predisposing causes include hypertension, heart disease,

diabetes, raised serum lipids and smoking.

A new interest and vigour attaches to the problems of rehabilitating the survivors, though here it is noteworthy that psychiatrists take little part. Much of the disability resulting from strokes is mental rather than physical, and psychological influences are often paramount in determining what progress is made. Yet there have been few systematic surveys of the extent and nature of the psychiatric sequelae of stroke. This would appear to be largely a consequence of the way in which services for patients are organised, with the burden of care falling chiefly on the geriatrician, the general physician and specialists in physical rehabilitation.

In what follows the general background to cerebrovascular accidents will be briefly sketched before reviewing what is known of the psychological and psychiatric aftermaths.

FORMS OF CEREBROVASCULAR ACCIDENT

Virtually all enduring effects of vascular disease on the brain can be reduced to two essential pathological processes—infarction and haemorrhage. The common denominator of both from the clinical point of view is the 'stroke', which may be loosely defined as a focal neurological disorder of abrupt development and due to a pathological process in blood vessels (Committee of National Institute of Neurological Diseases and Blindness, 1958).

Infarction is commoner than haemorrhage in a ratio of approximately 3 to 1. It is not only more frequent as an acute development but very much more so as a source of enduring disability. Thus approximately three-quarters of patients with infarctions survive, whereas more than four-fifths of patients with cerebral haemorrhage die. Infarction may result from thrombosis of vessels or from emboli which come to lodge within them. Haemorrhage may be primarily into the substance of the brain or into the subarachnoid space.

In addition to examples of 'completed stroke' one must recognise the multitude of patients with episodes, often recurrent, which depend upon brief and transient ischaemia of the brain. Such 'transient ischaemic attacks' have attracted increasing attention, and the understanding of their pathophysiological basis has led to important therapeutic advances.

Cerebral Haemorrhage

Intracranial haemorrhage, representing some 25% of all strokes, may be divided into primary intracerebral haemorrhage and subarachnoid haemorrhage. The former is intimately associated with hypertension as the main aetiological factor, and the latter with rupture of an aneurysm or angioma. The differentiation is not always absolute, since bleeding may occur into brain tissue in the neighbourhood of a ruptured aneurysm, and blood may gain access to the ventricular system and subarachnoid space after primary intracerebral haemorrhage. The two disorders are, however, in the main distinct. Subarachnoid haemorrhage is dealt with separately on p. 334 et seq. because the sequelae have been studied especially closely from the psychiatric point of view.

Primary intracerebral haemorrhage is most common in patients between the ages of 60 and 80. For practical purposes it is almost always associated with hypertension. The precise mechanism whereby haemorrhage develops has been the subject of some controversy, but it seems probable that bleeding is often initiated from microaneurysms situated along the course of small arteries. These appear to develop in relation to hypertension in older subjects, and their distribution accords well with sites where haemorrhage is common (Russell, 1963).

The onset is often during exertion, and very rarely during sleep as with cerebral thrombosis. The patient is abruptly seized with an ill-defined sensation of something wrong within the head, and shortly thereafter develops hemiparesis, dysphasia or other form of neurological deficit. Headache and vomiting frequently occur. As the paralysis worsens mental confusion gives way to rapid impairment of consciousness. The picture characteristically worsens over one or more hours, usually to deep coma with stertorous breathing and a slow bounding pulse. Neck stiffness is common and the cerebrospinal fluid is often bloodstained.

The most common site of haemorrhage is in the putamen and internal capsule, from rupture of the lenticulostriate artery. A dense contralateral hemiplegia may be accompanied by deviation of the head and eyes away from the side of the lesion. The formation of a large intracerebral haematoma can lead to secondary effects due to tentorial herniation and brain stem compression. Another site of predilection is the cerebellum, leading to a similar picture but with vertigo and ataxia during the early stages. With haemorrhage into the pons consciousness is usually lost rapidly, the pupils are unequal or pinpoint, hyperpyrexia may occur, and quadriplegia is likely to be present.

Early mortality is extremely high, and survivors are usually severely crippled. Mild examples with only brief loss of consciousness may, however, make a reasonably good recovery. Medical treatment during the acute stages rests primarily on excellent nursing care. Steroids may be given to reduce cerebral swelling. Surgical evacuation of the clot has been undertaken in carefully selected cases but has proved in general to be of limited value. It is most likely to be of benefit when the haematoma is in the central white matter or the cerebellar hemisphere and the patient is not deeply unconscious at the time (Ransohoff et al., 1971).

Cerebral Infarction

Thrombosis is considerably more common than embolism as a cause of infarction. This has tended, however, to be used as the diagnostic category when no other cause is clinically evident for the stroke. The role of embolism has come to be recognised increasingly, and is now, for example, thought to account for about half of the cases of infarction in the internal carotid territory (Blackwood et al., 1969).

Cerebral thrombosis is mostly seen in patients over 60, but appears to be increasing in frequency among the middle aged. It has emerged as a rare but serious complication in young women taking the contraceptive pill. The principal cause is atherosclerosis, namely that form of arteriosclerosis in which lipid material accumulates beneath the intima of affected vessels. Hypertension aggravates the process, and this, like diabetes mellitus, may be an important contributory factor in younger subjects. As the plaques thicken the lumen narrows and flow becomes reduced. The vessels chiefly involved are the larger arteries—the aorta, carotids, middle cerebrals and vertebrobasilar arteries. The size of the infarct eventually produced will depend on the vessels principally involved and also on the efficiency of the collateral circulation.

An important factor in precipitating thrombosis may often be a transient fall in blood pressure, further compromising the flow in vessels already critically affected. Thus an abrupt reduction of cardiac output, as after myocardial infarction or episodes of ventricular fibrillation, may present with cerebral symptoms. The reduction of blood pressure which occurs during sleep may sometimes be enough to tip the scales (Walton, 1982).

Interest has been revived in the minute 'lacunar infarcts' which develop deep in the brain substance from occlusion of small penetrating arteries supplying the basal ganglia, thalamus, internal capsule, optic radiation or pons (Fisher, 1965, 1968, 1971; Weisberg, 1982). Such infarcts may be multiple and almost microscopic in size. They have been found to outnumber all other strokes combined at autopsy. Hypertension appears to be an associated finding in the great majority of cases.

The clinical picture in cerebral thrombosis usually develops abruptly, though less markedly so than with embolism. Occasionally the development is ingravescent, with the neurological deficit increasing over hours or days and progressing in a stepwise or saltatory fashion. Onset is often during sleep, with the patient waking to find paralysis, dysphasia, diplopia or other deficits. Headache may be present in the early stages but is often absent throughout. Some degree of mental confusion is common, but consciousness may be little if at all impaired. Much will depend on the size and location of the infarcted brain tissue. Large infarcts may be followed by swelling of the affected hemisphere, leading to coma and a picture closely resembling cerebral haemorrhage. An important differentiating feature may be a history of previous small episodes, rapidly clearing, and perhaps disregarded by the patient and his family at the time.

Cerebral embolism can in the majority of cases be traced to disease of the heart or great vessels. Fragments of thrombus may be derived from atheromatous plaques in the aorta or carotids, or consist of newly formed platelet aggregates ('white emboli') which have formed in relation to abnormal areas of the vessel wall (Russell, 1970). A cardiac origin is probable when there is atrial fibrillation, mitral stenosis, subacute bacterial endocarditis or a recent myocardial infarction. Rare forms include paradoxical embolism, in which a congenital cardiac malformation allows material from the veins of the legs to reach the brain by bypassing the pulmonary circulation. Cerebral fat embolism is closely linked to trauma.

The clinical picture is usually extremely acute in onset, developing within seconds or a minute and usually during activity. The neurological deficit is typically maximal from the outset, often with rapid resolution over the first few hours thereafter. Headache is usually absent. Consciousness is often relatively preserved, or even retained completely.

Rare cases have been reported of multiple microembolism, in which a fluctuating acute confusional state is punctuated by transient episodes of dysphasia, multiple pareses and episodes of visual disturbance, pursuing a progressive downhill course to death (McDonald, 1967). The source in the examples reported was an ulcerating atheromatous lesion in the aorta or internal carotid artery, the emboli consisting of multiple cholesterol crystals.

The prognosis for cerebral infarction is much better than for cerebral haemorrhage. Approximately 20% of patients die in the acute stage, 20% recover completely, and 60% are left with residual disability. Recovery from emboli is in general much quicker and more complete than after thrombosis, since collateral channels will usually be more readily available. In both, however, much will depend on the size of the infarct produced.

Treatment in the acute stage includes not only nursing care and physiotherapy as appropriate, but also evaluation of the patient's cardiovascular status. Possible sources of emboli must be sought out with care. Anti-coagulant therapy may be indicated where embolism is suspected, or operative intervention on a stenosed or atheromatous carotid artery, but these are matters for neurological assessment.

Cerebral Arterial Syndromes

The form which the neurological deficits take after thrombosis or embolism obviously depends on the vessels principally affected. It is now recognised, however, that much variation occurs from one individual to another, and that partial and incomplete syndromes are extremely common. The following can, however, be diagnosed with reasonable confidence:

Occlusion of the main trunk of the *middle cerebral artery* leads to a contralateral hemiparesis and sensory loss of cortical type, often with hemianopia due to involvement of the optic radiation. When the more distal parts of the artery are affected alone the weakness mainly involves the face, arm and hand. Dysphasia is common in dominant hemisphere lesions, and agnosic syndromes and body image disturbances with non-dominant hemisphere lesions. Infarction of the deep territory of the middle cerebral artery, which includes the posterior limb of the internal capsule, leads to a dense and global hemiplegia.

Mesulam *et al.* (1976) have drawn attention to the states of mental confusion which can follow middle cerebral infarctions on the right, sometimes leading to diagnostic difficulties in that focal signs may consist of little more than left sided cortical sensory loss and visual inattention. A toxic or metabolic cause for the acute organic reaction had often been suspected in their patients. Salient features were inattentiveness to relevant stimuli, and inability to maintain a coherent stream of thought or behaviour. Disorientation, anomia, incontinence, an abnormal gait and lack of concern for the illness were characteristic. An example was as follows:

A 61-year-old man was discovered in an incoherent agitated state, banging on doors and shouting in the night. He was disoriented in all spheres, very distractible, and with a severely diminished span of attention. His speech contained paraphasic errors and there were difficulties in naming objects. Gait was unsteady and he was incontinent and unkempt. Over the next few days the agitation gave way to an amiable placid state, but the incoherence and impaired attention span persisted for several weeks. Angiography showed occlusion of the right angular branch of the middle cerebral artery.

(Mesulam *et al.,* 1976)

Infarctions in the distribution of the *anterior cerebral artery* lead to contralateral hemiparesis affecting the leg more severely than the arm. There may be a grasp reflex in the hand. Cortical sensory loss and motor dysphasia are often present as well. Mental changes may resemble those of a global dementia and incontinence may be a prominent feature. Residual personality changes of frontal lobe type may occur. Involvement of the penetrating branch which supplies the anterior limb of the internal capsule (Heubner's artery) leads to paralysis of the contralateral side of the face and arm, often with sensory loss of spinothalamic type in the contralateral limbs.

Occlusion of the *internal carotid artery* can be entirely asymptomatic, emerging as a chance finding at autopsy. If the circulation should fail, infarction occurs principally in the territory of the middle cerebral artery, though the distribution of the anterior cerebral may be involved as well. Much depends on the efficiency of the collateral circulation and the patency of the circle of Willis. The common 'watershed infarct' lies at the borderland of the major arterial territories—a sickle-shaped zone on the lateral surface of the hemisphere (Fisher, 1968). The resulting clinical picture is often indistinguishable

from that of middle cerebral infarction. A common tell-tale sign is monocular blindness, fleeting or permanent, in the eye contralateral to the hemiplegia, due to interruption of blood flow in the ophthalmic or retinal arteries. Evidence of the source of infarction may also be obtained by noting a bruit over the bifurcation of the common carotid, loss of pulsation unilaterally in the neck, or decreased retinal arterial pressure on the affected side. An ipsilateral Horner's syndrome may result from involvement of the sympathetic fibres in the carotid sheath.

Sometimes mental symptoms may predominate with general slowing up, decreased spontaneous activity, dyspraxia and incontinence, all pointing to a frontal lobe deficit. If the abruptness of onset and fluctuation in the symptoms is not appreciated, the nature of the lesion may not be detected as in the following example reported by Fisher (1968):

A man of 68 had shown a change of personality some four months before, consisting of selfishness, overeating and impoliteness, combined with clumsiness, falling, spilling food, episodic difficulty in speaking and urinary incontinence. On examination he stared vacantly into space, spoke in a quiet voice, forgot quickly and was clumsy in all his movements. There were elements of dysphasia, both hands were dyspraxic, and he broke spasmodically into tears. Angiography showed left carotid occlusion but this was felt to be irrelevant. He died suddenly, however, and autopsy revealed an extensive watershed infarct in the left hemisphere.

The main effect of *posterior cerebral artery* infarction is a contralateral hemianopia, sometimes with visual hallucinations, visual agnosias or spatial disorientation. Visual perseveration may consist of a train of objects repeating within the affected field, or persistence of an image in the centre of the field after the object is removed (Caplan, 1980). Alexia without agraphia occurs when damage has affected the dominant occipital lobe along with the splenium of the corpus callosum (p. 43, Chapter 2). Involvement of the perforating branches to the thalamus and brain stem may lead to a contralateral thalamic syndrome, or mild contralateral hemiparesis and cerebellar ataxia. Bilateral infarctions may lead to cortical blindness, sometimes with conspicuous denial of disability (Anton's syndrome).

Adams and Hurwitz (1974) stress that psychological disturbances are frequent with posterior cerebral infarctions. Transient mental confusion may be the only manifestation apart from a hemianopia which is difficult to demonstrate. Amnesic syndromes may also figure prominently when the hippocampus and other limbic structures are involved bilaterally on the inferomedial surfaces of the temporal lobes (Victor *et al.*, 1961; Benson *et al.*, 1974). The question of whether amnesia can occur after strictly unilateral infarctions in the posterior cerebral territory is reviewed by Benson *et al.* (1974), likewise the problem of whether amnesia can ever be the sole manifestation. Both are questions which cannot be anwered decisively at present.

Strokes in the distribution of *the vertebrobasilar system* are extremely diverse in their manifestations. The vertebrals unite to form the basilar artery which in turn feeds the posterior cerebral arteries; from this system perforating branches supply the brain stem and cerebellum.

Total occlusion of the basilar artery is usually rapidly fatal with loss of consciousness, a decerebrate state and quadriplegia. Partial occlusions of the system, with infarctions in the territory of individual branches, can lead to a multitude of pictures. The hall-mark is brain stem involvement, with bilateral or unilateral pyramidal signs and a variety of ipsilateral cranial nerve palsies. Ipsilateral cerebellar deficits may also be present. Common signs therefore include weakness or paralysis of one or all four limbs, long tract sensory deficits which may be contralateral to the hemiparesis, diplopia, pupillary changes, Horner's syndrome, facial numbness, vertigo, unilateral or bilateral deafness, dysarthria, dysphagia, cerebellar ataxia and visual field defects. Major obstacles to recovery include disturbances of balance and persistent dizziness. Intellectual processes are usually little if at all affected.

The various pictures of coma, decerebration and akinetic mutism which may follow brain stem infarction are described by Plum and Posner (1972). One rare but striking picture is the so-called 'locked-in' syndrome which follows a circumscribed infarction affecting the descending motor pathways in the ventral part of the pons. This is compatible with full wakefulness and alertness, despite aphonia and total paralysis of the limbs, trunk and lower cranial nerves. Such patients are responsive and sentient, although their repertoire of responses is limited to blinking, and jaw and eye movements. Feldman's (1971) patient was able to learn to employ blinks and eye movements, using morse code, to communicate with those around her, displaying preserved memory and appropriate awareness of her environment.

Caplan (1980) reviews further striking pictures with prominent behavioural change following occlu-sion of the rostral branches of the basilar artery (the 'top of the basilar' syndrome). The result is infarction in the midbrain, thalamus and portions of the temporal and occipital lobes, producing an array of visual, oculomotor and behavioural abnormalities. Motor dysfunction can be minimal, leading to difficulties with diagnosis. The remarkable syndrome of '*peduncular hallucinosis*' consists of vivid, well-formed hallucinations, sometimes confined to a half-field of vision and occurring with or without visual field defects. The hallucinations are recognised by the patient as unreal despite their dramatic nature. Caplan's patient saw a parrot in beautiful plumage to the right, and pictures of a relative flashed on the wall to the left. Others have reported vivid hallucinations of animals, of children at play with toys, fleeting images of the head of a dog or intricate lines and colours lasting for an hour or two at a time. States of *bizarre disorientation* accompanied by somnolence may likewise reflect disturbance in the rostral portions of the brain-stem reticular formation. In response to questions one patient said she was lying on a beach at Nice, another that she was speaking to friends on the telephone. Such answers, entirely divorced from the current reality, may appear as an extraordinary form of confabulation. Other patients may dream excessively, with inability to distinguish the dreams from reality. Oculomotor disturbances and pupillary abnormalities will usually betray the origins of such abnormal mental states.

Lacunar Infarcts

The syndromes associated with *lacunar infarcts* are outlined by Fisher (1968, 1971). Very small lacunes may be asymptomatic, but those 0·5–1·5 cm in diameter are likely to produce deficits, especially when situated along the corticobulbar-spinal-motor system or long sensory tracts. Lacunes in the posterior limb of the internal capsule or pons may lead to a pure motor hemiparesis, those in the posterolateral thalamus to a pure sensory stroke. Others are associated with ataxia, dysarthria and a variety of cranial nerve palsies. The deficits resulting from lacunar infarcts are usually slight and recover rapidly, but the effects of successive small lesions may sometimes be cumulative, leading eventually to dementia and pseudobulbar palsy as described on pp. 327 and 387.

Transient Cerebral Ischaemic Attacks

Vasospasm was formerly invoked to explain short-lived attacks of hemiparesis, dysphasia or other neurological disturbance, though clear evidence for such a basis was not forthcoming. Attacks of this nature were commonly recurrent, with complete recovery between episodes, yet leading ultimately in a proportion of cases to a full-blown stroke.

Such episodes are now designated transient ischaemic attacks ('TIAs') and the mechanisms behind their occurrence are more clearly understood (Russell, 1970; Marshall, 1973). The feature common to all is a temporary reduction of the blood supply to a small area of the brain, long enough to cause manifest loss of function but not enough to lead to infarction. In some cases the reduction is occasioned by temporary occlusion of vessels, and in others by reduction of flow while the patency remains unimpaired.

The occlusive variety appears mainly to be due to microemboli derived from extracranial sources in the heart or great vessels. Atheromatous plaques on the wall of the internal carotid artery itself are frequently the source. The emboli may consist of platelet aggregates, cholesterol, or small fragments of thrombus which come to lodge in small end-arteries within the brain. In other cases haemodynamic factors are essentially responsible and emboli cannot be blamed. Thus a sudden fall in cardiac output, or systemic hypotension due to any cause, may compromise flow in vessels already critically narrowed by atherosclerosis. Occasionally the flow is reduced by kinking of the carotid artery on rotation of the head, or by compression of the vertebrals by osteophytes associated with cervical spondylosis. Sometimes the responsible lesion is an occlusive or stenotic lesion of the subclavian artery proximal to the origin of the vertebrals, leading to 'stealing' of blood from the vertebral distribution. The blood pressure is then found to be different in the two arms and a bruit may be detectable in the supraclavicular fossa. Anaemia or polycythaemia may be background factors facilitating the development of attacks.

Clearly a multitude of factors may be responsible and require careful investigation in every case. The tendency for the same vascular territory to be involved in successive attacks is explained in the haemodynamic group by the sites of maximal atheroma in cerebral vessels. In the embolic group the predilection for certain territories may rest on the fact that flow in vessels appears to adopt a uniform laminar pattern, so that emboli entering circulation at a particular point will tend to follow the same route to their eventual destination.

TIAs are commonly very brief, most lasting less than an hour and sometimes for a few minutes only. They may occur at frequent intervals over days, weeks or months, or alternatively as isolated and widely spaced attacks over many years. After a number of attacks complete resolution becomes less likely and increasing deficit is liable to develop. The symptoms produced are extremely variable depending on the territory of the brain which has been rendered ischaemic. A broad division may be made into those implicating the territory of the internal carotid and its branches, and those involving the areas of supply of the vertebrobasilar system.

TIAs in the carotid territory typically show contralateral pareses, paraesthesiae, hemianopias or dysphasia, sometimes with transient blurring or even episodes of total blindness in the ipsilateral eye (amaurosis fugax). Microemboli may actually be observed in the retinal arteries on ophthalmoscopy in such cases. Motor impairments may take the form of a brief monoparesis involving only part of a limb. Transient numbness of the face or arm is a common variety. Mental confusion may occasionally be marked, and in some cases the recurrent motor and sensory symptoms are merely the more dramatic part of a picture which contains other evidence of accumulating frontal and parietal lobe damage (Adams and Hurwitz, 1974). Relatives may have noted signs of deterioration in intellect, memory and personality as the attacks continue. Alvarez (1966) similarly stressed the mental deterioration which could follow in the wake of 'little strokes', presenting numerous case vignettes of people who lost their efficiency and ability over the years, gradually becoming untidy, irascible and difficult to live with. Only a careful history could trace this change to a sudden point in time when some 'dizzy spell' or transient neurological deficit had been declared, often recurring thereafter as the deterioration progressed.

Vertebrobasilar TIAs present with a multitude of pictures. Spells of vertigo, tinnitus or diplopia are typical. Episodes of paresis or numbness may involve different sides of the body in successive attacks. Drop attacks are commonly attributable to such a cause in the elderly—the person falls abruptly to the ground without loss of consciousness then can rise immediately, as a result of acute and transient failure of the antigravity muscles. Sometimes a staggering ataxia may be combined with dysarthria and drowsiness, leading to an impression of drunkenness. Visual phenomena include blurred vision, altitudinal or homonymous hemianopias, or scintillation scotomata. Transient bilateral blindness may occur when both posterior cerebral arteries are implicated.

TIAs may at first be mistaken for epileptic seizures, migraine, simple faints, labyrinthine disease or the early symptoms of cerebral tumour. They may be so slight and transient as to be overlooked entirely. It is important, however, that the significance of the symptoms should be recognised as early as possible so that appropriate investigation and treatment can be started.

Follow-up of such patients has shown that they have an increased risk of developing a frank cerebral infarction. In Acheson and Hutchinson's (1971) series half had developed strokes within 3 years and two-thirds within 5 years. The outlook is in general more favourable for vertebrobasilar than carotid attacks, and the prognosis appears to be particularly benign where symptoms are confined to vertigo, disturbed vision, diplopia or drop attacks (Marshall, 1964).

Angiography may reveal a surgically remediable lesion, usually stenosis or atheromatous deposits in the internal carotid artery, in up to 20% of cases (Marshall, 1971). Vertebral angiography carries special hazards in this situation and is usually contraindicated. For cases not amenable to surgery anticoagulants may be indicated, or treatment with drugs such as aspirin to reduce platelet aggregation. Attention may need to be directed to hypertension, anaemia, polycythaemia, diabetes, episodes of cardiac dysrhythmia or other aspects of heart disease.

THE SEQUELAE OF STROKES

The disablement resulting from strokes is frequently an admixture of physical and mental problems. The latter may be attributable directly to the brain damage sustained, or largely represent the individual's reaction to the handicaps imposed upon him. In either event his personality make-up and his life situation can have a profound effect on overall adjustment to the disability, and the mental components of the picture will often be decisive in determining the level of success achieved in rehabilitation. It is therefore unfortunate that little attention has been directed specifically at the problem of the psychiatric aftermaths of strokes, and of the ways in which these interact with the physical disabilities. The studies of Adams and Hurwitz are important exceptions in this regard, and have highlighted the practical value of paying due regard to matters other than the purely physical sequelae (Adams and Hurwitz, 1963; Adams, 1967; Hurwitz and Adams, 1972; Adams and Hurwitz, 1974).

In what follows an attempt will be made to review the principal components of psychiatric disability after stroke, but first the question of overall prognosis will be considered. The general picture of the incidence of defects and quality of survival provides the framework against which to view the range and extent of the problems encountered.

Overall Prognosis

Marquardsen (1969) analysed the mortality and long-term morbidity of 769 patients admitted to hospital with acute cerebral infarcts and haemorrhages. The immediate mortality was high, almost half dying within the first three weeks. Of the 407 survivors 52% were restored to independence and self-care, a further 15% were able to walk unaided but required some assistance with personal needs, and the remaining 33% failed to achieve independence in either walking or self-care. Factors indicative from the outset of a poor prognosis for functional recovery were age over 70, extracerebral complications, and indices of the extent of cerebral damage such as severe motor deficit, conjugate ocular deviation, prolonged impairment of consciousness, incontinence, and persistent confusion or apathy.

Improvement in motor function, once started in hospital, usually continued for several months. Contrary to general belief, patients with right hemisphere lesions fared less well than patients with left sided lesions in terms of recovery of independence; the accompanying visuospatial and allied difficulties appeared to provide a greater handicap to rehabilitation than dysphasia. Patients who survived after brain stem lesions did somewhat better overall than patients with hemisphere strokes, presumably because of the absence of cortical deficits.

At one year after the stroke two-thirds still had residual hemiplegia, a quarter had substantial mental impairment, and 40% had other cerebral symptoms such as dysphasia, vertigo or cranial nerve palsies. As to the predominance of the various deficits, residual hemiplegia was the main problem in approximately half, a third were mainly handicapped by other cerebral symptoms including dementia, and in most of the remainder the clinical picture was dominated by cardiac disabilities such as angina or dyspnoea. Very few were entirely symptom free.

Follow-up showed further cerebrovascular accidents in a third, occurring at a mean interval of 3 years after the primary stroke. Recurrent epileptic convulsions developed in 6%. Forty-six per cent had died within 3 years compared to an expected 12%

for the general population. The principal causes of death were cardiac failure, bronchopneumonia, recurrent stroke, myocardial infarction, pulmonary infarction and uraemia.

The general conclusion was that the majority of strokes appeared merely as incidents in the progress of a generalised vascular disorder, either atherosclerotic or hypertensive vascular disease, the extent of which essentially determined the long-term prognosis. With regard to the aims of rehabilitation, the realistic goal was usually not re-employment but independence in self-care and domestic resettlement. Of the younger patients in employment at the time of the stroke only a third were able to return to work.

Marquardsen's survey was based on patients admitted to hospital. Gresham *et al.* (1975) attempted to gauge the magnitude of long-term stroke disability by tracing 123 survivors of cerebrovascular accidents from a large community-based study, and comparing them with controls matched for age and sex. The mean age at which the strokes had occurred was 64, and the mean interval to re-examination 7 years. Eighty-four per cent of the stroke survivors were living at home, 80% were independent in mobility, and 69% were rated as independent with regard to activities of daily living (compared to 97%, 95% and 92% of controls respectively). Sixty-two per cent showed decreased socialisation compared to 31% of controls. Comparisons with controls showed in each case significantly greater disability than would be expected from age alone; but the differences were less than might have been anticipated on account of the widespread functional limitations accruing from other causes in the elderly population.

Cognitive Impairments After Stroke

Defect in intellect or other higher cortical function is among the more serious of the sequelae of stroke, delaying and often gravely compromising attempts at rehabilitation. Such elements in the clinical picture may be less immediately obvious than the hemiplegia or other physical handicap, yet often prove to be the factors which are truly responsible for failure to regain independence. Thus among patients who become long-stay invalids, permanently confined to chair or bed, paralysis by itself rather seldom accounts for their incapacity and may even contribute little towards it (Adams and Hurwitz, 1963, 1974).

In a review of 45 bedfast hemiplegics, Adams and Hurwitz (1963) showed that physical disability, such as dense paralysis or limited exercise tolerance, accounted for failure in less than half. In 18 patients severe residual paralysis and sensory defect were accompanied by varying degrees of generalised intellectual impairment and a correspondingly high rate of incontinence. Failure to respond to treatment seemed to derive from impaired comprehension, difficulties in communication, inattentiveness and lack of spontaneous effort. They were frustrated by perseveration and could not assimilate or retain instructions. Insight into their illnesses had been lacking in the critical early months. Most of these infarctions had occurred in the distribution of the middle cerebral artery of the dominant hemisphere. Ten further patients showed neglect of the affected limbs or even denied that they were in any way abnormal. Some disowned their hemiplegic limbs or complained of bizarre changes within them. The latter had at first given a superficial impression of alert and responsible behaviour, which was later belied by defective grasp, inattentive lapses and persistent incontinence. Seven were mainly incapacitated by postural imbalance which had often led to profound loss of confidence. Other patients showed severe receptive dysphasia, apraxia of gait, or emotional disturbance with catastrophic reactions.

The mental impairment that may follow a single stroke usually proves to be focal in nature once the initial clouding of consciousness has cleared. For some time, however, global confusion and disorientation may be much in evidence, and can be slow to clear when the cerebral damage has been extensive. It may be aggravated by anoxia from congestive cardiac failure or respiratory infection, or be attributable in part to the patient's difficulty in coping with new-found barriers to communication with his environment. As the situation improves the true extent of cognitive dysfunction is revealed. The longer clouding of consciousness has persisted the more likely will it be that residual mental deficits are severe and extensive.

Considerable difficulty may be encountered in assessing the extent of global intellectual impairment, particularly if the patient is dysphasic or with marked constructional difficulties. Hurwitz and Adams (1972) suggest that sometimes the best early indication is an alert glint in the patient's eye, and the nurses' opinion that the patient is 'with it'. Agitation, depression or apathy in the early stages may give a false impression of dementia. Likewise behaviour resulting from visual disorientation or agnosic difficulties. A circumscribed amnesic syndrome due to posterior cerebral infarction may not at first be appreciated as such.

Much of our understanding of the classical focal cortical syndromes—the dysphasias, apraxias and body image disturbances—has come from studies of stroke survivors. The essentials of such disorders have been outlined in Chapter 2 and will not be recapitulated here. Disturbances of language accompany some two-thirds of right hemiplegias, or may be found without paralysis. They contribute a large added handicap and source of frustration, frequently outlasting recovery of motor function. Patients with expressive loss but good comprehension will in general make much better adjustment than when understanding is faulty. Apraxic disturbances may persist as a barrier to rehabilitation when motor paralysis has cleared, particularly an apraxia of gait. Thus occasional patients with dominant hemisphere infarction appear to make a quick recovery from hemiparesis, but fail to regain a normal pattern of walking and postural control; they shuffle shakily, tend to fall backwards, and their feet seem to 'stick to the floor' (Adams, 1967).

Disturbed awareness of the self or of space more commonly occurs after right hemisphere lesions than left. Neglect of the left half of external space may be accompanied by left sensory inattention, neglect or unawareness of body parts, or frank denial of disability. Occasionally, however, exceptions are found and such symptoms result from left hemisphere lesions leading to a complex admixture of deficits:

Welman (1969) for example reported a right-handed man who had a left parietotemporal infarction. This led to a right hemiplegia, aphasia for some hours, apraxia, hemisomatognosia and anosognosia for the right side of the body, left unilateral spatial agnosia, visual-constructive apraxia, left-right disorientation, loss of memory and finger agnosia in both hands.

The more florid aspects of anosognosia, involving verbal denial or disowning of paralysed limbs, usually subside over several weeks, but neglect and inattention may endure. After severe infarction in the non-dominant hemisphere a characteristic pattern may emerge, providing immense difficulties for effective rehabilitation—the patient has a dense hemianopia, hemiplegia and hemianaesthesia but lacks insight into his predicament, may admit to nothing wrong with the left limbs or disown the arm (Adams, 1967). Sometimes this persists even after quite good recovery of power and the patient makes no constructive attempts to walk. Persistent incontinence is a common accompaniment, adding to the poor progosis for recovery of independence and social reliability.

Improvement over time in specific cognitive and perceptual disabilities may be expected to follow the course of a decelerating learning curve, the percentage return of function gradually diminishing as time after stroke increases. In general most improvement can be expected within the first 6 months, but wide variation is seen. The influence of affective or motivational factors is often profound, delaying full recovery until several years have gone by.

A considerably longer period must usually be allowed for the optimal resolution of dysphasia, visuospatial or topographical defects than of physical disabilities such as hemiplegia. The ultimate level achieved will depend crucially on the amount of brain tissue destroyed, the number of separate deficits involved, and on the multitude of factors peculiar to the individual which dictate his adaptive capacity.

Dementia

While it is rare for a truly global dementia to follow a single cerebrovascular accident, multiple strokes may combine to produce such a picture. Each episode is accompanied by some further loss of mental ability, accruing over time in a step-like fashion to lead to a more or less global deterioration of memory, intellect and personality. This is the 'arteriosclerotic' or 'multi-infarct' form of dementia as described in Chapter 10. A careful history will usually make it evident that infarctions have occurred, from the tempo of events combined with episodes of neurological disorder. The latter, however, may be slight and transient, at least in the early stages, and the dementia will then emerge as the dominant symptom.

The *role of 'lacunar' infarcts* in producing dementia is discussed by Fisher (1965, 1968). The deficits resulting from each such minor stroke are often mild and recover rapidly, but as their number increases the effects may be cumulative leading to the so-called 'état lacunaire' with dementia and some degree of pseudobulbar palsy. The mental deterioration generally lags behind physical changes of weakness, slowness, dysarthria, dysphagia, a small-stepped gait, and neurological evidence of bilateral pyramidal involvement. Very occasionally, however, the dementia may emerge in a gradual fashion, resembling a primary degenerative dementia and without sudden infarcts to betray the minor strokes (Fisher, 1968; Weisberg, 1982). This is probably rare, though with increasingly sensitive CT scan studies such patients are now being detected. If the history fails the neurological findings will usually be decisive.

Weisberg (1982), however, has described a small group of patients with bilateral capsular lacunae and gradual mental deterioration who showed no neurological deficits whatsoever. Emotional lability with spasmodic laughing and crying also serves to make the differentiation from Alzheimer's disease, being rare in the latter but frequent in the lacunar state.

In rare cases dementia had been attributed to *vascular lesions of the thalamus*, much as may occur with tumours in this location (p. 198). De Boucaud *et al.* (1968) reported a patient of 59 with dementia of a year's duration accompanied by incontinence and overactivity. The gait was hesitant and awkward but there were few clear neurological signs. Autopsy showed an old haemorrhagic softening affecting a large part of the right thalamus along with a smaller similar lesion of the left. The cerebral cortex was free from pathological changes.

The possible *role of carotico-vertebral stenosis* in leading to dementia has also attracted attention. At one time there were hopes that surgical intervention on narrowed or occluded carotid arteries might help to remedy diminished blood flow to the brain, and thereby improve the mental functioning of patients, but results in general have been disappointing.

Thus Clarke and Harrison (1956), reviewing the cases of bilateral carotid occlusion in the literature, found that mental changes were encountered in almost a third, often taking the form of a progressive dementia. Neurological accompaniments such as hemiplegia or visual difficulties were frequent but often transient, and in the early stages neurological signs could be entirely absent. Fisher (1951, 1954) described examples of carotid occlusion associated with progressive cerebral deterioration, and cautiously proposed that sometimes this may have been the cause of the dementia rather than a coincidental finding; chronic cerebral ischaemia on such a basis may have explained some cases of senile dementia not previously attributed to cerebrovascular lesions.

Subsequent experience has now shown that this is very unlikely. Stenosis or occlusion of the carotids is not uncommon in unselected series of autopsies past middle age (Schwartz and Mitchell, 1961). And Corsellis and Evans (1965) have demonstrated that when the entire vascular tree from the heart to the brain is examined, whether in demented or non-demented subjects, the cerebral and extracerebral vessels are usually found to be spared or to be involved in stenosis to roughly the same extent. Altogether there was little to suggest that structural interference with blood supply in the neck had any special or unique role to play in contributing to dementia. There also appeared to be little lee-way for the re-establishment of improved cerebral circulation by operative procedures.

The present consensus of opinion is therefore that it is most unlikely that chronic marginal ischaemia from carotid stenosis can lead to a progressive deterioration resembling Alzheimer's senile dementia. When dementing symptoms are attributable to carotid occlusion infarctions will have occurred within the hemispheres, and there will almost invariably be motor and sensory signs to indicate the nature of the process (Fisher, 1968).

Organic Personality Change

Personality changes attributable to brain damage are among the most troublesome of the sequelae of stroke, and may overshadow the intellectual deficits. Most are probably attributable to widespread changes of an arteriosclerotic nature within the damaged brain, and as such they may progress even though the focal sequelae of the stroke improve. Usually they prove to be the prelude to a progressive dementing illness.

A woman of 69 had a very mild stroke affecting the left arm transiently. She seemed well for a while thereafter, but gradually changed, becoming irritable, hard to please, and with vague complaints of headache and giddiness. She became anxious and did not want to be left alone. Loss of interests and slowing were accompanied by episodes of confusion and disorientation. On examination fifteen months after the stroke she was not grossly demented, but showed some difficulty in understanding questions and had only a vague idea of the date. There was a residual left hemiparesis, a left homonymous hemianopia, some dyscalculia and a mild nominal dysphasia. Her affective state was, however, worse than her intellect—she was mostly apathetic and dull, though cheerful in a facile way at times. Eventually she needed long-term hospitalisation.

(Slater, 1962)

Slater (1962) outlines the range of problems encountered. Typically one sees a 'reduction of margins'. The patient cannot adjust to anything out of the way, and small matters make him anxious, irritable or depressed. Consciously or unconsciously he avoids new experiences and restricts himself to an unvarying routine. The barriers this can impose to rehabilitation are obvious. Confrontations with a task or with social demands carries the risk of provoking a catastrophic reaction. He may become irritable, abusive and uncooperative if asked to make any effort, yet be affable and obliging when left in peace.

Minor bodily ills are apt to be felt as oppressive, and hypochondriacal concern may centre around sleep or bowels. The picture may bear a deceptively neurotic appearance until evidence of cognitive impairment is detected. Constitutional predispositions may also be revealed or accentuated: a previously lonely person may become suspicious or frankly paranoid, or cyclothymic tendencies may have issue in endogenous depression.

At a later stage the emotional state is recognisably abnormal, with dulled and flattened responsiveness, marked irritability, and emotional reactions which are stereotyped and lacking in flexibility. The patient is unmoved by pleasure or dismay where the interests of others are concerned, but if his own security is threatened the emotional reaction is severe and prolonged. These changes may be in evidence for some time, hindering rehabilitation and providing a considerable burden for relatives, before more decisive evidence of failing memory and impoverishment of thought supervene.

Depression

It is scarcely surprising that depressive reactions should be common in survivors of strokes. Ullman (1962) vividly describes the subjective impact which the experience may have. The patient finds himself abruptly in the grip of something novel, frightening, and ill-understood. He may well not be in a position to evaluate the situation objectively, but may project the blame outwards or alternatively against himself. Even slight interference in free communication with those around will greatly intensify feelings of isolation, threat or loss.

When the acute stage is over there are a variety of factors around which depression may come to be organised—the frustrations of physical handicaps, uncertainty about the prospects of their resolution, the enforced dependency and imposition of the invalid role. In the longer-term the patient may face loss of job and status, financial insecurity, a sense of uselessness, or the prospect of permanent loss of independence. Robinson and Price (1982), in a survey of 103 patients attending a stroke clinic, found that one-third were depressed, the majority remaining so for at least 6 months. The peak incidence of depression was in the period 6 months to 2 years after the stroke had occurred.

The reaction to the situation will be strongly determined by aspects of the premorbid personality. Patients of striving and self-sufficient disposition may react more adversely to handicap than those with strong dependency needs. Those who have experienced anxiety and depressive reactions under previous stress will be at increased risk. Much will also depend on the family setting and relationships with which the patient is surrounded. Quite frequently, at the era of life in which most strokes occur, the patient is relatively unsupported—the spouse may have died or herself be infirm, and children will have moved away.

Others may experience depression of an endogenous type, sometimes precipitated by strokes of a relatively minor nature and persisting after excellent recovery from the more immediate disabilities. Complaints of difficulty with memory and concentration, and inability to take up the threads of life again, may then give a false impression of the severity of residual brain damage. Insomnia, feelings of hopelessness, and hypochondriacal concern over minor handicaps, may greatly retard the resumption of normal activities.

The interesting suggestion has recently come forward that there may be a special relationship between strokes and depression, depending at least in part on the direct effects of the cerebral lesion. Thus stroke patients have been found to show a higher incidence of depression than orthopaedic controls or patients suffering from traumatic brain injuries, despite equivalent levels of disability in terms of 'activities of daily living' or cognitive dysfunction (Folstein et al., 1977; Robinson and Szetela, 1981). Moreover, the location of infarction may be a significant factor. Left hemisphere strokes appear to yield significantly more depression than right hemisphere or brain stem strokes (Robinson and Price, 1982); and within the left hemisphere the proximity of the lesion to the frontal pole has emerged as an important factor (Robinson and Benson, 1981; Robinson and Szetela, 1981; Lipsey et al., 1983). In effect, left anterior brain lesions seem to produce more depression than lesions in any other location.

It has been suggested that this may be related to the anatomical disposition of catecholamine-containing pathways in the brain, which pass from subcortical centres through the frontal cortex en route to their diffuse projections elsewhere. Related animal experiments have demonstrated depletion in whole brain catecholamines following focal infarctions (Robinson and Bloom, 1977; Robinson et al., 1980). The preponderance of depression with left-sided infarcts is not, however, explained, and may yet prove to depend on special aspects of cognitive dysfunction in such patients. Moreover, the studies revealing these anatomical associations have not so far controlled for levels of premorbid risk among the patients studied.

The importance of recognising the depression need not be stressed. On occasion this can be very difficult, especially when the development has been insidious. Sometimes it is masked by stoical attitudes, or absorbed into habitual or automatic patterns of behaviour. It may lead to lack of cooperation or poor motivation for rehabilitation, and aggravate dysphasic and similar difficulties. In all such circumstances appropriate treatment can be quickly rewarding. It is important, however, to distinguish depressive disorder from simple loss of confidence, or from the emotional lability associated with intellectual impairment. It is also necessary to remain sensitively aware that sometimes, in severely disabled patients, feelings of resignation and futility are realistically based; some elderly patients really are so frail, and the odds so genuinely against them, that their wish 'not to bother' deserves to be treated with the proper respect. Needless to say this is an aspect of differential 'diagnosis' which requires the utmost care.

Psychoses After Stroke

There are no figures against which to gauge the incidence of functional psychoses after cerebrovascular accidents. A severe endogenous depression may be provoked in susceptible subjects, as mentioned above. Hypomanic syndromes have also been reported, though rarely with convincing time relationships to the stroke (van der Lugt and Visser, 1967).

Davison and Bagley (1969) review the evidence concerning the relationship between psychotic disorder and cerebrovascular disease. There was some suggestion that late onset schizophrenia might be significantly associated with cerebral atheroma and its complications, but insufficient information on which to base firm conclusions. Davison and Bagley also mention reports of paranoid-hallucinatory syndromes developing shortly after cerebrovascular catastrophes. One such example, at first thought to be a functional illness but later recognised as organic, was reported by Shapiro (1959) in association with carotid artery occlusion:

A woman of 60 developed a psychosis of acute onset, with hallucinations and delusions that people were saying she had married her husband for his money. She was hyper-

tensive but showed no abnormal neurological signs. Improvement occurred with eight ECTs, and she became normal for a week, but then relapsed with confusion and a return of hallucinations. She developed a transient left hemiparesis, and angiography showed right carotid occlusion. Two days later she died, and at autopsy bilateral carotid occlusions were revealed.

Levine and Finklestein (1982) have noted an apparent relationship between cerebrovascular lesions of the right hemisphere, specifically of the right temporo-parieto-occipital areas, and the development of psychotic illnesses some time later. Eight patients were described, with the psychoses appearing some weeks or years after the stroke. All but one had developed seizures in the interim which may have been a connecting factor. The psychoses developed acutely, with formed auditory and visual hallucinations; the majority of patients showed agitation, persecutory delusions and confusion, but in some the hallucinosis was relatively pure. All had constructional apraxia, and most a variety of other neurological residua. The right-sided location in every case may have reflected the freedom from dysphasia, allowing the psychoses to be revealed, or alternatively may have reflected the predisposing effects of spatial disabilities in leading to environmental misinterpretations.

Other Psychiatric Sequelae

Other significant developments include a variety of psychological reactions which may greatly impede convalescence and prove an enormous burden to relatives. An accentuation of paranoid traits is common. Some patients develop rebellious aggressive attitudes and unwillingness to conform to medical régimes and treatment, others become hostile, vindictive and spiteful (Rees, 1961). The predominant factor will usually lie in the patient's response to his disabilities, often aggravated or brought to the fore by the brain damage which has occurred.

Two main channels into which irrational modes of adaptation may flow are unrealistic strivings for independence and unrealistic dependency (Ullman, 1962). Thus the patient may attempt to deny his limitations and refuse the provision of simple aids. Or an overzealous impatient attitude may interfere with progress. Others, by contrast, regress considerably and succumb to invalidism to an unnecessary degree. Here a profound loss of confidence may be the essential ingredient, or there may be elements of secondary gain. Manipulative tendencies may be effective within the family circle because of the feelings of guilt they arouse. In this way the patient may evade responsibilities and exploit his disabilities, perhaps protesting against dependence while renouncing many of the things he could do for himself.

Psychological problems can be severe when the life situation is profoundly altered as a consequence of the stroke. Many important sources of gratification, pleasure and interest may be lost both for the patient and other family members. There are often far-reaching domestic upheavals, particularly in younger patients—the wife may need to work and the husband adjust to a new domestic role. Marital problems may come to the fore, with rejection or even desertion by the spouse. Sexual sequelae, commonly impotence in the face of continuing desire, can have highly distressing repercussions.

Many components will therefore enter into the success or failure of the adaptation which is made to the sequelae of stroke, and will combine to determine the change of life pattern that follows. Ullman (1962) provides several case histories which illustrate the social, psychological and physical variables which can contribute to the final adaptive response on the part of the victim and his family.

REHABILITATION AFTER STROKE

The management of the acute phases of stroke is a matter for the medical and neurological team, an integral part being attention to differential diagnosis and the mounting of appropriate investigations. Thereafter skilled nursing care is of the utmost importance. Steroids may have a part to play in reducing cerebral oedema, but vasodilator drugs have not proved their value. Decisions may be required over anticoagulants; these find little place in the management of completed stroke, but can be of prophylactic importance in transient ischaemic attacks or when sources of emboli are discovered in the heart and great vessels. The use of aspirin as a prophylactic has perhaps more evidence to commend it (The Canadian Cooperative Study Group, 1978) and extensive further trials are under way.

Correct management of hypertension is of great importance, and has been shown to be effective in delaying mortality and recurrence among younger survivors of stroke (Carter, 1970). Even so antihypertensive therapy must be carried out with care. When the evidence points to infarction rather than haemorrhage it will usually be prudent to defer any lowering of blood pressure at least until the acute phase of the stroke is over.

Operative intervention may be considered in certain circumstances. Carotid endarterectomy has enthusiastic advocates, likewise extracranial-intra-cranial bypass operations in certain circumstances. Their value in preventing further ischaemic attacks or strokes, or in ameliorating existing deficits, requires careful further appraisal (Harrison, 1980; *Lancet*, 1981).

Details of medical management are summarised by Isaacs (1973) and Russell and Harrison (1973), and set out in full by Marshall (1976). Here attention will be restricted to the longer-term problems of rehabilitation which must be tackled once the acute phase is over. Three stages can usually be envisaged in the process of recovery—2 weeks concerned with survival, 8–12 weeks of effort to restore activity and independence in standing, walking and self-care, then often 2 years more before the full capacity of the patient to participate in normal social activities is realised (Hurwitz and Adams, 1972).

The processes of recovery are largely spontaneous and usually slow. Rehabilitation implies efforts aimed at promoting recovery and the optimal utilization of residual functions (Isaacs, 1973). The mechanisms underlying such changes over time are undoubtedly complex and incompletely understood. In part there would appear to be transfer of lost functions to unaffected brain areas, reorganisation within the brain to allow other areas to contribute more, and perhaps removal of inhibitory influences from elements which are still intact. Key structures such as the anterior horn cells may improve their ability to modify influences playing upon them. Better utilization of unaffected body parts will help with substitute performances.

Rehabilitation in any extensive sense requires a team of several workers. It may proceed in the hospital, the home, or specialised rehabilitation units, depending on circumstances and the severity of the problems involved. Commonly it will be a prolonged and multi-stage exercise, drawing on the patience and persistence of all concerned and not least that of the patient himself. Proper liaison among the different people involved is essential for success, also adequate continuing care when the patient is discharged home.

Isaacs (1971) offers a useful practical guide to the planning of rehabilitation by classifying stroke disability into four principal categories—motor deficit alone, major disorder in communication, major perceptual disorder, and major cognitive disturbance. Among 115 patients in his practice 23 showed a motor deficit alone, 43 a major disorder of communication with or without perceptual or cognitive disturbance, 31 major perceptual disorder without disturbance of communication, and 18 major cognitive disturbance without perceptual or communication deficits.

Motor deficits require physiotherapy from the earliest stages. Voluntary movements should be encouraged while the patient is still confined to bed, and a full range of passive movements will help to prevent contractures and joint immobility in the affected limbs. Exercises in standing and balancing from the early weeks will do much to achieve a correct postural background for the walking exercises which follow. These must often be pursued over many months in an atmosphere of optimism and constant encouragement. Fundamental to success is the gradual restoration of the patient's self-confidence, and hence his motivation to help himself further.

The occupational therapist will concentrate on matters of fine motor control, particularly in the upper limbs. Restoration of function after hemiplegia is commonly much less complete in the arm than the leg, so that patients with excellent mobility remain at risk of dependence on others. Re-training may be needed over activities of daily living—how to dress, feed, wash and cook despite the handicaps which persist. The provision of simple mechanical aids for such purposes can be of immense help in restoring capabilities which would otherwise be lost. The carefully graded occupational therapy programme is thus a further important boost to morale.

Sensory handicaps gravely complicate rehabilitation, particularly sensory impairments in paralysed limbs. Loss of position sense which persists after the early weeks carries a bad prognosis in hemiplegic patients, and may need special training under visual and tactile control to counteract it. Constant emphasis is required on the existence and position in space of the limbs. Cortical sensory loss, with defective discrimination, adds to the difficulties with fine manipulations of the fingers.

Hemianopic or quadrantic field defects tend to resolve with time, or the alert patient learns to compensate for them. In the early stages, however, or when there is mental impairment, care must be taken to approach the patient from the sound side, and to arrange the disposition of belongings and work materials accordingly. A tendency to ignore the left half of space may be a greater barrier, contributing to falls and mishaps and hindering mastery of a new environment.

Refractive errors or defective hearing must not be overlooked as remediable sources of extra difficulty.

Disturbed body awareness when long continued can provide serious obstacles to progress. Neglect, disuse, or seeming unawareness of the hemiplegic limbs must be vigorously countered by appropriate stimulation and exercises. Frequently body image disturbance and anosognosia are complicated by sensory deficits in the limbs of the type described above. Persistent denial or disowning of hemiplegic limbs carries an especially poor prognosis for recovery of independence, and is often accompanied by prolonged incontinence. Over many months, however, the situation may improve (Adams and Hurwitz, 1974). Repeated testing of the limits of what can and cannot be done may ultimately help to rectify body image disturbances, and help the patient to maximise his residual functioning potential (Rigoni, 1969). The incontinence may respond to careful régimes of toilet training, together with the general mental stimulus derived from activities and interests. Nevertheless it would seem to be deficits such as these which make an important contribution to the poorer overall prognosis of right hemisphere strokes than left, even despite the absence of dysphasic difficulties.

Communication disorders warrant attention from the moment they are declared. It must be remembered that the dysphasic patient has lost not only his ability to speak but also his primary means of relating with those around. Once he knows that he can communicate, however little, frustration and fear begin to diminish.

In addition to inducing feelings of isolation and frustration language difficulties play a central role in impairing other aspects of progress. The patient may have lost the means of stabilising internally the events which are occurring around him, and will be at a grave disadvantage in relearning other patterns of behaviour and activities (Hagen, 1969). Without personal understanding of the requisite goals it will be hard for him to muster and sustain effort towards those goals.

A first aim must be to establish emotional contact with the patient, using whatever channels of communication are most intact. Pictures may be used with which he can indicate requests, even though he cannot read or speak. Cards with words or short phrases may be useful later on. Gestures or visual signs may be employed when verbal understanding is very poor, coupled with one or two concrete words but avoiding a confusing flow of speech. Later in recovery instructions must be carefully spaced, given slowly, and as far as possible in the same manner on each occasion. Thus a special approach is needed from all the staff. Every attempt must be made to avoid withdrawal after early failures, to keep the patient involved and active, and to stimulate a continuing desire to communicate.

Formal speech therapy has rarely been rigorously tested, which is surprising in view of the magnitude of the problem. Whether the final level achieved exceeds that which would have occurred spontaneously is unknown, but few doubt the effects of retraining programmes on emotional adjustment and morale. Butfield and Zangwill (1946) obtained some evidence that training begun early was more effective than that begun late, and that predominantly expressive dysphasias did better than receptive or mixed dysphasias. Speech fared better than reading or writing, and mathematical ability did particularly badly. Darley (1970) reviews other attempts to gauge the efficacy of retraining programmes, sometimes with results suggesting that measurable gains are attributable to therapy, but, it must be admitted, on rather slender grounds.

The role of the speech therapist is outlined by Leche (1972). After establishing the range of the deficits, re-education must aim at maximising spontaneous recovery, sustaining incentives, and preventing the development of undesirable speech habits. Throughout the process the patient is reassured to know that his difficulties are understood, and his own attention is focused constructively upon them. Later, group therapy can have an important part to play, also the counselling of relatives about optimal means of overcoming the communication problem.

Impairment of memory must be specially catered for with a more gradual programme, frequent rehearsals, and the provision of props and supports by way of notes and written instructions. The relative preservation of old memories may initially produce a misleading impression until ability to acquire new knowledge is specifically tested.

Other intellectual impairments are a serious barrier to progress when at all extensive. Ill-sustained attention, perseveration, fatiguability, and failure to grasp instructions may combine to render attempts at rehabilitation fruitless. To maximise the chances of success, verbal instructions must be presented in simple language, with deliberate methodical repetition to hold wandering attention and memory. Practical demonstrations of what is expected may

get the ideas across when other methods have failed. The pace will necessarily be slow, and allowance must be made for variability in performance from day to day.

Much ingenuity is obviously required in devising special methods of treatment to counteract these various obstacles to recovery. It is here that the studies of Hurwitz and Adams have been particularly valuable in drawing attention to the 'mental barriers' which may impede progress and which can all too easily be overlooked. Defective comprehension, impaired memory, apraxia, loss of sensation and disturbed body awareness may not be appreciated as such, and the patient's failure is attributed simply to inadequate motivation or to generalised dementia. He seldom has the insight to appreciate or complain about such difficulties himself, so they must be sought out with care by systematic examination. Adams (1967) reports remarkably improved results in the rehabilitation of hemiplegics since routinely searching for barriers of this nature. Whereas 42% of an earlier series regained independence in self-care and walking, 59% of a more recent series did so. Thirty-eight per cent of the former remained chronic invalids compared to 26% of the latter. Thus a 4% difference between recovery and failure in the earlier series was converted to a 33% difference as a result or improved awareness of special needs.

Motivation itself is nevertheless among the most crucial determinants of progress and every means must be taken to optimise and maintain it. The day to day enthusiasm and encouragement of the therapeutic team is an essential ingredient. The patient's own awareness of his progress then plays back powerfully to reinforce it. All through, he needs some central figure in the team who can be relied upon, and proper communication must be maintained so that he is aware of the plans and goals at every stage.

A watch must be kept for evidence of depression, which will commonly respond to appropriate medication. It is a serious mistake to overlook such a source of impaired cooperation or zeal. Tactful handling may be required in the face of discouragement, or when regressive or obstinate behaviour emerges. Clear guidelines must sometimes be laid down, especially for patients with intellectual impairment, who will usually respond to a structured environment in which they are not left to work out for themselves what is expected of them. By contrast, flexibility must be built into the programme to allow for patients of differing needs and personalities. Rigid conformity to set standards cannot always be expected, and in some persons will be counter-productive.

Attention must also be devoted to the relatives of the patient. They too will need full discussion of aims and procedures, and help in adjusting to the disabilities that are likely to remain. Skilful physical rehabilitation may be doomed to failure if insufficient attention has been given to the family situation and to the impact of the problem on family dynamics. Here the social worker has a vital part to play, and should be brought into the picture at an early stage. Much work may be needed to allay unrealistic expectations or needless anxieties and fears. The stroke and its repercussions may have had a far-reaching effect on many members of the household, disturbing family equilibrium and requiring a reorganisation of roles. The range of the problems encountered, and the value of counselling in surmounting them, are illustrated by de la Mata *et al.* (1960), Collins (1961), Overs and Healy (1973) and Holbrook (1982).

Preparations for discharge must be made well in advance, on a practical as well as an emotional level. The patient's assets and liabilities must be carefully assessed, likewise the family and community resources available to help. Physical adaptations may be needed in the home by way of ramps or simple supports. Proper liaison will be required with local authority and voluntary services.

Where work is to be considered the Disablement Resettlement Officer will often have an important part to play, and the services of Industrial Resettlement Units may need to be exploited to the full. Extended workshop evaluation and training will usually be invaluable for determining employability in difficult cases. Sheltered employment may need to be found when the patient is too disabled to cope on the open market.

In older patients, and those severely disabled, attendance at a day hospital, occupation centre or social club may need to be organised. Transport problems in particular will need attention. For those who remain at home every effort must be made to combat feelings of loneliness and isolation, by building new contacts, encouraging a return to hobbies, and mobilising community resources for visits and outings.

Sadly, some patients will need to remain in institutions, usually by virtue of extensive mental impairments in addition to their neurological defects. Others will have complicating pathologies, such as heart disease or arthritis, which have conspired to make effective rehabilitation impossible. Here

nursing care and occupational therapy will be required long-term if the quality of life is to be maintained at the optimum. A reasonable level of stimulation must be ensured, with routines that are as varied, useful and congenial as possible. Psychotropic medication will occasionally be required to combat anxiety and depression.

The effectiveness of antidepressants in relieving post-stroke depression has been documented (Lipsey *et al.*, 1984). Tricyclic antidepressants have also been shown to be remarkably effective in patients who develop 'emotional incontinence' with pathological laughing and crying, whether or not this is associated with other features of pseudobulbar palsy (Lawson and MacLeod, 1969; Ross and Rush, 1981). Lawson and MacLeod found that even in the absence of subjective depression such medication could apparently alleviate the disruptive and socially embarrassing effects of the disorder to a considerable extent.

Subarachnoid Haemorrhage

It is estimated that subarachnoid haemorrhage makes up some 8% of cerebrovascular catastrophes. It is particularly important in that it affects a younger age group than other strokes, and because correct management can substantially reduce mortality. Since the site of origin of the haemorrhage is often demonstrable on angiography, and the ensuing brain damage commonly localised, the mental sequelae have attracted detailed attention. Moreover the pictures which are produced are less liable than with other strokes to be contaminated by the effects of diffuse cerebrovascular disease.

The usual cause is rupture of an intracranial aneurysm, estimated to account for some 60% of cases. A smaller group derive from ruptured angiomas (5–10%). In 15–20% no structural cause for the bleeding can be found, and it is in this group that hypertensive crises due to monoamine oxidase inhibitor drugs may occasionally be to blame. During a 2 year period Villiers (1966) found 16 patients who had developed subarachnoid haemorrhage while taking monoamine oxidase inhibitors; it was estimated that 3·3% of unexplained subarachnoid haemorrhages occurred in patients on such drugs, the ingestion of cheese or other tyramine containing foods commonly being the precipitant. Rare additional causes include bleeds from intracranial and spinal tumours, blood dyscrasias, or inflammatory conditions of the brain and meninges. Others represent primary intracerebral or cerebellar haemorrhages which have bled into the ventricular system and thereby reached the subarachnoid space.

Aneurysms arise from congenital defects in the media, usually at the forks of the cerebral arteries. The great majority arise close to the circle of Willis at the base of the brain. Common sites are on the anterior cerebral or anterior communicating arteries, at the point of division of the middle cerebral arteries, or where the posterior communicating artery arises from the upper end of the internal carotid artery. Another common site is on the intracavernous part of the internal carotid, but this more often leads to local pressure effects than to subarachnoid haemorrhage (p. 357). Rupture occurs spontaneously and suddenly, with bleeding directly into the subarachnoid space and often into the adjacent brain substance as well. Spasm of adjacent vessels may lead to infarction in their territories of supply.

Anterior communicating aneurysms lie between the frontal lobes and near to the anterior hypothalamus. Rupture is often unaccompanied by localising signs, but ischaemia can be extensive in one or both frontal lobes due to occlusion or spasm of the anterior cerebral arteries. Middle cerebral aneurysms lie in the Sylvian fissure or embedded in the frontal or temporal lobes nearby. Rupture is often accompanied by hemiparesis due to vascular spasm in the territory of the middle cerebral, or haematoma formation. Posterior communicating aneurysms lie medial to the uncus of the temporal lobe. They often bleed directly into the subarachnoid space, but infarction can be widespread in the territory of the middle cerebral arteries, and there may also be interference with the fine perforating vessels to the basal ganglia and hypothalamus.

Whatever the site of the bleed, vasospasm may develop focally or diffusely, involving vessels near to or distant from the site of rupture. Local vasospasm leads to evanescent symptoms, but widespread involvement carries a grave prognosis.

(Saito *et al.*, 1977)

Acute Clinical Picture

The patient is usually between 40 and 60 though cases can be seen at an early age. The onset is abrupt with intense, often catastrophic pain in the head, mainly in the occipital region but radiating into the neck and later becoming generalised. Vomiting, photophobia and fits may occur. Consciousness may be lost from the outset though some patients retain full awareness throughout. Others are drowsy, confused and irritable. Sometimes the mental symptoms overshadow the headache to such an extent that the diagnosis is not immediately apparent. Walton (1956) mentioned three patients who had been accused of drunkeness at the onset, and two who were regarded as hysterical on first admission to hospital.

Neck stiffness generally becomes intense. The tendon reflexes are diminished and the plantars extensor. Papilloedema may develop immediately or within a few days, and subhyaloid haemorrhages may be observed spreading from the edge of the optic discs. Focal ophthalmoplegias are common, and aphasia or hemiplegia may result from arterial spasm or intracerebral extension. Lumbar puncture shows uniformly bloodstained cerebrospinal fluid, usually under increased pressure, becoming xanthochromic after 36–45 hours. CT scanning performed within a week of the bleed may obviate the need for lumbar puncture by demonstrating the presence of blood in the cerebrospinal fluid directly (Moseley, 1981). Small aneurysms will often escape detection on the scan, but any intracerebral bleeding is usually clearly shown.

Immediate bed rest is mandatory with sedation and analgesics. A recurrence of the bleed is particularly likely during the first two weeks and the risk diminishes considerably thereafter. The delicate question of operative intervention is discussed by Richardson (1969, 1973). Techniques available include occlusion of the neck of the aneurysm or the feeding vessels, reinforcement of the wall by gauze or acrylic compounds, or ligation of the common carotid artery in the neck. Complications such as intracerebral haematomas may need surgical treatment in their own right.

Coma persisting for more than 24 hours is a bad prognostic sign. Altogether some 40–50% of cases may be expected to die from a first bleed, and a further 20% from recurrences during the ensuing months or years (Walton, 1982). Of survivors approximately one-third are symptom free, one-third show some disability, and one-third are left with moderate or severe disability. In patients with no aneurysm demonstrable on angiography the mortality and morbidity rates are considerably lower.

PSYCHIATRIC SEQUELAE OF SUBARACHNOID HAEMORRHAGE

Mental symptoms in the wake of subarachnoid haemorrhage had received remarkably scant attention until Walton (1952, 1956) emphasised their importance as a source of persistent disability. Among 120 survivors, examined 2–11 years later, he found that important residua included paresis in

10%, epilepsy in 13% and persistent headache in 23%; also organic mental symptoms in 9% and anxiety symptoms in 27%. The anxiety was occasionally severely disabling, resulting in chronic psychiatric invalidism.

More recently two large series of patients have been reported with attention directed primarily at the psychiatric sequelae. Storey (1967, 1970, 1972) studied 261 patients who had had a subarachnoid haemorrhage 6 months to 6 years earlier, noting the site of the responsible aneurysm and correlating this with the psychiatric aftermaths. Eighty-one patients had bled from anterior communicating aneurysms, 71 from middle cerebral aneurysms, 72 from posterior communicating aneurysms and 7 from multiple aneurysms, while in the remaining 30 no aneurysm could be detected. Logue *et al.* (1968) confined attention to 79 survivors of haemorrhages from anterior cerebral aneurysms, studied 6 months to $8\frac{1}{2}$ years later.

Both studies confirmed the high incidence of mental disablement among survivors, especially as a result of organic mental impairments and personality change attributable to brain damage. Rather surprisingly both have also stressed that improvement in personality can occur in occasional survivors, mainly evident to relatives but sometimes also to the patients themselves.

Cognitive Impairments

Severe confusion and states of akinetic mutism can be seen in the early stages of recovery. Most are transient, but when substantial brain damage has occurred there may be enduring cognitive sequelae. These range from mild difficulties with memory to gross and disabling dementia. Focal dysphasic symptoms may be prominent.

Storey (1967) found persistent intellectual difficulties in about 40% of patients as judged by simple clinical criteria. They were rated as moderate to severe in some 10% of cases, and occasional patients remained grossly demented and bedfast. Those with middle cerebral aneurysms fared considerably worse than other groups, while patients with no demonstrable aneurysms had the lowest morbidity of all. Logue *et al.*'s (1968) patients with anterior cerebral aneurysms showed 10% with global dementia but many more with minor persistent defects. 40 per cent showed dysphasic errors on detailed testing. Memory was often more impaired than intelligence, perhaps by virtue of the close proximity of these anterior aneurysms to the base of the third ventricle.

Intellectual impairment when severe is usually associated with other evidence of residual brain damage by way of neurological deficits. Occasional examples may owe their origin to the development of 'normal pressure hydrocephalus' (p. 639), as a result of obstruction of the flow of cerebrospinal fluid by organisation of exudate at the base of the brain. Ojemann (1971) reviews the evidence that ventricular enlargement can follow a progressive course over months or years after subarachnoid haemorrhage. In his own material of 12 such cases improvement was usually evident within a few days of inserting a ventriculovenous shunt. Focal neurological deficits were rarely alleviated, but one patient experienced immediate improvement in a focal speech defect.

Amnesic Syndromes

A picture resembling Korsakoff's psychosis may emerge shortly after the haemorrhage, with disorientation, confabulation and marked memory difficulties. Tarachow (1939) and Walton (1953) recorded several examples, often developing after a latent interval of several days or weeks. The disorder was always temporary, usually recovering gradually over a few weeks but occasionally with abrupt resolution overnight. Speculations as to the cause included diffuse brain damage, hydrocephalus, or the possibility of some toxic factor derived from disintegration products of the blood in the subarachnoid space. It was hard to explain the syndrome on the basis of focal brain damage because of the frequent latent interval and the examples of abrupt recovery.

Theander and Granholm (1967), reviewing 56 survivors of subarachnoid haemorrhage, demonstrated communicating hydrocephalus in 5, 4 of whom had had severe dysmnesic syndromes lasting months or years. Intraventricular pressure was normal. The hydrocephalus was attributed to obstruction of CSF circulation, and 3 of the 4 improved remarkably on shunting.

It is therefore possible that some of the earlier transient examples may have been due to similar mechanisms. Tarachow explicitly described hydrocephalus on air encephalography in two of his three patients, and commented on the lack of air in the subarachnoid spaces in one of them. The latent interval may have been attributable to the time required for the development of adhesive arachnoiditis, and the subsequent improvement to the eventual freeing of CSF circulation. The abrupt resolution occasionally noted by Walton suggests such a mechanism. In Theander and Granholm's cases, by contrast, the obstructions had become permanent and required operative intervention. The dramatic success achieved is indicated in the following example:

A 57-year-old woman had a subarachnoid haemorrhage, and on recovery of consciousness showed signs of severe cerebral injury with disorientation. She was transferred to a home for the chronic sick. At examination 3 years after the haemorrhage she was bedridden with contractures of the hips and knees—lively, talkative, almost euphoric, but completely disoriented in time and place. She could not remember having fallen ill and was unaware of her disease. Encephalography showed severe hydrocephalus due to obstruction of CSF circulation in the basal cisterns. A shunt operation produced rapid improvement. She became fully oriented and her ability to add to her store of new memories became virtually normal. An amnesic gap persisted, however, for the 3 years between the bleeding and the shunt. Extensive orthopaedic treatment and rehabilitation eventually allowed her discharge home.

(Theander and Granholm, 1967)

A distinct group would seem after all to owe their amnesia to focal brain damage, particularly after rupture of anterior communicating aneurysms. Transient confabulation was noted in almost a quarter of Logue et al.'s (1968) cases, and two striking examples of enduring memory difficulties have been reported after operative intervention on aneurysms in this location (Sweet et al., 1966; Talland et al., 1967):

Pre-operatively both patients had been severely confused and apathetic, but immediately post-operatively they showed severe disorientation, nonsensical confabulation, some retrograde and virtually complete anterograde amnesia. The disorientation improved considerably within a few weeks, and at the same time their confabulation changed from fantastic fabrications to temporal misplacement of actual incidents. Over the next three years the memory disorder became chronic, together with impotence in both and marked lack of initiative in one. The lesions seen at operation had involved the postero-medial aspects of the orbital surface of both frontal lobes and the adjoining medial surface of the hemispheres—the so-called septal region in front of the lamina terminalis and anterior commissure. The crucial region was thought to lie in the septal region bilaterally, and it was suggested that this should be added to those parts of the brain implicated in memory functions in man.

Lindqvist and Norlen (1966) reported similar amnesic syndromes in 17 of 33 patients after operations on anterior communicating aneurysms. Eleven improved markedly within 6 months, but 5 appeared destined to be permanent. The memory disorder was accompanied by elevation of mood, indifference and apathy, and even in those which resolved there was sometimes persistent emotional shallowness.

It seems hard to escape the conclusion that operative intervention may play a part in the development of such changes, especially from some of the case histories presented by Lindqvist and Norlen. Gade (1982) has reported persistent amnesic syndromes very much more commonly after 'trapping' than after ligations confined to the neck of anterior communicating aneurysms. 'Trapping' involves ligatures placed on the anterior communicating artery on either side of the aneurysm, thus depriving blood supply to the fine perforating branches which supply structures along the anterior wall of the third ventricle—regions known to be implicated in memory functions.

Personality Changes

Personality deterioration after subarachnoid haemorrhage usually has an obvious organic stamp in a setting of intellectual impairment. Prominent changes include loss of drive and vitality, decreased interest and initiative, withdrawal, irritability and easily provoked anxiety. Emotional lability and catastrophic tendencies may be marked. Storey (1970) describes a picture of 'organic moodiness' with chronic shallow depression, often lifting quickly in response to some new stimulus but rapidly falling back again with boredom, loss of interest and easy fatigue. Changes reminiscent of the frontal lobe syndrome may occur, with uninhibited selfish behaviour, tactlessness, or elevation of mood and a decreased tendency to worry. Some of these aspects can be construed as improvements in personality as discussed below.

Personality impairment was rated as moderate or severe in 19% of Storey's patients, and mild in 22% more. It was most common after rupture of middle cerebral aneurysms, and in general the incidence paralleled that of intellectual impairment and neurological disability. The exception was a significant tendency for anterior communicating aneurysms to show relatively less intellectual impairment in the presence of personality deterioration. Descriptions of uninhibited behaviour, lessened worry and lessened irritability were commoner with anterior aneurysms than other groups, lending support to the classical idea of a frontal lobe syndrome. Logue *et al.* (1968), in a factor analysis of symptoms, similarly found a relatively independent component of elevation of mood and reduction of anxiety which could occasionally occur without anything at all by way of intellectual impairment.

Improvement in personality was noted by relatives in 13 of Storey's patients, 8 after bleeds from anterior aneurysms. The same was seen in 9 of Logue *et al.*'s patients. In both series, therefore, approximately 10% of patients with anterior bleeds showed a favourable outcome of this nature. Storey's patients were described as being more pleasant to live with, less sarcastic and irritable, less anxious and fussy, and often more affectionate and tolerant. Most were aware of increased well-being subjectively. The majority had previously been tense, perfectionistic or inhibited. Two who had been gloomy and readily fatigued became cheerful, vigorous, and lost their tension headaches. Another lost compulsive rituals of long-standing. Two of the 13 showed minor forgetfulness, but in the remainder there was no detectable intellectual impairment. None showed loss of drive or fall-off in work ability.

By contrast Logue *et al.* found that a price was usually paid for the improvements, in terms of memory impairment or an increase in irritability or outspokenness. The improvements consisted mainly of a decreased tendency to worry or get depressed. In three patients there was relief of a pre-existing endogenous depression, and another showed virtual relief of an obsessional neurosis. Both Storey and Logue attributed the improvements to a 'leucotomy effect' consequent upon frontal lobe damage or ischaemia.

Anxiety and Depression

Walton (1952) emphasised anxiety symptoms in 27% of his cases, half with premorbid neurotic tendencies and half without. The anxiety was often severe and incapacitating, centering largely on fear of recurrence of the haemorrhage. Some patients were afraid for months afterwards to leave the house, or retired to bed immediately they had a headache. In some instances the situation had been worsened by medical advice to avoid exertion.

Storey (1972) found symptoms of anxiety or depression in a quarter of patients, being moderate or severe in 14%. Such symptoms showed an association with indices of brain damage, but depression could also be severe when there was no evidence of brain damage whatever. The depressives without

neurological signs had been more neurotic and prone to depression in their premorbid personalities, while those with brain damage had more often been energetic and were therefore perhaps reacting to their losses of function. The patients in whom aneurysms had not been detected appeared to form a special group, with a similar incidence of depression to the remainder despite considerably less evidence of intellectual impairment or neurological disability. Depression was commonest of all, and more liable to be severe and persistent, in patients with posterior communicating aneurysms, where rupture is known to interfere with the fine perforating vessels to the hypothalamus.

Other Disturbances

'Neurasthenic' symptoms can occasionally be marked with fatigue, headache, dizziness and sensitivity to noise. These were persistent and incapacitating in 7 of 56 patients followed by Theander and Granholm (1967), and present in mild degree in many more. Their origin was obscure and showed no relation to the duration of loss of consciousness. Walton (1952) commented on the general similarity between such symptoms after subarachnoid haemorrhage and after head injury.

Psychotic developments appear to be rare. Silverman (1949) reviewed occasional examples, and reported a patient of his own who became paranoid for several weeks despite normal orientation. Walton (1953) observed paranoid developments in two patients, one in association with a Korsakoff psychosis. Storey (1972), however, found no examples of psychosis among 261 patients who were studied closely from the psychiatric point of view. One of his patients developed schizophrenia a year later, but the illness seemed unrelated to the haemorrhage.

EMOTIONAL PRECIPITATION OF SUBARACHNOID HAEMORRHAGE

Occasional examples are reported of cerebrovascular accidents which show a striking temporal relationship to emotionally stressful events. The question has attracted some interest, since the development of a stroke at a given point in time may well depend on general circulatory as well as local occlusive processes. Ecker (1954) regarded a high proportion of his cases as having some special emotional stress immediately preceding their strokes. In Ullman's (1962) series there were occasional cases where the stroke was closely associated with an unusual and deeply disturbing life event, for example in a woman who had just returned from visiting her son who was being held on a charge of homicide, and in another on the night before being admitted to hospital for a mitral valvotomy which she dreaded. Adler *et al.* (1971), in a retrospective study, found that strokes typically occurred during a period of sustained or intermittent emotional disturbance which had been going on for weeks or months, and which sometimes had become intensified shortly before the stroke occurred.

The most dramatic instances, however, appear to involve patients with subarachnoid haemorrhage. Particularly striking examples have been recorded by Storey (1969, 1972) in which the haemorrhage followed immediately upon some emotionally traumatic event, presumably by virtue of the rise of blood pressure engendered. Thus a woman answered the door to a policeman who told her that the woman next door, her closest friend, had hanged herself—she said 'Oh, my God' and forthwith had her haemorrhage. Another woman was watching television when an aeroplane on a test flight was shown exploding in the air; she believed (erroneously as it turned out) that her son was on it, put her hands to her head and had the haemorrhage within seconds of the disaster. Another had a subarachnoid haemorrhage within a minute of being told by her husband that he knew of her adultery and was going to divorce her.

Altogether Storey found evidence of a striking emotional precipitant in four of his original 261 patients, and two further less dramatic examples. All were in women, although 43% of the series were male. Such precipitation appeared to be markedly more common in patients with no obvious source for the haemorrhage than in patients with aneurysms demonstrable on angiography. A history of affective disorder antedating the haemorrhage was also more common in the non-aneurysm cases.

Exploring this further, Penrose and Storey (1970) carried out a blind prospective study by interviewing the relatives of 56 patients admitted with subarachnoid haemorrhage before the results of angiography were known. Significantly more emotional disturbance immediately antedating the haemorrhage was confirmed in the patients with normal angiograms. A standardised life events schedule also showed a significant increase in the number of upsetting life experiences during the three weeks prior to haemorrhage in patients without aneurysms (Penrose, 1972).

The reason for a greater incidence of emotional precipitation in patients with normal angiograms is intriguing and not immediately clear. Part of the explanation may be that they are less often engaged in physical activity at the onset than are patients who bleed from aneurysms, or they may represent persons with unusually labile blood pressures and unusual reactivity to emotional traumata.

Mention must finally be made of 2 patients described by Engel (1972) in whom there was an astonishing conjunction between the timing of subarachnoid haemorrhage and antecedent events:

A 17-year-old boy collapsed and died at 6 a.m. from a ruptured aneurysm of the anterior communicating artery. Exactly one year earlier his brother had died at 5.12 a.m., a few hours after a car crash. The family had heard the boy stirring in his room around 5 a.m., earlier than he normally arose.

In the second case a man of 46 had his subarachnoid haemorrhage on the same date and in the same hospital as his father, who had died of a subarachnoid haemorrhage when 46 after a quarrel with the patient who was then a boy of 15. The patient had felt himself impelled to provoke a quarrel with his own teenage son on the day prior to his own subarachnoid haemorrhage.

Hypertension

Hypertension attracts psychiatric interest on several grounds. First there is the intriguing possibility that essential hypertension may owe its aetiology, at least in part, to psychological factors. The question of a relationship to stress, or of an association between hypertension and certain personality attributes has therefore received a good deal of attention. Secondly, the more discriminating assessment of common 'symptoms' of hypertension, such as headache and fatigue, has shown that they appear often to arise secondarily to knowledge of the disorder, rather than being attributable to elevation of the blood pressure *per se*. Thirdly, iatrogenic psychiatric effects can figure prominently in the use of antihypertensive drugs and must be taken carefully into account in treatment. Fourthly, clinical syndromes such as hypertensive encephalopathy may develop in the course of the disorder and present with marked mental changes. All of this is additional to the important role of hypertension in contributing to cerebrovascular disease and stroke which has already been considered.

Psychological Factors in Causation

The precise aetiology of hypertension remains elusive in the great majority of cases. Rather less than 10% of patients show some specific causative pathology such as chronic renal disease, renal artery stenosis or, more rarely, a primary adrenal disorder. In the remainder, with so-called 'essential' hypertension, there is probably multifactorial causation involving genetic and other factors. A model frequently proposed envisages such persons as unusually susceptible to vasomotor reactions resulting from a stressful environment, by virtue of inherited traits, intrinsic emotional instability, or a hyperreactive peripheral vasculature. The frequent excessive rises of blood pressure so provoked lead on to changes in small blood vessels, and thereby to secondary humoral mechanisms originating in the kidneys which maintain the blood pressure at sustained excessive levels. Claims for including essential hypertension among the psychosomatic disorders in this way merit the closest examination, in view of its high incidence and associated mortality. Two facets warrant exploration here—the relationship to stress, and predisposition in terms of specific personality features.

There is a wealth of evidence that transient rises of blood pressure accompany psychological stimuli and stress, as reviewed by McGinn *et al.* (1964). The relationship has been shown to be extremely sensitive, with short-lived rises accompanying such matters as telling a lie, discussing life problems or dealing with material of threatening significance. The problem is whether lasting elevation of blood pressure may be related to stress, and here the evidence is necessarily indirect. Chronically stressed animals may develop hypertension, persisting for several months after exposure to the stressful situation. In man, Graham (1945) observed symptomless hypertension in 27% of soldiers resting after a year in active field operations, with diastolic pressures over 100 mm Hg which lasted for several weeks or months. Following the severe explosion in Texas City in 1947 diastolic hypertension was present in more than half of the patients observed, often persisting for one or two weeks or even longer (Ruskin *et al.*, 1948). Cruz-Coke (1960) drew attention to possible cultural stress influences, showing that blood pressure levels were significantly raised in a sub-section of the population of Lima who were in rapid cultural transition from a primitive society to the stress of 'Western'-type civilization.

An interesting model for exploring the question was utilised by Heine *et al.* (1969). They argued that persons who had undergone the emotional disturbance of an agitated depressive illness, severe enough to warrant ECT, might be expected to show an irreversible increase of blood pressure on recovery, and that the levels would be proportional to the duration of distress. Examining twenty-five such patients, they found a significant correlation between the blood pressure on recovery and both the duration and number of spells of illness, thus confirming their hypothesis. It seemed unlikely from the data that the results could be explained by common genetic determinants for depression and hypertension, or that pre-existing hypertension had predisposed to the depressive episodes. It should be noted, however that the levels of hypertension observed were relatively low in comparison with those of patients seeking treatment for raised blood pressure.

Direct approaches to evaluating stress in the lives of established hypertensive patients have rarely been undertaken on any comprehensive scale. Reiser *et al.* (1951) reported an uncontrolled investigation of patients entering the malignant phase of hypertension, and felt that a close chronological correlation could be observed with emotionally charged life situations occurring at the time. Others, however, have found no difference between hypertensives and controls with regard to preceding life events, in particular when community based samples have been studied (Wheatley *et al.*, 1975). Stressful occupations have been examined, sometimes with highly suggestive findings. Cobb and Rose (1973), for example, found that the incidence of hypertension at annual physical examination was many times greater among air traffic controllers than among second-class airmen whose jobs were considerably less stressful. Moreover those controllers working with high traffic densities showed more cases of hypertension than those working at low densities, and developed the disorder at an earlier age.

Thus the sum total of evidence rather strongly suggests that stress may be related to the development of sustained hypertension in certain situations. It is not inconceivable that stress may operate in this way in the hypertensive population generally. It is therefore necessary also to examine whether those who fall victim to hypertension are in any way unusual in their constitutional reactivity to environmental or interpersonal stresses. This has involved studies of vasomotor reactivity and of certain personality features in hypertensive patients.

Emotionally stressful situations have been shown to produce higher rises in blood pressure in hypertensive than normotensive persons, both in absolute terms and as a proportion of the original level (Robinson, 1963). This, however, could be a feature secondary to the hypertensive process itself, rather than reflecting an innate tendency. Thus it seems to apply equally in renal and essential hypertension (Ostfeld and Lebovits, 1958). 'Neuroticism', as a feature in the personality, has often emerged as high in hypertensives, and has connotations for emotional lability, emotional over-responsiveness and perhaps vasomotor reactivity. Here, however, there has been difficulty in deciding how far the association is causal, coincidental, or secondary to knowledge of having the disorder.

Sainsbury (1964) found that hypertensives attending an out-patient clinic obtained high neuroticism scores on the Maudsley Personality Inventory, being similar to 'psychosomatic' groups but scoring significantly higher than non-psychosomatic patients. Robinson (1963) found similar evidence among hospital attenders, but in a community survey found little relationship between neuroticism and the level of the blood pressure. He concluded that patients attending hospital were open to special selection, probably by their general practitioners. Cochrane (1969) compared the neuroticism scores of patients discovered to be hypertensive by general practitioners with those discovered to be normotensive in the same practices, and found no difference between them. The hypertensives had virtually normal neuroticism scores. He suggested that the results in Sainsbury's and Robinson's out-patient surveys may have been partly due to the use of rauwolfia at that time, which may have led to artificially elevated responses on the neuroticism scale. Kidson (1973) compared hypertensive clinic attenders with persons randomly selected from industry and found to have elevated or normal blood pressures. On a range of personality measures the hypertensive patients were strikingly different from the non-patient subjects, with higher neuroticism, more insecurity, more tension, and higher total scores for somatic discomfort on the Cornell Medical Index. But among the nonpatient groups, hypertensives and normotensives were in most respects similar on psychological variables. Thus the 'neurosis' of the hospital attenders appeared more likely to be a reaction to knowledge of the disease, or a by-product of treatment, rather than representing a psychological precursor of the hypertensive process.

The lack of any innate relationship between psychological factors and raised blood pressure has recently been strongly confirmed in the course of a large treatment trial for mild to moderate hypertension (Mann, 1977, 1981, 1984). Psychiatric morbidity was assessed by means of the General Health Questionnaire in over 2000 persons attending screening clinics, before the blood pressure was taken. No significant differences emerged in the scores of those subsequently found to be normotensive or hypertensive. Interestingly moreover, when trial entrants were followed over the first year of treatment their level of psychiatric morbidity fell in relation to normotensive controls; the evidence suggested that this was attributable to the support derived from regular clinic attendance rather than to more specific factors such as the effects of medication or control of the hypertension.

A specific personality attribute claimed to characterise hypertensive patients is the chronic inhibition of aggressive, hostile impulses. Alexander (1939) suggested that a central feature was their inability to freely resolve either of two opposing tendencies—passive dependent needs on the one hand, and overcompensatory aggressive impulses on the other. Such conflict was often brought to the fore by the culturally determined complexities of present civilisation. Saul (1939) similarly found intense, chronic and unexpressed hostility in his patients, along with marked inhibition and anxiety over heterosexuality. These, however, were uncontrolled observations in patients selected for psychoanalysis. Mann's (1977, 1984) study, referred to above, has indeed indicated a precisely opposite tendency, with hypertensive patients showing more overt hostility and reduced self-criticism when compared to normotensive controls. Altogether the evidence in favour of specific predisposing personality patterns must be judged as very slender.

We are left, therefore, with highly suggestive findings that stress may be important in the aetiology of hypertension, but with rather little to support the notion that personality attributes make a definite contribution. The factors which select out the peripheral vasculature, and hence the blood pressure, as the system to be affected remain to be determined.

The Symptoms of Hypertension

The repeated finding that hypertensives attending out-patient clinics score highly on indices of neurosis, whereas those discovered in the community do not, must call into question many of the symptoms which in the past have been attributed to elevation of blood pressure. Robinson (1963) pointed out that many of the so-called symptoms of hypertension are similar to those of emotional disorder—symptoms such as headache, dizziness, fatigue, palpitations, insomnia, depression and anxiety. Of the patients who are sent to hospital with complaints of this nature, those with elevated blood pressure will often tend to be directed to medical clinics and those without to psychiatric clinics, yet in both groups the symptoms may be founded equivalently in anxiety.

Stewart (1953) made a careful comparison between two groups of patients with hypertension of comparable severity—those who were unaware and those who were aware of the elevation of their blood pressure. Only 16% of the former had headache and only 3% complained of this spontaneously, compared with 74% of those who had knowledge of their hypertension. Most of the latter described it in terms characteristic of anxiety. It was only in a very small group that headache appeared to be attributable directly to the elevation of blood pressure, and in character this closely resembled migraine. Robinson (1969) compared groups of patients attending their general practitioners, noting whether or not the blood pressure had been measured and whether this was high or normal. Again little evidence emerged for linking headache, or any other symptom, to elevation of the blood pressure *per se*.

Thus the present consensus of opinion is that hypertension is essentially a symptomless disorder until complications occur. Frequently, however, there will be superadded anxiety with its attendant somatic complaints. The development of exceedingly high levels in the malignant phase is a different matter. Headache is then often severe, and may be associated with raised intracranial pressure and visual failure.

Iatrogenic Effects of Treatment

It is now well established that the prognosis of essential hypertension is considerably improved when the blood pressure is lowered by means of drugs. Treatment should therefore be offered to all patients with moderate or severe hypertension and must usually be continued indefinitely. Unfortunately such treatment is not without side effects, including adverse psychological reactions. The newer drugs now available represent a distinct improvement in this regard, but still carry hazards which must be borne in mind.

The introduction of rauwolfia alkaloids led to an outbreak of iatrogenic depression, often of considerable severity and occurring in up to one-third of patients in some series. Rauwolfia depletes stores of noradrenaline and other amines both centrally and at peripheral adrenergic nerve terminals. The depressive effect was so marked that research was directly stimulated into the possible biochemical basis of naturally occurring depressive illnesses. Nowadays the pure form, reserpine, is still used occasionally, but only in low dosage. It can be given with reasonable safety if patients with a past history of depression are excluded, if there has been no recent bereavement, and if the patient is warned of the possibility of depression (Simpson and Waal-Manning, 1971). Needless to say treatment must be closely monitored, especially since depression is liable to come on slowly and insidiously at the low dosages employed.

Methyldopa (aldomet), a commonly prescribed hypotensive agent, is given with or without thiazide diuretics. It has a central action analogous to that of rauwolfia, depleting the brain of noradrenaline, serotonin and dopamine, and early reports suggested that it too could induce depression. It seems, however, that fears in this regard were overstated. Controlled trials have shown no higher incidence of depression with methyldopa than with postganglionic sympathetic blockers (Pritchard *et al.*, 1968). Surveys in general practice have also on the whole been reassuring (Snaith and McCoubrie, 1974). It is nonetheless considered wise to avoid methyldopa when there is a past history of depressive illness. The most troublesome and definite side effects are tiredness, drowsiness and limb weakness, which tend to pass off after the early stages. Nightmares and hallucinations have occasionally been reported.

Drugs such as guanethidine, bethanidine and debrisoquine block transmission in postganglionic sympathetic neurones but have no demonstrable central effects. These rarely cause depression, but are liable to prevent ejaculation and may lead to impotence. They may also produce troublesome postural hypotension which can be serious in the elderly patient with cerebral atherosclerosis.

Beta-adreno receptor blockers (propanolol, practolol, oxprenolol) act by competition at beta nerve endings, but may also exert a central effect. Some tendency to lead to depression is suspected.

Clonidine has mixed central and peripheral actions which are incompletely understood. Depression is occasionally reported, so this too is best avoided if there is a past history of depressive illness.

Drugs such as pentolinium, hexamethonium, mecamylamine and pempidine act by non-selective blockade of nerve impulse transmission in autonomic ganglia. Accordingly they have widespread side effects and are now rarely used. An exception is in emergency situations, such as hypertensive encephalopathy, when hexamethonium bromide may be given intravenously or pentolinium subcutaneously.

With the range of drugs available there is considerable lee-way for choice of the most suitable agent. Most difficulty is likely to be encountered in the not uncommon situation when a patient is both hypertensive and depressed. The relative urgencies of treating the two conditions must sometimes be carefully assessed, since drugs used for each may disrupt the other (Simpson and Waal-Manning, 1971; *Drug and Therapeutics Bulletin*, 1975). Tricyclic antidepressants antagonise the hypotensive effect of postganglionic sympathetic blockers such as guanethidine, which might otherwise have been the treatment of choice in that they seldom cause depression. Clonidine is also rendered less effective. A change of medication to a thiazide diuretic or propanolol is therefore indicated before commencing tricyclic antidepressants, accepting the small risk of the propanolol aggravating the depression. Alternatively, mianserin (Bolvidon, Norval) may be used as the antidepressant drug since this is compatible with most antihypertensive agents (*British National Formulary*, 1985). Monoamine oxidase inhibitors are contraindicated in view of their liability to interact dangerously with other drugs. With methyldopa they may exert a central stimulating effect and lead to a dangerous rise of blood pressure; they potentiate the hypotensive effect of sympathetic blockers; and hypertensive patients are particularly susceptible to hypertensive crises with monoamine oxidase inhibitors if they take tyramine containing foods.

Depression may of course also arise as a reaction to unwanted side effects of hypotensive medication, such as weakness, fainting on standing, loss of libido and sexual failure. Such an origin must not be overlooked since the way may be open for change to less troublesome medication. Nevertheless a considerable range of side effects must often be tolerated for the sake of adequate blood pressure control. The frequency of symptoms encountered in patients attending a hypertensive clinic was illustrated by Bulpitt and Dollery's (1973) survey. The largest group was made up of patients taking methyldopa with or without a diuretic, who experienced symptoms as follows: sleepiness in 57%, dryness of the mouth 41%, impotence 36%, slowed walking 35%, postural hypotension 32%, depression 30%, weak limbs 27%, diarrhoea 27%, blurred vision

19%, and failure of ejaculation 19%. Though not all symptoms in every patient would be directly attributable to medication the range and incidence of discomforts is clearly very high.

Hypertensive Encephalopathy

This was never a common condition, and is now even rarer as a result of management of hypertension which prevents the malignant phase. When it does arise it is always a serious medical emergency. Very occasionally it may be the presenting manifestation of the hypertension.

Onset is acute with headache, drowsiness, apprehension and mental confusion. Epileptic fits frequently occur. The disorder evolves rapidly, often within the space of twenty-four hours, and if untreated progresses to coma with a fatal outcome in a high proportion of cases. The diastolic blood pressure is extremely high, often exceeding 140 mm Hg. Vomiting may occur and papilloedema frequently develops. Differentiation from a tumour or abscess may not be easy (Marshall, 1976). Advanced retinopathy is invariably present, and threatening kidney or heart failure are common.

Focal signs such as nystagmus, cortical blindness or limb weakness are variable and tend to come and go. Usually, however, focal neurological signs are not a part of the picture. When present they imply complicating factors such as thrombosis, embolism or haemorrhage. Many focal syndromes previously labelled as hypertensive encephalopathy were probably transient cerebral ischaemic attacks occurring in severely hypertensive patients.

Pathological examination may reveal a normal brain, but usually there is marked oedema or petechial haemorrhages and micro-infarcts. Byrom (1954) has shown that in hypertension of advanced degree there is intense segmental constriction of cerebral arterioles, attributable to attempts at autoregulation which fail when the pressure exceeds a certain limit. Dilatation occurs between the constricted segments and the vessel wall is damaged, leading to hyperperfusion and cerebral oedema which appear to be the essential factors underlying hypertensive encephalopathy (Skinhoj and Strandgaard, 1973).

Migraine

Migraine is a common and sometimes severely incapacitating disorder, estimated to affect 5–10 per cent of the population at some time or another.

Comprehensive reviews of the condition are provided by Pearce (1969), Sacks (1970) and Lance (1982). Psychological factors can play an important role in the precipitation of attacks and psychiatric phenomena may feature prominently in the course of the attacks. Psychological aspects of management often prove to be of great importance, especially in recalcitrant cases.

The syndrome is hard to delineate precisely since to some extent boundaries are blurred between this and other forms of vascular headache. Many variations occur and several subtypes have come to be established. The Research Group on Migraine and Headache of the World Federation of Neurology defined migraine as a familial disorder, characterised by recurrent attacks of headache widely variable in intensity, frequency and duration, commonly unilateral, usually associated with anorexia, nausea and vomiting, and sometimes preceded by or associated with neurological and mood disturbances (Critchley, 1969). Others have chosen a more empirical approach to definition. Whitty *et al.* (1966), for example, used the criteria of recurrent throbbing headaches together with two of the following five features—unilateral headache, an association with nausea or vomiting, a visual or other sensory aura, a history of cyclical vomiting in childhood, or a family history of migraine.

Clinical Features

The disorder is commoner in women than men in a ratio of two or three to one. Onset is usually in childhood or early adult life, some 25% of cases beginning before the age of 10 and very few after 45. A childhood history of cyclical vomiting with abdominal pain can sometimes be traced as a precursor. Affected individuals show an increased incidence of allergic disorders such as asthma or hay fever, and very probably an increased incidence of epilepsy. A family history of migraine is reported in some two-thirds of cases.

Headache is the most constant element, lasting usually for 8 to 24 hours though occasionally several days, and varying from mild discomfort to pain of incapacitating violence. It is mostly unilateral at onset, though tending to become diffuse later in the attack. The chief focus may be temporal, supraorbital, retrobulbar, or more rarely over the parietal or occipital regions. Throbbing is common at least initially, with aggravation on coughing or jolting. Anorexia, nausea and vomiting usually develop, also photophobia and intolerance of noise. Autonomic changes may include pallor, facial oedema, conjunctival injection, abdominal distension or the passing of one or more loose stools. In attacks of any severity the patient is usually obliged to lie down until the episode has passed.

This variety is designated *'common migraine'*. Difficulty will be encountered in certain cases in distinguishing it from tension headache (p. 353). In perhaps a third of cases the headache is preceded by more dramatic phenomena in the form of a visual aura, the syndrome then being known as *'classical migraine'*. Here visual disturbance is the first indication of an impending attack, lasting some 10–60 minutes and subsiding as the headache sets in. Most typical are the well-known 'fortification spectra' ('teichopsia'), starting near the fixation point in one half field and expanding to the periphery as a semicircle of shimmering highly-coloured zig-zag lights. Hare (1973) has drawn attention to the remarkably constant duration of 20 minutes for such classical spectra. Other forms consist of moving coils, curving lights, or rippling sensations in the visual field. Not all are confined to one half field of vision. A negative scotoma may follow in their wake, or constitute the whole of the aura in itself. Other disturbances include micropsia, macropsia, distortions of shape and position, 'zoom vision' and 'mosaic vision'. Occasionally there are hallucinations and distortions of taste, smell and hearing. Tactile paraesthesiae may co-exist with the visual disturbances or occur alone. Body image disturbances, though rare, can take fascinating forms as discussed on page 348.

A not uncommon variant is *'basilar artery migraine'* (Bickerstaff, 1961a, 1961b). The attacks begin with a visual aura, sometimes extending to both half fields and obscuring vision, then proceed to symptoms of brain stem dysfunction such as vertigo, dysarthria, ataxia, tinnitus, and sensory symptoms distally in the limbs and around the lips and tongue. After several minutes to three quarters of an hour these give way to throbbing headache, usually of occipital distribution. Loss of consciousness may be interposed between the brain stem symptoms and headache, lasting sometimes for up to half an hour and presumably due to ischaemia of the reticular formation. The impairment is gradual in onset, resembling deep sleep rather than syncope. Attacks of basilar migraine appear to be especially common in adolescent girls and carry a strong family history of migraine. The episodes are usually infrequent and interspersed among classical attacks.

More marked neurological phenomena can occur in patients with so-called *'complicated migraine'*.

With '*hemiplegic migraine*' unilateral motor (or sensory) disturbances in the limbs accompany or replace the visual aura, or may appear in the later stages of the attack. Dysphasia can accompany the paresis when the dominant side is affected, and consciousness is sometimes impaired (Whitty, 1953; Bradshaw and Parsons, 1965). The neurological signs may outlast other components of the attack, sometimes persisting for several days. In such cases there tends to be a strong family history of similar attacks. In '*ophthalmoplegic migraine*' attacks are accompanied by paresis of external ocular movement, again often outlasting the headache.

Other variants include '*facial migraine*' ('*lower half headache*') in which episodes of unilateral facial pain are associated with typical migrainous phenomena, starting in the cheek or palate and spreading to the ear or neck. '*Migrainous neuralgia*' ('*cluster headaches*') consists of severe unilateral head or face pain, usually periorbital, typically occurring in bouts over a period of several weeks, and often appearing at exactly the same time each day. Attacks are accompanied by lachrymation and nasal blockage on the ipsilateral side, and sometimes by a Horner's syndrome. Some consider this to be a distinct entity rather than a variant of migraine.

A further variation consists of attacks in which components other than headache dominate the clinical picture ('*migraine equivalents*'). The headache may be mild or even totally absent, leading to considerable diagnostic difficulty if a history of more typical attacks is not forthcoming. Thus the visual aura or other neurological disturbance may occur alone, or there may be episodes of nausea and vomiting, abdominal pain or drowsiness. Some of the mental phenomena which may constitute equivalents are discussed below.

Course and Outcome

Once established migraine is commonly a life-long complaint, though spells of relief may occur for years at a time. The frequency and severity of attacks vary greatly from one patient to another. Some are affected at fairly regular intervals, and a small number of women are especially susceptible around the time of the menstrual periods. Temporary relief during pregnancy is well attested in approximately 60% of cases. Improvement at the menopause may occur but is less regularly observed. A general indication of outcome is given by Whitty and Hockaday (1968) who reviewed a large group of patients 15 to 20 years after their first attendance at a clinic.

Attacks had ceased in a third, improved over time in half, and continued without improvement in the remainder. Changing patterns over time were not uncommon, also dissociation between the auras and the headaches so that either could occur alone.

Psychological precipitants (p. 348) are universally recognised and in some patients play a major role in determining the frequency and timing of attacks. Dietary factors may also be blamed, including alcohol, cheese, chocolate and fatty foods. In some patients missing a meal or going without sleep appears regularly to precipitate attacks. Oral contraceptives have been found to exacerbate migraine, or indeed to induce its first appearance (Whitty *et al.*, 1966; Bickerstaff and Holmes, 1967).

Permanent sequelae to attacks are extremely uncommon and constitute clinical rarities. Nevertheless Davis-Jones *et al.* (1973) refer to 145 cases in the literature and add fourteen more of their own. Most frequent are enduring visual field defects, attributable to retinal or cerebral lesions, also pareses, dysphasia, ophthalmoplegias and oculosympathetic lesions. The occasional cases of dementia in association with migraine are discussed below (p. 351).

Findings of possible relevance have come from recent CT scan studies. Among 53 patients with very severe migraine Hungerford *et al.* (1976) found 6 with generalised and 8 with focal atrophy, usually mild in degree. Probably of more significance, 6 patients showed evidence of infarcts, 3 corresponding in site to aspects of the clinical history. Of the 13 patients with permanent neurological sequaelae 11 showed some abnormality on the scan. Dorfman *et al.* (1979) demonstrated infarctions by angiography or CT scan in 4 young adults with migraine, one representing a posterior cerebral artery occlusion and 3 infarctions in the middle cerebral territory. Thus at least in complicated migraine cerebral changes may be not uncommon. Determination of their true incidence will obviously require careful controlled studies, in groups of patients who have not been specially selected for their atypical features.

Aetiology and Pathology

The precise cause of migraine remains uncertain. An inherited predisposition seems likely in view of the high familial concentrations reported (Dalsgaard-Nielsen, 1965), though careful epidemiological surveys suggest that this may have been overstressed (Waters, 1971). Allergic factors have often been proposed but rarely upheld. Hormonal influences are suggested by the high remission rate in pregnancy, the exacerbation on taking the contraceptive pill, and the small group of cases with attacks clearly related to the menstrual periods. Even in the latter, however, precise correlations with hormonal levels remain elusive (Epstein *et al.*, 1975). There is often evidence of sodium and water retention with attacks, patients noticing weight gain and oedema beforehand and polyuria as the headache subsides, yet diuretics have little prophylactic value. The role of hypoglycaemia has been studied in cases provoked by fasting and cases preceded by abnormal sensations of hunger; no clear correlations have emerged with blood glucose levels, but there are indirect indications of an abnormal central response to carbohydrate depletion in certain subjects (Hockaday *et al.*, 1971, 1973; Rao and Pearce, 1971).

Much of the above therefore appears to be dealing with epiphenomena to attacks rather than revealing the fundamentals of the disturbance. Pearce (1969) suggests that the basic abnormality may lie in a periodic central disturbance, or functionally labile threshold, of hypothalamic activity. This could have effects on the autonomic control of the vasculature, and at the same time provide a mechanism whereby emotional disturbance could influence the pattern and timing of attacks. As yet, however, direct support for the hypothesis has not been forthcoming.

The pathophysiological mechanisms responsible for the headache have been explored in a long series of studies summarised by Lance (1982). There is good evidence that headache is associated with dilatation of the cranial arteries, the principal component coming from the *extracranial* or scalp arteries. An important additional factor appears to be the development, later in the attack, of a sterile inflammatory reaction in and around the affected vessels, with the accumulation of substances which sensitize them to pain. Pain may also be derived in part from meningeal and other intracranial vessels, accounting for accentuation by coughing, sneezing and head movement (Blau and Davis, 1970).

The mechanisms behind the production of neurological prodromata are less completely understood. There is evidence of intracranial vasoconstriction as a prelude to the extracranial vasodilatation, but this is unlikely to be the complete explanation. Cerebral blood flow studies carried out during the course of migraine attacks have shown oligaemic changes, starting posteriorly and spreading forwards over the course of 15–45 minutes (Lance, 1982). However, focal cerebral symptoms had often preceded this oligaemic phase. Moreover vasoconstrictors (such as

ergotamine) given early in the attack can sometimes cut short the aura as well as preventing the headache. It is also difficult to explain the distribution and rate of progress of classical visual spectra on the basis of cortical ischaemia alone. Vasoconstriction may be the initiating change, but a secondary process of spreading depolarisation ('spreading depression') may then be set in motion over the cortex. Or in the case of prolonged neurological phenomena, as in hemiplegic migraine, local oedema ensuing on the spasm may be responsible for the symptoms (Whitty, 1953).

The site of the changes responsible for auras must differ widely from one form to another. Teichopsia and homonymous field defects almost certainly originate in the occipital lobes, illusions of altered size, shape and position in the optic radiations, and bitemporal hemianopias from disturbance of chiasmatic vessels. The retinal vessels are clearly involved in some cases of monocular scotoma and occlusion of retinal arteries has been directly observed. The middle cerebral or internal carotids are likely to be involved in hemiplegic migraine, and the vertebrobasilar system in patients with brain stem manifestations. In fact it is probable that in many attacks a large part of the cerebral vasculature is affected diffusely, the focal symptoms merely reflecting ischaemia in the territory most severely involved— hence the vague but definite symptoms of slowed cerebration and somnolence which are common in attacks.

Biochemical alterations have been identified along with the vascular changes and could conceivably play a primary role in the genesis of attacks. In the early stages catabolites of norepinephrine and serotonin are excreted in excess in the urine, and plasma serotonin has been shown to fall abruptly at the onset of the headache phase. Serotonin is known to constrict scalp arteries, so the fall could be responsible for the vasodilatation of the headache. It remains to be explained, however, why attacks should commonly be unilateral in distribution, and some constitutional vascular instability or hypersensitivity to humoral agents must still be postulated.

PSYCHIATRIC ASPECTS OF MIGRAINE

Virtually all observers, neurologists and psychiatrists alike, stress the influence which psychological factors may have in migraine and the importance attaching to them in treatment. Migraine is indeed often seen as a model for 'psychosomatic' disorders. A considerable literature has accumulated concerning the personality of migraine sufferers, and the role of emotions and conflicts in precipitating attacks. Mental phenomena are also recognised as common accompaniments of the disorder, and may sometimes assume bizarre expression leading to diagnostic difficulty. These aspects will be briefly reviewed.

Personality in Migraine

Many accounts stress the driving conscientious personality of migraine sufferers, often with marked obsessional traits and above average intelligence. Such a picture originated with the work of Wolff (1937, 1963) and has clearly accorded with the experience of others (Alvarez, 1947; Fine, 1969).

Wolff's migraineurs were described as delicate and shy in childhood, overtly obedient but with contrasting traits of stubbornness and inflexibility. In adult life certain features were seen in marked degree— 90 per cent were ambitious and preoccupied with achievement and success, almost all attempted to dominate their enviromnents, and most were persistent, exacting and meticulous. A poised external appearance hid inner tensions. Many harboured strong resentments which were linked to their intolerance of frustration and superabundance of drive. Sexual maladjustment and dissatisfaction were common. Such features were not universal or pathognomonic for the disorder, but when present appeared to furnish optimal conditions for the precipitation of attacks.

Psychoanalysts, from intensive observation of small numbers of cases, have highlighted certain other constellations in the personality. Fromm-Reichmann (1937) stressed the role of repressed hostility and inability to face unresolved ambivalence against loved persons. Sperling (1964) described oral fixation, with low tolerance for frustration and strongly developed anal-sadism resulting in compulsive behaviour, tenseness and rigidity. The choice of the head, as a physical expression of repressed conflicts, was attributed to specific pre-genital fantasies and impulses of attacking the frustrating object, or destroying the loved person's intellectuality. This often appeared to be a 'castration tendency' displaced upwards from below. Others have emphasised the significance of sexual conflicts, and confusions over sexual identification. The startling visual prodromes and scotomata have been attributed to repression of early psychological traumata that were experienced visually (Fine, 1969).

It seems unlikely, however, that generalisations can be made about the personality make-up of migraine patients. Sacks (1970) illustrates the variety of emotional needs which attacks appear to fulfil, and found it impossible to fit his material into stereotypes of obsessive personality or chronically repressed hostility. Special selection would appear often to have been at work where earlier reports were concerned. Selby and Lance (1960) made a rough categorisation of their patients, and considered that the personality range differed little from what occurs in the population generally—23% showed obsessional trends, 22% were hyperactive and found it hard to relax, 13% showed overt anxiety symptoms, and 42% were considered 'normal'. Dalsgaard-Nielsen (1965) estimated that a third showed pathological personality configurations, a third showed minor peculiarities, being sensitive, perfectionistic and inclined to bottle up feelings, while a third showed no abnormal traits whatever. Ross and McNaughton (1945), using Rorschach protocols, obtained some confirmation that migraine patients tended to be particularly inflexible and striving, but on purely objective indices of scoring they were largely indistinguishable from other groups.

Attempts at achieving unbiased samples of migraine sufferers have in fact been unable to uphold many of the personality features traditionally linked to the disorder. Henryk-Gutt and Rees (1973) surveyed a large population of government employees and matched the migraine sufferers with carefully chosen controls, thus overcoming the selective processes involved in medical referral. Semi-structured interviews and personality inventories were used to explore psychological aspects of the disorder. They obtained no evidence of increased ambitiousness, striving or obsessionality among the migraine subjects, though a history of suppressive parental discipline was significantly commoner than among the controls. Hostility and guilt scores on the inventories showed no clear relationship to migraine. However 'neuroticism', as measured by the Eysenck Personality Inventory, was significantly higher than among controls, likewise indices of emotionality as manifest in current nervous symptoms, current emotional difficulties, liability to mood swings and tendencies to bottle up anger and resentments. They concluded that while migraine subjects were no more ambitious or obsessional than non-migraine subjects, they were constitutionally predisposed towards increased emotional reactivity, and thus to experience a greater than average reaction to a given quantity of stress. This increased reactivity of the autonomic nervous system could conceivably provide the predisposing factor for the devolopment of attacks.

Waters' (1971) survey of a community-based sample has also been informative. No evidence was found to support the contention that migraine is especially common among persons of higher intelligence, though it was noted that a higher proportion of the more intelligent sufferers had consulted doctors about their headaches. Similarly, there was no indication that migraine was especially frequent among persons in social classes I and II, but again there was a tendency for a higher proportion of migraineurs in these social classes to have consulted their doctors.

A failure to corroborate specific personality features among migraine sufferers as a group does not of course diminish the importance which may attach to such features when they are apparent in the individual. Clearly the type of personality structure outlined by Wolff and others will, when present, readily lead to conflicts and contradictions with the environment. And as described immediately below, psychological precipitants can be closely relevant to the pattern and timing of attacks.

Psychological Precipitants

Many observers place psychological factors high on the list of features that may provoke episodes of migraine. It is common to find that periods of stress, or the anticipation of stress, are associated with attacks. Sustained emotional tension of this nature seems to be more important than acute emotional disturbance, the crucial factor being the degree to which feelings are sustained, bottled up and inadequately expressed (Rees, 1971). Frustrations and resentments may operate powerfully in this way. Another well-documented finding is the tendency for some patients to develop attacks during the 'let down period' after intense activity and striving. Consequently some have attacks quite regularly when a harassing day is over, at weekends, or on the first day of a holiday. Many patients however insist that the majority of their attacks are entirely without discernible precipitants. Emotional disturbance therefore appears to be a common, but by no means a universal factor. Its role is quite possibly subsidiary, or no more than complementary, to other matters which so far remain elusive.

Some two-thirds of clinic based samples report that emotional precipitants are important, though rarely as the sole invariant factor (Selby and Lance, 1960; Dalsgaard-Nielsen, 1965). Henryk-Gutt and Rees (1973), in their community survey, found about 60% in whom problems at work or with interpersonal relationships were regarded as direct precipitants. Relief from strain was noted as a factor in about a third. In controls with non-migrainous headaches such features were less commonly blamed. Moreover in almost half of the migraine subjects the disorder had had its onset during a period of emotional stress. The subjects were then asked to keep records of their attacks for a two month period, noting any special events or emotions coinciding in time with the attacks. Over half of the episodes recorded proved to be related to emotionally stressful events. Other precipitants such as alcohol, food or hunger were by comparison very rare. In approximately one-third of attacks no cause whatever could be discerned.

Psychiatric Features Associated with Attacks

Feelings of irritability and anxiety may last for several hours as a prelude to attacks. More rarely patients may experience unusual health and vigour, amounting to elation, with hyperactivity and pressure of speech. A rebound of energy is also described in the wake of attacks, with feelings of buoyancy and increased drive. Others by contrast remain listless and fatigued for several days. Such swings may sometimes occur with sufficient regularity to suggest that they are part and parcel of the pathophysiology of the disorder, rather than simply reactions to the episodes themselves.

In the course of attacks mental changes in some degree are almost universal. Anxiety and irritability are common early on, with drowsiness, lethargy and apathy as the headache continues. Depression may be mixed with angry resentment and sullen hostility. Cerebration is typically slowed, with poor concentration and poor ability to formulate ideas. Any of these features can occasionally be marked, even to the extent of dominating the clinical picture.

Moersch (1924) estimated that 15–25% of migraine sufferers presented definite psychological disturbances in association with attacks at some time or another. Klee (1968) made a detailed analysis of patients with migraine severe enough to warrant hospitalisation, and found that attacks were accompanied by marked impairment of memory in 10%, clouding of consciousness or delirium in 8%, pronounced anxiety in 8%, complex visual and auditory hallucinations in 6%, changes of body image in 6%, and severe depression in 4%. Altogether 22% of patients experienced at least one mental symptom severely enough to affect them greatly in the course of their attacks.

Alterations of consciousness range from the common blunting of alertness, through states of marked lethargy and drowsiness to frank loss of consciousness. The latter is the so-called 'migrainous syncope', sometimes occurring during the aura and sometimes later in the attack. Typically the patient lapses into unconsciousness over a period of several minutes, appears as though sleeping deeply, then emerges from the episode in the same gradual fashion. Such attacks have been described as characteristic of basilar artery migraine (Bickerstaff, 1961b) but can also be seen with hemiplegic migraine and other varieties (Hockaday and Whitty, 1969). On rare occasions there may be short-lived periods of coma with incontinence or even epileptic fits at the height of attacks.

Mental 'confusion' can be marked, occurring with or without impairment of consciousness. Sometimes it represents a focal disturbance of cerebral function with dysphasic, apraxic or agnosic manifestations. Disturbance of memory may be the main component as described below. Or there may be elaborate 'dreamy states', probably reflecting temporal lobe dysfunction, with feelings of déjà-vu, timelessness, depersonalisation or forced reminiscence:

A 44-year-old man suffered very occasional attacks of migraine from adolescence, ushered in by scintillation scotomata. In one attack a profound dream-like state followed the visual phenomena thus—'First I couldn't think where I was, and then I suddenly realised that I was back in California. . . . It was a hot summer day. I saw my wife moving about on the verandah, and I called her to bring me a coke. She turned to me with an odd look on her face, and said 'Are you sick or something?' I suddenly seemed to wake up, and realised that it was a winter's day in New York, and there was no verandah and that it wasn't my wife but my secretary who was standing in the office looking strangely at me'.

(Sacks, 1970)

Other examples clearly represent acute organic reactions due to generalised cerebral dysfunction, with disorientation and clouding of consciousness. Medicaments administered for treatment of the attack may sometimes be partly responsible. Such states may be coloured by anxiety, restlessness, and complex visual and auditory hallucinations. A paranoid element may be marked. The condition may amount to a frank delirium, lasting throughout the ensuing headache for several hours or days. Very occasionally the headache fails to materialise and the transient mental disturbance then appears as a psychotic episode in itself ('mental migraine equivalent'). The range and diversity of the pictures seen is illustrated in the examples below:

A 50-year-old woman had suffered migraine from the age of 16, increasing in severity from the age of 43. For the past 5 years pronounced mental changes had accompanied attacks, in that her memory became faulty and she felt extremely depressed and hopeless. In particularly severe examples consciousness was clouded, with disorientation and restlessness. During several of her severe attacks she had had the experience of seeing her deceased adoptive mother, and in one attack imagined that she saw and talked to her deceased biological mother, lying in a hospital bed as she had done when last she saw her. During the course of these hallucinations she was very anxious, definite about the experiences but unable to remember all the details afterwards. Since the onset of the mental components she had noticed that some reduction in memory tended to persist between attacks.

(Klee, 1968)

A boy of 16 had been prone to migraine attacks since childhood, taking many different forms. Commonly they started with paraesthesiae in the left leg and right hand. As these died away he developed distortions of hearing then bilateral scintillation scotomata in both lower halffields of vision. Other attacks started with tingling in the epigastrium associated with an intense sense of foreboding. Those occurring at night often had a nightmarish quality with feelings of compulsion and restlessness leading on to a profound hallucinatory state—hallucinations of being trapped in a speeding car and of figures made of metal advancing upon him. As he emerged from these he became conscious of paraesthesiae then intense headache. This patient also suffered 'syncopal' attacks during severe auras, with simultaneous fading away of sight and vision, a sense of faintness and then unconsciousness.

(Sacks, 1970)

A 37-year-old housewife had suffered attacks of migraine from 19, increasing in severity since the age of 32. Attacks began with headache, later proceeding to paraesthesiae in the right hand and leg with weakness of the limbs and a variety of visual phenomena. They often lasted for 3 or 4 days. During a particularly severe attack which lasted for a week she had to be admitted to a mental hospital. On the preceding day she had become increasingly restless with clouding of consciousness, had heard neighbours making unpleasant comments about her and believed she had been stuck with knives. For the first few days in hospital she was disoriented, restless and appeared hallucinated both visually and aurally. She heard children's voices and the voice of her general practitioner, and believed her legs had been amputated. This psychotic episode disappeared within a few days and she was amnesic for it afterwards. Her last clear memory was of lying down to sleep at home, and the next of waking in hospital.

(Klee, 1968)

The hallucinatory elements may sometimes be the dominant feature, as in one of Klee's patients who saw greyish-coloured Red Indians, 20 cm high, crowding round in the room in which he lay. On another occasion picked up hallucinatory musical instruments from the floor. Another patient saw 'white living creatures', stationary and rather indistinct, apparently unaccompanied by clouding of consciousness or disorientation.

Florid examples of confusion are probably rare, at least in adults. But in children it may not be uncommon for migraine to present in this fashion. Gascon and Barlow (1970) observed 4 children who showed acute organic reactions lasting from 6 to 24 hours, often resembling the pictures seen with drug intoxication, metabolic disorders or encephalitis. Although headache developed in every case it was usually not detected until the mental disturbance had receded. Ehyai and Fenichel (1978) found 5 similar examples among 100 consecutive cases of childhood migraine, with episodes of agitated confusion lasting from several minutes to hours, and succeeded by diffuse EEG changes indicative of cerebral ischaemia. Such attacks tended to recur on follow-up but were eventually replaced by typical migraine.

Amnesia may feature prominently in some episodes, either along with the visual aura or as a variant of classical attacks. When occurring as a relatively isolated phenomenon it may betoken ischaemia in the hypothalamic or hippocampal regions. Nielsen (1930, 1958) described examples lasting from 20 minutes to several hours, sometimes associated with typical headache but sometimes occurring as migraine equivalents. During attacks it was common to find that isolated thoughts and ideas came to the mind unbidden while wanted material could not be recalled. Islands of thought failed to associate one with another leading to patchiness of memory:

A doctor of 37 complained of episodes of mental disturbance lasting 3–6 hours at a time, and occurring once or twice per year from the age of 18. They began with a feeling of mild depression, then strangeness, then mental confusion. Throughout the attack he remained perfectly oriented, yet was unable to organise his thinking and had large defects in his memory. Facts and events seemed isolated and devoid of normal associations. He was unable to remember things for more than half a minute and found it difficult to converse as a result, repeating questions and appearing absent-minded to onlookers. Close questioning revealed migraine attacks with scotomata and fortification spectra occurring in between such episodes. The more typical attacks were also associated with very mild confusion.

(Nielsen, 1930)

A woman of 24 had attacks beginning with fortification spectra in the right half field, leading after a few minutes to severe anterograde amnesia and inability to direct her thoughts. Independent ideas came to the mind spontaneously, but she was unable to follow them through or gain associations before they disappeared again. Everything looked strange, and topographical orientation was considerably disturbed. This would last for 20 minutes then merge with headache, nausea and vomiting if the attack was to be complete. More commonly however the attacks consisted of the mental disturbance alone, following the visual spectra but without further progression thereafter.

(Nielsen, 1958)

Caplan *et al*. (1981) have recently reported an association between the syndrome of 'transient global amnesia' (p. 357) and migraine, describing 12 migraineurs who experienced a typical amnesic episode. Six were cases of common and 6 of classical migraine. Of the latter, 3 experienced their classical aura accompanying the attack and headache followed it; 2 more had pounding headache during the attack. Altogether 9 of the 12 experienced headache in the course of the amnesic episode.

Body image disturbances may occur just before, during or after attacks of headache, portions of the body being felt to be magnified, diminished, distorted, reduplicated or absent. Some examples were described in Chapter 2 (pp. 64 and 65). Lippman (1952) reported several examples, all in classical migraine, including patients in whom the abnormal sensations could constitute the entire attack without headache developing. One patient felt as though the neck or the hip were extending out on one side, another that the left ear was ballooning out for six inches or more, another that the head had grown to tremendous proportions and become light, floating up to the ceiling. One patient felt alternating enlargements and diminutions in the size of the right half of the body, coming and going throughout the headache period. Patients who felt exceedingly tall or extremely minute during attacks were suggestive of Alice in Wonderland, and Lewis Carroll was known to have suffered from migraine.

Lippman (1953) also drew attention to experiences of physical duality ('autoscopy', p. 65) in association with migraine. During attacks such patients felt a conviction of having two bodies, usually for several seconds at a time, before, during or after the headache. Qualities such as observation, judgement and perception were typically transferred to the 'other' body which for the moment seemed the more real of the two, but throughout the experience the patient remained aware of the actual body and its position in space. Feelings of fear, mild wonder or amazement were common accompaniments. This striking phenomenon is best illustrated by some of Lippman's examples:

A woman of 37 wrote: 'Until . . . 5 years ago, I felt the queer sensation of being two persons. This sensation came just before a violent headache attack and at no other time. Very often it came as I was serving breakfast. There would be my husband and children, just as usual, and in a flash they didn't seem to be quite the same. They were my husband and children all right—but they certainly weren't the same. . . . There was something queer about it all. I felt as if I were standing on an inclined plane, looking down on them from a height of a few feet watching myself serve breakfast. It was as if I were in another dimension, looking at myself and them. I was not afraid, just amazed. I always knew that I was really with them. Yet there was "I" and there was "me"—and in a moment I was one again!'

Another patient might develop attacks when walking. She would feel as if from the hips downwards the walking continued but with no volition or direction—the 'control' was in the upper self, way up above, totally indifferent to the legs' destination. During such experiences she would try to move over to a doorway or building until she could focus on 'myself' and become one again. Such episodes always occurred during episodes of headache or just after recovery.

Another patient while performing some habitual activity had the distinct impression of being two people—one going through the actions of eating or reading, the other suspended above and to one side, perceiving or contemplating herself in a detached way. This experience would come and go in a flash.

(Lippman, 1953)

Affective disturbance may sometimes greatly exceed the usual irritability, anxiety and depression of attacks. It is uncertain to what extent this depends on the patient's constitution, or how far both the migraine and the emotional disturbance may derive from the same pathophysiological process at the meso-diencephalic level. Klee (1968) noted examples of profound anxiety and depression. Sacks (1970) referred to sudden eruptions of 'forced mood' occurring in the course of an aura—feelings of great foreboding, or states of awe, rapture or sudden hilarity. They were marked by the suddenness of onset, their senselessness and their overwhelming quality.

Most were brief, lasting for only a minute at a time.

Periodic mood changes have also been described in the interictal phases of patients who experience affective disturbance as part of their attacks. Episodes of depression or elation may occur as isolated symptoms, lasting for several hours or days at a time and differing from manic-depressive mood swings chiefly by their brevity (Moersch, 1924; Sacks, 1970). These have been interpreted as representing the affective component of attacks devoid of headache or other aural manifestations. Clearly however the distinction from primary emotional disorders will often be difficult in such cases.

Other psychiatric abnormalities have been described, usually as rarities or striking instances. The literature is reviewed by Moersch (1924) and Bruyn (1968a). Conversion hysteria may be seen at the height of attacks, or states of dissociation with multiple personality. Automatisms have been described, apparently similar to those occurring with epilepsy except for a more gradual onset and the accompanying headache and malaise (Nielsen, 1958). Disinhibition, obsessions, phobias and compulsions may occur in association with attacks. Kleptomania has sometimes been claimed as an integral part of the periodic disturbance, either occurring in association with headache or as a migraine equivalent.

Progressive mental impairment has occasionally been noted in sufferers from severe migraine, though a causal connection has not been clearly established. The association would certainly appear to be rare. Symonds (1951) considered it probable that in some cases there might be slight but cumulative brain damage as a result of successive small infarctions. An example is reported by Bradshaw and Parsons (1965):

A 39-year-old nursing sister had had migraine from the age of seven, increasing after a period of worry some years before. After injecting herself with ergotamine tartrate during one attack she developed a right hemiplegic episode with dysphasia. This improved slowly over 5 weeks but left a slight residual deficit. Angiography and other investigations showed no abnormalities. Follow-up showed unequivocal evidence of progressive impairment of mental faculties, leading to memory impairment, falling standards of work, lack of insight and emotional instability. Further migraine attacks had continued, some with right-sided paraesthesiae. Her mother had had right hemiplegic migraine, and from the age of 52 had shown mental changes which progressed to gross dementia over the course of several years.

Gowers (1888) stated that some permanent failure

of mental power could occasionally be observed after many attacks attended by intellectual difficulties, and Flatau (1912) reported several patients with restricted powers of concentration and memory continuing between attacks. Klee and Willanger (1966) found evidence of slight intellectual impairment on psychological testing in 6 out of 8 patients with severe migraine, ranging in age from 35 to 55. The intellectual impairment appeared to have developed gradually as the migraine increased in severity. The findings from recent CT scan studies (p. 345) may be relevant in such cases.

'Chronic Migrainous Disability'

Occasional sufferers from migraine may enter a phase in which very frequent, severe and unremitting headaches develop. Typically this is coupled with malaise, anorexia, sleeplessness and loss of weight. Depression of considerable severity is usually an integral part of the picture. Over-medication may prove to be partly responsible, but in many cases psychological influences are clearly at work in initiating or perpetuating the disorder.

The deterioration may be decisively linked to the development of a circumscribed depressive illness, the migraine and the affective disorder thereafter reinforcing each other. In other patients it may be difficult to discern which components have been primary in initiating the vicious circle once the condition has become entrenched. Some will prove to have been 'caught in a malignant emotional bind of one sort or another' and to be reacting to chronically difficult, intolerable life situations (Sacks, 1970). The attacks may then be observed to bring about a range of reactions—regression, withdrawal or exploitation—which in turn may initiate autonomic and other pathological mechanisms which exacerbate and perpetuate the condition.

The interdependence of emotional disturbance and migraine is highlighted in such examples, and a conjoint approach by psychological and physical measures is usually essential for resolution of the situation.

DIFFERENTIAL DIAGNOSIS OF MIGRAINE

Migraine headaches must first be differentiated from other causes of pain in the head and face—chronic sinus disease, glaucoma, hypertension and raised intracranial pressure. In the majority of cases the history will be sufficient to allow such a distinction, aided by physical examination or simple investig-

ations. More difficulty may be encountered in making a firm distinction between migraine and tension headaches, both of which are common, chronic and frequently incapacitating. This issue is considered separately below.

Problems with neurological diagnosis are likely to arise in cases of 'complicated migraine' where marked neurological deficits accompany or follow attacks. Here a neurological opinion is essential, even though a basis in structural cerebral pathology will emerge in only a minute proportion of cases. An angioma must be considered when the deficits well outlast the headache, and especially when attacks of hemiplegic migraine involve one side of the body exclusively. Ophthalmoplegic attacks limited to one side will similarly raise the possibility of an aneurysm of the internal carotid or posterior communicating arteries. In basilar migraine the prominence of brain stem deficits may suggest the possibility of some brain stem lesion. And even classical migraine attacks may warrant investigation if they first declare themselves in adult life, particularly if the auras tend to occur alone without much by way of headache.

On occasion difficulty can arise in distinguishing migraine from epilepsy, and indeed the two may occur together. When loss of consciousness occurs with migraine it is usually gradual in onset and a good deal less profound than in epilepsy. Even when sudden, it is usually succeeded by headache far exceeding that which follows an epileptic attack. Doubt can also arise over the complex auras of migraine, especially when these occur as isolated events. However visual phenomena are far commoner in migraine than in epilepsy and often assume their highly specific form. Paraesthesiae are rarely bilateral in epilepsy, and proceed with much greater rapidity than in migraine. The most ambiguous region is represented by the rare dreamlike states of migraine, especially when accompanied by depersonalisation, terror, rapture or other alterations suggestive of psychomotor attacks (Sacks, 1970).

Patients presenting with episodes of confusion may be suspected of delirium due to toxic or metabolic factors. Long-lasting acute organic reactions may be diagnosed as transient paranoid reactions. Episodes coloured by marked mood disturbance may resemble the swings of manic-depressive disorder, especially when preceded or followed by a rebound of elation and hyperactivity. Episodes of syncope in migraine may be regarded as hysterical dissociation, particularly when the impairment of consciousness is not profound and is preceded by a dramatic train of symptoms. In all such variants the true situation is usually revealed by the development of headache later in the attack, or by the history of more typical migraine attacks in the past.

Migraine Versus Tension headaches

Tension (or 'muscle contraction') headache is probably almost as frequent as migraine. Moreover the two may coexist in a substantial proportion of patients. The difficulties which may be encountered in making a clear distinction are widely recognised, yet the differentiation must be attempted if specific anti-migrainous therapy is to be employed. Diagnostic difficulty is most likely to arise with common migraine where characteristic prodromata to attacks are lacking.

While emotional factors are important in the genesis of both forms of headache the mechanism of their operation is different. Tension headache seems to depend essentially on sustained contraction in the muscles of the scalp, forehead and neck. The intracranial and extracranial vasculature is not primarily involved, though additional factors such as vascular reactivity within the muscles, or the accumulation of pain provoking substances, may yet prove to make a contribution.

Comprehensive accounts are provided by Friedman et al. (1954), Martin (1966) and Lance (1982). Tension headache usually arises and coexists with emotional conflicts or states of anxiety and depression. The patient himself may be aware of such a derivation, though in long-lasting examples the emotional disorder may come to be regarded as secondary to the headaches themselves. Frequent concomitants are complaints of fatigue, insomnia, lack of interest and difficulty with concentration. Close questioning will often reveal evidence of tension or depression persisting between the headaches, whereas attacks of migraine usually occur against a background of relative well-being. In migraine moreover there is often a long history of intermittent attacks dating well back to childhood or adolescence.

Tension headaches, like migraine, vary widely in intensity, frequency and duration but certain characteristics help in the distinction. There are usually no prodromata, and onset and offset tend to be gradual. Tension headaches are commonly of daily occurrence, which is very rare in migraine, and they are often day-long in duration. Undulations in severity may occur throughout the day, diurnal variation sometimes being the key to an origin in depressive disorder. They are usually bilateral in distribution, generalised over the head or with an accent on the frontal, occipital or posterior cervical regions. Examnination may reveal tenderness over the scalp, or on palpation of the trapezius and posterior cervical muscles.

The quality is typically dull and steady, described as a sensation of tightness, pressure or constriction around the head. Again many variations may be seen on the classical picture. Sudden jabs of pain can be superimposed upon a steady ache, or a throbbing character may be assumed at times. Anorexia is common, and nausea may be felt when the headache is severe though actual vomiting is rare. Some degree of photophobia may be present. Pronounced relief may be obtained with alcohol, whereas migraine headaches are almost invariably worsened by this.

The points of value in distinguishing between migraine and tension headaches are indicated in Friedman et al.'s (1954) analysis of 1000 cases of each. A family history of headache was present in 65% of migraine sufferers and 40% of patients with tension headaches. Onset had been over the age of 20 in 45% of the former and 70% of the latter. The frequency was daily in only 3% of migraine yet 50% of tension headaches, and less than once per week in 60% and 15% respectively. Prodromata occurred in 60% of migraine patients but only 10% of patients with tension headaches. The character was throbbing in 80% and 30% respectively, and the distribution bilateral in 20% and 90%. Vomiting occurred in 50% of migraine patients and 10% of tension headache patients. No differences could be found with regard to precipitants, mood changes or the gradualness of onset or ending. In all cases of tension headache emotional causes could be identified, usually environmental demands which exceeded the capacity of the patient's personality to cope. As with migraine the conflicts were very variable in nature but often seemed to centre around the control of hostile impulses.

TREATMENT OF MIGRAINE

Medical details of treatment and prophylaxis are dealt with in neurological text books but may be briefly outlined here. Many attacks are adequately controlled by rest and simple analgesics provided these are instituted at an early stage. Ergotamine tartrate usually gives pronounced relief for more severe attacks, again when taken early enough in the course. Preparations are available for use sublingually, by inhaler, or by suppository. Oral preparations may contain certain adjuvants in addition to ergotamine, such as caffeine (in Cafergot) or caffeine and cyclizine (in Migril). Patients commonly appear to find some preparation which suits them better than others. Chlorpromazine, prochlorperazine (Stemetil) or metoclopramide (Maxolon) may occasionally be needed to control nausea and vomiting.

Ergotamine preparations must be avoided in patients with peripheral vascular or coronary disease, in hypertension and in pregnancy. The dose must be carefully controlled. Pearce (1969) recommends a maximum of 6 mg in any one day, or 12 mg in a week. In addition to the well-known toxic effects of overdosage there is risk of habituation and tolerance from excessive self-medication. A paradoxical effect may indeed emerge in which the drug relieves the headache for which it is given, but at the same time leads to increasing frequency of headaches so that consumption steadily rises (Friedman *et al.*, 1955). Lucas and Falkowski (1973) draw attention to the special dangers of such a course in emotionally disturbed patients, and illustrate the benefit which can result from withdrawal of medication.

Prophylactic drug therapy may be indicated during spells when attacks are frequent and severe. Minor tranquillisers such as chlordiazepoxide or diazepam are usually the first to be tried. Amitriptyline has also been shown to be successful in controlled trials even when clinical evidence of depression is absent (Gomersall and Stuart, 1973). Belladonna alkaloids have a traditional though unproved place in prophylaxis, usually combined with a small dose of phenobarbitone and ergotamine as in Bellergal tablets. Propanolol (Inderal) and atenolol (Tenormin) have shown encouraging results as prophylactics (*Drug and Therapeutics Bulletin*, 1981).

The most potent prophylactic is methysergide (Deseril), a serotonin antagonist. It proves capable of preventing attacks in a high proportion of regular sufferers, even though it has no effect when taken during the attack itself. Caution must always be exercised when using the drug on account of two principal dangers—retroperitoneal fibrosis, and peripheral vasoconstriction which may affect a single large vessel alone. These can be prevented by proper régimes of treatment; it must be given for no more than a few months at a time and only under close supervision. Clonidine (Dixarit) and pizotifen (Sanomigran) are other drugs which may prove beneficial when taken regularly.

Pharmacological aspects are, however, merely a part of the total management required in patients with migraine of any severity. Attention may need to be directed towards a host of factors specific to the individual—regularisation of sleep and meal times, judicious avoidance of stress where this is possible, and perhaps attention to provocative substances in the diet. In addition social and psychological factors will usually warrant close consideration; where attacks have become frequent and incapacitating, problems in such areas will usually be found to be aggravating the condition.

Psychotherapy in the formal sense would appear to be indicated in only a small proportion of patients. What is more commonly required is a sound doctor-patient relationship, through which an understanding can be gained of the emotional problems and life situations which provide the settings for attacks. The ability of the patient to handle emotional tension, and to learn how to obviate situations conducive' towards it, will often prove to be major factors in preventing attacks or in breaking a vicious circle when this has become entrenched. It will usually be an unrealistic aim to seek to persuade a driving and over-committed person to change a life style which is part and parcel of his personality. But during exacerbations of the disorder he may respond to advice to moderate his work, to delegate duties, or at least to arrange for regular periods of rest and relaxation.

It is essential to be alert to the development of depressive disorders and anxiety neuroses which may powerfully aggravate the situation. These will require treatment in their own right, and the migraine may be expected to benefit thereby. One must similarly be sensitive to sources of emotional turmoil which have arisen in the patient's life, especially conflicts at work or in interpersonal relationships. When the patient's personality and life situation are well understood, the attacks will sometimes be seen to provide an oblique expression of feelings and needs which are denied expression in other ways. Major strategic roles which may be encountered include attacks which serve for recuperation, imposing a halt after prolonged physical and emotional activity; those which allow temporary regression or dissociation while the patient works through an accumulation of stresses and conflicts; those which provide an expression of repressed anger and hostility; and those which are self-punitive in masochistic and chronically depressed individuals (Sacks, 1970). The principal motivational determinants are often apparent without recourse to intensive psychotherapy, but in some instances there may be indications for embarking on this. Examples of striking success from analytically oriented therapy have been reported in selected groups of patients by Fromm-Reichmann (1937) and Sperling (1964).

Mitchell (1971) has indicated the value which may be obtained from behaviourally oriented techniques in reducing the frequency and severity of attacks. Small groups of patients were treated by relaxation training, with or without systematic desensitisation and assertive training. The desensitisation was aimed at reducing anxiety and hostility, while assertive therapy involved the planning of daily tasks to overcome problems in sexual, interpersonal and vocational areas. Significant improvement was observed in the fully treated group, relative to controls. It remained uncertain which components of the treatment régime were responsible for the benefits obtained, but similar approaches would seem worth exploration in patients habitually incapacitated by their disorder.

Finally biofeedback techniques have been reported to show striking success with certain patients (Kogeorgos and Scott, 1981; Fischer-Williams *et al.*, 1981), though the coincident use of relaxation makes the specificity of such treatment uncertain. Electromyographic feedback, of value with tension headaches, often fails with migraine; electrothermal feedback, in which for example the patient is trained to raise the distal finger temperature, appears to be the most promising technique with headaches of vascular origin.

Subdural Haematoma

The majority of subdural haematomas follow head injury, though spontaneous cases occasionally arise in patients with blood dyscrasias or on anticoagulants. Blood accumulates in the subdural space from rupture of veins running between the cortex and the dural venous sinuses. It becomes encysted between the dura and arachnoid and may swell by osmosis to reach a very large size. Localising signs often remain minimal, however, since the brain is compressed from without. The collections usually lie over the frontal or parietal lobes and are bilateral in a third to a half of cases.

Those which declare themselves acutely after head injury present either with failure to regain consciousness, or with fluctuating confusion and torpor often lapsing into coma. Hemiparesis and ocular changes are usually evident, but neurological deficits can be surprisingly slight and overshadowed by the mental disturbance. Quite often the haematoma is suspected only because the patient's recovery from the injury is slower than expected.

It is the chronic subdural haematoma, however, which is notorious for leading to mistakes in diagnosis, particularly among the elderly. The antecedent head injury may be trivial and go unrecognised, and there may be few clear pointers to the presence of a space occupying lesion within the skull. Quite often there is a latent interval of days, weeks or months after injury before the declaration of symptoms. Very occasionally a year or more may elapse.

In classical examples there is vague headache which sets in gradually and may or may not be localised. It may be present only intermittently, or occasionally be quite absent. Dullness, sluggishness and difficulty with concentration slowly increase in severity. Lapses of memory and episodes of mental aberration occur. The level of consciousness fluctuates widely, with periods of apparent normality alternating with periods of drowsiness, changing from day to day or even from hour to hour. The variability in the mental state is often the most important indicator of the condition. Physical signs may be few, with inequality of the pupils, transient ocular paralyses or up-going plantar responses. Pyramidal tract involvement may progress to hemiparesis, and a grasp reflex may be present. Papilloedema remains absent in a large proportion of cases. Epileptic fits may occur but are rare. Ultimately the patient lapses into intermittent mutism or semi-coma, but even at this stage evidence of neurological involvement can be surprisingly slight.

Wide variation may be seen from the typical picture, however. Occasional patients present with severe headache but no physical signs, others with episodes of confusion and restlessness. In long-standing cases there may be insidious failure of intellect progressing to generalised dementia. Problems with diagnosis are particularly severe among the elderly where the classical picture has been found to be the exception rather than the rule, occurring in only 5 of 52 examples reported by Bedford (1958). The typical story was of an aged person, already somewhat enfeebled, recently becoming mentally confused. Drowsiness was not always present, and concomitant disease such as pneumonia, uraemia or cardiac failure provided further diagnostic distractions. Stuteville and Welch (1958) found that a history of trauma could not be elicited in almost a quarter of patients, or when present it was often trivial and considered a symptom rather than the cause. Falls are commonplace in old age, likewise minor neurological signs such as a positive Babinski response or pupillary abnormalities. The diagnosis may therefore be overlooked until the patient declines and becomes somnolent or comatose. Despite the utmost vigilance only 40% of Bedford's cases were diagnosed during life.

In a mental hospital autopsy study Cole (1978) found subdural haematomas to be the commonest form of space occupying lesion. Six acute and 8 chronic haematomas were discovered among 200 routine autopsies, yet the diagnosis had been made before death only once. In the chronic cases, particularly, signs were often minimal, and fluctuation of consciousness had rarely been conspicuous. A terminal seizure or sudden death had sometimes been the first indication of a change in the patient's condition. In the elderly a cerebrovascular accident had often been held responsible when neurological deficits were present.

Apart from dementia, differentiation must be made from cerebral infarction, cerebral tumour and alcoholism. Important features distinguishing subdural haematomas from strokes are the slow steady increase in neurological deficit, the presence of some lack of responsiveness, and lack of improvement mentally despite comparatively slight physical disability (Carter, 1972). Sometimes the two occur together when cerebral infarction has led to a fall with striking of the head. Cerebral tumour may be closely simulated when there is evidence of raised intracranial pressure. The fluctuating course of the drowsiness and mental confusion can then be an important differentiating feature. Chronic alcoholism may lead to similar drowsiness and intermittent mental aberration, and alcoholics are liable to head injuries which are then forgotten. Thus 7 of the 14 cases of subdural haematoma discovered by Selecki (1965) among patients admitted to a mental hospital were deteriorated chronic alcoholics.

Further examples of diagnostic difficulty are provided by Chambers (1955):

A man in his 40s entered hospital twice on account of severe intractable headache. Because of certain tensions in his environment he was at first diagnosed as suffering from tension headaches. The cerebrospinal fluid was normal in content and under normal pressure. The only neurological sign was drift of the left arm. When closely questioned his family admitted that he had behaved oddly, on one occasion for example walking naked through the house in front of the children. Air encephalography showed lack of subarachnoid air on the right, and on the authority of these few findings burr holes were made. A

subdural haematoma two inches thick was removed from the right frontal area and he made a complete recovery.

A 70-year-old mother became excited on hearing that for the first time her family were not coming to visit at Christmas. She fell backwards from a rocking chair, striking her head, but was not rendered unconscious. Over the next few weeks she became depressed, sullen, somnolent and lacking in appetite. For 3 months she was treated as a case of depression superimposed on senility until she finally had a convulsion. A large subdural haematoma was then disclosed.

Investigations are usually crucial for the diagnosis. Skull X-ray or echoencephalography may reveal shift of the midline structures. The electroencephalogram is abnormal in 90% of patients, with diminution or suppression of alpha rhythms over the affected hemisphere or unilateral slow activity (Kiloh *et al.*, 1981). It is a guide to laterality in 75% of cases, but there can be abnormal rhythms bilaterally or even localisation to the wrong side of the head.

The CT scan will usually provide definitive evidence, showing displacement of midline structures, obliteration of the ventricle on the ipsilateral side, and a low density area underlying the skull. Care must be taken, however, particularly with bilateral haematomas which can sometimes be missed on the scan. The acute haematoma is initially denser than brain, becoming hypodense as it liquefies; it therefore passes through an isodense phase during the transitional period.

Additional investigations must accordingly be carried out when the CT scan is negative and the index of suspicion high. Conray enhancement may reveal the capsule, or a radioisotope scan show crescentic uptake over the hemisphere. Angiography can show characteristic displacement of vessels. Exploratory burr holes will sometimes be needed to resolve the issue decisively.

Lumbar puncture should be avoided when a subdural haematoma is suspected. The cerebrospinal fluid is often under increased pressure but may be otherwise normal. The protein may be raised and xanthochromia may be present. Red blood corpuscles are found if a leak has occurred into the subarachnoid space.

Evacuation of the haematoma can lead to excellent results, particularly in early cases. Much depends, however, on the presence of complicating pathologies, and the prognosis often proves to be poor in the elderly. Forty-three per cent of Stuteville and Welch's (1958) cases died post-operatively. Among

30 survivors Wortis *et al.* (1943) found that half recovered virtually completely, though some of these were left with slight emotional dullness. The remainder showed impairments of memory and intellect, dysphasia, or persistent euphoria with severely impaired behaviour. Mehta (1965) has similarly stressed the high morbidity among survivors, particularly by way of organic mental impairments.

Giant Cerebral Aneurysms

The great majority of aneurysms giving rise to subarachnoid haemorrhage are small, rarely exceeding 1 or 2 cm in diameter. Massive aneurysms are distinctly uncommon, but when present can give rise to much diagnostic confusion and are often not even considered in differential diagnosis.

Best known is the aneurysm of the intracavernous portion of the internal carotid artery, which may compress surrounding nerves leading to ophthalmoplegias and sensory loss of trigeminal distribution, It occasionally ruptures to give rise to a pulsating exophthalmos.

Those situated on the circle of Willis at the base of the brain rarely rupture, but can produce local pressure effects simulating basal space-occupying lesions. Bull (1969) reported 22 such cases collected over a similar number of years. Common complaints were of visual disturbance or headache. In 6 patients, however, mental changes predominated; dementia was the presenting feature, usually but not invariably accompanied by neurological signs such as cranial nerve deficits or hemiparesis.

Morley (1967) reviewed the literature concerning unruptured vertebrobasilar aneurysms, which can lead to a variety of pictures simulating multiple sclerosis, posterior fossa tumours or vertebrobasilar ischaemia. Three of his own five cases had at first been diagnosed as psychiatrically unwell—vague symptoms of headache, nondescript dizziness, slowed speech and a muted facial expression had led to an impression of depressive illness. Mental impairment was also sometimes evident.

Transient Global Amnesia

The syndrome of transient global amnesia consists of episodes, abrupt in onset, in which the patient displays profound memory difficulties despite remaining alert and responsive to his environment. Attacks usually last for several hours after which memory functions gradually return to normal. The pathogenesis has not been established with certainty though a vascular basis is probable. Attention was first drawn to the condition by Bender (1956, 1960) and Poser and Ziegler (1960). It was independently described by Fisher and Adams (1958, 1964) who gave it its name. The condition appears to be not uncommon and derives much of its importance to neurologists and psychiatrists from the mistakes in diagnosis which are liable to be made.

Clinical Features

Most patients are affected in late middle or old age, and males appear to outnumber females. Abruptly and entirely without warning the memory apparatus ceases to function, with the result that current experiences are not recorded in memory. The patient may himself sense that something is wrong, or merely betray the abnormality to onlookers by his remarks or behaviour. As the attack continues it becomes evident that the patient cannot memorise the events of his immediate situation, also that he has a patchy retrograde amnesia for the days, weeks or even years preceding the onset of the attack. Thus he has difficulty in locating himself in time or place, and in ascertaining his relationship to what is happening around him. Furthermore whatever information is given cannot be held for long in mind. A state of anxious bewilderment typically results, with repeated stereotyped questioning of those around and sometimes expressions of considerable fear and concern. Some patients, however, appear to lack insight and sit quietly, though puzzled, through most of the attack.

In contrast to the difficulty with recent memory and the inability to store new information, recall appears to be normal for events from the distant past. Knowledge of personal identity remains unimpaired, and relatives and acquaintances of long standing are recognised normally. The memory deficit is 'global' in the sense of affecting all modalities—visual impressions, verbal material, thoughts, events, etcetera. Confabulation is rarely observed.

The detailed descriptions of Fisher and Adams (1964) indicate that most functions other than memory remain substantially intact throughout the attack. There is no drowsiness, inattentiveness or other evidence of impairment of consciousness. The attention span is normal as judged by the digit repetition test. The patient may be able to continue working for some minutes on an assigned task. Thinking appears to be coherent within the limits allowed by the memory disorder. Understanding and production of language are normal, and perceptual competence well preserved. Habitual acts such as dressing, eating and even driving are performed without difficulty. Most patients have found their way normally about familiar environments, and several have driven home while attacks were continuing.

Gordon and Marin (1979) were able to make detailed observations on a patient during an attack. He showed normal immediate recall, as tested by the digit span, but an almost total inability to store new information. Cueing was of no help with this anterograde amnesia. There was an extensive though patchy retrograde gap, with no knowledge of the President of the USA or his predecessor, and vague awareness of a 'catastrophe' affecting President Kennedy (13 years before) but no knowledge of its nature. Other cognitive functions were carried out normally. The failure to recall or recognise information from the distant past, which was perfectly available to the patient when the attack was over, implied an impairment of retrieval as well as of consolidation.

The episode commonly lasts from one to several hours or rarely for several days. As it begins to subside the retrograde gap shrinks, distant events returning before those most closely related to the onset, and the patient gradually shows evidence that current experiences are beginning to register. A further hour or more may elapse before memory is fully restored to normal. After complete recovery an amnesic gap remains for the period of the episode, together with a permanent retrograde amnesia of several minutes to several hours. Other than this there are no enduring sequelae in the typical case.

Thus the attacks are in essence a highly circumscribed failure of the memory apparatus, lasting usually for several hours and proving to be reversible. Other accompaniments, by way of neurological signs or systemic disturbances, have in most cases been conspicuous by their absence. Occasionally, however, when opportunities have arisen for detailed observation, there has been evidence of dizziness, tinnitus, headache, mild paraesthesiae or some reflex asymmetry.

Typical examples are as follows:

A man of 67 developed his attack immediately after a prolonged interview with two journalists who had noticed nothing amiss. He turned to his family after bidding the visitors goodbye, looking puzzled and asking 'Who are they? What are they doing here?' He then asked how it happened that certain members of his family were present (they had come for a visit the previous day). He was obviously worried and appreciated that he could not remember or collect his thoughts. For the next hour and a half he repeatedly asked similar questions—'What are they doing here? What are you doing here? Do you see anything wrong with me?' There was no dysarthria or dysphasia. He tested his arms and legs periodically to assure himself that they functioned normally. He did not remember that the journalists had made their appointment a few weeks previously, nor did he recall special events of the day before or of the morning hours preceding the interview.

As recovery occurred he first recalled the events of the day before, then of the evening before, and finally he recalled fetching wood for the fire one hour prior to the interview. After $1\frac{1}{2}$ hours he lay down and slept for an hour, following which he appeared to have recovered fully. A retrograde anmesia remained permanently for the period of the interview (one and a half hours), and the hour prior to this. He also proved subsequently to remember very little of the day following the attack, although he appeared to his family to have recovered in three hours.

(Fisher and Adams, 1964)

A 76-year-old housewife was in good health when, without premonitory symptoms, she suddenly appeared confused and disoriented, asking questions such as 'Where am I?', 'What happened?', etc. There was no disturbance of sight, speech or motor power. When admitted to hospital 3 hours after the onset she was fully alert, and answered routine questions about her family and past history correctly, but was restless and anxious, frequently interrupting the conversation with stereotyped questions such as the above. She did not know where she was and forgot immediately after being told. She was muddled as to the time, date and year. After the initial examination the doctor left the room for a few minutes and when he returned she did not recognise him. A retrograde amnesia was present, covering the preceding week, whereas memory for remote events was intact. The patient seemed to be aware of the memory defect and did not confabulate. No abnormal signs were found on neurological examination. Ten hours after admission the patient's memory functions began to return, and during the following 2 days the retrograde amnesia cleared.

(Bolwig, 1968)

Another case, reported in detail by Fisher and Adams, showed that the patient was able to make astute observations concerning his state during the amnesic period. The attack was unusual in that there was seemingly an auditory hallucination at the onset, although it was not clear whether this was actually experienced or merely offered as an excuse for the patient's inability to take a telephone message:

A physician aged 55 was examining a patient he had known for some 20 years when the telephone rang. He showed obvious difficulty in taking the message, became flushed, anxious and perplexed, and complained of a riveting sound outside the window although no such disturbance was occurring. He told his patient he was having a lapse of memory, asked her who she was and why she was there. He asked over and again what day it was and why his secretary was not available (he had given permission for a vacation ten days before). Ultimately his wife called at the office bringing his daughter and granddaughter who were scheduled to be taken to the airport. He had forgotten the arrangement and remained perplexed, asking reiterative questions as they drove to the airport. There he met an old friend, greeted him by name and was proper in his responses. Another friend was called to come over and give advice. When he arrived the patient knew why he had come and said he was feeling unwell and confused. He insisted on returning to his office to look at his appointments book and try to reconstruct events, then agreed to be seen by a physician. He named the doctor of his choice and recalled the number of the hospital where he could be contacted. Meanwhile he was able to make appropriate observations about his condition, worrying that he might have a brain tumour or epilepsy. He said that at his age a seizure could mean a tumour and that it could be the only symptom.

At the hospital, some 4 hours after the onset, he was perplexed and restless and said that he could remember hardly anything that had occurred throughout the day. But he recognised the physician immediately and reminded him of a case they had discussed some 3 or 4 years before. He vaguely recalled seeing his granddaughter first thing that morning, seemed to realise he had seen a woman patient and remembered her name, and vaguely recalled seeing his daughter and granddaughter off on the plane. He remembered having a discussion about obtaining a medical consultation but did not recall the journey to his office or to the hospital.

He was repetitious of certain accounts as though he had not told them before. He repeated 6 or 7 times the circumstances of his sister's death 10 months before. He gave the day and date correctly and knew where he was. The digit span was 6 forwards and 6 backwards. He could recall nothing of a name and address after 10 minutes and had no recollection of being asked to remember them. Speech was normal and mathematical ability unimpaired. No abnormal signs were found on neurological examination.

When re-examined a few hours later some of the memory of the day's events was returning in a rather patchy manner. He could now remember the purpose of the visit of the patient whom he was examining when the attack began, but could not recall his findings on examination. He could also recall various activities of the morning preceding the attack. The following day further islands of memory had returned for events both before and after the attack, but he could not arrange such memories in chronological order.

Subsequently he remained well, though with permanent amnesia for the 2 hours preceding the attack and for most of the events during the 8 hours following it.

(Fisher and Adams, 1964)

Of the original 17 cases reported by Fisher and Adams (1964) all but one suffered a single attack only. The other had three attacks over a 6 year period. The condition appeared to carry a benign prognosis—follow-up for an average of 3 years revealed a stroke 7 months later in one patient but no adverse developments in the others. Since that time many similar cases have been reported, in general underlining this favourable course and outcome (Shuttleworth and Morris, 1966; Cunningham, 1968; Bolwig, 1968; Martin, 1970). Others, however, have observed patients with several recurrent attacks, and sometimes leaving significant residual disability. Lou (1968) reported one patient with nine and another with three attacks over periods of several months. Out of 19 patients seen by Heathfield et al. (1973) 8 had recurrent episodes at intervals varying from several days to several years. Steinmetz and Vroom (1972) described a patient whose fifth attack resulted in persistent memory difficulties. Mathew and Meyer (1974) found that all 8 of their patients with more than one attack developed signs of permanent memory impairment, occasionally with evidence of global involvement of other intellectual functions as well. Mazzucchi et al.'s (1980) report of psychometric impairment after single attacks perhaps reveals minor deficits which are not uncommon but tend to be overlooked on clinical examination. A group of 16 patients who had suffered isolated episodes were tested on average 8 months later; their verbal intelligence scores were significantly lower than performance intelligence scores, and in comparison to carefully selected controls they performed less well on tests of verbal long-term memory.

Differential Diagnosis

Though varying as to detail, the main features of the attacks are remarkably similar from one example to another. Unless one is conversant with the syndrome, however, a range of diagnoses will usually be considered.

A short-lived episode may raise the possibility of temporal lobe epilepsy. Psychomotor seizures begin abruptly in a similar fashion, involve a suspension of memory recording and leave an enduring amnesic gap. Patients with repeated episodes will be particularly suspected of epilepsy. Several, moreover, have shown electroencephalographic abnormalities in the region of the temporal lobes (Steinmetz and Vroom, 1972; Heathfield *et al.*, 1973). However most psychomotor attacks are brief, lasting minutes rather than hours, and may be ushered in by aural manifestations which are totally lacking in transient global amnesia. During a psychomotor seizure there is usually evidence of clouding of consciousness, poor appreciation of the environment, and purposeless or 'automatic' behaviour. By contrast, the patient with transient global amnesia remains fully in touch with his surroundings, is alert, and shows evidence of awareness of what he is doing and experiencing. He responds to questions appropriately and behaves normally apart from his obvious memory defects. Recovery of normal mental function is gradual after an attack of transient global amnesia whereas it is usually abrupt after a psychomotor seizure.

Hypoglycaemic attacks may likewise set in abruptly, lead to a period of confused behaviour, and leave an amnesic gap for what has transpired. However behaviour is usually inappropriate or even disorderly during the attack, and motor coordination is likely to be impaired with ataxia, clumsiness or dysarthria. Nevertheless, when a patient is seen in the course of an attack, hypoglycaemia should be excluded, and when there is room for doubt glucose should be administered.

Many patients will be suspected of suffering from minor strokes. Cerebral ischaemia on a vascular basis may indeed be the mechanism behind the majority of episodes, as discussed below. It should be noted, however, that attacks of transient global amnesia only rarely show ancillary evidence of cerebral ischaemia by way of associated neurological deficits, and that strokes rarely lead to extensive temporary amnesia unless other manifestations are marked.

A brief episode of delirium or some acute intoxication may at first be considered a possibility. Alcoholism will sometimes be suspected. However the suddenness of onset in persons who were normal a moment before, the restriction of the abnormalities to memory defects, and the lack of clouding of consciousness or perceptual disturbance should allow a differentiation. When the history of the onset is not available a period of post-traumatic confusion may be suspected. Very occasionally, episodes of amnesia may be the presenting feature of an encephalitic illness.

A psychological origin for the amnesias is probably quite often entertained, especially since follow-up commonly fails to reveal the development of organic disease. However the setting and the manifestations of the attacks are quite unlike amnesic episodes due to psychological causes. A stereotyped setting will of course raise the strong possibility of psychogenesis as in the following example:

A 28-year-old man experienced five amnesic episodes over the course of a year, lasting from 30 minutes to 14 hours at a time. None were witnessed, and all had occurred from the moment of locking his office door after a stressful day at work. After three of the attacks he regained awareness while sitting on a railway station awaiting a train to Aylesbury. After another he regained a vague recollection of being in Aylesbury and visiting his old home there. He could not be encouraged to divulge reasons for the recurrent preoccupation with Aylesbury, but readily accepted that it indicated a psychogenic basis for the attacks. He had lived there until moving to Kent $2\frac{1}{2}$ years previously. Current stresses included serious illness in his father, his wife's second pregnancy, and a threat of foreclosure on the mortgage involving his new home.

Psychogenic amnesia is uncommon in the age group principally affected by transient global amnesia, obvious psychological precipitants do not come to light, and most patients are said to have been of normal personality and good premorbid stability. The structure of the memory defect itself, with demonstrably faulty new learning and a time-related retrograde gap, is entirely consistent with an organic origin. The retention of knowledge of personal identity throughout the attack is also at variance with what is commonly found during psychogenic amnesias. The memory difficulties are not restricted to matters of personal concern or specific themes, there are no inconsistencies in performance, and no evidence of gain. The patients are not suggestible during attacks, but behave appropriately and typically seek to remedy the amnesic gaps by anxious questioning.

Croft *et al.* (1973) showed the relative frequency of transient global amnesia among 39 patients referred by general practitioners to a neurological clinic. All had experienced a transient amnesic episode. Twenty-four (62%) proved to be examples of transient global amnesia, 7 were epileptic, 2 had occurred in the context of migraine and 2 were the prelude to encephalitic illnesses. Only 4 were considered psychogenic in origin, but this may have reflected the special selection inherent in neurological referral.

The Nature of the Disorder

So far there has been no autopsy material and the

cause of the attacks has not been conclusively established. Fisher and Adams considered that both an unusual type of local cerebral seizure and a transient ischaemia of the hippocampal-hypothalamic system were tenable hypotheses, though there were difficulties in the way of either interpretation. If epileptic in origin the attacks were distinctly unusual in form, as already outlined. Many, perhaps the majority, do not recur over follow-up periods of several months or years. And epilepsy beginning so late in life would be expected often to have a lesional basis yet such is not revealed.

The evidence for a basis in cerebral ischaemia has become firmer as fresh series have been reported. Thus the great majority of patients are elderly, recurrence has proved to be less unusual than was at first supposed, and attacks are now known occasionally to proceed to permanent impairments (Steinmetz and Vroom, 1972; Mathew and Meyer, 1974). Precipitating factors, though inconstant, have quite often included features which might suggest a vascular aetiology—physical exertion, exposure to cold as in sea bathing, or to heat as when taking a bath. More directly, Heathfield et al. (1973) found that almost half of their 19 patients showed strong ancillary evidence that attacks were due to cerebral ischaemia. Several had hypertension or generalised vascular disease, and four showed symptoms or signs of infarction in the distribution of the basilar artery or posterior cerebral circulation. One patient, for example, developed ataxia immediately after her amnesic episode, and this persisted for several weeks with a right up-going plantar reflex. Another showed a resolving posterior temporal EEG abnormality over several months following a series of attacks, compatible with infarction of the left posterior cerebral artery. The nature of the transient amnesias in such patients was no different from that in patients without evidence of cerebrovascular involvement.

Mathew and Meyer (1974) produced considerable evidence for a basis in cerebrovascular disease in their 14 examples of the syndrome. Thirteen showed one or more risk factors for cerebrovascular disease, such as hypertension (9 cases), cardiac abnormalities (11 cases), diabetes (4 cases) or hyperlipidaemia (4 cases). There had been clinical indications of vertebrobasilar insufficiency in 11 patients, such as periods of light-headedness, dizziness, blurred vision, ataxia, paraesthesiae or occipital headache. These mainly occurred between amnesic episodes, though in 4 cases actually during attacks. Four-vessel arteriography showed atherosclerotic, stenotic or occlusive lesions in 11 cases, predominantly in the vertebrobasilar or posterior cerebral systems. Two of the patients on follow-up developed frank infarctions in the territory of the posterior cerebral arteries. In the remarkable family reported by Corston and Godwin-Austen (1982), where 4 brothers had suffered attacks, it seemed likely that the reason was a summation in the family of risk factors for cerebrovascular disease—hypertension, diabetes and cardiac disease.

It therefore seems very likely that cerebral ischaemia in the distribution of the posterior cerebral circulation is responsible for the majority of examples of the syndrome. Temporary insufficiency of the circulation, rather than actual infarction, is probably usually responsible, in view of the short-lived nature of the episodes and their complete resolution. This may be attributable to emboli or to haemodynamic factors as in transient cerebral ischaemic attacks generally (p. 323).

It remains difficult, however, to account for the relative rarity of other associated neurological deficits when at the same time the amnesia is so very profound. On the basis of present anatomical knowledge of the memory apparatus, one would expect the ischaemic territory to involve the diencephalic-hypothalamic system or the inferomedial parts of both temporal lobes. Occlusion of the arteries supplying such structures would be expected more often to give rise to other associated deficits, particularly visual field or brain stem signs. Certainly the lesions of the posterior cerebral arteries which give rise to *permanent* amnesic states appear always to be associated with such additional deficits (Benson et al., 1974). It is especially hard to conceive of a single vascular lesion which could affect both temporal lobes simultaneously and sometimes repeatedly. Steinmetz and Vroom (1972) suggest that in cases with repeated attacks there may often be silent infarction in one temporal lobe with episodes of transient ischaemia in the other.

In a minority of cases other mechanisms may be responsible. Occasional examples have shown a relationship to migraine attacks (p. 350), and one followed an overdose of diazepam (Evans, 1966; Gilbert and Benson, 1972). Fisher's (1966) case of severe transient amnesia following head injury but without loss of consciousness may represent an example attributable to trauma.

Systemic Lupus Erythematosus

Systemic lupus erythematosus ('SLE') is a member of the so-called 'collagen diseases' or 'connective tissue disorders', along with rheumatoid arthritis, rheumatic fever, scleroderma, dermatomyositis and polyarteritis nodosa. To some extent there may be overlap between variants of SLE and these other conditions, though in the main it is established as a specific disease entity.

The change in our conception of the disease, from a fulminant and rapidly fatal disorder to one that can run a chronic course with relapses and remissions, owes much to the establishment of the 'LE test' as a diagnostic measure by Hargreaves *et al.* in 1948. It is now recognised as a not uncommon disease with markedly pleomorphic manifestations. Cerebral involvement has been reported increasingly, and mental symptoms are known to be prominent in a high proportion of cases. It is evident, moreover, that very occasionally neuropsychiatric complications can set in early before involvement of other systems is clinically obvious. Hence it has become important to include appropriate screening tests in the detailed evaluation of certain neurological and psychiatric patients as described below.

The aetiology remains incompletely understood. An inherited predisposition may be partly at work, and a great deal of evidence supports an immunological basis for the development of tissue lesions. Whether the hypersensitivity reactions are to external toxins, or the result of an autologous autoimmune process, is not entirely clear, though the latter is increasingly favoured. Many of the pathological features of the disease appear to be due to deposition of antibody–antigen complexes with resultant complement fixation and inflammation of the tissues.

General Clinical Features

The disease is markedly more common in females with a female/male ratio of 9:1. It mainly occurs in young adult life, with a mean age of onset of 30, but the range is wide.

The clinical manifestations are described by Dubois (1966) and Byron and Hughes (1983). The onset is usually insidious with the development of fatigue, malaise and low-grade intermittent fever. A migratory arthritis or arthralgia ultimately develops in the majority of cases, closely resembling that of rheumatoid arthritis or rheumatic fever. Diffuse muscle aching is a common accompaniment. Skin changes are frequent, though the classical butterfly eruption over the nose and cheeks is by no means always seen. SLE and discoid lupus erythematosus are now regarded as poles of a spectrum, sometimes occurring separately and sometimes with an admixture or transitional forms in the same patient. Other skin manifestations include purpura, Raynaud's phenomenon and alopecia. Photosensitivity of the skin may be pronounced.

Lymphadenopathy, oedema and anaemia are often disclosed. Of the viscera the kidneys are probably most frequently involved, also the pleura, lungs, heart and pericardium. Liver involvement is exceptional and gross splenomegaly rare. Anorexia, nausea, abdominal pain and vomiting are common. Hypertension is often considerable in degree and retinopathy may develop.

Thus SLE is a multisystem disease, the majority of its manifestations being attributable to vascular lesions or more directly to disturbances of connective tissue. Its manifestations are polymorphous, sometimes involving one organ or system predominantly and often changing considerably over time. Nervous system involvement, as described below, is no exception in this regard.

The course of the disease may be acute, subacute or chronic. Chronic progression with repeated exacerbations and remissions appears to be a frequent pattern, and treatment with steroids is usually successful in tiding the patient over crises and perhaps in delaying fresh progressions. It can be a recurrent mild illness with prolonged asymptomatic intervals. Five year survivals of 95% are now being recorded, perhaps chiefly on account of more frequent recognition of mild forms of the disease (Bresnihan, 1979). Nevertheless in Estes and Christian's (1971) study of 150 patients one-third had died over an 8 year period, the commonest causes of death being renal failure and central nervous system involvement.

Laboratory Investigations

Anaemia is often accompanied by leucopaenia and occasionally thrombocytopaenia. The erythrocyte sedimentation rate is raised in about 90% of cases, showing an approximate correlation with the current stage of activity of the disease. Occasionally however it can remain high when the disorder is in full remission and all other laboratory tests are normal, and very occasionally a normal ESR is found in the presence of active SLE (Dubois, 1966). Plasma protein abnormalities are common, with lowered serum albumin and raised serum globulins. Serological tests for syphilis such as the WR, TPHA and VDRL (pp. 284–5) are liable to give false positive results in 10% of cases though the TPI and FTA will be negative. Examination of the urine will often reveal proteinuria or abnormal sediments.

The 'LE cell' test is positive in 75–80% of cases, again in general being more often positive when the disease is active. When carefully carried out it has a high degree of specificity for SLE, though weak positive results may also be obtained in patients with rheumatoid arthritis, generalised scleroderma and dermatomyositis. The test consists in looking for characteristic changes in polymorph leucocytes after *in vitro* incubation of the patient's blood—the nucleus swells, becomes basophilic, then detaches from the cytoplasm and is engulfed by phagocytic cells to form the 'LE cell'. The responsible factor present in the plasma of affected patients is now identified as a gamma globulin (IgG). It is an antibody to nucleoprotein, a nuclear antigen (Burton *et al.*, 1971).

The estimation of 'antinuclear antibodies' is now more often used, particularly as a screening test. Antinuclear serum reactions can be positive before the LE cell test is positive, and a negative result almost excludes a diagnosis of SLE. The introduction of an immunoassay for the detection of antibodies directed against double-stranded DNA has provided the most specific test to date (Bryon and Hughes, 1983). Biopsy of skin lesions, or occasionally renal biopsy, may give valuable confirmation of the diagnosis.

Electroencephalographic changes are common whether or not neuropsychiatric changes are present. They are usually diffuse and non-specific though focal changes may occur (Dubois, 1966). The cerebrospinal fluid shows an elevated protein and occasional lymphocytes in approximately half of the patients with neuropsychiatric manifestations (Johnson and Richardson, 1968).

INVOLVEMENT OF THE NERVOUS SYSTEM

Neuropsychiatric manifestations are now being reported in up to 60% of patients with SLE, when comprehensively studied and followed for reasonably long periods of time. Indeed Hughes (1974) suggests that central nervous system involvement may be overtaking renal disease as the major clinical problem in the disorder, in that it carries a high mortality and the response to treatment is uncertain.

Valuable reviews of the psychiatric and neurological features are provided by Dubois (1966), O'Connor and Musher (1966), Johnson and Richardson (1968), Estes and Christian (1971), and Bennett *et al.* (1972). Mental disorders are repeatedly stressed as the commonest of neuropsychiatric manifest-

ations, with acute and chronic organic reactions, functional psychoses, changes of personality and a variety of neurotic reactions. The majority of mental disturbances appear to be transient, usually clearing within 6 weeks and rarely outlasting 6 months, though episodes are often recurrent (Gurland *et al.*, 1972). Seizures are also common. Neurological findings may include cranial nerve palsies, peripheral neuropathy, movement disorders, hemiparesis, aphasia, or more rarely spinal cord involvement leading to paraparesis.

The relative incidence of such changes is shown by Estes and Christian's (1971) survey of 150 patients followed closely over several years. Forty-two per cent showed disorders of mental function, with organic mental syndromes in 21%, functional psychoses in 16% and neurotic reactions in 5%. Seizures occurred in 26%, cranial nerve abnormalities in 5%, peripheral neuropathy in 7%, tremor in 5% and hemiparesis in 5%.

It is clear that the neurological and psychiatric features of SLE lack any characteristic form or pattern but are as varied as other manifestations of the disease. The most that can be said is that they show a tendency to appear in the later stages, and to develop during relapses of the disorder when other systemic features are in evidence. This is not invariable, however, and central nervous system involvement can sometimes be the primary manifestation, antedating other clear-cut evidence of the disease by months or years (Siekert and Clark, 1955).

Multiple neuropsychiatric manifestations often occur together. The bizarre nature of the syndromes produced can readily lead to mistakes in diagnosis unless the possibility of the disease is borne in mind and appropriate investigations carried out. Patients presenting with neurological symptoms may be suspected of multiple sclerosis, sometimes for several years before multi-system involvement is noted (Dubois, 1966). Psychotic developments may similarly be misinterpreted in the early stages, or lead to diagnostic difficulty when they appear in a patient who is apparently in full remission. Fessel and Solomon (1960) suggest that all psychotic patients who have a raised ESR and positive serology for syphilis, with no apparent reason, should be fully explored immediately for SLE.

Organic mental syndromes are the most frequent of the mental abnormalities, occurring at some time or another in approximately 30% of patients (Heine, 1969). Acute organic reactions account for the great majority. These are usually brief, lasting for hours or days then subsiding completely. They are often recurrent, appearing with fresh relapses of the disease and clearing as it goes into remission. The picture may be of quiet confusion and clouding of consciousness, or more florid delirium with visual and auditory hallucinations and excessive motor activity (Johnson and Richardson, 1968). Paranoid delusions, mood disturbances and hallucinations may be in the foreground, leading to a diagnosis of schizophrenia if the organic mental features are overlooked (Guze, 1967). The degree of disorientation and memory impairment may fluctuate markedly from time to time.

Chronic cerebral dysfunction is a good deal less common, but general deterioration of intellect and memory may occasionally progress to a picture of dementia (Johnson and Richardson, 1968; Burton *et al.*, 1971). Clark and Bailey (1956) found memory deficits in many patients, often associated with changes of personality, anxiety and emotional lability.

Dubois (1966) emphasised the management problem presented by patients with slight organic brain damage, resulting in personality difficulties and impaired judgement which could render home life intolerable. 'The patient is in a never-never land of not being psychotic enough to be declared mentally incompetent and yet truly not being able to handle her own affairs effectively'. Often with such patients it can be hard to decide how much is attributable to brain damage and how much is the reaction to a chronic illness and physical exhaustion.

Functional psychoses may be depressive, schizophrenic or occasionally hypomanic in nature. Their incidence is substantially less than that of acute organic reactions. The pictures are often hard to classify with precision since an admixture of functional and organic features may occur together. Clearly, however, classical affective or schizophrenic illnesses can occur.

Chronic psychotic depressions appear to be much commoner than schizophrenia-like states. Thus Guze (1967) found 10 episodes of affective illness and 5 of schizophrenia-like disorder in 101 patients. Others who have reported a high incidence of schizophrenia may have overlooked the presence of minor memory deficits or clouding of consciousness in patients with paranoid delusions.

Neurotic reactions are probably a good deal commoner than their reported incidence. Anxiety, depression, withdrawal, and episodes of depersonalisation have all been stressed. O'Connor and Musher (1966) observed severe anxiety and depression in 19 of 150 patients, and a further 2 had episodes of 'hysteria'. Such acute neurotic reactions were usually short-lived. The anxiety may fluctuate markedly from day to day, without associated change in the physical condition and without clear relation to the current life situation (Clark and Yoss, 1956; O'Connor, 1959). Similarly patients may complain of overwhelming feelings of impending disaster which are quite unwarranted by the state of their disease (Clark and Bailey, 1956).

Depressive reactions tend to be more gradual in onset, lasting several weeks or months then resolving slowly (Heine, 1969). Ganz *et al.* (1972) compared patients with SLE and with rheumatoid arthritis, and showed that depressive symptoms were chiefly responsible for the increased incidence of psychiatric disorder in the former disease. They were twice as common as organic mental symptoms, occurring in 51% and 22% of SLE patients respectively.

Seizures have been reported in up to 50% of cases, usually grand mal but also focal epilepsy and temporal lobe seizures. Status epilepticus can lead directly to death. They are most common in the terminal stages but some appear early in the disease. Occasionally they accompany an acute exacerbation then do not occur again (Dubois, 1966). A rare source of diagnostic uncertainty is the occasional epileptic patient on treatment with hydantoins or primidone who develops an SLE-like syndrome which regresses on withdrawal of the drug.

Cranial nerve disorders are among the commonest neurological signs. Usually they set in suddenly without prodromata and most are transient disturbances. Disorders of external ocular movement, pupillary abnormalities and vertigo are the most frequent, more rarely disorders of the fifth, seventh and bulbar nerves. Visual field defects are often partly due to retinal changes. Papilloedema may result from a local retinal lesion and optic atrophy may follow.

Peripheral neuropathy is usually symmetrical and distal, with both sensory and motor deficits. A Guillain-Barré form may occur, or occasionally a mononeuropathy.

Movement disorders include tremors, parkinsonian rigidity, ataxia due to brain stem lesions, and choreoathetosis. All are relatively rare. Choreiform movements in association with SLE may at first be diagnosed as Sydenham's chorea.

Hemiparesis is rare. Most examples arise in the course of the disease but it can be the initial manifestation (Bennett *et al.*, 1972). Dysphasia is occasionally seen. Paraparesis due to transverse 'myelitis' of the cord is also infrequent.

Aetiology of Neuropsychiatric Manifestations

Pathological changes in the brain have been abundantly described in SLE, chiefly in the form of disease of the small blood vessels leading to scattered infarctions and haemorrhages. The smaller arterioles and capillaries are principally affected with evidence of inflammatory, destructive and proliferative changes. A true 'vasculitis' is rare, the usual finding being fibrinoid degeneration in the vessel walls, or hyalinisation with necrosis (Johnson and Richardson, 1968). This may be associated with microglial proliferation around the capillaries, or microhaemorrhages due to extravasation of erythocytes and fibrin. The vascular changes are especially prevalent in the cortex and brain stem. Infarcted areas are usually small and multiple, though extensive areas of softening and large intracerebral haemorrhages occasionally occur.

Many of the neuropsychiatric manifestations clearly depend directly on the cerebral pathology. Johnson and Richardson (1968) observed a correlation between seizures and microinfarcts of the cortex, and between cranial nerve lesions and infarcts in the brain stem. The small size of the typical lesions accorded with the transient nature of the clinical symptoms. Johnson and Richardson further hypothesised a relationship between acute confusional states and widespread cortical pathology. A higher incidence of cerebral atrophy has been shown on the CT scan in the presence of neuropsychiatric features (Ostrov *et al.*, 1982), similarly more severe abnormalities of cerebral blood flow and regional cerebral metabolism (Bresnihan *et al.*, 1979).

Clinico-pathological correlations at autopsy are, however, far from exact. O'Connor and Musher (1966) found that gross impairment of CNS function could exist with no demonstrable lesions at autopsy, and conversely patients without neuropsychiatric manifestations could show widespread cerebral pathology. Other factors such as uraemia, electrolyte disturbance and hypertension must therefore make their own contributions to mental disturbance.

An additional mechanism was suggested by Atkins *et al.* (1972), who demonstrated gamma globulin deposits in the choroid plexus of two patients with mental disturbance but not in controls. These appeared to be immune complexes, probably derived from the blood, and similar to those deposited in the glomerulus in lupus nephritis. More recent immunological studies have indicated a potential role for lymphocytotoxic antibodies derived from the blood with special affinity for neural tissue (Bluestein and Zvaifler, 1976; Bresnihan *et al.*, 1979). Thus levels of lymphocytotoxic antibodies have proved to be higher in patients with cerebral manifestations than in those without, and they are absorbed by cerebral tissue. Anti-neuronal antibodies have also been found in the serum. A model is therefore proposed whereby episodes of cerebral vasculitis may allow brain reactive antibodies to gain access to the cerebral parenchymal structures, thus accounting at least in part for neuropsychiatric manifestations.

Considerable attention has been given to the possible role of steroids in precipitating confusional episodes, with a consensus of opinion that they can only rarely be held responsible (O'Connor and Musher, 1966; Dubois, 1966; Guze, 1967). Thus similar episodes were often reported before steroids were introduced, they continue to be reported in patients not having such treatment, lowering of the dose has an inconsistent effect, and episodes do not necessarily recur when steroids are given again during later relapses of the disease. Nevertheless the possibility must still be borne in mind that on occasion steroids may have an aggravating or precipitating effect.

The genesis of functional mental symptoms in the disease remains obscure. The incidence of affective disorders and neurotic reactions has seemed higher than would be expected in general medical patients, and to be more than merely a reflection of the stress of a severe disease or an intensification of pre-existent psychopathology (Baker, 1973). The reversibility of such disorders, and their reappearance later in the illness, have similarly suggested that they may be intrinsically related to the disease process itself. On the other hand much of the emotional disturbance can be seen as an understandable response to the trials of the illness, and any contributory cerebral pathology may do little more than actualise such reactions. Gurland *et al.* (1972) emphasise the difficulty in speculating about mechanisms when there is so much uncertainty about the frequency and form of psychiatric symptoms in SLE, and when sampling problems are clearly implicit in most studies to date.

Finally, Otto and MacKay (1967) have hinted at the possibility of a special psychological vulnerability, not merely to emotional complications but to the development of SLE itself. This small study does not, however, appear to have been replicated.

Treatment

The management of the neuropsychiatric manifestations can prove difficult, though fortunately most episodes are transient and self-limiting at least in the early stages. Assessment must be thorough, with special attention to underlying clouding of consciousness or mild intellectual impairment in what appear at first sight to be purely functional disturbances. The EEG and examination of the CSF can be helpful in deciding on the likelihood of an organic cerebral cause for the symptoms, but are not an accurate guide in every case (Bennett *et al.*, 1972). Other causes must always be carefully considered— uraemia, hyponatraemia, hypopotassaemia, hypertension or steroid administration. The patient's current physical status and psychosocial situation must equally be taken into account.

Steroids are the mainstay of treatment for the systemic effects of the disease and may also be important with regard to certain mental developments. When confusion or delirium appear with fresh relapses of the disorder, steroids may help considerably in their resolution. Dubois (1966) has been an enthusiastic advocate of massive doses of steroids in this situation. Bennett *et al.* (1972) recommend an intravenous infusion of hydrocortisone when fits are recurrent or when disturbance of consciousness is profound, otherwise oral prednisone is given for less acute cases. On other occasions, however, steroids may stand to aggravate rather than help the mental picture, particularly in patients with functional psychiatric disorders. Sergent *et al.* (1975), for example, found that functional psychoses were often precipitated by steroid therapy and responded to a reduction in dosage. Altogether, therefore, there is much to commend O'Connor and Musher's (1966) suggestion that the decision regarding steroids should depend on the entire clinical status of the patient and not on the psychiatric picture alone.

Particular difficulty arises when a patient in good remission on steroids develops a marked personality change or psychosis. Dubois (1966) then recommends an initial attempt at withdrawing the steroids gradually, but with readiness to give large doses immediately if the psychosis becomes worse along with a return of fever, arthralgia and other systemic recrudescence. The monitoring of DNA antibodies can also be useful here. With suppression of the disease the titres generally fall to normal, so the finding of a high titre when the patient is already on steroids is a help in deciding between a steroid induced psychosis and a psychosis attributable to the disease process itself (Bennett *et al.*, 1972).

Immunosuppressive drugs such as cyclophospha-

mide and azathioprine have occasionally been found to help when steroids have failed, both with systemic manifestations and with acute organic psychoses (Brook and Evans, 1969). Phenothiazines may be indicated for functional psychiatric disturbances or grossly abnormal behaviour. Antidepressants may be required, and electroconvulsive therapy is not contraindicated.

Periarteritis Nodosa
(polyarteritis nodosa, panarteritis nodosa)

Periarteritis nodosa is another member of the 'collagen diseases', characterised like systemic lupus erythematosus by involvement of many systems of the body and not infrequently implicating the nervous system. The cause is unknown but a hypersensitivity or autoimmune reaction is suspected. The lesions are in some ways analogous to those of serum sickness. There may be a preceding history of streptococcal infection, and on rare occasions it may follow the administration of phenytoin, sulphonamides or other drugs.

The underlying pathology is a focal arteritis of the small and medium sized vessels. The larger arteries may also suffer due to involvement of their nutrient vessels. Highly characteristic focal dilatations are seen along affected vessels and whitish-grey nodules may be apparent macroscopically. A cellular reaction occurs at the site of the changes in and around the vessel walls. Necrosis of the artery wall leads to rupture, and intimal proliferation causes thrombosis.

The onset is usually in middle age but the range is wide. Males predominate over females. The disorder may declare itself abruptly or insidiously, and tends to run a subacute or chronic course with relapses and remissions. Aita (1972) summarises the clinical features as follows:

Early symptoms consist of headache, malaise, weakness and a low-grade intermittent fever. Rhinorrhoea, coughing and wheezing are frequent. Weight loss may be profound and multisystem involvement is usually soon apparent. Renal insufficiency leads to severe hypertension in a high proportion of cases, and crises of abdominal pain result from infarctions in the mesenteric vessels and their tributaries. Arthritis and myositis are common. Pleuritic pain and pneumonitis may develop, and cardiac involvement leads to myocardial infarction, congestive cardiac failure and pericarditis.

Skin lesions include purpura, ecchymoses, subcutaneous nodules, necrotic ulcers and superficial gangrene. In addition to hypertensive retinopathy the eyes may show evidence of scleritis, keratitis, choroiditis, retinal artery occlusion or optic atrophy.

Laboratory investigations usually disclose anaemia, a raised ESR, and reversal of the albumin-globulin ratio. Leucocytosis is common, sometimes with eosinophilia. Most cases show uraemia, albuminuria and abnormal sediment in the urine. The chest X-ray may show pulmonary infiltration or a pleural reaction. The cerebrospinal fluid is sometimes under increased pressure, with elevation of protein, pleocytosis or xanthochromia. Arteriography via the aorta may reveal a diagnostic picture by way of multiple small aneurysms, focal dilatations, or infarcted areas in the kidneys or other abdominal organs. Biopsies from skin, liver, kidney or small nerves serve to confirm the diagnosis.

Death often occurs within months or years of onset, though recent reports suggest a more encouraging long-term prognosis among those who survive the acute stages (Travers, 1979). Death is usually attributable to renal failure or to coronary, mesenteric or cerebral infarction. Treatment with steroids and immunosuppressive drugs meets with modest success in prolonging survival. Hypertension warrants vigorous management and anticoagulants may be indicated.

Nervous System Involvement

Peripheral neuropathy is the most frequent neurological finding and is more often seen with periarteritis nodosa than with any other collagen disease (Aita, 1972). It is quite commonly a presenting feature. The nerves suffer via their nutrient arteries, leading to multiple infarctions along their course. The result is usually a mononeuropathy or multiple mononeuropathy, with paraesthesiae, weakness and wasting. Symmetrical polyneuropathy occurs more rarely.

Cerebral manifestations appear in up to half of cases eventually but usually in the later part of the illness. Cranial nerve lesions are common, especially blurring of vision, vertigo, tinnitus, and disorders of external ocular movement. Focal cerebral or cerebellar infarctions may lead to hemianopia, hemiparesis or ataxia. A local mass of brain necrosis may simulate a tumour, and spontaneous subarachnoid haemorrhage may occur. Headache is common, sometimes attributable to hypertension and sometimes to arachnoiditis at the base of the brain. Epileptic seizures may result from uraemia, hypertension or focal lesions in the brain.

Mental changes may figure prominently and occurred in 26 of 114 cases from the Mayo Clinic (Ford and Siekert, 1965). The usual picture was of confusion and disorientation, sometimes with visual hallucinations and delusions. Delirium, 'mania' and paranoia were seen occasionally. Forgetfulness was noted in many patients, and seven showed marked intellectual deterioration. Eight showed a fluctuating impairment of consciousness varying from somnolence to coma.

Occasional cases are reported in which periarteritis nodosa appears to be largely confined to the nervous system. MacKay *et al.* (1950) described a patient who for two years showed intermittent diplopia, hemiparesis and cranial nerve disorders accompanied by a low pyrexia, then developed restlessness, depression and progressive dementia leading to death over several months. At autopsy the typical changes of periarteritis nodosa were largely confined to the brain and cord.

Other Collagen Diseases

Temporal arteritis ('cranial arteritis', 'giant cell arteritis') is a disease of later years appearing rarely before 60 and with a mean age of onset at 70. The temporal arteries are the site of a subacute inflammatory reaction with necrosis, granulation and giant cell formation. Intimal proliferation leads to thrombosis. The ciliary arteries, which supply the optic nerve and disc, are involved in about 30 per cent of cases. The occipital vessels and the aorta and its main branches may also be affected.

Clinically there is often a prodromal phase of vague malaise with muscle and joint pains lasting for several weeks or months. A low pyrexia may develop and weight loss and depression may be marked. Characteristic headache then appears, sometimes abruptly, situated principally over the affected vessels in the temporal region. The temporal arteries may be palpable and exquisitely tender. Suffering is usually intense, with throbbing or lancinating pain and severe insomnia.

The acute stage lasts for a week or two but tenderness may persist rather longer. At any time in the early days or weeks the serious complication of ciliary artery obstruction may follow, leading to impairment or loss of vision in one or both eyes. Hence the importance of prompt diagnosis and treatment. Ophthalmoplegias may also occur. The systemic disturbance continues throughout the stage of headache and visual complications, and may last for many months more. Peripheral neuropathy and muscle pain and wasting may occur. Infarctions can follow from involvement of the carotid or vertebral vessels. McCormick and Neuberger (1958) describe the brain lesions which may be observed at autopsy, including involvement of small intracerebral vessels by giant cell arteritis.

Mental disturbances sometimes feature prominently during the illness, with confusion, delirium, memory impairment, and drowsiness proceeding to coma (Cloake, 1951). Vereker (1952) described examples in the literature with restlessness, disorientation, severe memory difficulties and episodes of delirium, often with abrupt resolution after several weeks. Coma is a serious development, but can recover after several days. Vereker also stressed the frequency of severe depression in the disease, and considered that in many examples it was attributable to cerebral arterial disease rather than being secondary to the headache. Russell (1959) found that 7 of 35 patients were depressed and 4 were confused during the stage of headache.

The erythrocyte sedimentation rate is greatly raised and there may be a leucocytosis. Biopsy of an inflamed artery can serve to confirm the diagnosis. Steroids meet with dramatic success in treatment and must not be delayed. They are given in high dosage initially then reduced after 1–2 weeks to maintenance levels which are continued for 6–12 months or in some patients indefinitely. Graham *et al.* (1981) found that approximately one-third of cases needed very long-term treatment to prevent future relapses. Anticoagulants may also be indicated in the acute stages.

Thrombotic thrombocytopaenic purpura is a rare disorder with fever, haemolytic anaemia and widespread small vessel occlusions in many organs. It usually runs a fulminant course. Neuropsychiatric features can be conspicuous, with convulsions, confusion and pareses of the limbs, resulting from blockage of cerebral capillaries by platelet thrombi (Walton, 1982). Symmetrical cranial nerve involvement is rather characteristic, and delirium and stupor may simulate encephalitis (Miller, 1966b). Steroids are often ineffective and mortality is high.

Other collagen-vascular disorders may be suspected in certain neuropsychiatric syndromes even though definite confirmation is lacking. This was so in the three cases of dementia reported by Chynoweth and Foley (1969) which responded to steroid therapy. The authors postulated some collagen disorder or possibly cerebral sarcoidosis (p. 651) as a basis for the illnesses, on account of the raised ESR and altered serum proteins and the gratifying response of all three patients to steroids. Other features indicative of collagen vascular disorder included fluctuating confusion, headaches, muscle cramps, transient disturbances of vision and variable neurological signs. In view of the importance of detecting treatable causes of dementia an example from their series is given below, illustrating the rather minor clues which led to a trial of steroid therapy:

A woman of 58 complained of headaches and epistaxes which were attributed to sinus infection. The following year she developed cramp-like pains in the limbs and back, double vision and occasional difficulty with speech. Transient episodes of disorientation occurred during which she failed to recognise her friends or her own bedroom. Examination showed mild nominal dysphasia with impairment of memory and difficulty in performing simple calculations. Deterioration occurred, with bouts of trembling and falling and increasing depression.

In hospital, 2 years from onset, the ESR was raised at 30 mm/hour and an air encephalogram showed cortical atrophy. Her mental state fluctuated considerably, with a return to normal over several weeks but relapse soon thereafter. She became distractible, disoriented and with marked memory difficulties. The ESR remained elevated and the cerebrospinal fluid showed 2 lymphocytes, a protein of 75 mg per 100 ml and a positive Pandy test. The EEG showed diffuse abnormalities with paroxysmal slow waves. Serum proteins were normal and no LE cells were found.

An episode of dysphasia was followed by confusion for several days, and over the next few months she became progressively confused with confabulation and paranoid delusional ideas. Fluctuation continued but with overall deterioration. Ultimately she was doubly incontinent, abusive, aggressive and with complete loss of orientation and memory. A diagnosis of presenile dementia secondary to cerebrovascular disease was made.

After two months in her local mental hospital the ESR remained elevated at 19 mm/h, there was a slight polymorph leucocytosis, and electrophoresis of serum proteins now showed an increase in alpha-2 globulin and mucoprotein. A trial of steroids was considered worthwhile. Hydrocortisone was commenced intramuscularly for one week then followed by prednisone orally. Within twenty-four hours of starting treatment her mind felt clearer and she felt well and recognised her surroundings. Within one week she was up and about and appeared to have recovered completely. The EEG showed progressive improvement, and psychological testing confirmed normal memory functioning though with slight residual impairment of visuospatial memory. She was discharged and remained well one year later, still taking prednisone 5 mg daily.

(Chynoweth and Foley, 1969)

Thrombo-Angiitis Obliterans
('Buerger's disease')

Thrombo-angiitis obliterans is virtually confined to males and presents usually between 25 and 40 years of age. The cause is unknown, but tobacco smoking shows a strong association with the development of the disorder and markedly aggravates the symptoms.

The pathology consists of a pan-arteritis affecting all layers of the vessels and implicating both arteries and veins. The medium sized vessels of the legs are predominantly affected. An acute inflammatory response is followed by fibrosis and scarring. Intimal proliferation leads to thrombosis, often with recanalisation later. A relapsing-remitting course is characteristic, affecting short segments of the vessels at a time so that lesions in all stages of activity are to be found at different sites.

The common presentation is with intermittent claudication, leading eventually to gangrene of the toes. Superficial venous thromboses frequently occur. The affected limb is pulseless, cyanosed and cold. Nocturnal pain is typically relieved by hanging the leg downwards out of bed.

Many cases remain confined to the peripheral circulation but cardiac, visceral and cerebral involvement can occur. A chronic intermittent course is usual, extending over many years with remissions and fresh progressions, though ultimately with considerable residual disability. The blood pressure remains normal throughout.

Cerebral involvement is rare but well attested. The literature is reviewed by Perk (1947), Davis and Perret (1947) and Cloake (1951). In some reported cases the nature of the responsible pathology in the cerebral vessels must be open to doubt, but in others clear confirmation has been obtained at autopsy of typical changes in the arteries of the brain.

Usually cerebral manifestations appear only when the peripheral disease is well established, though in occasional cases they have been the presenting feature. The possibility of the disease should therefore be borne in mind when young adult males develop cerebrovascular symptoms, especially in the absence of hypertension. It further seems possible that in occasional cases a cerebral form of the disease may exist alone.

The vessels principally affected are the internal carotids and the anterior and middle cerebral arteries (Cloake, 1951). Infarctions follow in the corresponding territories. In the early stages the deficits may be slight and transient, suggesting that they are due to episodes of spasm or emboli. Transient pareses and paraesthesias may be accompanied by confusion and memory impairment. Episodes of giddiness, diplopia, visual flickering or speech disturbance may last for minutes or days and recur in different forms. Epileptic fits are common and headache of migrainous type may occur. Later there are major and more lasting syndromes of cerebral infarction, and a trend towards increasing emotional and intellectual deterioration. Dementia can ultimately be profound with an endstate similar to that of cerebral arteriosclerosis.

Very occasionally mental disorders are florid in the course of the disease, with acute organic psychoses, paranoia or psychotic depression. Perk's (1947) case showed a predominantly manic picture, lasting for many months along with transient diplopia, fits and episodes of unconsciousness.

The course is variable once cerebral symptoms have been declared. Survival may sometimes be seen for up to fifteen years, though few patients are reported to survive for more than five.

Chapter 10. The Senile Dementias, Presenile Dementias and Pseudodementias

The clinical syndrome of dementia has many causes, both cerebral and extra-cerebral, as outlined in the table on p. 130. Prominent among them are certain intrinsic degenerative diseases of the brain occurring in middle or late life which have attained the title of dementia as signifying specific disease entities. These, the so-called 'primary dementias', will be the subject of the present chapter. Later in the chapter the 'pseudodementias' will also be discussed—an important group of conditions in which an apparent dementia occurs in the absence of physical pathology and in the context of non-organic psychiatric disorder.

By far the commonest of the primary dementias is Alzheimer's disease, chiefly by virtue of its sharply rising incidence with age. Among 'presenile dementias', *viz* those with onset before the age of 65, it is also probable that Alzheimer's disease is more frequent than other varieties. Next in frequency is arteriosclerotic or 'multi-infarct' dementia, both in the senile and presenile age ranges. This is traditionally discussed along with the primary dementias, even though strictly speaking it represents a secondary rather than a primary degenerative brain process. Pick's disease, Huntington's chorea and Creutzfeldt–Jakob disease constitute the best-known of the remaining primary dementias and are all very much less common. When the distinctive pathologies of the above conditions fail to be revealed at autopsy in a patient with a primary dementing illness it is usual to speak of a 'simple' or 'non-specific' primary dementia.

The general clinical picture is similar in all—a progressive disintegration of intellect, memory and personality, with symptoms of the chronic organic reaction as described in Chapter 1. The different conditions are distinguished to some extent by the rapidity of their course or by associated symptoms and signs, as will be described when the individual disorders are considered in turn. Quite often, however, the precise diagnostic category is revealed only by careful post-mortem examination of the brain, and even then a measure of uncertainty can remain in some cases. There is considerable dispute over the nosological distinctions which can be made among several of the rarer sub-varieties; and some uncertainty persists over whether distinctions should be drawn between Alzheimer's disease developing in the senile and presenile age periods. Future work may be expected to clarify these issues, but unfortunately clinical information is all too often sparse by the time the brain comes to histological or biochemical examination.

All of these diseases share a uniformly hopeless prognosis and the chief aim in diagnostic practice must be to distinguish them from the 'secondary dementias', that is to search for the other causes of chronic organic reactions which may have some therapeutic issue.

It is perhaps because of this emphasis in clinical enquiry that the primary dementias have traditionally been neglected in neurological and psychiatric research. No doubt enthusiastic enquiry into their aetiology has also been impeded by the evidence of genetic predisposition where several are concerned, and by the similarities in pathology with the normal processes of senescence. Thus Gowers' concept of 'abiotrophy' has often been applied, with the implication that they represent merely a precocious ageing of the central nervous system, sometimes on a familial basis, and due to limited viability of the cells concerned. There is a risk, however, of falling into error here, since diseases may represent an intensification of the ageing process without owing much, or anything, directly to it. Recently there has been a start with more intensive research, particularly in relation to Alzheimer's disease, and some lines of enquiry are afoot which may ultimately prove to be fruitful. These are outlined in some detail on pp. 381 to 385.

In the first place experience with other disorders has shown that genetic causation is not incompatible with possibilities for therapeutic intervention. Where a single dominant gene is responsible, as in Pick's disease and Huntington's chorea, a specific biochemical abnormality may yet be discovered and prove to be remediable. Where polygenic inheritance is possible, as in Alzheimer's disease, the genetic factor is likely to be quantitatively graded in severity, and some additional exogenous cause may be required before the disease becomes manifest. With regard to the parallels drawn with senescence, recent studies have served to sharpen the distinctions between normal ageing and the dementing diseases on both clinical and pathological grounds, even in Alzheimer's disease where the parallels in pathology were always most readily drawn. Most hopefully of all, the traditionally static techniques of neuropathological examination are being supplemented by detailed neurochemistry and other neurobiological approaches, which seek to explore the genesis of the salient changes in the nervous system. Altogether it has now become clear that causation could lie at least in part in biochemical aberration, toxic influences or subtle deprivations which may one day prove to be remediable. The possibility even of infection with some 'slow viral' organism has been raised, since some cases of Creutzfeldt–Jakob disease have proved to be transmissible by brain inoculation. All of these and related matters will be considered in further detail below.

The Senile Dementias

Dementia setting in after the age of 65 has usually been considered separately from that occurring in younger patients. The organisation of clinical services for the elderly, and the development of the specialities of geriatrics and psychogeriatrics, have served to reinforce the practice. Unfortunately, in consequence, 'senile dementia' has tended to acquire nosological status as a separate and distinct entity in clinical and even in some research writing. In fact the dementias of the elderly can have several causes, as at any other age, and with advancing age multiple causes will sometimes be operative together.

The most common pathology displayed at autopsy in elderly demented patients is closely similar to, if not identical with, that of Alzheimer's disease in younger persons. Formerly this was labelled as 'parenchymatous senile dementia', but more recent practice is to speak of 'senile dementia of the Alzheimer type' ('SDAT'). The change in terminology reflects the increasing body of evidence that the conditions are likely to be identical whether setting in before or after the age of 65. A second large group consists of the arteriosclerotic or multi-infarct dementias, whereas a third is determined by an admixture of these two common forms of pathology. The relatively small remainder of cases is likely to show a range of other causative pathologies, or

the brain may be normal apart from the changes expected with age.

The difficulty in applying precise nosological labels during life has impeded clarification of the clinical, genetic and other allegiances of the dementias of the elderly. Opportunities have been rare for the long-term follow-up of patients to allow clinico-pathological correlations on any extensive scale. Special difficulties arise, moreover, from the fact that plaques and tangles accumulate in the brain as age advances, even in the healthy aged population. This has led to uncertain lines of demarcation, even at the pathological level, between what should be regarded as relevant or irrelevant to the development of dementia as older age groups are considered.

In the present chapter the sections on Alzheimer's disease and arteriosclerotic dementia will describe the clinical picture and underlying pathology of these conditions in some detail. First, however, it will be useful to consider certain aspects of the dementias of the elderly separately, bearing in mind that the major proportion of such cases is likely to represent 'senile dementia of the Alzheimer type'. This will be referred to for economy as 'SDAT'.

Prevalence and Forms of Senile Dementia

Epidemiological studies show that the prevalence of dementia rises markedly with age, from about 2% in persons aged 65–70 to approximately 20% in those over 80 (Royal College of Physicians, 1981). In addition to such cases of 'moderate to severe' dementia there are perhaps two to three times as many patients at any one time with mild forms of the disorder. As a consequence of increasing longevity in the population the prevalence of dementia has therefore risen and continues to rise alarmingly. Terry and Katzman (1983) estimate that there are now approximately 1·3 million persons with severe dementia in the USA, viz with a degree of impairment that precludes independent living, and a further 2·8 million who are still able to live semi-independently. Altogether dementia now probably ranks as the fourth or fifth most common cause of death in the USA (Katzman, 1976).

The implications of a problem on such a scale for the cost and provision of care are clearly enormous. Kay et al. (1970) were able to show that admission rates to hospital for the elderly demented exceeded the rates for all other psychoses combined, likewise that their demands on hospital and residential facilities outstripped those due to all other forms of disability in old age. Yet statistics from institutions underestimate the size of the problem. The Newcastle-upon-Tyne survey of a random sample of people living at home, coupled with a census of institutions in the same area, disclosed that fewer than one-fifth even of the more severe cases were in hospitals or homes for the elderly (Kay *et al.*, 1964). Of demented patients in the community, moreover, only a small proportion are known to their general practitioners (Williamson *et al.*, 1964).

Accurate data on the relative prevalence of different forms of dementia in the elderly are obviously hard to obtain. Autopsy information, based largely on hospitalised patients, has consistently shown that an Alzheimer pathology is the most common variety encountered and occurs in some half to two-thirds of patients. An arteriosclerotic basis is present in perhaps a quarter; this will sometimes co-exist with Alzheimer changes, each contributing to the dementia. Thus Tomlinson *et al.* (1970) found the following distribution in their autopsy material on 50 patients: definite Alzheimer pathology in 50%; definite arteriosclerosis in 12% and probable arteriosclerosis in 6% more; and a mixture of Alzheimer and arteriosclerotic pathology in 18%. The remaining 14% could not be classified into any of the above three categories, some representing probable Alzheimer's disease (6%), some showing no evident pathology (4%), and the others a probable traumatic or Wernicke basis (4%).

It is difficult, however, to judge how far these findings may be extrapolated to the elderly demented generally. Different forms of institution tend to cater for different types of patient; those dying in geriatric and psychiatric facilities, for example, may not be strictly comparable with each other, and those who remain in the community may present a different spectrum again. The nosological status of patients with less severe and less rapidly progressive forms of dementia has not been clarified directly. Nevertheless the clinical impression remains that SDAT and arteriosclerotic dementia account between them for the great majority of cases, other varieties being distinctly uncommon after the age of 65. Those patients in whom no clear pathological basis for their dementia can be demonstrated at autopsy—4% in Tomlinson *et al.*'s (1970) series, and 12% among those reported by Blessed (1980)—remain puzzling and a challenge to further research.

Aetiology of SDAT

Despite the close neuropathological similarities between SDAT and the brain changes seen with normal ageing, it can now scarcely be doubted that a disease process is involved. Thus epidemiological surveys show that even in extreme old age the great majority of persons remain free from clinical evidence of dementia; it seems probable that there are genetic determinants for its development; and most persuasively of all there are ever-increasing indications that SDAT is similar in virtually all essentials to Alzheimer's disease occurring in younger persons. Key factors in the aetiology of the one are therefore likely to apply to the other, hence the current emphasis of research in many centres into the origins of such pathology.

The rival theories concerning the pathogenesis of Alzheimer's disease are outlined on p. 381 *et seq.* Here it is only necessary to note that where opportunities have arisen to compare research findings in presenile and senile cases the results have been very similar. Detailed observations concerning the structure of plaques and tangles yield equivalent results whatever the age of the patient, and cholinergic deficits are pre-eminent among the brain biochemical changes. Certain exceptions in the biochemical data are discussed on p. 383 but do not yet amount to a serious challenge to the unitary nature of the disorder. Whatever may ultimately emerge as decisive for the pathogenesis of presenile Alzheimer's disease may therefore be expected to apply with equal force to SDAT as well.

Genetic studies have had to contend with a measure of diagnostic uncertainty, especially when based on living probands. Nevertheless evidence of genetic predisposition for SDAT has been forthcoming. Kallmann's (1956) investigation of 108 twin pairs showed that 43% of monozygotic twins were concordant for 'parenchymatous senile dementia', compared with 8% of dizygotic twins and 7% of siblings. Larsson *et al.* (1963) studied the incidence of the disorder in the first-degree relatives of 377 cases, with the striking finding that their morbidity risk was about four times that of corresponding age groups in the general population. The increased incidence among relatives was not simply due to longevity in certain families, since there was no more than average longevity in the relatives of index patients. They concluded that a dominant autosomal gene was probably responsible, with partial penetrance. Polygenic inheritance seemed unlikely since forms intermediate between dementia and normal ageing were not found among the relatives.

Other significant findings from Larsson *et al.*'s survey were that there was no increased risk for other psychoses among the relatives, and that the incidence of arteriosclerotic dementia was actually lowered. A puzzling feature was the lack of presenile Alzheimer's disease in over 2000 first-degree relatives in Larsson et al.'s study; others, however, have found such cases (Constantinidis et al., 1962), also cases of SDAT among the relatives of patients with presenile Alzheimer's disease (Lauter and Meyer, 1968).

Heston et al.'s (1981) careful genetic survey took origin from 125 probands, all with autopsy proof of Alzheimer-type pathology. The onset had been below 65 in approximately 40% of cases and at 65 or over in the remainder. The risk for parents and siblings proved again to be elevated some four-fold over general population estimates. Here, however, age of onset appeared to be an important consideration, in that a relatively early onset (below 70) together with the presence of an affected parent greatly increased the risk to sibs; conversely when the illness began only after the age of 70 the risk to sibs appeared to be little if at all elevated. This important study is discussed further on p. 377. Preliminary evidence that certain clinical features of the dementia may indicate special genetic risk await confirmation; Breitner and Folstein (1984) suggest that familial aggregations of dementia may be largely confined to patients who show language disorder and apraxia as part of the clinical picture.

Attention has been directed at the possibility of loss of chromosomal material in elderly demented patients by searching for hypodiploid cells in peripheral lymphocytes. Hypodiploidy has been found to increase with age in females, and less certainly in males (Martin, 1982). Several studies have reported a further increase in females suffering from dementia (Nielsen, 1968, 1970a; Jarvik et al., 1974a, b), though this has not been uniformly confirmed (Martin et al., 1981).

Interesting findings have also emerged from the neurophysiological work of Levy et al. (1970, 1971), which raises the possibility that the dementia may represent only one facet of a more general degenerative process affecting the nervous system at several levels. Patients with SDAT, when compared with patients of the same age without organic mental impairment, were found to have slowing of motor conduction along the ulnar nerve distally in the arm. There was a high correlation between the severity of the dementia and the degree of peripheral slowing, and re-testing one year later showed that increase in dementia was associated significantly with further slowing. The latencies and morphological characteristics of somatosensory evoked responses were also found to be altered in SDAT, though here the site of slowing was probably within the brain itself rather than in peripheral pathways.

The frequent finding of folate deficiency among elderly persons is discussed in Chapter 12, but it is unlikely that this contributes on any widespread scale to the development of dementia in old age. A role for cerebral anoxia has sometimes been championed, especially in view of the frequency of cardiac disease and dysrhythmias in the elderly (Lancet, 1977), but evidence for an aetiological connection between cardiac disorder and SDAT had not been forthcoming (Emerson et al., 1981). Socioeconomic factors are certainly important in dictating admission to hospital and residential care (Sainsbury et al., 1965) but do not seem to influence the incidence of the disease.

Clinical Features of SDAT

The onset is usually in the 70s or 80s and females preponderate over males to a considerable extent. In Larsson et al.'s (1963) large Swedish material the mean age of onset was 73 for males and 75 for females. The early stages are rarely seen in hospitals or clinics and many patients already have advanced dementia by the time they come to attention.

The general clinical picture follows that described for Alzheimer's disease on p. 378 et seq., except that the onset may be particularly hard to discern and parietal lobe symptomatology is less regularly conspicuous. Among older patients it is probable that the disorder can sometimes follow a relatively protracted course as a result of more 'benign' development of the pathological changes.

The early stages are commonly overlooked by relatives and even by medical attendants. Failing memory and lack of initiative and interest tend to be regarded as no more than an accentuation of the normal processes of ageing. An exaggeration of such traits as obstinacy, egocentricity and rigid adherence to old habits may be viewed likewise. Thus the family will often adapt insensibly to the patient's gradual decline in a manner that scarcely impinges on their attention. Old people, moreover, may already have adopted a circumscribed routine within which cognitive failure is slow to be exposed.

The diagnosis of dementia in such early stages can present considerable problems. Follow-up of a large community cohort of elderly persons 2–4 years later showed that only 6 of 20 'borderline demented' subjects had indeed progressed to unequivocal dementia (Bergmann, 1977). The misdiagnoses had mostly occurred in persons of low social class and low intelligence, and those who were relatively incoherent at interview. The distinction from depression will often be far from clear-cut, likewise the discernment of what may be expected by way of memory failure with age.

In this last respect Kral (1962) has attempted to distinguish a 'benign' form of memory failure ('benign senescent forgetfulness') from that due to dementia. The former is said to be patchy and variable, with difficulty over the recall of names and places but with relative ease of recall of experiences. In dementia, by contrast, the memory disturbances are soon more severe. At first they may selectively affect recent rather than remote events but this distinction rapidly becomes obscured. Whole segments of experience are blotted out and the patient becomes increasingly disoriented in time and place. He may imagine he is living in the remote past or in some other location, forget the names of his children or spouse or the death of close relatives and friends. Islands of memory may stand out for a time, but are frequently displaced in time and distorted in context.

In a follow-up over 4 years of 40 normal elderly persons, 20 patients with benign forgetfulness and 34 patients with dementia, Kral (1978) has indicated that valid distinctions can be drawn. Those with benign forgetfulness showed similar mortality rates and longevity to the normal group, with mean survival times of 24 and 25 months respectively, whereas the demented patients fared significantly worse with an average survival of 15 months.

While the onset of dementia is insidious it not infrequently comes to attention as a result of some acute disturbance. An intercurrent illness may have taxed the reserves of the failing brain beyond their limit or resulted in an acute episode of delirium. Or a sudden change of environment or the loss of a partner may have abruptly revealed the inroads made by the disorder. Other cases come to notice as a result of the social disorganisation produced by the dementing process—the patient may wander away and get lost, become suddenly abusive on account of paranoid delusions, or harm himself due to some clumsiness or accident.

Once firmly established the disintegration of intellect and personality proceeds relentlessly. Episodes of confusion and delirium may occur at night and the patient sleeps badly. Repetitive futile behaviour is characteristic and restlessness may become extreme. Psychotic features are common, usually of a paranoid nature and sometimes with grotesque hypochondriacal delusions. Emotions become blunted, though outbursts of anger may occur if routines are disturbed. Habits deteriorate with loss of sphincter control, so that the patient is sometimes found to have been living in appalling conditions by the time he is admitted to hospital. The appearance becomes decrepit and shrunken, and the gait slow, shuffling and tottery. The general physical enfeeblement is said to be in contrast to presenile Alzheimer's disease, in which physical deterioration is often delayed until the dementia has reached a very advanced degree.

It was formerly considered that focal symptomatology was rare in 'senile dementia' but this has now been reconsidered. Lauter and Meyer (1968) reported a high incidence of dysphasia, apraxia, agnosia and disturbance of spatial orientation when patients were examined systematically. In Blessed's (1980) series, followed to autopsy almost a third of those with typical Alzheimer pathology had shown evidence of parietal lobe symptomatology during life. It is clear therefore that these features are common, though not universal in SDAT. Seltzer and Sherwin (1983) have attempted a direct comparison between patients with onset of Alzheimer's disease before or after the age of 65, confirming a higher prevalence of language disorder among the younger patients. However, much may depend on the severity with which the disease process is developed, the more severe afflictions tending to compromise the parietal lobe to an extent that has issue in clinical symptoms. McDonald (1969) was able to show that parietal lobe symptoms were commoner among the rather younger patients who developed the disease and conferred a poorer overall prognosis. Hare (1978) similarly found a poorer outcome in their presence, and Naguib and Levy (1982a) have shown that survival may be shorter when there is decreased absorption density in the parietal region on CT scans.

Such observations deserve attention because they are relevant to the question of the distinction between the presenile and senile forms of Alzheimer's disease as discussed on p. 385. Those who see no reason for the distinction are not surprised at the occurrence of focal parietal lobe symptomatology in SDAT. Those who have wished to uphold the distinction, such as Sourander and Sjögren (1970), separate off those patients who display marked focal signs as 'late onset Alzheimer's disease' and place the remainder in a distinct nosological category. The latter may be designated as 'parenchymatous' or 'simple' senile dementia.

The relationship between SDAT and functional psychiatric illness in late life has been discussed by Post (1968). His studies have discounted the idea that neurotic or depressive symptomatology is a frequent prodromal manifestation of SDAT. Nor does he regard SDAT as an important cause of sexual transgression against juveniles in old men. The late appearance of paraphrenic symptoms is perhaps more commonly associated with SDAT, but this may be partly due to the difficulty sometimes encountered in distinguishing clinically between the early stages of the two disease processes.

Rather more suggestive findings emerge in relation to premorbid personality adjustment. When the dementia is accompanied by florid paranoid or affective symptoms the subject will more commonly have shown evidence of an abnormal personality early in life; those whose dementia pursues a simple downward course are found to have been more stable (Post, 1944). Thus the clinical features of the illness appear to be influenced pathoplastically by factors in the previous personality. Both Post (1968) and Oakley (1965) have also stressed the frequency with which obsessional traits emerge in the history, such as rigidity of outlook, obstinacy and overconscientiousness. The validity of such associations must, however, wait upon proper random comparisons of unselected series of patients, since special features in the personality may obviously dictate referral to hospitals and other institutions.

The electroencephalogram usually shows little more than an accentuation of the normal changes with ageing. With increasing age alpha activity is reduced in frequency and abundance, theta tends to appear in the temporal regions, and even random delta may emerge (Kugler, 1964; Kiloh et al., 1981). In SDAT such changes may be marked, sometimes with total abolition of alpha and prominent theta and delta activity. However the changes lack specificity, and occasionally advanced dementia can exist alongside a normal EEG. Localised theta in the temporal regions of elderly subjects must always be interpreted with caution, and will usually warrant no definite conclusion about the presence of cerebral pathology.

Course and Outcome of SDAT

The overall course is usually steadily and smoothly progressive, in contrast to the step-like progression often seen in arteriosclerotic dementia. Death tends to follow within 5 to 7 years of the appearance of the disease, but precise estimates are difficult to obtain because many cases are not seen in hospitals. Certainly among those admitted to psychiatric hospitals the life expectancy is very poor, Roth (1955) finding that almost 60 per cent were dead within six months and 80 per cent within 2 years. More recently Shah et al. (1969) have reported rather better survival times, at least where female patients are concerned, and Blessed and Wilson (1982) have documented further recent gains. Heston et al.'s (1981) elderly patients with SDAT usually survived for less than 7 years, but occasional cases could live for more than 20 after the first appearance of the disease (p. 373).

Death is often due to intercurrent infection, or may follow upon a gradual period of 'vegetative extinction' which cannot be attributed to any exact cause. In consequence death certification may fail to document the existence of dementia, reporting only pneumonia, cardiac failure or some other psysical disorder occurring prior to death. At autopsy the body and viscera are said commonly to be atrophied in addition to the changes within the brain.

Pathology of SDAT

The pathological changes within the brain appear to be identical in form and distribution to those occurring in presenile Alzheimer's disease as described on p. 380. Here it may be noted, however, that they are said to be generally *less* severely developed in elderly demented persons. Sourander and Sjögren (1970) made detailed comparisons between the pathological findings in patients with presenile Alzheimer's disease, patients with 'parenchymatous senile dementia', and elderly patients dying from other causes. A striking finding was that the reduction in brain weight was much more severe in presenile Alzheimer's disease than in the elderly dements. A quantitative assessment of the frequency of neurofibrillary tangles showed them to be considerably more frequent in all brain regions studied in the presenile patients, and the differences persisted when the youngest group of Alzheimer's patients were compared with the oldest group of senile dements.

Vascular changes may co-exist with the Alzheimer pathology as in old age generally—arteriosclerosis of large vessels and hyaline degeneration of small vessels, though these are by no means characteristic of the brain in SDAT. Amyloid changes may also be observed in small cortical arterioles in which the entire vessel wall has the appearance of a thick almost homogeneous tube (Corsellis, 1969b). Occasional small infarcts are probably not uncommon as a result. In some cases, perhaps 10–20 per cent of elderly dements generally, a clear admixture of

Alzheimer change and arteriosclerotic pathology will be found to have contributed to the picture as described on p. 372.

The changes in cerebral blood flow which have been demonstrated during life are probably secondary to lowered cerebral metabolism. Ingvar (1970) and Simard (1971) showed reductions of cerebral oxygen uptake and regional blood flow in proportion to the degree of intellectual impairment, which has been confirmed by more recent PET-scan studies (Frackowiak et al., 1980). These have also confirmed the close coupling of blood flow to oxygen utilisation in all brain areas studied, with falls of about 30% in grey matter and 23% in white matter, in proportion to the severity of dementia. Parietal and temporal reductions were most pronounced in the less severely demented subjects, while profound frontal losses appeared when deterioration was advanced.

Distinction Between SDAT and Normal Ageing

All components of the cerebral pathology of SDAT may also be found in aged persons who have appeared to be mentally intact up to the time of death. Thus it has been argued that cerebral atrophy and its attendant histological changes are so common in later life that the structural state of the brain, as at present revealed, is of doubtful significance in relation to the disease process (Rothschild, 1956). Some other qualitative differences might wait to be discovered, or alternatively it might be the mode of the patient's reaction to the ageing processes within the brain which holds the key to dementia. The problem has recently been clarified, first from the comprehensive studies of Corsellis (1962), and more recently from the series of reports from Newcastle upon Tyne (Roth et al., 1967; Blessed et al., 1968; Tomlinson et al., 1968, 1970; summarised by Roth, 1971).

Corsellis (1962) examined the brains of a large group of aged patients who had died in a mental hospital, and found a high level of agreement between the clinical diagnosis during life and the severity of the neuropathological changes. Both parenchymatous and vascular changes tended to become more common with advancing age, but the great majority of those diagnosed as suffering from dementia showed cerebral pathology of at least moderate severity compared to only a quarter of those who had suffered from functional mental disorders. It was possible to conclude that the occurrence of a progressive dementia was more often than not reflected in the ultimate appearance of the brain when fully and comprehensively examined.

The Newcastle workers undertook prospective studies, beginning with clinical and psychometric observations during life, and comparing these with quantitative measures of neuropathological changes after death. The subjects included elderly dementing patients, patients with functional psychiatric illness, and mentally well-preserved persons who died from accidents or other acute illnesses. The non-dementing elderly subjects frequently showed senile plaques in the cortex, and neurofibrillary changes in the hippocampi. Outfall of cells and granulovacuolar degeneration were also seen in some degree in the absence of dementia. But quantitative estimates of the number of plaques, or of the severity of neurofibrillary changes, proved to correlate very highly indeed with scores of intellectual and personality impairment. In fact the relationship between impairment and mean plaque count was broadly linear. Moreover, plaques were present in all layers of the cortex in demented subjects, but often restricted to the superficial layers in those who had shown no intellectual decline. Very large conglomerate plaques were far commoner in the demented than in the normal subjects.

Wilcock and Esiri (1982) have recently confirmed the Newcastle findings and have focused particular attention on the significance of neurofibrillary change. Ball (1976) had already demonstrated an enormous increase in the number of tangle-bearing neurones in the hippocampi when SDAT patients were compared with age-matched controls, and Wilcock and Esiri sought to relate this to the severity of the dementia. Counts of both plaques and tangles were made in the cortex and hippocampi in patients with SDAT and in controls of equivalent age. Tangle formation proved to be highly correlated with the severity of dementia prior to death in the majority of areas sampled, in addition to distinguishing reliably between demented and non-demented subjects. Plaque counts showed significant associations of a similar nature but less impressively so. It would appear, therefore, that the extensive development of neurofibrillary tangles may be of particular significance as a histological marker of SDAT. Tomlinson (1982) concludes from his considerable experience that while tangles can be found in the hippocampal pyramidal layer and occasionally in the hippocampal gyrus in healthy aged subjects, it is extremely rare to find them in the neocortex at any age in the absence of dementia.

Thus it appears that SDAT arises clinically when

the pathological changes of senescence develop beyond a certain degree of severity. Thresholds in terms of mean plaque counts or neurofibrillary change could be established with reasonable clarity in the Newcastle studies, below which destructive changes appeared to be accommodated within the reserve capacity of the brain and above which dementia became manifest. The finding of such quantitative relationships is impressive evidence for upholding the significance to be attached to the neuropathological changes, and the demonstration of regional effects goes some way to supporting a distinction between SDAT and normal ageing.

It remains possible, of course, that additional differences remain to be discovered and that these will highlight even more clearly the distinctions that can be drawn. As discussed on p. 382 there is increasingly clear evidence of profound cell loss from the cortex when SDAT patients are compared with age-matched controls (Terry et al., 1981; Terry and Katzman, 1983). Changes in the morphology of dendrites (Scheibel, 1978) and reductions in their fields of arborisation (Buell and Coleman, 1979) may prove to be of especial significance for dementia (p. 382). The biochemical changes found in SDAT are described on p. 382 et seq. Here again it is noteworthy that while cholinergic function declines with age, the scale of the deficits found in dementia outstrips in large degree what might be expected from ageing processes alone.

Other evidence which may be presented for regarding SDAT as distinct from normal ageing includes the genetic information outlined on pp. 372–3, as well as the more dubious distinctions that can be drawn between the nature of the psychological disabilities seen in the two conditions. Dorken (1958) has contrasted the orderly relationship in the decline of various abilities in normal old age with the more chaotic state of affairs in senile dementia, and Botwinick and Birren (1951) point out that the intellectual skills most vulnerable in normal senescence are not necessarily those which differentiate between normal and demented subjects. The issues involved are comprehensively discussed by Miller (1974, 1977) who concludes that it is unlikely that the psychological changes in dementia are merely analogous to accelerated ageing.

The problems which surround the distinction between SDAT and arteriosclerotic dementia are discussed on pp. 388–9.

Alzheimer's Disease

Alzheimer's disease was first described early in this century (Alzheimer, 1907, 1911) and is now believed to be the commonest of the primary dementing illnesses. Characteristics of the disorder when it appears in the elderly have been described just above. In what follows, presenile Alzheimer's disease will be given special consideration.

Aetiology

The great majority of cases appear to arise sporadically, though a slight but definite familial tendency has emerged when large series have been investigated. Sjögren et al.'s (1952) evidence suggested a multifactorial mode of inheritance. Much more rarely it seems to be transmitted as a regularly manifest dominant trait in occasional families (Pratt, 1967). Here the usual female preponderance is said not to occur, and there are sometimes features peculiar to the family concerned—muscular twitching, spastic paraplegia, or marked amyloidosis of cerebral vessels. An example has now been described in a mother and identical twin sons who died in early adulthood after rapidly progressive dementia (Sharman et al., 1979).

Heston et al.'s (1981) genetic study, taking origin from autopsy-proven cases of Alzheimer's disease, revealed secondary cases among first-degree relatives in 51 of 125 families. Sixty per cent of the probands were thus isolated cases despite large family memberships in certain instances. The increased risk to relatives was largely confined to patients whose dementia had begun below the age of 70, but was then increased 4-fold; indeed the risk to siblings when onset had been before 70 years of age and when a parent had already shown the disease approached 50 per cent, resembling autosomal dominant inheritance in these unusual families. Interesting further associations emerged: among the relatives of younger probands there appeared to be an increased risk of Down's syndrome, of myeloproliferative disorders such as lymphosarcoma, reticulum cell sarcoma and Hodgkin's disease, and of immune system disorders. Heyman et al. (1983) have confirmed a significant increase in Down's syndrome in the families of probands, and point also to a possibly increased incidence of thyroid disorder in the past histories of affected females. It would seem, therefore, that presenile Alzheimer's disease may be associated with a genetic factor leading occasionally to substantial familial aggregations of dementia, and conferring vulnerability to other disorders as well.

The association with Down's syndrome is particularly striking in that patients with mongolism are unusually prone to develop the neuropathological features of Alzheimer's disease, including the typical paired helical filaments in neurofibrillary tangles (Jervis, 1948; Malamud, 1964, 1972; Olson and Shaw, 1969; Burger and Vogel, 1973; Ball and Nuttall, 1980). It has been claimed, indeed, that it is rare for Down's syndrome patients to survive beyond middle age without such features developing in the brain. Wisniewski *et al.* (1978) have obtained some evidence of deterioration in institutionalised Down's syndrome patients over the age of 35 which may reflect this developing pathology, and Yates *et al.* (1980a) have shown cholinergic deficits in the brain similar to those occurring in Alzheimer's disease (p. 382).

The interesting suggestion has been made that an underlying defect in microtubule organisation, reflecting a disturbance of tubulin protein, may explain this association. Erratic functioning of the spindle mechanism could lead to the initial disturbance of chromosome division producing mongolism, and equally have issue in the development of neurofibrillary tangles. The increased incidence of chromosomal aneuploidy in Alzheimer's disease could be further evidence of the basic defect (Cook *et al.*, 1979; Nordenson *et al.*, 1980).

McMenemy (1963a) suggests that the genetic tendency may operate by allowing other extrinsic influences to bring the disease process into being. It is such additional influences which may ultimately be identified, and which are now being vigorously pursued along a number of research pathways. These important and mostly relatively recent developments are described in some detail on p. 381 *et seq.*

The question of precipitation is not uncommonly raised by relatives who may note an apparent onset after head injury, operations, or admission to hospital for other causes. A detailed history will then usually show that the illness had already been in existence, and the so-called precipitant has merely revealed the true state of affairs. The possibility must be recognised, however, that minimal brain damage from head injury, infection or anaesthesia may sometimes have served to worsen the situation, and have been decisive in pushing the patient below a threshold at which he was previously coping. A report by Hollander and Strich (1970) is also of interest in this regard. Six patients were described in whom dementia of acute onset became manifest within hours or days of some catastrophic illness such as subarachnoid haemorrhage, head injury or major cardiac surgery. The brains showed the pathological features of Alzheimer's disease along with widespread amyloid angiopathy. It seemed that the acute illness had probably played some part in the

sudden mental deterioration which had occurred, and the amyloid changes, at least, appeared to have been of very rapid evolution. Hollander and Strich suggest that generalised metabolic precipitants, or disturbance of the cerebral circulation, should more often be taken into account in assessing the aetiology of Alzheimer's disease.

Clinical Features

The onset of presenile Alzheimer's disease is usually after 40, though rare cases have been reported at younger ages. Females preponderate over males in a ratio of 2 or 3 to 1.

The beginning is usually insidious and can be dated only imprecisely. The slow development of the intellectual deterioration often allows the patient to preserve considerable social competence until the disease is well advanced. Fortunately it is usual for the patient to lose insight into the changes within himself from a very early stage.

Three main phases to the disease are commonly distinguished. The first, often lasting for 2 or 3 years, is characterised by failing memory, muddled inefficiency over the tasks of everyday life, and spatial disorientation. Disturbances of mood may be prominent but psychotic features are rare. The mood disorder may take the form of perplexity, agitation and restless hyperactivity. Others by contrast have stressed aspontaneity and apathy from the early stages (Sjögren *et al.*, 1952).

The second stage brings more rapid progress of intellectual and personality deterioration and focal symptoms appear. An accent on the parietal lobes is common with dysphasia, apraxia, agnosia and acalculia. Extrapyramidal disorders are also characteristic with disturbance of posture and gait, increase of muscle tone and other typical features of parkinsonism. Such parkinsonian signs were present in almost two-thirds of Pearce and Miller's (1973) patients. Extensor plantar responses may be seen and facial weakness is not uncommon. Florid psychotic symptoms of a delusional or hallucinatory nature may occur, but usually only when the dementia is very far advanced.

The third or terminal stage consists of profound apathetic dementia in which the patient becomes bedridden and doubly incontinent. Gross neurological disability may sometimes develop, such as spastic hemiparesis or severe striatal rigidity and tremor. Forced grasping and groping may be seen, along with sucking reflexes. Grand mal fits are not uncommon. In the terminal phase of the disease bodily wasting may be astonishingly rapid despite adequate preservation of appetite. Before this, however, somatic manifestations of senility usually remain in abeyance despite the steadily progressive dementia.

The clinical features which have been stressed as distinguishing Alzheimer's disease from other forms of presenile dementia include the following:

Memory difficulties are reported as the earliest feature more regularly than in any other presenile dementing process, and are said to precede changes in mood and behaviour in virtually every case. This was confirmed in the important study by Sim *et al.* (1966) who used cerebral biopsy to establish the pathological diagnosis in a large series of patients. Emotional changes such as anxious hyperexcitability or aspontaneity have also been regarded as characteristic, likewise dysphasic, apraxic and agnosic difficulties. Lauter and Meyer (1968) found the latter in virtually every case below 59 years of age, though progressively less often in older age groups. Disturbances of gait and other extrapyramidal manifestations are regarded as equally typical of Alzheimer's disease. Other features regarded as characteristic include early spatial disorientation, a progressive reduction in spontaneity of speech, and increased muscular tension. Gustafson and Nilsson (1982) have partially validated a weighted scale, using these and other features, for distinguishing Alzheimer's disease from other forms of presenile dementia.

The frequency of epilepsy has sometimes been quoted as a distinctive feature and has been reported in up to 75% of cases. Minor seizures may occur early in the disease, though grand mal fits appear to be mainly a late development. Sim *et al.* (1966) found that *early* fits were actually more frequent in presenile dementias other than Alzheimer's disease.

Sourander and Sjögren (1970) have recently drawn attention to the frequency of behavioural abnormalities suggestive of temporal lobe dysfunction in presenile Alzheimer's disease, particularly phenomena reminiscent of the Klüver Bucy syndrome in animals after bilateral temporal lobe excision (Chapter 2, p. 23). Visual agnosic difficulties were often the first focal deficits to be noted, especially inability to recognise the faces of relatives or the self in a mirror. Late phenomena included strong tendencies to examine and touch objects with the mouth ('hyperorality'), and tendencies to be stimulus-bound to contact and touch every object in sight ('hypermetamorphosis'). Hyperphagia was often a terminal phenomenon, with indiscriminate eating of any material available. The emotional changes of apathy and dullness were similarly reminiscent of the pathological tameness of monkeys with the Klüver Bucy syndrome. Such manifestations were observed in over three-quarters of patients with Alzheimer's disease, and in some of them the full gamut of phenomena was displayed. The human counterpart of the Klüver Bucy syndrome has been occasionally observed with other cerebral disorders such as arteriosclerosis, Pick's disease and cerebral tumours, but Sourander and Sjögren consider that in most cases it forms an essential part of the symptomatology of Alzheimer's disease. They also stress that the seizures which occur are often temporal lobe in origin with characteristic chewing, smacking and lip-licking movements.

The electroencephalogram shows abnormalities more frequently in Alzheimer's disease than in any other form of dementia. Several investigations have demonstrated abnormal records in every case (Lidell, 1958; Letemendia and Pampiglione, 1958; and Swain, 1959), and Gordon and Sim (1967) have confirmed that changes are likely to be seen even in very early examples with minimal dementia. The early stage consists of reduction of alpha activity which may sometimes disappear entirely. This is particularly characteristic of Alzheimer's disease and is perhaps of some value in distinguishing it from other varieties. Later diffuse slow waves appear, typically irregular theta activity with superimposed runs of delta. Focal or paroxysmal features are rare, even in patients with epileptic fits. The degree of abnormality appears to be more marked in patients in whom the disease is rapidly progressive (Swain, 1959), and to worsen with the increase in dementia (Gordon and Sim, 1967; Gordon, 1968).

Finally the overall findings of Sim *et al.* (1966) may be quoted as providing the best available comparison of the early and late manifestations of Alzheimer's disease in relation to other forms of presenile dementia. Biopsy during life allowed 35 patients with Alzheimer's disease to be compared with 21 patients suffering from other dementing processes. The non-Alzheimer patients were considered to represent a mixture of Pick's disease and several other forms. Features occurring early in Alzheimer's disease but often late in the other group included impairment of memory, apraxia, and generalised disturbances in the electroencephalogram. Features occurring late in Alzheimer's disease but early in other cases included fits, incontinence, confabulation, personality change, delusions and hallucinations, and gross focal neurological disturbances such as spasticity, hemiparesis, striatal rigidity and tremor.

Course and Outcome

The disease runs a progressive course with death following some 2–8 years after onset. In Heston *et al.*'s (1981) material a trend could be seen for survival to increase a little from a mean of 7 years in those under 49, to $8\frac{1}{2}$ years for those aged 55 to 74. In more elderly groups the survival was on average shorter, presumably due to deaths from competing causes, but even so the span could sometimes exceed 20 years. Seltzer and Sherwin (1983) made direct comparisons of 'relative survival time' between patients with onset before and after the age of 65 (by comparing observed length of survival for each individual with his expected survival from actuarial tables), and found significantly shorter survival for those in the presenile category.

Rare cases are described in which the disorder becomes arrested for a time, but these must be regarded as exceptional. Neither remissions nor fluctuations characterise the disease.

Pathology of Alzheimer's Disease

The typical picture is of a grossly atrophied brain, without immediately obvious variation from one cortical region to another. Histologically there is extensive degeneration and loss of nerve cells accompanied by secondary glial proliferation. The striking features of senile plaques and neurofibrillary tangles are much in evidence. The vascular system is usually normal or displays only minimal changes, though sometimes amyloid angiopathy may be seen as described below.

The cortical atrophy, though generalised, tends to affect the frontal and temporal lobes more severely than the parieto-occipital regions. Variants on the typical picture are very occasionally seen, for example restricted lobar atrophy similar to that in Pick's disease, or a lack of any gross shrinkage despite extensive microscopic degeneration. Neuronal degeneration affects the outer three cortical layers particularly. An accent is often found on the limbic areas and especially on the hippocampi and amygdaloid nuclei. Affected neurones may show an accumulation of lipofuscin pigment, or granulovacuolar degeneration in which minute vacuoles surround a central granule in the cytoplasm. The white matter shows axonal degeneration, hyperplasia of astrocytes and fibrous gliosis.

Senile plaques are almost universally seen in Alzheimer's disease. They are usually found densely throughout the cortex and can readily be identified by silver staining. The hippocampi and amygdaloid nuclei are again particularly affected, the latter perhaps more severely than any other part of the brain (Corsellis, 1970). The subcortical grey matter is much less severely affected, and plaques are not seen in the white matter itself. They appear as irregular masses ranging from 5–100 μm in diameter. A central argyrophilic core is usually surrounded by a clear halo and then an outer ring of filamentous material. Amyloid material is present in the core. Microglial cells can often be identified within the disintegrating tissue of the plaque, and astrocytes tend to collect around its margin. Within the substance of the plaque unmyelinated neuronal processes, including synaptic boutons, have been identified by electron microscopy (Terry and Wisniewski, 1970). These may contain bundles of twisted tubules similar to those of the neurofibrillary tangles.

Neurofibrillary tangles are also present and are usually considered essential for the diagnosis. They are again shown by silver impregnation, and occur diffusely in the grey matter and particularly in the hippocampi. They lie within the nerve cells themselves, often displacing the nucleus or filling the cell body entirely.

Another focus of interest has been the occurrence of amyloid-like material in the brains of patients with Alzheimer's disease. This is most readily shown after treatment with Congo red when the material becomes birefringent. Divry (1927) first demonstrated the material in the centre of the senile plaque, and it has since been found in the neurofibrillary tangles and in the walls of intracortical arterioles. Heavy involvement of the vasculature ('amyloid angiopathy', 'congophilic angiopathy') has formed a special feature of certain familiarly occurring variants (Corsellis and Brierley, 1954). It is, however, only in the core of the plaques that the material has been firmly established as amyloid in nature; on electron-microscopy even the smallest plaques are found to contain wisps of the material, whereas larger (and presumably older) plaques may simply consist of amyloid alone (Terry and Wisniewski, 1970).

Extracerebral pathology has been remarkably little studied in Alzheimer's disease. The reason for the striking terminal loss in weight, often unrelated to inadequate intake of food, is unknown. Whether this depends on endocrine factors, or possibly on hypothalamic pathology remains to be explored.

Research Findings in Alzheimer's Disease

The past decade has witnessed an accelerating investment of research into Alzheimer's disease, spurred on no doubt by the realisation that this is the common cause of dementia among the elderly, and by the emergence of a number of promising leads. The Medical Research Council in the UK nominated research into the dementias as a priority area (Medical Research Council, 1977) and the Royal College of Physicians has commissioned a review of the current state of knowledge (Royal College of Physicians, 1981). There is now no dearth of avenues for study—the difficulty is rather to choose from among a number of quite different pointers towards the pathogenesis of the disorder. Toxic, biochemical, infective and immunological theories can find support, but none at the moment can claim primacy over the others. Research proceeds in parallel into presenile and senile Alzheimer's disease, though with the latter providing the more abundant clinical material.

Histological studies continue with the aim of determining what are the significant tissue elements involved in the disorder and how far these diverge from age-dependent changes. The intensity of development of senile plaques and neurofibrillary tangles correlates closely with the severity of the dementia (Tomlinson *et al.*, 1970; Wilcock and Esiri, 1982), but their true significance for the disease process still remains uncertain. Questions of nerve cell and synaptic loss can now be approached directly by quantitative techniques and may clarify the extent to which neuronal elements are primarily affected.

Both tangles and plaques have been studied in detail in the hope of throwing light upon their genesis. Electron-microscopy shows that the tangles of Alzheimer's disease consist of twisted bundles of paired helical filaments, chemically and immunologically closely related to the normal neurotubules and neurofilaments of the cell (Iqbal *et al.*, 1978; Grundke-Iqbal *et al.*, 1979). Tangles of this nature are not, however, unique to Alzheimer's disease— they are found in dementia pugilistica, post-encephalitic parkinsonism, subacute sclerosing panencephalitis and Down's syndrome, indicating that a variety of pathological processes can produce them. Those seen in other conditions, for example progressive supranuclear palsy, are now known to be distinct, consisting of straight filaments alone.

The significance to be attached to the tangles of Alzheimer's disease therefore remains uncertain— they could reflect some fundamental derangement unique to the disease, or merely represent a secondary and non-specific reaction within the cell.

The senile plaques could take origin from metabolic processes within the neuropil since histochemical studies show increased enzyme activity around their margins (Friede, 1965). Their frequent proximity to blood vessels and their amyloid content have suggested that immunological processes could be important to their development. Terry and Wisniewski (1970, 1972), however, favour the view that the nidus of formation is the damaged neurite itself. Ultrastructural studies of material from cortical biopsies suggest that the first stage of plaque formation may be the aggregation of small groups of degenerating terminal dendrites containing large numbers of mitochondria. Amyloid material then appears in the form of wisps between the neurites and condenses to form the central core. In this view it may well be that the twisted tubules of the neurofibrillary tangles are the primary structural abnormality, embarrassing cell function centrally and, by interfering with axoplasmic flow, causing the neuritic processes to degenerate and contribute to plaque formation. Precise details clearly remain to be discovered, but it is now abundantly evident that both plaques and tangles may reflect metabolic or other disturbances in the neurones and neuropil.

Cell counting within the brain is a laborious exercise, recently speeded by semi-automated techniques. It has seemed crucial to determine whether cell loss in Alzheimer's disease, and especially the senile form, exceeds that to be expected as a result of ageing alone. If it does not there could be reason to doubt whether Alzeimer's disease represents a primary neuronal disorder; whereas if cell loss is indubitable the development of tangles and plaques would take secondary importance and could even be epiphenomenal. The relation of cell loss to age has itself turned out to be complex, with certain brain regions showing different stability from others. Brody (1955) claimed substantial decrements in the cortex from childhood to the eighth decade, some areas such as the superior temporal gyrus showing losses of up to 50 per cent while others such as the post-central gyrus were relatively stable. Henderson *et al.* (1980), using an automated technique, found losses of up to 60 per cent for large neurones in all cortical areas sampled over an equivalent age range, and without this regional variability. The Purkinje cells of the cerebellum clearly decline with age (Hall *et al.*, 1975), but in the brain stem the situation is variable—losses occur in the locus caeruleus, whereas counts in many cranial nerve nuclei appear to change very little (Brody, 1978; Tomlinson, 1979).

In presenile Alzheimer's disease substantial cortical cell losses relative to controls have been reported (Colon, 1973; Brun and Englund, 1981), but among elderly patients the situation was initially unclear. Shefer (1973) found substantial decrements in patients with SDAT, but Terry and co-workers were at first unable to confirm this (Terry *et al.*, 1977; Terry, 1979). More recent studies, however, are unequivocal—major neuronal losses are found in frontal, parietal and temporal areas in SDAT, affecting mainly the larger neurones and amounting to a reduction of some 40% relative to age-matched controls (Terry *et al.*, 1981; Terry and Katzman, 1983). Mountjoy *et al.* (1983) have reported similar findings to Terry, though with the interesting observation that cell loss is less marked in the most elderly dements of their series, no longer being significant in those exceeding 80 years of age.

Dendritic changes have been reported with age and in dementia and could be of special significance. The dendritic tree represents 70–90 per cent of the total membrane area of the neurone, and any curtailment will stand markedly to diminish synaptic connectivity. Scheibel (1978) has described loss of spines, degeneration of basal branches and later of terminal arches, as a widespread affection of pyramidal cells in the frontal and temporal cortex of elderly deteriorated patients. Furthermore, in cases of presenile Alzheimer's disease, clusters of new dendritic growth have been observed, perhaps in an attempt at compensation, but organised in a haphazard and 'lawless' fashion (Scheibel and Tomiyasu, 1978).

Automated methods have been employed for tracing the extent and complexity of the dendritic trees deriving from individual nerve cells, with particularly interesting results. Buell and Coleman (1979) have obtained strong indications that in healthy elderly persons the dendritic domain becomes *more* extensive, with increased branching and larger terminal segments than in persons of middle age. This would seem to imply a continuing growth of the dendritic trees attaching to neurones which remain healthy, extending well into old age and perhaps compensating for the decline in total neuronal numbers. In elderly dements, however, the size of the dendritic trees was significantly reduced, compared to those found in both middle-aged and elderly controls. SDAT, therefore, appears to represent a failure of normal dendritic growth, or perhaps even a net regression of existing dendritic domains. The factors which govern dendritic extension and division may thus be fundamentally at fault.

Biochemical studies of brain tissue obtained at autopsy, chiefly from patients with SDAT, have clarified key changes that occur in brain proteins, enzymes and other constituents. Bowen *et al.* (1973) found lack of a specific brain protein (neuronin S-6) in the cortex, and Iqbal *et al.* (1974) showed that tangle-bearing neurones contain a new protein of abnormal type. Biochemical indices reflecting neuronal cell loss and glial reactivity have also been described (Bowen *et al.*, 1979). The most promising approach, however, has been the study of enzymes involved in synaptic transmission, culminating in the focus of attention on the cholinergic system.

Investigations from several centres have combined to highlight a widespread deficiency in cholinergic transmission, both in presenile and senile Alzheimer's disease (Davies, 1977; Perry *et al.*, 1977; Spillane *et al.*, 1977; White *et al.*, 1977). The enzymes responsible for the synthesis of acetylcholine (choline acetyl transferase, CAT) and for its degradation (acetylcholinesterase, AChE) have emerged as remarkably deficient, with reductions amounting to 30 per cent of normal levels in many areas. The balance of evidence suggests, moreover, that the density of receptor-binding sites remains relatively normal (Bowen, 1981). This latter observation has opened up prospects for remediation with cholinergic substances, as described on p. 425.

CAT levels appear to decline with age, at least in the hippocampus, but not to an extent that could account for the decrements seen in SDAT (Perry *et al.*, 1977). In arteriosclerotic dementia analogous deficits do not occur (Perry *et al.*, 1978; Wilcock *et al.*, 1982). The reduction in CAT has been demonstrated in biopsy as well as autopsy samples (Spillane *et al.*, 1977; Bowen *et al.*, 1979); and in fresh tissue samples a parallel reduction in acetylcholine synthesis has been confirmed (Sims *et al.*, 1980). CAT is reduced in proportion to the severity of the dementia prior to death, and in relation to the concentration of senile plaques and neurofibrillary tangles displayed on histological examination (Perry *et al.*, 1978; Wilcock *et al.*, 1982). The evidence combines to suggest, therefore, that cholinergic deficits are an integral and meaningful part of the Alzheimer disease process, not merely related to non-specific agonal factors.

There may well be deficits in other neurotransmitters too, though to date these have shown less impressive associations with key aspects of the disorder. Noradrenaline appears to be depleted in many brain regions, the levels in some areas being significantly related to the severity of dementia prior to death (Adolfsson *et al.*, 1979; Mann *et al.*, 1980; Rossor *et al.*, 1984). Dopamine-β-hydroxylase, the marker enzyme for noradrenaline, is also reduced, though not consistently so in all patients studied (Cross *et al.*, 1981). Low concentrations of dopamine and gamma-aminobutyric acid have similarly been reported in relation to age-matched controls. It is clear that to date only a small proportion of the putative neurotransmitters have been adequately explored, and further findings of significance may yet be expected to emerge.

A recent development has been to view these deficiencies as possibly reflecting, not cell loss in the cortex, but in the subcortical nuclear masses which give rise to ascending cortical projections. In the case of the cholinergic system it was apparent that the severity of the reductions in CAT greatly exceed estimates of cell loss in the cortex, indicating that cholinergic *terminals* in the cortex might be principally involved. It is therefore of interest that cell counts in the nucleus basalis of Meynert show pronounced reductions to less than 25% of normal numbers in Alzheimer's disease (Whitehouse *et al.*, 1982). The nucleus basalis, lying below the globus pallidus in the substantia innominata of the forebrain, provides the main cholinergic input to the neocortex (Emson and Lindvall, 1979). The extent of cell depletion discovered here closely parallels the degree of reduction of CAT in the cortex. It seems possible therefore that this may represent the major source of the widespread cholinergic deficits of Alzheimer's disease, in other words that this component of its pathophysiology may be in large measure focal.

Equivalent evidence has emerged in relation to noradrenergic deficits as well. Significant reductions in the cells of the locus caeruleus have been established in SDAT, exceeding that to be expected with age alone (Tomlinson *et al.*, 1981). The locus caeruleus provides the main noradrenergic innervation of the cortex. Surviving cells in the nucleus, moreover, show reduced nucleolar volume and reduced cytoplasmic RNA indicative of diminished activity (Mann *et al.*, 1980).

From such observations Rossor (1981) postulates a model whereby Alzheimer's disease may be viewed as a disease of the 'isodendritic core', i.e. of subcortical neurone systems which constitute major projections to the cerebral cortex along biochemically distinct pathways. Cholinergic projections from the septal region and substantia innominata, and noradrenergic projections from the locus caeruleus, may be the earliest and principal casualties of the disease process. Cell degeneration in the cortex may be largely secondary, due to transsynaptic degeneration consequent upon loss of ascending inputs. What has long been viewed as an essentially cortical disease process may thus have its roots elsewhere. Parkinson's disease can be viewed similarly as a disease of the isodendritic core; this time of the dopaminergic projections from the substantia nigra to the corpus striatum; with progression of either disease extension may tend to occur to the other neuronal projections, accounting for the later appearance of dementia in some Parkinson's patients (p. 556) and of extrapyramidal dysfunction in Alzheimer's disease (p. 378).

As more detailed biochemical evidence has begun to emerge it seems probable that the deficits encountered are more severe in younger than older Alzheimer patients. Thus Rossor *et al.* (1981, 1982, 1984) have shown that patients dying in their 80s or 90s have a relatively pure cholinergic defect, principally involving the temporal lobe and hippocampus, whereas those dying in their 60s and 70s have more severe and widespread deficits extending to the frontal cortex as well. The younger group also showed depletions in noradrenaline, gamma-aminobutyric acid and somatostatin which were rarely reduced in the very old. Tagliavini and Pilleri (1983) have found that neuronal losses from the nucleus basalis of Meynert are more profound in presenile than senile Alzheimer's disease (while present in both), and no losses whatever could be detected in a small group of very elderly patients with 'simple' senile dementia. Bondareff *et al.* (1981b, 1982), investigating neurone counts in the locus caeruleus, have found a bimodal distribution, those with low counts being significantly younger at death than those in whom counts were normal. It is difficult to decide, on present evidence, how far these age-related differences merely reflect the more 'malignant' course of the disease process when it occurs at a younger age, or whether in time they will point to subdivisions within a 'syndrome' of Alzheimer's disease. Particular interest will attach to the clinical-biochemical correlations which emerge from further studies, and to the impact the findings may have on the current unitary theory of presenile and senile Alzheimer's disease.

Toxicity from aluminium has been suspected, since intracerebral injections of aluminium salts induce neuronal tangles in the cat and rabbit. This seemed at one time to offer a potential animal model of Alzheimer's disease. Crapper *et al.* (1978) showed that similar tangles were induced when aluminium was added to cultured human foetal cortical neurones. Moreover, elevated aluminium levels were demonstrated in the brain in Alzheimer's disease, the levels being highest in regions markedly affected by neurofibrillary tangles (Crapper *et al.*, 1976). Perl and Brody (1980), using a spectrometric method, were able to detect foci of aluminium actually within the nuclei of hippocampal neurones affected by neurofibrillary degeneration, adjacent tangle-free neurones being unaffected. Further evidence came from reports of progressive dementia in patients exposed to high aluminium levels, and from the realisation that aluminium is responsible for the deterioration seen in patients suffering from dialysis encephalopathy as discussed on p. 475.

However, electron microscopy has now shown that experimentally induced tangles consist of straight filaments, not the paired helical filaments of Alzheimer's disease. Examination of the brain in patients dying from dialysis encephalopathy does not reveal neurofibrillary degeneration, and McDermott *et al.* (1979) suggest that the high levels of aluminium detected in Alzheimer's disease are attributable to ageing rather than to the disease process itself. The present consensus of opinion is therefore that aluminium tends to accumulate as a secondary effect in ageing or damaged neurones, rather than playing a primary aetiological role in the genesis of the dementia. It is intriguing, nonetheless, that aluminium and silicon have now been identified in high concentration in the cores of senile plaques (Candy *et al.*, 1986). The association of aluminium with both major neuropathological features of Alzheimer's disease remains a striking finding.

An infective aetiology for Alzheimer's disease has been considered in view of the known transmissibility of Creutzfeldt–Jakob disease (p. 400). The evidence so far is, however, slender and the leads obtained to date must be viewed with caution. In Gajdusek's laboratory 3 out of 35 cases of Alzheimer's disease proved to be transmissible to chimpanzees, 2 being examples of familial Alzheimer's disease and all having shown atypical features in one way or another (Traub *et al.*, 1977). All, moreover, produced on transmission the picture of spongiform encephalopathy, typical of Creutzfeldt–Jakob disease, not the histological features of Alzheimer's disease itself. Three other aberrant transmissions were obtained from cases of progressive supranuclear palsy, Leigh's disease and dementia of an unknown type (Goudsmit *et al.*, 1980). The possibility therefore arises that the inocula may have been contaminated, or alternatively that the Creutzfeldt–Jakob agent may sometimes be found as a secondary pathogen in a brain already damaged by other disease. The conclusion at present must be that transmissibility in Alzheimer's disease has not yet been demonstrated with any reasonable certainty.

Other lines of evidence are, however, intriguing. Wisniewski *et al.* (1975) have shown that plaques similar to those of Alzheimer's disease can be induced in mice by inoculation with the 'scrapie' agent, another slow virus analogous to that causing Creutzfeldt–Jakob disease. Moreover, the brains so infected show a reduction in CAT activity similar to that occurring in Alzheimer's disease (McDermott *et al.*, 1978a). The remote possibility therefore remains that species-specific factors may have prevented the demonstration of Alzheimer pathology in the chimpanzee in the experiments described just above.

Interest also attaches to the demonstration of neurofibrillary tangles in tissue cultures of human foetal cortex, after adding extracts of brain tissue or cerebrospinal fluid from patients with Alzheimer's disease (De Boni and Crapper, 1978; Crapper-McLachlan and De Boni, 1980). The latent interval observed has seemed consistent with the presence of some infectious agent, though spontaneous degenerative processes in the cultures cannot be excluded.

Immunological factors have been suspected from several lines of evidence. Ageing is associated with a decline in both cell-mediated and humoral-mediated immune mechanisms, and Alzheimer's disease might conceivably represent a profound accentuation of such a process (Nandy, 1978).

Amyloid has long been recognised as an integral part of the neuropathological picture, in the core of plaques, in neurofibrillary tangles and in the walls of blood vessels. It is occasionally found in other primary dementias, and in old age in the absence of dementia, but it occurs with especial frequency in Alzheimer's disease (van Bogaert, 1970). There is a great deal of evidence that amyloid is deposited in tissues under conditions of altered immunity, and immunoglobulins have been identified in the amyloid of the plaques (Ishii and Haga, 1976). Moreover the close relationship of plaques to blood vessels, especially when these are heavily affected, suggests that the deposition may originate from the bloodstream (Behan and Behan, 1979). Abnormalities in certain serum protein fractions have been identified in patients with Alzheimer's disease, similar to those which occur in primary and secondary amyloidosis (Behan and Feldman, 1970). In generalised amyloidosis the brain is very rarely affected, but in Alzheimer's disease there may be some concurrent disruption of the blood/brain barrier.

Abnormalities of serum immunoglobulins have been reported in patients with SDAT when compared with age-matched controls, and some significant correlations have emerged between immunoglobulin levels and tests of cognitive function (Eisdorfer *et al.*, 1978; Eisdorfer and Cohen, 1980; Cohen and Eisdorfer, 1980). There are also indications of an age-related increase in anti-neural antibodies in the serum, with higher titres in dements than in age-matched controls (Nandy 1981). It is difficult, however, to decide whether such findings may be secondary to the cerebral pathology rather than reflecting primary aetiological mechanisms.

Finally the study of HLA typing in Alzheimer's disease has pointed to certain unusual distributions of HLA sub-types (Behan and Behan, 1979; Harris 1982). It is possible, therefore, that some immunological deficit predisposing to the disorder may be conferred by the patient's genetic constitution. The recent demonstration of an increased incidence of immune system disorders among the relatives of patients with Alzheimer's disease (Heston *et al.*, 1981), and of an increased incidence of thyroiditis, hypothyroidism and Grave's disease in the histories of female probands (Heyman *et al.*, 1983), lends some support to the hypothesis that autoimmune factors may play a part in the genesis of the disorder (p. 377).

Distinction Between Alzheimer's Disease and SDAT

Many authorities hold the view that Alzheimer's disease and 'parenchymatous senile dementia' are identical in all respects other than age of onset (Lauter and Meyer, 1968; Corsellis, 1969b; Terry and Katzman, 1983). In the neuropathological picture no distinguishing features, taken individually, have come to light, and certainly few neuropathologists would claim to be able to distinguish between the two on examination of the brain. Hence the present practice of referring to 'presenile Alzheimer's disease' and 'senile dementia of the Alzheimer type' as explained on p. 371.

Nonetheless Sourander and Sjögren (1970) believe that distinctions can be drawn. Their comparisons between the pathological findings among older and younger patients are discussed on p. 375, with

indications of less severe cerebral atrophy and less intense pathological change among the elderly. They were led to conclude that Alzheimer's disease represents something other than merely an early occurrence of senile dementia, at least in so far as the intensity of neuropathological features is concerned.

Recent neurochemical findings have also pointed to differences between younger and older patients, the former tending to show more severe and widespread cholinergic deficits and more definite depletions in other neurotransmitters (p. 383). Differences are also suspected in certain key subcortical nuclei which play an important role in relation to brain biochemistry (p. 383). As with the neurohistological features, however, it is hard to exclude the possibility that all such findings merely reflect a greater overall severity of the dementing disease process in the young compared to the old. How far further biochemical and ultrastructural studies will challenge the basic similarities between presenile and senile Alzheimer's disease remains to be seen, though present indications still tend to favour a unitary disorder.

Other strands of evidence which may indicate a difference are equally debatable, but may be summarised as follows:

Certain genetic evidence has implied a distinction as discussed on pp. 372–3. Physical senescence is said to be absent in Alzheimer's disease until the terminal stage of rapid emaciation, whereas in SDAT physical deterioration often parallels the mental disintegration throughout. This, however, may be no more than a reflection of the greater impact on physical health of any disease process in persons of advanced age. It was formerly taught that disturbances such as dysphasia and apraxia were characteristic only of presenile Alzheimer's disease, though this view has recently come under review (p. 374). Seltzer and Sherwin (1983) have nevertheless found that language disorder is significantly more common, and length of survival reduced, in patients with presenile as compared to senile Alzheimer's disease. It remains to be seen whether the frequency of Klüver Bucy symptoms in presenile Alzheimer's disease (p. 379) is similarly found in SDAT when random groups are carefully investigated.

Arteriosclerotic Dementia
('Multi-infarct dementia'; 'Vascular dementia'; 'Arteriopathic dementia')

The dementias which rest on a vascular basis are considered here rather than in the chapter on cerebrovascular disorders since they enter into the differential diagnosis of other dementing illnesses. Both in the senile and presenile age ranges they appear to be second only to Alzheimer's disease as a cause of progressive intellectual impairment. It is probable, however, that there is a considerable tendency to overdiagnose this category during life. Corsellis (1969b) points out that in the middle-aged adult the clinical diagnosis is encountered much more often than is justified by the eventual pathological findings. And in the aged patient with SDAT the diagnosis may also be made erroneously, since the relatively common minor infarctions of later life will readily produce clinical evidence of focal disorder when the reserves of the brain are reduced.

The presence of arteriosclerosis in the peripheral or retinal vessels cannot be taken as a firm guide towards the diagnosis. Peripheral changes are common with advancing age and will frequently be found when the dementia has some other basis; conversely, after middle age, cerebral arterial pathology cannot be excluded even when there is no evidence of arteriosclerosis elsewhere. Hypertension is perhaps a more reliable guide but can similarly be misleading. Corsellis (1969b) reported that it was most unusual for autopsy to reveal a vascular basis for dementia in the absence of marked hypertension (over 210/110 mm/Hg). In St. Clair and Whalley's (1983) survey of autopsy-proven cases the blood pressure had been significantly higher in those with multi-infarct dementia (mean 173/98) than in those with Alzheimer's disease (mean 137/85).

A major difficulty in clarifying the pictures to be expected lies with the pleomorphic forms which the vascular dementias may take. One large and prominent group rests on major infarctions of cerebral tissue, sometimes few in number but strategically placed to disrupt key cortical systems. Alternatively there may be numerous scattered softenings, individually small in effect but combining together to produce an additive result. In the latter category the accent of pathology may be cortical, subcortical or both. When the subcortical 'lacunar state' is responsible for the dementia this may be expected to have distinctive associated features (p. 387). Rarer subvarieties include dementias which probably owe much to diffuse white matter demyelination ('subcortical arteriosclerotic encephalopathy') as discussed on (p. 390).

Aetiology

The ultimate cause will usually lie with the causes of atheromatous disease and hypertension generally, for which text books of medicine should be consulted. Hachinski *et al.* (1974) stressed that the evolution of the dementia depends not on progressive chronic ischaemia, i.e. a relentless strangulation of the brain's blood supply, but essentially on the accumulation of deficits from infarcts large and small. Hence they preferred the term 'multi-infarct dementia' to 'arteriosclerotic dementia', in order to underline such a pathogenic mechanism. They concluded, moreover, that the majority of infarcts were due to thromboembolism from the extracranial arteries and the heart, and that only in a small minority of cases could atherosclerosis of the cerebral arteries be primarily blamed for the cerebral softenings. In Tomlinson *et al.*'s (1970) autopsy-proven cases ischaemic cortical lesions involving the territories of the middle and posterior cerebral arteries appeared to be particularly significant.

Others, however, have laid emphasis on the role of hypertensive small vessel disease in leading to dementia. Hypertension is associated with fibrinoid necrosis and microaneurysm formation along the walls of small arteries and arterioles, leading on to local occlusions and perianeurysmal haemorrhages. It affects particularly the long perforating arteries to the deep white matter and subcortical nuclear masses, resulting in numerous 'lacunar' infarcts in the central brain substance. The relative incidence of these two main forms of pathogenesis remains debatable, as discussed in Liston and La Rue's (1983) careful review. Not uncommonly both forms of pathology will be found together, since hypertension itself predisposes to widespread atherosclerosis.

Other associated disease processes may contribute to the arterial pathology in certain cases, diabetes mellitus being prominent among them. Collagen vascular disorders, leukaemia or polycythaemia may occasionally play a part. Cardiac conditions predisposing to embolisation include rheumatic valvular disease and atrial fibrillation; carotid stenosis or occlusion is another important source.

Clinical Features

Arteriosclerotic dementia is found with almost equal frequency in males and females, with perhaps a slight excess in males. It usually begins during the late 60s and 70s, though well-confirmed examples are occasionally seen in patients in their 40s.

Arteriosclerosis will often be obvious in the peripheral and retinal vessels and hypertension will usually be severe, but these alone do not provide firm guidelines to the diagnosis. Attempts have been made to define the characteristics of the dementing process itself which will enable it to be distinguished from other forms of senile and presenile dementia, notably by Rothschild (1941) and Birkett (1972) after obtaining pathological confirmation at autopsy. Their findings are incorporated in the description below, but in fact the clinical distinctions remain far from well established.

The onset is frequently more acute than in Alzheimer's disease, and a substantial number of cases only come to medical attention after a frank cerebrovascular accident has occurred. When the onset is gradual, emotional or personality changes may antedate definite evidence of memory and intellectual impairment. Other common early features include somatic symptoms such as headache, dizziness, tinnitus and syncope which may be the main complaints for some considerable time.

Once established the cognitive impairments characteristically fluctuate in severity, varying from day to day and sometimes even from hour to hour. In large measure this may be due to episodes of clouding of consciousness which are a feature from the early stages. Clouding is common towards nightfall and may lead to florid nocturnal delirium. Birkett (1972) confirmed that fluctuations tended to distinguish arteriosclerotic dementia from SDAT, but even so two of his patients who showed striking fluctuations proved ultimately to have the latter disease.

Apoplectiform features punctuate the progress of the disorder and are due to episodes of cerebral infarction. Commonly they consist of abrupt episodes of hemiparesis, sensory change, dysphasia or visual disturbances. At first they are transient and followed by gradual restitution of function, but later each leaves more permanent neurological deficits in its wake. Each episode is usually followed by an abrupt increase in the severity of the dementia. Lacunar infarcts may lead to a variety of neurological defects including ataxia, dysarthria and motor and sensory disturbances, culminating in the picture of pseudobulbar palsy (dysarthria, dysphagia, and emotional incontinence) together with bradykinesia and marche à petit pas. Very occasionally, however, lacunes may be associated with gradual mental deterioration without conspicuous focal signs (p. 327).

Other features which suggest arteriosclerotic dementia include the patchy nature of the psychological deficits which result. Thus the basic personality may be well preserved until late in the disease, whereas in other dementing illnesses this is undermined from an early stage. Capacity for judgement may persist for a surprisingly long time, and a remarkable degree of insight is sometimes maintained. As a result the patient often reacts to awareness of his decline by severe anxiety and depression which are seldom prominent in Alzheimer's disease (Rothschild, 1941).

Other emotional changes include lability, no doubt due to lesions in the basal parts of the brain, and a tendency towards explosive emotional outbursts. Episodes of noisy weeping or laughing may occur on minor provocation, often without accompanying subjective distress or elation.

Birkett (1972) found that neurological abnormalities predicted arteriosclerosis more accurately than any mental feature. Even in the absence of gross defects, such as dysphasia or hemiparesis, there will often be minor focal signs. The tendon reflexes are often unequal, the plantars extensor or the pupil reactions impaired. Parkinsonian features may be conspicuous, likewise evidence of pseudobulbar palsy as described above. Epileptic seizures are found in about 20% of cases, and attacks of syncope are common.

The electroencephalogram shows a picture similar to that of Alzheimer's disease (p. 379), but the changes tend to be more severe. Advanced examples can, however, sometimes show normal records. A distinctive feature may be the appearance of focal abnormalities in the region of local cerebral thromboses—a low amplitude delta focus may emerge if the infarction is sufficiently extensive and some asymmetry may persist for several weeks thereafter. Frontal delta activity may appear when there are episodes of delirium. Nevin (1967) suggests that the EEG can be helpful in distinguishing arteriosclerotic dementia from Alzheimer's disease; in the former alpha activity tends to be longer retained, and slow activity is more variable and asymmetrical. Paroxysmal activity is also more often seen. Harrison et al. (1979) found that the EEG more often showed focal or lateralising abnormalities in patients diagnosed as multi-infarct dementia than in equivalently impaired patients with Alzheimer's disease.

The CT scan will usually show evidence of cerebral atrophy, sometimes marked in degree. Areas of low attenuation, consistent with old and recent infarctions, may be revealed. Multiple small lacunar infarcts will often escape direct detection, but loss of central brain substance shows as ventricular dilatation. Radue et al. (1978) found that in general the CT scan was unreliable in differentiating multi-infarct dementia from Alzheimer's disease, though patients with the former were more likely to show low attenuation areas, unequal Sylvian fissures, and focal enlargements of the ventricles. Altogether the scan findings were equivocal in 80 per cent of patients, though useful in predicting the type of dementia in the remainder. Angiography can sometimes give added evidence by demonstrating irregularities of the walls of major cerebral vessels and ischaemic areas within the brain parenchyma (Harrison *et al.*, 1979), though again such findings are far from reliable.

The cerebrospinal fluid shows an elevated protein in perhaps a quarter of cases, especially when there has been a recent episode of cerebral infarction or in the presence of uraemia or congestive cardiac failure.

Course and Outcome

Perhaps the most reliable distinguishing characteristic of arteriosclerotic dementia is the course which it pursues. This is rarely smoothly progressive as in Alzheimer's disease, but punctuated by abrupt step-like progressions. Acute exacerbations are sometimes followed by improvement for a time, and in the early stages at least periods of remission may last for months at a time. These features depend on the pathogenesis of the disorder in terms of repeated cerebral infarctions.

The time to death varies widely. Sometimes the course is brief and stormy, but in general progress is slower than in Alzheimer's disease. The average duration after diagnosis is perhaps some 5 to 7 years, though many cases survive much longer. Among patients admitted to psychiatric hospitals Roth (1955) was able to demonstrate an improved survival compared to SDAT after 6 months, though by 2 years the differences were diminished and 70% of the arteriosclerotic patients were dead. Shah *et al.* (1969) confirmed improved survival among arteriosclerotic dementias where females were concerned, with 65% of hospitalised females surviving at 2 years (compared to 32% of females with SDAT). Death is attributable to ischaemic heart disease in approximately 50% of patients, others dying of cerebral thrombosis or renal complications.

Pathology of Arteriosclerotic Dementia

The brain may show localised or generalised atrophy, with thickened adherent meninges and sometimes with evidence of subdural haemorrhage. The ventricles are dilated, and cyst formation may be evident to the naked eye. Scattered infarctions are seen with areas of softening and scarring. Sometimes occlusion of a major vessel will have affected a large part of a hemisphere.

The detailed picture is summarised by Corsellis (1969b). Vessels of all sizes are usually implicated in the arteriosclerotic process. The main arteries at the base of the brain are thickened, tortuous and rigid, often with yellowish patches and nodular expansions of the wall. Their lumina are greatly reduced or even obliterated by intimal thickening and subintimal plaques of atheromatous material. Small vessels within the substance of the brain show greatly thickened walls with a fibrosed or 'onion skin' appearance. Frequently the walls are necrotic and disintegrated. Perivascular rarefaction may produce a sieve-like appearance, particularly in the striatum and thalamus.

Microscopy shows the effects of both ischaemia and infarction. Loss and chromatolysis of nerve cells is extensive, sometimes occurring in streaks or patches within the cortex. Irregular patches of demyelination may be seen in the white matter. Small scattered infarcts are revealed, with cyst formation and reactive gliosis. Small cystic softenings are particularly common in the pons, and micro-infarcts in the hippocampi. In the 'lacunar state' multiple cavities with irregular contours are found in the central brain regions, particularly in the basal ganglia, internal capsules and thalamus. Larger areas of infarcted brain tissue show necrotic degeneration with masses of granular phagocytes, or at a later stage sclerosis with dense glial and fibrocytic infiltration and distortion of brain substance.

Arteriosclerotic changes are likely to be seen elsewhere in the body, especially in the heart and kidneys, and the heart is commonly enlarged at post-mortem. Quite often one or more of the main arteries supplying the brain is found to be stenosed and atherosclerotic, either the carotids in the neck or the vertebrals within the bony channels of the skull.

Distinction Between Arteriosclerotic Dementia and Alzheimer's Disease

The distinction between arteriosclerotic dementia and Alzheimer's disease can be unclear during life, particularly in the elderly, and has also been debated in terms of neuropathology. It has been suggested that vascular and parenchymatous changes occur so commonly together with advancing age that a valid distinction is hard to maintain. The situation has again been clarified by the investigations of Corsellis and Tomlinson as described on p. 376.

Corsellis (1962) concluded that in the majority of elderly patients the parenchymatous and arteriosclerotic forms of dementia could be broadly distinguished from each other in terms of the neuropathological findings. When the severity of each type of pathological process was examined in his material, overlap was found in only 20% of the brains examined. The Newcastle studies reported by Tomlinson *et al.* (1970) and Roth (1971) support this conclusion. First of all, within the group of subjects diagnosed on clinical grounds as having arteriosclerotic dementia, it was possible to show a quantitative relationship between the dementia score during life and the extent of cerebral softening measured at autopsy. A marked threshold effect was seen, 50 ml of softening differentiating to a high degree between arteriosclerotic dements and non-dements. This measure allowed an assessment to be made of the contribution which vascular changes might make to the cerebral disorder in SDAT. In fact a high level of discrimination was found—94% of patients diagnosed as parenchymatous dementia had less than a total of 50 ml of softening, whereas 73% of patients diagnosed as arteriosclerotic dementia had more than 50 ml of softening. There was, of course, some degree of overlap, as might be expected from two such relatively common degenerative processes of old age. Thus cases diagnosed clinically as having vascular dementia, but proving at autopsy to have less than 50 ml of softening, frequently also showed plaque formation to a substantial degree. There was also evidence that the two types of pathological change, when appearing together, could augment each other to a significant extent in the production of dementia. In Tomlinson *et al.*'s (1970) material the principal softenings in patients with vascular dementia were cortical in location; lacunar infarcts could often be present as well but these were also frequent in elderly patients without dementia.

The other evidence supporting a distinction between arteriosclerotic dementia and Alzheimer's disease may be summarised as follows:

There is evidence of a genetic contribution to SDAT, yet no excess of arteriosclerotic dementia among the relatives of probands studied (Larsson *et al.*, 1963); females are affected in excess of males in SDAT but not in arteriosclerotic dementia, though this may represent no more than the greater tendency to longevity in females; the length of survival after hospitalisation is rather longer in arteriosclerotic dementia than SDAT, and whereas the cause of death in the former is frequently ischaemic heart disease or definable arteriosclerosis in other organs, the precise cause is often uncertain in SDAT.

Distinguishing clinical features may be summarised thus: a relatively sudden onset favours arteriosclerotic dementia; the step-like course is characteristic, and is seen from an early stage in conjunction with episodes of cerebral infarction which leave transient or permanent neurological deficits. In Alzheimer's disease, by contrast, the course is smoother and more gradual. Acute episodes of clouding of consciousness or delirium are much commoner in arteriosclerotic dementia. Psychological deficits tend to be patchy, with for example good preservation of insight and personality, whereas the disintegration in Alzheimer's disease is global. There is greater mood lability with arteriosclerotic dementia, and a greater tendency towards conspicuous depression and anxiety. Hypertension and fits are much commoner in arteriosclerotic dementia than Alzheimer's disease, and somatic complaints such as headache and dizziness feature more often in the history. On neurological examination both gross and subtle evidence of focal cerebral disorder is common, likewise evidence of arteriosclerosis elsewhere in the body.

The 'ischaemic index' drawn up by Hachinski *et al.* (1975) has been widely employed as a guide to distinguishing between arteriosclerotic dementia and Alzheimer's disease. Features in the clinical history and on examination are given a weighted score as follows: abrupt onset (2), step-wise deterioration (1), fluctuating course (2), nocturnal confusion (1), relative preservation of personality (1), depression (1), somatic complaints (1), emotional incontinence (1), history of hypertension (1), history of strokes (2), evidence of associated atherosclerosis (1), focal neurological symptoms (2), and focal neurological signs (2). Patients scoring 7 or above are classified as arteriosclerotic dementia and those scoring 4 or below as parenchymatous dementia. The separation of patients on such a basis can be valuable in refining groups for research purposes, and when used with caution can give some guidance to diagnosis in the individual case. The index was drawn up, however, on relatively young and mildly affected patients; a very considerable degree of overlap may be expected in the elderly and when the dementia is more advanced.

Radue *et al.* (1978) and Harrison *et al.* (1979) have shown certain broad differences in EEG, angiographic and CT scan findings when patients are separated on the basis of the Hachinski index (pp. 387–8), though cerebral blood flow studies have given conflicting results. Hachinski *et al*.'s (1975) own study, using the intracarotid xenon method, showed significant reductions in overall blood flow among patients scoring in the multi-infarct dementia range, and this was confirmed by Harrison *et al*. (1979). Frackowiak *et al*. (1981), however, found no difference in cerebral blood flow or oxygen utilisation using positron emission tomography when patients were separated in this manner. Unfortunately there has not yet been a comprehensive attempt at validation of the index on autopsy-proven material. Rosen *et al*. (1980) and Gustafson and Nilsson (1982) have attempted such an exercise on very small groups of patients, demonstrating reasonable predictive accuracy but also revealing considerable room for further refinement of the items to be included. Rosen *et al*. (1980), for example, found no value attaching to depression, fluctuating course, nocturnal confusion or the presence of atherosclerosis elsewhere; prediction was improved when such items were excluded.

SUBCORTICAL ARTERIOSCLEROTIC ENCEPHALOPATHY

('Chronic subcortical leucoencephalopathy'; 'Binswanger's disease')

This rare variant of arteriosclerotic dementia was first described by Binswanger (1894) under the title 'encephalitis subcorticalis chronica progressiva'. It has recently come into greater prominence as a result of certain distinctive findings on the CT scan, and the realisation that diffuse white matter damage is probably commoner than previously suspected in patients with dementia. The cognitive failure in such patients seems to be attributable to the pronounced white matter changes since the cerebral cortex is often little if at all affected.

Olszewski (1962) suggested the name now commonly in use for the condition in his review of the earlier literature. It appears to derive from pathological changes affecting the long perforating vessels to the deep white matter and subcortical nuclear masses, resulting in multiple small areas of infarction ('lacunes') together with diffuse demyelination of the white matter. The arcuate fibres beneath the sulci are by contrast spared, and the cortex itself is substantially intact. The white matter changes are usually extensive, demyelination being associated with pronounced fibrillary gliosis. Possible patho-

genic mechanisms include diffuse ischaemia consequent on subacute hypertensive encephalopathy (Caplan and Schoene, 1978), or chronic hypoperfusion in the watershed area between the territories of the cortical medullary arteries and the long perforating branches to the white matter (Loizou *et al*., 1981).

Clinical features stressed from the outset were of a slowly evolving dementia associated with focal neurological deficits, usually in hypertensive patients in their 50s or 60s. Caplan and Schoene (1978) clarified the picture from a description of autopsy-proven cases. They noted persistent hypertension, a history of acute strokes, a lengthy course, and dementia accompanied by prominent motor signs and usually by pseudobulbar palsy. The distinctive clinical manifestation, however, was the *subacute* progression of focal neurological deficits. Such deficits commonly developed in a gradual fashion over some weeks or months, the picture then stabilising with long plateau periods lasting for months or occasionally years. This feature appeared to separate the Binswanger patients from those whose dementia rested on large vessel occlusions or on a lacunar state without accompanying white matter demyelination. The dementia varied considerably in its manifestations—some patients showed a phase of ebullience and lack of inhibition, others progressive loss of spontaneity. Memory disorder was not invariably prominent as in senile dementia of the Alzheimer type.

The interest has been to relate this apparently rare condition to the intriguing observation of diffuse white matter translucency on the CT scan in certain dementing patients. Previously the diagnosis had necessarily been based on autopsy findings alone. Valentine *et al*. (1980) reported white matter translucency in approximately 2 per cent of routine scans on patients with cerebral atrophy, most of those affected being hypertensive and two-thirds having evidence of dementia. The white matter low attenuation was bilateral and usually symmetrical, always affecting the regions around the frontal horns and usually spreading backwards to involve parietal and central regions as well. The cerebral atrophy in such patients tended to be relatively mild. Zeumer *et al*. (1980) found similar CT scan changes in 15 patients, all with progressive dementia and histories of transient, usually recurrent neurological deficits. All but one were hypertensive and two showed pseudobulbar palsy. Micro-infarcts were visible in the basal ganglia in 5 of the patients. One came to autopsy and showed the histological features of Binswanger's disease. It seems likely, therefore, that at least a proportion of patients with this unusual scan appearance are suffering from the disorder under consideration.

Loizou *et al.* (1981) have attempted to identify patients with the syndrome using a combination of Caplan and Schoene's (1978) clinical features and the above CT scan appearances. Fifteen patients were found, showing the following characteristics:

The onset was between 50 and 70, with a slight male preponderance and durations varying from 1 to 12 years. Twelve of the 15 patients were hypertensive. Eight had presented with neurological features (acute or resolving strokes, ataxia or apraxia) and were found to be demented, and 7 had presented with dementia (all with neurological deficits). The dementia commonly showed an insidious loss of memory, slowly evolving to global intellectual impairment with prominent affective changes. It was often less incapacitating than motor symptoms such as gait disturbance, dysarthria, or the full picture of pseudobulbar palsy. The neurological deficits could arise in an acute or subacute fashion, and stepwise deterioration in motor and mental functions was often observed.

White matter low attenuation was present on all CT scans and could sometimes be observed to progress over 6–18 months despite hypotensive treatment. In addition, 9 patients showed subcortical lacunar infarcts in the internal capsule and basal ganglia, and 3 showed infarcts in the cortex. Ventricular dilatation was common, but the cortical sulci were normal in 6 and only mildly to moderately enlarged in the remainder.

In discussing differential diagnosis Loizou *et al.* point out that the clinical picture is very similar to that of pseudobulbar palsy resulting from the subcortical lacunar state (p. 327). The CT scan appearances appear to be distinctive, but it remains possible that the two conditions may merely represent different stages in the natural history of subcortical arteriosclerosis. Patients with multi-infarct dementia due to extracranial thromboembolism may also present with a not dissimilar picture; 5 of Loizou *et al.*'s patients had initially been diagnosed as such, then reclassified in view of the subacute evolution of the neurological deficits and the CT scan appearances. The slow and insidious development of the dementia may cause confusion for a time with Alzheimer's disease, and it is noteworthy that this had been the ante-mortem diagnosis in 2 out of 7 of Janota's (1981) autopsy-proven cases.

Pick's Disease

Pick's disease is a great deal less common than Alzheimer's disease, though it was first described earlier in 1892. It is now established as a separate disease entity, with a distinct hereditary pattern and neuropathological picture. The relative incidence of Pick's and Alzheimer's diseases has varied considerably in different reports, from 1 in 3 in Minnesota, to 1 in 5 in Sweden, 1 in 7 in Scotland and 1 in 50 in New York (Glen and Christie, 1979). Interesting geographical differences between the two disorders have been described in Sweden, with most cases of Pick's disease coming from the region of Stockholm and most Alzheimer's from near Gothenburg (Sjögren *et al.*, 1952).

There have been few clues towards causation apart from the evidence of strong genetic allegiances in certain families. Sjögren *et al.* (1952) suggested determination by a single autosomal dominant gene, possibly along with other genes which modify its manifestations. Most cases, however, appear to arise sporadically. In a family study of 11 autopsy-proven cases Heston (1978) found evidence of dominant inheritance in one family but not in any other. Groen and Endtz (1982) have been able to report 25 patients, 14 with proof at autopsy, in a single large family followed over six generations.

With regard to the pathophysiology of the disorder Constantinidis *et al.* (1977) found increased concentrations of zinc in the brain and red blood corpuscles in several cases, together with increased excretion of zinc in the urine. Biochemical studies have failed to show the cholinergic brain deficits typical of Alzheimer's disease (*viz* loss of choline acetyltransferase and acetylcholinesterase), though muscarinic cholinergic binding sites may be reduced (Yates *et al.*, 1980b).

Clinical Features

Women are affected almost twice as frequently as men. The onset tends to be rather later than in presenile Alzheimer's disease, with a peak between 50 and 60, though cases have been reported at all ages from the 20s onwards. The course of the illness is also said to be somewhat slower, though accurate data on a large number of cases are unavailable.

The most distinctive clinical feature is a tendency to begin with changes indicative of frontal lobe damage. Thus the early abnormalities often concern changes of character and social behaviour rather than impairment of memory and intellect. Drive becomes diminished and episodes of tactless or grossly insensitive behaviour may occur. Lack of restraint may lead to stealing, alcoholism, sexual misadventures or other ill-judged social conduct. From an early stage the expression becomes fatuous and vacant, manners deteriorate and indolence may become extreme. A tendency to indulge in foolish jokes and pranks has often been noted. Insight is impaired early and to a severe degree.

With progress of the disease, impairment of intellect and memory become obvious and slowly increase in severity. The predominant mood often remains as a fatuous euphoria, or apathy may be interspersed with brief periods of restless over-activity. Delusions or hallucinations are relatively rare and epileptic fits uncommon.

Speech becomes markedly perseverative, and a prominent reduction in vocabulary with stereotyped repetition of brief words or phrases is said to be characteristic. Dysphasic disturbances may progress to jargon, and periods of mutism may occur. Apraxia and agnosia sometimes appear, but less commonly than in presenile Alzheimer's disease. Gait and muscle tone are also less frequently affected, but occasional cases show marked parkinsonian features in association with an accent of the pathological changes on the basal ganglia. Robertson et al. (1958) have reported transient attacks of hyperalgesia similar to that of the 'thalamic syndrome', but how far this is characteristic of Pick's disease is uncertain. Cummings and Duchen (1981) have stressed the early appearance of features of the Klüver Bucy syndrome—oral tendencies, overeating with weight gain, and tendencies to touch and seize objects within the field of vision—contrasting this with its late appearance in Alzheimer's disease (p. 379). In the late stages the general disintegration of intellect and personality is indistinguishable from that of other advanced dementing processes.

The electroencephalogram shows a considerably lower incidence of abnormalities than in Alzheimer's disease (Swain, 1959; Gordon and Sim, 1967; Johannesson et al., 1979). The record may be entirely normal, or when abnormalities are found they are often mild in degree. The general picture is similar in form to that of Alzheimer's disease (p. 379) but the reported changes do not conform to any consistent pattern. Contrary to expectation there is usually little discernible accent on the frontal or temporal regions.

The CT scan appearance may sometimes be sufficiently characteristic to suggest the diagnosis (McGeachie et al., 1979). In typical cases marked atrophy affects the anterior portions of the frontal and temporal lobes, with considerable enlargement of the frontal horns; by contrast, the bodies of the lateral ventricles and the sulci over the parietal and occipital lobes are much less affected. The scan may, however, resemble that seen in Huntington's chorea, especially when caudate atrophy is marked. Groen and Endtz (1982) have made the interesting observation of frontal atrophy in 4 out of 12 offspring in a large family affected by hereditary Pick's disease, 1 of the 4 developing clinical evidence of the disorder a year later.

Pathology of Pick's Disease

In classical cases the gross appearance of the brain is characteristic. Some degree of generalised atrophy is combined with striking circumscribed shrinkage of certain lobes, most commonly the frontal and temporal. In the frontal lobes the convexity or the orbital surface may be affected alone, and in the temporal lobe the posterior half of the superior temporal gyrus may stand out as relatively spared. The distribution of atrophy varies considerably from case to case, but major involvement of the parietal lobes is unusual and occipital atrophy extremely rare. The gyri are roughened and brownish, often with a characteristic 'knife-blade' appearance.

The ventricles are dilated, often with great enlargement of the horn of the lateral ventricle beneath the site of maximal cortical atrophy. The basal ganglia and thalamus also show atrophy, sometimes pronounced in the caudate nucleus, but the cerebellum is usually spared.

Microscopy shows neuronal loss, accompanied by dense astrocytic proliferation and fibrous gliosis in the cortex and underlying white matter, hence the older term of 'lobar sclerosis'. The neuronal loss is chiefly in the outer layers of the cortex in affected areas, and a striking feature may be the presence of normal neurones quite near to severely degenerated cells. Characteristic 'balloon cells' may be seen but are not a constant feature—the affected neurones are swollen and oval in shape, with loss of Nissl substance and irregularly shaped argentophilic inclusions ('Pick bodies') which displace the nucleus towards the periphery. Eosinophilic inclusions ('Hirano bodies') may also be seen, also granulo-vacuolar changes.

In the majority of cases senile plaques and neuro-fibrillary tangles are conspicuous by their absence. Vascular changes are not characteristic. The middle cortical layers may have a spongy appearance similar to that in Creutzfeldt–Jakob disease. Loss of myelin in the white matter of affected lobes is usually considerable.

A variant of the typical picture has been described as 'Pick's Disease Type II' or 'Progressive Subcortical Gliosis' (Neumann and Cohn, 1967). Histological examination shows pronounced and severe gliosis in the subcortical white matter, while that within the cortex itself is less marked than in the classical disease. Glial proliferation is also marked in the subcortical nuclear masses, the brain stem and the ventral columns of the cord. Loss of cortical neurones is not a prominent feature, and those which are affected are shrunken rather than swollen.

Constantinidis et al. (1974) have suggested a division based on the presence or absence of argyrophilic inclusions and neuronal swellings. Patients with both features had predominant atrophy of the temporal lobes, those with swellings but no inclusions had atrophy mainly affecting the frontal lobes, whereas those with neither feature could have atrophy in either location. The last group corresponded to the Type II cases of Neumann and Cohn.

The usefulness of noting these variants lies in the clues they may provide to aetiology. In Type II Pick's disease the primary change would appear to be the overwhelming proliferation of astrocytes in the subcortex and elsewhere, with only secondary embarrassment of neuronal function.

Distinction Between Pick's Disease and Alzheimer's Disease

In addition to the distinctions which can be drawn on genetic and pathological grounds, certain differences in the clinical picture have traditionally been emphasised. In most cases, however, the true diagnosis is revealed only at autopsy.

In Pick's disease changes of character and disposition are often noted from the onset, whereas memory disturbance is almost invariably the presenting feature in Alzheimer's disease. Incontinence occurring early in the course of the dementia has also been regarded as indicative of Pick's disease, and may similarly be due to the accent of pathology on the frontal lobes.

Parietal lobe symptomatology in the form of dysphasia, apraxia and agnosia is said to be much less common in Pick's than Alzheimer's disease, likewise disturbances of gait and other extrapyramidal features. Aspects of the Klüver Bucy syndrome may be detected early in Pick's disease but are in general a late development in Alzheimer patients (Cummings and Duchen, 1981).

The facile hilarity and aspontaneity of Pick's disease has been contrasted with the depressed anxious mood and overactivity of Alzheimer's disease (Stengel, 1943b), though Sjögren et al. (1952) have emphasised aspontaneity in the latter condition also.

The preservation of a normal electroencephalogram, even in the presence of moderately advanced dementia, will suggest Pick's disease, likewise atrophy restricted to the anterior half of the brain as revealed by CT scanning. Intermediate pictures will, however, quite often be encountered.

It appears, therefore, to be chiefly in the mode of onset of the disorder and in the neurological concomitants that a clinical differentiation is to be sought. The differentiation is more easily made in the earlier than the later stages, since ultimately any differences become submerged.

Huntington's Chorea

This disease, though rare, has attracted a great deal of interest and attention. Choreiform movements are combined with the dementia, serving as a clinical marker which has allowed its genetic background to be studied with care. Since Huntington's original account in 1872 cases have been reported from all over the world and no race appears to be immune. The responsible mutation has clearly arisen repeatedly.

Prevalence varies markedly from one investigation to another. Very high figures have been reported from Tasmania, while in parts of Japan the disease appears to be extremely rare. Myrianthopoulos (1966) considers that 4 to 7 cases per 100,000 of the population is a reasonable overall estimate. In the United Kingdom, surveys have indicated 5.2 cases per 100,000 for the West of Scotland (Bolt, 1970), and 6.3 per 100,000 in Northamptonshire where detailed pedigrees have been kept for many years (Oliver, 1970). An astonishingly dense focus is known to have existed for a long time in the Moray Firth area of Scotland, with the equivalent of 560 cases per 100,000 in a small fishing community on the east coast of Ross-shire (Lyon, 1962).

Aetiology

The disease is associated with a single autosomal dominant gene with virtually 100% rate of manifestation. Approximately half of the offspring of an affected person can therefore be expected to develop the disorder, with equal incidence in males and females. It is only very rarely known to have skipped a generation. Cases in Massachusetts and Connecticut have been traced back to emigrants from England, principally to three men and their wives who left from Bures in Suffolk in 1630 and thereafter produced eleven generations of choreics (Vessie, 1932).

Nevertheless, a family history is not always forthcoming, even among classical examples. In Heathfield's (1967) North London survey a family history was lacking in one-fifth of cases. This may be the result of several factors—the early death of a parent, illegitimacy, lack of an adequate history, or concealed and circumscribed knowledge within the immediate family circle. The spontaneous appearance of new mutations from time to time is also very probable.

Genetic counselling is the only method at present available for curtailing the disease and is indicated on humanitarian and economic grounds. In Barette and Marsden's (1979) survey most relatives stated that they preferred to know the painful facts as soon as possible, and the majority were then prepared to restrict their families or have no children whatever. Only 7% said that they would have preferred to remain in ignorance. Unfortunately, however, the major part of reproductive life is often over when the disease comes to medical attention, and there are some indications that fertility may be increased among affected as compared to unaffected sibs. As the patient deteriorates he is less likely to use contraception and hypersexuality is said sometimes to occur. This, added to the social disorganisation often encountered in Huntington's families, can make effective prevention a most difficult task. In Bolt's (1970) survey, for example, 15 children were found to have been produced by 3 of the patients since the onset of their disease. Despite such difficulties a fall in the number of births at risk has been documented in a South Wales population followed prospectively, and this may have owed a good deal to regular support and counselling (Harper et al., 1981).

There are as yet no acceptable guidelines for the identification of carriers of the gene, and the probability of 1 in 2 is usually the most that can be offered when relatives seek advice. This probability is of course reduced proportionately according to the length of time an individual has outlived a part of the danger period. The question of genetic counselling, and the procedures and logic to be applied to it, are usefully discussed by Slater and Cowie (1971) and Baraitser (1981). Therapeutic abortion is generally considered to be indicated when requested by the offspring or siblings of an affected person.

Attempts at Carrier Identification

Many lines have been pursued in the attempt to identify carriers of the gene before the disease becomes manifest, but so far with little definite result. Thomas (1982) discusses the difficult ethical issues involved should such a test become available. Without it, non-carriers of the gene can have a lifetime of distress and anxiety falsely engendered by counselling; yet with a predictive test the non-carrier's peace of mind would be at the expense of the carrier's certainty that they stand to develop or transmit the disease. Surveys, nevertheless, have shown how widely a *reliable* predictive test would be welcomed among the relatives of patients (Stern and Eldridge 1975; Barette and Marsden, 1979).

A close resemblance in appearance and personality between carriers and the affected parent has been claimed but is not well substantiated. It has also been suggested that the premorbid personality of gene carriers tends to be more abnormal than that of unaffected sibs, but the evidence is certainly not clear enough to lead to usable conclusions. Disordered behaviour and severe disturbance of personality may long antedate the onset of the disease in affected individuals, but appear to be common in unaffected siblings also (p. 399).

Psychometric testing has shown some predictive value, notably in surveys carried out by Lyle and Quast (1976) and Lyle and Gottesman (1977). A large group of persons at risk, and who had been tested extensively in their early 30s, were followed up 15–20 years later. Results of the Wechsler Intelligence Test, the Shipley-Hartford Retreat Scale and the Bender Visual-Motor Gestalt Test showed significant differences between those who later developed Huntington's chorea and those who did not, the choreics' performance being inferior on each of the tests. It appears, therefore, that the effects of the gene may be detectable on group comparisons many years before the disease is overt. The reliability with which prediction can be made is nonetheless too low to be of use in individual cases.

Electroencephalographic changes were at one time thought to hold promise. Abnormalities have been reported in unaffected relatives, sometimes in three-quarters of those examined (Patterson et al., 1948), but these consist of a great variety of changes and have not proved useful in the prediction of the disorder (Chandler, 1966). Other approaches reviewed by Myrianthopoulos (1966) include blood grouping, finger printing and analysis of tremor recording, but all so far without result.

A recent approach has involved giving levodopa to persons suspected of harbouring the gene, on the grounds that Huntington's chorea might be due to an abnormal response of the caudate nucleus neurones to dopamine (*British Medical Journal*, 1972). Stimulation with levodopa might therefore be expected to elicit chorea in asymptomatic individuals who are later to develop the disease. Klawans *et al.* (1973) reported their experience with 30 subjects who were the offspring of families with Huntington's chorea, tested along with normal controls. After giving levodopa for periods of up to 10 weeks, a third of those genetically at risk developed clear-cut facial chorea and/or limb dyskinesia, whereas no controls were affected. The movements disappeared rapidly when levodopa was discontinued. Follow-up 8 years later showed that 5 of the 10 positive reactors had later developed Huntington's chorea, whereas only 1 of the 20 non-reactors did so (Klawans *et al.*, 1980). The possibility of even one false negative is, however, disturbing and further follow-up has now revealed two more (Myers *et al.*, 1982). This, together with the continuing possibility of false positive results has led to the test being abandoned.

New promise attaches to the development of polymorphic DNA markers which, in the presence of adequate information on other affected and unaffected family members, may allow prediction of persons at risk. The Huntington's disease gene has already been confined to chromosome 4 and one closely linked DNA probe identified. This important recent development is described by Gusella *et al.* (1983) and Harper (1986).

Biochemical Studies

Biochemical enquiries would be expected to be a fruitful approach, both for the detection of carriers and for exploring possible metabolic aberrations in the established disease. The clear genetic determination immediately suggests an inborn error of metabolism, perhaps derived from abnormality in a specific enzyme process controlled by a gene. Extensive searches have sometimes uncovered isolated abnormalities, but until recently most biochemical studies have proved disappointing:

Earlier findings are reviewed by Myrianthopoulos (1966) and Slater and Cowie (1971). Calcium, magnesium and trace elements such as copper have been investigated, the latter by analogy with Wilson's disease, but the total evidence remains contradictory. Phospholipids, glycolipids, neutral lipids and acid mucopolysaccharides have been found to be normal in the blood, whereas alterations in brain lipids are almost certainly secondary to the neuropathological changes. Urinary aminoacids have shown no consistent abnormalities, and Cowie and Seakins' (1962) discovery of raised serum alanine in two sons of an affected woman was unconfirmed in further cases. Perry *et al.* (1969) have found low levels of certain aminoacids in the serum, including tyrosine, and Ottosson and Rapp (1971) showed significant lowering of phenylalanine and tyrosine in patients with the established disease, but such changes may prove to be secondary rather than causative. Immunological studies have shown elevation of various globulin fractions, but so many different fractions are implicated that the changes are likely to be non-specific.

More recent studies on brain material obtained at autopsy have produced more encouraging and interesting findings. Perry *et al.* (1973) found reduced levels of gamma aminobutyric acid (GABA) in the basal ganglia and substantia nigra of 8 brains from patients with Huntington's chorea, when compared to brains from neurologically normal persons. GABA is a possible inhibitory synaptic transmitter, so its lack could be significant in relation to the movement disorder. Bird *et al.* (1973) and Bird and Iverson (1974) have confirmed the deficiency in 38 patients when compared with controls, and have shown a marked reduction of the enzyme responsible for the synthesis of GABA (glutamic acid decarboxylase, GAD) in the putamen and globus pallidus. Levels were normal in the frontal cortex, thus indicating a selective loss of GABA-containing neurones from the basal ganglia.

Cholinergic neurones have also been found to be severely deficient in the striatum, as reflected in low levels of choline acetyltransferase (CAT) and of cholinergic receptors. The dopaminergic system is, by contrast, spared (Spokes, 1980). Indeed dopamine (and noradrenaline) have proved to be elevated in the striatum and substantia nigra, perhaps as a consequence of the low GABA levels since GABA is known to inhibit release of dopamine in the nigrostriatal system.

A model is therefore proposed whereby the intact nigrostriatal pathway in Huntington's chorea releases approximately normal quantities of dopamine on to a considerably reduced population of striatal neurones, leading to net dopamine overstimulation of those that remain (Spokes, 1980; Marsden, 1982). Dopamine over-activity in the striatum is known to provoke chorea (p. 554). This could therefore be the key neuropharmacological feature of Huntington's chorea, at least where the movement disorder is concerned; and a similar excess of dopamine in the mesolimbic system may underlie the behavioural manifestations and psychoses seen with the disease. Further biochemical changes could, however, prove to be involved. The levels of peptides such as substance P and angiotensin-converting enzyme are also low in the basal ganglia, though the functions of such substances in this location remain at present unknown.

Clinical Features

The onset is usually between the ages of 25 and 50, with an average in the mid forties. Variation is wide, however, and onset has been reported in childhood and in extreme old age. In general the age of onset among sibs tends to be closer than among members of different families, but the correlation is not sufficiently close to be of value in genetic counselling. There is evidence that the disease follows a more severe course when onset is early rather than late, also that emotional disturbance is more prominent as a premonitory feature. There is some suggestion of other changes in manifestation with age of onset, striate rigidity predominating in the early 20s, choreic symptoms in middle age, and intention tremor after 60. Special features of the disease in childhood will be considered below.

Considerable variations may be seen in the relationship between the neurological and psychiatric features. In the typical case involuntary movements precede dementia, though the reverse can also be seen. Occasionally several years may separate the appearance of the two components, or the two may begin and proceed throughout together. Certainly once both are well established each tends to worsen in conformity with the other.

Very occasionally chorea may be the sole manifestation. Dementia without chorea has similarly been recorded, even when chorea was prominent in previous generations of the family. Other variations include the form the neurological abnormalities take, progressive rigidity with parkinsonism replacing the typical choreic movements in up to 10% of cases. All such variations usually appear sporadically; despite some indications in the literature it is not well established that in different families the form of the disease tends to breed true.

The presenting symptoms were almost equally divided between neurological and psychiatric features in Heathfield's (1967) survey. Neurological presentations were usually with choreiform movements, or less often with unsteadiness of gait, a tendency to fall, or general clumsiness. Psychiatric presentations could be with symptoms of incipient dementia, but even more commonly with change of disposition, emotional disturbance and paranoia.

Most observers agree that psychiatric changes are often present for some considerable time before chorea or intellectual impairment develops. A change in personality may be marked, the patient becoming morose and quarrelsome, or slowed, apathetic, and neglectful of home and person. These are well recognised as premonitory symptoms by those who have practical dealings with communities in which the disease is rife (Lyon, 1962). Paranoid developments may be the earliest change, with marked sensitivity and ideas of reference. Sometimes a florid schizophrenic illness may be present for several years before the true diagnosis becomes apparent. Depression and anxiety may be marked from the outset, perhaps appearing abruptly and being ascribed to some stressful event.

The neurological features often go unrecognised at their first appearance. The typical early choreic movements consist of randomly distributed and irregularly timed muscle jerks, brief in duration and unpredictable in their appearance. At first the patient is merely thought to be clumsy or fidgety. Early movements may be no more than the twitching of a finger, or fleeting facial grimaces which pass for mannerisms. The movements usually start in the muscles of the face, hands or shoulders, or are first manifest in subtle changes of gait. Speech is often affected early with slight dysarthria. For some time the patient may conceal the involuntary nature of the movements by exploiting them to perform some habitual activity such as smoothing the hair or the clothes.

With worsening of the disease the pathological nature of the disturbance becomes abundantly obvious. The movements are abrupt, jerky, rapid and repetitive but variable from one muscle group to another. They may be aggravated by voluntary movement but also occur spontaneously. The face shows fleeting changes of expression and constant writhing contortions which give a grotesque appearance. The fingers twitch, the arms develop athetoid twisting movements, and the proximal musculature is affected with shrugging of the shoulders. The gait is sometimes affected by a curious dance-like ataxia which results from the variable choreic influences on the lower limbs—the weight tends to be carried on the heels while the toes are dorsiflexed, and often a foot will remain suspended off the ground for longer than usual. Eventually the patient walks with a wide base, exaggerated lumbar lordosis, wide arm abduction and zigzag progression due to lurching of the trunk. Progress is interrupted by pauses and even backward steps, and accompanied by a great increase in choreiform movements of the upper limbs.

Hemichorea, massively affecting one half of the body, may be seen. Involvement of the diaphragm and bulbar muscles may lead to jerky breathing, explosive or staccato speech, dysphagia, and difficulty in protruding the tongue.

In addition to such involuntary movements extrapyramidal rigidity may be present, or spasticity with pyramidal signs. As mentioned above some cases develop striate rigidity rather than chorea, perhaps especially when the onset is at an early age ("Westphal variant"). This is commonly associated with akinesia, tremor and cogwheel rigidity, and occasionally progresses to torsion dystonia. Fits are more frequent in this variety than in the generality of cases (16% compared to 3%, Myrianthopoulos, 1966).

The dementia is commonly very insidious in development. General inefficiency at work and in the management of daily affairs is usually the presenting feature, rather than obvious memory impairment. A prevailing apathy, setting in early and impeding cognitive functioning has been stressed as characteristic (McHugh and Folstein, 1975). In consequence the patient's performance on everyday tasks is usually more slip-shod than psychological testing would predict during the early stages of the disorder.

Memory impairment can usually be clearly demonstrated when carefully sought out, even in patients examined within a year of onset of the chorea (Butters *et al.*, 1978). But it is rarely conspicuous as in Alzheimer's disease, and gradually becomes submerged in general difficulties with attention, concentration and organisation of thought. The relative sparing of memory as the disease progresses is consonant with the pathological finding that the limbic areas of the brain are often less affected than in other dementing processes. Disorientation in time and place tends similarly to be a late development.

Focal psychological features are also rare in comparison with other primary dementias (Bruyn, 1968b; McHugh and Folstein, 1975). Word-finding difficulties can occur, but dysphasia, dyslexia, apraxia and agnosia are seldom detected. Judgement is often severely impaired as part of the widespread intellectual decline, but insight is commonly retained for a considerable length of time. The patient may thus be aware of his mental changes, complaining that he feels dulled, slow and forgetful and that his thinking is muddled.

These clinical impressions have been confirmed by Aminoff *et al.* (1975), who examined 11 patients with the disease an average of 6 years after onset, and when all were sufficiently impaired to have warranted premature retirement from work. The intellectual deterioration was found to be global, with a pattern of results on psychometric testing which approximated to that of the decline normally occurring in old age. Memory was not selectively impaired, and no patient showed focal symptoms such as dysphasia or dyspraxia. Seven of the 11 were fully oriented for time, place and person, and 9 retained full insight into their condition.

Distractibility is a marked and characteristic feature, and can be seen as the counterpart of the disturbed motor patterns. Depression may be severe, especially while insight is retained, and suicide is a considerable risk in the early stages. The eventual mood, however, is of apathy or fatuous euphoria, and inertia and self-neglect become pronounced. Episodes of restlessness and irritability or outbursts of excitement may occur from time to time, and some patients become difficult to manage on account of spiteful, quarrelsome or violent behaviour. A picture resembling akinetic mutism may mark the terminal stages.

The special features of the dementia in Huntington's chorea—poor cognitive ability generally but a lack of language disorder or other focal cortical deficits—has suggested that it owes much to subcortical rather than cortical pathology. The pronounced apathy which accompanies and develops along with it is also typical of 'subcortical dementia' as outlined on p. 568.

Psychotic features become obtrusive in many cases, often early in the course or even preceding the onset of chorea or dementia. Most common is a depressive psychosis, sometimes recurrent and usually responsive to drugs or electroconvulsive therapy. A schizophrenic or paraphrenic picture may also be seen. Delusions of persecution can be pronounced, with religiosity and sometimes grandiosity. Ideas of reference are perhaps accentuated by the attention attracted by the involuntary movements and bizarre facial expressions.

Folstein *et al.* (1983) have recently surveyed the incidence of affective disorder among 88 patients (from 63 kindreds) drawn from a defined geographical area in Maryland. Forty-one per cent showed major affective disorder, 32 per cent being depressive and 9 per cent bipolar. This development had antedated the Huntington's chorea by 2–20 years in almost two-thirds of cases. It appeared, moreover, to be confined to certain families, suggesting that the association may represent genetic heterogeneity within Huntington's chorea. Five probands with affective disorder and five without were subjected to detailed family studies; affective disorder accompanied the Huntington's chorea significantly more often in the families of the former than the latter, and was also somewhat commoner among unaffected family members.

The schizophrenia-like pictures can also be an early development. McHugh and Folstein (1975) prefer the term 'delusional-hallucinatory states', noting the emergence of psychotic symptoms from a pervasive delusional mood. They describe the typical progression as follows: the patient is overwhelmed by a vague impression of an uncanny change in reality which becomes laden with meaning of an uncertain nature. Delusions and hallucinations distil from this, often welling up suddenly and usually lasting for several months. Treatment with neuroleptics can lead to considerable improvement. McHugh and Folstein suggest that the admixture of dementia with such a picture may account for many of the reports of severe personality change and paranoid features among patients with Huntington's chorea.

The electroencephalogram characteristically shows poorly developed or complete loss of alpha rhythms. There may be generalised low voltage fast activity or random slow activity, but this too may disappear as the disease progresses. In consequence the record may become entirely flat. Occasionally, however, a normal record may be obtained even in the presence of advanced dementia.

The CT scan shows dilated ventricles, often particularly affecting the frontal regions. Atrophy of the caudate nuclei may be clearly apparent, with loss of the normal convex bulging into the lateral walls of the frontal horns. Various linear measures have been proposed for establishing this feature as an aid to diagnosis, but they are not sufficiently specific to be of value in the individual case (Shoulson and Plassche, 1980).

Course and Outcome

The course after the first definitive manifestations is generally much longer than with other primary dementing illnesses. The average duration is reported as 13 to 16 years, but with wide variation, some cases showing very slow progression over several decades.

Special Features in Childhood

Huntington's chorea may occasionally set in during childhood, though the true diagnosis will often only be made post mortem. In several respects the disease tends to differ from the adult form, yet the pathological changes at autopsy are typical and the same genetic mechanisms appear to be responsible. Muscular rigidity and tremor are commoner than choreiform movements, the mental deterioration tends to be rapid, and epileptic fits occur in more than half of the cases. Death occurs at a mean of 8 years from the onset.

After developing normally the child becomes clumsy, ataxic, dysarthric and mentally backward. The absence of chorea readily leads to other diagnoses even in families known to harbour the disease. Friedreich's ataxia may be suspected, or Wilson's disease, or post-encephalitic parkinsonism.

The death rate of children in the first decade is known to be high in Huntington's families, and has often been vaguely ascribed to 'mental deficiency', or 'spinal paralysis' (Oliver and Dewhurst, 1969). The infant mortality is also high, and Oliver and Dewhurst suggest that this may be partially due to undiagnosed cases occurring even in infancy. Such deaths are often attributed to birth injury, spasticity or quadriplegia. Social factors, however, are likely to be important in contributing to the infant mortality, since the children of Huntington's families are sometimes the victims of a disorganised or even brutal home environment (see below).

Other Psychiatric Associations of the Disease

The frequent occurrence of change of personality and emotional disturbance as premonitory symptoms of the disease has already been mentioned, also the marked psychotic features which may accompany the dementia. The association with severe depressive illness may have special genetic determinants. In addition certain other psychiatric associations deserve emphasis.

A large number of psychiatric abnormalities, sometimes severe in degree, are reported when detailed studies of Huntington's families are undertaken. A picture is painted of families severely disorganised on account of a multitude of pathologies, involving both the patients themselves and their relatives. Epilepsy, schizophrenia, mental defect and a variety of other degenerative brain diseases have been reported. How far these may represent common genetic determinants remains to be established. It is possible that to some extent assortative mating between patients from Huntington's families and those with other physical and psychiatric handicaps may contribute to the frequency of such disabilities.

Minski and Guttmann (1938) noted a variety of psychopathological features in the relatives of cases, particularly a personality characterised by explosive irritability, readiness to take offence and tendencies towards violence. Suicide was already stressed by Huntington (1910) and has been reported to be frequent even among members unaffected directly by the disease (Bickford and Ellison, 1953). It is unclear how far this may be due to endogenous mental illness or the result of knowledge of the consequences of the disease. Suicide is certainly common among the patients themselves, accounting for 7% of the deaths among those not hospitalised (Reed and Chandler, 1958).

Dewhurst et al.'s (1970) study of 102 patients illustrates vividly the psychosocial consequences of the disorder. Ten attempted suicide and 13 self-mutilation. Nineteen were alcoholics and 18 had had convictions for serious criminal offences. Of those who had married 38% subsequently divorced or separated, usually because of social or intellectual deterioration in the patient. Sexual disturbances were common—excessive demands, violence on rebuff, sexual assault, sexual deviation, impotence and frigidity. Notably there was often a history of promiscuity with the production of illegitimate offspring. The children were found to be much at risk from their parents with frequent examples of serious neglect.

Oliver (1970) showed that unaffected siblings from Huntington's families also became victims of their disturbed environment. Ninety-three out of 150 either died young, became psychotic, or suffered such disturbance as psychopathy, chronic alcoholism, criminality or divorce.

Mistakes in Diagnosis

Huntington's chorea may be mistaken for many other psychiatric and neurological illnesses, certainly in the early stages. Surveys have shown that between a third and two-thirds of cases are wrongly diagnosed initially (Bolt, 1970; Dewhurst et al., 1970).

Psychiatric misdiagnoses are the most common, especially a label of schizophrenia or paranoid psychosis. When schizophrenic features are the most obtrusive abnormality the chorea may readily be ascribed to 'schizophrenic mannerisms'. Affective

psychosis, anxiety state and personality disorder may be the initial diagnosis. Oliver (1970) found that some cases had been receiving army pensions for 'shell shock', or psychotherapy for 'hysteria'. Other forms of dementia will often be suspected when a family history is not forthcoming, and the motor abnormalities which develop may then be ascribed to dyskinesia induced by phenothiazine medication.

Bolt (1970) found that diagnoses of neurosis or affective psychosis were almost invariably revised before the patient's death, but sometimes a diagnosis of schizophrenia or paranoid psychosis was not. A diagnosis of some other form of dementia or of neurological disease was much less likely to be corrected.

Neurological mistakes include multiple sclerosis, Wilson's disease, Parkinson's disease, neurosyphilis, cerebellar disorders, and ataxia due to drug abuse. Arteriosclerotic or senile chorea may be misleading in the elderly—distinguishing features include the absence of a family history, and mental changes which are less conspicuous or progressive; moreover these are often vascular in origin and can therefore be abrupt in onset and with a tendency towards resolution. The rare syndrome of 'hereditary chorea without dementia' may also be misleading; Behan and Bone (1977) have described the affection in three generations of a family, beginning in childhood and apparently transmitted as a Mendelian dominant.

The childhood form is liable to be mistaken for mental subnormality, Friedreich's ataxia, Wilson's disease, epilepsy, spasticity or birth injury. Sydenham's chorea may be simulated, but is usually sudden in onset and associated with other rheumatic manifestations.

Pathology of Huntington's Chorea

The brain is usually small and atrophic though this varies much in degree. It is in general hard to correlate the intensity of pathological changes with the severity of mental symptoms. The frontal lobes are often the site of maximal change. Marked dilatation of the ventricular system is characteristic, especially of the frontal horns, along with striking atrophy of the caudate nuclei. Instead of bulging into the lateral ventricles these may be represented by a mere rim of tissue along the ventrolateral edge of the dilated anterior horns. The putamen is also atrophic, though the globus pallidus usually escapes in large degree.

Microscopic examination shows cell loss accompanied by gliosis. This can usually be detected in the cortex even when atrophy is not severe. It is particularly marked in the frontal lobes. Severe cell loss is invariably present in the caudate and putamen together with much astrocytic proliferation. The loss of small nerve cells is particularly striking. Similar changes of less degree are sometimes found in the globus pallidus, substantia nigra or cerebellar nuclei.

The white matter shows diffuse loss of nerve fibres, often with consequent narrowing of the corpus callosum. Vascular changes are not marked and cannot be incriminated in the pathogenesis of the disorder.

Creutzfeldt–Jakob Disease

This rare disease was first described by Creutzfeldt in 1920 and by Jakob in 1921. It is now estimated that in the UK there may be some 20 new cases per year. Siedler and Malamud's (1963) important contribution reviewed the cases reported to that date. The disorder consists essentially of a dementing illness which runs a very rapid course, usually accompanied by a number of prominent neurological symptoms and signs. Florid psychiatric symptoms, by way of delusions or hallucinations, are also often seen. The neuropathological changes typically include an accent on structures additional to the cerebral cortex itself—the subcortical nuclear masses, cerebellum, brain stem and cord, though a good deal of variability is seen from one example to another.

So many different pictures have been reported that the nosological status of the disease has often been in doubt. To some extent the term has run the risk of being applied to any atypical presenile dementia which runs an unusually rapid course. More recently, however, careful attempts have been made to group together small numbers of cases with features in common, and under the focus of present interest greater clarity is being obtained.

Aetiology

The disease usually arises sporadically, though review of a large case material world-wide shows that a positive family history is obtained in about 15% of cases (Masters et al., 1979). This may indicate vertical transmission in certain families, or alternatively lateral transmission of the infective agent in genetically susceptible hosts. The distinction is difficult to make on present evidence as discussed below.

A chief stimulus to interest in the condition has come from the demonstration that a transmissible agent may be involved (Gibbs et al., 1968). Certain similarities between kuru (p. 645) and Creutzfeldt-Jakob disease had suggested that since the former was transmissible to chimpanzees by brain inoculation the latter should be investigated similarly. A homogenate of brain tissue obtained at biopsy from a patient was accordingly inoculated both intracerebrally and intravenously into a chimpanzee, and the animal developed a fatal neurological disease 13 months later. The clinical and neuropathological pictures were remarkably similar in man and animal and appeared to represent essentially the same disease (Beck et al., 1969a, 1969b). These observations have since been amply confirmed with biopsy material from further human cases, with transmissions to chimpanzees, Old and New World monkeys, cats, guinea-pigs, mice and hamsters (Gajdusek, 1977). Serial passage from animal to animal has been successful, including transmission through purely peripheral routes—intravenously, intramuscularly, subcutaneously and intraperitoneally. Some evidence of oral transmission in the squirrel monkey has also been forthcoming (Gibbs et al., 1980).

The precise nature of the transmissible agent remains elusive. It belongs to the category of 'unconventional' or 'slow' viruses involved in other central nervous system disorders, including Creutzfeldt–Jakob disease and kuru in man, scrapie in sheep and goats, and transmissible mink encephalopathy. All show transmissibility to experimental animals, long incubation periods, and lead to closely similar pathological changes in the brain. The possibility even arises that they may represent different strains or variants of a single agent (Gajdusek, 1977). Other properties shared in common include unique physico-chemical characteristics. The agents pass a 100 nm filter but have not been visualised with certainty by electron-microscopy; they are remarkably resistant to heat, formalin, ultra-violet light and X-rays, do not evoke an immune response, and do not have a cytopathic effect in tissue cultures. In these respects they differ markedly from conventional viruses. An analogy can be drawn with 'viroids'—naked pieces of ribonucleic acid without protein which are responsible for certain plant diseases and which represent another unusual variant of the traditional virus—though the analogy cannot be drawn closely (Roos, 1981). More recent evidence has pointed to 'prions' as possible agents—small rod-shaped objects consisting of glycoprotein particles without either RNA or DNA (Prusiner, 1984; Bockman et al., 1985). These now appear to have been identified in purified extracts of brain, both in scrapie and in Creutzfeldt–Jakob disease.

Though degenerative changes are confined to the central nervous system, the responsible agent appears to be present in many organs and tissues during the incubation phase in animals. Infectivity has been shown from lymph nodes, spleen, liver, kidney and lungs before the agent reaches the cerebrospinal fluid. Blood from the infected guinea-pig can transmit the disease to others (Manuelidis et al., 1978). Concern has accordingly arisen that Creutzfeldt–Jakob disease may be transmitted by an 'infective' process in man, possibly with a reservoir of infection existing in other species. The evidence remains indirect and far from conclusive, but certain interesting observations have been made.

Thus small but apparently definite geographical clusters of cases have been reported in persons unrelated genetically to one another. Matthews' (1975) survey of 46 cases in England and Wales showed a markedly uneven geographical distribution, with several clusters which bore no relation to urban density. A small rural community in the Midlands produced 3 patients who had probably had contact with one another, and an area in Eastern England yielded 5. Mayer et al. (1977) have reported 3 patients who developed the disease within a period of 4 years, all living in villages 10 km apart in Czechoslovakia. Galvez et al. (1980) found familial clustering in Santiago, Chile, plus a remarkable example of a woman who developed the disease after marrying into a family with several affected members. Such evidence is little more than anecdotal, but rather striking in view of the rarity of the disease. Epidemiological surveys must contend, moreover, with the likelihood that incubation periods often last for many years. Taken altogether the evidence does not yet amount to proof that intimate exposure is in itself sufficient to cause the disease; but the possibility remains that it may contribute in persons who have inherited special genetic susceptibility. If so a reservoir of infection is likely to exist, since the disease is too rare to survive by case to case transmission alone. This may take the form of widespread latent infection in man, or exist in other animal species (Matthews et al., 1979).

The possibility of contracting the disease through eating animal products has been raised by analogy with scrapie in sheep (Gibbs et al., 1980; Roos, 1981). Firm evidence has not, however, been forthcoming. Bobowick et al. (1973) questioned relatives of patients in detail, using friends of the patients as matched controls, and found some small indication that the eating of brains had been more frequent among the persons affected. Concern also arose at Kahana et al.'s (1974) discovery of a very high incidence of Creutzfeldt–Jakob disease among Libyan Jewish immigrants to Israel, thought possibly to be related to the eating of sheep's eyeballs, but significant familial clusterings were ultimately shown to account for the excess (Alter et al., 1978; Neugut et al., 1979).

It is only in the field of surgical transmission that worrying evidence has been forthcoming. It now seems incontrovertible that Creutzfeldt–Jakob disease has several times been accidentally transmitted from patient to patient by ophthalmic or neurosurgical procedures. Duffy et al. (1974) reported transmission in one case by corneal transplantation, and Bernoulli et al. (1977) two further examples in young epileptic patients after using contaminated depth electrodes. Foncin et al. (1980) reported a patient who developed the disease 28 months after an intracranial operation carried out in the same theatre, and probably with the same instruments, that had been used three days earlier on a patient with the disease. Retrospective evidence now strongly incriminates similar neurosurgical transmission in 3 of the 8 patients included in Nevin et al.'s (1960) report (Masters et al., 1979; Will and Matthews, 1982).

Short of direct intracranial transmission, however, the risk of acquiring the disease by day to day infection appears to be remote. There are no controlled studies to show that health professionals, farmers or butchers are specially at risk, even though persons with such occupations have contracted the disease from time to time (Masters et al., 1979). It is perhaps especially noteworthy that there is no recorded example of a neuropathologist developing Creutzfeldt–Jakob dementia (Matthews, 1981), and no report of an excess of dementias generally among pathologists or their assistants (Corsellis, 1979). Masters et al. (1979) conclude from their vast experience that the potential for transmission by noninvasive bodily contact must be judged as very low. Certain reasonable precautions are recommended, nonetheless, in those who come into contact with patients with the disease (Gajdusek et al., 1977; Corsellis, 1979; Advisory Group on the Management of Patients with Spongiform Encephalopathy (Creutzfeldt–Jakob Disease), 1981):

The isolation or barrier-nursing of patients is not considered to be necessary. However, wounds and sores must be dressed with strict sterile precautions, similar care being observed when taking blood or cerebrospinal fluid. Equipment must not be reused thereafter and should be incinerated. Attendants should wash thoroughly if exposed to saliva, nasopharyngeal secretions, urine or faeces, and skin puncture in attendants must be strictly avoided.

At operation or autopsy tissues must be handled with special care, likewise blood, cerebrospinal fluid or biopsy material obtained from patients. Even formalin-fixed specimens should be regarded as potentially infective. Disposable drapes, dressings and where possible disposable instruments, should be used for any operation; for operations on brain, cord or eye even non-disposable instruments must be immediately destroyed. Otherwise autoclaving at specially prescribed temperatures and pressures is recommended for sterilising equipment, or sodium hypochlorite solution for use on contaminated surfaces.

Even suspected patients must not be used as blood, tissue or organ donors. Corneal grafts are not to be taken from any demented patient, from those dying in psychiatric hospitals, or from patients who die from obscure undiagnosed neurological diseases.

Clinical Features

Males are affected as often as females. The onset is usually between the ages of 40 and 60 but cases are reported with onset at any adult age.

The clinical features are very diverse from case to case and are well reviewed by May (1968). A prodromal stage is usually described, lasting weeks or months and characterised by neurasthenic symptoms. The patient complains of fatigue, insomnia, anxiety and depression, and shows a gradual change towards mental slowness and unpredictability of behaviour. Occasionally the mood is mildly elevated with loquacity and inappropriate laughter. Already at this stage there may be evidence of impaired memory and concentration, the limbs may appear to be weak and the gait unsteady. Frequently, however, objective findings are lacking and a functional psychiatric disorder is suspected. This is especially likely in cases in which the early symptoms remit for several weeks at a time.

Soon intellectual deterioration or neurological defects become prominent. The latter are extremely variable but are liable to involve motor functions, speech or vision. There may be ataxia of cerebellar type, spasticity of limbs with progressive paralysis, extrapyramidal rigidity, tremor or choreoathetoid movements, depending on the brain regions principally involved. Involvement of the anterior horn cells of the cord may lead to muscular fibrillation and atrophy, especially of the small hand muscles, resembling amyotrophic lateral sclerosis. Speech disturbances are common with dysphasia and dysarthria, likewise parietal lobe symptoms such as right-left disorientation, dyscalculia and finger agnosia. Vision may be severely affected with rapidly progressive cortical blindness. Apart from this, sensory changes are usually absent. Brain stem involvement may lead to nystagmus, dysphagia, or bouts of uncontrollable laughing and crying. Myoclonic jerks are frequently seen and epileptic fits may occur.

Attempts have been made to classify this bewildering variety of phenomena though with little success. A given case may show a succession of different neurological features as the disease progresses. A broad classification into those which begin with cerebellar symptoms and those with parietal lobe symptoms has been suggested, similarly into cases with and without spinal cord or visual cortex involvement.

Intellectual deterioration follows or appears along with the neurological defects and evolves with great rapidity. An acute organic picture may be present initially with clouding of consciousness or frank delirium. Auditory hallucinations and delusions may be marked, and confabulation is often seen. Ultimately a state of profound dementia is reached, accompanied by gross rigidity or spastic paralysis and often a decorticate or decerebrate posture. Repetitive myoclonic jerking of muscle groups is often still evident late in the disease. Emaciation is usually profound by the time death occurs.

The cerebrospinal fluid is usually normal throughout, though the protein is very occasionally elevated. The CT scan may show cortical atrophy and ventricular enlargement but this is rarely gross in degree. Indeed the CT scan can be essentially normal when the dementia is well advanced, a feature which may be of some importance in differential diagnosis (Galvez and Cartier, 1984). The electro-encephalogram is almost always markedly abnormal. A variety of changes have been reported and different findings may emerge in different stages of the illness. Initially there is some diffuse or focal slowing. Later repetitive sharp waves or slow spike and wave discharges appear; these are bilaterally synchronous and may accompany the myoclonic jerks. Ultimately a characteristic pattern emerges of synchronous triphasic sharp wave complexes, superimposed on progressive suppression of cortical background activity (May, 1968; Elliott et al., 1974). The triphasic discharges are at first intermittent, but evolve to a periodic picture at rates of one to two per second. The latter changes may be helpful in diagnosis, though usually only late in the course of the disease.

Course and Outcome

The course is a good deal more rapid than with most other primary dementing illnesses. Over half of the patients are dead within 9 months and the great majority within 2 years. Death is usually preceded by a period of deepening coma which lasts for several weeks.

Pathology of Creutzfeldt–Jakob Disease

The brain may appear to be somewhat atrophied but often there is little abnormal to detect macroscopically. Histological examination shows great variability from case to case, but the essential features consist of neuronal degeneration, great proliferation of astrocytes, and frequently a characteristic spongy appearance of the grey matter. In some varieties the latter may be so pronounced that it is visible to the naked eye. The degenerated neurones often show an accumulation of lipid material.

The accent of the pathology may fall on different regions, accounting for the various clinical pictures that are seen. The cortex is nearly always involved, though often with relative sparing of the parietal and occipital lobes. The hippocampi may also escape. In different cases there may be a marked emphasis on the corpus striatum, thalamus, cerebellum, substantia nigra, brain stem and spinal cord. The corticospinal tracts and also the extrapyramidal pathways are often severely degenerated.

The 'status spongiosus' of the cortex is highly characteristic, showing as a finely meshed vacuolation under the microscope. Severely affected areas have the appearance of being riddled with tiny cavities. In some varieties this is widely disseminated, but much uncertainty surrounds its pathogenesis. Occasionally the condition has been found in biopsy specimens during life but has been absent at autopsy, and vice versa. It has been suggested that astrocyte proliferation may be the primary change, and that the spongy appearance results from their degeneration. Electron microscopy shows the presence of vacuoles within the cytoplasm of both neurones and astrocytes. Status spongiosus is not entirely pathognomonic for Creutzfeldt–Jakob disease but has occasionally been reported in senile dementia of the Alzheimer type, Pick's disease, Wilson's disease and other degenerative conditions.

There are usually no senile plaques or neurofibrillary tangles as in Alzheimer's disease, no massive circumscribed atrophy as in Pick's disease, and no evidence of an inflammatory reaction. The cerebral vessels appear healthy, or if cerebrovascular disease is present this appears to be incidental.

Sub-varieties of the Disease

Several sub-varieties have been described, depending partly on the detailed neuropathological picture and partly on clinical features. Present views on classification are far from unanimous, however, and some varieties may yet prove to be distinct clinical entities.

One in particular has been labelled *Subacute Spongiform Encephalopathy* (Jones and Nevin, 1954; Nevin, 1967). The age of onset is some 10 years later than that of the classical disease, and the beginning tends to be abrupt without the usual prodromata. The course is extremely rapid with a fatal ending after 3–6 months. Visual failure due to degeneration of the striate cortex has been a prominent feature in over a third of reported cases. Extrapyramidal changes are well developed, with progressive hypertonus, likewise irregular shock-like myoclonic jerks which come to involve the entire body musculature. The electroencephalogram is always markedly abnormal as described above.

At autopsy the brain shows more severe and widespread cortical atrophy than in other forms of Creutzfeldt–Jakob disease, and an emphasis is seen on the occipital lobes which is otherwise exceptional. The brain stem and cord are spared. Status spongiosus is widely disseminated in the grey matter and usually extremely well developed.

Another very rapid form has been named the *Ataxic Form of Subacute Presenile Polioencephalopathy* (Brownell and Oppenheimer, 1965). This is regarded as a nosological entity within the Creutzfeldt–Jakob group. It presents initially with rapidly progressive cerebellar ataxia. This is followed by dementia and abnormal motor movements in the form of rhythmic myoclonic jerking, leading ultimately to generalised muscular rigidity. The principal findings at autopsy are selective degeneration of cells in the granular layer of the cerebellum, variable status spongiosus, and cell loss and astrocytosis in the cortex, thalamus and striatum. It would appear to be this variety of the disease which first proved to be transmissible on intracerebral inoculation as described on (p. 400).

The amyotrophic form, which presents with muscle wasting, can sometimes run a relatively chronic course. This variety is also unusual in that it has not yet proved to be transmissible to animals (Masters *et al.*, 1979).

The possibilities of overlap with Alzheimer's disease in rare examples have also been stressed from time to time (Matthews, 1981, 1982). Cases diagnosed as Creutzfeldt–Jakob disease during life with dementia, myoclonous and the typical electroencephalographic changes, can occasionally show Alzheimer pathology and nothing more at autopsy. Conversely, Creutzfeldt–Jakob pathology may on rare occasions be detected in patients who have died after unremarkable dementing illnesses, with little to raise a suspicion of the disease during life.

The Pseudodementias

In a number of conditions a clinical picture resembling organic dementia presents for attention yet physical disease proves to be little if at all responsible. These disorders are conveniently grouped together as the 'pseudodementias'. The main varieties include the Ganser syndrome, hysterical pseudodementia, simulated dementia, depressive pseudodementia and other rarer forms as discussed below. The distinction from organic dementia can sometimes be difficult, at least for a time. It must also be remembered that in the early stages of organic brain disease a patient may occasionally react in such a way that his dementia is suspected of being more apparent than real—in other words a pseudo-dementia may turn out in fact to be a 'pseudo-pseudodementia'.

While it is helpful to consider the several varieties separately it must be stressed that the dividing lines between them are often far from clear. Several mechanisms may contribute to the genesis of the clinical picture, sometimes in relatively pure culture but sometimes in combination with one another. Thus mechanisms of hysterical dissociation may operate to some degree in depressive pseudodementia; covert affective disorder may make a contribution to hysterical pseudodementia; and conscious simulation will only rarely be entirely divorced from the operation of hysterical and other neurotic defensive mechanisms. In dealing with an individual case of pseudodementia, therefore, it will be necessary to keep several possible factors in mind. It will often not suffice to seek out simple pointers such as obvious motivation or coincident functional psychiatric illness as the total explanation. This has been illustrated particularly well by the chequered career of the Ganser syndrome, which is considered in some detail immediately below.

THE GANSER SYNDROME

In 1898 Ganser described three prisoners who showed an unusual clinical picture including the feature which now bears his name—the 'Ganser response' ('answering past the point', 'approximate answers', 'vorbeireden'). The condition has been the focus of interest, controversy and misunderstanding ever since, as reviewed by Whitlock (1967b) and Enoch *et al*. (1967). Uncertainty surrounds its nosological status and the mechanisms behind its appearance.

Clinical Features

The phenomenon which from the outset attracted most attention was that of answering past the point. A clear example occurs in one of Ganser's original cases:

'In what city are we? In Berlin, in Russia. What are you doing here? We wanted to go hunting, and we unhitched our horses. How many noses do you have? I don't know. Have you any nose at all? I do not know if I have a nose. Have you eyes? I have no eyes. How many fingers do you have? Eleven. How many ears? (He first touches his ears, and then he says: Two). How many legs does a horse have? Three. An elephant? Five. After being shown a coin and asked, What is that? the answer is: A map which a person hangs on his watch chain. Glancing at the eagle stamped on a coin: I don't know that person. Is it Kaiser Wilhelm ? He was shown a dollar and was asked: Do you know a dollar? He said, I don't know a dollar. That is a toy which one gives to children. What is your name? My name is Fürst (incorrect)'.

(Ganser 1898, translated by Schorer 1965)

Another example is provided by Kiloh (1961):

A man of 25 became fully accessible some hours after a head injury but for a period replied as follows to questions: What is the colour of your pyjamas?—Red (in fact they were blue). What is the colour of the chair in the corner?—What corner? I don't know what a corner is. I don't see a chair. Look again!—Red (yellow). What year is it?—1938 (1958). What year were you born?—1933. How old are you ?—That makes me five. What is the date?—the second day of the twelfth month (12th February). Which is the twelfth month?—January.

The patient's responses to questions are markedly inaccurate and often absurdly so. But they seem to betray a knowledge of the purpose of the question, and by their close approximation to the correct answer imply that this too was at some level available to the patient. Approximate answers may be seen in response to simple addition, counting, the naming of colours, or simple questions about everyday matters. Sometimes the patient may answer in a way quite contrary to the evidence before him, for example stating that it is midnight when the sun is shining clearly through the window. The absurd responses are usually given with full deliberation and apparently serious intent, and false responses may be quite inconsistently interspersed with accurate answers.

A difficulty with the concept of 'approximate answers' is that they require an element of subjective interpretation on the part of the examiner. In some rare examples, when asked to count fingers or add an ascending series of digits, the patient may consistently give one in excess or one less than the correct answer throughout the series, but such clear instances are rare. Short of this it can be difficult to decide how approximate an answer must be to deserve the appellation. Anderson and Mallinson (1941) foresaw a tendency for the term to be applied to any random answer, and proposed the definition: 'that false response of a patient to the examiner's question where the answer, although wrong, is never far wrong and bears a definite and obvious relation to the question, indicating clearly that the question has been grasped by the patient'. Moeli's (1888) early description was that 'the answer is wrong it is true, but it bears nevertheless some relationship to the sense of the question and shows that the sphere of appropriate concepts has been touched upon'.

Whitlock (1967b) has suggested that it is often not the approximateness but the absurdness of the answers which is so striking. The playful childish character of the responses may have something in common with the 'buffoonery syndrome' of schizophrenia. On other occasions the replies may be akin to other forms of schizophrenic thought disorder, or may resemble the confused responses seen in clouding of consciousness or early dementia. They may sometimes resemble confabulations, though usually the randomness and absurdity of the replies differs sharply from the factual and circumstantial detail of the confabulation response.

The apparent dementia which accompanies the approximate answers is usually incomplete, inconstant and often self-contradictory. Disorientation is invariably present, but the apparently gross disturbance of intellect fails to be reflected in the patient's overall behaviour. Thus he usually proves capable of adapting to the demands of daily life in a way

that the severe organic dement would not. Motor behaviour may range from dazed stupor to histrionic outbursts of excitement, and the mood may vary from apathetic indifference to anxious bewilderment.

Other features shown by Ganser's original patients are often overlooked. All had prominent hallucinatory experiences, hysterical stigmata of various types, and showed evidence of fluctuating disturbance of consciousness. Resolution of the disorder was abrupt, the abnormal mental state clearing suddenly along with the hysterical conversion symptoms. All were left with a complete amnesia for the period of the illness.

Nosological Status

Cases closely similar in all these respects have been reported from time to time, for example those described by May *et al.* (1960), but the complete syndrome is undoubtedly very rare. Much more commonly patients are reported who show approximate answers along with other mental abnormalities, or exhibit aspects of the syndrome superimposed upon other psychiatric disease processes. A partial or complete Ganser state may be seen in the course of depressive and schizophrenic psychoses, after head injury, in the course of early dementia, general paralysis of the insane, or a wide variety of toxic states including alcoholism. It seems, however, that it can also occasionally appear in subjects without other definable psychiatric disorder and in response to purely emotional traumata.

Hence the difficulty with the nosological status of the syndrome. It has been suggested that it should rank as a distinct nosological entity along with other excessively rare and exotic psychiatric disorders, or alternatively that it should be viewed as a preformed mode of reaction which is determined by the individual's defensive structure and which may be called forth by a variety of different stresses and disease processes. Either way the problem remains how much must be present to justify applying the label. There is much to commend Scott's (1965) distinction between the *Ganser symptom* (approximate answers) and the *Ganser syndrome,* the first being common and the second extremely rare, while both may be found in a wide variety of psychiatric illnesses. Whitlock (1967b) suggests that the diagnosis of the syndrome should imply, in addition to approximate answers, at least some evidence of impairment of consciousness, a sudden termination, and subsequent amnesia for the episode.

Mechanisms

With regard to the mechanisms underlying the development of Ganser symptoms these have been variously regarded as akin to hysterical conversion reactions, malingering, organic confusion, and psychotic thought disorder.

Ganser entitled his original contribution 'an unusual hysterical confusional state', and stressed the presence of a variety of other hysterical phenomena. He insisted, however, on the pleomorphism and severity of the acute illness episodes which he had witnessed, and did not commit himself to an hysterical aetiology for the total picture. Since then, the reporting of other examples in response to purely psychogenic stresses, and the appearance of approximate answers in patients with obvious hysterical pseudodementia, have led many authorities to view hysterical mechanisms as fundamental to the development of the condition. The hallucinations in most reported examples have seemed to be analogous to the pseudohallucinations of hysterical states, the content usually being immediately related to current conflicts in the patient's mind. It must be conceded that hysterical mechanisms are likely to contribute in large measure, but in many cases these may have been released by organic brain damage or functional psychiatric illness. It is unfortunate therefore that the 'Ganser syndrome' has often come to be regarded as synonymous with 'hysterical pseudodementia'.

The older and more restricted views of 'hysteria', with the implication of overt gain as a motivating force, will not of course always be found to apply. Gain may be obvious in prisoners awaiting trial, or in the considerable number of cases where compensation is at stake, but in many others more complex dynamic factors may be at work. Anderson and Mallinson (1941) claimed that the precipitating situation could be internal to the patient, sometimes no more than a 'wrathful conscience', and with no external threat or disgrace which could be identified. Other suggested motivations include the wish to be insane, the protection of self-esteem, or an essay at absolution (Scott, 1965). May *et al.* (1960) described Ganser patients who paradoxically had in common the prospect of release from freedom-restricting situations. Here what looked like imminent gain had apparently been perceived as threat. Obviously these expanded possibilities are to a large extent inferential, and must run the risk of sometimes being applied when other factors are primarily at work.

Many patients with the Ganser syndrome have been suspected of malingering, that is of deliberately feigning their approximate answers and other symptoms. The phenomenon of approximate answers has struck some observers as so bizarre that conscious simulation has seemed the only reasonable explanation. In fact Ganser was himself at pains to point out that he rejected any suspicion of deliberate simulation, and that the patients made an exceedingly convincing impression of being genuinely ill. He noted that they made no spontaneous absurd remarks, but only in response to questions. They seemed convinced that what they said was correct, and seemed unwilling to have anyone think their answers false or themselves foolish or simple minded.

Other observers have felt less able to absolve their patients from all trace of simulation, and motivation 'near the level of consciousness' has often been inferred even when the syndrome accompanies other frank psychiatric illness. The fact that Ganser's original three patients were prisoners has perhaps caused selective reporting of cases from the prison population, and this in turn may have given spurious emphasis to the possibilities of deliberate simulation. Ganser's syndrome has, indeed, sometimes been labelled 'prison psychosis'. Scott (1965) reports that it still occurs in English prisons but extremely rarely, typically in prisoners awaiting trial but also in sentenced prisoners who later develop schizophrenia. Most cases nowadays are in fact probably to be found in patients in mental hospitals, and include a fair proportion of law-abiding citizens.

The striking frequency with which the condition is found in conjunction with some form of trouble—domestic, sexual, financial, or legal—should not of course argue more in favour of simulation than of hysteria, nor should the two be regarded as mutually exclusive.

McGrath and McKenna (1961), in their interesting attempt at a psychological formulation of the mechanisms behind approximate answers, see them as the result of defence mechanisms of an unusual character, operating in patients who fail to carry through an initial wish to feign non-comprehension. 'The typical (approximate) answer is a compromise, simultaneously carrying on the original attempt to simulate and attempting to regain the lost reality by convincing both the patient himself and others that apprehension of the environment is still operating. The result of the message is a contradictory one, conveying "I am insane, yet sane". Hence the confusion in the diagnostic constructions put upon this relatively rare state'.

A contribution due to organic brain damage is

attested by the large number of cases reported after head injury, or occurring in the course of other acute and chronic organic reactions. Of Ganser's original three cases, two had suffered head injury and the third was recovering from typhus fever. Among the more typical cases in the literature evidence of fluctuating impairment of consciousness is found almost without exception, and a dense amnesia for the episode remains after it has resolved. In general it can be said that the organic character of much of the disturbance, as well as the organic antecedents, have impressed many observers. It is likely that in many cases an admixture of organic and psychogenic factors are operating together, the organic process serving to actualise whatever more complex mechanisms underlie the Ganser state. In this connection it is noteworthy that even in the presence of organic brain disease there is frequently a psychogenic setting to the development of the disorder.

The conjunction of typical Ganser states with functional psychotic illnesses, both schizophrenic and depressive, was increasingly reported after Ganser's original observations. Sometimes catatonic phenomena and other typical schizophrenic features have been found to accompany Ganser manifestations, and sometimes the Ganser state has appeared merely as a prelude to a developing schizophrenia. Hence the idea has gained ground that mechanisms akin to psychotic thought disorder might underlie the process. Schizophrenic thought disorder may occasionally come close to 'approximate answers'. Sometimes these seem to be due to a childish playful attitude on the part of the patient, as in the 'buffoonery syndrome'. In others they may represent catatonic phenomena of the nature of forced responsiveness, in that the patient is obliged to respond to the question immediately and says the first thing that comes into his head (Fish, 1962). Anderson and Mallinson (1941) reported three examples of the Ganser syndrome, two in the course of endogenous depression and one with schizophrenia, and suggested that here depersonalisation was the common factor which led to the development of Ganser symptoms. These ideas have not, however, stood the test of time, and hysterical or allied mechanisms continue to be given precedence, even in cases with obvious concomitant psychosis. The latter is seen merely to release the more specific Ganser tendency, and to colour it accordingly. Certainly Ganser episodes are mostly transitory when they occur in the course of other psychoses, and as with organic brain disease a psychogenic precipitant can frequently be discerned.

In summary, therefore, it may be said that the Ganser syndrome represents a definite but exceedingly rare disorder, characterised by approximate answers, some disturbance of consciousness, and subsequent dense amnesia for the episode. While the syndrome itself is rare the symptom of approximate answers is not. Both the Ganser syndrome and the Ganser symptom are more commonly found in association with other psychiatric disorders than in isolation, occurring in the course of organic brain disease and with functional psychotic illness. Evidence of psychogenesis is frequently to be found, even in cases complicated by organic or psychotic illness. The disorder would appear to rest principally on a complex psychogenic basis, in which hysterical mechanisms or mechanisms closely allied to them are largely responsible, though contributions due to organic brain dysfunction and psychotic thought disorder cannot be excluded in certain cases. It seems probable, however, that when organic or functional psychoses are seen in association with the Ganser manifestations they have served principally as releasers rather than as prime determinants of the condition.

HYSTERICAL PSEUDODEMENTIA

Of all the forms of pseudodementia there is probably least difficulty in distinguishing the typical case of hysterical pseudodementia from true organic dementia. On occasion, however, there may be protracted difficulty. There may also be an added psychogenic component in the early stages of organic brain disease, and it it then that most difficulty is likely to arise.

Hysterical pseudodementia is mostly seen in persons of limited intellectual endowment. Sometimes the patient is mute or monosyllabic in his replies. Short of this his account is grossly incoherent, he appears disorientated and fails on simple tests of cognitive function. The symptom of 'approximate answers' may be seen, but perseveration does not occur and clear examples of concrete thinking will rarely be detected.

Careful observation will usually soon reveal much that is inconsistent or self-contradictory in behaviour. Responses to commands may be grossly inaccurate, the patient producing an unconvincing and theatrical display of non-comprehension and inability to perform. The wrong reply or action may be followed later by the correct one, or patchy performance may fail to correspond to any hierarchy of increasing difficulty. The patient is usually found to be highly suggestible, so that the level of his performance is readily influenced by the way in which he is handled. Unlike organic dementias, memory may appear to be markedly deficient for the most elementary aspects of knowledge and experience, and even simple skills may apparently be lost. Most impressively of all, such patients may settle into ward routines and find their way about in a manner quite inconsistent with the degree of disability displayed at interview. Personal care, habits of eating, and standards generally may be observed to be little impaired, with normal competence in the everyday things of life.

Sometimes, though by no means invariably, other hysterical conversion symptoms will be present, such as sensory loss, paralysis, or other stigmata of classical type. In the great majority of cases the patient's attitude is bland and unconcerned, with an incurious detachment to his predicament ('belle indifference'). He may show a fatuous cheerfulness or a state of sullen apathy. In general his emotional responses are superficial and in large degree unconvincing.

In more severe degrees of 'hysterical puerilism' or 'hysterical infantilism' the patient may enact a desire to regress to the helpless state of infancy, lose ability to walk and talk, eat with his fingers, make inarticulate noises and wet his bed. Such florid states are relatively rare, and the abundant evidence of superficial motives and of previously unstable personality will usually serve to dispel real diagnostic difficulty.

Hysterical amnesia forms part and parcel of the picture in most cases of hysterical pseudodementia, though it may also occur in relative isolation. The cardinal features of psychogenic amnesia have already been described in Chapter 2 (p. 31) along with the points which serve to differentiate it from organic anmesic states. Kennedy and Neville's (1957) series of 74 patients presenting with abrupt failure of memory, with or without loss of personal identity, remains one of the most comprehensive surveys to date:

The patients had either presented themselves at hospital or at police stations and were examined in the acute phase of the disorder. In 43% psychogenic mechanisms appeared to operate alone, in 41% psychogenic and organic factors together, and in 16% organic factors alone. Sometimes organic brain disease was present along with an obvious psychological precipitant, and neither aetiology precluded the other. Altogether more than a third had some evidence of brain damage on complete examination; many had epilepsy but others were suffering from the effects of head injury, chronic encephalitis lethargica, early presenile dementia, multiple sclerosis, neurosyphilis or raised intracranial pressure.

Kennedy and Neville suggested that brain damage appeared to predispose to the development of primitive mental mechanisms of escape, or lower the threshold at which stress would bring them out. The flight was typically from simple situations to do with difficulties in marriage, bigamy or debt, but could also be from mental pain as in examples suffering from endogenous depression. The great majority of their cases of psychogenic amnesia, when seen and managed in the acute stage, recovered within a few hours or several days.

In cases of hysterical pseudodementia there is frequently an antecedent history of severe personality instability if not of previous hysterical conversion reactions. The problem, of course, is that such retrospective evidence is often not available when the patient first presents for attention. Typically the condition arises in response to emotionally traumatic events or personally threatening situations, though sometimes the psychogenic derivation may be complex and not immediately obvious. In routine civilian practice domestic disharmony, financial troubles, or complications of sexual encounters rank high on the list of causes, while in the army disciplinary measures will often be found to be pending. The patient may have wandered away in a fugue-like state, sometimes for several days on end, after which he presents for attention with loss of personal identity and other evidence of intellectual malfunction. At other times the condition may be witnessed to set in abruptly, as after head injury or when the patient is apprehended for some misdemeanour. Some of the most entrenched examples occur in head-injured patients when litigation is in progress over claims for compensation.

The points of difference between hysterical pseudodementia and the Ganser syndrome are implicit in the account of the latter given above. The presence of clouding of consciousness and abundant evidence of approximate answers will lead most observers to apply the term Ganser syndrome, and particularly so when the episode occurs in conjunction with organic or psychiatric disorder. Approximate answers alone should not, however, be used as the basis for the distinction. It is generally agreed that the whole reaction appears more superficial with hysterical pseudodementia than in the Ganser syndrome, and that some element of conscious malingering is more often to be detected along with it. Ganser episodes are typically brief, with sudden spontaneous termination even in patients who progress ultimately to schizophrenia or other mental illness, while hysterical pseudodementia not infrequently runs a prolonged and relapsing course, particularly when the underlying conflicts cannot be revealed or resolved.

The distinction of hysterical from depressive pseudodementia rests principally on the absence of melancholic changes or typical psychomotor retardation, and in the general superficiality of the emotional display. In depressive pseudodementia the cognitive disabilities are likely to appear more genuine, and can often be traced to the patient's difficulty with attention and concentration.

The features which may point to conscious simulation rather than hysterical pseudodementia are discussed in the section that follows.

SIMULATED DEMENTIA

Most authorities agree that entirely conscious simulation of dementia, or indeed of amnesia, is very rare indeed, though self-confessed cases have been recorded from time to time. Motivation is gross and obvious when adequate information is to hand, though of course this is likely to be carefully concealed from the examiner.

As with hysterical pseudodementia, careful observation usually soon reveals much that is out of keeping with genuine cognitive impairment. The simulant, after all, is presenting his own notion of the condition he seeks to portray, and through ignorance will usually fail to show the complete picture (Bluglass, 1976). An isolated symptom, such as loss of memory or loss of speech, will be more commonly encountered than a complex syndrome.

Formal examination may be impossible on account of mutism or total lack of cooperation, and it will then be necessary to judge the patient's behaviour when he feels he is under less careful scrutiny. He may be observed to cope with the necessities of daily life in a manner quite inconsistent with the impression made at interview. In more productive examples the patient will often overdo his part, mixing up incoherent and absurd answers with a theatrical demonstration of insanity and talking no sense at all.

Interesting attempts have been made to assess the responses of healthy subjects who have been asked to feign mental illness. The broad conclusion from such experiments is that convincing simulation of dementia for more than a very brief period is virtually impossible, even among reasonably sophisticated subjects. Anderson *et al.* (1959), for example, asked 18 psychology students to simulate mental disorder, and compared the results with the clinical picture shown by 25 patients with organic dementia

and 10 patients with hysterical pseudodementia. No normal subject was able to feign dementia in a convincing manner. The length and thoroughness of the examination was an important factor in revealing the spuriousness of the simulations; fatigue was observed to 'increase the pull of reality', and responses became more and more normal as examination progressed. A special focus of interest was the occurrence of approximate answers and confabulations; simple 'near miss' answers were given on occasion by all three groups but most often by the patients with hysterical pseudodementia, while gross confabulations occurred with almost equal frequency in the simulants, the dements and the pseudodements. Perseveration was a more useful distinguishing feature, being prominent in the organic cases but very rarely observed in simulation or pseudodementia.

Benton and Spreen (1961) discuss differences in performance on a visual memory test between subjects simulating brain damage and patients with true brain damage. Significant differences between the groups were observed where certain qualitative aspects of performance were concerned; the simulators made more errors of distortion than the patients in reproducing visual designs, and fewer errors of omission, perseveration and size. Hunt (1973) summarises work on certain scales incorporated in the Minnesota Multiphasic Personality Inventory which prove sensitive to experimentally induced malingering, and which could, at least in theory, have practical value in pointing towards deliberate attempts at feigning mental illness.

The distinction between simulation and hysteria usually provides most difficulty, and the decision reached will often depend to a considerable extent on the orientation of the examiner. The patient who is simulating will be likely to have a markedly abnormal personality, and hysterical mechanisms may be mobilised in his performance. Thus even the simulant may have a partial self-deception, with the result that the boundaries between fully conscious feigning of dementia and hysterical pseudodementia are probably far from definite, and the two will be inextricably mixed in many cases.

In attempting to apportion the roles of simulation and hysteria, Kräupl-Taylor (1966) makes the important clinical point that the malingerer is likely to be anxiously on guard to avoid inconsistencies in his behaviour, and will get angry or upset and attempt to explain away his slips when these are pointed out to him. With the self-deception of the hysterical pseudodement, on the other hand, there is often a carelessness about the inconsistencies which he shows, and his reaction may be bland, uncaring or even puzzled when these are brought to his attention. The inconsistencies themselves are likely to be more crude and obvious, and will often be closely tied to the conflict-inducing situation— the hysterical patient, for example, may recognise a neighbour while disclaiming recognition of his wife in a way that would not occur with conscious simulation.

Suggestibility is another feature which may help towards the differentiation. Kennedy and Neville (1957) found that their patients with psychogenic amnesia were markedly suggestible during interview, but the small group who later confessed to malingering had hardly been suggestible at all. Finally, the simulant is also much more likely than the hysterical patient to use his resources to defeat full inquiry, and to fail to cooperate in any close investigation.

As already stressed, however, the distinction will often be blurred, and the situation may fail to be resolved in a considerable proportion of cases. Kräupl-Taylor (1966) points out that even retrospectively the evidence can be equivocal—the dependence of the syndrome on a critical situation, and the fact that the patient has stood to gain from his behaviour, is likely to be found equally in hysterical pseudodementia and in malingering. Even a confession from the patient himself will not always be final proof, since some will confess under pressure when there is strong evidence of organic or psychogenic causation (Kennedy and Neville, 1957). It will often be helpful to keep the criteria of Farrell and Kaufman (1943) in mind before deciding firmly on a diagnosis of simulation—namely the absence of obvious disease, *a firm impression that the individual is consciously aware both of what he is doing and of his motive for so doing, and that he is fixed in carrying out a purpose to a preconceived result.*

DEPRESSIVE PSEUDODEMENTIA

Pseudodementia due to affective disorder is perhaps the form which most readily leads to mistakes in diagnosis. In depressive illness several situations may lead to a spurious impression of organic cognitive impairment. The affective disorder may activate hysterical mechanisms in the predisposed patient, so that signs of hysterical pseudodementia accompany the other manifestations of the illness. In some such patients successive attacks of depression may regularly produce a similar clinical picture. In other cases, and particularly in the elderly, the depressive illness occurs in a person whose neuronal reserves are already reduced and brings the level of functioning below a critical threshold; with antidepressant treatment, however, the previous level of functioning is restored.

Most commonly of all, however, the problem appears to have its roots neither in hysteria nor in covert brain disease, but in the general psychomotor retardation which accompanies depression and in the withdrawal of interest and attention from the environment. The patient becomes slow to grasp essentials, thinking is laboured, and behaviour becomes generally slipshod and inefficient. Events fail to register, either through lack of ability to attend and concentrate or on account of the patient's inner preoccupations. In consequence he may show faulty orientation, impairment of recent memory, and a markedly defective knowledge of current events. The impression of dementia is sometimes strengthened by the patient's decrepit appearance due to self-neglect and loss of weight (Kiloh, 1961), or when the elderly depressive becomes tremulous and assumes a shuffling gait (Post, 1965). Some patients tend to emphasise the physical components of the disorder in their complaints and fail to report the change of mood; or when depression and agitation are detected these may be regarded as secondary to the supposed dementing process.

Kendell (1974) analysed the stability of psychiatric diagnoses in England and Wales over a 5 year period as reflected in statistical returns to the Department of Health and Social Security, and found that 8% of the diagnoses of dementia were later changed to depression. Follow-up studies of patients discharged from hospital have shown even more pointedly how commonly mistakes may be made (Nott and Fleminger, 1975; Ron *et al.*, 1979). Thus in Ron *et al.*'s survey, described on pp. 414–15, 5 of 52 patients discharged with a firm diagnosis of presenile dementia were found later to have been suffering from affective disorder alone, and in several more depression had combined with other factors to give the misleading impression.

Post (1965) reports a typical example of severe cognitive impairment in the course of a depressive illness:

A retired schoolmaster had had a first depressive illness at 63, recovering with electroconvulsive therapy. At 69 he was readmitted with a six weeks' history of increasing agitation. He was very restless and apprehensive, looked perplexed and miserable, and believed that a cancer was closing up his throat. He also thought that the police were about to arrest him for some trivial sexual misdemeanour in his youth. There were no physical abnormalities, but the patient appeared to be organically confused: he did not know the name of the hospital, thought it was situated in Edenbridge instead of Eden Park, and that he had been previously admitted one year ago. He gave the year (1950) variously as 1918, and 1952. He failed to learn his psychiatrist's name. In addition he telescoped the date of various events in his life, placed the first world war correctly, but was unable to give the dates of the 1939 war, and thought MacDonald had preceded Churchill as Prime Minister. These failures were not due to lack of cooperation, as he was consistently able to repeat correctly eight digits forwards and six backwards, and he also gave excellent immediate renderings of a brief story. He recovered after four ECTs, and a week or two later his performance on tests of memory function was in keeping with his educational background and almost faultless. He continued to enjoy his retirement, but at the age of 73 had to be admitted once again on account of agitation and a fear that he had a growth in his neck. Cognitive impairment was again noted, clearing together with the agitated depression after 5 ECTs.

(Post, 1965)

Bourgeois *et al.* (1970) present further examples of apparent dementia in a setting of severe depression, all responding to ECT even where antidepressant medication had failed.

Precisely what factors govern the liability of some patients to manifest such prominent cognitive disturbance in association with depressive illness is not known. Those who do so may have some personal predisposition, since not infrequently the situation recurs in subsequent attacks. The problem may rest ultimately on matters of cerebral metabolism, levels of arousal, or other variants in the biological background of the depressive illness process. Impairment of cortical arousal, as measured by barbiturate sedation thresholds, has been studied in elderly depressives by Hemsi *et al.* (1968) and Cawley *et al.* (1973), and appears to provide a partial explanation for those who show cognitive difficulties.

The tendency is certainly particularly common in later life. Elderly depressives may sometimes score like patients with brain damage on tests of learning new material, even when not showing striking clinical signs of confusion. In consequence too great a reliance on the assessment of intellectual functions alone can be misleading in the depressed elderly patient, as already discussed in Chapter 3 (pp. 100–1). It is probable, moreover, that the biological processes of ageing within the brain are related to the development of cognitive failure with depression,

just as they appear sometimes to facilitate the emergence of depression itself. It has been shown, for example, that elderly depressives may have larger ventricles than controls (Jacoby and Levy, 1980b), and decreased brain absorption density as measured on CT scans (Jacoby *et al.*, 1983). Such features appear to characterise those patients whose first depression has only appeared in old age. Hendrickson *et al.* (1979) have shown delays in the latencies of auditory evoked responses in elderly depressed patients, similar in direction though less in degree to those seen in dementia. There is reason to suppose, therefore, that ageing processes affecting the brain, such as cerebral neuronal loss, may combine with the neurochemical concomitants of depression to lead to the cognitive failure.

The following clinical points may be helpful in making the important differentiation between depressive illness and degenerative brain disease in patients where the situation is uncertain (Post, 1965; Roth and Myers, 1969; Wells, 1979, 1982):

The onset of endogenous depression is typically acute and recent, whereas that of dementia is insidious. A careful history in depressive pseudodementia may strongly suggest that up to the time of appearance of depressive symptoms there had been no decline whatever in abilities or memory. The depressed patient will often communicate a sense of distress, whereas in dementia the emotions tend to be shallow. In particular, patients with depression will often complain of their cognitive difficulties with vigour and feeling in a manner distinctly unusual for dementia. In the standard interview it may be noted that questions about the presenting complaints are handled well and that large amounts of historical information are organised without difficulty, whereas replies to direct and specific questions meet with a strangely inadequate response. A tendency to counter questions by 'Don't know' responses is frequently observed, in contrast to the attempts to confabulate or make facile excuses for failure in the patient who is organically confused. Performance on tests of cognitive function may be inconsistent in depressive pseudodementia, with surprising preservation of certain areas and topics. Inattention will usually emerge as the principal defect, along with slowed mental processing and paucity of verbal elaboration (Caine, 1981). Defects of higher cortical function such as dysphasia or dyspraxia will be conspicuous by their absence. Finally in cases which most resemble dementia the family pattern of illness is often also atypical.

Mention must be made of the special problem

which exists when depressive illness complicates the picture in patients with organic brain damage. The situation in patients recovering from head injury is discussed in Chapter 5 (p. 159), but difficulty may also arise with other forms of cerebral insult as in the following case:

A 43-year-old woman of good previous intelligence and stable personality was referred to hospital with a 6 month history of insomnia, difficulty in thinking clearly, forgetfulness when shopping and difficulty in managing her home. Three weeks before admission she had developed an acute episode of agitation with incoherent and muddled speech, and from that time she had become progressively out of touch with those around her. On examination she was perplexed and anxious but showed no noteworthy evidence of depression. Her talk was incoherent, she was disoriented for time, and psychometric examination revealed a full scale IQ of 60 (verbal scale 68, performance scale 59). The electroencephalogram showed some reduction of activity over the right central area and slow waves in the posterior temporal regions. The air encephalogram showed dilation of the right lateral ventricle with some cortical atrophy over the surface. A diagnosis of presenile dementia was made, and after an unsuccessful trial at home she was transferred to a mental hospital in another part of the country. There she could be visited by her sisters while her husband continued to rear the children alone.

Some 6 years later she was re-referred for assessment at the request of her relatives. They had noted great variability in her condition, and although most of the time she had continued to be incoherent and perplexed she had not deteriorated further as expected. On week-end leaves from hospital in recent months she had even shown short-lived spells of near normal behaviour.

Examination now showed her to be slow, incoherent and perplexed as before, often losing the thread in simple sentences and with obvious difficulty in assembling her thoughts. Now, however, she was correctly oriented and showed definite evidence of mild depression. Her level of performance fluctuated remarkably from day to day, and sometimes she proved capable of answering questions and holding brief conversations on simple matters. The air encephalogram showed persistent cortical atrophy on the right and the ventricles were slightly larger than before, but repeat psychometric testing showed considerably better scores (full scale IQ = 91, verbal scale 97, performance scale 84). However, tests of new learning ability remained firmly in the organic range.

She was started on imipramine and this was followed by slow improvement. Later six ECTs were given with further improvement still. Lucid intervals became increasingly prolonged and she began for the first time to take some interest in her affairs and predicament. Unfortunately it emerged that in the intervening years her husband had established a liaison with his housekeeper and he now refused to have her home, but despite the distress of this discovery she achieved a job as a typist and eventually left hospital to live in a hostel nearby. She remained well during the next twelve months, apart from occasional brief relapses to her former incoherent state after particularly distressing episodes in relation to her family situation. She then died suddenly of a subarachnoid haemorrhage and autopsy was not obtained.

It would seem that in this patient some episode, possibly of a vascular nature, had led initially to the brain damage which was revealed and which had suggested the diagnosis of presenile dementia. Over the ensuing years her level of function had been still further impaired by affective disorder, which nonetheless responded gratifyingly to appropriate treatment and with substantial and sustained improvement in cognitive function.

Some patients can obviously present severe and protracted difficulties over the question of diagnosis, particularly those who are mute or bordering on stupor. When the true situation remains uncertain after careful in-patient observation, the response to light abreaction with intravenous sodium amytal can be informative. Abundant evidence of depressive thought content may be revealed, or memory difficulties may clear substantially, whereas in organic dementia the confusion would be exacerbated. Perry and Jacobs (1982) review the value of the procedure and give guidance over matters of technique.

Attempts at sleep deprivation have also been recommended in this situation (Letemendia et al., 1981). A period of 40 hours of maintained wakefulness can result in a temporary reversal of mood in depressive pseudodementia, and a dramatic return to normal intellectual function. Though only briefly maintained this can provide the decisive information on which to base future treatment strategies. Electroconvulsive therapy, as indicated above, can at times be effective when antidepressant medication has failed, and will frequently warrant a trial when results from these procedures are encouraging.

It is possible that certain advances in electrophysiological investigation may also prove to be of value in aiding the distinction between depression and dementia, particularly the study of event related potentials and other derivatives of the EEG. Goodin et al. (1978) have found that delay in the P_3 component of the auditory evoked response can be a sensitive indicator of dementia, and O'Connor et al. (1979) have shown that 'coherence' measures of EEG synchronisation between one brain region and another can distinguish broadly between depressed and demented elderly patients. The further exploration of such methods could result in clinically useful tools.

OTHER FORMS OF PSEUDODEMENTIA

Hypomania rather than depression may very occasionally produce a picture which is mistaken for dementia. Distractibility may be so severe that the patient cannot follow a coherent train of thought, and answers so random that he appears to be grossly disoriented and with failing memory. Playfulness may also lead him to give false replies to questions. When at the same time the affective component of the picture is incompletely developed, considerable difficulty with diagnosis may be encountered. Such cases are rare, but an example has been reported by Kiloh (1961):

A man of 58 had been behaving strangely for four weeks, claiming that he had won £100,000 on the football pools and extracting paste stones from cheap jewellery and attempting to sell them as valuable diamonds. He was restless and overactive and broke several windows on being ejected from his lodgings.

On admission to hospital he appeared grossly confused. He gave hopelessly inaccurate answers to calculations, to the date, and gave long rambling stories about his earlier activities, each totally different from the others. He was thought to be confabulating and the diagnosis of a Korsakoff state with an underlying dementia was made. On psychiatric examination it became apparent that he was elated and many of his ideas were distinctly grandiose in quality. Although he was dirty and neglected, behaviour was in most respects out of accord with his apparently gross memory defect. Furthermore he gave an accurate account of the facts leading up to his admission, even though he insisted that this had occurred nine years ago. He was clearly well in touch with his surroundings and his replies merely reflected a playfulness dependent on a somewhat simple sense of humour. He was, in fact, suffering from a manic illness and there was no real evidence of any intellectual impairment.

(Kiloh, 1961)

Episodes of mania in the elderly are particularly liable to produce a picture which at first sight suggests dementia (Carney, 1983). The overactivity is mistaken for agitation, and incoherence and physical deterioration can combine to suggest an organic cerebral process.

Schizophrenia may likewise lead to difficulty, for example when a patient with advanced schizophrenic deterioration presents for attention at a hospital where he is unknown. The poverty of ideas, blunting of emotion and unkempt appearance may strongly suggest dementia, especially when habits are deteriorated and hoarding rituals have become established. Elderly patients with late paraphrenia can present a particularly misleading picture (Roth, 1981). Years of self-induced isolation coupled with entrenched paranoid ideas may have led to a situation of chaos and disorganisation in their homes. Moreover their delusions and hallucinations can be so bizarre and insightless that dementia immediately springs to mind.

In schizophrenia both concrete thinking and perseveration may be much in evidence, and proper assessment of cognitive functions may be very difficult. The so-called 'buffoonery syndrome' perhaps comes closest to simulating dementia (Bleuler, 1924). As the name implies such patients show a tendency to clowning and fatuous jocularity, give bizarre inaccurate replies to questions, and fail hopelessly on tests of cognitive function. The distinction here from hysterical pseudodementia may be very difficult, and hysterical as well as schizophrenic mechanisms are probably operative in many examples.

In uncertain cases the clinical distinction between schizophrenia and dementia usually rests on identifying first rank symptoms of schizophrenic illness, or cardinal aspects of schizophrenic thought disorder. Schizophrenic thinking, although grossly disordered, is usually adequate for the day to day tasks of living, and the 'hard core' of basic cognitive functions which deteriorate early in organic dementia can usually be shown to be intact.

Forms of neurotic reaction other than hysterical dissociation may also lead to pictures resembling dementia. Severe obsessional ruminative states occasionally entrap the patient to an extent that leads to self-neglect, and may block his ability to demonstrate that intellectual functions are intact. In severe anxiety neurosis the patient may come to focus on minor defects of memory, difficulty with concentration and a host of physical symptoms, and be rendered incapable of co-operating fully on tests of cognitive ability. Reactive depression, in addition to liberating hysterical features, may also lead to states of pathological regression and dependence which fortify the impression of failing cognitive function; such an example was described in Chapter 5 (p. 166).

Assessment and Differential Diagnosis

Every patient suspected of a primary senile or presenile dementia requires full and comprehensive evaluation. This will in all cases require certain investigatory procedures in addition to the routines of history taking and clinical examination. The label of a primary dementing illness carries a hopeless prognosis, and unless every care is taken in applying it serious mistakes may later be revealed.

The principal aim must be to exclude a remediable cause for the patient's symptoms. Altogether the yield of treatable conditions is likely to be low, but those that are discovered are vitally important. Moreover, even if a primary dementing process is confirmed, other concomitant disorders may still be aggravating the situation, and will sometimes have caused the patient to present at this particular time.

Conditions amenable to treatment include pathologies within the skull such as cerebral tumour, subdural haematoma, normal pressure hydrocephalus and general paresis, also certain systemic disorders which may be impairing cerebral function indirectly. The latter include the several causes of cerebral anoxia, myxoedema, hypoglycaemia, metabolic derangements due to renal or hepatic disease, vitamin deficiencies, alcoholism, and intoxication due to various drugs and chemicals. The tendency, especially in the elderly, for a depressive illness to masquerade as dementia or to aggravate its manifestations must also be remembered.

This range, even of the commoner differential diagnoses, is very large, and cannot be adequately appraised in the out-patient clinic. In-patient evaluation should be regarded as mandatory for every patient suspected of presenile dementia; many patients with dementia in old age will likewise require admission, though in the very elderly it will not always be justified to pursue investigations to the limit as discussed on p. 419. In the hospital setting a more comprehensive history can be obtained, the patient's behaviour can be closely observed, and investigations can be planned and carried out more efficiently than on an out-patient basis.

The value of comprehensive in-patient evaluation has been shown by several surveys, as indicated in Table 14. These represent consecutive series of patients admitted to hospital with a presumptive diagnosis of dementia, from the UK (Marsden and Harrison, 1972), the USA (Freemon, 1976), Scotland (Victoratos et al., 1977) and Australia (Smith and Kiloh, 1981). Remarkably similar findings emerge with regard to the relative incidence of different forms of pathology. The series were from neurological units and represent a broad spectrum of patient ages, some 80% or more being below the age of 65; they should be interpreted therefore as indicating what might be expected in 'presenile' rather than 'senile' dementias.

The first point to note is that some 15 per cent of the patients were judged not to be demented after full evaluation, but to be suffering from some other organic psychosyndrome or from functional psychiatric disorder. Almost half of the total were presumed to have Alzheimer's disease, establishing this as the single most important cause of dementia. Arteriosclerotic dementia follows next, with an equal number where alcoholism is thought to have played a part. Huntington's chorea and Creutzfeldt–Jakob disease make a relatively small contribution to the total numbers.

Tumours and normal pressure hydrocephalus are not infrequent. Among the eight tumours in Marsden and Harrison's series three were benign, three had no abnormal neurological signs, and seven showed global impairment of intellect without focal psychological deficits. The rarity of examples of myxoedema, B_{12} deficiency and other well-recognised causes of dementia may have been the result of out-patient screening for more obvious medical illnesses.

Functional psychiatric disorder masquerading as dementia proves to be remarkably common in the UK and Australian series, and amounts to 8% of cases overall. Depression is most often responsible.

In discussing such results Wells (1978) concludes that potentially correctable disorders (depression, drug toxicity, hydrocephalus, benign intracranial masses) may be expected in some 15% of patients, with an additional 20–25% in whom some useful intervention will be possible—control of hypertension, withdrawal of alcohol, or genetic counselling. Thus prospects for helping are by no means rare when the precise diagnosis is pursued energetically. In elderly demented patients the results will of course be less impressive; Smith and Kiloh (1981) estimated that 21% of their patients below the age of 65 had potentially treatable conditions, compared with only 5% of the over 65s.

Analogous surveys of patients admitted to psychiatric hospitals are not available but might be expected to show an even higher incidence of functional psychiatric disorders. Two follow-up reports of patients *discharged* from psychiatric units with a firm diagnosis of presenile dementia have yielded striking results. Nott and Fleminger (1975) enquired into the long-term outcome of 50 patients discharged with such a diagnosis; of the 35 traced 5–25 years later, 15 had deteriorated as expected and many of these had died, but 2 remained unchanged and no less than 18 had actually improved. Thus the diagnosis had been erroneous in more than half of the patients. The presence of memory disorder on initial evaluation had been a central source of error, but abnormal results on psychometry and indications of atrophy on air-encephalography had also contributed. The patients wrongly diagnosed as demented consisted mainly of people with marked personality difficulties and severe neurotic or affective disorders, most of whom continued thereafter to show chronic psychiatric disability of a non-organic type.

Ron et al. (1979) carried out a similar 5–15 year follow-up, obtaining information on 51 patients discharged from the Bethlem Royal and Maudsley Hospitals with a diagnosis of presenile dementia. Eighteen were alive, and the diagnosis was rejected in 16 (31%). Seven of the 16 proved in retrospect to have been suffering from a functional psychiatric disorder alone, mostly affective illness. The other 9 showed non-progressive brain damage or Parkinson's disease, or had had transient acute organic reactions; many had had a complicating affective illness as well. The results of psychometry and air-encephalography had again often lent spurious support to the clinical impression of a progressive dementing process.

Both studies therefore illustrate the surprisingly large margin of error liable to occur in the diagnosis of dementia in psychiatric units, and the need to take special care over the evaluation of the total psychiatric setting in which the presumed dementia occurs. Ron et al. were able to show that certain key psychiatric features discriminated strongly between patients who had demented and those who had not—the presence of depressed mood during admission, a history of previous affective disorder, and evidence of an abnormal premorbid personality.

A broad attitude to the question of differential diagnosis must be maintained throughout all stages of the clinical enquiry. The history provides important clues, similarly the physical and mental state examinations. Psychometric assessment can be very helpful, especially in borderline cases, and in

TABLE 14. Final diagnosis in patients presumed to be demented

	Marsden and Harrison (1972)	Freemon (1976)	Victoratos et al. (1977)	Smith and Kiloh (1981)	Total	% of Total
Total cases admitted:	106	60	52	200	418	100%
Dementia confirmed						
Cause unknown						
(presumed Alzheimer's disease)	48	26	31	84	189	45%
Arteriosclerotic dementia	8	5	5	22	40	10%
Alcohol contributing	6	4	1	30	41	10%
Huntington's chorea	3	4	—	5	12	3%
Creutzfeldt–Jakob	3	—	1	—	4	<1%
Tumour or subdural haematoma	8	3	5	3	19	5%
Normal pressure hydrocephalus	5	7	1	8	21	5%
Post-head injury	1	1	1	5	8	<2%
Myxoedema/neurosyphilis/ post-encephalitis	1	3	1	3	8	<2%
Other	1	—	4	4	9★	2%
Total:	**84**	**53**	**50**	**164**	**351**	**84%**
Dementia uncertain:	6	—	—	—	6	1%
Diagnosis uncertain:	2	—	2	—	4	1%
Other organic psychosyndrome						
Korsakoff psychosis	—	—	—	11	11	3%
Drug toxicity	2	5	—	1	8	<2%
Delirium	—	—	—	2	2	<1%
Dysphasia/epilepsy/hepatic failure	1	1	—	2	4	<1%
Total:	**3**	**6**	—	**16**	**25**	**6%**
Functional psychiatric disorder						
Depression	9	1	—	11	21	5%
Hypomania/mania	1	—	—	2	3	<1%
Schizophrenia	—	—	—	7	7	<2%
Hysteria	1	—	—	—	1	<1%
Total:	**11**	**1**	—	**20**	**32**	**8%**

★ Includes 2 epilepsy, 2 cerebral anoxia, 1 post-subarachnoid haemorrhage, 1 giant aneurysm, 1 Parkinson's disease, 1 cerebellar degeneration, 1 Kufs' disease.

confirming or refuting the global nature of the patient's intellectual difficulties. Certain ancillary investigations will always be needed as set out below. In the majority of cases the definitive diagnosis will soon become apparent, but occasionally the picture will be perplexing and the search may need to be far ranging. The problem may then conveniently be considered in relation to the broad diagnostic categories outlined in Chapter 4—organic versus functional mental illness, acute versus chronic organic reactions, and diffuse versus focal lesions, before embarking on a systematic consideration of specific disease entities. With observation in hospital the functional psychiatric disorders which masquerade as dementia will usually be detected before investigations have proceeded very far, but this is not invariably so.

Occasionally complete investigation will leave one with probabilities rather than certainties, and it will then be necessary to see what course the disorder takes with time. In early cases of primary dementia all investigations can be negative. Lack of clear confirmation of the diagnosis will mean that it is essential to keep the patient under regular review, with readiness to investigate anew if later developments are in any way unusual.

History

The *family history* can be of prime importance in Huntington's chorea, particularly in very early cases and when the presentation is atypical. A family history may occasionally be forthcoming with other forms of primary dementia, but not sufficiently often to help materially with diagnosis. A marked family history of affective disorder may occasionally help towards the identification of depressive pseudodementia.

The *antecedent history* may contain clues of great significance. Even slight head injury can lead to a subdural haematoma, especially in elderly, arteriosclerotic or alcoholic subjects. This may declare itself only after a considerable latent interval. Normal pressure hydrocephalus may likewise be traceable to prior head injury, subarachnoid haemorrhage or meningitis.

Recent fits, faints or episodes of collapse will indicate the possibility of a cerebral tumour, a cerebral infarction, episodic hypoglycaemia, or an undiagnosed myocardial infarction which has led to cerebral anoxia. Previous episodes of transient neurological disturbance will raise the question of cerebral arteriosclerosis or multiple sclerosis.

Special care must be taken whenever there is a previous history of anaemia, heart disease or chronic pulmonary disorder which may now be leading to cerebral anoxia. The recent administration of an anaesthetic may be significant, or any episode of carbon monoxide poisoning or prolonged coma due to drug overdosage.

Recent illnesses must be viewed in relation to their effects on cerebral function, in particular hepatic or renal disease which may have led to metabolic disturbance, or infective processes which may have resulted in a cerebral abscess.

Dietary neglect may have produced vitamin B or folic acid deficiency, either as a primary aetiological factor or as a complication of the dementing process. A history of gastrectomy may be especially significant in relation to vitamin B_{12} deficiency.

Alcoholism deserves careful and sometimes pressing enquiry. The progressive inefficiency and deterioration of habits in alcoholic subjects can present as a possible dementing process, and Korsakoff's psychosis can at first sight be mistaken for global intellectual impairment. The possibility that a true alcoholic dementia may exist is discussed on p. 517. Drug abuse should be suspected when the picture fluctuates from time to time or when there is a history of similar episodes in the past. Medication recently prescribed should also always be determined. In obscure cases the patient's occupation warrants consideration, with enquiry about the possibility of chronic poisoning from lead, manganese or other chemicals.

Finally due attention should be paid to any history of markedly unstable traits in the previous personality, of previous episodes of functional mental illness, or of conflict situations antedating the onset of the illness. These may be the essential clues to certain cases of pseudodementia.

Certain symptoms are of importance. Headache, visual disturbance or vomiting will raise the possibility of a space occupying lesion. Epileptic fits, especially with a focal onset, must similarly be noted with care. Other complaints which may indicate focal rather than diffuse cerebral disease include special difficulty with language, trouble in recognising people or objects, or inability to carry out habitual acts and manipulations. Malaise, loss of energy and anorexia will suggest anaemia, uraemia or occult malignant disease. A cough of recent onset and severe loss of weight will suggest carcinoma of the lung, which can sometimes present with dementia in the absence of secondary cerebral deposits. Sensitivity to cold will immediately raise the possibility of myxoedema, and excessive thirst or bone pain may suggest parathyroid disorder.

The *mode of evolution of the illness* is of great diagnostic importance. Separate note must be taken of the nature of the principal early difficulties, the duration up to the time of presentation, the definiteness or indefiniteness of onset, and the steadiness or otherwise of progression.

An onset with memory disturbance is characteristic of most primary dementias, especially Alzheimer's disease which is the commonest form. In the elderly this may for a time be hard to distinguish from the 'normal' memory difficulties of old age; the dysmnesia of senescence typically progresses very slowly, and occurs in a setting of relative preservation of other cognitive processes, whereas in dementia other aspects of intellect usually soon come to be implicated. Any onset with symptoms other than memory disturbance should always raise suspicion. Marked affective disturbance or change of personality may be seen with Pick's disease or Huntington's chorea, but may equally be indicative of a frontal lobe tumour or general paresis.

A short duration immediately raises the possibility of a secondary dementia—due to cerebral tumour, covert cerebral infarction, or some extracranial cause. In most primary dementing illnesses the symptoms are of long duration, usually many months by the time the patient presents for attention.

A definite date for the onset is also rarely obtained in the primary dementias, which tend to begin so insidiously that neither the patient nor his family can give a precise timing to the earliest manifestations. With cerebral tumours, by contrast, there is usually some episode or symptom which can later be recalled as the first indication of the illness. This information can be important in tumours which are unaccompanied by headache or other evidence of raised intracranial pressure, or, for example, in frontal meningiomas which can present with global dementia and lack all focal signs.

An abrupt onset coupled with neurological defects which later resolve will strongly suggest a cerebrovascular accident. Alvarez (1966) has stressed the importance of 'little strokes' which may lead to intellectual impoverishment yet produce no identifiable focal signs whatever; here the clue is provided by the fact that the disturbance can be traced to a precise point in time. Caution is needed, however, before ascribing the patient's dementia entirely to such causes, and when rapid dementia follows a minute infarct some additional pathological process

such as the parenchymal changes of SDAT may be expected to be present as well.

Steady progression without fluctuation or remission is typical of all the primary dementias with the exception of arteriosclerotic dementia. Marked fluctuations from time to time immediately suggest that one may be dealing not with a chronic but an acute organic reaction, or at least with an acute component superimposed upon the basic dementing process. Rothschild (1941) rightly points out the difficulty which can be encountered in differentiating an acute organic reaction from dementia, especially arteriosclerotic dementia. The elderly are unusually vulnerable to the effects of anoxia or metabolic derangements, and the responsible somatic disease may not be very obvious. A markedly intermittent course, with periods of possible clouding or delirium, should therefore be noted with especial care, and will indicate the need for a scrupulous survey of the cardiac, pulmonary, renal, hepatic and endocrine systems. Fluctuations and periods of remission will also raise the possibility of a subdural haematoma or of drug abuse. An intermittent course with discrete episodes of abnormal behaviour may suggest hypoglycaemia, and when severe this can leave enduring dementia in its wake.

Examination

The *physical examination* is usually much more important than the mental state evaluation in pointing to remediable causes of dementia, or in revealing systemic disorders which may be aggravating the situation. The general appearance may suggest myxoedema or malnutrition. Inspection of the skin and tongue may indicate dehydration, vitamin depletion or anaemia. A patient who looks unwell will be suspected of metabolic disorder, malignant disease or some infective process. Common foci of infection in the elderly include low-grade pneumonia or bronchitis, and in women cystitis. A low-grade intermittent pyrexia may also raise the possibility of subacute encephalitis, cerebral abscess, collagen vascular disorder, or on rare occasions multiple embolisation in association with subacute bacterial endocarditis (Roth 1981). The cardiovascular state always requires appraisal with regard to hypertension, arteriosclerosis, congestive cardiac failure, and the patency of the carotid arteries in the neck. In elderly males the possibility of prostatic enlargement should be explored.

The *neurological examination* will rarely reveal marked localising signs in the primary dementias, with the exception of arteriosclerotic dementia and the rare cases of Creutzfeldt–Jakob disease. Evidence of focal paresis or sensory loss in association with a slowly progressive dementia therefore immediately raises the possibility of a space occupying lesion. Considerable care must sometimes be taken to exclude visual field defects or unilateral anosmia, and this can be difficult in patients who are less than fully cooperative.

Examination of the optic fundi may reveal evidence of raised intracranial pressure. The pupil reactions may betray general paresis, and nystagmus will suggest barbiturate intoxication. Tremors, incoordination and dysarthria may indicate bromism. Pronounced ataxia in association with memory disturbance will suggest the residue of Wernicke's encephalopathy, and peripheral neuropathy will raise the possibility of alcoholism or heavy metal poisoning.

Evidence of dysarthria, minor dysphagia, or a brisk jaw jerk may indicate early pseudobulbar palsy, and should be carefully assessed when cerebral arteriosclerosis is suspected.

Early incontinence and unsteadiness of gait are important pointers towards normal pressure hydrocephalus. Close observation may sometimes be required for the detection of the early choreiform movements of Huntington's chorea, and myoclonic jerking in association with dementia will raise the possibility of Creutzfeldt–Jakob disease. Evidence of Parkinson's disease or multiple sclerosis must not be overlooked.

The *mental state evaluation* is principally directed at establishing the global nature of the intellectual disorder. Care must be taken to avoid mistaking dysphasia, circumscribed amnesic difficulties or parietal lobe symptomatology for global dementia. Somnolence, in the absence of uraemia or other metabolic disorder will suggest hypothalamic damage. A marked degree of emotional lability with pathological laughing and crying will suggest an arteriosclerotic process with an accent on the basal regions of the brain. Any suspicion of clouding of consciousness will immediately raise the possibility that one is dealing with an acute organic reaction rather than dementia, or that there is some complicating toxic, infective or metabolic disorder present.

The mental state evaluation is equally important for the detection of pseudodementia. Inconsistencies in the patient's performance may raise the question of a Ganser state, hysterical pseudodementia, or even on rare occasions simulation. The patient's attitude to his symptoms, and the degree to which his purported disabilities interfere with his daily life can be observations of crucial importance. Affective changes sometimes need to be sought out with care. A marked depressive component may indicate depressive pseudodementia, or concurrent depression may be aggravating the situation in a patient with organic cerebral disease. The help that may sometimes be obtained by abreaction in reaching the correct diagnosis is discussed on p. 412. Careful interviewing may reveal schizophrenic symptomatology in the patient who is markedly withdrawn or bizarre in conduct.

Psychometric testing will often be of value (Chapter 3, p. 92). It may help in the distinction between organic and functional psychiatric illness and with the question of diffuse versus focal cerebral disorder. In very early cases psychometry provides a measured baseline against which future progress can be assessed.

Investigations

In the primary dementias there are no specific abnormalities in the blood, urine, cerebrospinal fluid or on skull X-ray. Investigations are therefore principally directed at detecting remediable conditions, or uncovering systemic disorders which may be worsening the clinical picture.

Every patient with dementia requires the following investigations as a minimum:

Estimation of haemoglobin, full blood count, erythrocyte sedimentation rate, serological tests for syphilis, blood urea, serum electrolytes, serum proteins and liver function tests. Routine urine examination should be supplemented by microscopy and where necessary culture. Chest X-ray should always be performed for the evaluation of cardiac and pulmonary status and as a screen for primary or secondary carcinoma. Skull X-ray is required for the detection of possible pineal shift or raised intracranial pressure. The electroencephalogram should be performed routinely; evidence may emerge to raise suspicion of a focal cerebral disorder, or the pictures seen with the primary dementias may be obtained and give some support to the diagnosis. The latter, however, lack specificity as discussed in Chapter 3 (pp. 113–14), and must never be relied upon alone. An entirely normal EEG will lead one at least to reconsider the possibility of a pseudodementia.

Where CT scanning is available this should also be carried out routinely, though pressures on services for the elderly still make this impractical in many centres. Special indications will include any remote suspicion of a cerebral tumour or subdural haematoma, the presence of focal neurological signs, a history suggestive of cerebral infarction or head injury, or clinical pointers towards normal pressure hydrocephalus. In the primary dementias cerebral atrophy will be revealed in a high proportion of cases, with ventricular dilatation and prominence of cortical sulci but without distortion or displacement of the ventricular system. The distribution of atrophy may point towards a diagnosis of Pick's disease, as described on p. 392, or marked shrinkage of the caudate nuclei may indicate Huntington's chorea (p. 398). Evidence of old and recent cerebral infarctions may suggest a vascular basis for the dementia. Sometimes, however, the CT scan may be entirely normal, especially in early cases, and conversely some degree of atrophy may be found in persons not suffering from dementia. The results can be interpreted only in conjunction with the total clinical findings, and the latter must be given precedence when discordant results emerge. The question of the significance of cerebral atrophy as revealed by radiological procedures is discussed further in Chapter 3 (p. 119 et seq.).

Further tests will very often be required and many clinicians will wish to include several of the following as a routine when facilities are available:

Estimation of serum B_{12}, folate, sugar, T3 and T4, cholesterol, lipids, calcium, phosphorus, and barbiturate levels. Serum protein electrophoresis may be indicated, also immunoglobulin assay and estimation of antinuclear antibodies. The electrocardiogram may show evidence of dysrhythmia, heart block, or recent myocardial infarction. Guidance to the choice of these more extended investigations will have been obtained from the history and clinical examination.

Lumbar puncture should be undertaken if the cause for the dementia remains uncertain and when there is no reason to suspect a cerebral tumour or raised intracranial pressure. Examination of the cerebrospinal fluid can be decisive in the diagnosis of general paresis in cases when the blood serology has been negative. Dementia can also occur with syphilitic arteritis which has produced scattered cerebral infarcts. The first indication of a subdural haematoma may come from an elevated cerebrospinal fluid pressure, increased protein or xanthochromia. Xanthochromia may also betray the very rare cases of leakage from a giant cerebral aneurysm which is producing dementia. Subacute and chronic forms of encephalitis may likewise be detected only after examination of the fluid.

In most cases of primary dementia the cerebrospinal fluid is entirely normal. It has been uniformly normal in autopsy-proven cases of Alzheimer's disease, though occasionally the protein may be elevated in Creutzfeldt–Jakob disease, and sometimes in cases of arteriosclerotic dementia when there has been a recent cerebral infarction, uraemia or congestive cardiac failure.

Most of the above procedures cause relatively little discomfort or inconvenience and are readily carried out. The chief difficulty usually arises when CT scanning is not available and a decision must be made about further radiological procedures which are upsetting to the patient. Echoencephalography may be undertaken as a screening test for focal brain lesions, or alternatively a radioisotope scan. But arteriography or air-encephalography may then be needed, the latter remaining the definitive investigation for excluding a cerebral tumour or normal pressure hydrocephalus.

Air-encephalography will be required for the complete investigation of younger demented patients in the absence of facilities for a CT scan; in the elderly, however, it must be performed more circumspectly, especially when the physical condition is poor. When all other evidence is consonant with a primary dementing process, and there is no focal component to the clinical picture, it will usually be judged unwarranted to subject a frail and elderly person to the distress of the investigation.

The further investigations required when normal pressure hydrocephalus is strongly suspected—risa cisternography and intracranial pressure monitoring—are discussed on pp. 117 and 640.

Very occasionally it may be deemed advisable to exclude other rare conditions which can give rise to dementia. Metachromatic leucodystrophy is detected by the estimation of arylsulphatase in the blood or urine or by biopsies of peripheral nerve or rectal wall (p. 649), Kufs' disease by skeletal muscle or rectal biopsy (p. 649), and Whipple's disease by lymph node or jejunal biopsy (p. 650).

Finally, cerebral biopsy is very occasionally used as an aid to diagnosis. Changes typical of Alzheimer's disease may be revealed, or on rare occasions Creutzfeldt–Jakob disease or subacute encephalitis may be discovered. Short of cerebral biopsy there is no investigatory procedure which can give information of much value in differentiating one form of primary dementing illness from another, but in the present state of knowledge such distinctions are of little practical value to the patient. If future research should bring promising leads in the treatment of individual conditions biopsy may ultimately become better justified and more widely practised.

Management of the Senile and Presenile Dementias

The first step in management is always full medical evaluation along the lines already discussed. This is necessary for the firm establishment of the diagnosis, the exclusion of remediable conditions which have masqueraded as primary dementia, and to check on any concurrent disease which may be aggravating the symptoms. In cases where the first evaluation has given equivocal results it is essential that this be borne in mind during follow-up, with readiness to investigate anew at a later stage if the course is in any way unusual.

Early Problems in Management

After establishing the diagnosis, both the disease and the person suffering from it must be clearly kept in mind. In early cases, particularly of presenile dementia, difficult decisions will often have to be made over such questions as continuation with work and how fully to explain about prognosis. On both issues much will depend on factors specific to the individual and his family.

Continuation with employment may occasionally be possible for a surprising length of time when the work makes little demand on intellect and social competence is preserved. Simple assembly work, for example, may continue to be feasible even though memory lapses are occurring in unfamiliar situations. Unfortunately, however, it is often in the field of work that the earliest evidence of the disease has emerged. Certainly work involving responsibility or the need for informed decisions should be terminated as soon as the diagnosis is unequivocally established.

A housewife may continue to cope for some considerable time with the help of simple props and tactful aid from other members of the family. Advice at a very simple level, such as the provision of shopping lists or the setting aside of more time for routine tasks, may delay the point when independence must be relinquished. Regular visits from a friendly neighbour during the day can similarly be invaluable.

On the question of prognosis there is usually little to be gained by attempting to explain this in detail to the patient. Often he will not raise the subject at all; quite commonly the difficulty is in trying to persuade him that something is amiss and that an alteration is needed in his way of life. Some simple formula is usually most appropriate and kindest to the patient, telling him for example that 'there appears to be some trouble with the circulation which has caused your memory to be faulty, and we are going to try to remedy it'. More detailed explanations are likely to be forgotten. If, however, the affective tone of the consultation is gloomy this may well persist and colour the patient's attitude to his disability.

With the relatives it will usually be necessary to be entirely frank, particularly if long-term family decisions are to be made. Here again, much will depend on a sensitive appreciation of the nature of the person who will have to bear responsibility for the patient. Some will genuinely want to know the outlook, others will find it easier to learn about it gradually from the course of events. Since one cannot hope to be accurate it is wise and humane to err in the direction of too favourable rather than too pessimistic a forecast; the latter may needlessly destroy morale just when it is most needed in the earlier phases of the disorder. Thus it is reasonable to emphasise the variability in the rate of progress of such disorders from one patient to another, and to stress that one can only wait to observe what course is followed in each particular example.

It is important, if the point is pressed, to emphasise how commonly the patient's own appreciation of his decline becomes blunted with the progress of the disease.

Social Work Care

The management of the dementing patient and his family is an area in which the social worker can give a great deal of help. At a practical level maintenance in employment may be secured for a while. An understanding employer may be persuaded to make allowances, or to readjust the nature of the demands made upon the patient. When gainful occupation is no longer feasible attendance at a day centre may be arranged, improving at the same time the morale of the patient and his family.

Among the elderly, in particular, there will often be a need to exploit community resources to the full, with provision of home helps, 'meals on wheels' or domiciliary laundry services. The assistance of community nurses or health visitors may be required. Voluntary organisations can provide invaluable help, such as the local branches of the National Association for Mental Health ('MIND'), or local church and community groups. These will more readily offer help when the social worker is at hand to advise and coordinate activities. Much will depend on knowledge of what is available in the vicinity.

In addition, and very importantly, the family can be helped in their own understanding and management of the patient. It is essential to explain in some detail the nature of the patient's disabilities and the areas in which he is liable to fail. The need to avoid sudden changes of surroundings and routines should always be stressed, and the family's natural inclination to take the patient for a holiday or complete change of scene must sometimes be discouraged. A proper appreciation of the causes of failure and of aberrant behaviour will do much to relieve the onlooker's distress. Unhelpful attitudes of irritability or hostility towards the patient may be prevented, likewise attitudes of excessive compassion and concern. Valuable support and advice can be obtained by relatives from organizations such as the Alzheimer's Disease Society in the UK, and the Alzheimer's Disease and Related Disorders Association in the USA. Many families will benefit from the detailed practical advice on the management of day-to-day problems contained in the family guide prepared by Mace and Rabins (1981).

Macmillan (1960) has discussed the common progression seen in the families of elderly demented patients, whereby responsibility is at first willingly accepted but later this becomes increasingly irksome. A similar pattern may be discerned with presenile dementia. A state of partial rejection ultimately develops, and this then suddenly becomes intensified by some incident such as wandering away, nocturnal restlessness or paranoid accusations. The situation can be greatly ameliorated by on-going social work support, and the need for institutionalisation may then be considerably delayed. It is essential, however, that the family should know that when it is finally necessary, admission to hospital or some other form of care will be arranged. Temporary admissions at holiday periods may also help the family to cope, or better still attendance at a day hospital or occupation centre from an early stage.

When the patient can no longer be managed at home optimal placement must be arranged. Much will again depend on local facilities and the degree to which social, psychiatric and geriatric services have become organised. Preparation should ideally be made well in advance of the time when this is likely to be required, though such is not always possible. Alternatives to hospitalisation will often suffice, since after full evaluation and attention to remediable abnormalities most patients need little by way of direct medical attention. The more expensive models of hospital care are not always optimal and may indeed sometimes be counter-productive; small living units may do much more to maintain self-help skills and delay total dependence. An old people's home or nursing home is often ideal, and sometimes night-hostel accommodation is all that is required for a time. Sheltered accommodation for married couples is sometimes a possibility. The needs of different patients are widely variable, and should ideally be matched by an equally varied range of resources.

Psychological Aspects of Management

In the early stages supportive care can do much to help the patient. A positive relationship with a trusted physician or general practitioner has an important part to play in alleviating distress, and while insight is retained the patient should not be allowed to feel abandoned. Skilled help may be required to enable him to reach a new adjustment, and to persuade him to relinquish tasks which are no longer possible. The aim must be to achieve such things without a catastrophic lowering of self-esteem.

Kennedy (1959) describes how dementing patients commonly develop a sense of ill-formulated inferiority, and react thereto in a variety of ways. Intimate knowledge of the patient and of his style of coping can often help to avert, or at least defer, the more florid forms of reaction.

Some patients tend to react by what Kennedy describes as 'dependent decline', with greater than necessary dependence on those around and premature abdication of responsibility. Others react by 'defensive limitation' with restriction of activities, hoarding of material assets, suspicious attitudes and self-isolation. Others 'over-compensate', becoming interfering and dogmatic, and tend to dwell on the past with insistent repetition of anecdotes. Some 'retreat from reality', with refusal to retire from work. 'Projective decline' involves the blaming of others for mistakes and transgressions, and in more florid form extends to the development of frank paranoid delusions. Other forms of maladaptation involve egocentric demanding behaviour, exaggeration of deafness or immobility, reactive depression, hypochondriasis, or paranoia.

Of central importance is the handling the patient receives from those in daily contact with him, whether members of his family, nurses or occupational therapists. Wells (1971b) usefully distinguishes three aims in management—the restitution of lost functions, the reduction of the patient's need for functions irretrievably impaired, and the optimal utilisation of those which remain.

The first, *the restitution of lost functions*, is unfortunately rarely possible. It is largely a matter of medical treatment as discussed below, with measures to promote optimal physical health and some rather dubious benefits which may accrue from certain drugs. But with the others, the reduction of need for functions lost and the optimal use of those which remain, considerable headway can be made by skilled and tactful interaction with the patient.

Reduction of need for functions lost: An accurate assessment of functions irretrievably lost is essential, so that the patient may be steered away from attempts to perform impossible tasks. Immediate stress is often the determinant of symptomatology in the form of anxiety, outbursts of aggression or paranoid reactions. An anonymous author writing in *the Lancet* (1950) describes with great sensitivity her interactions with her dementing father, and how the origin of illusions, delusions and episodes of grossly disturbed behaviour could be helped by the correct approach:

'He was still potentially rational. His delusions were not determined by a warped mental outlook, but were a reasonable attempt to make sense out of what was subjectively a hopelessly confusing situation. In days gone by I had learned to follow his train of thought intuitively, and could still keep close to him in spite of his difficulty with speech. I found that if I got him away from other people and steered his mind to topics which he had handled with ease in the past he became rational quite quickly. I sometimes led him into interesting discussions on subjects which he knew and cared about, and when he got the sense of being on familiar ground, where he could still tread firmly, the black cloud of depression lifted and he became his old self. As soon as he returned to the strain of new and unfamiliar situations he relapsed.'

Thus whenever possible conversation should be restricted to subjects within the patient's capability, and his own leads should be followed rather than venturing upon new topics. New and disturbing experiences should be kept to a minimum, and the daily routine structured within the patient's capabilities. Extra time must be set aside for necessary tasks, preferably with someone at hand to remind the patient what to do and how to do it.

The environment should be manipulated as far as possible to maintain calm and non-taxing surroundings, and matters arranged so that the patient is rarely confronted by his inadequacies. Things frequently required can be placed prominently and near at hand. The disposition of furniture in the room should not be changed, and a clock and a calendar should be hung conspicuously on the wall. It may be helpful to label the lavatory with a printed notice. Goldfarb (1972) discusses the ordered use of such props and supports; the more protective the setting the less will be the occasions on which the patient's autonomy and self-esteem are challenged.

Williams (1956) has shown experimentally that in dealing with demented patients the provision of extra cues can help to maintain behaviour at an improved level. Such cues may be the repetition of orders, or the supplementing of instructions by visual example. What the patient lacks is often not so much the ability to behave in a fitting manner, as the ability to select or abstract what is relevant from all the information available. Thus in Williams' experiments the performance of patients could often be greatly improved on tests of perception, or even of intellectual activity, when they were supplied with additional cues or helped to focus attention upon those normally available.

Clearly these requirements will at some point be better met in a hospital or nursing home than in the patient's own home. The strain imposed on the family must not be allowed to continue too long on the false assumption that he will be happier there. Skilled supervision ultimately becomes essential, and in the correct milieu these principles of management can be carried out much more effectively and extensively. The nurse or attendant must be prepared to repeat instructions, explain surroundings with a minimum of words, repeatedly say who she is, and become the focal point around which the patient can orient his thoughts (Kennedy, 1959). Again the environment must be stabilised as far as possible, with the minimum of changes of staff. Strong multi-colour decorations may help to improve orientation. Similarly the patient should be allowed to have familiar possessions around him.

The optimal use of residual functions is a separate aim. The patient should be encouraged to continue with social activities and to take regular exercise. Adequate periods of rest must be interspersed with gentle urging towards activity. His surroundings should be stimulating within his restricted range of abilities and despite his need for constancy. Without this his own diminished self-motivation can easily lead to under-utilisation of faculties which remain.

Occupational therapy requires a skilful selection

of tasks in order to avert frustration and help in the readaptation of the failing brain. The skill lies in helping towards disengagement from work beyond the patient's capabilities, and guidance towards substitute activities which are still within his range. It is thus the reverse of the common occupational therapy aims in patients who are being rehabilitated for work. Simple domestic tasks are often most fitting, or repetitive craft work which can give a sense of achievement without making demands on intellect or memory.

Attempts must be made to combat social isolation. Continuing ties with the family should be encouraged, even when institutionalisation has become mandatory. Socialisation may be fostered and communication improved by conjoint tasks and group activities. Simple games, quizzes and assembly work in groups can be of considerable benefit.

Cosin *et al.* (1958) were able to demonstrate the effectiveness of simple occupational and social activities in improving, at least in the short-term, the general level of behaviour of elderly patients with dementia. Domestic activities, particularly when involving cooperation with others, produced the most noticeable stimulation and satisfaction. Bower (1967) similarly reported the effects of an enriched environment in slowing, or even reversing outward evidence of the dementing process for a time.

'*Reality orientation*' and related programmes of management have been introduced in many centres where the long-term care of demented patients is undertaken. Such enterprises hinge largely on the principles outlined above, but seek to involve the staff in regularly prescribed periods of intensive interaction with the patients. These in turn have the aim of stimulating the patient into re-using neglected patterns of functioning, of re-orienting him to his environment and of restoring a sense of purpose and identity.

Informal reality orientation involves only the day to day interactions between staff and patients; repeated opportunities are taken to remind the patient who and where he is, of the time and day, and of what is happening around him. The repeated communications with the patient must be slow, clear and direct. In effect he re-learns then continually rehearses essential items of information. More formal treatment takes place in groups, occupying perhaps half an hour per day and usually in a specially set-aside room. Here stimulating materials are kept to hand, with large colourful illustrations of everyday objects and the day, month and year clearly displayed to view. During reality orientation sessions the patients are encouraged to greet one another, rehearse names and dates, identify objects, and where possible discuss outstanding items of news. A daily diary of basic information may be kept, followed by

spelling and counting games and simple group activities. The precise techniques adopted must be geared to the levels of ability of the patients concerned.

Brook *et al.* (1975) have described the effectiveness of sessions such as these in improving socialisation in the ward and sometimes even in diminishing incontinence. The active engagement of the therapists with the patients was shown to be important for success. Woods (1979) compared reality orientation sessions with unstructured discussion groups in which equivalent staff attention was given, and found that the former led to greater improvement on tests of information, orientation and memory. In general, however, the gains from treatment tend to be small and evanescent, and improvements in cognitive function usually prove to be closely tied to the content of the training sessions. Generalisation to other aspects of behaviour and to other situations has often been disappointing in the long-term view. Powell-Proctor and Miller (1982) provide a comprehensive review of the techniques and the benefits which may be expected.

Other procedures include 'reminiscence group therapy', in which patients are specifically encouraged to engage in familiar over-learned activities, listen to familiar music and re-enact well practised social situations. Bewilderment may be lessened and group cohesion improved. Miller (1977) and Woods and Britton (1977) review further specialised treatment approaches, including attempts at behavioural modification by token economy régimes. All share common factors, including the active participation of both staff and patients, the need for a consistent approach, and the desirability of near-continuous operation if maximal gains are to be achieved. The importance of these newer treatment approaches lies in the demonstration that dementing patients are capable of responding to properly structured interactions with those who care for them, and hopefully thereby of attaining improvement in the quality of their day to day existence.

Medical Aspects of Management

The strictly medical aspects of management must not be neglected. Optimal physical health must be maintained if the patient's deterioration is to be slowed and the best use made of residual functions at any given stage. Attention to adequate nutrition, hydration and vitamin replacement can sometimes meet with gratifying improvement. The elimination of infection is a matter for repeated checks, particularly chronic infection within the lungs or urinary tract. Any tendency towards congestive cardiac failure, cardiac arrhythmia or anaemia must be treated energetically. Hypertension, when severe, will warrant appropriate management. Special care must be taken to guard against iatrogenic disorders, particularly electrolyte imbalance due to diuretics and toxicity from other drugs. In multi-infarct dementia there will often be a special case for strict control of hypertension, and sometimes for treatment with anticoagulants or aspirin to guard against embolisation.

Adequate physical exercise must be encouraged, sometimes with the aid of physiotherapy. Orthopaedic complications may need attention in the elderly. Adequate daily activity will induce normal fatigue and lessen the incidence of disturbed and restless nights. It will also help defer the time when nursing in bed, and hence the terminal stages, are reached.

Psychotropic medication will often be needed to allay agitation and depression. In general, however, one will wish to avoid using drugs with strong anticholinergic effects for prolonged periods of time, in view of the known cholinergic deficits in Alzheimer's disease. Phenothiazines may transform the problems of management in a disturbed and restless patient, and paranoid symptoms may lose distressing force and intensity. Unlike barbiturates, phenothiazines are relatively safe among elderly and brain-damaged subjects, and less likely to aggravate confusion. A very small dose of haloperidol can be useful for short periods of time. Antidepressant and anxiolytic drugs can also be effective, especially in multi-infarct dementia where emotional instability and depression are particularly common.

For sedation at night chloral hydrate, dichloralphenazone (Welldorm), phenergan or diazepam are greatly preferable to barbiturates or nitrazepam. Chlormethiazole (Heminevrin) can also be employed. Pearce and Miller (1973) make the further important point that restlessness and insomnia are often prompted by pain, and simple analgesics are more effective than hypnotics if a painful hip, knee or back is keeping the patient awake. Similarly faecal impaction or a distended bladder may require attention and should be borne in mind when agitation appears without obvious cause.

Specific drug treatment, aimed at delaying the degenerative process or improving cognitive performance, has so far proved to be disappointing. Numerous claims have been made, but to date no substance has proved its worth in routine clinical practice. Where gains have been reported these appear to have been evanescent and usually minimal in degree. The more enthusiastic reports have often been from uncontrolled or poorly controlled investigations, and of course even severely demented subjects will demonstrate placebo effects when exposed to increased attention, encouragement and stimulation. Nevertheless there is a place for trying

the effects of some of the less expensive preparations, certainly in the early stages and even if for little more than the benefit of their placebo effects.

High potency vitamin preparations have been advocated enthusiastically from time to time. Krawiecki *et al.* (1957) reported memory improvement after intramuscular Parentrovite in a double-blind study on elderly patients with dementia, also some increase in activity, spontaneity and interest.

Ribonucleic acid has been given in attempts to encourage cell regeneration and revival. Improvements have been claimed in patients with dementia, especially arteriosclerotic dementia (Cameron and Solyom, 1961; Cameron, 1963; Cameron *et al.*, 1963). Memory, self-care and emotional stability were said to improve. However, a carefully controlled attempt to reproduce these findings was not successful (Nodine *et al.*, 1967). Magnesium pemoline is another interesting substance thought to act as a catalyst to ribonucleic acid and said to assist learning in small animals. This too has been reported to lead to improvement in dementia (Cameron, 1967), but the situation is again far from clearly established.

Anticoagulants have sometimes been advocated (Walsh 1969a, 1969b) but their value is unproven. Moreover they are associated with risk of haemorrhage, particularly in the elderly.

Hyperoxygenation has attracted interest as a result of the work of Jacobs *et al.* (1969). Thirteen elderly demented patients were exposed to oxygen under 2.5 atmospheres of pressure, for 90 minutes twice a day for 15 days. A double-blind crossover trial showed significant improvements in psychological test scores and ward behaviour, persisting well beyond the increase of pO_2 in the blood or tissues. Similar findings were reported in less severely affected out-patients by Edwards and Hart (1974). Thompson *et al.* (1976) however found entirely negative results.

Central nervous system stimulants have been tried in small groups of patients. Pentylenetetrazol (Metrazol) was shown to increase visual discrimination learning in mice, bringing renewed interest to its use in geriatric patients. Prien (1973) lists the many studies in man, some finding beneficial effects and others not. Leckman *et al.* (1971) report the only controlled trial with a trend towards positive results where intellectual functions are concerned. Rather more positive findings have emerged with pipradol (Meretran), though this has been less extensively evaluated. Turek *et al.* (1969) showed in a controlled trial that it produced significant improvement in ward behaviour among hospitalised elderly patients with dementia.

Other treatments are discussed by Villa and Ciompi (1968), including procaine and novocaine injections, pyrithoxin (Encephabol), the nucleosides cytidine and uridine, and meclofenoxate (centrophenoxine, clofenoxine, ANP_{235}, Lucidril). The last has been shown to bring about the disappearance of the lipofuscin granules which accompany age changes in the neurones of the guinea-pig (Nandy and Bourne, 1966; Nandy, 1968), and there are reports that in senile patients it may reduce confusion, apathy and memory disturbance. Gedye *et al.* (1972) showed a small but significant improvement with meclofenoxate on an automated learning task in a small group of patients with mild to moderate dementia. Other drugs with similar actions on lipofuscin deposition include kavain and magnesium orotate (*Lancet*, 1970). So far the value of all these agents remains unproven.

A large number of *vasodilator substances* have been tried, both in arteriosclerotic and other forms of dementia. Two in particular, cyclandelate and hydergine, have been subjected to careful studies. *Cyclandelate* (Cyclospasmol) was used in a double-blind crossover trial by Fine *et al.* (1970) on 40 elderly patients with dementia considered to be due to cerebral arteriosclerosis. Significant improvements were observed in orientation, communication and socialisation. Young *et al.* (1974), in a similar trial on patients with arteriosclerotic dementia, found slight improvements in memory, apraxia and certain sub-tests of the WAIS, and concluded that a modest but real gain in ability to cope with everyday life was achieved. Davies *et al.* (1977), however, were unable to confirm such benefits. It appears that the drug increases cortical perfusion rates, and there are claims that it brings about a redistribution of blood flow to especially ischaemic areas.

Hydergine is the proprietary name for a combination of several hydrogenated ergot alkaloids. Several double-blind trials on patients with arteriosclerotic dementia and SDAT have indicated significant improvements in mood and attitude, self-care, and the relief of physical symptoms such as anorexia, dizziness and incoordination (Gerin, 1969; Triboletti and Ferri, 1969; Banen, 1972). Improvement in cognitive functioning has been less consistently reported, but there have been claims of improved alertness, memory and orientation (Ditch *et al.*, 1971; Jennings, 1972; Rao and Norris, 1972). Roubicek *et al.* (1972) noted concurrent improvement in EEG patterns. Yesevage *et al.* (1979) and Wittenborn (1981) provide further recent reviews. Hydergine is thought to improve neuronal metabolism through its influence on enzyme systems, thereby increasing cerebral blood flow as a secondary effect.

Naftidrofuryl (Praxilene) is another vasodilator which has attracted some favourable reports (*Drug and Therapeutics Bulletin*, 1972). Judge and Urquhart (1972) carried out a double-blind trial on geriatric patients with severe intellectual impairment, and found improved scores on certain tests of cognitive function but no benefit on activities of daily living or recent memory. Gerin (1974) found improved social behaviour and memory in a small group of patients with cerebral arteriosclerosis.

In Europe *piracetam* (1-acetamide-2-pyrrolidine, 'Nootropil'), a cyclical derivative of GABA, has been widely promoted for use in dementia, largely on the basis of observed effects in animals. It has been shown to improve animal learning, to protect from anoxia, and to increase the amplitude of transcallosal evoked potentials, thus possibly enhancing associative cognitive functioning. Controlled trials in patients with dementia have produced equivocal results, some indicating improvement and some showing no benefit whatever (Gustafson *et al.*, 1978). It is possible that it may have some stimulant effect on attention and memory in mildly affected patients (Reisberg *et al.*, 1981), and recent studies (p. 426) suggest that it may enhance the effects of choline when the two are given together.

Cholinergic treatment has attracted a good deal of attention following the demonstration that cholinergic transmission is profoundly affected in Alzheimer's disease (p. 382). Measures designed to augment brain acetylcholine levels have been pursued with vigour, especially since it seems that the cholinergic receptors are largely intact. There is evidence, moreover, that the cholinergic system is important in relation to memory functions even in healthy persons, giving added weight to its relevance in dementia:

Drachman and Leavitt (1974) found that central cholinergic blockade with scopolamine impaired learning and retention in normal subjects, producing deficits similar to those seen in aged drug-free controls. Sitaram *et al.* (1978) confirmed this, and also showed that the learning of word lists was slightly but significantly enhanced after orally administered choline or injected arecholine. Mohs *et al.* (1979) have demonstrated similar improvement in the memory of healthy volunteers during the slow intravenous infusion of physostigmine, an anticholinesterase which crosses the blood–brain barrier and impedes the breakdown of brain acetylcholine. All such effects are slight and transient, but illustrate how manipulation of the central cholinergic system can influence memory processes.

Unfortunately, however, attempts at remedying the cholinergic deficits in patients with Alzheimer's disease have so far met with very limited success. The numerous trials reported in Corkin *et al.* (1982) show that little benefit can be expected from feeding choline or lecithin (phosphatidyl choline), though in most trials to date the substances have been given for relatively brief periods and to patients with advanced disease. Sporadic improvements have sometimes been observed but have generally been of minor degree. Dimethylaminoethanol (Deanol), a choline agonist, has been tried with similarly negative results (Worral and Dewhurst, 1979). More recently choline and piracetam have been given together, following leads from animal studies, and greater effectiveness has been reported (Friedman *et al.*, 1981; Bartus *et al.*, 1982; Ferris *et al.*, 1982). Physostigmine infusions have also yielded short-lived benefit in demented patients (Smith and Swash, 1980; Davis and Mohs, 1982), but not in a manner that could be useful therapeutically. Possibilities of giving physostigmine orally, with or without lecithin supplements, are also being explored.

Studies concentrating on patients in the earlier stages of dementia might yet bring more encouraging results; and more effective methods may yet be discovered for augmenting cholinergic function over sustained periods of time. It seems likely, however, that replacement of more than one neurotransmitter may be required before decisive improvements in dementia can be obtained.

Patients suspected of subacute sclerosing panencephalitis will warrant a trial of treatment on *steroids* (p. 306), similarly patients whose dementia is thought to be based in some collagen vascular disorder. Examples of the latter reported by Chynoweth and Foley (1969) are described on p. 368. Mention must also be made of the attempts to demonstrate improvement in primary dementing illnesses after *ventriculo-atrial shunting operations* of the type used in normal pressure hydrocephalus (Appenzeller and Salmon, 1967; Salmon and Armitage, 1968; Salmon *et al.*, 1971). The results reported to date are not sufficiently convincing to commend the procedure in the absence of definite evidence of obstruction to the cerebrospinal fluid circulation.

Huntington's chorea: Further specific treatment may help in Huntington's chorea for the control of choreiform movements. Phenothiazines are widely employed for this purpose and have been shown to be effective. Trifluoperazine, thiopropazate and fluphenazine have been especially commended. Several reports have stressed the value of haloperidol and of pimozide. Tetrabenazine (Nitoman) has been found to help decisively but can cause severe depression. It is unclear whether such agents act merely by calming emotional tension, and perhaps by creating an element of muscular rigidity which opposes the choreic movements, or whether their central neurochemical actions are beneficial in a more direct

fashion. The phenothiazines and butyrophenones may exert their effect by dopamine receptor blockade, whereas tetrabenazine depletes central stores of dopamine and other amines as well.

Chlordiazepoxide and diazepam have been recommended, both for control of chorea and emotional lability. Here there is little to suggest any direct central action on the basal ganglia. Chelating agents, such as dimercaprol and penicillamine, have been tried by analogy with Wilson's disease, but with little consistent or proven effect (Nielsen and Butt, 1955; Haslam, 1967). Aminoff and Marshall (1974) were unable to confirm the occasional reports that lithium might be of value. Sodium valproate has been given in view of its effect in elevating GABA levels in the brain, but without successful result. Anti-cholinergic drugs are contra-indicated since they exacerbate the chorea.

Pallidectomy and thalamotomy have been tried, occasionally with excellent results on the control of abnormal motor movements. Heathfield (1967) considered that such operations had a place in younger patients with minimal mental changes, good insight and severe chorea. Unfortunately they appear to carry some risk of aggravating the dementia.

Creutzfeldt–Jakob disease: In Creutzfeldt–Jakob disease there have been occasional reports of benefit from treatment with amantadine, one patient at least appearing to have been cured completely. Unfortunately, however, negative results are also frequently observed, and it is hard to be entirely certain about the diagnosis in patients who have responded. A trial of treatment with the drug is nevertheless well worth consideration since the outlook is otherwise hopeless.

Braham (1971) first reported a patient with the disease who showed temporary improvement on the drug. The clinical course and electroencephalographic findings had been typical of the disorder, and the patient was stuporose by the time treatment with amantadine was commenced. Marked improvement began two days later, relapse accompanied a few days' interruption of the drug, and improvement occurred again on restarting it. The rapidity of the effect suggested a biochemical rather than an antiviral action in producing these results, despite the evidence that a transmissible agent is involved in the disease.

Sanders and Dunn (1973) reported two further patients treated with some success. One who showed temporary improvement had the disease confirmed later at autopsy; the other, in whom the disease was never proven, appears to have been cured:

A man of 69 had a rapid onset of confusion and loss of memory, and within 6 weeks became stuporose and incontinent with extrapyramidal rigidity in the limbs, increased tendon reflexes in the legs, and widespread muscular fasciculation. The cerebrospinal fluid was normal and the EEG showed diffuse slow activity. Amantadine, 200 mg per day, produced a markedly beneficial response within several days. The extrapyramidal rigidity lessened, and within four days he was eating and drinking and talking rationally, though his speech was rapid and indistinct. The improvement was sustained for 2 months and he became able to walk unaided. Thereafter he deteriorated, coincidentally with the development of a carbuncle, and pursued a downhill course over the next two months despite increasing doses of amantadine. At autopsy, histological examination of the brain showed changes consistent with early Creutzfeldt–Jakob disease.

A woman of 55 developed a more protracted illness with listlessness, depression and obvious intellectual impairment. She developed diplopia and later became ataxic with frequent falls. A year after onset there were pyramidal signs in the legs, the CSF was normal and the EEG showed runs of theta and frontal delta waves. Marked tremor appeared in the limbs and tongue. She was agitated, emotionally labile, and with confusion and disorientation which fluctuated from day to day. Eighteen months after onset she was severely demented and doubly incontinent, with extrapyramidal rigidity in the legs. Her speech was rapid and indistinct, and she was unable to stand, walk, dress, or feed herself. Four days after starting amantadine she was more alert, and after 10 days she was beginning to walk. After 2 weeks she was well oriented and able to carry on a rational conversation. Progressive improvement led to the disappearance of all abnormal signs within 2 months. Follow-up showed maintained improvement, normal results from psychological testing, and a normal EEG. After 18 months the amantadine was stopped and she remained well one year later. Further follow-up (Sanders, 1979) has shown that she still remains well.

Sanders and Dunn, like Braham, felt that a metabolic rather than an antiviral action of the drug was involved in these patients, especially since in the first the response appeared to be dose related. Sanders (1979) has reported a further example of considerable temporary improvement in a man of 56, who died 5 years later with autopsy confirmation of the disease. Others, however, have found no benefit (Ratcliffe et al., 1975; Kovanen et al., 1980). Interferon has also been tried without success. Further experience may clarify whether positive responders are truly examples of Creutzfeldt–Jakob disease or represent some closely related variant.

Chapter 11. Endocrine Diseases and Metabolic Disorders

The relationship between endocrinology and psychiatry has attracted a good deal of attention for obvious reasons. Endocrine disorder can be accompanied by prominent mental abnormalities, as for example in myxoedema and hyperthyroidism, and epochs of life marked by endocrine change such as pregnancy and the menopause have appeared to be associated with special liability to mental disturbance. In the reverse direction it is now clear that primary emotional disturbance is accompanied by marked changes in neuroendocrine regulatory functions of a highly complex nature.

Historically it.is interesting to note that treatment by means of hormones has often been hoped for in psychiatry. Kraepelin (1896) at one time proposed that dementia praecox was basically an endocrine disorder. Others have speculated on the role of hormones in regulating the 'biological background of psychic life', noting their influence on such matters as impulsivity, attention, arousal, and their role in numerous drives in animals as well as man (Bleuler, 1967). Patients on substitution therapy are said to 'lose something in their personal profile' due to lack of the complex interplay between emotions and hormonal levels. On this general question, however, there is as yet no clear evidence.

A relatively new area of interest centres on the way hormonal influences during intrauterine life and immediately after birth can come to alter fundamental aspects of behaviour in the long-term view. The role of thyroxine in early cerebral development has been studied in detail (Eayrs, 1968), but experimental work in animals has also shown the decisive influence of prenatal steroid hormones on later sexual development. This has now been investigated in human beings. Money and Ehrhardt (1968) report that girls affected by androgens *in utero,* either due to spontaneous hyperadrenocortical activity or as a result of progesterone given to pregnant mothers, show an increased developmental tendency towards tomboyish behaviour later in their development. Such findings, if well confirmed, may open a further chapter in the relationship between endocrinology and psychological functions.

In the past decade there has been an explosion of interest in peptide hormones, their regulation and their possible relevance to psychiatry. Thyrotrophin-releasing hormone (TRH), corticotrophin (ACTH) and other hypothalamic peptides have proved to be under delicate control from neural as well as endocrine feed-back processes. The activity of the hypothalamic-pituitary axis has come under detailed scrutiny in mental disorder, with evidence, for example, of impaired cortisol production in response to dexamethasone (Carroll, 1976a; Carroll *et al.*, 1981) and impaired growth-hormone response to clonidine in endogenous depressive illness (Checkley *et al.*, 1981, 1984). Such disturbances appear to reflect central, presumably hypothalamic, alterations accompanying the emotional disorder. Pituitary neuropeptides related to ACTH and vasopressin are now known to affect learned behaviour (De Wied *et al.*, 1976). Through them it can be expected that the pituitary plays an important role in motivational, learning and memory processes. The opiate peptides (the endorphins and enkephalins) are obviously an immensely important discovery with potential relevance to addictive behaviour and the control of chronic pain (Rees, 1981).

The purpose in what follows is not to explore these many aspects in detail, but rather to concentrate on the clinical psychiatric manifestations of primary endocrine disorder. It may be said that in all of the conditions considered below, occasional individuals will react in such a way that psychiatric manifestations gain prior attention and the endocrine disturbance goes unnoticed. With some, for example myxoedema and Addison's disease, the psychiatric abnormalities are regularly intrusive to such a degree that there is a constant risk of mistaken diagnoses.

The other metabolic disorders to be discussed—hypoglycaemia, anoxia, uraemia, electrolyte disturbance and hepatic disorder—similarly illustrate the importance of the correct biochemical milieu for the proper functioning of the central nervous system. They are quite often encountered by psychiatrists working in general hospital units, and their psychological manifestations have accordingly received increasing attention in recent years. Porphyria is included as a rare but striking example of an inborn error of metabolism with important psychiatric features.

Hyperthyroidism

Hyperthyroidism affects females much more commonly than males in a ratio of approximately 6 to 1. It is commonest in the second and third decades of life but the range is wide. The cause may lie in a hyperplastic nodule or secreting adenoma of the thyroid gland, but more commonly the gland is diffusely overactive. Goitrous enlargement may or may not be present.

Attention has been directed to the role of stress and emotional disturbance in precipitating hyperthyroidism, also to the psychological constitution of those who develop the disorder. The onset is often abrupt and may be seen to follow directly some stressful event or emotional crisis. Michael and Gibbons (1963) concluded from the large literature on the subject that in many cases psychological factors may indeed be precipitants. The difficulty here is in excluding the possibility that emotional traumata at the time of onset may themselves have been the byproducts of early and unsuspected thyroid overactivity.

With regard to predisposition opinions have varied widely. Mandelbrote and Wittkower (1955) emphasised the instability of premorbid personality in persons subject to hyperthyroidism, and attempted to outline the psychodynamic mechanisms which could underlie the disorder. Robbins and Vinson (1960) however considered that the role of personality factors had been overstressed. Gurney et al. (1967) found that hyperthyroid patients as a group fell somewhere between neurotics and normals in previous stability, with a similar family and personal history of psychiatric disorder to the neurotics but with greater previous stability on a number of other indices. It would seem, therefore, that some degree of emotional instability characterises a significant proportion of subjects liable to hyperthyroidism, and it is perhaps in these cases that psychological precipitants play a special part in the genesis of the disorder. Such vulnerability may further explain why some hyperthyroid patients remain emotionally unstable after resolution of the endocrine disorder.

Common Psychological Accompaniments

Psychological disturbance in some degree is universal with thyroid overactivity. The patient becomes restless, overactive and irritable, sometimes with hyperacuity of perception and over-reaction to noise. Heightened tension leads to impatience and intolerance of frustration, and there may be emotional lability with unreasonable or histrionic behaviour. Fluctuating depression is occasionally a prominent feature, though unaccompanied by retardation. In very rare instances there may be marked apathy and inertia ('apathetic hyperthyroidism'; Lahey, 1931). This is discussed on p. 431.

The over-arousal leads to distractibility so that concentration is impaired and effort cannot be sustained. In addition, careful examination may reveal definite cognitive impairments of which the patient is unaware, in the form of difficulty with simple arithmetic or difficulty with recent memory (Whybrow et al., 1969).

The emotional disturbance can reach a degree which leads to difficulty in clinical management, though modern antithyroid drugs have proved invaluable in circumventing the problems which arose when urgent thyroidectomy was the treatment of choice. States of extreme anxiety or hostile irritability may emerge as a direct extension of the heightened emotional tension, or paranoid features may appear as part and parcel of the disturbed mental state. Whybrow et al. (1969) found that 7 out of 10 consecutive hyperthyroid patients in a general hospital showed psychiatric abnormalities severe enough to constitute a 'psychiatric illness', even though none had been referred or considered as 'psychiatric problems'. Nevertheless hyperthyroidism does not appear to be exceptionally frequent among hospitalised psychiatric patients. McLarty et al. (1978) found 8 patients with thyrotoxicosis after surveying the entire population of two psychiatric hospitals, a total of over 1200 persons in all. In 6 the hyperthyroidism had been unsuspected prior to the survey, and in 5 it seemed to be contributing to the mental illness.

Psychoses with Hyperthyroidism

Other developments are the organic and functional psychoses which sometimes accompany hyperthyroidism. Occasionally these are the presenting feature and lead directly to psychiatric referral.

Acute organic reactions accompany 'thyroid crises' and show the picture typical of delirium, usually accompanied by fever. They were formerly one of the commonest forms of major mental illness encountered in the disease, but are now relatively rare owing to modern possibilities of treatment.

They constitute a grave emergency which warrants urgent intervention. Diagnostic confusion is unlikely to arise on account of the abundant evidence of hyperthyroidism which accompanies their development. The rare 'apathetic hyperthyroidism', however, can sometimes progress to stupor or coma, and here diagnostic difficulties may be encountered.

Affective and schizophrenic psychoses are sometimes indistinguishable from the naturally occurring functional psychotic disorders. Mania is said to be more frequent than depression, and often the progression to mania can be seen as a direct outgrowth from the characteristic mental changes of the endocrine disorder. Schizophrenic illnesses of all types have been reported—hebephrenic, catatonic and paranoid, and have sometimes been found to outnumber affective psychoses.

It is no longer believed that a specific 'thyroid psychosis' exists, but it is generally agreed that a distinctive colouring may be lent by the hyperthyroidism. Thus a manic component may accompany otherwise typical schizophrenic symptomatology, and agitation is often profound in the presence of depression. Most observers are also agreed that paranoid features are especially common whatever form the psychosis may take.

The diagnostic distinctions between the affective and schizophrenic reactions are often blurred, and an admixture of organic psychiatric features is relatively common. A seemingly schizophrenic psychosis may sometimes represent covert organic disorder, the essential evidence for which may easily be overlooked as in the case reported by Greer and Parsons (1968):

A man of 28 developed a short-lived schizophrenia-like illness with a paranoid delusional system, ideas of reference and influence, and auditory and visual hallucinations. Orientation and memory were apparently intact, but a contribution due to organic cerebral disorder was suggested by the presence of déjà vu and panoramic memory at the height of the illness.

Psychotic developments have been reported in up to 20% of cases, though this may reflect matters of special selection and the inclusion of acute organic reactions in earlier series. Johnson (1928) found only 24 examples of psychosis among over 2000 patients referred for thyroidectomy, when patients with obvious confusion or delirium were excluded. Most were depressive states with hallucinations and delusions. The majority had a personal or family history of mental disorder, and the psychosis had usually been in evidence long before symptoms of hyperthyroidism appeared. This incidence, at little more than 1%, would suggest a chance association in most instances, with the hyperthyroidism aggravating an established mental disorder rather than bringing it into being. In a careful survey of a number of patients with manic-depressive psychosis who had also had thyrotoxicosis, Checkley (1978) was unable to detect clear time relationships suggestive of a link between the two. He argued that if the hyperthyroidism had so little effect on the course of the affective disorder in patients long subject to manic-depressive episodes, it would seem unlikely to serve as a precipitant in patients without such constitutional liability.

Dunlap and Moersch (1935) reported 143 patients with mental disturbance accompanying hyperthyroidism; over 70% were organic psychosyndromes, but 26 patients showed manic-depressive psychosis (mostly depressions), 2 had dementia praecox and 2 were paranoid. Bursten (1961) found 10 examples of psychosis among 54 hyperthyroid patients seen in a general hospital during a four year period. Five were schizophrenic, 3 were organic reactions, one was a depressive illness and one a psychosis of undetermined type. From the same source of referral 6 examples of psychosis were observed among an equivalent number of cases of diabetes matched for age and sex, and only 2 among an equivalent number of cases of cholecystitis.

Investigations

Laboratory investigations are essential for confirming the diagnosis of hyperthyroidism. In the majority of cases they give unequivocal results: raised serum thyroxine (T4) and triiodothyronine (T3) as measured by radio-immunoassay, coupled with a raised 'free-thyroxine index'. The latter is calculated when the free T4 cannot be measured directly, since total T4 is much influenced by the levels of thyroxine-binding proteins in the serum.

In a small number of cases, however, the results may be borderline or even self-contradictory. The clinical features then require careful appraisal, and referral for specialist investigation is usually indicated. In general terms such borderline cases mostly prove to be suffering from primary emotional disorder rather than hyperthyroidism, but further tests are nonetheless essential.

In doubtful cases it can be valuable to estimate the serum TSH, alone or in response to an injection of thyrotrophin-releasing hormone (TRH). Lack of a TSH response to TRH supports, but cannot prove, the presence of hyperthyroidism; on the other hand a positive response effectively excludes the condition (Hoffenberg, 1983), and this on occasion can be extremely useful.

In the syndrome of 'T3 toxicosis' there is an isolated excess of triiodothyronine which can produce clinical signs of thyrotoxicosis despite normal levels of total and free serum T4.

Differential Diagnosis

The differential diagnosis between hyperthyroidism and anxiety neurosis is a classical and often a difficult exercise. Physicians and psychiatrists need equally to be aware of the pitfalls. The presenting mental symptoms can be virtually identical in both conditions; both show tachycardia, fine finger tremor, palpitations and loss of weight, and both may appear to have been precipitated by stressful events. The frequency of previous neurotic symptomatology in thyrotoxic patients and their families leads to further blurring of the diagnostic criteria between the two conditions.

Careful analysis of the features shown by large numbers of patients with hyperthyroidism has clarified the physical symptoms and signs which are of most importance in indicating this disorder (Wayne, 1960) and it is useful to refer to such data in doubtful cases. The symptoms, in descending order of discriminating value, were sensitivity to heat and preference for cold, increased appetite, loss of weight, sweating, palpitations, tiredness, 'nervousness', and dyspnoea on effort. The signs, in order of importance, were cardiac dysrhythmias (chiefly auricular fibrillation), hyperkinetic movements, tachycardia exceeding ninety per minute, a palpable thyroid gland, a bruit audible over the thyroid, exophthalmos, lid retraction, hot hands, lid-lag, and fine finger tremor. These lists show how closely anxiety neurosis may be simulated.

Gurney et al. (1967) have focused more closely on the problem by reviewing the features found in euthyroid patients with psychiatric disorder but who were initially referred with suspected thyrotoxicosis. Such patients, when compared with thyrotoxics, had an increased frequency of psychological precipitants for the illness, a lower age of onset, more frequent hysterical symptoms and panic attacks, and more neurotic features in the personality.

Thus hyperthyroidism will usually be readily suspected when the patient gives a clear history of sensitivity to heat and a preference for cold, and this deserves careful specific enquiry. Similarly the classical signs of exophthalmos, lid retraction and lid-lag will clarify the situation when such are present. Precipitation by stress will be found more commonly and more impressively in anxiety neurosis. But perhaps the most decisive feature in differentiating the two conditions is the preservation or otherwise of appetite in face of steady loss of weight; in hyperthyroidism appetite is characteristically increased whereas in anxiety states it is reduced.

In the presence of frank psychosis diagnostic difficulties are liable to be increased, and the hyperthyroidism may sometimes go unrecognised for a considerable time. It is necessary to beware of the occasional case of hyperthyroidism in which fluctuations occur with periods of spontaneous resolution. Repeated episodes of affective disorder may be particularly misleading:

A man of 40 was admitted to hospital with a typical attack of hypomania which responded satisfactorily to chlorpromazine during the next three weeks. Ten days later he was re-admitted with a relapse after discontinuing his medication, but once again he responded rapidly to chlorpromazine. Three months later he developed marked weakness and depression, and for the first time appeared to be physically unwell. It was noted that he had a persistent tachycardia, a warm moist skin, and possibly an enlarged thyroid gland. Investigations confirmed hyperthyroidism, and retrospective enquiry revealed steady loss of weight and increased appetite since shortly before the first episode of hypomania. The admission notes on the two previous occasions had shown a tachycardia which had been overlooked at the time.

Special diagnostic difficulty is likely to be encountered when thyrotoxicosis is accompanied by depression. 'Apathetic hyperthyroidism', though rare, may easily be overlooked. The typical picture is of a middle-aged or elderly patient with considerable weight loss and apathy or depression (Lahey, 1931; Thomas et al., 1970). Cardiovascular symptoms may overshadow other evidence of thyrotoxicosis, and eye signs in particular tend to be absent. The physical appearance may be of senility. In younger patients, too, depression can be the presenting feature. Folks and Petrie (1982) describe a woman of 23 presenting with depression, insomnia and early morning waking, who after an overdose of amitriptyline was found to be thyrotoxic. The affective disorder resolved as the hyperthyroidism came under control. Taylor (1975) reported a patient who was found to be thyrotoxic during a second attack of psychotic depression, the first having responded to electroconvulsive therapy; here the depression likewise abated when the thyroid disorder was treated.

Alcoholism may be wrongly blamed for the tremulousness and emotional lability of hyperthyroid patients. Davis *et al.* (1971) have reported three men with previously stable records who were found to have been indicted for larceny shortly after the onset of thyrotoxicosis. In two of them alcoholism had been suspected by the employers on account of tremulousness, weakness and inattention at work, and loss or threatened loss of employment had precipitated their crimes.

Aetiology of Mental Disturbances

The common psychological accompaniments of hyperthyroidism are probably the direct result of increased thyroxine levels, and subsequent metabolic derangements within the central nervous system. This is supported by the uniformity of the common mental changes from case to case, their fluctuations with exacerbations of the disorder, and the rapid subsidence of symptoms with antithyroid treatment. Cerebral catecholamines may be intimately involved in such changes. The acute organic reactions are likely to have a similar origin and usually appear only at peaks of thyrotoxicosis.

The precise aetiology of other psychotic developments is incompletely understood. Constitutional predisposition is usually invoked to explain affective and schizophrenic developments, but even so the situation may be complex. The psychosis may be precipitated by the metabolic derangement, or by the resulting emotional turmoil; alternatively an ingravescent psychosis may have served to precipitate the thyrotoxicosis; or as Bursten (1961) suggests, both thyrotoxicosis and psychosis may be simultaneously produced by shifts in psychodynamic equilibrium in specially vulnerable individuals. Simple coincidence may account for the two developments, but the parallel course which they sometimes pursue suggests that a causal relationship of some sort is likely to exist quite commonly. At all events, once the processes are under way they doubtless augment one another.

During treatment with antithyroid drugs, such as carbimazole, an acute organic psychosis may make its first appearance, presumably in response to the toxic effects of the drug or a period of drug-induced hypothyroidism (Herridge and Abey-Wickrama, 1969; Brewer, 1969). Other cases are reported in which schizophrenia-like psychoses make an appearance at such a time. Bewsher *et al.*'s (1971) case illustrates the difficulties which can be encountered in deciding on the precise aetiological factors at work:

During the fifth week of treatment with carbimazole a woman became acutely psychotic with paranoid delusions, auditory hallucinations and marked overactivity, producing bursts of song and whoops of excitement. Initially she was febrile (100°F) and showed a tachycardia, but there was no evidence of recurrence of thyrotoxicosis. Memory and orientation were normal throughout and the level of consciousness was unimpaired. The paranoid delusions slowly resolved over several months during which chlorpromazine was given and carbimazole continued. The patient was euthyroid at the time the psychosis developed and remained so throughout its resolution. Follow-up over the next 2 years showed no recurrence. It was suggested that the psychosis had been precipitated by the fairly rapid alteration in the level of circulating thyroxine from severe excess to normality over the preceding four weeks, and perhaps by virtue of the effects of this transition on cerebral catecholamines.

Outcome of Mental Disturbances

The result of treatment is in general satisfactory, with resolution of emotional disorder as the patient is rendered euthyroid. Sometimes, however, emotional instability persists, and in most cases is probably attributable to premorbid tendencies in this direction. The acute organic psychoses respond rapidly as the thyrotoxicosis comes under control, but affective and schizophrenic illnesses run a more variable course. These may need additional treatment in their own right, and the final outcome will vary according to the degree of constitutional vulnerability which contributed to the appearance of the psychosis. As with other psychoses in which a precipitating cause has been apparent, the prognosis will usually be better than for equivalent illnesses which arise spontaneously.

Hypothyroidism (Myxoedema)

Myxoedema is of great importance in psychiatric practice and notorious for leading to mistakes in diagnosis. It is liable to be overlooked on account of its insidious development, and the minor and diffuse nature of the early complaints. Mental symptoms are universally present by the time the patient seeks advice, and many examples come before the psychiatrist. It is only by keeping the disorder in mind that early cases, or sometimes even advanced examples, will be detected.

As with hyperthyroidism, myxoedema is very much commoner in females than males in a ratio of approximately 8 to 1. It presents most frequently in middle age though the range is wide. The physical accompaniments deserve first consideration since these will usually prove to be the features which raise suspicion.

Physical Features

The appearance is characteristic, with a pale puffy complexion and baggy eyelids. The skin is dry and rough, with a non-pitting oedematous appearance over the face and limbs and in the supraclavicular fossae. The patient may have noticed increased loss of hair, which has become lank and dry in texture. Speech is slow, and the voice often coarse, thick and toneless. The whole disposition of the patient is sluggish and inert.

The pulse is slowed and angina not infrequent. Appetite is diminished, the patient is constipated, and hearing, taste and smell may be impaired due to deposits of mucoid material. Menorrhagia is common in females, and impotence in males. Vague generalised aches and pains of a rheumatic nature are often a prominent complaint. Very occasionally muscular weakness may be the initial manifestation. On examination the ankle reflex may be slowed with marked delay in the relaxation phase.

Common Psychological Accompaniments

The typical picture is of mental lethargy, general dulling of the personality, and slowing of all cognitive functions. In the earlier stages the patient is subjectively aware of such changes, and complains of a thickness in the head or of 'feeling in a fog'. Ready fatigue may be a conspicuous feature, and relatives may have noted increasing psychomotor retardation with the patient taking progressively longer to eat or perform routine tasks. Memory is often affected from an early stage, with failure to register events and forgetfulness for day-to-day happenings.

With further progression there is marked inability to sustain mental exertion, and increasing slowness of uptake and grasp. The profound loss of interest and initiative carries the risk of delaying medical attention, since the patient may cease to complain and come to spend her time in a state of sluggish indifference.

The typical mood change is towards apathy rather than depression, though the distinction is not clear cut. Irritability is a frequent feature, and some patients become markedly agitated and aggressive.

Psychoses and Dementia with Myxoedema

It is against the background of these universal changes that the more severe psychiatric illnesses of myxoedema occur. The commonest is an organic psychosis, sometimes developing acutely or sometimes running a subacute course over several weeks or months. In other cases a picture of dementia develops insidiously and may progress over several years to an advanced degree. More rarely a severe depressive psychosis may emerge, or a typical schizophrenia may be precipitated. It is generally agreed that there is no form of psychosis specific to myxoedema, but rather a variety of 'reaction types' which may be called forth differently in different individuals. The only unifying feature, upheld by many observers, is the frequency of a paranoid colouring whatever form the psychosis may take.

In Asher's (1949) classical paper on 'myxoedematous madness' 5 patients showed an organic reaction with hallucinations and persecutory ideas, 5 showed the picture of schizophrenia with a marked paranoid colouring, 2 presented as advanced dementia and 2 with depressive features.

The common organic psychosis usually shows the features of delirium, with florid delusions and hallucinations, mental confusion, and impairment of consciousness. Delusions of persecution may be gross and bizarre. Auditory hallucinations appear to be particularly common. The condition may run a fluctuating course, but even when clouding of consciousness cannot be established there is usually evidence of impairment of cognitive function and particularly of recent memory.

Dementia develops as an extension of the mental impairment characteristic of the condition generally. It progresses insidiously in a manner indistinguishable from primary presenile dementia, and may have reached an advanced degree by the time the diagnosis is made. Olivarus and Röder (1970) consider myxoedema to be the most important, and the most frequently overlooked, of the metabolic causes of reversible organic intellectual impairment.

A 53-year-old woman developed dizziness and a constant diffuse headache after a mild head injury. Four months later she was admitted to hospital for repair of a rectal prolapse, but the operation was deferred because she was found to be confused and deluded. The electroencephalogram revealed diffuse slow activity with occasional sharp waves in the fronto-temporal regions.

Full examination of the mental state showed her to be mentally sluggish, slightly depressed, and with marked intellectual impairment. This was confirmed on psychological testing. There was slight left facial weakness and incoordination of the left arm. Her husband explained that in recent years she had had increasing difficulties with her job as a teacher, mainly because the pupils made fun of her lapses of memory. In the last four months she had become slowed and sluggish, with increasing inability to concentrate or remember.

Angiography failed to reveal a cerebral tumour and a diagnosis of presenile dementia was seriously considered. Air encephalography, however, showed little evidence of cortical atrophy. Signs of myxoedema were then noted and the diagnosis was confirmed.

Within 3 weeks of starting replacement therapy she reported improvement, with decreased fatigue and improved memory. She was able to do crossword puzzles which she had given up several years before. Two months later psychometric testing confirmed marked intellectual improvement and showed only slight residual impairment of memory. She resumed her work without difficulty and remained well on follow-up.

(Olivarus and Röder, 1970)

Depressive and schizophrenic psychoses may or may not be accompanied by organic mental features, though these are usually found when sought out with care. Paranoid symptoms again figure prominently. The depressive psychoses are often severe, with agitation or bizarre hypochondriasis, and may prove to be particularly resistant to treatment until the myxoedema is discovered. Schizophrenic psychoses will in general be coloured by mental slowing, and often include features indicative of organic cerebral impairment.

Neurological Abnormalities in Myxoedema

The slowing of the tendon reflexes has already been mentioned. This may serve as a useful confirmatorysign, and with careful measurement has been used to monitor the progress of treatment.

Jellinek (1962) has drawn attention to the occurrence of fits, faints and cerebrovascular accidents in myxoedematous patients. Four patients were reported with grand mal attacks which responded to thyroid replacement, others with attacks of syncope, and others with unusual confusional episodes which suggested temporal lobe dysfunction.

A man of 57 had sudden attacks which lasted a few minutes and consisted of varying sensations of familiarity and unfamiliarity: 'You know where you are but things face the wrong way'. On one occasion, when quite near home,

he crossed the road away from his intended route and walked straight into a flow of moving traffic. He came to, in a state of panic, in the centre of the road. The attacks stopped when thyroxine was commenced.

Another patient had 'blackouts' in which she would become briefly confused and talk nonsense. On one occasion she was accused of being drunk by a taxi driver when she refused to pay her fare. These attacks also ceased when she started thyroid therapy.

(Jellinek, 1962)

Cerebrovascular accidents were found to have occurred in several patients, and evidence of attacks of transient cerebral ischaemia in several more.

Jellinek and Kelly (1960) have described other cases of myxoedema presenting with cerebellar disturbance in the form of ataxia, tremor, dysarthria and nystagmus, and remitting promptly with replacement therapy.

Myxoedema coma is a grave condition which carries a high mortality. It should be suspected in any patient with severe impairment of consciousness and hypothermia. The skin feels icy cold, and a low-reading rectal thermometer is required to confirm the hypothermia. Respiration may be sluggish, and cardiac failure or arrhythmia are features of serious significance.

Investigations

As with hyperthyroidism it is essential to confirm the diagnosis by laboratory tests before starting treatment. The levels of T4 and T3 are low, after appropriate correction for the levels of thyroxine-binding proteins in the serum. Elevated plasma TSH will indicate primary thyroid failure in distinction to hypopituitarism. A TRH stimulation test may be useful in doubtful cases; failure of TRH to produce a marked elevation of TSH excludes hypothyroidism, unless this is secondary to pituitary disease (Hoffenberg, 1983). Estimation of anti-thyroid antibodies may help to establish the cause, these being found in particularly high dilution in Hashimoto's thyroiditis.

The serum cholesterol is elevated, the heart is usually enlarged, and the electrocardiogram shows a low-voltage tracing with flattened or inverted T-waves. The electroencephalogram shows lowered voltage and slowing of the dominant frequencies; occasionally it is normal despite severe myxoedema but this is rare. The protein in the cerebrospinal fluid may be moderately raised.

Differential Diagnosis

Not uncommonly the myxoedema is first recognised only after a considerable lapse of time. Early dementia or intractable depression are probably the diagnoses most frequently entertained, or the patient may have been labelled as neurotic, hypochondriacal or personality disordered. Occasionally such patients are found to have spent some time in a vain quest for medical help before the correct diagnosis is made.

The suspicion of myxoedema is usually derived from the characteristic facial appearance or other physical symptoms and signs, but unless the disorder is specifically considered these may easily be overlooked. In the 14 cases reported by Asher (1949), all with florid mental illnesses, the myxoedema had been missed by the referring doctor in every case. In the more severe psychotic illnesses organic features are usually evident in the mental state but not invariably so.

Even without overt evidence of myxoedema, psychiatric patients may warrant investigation if they have a history of thyroidectomy or of having required thyroid medication in the past. These were the factors which prompted investigation in 5 of 18 myxoedematous patients surveyed by Tonks (1964) in a psychiatric hospital. Patients on long-term lithium therapy are also at increased risk of developing hypothyroidism and require periodic checks of serum thyroxine levels.

Aetiology of Mental Disturbances

The mental symptomatology in myxoedema can be largely ascribed to changes in cerebral metabolism. Such changes are reflected in the electroencephalographic findings described above, and these can be observed to improve with substitution therapy. Cerebral blood flow has been shown to be considerably reduced as a result of diminished cardiac output, while the cerebral metabolic demands for oxygen and glucose are unaltered (Scheinberg et al., 1950; Sensenbach et al., 1954; O'Brien and Harris, 1968). The relative cerebral hypoxia which results is worsened by the anaemia which frequently coexists. The cerebral changes therefore appear to be largely secondary to the effects of thyroxine deprivation on other organs such as the heart, rather than the direct result of thyroxine-lack on the brain itself.

Such abnormalities probably go much of the way towards explaining the mental slowing and dulling which form an integral part of the disorder. The acute organic psychoses are likely to be due to some additional aspect of the intracerebral metabolic disturbance. Distinctive colouring by way of mood disorder or paranoia will usually be derived from pre-morbid personality factors. When long-continued the chronic dementing illnesses can obviously result in fixed and permanent brain damage, but so far specific neuropathological changes do not appear to have been described in myxoedema (Michael and Gibbons, 1963).

Cases of affective disorder and schizophrenia are likely to owe a good deal both to organic factors and to matters of constitutional vulnerability. In the rare examples where organic features are entirely absent from the mental state the cerebral metabolic defect has probably served merely as a precipitant. But the situation is not entirely straightforward, since occasional cases with purely depressive symptomatology have been found to respond to thyroxine after other forms of treatment have failed entirely (Michael and Gibbons, 1963). Whether such affective changes can be tied directly to altered cerebral metabolism remains to be determined; electrolyte changes and catecholamine disturbances are obvious possibilities.

'Non-Myxoedematous Hypometabolism'

Kurland et al. (1955) reported a syndrome of 'metabolic insufficiency', in which the basal metabolic rate was low in spite of a normal serum protein-bound iodine and radioactive iodine uptake. Such patients frequently complained of fatigue, lethargy, sensitivity to cold, musculoskeletal pain and diminished sexual potency. Treatment with thyroxine was ineffective, but triiodothyronine was said to raise the basal metabolic rate and lead to striking clinical improvement. The condition gained popularity and came to be rather commonly diagnosed.

Levin (1960), however, performed a careful double-blind trial of thyroxine, triiodothyronine and placebo in patients fulfilling the diagnostic criteria, and neither treatment could be shown to have definite effects on symptoms or on the basal metabolic rates. The patients' complaints were more typical of neurotic disorder than of myxoedema, and M.M.P.I. scores showed a high degree of psychological maladjustment in the individuals concerned. It would seem, therefore, that the syndrome is unlikely to be a clinical reality, and that triiodothyronine is not effective treatment. Some neurotic patients clearly have low basal metabolic rates, but so also do some members of the general population.

Outcome of Mental Disturbances in Myxoedema

The treatment of myxoedema is usually highly rewarding. The patient gradually regains vitality, physical symptoms diminish, and mental processes return to their usual speed and efficiency.

The great majority of patients with serious psychiatric developments can also be expected to respond, even those with overt dementia provided too long an interval has not elapsed. Jellinek (1962), however, stressed that several of his cases were left with measurable defects of intellect and memory after being rendered euthyroid, mostly those who had remained undiagnosed for very long periods of time or where treatment had been inadequate.

Where response to thyroxine itself is concerned, the frankly organic psychoses can in general be expected to do better than psychoses with predominantly functional symptomatology. This was confirmed by Tonks (1964), who surveyed 18 hypothyroid patients in a psychiatric hospital during a period of treatment with thyroid preparations alone; the proportion who made complete and lasting recoveries was much higher among patients who showed evidence of disturbance of consciousness, in the form of disorientation or confusion, than among those who did not. The duration of the illnesses was also important, in that no patient with a mental illness exceeding 2 years made a satisfactory response to the trial of thyroid replacement therapy alone. The only clearly organic condition which failed to respond was a patient with chronic progressive dementia and aphasia of 7 years duration.

Additional measures in the form of phenothiazines, antidepressant medication or electroconvulsive therapy, may be necessary in severe psychotic disorders, and particularly so when organic features are absent from the mental state. It must be borne in mind, however, that phenothiazines carry some risk of precipitating hypothermic coma in hypothyroid patients, as in the case reported by Mitchell *et al.* (1959).

It is necessary to introduce thyroxine with caution at the beginning of treatment because of the possibility of myocardial damage. The starting dose of l-thyroxine sodium should not exceed 50 μg per day. If there is no evidence of cardiac failure or angina this may be increased by 25–50 μg per day every 2–3 weeks until the maintenance dose of 100–200 μg per day is reached.

Cushing's Syndrome

Cushing's syndrome is commoner in women than in men, usually starting in young middle-age though the range of onset is wide. A tendency has been noted for the disorder to start during pregnancy, at the menopause or at puberty, or while the subject is undergoing a prolonged period of psychological stress.

In the majority of cases, perhaps some 80%, it is due to pituitary overproduction of ACTH, resulting in secondary bilateral hyperplasia of the adrenal cortices. How far this in turn is due to a primary abnormality of the pituitary, or a primary hypothalamic disturbance affecting the mechanisms of corticotrophin release, is still not entirely clear, though small pituitary microadenomas are demonstrable in a very high proportion of cases (Burke, 1983). Occasionally there may be a radiologically demonstrable pituitary basophil adenoma, though this is rarely large enough to cause chiasmatic compression or raised intracranial pressure. Rarer causes include adrenal tumours—benign adenomas or malignant carcinomas—or ectopic ACTH production from malignant tumours elsewhere. Apart from differing levels of circulating ACTH, the endocrine abnormalities are the same whether due to adrenal or pituitary disease—a sustained excessive production of cortisol, obliterating the normal diurnal rhythm, and usually excessive production of adrenal androgens as well. Chronic alcoholics may occasionally develop a typical Cushing's syndrome which resolves within days or weeks when the alcohol intake stops (Smals *et al.*, 1976; Morgan, 1982); it can therefore be wise to rule out alcoholism as a cause.

The great majority of cases present for medical attention on account of the physical disorder which develops, but psychiatric features are strikingly frequent and can be severe. Moreover occasional cases have been reported to present with psychiatric illnesses from the outset as discussed below, and the endocrine disorder may then be recognised only after a considerable delay.

Physical Features

The physical changes include the well-known moon face, buffalo hump and purple striae on the abdomenand thighs. Truncal obesity is almost always present, and insidious weight gain is often the earliest sign. The complexion is plethoric and hirsuties may be marked. Excessive bruising is common. Skin pigmentation may develop from the direct action of excessive ACTH on melanocytes. Hypertension is often severe and mild glycosuria may appear. Amenorrhoea is usual in the female, and impotence, testicular atrophy or gynaecomastia in the male. Other noteworthy features include liability to intercurrent infections, osteoporosis leading to backache or vertebral collapse, and muscular weakness which can sometimes be extreme.

Psychiatric Disorders

Among patients reported from general hospitals, psychiatric disturbance has often been found in more than 50% of cases (Michael and Gibbons, 1963). Trethowan and Cobb's (1952) series of 25 consecutive patients seen in a general hospital is typical—4 were severely disturbed and psychotic, 6 moderately disturbed, and 8 mildly disturbed; 3 had relatively insignificant psychiatric symptoms but only 4 could be declared mentally normal. Jeffcoate et al. (1979) surveyed 40 patients of whom 22 were depressed, 5 severely, and 4 showed other psychiatric disorders (mania, chronic anxiety and an acute organic reaction). Only a third were judged to be free from mental disorder. Whybrow and Hurwitz (1976), in a review of the literature up to that time, suggested that some 35 per cent of patients develop depression, 16% disturbed cognition, and 9% psychotic illness. Less than 4% appeared to show euphoria, in contrast to the situation when exogenous steroids are administered for therapeutic purposes (p. 535).

Depression is undoubtedly the most frequent psychiatric symptom, and paranoid features are also very common. A wide range of other mental abnormalities is seen—emotional lability with gross overreaction to emotional stimuli, uncooperative behaviour, or sudden outbursts of restless hyperactivity. These may be noted from very early in the development of the illness. Acute anxiety may also figure prominently, or states of apathy verging on stupor. Fatigue and asthenia derived from the physical disorder often colour the psychiatric picture.

Cohen's (1980) recent study is important in that a consecutive and unselected series of 29 patients with Cushing's syndrome were examined closely from the psychiatric point of view. Twenty-five of them (86%) showed a significant degree of depression, this being mild in 7, moderate in 13 and severe in 5. Almost half of the series had a family history of depression or suicide, or a past history of early bereavement or separation; 6 had had a major emotional disturbance shortly preceding the onset of the endocrine disorder, and in 5 this had consisted

of a loss (bereavement, separation, or broken engagement). These are all factors of known importance in the genesis of depression, raising at least the possibility of an aetiological link between Cushing's syndrome and depressive illness. Moreover, depression was particularly common among the 21 patients with a pituitary origin for their Cushing's syndrome; and all 6 patients with a disturbing life event preceding it fell into this group. It was, by contrast, uncommon to find severe psychiatric disturbance in the 8 patients with adrenal adenomas or carcinomas.

The severe psychoses accompanying Cushing's syndrome are again mostly depressive in nature. Typically they are florid illnesses with delusions and auditory hallucinations and often with paranoid symptoms. Retardation tends to be severe, sometimes bordering on stupor. Anxious agitation may replace the retardation in other cases, or there may be acute brief episodes of grossly disturbed behaviour. Marked fluctuations in the severity of the condition appear to be characteristic.

Acute organic reactions are rare, but an element of disorientation or transient impairment of consciousness may be detected in severe examples of the disease. Classical schizophrenic psychoses are also rather uncommon though a schizophrenic colouring may be lent to the total picture. Johnson (1975) reviews the occasional cases of schizophrenia in the literature and presents an unusual example of his own:

A woman of 50 had had a chronic schizophrenic illness with first rank symptoms for 25 years. This had been extensively treated with insulin comas and electroconvulsive therapy. Signs perhaps suggestive of Cushing's syndrome—excessive bruising and pigmentation—had been noted some 19 years before the florid endocrine illness was declared. Despite the length of the psychiatric history, bilateral adrenalectomy led to a dramatic and sustained improvement in her mental state. It was concluded that in all likelihood she had had a primary schizophrenic illness, partly in remission as a result of earlier treatment, then exacerbated by the developing Cushing's syndrome.

(Johnson, 1975)

The chief diagnostic hazard lies with those patients who develop psychotic features early in the illness. These may dominate the picture to such an extent that the endocrine disorder goes unnoticed. Two of Spillane's (1951) patients were apparently psychotic from the outset and long before the physical changes were sufficiently marked to suggest Cushing's syndrome.

One of Spillane's patients, a man of 26, had developed a paranoid psychosis which was treated with electroconvulsive therapy and continuous narcosis. It was not until two years after the first hospitalisation that Cushing's syndrome was diagnosed. It was on his return home after being invalided from the army that his mother noted a pronounced change in his appearance, with obesity, a bull-neck and a plethoric complexion.

Trethowan and Cobb (1952) similarly reported a woman of 31 who had developed obesity, marked muscular weakness and amenorrhoea for a year before becoming excited, overactive and disoriented. Two further acute psychotic episodes occurred before Cushing's syndrome was diagnosed. Another of their patients was diagnosed as schizophrenic for several months, and another as hysterical for a year before the physical changes led to investigation of Cushing's syndrome.

Cognitive impairments have rarely been investigated systematically in Cushing's syndrome. A report by Whelan et al. (1980), involving neuropsychological testing of 35 unselected patients before treatment, has indicated some degree of diffuse cerebral dysfunction in almost two-thirds of the sample. Thirteen patients showed essentially normal results on an extensive battery of tests, 10 showed mild impairments, 8 moderate, and 4 severe and frequent deficits. No aspect of cognitive functioning was spared, though impairments tended to be more marked on non-verbal tests (visuo-ideational, spatial-constructional and visual memory tasks) than in the field of language and verbal reasoning. Patients may therefore be more impaired in cerebral functioning than is evident in conversation or on purely verbal assessments. The deficits sometimes extended beyond purely cognitive functions, with poor performance on tests of manual dexterity and somatosensory discrimination.

Radiological evidence of cerebral atrophy has also been forthcoming in a considerable proportion of patients (Momose et al. 1971), occurring as commonly in those below 40 as in older groups. Cerebellar atrophy was often conspicuous despite a lack of clinical signs. CT scanning has shown atrophy, reversible with treatment and perhaps attributable to electrolyte and fluid changes or protein loss (Heinz et al., 1977). Ventricular enlargement and cortical atrophy have also been reported at autopsy (Soffer et al., 1961).

Aetiology of Mental Disturbances

The depression so characteristic of Cushing's syndrome is doubtless partly reactive to the physical disfigurements and discomforts produced by the disease. But a more direct connection is suggested in those cases where affective disorder is an early or even presenting feature, and by the frequency with which the depression reaches 'psychotic' intensity.

Cohen's (1980) observations (p. 437) are particularly interesting in this regard. The high incidence of factors predisposing to depression in the histories of his patients may merely illustrate their vulnerability to depression in the face of physical illness; or it may indicate something more—a close pathophysiological link between the genesis of depression and the genesis of some forms of Cushing's syndrome. Thus it is noteworthy in his series that depression was significantly more common in primary pituitary than primary adrenal forms of the syndrome, a difference that had already been discerned by Carroll (1976b) from cases in the literature. Disturbing life events, antecedent to the development of the endocrine disorder, were confined to this form of the disease. More discriminating controlled studies will be necessary, however, before concluding that Cushing's syndrome may sometimes be stress-induced.

The depression of Cushing's syndrome has often been contrasted with the elevation of mood characteristically seen when steroids or ACTH are administered for therapeutic purposes. Whether the difference is due to differing plasma levels of biologically active steroids, or to the long-continued chronic elevation of steroids in Cushing's syndrome is not known. Neither Cohen (1980) nor Kelly et al. (1983) could relate the severity of depression to the levels of circulating cortisol in their patients; yet its alleviation after surgical removal of the hyperplastic adrenals suggests that it must owe a good deal to some substance they produce. Hypothalamic factors may also be presumed to play a part, in view of the complex neuro-endocrine relationships now being discovered in the control and regulation of the hypothalamic-pituitary axis (p. 428).

Outcome

A successful psychiatric outcome can be expected when the endocrine disorder is effectively treated. The physical and mental symptoms usually improve in parallel until the patient regains her former stability. Depression is regularly observed to recede after adrenalectomy or treatment with metyrapone, often starting to abate within days or weeks though sometimes taking as long as a year to clear completely (Jeffcoate et al., 1979; Cohen, 1980; Kelly et al.,

1983). Needless to say, when psychiatric disturbance has long antedated the Cushing's syndrome there may be little or no change when the latter is remedied.

With florid psychotic illnesses the results can be dramatic, as in the following examples:

A woman presented initially with physical symptoms of Cushing's syndrome, but on admission to hospital developed an acute psychotic picture with auditory and visual hallucinations and delusions about changing her sex. This was thought to have been precipitated partly by the mounting anxiety surrounding her admission to hospital. She became markedly paranoid and agitated, developed confusional episodes, and showed bizarre catatonic motor phenomena. The entire condition responded well to bilateral extirpation of hyperplastic adrenal glands and the mental state returned to normal within a few days of the operation. Follow-up three years later showed that she remained entirely well.

(Hickman *et al.*, 1961)

A soldier of 23 with a good service record became abruptly confused and hallucinated, and showed severely disturbed behaviour with grandiose and religious delusions. He was diagnosed as schizophrenic and treated extensively with electroconvulsive therapy. It was not until one year from the start that Cushing's syndrome was diagnosed. He continued to be severely disturbed, but pituitary irradiation eighteen months and two years after onset led to transitory amelioration of the psychotic symptoms. Two and a half years after onset bilateral adrenalectomy was performed, and thereafter there was steady and gradual improvement until full premorbid stability was regained.

(Hertz *et al.*, 1955)

Details of management of the endocrine disorder, and of the distinction between pituitary and adrenal causes, will not be dealt with here. There are rival claims and special indications for bilateral adrenalectomy, pituitary operation and pituitary irradiation. Metyrapone can be useful in suppressing cortisol production.

Addison's Disease

Addison's disease usually presents in early adult or middle life and is commoner in males than females. It results from primary atrophy of the adrenal cortices, or diseases such as tuberculosis which involve the glands bilaterally. The output of all adrenal steroids is low—cortisol, aldosterone, corticosterone and androgens. Loss of sodium is accompanied by retention of potassium and extracellular dehydration. The blood sugar is usually low.

Physical Features

The onset of symptoms is gradual, and the usual presentation is with general weakness, loss of appetite, and loss of weight. Tiredness is an almost universal complaint. Pigmentation develops mainly on exposed skin surfaces. The voice is often soft and whining. Loss of libido is common, with impotence in the male and amenorrhoea in the female. Resistance to stress is lowered and sensitivity to infections increased. There is often pronounced intolerance of cold and the body temperature is usually subnormal. Hypotension is almost always present, syncope is common, and symptoms of hypoglycaemia may appear at higher levels of blood sugar than is usual. There is an increased liability to convulsions, and the electroencephalogram is often abnormal with diffuse high-amplitude slow activity.

These several features deserve emphasis because the correct diagnosis is often delayed, sometimes until a severe 'Addisonian crisis' has occurred with considerable threat to life. The Addisonian crisis consists of a sudden exacerbation of symptoms with pyrexia, vomiting, epigastric pain, dehydration and profound hypotension. It may occur spontaneously or in response to infection, chilling, or drugs such as morphine or anaesthetic agents.

Psychiatric Features

Psychiatric abnormalities are present almost without exception in patients with Addison's disease. The commonest changes are those which might be expected in persons suffering from chronic physical exhaustion—depression, emotional withdrawal, apathy, and loss of drive and initiative. There are sometimes sudden fluctuations of mood, or episodes of marked anxiety and irritability. Based on his own experience and on cases from the literature, Cleghorn (1965) described the mental symptoms as apathy and negativism in 80% of cases, depressive withdrawal and irritability in 50%, suspiciousness in 15%, agitated behaviour in 10% and paranoia with delusions in 5%.

Difficulties with memory form a major feature in up to three-quarters of cases (Michael and Gibbons, 1963). Early dementia may be simulated on account of the mental anergia, poverty of thought and general air of indifference. Drowsiness can be conspicuous though some patients show restlessness and insomnia. The severity of the changes may fluctuate from time to time, varying directly with the severity of the endocrine disorder.

Addisonian crises are sometimes preceded by increasing irritability and apprehension. Nightmares and episodes of panic lead on to acute organic reactions with clouding of consciousness, delirium, stupor and epileptic fits. In Addisonian stupor the patient is obviously unwell, lies curled up in bed resenting interference, and is collapsed and cold with dehydration, falling blood pressure and peripheral circulatory failure.

Psychotic pictures of a depressive or schizophrenic nature are rare in contrast to the situation in Cushing's disease. Cleghorn (1951), however, reported examples of acute and chronic paranoia, hallucinatory states and schizophreniform psychoses. Such disturbances may be evanescent. They are sometimes intimately related to impending crises. McFarland (1963) reviewed reports of 10 patients with schizophrenia, 6 with affective psychosis and one with organic psychosis, concluding that the form of psychotic development is unpredictable. One of his patients presented with hypomania; this masked the adrenal disorder until the patient lapsed into coma after electroconvulsive treatment, when severe hyponatraemia was discovered.

Differential Diagnosis

Addison's disease must be differentiated from hypopituitarism and from other chronic debilitating diseases. Weight loss, hypotension and pigmentation may all be seen, for example, in carcinoma, tuberculosis, malabsorption or malnutrition. It is therefore essential to investigate adrenal function adequately before making the diagnosis. Plasma cortisol estimations should be carried out at 9 a.m. and 11 p.m. to observe the presence or absence of the normal diurnal rhythm of cortisol secretion. The 'synacthen test' consists of the intramuscular injection of tetracosactrin, an ACTH analogue, then examining the rise in plasma cortisol that follows. In primary adrenal failure there is little or no response; with hypoadrenalism secondary to pituitary failure the response is abnormal or delayed.

From the psychiatric point of view an erroneous diagnosis of neurosis or early dementia may easily be made. The depression and generalised weakness is often attributed to 'neurasthenia', especially when pigmentation is slight and the serum electrolytes are normal. The impression of neurosis is strengthened by the anorexia, irritability and diminished libido, and by the fluctuations which occur from time to time. Dementia, or a chronic amnesic syndrome, is suggested when memory difficulties are in the forefront of the picture.

Outcome

Adequate replacement therapy is usually highly successful in alleviating both physical and mental disturbances. The patient's sense of well-being is quickly restored, and appetite and energy gradually return to normal. It has been observed that Addisonian patients are unusually sensitive to the mood elevating effect of steroids (Cleghorn, 1965). Glucocorticoids appear to be more important than mineralcorticoids for reversing the mental symptoms and abolishing the electroencephalographic abnormalities, indicating that these do not rest entirely on disturbances of electrolyte and water balance (Reichlin, 1968). Cleghorn (1951) found that apathy, depression and irritability often persisted on treatment with desoxycorticosterone acetate and salt alone, but could resolve when cortisone was added later. Further treatment with androgens appears to give no additional benefit.

Phaeochromocytoma

Phaeochromocytomas are tumours of the chromaffin cells of the adrenal medulla. Occasionally they are found ectopically in relation to the sympathetic ganglia lying along the aorta or in the cervical and thoracic chains. Most are benign and some occur familially. Some association with neurofibromatosis has been noted; also with hyperparathyroidism and medullary carcinoma of the thyroid ('multiple endocrine adenomatosis', 'MEA type 2', pp. 447–8). In Hutchison et al.'s (1958) series the age of presentation varied from 9 to 51.

Clinical Features

The tumours secrete an excess of adrenaline and noradrenaline, the relative proportions differing in different cases. The output may be paroxysmal or continuous. Accordingly the clinical features are subject to great variation.

Hypertension is always present during attacks and commonly persists in between (Ross, 1972a, 1972b). The paroxysms which occur are usually the presenting feature. They last anything from five minutes to several hours at a time, and consist usually of severe palpitations, flushing or blanching, sweating, dizziness and tremulousness. A violent tachycardia is common, sometimes with substernal pain and acute dyspnoea. Nausea and vomiting may occur. The acute rise of blood pressure can be accompanied by agonising headache and may precipitate a cerebro-vascular accident, epileptic fit or myocardial infarction. Death may result from ventricular fibrillation. After a severe attack the patient is left exhausted for hours or sometimes days.

Marked mental symptoms regularly accompany attacks. Intense fear is often present at the start and the patient may be overwhelmed with a feeling of impending death. Anxiety usually remains severe throughout the attack, and a period of excitability and confusion can follow. Attacks are precipitated by physical exertion, change of posture or raised intra-abdominal pressure, but also sometimes by emotional factors. Quite commonly they are triggered by a recognisable stimulus such as excitement, shock or panic. Sometimes, however, there are no discernible precipitants.

While the above is the classical picture, with well-marked episodes, cases may also present surreptitiously. Attacks are sometimes minor in nature, or mentioned only in passing as feelings of faintness, palpitations or episodes of sudden anxiety. Hence the great importance of carrying out appropriate investigations whenever the disorder is remotely suspected.

Examination reveals marked hypertension during attacks and usually also in between. Papilloedema may very occasionally be present, with haemorrhages and exudates in the retina. Transient glycosuria may accompany the attacks, and a considerable proportion of patients show diabetes mellitus (Hutchison et al., 1958).

Investigations

The essential investigation is the demonstration of greatly increased levels of catecholamines in the blood or urine, or of their metabolites in 24 hour samples of urine (metadrenaline, metnoradrenaline and vanilmandelic acid). When the index of suspicion is high, repeat estimations may have to be undertaken. In the presence of hypertension a blocking test is useful: phentolamine ('Rogitine') given intravenously causes an immediate fall in blood pressure when a phaeochromocytoma is present. Provocation tests formerly utilised various procedures to demonstrate an abrupt rise of blood pressure; these have now been largely abandoned since they can give misleading results and are potentially dangerous.

Differential Diagnosis

Many patients referred as possible cases of phaeochromocytoma prove to be suffering from some other condition. In Evan et al.'s (1951) series, 10 out of 20 suspected cases were suffering from anxiety or hysteria, often with episodes of hyperventilation. Other cases prove to be suffering from vascular headache, epilepsy, agitated depression or alcoholism (Hutchison et al., 1958).

More serious mistakes may occur in the reverse direction, in that the phaeochromocytoma is missed. Essential or renal hypertension are probably the commonest misdiagnoses. Hyperthyroidism is often suggested by the patient's hypermetabolic state and associated heat intolerance. Any patient with hypertension in whom hyperthyroidism is suspected should immediately be screened for phaeochromocytoma. Other misdiagnoses include temporal lobe epilepsy, hypoglycaemic attacks, and paroxysmal cardiac arrhythmias (Ross, 1972b).

From the psychiatric point of view an anxiety state may be very closely simulated, especially when emotional factors are known to trigger attacks. In two patients reported by Doust (1958) anxiety states of considerable duration had been attributed to psychological factors alone. One showed no obvious acute episodes and was normotensive. In a patient described by Gillmer (1972) a diagnosis of endogenous depression was made initially and the true condition was revealed in an unusual manner:

A woman of 61 with a strong family history of affective disorder complained of depression and anxiety for 18 months which had recently intensified greatly. She had severe insomnia and marked psychomotor retardation alternating with periods of acute anxiety and agitation. Blood pressure was 180/100 and there were minor hypertensive retinal changes. Treatment with antidepressants, chlordiazepoxide and ECT was commenced. After the first ECT she complained of severe headache associated with sweating and tachycardia, and the blood pressure was found to be 120/60. In view of the drop in blood pressure six-hourly recordings were instituted before further ECT was given. During the period of observation it was found that bouts of severe headache, dizziness and sweating were associated with peaks of greatly elevated blood pressure, for example to 300/170. A phaeochromocytoma was confirmed and removed successfully.

A patient seen personally illustrates another unusual mode of presentation, and underlines the importance of screening tests:

A 57-year-old man presented with a one year history of decline in work performance, loss of confidence, and a change towards becoming quiet and subdued. This appeared to follow an accident at work when, as a senior ship's pilot, he had grounded a large vessel. After a second similar accident he was referred for investigation.

There was a 13 year history of diabetes mellitus, often difficult to control, and currently being treated with 44 units of insulin per day. Two years previously he had been treated briefly for hypertension with propanolol. Searching questions revealed two possible episodes of transient neurological dysfunction; for a few days after the first grounding he had appeared disoriented and had shown problems with direction when driving, and a year before that there had been tingling in the left arm and dragging of the left foot for a few hours.

On examination he was found to be depressed, apathetic, and poorly informed about recent items of news. He was fully oriented but performed poorly on tests of memory and showed word finding difficulties. The blood pressure varied from 140/95 to 180/130. There were no neurological abnormalities.

The CT scan showed some diffuse cerebral atrophy, generalised white matter low attenuation, and two small cerebral infarctions, in the head of the right caudate nucleus and in the right cerebellar hemisphere. It was considered that the likely diagnosis was an early multi-infarct dementia in the setting of hypertension and diabetes mellitus.

As part of a thorough screening procedure 24 hour urine collections were obtained and showed greatly elevated levels of vanilmandelic acid, metadrenaline and metnoradrenaline. A body scan showed bilateral suprarenal masses.

At operation bilateral phaeochromocytomas were removed. Evidence of diabetic retinopathy rapidly receded thereafter and he was soon able to dispense with hypoglycaemic agents. The blood pressure remained within normal limits or only mildly elevated without antihypertensive treatment. Repeat psychometric testing showed steady gains in general intellectual competence, the full scale IQ rising from 99 to 114 during the first post-operative year. Word finding difficulties resolved completely, though difficulties with new learning persisted. In terms of his general demeanour he regained a good deal of his former vitality though remaining quieter than formerly. Repetition of the CT scan showed persistence of the white matter low attentuation, and some dilatation of the anterior horn of the right lateral ventricle adjacent to the infarct in the caudate nucleus.

In this patient the phaeochromocytomas had clearly been responsible for diabetes of many years standing, and for hypertension which had more recently been discovered. The diagnosis was only made, however, after episodes of silent cerebral infarction had led to difficulties in a demanding work situation. There had at no point been indications of episodic changes in blood pressure or anything remotely resembling anxiety attacks.

Acromegaly

Overproduction of the pituitary growth hormone results from an adenoma, or rarely simple hyperplasia, of the eosinophil cells of the anterior pituitary gland. Skeletal overgrowth develops insidiously, affecting mainly the hands, feet, skull and lower jaw. Headache is often severe and incapacitating, kyphosis is common and joint pain may be severe. Hypertension, hypogonadism and diabetes mellitus usually occur. Chiasmatic compression is relatively rare.

The psychological accompaniments of the disease do not appear to have been studied systematically, though apathy and lack of initiative are said to characterise the disorder from an early stage. Patients are often described as pleasant and easygoing though with marked traits of obstinacy. In some cases lability of mood may be a feature, and difficulty with recent memory can be striking.

Many of the mental symptoms seen in the disorder are understandable as reactions to the physical disfigurement, headache and pain in the limbs. The patients are sometimes reserved, touchy and irritable, and depression is common.

Margo (1981) reported a 53-year-old woman with a chronic depressive illness beginning 12 years before the acromegaly was diagnosed. It was notable that from the outset she had shown prominent psychomotor retardation, remaining sluggish and lacking in confidence despite attempts at treatment. She had experienced a good deal of chronic headache. Pituitary fossa irradiation ultimately led to some improvement.

Avery (1973) described an adolescent girl whose initial presentation was with symptoms of anxiety and depression, coupled with loss of self-confidence, guilt and concern over body size.

Other patients by contrast remain surprisingly cheerful as long as their disabilities cause no physical discomfort. Some appear to show little concern about the disease even when it is considerably advanced. How far these psychological reactions may also depend upon metabolic changes or on basal brain compression has not been clarified.

Hypopituitarism
(Simmond's Disease)

The commonest cause of hypopituitarism was formerly ischaemic necrosis of the anterior pituitary gland as a result of post-partum haemorrhage (Sheehan's syndrome). The cause is now usually a pituitary tumour, in particular a prolactin-secreting tumour in adults or a craniopharyngioma in children. A rare cause is head injury with fracture of the base of the skull.

Physical Features

The condition is commonly of long duration, sometimes extending over many years when first presenting for attention. Leading symptoms include weakness, ready fatigue and marked sensitivity to cold. There is loss of libido, with amenorrhoea in the female and impotence in the male. Loss of weight is common, but despite the earlier name of 'pituitary cachexia' it is not universal. Nor is it extreme until the terminal stages of the disorder (Sheehan and Summers, 1949). In cases with pituitary neoplasms weight may actually be gained if hypothalamic function is disturbed. Anorexia is common but in some cases appetite is very well preserved.

Cardinal signs on examination are a thin dry skin, which fails to tan normally and may become wrinkled as in premature ageing; a dull expressionless face, and loss of pubic and axillary hair. The body temperature is often subnormal, the pulse slow, and the blood pressure low.

Psychiatric Features

The mental picture can be equally striking. The frequency of psychiatric disorder was shown by Kind's (1958) survey of cases from the literature and from his own experience. Ninety per cent showed psychiatric symptoms and in half these were severe.

Depression may be marked, sometimes with outbursts of irritability. Drive and initiative are impaired, and the patient comes to spend progressively longer in bed. Virtually all patients show apathy, inertia and somnolence in some degree. Ultimately most are dull and drowsy, prone to self-neglect and indifferent about their state. The degree of psychological change commonly seen is greater than in other chronic debilitating diseases, and the patient's poor physical condition is therefore unlikely to be the complete explanation.

Impairment of memory may occasionally figure prominently and give rise to an impression of a dementing process. Other severe psychiatric complications include episodes of delirium in relation to impending metabolic crises, or more rarely chronic paranoid hallucinatory psychoses.

Metabolic crises may lead on from delirium to hypopituitary stupor or coma which is always a grave complication. Such severe developments usually set in only several years after the physical disorder has made its first appearance. The following case reported by Blau and Hinton (1960) illustrates the problems which may arise:

A woman of 46 was admitted with drowsiness, neck stiffness and a moderate pyrexia of two days duration. She opened her eyes to her name but would not obey commands and resisted examination. Meningitis was diagnosed at first, but scanty pubic and axillary hair soon led to the diagnosis of Simmond's disease.

Falling blood pressure required intravenous noradrenaline in addition to intravenous glucose and hydrocortisone. She emerged from the semicomatose state but remained incontinent and uncooperative, and proved to be deluded about her attendants. Violent behaviour necessitated transfer to a psychiatric hospital 2 weeks later, and over the next month she fluctuated from apathy to outbursts of restlessness with aggressive shouting. Memory and orientation were very faulty and she was unable to concentrate for long. In the next few weeks she settled into a calm rather foolish euphoria and was correctly oriented for most of the time.

She was followed up on regular treatment with cortisone. Three months after recovery from the coma her mental state and intellectual functions were back to normal. She had recovered her libido, which had deteriorated along with her general health since the birth of her child 10 years previously.

In this case the episode of coma appeared to result from a combination of intercurrent infection, hypoglycaemia, hypotension, and hypocorticoidism. The transient organic psychosis which followed it was probably due to reversible cortical damage resulting from some of the latter factors.

Thus, as with adrenal cortex hypofunction, hypopituitarism rarely leads to functional psychoses, but commonly to acute organic reactions in association with crises of metabolic disturbance. In both endocrine conditions alterations of mood form an integral part of the clinical picture and take the form of apathy, anergia and indifference. In all these respects the psychiatric accompaniments and complications are in contrast to those of Cushing's disease, where functional psychoses are common and where the usual mood change is towards depression and emotional lability.

Differential Diagnosis

Hypopituitarism must be differentiated from myxoedema, in which the facial appearance of the patient is very different, and from Addison's disease in which pigmentation is a prominent feature. In questionable cases full endocrine assessment is essential before embarking on the appropriate replacement therapy.

From the psychiatric point of view, neurosis and dementia may sometimes be closely simulated, but the principal differential diagnosis is from anorexia nervosa. Many of the early reported cases of hypopituitarism seem in retrospect to have been anorexia nervosa. Many of the early reported cases of hypopituitarism seem in retrospect to have been anorexia however, there is rarely clinical doubt, even though both share the cardinal feature of amenorrhoea. *Severe* weight loss is rare except terminally in hypopituitarism, whereas it is usually a presenting feature in anorexia nervosa. Similarly appetite may sometimes be well preserved in hypopituitarism. Loss of pubic and axillary hair is unusual in anorexia nervosa, and the fine downy facial hair of anorexia nervosa is rare in hypopituitarism. The psychological features of the two conditions are also very different: in hypopituitarism the patient is dull, apathetic and somnolent, whereas in anorexia nervosa she is typically restless and surprisingly active; distinctive attitudes to food and to the body image are lacking in hypopituitarism, whereas they form an important constellation of symptoms in anorexia nervosa. When serious doubt exists full endocrine assessment will clarify the differential diagnosis.

Outcome

Response to replacement therapy is usually good. Within a few days the patient experiences return of interest and energy, and most lose their symptoms entirely. In cases of very long duration, however, apathy and lack of drive may persist in some degree. Cortisol or prednisolone alone may suffice, though thyroxine is sometimes given in addition. Gonadal steroids may be required to restore libido and potency in the male. Textbooks of medicine should be consulted for further details.

Diabetes Insipidus

The syndrome of diabetes insipidus consists of polyuria with secondary polydipsia, resulting either from a deficiency of circulating antidiuretic hormone or a lack of action of the hormone on the kidney. Antidiuretic hormone (ADH, vasopressin) is synthesised in the supraoptic and paraventricular nuclei of the hypothalamus, whence it is transported to the posterior lobe of the pituitary then gains access to the circulation. It acts to increase the reabsorption of water by the distal convoluted tubules of the kidney, resulting in the production of a more concentrated urine.

In cranial (neurogenic) diabetes insipidus ADH is produced in insufficient quantity. In the nephrogenic form the kidney fails to respond normally to that available. Both result in the production of large volumes of dilute urine, normally accompanied by thirst. The urine osmolality is low, but the plasma osmolality is usually only slightly raised provided the thirst mechanisms are intact and the patient drinks adequately. If thirst does not occur, or if fluid intake is prevented, a dangerous degree of hypernatraemia and dehydration may develop.

Cranial diabetes insipidus can set in at any age without apparent cause, usually as an isolated abnormality but occasionally with other indications of hypothalamic disorder. The onset is typically abrupt. In very rare examples the condition is familial, being inherited as a Mendelian dominant. Other cases result from head injury with damage to the pituitary stalk, then often being transient, or follow pituitary surgery or yttrium implantations. Primary or secondary tumours involving the hypothalamus may be responsible.

Nephrogenic diabetes insipidus can occur as a rare sex-linked recessive disorder affecting males, and usually presenting soon after birth. Causes in adults include hypercalcaemia, potassium depletion, and the prolonged intake of excessive amounts of water, all of which can impair the action of ADH on the nephron. A variety of drugs, including lithium, may also be responsible. Polyuria from lithium treatment can develop when plasma levels are within the therapeutic range; some 40 per cent of patients on lithium experience thirst, with perhaps 12 per cent developing polyuria (Ledingham, 1983). In most cases this resolves within several weeks of withdrawing the drug.

The differential diagnosis of diabetes insipidus must include primary renal disease, diabetes mellitus, and the polydipsias induced by drugs such as chlorpromazine or thoridazine which may stimulate drinking by a direct action on the hypothalamus. The major diagnostic problem, however, is to distinguish diabetes insipidus from compulsive water drinking as described below.

The treatment of neurogenic diabetes insipidus consists of administering vasopressin. For transient states, as after head injury, aqueous vasopressin may be given subcutaneously. In the chronic condition the synthetic analogue DDAVP (1-desamino-8-D'-

arginine vasopressin) is preferable on account of its longer duration of action and diminished pressor activity. This can be administered as a nasal spray. Nephrogenic diabetes insipidus is treated by thiazide diuretics; their mechanism of action in this situation is unclear.

Compulsive Water Drinking ('psychogenic polydipsia')

Compulsive water drinking may be associated with a wide range of psychopathology—neurosis, personality disorder or psychosis. In psychotic patients it is frequently delusionally motivated. Among the nine examples described by Barlow and De Wardener (1959), long-standing personality disorder was common, often with hypochondriasis and depression. Six of the patients had had hysterical conversion episodes and some had histories of compulsive eating. Denial and evasion were sometimes a prominent part of the picture.

The clinical syndrome that results can simulate diabetes insipidus closely. In both conditions the fluid intake and output are raised and the urine osmolality is low. With compulsive water drinking, however, the plasma osmolality is also likely to be low. Hyponatraemia may develop when the water intake is so excessive that it exceeds the kidneys' ability to excrete it. There may be other evidence of psychiatric disorder to give the clue, or the onset may be clearly related to a depressive phase or period of emotional stress. The onset will often be gradual rather than abrupt, and consumption may tend to fluctuate from hour to hour or day to day in contrast to the steadily increased intake of diabetes insipidus. Nocturnal polyuria will often prove to be absent.

Not infrequently, however, the distinction can be difficult, and such difficulty can persist during fluid deprivation studies. In normal subjects fluid deprivation over an 8 hour period leaves the plasma osmolality unchanged, while the urine osmolality rises to twice that of the plasma (Hall, 1983). In diabetes insipidus the plasma osmolality rises, but that of the urine remains relatively low. The test may indeed have to be discontinued if the patient loses more than 3% of body weight. In compulsive water drinking the initial plasma and urine osmolality are low, and the plasma osmolality rises to normal at the end of the test. However, the urine osmolality may fail to rise to twice that of the plasma, since the prolonged excessive water intake may have led to a secondary nephrogenic diabetes insipidus. For the same reason response may be inadequate to a

trial injection of vasopressin. Prolonged water deprivation (carefully monitored) for 2–4 days may be necessary to allow the return of normal renal function, or this may even be longer delayed. Hypertonic saline infusion with measurement of the plasma ADH response may ultimately help towards clarifying the diagnosis.

When compulsive water drinking is mistaken for diabetes insipidus and treated with ADH, hyponatraemia and symptoms of water intoxication (p. 476) can develop. Water intoxication also seems to be a special hazard in compulsive water drinking associated with psychosis; numerous examples of such a complication have been described in schizophrenic patients, sometimes presenting acutely with vomiting, impairment of consciousness or fits (Fowler et al., 1977; Khamnei, 1984; Singh et al., 1985). Khamnei noted that 17 of 23 reported cases of water intoxication due to polydipsia were psychotic, and that sometimes there was clear evidence of inappropriate ADH secretion. How far the latter may reflect hypothalamic disorder intrinsic to the psychosis is, however, uncertain. Multiple factors may often be at work including the effects of other medical illnesses or drugs (Fowler et al., 1977). Both amitriptyline and thiothixine, for example, have been implicated in leading to inappropriate ADH secretion. Fatalities have been reported from time to time, and Shevitz et al. (1980) stress the danger of giving neuroleptics before the water intake is controlled.

It is clearly important to enquire for a history of polydipsia in any psychotic patient who presents with seizures or lowering of consciousness. Similarly the discovery of polyuria with a low urinary specific gravity should always lead to careful observation of the patient's water intake. This may on occasion be skilfully concealed.

Klinefelter's Syndrome

Klinefelter's syndrome results from the presence of at least one additional X chromosome in the nucleus in the male. It may present with infertility or delayed sexual maturation, or the hypogonadism may be discovered on routine examination. The usual karyotye is 47 XXY, revealed on buccal smear examination. Other variants occur, however, and in mosaicism the abnormal cell line may be restricted to testicular or other tissue.

Examination shows small testes and a variable degree of androgen deficiency, manifest as gynaecomastia or scanty beard growth. Azoospermia or oligospermia are always present and irreversible.

The urinary gonadotrophin levels are raised.

Psychiatric Features

A high incidence of psychiatric disorder has emerged in the condition. Intelligence is often low, personality and behaviour are frequently abnormal, and there is a probable excess of psychotic illness. Some psychiatric features appear to be attributable to the endocrine disorder, others to be more directly related to the chromosomal abnormality.

Early reports of an excess of Klinefelter's syndrome among patients in mental subnormality hospitals led to the view that severe impairment of intellect was characteristic. It is now appreciated, however, that even superior intelligence may occasionally be encountered (Swanson and Stipes, 1969). The usual picture is of mild impairment only, though perhaps a quarter of patients presenting at infertility clinics fall within the subnormal range. The greater the number of additional X chromosomes in the karyotype the more severe the mental retardation (Forssman, 1970).

It seems clear that genetic rather than hormonal factors are operative in reducing the level of intelligence. No relationship has emerged between the degree of hypogonadism and the IQ levels obtained; and patients with hypogonadism due to other causes tend to show intelligence within the normal range. Pasqualini et al. (1957) and Wakeling (1972) found a mean IQ of approximately 80 among their Klinefelter patients, compared with a mean of 100 among the hypogonadal patients, despite a tendency towards more severe endocrine disorder in the latter.

The lowered intellectual capacity may be due at least in part to impaired cerebral maturation or other brain abnormality consequent upon the genetic defect. A high incidence of EEG abnormalities has been reported in the condition, chiefly slowed alpha frequencies but also slow wave dysrhythmias and paroxysmal features (Hambert and Frey, 1964). Epilepsy is also commoner than chance expectation.

The personality in Klinefelter patients is frequently abnormal. A variety of pictures has been described, ranging from markedly antisocial conduct to passivity and social withdrawal. Common descriptions are of patients lacking in drive and initiative, with severe restriction of interests and generally indolent, insecure and dependent. At the same time tolerance of frustration tends to be impaired, with explosive irritability and outbursts of aggression. Poor school and work records, marital instability and impoverished social relationships are common.

Nielsen's (1969) review showed histories of alcoholism in 6% and of criminal behaviour in 12% of patients. A small excess of XXY patients has emerged in surveys of institutions caring for severely disturbed criminals, along with the more usual excess of XYY or XXYY karyotypes (Swanson and Stipes, 1969).

The endocrine disorder may play a considerable part in hindering personality maturation and contributing to some aspects of the problem. Thus patients with hypogonadism due to other causes are typically shy, timid and markedly lacking in drive. They tend, however, to show more stable histories and temperaments than Klinefelter patients, and lack the excess of criminal behaviours. Wakeling (1972) compared 11 Klinefelter patients and 9 other hypogonadal patients seen in a psychiatric hospital; both groups showed insecurity and low tolerance of frustration, but passivity was more marked in the hypogonadal patients and impulsive erratic behaviour in the Klinefelters. The latter, moreover, frequently had histories of pre-pubertal maladjustment, with a higher incidence of unsettled schooling, neurosis and behaviour disorder in childhood. It appears therefore that in Klinefelter's syndrome delayed cerebral maturation may make a contribution, over and above the androgen deficiency, to poor social adjustment and disturbed personality functioning.

Sexual problems, as might be expected, are not uncommon. Potency tends to be low and to show an early decline, especially when features of hypogonadism are marked (Pasqualini et al., 1957). The sexual drive is generally well-oriented, however, in contrast to the marked lack of libido and interest seen with hypogonadism due to other causes. Androgen treatment can be successful in restoring libido and potency (Beumont et al., 1972). Occasional reports have described homosexuality, transvestism, exhibitionism and paedophilia in Klinefelter patients, but there is little to suggest that deviation is characteristic of the syndrome (Orwin et al., 1974). Sexual pathology, when it occurs, probably again reflects the restricted personality development and incapacity for deep interpersonal relationships. The more extreme examples of deviant sexual practice have usually occurred in severely antisocial or psychotic individuals.

Mental hospital surveys, reviewed by Forssman (1970), indicate a 3-fold increase in Klinefelter patients compared with the general population. This appears to be mainly due to psychotic illnesses of a schizophrenic nature. Nielsen (1969) found that 6%

of patients recorded in the psychiatric literature had been given a diagnosis of schizophrenia, and another 7% had psychoses of an uncertain type but almost all with paranoid delusions. Well documented examples of schizophrenia in association with Klinefelter's syndrome are provided by Pomeroy (1980) and Roy (1981). The increased risk of mental illness may represent another facet of the increased vulnerability to stress of the Klinefelter patient, or may have more direct genetic determinants.

There is little to suggest an increased incidence of organic psychiatric illness. Jablensky et al. (1970) have described a patient who demented rapidly in his early 40s, showing diffuse white matter degeneration and adrenal cortical atrophy at autopsy; this, however, may well have represented a chance association with Klinefelter's syndrome.

Turner's Syndrome

The XO karyotype is associated with oestrogen deficiency and hence failure of sexual maturation. Primary amenorrhoea is accompanied by short stature and a variety of skeletal abnormalities including cubitus valgus and arching of the palate. The facial appearance may be characteristic with a small jaw, fish-like mouth and low set ears. The neck is short and may be webbed. Congenital renal abnormalities and coarctation of the aorta are common. The classical case shows a 45 XO karyotype, though other X chromosome abnormalities occur. The FSH concentration in the urine is raised.

Psychiatric interest in the condition has largely centred on the cognitive functioning of such patients. Mental retardation, chiefly mild in degree, was once regarded as common, but it now seems probable that verbal intelligence, at least, is normally distributed. Superior intelligence can certainly be encountered.

Money (1963, 1964) drew attention to the common finding of lower performance than verbal intelligence in patients with the syndrome, the means in his sample being 88 and 105 respectively (on the WISC or WAIS). This was paralleled by inferior scores on tests of perceptual organisation when compared with scores on verbal comprehension—discrepancies which became more marked at the higher intelligence levels. Visuospatial ability appeared to be particularly poor.

In some respects this disparity can be seen as an accentuation of the usual female as opposed to male pattern of differential cognitive abilities, which brings interest to Money's suggestion that it might

be a specific cognitive consequence of the abnormal chromosomal condition. Garron and Vander Stoep (1969) review further evidence that Turner's patients have poor ability at drawing geometrical designs from memory, at drawing human figures and in certain aspects of left-right orientation. Virtually all tasks that are primarily non-verbal appear to be impaired in some degree, while verbal abilities are preserved at normal levels. How far this may reflect an underlying impairment of cerebral maturation is uncertain; but several reports on small groups of patients have suggested a high incidence of electroencephalographic abnormalities (Christodorescu et al., 1970).

With regard to personality, feminine sexual identification and interests are usual, and gross psychopathology appears to be rare (Garron and Vander Stoep, 1969). Libido tends to be low, however, and many descriptions stress childish, meek and overcompliant behaviour. Traits of passivity and immaturity in the personality are congruent with failure of sexual maturation (Kihlbom, 1969; Nielsen, 1970b). Such features may also be partly determined by the infantilizing responses called forth by the patients' short stature and child-like appearance.

Neurotic traits may emerge, but severe emotional disorder appears to be rare despite the handicaps imposed by the physical defects and sterility. In contrast to the situation in Klinefelter's syndrome, there is no suggestion of an increased incidence of antisocial behaviour or of psychotic illness. It would seem, therefore, that the lack of an X chromosome has substantially less effect than the possession of an additional X where mental health is concerned (Forssman, 1970).

Hyperparathyroidism

Hyperparathyroidism has gained recognition as a rather rare but very important cause of psychiatric morbidity. It is important because the diagnosis may be missed, resulting in many years of chronic mental ill-health, yet treatment of the endocrine disorder can bring prompt relief. The cause is usually a benign adenoma of one of the parathyroid glands. Sometimes multiple tumours are present, and occasionally the condition may occur familially. More rarely there may be diffuse hyperplasia of all parathyroid tissue. In 'multiple endocrine adenomatosis', parathyroid adenomas are accompanied by endocrine tumours of the pancreas and pituitary ('MEA Type 1'), or by phaeochromocytomas and medullary carcinoma of the thyroid ('MEA Type 2').

Women are affected more often than men. Cases usually present in middle age though the range of onset is wide. Calcium and phosphorous are mobilised from the bones and excreted in excess in the urine.

Physical Features

Renal calcification is present in about two-thirds of cases in the form of renal calculi or as diffuse nephrocalcinosis. The typical X-ray changes of osteitis fibrosa are present in many of the remainder.

In the great majority physical complaints are the predominant feature, with pain, fracture or deformity of bones, renal colic, or profound muscular weakness. The myopathic syndrome consists of proximal muscular weakness and wasting, hypotonia, and discomfort on movement. Other common symptoms which may suggest the condition are increased thirst, polyuria, dull diffuse headache, anorexia and nausea. On examination corneal calcification may be seen close to the corneo-scleral junction as linear aggregations of granular material.

Psychiatric Features

Mental symptoms are also common and were found in two-thirds of Petersen's (1968) series, even after excluding patients who had been referred specifically on account of psychiatric disturbance. In a third the mental abnormalities were severe. Watson (1968) found that a very small but important group presented with mental symptoms alone, and showed neither renal stones nor bone disease. In Karpati and Frame's (1964) series 4 out of 33 cases had psychiatric complaints which dominated the picture to the extent that they had been referred initially for psychiatric or neurological consultation:

A woman of 40 presented with depression which had proved resistant to drugs and psychotherapy for several years before hyperparathyroidism was diagnosed. A woman of 64 had a 2 year history of agitated depression with tremulousness, disorientation, confusion and severe headache. A man of 43 presented with increasing nervousness and obsessive-compulsive features which subsided after operation. The fourth patient presented with a confusional state accompanied by severe headache.

Gatewood *et al.* (1975) have reported five further examples, all presenting with problems that seemed to be mainly psychiatric, and four of them showing no evidence of bone or renal pathology:

A 63-year-old man developed persistent confusion following a cholecystectomy, which subsided within 2 weeks of discovering and removing a parathyroid adenoma. A 65-year-old man presented with a 14 month history of progressive depression, fatigue, lethargy and periods of confusion, and was similarly cured. A 56-year-old woman had been treated for 4 months for catatonic schizophrenia and improved gradually without medication after operation. A 74-year-old woman with endogenous depression similarly recovered without antidepressants. And a 75-year-old diabetic with a recent history of syncope, confusion and drowsiness made a remarkable recovery from what had initially been thought to be a cerebrovascular accident.

The commonest mental change is depression with anergia. The patient gradually becomes tired, listless and dull, with marked lack of initiative and spontaneity. In Petersen's (1968) series 36% of patients showed such changes, and almost all of these had been unable to work on account of lack of energy during the months preceding operation. Tension and irritability sometimes accompanied the depression, and explosive outbursts were occasionally seen.

Even among patients who do not complain of such symptoms at the time, they can often be recognised retrospectively when operation has restored the metabolic state to normal. Anderson (1968) found that three-quarters of patients reported that they felt better post-operatively, with higher spirits and greater energy than for many years before. It seemed that the chronicity of the disorder, which had often been present for ten or more years when diagnosed, had made it difficult for the patient to appreciate the mental changes subjectively at the time.

Organic mental symptoms were present in 12% of Petersen's cases, chiefly impairment of memory or general mental slowing. This may be an insidious and chronic development, or may herald an acute organic reaction as part of a 'parathyroid crisis'. Such acute organic psychoses occurred in 5% of cases, with spells of mental confusion, or acute delirious episodes with hallucinations, paranoia and aggressive behaviour. Stuporose states may also occur, or recurrent convulsions leading to coma. Hockaday *et al.* (1966) have described a patient who presented with stupor, and Cooper and Shapira (1973) report a patient in whom stupor supervened during the course of a depressive illness. Both of these showed flexibilitas cerea at some point in their course.

Very occasionally the degree of intellectual impairment can give rise to a mistaken diagnosis of presenile dementia as in the following case:

A schoolmaster of 65 was admitted to hospital for investigation of spells of mental confusion of four months duration. A diagnosis of presenile dementia had been made elsewhere. At the outset he had developed unsteadiness of gait, and thereafter showed a gradual decline in mental abilities. By the time of admission it was difficult to get a coherent history, but it appeared that he had complained of excessive thirst and sudden episodes of muscular weakness. The episodes of confusion had tended to be intermittent.

On examination he showed gross mental confusion interspersed with periods of lucidity. He was drowsy with some muscular weakness, and was drinking $2\frac{1}{2}$–3 litres of fluid per day. Carotid arteriography and ventriculography showed mild cerebral atrophy consistent with his age, but after the ventriculogram he developed a severe fall of blood pressure and failed to recover consciousness. At autopsy the immediate cause of death was found to be fulminating acute pancreatitis. A parathyroid tumour was also discovered. The result of his serum calcium (16·2 mg/100 ml) was received only after he had died. Microscopic examination of the brain showed fine symmetrical calcification in the basal ganglia and hippocampi.

(Duchen, 1972)

Non-organic psychoses appear to be rare in hyperparathyroidism, and when present are probably coincidental.

Investigations

Confirmation of the disease is usually obtained by finding a raised serum calcium. Repeat estimations may sometimes be required. The serum phosphate may be low but is sometimes normal. Blood must be taken while the patient is fasting and without venestasis, and account must be taken of the serum albumin level. Radioimmunoassay for parathyroid hormone levels can provide further confirmatory evidence, though a normal result does not exclude the condition. A hydrocortisone supression test can also be useful—in hyperparathyroidism the administration of steroids usually fails to lower the plasma calcium, whereas this occurs in hypercalcaemias of other origin.

The serum alkaline phosphatase is raised when the bones are involved. Renal stones or calcification may be detected on X-ray, and typical changes may be seen in the bones. The hand X-ray can be particularly informative. Radiography of the skull may occasionally show calcification in the caudate nuclei and frontal lobes, though this is very much less common than in hypoparathyroidism since the calcium deposits are usually finely distributed. The electroencephalogram shows widespread slow activity, sometimes with paroxysms of frontal delta waves at high levels of serum calcium.

Differential Diagnosis

The disorder should be borne in mind in patients who show chronic affective disorder, neurotic disability or minor intellectual impairment in association with suspicious physical symptoms. Neurotic ill-health together with polydipsia and polyuria is a not uncommon mode of presentation. Petersen (1968) suggested that hyperparathyroidism should always be considered 'when lack of initiative, depression and thirst appear during a prolonged, insidiously developing and diagnostically unclear change of personality'.

Patients with fluctuating confusion or delirium may cause special diagnostic difficulties. When the acute organic reaction is recognised the main hazard is concentrating on a fruitless search for some intra-cranial cause (Henson, 1966). In the presence of stupor, the electroencephalographic finding of widespread slow waves may provide the important clue to the metabolic derangement (Moure, 1967; Cooper and Shapira, 1973).

Neurological disorders are more frequently simulated. Headache, vomiting, fits and drowsiness can lead to a suspicion of cerebral tumour, or profound muscular weakness may suggest a primary muscular disorder. Cerebral arteriosclerosis, subdural haematoma, uraemia, and phaeochromocytoma are other misdiagnoses which have been reported.

Aetiology of Mental Disturbances

The cause of the psychiatric disturbance appears to lie chiefly or even exclusively with the elevation of serum calcium. Unlike the other endocrinopathies a relatively straightforward quantitative relationship is found between the severity of psychological disturbance and this simple measure of serum chemistry. In Petersen's (1968) careful review, affective disorder and disturbances of drive corresponded to a serum calcium of 12–16 mg/100 ml, acute organic reactions with florid delirium appeared at 16–19 mg/100 ml, and somnolence and coma were found with levels exceeding 19 mg/100 ml. Such a sequence of changes could sometimes be traced in the single patient. Bleuler (1967) points out that the psychiatric disorders of hyperparathyroidism are more constant from person to person, and less dependent on the dynamics of the personality, than are the psychiatric pictures seen with most other endocrine disorders. This is no doubt because they depend upon a widespread ionic intermediary, and not upon the direct cerebral effects of a hormone which can influence brain functions and emotions physiologically.

The level of circulating parathormone does not appear to be directly responsible, since mental symptoms can improve rapidly when the serum calcium is lowered by peritoneal dialysis (Petersen, 1968). Nor can a relationship be discerned with the level of serum phosphorus or serum alkaline phosphatase, or with the duration of the disorder. The possible role of hypomagnesaemia has not been fully explored. Other factors may make a contribution, such as hypertension or renal failure due to nephrocalcinosis, but in the majority of cases these are clearly of subsidiary importance (Karpati and Frame, 1964).

Outcome

Removal of the parathyroid adenoma usually brings relief to disorders of affect and drive, also to acute organic psychoses. The mental disorder is commonly found to be wholly reversible, with rapid resumption of former mental health. Headache is abolished, and muscular strength increased. The time to recovery has been found to be independent of the duration of the disease and of the severity of the mental changes, and to parallel closely the fall in serum calcium. The rare psychotic states of long duration, with thought disorder and paranoia, may respond less satisfactorily, but probably owe a good deal to premorbid vulnerability. With severe depressive illness antidepressant medication may be required to obtain complete resolution as in a patient described by Noble (1974):

A woman of 50 developed a severe depressive illness for the first time in her life. This responded well to electroconvulsive therapy. Eighteen months later she became apathetic and retarded, failed to respond to antidepressants, and during a course of ECT became dehydrated and incontinent. A parathyroid adenoma was discovered while this was being investigated. Its removal, however, left her profoundly apathetic and unwell, despite the return of the plasma calcium to normal. After 4 weeks she was started again on tricyclic antidepressants which now led to progressive and full recovery.

Post-operatively care is needed to guard against hypocalcaemia. Pre-operative preparation is required with the administration of vitamin D. Acute anxiety may herald tetany, usually between the tenth and fourteenth post-operative days. Sometimes short-lived psychiatric disturbance sets in within a few days of the operation even though hypocalcaemia cannot be demonstrated, presumably occasioned by the abrupt drop in extracellular calcium which has occurred. Karpati and Frame (1964) report such examples showing catatonia, acute agitation or mental confusion.

Hypoparathyroidism

Hypo- like hyperparathyroidism has come to be recognised as a cause of remediable psychiatric disorder, especially since the comprehensive survey of the literature by Denko and Kaelbling (1962). This is replete with examples of failure to diagnose the condition, sometimes over very many years, yet treatment offers an excellent chance of reversing both the physical and psychiatric changes.

The commonest cause is removal of the parathyroid glands at thyroidectomy, or interference with their blood supply in the course of other operations on the neck. In other cases the aetiology is obscure; the parathyroids are found to be absent or degenerated, sometimes in more than one member of a family and occasionally in association with Addison's disease ('idiopathic hypoparathyroidism'). The deficiency of parathormone leads to a low serum calcium and a raised serum phosphate. Calcium deposits may occur in the skin and the brain.

Two allied conditions occur more rarely. In 'pseudo-hypoparathyroidism' the parathyroid glands function normally but the tissues are for some reason resistant to the effects of parathormone. The same abnormalities are found in the serum chemistry and calcium deposits are found similarly in the soft tissues including the brain. But there are frequently additional traits of short stature, marked shortening of some of the metacarpals, and a characteristic rounded facies. The condition usually presents in the first three decades of life, is often familial, and is presumably congenital in origin. 'Pseudo-pseudo-hypoparathyroidism' is a rare disorder, identical to pseudo-hyperparathyroidism in the associated traits, but with normal serum calcium and phosphate. It also presents early and occurs familially, and may be an abortive form of pseudo-hypoparathyroidism which lacks full expression of the biochemical abnormality.

Physical Features

Hypoparathyroidism should be suspected in patients with symptoms of chronic tetany, or when ocular cataracts develop at an unusually young age. A history of operation on the neck should bring the possibility of the condition to mind.

Tetany occurs in the form of numbness and tingling in the hands and feet or around the mouth. With more severe degrees the patient experiences muscular cramps and stiffness in the limbs, carpo-pedal spasms or laryngeal stridor. In carpo-pedal spasms the metacarpophalangeal joints are flexed and the interphalangeal joints of the thumb and fingers extended to produce a characteristic posture of the hand ('main d'accoucheur'). Epilepsy can be the first and sometimes the only manifestation.

In addition to cataracts the patients may have a dry coarse skin, scanty hair, trophic changes in the nails and poor dental development. Calcium deposits may be detected in the skin, or appear on skull X-ray as calcification in the region of the basal ganglia. Clinically useful signs include twitching of the facial muscles on tapping the facial nerve below the zygoma (Chvostek's sign), and the production of carpo-pedal spasm by temporarily occluding the circulation to the arm (Trousseau's sign). Very occasionally papilloedema may be observed.

Psychiatric Features

A wide variety and a high incidence of psychiatric disturbances have emerged in hypoparathyroidism. Denko and Kaelbling (1962) estimate that at least half of the cases attributable to surgery have psychiatric symptoms, and that the incidence is probably higher still in idiopathic hypoparathyroidism.

The most frequent disturbances are organic psychiatric syndromes. Acute organic reactions with features typical of delirium are prone to develop in surgical cases, where the biochemical changes are likely to be abrupt. More chronic and insidious developments are not uncommon in idiopathic hypoparathyroidism, where the biochemical changes have developed gradually and been much longer in operation. Such patients may show sustained difficulty with concentration, emotional lability, and impairment of intellectual functions. Robinson *et al.* (1954) reported a case of idiopathic hypoparathyroidism which presented first as status epilepticus and seeming presenile dementia, and which illustrates the clinical problems involved:

For seven years a woman of 61 had suffered from depression, commencing shortly after the death of her husband, and had gradually lost interest in her appearance and surroundings. Sometime after the onset bilateral cataracts had been removed. For several years she had experienced occasional numbness and tingling in the legs, and some 3 years previously skull X-ray had shown calcification in the basal ganglia. However she had not reattended hospital for follow-up at this time. For 2 years there had been episodes of urinary incontinence, and for six months 'fainting spells' in some of which twitching of the limbs had been observed. For 5 weeks there had been considerable mental deterioration with confusion and loss of memory.

On admission to hospital the status epilepticus subsided with treatment and she was found to be disoriented, apathetic and doubly incontinent. No rational history or conversation was possible. Evidence of self-neglect was extreme. She showed dysarthria, fine lateral nystagmus, diminished tendon jerks and feebly extensor plantar responses. On the tenth day she showed attacks of tetany and carpo-pedal spasm, and Chvostek's sign was positive. The electrocardiogram showed prolonged Q-T intervals and low T waves. She was treated with intravenous calcium gluconate, oral dihydrotachysterol (A.T.10) and calcium lactate. Within a few days she had improved, becoming continent, oriented, and taking an intelligent interest in her surroundings and her own person.

She remained well and her mental state did not deteriorate, but three months after treatment she developed choreiform jerks of the limbs and twitching in the face, presumably as a result of lesions in the calcified basal ganglia.

An important point stressed by the authors was that the patient showed no evidence of tetany on clinical examination until 10 days after her acute presentation.

Another remarkable example was reported by Eraut (1974):

An 80-year-old man was admitted to hospital on account of numerous falls at home. He could give no account of himself, but his wife reported that he had been deteriorating for many months and had been confused and forgetful for a long time. Bilateral cataracts had been extracted 14 and 20 months previously. While in hospital the previous year mild dementia had been noted.

He was disoriented in time and place, could answer simple questions but could not respond to commands. There were no neurological abnormalities. A chest infection responded to antibiotics, but he remained demented. Three weeks after admission he had a grand mal fit, and when started on phenytoin became tremulous and totally unresponsive. This was followed by tetanic spasm of the left hand and laryngeal stridor, whereupon tests confirmed the presence of idiopathic hypoparathyroidism.

Treatment with dihydrotachysterol led to considerable improvement within a few days. He was discharged well recovered mentally, capable of lucid conversation and showing reasonable memory for recent and past events.

'Pseudo-neurosis' is described as the next most common change, both in surgical and idiopathic hypoparathyroidism, and occurring in all age groups. Children show temper tantrums and night terrors, and adults become depressed, nervous and irritable with frequent crying spells and marked social withdrawal. The emotional disturbances may fluctuate in degree or show periods of spontaneous resolution.

In this connection the concept of 'partial parathyroid insufficiency' is interesting. Fourman *et al.* (1963) showed that in a quarter of patients who had undergone thyroidectomy the plasma calcium was merely at the lower limit of normal, but could be provoked to fall to definitely subnormal values by calcium deprivation or intravenous administration of edetic acid. About half such patients had mental symptoms in the form of tension and anxiety, panic attacks, depression and lassitude. Often there were no other pointers to parathyroid insufficiency and the symptoms were therefore indistinguishable from those commonly found in middle-aged neurotic women. Fourman *et al.* (1967) have since assessed the relevance of such symptoms by a double-blind trial of calcium citrate tablets and placebo, and have confirmed that calcium is significantly effective in reducing psychiatric symptom scores. The most consistent changes were with regard to depression and diminution of appetite.

More rarely psychotic illnesses of manic-depressive or schizophrenic type may be seen, particularly in cases due to surgery. Again spontaneous remissions or response to other forms of treatment may delay diagnosis of the underlying condition.

In pseudo-hypoparathyroidism and pseudo-pseudo-hypoparathyroidism intellectual impairment is by far the most frequent psychiatric abnormality, occurring in approximately half of all reported cases. Several such patients have been discovered in hospitals for the feeble-minded, and Denko and Kaelbling suggest that the serum calcium should be investigated in every patient with mental retardation.

Investigations

The serum calcium is low, the serum phosphate raised, and the urinary excretion of calcium and phosphate diminished. The serum alkaline phosphatase is normal. Skull X-ray frequently shows calcification in the region of the basal ganglia as symmetrical bilateral punctate opacities. Electroencephalographic abnormalities may be present even in the absence of epilepsy, usually generalised but sometimes surprisingly focal (Watson, 1972).

In pseudo-hypoparathyroidism the same abnormalities of serum chemistry are found, but a distinction can now be made by examining the effect of an infusion of parathyroid hormone on the excretion of 3'-5'-cyclic adenosine monophosphate in the urine (O'Riordan, 1972).

Differential Diagnosis

The diagnoses which may be mistakenly entertained include mental retardation, presenile dementia, neurosis, hysteria, idiopathic epilepsy and cerebral tumour.

A diagnosis of neurosis or hysteria is suggested by the peculiar and intermittent nature of the symptoms, including bizarre paraesthesiae and muscular spasms. Moreover the patient may give a vague and perplexing account, with obvious difficulty in observing and describing the symptoms accurately. Attacks may be triggered by emotional influences, since hyperventilation will lead unusually readily to tetanic symptoms. Hypochondriasis is readily suggested by the generally heightened level of anxiety, the vagueness of the complaints and the occurrence of periods of spontaneous remission. As a result, patients with hypoparathyroidism are sometimes found to have carried a label of psychogenic disorder for several years before the true diagnosis is made. In other cases well-defined mood swings have led to an initial diagnosis of manic-depressive disorder (Denko and Kaelbling, 1962).

Epileptic attacks may be thought to be idiopathic in origin, and the serum calcium should be determined in every epileptic patient when the precise cause of the attacks remains uncertain. In the rare cases of hypoparathyroidism with papilloedema and raised intracranial pressure, cerebral tumour may be closely simulated, especially when fits are present and alteration of personality has occurred.

Outcome

The response to correction of the serum biochemistry is usually gratifying. Neurotic symptoms are reported to clear up in the majority of patients even though some weeks may elapse before the patient feels entirely well. It is probable that an element of secondary neurotic disorder often becomes established in response to the chronically undiagnosed physical complaints, and it is not surprising that some time may be needed for complete recovery.

Acute organic reactions may be expected to improve promptly. Chronic intellectual impairments may also be completely reversed. Denko and Kaelbling (1962) noted that when adequate details were given, about half the cases of idiopathic hypoparathyroidism with intellectual impairment were reported to improve whereas very few cases were unchanged or worse. Patients with pseudohypoparathyroidism may also improve in intellectual status when the serum chemistry is corrected, but rarely to a spectacular extent. This is perhaps because such patients have been damaged intellectually while still immature, or perhaps because there is an associated genetic cause for their intellectual impairment.

Details of long-term management will not be dealt with here. This usually requires vitamin D or equivalent preparations such as dihydrotachysterol in addition to oral calcium.

Diabetes Mellitus

Diabetes mellitus results from an absolute or relative deficiency of insulin production by the pancreas, causing disturbed carbohydrate metabolism with hyperglycaemia and glycosuria. Secondary changes are prone to occur in the metabolism of protein and fat, the latter leading to ketosis and acidosis. It is a syndrome rather than a disease entity. The requirements of insulin are commonly found to be much in excess of normal pancreatic production, owing to resistance to the action of insulin or excessive gluconeogenesis. Hence it is probable that factors other than decreased insulin production contribute to the severity of diabetes in many patients, with the anterior pituitary and adrenal glands also playing a part.

It is well established that genetic mechanisms are operative though the precise modes of inheritance have not been clarified. Obesity has an important relationship to the development of the disease in middle life.

The onset can be at any age from infancy to old age, with approximately half the cases appearing before 50 and another quarter between 50 and 60. The disorder tends to be rapid in onset in the young, but usually insidious in development and milder in older persons. Textbooks of medicine should be consulted for the general clinical associations of the disorder and the principles of management by diet, insulin and oral hypoglycaemic agents.

Psychiatric attention to diabetes has been sporadic, and few systematic surveys have been made of the emotional and other mental complica-

tions. Two valuable recent reviews have, however, been produced (Wilkinson, 1981; Tattersall, 1981). In clinical practice it is clear that the diabetic who is poorly endowed or emotionally unstable can pose a considerable therapeutic problem, since his cooperation in treatment is essential if adequate control is to be achieved. Moreover there are indications that psychological stresses can be important in aggravating the disorder or precipitating episodes of loss of control, and even suggestions that emotional factors may sometimes bring the disorder into being.

These issues will be discussed below, along with the question of brain damage in diabetic patients. When evidence of brain damage emerges this may be attributable to episodes of hypoglycaemia or diabetic coma, or alternatively to the high incidence of atherosclerosis which exists in diabetics. The picture of diabetic coma, and certain common neurological complications, will also be briefly described.

Emotional Influences on the Course of Diabetes

A considerable body of evidence shows that emotionally stressful experiences can produce fluctuations in levels of blood glucose and ketone bodies, both in diabetic and non-diabetic persons. Experimental observations in this area are summarised by Hinkle and Wolf (1952a, 1952b). The magnitude of such changes is much greater in diabetics, and if of long enough duration they appear capable of leading to ketosis and hyperglycaemia in some cases and to hypoglycaemia in others. It has proved difficult, however, to define the extent to which such factors may be operative in the actual disease.

Stress, either physical or emotional, has often been blamed as the initial cause. Examples of the sudden manifestation of diabetes in relation to dramatic stresses are scattered throughout the literature, also attempts at constructing a characteristic personality profile which has rendered the diabetic unusually susceptible to stress. Treuting (1962) reviews the theories which have been elaborated, suggesting for example that diabetes is a disorder of adaptation and that persons showing it have reacted to various life stresses with a physiological response that is appropriate to starvation. The pathway for such an emotional origin would be via hypothalamic-autonomic or pituitary-endocrine relationships. However no increased incidence of the disorder emerged in battle casualties from the first and second world wars, and it now seems most unlikely that stress can bring the disorder into being in people who would otherwise never have developed it. It remains possible, nonetheless, that stress may sometimes change a latent case of diabetes into an active one, i.e. that physical or emotional stresses may play a part in determining the time at which the disorder is declared.

A rather less controversial area is the effect of emotional influences on the course of the established disease. Diabetic patients may sometimes show a close relationship between disturbing life experiences and episodes of loss of control, even to the extent of developing ketotic coma. Hinkle and Wolf (1952a, 1952b) observed 64 diabetics with special attention to their prevailing attitudes and the persons and relationships important to their emotional security. In long-term studies extending over several years, periods of exacerbation and remission were correlated with events in the life situation. Events which were consciously or unconsciously interpreted by the patients as threatening to their security appeared to be particularly liable to lead to loss of control. Case histories were presented to illustrate how admissions to hospital for coma could regularly follow stressful life situations, as in the following example:

An adolescent girl from a disturbed home background had twelve admissions for diabetic acidosis and coma during five years, all following acutely stressful life situations. 'To each of these stresses—fights between her parents, arguments with her mother, change to a new school, the departure of her sister ("the only one who loved me")— she reacted as if it were a threatened deprivation of love and security. They aroused in her resentment, which she felt afraid to express, and were accompanied by the rapid development of thirst, polyuria, ketosis, and coma. On several occasions . . . she expressed her hopelessness and rebellion by stopping her insulin when the ketosis developed. On other occasions she expressed her resentment and hopelessness by failing to sterilise her equipment, and the subsequent infections led to hospital admissions. In half of these instances, however, diabetic coma followed swiftly upon the onset of a stressful life situation, despite the fact that no infection was present, and the insulin dose was not altered. It may be remarked in passing that this patient was typical of the group in that the exacerbations of the diabetic state were in all instances closely related to situational and interpersonal conflicts . . .'. Close supervision and help with her emotional problems led in this case to better control of the diabetes.

(Hinkle and Wolf, 1952b)

The uncertainty in such examples concerns the extent to which the direct metabolic consequences of the emotional upheavals are responsible, rather than secondary effects due to abandoning dietary régimes or insulin requirements. Thus some patients may overeat or resort to alcohol when under stress, and others may omit insulin or neglect sterile precautions. In occasional cases comas may be deliberately induced to secure attention or as a means of escape into the shelter of hospital. Indeed, Tattersall (1981) has termed insulin-dependent diabetes 'the manipulator's delight'.

Hinkle and Wolf, however, argued strongly for a more direct influence of life experiences upon the metabolic disorder and hence on the course of the disease. When it appeared that a certain personal conflict was connected with variations in the diabetic state, they tested this in short-term experimental settings. Base-line observations were made, then the suspected topic of conflict was vigorously introduced into discussion. Control studies were made in which neutral topics were discussed. In this way psychological stress was shown to lead to ketonaemia and increased water, glucose and chloride excretion, in addition to alterations in fasting blood sugar levels.

Baker and Barcai (1970) felt able to demarcate a small number of 'super-labile' juvenile diabetics in whom emotional arousal led directly to ketoacedosis, mediated by an increased ketone response to endogenous catecholamines. β-adrenergic blockade was apparently successful in inhibiting the metabolic decompensation in such patients, producing marked therapeutic benefit. Tattersall (1981), however, doubts whether organic a priori causes are common. In the usual 'brittle diabetic', whose life is constantly disrupted by episodes of hyper- and hypoglycaemia, physiological, psychological and social problems come in time to be inextricably intertwined. Depression and reactions of frustration and futility breed carelessness in self-management and distrust of prescribed routines. An emotional origin often appears to be paramount in leading to this vicious circle.

Whatever the mechanisms, many agree that life experiences and emotional factors can have an important bearing on the course of diabetes, and that this is particularly important in juveniles and adolescents (Treuting, 1962). Attempts at demonstrating the influence of 'life events' have indeed been partially successful despite difficulties in methodology. Grant et al. (1974) studied 37 adults over 8— 18 months, and found a trend towards an association between important life events, particularly those of an unpleasant nature, and fluctuations in diabetic control. Bradley (1979) reviewed 114 patients retrospectively, and found a significant association between the number of life events experienced over a 12 month period and the incidence of glycosuria, changes in prescription and number of clinic attendances. Insulin-treated patients appeared more vulnerable in this regard than those receiving oral hypoglycaemic agents. Accordingly it may sometimes be necessary to pay careful attention to psychological and psychosocial aspects of the patient's situation if optimal control of the diabetes is to be achieved.

Psychological Problems in Diabetes

In several ways the situation imposed by diabetes is unusual in comparison with other chronic diseases. The patient must often face interminable dietary restrictions and daily self-administered injections, yet is usually symptom-free so gets no perceptible reward. He has responsibility, which is rare in other illnesses, for judging unusual situations and adjusting the dose of insulin required. Repeated hospitalisations can stigmatise him from an early age. Such factors can contribute to neurotic developments or disturbed family relationships, and hypochondriacal attitudes may come to be established.

Certain types of behaviour are said to be common in diabetics, but many are of a nature which would be unremarkable but for the fact that they complicate therapy. Thus some show an unusual need to eat and find great difficulty in adhering to dietary régimes. This may be intensified during periods of loneliness, depression or tension. Explosive rebellion may be seen in adolescents, with wilful neglect of treatment.

In children the disorder lends itself to incorporation in disturbed parent-child relationships. The anxiety of the parents may be transferred to the young child, or a perfectionistic mother may gain control over the illness at the cost of behaviour difficulties. The child on his part may utilise the diabetes to manipulate the home environment, using food as a weapon or form of retaliation. Surveys of diabetic children have been undertaken to explore possible psychological effects in detail, though with varying results (Sterky, 1963; Swift et al., 1967; Gath et al., 1980). In general adjustment has seemed remarkably good, though the sample investigated by Swift et al. showed minor abnormalities on measures of dependence/independence, self-perception, manifest and latent anxiety and sexual identification.

In adult life employment or marriage prospects may stand to be affected. Pruritis and decreased sexual interest may contribute to emotional complications, and impotence and amenorrhoea can be early complaints even in undiagnosed diabetics. Surridge et al. (1984) have found indications of delayed psychosexual development when diabetes sets in at an early age. Earlier reports of the frequency of impotence in men and anorgasmia in women (Kolodny, 1971; Kolodny et al., 1974) may have been an overestimate, but there can be little doubt that such problems often occur. Disturbances of ejaculation are also probably common (Fairburn et al., 1982). The physical handicaps later imposed by ocular and other complications bring further problems of their own.

A major fear among many insulin takers is the occurrence of a hypoglycaemic attack. They particularly dread attacks which lack the adrenergic warning, and in which loss of self-control or bizarre behaviour may occur. It now seems clear, moreover, that 'subclinical' hypoglycaemia is commoner than previously suspected in diabetics, as a result of overtreatment, and that this may account for considerable chronic disability.

Thus Gale and Tattersall (1979) found, from overnight metabolic studies, that nocturnal hypoglycaemia occurred in 22 of 39 poorly controlled insulin treated patients. This was often sustained for periods of several hours. Overt hypoglycaemic symptoms by day had been very mild or absent. The features occurring in such a situation included lassitude and depression in 15 patients, undue difficulty in waking in 11, early morning headache in 7 and nocturnal fits in 2. By day the worst affected appeared pale, apathetic, torpid and demoralised. Others complained of lethargy, depression and difficulty in concentration. Reduction of insulin dosage relieved or abolished all such problems without loss of overall diabetic control. Schwandt et al. (1979) have described similar examples. Nine out of 45 unstable diabetics turned out to have been chronically overtreated with insulin; their symptoms included excessive appetite, polydipsia, vertigo, mood swings, irritability and chronic fatigue.

Descriptive studies have shown that all forms of mental illness may occur in association with diabetes but there is little evidence about prevalence and forms. Apart from disturbances associated with overt or covert hypoglycaemia there is probably little that is specific. Increased fatigue and diminished energy were the most prominent mental symptoms in Surridge et al.'s (1984) survey, also depression and irritability. Carefully controlled observations have not, however, been carried out. Surveys of mental hospital populations have sometimes indicated a higher prevalence than expected of diabetes mellitus

(Waitzkin, 1966a, 1966b; Clayer and Dumbrill, 1967), but chiefly of the late-onset non-insulin-dependent form. This may merely reflect the age and tendency to obesity among long-stay patients; chlorpromazine, moreover, may lead to hyperglycaemic responses on the glucose tolerance test.

Finally, in the management of manic-depressive illness in diabetics it may sometimes be necessary to consider the possibility that insulin requirements increase during markedly depressive phases:

Crammer and Gillies (1981) report a woman with long-standing manic-depressive disorder which for some years had been cyclical, occurring approximately every 20 weeks. For several years she had also had late-onset diabetes, well controlled with oral hypoglycaemic drugs. During a particularly severe depressive episode the diabetes became out of control, requiring soluble insulin injections. Electroconvulsive therapy relieved the depression, but coincidentally the insulin requirement declined dramatically. With recurrence of the depression the same changes were seen, again resolving on recovery. During her manic phases, by contrast, no changes in diabetic treatment were required.

Kronfol *et al.* (1981) report a similar example of a patient who required increased insulin during recurrent phases of a depressive illness.

Brain Damage in Diabetes

When a diabetic patient develops organic psychiatric disorder the question arises how far this may be attributable to some aspect of the diabetic process. Episodes of hypoglycaemia or diabetic coma may have contributed to brain damage, or associated atherosclerosis may be responsible.

In very young children Ack *et al.* (1961) have produced some evidence that intelligence may be impaired, possibly as a result of damage to the immature brain by episodes of hypoglycaemia or acidosis. Thirty-eight diabetic children were compared with their siblings on the Stanford Binet test, and those with onset below the age of 5 were found to score an average of 10 points lower than the controls. By contrast those with onset over the age of 5 were unaffected. The result may have reflected some degree of brain damage, or merely the psychological impact of a chronic disease at such a young age.

Ives (1963) surveyed 380 adult diabetics in a general hospital and found that 45 were mentally abnormal. Eighteen showed 'organic brain syndromes', 14 were mentally deteriorated, 9 had personality disorders and 4 were psychotic. Hypertension was commoner in the mentally impaired patients than in the group as a whole, suggesting that cerebral atherosclerosis was probably the responsible factor. In others the mental abnormalities may have been coincidental, but episodes of diabetic coma and hypoglycaemia had been more frequent in the total group of 45 than in the remainder.

Bale (1973) compared 100 patients from a diabetic clinic with age and sex matched controls drawn from visitors to the hospital. All patients were under 65 years of age and had had diabetes for 15 years or more. On the Walton Black New Word Learning Test 17 diabetics, but no controls, scored in the brain damaged range. A significant relationship was observed between low scores on the test and the apparent severity of past hypoglycaemic episodes. The incidence of cerebrovascular accidents was higher in the diabetic group than the controls, but only one patient with a cerebrovascular accident scored within the brain damaged range. It thus appeared that mild cognitive difficulty was not uncommon in long-standing diabetics, and that hypoglycaemic episodes rather than cerebrovascular disorder might be the principal factor responsible. Bale's findings, while strongly suggestive, are not of course conclusive. It is possible that the association between impaired cognitive capacity and hypoglycaemic episodes may merely reflect the fact that patients with poor endowment manage their diabetes less well. Prospective follow-up studies will be needed to clarify the situation.

The role of arterial disease is clear in patients who develop cerebrovascular accidents and will often be incriminated in those who develop dementia. An increased incidence of vascular lesions has long been recognised in the heart and lower extremities of diabetic subjects, but the situation with regard to cerebrovascular disease remained uncertain until careful autopsy studies were performed. Alex *et al.* (1962) showed that cerebral infarctions were one and a half times as common in diabetics as controls, with a greatly increased incidence of proliferative lesions in the small cerebral vessels. Grunnet (1963) graded the severity of atheroma in the circle of Willis in 107 cases, and showed an increased frequency and severity in all age groups when compared to controls. Between the ages of 30 and 70 the incidence was almost doubled. The duration of diabetes and the presence or absence of hypertension were not closely correlated with the severity of such changes, but they seemed to be related to high blood cholesterol levels and frequent acetonuria.

Cerebral blood flow studies have indicated another mechanism whereby the risk of cerebrovascular damage may be increased in diabetics (Dandona *et al.*, 1978). Even when resting levels are normal, the reactivity of the vessels to carbon dioxide inhalation is unusual in a high percentage of patients. The expected increase in cerebral blood flow may fail to occur, or paradoxically this may show a substantial fall. This failure to compensate appropriately in response to increased cerebral metabolic demands may in the long term make its own contribution to brain damage.

Reske-Nielsen and Lundbaek (1963) found both diffuse and focal changes in the brains of long-standing diabetics, partly attributable to vascular disease and hypertension but possibly also deriving in part from the effects of metabolic disturbances on the neurones. Diffuse degeneration was observed in neurones and nerve fibres of the cerebrum, cerebellum and brain stem, and gliosis was often considerable.

Diabetic Coma

The development of diabetic ('ketotic') coma is a serious medical emergency. Very occasionally patients may present in this way without being known diabetics, but usually the coma develops in a patient with the established disorder which has got out of control. Insulin may have been omitted, or there may have been precipitants by way of infection, physical trauma, gastrointestinal disturbance or alcohol excess. The role which has been claimed for emotional precipitants has already been discussed.

Prodromal symptoms consist of weakness, thirst, dull headache, abdominal pain, nausea, vomiting and drowsiness. The onset may be abrupt or insidious. It is sometimes very gradual over several hours, so that a patient with a dangerous level of ketosis may still be fully ambulant. Air hunger and heavy laboured breathing develop. The patient becomes increasingly listless and slowly sinks into coma, sometimes after a period of restlessness, irritability and confusion.

The pulse is rapid and feeble and the blood pressure low. Dehydration is marked, the face flushed, and acetone may be smelled on the breath. Investigations reveal large amounts of sugar and acetone in the urine, and elevated sugar and ketone bodies in the blood. Acidosis is marked and the blood urea raised.

On initial examination the picture may be hard to distinguish from hypoglycaemic coma or from advanced renal failure. Overdosage with salicylates can also give a closely similar picture. In older subjects the differential diagnosis must sometimes in-clude a cerebrovascular accident, since glycosuria may also occur in such a situation.

Neurological Complications

Peripheral neuropathy can be a severe and distressing complication. In the middle-aged and elderly sensory changes usually predominate, with paraesthesiae, pain and cramps in the calves, absent knee and ankle reflexes and diminished vibration sense. Loss of postural sense may lead to ataxia. Atherosclerosis of the vasa nervorum is thought to be mainly responsible. In younger patients the affection may be more severe, with both motor and sensory disturbances involving all four limbs. Some as yet unidentified metabolic complication may be responsible (Walton, 1982). Both forms tend to improve when the diabetes is properly controlled.

Isolated 3rd or 6th cranial nerve palsies are not uncommon, and are probably attributable to focal infarctions in the cranial nerve trunks. These usually clear spontaneously after a few weeks or months. In elderly diabetics pupillary changes may include miosis, irregularity and a sluggish reaction to light, sometimes amounting to the classical Argyll-Robertson pupil ('pseudo tabes'). Lesions in the mid-brain are presumably the cause.

Rare complications include a variety of forms of amyotrophy, myelopathy, and autonomic disturbances.

Insulinomas and Other Forms of Hypoglycaemia

Though rare, insulin secreting tumours of the pancreas are the most important cause of hypoglycaemia, especially to the psychiatrist. The disorders which they produce are extremely varied and usually intermittent with normal health between attacks. Problems of differential diagnosis are therefore considerable and will be dealt with in some detail. The discovery of the condition is often long-delayed, resulting in prolonged ill-health and very occasionally in irreversible brain damage.

Pathology and Pathophysiology of Insulinomas

Insulin secreting tumours gained recognition in the late 1920s. By far the most common are benign adenomas of the islet cells. Those found during life are usually 1–2 cm in diameter, whereas those seen at autopsy are often microscopic in size. A tumour too small to be palpated at operation may therefore be responsible for symptoms. Two-thirds are found in the body and tail of the pancreas rather than the head, and multiple tumours are common. Rarely ectopic insulinomas occur in the vicinity of the duodenum or porta hepatis.

The great majority are benign, but approximately 10% are malignant and can metastasise to other parts of the body. Microadenomatosis throughout the pancreatic tissue is another rare possibility, or diffuse insular hyperplasia without tumour formation. These latter conditions sometimes occur familially along with adenomas of the parathyroid, pituitary or other endocrine glands as part of the 'pluriglandular syndrome' ('MEA Type 1').

The type of tumour which produces insulin is composed of beta cells. Other forms of islet-cell tumour may be non-functioning or 'ulcerogenic', the latter being associated with gastric hypersecretion and peptic ulceration (Zollinger-Ellison syndrome).

The primary defect in insulin secreting tumours appears to be inability to control the storage and release of insulin, rather than simply excessive production. The result is a constant slow excessive release coupled, for unknown reasons, with sudden excessive discharges. In consequence the plasma insulin level shows large and abrupt fluctuations.

Syndromes of Hypoglycaemia

Marks (1981a), from whom much of the present account is taken, demarcates four categories of disturbance all of which may be seen with insulinomas. He prefers the term 'neuroglycopaenia' when referring to clinical syndromes, and reserves the term 'hypoglycaemia' to describe the level of sugar in the blood. Correlations between the two are not exact, and occasionally profound lowering of blood sugar may be found without apparent effect on brain function.

Acute neuroglycopaenia: This is the common syndrome that follows overdosage with insulin or oral hypoglycaemic agents, though similar attacks may occur with insulinomas. The patient experiences vague malaise with anxiety and panic, or an unnatural detached feeling akin to depersonalisation. This is accompanied by feelings of hunger, palpitations and restlessness, and is shown objectively by tachycardia, tremor, flushing, sweating and ataxic gait. Angina may be precipitated if coronary artery

disease exists. Brief episodes of unconsciousness may occur and epileptic attacks can be provoked. Occasionally focal neurological disturbances such as diplopia, hemiparesis or dysphasia may be seen without obvious diffuse cerebral disturbance. In severe examples progression occurs to coma.

Subacute neuroglycopaenia: This also occurs episodically and is more characteristic of insulinomas. Subjective symptoms are slight, and all of the above features may be only minimally developed. Instead there is clumsy performance at habitual tasks, and behaviour which is out of character for the person affected. He may behave in a disinhibited, foolhardy or aggressive manner which closely resembles alcoholic intoxication. Others become apathetic and withdrawn, with slurred speech and somnolence. Disorientation and mental confusion are usually in evidence but consciousness is retained until late.

The degree of functional impairment is out of proportion to subjective discomfort, and the person typically lacks realisation of the changes within himself. Moreover negativism is a common feature, so that he may fail to seek help or take appropriate action even if partially aware of the disturbance. Often it is only after recovery that the person realises he has been unwell at all.

Chronic neuroglycopaenia: This, though rare, is virtually confined to patients with insulinomas. There are no dramatic symptoms or signs but an organic change of personality develops insidiously. Defective memory and intellectual deterioration ultimately lead to severe dementia. Emotional changes may be prominent, with irritability, apathy or emotional lability, and psychotic features with paranoid delusions may develop. The course may be punctuated with episodes of acute or subacute neuroglycopaenia, or may be uniformly smooth so that the possibility of hypoglycaemia goes unsuspected. The symptoms and signs are unaltered by food, and little further deterioration is observed with fasting unless this is very prolonged.

Hyperinsulin neuronopathy: Peripheral neuropathy may develop, with paraesthesiae in the hands and feet and wasting of muscles. The wasting is usually in the distal musculature but can sometimes be proximal. The cause of the hypoglycaemia is almost always an insulinoma. It may occasionally be the presenting feature of the illness, but is more commonly overshadowed by preceding coma or other acute disturbances.

CLINICAL MANIFESTATIONS OF INSULINOMAS

Insulinomas occur equally in males and females. They present usually between 20 and 50 though cases are reported at all ages including childhood. Familial examples are described, perhaps as part of the pluriglandular syndrome. Episodes of odd behaviour and disturbances of consciousness are the main reasons for referral. Symptoms have commonly been present for months or years by the time the diagnosis is made, sometimes for as long as 30 years. Very occasionally long remissions may be detected in the histories.

Almost any psychiatric syndrome may be simulated, depending partly no doubt on the make-up of the individual. The detailed content of attacks may differ from one occasion to another and diagnostic confusion is common. The essential clue usually lies in the episodic and recurrent nature of the attacks. An added difficulty is that organic features are not always in evidence, the change of consciousness sometimes being so slight that it passes unnoticed except to those familiar with the patient.

Typically attacks of subacute, or less often acute neuroglycopaenia occur as described above. These gradually increase in frequency, initially occurring at intervals of several weeks or months but often occurring several times per week by the time of presentation. Attacks may commence abruptly, or with a slow build-up of weakness, ataxia and increasing confusion. During witnessed attacks one may see sweating, nystagmus, incoordination, or focal neurological signs such as hemiparesis or positive Babinski responses. Actual coma is rare except in the most severe episodes.

At first attacks are commonest at noon or late afternoon, and only later do they occur more characteristically before breakfast and during the night. Only a quarter of patients give a clear history of relation to fasting and only 10% to exercise, while relief by eating is even more rarely noticed by the patient (Marks, 1981b).

Typically the patient has complete amnesia for the content of the attacks, and occasionally for additional periods during which behaviour was seemingly normal. Between attacks he usually feels quite well.

In a small proportion there is progressive mental or physical disability with little or no history of episodic disturbance. This has already been described under the heading of chronic neuroglycopaenia.

The diagnostic problems are well illustrated by cases in the literature:

A man of 44 suffered from attacks of confusion with bizarre behaviour over a 5 year period, each lasting from a few minutes to several hours, and increasing in frequency until they were occurring four or five times a week. He had a partial or complete amnesia for most of what happened during attacks. Initially they were interpreted as hysterical fugue states.

On one occasion, when motoring home from a funeral, he abruptly began to drive at breakneck speed and seemed quite unaware of his passenger. On another he wandered in a semi-confused condition about the corridors at work for 2 hours, carrying on coherent conversations with certain people he met but ultimately removing his shirt and staring foolishly at people who tried to talk to him. Once when chopping wood he suddenly clutched his axe in a menacing manner and wandered about the neighbourhood with a dazed and glassy-eyed expression; after this he was taken to hospital where his speech was confused and mumbling and he showed constant grotesque and purposeless movements. He then abruptly recovered with amnesia for the entire episode. In the attack which led to the correct diagnosis he had frightened a fellow employee by brandishing a knife. This informant was able to give a clear description of many episodes, describing marked pallor, sweating, limpness, unsteady drunken behaviour and double vision, and emphasising their liability to occur after excessive exertion or towards the end of the morning.

Before removal of the insulinoma, detailed studies were made of the interrelationships between the patient's behaviour and blood sugar levels. During prolonged starvation experiments it was possible to demonstrate intermittent disturbances of awareness which became progressively more marked even though the blood sugar values were essentially unchanged. Periods of acute motor excitement with confusion and aggressive behaviour could similarly begin and end without significant changes in the blood sugar.

(Romano and Coon, 1942)

A 27-year-old man was referred as a psychiatric emergency on account of bouts of aggressive and destructive behaviour. He showed disorientation and inappropriate behaviour during attacks, with sweating and violent tremor, and had no subsequent recollection of what occurred. He had always been backward and had had a head injury at 18. His father had shown similar bouts of violent behaviour.

The initial differential diagnosis had included aggressive psychopathy, mental subnormality with behaviour disturbance, and post-traumatic epilepsy. Prolonged fasting provoked a typical attack at 16 hours, associated with hypoglycaemia and relieved by glucose. At laparotomy multiple islet cell tumours were found. A diagnosis of multiple adenomatosis (pluriglandular syndrome) was made since hyperparathyroidism was also present. His father had died with 'islet cell secreting tumour of the pancreas and calcification of the kidneys'.

(Carney et al., 1971)

A physicist of 32 had attacks consisting of inappropriate aggressive behaviour, sometimes involving attacks on people or destruction of his own belongings. Attacks might last for 30 minutes to one hour and were covered by dense amnesia. If they did not end in an epileptic fit or simple unconsciousness, they would lead on to a period of emotional disturbance and confusion for which memory would subsequently be incomplete and fragmentary. The electroencephalogram showed some inconstant theta activity arising mainly in the temporal leads. A 12 hour fasting blood sugar was normal at 84 mg/100 ml.

He was regarded as suffering from temporal lobe epilepsy but anticonvulsant treatment was ineffective. Subsequent and more thorough blood sugar studies indicated an islet cell tumour and this was confirmed at operation.

(Whitty and Lishman, 1966)

Investigation of Insulinomas

The finding of a low blood glucose is essential to the diagnosis. The exact level at which symptoms of cerebral dysfunction may be expected is somewhat variable, but they usually do not appear until the level is below 2.2 mmol/l (Marks, 1981c). The range is wide, however, depending on the rate of fall and other concurrent metabolic factors.

If an actual attack is witnessed blood should be taken immediately for glucose estimation, also where possible for the measurement of plasma insulin and C-peptide levels (see below). The ability of intravenous glucose to bring prompt relief should then be assessed. If spontaneous attacks do not occur while the patient is under observation, an attempt may be made to provoke an attack by fasting, coupled if necessary with exercise. Routine overnight fasts may need to be repeated on a number of occasions, but will fail to reveal significant changes in perhaps 10 per cent of cases; the fast may then need to be prolonged for up to 72 hours. Close supervision is of course necessary, and with any attack that occurs the efficacy of intravenous glucose to terminate it should be tried immediately blood has been withdrawn. The hypoglycaemia seen with insulinomas is characterised by inappropriately high levels of plasma insulin and C-peptide. C-peptide is secreted molecule for molecule along with insulin by the pancreas, providing a very useful measure of pancreatic β-cell function.

An insulin-tolerance test may circumvent the need for prolonged fasting and brings important evidence of its own. Patients with insulinomas show increased sensitivity to injected insulin, with extended maintenance of the hypoglycaemic response. Moreover, plasma C-peptide levels are not suppressed in the normal manner.

The availability of refined plasma immunoreactive insulin measurements and C-peptide assays has rendered most other provocation and suppression tests (tolbutamide, 1-leucine and diazoxide tests) superfluous. They retain a place in difficult problems of differential diagnosis, however, as discussed by Marks (1981c). It should only rarely be necessary nowadays to do an exploratory laporotomy to search for an undisclosed tumour.

Electroencephalography

The earliest change to be detected is the appearance of delta rhythms on overbreathing. Then spontaneous theta and delta waves occur, and later asynchronous irregular waves and a flattened tracing. The abnormalities are often most marked over the temporal lobes. In hypoglycaemic coma the EEG consists of high voltage delta waves as in other comas of metabolic origin. After severe hypoglycaemic episodes, abnormalities may persist in the EEG for several days and then revert to normal.

These sequential changes have been studied in the course of therapeutic insulin comas, formerly used for the treatment of schizophrenia. The electroencephalographic response to hypoglycaemia appears to vary considerably in different subjects, though the same individual may show closely similar responses in each episode of a series. In general the correlation between the symptoms provoked and the electroencephalographic changes is closer than that between symptoms and blood sugar levels.

The value of the EEG in helping towards a diagnosis of insulinoma is controversial. Rose (1981) considers it useful to take serial records during fasting, and if symptoms occur with a low blood sugar and an abnormal tracing intravenous glucose can then be shown to restore the record to normal within minutes.

After removal of the insulinoma the electroencephalogram soon returns to normal, including the response to overbreathing.

Differential Diagnosis of Insulinomas

The following psychiatric and neurological conditions may often be suspected before the true diagnosis is revealed:

Neurotic disorder is suggested by the occurrence of transient symptoms which are described vaguely and diffusely, often variable from time to time, and unbacked by physical signs when the patient is examined between attacks. Episodes of anxiety, panic and depersonalisation may suggest anxiety neurosis; transient disturbances of consciousness with periods of amnesia may suggest hysteria. The latter may also be diagnosed when transient neurological features such as dysphasia or hemiparesis follow attacks. The differentiation between neurosis and essential reactive hypoglycaemia is discussed on p. 462.

Personality disorder may be suggested by a history of episodes of aggressive or antisocial conduct, for which the patient claims amnesia or only a hazy recollection. Aggressive psychopathy may be diagnosed in more extreme examples.

Manic-depressive or schizophrenic psychoses may very occasionally be diagnosed. Rare cases of insulinoma have been reported to present with acute depressive psychoses, no doubt as a result of individual predisposition. In other cases the bizarre nature of the behaviour during attacks may suggest an ingravescent schizophrenia, and in chronic neuroglycopaenia thought disorder and paranoid delusions may be prominent.

Presenile or senile dementia may be closely simulated in cases with chronic deterioration of intellect and personality. Superimposed episodes of acute and transient disturbance may resemble the step-like course of arteriosclerotic dementia. These are serious diagnostic mistakes since the brain damage which occurs may ultimately become irreversible.

A space occupying lesion may be suspected when attacks provoke epilepsy, or when headache and focal neurological symptoms accompany clouding of consciousness. Subdural haematoma may be considered in view of the negative or equivocal neurological findings between attacks.

Carotid artery stenosis may be suggested by attacks of dysphasia or hemiplegia, or vertebrobasilar insufficiency when vertigo and diplopia are prominent features.

Epilepsy is a relatively rare form of presentation of hypoglycaemia except in childhood. But any episodic and recurrent neurological disorder is likely to raise the question of epilepsy, and the content of attacks may closely resemble the automatisms of temporal lobe seizures.

Intoxication with alcohol is often suspected when attacks are witnessed by on-lookers and the picture may be very similar indeed. When the patient is known to be alcoholic, episodes of amnesia may be ascribed to 'alcoholic blackouts'. Intoxication with barbiturates may similarly be suspected.

Other metabolic disorders such as uraemia or liver failure may be closely simulated, or endocrine disorders such as thyrotoxicosis, hypoparathyroidism, or phaeochromocytoma.

Peripheral neuropathy has already been mentioned as a rare form of presentation. Narcolepsy may sometimes be considered, or attacks of somnolence may suggest the Kleine-Levin syndrome.

Among disorders of the cardiovascular system, angina, vasovagal attacks, orthostatic hypotension, and Stokes-Adams attacks may all come under suspicion.

The differential diagnosis from other forms of hypoglycaemia is considered below. Of particular importance in psychiatric practice are *essential reactive, alcohol-induced* and *factitious hypoglycaemia*.

OTHER FORMS OF HYPOGLYCAEMIA

An important step when hypoglycaemia is confirmed is to differentiate between the various conditions with which it may be associated. The old classification into organic and functional hypoglycaemia has outgrown its usefulness, since the former rests entirely on finding some identifiable cause. When an insulinoma was missed at operation the case would have been erroneously labelled as functional; and the cause remains elusive in some of the organic forms which are important in general medicine.

The most useful classification in practice is into hypoglycaemias which are provoked by fasting and those which are not. The latter are labelled the 'stimulative hypoglycaemias' since they develop only in response to some identifiable stimulus. The distinction is helpful since attempted provocation by fasting always forms the first step in investigation.

Fasting Hypoglycaemias

The fasting hypoglycaemias include those due to insulinomas and those associated with liver disease and endocrine disorder. Fasting hypoglycaemia may occur with all varieties of liver disease, both trivial and serious, and shows little correlation with the severity of the hepatic disorder. Among endocrine disorders Addison's disease and hypopituitarism are the commonest causes.

Other causes, unlikely to come before the psychiatrist, include glycogen storage disease, neonatal hypoglycaemia, and the so-called idiopathic hypoglycaemia of childhood. The differentiation of these conditions from insulinoma requires careful medical investigation; the absence of raised plasma insulin levels during fasting, and the presence of normal C-peptide suppression after insulin administration, ultimately provide the decisive distinction.

'Essential Reactive Hypoglycaemia'

This is the commonest form of stimulation hypoglycaemia and must be carefully distinguished from insulinoma. The most important clinical difference is that symptoms resembling acute neuroglycopaenia occur after ingesting food but are not provoked by fasting. They do not occur before breakfast, whereas this is common with insulinoma. In effect the disorder represents an exaggeration of the normal physiological response to the ingestion of carbohydrate.

Females are affected more frequently than males, and most cases occur between the ages of 30 and 40. It appears to occur particularly in asthenic and emotionally labile persons, and may be associated with minor psychiatric instability in a manner which initiates a vicious circle.

Common symptoms are episodes of weakness, faintness, palpitation and irritability, often in association with feelings of hunger, nausea, headache and vertigo. The patient may complain of 'blackouts', but objective evidence of impairment of consciousness is rare. An interesting medico-legal example, in which a patient committed a serious offence but had no knowledge of it afterwards, is described by Bovill (1973). The symptoms are commonest in mid-morning, usually 2–5 hours following food, though the patient rarely comments spontaneously on such an association. Exercise may provoke or aggravate the symptoms, but food or glucose do not bring decisive relief. Between attacks the patient often reports that he feels run down and is functioning below his optimum. The episodes may occur intermittently over several years, but do not show the progression in frequency and severity characteristic of insulinomas.

Fasting blood glucose levels are normal, but a 6 hour glucose tolerance test will show an excessive fall $1\frac{1}{2}$–4 hours after glucose ingestion. The diagnosis should be made only when both hypoglycaemia and symptoms of neuroglycopaenia are reproduced during the procedure. A pronounced rise of plasma cortisol in response to the rebound hypoglycaemia will add confidence to the diagnosis.

It is often uncertain whether the degree of reactive hypoglycaemia demonstrated in such patients should be considered abnormal. Many authorities suggest that only a minority have a true defect of glucose homeostasis as a cause of symptoms. A number of examples probably represent neurotic disorder, and since reactive hypoglycaemia in some degree is just as likely to occur in neurotic as non-neurotic individuals one must be cautious in attributing the symptoms to the blood sugar changes which are demonstrated.

Ford et al. (1976), for example, found that among 30 patients referred as possible examples of the syndrome, only 18 showed reactive hypoglycaemia on testing. Moreover, half of the sample were markedly psychiatrically unwell, mostly with depression or anxiety neurosis. Many showed hysterical or obsessional personality patterns. While the patients attributed their emotional distress to hypoglycaemia the overall findings ran counter to this. Thus the number and severity of symptoms experienced—emotional lability, depression, headache, tremor, tachycardia, weakness, dizziness—were unrelated to the degree of hypoglycaemia shown on glucose tolerance tests. And whether or not they had demonstrated reactive hypoglycaemia their scores for emotional disturbance on the MMPI were similar. Careful histories often showed a close association between the onset of the complaints and some precipitating stress. Ford et al. conclude that while essential reactive hypoglycaemia remains a definite clinical entity, causing genuine somatic discomfort, it is nevertheless considerably overdiagnosed in the face of multiple non-specific complaints. Patients with hysterical or obsessional personalities may come forward with symptoms that would be tolerated with less anxiety by persons of stable temperament; when a glucose tolerance test is then performed the symptoms may all too easily come to be attributed to any hypoglycaemia revealed, incidental though this may be.

Finally, Rennie and Howard (1942) described a group of patients suffering from tension states and depression in whom the reactive hypoglycaemia appeared, in fact, to be secondary to the psychiatric disorder. After appropriate psychiatric treatment the patients were found to have lost their presenting symptoms, but in addition repetition of glucose tolerance tests often showed that these too had returned to normal.

Clearly therefore the interrelationships between psychiatric disorder, physical symptoms, and low blood sugar levels are complex. It is nevertheless worth trying the effect of a high-protein low-carbohydrate diet in the more marked examples of the disorder, and especially when there is no overt neurotic disorder towards which treatment can be directed.

Alcohol-induced Hypoglycaemia

Hypoglycaemia may occur in response to various drugs and poisons of which alcohol is the most important. Inhibition of gluconeogenesis by alcohol appears to be the predominant factor, though impaired response of the pituitary-adrenal axis, and enhanced insulin secretion following an oral glucose load, can also play a part.

The true importance of alcohol-induced hypoglycaemia has been recognised relatively recently. It occurs mostly in chronic alcoholics, usually 6–36 hours after a large intake, and quite often presents with hypoglycaemic coma. It may sometimes develop sooner, then running a considerable risk of being overlooked in the face of obvious intoxication. Recovery is usually prompt after the administration of glucose though hydrocortisone may be required as well. It is possible that the condition accounts for a considerable number of deaths in alcoholic subjects.

Recurrent attacks are rare but have been reported (Fredericks and Lazor, 1963; de Moura et al., 1967). It is uncertain whether some special sensitivity to alcohol has been acquired in such cases, since the alcoholic history is often of long duration before the complication makes its appearance.

An especially severe form of alcohol-induced hypoglycaemia is liable to occur in insulin-dependent diabetics. Arky et al. (1968) first drew attention to this, reporting patients who were repeatedly admitted to hospital in hypoglycaemic states after an alcoholic debauch. Their 5 patients illustrated the severity of the neurological damage which could result from hypoglycaemia of such combined origin—2 died without recovery from coma, and 3 were left with permanent memory impairments or dementia.

Factitious Hypoglycaemia

The clandestine use of insulin or sulphonylureas to induce hypoglycaemic symptoms can pose a difficult diagnostic problem. It is seen predominantly among nurses and other paramedical personnel, or in close relatives of diabetics who have access to the agents. It has also been noted among teenage female diabetics who misuse their insulin (Lancet, 1978). Some patients addicted to heroin have described

obtaining insulin from the same sources of supply.

The hypoglycaemias may be induced for the benefit of the symptoms experienced or as part of attention-seeking behaviour. Sometimes the practice appears allied to Munchausen's syndrome, the patients submitting to laparotomy and even sub-total pancreatectomy.

The presentation is with symptoms suggestive of insulinoma. Many patients are admitted in coma. Scarlett et al. (1977) found that symptoms had been present for 2 months to 6 years among their 7 insulin abusers, 2 of whom had had subtotal pancreatectomies before the true cause was discovered. One had been diagnosed as diabetic for 17 years and this had probably always been erroneous. Another described the exquisite pleasure of going to sleep after injecting insulin, not knowing whether she would regain consciousness. A sinister facet of Scarlett et al.'s series was that 2 patients had also given insulin to their children, one with a fatal result.

Jordan et al. (1977) describe patients abusing sulphonylurea and presenting in a similar manner. One of their patients began taking her husband's chlorpropamide while severely depressed, another was an alcoholic whose hypoglycaemia was at first ascribed to alcohol. Jordan et al. estimated that the problem had become as common as genuine insulinoma, requiring therefore the utmost care to screen for factitious hypoglycaemia before such a diagnosis was made.

The risk of error is increased by the finding of inappropriately raised plasma insulin during the hypoglycaemic episodes, both with insulin and sulphonylurea abuse. However, C-peptide levels (p. 460) will be low when exogenous insulin has been taken, and this will immediately raise suspicion of the practice. After oral hypoglycaemic agents the picture can be virtually indistinguishable from insulinoma since C-peptide levels are likely to be raised as a result of β-cell stimulation; the diagnosis must then be made by demonstrating the drugs in the blood or urine.

Under the heading of 'pseudoneuroglycopaenia' Marks (1981a) describes a quite separate group of patients with disturbed personalities, also paramedical workers or relatives of diabetics, who present with attacks simulating acute neuroglycopaenia, sometimes gradually proceeding to coma. Here the blood glucose and electroencephalogram remain normal throughout the episodes. Recovery occurs spontaneously or may be provoked by saline injection. The situation is considered to represent an hysterical conversion reaction.

Other Stimulative Hypoglycaemias

After gastrectomy the 'dumping syndrome' occurs during or immediately after a meal; other similar forms of disturbance may be some hours delayed. The symptoms resemble those of essential reactive hypoglycaemia. Glucose tolerance tests again often produce conflicting results, and the true relationship of symptoms to reactive lowering of blood sugar remains uncertain.

A number of drugs other than alcohol may provoke hypoglycaemia. The effect of salicylates can be profound, especially in children, leading occasionally to fatal results. They potentiate the effect of oral hypoglycaemic agents. Propanolol and other non-selective β-blockers can have a similar effect. Among poisons those present in certain toadstools are markedly hypoglycaemic.

Finally under the heading of stimulative hypoglycaemia the reactions liable to occur in insulin-treated diabetics must be remembered. Some diabetics are particularly prone to insulin-induced hypoglycaemias and others are incautious of diet.

In the stimulative hypoglycaemias fasting fails to produce abnormal blood sugar levels and the other confirmatory tests for insulinoma will be negative, the sole exception being sulphonylurea abuse as described above.

TREATMENT OF HYPOGLYCAEMIA

Sugar or glucose tablets should be carried by patients awaiting investigation when hypoglycaemic attacks are known to occur, and relatives should be instructed about the urgent need to give glucose in the earliest stages of an attack. In severe reactions, or if the patient is comatose, glucose should be given intravenously, 10–20 g as a $33\frac{1}{3}\%$ or 50% solution.

Treatment of hypoglycaemia coma is always a grave emergency. Whenever it is considered a possibility intravenous glucose should be given immediately after withdrawing blood for laboratory investigations. The response is usually rapid, though it may sometimes be slow if the coma has been of long duration or the patient is markedly hypothermic. The possibility of coincident hypoadrenalism or hypopituitarism must then be borne in mind, and parenteral hydrocortisone should be tried. The response may be dramatic if irreversible brain damage has not occurred.

The essential treatment for insulinoma is surgical removal at the earliest opportunity after the diagnosis is established. Sometimes more than one adenoma is present and re-operation may occasionally be necessary. When the diagnosis of hyperinsulinism has been fully confirmed by tests yet no tumour is palpable, subtotal pancreatectomy is indicated. If operation is refused, or if the tumour proves to be malignant, palliative treatment may help for a while in the form of large doses of steroids or diazoxide, together with constant food intake at three hourly intervals during the day.

Patients with essential reactive hypoglycaemia should not be given repeated doses of glucose, but must be encouraged to take frequent meals which are high in protein and fat.

OUTCOME OF HYPOGLYCAEMIA

The immediate outcome for most attacks is excellent. The symptoms usually resolve spontaneously even without specific treatment. Sometimes, however, neurological and psychiatric manifestations may outlast the actual period of hypoglycaemia. Dysphasia, hemiparesis and stupor have been reported to persist for hours or even weeks after restoring the blood sugar to normal, also negativism, restlessness, apathy and prolonged behaviour disorder (Markowitz *et al.*, 1961). Such disturbances are thought to rest on a vascular basis which ultimately resolves. Recovery from hypoglycaemic coma may similarly be delayed for hours or even weeks in occasional cases. After prolonged coma recovery may be incomplete, with evidence of permanent brain damage and dementia (Arky *et al.*, 1968).

The outcome after surgery for insulinoma is excellent in the great majority of cases. The typical patient who has presented with intermittent episodes of neuroglycopaenia ceases to have such attacks, whatever form they have taken, and normal health is restored.

While this is the experience of most observers, occasional reports have indicated a less favourable picture on prolonged follow-up. Markowitz *et al.* (1961) followed 6 early cases after a lapse of 25 years, and found that five had shown either persisting or newly acquired mental disturbances in the interim. These were sometimes severe, including manic-depressive psychosis, irrational or erratic behaviour and other aberrations of personality, and were thought possibly to represent the aftermath of brain damage which had accrued from the hypoglycaemic episodes. A surprisingly high incidence of peptic ulceration and haemorrhage had also developed, even though ulcerogenic pancreatic tumours had not appeared to be present.

The rarer presentations in the form of chronic psychosis or intellectual deterioration may be expected to improve to some degree after operation, but here recovery is seldom complete. In these cases, as after prolonged episodes of hypoglycaemic coma, irreversible brain damage often proves to have occurred. Thus among 100 patients with psychosis or 'long-term insanity' in the detailed review by Laurent *et al.* (1971), 37 showed little or no improvement after removal of the hypoglycaemic tumour. The longer the duration of symptoms before the diagnosis, the greater was the risk of permanent mental disability.

Cerebral Pathology

The pathological changes in the brain after acute episodes of hypoglycaemia have mostly been studied in cases of insulin shock. The brain may show oedema and vascular congestion. Survival after profound hypoglycaemic coma may be associated with ventricular dilatation, cortical atrophy and shrinkage of the hippocampi.

Microscopically the neurones show ischaemic cell changes and associated gliosis. The cell damage may occur in scattered foci, but is more typically laminar with emphasis on the third and fifth layers (Brierley, 1981). Relative sparing of the visual cortex is usual, but the corpus striatum and hippocampus appear to be especially vulnerable, much as in anoxia (p. 467). However, with hypoglycaemia the Purkinje cells of the cerebellum are less prone to be affected (Richardson *et al.*, 1959).

The precise pathology which may be produced by intermittent hypoglycaemia of less degree has not been documented, nor the changes which result from long-continued chronic neuroglycopaenia. The pathological basis for the rare examples of persistent neuropsychiatric disability short of gross dementia is therefore incompletely understood.

Cerebral Anoxia

Barcroft (1920) distinguished four main varieties of anoxia—anoxic, anaemic, stagnant and metabolic—which serve as a framework for reviewing the clinical conditions in which cerebral anoxia can occur. These are shown in Table 15 along with a fifth category of 'overutilisation anoxia'.

'*Anoxic anoxia*' is due to deficient oxygenation of the arterial blood. It may result from respiratory insufficiency in pulmonary diseases such as chronic bronchitis, emphysema or pneumonia, from the administration of general anaesthetics, from asphyxia or drowning, or from lack of oxygen in the inspired air at high altitudes.

A respiratory cause, and particularly a respiratory infection, must be constantly borne in mind when unexplained mental confusion appears in the elderly, or when a fluctuating acute organic reaction is superimposed upon a known dementing process. The anoxia which results from respiratory disease is often further complicated by the accumulation of carbon dioxide ('hypercapnia') as described on p. 479.

General anaesthesia inevitably carries a hazard of anoxia. In particular, minor degrees which would be tolerated by a fit person may prove disastrous when the blood volume is low (Dinnick, 1964). Thus anaesthesia contributes to some of the acute delirious episodes which appear post-operatively, especially those which emerge immediately upon recovery. A mild degree of persistent dementia may likewise make its first appearance after the administration of an anaesthetic for some relatively minor surgical procedure. This is particularly likely in the elderly or arteriosclerotic in whom the reserves of cerebral function have already been precarious. Bedford (1955) reviewed a population of over a thousand geriatric subjects who had had operations in the preceding 15 years, and found that in more than a third the relatives claimed that the patients had 'never been the same again'. The statement proved to be unjustified in the majority, but in approximately one case in ten there was reason to think that the anaesthetic may have contributed to memory difficulties or intellectual impairment. In eighteen cases seen personally Bedford found a severe dementia which appeared to have followed anaesthesia directly. Other more minor forms of intellectual disability were found, as in the case of a surgeon who had been obliged to cease work on account of memory difficulties.

'*Anaemic anoxia*' results from deficient oxygen carrying power of the blood as in carbon monoxide poisoning. Abrupt blood loss may be the cause as in haematemesis or unsuspected gastrointestinal haemorrhage. Severe anaemia is an important cause which runs an especial risk of being overlooked:

A man of 70 was admitted to hospital with a 12 month history of jerking movements of the head and arms, and loss of weight and appetite for 2 years. He was noisy and restless by day and night, and emotionally labile with frequent laughing and crying. At night he was agitated and confused and moaned continually. There were incessant coarse movements of the limbs and head but no definite parkinsonian features. The electroencephalogram was

TABLE 15. Causes of cerebral anoxia

Anoxic anoxia	—chronic bronchitis, emphysema, pneumonia, general anaesthesia, asphyxia, drowning, high altitudes
Anaemic anoxia	—carbon monoxide poisoning, gastrointestinal bleeding, severe anaemia
Stagnant anoxia	—cerebral arteriosclerosis, peripheral circulatory failure (shock), congestive cardiac failure, cardiac arrest, paroxysmal dysrhythmias, myocardial infarction
Metabolic (toxic) anoxia	—hypoglycaemia, cyanide poisoning, carbon disulphide poisoning
Overutilisation anoxia	—epileptic seizures

markedly abnormal with a diffuse excess of theta and paroxysmal delta activity. He was thought to be suffering from presenile dementia secondary to cerebral arterio-sclerosis.

His haemoglobin was found to be only 6·1 g/100 ml, probably as a result of chronically bleeding haemorrhoids. Three pints of blood were transfused and he improved remarkably, with resolution of the involuntary movements and of the mental abnormalities.

Four months later the appearances of dementia and the motor abnormalities returned in the course of a transient depressive illness, but on this occasion responded well to antidepressant medication. The electroencephalogram now showed only mild abnormalities in the form of gener-alised theta activity on over-breathing. He remained well when followed up during the next 2 years.

Carbon monoxide produces much of its effect by inactivating the oxygen carrying power of the haemoglobin molecule. Since carboxyhaemoglobin is relatively stable the effects of exposure to carbon monoxide may be longer-lasting and more profound than a transient reduction in oxygen supply per se. But carbon monoxide also acts directly on tissue cells by inhibiting the oxydo-reduction enzyme system, contributing an element of metabolic anoxia in addition.

'Stagnant anoxia' is due to arrest or reduction of blood flow. It occurs in cerebral arteriosclerosis, or more acutely in peripheral circulatory failure due to shock. Important cardiac causes are congestive cardiac failure, temporary cardiac arrest, episodes of severe dysrhythmia as in paroxysmal ventricular tachycardia, and myocardial infarction. A silent coronary infarction can be particularly misleading. Abrupt loss of consciousness at the onset may be mis-diagnosed as a cerebrovascular accident, especially if epileptiform jerking has occurred. An episode of severe collapse followed by confusion, but leaving behind no residual neurological signs, should therefore be viewed with suspicion (Slater and Roth, 1969). The myocardial infarction is especially prone

to be overlooked in hypertensive patients whose blood pressure may drop to normal levels after the episode.

With stagnant anoxias there are additional compli-cating factors. In addition to oxygen lack there is a deficiency of glucose supply to the brain, and accumulation of waste products leading to acidosis and other local metabolic derangements.

'Metabolic' or 'toxic anoxia' occurs when there are factors which interfere with the utilisation of oxygen by the tissues even though there is no lack of oxygen supply. This is seen with hypoglycaemia, and with poisoning by substances such as cyanide or carbon disulphide. As mentioned above carbon monoxide has a histotoxic effect in addition to reducing the oxygen carrying capacity of the blood.

'Overutilisation anoxia' exists when there is an increased demand in relation to supply. This occurs locally in the brain during epileptic seizures.

Clinical Features in Anoxia

The clinical picture varies with the individual situa-tion, depending on the rate at which anoxia develops, its duration and the degree of concomitant physical exertion. Individual tolerance also varies widely, with more severe effects and a greater likelihood of sequelae in persons who are already existing near the threshold of neuronal reserve. Co-existing hypotension is often an important, and sometimes a crucial factor in determining the severity of brain damage, as after temporary cardiac arrest (Brierley, 1970).

Most forms of cerebral anoxia are transient events, presenting with impairment of consciousness of varying severity, confusion, disorientation or deli-rium. There may be muscular twitching or tremor, and epileptic fits may occur. In sustained hypoxia, as at high altitudes, mental obfuscation may develop more gradually and personality change may be the obtrusive feature as described below. In either event the diffuse nature of the cerebral affection is apparent.

Unless the anoxia is sufficiently prolonged or severe to cause death there are rarely enduring sequelae. A dense amnesic gap for the acute condition is usually all that remains. In a minority, however, permanent memory difficulties may result, or more global impairment of intellect extending even to severe dementia. Neurological sequelae may consist of extrapyramidal disturbances with parkinsonism or athetosis. Hemiplegia, blindness or pseudobulbar palsy may very occasionally remain. After the anoxia which follows abrupt systemic hypotension there may be a monoplegia and sensory loss affecting the arm predominantly, due to the selective involvement of neurones at the borderland territories of supply of the anterior and middle cerebral arteries (see p. 321). Parietal lobe deficits may also be severe.

The psychological changes produced at high altitudes and the clinical complications of carbon monoxide poisoning are considered in more detail below.

Cerebral Pathology in Cerebral Anoxia

The pathological changes in the central nervous system in fatal cases have been described by Hoff *et al.* (1945) and Richardson *et al.* (1959). They are usually remarkably similar regardless of the cause, and resemble those seen after hypoglycaemia (p. 465). Brierley (1976) presents a comprehensive review.

If death occurs within a few minutes there is little to be detected other than scattered petechial haemorrhages. Cerebral oedema occurs early, and changes in cerebral blood flow raise the intracranial pressure further in a manner which aggravates the situation (Brock, 1971). If the patient survives long enough there may be widespread degeneration and necrosis of nerve cells with corresponding glial proliferation. The cells of the 3rd, 4th and 5th cortical layers are particularly susceptible ('laminar cortical necrosis'), also the Purkinje cells of the cerebellum and the cells of the corpus striatum. Bilateral necrosis of the globus pallidus is often a marked feature. The hippocampus and the parastriate cortex are also characteristically affected severely. Areas of subcortical demyelination eventually become apparent if the patient survives for more than a few weeks. The subcortical U-fibres are, however, characteristically spared.

A different pathological picture results when blood flow to the brain has been abruptly curtailed despite a sustained normal arterial oxygen tension. Thus the sudden systemic hypotension occasioned by temporary cardiac arrest, or severe myocardial infarction, may lead to ischaemic neuronal destruction largely confined to the boundary zones between major arterial territories in the cerebrum and cerebellum. Brierley (1970, 1976) reviews the experimental and clinical evidence on the matter. Changes are minimal or absent in the hippocampi and diffuse laminar cortical necrosis does not occur. Boundary zone necrosis is often most severe in the parieto-occipital regions where the territories of the anterior, middle and posterior cerebral arteries meet. Involvement of the subcortical white matter is roughly proportional to the severity of the cortical lesion, sometimes extending inwards as far as the wall of the lateral ventricle. Accompanying lesions in the basal ganglia are variable but often circumscribed and severe. In the cerebellum the lesion is at the junction of the superior and posterior inferior cerebellar arteries, forming a wedge with its base at the cortical surface and its apex in the central white matter.

Such classical boundary zone lesions may sometimes be combined with diffuse ischaemic changes, depending on the speed of development and severity of the hypotension. If the fall in cerebral perfusion pressure is abrupt and considerable, ischaemic necrosis will tend to be confined to the boundary zones; if it is slow and relatively moderate the changes will often be more generalised, since the accompanying vasodilation will allow a more uniform distribution of the available but inadequate blood flow. Coincident respiratory failure will often also have occurred in examples encountered clinically, and a combination of the two factors—primary hypoxia and systemic hypotension—will often have been operative together.

The electroencephalographic changes in anoxia are identical with those of hypoglycaemia as described on p. 460.

ANOXIA AT HIGH ALTITUDES

The psychological changes produced at high altitudes have been studied extensively. Important early observations were made on expeditions such as the International High Altitude Expedition to Chile (McFarland, 1932, 1937), and in experiments conducted in low pressure chambers where high altitudes could be simulated (Haldane *et al.*, 1919;

Barcroft, 1925). Aviation experiences, particularly during the first world war, underlined the importance of this area of study. The subject is comprehensively reviewed by Van Liere and Stickney (1963).

The slow ascent in mountaineers allows a process of adaptation. Individual variability is marked, some subjects being affected at 8000 and some only at 14,000 feet. Hypoxia due to the decline in partial pressure of oxygen in the inspired air is accepted as the principal cause, though fatigue, alkalosis, mountain glare and isolation will also contribute to the picture.

At first there is often a feeling of exceptional well-being, which gradually gives way to lassitude and mental sluggishness. Headache, nausea, anorexia, dyspnoea and tachycardia are usual accompaniments. Tasks become effortful, concentration cannot be sustained and reasoning becomes slowed and faulty. Judgement is impaired and imposes a serious risk to the climber. Marked difficulty with short-term memory may be apparent. Emotional changes consist of irritability and often a readiness to take offence or criticise others for little or no reason.

A prolonged stay at high altitudes may be accompanied by an entire change of personality. Along with episodes of mental confusion there is progressive indifference and apathy, mild depression and persistent inability to concentrate. Refreshing sleep is hard to obtain, and insomnia worsens the emotional and intellectual abnormalities. Dreams are frequently of an unpleasant and frightening nature, though at still higher altitudes dreaming apparently ceases to occur.

On return to normal altitudes there are rarely enduring defects. Pugh and Ward (1956), however, reported eight mountaineers who climbed to 28,000 feet without additional oxygen, one showing residual mental difficulties in the form of impaired ability to memorise.

Among aviators the onset of symptoms is more dramatic, appearing often at 9000 feet though depending again on the rate of ascent and individual susceptibility. Difficulties are universal above 20,000 feet without additional oxygen, and complete loss of consciousness is likely to occur at 25,000 feet. The first manifestations are variable—fatigue and mental slowing, euphoria, or surly and pugnacious behaviour. Headache, nausea and vomiting are again usually in evidence. Motor control soon becomes impaired and reaction times are slowed.

The subject is typically unaware of the change in himself and becomes oblivious of danger. He may feel his mind to be unusually keen and develop a dangerous fixity of purpose from which he cannot be dissuaded. Thus foolhardy and reckless behaviour is common. Birley (1920) reports some interesting examples of altered judgement in pilots during the 1914–18 war. One returned from a high photographic reconnaissance flight well pleased with his effort until it was found that he had taken eighteen exposures on the same plate; others had attacked enemy formations without any plan of campaign, making tactical errors of which they would never be guilty under ordinary circumstances. One officer had been known to wave his hand in friendly greeting to the enemy.

After such exposures there is only a muddled and confused recall of what happened during the flight. The after-effects are usually transient, with headache, nausea and emotional instability which may last for a few hours or days. Kossmann (1947), however, reported a pilot who experienced severe hypoxia during a bombing mission and showed slowed cerebration and impairment of memory even three weeks after return, though with later recovery.

Experimental observations in the decompression chamber, or with re-breathing apparatus, have amply confirmed these changes and shown their essential dependence on cerebral hypoxia. Severe exposures can lead to loss of consciousness without warning. Less severe degrees produce a picture closely resembling alcoholic intoxication, with headache, drowsiness, confusion, muscular weakness and incoordination. An initial stage of euphoria is again often seen with feelings of self-satisfaction and unusual power. The lifting of inhibitions sometimes leads to hilarious silly behaviour, anger, or outbursts of uncontrolled laughter. Both the quantity and quality of mental work are affected; reasoning is slow, calculations faulty, and writing shows perseverative errors. Distractibility becomes marked and attention to detail is lost. Choice reaction times are affected earlier than simple reaction times, but these too are slowed as neuromuscular control deteriorates. Visual and kinaesthetic perception are impaired, and later auditory perception also. Memory and learning ability can be shown to decline from an early stage. The lack of subjective awareness of the changes and the dangerous loss of initiative which accompanies them have also been fully confirmed.

Tune (1964) provides a detailed review of the psychological effects of hypoxia and its impact on performance at a variety of standardised tests measuring sensory functions, performance and cognitive skills. Burns (1959) has shown the special vulnerability of memory functions; subjects exposed to 40% nitrous oxide were unable to retain new information, such as a number on a card, for more than a minute, yet could carry on intelligent discussion. In consequence it could be hard to tell that there was anything abnormal unless conversation concerned some recent change in the environment. Time judgement was also markedly faulty.

CARBON MONOXIDE POISONING

In addition to attempted suicide with domestic gas supplies, carbon monoxide poisoning may occur accidentally in connection with slow combustion stoves, bathroom geysers and car exhaust fumes in enclosed spaces. Domestic risks have now been greatly diminished in the UK since the introduction of North Sea gas. In industry it is seen in connection with blast furnaces and when explosions occur in mines.

The clinical picture has been fully documented by Bour *et al.* (1967). Lowered efficiency and self-control lead imperceptibly to loss of consciousness without any intervening delirium. Complete unconsciousness is usually rapidly attained, resulting in coma of variable duration. Diffuse hypertonicity is common, with trismus and up-going plantar responses. Paroxysms of decerebrate rigidity may occur. Hypotonic forms are rare and carry a graver prognosis. Sphincter and swallowing difficulties are often present, and the corneal and pupillary reflexes may be abolished. The complexion is plethoric, and hyperpnoea is often extreme with a forceful expiratory phase. The classical 'cherry red' colour is in fact rare. The cerebrospinal fluid is normal.

In Shillito *et al.*'s (1936) series of 21,000 cases two-thirds were successfully resuscitated. If death is to follow this is usually within a few days, but sometimes survival extends for several weeks or months. Very occasionally the patient recovers for 10–15 days before a fatal relapse. Long persistence of coma after removal from the contaminated atmosphere carries an unfavourable prognosis, likewise prolonged circulatory collapse, fluctuating pyrexia, hyperglycaemia, uraemia or acidosis.

After Effects

As coma regresses the patient shows a period of disorientation and confusion. Sometimes there is a brief phase of irritability and restlessness, but usually the predominant features are apathy and general inertia. Approximately one-fifth of patients

show prolonged delirium, ranging from several hours to several weeks (Smith and Brandon, 1970). Hallucinations and delusions are conspicuous by their absence (Shillito *et al.*, 1936). Speech is slowed and difficult for a time, and thought processes reduced. Amnesic difficulties are usually much in evidence and often the last to clear:

A woman of 70 was admitted in coma and only several weeks later had recovered sufficiently to respond to simple commands and reply to questions. For the next two weeks she was grossly disoriented in time, giving the year variously as 1888 or 1918, and being equally wide of the mark for her age. Another week passed before she realised she was in hospital, yet insisted it was in Armagh, the place of her childhood, though in fact she was in Belfast. At this stage she was able to repeat the months of the year correctly, and could repeat four digits, but could retain nothing of a name and address after a 3 minute interval. She could remember the names of her brothers and sisters and recall some episodes from her childhood. Two weeks later she had improved remarkably. She was then consistently orientated in time and place, had good general insight, and was able to recall the circumstances leading right up to her accidental coal gas poisoning.

(Allison, 1961)

Sometimes a classical Korsakoff psychosis emerges, or alternatively the patient's profound inertia, indifference and slowing of cerebration may cause the memory to appear to be more defective than is really the case ('une sorte d'indifférence amnestique'—Ajuriaguerra and Rouault de la Vigne, 1946). Agnosia, constructional apraxia or dysphasia may also be seen later in recovery.

Extrapyramidal signs which are absent during the stage of coma may emerge on recovery, with cogwheel rigidity of the musculature, athetosis or immobility of facial expression. Transient hemiplegia is not uncommon, and eighth nerve affections may produce deafness and vertigo. In most cases the neurological abnormalities gradually clear along with the psychological disturbances, though sometimes this may take several weeks or months. The degree of recovery from early severe disability can sometimes be remarkable:

A 24-year-old woman was admitted to hospital in deep coma. There were repeated tonic seizures, breathing was laboured, and she required a tracheotomy. After several days in coma she passed into a muttering resistive state for some weeks, then became mute and unresponsive for three weeks more. At this stage she showed a quadriparesis and bilateral extensor plantar responses. Six weeks later she began to show some recovery of consciousness and ability to move, but remained confused and severely aphasic. Four months after the initial exposure, however, there had been a good deal of recovery; she was then talking well and was discharged from hospital. She continued to improve in a remarkable fashion, and by eight months there was only a moderate hemiparesis and slight mental impairment.

(Richardson *et al.*, 1959)

Latent Interval

A strange feature, repeatedly noted in a large series of cases, is the occurrence of a latent period between recovery from coma and the onset of profound neurological or mental disorder (Shillito *et al.*, 1936; Ajuriaguerra and Rouault de la Vigne, 1946; Bour *et al.*, 1967). This may also follow other forms of cerebral anoxia, as after anaesthesia or cardiac arrest (Plum *et al.*, 1962). Apparently normal health is regained, but 2-10 days later, or even after several weeks, there is an abrupt relapse with the appearance of extrapyramidal disturbance, delirium or a return of coma. Sometimes the patients have been discharged or even returned to their jobs in the interim. A progressive vascular pathology has been postulated as the basis (Richardson *et al.*, 1959), but nonetheless complete recovery is again often attained:

A man of 37 was accidentally gassed while intoxicated. He was unconscious for two days but for the rest of the week seemed entirely recovered. On the seventh day he began to act peculiarly, became unresponsive to questions and the right plantar response was found to be up-going. Several weeks later he was still dull, apathetic and disoriented, but thereafter improved and was ultimately discharged fully recovered.

A woman of 51 was unconscious for 2 days, but was discharged at the end of a week fully recovered apart from a general feeling of weakness. After 2 weeks, however, her gait became unsteady, and she became confused and bewildered. Her face was blank and expressionless and she developed a coarse tremor of the hands. She gradually improved over the next few months, with disappearance of the mental and neurological abnormalities.

(Shillito *et al.*, 1936)

In cases which progress to severe neurological disability and dementia, demyelination is usually extensive in the cerebral hemispheres and neuronal damage can be remarkably slight or absent (Plum *et al.*, 1962).

Enduring Sequelae

The majority of patients are left only with an amnesic gap for the period of coma, together with a variable amount of retrograde amnesia and patchy memory for part of the period of recovery. The commonest neurological sequelae are extrapyramidal disturbances, usually parkinsonian in nature or sometimes athetotic. Global impairment of intellect is uncommon but permanent defects of memorising may be seen. Neurological disabilities are almost invariably evident when gross mental impairments remain.

It has usually been claimed that persistent sequelae are remarkably rare. Thus over a ten year period Shillito *et al.* (1936) found that 21,000 cases of carbon monoxide poisoning had occurred in New York City with 14,500 recoveries, but only 39 patients (0·27% of survivors) could be identified who had been hospitalised with enduring defects. It seemed, therefore, that the great majority of patients either succumbed or recovered completely. Most of those with permanent sequelae had been deeply comatose for hours or days, and had often required long periods of assisted respiration when first discovered. Van Amberg (1942) found that recovery within an hour of removal from the contaminated atmosphere carried a uniformly good prognosis.

The investigations of Smith and Brandon (1970, 1973), however, revealed a more serious picture. Two hundred and six cases of carbon monoxide poisoning were traced from a defined geographical area (Newcastle-upon-Tyne), 42% being accidental and 58% due to suicide attempts. Of the 135 survivors, 3 patients (2·2%) were severely affected at the time of discharge, all showing dementia and one with parkinsonism in addition. Two others had spastic hemiplegia, though it was possible that this had developed immediately before exposure.

Follow-up was then undertaken among those who had been domiciled within the city at the time of poisoning. Seventy-four patients were traced at an average of 3 years after the event. Eleven had died (15%), 3 from suicide and 8 from other causes. Eight (11%) had evidence of gross neuropsychiatric damage which was directly attributable to the poisoning, in the form of cognitive disability, personality change, or frank neurological abnormalities. In some cases defects such as parkinsonism, dementia or personality change had become evident only after discharge from hospital, emphasising the importance of following every case for sufficient time to allow for the emergence of delayed sequelae. Five of the 8 showed a severe global deterioration of intellect.

Of the 63 alive at follow-up, 27 patients (43%) complained of impaired memory and this correlated highly with objective deficits on the Wechsler

Memory Scale. Twenty-one (33%) showed a deterioration of personality subsequent to the poisoning, with a marked association between personality and memory deficits. The commonest personality change was towards increased irritability, verbal aggressiveness, violence, impulsiveness and moodiness, a constellation described by the authors as 'affective incontinence'. Thus, over and above the 11% with gross sequelae, a large number appeared to have suffered milder brain damage, resulting in personality and affective change with associated mild cognitive impairment. This was a great deal more common than in a matched control group of patients who had survived barbiturate overdosage. The level of consciousness on admission to hospital correlated significantly with the development of gross neuropsychiatric sequelae and with complaints of memory impairment.

An example from Smith and Brandon's (1973) series with severe personality change was as follows:

A 33-year-old miner of good premorbid stability was accidentally exposed to carbon monoxide in a coal mine explosion. He was comatose when found some minutes later, and subsequently was delirious, irritable and aggressive for four hours. Oxygen therapy was given and he was discharged from hospital the same day. Subsequently he was forgetful, had difficulty in coping with his previous level of work, was increasingly irritable, restless and argumentative, and on occasion was violent towards his wife. He was more impulsive and outspoken, more anxious, and more prone to paranoid misinterpretations. His physical energy was markedly diminished. In the month before interview he had been charged with indecent assault on five young girls. His wife verified his previous mental stability and the deterioration of memory and personality change subsequent to exposure. An independent witness, unaware of the patient's fate after the accident, attested to his previously stable personality. Financial compensation had never been considered.

Cerebral Pathology in Carbon Monoxide Poisoning

Lapresle and Fardeau (1967) describe the characteristic changes in the brain in cases which come to autopsy. The most frequent lesion is necrosis of the globus pallidus, sometimes limited to a small and circumscribed portion bilaterally. Similar lesions are common in Ammon's horn, again variable in extent and sometimes affecting Sommer's sector only. The cerebral cortex shows necrotic foci with intense capillary proliferation and degeneration or disappearance of nerve cells, but the typical laminar cortical damage seen with other forms of anoxia is rare. The cere-bellum also shows necrosis but the Purkinje cells are relatively spared, again in contrast to their special vulnerability in other forms of anoxia.

Lesions are very common in the white matter of the centrum ovale. Here foci of necrosis can be extensive and coalescent with areas of demyelination. The latter appears to be particularly characteristic of cases which have shown a latent interval during their clinical course.

Vascular lesions are widespread, with endothelial swelling leading to thrombosis and miliary diapedetic haemorrhages. Sometimes there is marked general vasodilation. Cerebral oedema occurs regularly in the early stages and may contribute to the ischaemic changes. The lesions of the globus pallidus and Ammon's horn are thought to rest on a common vascular basis.

Brucher (1967) discusses the aetiology of the lesions. The cerebral pathology differs from that of anoxia due to other causes in certain important respects—laminar cortical damage is rare, the Purkinje cells are relatively preserved, and lesions are prominent in the white matter. This suggests that carbon monoxide may have a specific histotoxic action in addition to its effect of reducing the oxygen carrying capacity of the blood.

Chronic Carbon Monoxide Poisoning

From time to time it has been claimed that intermittent exposures to low concentrations of carbon monoxide can have a cumulative effect, resulting in chronic disability. In Scandinavian countries during the 1939–45 war this became a focus of concern among persons handling 'producer gas' or driving vehicles in which this was the source of power (Grut, 1949). Other industrial settings are among foundrymen, gas-workers and blast-furnace workers.

Proponents of the disorder point out that breathing as little as 0·05% of carbon monoxide in the inspired air leads to symptoms after several hours, and that experiments with animals show pathological changes in the central nervous system after prolonged sub-lethal exposures (Beck, 1936). Beck reported 97 patients who had suffered many weeks or months of exposure to domestic gas, vehicle exhaust, or blast furnace fumes, and concluded that a definite clinical syndrome was produced. The chief complaints were of dull frontal headache, vertigo, nervousness, generalised weakness, neuromuscular pains, anorexia, digestive disturbances, dyspnoea, palpitations, tremulousness, weakness of the legs with ataxia, and paraesthesiae of the extremities.

Almost all showed prominent mental manifestations and many were 'confirmed neurotics'. Psychological symptoms included depression, restlessness, anxiety, mental retardation, memory defects and periods of confusion. Drowsiness and insomnia were common. Some showed speech defects, tinnitus, visual disturbances or impairment of the sense of smell. Four patients showed parkinsonian features.

The syndrome, however, has come heavily under suspicion (Lindgren, 1961), and evidence for an objective physical basis has not been forthcoming (Slater and Roth, 1969). Hunter (1978) points out that carbon monoxide is not a cumulative poison and that small amounts are readily ventilated out of the blood; he therefore concludes that there is no such clinical condition as chronic carbon monoxide poisoning. The subject remains under careful review, however, in view of current risks to health from urban atmospheric contamination (e.g. Goldsmith and Landaw, 1968). Evidence incriminating intermittent exposure to carbon monoxide as the cause of increased liability to atherosclerosis in smokers is also relevant in this regard (Astrup, 1972).

Uraemia

Uraemia may result from primary disease of the kidneys or from extrarenal causes. Anything which causes a prolonged and severe reduction of blood flow through the kidneys can produce a potentially reversible renal failure due to tubular damage, for example shock or dehydration following operations, burns or crush injuries. The uraemia is then often aggravated by the increased protein catabolism that ensues.

Disordered mental functioning forms a prominent part of the syndrome of uraemia, both in chronic renal failure and in these more acute disturbances. In Stenbäck and Haapanen's (1967) large consecutive series of patients seen in a renal unit, mental manifestations occurred in 60%, rising to 75% when the blood urea exceeded 250 mg/100 ml. Mental changes were as common in the acute as in the chronic uraemic patients.

Presentation with Psychiatric Features

Uraemic patients are usually obviously unwell, but occasionally the mental changes can be the first manifestation and lead directly to psychiatric consultation. This is more likely when the uraemia has developed slowly. The picture may simulate neurasthenia with symptoms of lethargy, anorexia and depression. Or early dementia may be suspected in view of sluggish comprehension and difficulty with memory. Elderly demented patients may suffer additional mental impairment from unsuspected uraemia, sometimes as a result of prostatic hypertrophy and the associated hydronephrosis. More rarely an acute organic reaction may be the first indication, and uraemia must be constantly borne in mind in the differential diagnosis of delirium of uncertain aetiology.

Common Psychological Accompaniments

By far the commonest mental disturbance is progressive torpor and drowsiness with the insidious development of intellectual impairment. Stenbäck and Haapanen describe the following sequence of changes:

The first complaint is usually of feeling generally unwell, with fatigue and incapacity for physical or mental effort. The difficulty with concentration is characteristically episodic, so that the patient performs well for short periods of time but cannot sustain mental activity. There may be no other definite features on examination at this stage, though headache and anorexia are usually prominent complaints.

With further progression memory becomes obviously impaired, and episodes of disorientation and confusion appear. Listlessness and apathy prevail but an anxious restlessness may sometimes be seen. Depression and emotional withdrawal are usually marked. There may be petulant demanding behaviour, with negative attitudes towards treatment and hostility towards attendants, which later clears with clinical improvement. Both the impairment of consciousness and the changes of mood typically fluctuate markedly, with lucid periods during which behaviour returns to normal. Neurological accompaniments include fascicular twitching, myoclonic jerks, tremor and muscle cramps. Flapping tremor of the outstretched hands may be observed, similar to that of hepatic encephalopathy (p. 480). On recovery there is patchy or complete amnesia for the periods of disorientation and confusion.

Episodes of acute delirium appear in a third of cases, with apprehension, bewilderment, and fleeting hallucinations which may be terrifying in content. As with delirium due to other causes the picture changes rapidly from time to time and paranoid developments are common. Eventually more profound impairment of consciousness develops with increasingly sluggish comprehension and reaction, slurring of speech, incontinence and ultimately coma.

Epileptic fits develop in about a third of cases, more frequently in acute than chronic uraemia. They are usually a late feature unless hypertension is present at an early stage. When the blood pressure is very high there may be episodes of hypertensive encephalopathy, with severe headache and transient attacks of blindness, dysphasia or monoplegia.

Peripheral neuropathy is common in chronic renal failure. Sensation is impaired distally and symmetrically, reflexes are diminished and intense painful paraesthesiae sometimes occur (Mawdsley, 1972). Even in the absence of clinically overt neuropathy impairment of nervous conduction can often be shown.

Functional Psychoses with Uraemia

Occasionally, and presumably depending on the premorbid constitution, the picture may closely simulate functional mental illness. Baker and Knutson (1946) reported a patient initially diagnosed as suffering from catatonic schizophrenia, but with rapid fluctuations between psychotic and normal periods. Menninger's (1924) patient presented with mounting paranoia over many months, culminating in a florid psychotic illness with clear organic features. Psychotic depression may likewise occur, and occasional manic reactions have been observed. In all of these, close examination will usually betray organic mental symptoms. The obvious impairment of physical health, with weakness, weight loss and anorexia, should alert one to the true situation.

Depression may usually be treated safely with tricyclic antidepressants, though patients receiving dialysis will warrant careful monitoring of blood levels (Rosser, 1976). Phenothiazines should where possible be avoided on account of their enhanced liability to induce marked dystonia and other movement disorders in the presence of uraemia.

'Acute Azotaemic Psychotic Encephalitis'

At one time it was believed that certain conditions existed in which an acute psychotic illness was accompanied by uraemia but was not directly caused by it. A primary cerebral pathology was thought to lead on the one hand to the psychosis and on the other to the uraemia. In the French literature an 'acute azotaemic psychotic encephalitis' was described, presenting with acute delirium and fever and progressing to coma and usually death, with evidence of degenerative and inflammatory lesions in the central nervous system. The case was vigorously argued that the uraemia was secondary to lesions in vegetative centres of the nervous system rather than their cause, just as uraemia might occasionally complicate epidemic encephalitis or delirium tremens (Marchand, 1953). The 'fatal catatonia' of German workers was viewed similarly (Stauder, 1934; Arnold, 1949).

More recent knowledge of physiology would allow most of these cases to be seen as examples of acute renal failure secondary to extrarenal causes, with the psychotic manifestations being attributable to the uraemia in the usual way. Alternatively, acute renal failure may have complicated a psychosis already brought about by other factors. It is noteworthy that the illnesses often followed operations, deliveries, or acute infections.

Investigations

The blood urea is raised and electrolyte disturbances are common. Sodium depletion can be marked, the serum phosphate elevated, and bicarbonate and calcium reduced. In the later stages the serum potassium may rise. Anaemia is often considerable in patients with chronic uraemia.

Electroencephalographic changes develop roughly in proportion to the severity of the clinical condition, and are rarely absent when the blood urea exceeds 60 mg/100 ml (Tyler, 1968). They resemble the changes seen in hepatic decompensation, namely lowering of voltage with loss of well-developed alpha, then progressive slowing and disorganisation with runs of 5–7 per second waves which ultimately replace all other activity. Epileptic disturbances frequently appear.

The pressure of the cerebrospinal fluid is usually slightly raised, sometimes with moderate elevation of protein but without increase of cells.

Aetiology of Mental Disturbances

Mental and neurological changes become commoner with increasing elevation of the blood urea, but there is by no means a simple linear relationship (Stenbäck and Haapanen, 1967). Nor can urea be regarded as responsible for all or even the majority of the symptoms which result; considerable improvement can follow dialysis when urea is present in the dialysis bath, and experimentally urea has not been found to have a strong neurotoxic effect. Other abnormalities must therefore play a direct aetiological role, with the level of blood urea serving mainly as an indicator of the severity of overall metabolic disturbance. Nevertheless estimation of the blood urea remains an important clinical indicator for monitoring the progress of the condition as a whole.

Other derivatives of protein such as uric acid may play a part, or other toxins so far unidentified. Electrolyte disturbances are certainly important in many cases though generalisations are difficult to make. Changes in sodium, potassium, calcium, chloride, phosphate, acid/base balance and osmolality can all be blamed in individual instances. The rapidity of the shifts appears to be the essential factor, whether this is in the direction of normality or abnormality (Tyler, 1968).

Drugs have been strongly incriminated among the causes of neuropsychiatric disturbance in patients with chronic renal failure, accounting for over a third of the episodes in some series (Richet and Vachon, 1966; Richet et al., 1970). Sedatives and antibiotics appear to be mainly responsible, either by virtue of accumulation when the drug is excreted by the kidneys, or as a result of increased susceptibility of the central nervous system in the uraemic patient.

Arterial hypertension brings its own contribution by way of transient neurological disturbances, fits and headache. In many cases a part is played by raised intracranial pressure, changes in cerebral blood flow and cerebral oxygen utilisation, and altered permeability of small blood vessels.

Neary (1976) draws attention to other causes of neuropsychiatric disturbance in patients with chronic renal failure. The risk of intracranial infection is increased in uraemia, especially when immunosuppressive drugs are used after renal transplantation; encephalitis due to herpes simplex or cytomegalovirus may be hard to diagnose in the prodromal stages, leading to behavioural disturbance and change of personality. Low-grade meningitis can lack the typical physical signs and present as depression with chronic headache. The use of anticoagulants in maintenance haemodialysis may lead to a subdural haematoma.

The psychological stresses associated with haemodialysis or transplantation bring a range of problems of their own. Salmons (1980) reviews the problems involved in the modern management of chronic renal failure, with disruptions in work, daily life and family relationships. Not surprisingly there is a high incidence of depression, anxiety and disturbed sexual functioning among such patients. Short-lived psychotic episodes may be observed, usually in clear consciousness but often marked by 'organic' features such as visual hallucinations or loosely held delusions. Steroids administered after transplantation may make an important contribution to such developments (p. 535).

Disturbances Occasioned by Dialysis

Gradual improvement usually follows dialysis, with return of mental clarity a short while after chemical normality has been achieved. Occasionally however the time lag may be several days in duration.

If the patient is lucid beforehand he usually remains so, provided time is taken over the procedure. However too rapid dialysis carries a hazard of worsening the clinical situation. Headache, muscle twitching, fits and confusion may develop, sometimes progressing to coma with signs of brain stem compression (Kennedy et al., 1962; Peterson and Swanson, 1964; Mawdsley, 1972). This is commoner when the initial level of blood urea has been very high, and usually occurs towards the end of the dialysis.

The exact cause is unknown, but is probably related to rapid changes in blood biochemistry and acid/base balance. In some cases the cause appears to lie in the more rapid clearance of urea from the blood than from the central nervous system, resulting in an osmotic gradient which draws water into the brain and cerebrospinal fluid sufficiently to raise the intracranial pressure. Electroencephalography carried out during dialysis shows changes consistent with such an hypothesis and reversible with hypertonic fructose (Kennedy et al., 1963). Similar disturbance may result from quite another mechanism, when glucose enters the blood from the dialysing solution and provokes reactive hypoglycaemia (Rigg and Bercu, 1967).

Another serious complication of dialysis has been traced to the aluminium content of the water used in preparing the dialysate. This, known as 'dialysis encephalopathy' or 'dialysis dementia', was formerly one of the commonest causes of death in certain units (Burks et al., 1976). The earliest signs were difficulty with speech or episodes of confusion appearing during the dialysis procedure. Over time the mental difficulties became permanent, with dysarthria, dysphasia, apraxia and slowly progressive generalised dementia. Paranoia, bizarre behaviour and episodes of delirium were sometimes prominent. Neurological accompaniments were flapping tremor, facial grimacing and myoclonus. Focal seizures and various pareses often occurred.

Slow worsening of the disorder usually led to death. Treatment was ineffective and progression could continue despite restoration of normal renal function by transplantation. At autopsy the changes in the brain were slight and non-specific.

Most patients developing the disorder had been on haemodialysis for several years. It was found that the aluminium content of the brain, and especially the grey matter, was increased 4-fold in such patients compared with uraemics dying from other causes (Alfrey et al., 1976; McDermott et al., 1978b). This was at first ascribed to the aluminium in the phosphate-binding gels employed, but it eventually emerged that the regional incidence of encephalopathy in various centres correlated with the aluminium content of the water used as dialysate (Parkinson et al., 1979). Since taking steps to circumvent the problem the disease has now virtually disappeared.

In areas where the incidence was high an association could be shown between duration of time on dialysis and certain measures of cognitive impairment, even before the disease was declared (English et al., 1978). The electroencephalogram was similarly often markedly abnormal for many months before signs appeared.

Cerebral Pathology in Uraemia

Gross lesions in the central nervous system are rare in the absence of marked hypertension. The most constant change is scattered neuronal degeneration, with chromatolysis and vacuolisation of the cells. In chronic cases this progresses to pyknosis and areas of cell loss. Olsen (1961) systematically examined the brains of 104 patients dying of uraemia, and found such changes most frequently in the brain stem nuclei, reticular formation and cortex, though variable in location from case to case. He was unable to confirm other features which have traditionally been emphasised, such as focal glial proliferation, areas of demyelination and cerebral oedema.

Changes in the cerebral vessels with thrombosis and infarction are common, but correspond to hypertension and arteriosclerosis rather than to uraemia itself. A general haemorrhagic tendency may be seen when other factors are present to explain it.

In general, therefore, the cerebral pathology shows little that is specific for uraemia, and the picture is dominated to a high degree by the disease processes responsible for the uraemia and the secondary complications which develop.

Electrolyte Disturbances

A delicate balance must be maintained in the chemical environment, both intracellularly and extracellularly, to maintain the proper functioning of the central nervous system. In this certain relatively simple components have been identified: the correct acid/base balance must be preserved, the proper gradient of sodium and potassium across the cell membrane, and the correct concentration of calcium and perhaps magnesium ions. These factors may be disturbed severally or together in many disease processes and mental symptoms may follow.

The metabolic dynamics involved in the production of mental symptoms are often complex, since disturbance of one aspect of the balance can have repercussions upon others. Alterations in cerebral blood flow may follow and complicate the situation further. Nevertheless the correct appreciation of the primary disturbance is of the utmost importance if appropriate treatment is to follow.

Electrolyte disturbance plays a prominent part in certain endocrine disorders and in uraemia as already described. It complicates respiratory disorders, and can assume great importance post-operatively when the patient is maintained on intravenous fluids for long periods of time. A variety of other causes will be mentioned below where appropriate.

Water Depletion

Water depletion can arise from simple unavailability as in shipwreck, and may be seen clinically in the presence of severe weakness from any physical illness, in severe dysphagia, and in coma. Intense thirst and dryness of the mouth is coupled with a greyish ill appearance and loss of weight. Signs of dehydration are less obvious than in sodium depletion since the greatest loss is from the intracellular compartment. The plasma sodium, chloride and urea tend to rise. Increasing mental confusion gives way to delirium and coma. The administration of water relieves the situation, but if intravenous fluids are required a 5% glucose solution should be given.

The elderly are especially at risk in view of their narrow limits of physiological balance, diminished capacity for renal tubular absorption, and liability to chronic debilitating disease. Jana and Romano-Jana (1973) have described 4 cases of 'hypernatraemic psychosis' in which elderly patients were admitted to a psychiatric hospital in a confused and disorientated state. Discovery of a raised serum sodium led to the intravenous administration of hypotonic fluids with rapid restoration of normal mental function. All four had been ambulatory on admission and did not complain of excessive thirst. The cause of the dehydration remained uncertain, but diminished fluid intake may have been occasioned by some degree of primary emotional lability and cognitive change.

Water Intoxication

Over-hydration may result from excessive infusion of 5% glucose solution post-operatively, from the administration of excessive quantities of vasopressin, or if too much water is drunk in the presence of renal failure. An important cause in psychiatric patients can be compulsive water drinking, as described on p. 445. The serum osmolality and sodium are low.

Anorexia, nausea and vomiting are early signs, with marked lassitude and changes of mood. Headache and blurring of vision may occur. Later there is impairment of consciousness, delirium and coma. Muscle cramps and twitches are sometimes seen, and epileptic fits are common.

Sodium Depletion

Sodium depletion occurs in tropical climates when common salt is omitted during the process of acclimatisation. Clinically it is seen after severe vomiting and diarrhoea from any cause, in Addison's disease, in salt-losing nephritis and pyelonephritis, and post-operatively when patients are maintained on intravenous glucose alone. The syndrome of 'inappropriate anti-diuretic hormone secretion' ('SIADH') has many causes, chief among which is bronchial carcinoma; hyponatraemia and hypotonicity of the plasma are accompanied by continuing excretion of sodium in the urine.

The classical symptoms and signs of heat exhaustion include weakness, dizziness, pallor, profuse sweating, diminution of urine, rapid pulse and respiration, low blood pressure and cramping pains in the abdomen and limbs. The onset is usually sudden, and the response to sodium chloride by mouth is dramatic. However the picture can be misleading when it sets in very gradually. Saphir (1945) described ten cases which were missed until the serum chloride was estimated. The resemblance to

neurosis was striking, and in some patients malingering had been suspected. Prominent mental complaints included irritability, depression without cause, and intense anxiety.

When associated with medical diseases the presenting features are usually of lassitude, apathy and weakness. Giddiness and hypotensive faints are common, with muscle weakness of a myasthenic character (Slater and Roth, 1969). Later anorexia develops with nausea, vomiting and severe muscle cramps. The patient appears dehydrated but thirst is rarely a prominent complaint. Mental confusion ultimately appears with disorientation, delusions and hallucinations. If untreated the condition progresses to coma.

Treatment consists of giving salt by mouth, or when necessary intravenous saline. The administration of water alone or glucose in water can be dangerous, as the hypotonicity is aggravated further.

Potassium Depletion

The normal renal mechanisms for the conservation of potassium are relatively inefficient, and accordingly potassium deficiency is liable to develop in any disease associated with chronic starvation or anorexia. The commonest cause is again inadequate intake when patients are maintained post-operatively on intravenous fluids. Gastrointestinal causes include hyperemesis gravidarum, chronic diarrhoea due to ulcerative colitis, malabsorption syndromes such as steatorrhoea, or the long-continued use of purgatives. Other causes include Cushing's disease, the massive diuresis which may arise in diabetes mellitus, the diuretic phase of acute renal insufficiency, or the rarer potassium-losing nephritis and renal tubular acidosis. It may also result from the administration of diuretics, ACTH, or adrenal steroids. Excessive transfer of potassium into the cells occurs in familial periodic paralysis and when diabetic ketosis is treated vigorously with glucose and insulin.

Judge (1968) has reported that potassium deficiency may arise in elderly persons simply because their diet contains inadequate amounts. Depression, apathy, weakness, paranoid ideation and disturbance of sleep rhythm follow. The serum potassium level may sometimes be normal, yet improvement in mood, alertness and activity follows supplementation. Others may have just sufficient potassium in the diet, but a secondary deficiency is produced by an attack of diarrhoea and vomiting, an acute infection, or a small cerebrovascular accident. In addition such persons may take a purgative or be given a diuretic which aggravates the deficiency.

The usual presentation in all cases is with lethargy, apathy and depression which can be profound in degree. Anorexia, constipation and abdominal distension are common accompaniments and paralytic ileus may develop. Severe muscle weakness may extend to flaccid paralysis.

Hysteria may be diagnosed, especially since the tendon reflexes are sometimes preserved until very low potassium levels are reached. Moreover in familial periodic paralysis emotional stress may precipitate an attack. Mitchell and Feldman (1968) report an example of a patient with renal tubular acidosis who was first thought to show conversion hysteria:

A woman of 30 complained of marked weakness of the arms and legs after a fall some hours earlier, and was unable to walk. There was a long previous history of anorexia, occasional vomiting, constipation and muscle spasm, and there had been several similar falls in preceding months. Marital difficulties were prominent and a hysterical conversion reaction was diagnosed. She slowly regained strength and was discharged after four days.

One month later she was readmitted with extreme weakness of several hours duration, and complained of sleeping excessively and frequent headaches. The serum potassium was low at 2·4 mEq/litre but again spontaneous recovery occurred. Two days later there were similar complaints, the serum potassium was 1·8 mEq/litre and the electrocardiogram showed typical changes. There had been no evidence of impairment of consciousness at any stage.

Apprehension and irritability are sometimes marked and an anxiety state may be simulated. Emotionally induced hyperventilation may be thought to be responsible for paraesthesiae, vague muscle discomfort and transient visual disturbances. Very occasionally a typical acute organic reaction is seen with disorientation, confusion, impairment of memory and delirium.

The electrocardiogram shows characteristic changes which may alert one to the situation—a small T wave, prolongation of the Q-T interval, and depression of the ST segment. A low serum potassium confirms the diagnosis but is not always found in the early stages.

Potassium citrate should be given orally, 10–15 g per day. Intravenous infusion of potassium chloride may be needed if oral intake is impossible, but must be undertaken with care.

Potassium Excess

Potassium excess occurs with acute renal failure, in severe crises of Addison's disease and in diabetic coma. The patient is dull, lethargic and confused, and asthenia progresses to flaccid paralysis in a manner indistinguishable from potassium depletion. Bradycardia develops due to heart block and ventricular standstill may ultimately occur.

Hypercalcaemia

The clinical manifestations of hypercalcaemia have already been described in the section on hyperparathyroidism (p. 447). Malignancy is another important cause—carcinoma with secondary bone deposits, multiple myeloma and Hodgkin's disease. Other causes include sarcoidosis, hyperthyroidism, the excessive administration of vitamin D, and the prolonged ingestion of calcium especially when taken as milk with an antacid (the 'milk-alkali syndrome'). Long-term treatment with lithium may very occasionally produce hypercalcaemia by elevating the level of parathyroid hormone (Christiansen et al., 1976).

Petersen (1968) reported six examples, mostly due to Vitamin D intoxication, with clinical pictures similar to those seen with hyperparathyroidism. Thirst, asthenia, depression and tension states were the main manifestations, and 3 patients showed acute organic psychoses. Weizman et al. (1979) found that 7 of 12 patients with hypercalcaemia due to malignant disease had prominent psychiatric symptoms. Three showed depression or anxiety, sometimes severe, 3 developed acute organic reactions, and one an acute paranoid psychosis. In all cases the mental symptoms disappeared within 2–6 days when the serum calcium was restored to normal. There is obvious risk of viewing the emotional disorder as a reaction to the basic disease, or of ascribing organic mental symptoms to intracerebral complications.

Hypocalcaemia

Hypocalcaemia may result from a deficiency of calcium or vitamin D in the diet, producing rickets in children and osteomalacia in adults. Hypoparathyroidism, chronic steatorrhoea and chronic nephritis are other possible causes. Anticonvulsant therapy leads to hypocalcaemia in a substantial proportion of epileptic patients.

In children there is a characteristic triad of convulsions, laryngeal stridor and carpopedal spasm

(p. 451). In adults the usual complaint is merely of painful cramps or tingling paraesthesiae in the limbs. The characteristic signs of latent tetany and the common mental manifestations are described in the section on hypoparathyroidism (p. 451).

The tetany due to alkalosis is described below.

Hypomagnesaemia

The clinical pictures attributable to magnesium depletion are ill-defined and controversial, largely because magnesium deficiency is usually associated with other concurrent metabolic derangements. It may arise after prolonged parenteral feeding, in chronic alcoholism, in delirium tremens, and in cases of severe malnutrition or malabsorption associated with diarrhoea and vomiting.

Vallee *et al.* (1960) claimed that a picture identical with hypocalcaemic tetany could result, with convulsions, carpopedal spasm, Chvostek's and Trousseau's signs, and athetoid movements of the limbs. They described such cases in which the serum calcium was normal and parenteral magnesium sulphate promptly abolished the symptoms. But Hanna *et al.* (1960) have questioned these findings, and presented three cases of pure magnesium deficiency with a rather different picture. Convulsions were present, but tetany in the sense of spontaneous muscle cramps was absent. The most marked manifestations were depression, irritability, vertigo, ataxia and muscle weakness. Other reports have included tremors, fasciculation, choreiform movements, mild confusion and disorientation, delirium of sudden onset with wild combative behaviour, and stupor, all of which may be reversed by intramuscular magnesium sulphate (Flink, 1956; Hammarsten and Smith, 1957; Randall *et al.*, 1959). More recent evidence on the subject is reviewed by Tucci (1981).

A number of workers have investigated serum magnesium levels in patients with schizophrenia. Elevated magnesium has often been reported, but also lowered levels or no difference from controls. Alexander and Jackson (1981) review the inconsistent findings in the literature.

Low Serum Zinc

Zinc deficiency is rare, but occurs in certain malnourished populations and in countries where bread with a high phytate content is consumed. It can be found with regional enteritis and with malabsorption syndromes. The excretion of zinc is increased in liver disease, diabetes, some renal diseases and with certain drugs (*Lancet*, 1973).

The syndrome most closely tied to low serum zinc is diminished acuity of taste and smell (hyposmia, hypogeusia), first described by Henkin *et al.* (1971) and shown to be responsive to the administration of oral zinc sulphate. Many such patients had developed the hypogeusia soon after a respiratory illness, while in others it appeared spontaneously. The strong perversions of taste and smell that were sometimes present could precipitate emotional disturbance including profound depression.

Henkin *et al.* (1975) monitored the low serum zinc produced by histidine in the treatment of 6 patients with progressive systemic sclerosis. They were able to follow the sequential appearance of anorexia, dysfunction of taste and smell, and ultimately the development of neurological and psychiatric features. The patients became dizzy and unsteady, with cerebellar symptoms in the form of ataxic gait and intention tremor. Several were irritable and easily upset, with depression and periods of weeping. Others showed memory impairments, lethargy, auditory and visual hallucinations and pronounced emotional lability. The disturbances correlated with the degree of lowering of serum zinc and with indicators of total body zinc loss. All were quickly reversed following the administration of zinc sulphate.

Staton *et al.* (1976) have described a young male patient presenting with a picture resembling catatonic schizophrenia who responded rapidly to zinc administration after failing to respond to other treatments. He had presented with auditory and visual hallucinations, loose associations, blunted affect and disorientation in time and place. Drooling, negativism and catatonic postures became established. Phenothiazines were ineffective and led to severe extrapyramidal disturbance. After some months electroconvulsive therapy was tried and produced only transient improvement. A low serum zinc and high serum copper were discovered and oral zinc sulphate and pyridoxine were commenced. Thenceforward he made excellent progress and remained well one year later.

Alkalosis

Metabolic alkalosis results from repeated vomiting as in pyloric stenosis, or the ingestion of large quantities of sodium bicarbonate given, for example, in the treatment of peptic ulcer. An important cause from the psychiatric point of view is the respiratory alkalosis which results from overbreathing. Attacks of hyperventilation are common in states of anxiety and in histrionic patients under stress. Hyperventilation also follows the ingestion of large quantities of salicylates.

In the cases associated with vomiting there is often apathy, delirium and stupor, but concomitant potassium and water depletion may often play a part. Tetany is liable to occur, because the proportion of ionised calcium is reduced even though the total serum calcium is normal.

The sequence of changes seen with hyperventilation are reviewed by Wyke (1963). Experimental studies show that hyperventilation facilitates the induction of hypnosis and increases the suggestibility of the subject. At an early stage perception is increased, but later dulled. As consciousness becomes impaired and awareness of the environment diminishes the electroencephalogram begins to slow, and high voltage delta waves ultimately appear. Impairment of memory and calculation develop when the dominant frequency reaches 5 Hz. Psychological studies show impaired performance on tests of reaction time, manual coordination and word association, and there is often a subsequent amnesia for events of the period.

When hyperventilation accompanies anxiety the emotional instability is increased, creating a vicious circle. Vertigo and paraesthesiae further reinforce the patient's concern. Mental confusion may become marked, and myoclonic jerks or epileptic phenomena may be precipitated. In severe cases the condition may progress to loss of consciousness.

It is uncertain whether these clinical phenomena depend directly on the lowering of carbon dioxide tension in the blood, or on the pH and other metabolic changes in the environment of the neurones. Hypoxia resulting from vasoconstriction of the cerebral arterioles may make a further contribution. The decrease in the ionised calcium of the blood is almost certainly responsible for the tetanic phenomena.

Acidosis

Metabolic acidosis may result from renal failure or from diabetes mellitus with ketosis. In chronic diarrhoea there may be loss of sodium bicarbonate in the stools. Respiratory disorders such as emphysema or status asthmaticus which lead to underventilation similarly cause acidosis due to carbon dioxide retention.

In metabolic acidosis the most prominent result is stimulation of the respiratory centre with deep and rapid respiration. Consciousness is progressively impaired and mental confusion or delirium are seen in varying degree. The precise clinical picture in the individual case is largely determined by the underlying condition and other associated metabolic derangements.

Respiratory acidosis (*hypercapnia*) provides a more distinctive clinical picture. Inhalation of 6–7% carbon dioxide can be shown to impair psychological functioning and lead to perseverative responses. In chronic respiratory disease mental dulling and drowsiness are common, and it has long been known that if oxygen is given alone this can sometimes impair consciousness further and precipitate mental confusion and irrational behaviour. This was at first ascribed to over-oxygenation, but is now recognised to result from the increased carbon dioxide retention which occurs as dyspnoea is relieved.

Westlake *et al.* (1955) reviewed the clinical findings in carbon dioxide retention due to emphysema. Mental disturbances were usually present when the blood pH was below 7·2 or the arterial tension of carbon dioxide above 100 mmHg, ranging from mild impairment of consciousness with irritability, disorientation and confusion, to delirium with auditory and visual hallucinations. Headache, muscle twitching and sweating were common accompaniments. When the pH fell below 7·1 or the tension of carbon dioxide rose above 120 mmHg, there was increasing lethargy and drowsiness leading ultimately to coma. The intracranial pressure was often raised, and papilloedema was sometimes seen. The disturbances were usually transient, because the pH is ultimately restored by renal activity, but in a minority of cases the outcome could be fatal.

The mental changes are thought to be due to the direct action of acidaemia or hypercapnia on the metabolism of cortical neurones. The rise of intracranial pressure is ascribed to the accompanying cerebral vasodilation. The electroencephalogram shows delta waves, sometimes paroxysmal or episodic, at high arterial levels of carbon dioxide.

Hepatic Disorder

Striking neurological and psychiatric changes may be seen in patients with liver disease. The range and extent of these features were clearly defined in the classical paper by Summerskill *et al.* in 1956. An important point was the demonstration that neuropsychiatric disorder could sometimes dominate the picture, even when unequivocal evidence of liver disease was not immediately obvious. The correct diagnosis might therefore easily be overlooked.

Seventeen patients were reported, mostly with portal cirrhosis. Neuropsychiatric symptoms were the presenting feature in 8 patients in whom liver disease had not previously been suspected. Four had been admitted to mental hospital initially, and in 3 others a psychiatric opinion had been sought. Only 3 were jaundiced and only 7 had large livers. Five showed little biochemical evidence of liver dysfunction. The signs of most value in supporting the diagnosis were palmar erythema, spider naevi, finger clubbing and loss of body hair. Foetor hepaticus was prominent in every patient and the spleen was constantly enlarged.

Psychiatric Features

The manifestations are extremely variable, making it hard to demarcate a single entity of 'hepatic encephalopathy'. Essentially the picture is of a chronic organic reaction, characterised by acute exacerbations and remissions, and accompanied by neurological abnormalities which wax and wane with the disorder. Functional neurotic or psychotic features may be prominent, depending on the premorbid personality, and change of personality may feature to a large degree. The disturbances may persist for many years, sometimes with complete remissions for long periods of time, or the condition may become chronic and constant.

Impairment of consciousness is always present during episodes of the disorder. Warning signs are a fixed staring appearance and reduction of spontaneous movements. Hypersomnia is an early feature, sometimes with overpowering attacks of sleepiness by day and inversion of sleep rhythm. Later this progresses to periods of marked confusion, semi-coma or coma, though deterioration can be arrested at any level. Coma at first resembles normal sleep, but later progresses to total unresponsiveness.

Rapid changes in the level of consciousness are accompanied by delirium with hallucinations, mainly in the visual modality. Episodic 'twilight' states with sudden onset and ending may also occur. One patient reported by Summerskill *et al.* (1956) experienced panoramic scenes in bright colours of frightening bears and wolves, and synaesthesia so that a dripping tap in the right peripheral field of vision was experienced as a cold drip on the right cheek. Recent memory is impaired in proportion to the impairment of consciousness, and confabulation is sometimes much in evidence. Dense amnesias with retrograde loss follow periods of coma.

The mood often shows abrupt swings, sometimes with depression, sometimes euphoria. Personality changes may be marked and are sometimes the presenting feature. During exacerbations uninhibited behaviour may be released, or previous traits of irritability or joviality are exaggerated. Between exacerbations an enduring disturbance of personality is characteristically seen, reminiscent of frontal lobe disorder with blunted affect, loss of drive and initiative, incongruous jocularity, tactlessness, defective insight, and loss of finer aspects of social judgement. Murphy *et al.* (1948) noted similar changes and found that 'the jaundiced, pot-bellied cirrhotic patients are usually the jovial clowns of the ward'. Such patients would often insist on going home or claim perfect health despite all evidence to the contrary.

Features attributable to the premorbid personality include short-lived depressive episodes, hypomanic reactions, anxiety attacks or obsessive-compulsive behaviour. Occasionally paranoid reactions which have set in during episodes of confusion persist on recovery.

Episodes of typical acute schizophrenia or hypomania have also been reported, sometimes in the absence of impairment of consciousness, but usually accompanied by other signs of hepatic encephalopathy (Read *et al.*, 1967). These may develop as little as weeks or months after porto-caval anastomotic operations. They are rare, however, and their causal relationship to liver dysfunction remains in doubt.

Neurological Features

The neurological abnormalities are more specific, and tend to worsen or remit in parallel with the psychiatric symptoms.

Motor disorders are the outstanding feature. There may be little to detect in remission other than mild exaggeration of tendon reflexes, unobtrusive tremor, and a characteristic blank or grimacing facial expression. But at some stage almost every patient shows the characteristic *flapping tremor* ('asterixis') which is brought into evidence when the arms are held outstretched. This consists of rapid bursts of flexion-extension movements at the metacarpophalangeal and wrist joints, superimposed upon a fine 6–9 per second tremor. It is aggravated by fatigue, anxiety and excitement but is absent at rest. The disorder is characteristic but not entirely specific for hepatic encephalopathy, and is occasionally seen in uraemia, respiratory failure and severe cardiac failure (Sherlock, 1981).

Deterioration is accompanied by a combination of extrapyramidal and pyramidal features—dysarthria, ataxia, gross tremor, muscular rigidity, hyperreflexia and clonus. The plantar reflexes usually remain flexor until the stage of coma is reached, so that the unusual combination of rigidity, clonus and down-going plantar responses is frequently seen. In deep coma the muscles become flaccid and reflexes may be abolished.

These gross neurological disorders can remit abruptly and dramatically from one day to the next along with the psychiatric features. Serial tests of handwriting may serve as an indicator of progress. Other neurological abnormalities include dysphasia with perseverative speech disturbances, blurring of vision, diplopia and nystagmus. Constructional apraxia has been stressed as an early and sometimes a persistent feature.

Read et al. (1967) have described some less common syndromes of neurological defect. One small group of patients developed progressive paraplegia, and another cerebellar dysfunction along with parkinsonian features. Occasional patients developed epilepsy or myoclonic spasms, or were at first suspected of cerebral tumours on account of dementia coupled with focal neurological signs.

Investigations

Biochemical evidence of liver dysfunction will usually be found but may sometimes be relatively slight.

The electroencephalogram can be of help in diagnosis and prognosis and shows a close correlation with the grades of neuropsychiatric disturbance (Parsons-Smith et al., 1957; Kennedy et al., 1973). Changes occur early in the progression towards coma, and even before psychological abnormalities have appeared. The earliest change is slowing of the alpha rhythm and the appearance of 5–7 per second theta waves, most marked in the frontal and temporal regions. Theta comes to replace the alpha activity completely as consciousness is progressively impaired. Later characteristic triphasic waves are seen, the appearance of which suggests a poor prognosis. Further deterioration is shown by decrease in amplitude, blunting of the triphasic waves, and periods of flattening.

These changes are not specific for hepatic failure, but occur with many other metabolic derange-ments—uraemia, hypokalaemia, anoxia, carbon dioxide retention, hypoglycaemia, B_{12} deficiency, and in the early phases of raised intracranial pressure—but in the conscious patient with liver disease they are virtually diagnostic of impending coma.

Lumbar puncture reveals cerebrospinal fluid under normal pressure. The protein is sometimes raised during coma, but there is no pleocytosis (Sherlock, 1981).

Differential Diagnosis

Summerskill et al.'s (1956) original patients had received various diagnostic labels including anxiety state, hysterical ataxia, depression, frontal lobe tumour, cerebral arteriosclerosis, narcolepsy, psychomotor epilepsy, multiple sclerosis, Wilson's disease and parkinsonism.

The fluctuations in severity differentiate the condition from dementia, but may closely simulate chronic barbiturate intoxication. The distinction from Wilson's disease (p. 563) can be important; the neurological disturbance is then non-fluctuating, the motor abnormalities usually consist of choreoathe-toid movements rather than a flapping tremor, and a Kayser–Fleischer corneal ring is virtually always present.

Delirious episodes may at first suggest delirium tremens, though hallucinations are less vivid and the patient is rarely fearful. The differentiation from alcoholic intoxication can be difficult because the two may coexist.

Depression may be misdiagnosed in view of the fixed facial expression, psychomotor retardation, and depressive swings of mood. Catatonia may be suggested by episodes of mutism and stupor. Moreover functional psychoses of an affective, schizophrenic or paranoid type may be precipitated at an early stage.

Finally, in the presence of known liver disorder which is under treatment, the disturbances must be distinguished from those due to hyponatremia caused by a low sodium diet and the administration of diuretics.

Aetiology of Mental Disturbances

It is now established that the neuropsychiatric disturbances are similar whatever the underlying liver pathology. Hepatocellular failure, portal hypertension or surgically induced porto-caval anastomosis all lead to essentially similar pictures. The feature which they share is a circulatory pathway by which portal blood may enter systemic veins and reach the brain without being metabolised by the liver (Sherlock, 1981). In primary hepatocellular failure the shunt is through the liver itself, because the cells cannot metabolise the contents of the portal blood completely. In cirrhosis the shunt is via the collateral vessels which become established. The mental disturbance is therefore essentially due to cerebral intoxication by intestinal contents which have failed to be metabolised by the liver.

The precise toxin responsible is uncertain, but it is clearly nitrogenous in nature. Thus the picture can be decisively influenced by the level of protein in the diet. A large intake of protein produces exacerbations and may even precipitate coma, while rigid protein restriction ameliorates the condition. The assessment of nitrogen intolerance by the administration of ammonium chloride has been used as a sensitive clinical indicator for confirming the diagnosis. The ammonium ion itself was at one time thought to be directly responsible, but this now appears unlikely.

Other metabolic disturbances may aggravate the situation by making the brain more susceptible to toxic influences. Acid/base imbalance, electrolyte disturbance, hypotension and anoxia may all contribute in this way. Not uncommonly acute episodes are found to have been precipitated by haemorrhage into the gastrointestinal tract, by infection, injudicious sedation, or the administration of a potent diuretic.

Treatment

Treatment is a matter for specialist medical supervision and is described by Sherlock (1981). The fundamental requirement is rigid restriction of dietary protein, often coupled with oral antibiotics to decrease bacterial ammonia formation in the gut. Enemas and purgation may help. Lactulose has proved to be highly beneficial. Levodopa or bromocriptine are employed in the rare patient with chronic encephalopathy who proves resistant to dietary restriction and lactulose.

Outcome

In the early stages at least the mental and neurological features are usually found to be reversible, including quite severe degrees of intellectual impairment. Frequently the therapeutic result is excellent. The prognosis depends principally on the extent of liver cell failure. Acute hepatitis has the worst prognosis, whereas a favourable outcome can be expected in chronic disorders with relatively good liver cell function but extensive collateral circulation. The prognosis is always better if a precipitant such as infection or haemorrhage can be identified and treated.

Cerebral Pathology

In cases which come to autopsy the brain is usually normal macroscopically. The most striking histological change is diffuse proliferation and enlargement of astrocytes in the cerebrum, cerebellum, putamen and globus pallidus. The neurones themselves show relatively minor alterations.

Such a picture appears to be virtually specific for liver disease. It can develop within a few days of the onset of encephalopathy, and bears an approximate relationship to the duration and severity of neuropsychiatric symptoms. In chronic cases there may be cerebral softening with cortical thinning, and neuronal degeneration most marked in the deeper layers of the cortex (Victor et al., 1965).

Acute Porphyria

The classification of the several varieties of porphyria is discussed by Goldberg et al. (1983). The commonest form in Britain is the Swedish or 'acute intermittent type', in which an inborn error of metabolism leads to a defect in the enzymic biosynthesis of porphyrins. It is inherited as a dominant autosomal gene with incomplete penetrance. The other major form is the South African type, 'porphyria variegata', with a similar though genetically distinct basis. This can declare itself either by light-sensitive skin lesions or in a manner similar to the acute intermittent type. When in the latter form this too is occasionally seen in European countries. Other rare varieties of little relevance to psychiatry include the 'symptomatic porphyria' secondary to severe liver disease, and 'erythropoietic porphyria' which is associated with skin lesions and haemolytic anaemia.

The historical researches of Macalpine and Hunter (1966) and Macalpine et al. (1968) have brought special interest to the disorder. Evidence has been presented which suggests that George III's prolonged and puzzling mental illness may have been associated with porphyria, and the disease has been traced in the Royal Houses of Stuart, Hanover and Prussia back to Mary Queen of Scots.

Clinical Features of Acute Intermittent Porphyria

The clinical features of the acute intermittent type declare themselves at any age from puberty onwards, but mostly in the third decade. Penetrance of the responsible gene is incomplete, so that the disease often exists in a latent form and a family history may not be forthcoming.

Attacks may take many forms which renders diagnosis difficult. Valuable reviews of the clinical features are provided by Goldberg (1959) and Stein and Tschudy (1970). Typical symptoms consist of acute abdominal pain, or pain in the limbs or back, often associated with nausea, vomiting, headache and severe constipation. Epileptic fits occur in some 20 per cent of cases, and status epilepticus may develop. A rapidly developing and predominantly motor peripheral neuropathy may ensue or can be the presenting feature, with weakness, numbness, paraesthesiae or pain in the limbs. This can progress to severe paralysis with embarrassment of respiration. After an attack weakness or wasting may occasionally persist as an enduring disability.

Mental disorder accompanies attacks in a quarter to three-quarters of cases, and psychiatric symptoms can dominate the picture. The patient becomes emotionally disturbed, sometimes acutely depressed and sometimes restless and violent. Marked emotional lability is common with histrionic, demonstrative behaviour. Clouding of consciousness and confusion may progress to delirium, with hallucinations, delusions and noisy disturbed behaviour. Coma sometimes develops abruptly. Psychotic developments may resemble schizophrenia and paranoid reactions are not uncommon.

Precipitation of Attacks

Attacks can be precipitated by acute infection, alcohol and certain drugs. Barbiturates are notorious in this respect and carry the grave risk of aggravating the disorder if given in an acute attack to sedate the patient. Thiopentone given in the course of laparotomy may endanger life by precipitating paralysis and respiratory failure. Other drugs which may precipitate or worsen attacks include amitriptyline, carbamazepine, phenytoin, nitrazepam, steroids, tetracyclines, sulphonamides, oestrogens, the contraceptive pill, dichloralphenazone ('Welldorm') and methyldopa (Goldberg *et al.*, 1983).

There has been much discussion of the role played by emotional disturbance in precipitating attacks. This is reviewed by Ackner *et al.* (1962) who found the evidence to be inconclusive. In their group of twelve patients, only three of the many episodes occurred at times of acute or chronic emotional stress. The patients and their relatives did not consider stress to be causally related, and detailed enquiry revealed many stresses in the past which had failed to provoke attacks. On the other hand, in a few of their patients there were grounds for thinking that psychogenic rather than organic factors were responsible for some of the psychiatric symptomatology observed during their periods in hospital.

Premorbid Stability

Similar controversy surrounds the background of emotional instability which has been said to characterise porphyric patients. It has been claimed, for instance, that porphyria occurs specifically if not exclusively in patients with severe neurosis or personality disorder, and that a family history of psychiatric disorder is very common (Roth, 1945).

Ackner *et al.* (1962) failed to confirm these features. The previous mental health and stability of their patients was unremarkable between attacks, and only one had a family history of mental illness. There was no strong evidence of abnormal personalities among the relatives. Ackner *et al.* suggest that the evidence for personality disorder is often confused with evidence of episodic disturbed behaviour during attacks, and that the latter is liable to add to a general impression of emotional instability. In fact it was surprising how little effect the disabling and capricious disease had had upon most of the patients in their series, despite frequent hospitalisation with mistaken labels of hysteria and personality disorder.

Investigations

The diagnosis is confirmed by the detection of excess porphobilinogen in the urine.

Porphobilinogen is itself colourless, but may change to a red uroporphyrin after standing, acidification or heating. Freshly voided urine may therefore be colourless, or pale pink varying to deep mahogany depencing on conditions at the time. In any case the presence of porphyrins may be established by adding the urine to Ehrlich's aldehyde reagent and sodium acetate, which produces a reddish purple colour not extractable by chloroform.

In the South African variety examination of the stools is more reliable than the urine, a brilliant pink fluorescence being produced by extracts from the stool under ultra-violet light.

In the acute intermittent variety there is a general tendency for the porphyrin metabolites to reach a peak during exacerbations of the disorder and to decrease to low or negligible levels between attacks. This, however, is by no means invariable and persistently elevated levels may occur. Ackner *et al.* (1961, 1962) failed to find a clear relationship between the levels of porphobilinogen and d-amino-laevulinic acid in the urine and the presence or absence of symptoms. The excretion of the two compounds fluctuated considerably over time, sometimes with quite high levels in symptomless cases and sometimes with no marked increase in output during mild attacks.

The widespread belief that there is a necessary association between increased excretion and acute attacks therefore appears to be erroneous. It may have arisen because the chance production of coloured urine is quite often the first pointer to the diagnosis in patients who have suffered from unexplained symptoms for a considerable time. In any case a coloured urine should not necessarily be expected in acute attacks, since the colour depends on physical characteristics of the urine and does not reflect the levels of excretion.

Thus the finding of high levels in a patient with suggestive symptoms certainly indicates the presence of the metabolic disorder, but does not absolutely confirm that an attack is occurring. Caution is also required on account of the false positive results which can occur with certain febrile illnesses, in lead poisoning, and in patients receiving phenothiazine drugs (Reio and Wetterberg, 1969). The diagnosis of a mild attack presenting without classical signs and symptoms is therefore still a matter for clinical judgement, and complete reliance must not be placed on an isolated finding in the urine. Conversely a negative finding between attacks does not entirely rule out the possibility that the patient has the disease.

The more sensitive methods of paper chromatography can be used to identify carriers of the gene in whom penetrance is incomplete. Demonstrable abnormalities of porphyrin excretion are revealed, and this may be useful in genetic counselling.

The electroencephalogram often shows abnormalities during attacks, with slowing of dominant frequencies and an excess of intermediate slow activity. Sometimes, however, it remains entirely normal. Isolated records are therefore of little help in the diagnosis, but serial recordings can occasionally be useful in confirming the organic origin of symptoms in attacks of uncertain nature.

Differential Diagnosis

Porphyria is notorious for leading to mistakes in diagnosis, and patients are sometimes admitted repeatedly to psychiatric units before the condition is discovered.

An impression of functional psychiatric illness is reinforced by the patient's emotional instability during attacks, and the long history of intermittent physical complaints for which no cause has previously emerged. Diagnoses of personality disorder or severe neurosis are commonly made. Hysteria may be suspected when the patient complains of weakness of the limbs and varied aches and pains unbacked by physical signs. Psychotic developments may likewise obscure other aspects of the disorder and lead to a primary diagnosis of depressive illness or acute schizophrenia.

Other patients are admitted to general medical wards with suspected appendicitis on account of abdominal pain and vomiting. Intestinal obstruction may be diagnosed when there is severe constipation. Laparotomy therefore features in the history of many porphyric patients. Other cases may be mistaken for the acute ascending polyneuropathy of Guillain-Barré, or the combination of fits and hypertension may suggest hypertensive encephalopathy.

Treatment and Outcome

There is no specific treatment for the disorder. The chief aim must be prevention of attacks by educating the patient about the drugs which must be avoided. Total abstention from alcohol should be advised. Any infection which arises must be treated immediately.

The symptomatic treatment of the acute attack is described by Goldberg *et al.* (1983). Vomiting may be controlled with promazine, and pain with pethidine, dihydrocodeine or, if necessary, morphine. The drugs of choice for emotional disturbance are chlorpromazine, promazine or trifluoperazine. Epileptic seizures are treated with diazepam or chlormethiazole. Barbiturates must be avoided under all circumstances.

Electrolyte imbalance may need attention, especially lowering of the serum sodium and chloride in the face of persistent vomiting. It is known that inappropriate secretion of antidiuretic hormone is liable to accompany attacks. A careful watch must also be kept for threatened respiratory embarrassment. Tracheotomy and assisted respiration may occasionally be needed in the more severe attacks.

The majority of attacks subside completely without enduring defects. Some patients, however, are left severely crippled with weakness or muscular wasting, and some remain psychotic for long periods of time. Ultimately there is usually full physical and mental recovery.

Chapter 12. Vitamin Deficiencies

Severe chronic malnutrition is accompanied by well-known psychological changes—apathy, emotional lability, retardation, impairment of memory and sometimes acute psychotic illness. Such manifestations have been described in prisoners of war by Helweg-Larsen *et al.* (1952). During periods of famine interest becomes focused on food alone and cultural and social inhibitions are prone to disappear. In adults all such effects usually prove to be reversible when the deprivation is relieved. Infants and young children, by contrast, may show permanent sequelae. Winick (1976, 1979) reviews the evidence that early malnutrition can retard brain growth substantially with curtailment of cell division, myelination and the arborization of dendrites. All brain regions appear to be vulnerable. Enduring effects on intellectual development are probable, especially when the malnutrition has dated from the early months of life.

Under normal circumstances malnutrition of this degree is rarely encountered in Western societies. But even in populations where the general standard of nutrition is high there are persons prone to inadequate or imbalanced intake of food who may present with vitamin depletion. The mentally retarded and the chronically mentally sick often live precariously in the community and vitamin deficiencies may add to their symptomatology. The aged population is similarly at risk, especially when depression or early senile changes impair standards of self-care. Alcoholics face the multiple hazards of inadequate intake, poor absorption and special demands made on vitamin reserves for the metabolism of alcohol. These are all groups of persons who are particularly liable to come before psychiatric attention. Patients with chronic gastrointestinal disease and malabsorption are another group at risk, while any physical illness may deplete reserves. Profound deficiencies may be revealed post-operatively, especially in patients maintained for a considerable time on intravenous fluids.

Of all the vitamins it is the members of the B complex, and particularly thiamine and nicotinic acid, which have proved to be of most importance in psychiatric practice. Other deficiencies will often co-exist in chronic malnutrition, but specific roles for vitamins A, C and D have not been clearly identified in relation to mental disorder. Vitamin B_{12} and folic acid have been increasingly studied in relation to psychiatric illness and this evidence will also be reviewed.

Vitamin B Deficiency

Laboratory studies provide a firm basis for expecting functional and pathological changes in the central nervous system as a result of vitamin B deprivation. Many components of the B complex are known to play an essential role in metabolic processes within the brain: thiamine pyrophosphate is a co-enzyme involved in carbohydrate metabolism, particularly the oxidation of pyruvate, and may also be necessary for the proper transmission of nerve impulses; nicotinic acid and its amide act as constituent parts of co-enzymes which are necessary for glucose metabolism; riboflavine acts similarly; pantothenic acid is concerned with the formation of acetylcholine; and pyridoxine becomes converted into pyridoxal-phosphate which is a co-enzyme fundamental to several enzyme systems concerned in brain metabolic processes.

It was not until the 1930s that the full significance of vitamin B deficiency in relation to psychiatric disorder began to be appreciated, although mental disorder had been recognised as an integral part of the syndrome of pellagra from its earliest descriptions. In the 1930s, however, the various constituents of the B complex were identified, and careful observation soon extended awareness of their functions. Experimental studies showed that deprivation could lead to psychological symptoms well before definitive manifestations were declared in other systems of the body. Acute and severe depletion of vitamin reserves also proved to be responsible for fulminating neuropsychiatric disorders which had not previously been thought to be nutritional in origin.

The wide natural dispersion of the B vitamins has made it difficult to work out precise relationships in naturally occurring disorders, and multiple deficiencies will often operate together. Sometimes, however, the evidence linking specific deficiencies to specific clinical pictures has been clarified by noting the therapeutic response to vitamins given singly. Thiamine and nicotinic acid have emerged as the vitamins of greatest importance in neuro-psychiatric disorders, with others such as pyridoxine, pantothenic acid and riboflavine contributing mainly to ancillary symptoms. Moreover with both thiamine and nicotinic acid it is clear that different syndromes of deficiency can follow, depending on the severity of depletion and the time over which it has operated.

Thiamine deficiency classically leads to beriberi, with neuropathy, cardiac failure or peripheral oedema. This is the picture that results from chronic depletion of fairly severe degree. Over shorter time spans a neurasthenic picture may result, with fatigue, weakness and emotional disturbance, well before these physical features have been declared. Acute and fulminating depletion can lead instead to the picture of Wernicke's encephalopathy (p. 491), usually when overwhelming demands have been made on reserves which are already low. The changes in Wernicke's encephalopathy may be confined to the central nervous system, and other evidence of vitamin lack may be entirely absent.

Nicotinic acid deficiency shows a similar range of disorders. Subacute deficiency produces the syndrome of pellagra (p. 488) with gastrointestinal symptoms, skin lesions and psychiatric disturbance. In the early stages, however, a neurasthenic picture may be seen in relative isolation. Acute and sudden depletion may again lead to a picture of 'encephalopathy' (p. 489), often with little or nothing in other systems to provide the clue to vitamin deficiency.

Pyridoxine deficiency can lead to convulsions in infants, either in those on deficient diets or in those with unusually high requirements. Pronounced abnormalities appear in the electroencephalogram and mental deterioration may ensue. Both the symptoms and the electrical changes may resolve within minutes of injection of the vitamin. Experimental deficiency in adults, or the feeding of pyridoxine antagonists, has been found to lead to irritability, confusion and lethargy (Fabrykant, 1960). More recently, with the availability of sensitive and reliable assays, pyridoxine deficiency has been suspected of playing a part in contributing to depressive illness (Carney *et al.*, 1979, 1982). Among patients admitted to a psychiatric unit deficiencies of pyridoxine, and perhaps of riboflavine, have emerged in a higher proportion of those with affective disorder than with other psychiatric conditions.

Pyridoxine deficiency has also been incriminated as the mechanism leading to depression in patients taking oral contraceptives; in such a context pyridoxine replacement was shown to be effective in relieving the depression in a double-blind cross-over trial (Adams *et al.*, 1973).

Riboflavine deficiency produces glossitis, angular stomatitis, lachrymation and photophobia. In an experimental study of severe and specific riboflavine restriction in healthy volunteers, Sterner and Price (1973) found weakened hand grip on dynamometer tests after several weeks, and 'personality changes' as reflected in scores on the Minnesota Multiphasic Personality Inventory. Changes in hypochondriasis, depression and hysteria scores appeared to reflect increasing lethargy, hypersensitivity and a multitude of minor somatic complaints.

Pantothenic acid deficiency has been incriminated in leading to the 'burning feet syndrome'. However, as in the case of riboflavine, a role in naturally occurring neurological or psychiatric disorder has not yet been clearly established.

It is important to note that various aspects of vitamin B deficiency may prove to be commoner than expected among a wide range of psychiatric patients (Carney *et al.*, 1979, 1982). Among 172 successive admissions to a psychiatric unit, 30% were considered to be deficient in thiamine, 27% in riboflavine and 9% in pyridoxine as assessed by red cell enzyme functions (p. 488). More than half were deficient in at least one of the three, despite being drawn from a reasonably affluent community. Thiamine deficiency was mainly encountered in patients who could be expected to have neglected their diets—alcoholics, drug addicts, schizophrenics and depressives. Those with pyridoxine deficiency, by contrast, often showed little evidence of malnutrition, and as mentioned above there was a significant association with endogenous and neurotic depression. Controlled studies will be required to determine whether such vitamin deficiencies may sometimes play an aetiological role in the genesis of depressive disorder, or indeed in contributing more widely to psychiatric morbidity.

In clinical practice, thiamine deficiency can be investigated by means of the pyruvate tolerance test. The fasting pyruvate level may be raised or normal, but after glucose administration it rises excessively. However, the test is of limited value since pyruvate metabolism may be blocked in a number of other conditions—thyrotoxicosis, pyrexia, congestive cardiac failure, anoxia and various intoxications (Thompson, 1967). Whole blood thiamine estimations can be performed by microbiological methods, but the measurement of red cell transketolase is a simpler and perhaps more reliable procedure (Williams, 1976). Moreover, the red cell enzyme activity can be measured with and without the presence of added thiamine *in vitro,* providing an indication of the extent to which bodily stores have been chronically depleted. Equivalent assessments of other vitamin-dependent red cell enzymes can reveal riboflavine deficiency (glutathione reductase) or pyridoxine deficiency (aspartate aminotransferase).

Experimental Studies of Vitamin B Deficiency

Experimental subjects have been kept on diets deficient in B vitamins, with the object of determining the earliest clinical features of deprivation. The findings are in broad agreement from one study to another, particularly in emphasising the prominence of mental symptoms. Jolliffe *et al.* (1939) observed anorexia, lassitude, precordial pain, palpitations, dyspnoea and muscle cramps, but were unable to induce the neuritic symptoms of beriberi. Elsom *et al.* (1940) observed a marked psychological disturbance in one subject who became depressed and irritable, wept frequently without cause and withdrew from social contacts. Defective memory and difficulty with concentration were prominent complaints. This was considered to represent more than a simple reaction to physical malaise, and to reflect a true change in cerebral functioning. Riboflavine was without effect on the symptoms, thiamine caused partial improvement, but full relief was only obtained on giving yeast containing all components of the B complex. O'Shea *et al.* (1942) in a similar experiment found measurable cognitive impairment on Porteus Maze scores which was relieved by thiamine and by yeast.

Williams *et al.* (1940, 1943) carried out a series of experiments with a diet severely deficient in thiamine but considered to contain adequate amounts of other vitamins. After several weeks all subjects developed symptoms closely simulating neurasthenia—generalised weakness, depression, anorexia and insomnia. A few developed apathy, forgetfulness, and difficulty with thinking, while others reported giddiness, paraesthesiae and soreness of muscles. Physical activity was greatly decreased and capacity for work fell progressively. Less severe but more prolonged deficiency led to emotional instability with moodiness, quarrelsomeness, depression, and numerous somatic complaints.

The patients were made to serve as their own controls during periods with and without thiamine replacement, and a valid relationship between mental symptoms and thiamine deficiency was upheld.

Brozek and Caster (1957) confirmed such psychological effects by more precise dietary techniques for producing severe thiamine depletion. General weakness and extreme anorexia were associated with marked irritability and depression, and scores on the hysteria, hypochondriasis and depression scales of the Minnesota Multiphasic Personality Inventory deteriorated considerably. Continuation of the diet led ultimately to peripheral neuropathy. Tests of manual speed, coordination and reaction time were impaired, but general intelligence was unaffected. The reintroduction of thiamine restored appetite promptly and produced a dramatic change in the attitude of the subjects, but the peripheral neuropathy was slower to improve.

Kreisler *et al.*'s (1948) study appears to be unique in attempting to evaluate the effects of induced vitamin B deficiency in patients already mentally ill. This was a prolonged experiment with chronically hospitalised schizophrenic and demented patients. The observations were largely impressionistic, but indicated both aggravation of pre-existing psychotic disorder and the development of new mental changes. Moderate restriction over 1–2 years was associated with gradual diminution of activity, dulling of affect and loss of interests. Severe restriction sometimes led to the explosive onset of serious emotional disturbances with loss of inhibitory control, exaggeration of pre-existing hypomanic or depressive features, and the emergence of paranoid trends. Recovery on giving yeast extract containing the full range of B vitamins was said to be often dramatic and sudden. Clearly these interesting findings would require confirmation by properly controlled investigation, though the ethical problems raised would be considerable.

Mental Changes in Pellagra

Multiple vitamin deficiences are probably operative in pellagra, but nicotinic acid is by far the most important and this can rapidly relieve the symptoms. The characteristic triad includes gastrointestinal disorder, skin lesions and psychiatric disturbance. Skin changes include roughening and reddening of the dorsum of the hands and pigmentation over bony prominences. Stomatitis and glossitis are also often seen.

The prodromal features are similar to those encountered in experimental thiamine deficiency. General deterioration of mental and physical health may antedate more definite manifestations by weeks or months, and indeed pellagra was sometimes thought to be a neurotic disorder before its relationship to vitamin deficiency was discovered. Most prominent is a subjective feeling of incapacity for mental and physical effort, coupled with a multiplicity of other vague complaints—anorexia, insomnia, nervousness, apprehension, dizziness, headache, palpitations and paraesthesiae. Characteristically these fluctuate markedly from one day to the next. Irritability and emotional instability may dominate the picture. Depression can be severe with considerable risk of suicide. At a later stage the mental processes are obviously retarded, memory is faulty and confabulation appears.

Such changes are well known in areas where pellagra is endemic, and the patients themselves often recognise them as prodromes of the more florid manifestations of the disease. They are likely to be misconstrued, however, when sporadic cases arise. Spies *et al.* (1938) made careful observations on patients attending a pellagra clinic who had recurrences each spring over a number of years, and were able to confirm the prompt response of such 'neurotic' symptoms to nicotinic acid. Discontinuation of treatment without the patients' knowledge caused recurrence of the complaints. Thiamine by contrast helped peripheral neuritis when this was present, but not the subjective complaints and emotional disturbances.

Longer continued and more severe nicotinic acid deficiency leads to the florid psychiatric manifestations of pellagra. These sometimes develop without the above prodromata. They are often associated with gastrointestinal and skin changes but may nonetheless dominate the picture. The commonest is an acute organic reaction with disorientation, confusion and impairment of memory. Wild excitement and outbursts of violent behaviour may occur, depression is often conspicuous, or paranoia may develop with hallucinations and delusions of persecution. Occasionally chronic untreated pellagra may progress with a picture akin to Korsakoff's psychosis, or as a slowly increasing generalised dementia.

The acute psychotic pictures again respond to nicotinic acid, often in a dramatic fashion. Calm and rational behaviour may be restored within hours of vitamin replacement, or more commonly over the course of several days. It is very rare indeed for treatment to fail in acute cases, though with chronic mental disablement less success can be expected (Spies *et al.*, 1938; McLester, 1943).

The early symptoms of pellagra presumably depend on reversible biochemical changes within the neurones, but these can ultimately lead to structural changes. In established pellagra the pathognomonic finding is central chromatolysis ('retrograde cell degeneration') in the Betz cells of the motor cortex, usually also involving cells of the pontine, dorsal vagal, gracile and cuneate nuclei (Leigh, 1952). The nuclei of the affected neurones are displaced to the periphery and Nissl bodies disappear from the centres. Other brain stem neurones may be involved, likewise the anterior horn cells of the cord. The Purkinje cells of the cerebellum are by contrast spared. Degeneration of the posterior and lateral columns of the spinal cord is sometimes a prominent feature (Spillane, 1947).

Hartnup Disease

This rare inborn error of metabolism results in nicotinic acid deficiency despite a normal dietary intake. Pellagra-like features occur as episodic attacks during childhood, then tend to subside during adult life. Increased renal clearance of neutral amino acids, including tryptophan, is accompanied by defective absorption of tryptophan from the gut. The abnormal amino-aciduria is the most constant diagnostic feature; large amounts of indican also appear in the urine, derived from the metabolism of unabsorbed tryptophan by the intestinal flora (Watts, 1983).

Some cases are asymptomatic and discovered only on routine screening. Others present with a photosensitive skin rash, often accompanied by psychiatric disturbance, cerebellar ataxia or other neurological abnormalities. Oral nicotinamide helps substantially during attacks, though these tend to subside spontaneously.

Psychiatric features range from emotional lability in the milder cases to apathy, irritability, depression, confusion and delirium in the more marked examples (Hersov and Rodnight, 1960). The co-existent photosensitive skin rash is an important clue to the underlying biochemical abnormality.

Acute Nicotinic Acid Deficiency Encephalopathy

This syndrome gained recognition as a result of a

series of reports of patients who presented with various forms of acute organic reaction, and proved to show an excellent response to large doses of nicotinic acid (Cleckley et al., 1939; Jolliffe et al., 1940; Sydenstricker, 1943; and Gottlieb, 1944). Since that time it seems largely to have disappeared from the British and American literature, though there is evidence, discussed below, that examples are still quite frequent in countries where nicotinic acid is not given routinely as part of parenteral multi-vitamin therapy.

Nicotinic acid was initially tried quite empirically because some of the patients had shown glossitis, but other evidence of vitamin depletion was not invariably present. A great number were chronic alcoholics, and others were the elderly infirm who had been living alone on inadequate diets. A third important group were patients without a clear history of dietary deficiency, who developed the disorder in the course of acute physical illness or after surgical operations or delivery.

The picture was of stupor or delirium, often catastrophic in development and carrying a high mortality. Weakness and lethargy were common but anxiety and agitation could be marked. A noteworthy feature was the development of extrapyramidal disturbance, with cogwheel rigidity and often grasping and sucking reflexes. Glossitis or stomatitis were frequently but not invariably present. In some patients the neuropsychiatric picture was the sole manifestation.

Cleckley et al.'s (1939) patients all had a history of malnutrition. The majority were elderly and suffering from other organic diseases which might easily have been considered an adequate cause for the mental symptoms. More than half had advanced arterio-sclerosis. Nicotinic acid was found to produce a striking and dramatic improvement, and was felt to be life saving in many cases:

A man of 78 was admitted to hospital after several weeks of increasing weakness and lethargy. For 8 days he had been bedfast and stuporose. He was found to be mildly delirious with a slight pyrexia, and showed marked hypertension, advanced arteriosclerosis and right-sided heart failure. The tongue was dry, bright red and atrophic. A liquid high-vitamin diet with intravenous dextrose and digitalis had no effect on his mental state. Sodium nicotinate was commenced, 100 mg intravenously, and on the second day he became alert and attentive. By the fourth day the mental state had returned to normal and all signs of glossitis had disappeared. He remained well until he died of a cerebral haemorrhage three months later.

Jolliffe et al. (1940) were able to report 150 cases

from Bellevue Hospital, New York. All were alcoholics who had been admitted with severe impairment of consciousness or delirium. Half showed stomatitis or other evidence of a partial pellagrinous state. Some had evidence of scurvy, polyneuritis, or oculomotor disturbance as in Wernicke's encephalopathy but this was by no means invariable. Cogwheel rigidity of the limbs was a marked part of the picture in many cases. Thiamine was without effect, but nicotinic acid in large dosage produced recovery usually in 3–5 days. Mortality was drastically reduced by such treatment, from 90% to 14%. Those who survived could often be left with memory deficits. The syndrome was ascribed to a marked depletion of nicotinic acid, developing acutely in patients already partially depleted but before classical pellagrinous manifestations had become established.

Sydenstricker (1943) referred to analogous cases seen in general hospitals, often post-operatively or after delivery, or when fever and infection had suddenly imposed increased metabolic demands. Some had been suffering from gastrointestinal diseases and some had been maintained for several days on intravenous fluids. After a short period of confusion the patient developed acute delirium with excitement and hallucinations. The tongue was often dry and red, but there were sometimes no physical signs of vitamin deficiency whatever. The response to nicotinic acid or nicotinamide was again rapid. These cases were considered to represent the most severe and acute examples of nicotinic acid deficiency, when sudden metabolic demands had exhausted scanty reserves.

Gottlieb (1944) confirmed these findings and added further cases seen in alcoholics, in the elderly malnourished and post-operatively:

A woman of 56 was admitted in alcoholic coma and revived. Three days later she became confused, restless and irrational, and deteriorated over the next 3 days with noisy behaviour and gross disorientation. Apart from nystagmus there was no physical abnormality. Nicotinic acid produced dramatic improvement within 24 hours and she remained well thereafter.

A woman of 62 was admitted with confusion, disorientation and incontinence of urine. Her memory had been failing for 2 weeks. Her tongue had been sore for 10 days and the angles of her mouth had been cracked for some 3 months. There was no history of alcoholism but she had been neglecting her food since the death of her son one year earlier. She was given oral thiamine and nicotinic acid for 10 days without improvement, but then responded rapidly to nicotinic acid given intramuscularly.

A case reported by Slater (1942) is important because evidence of organic brain dysfunction was minimal:

A man of 52 was admitted with complaints of numbness in the legs but there was no evidence of peripheral neuritis on examination. In hospital he became acutely psychotic, believing he was to be punished for his sins and that there was a spirit under the counterpane. He showed flexibilitas cerea and echopraxia, and the picture simulated schizophrenia closely. He remained fully oriented and without intellectual impairment, but a clue to the organic nature of the psychosis was provided by marked perseveration and some dysarthria. He deteriorated physically, with abdominal distension, diarrhoea and the development of a raw red tongue. Dramatic improvement followed the administration of nicotinic acid and ascorbic acid, with resolution of the psychotic illness. Prior to the illness he had had a period of prolonged malnourishment on account of a gastroenterostomy and subsequent gastrectomy.

It is interesting that reports of the syndrome are now so rare. Its apparent demise in the United Kingdom and North America is possibly because nowadays high potency vitamin therapy almost invariably consists of multiple vitamin replacement (Lishman, 1981). This became established as a routine from the 1950s onwards. Parentrovite injections in the UK, and Solu-B or Bejectal in the USA, contain ample nicotinamide in addition to thiamine. In the treatment of alcoholics and other depleted patients the syndrome may therefore be concealed.

It appears, nonetheless, to be still evident in other countries. Kayatekin (1981) has observed 3 patients in Turkey with severe and prolonged confusion in the wake of delirium tremens which cleared promptly on giving nicotinic acid. Treatment with parenteral thiamine, riboflavine and pyridoxine had been without effect. And Ishii and Nishihara (1981) have produced clear evidence that the syndrome persists in Japan. They discovered the classical brain changes of pellagra in 20 of 74 necropsies on alcoholics. The condition had gone unsuspected during life, presumably because most of the patients lacked skin lesions indicative of pellagra:

These patients had presented in a surprisingly uniform fashion. They had been hospitalised with a diagnosis of delirium tremens, then went on to develop extrapyramidal rigidity, hyperreflexia, gait disturbance and double incontinence. Gastrointestinal symptoms appeared in the form of diarrhoea, constipation or vomiting. Progressive deterioration led to death within a few weeks or months. The mental accompaniments were variable, including confusion, hallucinations, delirium, anxiety, depression, excitement and neurasthenia. Several patients had polyneuropathy but only one had shown signs of Wernicke's encephalopathy. Glossitis was a fairly common feature. Treatment with thiamine, pyridoxine and vitamin B_{12} had been ineffective. Nicotinic acid or nicotinamide had not been given.

Ishii and Nishihara suggest that when an alcoholic patient develops neurological signs, particularly extrapyramidal rigidity, in addition to mental and gastrointestinal symptoms, nicotinic acid deficiency must be strongly suspected even in the absence of skin lesions. Gait disturbance, incontinence and hyperreflexia are further important features differentiating the syndrome from uncomplicated delirium tremens. In many cases it may be expected that thiamine deficiency will be operative in addition; however, only 2 of Ishii and Nishihara's 20 patients showed the pathology of Wernicke's encephalopathy in addition to that of pellagra.

Wernicke's Encephalopathy

Wernicke's encephalopathy represents the acute neuropsychiatric reaction to severe thiamine defiency. It may be defined as a disorder of acute onset characterised by nystagmus, abducens and conjugate gaze palsies, ataxia of gait, and a global confusional state, occurring together or in various combinations (Victor et al., 1971). Wernicke first described the condition in 1881 under the title of 'polioencephalitis haemorrhagica superior', reporting two cases in chronic alcoholics and one in a patient with persistent vomiting after sulphuric acid poisoning. Initially it was ascribed to an inflammatory process in the central nervous system, but abundant evidence has since accumulated to show the role of thiamine deficiency. Alexander (1940) was able to demonstrate lesions in the brains of thiamine deficient pigeons which were similar in distribution and type to those of Wernicke's encephalopathy, and Jolliffe et al. (1941) clearly established the efficacy of thiamine in relieving the ophthalmoplegias and improving clouding of consciousness in human subjects. Nicotinic acid, by contrast, failed to do so. The precise relationship of Wernicke's encephalopathy to alcoholism, to beriberi, and to Korsakoff's psychosis remained, however, to be clarified.

Wernicke's Encephalopathy and Alcoholism

Alcoholism is an important but not an exclusive cause of the disorder. It leads to thiamine deficiency by several routes—the replacement of vitamin containing foods by alcohol, impaired absorption of thiamine from the gut, impairment of its storage and utilisation by the liver, and excessive requirements for the metabolism of alcohol. But Wernicke's encephalopathy is known to occur in a number of other conditions all closely connected with thiamine deficiency. Campbell and Russell (1941) could find a definite history of alcoholism in only 5 of 21 cases, and Spillane (1947) listed the following additional causes in his review of the literature—carcinoma of the stomach, pregnancy, toxaemia, pernicious anaemia, vomiting, diarrhoea and dietary deficiency. Very occasionally the condition has developed in association with anorexia nervosa (Ebels, 1978; Handler and Perkin, 1982), and it has recently been reported after a self-imposed 'hunger strike' in a paranoid patient (Pentland and Mawdsley, 1982).

Rimalovski and Aronson (1966) reported a large autopsy series and found that unequivocal evidence of alcoholism had been recorded in only 50% of patients. In most of the remainder the cause appeared to be carcinoma, especially of the oesophagus, or widespread tuberculosis. Nevertheless in the largest series reported from the USA, Victor *et al.* (1971) found that all but 2 of their 245 cases were suffering from established alcoholism. They therefore still regarded Wernicke's encephalopathy as essentially a disease of alcoholics, at least in American urban society.

It seems possible, however, that not all alcoholics are equally at risk. Blass and Gibson (1977) propose that those who develop the disorder may have inherited an unusually vulnerable metabolism which has rendered them particularly sensitive to thiamine deficiency. This would explain the relative rarity of the syndrome despite the great number of persons at risk. Specifically Blass and Gibson produced evidence that in Wernicke patients the enzyme transketolase showed a reduced affinity for its cofactor thiamine pyrophosphate (TPP). This was demonstrated in fibroblasts which had passed through serial tissue cultures in a medium containing an excess of thiamine and no alcohol, suggesting the presence of an inherited abnormality rather than some consequence of the disease.

Wernicke's Encephalopathy and Beriberi

The relationship with beriberi proved more of an embarrassment, since the classical neuritic and cardiac forms of the disease seemed rarely to be associated with encephalopathy despite their dependence on thiamine deficiency. During the war,

however, experience in prisoner of war camps gave ample opportunity for observing relatively acute deficiency syndromes in large numbers of subjects. In epidemics of beriberi psychological changes were often found to be marked, with irritability, depression and disturbance of memory (Cruickshank, 1961). More particularly De Wardener and Lennox (1947) were able to report 52 typical cases of Wernicke's encephalopathy from a prisoner of war camp in Singapore, most of whom at the same time showed neuritic, cardiac or oedematous signs of beriberi. Their classical paper was based on records which spent two years of the war buried in a Siamese cemetery; it was entitled 'Cerebral Beriberi (Wernicke's Encephalopathy)', and effectively bridged the gap between the two conditions.

Response to thiamine was in general excellent in this series. Gross examination of the brains in fatal cases confirmed pathological changes in the distribution typical of Wernicke's encephalopathy. The authors proposed that the encephalopathy appeared when particularly acute and severe thiamine depletion was superimposed upon partial deficiency, whereas other forms of beriberi generally resulted from less severe and more prolonged lack of the vitamin. In almost all of their cases the encephalopathy had set in when some other factor, such as epidemic diarrhoea, had intensified the vitamin deficiency. The situation was thus analogous to that seen with nicotinic acid, where severe acute depletion produces profound evidence of cerebral dysfunction and more chronic deficiency leads to the orthodox syndrome of pellagra.

Wernicke's Encephalopathy and Korsakoff's Psychosis

The relationship between Wernicke's encephalopathy and Korsakoff's psychosis has also gradually been clarified. Korsakoff gave the first comprehensive account of the amnesic syndrome which bears his name in 1887, shortly after Wernicke's description of his syndrome, but the close relationship between the two was not appreciated at the time.

All of Korsakoff's cases had polyneuritis which led him to propose the name 'psychosis polyneuritica'. The great majority of cases were reported in alcoholics and the cause was thought to be some toxic effect of alcohol. Shortly thereafter cases were reported without alcoholism or neuropathy in patients suffering from puerperal sepsis, typhoid or intestinal obstruction. By the 1930s other known causes included gastric carcinoma, intractable vomiting and severe dietary deficiency. Thiamine deficiency therefore came under suspicion as the common metabolic link. Bowman *et al.* (1939) tried the effect of parenteral thiamine and reported encouraging results; disorientation and confabulation responded in many cases, but the memory defects were largely unaltered.

Meanwhile evidence accumulated to suggest a clinical link between Wernicke's encephalopathy and Korsakoff's psychosis. Features of the two disorders were sometimes seen together, and the former was noted often to lead on to the latter. De Wardener and Lennox's (1947) cases were again important here, showing clear evidence of memory defects in association with ataxia and ophthalmoplegias. The acuteness of their cases also allowed the memory defects to respond unequivocally to thiamine in many cases. The link between the two conditions was finally consolidated when the site of the cerebral lesions in Korsakoff's psychosis was clarified. Malamud and Skillicorn (1956) eventually provided clear evidence that in patients dying with Korsakoff's psychosis the location of cerebral pathology appeared to be identical with that seen in Wernicke's encephalopathy, the two merely differing in the acuteness or chronicity of the pathological process.

The amnesic syndrome can, of course, result from a variety of brain lesions which have nothing to do with thiamine deficiency, as outlined on p. 25. But where the nutritionally depleted subject is concerned, Wernicke's encephalopathy and Korsakoff's psychosis now appeared to be merely different facets of the same pathological process. In effect, Wernicke's encephalopathy emerged as the acute organic reaction of which Korsakoff's psychosis represented the residual and sometimes permanent defect. Confirmation came from the comprehensive clinico-pathological study of Victor *et al.* (1971) which they published under the composite title of 'The Wernicke–Korsakoff Syndrome'. Of 186 alcoholic patients who survived the acute illness and were observed for long enough to assess the development of amnesia, 84 per cent developed a typical Korsakoff psychosis. Other cerebral pathology may make additional contributions to the fully developed picture, as discussed on p. 497, but lesions in the Wernicke location appear to be fundamental to the amnesic deficits displayed. The possibility that a direct toxic action of alcohol on the nervous system may also contribute to Korsakoff's psychosis is considered on p. 497.

Clinical Features

Victor *et al.*'s (1971) observations on 245 patients form the basis for much of the description that follows.

Wernicke's encephalopathy typically declares itself abruptly, though sometimes it may be several days before the full picture is manifest. The commonest presenting features are mental confusion or staggering gait. The patient may also be aware of ocular abnormalities with complaints of wavering vision or diplopia on looking to the side. This well-known triad of confusion, ataxia and ophthalmoplegia confers a highly characteristic stamp to the syndrome when it appears in full, but all parts are not always seen together.

Other common features include prodromal anorexia, nausea and vomiting. A marked disorder of memory is frequently in evidence and has been insufficiently emphasised in most descriptions. Special attention has also been called to lethargy and hypotension which, in the presence of an acute organic mental syndrome, may indicate Wernicke's encephalopathy despite the absence of other definitive signs (Cravioto *et al.*, 1961).

The age range is evenly distributed throughout adult life, with males affected approximately twice as often as females. This ratio is considerably lower than for alcoholism generally and may be partly a reflection of differences in patterns of drinking. The pattern which leads to Wernicke's encephalopathy appears to be steady drinking extending over months or years and coupled with inadequate intake of food. In Victor *et al.*'s (1971) series delirium tremens had occurred at some time in the past in 40% of cases, withdrawal fits in 10% and liver disease in 10%, indicating the general severity of alcohol abuse.

On examination Victor *et al.* observed the following signs:

Ocular abnormalities were present in 96% of patients on initial examination. The commonest findings were nystagmus, sixth nerve palsies producing lateral rectus weakness, or some form of conjugate gaze paralysis. The pupils usually showed little more than sluggishness of reactions. Ocular signs can be remarkably evanescent, resolving speedily with treatment or even on feeding thiamine-containing foods. This no doubt accounts for the much lower incidence of ocular abnormalities reported in cases viewed retrospectively.

Ataxia was observed in 87% of patients who were testable, varying from inability to stand without support to minor difficulties with heel-toe walking. By contrast intention tremor in the legs or arms was relatively rare.

Peripheral neuropathy was present in 82% of cases and usually confined to the legs. In addition to objective signs there were often subjective complaints of weakness, paraesthesiae and pain.

Serious malnutrition was evident in 84%. Common signs were redness or papillary atrophy of the tongue, cheilosis, angular stomatitis, telangiectases, and dryness and discolouration of the skin. Two-thirds of the patients showed evidence of liver disorder and a quarter were bedridden when first seen. Overt signs of beriberi were rare but resting tachycardia and dyspnoea on effort were common.

An abstinence syndrome was found at inception in 13%, with epileptic fits, hallucinoses or delirium tremens.

Mental abnormalities were observed in 90% of patients, the rest presenting with ataxia and ophthalmoplegia but remaining lucid throughout. The commonest mental disturbance was a state of *quiet global confusion* with disorientation, apathy and derangement of memory. Many were drowsy, sometimes falling asleep in mid-sentence, and others showed marked indifference and inattention to their surroundings. Against the prevailing view, however, almost all were readily rousable and impairment of consciousness was rarely profound or persistent.

In the typical case spontaneous activity and speech were minimal, and remarks irrational and inconsistent. Grasp, awareness and responsiveness were markedly impaired. Misidentifications were extremely common and made without hesitation. Physical and mental fatiguability was pronounced, and concentration was difficult for the simplest task. By contrast a small proportion were alert, responsive and voluble, despite obvious confusion and defects of memory.

Evidence of *mild delirium* was sometimes seen, with perceptual distortions, hallucinations, insomnia, agitation and autonomic overactivity. In a small number this amounted to frank delirium tremens, but was always evanescent and usually not severe. Hallucinations were rare in the remainder. Loosely knit delusions appeared occasionally and sometimes persisted for weeks after the confusion had cleared.

Assessment of memory was often difficult, but *in testable cases a defect of memorising was discovered or else became evident as soon as the major confusion subsided.* It was often hard to determine the point at which confusion of thought receded and the memory defect became the most prominent abnormality, since the two usually blended imperceptibly in the course of the illness. The memory disorder could easily be overlooked; while confused the patients were often markedly evasive, and later covered their defects by spontaneous facile chatter. In a small number a typical Korsakoff memory defect was clearly evident from the outset, being the only mental abnormality accompanying the ocular and ataxic signs.

Confabulation was common early in the disorder but was not found in every case. In those who showed it, moreover, it could not be elicited on every occasion. The origin could often be traced to confusion of thought or perceptual disorder, and it was sometimes hard to separate confabulations from misidentifications and misinterpretations. As the global confusion receded, and the memory defects became clearly established, the confabulation could often be traced to translocations in time of genuine past experiences.

Features more particularly stressed by de Wardener and Lennox (1947) included *emotional abnormalities* which appeared in two-thirds of their prisoner of war patients. Typically these set in soon after the ocular abnormalities had become well established. Apprehension was the common early change, with anxious insomnia and fear of the dark. Later this gave way to apathy, and later still to depression with emotional lability. Occasional patients showed marked excitability. De Wardener and Lennox's cases also more frequently experienced hallucinations, and more frequently progressed to coma.

Investigations

Diffuse slowing was found on electroencephalography in half of the patients tested by Victor *et al.* (1971). Sometimes, however, the tracings were entirely normal in marked and classical examples of the syndrome.

The cerebrospinal fluid may be abnormal with a mild elevation of protein. The blood pyruvate level may be expected to be raised in the acute phase of the disease. Transketolase studies can be informative, as described on p. 488.

Course and Response to Treatment

The unique value of Victor *et al.*'s (1971) series is that a substantial proportion of the patients who survived the acute stage remained under close medical observation for many months or years thereafter. Altogether 17% died during the acute stage, a quarter were followed for at least 2 months, and more than half were followed for periods of 2–13 years. The long-term outcome was accordingly greatly clarified.

Sixth nerve palsies always recovered, often starting to resolve within hours though sometimes taking several days or weeks to disappear completely. Other ocular abnormalities responded similarly, with the exception of horizontal nystagmus which was a permanent residuum in two-thirds of the patients. Ataxia usually began to improve within the first week, but often took a month or two for maximum resolution. In a quarter of patients the ataxia showed no improvement whatever, and altogether more than half were left with permanent unsteadiness of some degree. Thus residual ataxia and nystagmus can sometimes be useful signs in pointing to the origin of an obscure chronic amnesic syndrome. Polyneuropathy improved only very slowly over several months, and diminution or absence of tendon reflexes was another common permanent sequel.

The global confusion always recovered in survivors, beginning usually within 2–3 weeks and clearing completely within 1–2 months. As the confusion receded the amnesic defects stood out more prominently. Of 186 patients followed for long enough to assess the presence or absence of Korsakoff's psychosis, 84% developed the typical amnesic syndrome. The few who escaped had all shown relatively brief acute illnesses and had lost their confusion within a week. In addition the authors drew attention to the small but important group who presented with Korsakoff's psychosis from first contact along with ocular and ataxic signs (some 16% of the total), and their further very small group of 9 cases (3·7%) who had apparently developed Korsakoff's psychosis without ophthalmoplegia or ataxia at any time.

Follow-up of the Korsakoff patients showed complete recovery in a quarter, partial recovery in half, and no improvement whatever in the remainder. Complete recovery was observed even in some very severe examples. The onset of recovery was commonly delayed for several weeks or months, and once started it sometimes continued for as long as 2 years.

In the chronic amnesic stage anterograde and retrograde amnesia were the dominant features, but continuing minor impairments of perceptual and cognitive function could usually be discerned by careful examination. The retrograde amnesia was often of several years duration, though with islands of preservation and without a sharply demarcated beginning. Confabulation was rarely encountered in the chronic stage. The patients were typically inert, apathetic and lacking in insight, though fully alert and responsive to their surroundings. They were mostly neglectful of appearance, and tended to spend their days in complete idleness. A very few were gregarious or overtalkative. Most were placid, bland and detached in attitude, and emotional reactions were hard to arouse. Sustained anxiety or depression were rare, though brief periods of anger or irritability might be seen from time to time.

Pathology

The pathological changes are remarkable for their predilection for certain circumscribed parts of the brain. Symmetrical lesions are found predominantly in the neighbourhood of the walls of the third ventricle, the periaqueductal region, the floor of the fourth ventricle, certain thalamic nuclei (including especially the paraventricular parts of the medial dorsal nuclei, the anteromedial nuclei, and the pulvinar), the mamillary bodies, the terminal portions of the fornices, the brain stem, and the anterior lobe and superior vermis of the cerebellum. By contrast, obvious lesions are rarely seen in the cerebral cortex, corpus striatum, subthalamic and septal regions, cingulate gyri or hippocampal areas. Victor *et al.* (1971), however, found that convolutional atrophy was conspicuous enough to be remarked upon in 27% of their cases who came to autopsy.

Microscopically the lesions tend to involve all neural elements—neurones, axis cylinders, blood vessels and glia—but with variability from case to case and from one location to another. In general myelinated fibres tend to be affected more severely than the neurones themselves. Astrocytic and histiocytic proliferation is found in the areas of parenchymal loss. Proliferation of blood vessels and petechial haemorrhages may occur, but the latter may often represent terminal events.

The distribution of lesions is virtually identical in patients dying in the acute stages of Wernicke's encephalopathy and in patients who have shown chronic Korsakoff's psychosis, differing only in the chronicity of the glial and vascular reactions.

In seeking a correlation between symptoms and lesions, Victor *et al.* (1971) suggest that the ophthalmoplegias result from lesions in the 3rd and 6th cranial nerve nuclei and adjacent tegmentum, nystagmus from lesions of the vestibular nuclei, and ataxia from lesions of the vestibular nuclei and the anterior lobes and vermis of the cerebellum. Amnesia in their material appeared to be particularly closely associated with lesions in the medial dorsal nuclei and pulvinar of the thalamus; mamillary lesions which have traditionally been regarded as crucial for the development of amnesia were less constant (Victor, 1964; Victor *et al.*, 1971)

'Subclinical Wernicke's Encephalopathy'

The foregoing description applies to patients who have come dramatically to medical attention on account of an acute, often fulminating disorder. It seems probable, however, that milder variants may exist, or indeed that damage may sometimes develop surreptitiously in the Wernicke location without clear clinical indicators of the process (Lishman, 1981). The evidence is somewhat indirect but the pointers towards it deserve consideration.

Thus Cravioto *et al.* (1961) and Grunnet (1969) found patients with the classical lesion at autopsy who had died without exhibiting Wernicke's classical signs. Comparison of patients dying in the 1930s and 1960s suggested that the clinical presentations had become less severe, perhaps as a result of the wider availability and prescription of vitamins. The lesions at autopsy tended to be more circumscribed in the recent cases, and more often subacute or chronic in nature. Most significant of all, the condition could remain undiagnosed prior to death.

This last point has been strongly reinforced by Harper (1979, 1983). Over the course of 9 years in Perth, Australia, 131 cases of Wernicke's encephalopathy were diagnosed at autopsy, representing almost 3% of all brains examined in the hospital or referred by the city coroner. Only 26 of these 131 cases had been suspected during life, despite the fact that most had been examined in teaching hospitals. The great majority of affected persons were known to be alcoholics, and several had died suddenly and unexpectedly. A considerable range was encountered in the acuteness or chronicity of the lesions, with the not uncommon conjunction of acute histological changes superimposed on chronic pathology within the same brain regions. Two-thirds showed chronic pathological changes alone.

Some alcoholics may therefore harbour covert, undiagnosed pathology of the Wernicke type over a considerable period of time. Whether this evolves insidiously or in step-wise fashion is unknown. It may sometimes represent the cumulative effects of repeated minor episodes of Wernicke's encephalopathy which have largely gone unnoticed at the time.

In favour of the idea is the noted resistance to treatment of many alcoholic Korsakoff states, even when thiamine is administered from the earliest stages. This contrasts with the gratifying responses observed, for example, in De Wardener and Lennox's (1947) nutritionally depleted prisoners of war. The alcoholics appear often to have acquired an entrenched structural pathology which may well have been evolving for some time. Those cases in which Korsakoff's psychosis develops insidiously, without an obvious Wernicke episode (pp. 497–8), could equally be explained on such a basis. Finally, one might argue that a lesion dependent on biochemical changes secondary to vitamin deficiency is rather unlikely to obey an 'all or none' law, especially when the vitamin depletion has been operative for many years; that the lesion should either declare itself totally or fail to develop entirely would seem to be unlikely.

The issue is of potential therapeutic importance. If a substantial number of alcoholics develop a thiamine-dependent pathology well before it is clinically apparent, high potency vitamin therapy should find wider prophylactic application. The feasibility and desirability of routinely supplementing alcoholic beverages with thiamine has indeed received consideration (Centerwall and Criqui, 1978; Weinstein, 1978; Finlay-Jones, 1986). The identification of persons at special genetic risk (p. 492) could also prove important. These, however, are matters to be clarified by future research.

Treatment

Wernicke's encephalopathy represents an acute medical emergency and warrants energetic treatment from the moment the diagnosis is made. Doses of thiamine as small as 2–3 mg can modify the ophthalmoplegias, but much larger doses are indicated to minimise the chance of disabling sequelae, particularly since associated hepatic disorder may interfere with utilisation of the vitamin. 50 mg of thiamine hydrochloride should be given intravenously (after taking blood for pyruvate or transketolase estimation if the diagnosis is in doubt), and this should be accompanied by at least an equal amount intramuscularly. Intramuscular injections should be continued daily until a normal diet is resumed. In view of the possibility of other concurrent vitamin deficiencies, 'parentrovite' is often employed intravenously or intramuscularly in place of thiamine alone. Each injection of the 'high potency' preparation contains thiamine hydrochloride 250 mg, nicotinamide 160 mg, riboflavine 4 mg, pyridoxine hydrochloride 50 mg and ascorbic acid 500 mg. In the occasional patient who seems refractory to thiamine replacement, determination of the serum magnesium level may be indicated. Traviesa (1974) showed that hypomagnesaemia impaired both the biochemical and clinical response to treatment.

Other aspects of management must include attention to infection, dehydration, or electrolyte imbalance as a result of vomiting. Strict bed rest is mandatory in the acute stages, since sudden collapse and death can occur due to abrupt cardiac decompensation. Signs of congestive cardiac failure call for rapid digitalisation. Disturbed behaviour, and particularly that due to coincident delirium tremens, will require appropriate sedation (p. 517).

Oral vitamin supplements are usually continued for several weeks after the acute illness has resolved, though the value of this is uncertain. In patients with enduring ataxia, polyneuritis or memory disturbance, high potency vitamin injections should be pursued energetically as long as improvement is occurring.

KORSAKOFF'S PSYCHOSIS

The emergence of Korsakoff's psychosis as an often permanent aftermath of Wernicke's encephalopathy has been outlined above. The clinical picture and the neuropathological basis for the amnesic defects are described in Chapter 2 (pp. 28 to 30, and p. 25). Here, certain more recent considerations with regard to the pathogenesis and the nosology of the syndrome remain to be discussed.

First, it has become evident that the classical 'Wernicke' lesion at the base of the brain is often associated with more widespread cerebral pathology, including cortical shrinkage and ventricular dilatation. The contribution which this may make to certain aspects of the clinical picture warrants careful appraisal. Second, the rarity of a fully-fledged Korsakoff syndrome as a residue of thiamine deficiency in non-alcoholics raises the possibility that a direct neurotoxic action of alcohol may play some part in the evolution of the condition. Finally, there is evidence that Korsakoff's psychosis may be misdiagnosed to a considerable extent in clinical practice, and that an overlap with alcoholic dementia may be more widespread than is often appreciated.

Cortical Pathology in Korsakoff's Psychosis

Cortical pathology was widely described in the earlier literature before the diencephalic basal brain lesion came to be fully appreciated (Lishman, 1981).

Thereafter interest in cortical aspects showed a pronounced decline. It is noteworthy, however, that CT scan studies now re-emphasise that supratentroail atrophy is common (Cala and Mastaglia, 1980; Carlen *et al.*, 1981). On present evidence it is hard to judge whether this is greater in degree than in non-Korsakoff chronic alcoholics (see p. 519), but Carlen *et al.* (1981) considered that their Wernicke–Korsakoff group had developed sulcal atrophy and ventricular enlargement at a younger age than the remainder. At autopsy Victor *et al.* (1971) noted convolutional atrophy in a quarter of cases; Harper (1983) found ventricular dilatation and cortical atrophy in 34 per cent, the latter most commonly involving the frontal lobes.

A substantial cortical component to the pathology could be relevant to some of the striking clinical features of the syndrome, in particular the apathy, lack of initiative and profound lack of insight which the majority of patients display. As discussed on p. 30, such features are not inevitable concomitants of severe memory disorder, and can be entirely absent in amnesic syndromes of other aetiologies. It could be, moreover, that certain aspects of the memory disorder itself are influenced by the presence of cortical pathology: Butters (1984) reviews the evidence that frontal lobe damage may confer such matters as impairment of temporal recency judgements and failure to release from proactive interference on memory testing.

Neurotoxic Action of Alcohol

A role for the direct toxic action of alcohol in leading to Korsakoff's psychosis has been raised from time to time. It could be relevant to the aspects discussed just above, since a good deal of evidence points to alcohol neurotoxicity where cortical changes are concerned (p. 521). A more difficult question is how far thiamine deficiency alone can account for the chronic amnesic deficits which constitute the core feature of the syndrome. Certainly thiamine replacement is not regularly effective in reversing the memory difficulties; and as Freund (1973) points out there is a remarkable lack of evidence that permanent memory disorder can follow thiamine deficiency unaccompanied by alcohol abuse.

The inevitability of the link between Wernicke's encephalopathy and Korsakoff's psychosis may also be challenged on the basis of clinical experience. In many Korsakoff patients there is evidence of a pre-existing Wernicke's encephalopathy, as reported by Victor *et al.* (1971), but in others no such history is forthcoming. Some patients appear to develop their amnesic difficulties insidiously, in the context of chronic continuing inebriation. Such patients would be under-represented in Victor *et al.*'s sample, since most of their patients were incepted as cases of Wernicke's encephalopathy then followed through to the Korsakovian development.

Thus while the relationship between thiamine deficiency and Wernicke's encephalopathy cannot be doubted, there is less clear-cut evidence to incriminate thiamine lack in the chronic Korsakoff state. Alcohol neurotoxicity can vie with avitaminosis as a possible cause; or a conjunction of the two together may be necessary for the development of the fully fledged syndrome. An alternative explanation would be to view the amnesic difficulties as firmly linked to thiamine deficiency, but accepting that in alcoholics this may often have been operative over a considerable period of time. In other words alcoholism may tend to be associated with a 'subclinical' Wernicke pathology which, by the time it becomes overt, has led to fixed and irreversible structural changes (p. 496).

The Continuity Hypothesis

It is interesting in this connection that certain continuities are now being discerned between the memory deficits seen in Korsakoff's psychosis and those found in chronic alcoholics generally. Ryback (1971) was the first to point out that such were likely to exist. Butters and co-workers have reported detailed comparisons between alcoholic Korsakoff patients and groups of abstinent non-Korsakoff alcoholics on a wide range of memory tests (Ryan and Butters, 1980; Butters and Cermak, 1980). The non-Korsakoff alcoholics were divided into those with and without complaints of memory impairment. On standard memory tests (such as the Wechsler Memory Scale or the Benton Visual Retention Test) only those alcoholics who reported memory difficulties were impaired, overlapping in scores with the Korsakoff patients; the remainder performed well and were indistinguishable from controls. But on more demanding experimental memory tests (paired associate learning tests and the Brown–Peterson test), even the alcoholics who had no memory complaints were also significantly impaired.

Subtle but definite 'subclinical' memory deficits thus appear to be widespread in the alcoholic population, and these become more pronounced in alcoholics who complain of memory difficulties. In the latter the severity of the deficits can overlap in some degree with those seen in Korsakoff's psychosis. Either alcohol neurotoxicity or 'subclinical' thiamine deficiency could be the common link. Nevertheless there remain clear-cut differences between the Korsakoff and non-Korsakoff patients—the latter are aware of their memory deficits, make efforts to compensate for them, are not disoriented, and show little by way of a retrograde memory gap.

Diagnosis

For the diagnosis of Korsakoff's psychosis one should require clear evidence of a marked memory disorder along with good preservation of other cognitive functions. Subtle deficits will often be revealed by special testing as outlined on p. 30, particularly with regard to visuoperceptive functions and abstracting ability, but performance on standard intelligence tests should be substantially intact. This was well illustrated by Butters and Cermak's (1980) comparison of intelligence test scores (Wechsler Adult Intelligence Scale) in a group of Korsakoff patients and a group of intact normal controls. The latter were carefully matched for age, socioeconomic class and educational background. With the sole exception of the digit-symbol subtest, no significant differences could be discerned in any aspect of test performance. In measures such as the Wechsler Memory Scale, by contrast, Korsakoff patients can generally be expected to score some 20–30 points below the expectation derived from their IQs.

In clinical practice, however, such careful distinctions are not always observed. In a retrospective survey of 63 alcoholic patients admitted to the Maudsley Hospital, Cutting (1978b) found that 50 had been labelled as Korsakoff's psychosis and 13 as alcoholic dementia. The Korsakoff patients proved, however, to be heterogeneous. Those with a relatively acute onset were predominantly male, had an isolated memory deficit as expected, and showed a gloomy prognosis as judged by capacity to resume independent existence. In these respects they mirrored the classical syndrome. Seventeen of the 50, however, seemed closer in clinical picture to the alcoholic dements. Their symptoms had been several months in evolution, females predominated over males, they tended to be older, and some two-thirds were capable of improvement on follow-up. Psychological test profiles showed that the gradual onset group, like the alcoholic dements, were impaired across a wide range of cognitive functions in addition to their memory problems. It would therefore seem that Korsakoff's psychosis is quite commonly diagnosed when a label of 'alcoholic dementia' or 'reversible alcoholic cognitive deterioration' (p. 518) would have been appropriate. It is possible, furthermore, that continuities may exist between the two conditions.

Treatment

In the established chronic Korsakoff state treatment will often prove to be disappointing. Cutting (1978b) reviews the differing reports in the literature, some finding no patients whatsoever with a significant response to thiamine and others obtaining improvement in up to 70%. The results in Victor et al.'s (1971) large series are described on pp. 494–5. The possibility of occasional substantial improvement means, nevertheless, that high dosage thiamine replacement must always be attempted, by the parenteral route, and must be pursued over many months if benefit continues to be observed.

More recently McEntee and Mair (1980) have reported benefit in a double-blind trial of clonidine, a specific alpha noradrenergic agonist. A small but statistically significant improvement was obtained on measures of memory functioning in a group of chronic Korsakoff patients. This accords with the demonstration that the primary metabolite of noradrenaline (3-methoxy 4-hydroxy phenylglycol, MHPG) is substantially reduced in the cerebrospinal fluid of Korsakoff patients, the degree of lowering showing a significant correlation with the severity of memory impairment (McEntee and Mair, 1978; McEntee et al., 1984). The cerebrospinal fluid metabolites of dopamine and 5-hydroxytryptamine were also found to be reduced in comparison to controls, but less impressively so. The distribution of the lesions in the diencephalon and brain stem stands to disrupt the pathways of monoamine containing neurones, so these biochemical findings could reflect an important component in the genesis of the memory failure. Others, however, have failed to confirm any lowering of MHPG (Martin et al., 1984), and the situation remains in need of further investigation.

The occasional report that inhalation of vasopressin helps the Korsakoff memory impairment (Le Boeuf et al., 1978) likewise needs confirmation. This may well be a non-specific effect, since vasopressin has also been found to improve attention, concentration and memory in non-brain-damaged healthy volunteers (Legros et al., 1978). Gash and Thomas (1983) suggest indeed that vasopressin may primarily affect arousal and motivation rather than memory processes per se.

Other Nutritional Disorders Associated with Alcoholism

The syndrome of Wernicke's encephalopathy can be confidently ascribed to thiamine deficiency. Other disorders in alcoholics are suspected of being nutritional in origin though the evidence is less complete. Of those considered below peripheral neuropathy is almost certainly due in part to vitamin deficiency, but here and in the others a direct toxic effect of alcohol may also be responsible. The question of 'alcoholic dementia' raises special issues, so far unresolved, and is considered on p. 517 in Chapter 13.

Peripheral Neuropathy

Alcoholic peripheral neuropathy may sometimes be symptomless and manifest only by loss of the ankle jerks, but in most cases there are prominent complaints of sensory disturbance. It begins usually in the feet with numbness, pins and needles, burning sensations and pain. Weakness may progress ultimately to foot drop and a high stepping gait, with wasting of the leg muscles and absent knee and ankle reflexes. Cutaneous sensory loss is most marked peripherally in the hands and feet, and intense hyperaesthesia may be elicited on stroking the skin. The calf muscles are often very tender. Oedema of dependent parts may develop along with dystrophic changes of the skin and nails.

The condition often accompanies Wernicke's encephalopathy or Korsakoff's psychosis, and some 50% of patients with neuropathy show residua of these disorders. It may also present as an isolated abnormality, or in association with delirium tremens. The main cause appears to be deficiency of thiamine, though other deficiencies may be important as well (Fennelly et al., 1964). Pyridoxine and pantothenic acid deficiency can produce neuropathy and are likely to be involved in some alcoholics. A toxic role for alcohol itself, or other toxic substances in the alcoholic beverages, has been proposed, but slow recovery is usual with vitamin therapy even though drinking continues.

Cerebellar Degeneration

Victor et al. (1959) have described a remarkably uniform cerebellar syndrome in alcoholics, with ataxia of stance and gait as the principal abnormalities. The arms are little affected, and nystagmus and dysarthria may be absent. The typical course is gradual evolution over several weeks or months after which the disorder remains static for many years. More rarely slow progression occurs over a number of years. The resemblance to cerebellar degeneration seen with bronchial carcinoma can sometimes be close (p. 634), and a chest X-ray is obviously important in every case.

Pathological changes are largely restricted to the anterior and superior aspects of the vermis and cerebellar hemispheres. The cell loss affects the Purkinje cells especially. Victor *et al.* (1971) suggest that the ataxia of Wernicke's encephalopathy, at least in its chronic form, is based on a similar type of lesion. They therefore favour a nutritional cause, rather than a direct toxic effect of alcohol.

A similar cerebellar syndrome was reported by Skillicorn (1955) in alcoholics, with gross cerebellar atrophy demonstrable on air encephalography. Skillicorn's cases sometimes showed evidence of intellectual deterioration, and diffuse cerebral atrophy was found in addition to the cerebellar lesion.

Amblyopia

In rare cases retrobulbar neuritis may develop in alcoholics, progressing over one or two weeks but rarely extending to complete blindness. Dimness of central vision, especially for red and green, is the more common result. An associated peripheral neuropathy is usual. The smoking of strong pipe tobacco is often incriminated in addition to the alcoholism, and deficiencies of both thiamine and vitamin B_{12} appear to be responsible. Acute blindness is more commonly seen as a result of methyl alcohol consumption, and is then attributed to the direct toxic effects of the poison.

Marchiafava-Bignami Disease

This rare disorder was formerly thought to be restricted to Italian males but this is now known to be erroneous, likewise the belief that it was especially related to the drinking of wine. It presents with ataxia, dysarthria, epilepsy and severe impairment of consciousness, or in more slowly progressive forms with dementia and spastic paralysis of the limbs. Delmas-Marsalet *et al.* (1967) have reviewed the literature and presented cases with full neuro-pathological examination. Extensive demyelination

affects the corpus callosum, the optic tracts and the cerebellar peduncles. A nutritional origin is suggested by the symmetry and constancy of location of the lesions within the central nervous system, and the frequent history of dietary deprivation. The precise factors involved remain uncertain.

Central Pontine Myelinosis

This is an acute fatal complication of alcoholism, with pseudobulbar palsy, quadriplegia and loss of pain sensation in the limbs and trunk. Vomiting, confusion and coma are common accompaniments. The lesion consists essentially of demyelination involving the pyramidal tracts within the pons. A nutritional origin is again strongly suspected (Cole *et al.*, 1964) but no treatment is known to be effective.

Subacute Necrotizing Encephalomyelopathy ('Leigh's Disease')

The detailed pathogenesis of this rare disorder is still uncertain but some form of disturbance of thiamine metabolism is clearly implicated. It is inherited as an autosomal recessive. Leigh (1951) first described the condition in a 7-month-old infant who died after a rapidly progressive neurological disorder. At autopsy the pathology in the brain showed remarkable similarities to that of Wernicke's encephalopathy, both in form and location.

Many cases have since been reported, as reviewed by Monpetit *et al.* (1971) and Pincus (1972). Most have occurred in the first two years of life, though later childhood onset is occasionally seen. The picture is of progressive psychomotor retardation with feeding difficulties, respiratory disorder, hypotonia and weakness, leading to death usually within 4 years and often within a year. Neurological features are usually marked with oculomotor deficits, loss of vision, ataxia, cortico-spinal tract signs, seizures and movement disorders. The extreme variability of the picture makes diagnosis during life difficult unless the pathology has already been demonstrated in a sibling.

More recently several autopsy-proven cases have been reported in adults, as reviewed by Plaitakis *et al.* (1980). Their own patient showed the insidious development of strabismus, visual loss, a broad-based gait and impairment of intellect from early schooldays onwards, but remained active till he was

20. Thereafter he pursued a rapidly downhill course with death after a period of stupor.

A review of the large pedigree associated with this patient showed that several family members were affected and to a markedly variable degree. Mental retardation was commoner than specific neurological manifestations; some patients showed severe neurological affliction, others only subtle deficits. The onset could be abrupt or insidious, and in some cases the course was chronic and remittant. Plaitakis et al. suggest that the genetic defect has variable degrees of expression, resulting in a wide spectrum of disorder. Mild examples would stand to be missed at autopsy.

The site of the pathology in the classical Wernicke location suggests that thiamine metabolism may be at fault. Moreover a factor can be demonstrated in the blood and urine which inhibits the enzymatic synthesis of thiamine triphosphate. Its presence in the urine has been used as a diagnostic test, though false positives and negatives occur. There has been some suggestion that treatment with very large doses of thiamine and thiamine propyldisulphide can help to induce remissions, though without altering the overall course (Pincus et al., 1971). The tendency for onset or worsening to follow in the wake of metabolic stresses, such as infection, diarrhoea or vomiting, may reflect their tendency to compromise thiamine metabolism further.

Vitamin B_{12} Deficiency

Pernicious anaemia may be accompanied not only by the neurological complication of subacute combined degeneration of the cord, but also by mental abnormalities. Depression or anergia may be the earliest manifestation of the anaemia, and apathy and somnolence may be marked when anaemia is severe. In addition a number of other psychiatric disturbances have from time to time been attributed directly to the B_{12} deficiency—affective disorder, schizophrenia, paranoid states, episodes of disorientation and delirium, and progressive dementia. Interest was renewed in these phenomena by Holmes (1956) and Smith (1960) who reported several patients in whom mental symptoms apparently responded dramatically to B_{12} replacement. Moreover the mental manifestations had sometimes antedated the first signs of anaemia or cord disease by many months or years.

This is clearly an important subject for careful evaluation. If covert B_{12} deficiency can truly be responsible for mental disturbance, it will be impor-

tant to identify and treat it at the earliest opportunity before irreversible structural changes occur in the brain. Unfortunately it has proved difficult to establish firmly whether causal relationships exist and how widely they may apply, and the field remains controversial.

Surveys of psychiatric populations have often shown a very high incidence of patients with low serum B_{12} levels. Edwin et al. (1965) found that 15% of a large group of patients had values below 150 pg/ml and 6% below 100 pg/ml. Both organic and nonorganic types of mental illness featured among the patients with low values, and few had pernicious anaemia on examination of the blood. Carney and Sheffield (1970) found a similar incidence of low values among new psychiatric admissions. Shulman (1967a) found that 12% of new admissions to a psychogeriatric unit had values below 150 pg/ml, compared to 5% of elderly non-psychiatric patients assessed by the same laboratory. By contrast, however, Henderson et al. (1966) screened 1000 unselected psychiatric patients and found low B_{12} levels in only nine individuals, which is probably no higher than in the general population.

An additional difficulty is that the low B_{12}s which are discovered may sometimes be the consequence rather than the cause of the abnormal mental state, since B_{12} deficiency can result from inadequate nutrition. The daily requirements of B_{12} are small, and it would normally take many years before simple dietary lack became manifest in this way; but as Shulman points out a low serum iron or folic acid can contribute to lowering of the serum B_{12}, hence the latter may sometimes result from a mixed nutritional deficiency in depressed or demented patients who have neglected their diet.

In an attempt to resolve the problem, Zucker et al. (1981) have reviewed numerous case reports in the literature, using strictly defined criteria before accepting a causal link between B_{12} deficiency and psychiatric disturbance. As a result they found 15 patients where the relationship seemed well established. Among their requirements were the absence of other organic causes for the mental symptoms, a non-relapsing course, poor response to other treatments, and a positive and well maintained response to B_{12} administration. Criteria for the diagnosis of B_{12} deficiency were also specified with care. The psychiatric pictures in the patients so identified were heterogenous, though with a preponderance of organic mental symptoms, depression, paranoia, irritability and episodes of assaultive behaviour. Marked psychiatric disorder could sometimes occur in the absence of neurological abnormalities or anaemia. Zucker *et al.* concluded in particular that the combination of psychotic depression with organic mental symptoms should lead to screening tests for B_{12} deficiency.

Functional Psychiatric Disorders

Where affective disorders and schizophrenia are concerned there is a lack of critical evidence, other than that just cited, to support a causal relationship with B_{12} deficiency. Little has been done by way of controlled investigations. Minor mood disorder in association with pernicious anaemia may represent no more than a reaction to the non-specific effects of the physical disease. In cases of schizophrenia, severe affective disorder or paranoia, there may sometimes be no more than precipitation in the predisposed individual, or mere coincidence, or a secondary nutritional origin as outlined above. In many cases vitamin B_{12} has been administered along with other treatments so that its effectiveness in therapy is hard to determine.

Shulman (1967b) found four cases of affective disorder with low B_{12}s among his geriatric admissions, but all had shown considerable improvement with other forms of treatment before the results of the B_{12} estimations were known. In a separate study (Shulman, 1967c) a group of patients with pernicious anaemia was compared with a group suffering from other forms of anaemia after matching for age, sex and haemoglobin level. The overall incidence of psychiatric symptoms was similar in each, and several patients from both groups had had an initial psychiatric referral on account of symptoms which were regarded as neurotic in origin. Depression was sometimes marked, but showed no clear relationship to B_{12} lack; it often resolved before the first injection had been given, i.e. as soon as the patient was told the diagnosis and reassured about prognosis. In a retrospective survey such improvements might well have been attributed to replacement therapy. Nevertheless it was interesting that almost half of the patients with pernicious anaemia reported an increased sense of well-being when re-examined after treatment, whereas this was rare in patients with other forms of anaemia.

Organic Psychiatric Disorders

There is more convincing evidence that B_{12} lack is related to organic psychiatric symptoms. In Shulman's (1967c) prospective study approximately threequarters of the patients with pernicious anaemia showed objective impairment of memory on a simple learning test. On re-testing after treatment the majority had returned to normal, sometimes within 20 hours of the first injection.

Edwin *et al.* (1965) reviewed the evidence and concluded that low serum B_{12}s were more commonly found in elderly demented patients than in controls of similar age. Occasional patients with presenile dementia and low serum B_{12} have been reported to improve with replacement therapy (Henderson *et al.*, 1966; Hunter *et al.*, 1967a), though many failures are also recorded (Edwin *et al.*, 1965; Shulman, 1967b). Too much would not of course be expected of treatment when the dementia was of very long standing, even if B_{12} deficiency were the initial responsible cause. More short-lived disturbances should prove reversible, however, and an interesting example has been reported by Strachan and Henderson (1965):

A housewife of 60 was admitted with a provisional diagnosis of presenile dementia or stuporose depression. For four months she had complained of generalised weakness and vague epigastric discomfort, and had shown purposeless chewing and spitting movements. In recent weeks she had become distant and confused. On examination she lay silent in bed, was disoriented in all spheres, incontinent of urine and faeces, and able to obey only simple commands. There were no abnormal signs in the central nervous system, but the electroencephalogram was abnormal with diffuse theta and right centroparietal delta waves. The blood and cerebrospinal fluid were normal. On this occasion she improved spontaneously over the course of three weeks and returned to normal.

Five years later she was readmitted with a similar picture of one week's duration, and the electroencephalogram was even more abnormal with replacement of alpha rhythm by high voltage theta and delta waves. This time a low serum B_{12} of 64 pg/ml was discovered, along with a histamine fast achlorhydria but a normal blood and bone marrow. She again improved spontaneously and was discharged before the B_{12} result was known. On recall to the hospital she was now oriented, but her relatives noted that her memory remained poor and that she was lacking in interest in her home and pastimes. The electroencephalogram remained abnormal. Vitamin B_{12} produced gradual improvement with return of her normal energy, memory and interests, and this was paralleled by steady improvement in the EEG picture.

There is abundant evidence of cerebral disorder in B_{12} deficiency to serve as a basis for organic psychiatric disturbance. A cerebral pathology is known to occur in pernicious anaemia, similar to that which affects the cord in subacute combined degeneration (Adams and Kubik, 1944; Holmes, 1956). This consists essentially of diffuse and focal areas of degeneration in the white matter, with relatively little gliosis or change in the neurones, and should therefore be reversible at least in the early stages. The electroencephalogram in pernicious anaemia is abnormal in over 60% of cases (Walton et al., 1954). Mild abnormalities show as excessive theta activity, and severe abnormalities as delta activity which is sometimes paroxysmal or focal. Such abnormalities bear no simple relationship to the severity of the anaemia but appear to reflect a specific defect of cerebral metabolism. The majority of abnormal records are reversible with treatment, improvement sometimes starting within 7–10 days of the first B_{12} injection. Metabolic studies have also revealed impaired uptake of oxygen and glucose, especially in the presence of mental symptoms such as forgetfulness, confusion and disorientation, and again responding to replacement therapy (Scheinberg, 1951). These too were unrelated to the severity of anaemia and appeared to be a specific result of B_{12} deficiency. Similar disturbances of metabolism may accordingly be expected in patients with low serum B_{12} even in the absence of pernicious anaemia.

Such observations make it important to consider B_{12} deficiency in the differential diagnosis of all patients with unexplained acute organic reactions or dementing syndromes, and to pursue treatment vigorously at the earliest opportunity.

Routine Screening

It has been suggested that routine screening of psychiatric populations might bring to light remediable cases of B_{12} deficiency which would otherwise be missed. But the definitive investigation, namely estimation of the serum B_{12} level, clearly cannot be provided for every psychiatric patient.

Various preliminary screening procedures have been proposed. Shulman (1967a) recommends the routine estimation of haemoglobin and examination of blood films before selecting patients for complete investigation. This, however, would miss the cases which present with mental symptoms in the pre-anaemic phase. Strachan and Henderson (1965) suggest confining attention to patients with a histamine-fast achlorhydria, but this examination can be difficult to perform on psychiatric patients. Henderson et al. (1966) recommend a test of antigastric antibodies, which is essentially a serum test for the Addisonian state and only an indirect indicator of

B_{12} deficiency. It therefore applies only to patients with incipient pernicious anaemia, and not to those with other causes of B_{12} lack such as dietary deficiency. Moreover many false positives are obtained.

In practice the routine screening of psychiatric populations remains of doubtful value. It would seem preferable to confine attention to those at greatest risk, namely any patient with an organic psychiatric illness of uncertain cause, and those who complain of unexplained fatigue or are found to be anaemic. In addition Hunter et al. (1967b) have stressed the importance of assessing B_{12} levels in any psychiatric patient with a history of gastric surgery. Among 20 psychiatric patients with a history of gastrectomy they found 5 to have low B_{12}s, and in 4 the psychiatric illness was considered to be primarily due to this. The estimation would also be indicated in any patient who is known to have subsisted for a considerable time on a grossly inadequate diet.

Treatment

Hydroxocobalamin ('Neo-cytamen') has largely replaced cyanocobalamin ('Cytamen') in the treatment of B_{12} deficiency, since it is better retained in the body and maintenance injections are required less frequently. In the treatment of uncomplicated pernicious anaemia six intramuscular injections of 1 mg are usually given at three day intervals, before proceeding to maintenance therapy at 1 mg two-monthly. With subacute combined degeneration of the cord it is customary to give at least twice the loading dose in the early weeks of treatment, and this is equally advisable in patients with suspected cerebral involvement.

Folic Acid Deficiency

Folic acid deficiency has also become the focus of considerable psychiatric interest. Like B_{12} deficiency it may result in megaloblastic anaemia, though the metabolic interrelationships between the two vitamins are incompletely understood. It has become clear that megaloblastic anaemia due to folate deficiency is commoner in the UK than was previously thought, occurring particularly in pregnancy, in old people who are incapacitated, and in those suffering from psychiatric disorder (British Medical Journal, 1968b).

Accordingly surveys have been made of the incidence of folate deficiency in psychiatric populations with interesting results. 5 ng/ml is usually accepted as the lower level of normal for serum folic acid, with 2·5 ng/ml representing definite abnormality, though to some extent each laboratory must set its own cut-off point. Read *et al.* (1965) found that 80% of entrants to an old people's home showed values below 6 ng/ml, and Shulman (1967a) showed a similar proportion among elderly patients admitted to a psychiatric hospital. Hurdle and Picton-Williams (1966) found values below 5 ng/ml in 30% of elderly patients admitted to a geriatric unit with a variety of physical and mental disorders. Even allowing for a possible fall of serum folate with age these figures are remarkably high. The most common disorders associated with the deficiency appeared to be the organic psychosyndromes of old age.

In younger psychiatric patients low serum folates also appear to be common. Hunter *et al.* (1967a) found that half of a group of mental hospital admissions of all ages had values below 3 ng/ml. Carney (1967) surveyed 423 consecutive psychiatric admissions of all ages and found that 25% had values below 2 ng/ml. In the latter study a normal control group was selected from the hospital staff, and differences were significant not only for the patients with organic psychoses and epilepsy but also among those with endogenous depression.

In all such surveys it is hard to assess the causal significance of the low serum folates which are found. In the majority of cases deficient nutrition appears to have been responsible for the folate deficiency, and as with B_{12} deficiency this may often be secondary to the mental disorder itself. Or if a causal relationship does exist, the psychiatric disturbance must at least often establish a secondary vicious circle by impairing food intake further. Moreover the finding of a low serum folate may not always indicate clinically significant folate deficiency. Barbiturates and alcohol are known to depress serum folate levels, and other drugs including phenothiazines may do so as well. Nevertheless in a retrospective survey of a large number of patients, Carney and Sheffield (1970) found some evidence to suggest that greater improvement had occurred when the folate deficiency was treated than when it was ignored. The results were most clear where organic psychoses were concerned, but perhaps applied also to the quality and speed of recovery of patients with depression and schizophrenia. In the same population it could not be shown that the remedying of B_{12} deficiency was of benefit in the cases where this was discovered. It

seems possible, therefore, that even if not directly causal, the folate deficiency may often add its own contribution and worsen the clinical picture in a number of different conditions.

In addition to these general surveys, particular attention has been focused on folate deficiency in three conditions—depression, dementia, and epilepsy:

Depressive Illness

Carney's (1967) finding of significantly low folate levels in depressed patients has been supported by Reynolds *et al.* (1970). Among 100 patients with severe depressive illnesses one quarter were found to have serum folates below 2·5 ng/ml. The level of folate on admission could not be related convincingly to inadequate nutrition, nor to the taking of barbiturate drugs. There was also some indication that the folate-deficient depressives responded less well to antidepressant drugs or electroconvulsive therapy than the others, as judged by scores on depression inventories at the time of discharge. The differences, though small in size, were statistically significant. A more recent study of outpatient depressives attending a lithium clinic tends to support these findings; those patients with a lower range of serum folates showed a higher affective morbidity at the time of the folate assay and also over the preceding two years (Coppen and Abou-Saleh, 1982).

Shorvon *et al.* (1980) have paid special attention to the mental status of patients presenting in a general hospital with megaloblastic anaemia due to either B_{12} or folate deficiency. The commonest disturbance in the low folate group was depression which occurred in 50% of patients compared with only 20% of those with B_{12} deficiency.

Reynolds *et al.* (1970) point out that a causal relationship between folate deficiency and depression would be consistent with the biogenic theories of affective disorder, since folate deficiency could interfere with the synthesis of catecholamines and 5-hydroxytryptamine.

Dementia

The folate level in the cerebrospinal fluid is known to be two or three times higher than that in the serum (Reynolds, 1979), suggesting that folic acid may have considerable functional importance in cerebral metabolism. It is therefore interesting that occasional case reports have pointed to a close relationship between folic acid deficiency and organic psychiatric illness. Anand (1964) described a patient with megaloblastic anaemia, myelopathy, impairment of memory and moderate dementia of 'frontal lobe type', who showed no response to B_{12} but improved in all respects after starting folic acid. Read *et al.* (1965) similarly described an 82-year-old patient with megaloblastic anaemia due to nutritional deficiency in whom mental confusion and double incontinence improved with folic acid. Two further striking examples were provided by Strachan and Henderson (1967), both with advanced dementia. In each case the folate deficiency followed chronic malnutrition, and the dementia responded gradually to treatment with folic acid; there was a coincident megaloblastic anaemia in both cases but the blood picture returned to normal several months before the mental symptoms resolved:

A 70-year-old widow was seen in domiciliary consultation because of mental deterioration of several months duration. She was grossly disoriented for time and place and showed a severe defect of recent memory. She was living in dirty neglectful conditions and had been subsisting on tea and biscuits. In hospital she tended to lose herself in the ward and found it impossible to retain the names of members of staff even for a few minutes. There were no neurological abnormalities, the haemoglobin was 69% with a few macrocytes, and the sternal marrow showed megaloblasts. The serum B_{12} was normal, but the folic acid was 2·7 ng/ml. The electroencephalogram was moderately abnormal with slowed dominant activity at 7 Hz and fluctuating slower waves.

She was started on folic acid 20 mg daily by mouth together with ferrous sulphate. One month later she was discharged to an old people's home virtually unchanged. When re-examined 2 months later, however, there was considerable improvement—she was clean and tidy, oriented for time and place, recognised the nurses, and showed excellent awareness of current events. Learning ability was now within normal limits for her age. The electroencephalogram had improved. Nine months later she had maintained her improvement and detailed psychological testing showed further gains in cognitive function.

A 69-year-old widow was admitted with confusion of 3 months duration, and shortness of breath. She had been living for over a year on tea, toast and biscuits. She lay inert in bed, surveying the scene around in perplexed fashion, gave the year as 1891 and did not know her address. She could not cooperate on tests of memory and tended to confabulate. She was incontinent of urine and faeces.

The haemoglobin was 30% with many macrocytes, and the bone marrow was megaloblastic. The serum B_{12} was normal, and the folate 0·6 ng/ml. The electroencephalogram showed no normal activity but widespread theta and random irregular slow waves at 2 Hz. The blood urea, electrolytes and cerebrospinal fluid were normal.

Folic acid was given, 260 μg daily intramuscularly, and packed cells were transfused. After one month the haemoglobin had risen to 72% but there had been no definite improvement in the mental state. A month later she knew her age and date of birth, was oriented for time and place, and serial electroencephalograms showed progressively more normal records in parallel with her clinical improvement.

Six months later she was readmitted for assessment. She was neatly dressed, fully oriented, gave a good account of her life and previous medical history, and showed an excellent knowledge of current affairs. Psychological testing showed no evidence of intellectual loss. Her improvement was maintained when seen two years later.

(Strachan and Henderson, 1967)

Melamed (1979) reviews further examples of patients with organic mental syndromes, often in association with cord damage or peripheral neuropathy, who responded to folate replacement. Nevertheless the rarity of such patients is surprising in view of the frequency of nutritional folate deficiency. Melamed suggests that long-standing folate deficiency, or individual susceptibility, may need to be operative before such effects are declared. Or it may be necessary for the folate deficiency to be combined with other vitamin lack or coincident drug toxicity.

While severe mental impairment is rare, it seems possible that some degree of cerebral dysfunction may be commoner than generally suspected. Among patients presenting in a general hospital with very low folates, Reynolds *et al.* (1973) found that cognitive abnormalities were significantly more frequent than in controls. Shorvon *et al.* (1980) found that approximately a quarter of patients with megaloblastic anaemia showed organic mental changes, the proportion being similar when low folate and when low B_{12} were responsible. Botez *et al.* (1977) found some evidence pointing to minor CT scan changes in their low folate patients, and were able to demonstrate significant improvements on psychometric tests after folic acid replacement.

With regard to the general problem of dementia in the elderly, Sneath *et al.* (1973) studied 113 consecutive admissions to a geriatric unit, of whom 14 were diagnosed as suffering from dementia. These had significantly lower red cell folates than the remainder. Moreover, where red cell folates were low in the patients as a whole, there was a slight correlation between scores of mental impairment and the red cell folate level. The likely explanation seemed to be that dementia had led to the folate deficiency, by virtue of poor dietary intake, but the possibility could not be excluded that folate deficiency might of itself have led to impaired mental function.

Epilepsy

In epilepsy there is universal agreement that a low serum folate, with or without megaloblastic anaemia, can result from the administration of anticonvulsant drugs. Phenobarbitone, phenytoin and primidone appear all to be responsible, and it has been suggested that there may even be a causal relationship between their antifolate and anticonvulsant properties. In one series of treated epileptics attending an outpatient clinic over three-quarters showed subnormal serum folate levels, and over one-third had megaloblastic haemopoiesis. The serum B_{12}s were within the normal range but tended to be low when the folic acid was low (Reynolds, Chanarin *et al.*, 1966; Reynolds, Milner *et al.*, 1966).

Moreover, folate levels appear to be lower in mentally abnormal epileptics than in those who are free from psychiatric symptoms, whether measured in the serum, red blood corpuscles or cerebrospinal fluid (Reynolds *et al.*, 1969; Reynolds, Preece and Johnson, 1971). The differences have sometimes been found to be particularly large where dementia is concerned, but also to apply to schizophrenia-like psychoses. Snaith *et al.* (1970) found levels to be low in small groups suffering from schizophrenia, depression, neurosis and personality disorder when compared to mentally healthy epileptics, but could find no clear relationship to any particular form of psychiatric disturbance.

The usual difficulties are encountered in assessing the significance of these findings, and in deciding how far the folate levels may be causally related to the psychiatric abnormalities. Reynolds (1967a) treated a group of folate deficient epileptics with folic acid in an uncontrolled investigation, and found that the mental state improved over the ensuing months in the great majority. Improvement was seen in energy, drive, alertness and sociability, mood swings were lessened and aggressive behaviour reduced. But half of the patients showed a coincident increase in fit frequency or severity which sometimes necessitated termination of treatment. Reynolds (1967b) has also drawn attention to cases of temporal lobe epilepsy in which schizophrenia-like episodes have shown a possible relationship to disturbances of folate or B_{12} metabolism induced by treatment with anticonvulsant drugs.

Subsequent controlled trials have, however, so far failed to confirm these findings. Grant and Stores (1970) carried out a double-blind trial on in-patient epileptics with low serum folates, and found that folic acid was without significant effect on tests of speed of thought and action, personality, behaviour, or fit frequency. Norris and Pratt (1971) confirmed these negative findings where fit frequency was concerned, and suggested that the occasional examples even of status epilepticus on starting folic acid were probably due to chance. Smith and Obbens (1979) review the continuing uncertainty surrounding folate supplementation and seizures, concluding that while most patients are unaffected, individual epileptics can undoubtedly be adversely affected.

Thus while an association between lowered folate and mental disturbance in epileptics appears to be firmly established, a causal relationship remains to be definitely proved. The results of giving the vitamin are also uncertain. Blood-brain barrier effects appear to be important in determining the effects of administered folic acid, and differing durations of treatment may go some way towards explaining discrepant findings to date (Reynolds, 1973).

Routine Screening

Again the problem arises whether psychiatric patients should be screened routinely for folic acid deficiency. Estimation of serum folate would certainly seem to be indicated in any patient with an acute or chronic organic mental illness of uncertain aetiology, and a strong case can be made for including it as a routine investigation for every patient diagnosed as suffering from senile or presenile dementia. The same applies to epileptic patients on anticonvulsant drugs who show marked psychomotor retardation or psychiatric disturbance. The large number of patients with depressive illness makes routine screening impractical in most settings. But estimations of folic acid should be performed whenever there is a history of subsistence on an inadequate diet, of malabsorption syndromes such as steatorrhoea, or in the presence of megaloblastic anaemia.

Treatment

A trial of treatment with folic acid, 5 mg three times per day, is well worth while when deficient levels are found. It should however always be preceded by careful screening for B_{12} deficiency. The serum B_{12} tends to fall when folic acid is started (Reynolds, Wrighton *et al.*, 1971), suggesting that the two vitamins may be intimately involved in the metabolic disturbances and that some patients may need treatment with both. Moreover there is danger of precipitating or aggravating neurological disturbances by giving folic acid in patients with undiagnosed pernicious anaemia.

Chapter 13. Toxic Disorders

Alcohol, drugs and certain metals and chemicals are the exogenous toxins which will be considered in the present chapter. The effects of toxins derived from invading micro-organisms have been briefly considered on p. 313, and the toxic products of disordered metabolism in uraemia and hepatic dysfunction in Chapter 11.

Alcohol is the toxin most commonly encountered in psychiatric practice, though the effects of drug abuse must now be frequently considered in the differential diagnosis of acute psychiatric disturbance. Poisoning due to metals and other chemical compounds is largely the province of industrial medicine, but must also be borne in mind in occasional patients who present with psychiatric illness of uncertain aetiology.

Effects of Alcohol on the Nervous System

Alcohol is remarkable for the range of nervous system disorders which it can produce and for the diversity of mechanisms by which they come about. There are first the direct toxic effects of alcohol present within the body, which acts as a depressant of central nervous functioning; a further series of disorders including fits, hallucinoses and delirium tremens are largely due to alcohol withdrawal; associated nutritional defects lead to Wernicke's encephalopathy, Korsakoff's psychosis, peripheral neuropathy and perhaps cerebellar degeneration; and liver disorder or hypoglycaemia may ensue with their own neuropsychiatric complications. The distinction between these several mechanisms cannot be considered absolute for all of the syndromes concerned, but in general reaches broad agreement. The nutritional disorders associated with alcoholism have been considered in Chapter 12, and the direct toxic effects and withdrawal effects will be considered below.

ALCOHOL INTOXICATION

Alcohol acts as a central nervous system depressant in a manner analogous to that of anaesthetic agents, though acting very much more slowly and with a greatly reduced margin between the level which produces surgical anaesthesia and the level which depresses the respiratory centres to a dangerous extent. Its initial action is probably on the reticular formation, leading to increased excitability of the cortex. Later there are direct toxic effects on the cortical neurones as well.

The early effects are to produce 'inebriation', usually with subjective exhilaration, excitement and loquacity. Personality factors and environmental factors are important at this stage, lively company leading usually to boisterous cheerfulness, whereas alcohol taken alone may intensify feelings of loneliness and depression. Cultural influences are also clearly important in helping to shape the outward evidence of intoxication (Edwards, 1974).

Soon there is reduction of psychological efficiency and motor control, which may be at marked variance with subjective feelings of superiority and skill. Thinking becomes slowed and superficial, with poverty of associations and impaired judgement and reasoning. Learning and retention become faulty, and remote memory unreliable. Acuity of perception is reduced, attention impaired, and distractibility increased. Muscular control is impaired at an early stage and reaction times delayed. Later dysarthria, frank incoordination and ataxia appear.

With more severe intoxication there is progressive loss of restraint, self control becomes undermined and irregularities of behaviour appear. Emotions of hilarity, sadness or self-pity may gain the upper hand, or there may be marked irritability and hostility. With very high blood levels there is increasing drowsiness, leading finally to coma. In alcoholic coma the breathing is slow and stertorous and the temperature subnormal. The pupils may be contracted or widely dilated and the tendon reflexes weak or absent.

A fairly close relationship exists between the intensity of the effects and the level of alcohol in the blood. A level of 150-250 mg/100 ml is usually associated with very obvious signs of intoxication, and the legal maximum for drivers is set at 80 mg/

100 ml. The situation is complex, however, depending on the rate of rise to a given level and also the length of time that alcohol has been in the body. Thus a quick rise will produce effects at a lower level of blood alcohol than a gradual rise, and for a given rate of rise the effects will be less marked if alcohol has been present at a constant level for some time before. Isbell *et al.* (1955) found slowing of rhythms on the electroencephalogram when signs of clinical intoxication appeared, but later this effect diminished even though the blood level rose higher still. Tolerance within the central nervous system may be obvious in habituees, who absorb more quickly from the gastrointestinal tract yet at the same time become resistant to the early effects. Prolonged ingestion can also lead to metabolic adaptation; there is evidence to suggest that during periods of long-continued chronic intoxication the subject metabolises alcohol at an increased rate (Isbell *et al.*, 1955).

'Pathological Intoxication'

On occasion irrational combative behaviour may develop abruptly during the course of intoxication. In marked examples it presents as an outburst of uncontrollable rage and excitement leading to seriously destructive actions against other persons and property. This is the 'pathological reaction to alcohol', 'pathological intoxication', 'acute alcoholic paranoid state' or 'mania à potu', much discussed in the earlier literature. As typically described the behaviour is out of character for the individual concerned, the duration is short, and there is subsequently amnesia for the entire episode. Banay (1944) and May and Ebaugh (1953) review the condition.

It was sometimes maintained that such responses could follow the ingestion of relatively small amounts of alcohol, and that the normal associated phenomena of intoxication could be minimal or absent. The condition accordingly attained considerable medico-legal importance. It was regarded as an acute organic reaction or a short-lived paranoid psychosis released by alcohol in specially susceptible persons. Special attributes of personality were held to be responsible, or periods of strain or great exhaustion. Tendencies to epilepsy or hypoglycaemia were sometimes invoked.

There have, however, been few critical studies relating to the condition or its antecedents. Coid (1979), in an exceptionally thorough review, found virtually nothing to support the notion that small amounts of alcohol could trigger such outbursts, and little to suggest that they could develop in persons of stable disposition. The nosological status of the condition seemed very doubtful. He considered that the label should be dropped, and that the conception could be of little use in courts of law in cases of alcohol-related violence.

There is perhaps some evidence to suggest that brain damaged persons may be particularly liable to display reactions of this nature. Morozov *et al.* (1973) examined 105 persons who had committed infringements of the law in a condition of 'pathological intoxication' and 100 in 'simple intoxication'. Ninety-one per cent of the former showed evidence of organic changes in the central nervous system, mainly traumatic in origin, compared to 50% of the latter. This may, of course, reflect no more than the well-known increased susceptibility to severe intoxication in the presence of brain damage.

Attempts to study pathological intoxication directly have led to conflicting results. Bach-y-Rita *et al.* (1970) gave intravenous infusions of alcohol to 10 men with a history of violent outbursts when intoxicated, but in no case was the abnormal behaviour reproduced. In a similar experiment, however, Maletsky (1976) obtained the expected reactions in 15 of 22 cases. Nine became violent with inappropriate rage, 4 became psychotic with hallucinations and delusions, and 2 showed a mixture of both. The remainder developed normal intoxication only.

Maletsky's experiment is important in demonstrating that large amounts of alcohol were necessary before the disturbed behaviour occurred, the mean blood alcohol level at the time being 195 mg/100 ml. Many subjects showed changes in the EEG during the course of the infusion, but these did not correlate with the abnormal behavioural responses. In general the disturbed behaviour was superimposed on normal intoxication phenomena, but occasionally signs of the latter were slight. In some cases a witness to the disturbance could well have been blind to the aetiological agent. Maletsky's further impression that the behavioural responses were out of keeping with the personality of the subjects when sober is hard to evaluate. Further controlled studies would obviously be necessary to clarify the point.

The Alcoholic 'Blackout'

Special interest attaches to the abnormalities of memory which may follow a period of severe intoxication. An amnesic gap will of course follow any bout of drinking which is carried to the point of severe impairment of consciousness, but the alcoholic 'blackout' is a phenomenon of a more specific kind. It consists of a dense amnesia for signif-icant events which have occurred during a drinking episode, and when at the time outward behaviour perhaps seemed little disordered. Usually the gap extends for a period of several hours, but very occasionally it may cover several days. The subject may have carried on a conversation and gone through quite elaborate activities, for all of which there is no trace of memory next day. On rare occasions grossly abnormal or even criminal conduct may have occurred during the episode. The onset, as judged by subjective recall, is usually abrupt, and the end of the amnesic gap may be equally sharp if sleep does not follow directly.

Goodwin et al. (1969a, 1969b) have presented a detailed description of the nature of 'blackouts' in 64 alcoholic subjects. They confirm that behaviour during the episode is usually similar to behaviour during any heavy drinking bout, except that some subjects tended to travel long distances as in fugue states. Thus a quarter of their patients had found themselves in strange places with no recollection of how they got there. The wives of two patients claimed that they could tell when a blackout was in progress on account of a glassy stare, belligerent behaviour, or the repetition of questions which showed that experiences were failing to register. 'En bloc' blackouts, as just described, were distinguished from 'fragmentary' losses in which the subject was unaware that events had been forgotten until he was told about them later. Sometimes in this milder variety the memories might return with the passage of time, and sometimes recall was facilitated by further drinking. Thus many subjects had had the experience of hiding money or alcohol when drink-ing, forgetting it when sober, and later having the memory return in a subsequent drinking bout.

Such episodes can represent profoundly disturb-ing experiences for an alcoholic. They are commoner, apparently, after the ingestion of spirits than after wine or beer (World Health Organisation Report, 1955). The sharpness of the rise and fall of the blood alcohol level has been thought to be more important than the height which is achieved, and sometimes the episodes have been reported to follow the drinking of medium or even quite small amounts. Jellinek (1952) drew attention to their frequency in the histories of established alcoholics, usually dating from a time before the drinking had got out of control. He suggested that repeated experience of the phenomenon might be a prodromal sign of alcohol addiction, and that its occurrence after only medium alcohol intake represented heightened susceptibility or sensitivity to the effects of alcohol in the prospective addict. Goodwin et al. (1969a, 1969b) were unable to confirm these features in their careful study. The occurrence of blackouts was directly associated with the severity and duration of alcoholism. They appeared only late in the course of the illness, and well after physical dependence and loss of control had become established. Black-outs were very rarely seen unless large amounts of alcohol were being consumed, chiefly in the form of spirits. Goodwin et al. also noticed a fairly strong association with a prior history of head injury.

Tarter and Schneider (1976) investigated the possibility that alcoholics subject to blackouts might have some enduring impairment of memory when sober, but with negative results. Those with a high incidence of blackouts performed as well as those in whom blackouts were rare on a wide battery of memory measures. The quantity of intake on a given occasion again seemed to be the discriminating factor —the group with many blackouts had a significantly greater tendency to drink to intoxication or until falling asleep, and showed a significantly higher incidence of craving, tolerance and loss of control.

The pathogenesis of these episodes remains uncer-tain. They have been attributed to psychogenic mechanisms of repression, especially in view of the emotional setting in which some of the attacks are known to occur. Malingering has been suspected in the occasional cases where they have been used as a defence against charges of criminal behaviour. The majority, however, must be accepted as organically determined. An interesting suggestion is that they may represent the effects of 'state-dependent learn-ing'. It has been shown that animals trained in a drugged state may 'remember' their training better when retested in a comparable drugged state, indicating that learning depends for its optimum expression on restoration of the original conditions in which the learning was acquired. Goodwin et al. (1969c) have demonstrated an analogous situation in volunteers trained and tested under the effects of alcohol. For some tasks learning transfer proved to be better when the subject was intoxicated in both the first and the second test sessions, than when he was intoxicated in the first but sober in the second. This accords with the observation cited above that events during an alcoholic blackout may sometimes be recalled under subsequent alcoholic intoxication.

Another study has added further information by investigating short-term memory and 24 hour recall during a 2 week period of sustained intoxication (Tamerin et al., 1971):

Thirteen alcoholic patients, all with a long history of 'blackouts', were tested each day for registration (5 seconds recall) and short-term memory (1 and 5 minutes recall) of simple test material, and also asked a set of standard questions about the activities of the day before. During periods of moderate intoxication registration was substantially normal, but short-term memory was considerably impaired. More severe intoxication showed a significant fall in registration and a more profound decrement in short-term memory. Ability to recall the events of the preceding day was significantly reduced on days following moderate intoxication and more so on days following severe intoxication. The decrement was also related to the duration of intoxication, in that it tended to become worse as the days of the experiment went by. Defects in 24 hour recall were also more frequent and severe the worse the short-term memory had been when tested on the preceding day. Conversely 24 hour recall was always normal in subjects who had shown intact short-term memory the day before.

Marked individual susceptibility was revealed, however, the same blood alcohol level affecting different subjects to a different extent. Only 6 of the 13 subjects showed 'blackouts', defined as ability to answer less than 30% of the questions concerning the previous day's activities. Three of the subjects were particularly vulnerable in this regard. No relationship was discovered to factors commonly thought to be important such as age, intelligence, history of head injury, presence of EEG abnormalities, duration of drinking history, or history of delirium tremens.

This investigation therefore clearly reinstates the importance of an organic basis for the blackout. State-dependent effects were excluded in this particular setting because 24 hour recall was tested while the subjects were still intoxicated. The correlates of individual vulnerability remain an important question for further investigation.

Treatment of Intoxication

An acute episode of intoxication rarely calls for specific medical treatment, but severely intoxicated persons should be kept under close observation in case alcoholic coma should supervene. Gastric lavage is usually unnecessary since alcohol is rapidly absorbed from the stomach. If there is a possibility that drugs have been taken as well, however, lavage will be indicated. Episodes of combative behaviour may, on occasion, require sedation with major tranquillisers, but there are obvious hazards involved in adding one cerebral depressant to another. In actual management the most important factor is usually the handling which the patient receives from those around, who must attempt to react in as good-natured and unprovocative a way as possible. Kelly *et al.* (1971) have shown that intravenous injections of high potency vitamins B and C can reduce the subjective effects of intoxication and improve performance on reaction time tests, apparently by virtue of a direct effect on the central nervous system, but this will rarely need to be exploited in practice.

Alcoholic coma represents a medical emergency and should be managed in hospital. Care is needed to exclude coincident head injury and its complications, gastro-intestinal bleeding, hepatic failure, pneumonia or meningitis. Blood should be taken to confirm the presence of significant amounts of alcohol, and to exclude barbiturate intoxication or alcoholic hypoglycaemia (p. 463). A clear airway must be maintained, analeptic drugs may be indicated, and peripheral circulatory failure may require intravenous fluids, vasopressor drugs and steroids. If glucose-containing fluids are transfused thiamine must always be given in case Wernicke's encephalopathy should be precipitated.

ABSTINENCE OR WITHDRAWAL SYNDROMES

An important group of manifestations occur against a background of severe alcohol abuse but make their appearance usually after a period of complete or relative abstinence. It seems, therefore, that they depend not on the direct toxic effects of alcohol present at the time, but rather on a fall in the level circulating within the body (Victor and Adams, 1953; Isbell *et al.*, 1955). They include tremulousness, hallucinosis, fits, and most important of all delirium tremens.

The precise mechanisms underlying these disorders are far from clear. Where hallucinosis and delirium tremens are concerned several complex factors are probably at work. But all share in common the tendency to occur shortly after drinking has stopped or been abruptly curtailed. The clearest evidence comes from the experiments of Isbell *et al.* (1955), who kept 10 subjects continuously intoxicated for periods of 6–12 weeks while a high calorie diet was given along with full vitamin supplements. No fits or delirium occurred while consumption continued, but on withdrawal all developed an abstinence syndrome characterised by tremors, weakness, nausea, vomiting, hyperreflexia, and fever. Two had seizures, 2 experienced transient auditory and visual hallucinations, and 3 developed frank delirium tremens. The intensity of the withdrawal symptoms was related to the amount of alcohol that had been taken and the duration of consumption. Only one of the subjects who had persisted with continuous drinking beyond 7 weeks escaped without fits or hallucinations. Serial EEG records had shown slowing during the period of acute intoxication, but on withdrawal became normal for a while; 16 to 33 hours later the alpha rhythm diminished and random spikes and bursts of slow waves appeared coincidentally with the more severe withdrawal effects. This was therefore an unusually clear demonstration that withdrawal is a factor of prime importance in producing these phenomena, and also that nutritional deficiency is unlikely to be causally related.

The discovery of the different stages of sleep has brought new evidence concerning alcohol withdrawal (Greenberg and Pearlman, 1967; Gross and Goodenough, 1968). Increasing levels of alcohol suppress the rapid eye movement phase of sleep (REM sleep, p. 622) and the dreaming associated with it. With continuation of drinking some readjustment occurs, but on withdrawal an abrupt rebound is seen with a great excess of REM sleep. Immediately prior to an attack of delirium tremens REM sleep may occupy the whole of the sleeping time. It has been suggested that the vivid hallucinations of delirium tremens may represent a 'spilling over' of this active dream material into waking life. The essential mechanisms remain to be clarified, but certainly there appears to be an important relationship between the nature of the sleep disturbances associated with alcohol withdrawal and the clinical manifestations which occur.

A further interesting hypothesis has been put forward by Ballenger and Post (1978) who draw analogies with the phenomenon of 'kindling' in rats and other animals:

It has been shown that brief bursts of electrical brain stimulation, carried out at daily intervals and at constant intensity, can result in enduring changes in brain excitability (Goddard et al., 1969). Much theoretical interest attaches to the process. Stimulation which is initially subthreshold in its effect gradually acquires increased potency with daily repetition. After-discharges appear, increase, and spread widely to subcortical brain structures, eventually manifesting epileptiform spikes and then sustained epileptic discharges. Behavioural concomitants likewise develop, first in the form of motor automatisms then progressing to seizures in response to the stimulation. Stimulation within the limbic areas of the brain elicits kindling most reliably, and repeat stimulation at intervals of 24 hours appears to be the optimal rate for its development.

Ballenger and Post point out that similar kindling effects can result from the administration of metrazol and other drugs, and suggest that repeated heavy alcohol intake may have analogous effects. Intoxication and withdrawal are accompanied by minor dysrhythmias as described just above. Limbic system hyper-irritability accompanying each episode of withdrawal may thus conceivably increase by the kindling process and spread widely in subcortical structures. Long-term changes in neuronal excitability may accordingly underlie the progressive escalation of withdrawal symptoms from tremors, to seizures, and ultimately to delirium tremens. Direct electrophysiological evidence for the hypothesis is necessarily lacking in man, since depth electrode studies would be required. But Ballenger and Post present other data consistent with the hypothesis. In a survey of the incidence and forms of withdrawal phenomena in a large group of alcoholics, they demonstrate a stepwise escalation in the severity of the symptomatology as the years of alcohol abuse increase. Similar stepwise behavioural changes in response to stimulation are observed during kindling in animals.

From clinical evidence it would appear that tremulousness, nausea and transient hallucinations in clear consciousness are among the earliest withdrawal phenomena, occurring often within 3–12 hours of cessation of drinking. Fits occur somewhat later after an interval of 12–18 hours, and the full syndrome of delirium tremens usually only after 3 to 4 days (Victor and Adams, 1953). It is well established that a prolonged period of indulgence is necessary for the more severe effects to occur. With all withdrawal phenomena temporary alleviation follows the taking of alcohol again. All are essentially benign conditions with the exception of delirium tremens.

Alcoholic Tremor

This, the commonest withdrawal effect, is usually associated with general weakness, nausea and irritability. In mild form it can occur after a single night's abstinence and after a period of drinking of only several days. In severe form it usually occurs 12–24 hours after stopping, and only after several weeks of continuous drinking. The patient is alert, startles easily, suffers insomnia and craves the relief which further alcohol will bring. Usually the disorder subsides over several hours or days, but after severe attacks it may be one or two weeks before the patient is composed and can sleep without sedation.

Hallucinosis

Approximately a quarter of tremulous patients have disordered sense perception, ranging from transitory misperceptions of familiar objects to illusions and hallucinations (Victor and Adams, 1953). Hallucinations usually occur in both the visual and auditory modalities, are generally fleeting, and emerge in clear consciousness. The absence of disorientation, confusion and psychomotor overactivity is important in distinguishing the condition from delirium tremens. It is usually a benign condition, lasting often less than 24 hours and rarely for more than a few days.

Sabot *et al.* (1968) found that the hallucinations are often accompanied by simple auditory and visual sensory disturbances which seem to facilitate their appearance. Tinnitus is common with auditory hallucinations, antedating their appearance and persisting after they have cleared. Visual disturbances in the form of blurring, flashes and spots are usually reported by patients with formed visual hallucinations. The visual hallucinations are mostly of small animals such as rodents and insects, characteristically moving rapidly on the walls, floor or ceiling. Larger animals or human beings may also be seen, or fleeting half-formed images of faces.

As with tremulousness, withdrawal of alcohol appears to be the chief factor leading to transient hallucinations. Occasional patients, however, develop hallucinations while continuing to drink, and in these it has been suggested that thiamine deficiency may be a contributory cause (Morgan, 1968). Blackstock *et al.* (1972) have followed this possibility further, but were unable to demonstrate a significant difference in indicators of thiamine levels between alcoholics with or without a recent episode of hallucinatory disturbance.

The term '*alcoholic hallucinosis*' is sometimes used in a more restricted sense to refer to the relatively rare condition in which verbal auditory hallucinations occur alone, again in a setting of clear consciousness. Most examples clear within a few days, but the disorder may sometimes be prolonged. As such the picture may strongly resemble schizophrenia, and a good deal of discussion has centred on its nosological status.

The auditory hallucinations often commence as simple sounds such as buzzing, roaring, or the ringing of bells. Gradually they take on vocal form, usually the voices of friends or enemies who malign, threaten or reproach the patient. The hallucinations may consist of a single derogatory remark repeated with relentless persistence, or the patient may be assailed by a combination of accusations and admonitions. He may be discovered arguing angrily with his voices, or he may complain to the police about them. Sometimes the voices command the patient to do things against his will, and their compelling quality may be such that he is driven to a suicide attempt or to some episode of bizarre behaviour. Usually the patient is addressed directly by the voices, but sometimes they may converse with one another about him, referring to him in the third person as in schizophrenia. Secondary delusional interpretations follow upon the hallucinatory experiences, and the patient comes to believe firmly that he is watched, hounded or in danger.

The result is an illness which at first sight resembles acute paranoid schizophrenia. The delusions will be found, however, to follow only upon the hallucinatory experiences and not to arise autochthonously. Schizophrenic thought disorder is not seen, nor incongruity of affect, and insight is regained immediately the voices begin to wane. The syndrome must, of course, be viewed separately from the picture seen in established schizophrenic patients who also drink. Such patients may similarly develop abrupt auditory hallucinations when drinking and during withdrawal, since drinking bouts may aggravate the schizophrenic process. The distinction is made on the basis of the preceding history, and the features in the mental state as just outlined.

Victor and Hope (1958) have reviewed the divergent views about the implications of the illness, ranging from the belief that it represents a form of schizophrenia released by alcohol, to the view that it represents an independent psychosis induced by drinking for many years. Of their 76 examples 90% showed hallucinations which were benign and transient, the great majority clearing within a week. Hallucinations became chronic in only 8 patients, persisting then for months or years. In 4 of the latter the disorder ultimately resolved without the development of more serious psychiatric illness; only in the remaining 4 was there progression to a true schizophrenia-like illness with ideas of influence, emotional withdrawal and persistent paranoid delusions. Family histories gave no indication of special allegiance with schizophrenia, and the previous personality tended to be cyclothymic rather than schizoid. This applied even in those rare cases which did prove ultimately to develop a schizophrenia-like illness.

In these important respects the findings were in broad agreement with Benedetti's (1952) large series. Eighty per cent of 113 cases cleared within a few weeks or months, usually leaving no psychiatric defect whatever. The great majority of these cleared within a few hours or days. The remaining 23 became chronic, some developing typical schizophrenia and the others a chronic amnesic syndrome or dementia. Six months appeared to be the cut-off point beyond which remissions could not be expected. In the group as a whole a family history of schizophrenia was a great deal lower than among the relatives of schizophrenics, though possibly somewhat higher than in the general population.

There is therefore little to suggest that auditory hallucinosis is merely latent schizophrenia made manifest by alcohol. The mechanisms involved remain uncertain, beyond the fact that prolonged indulgence in alcohol is a necessary precursor and that abstinence is frequently observed prior to its onset. Of the 76 cases reported by Victor and Hope (1958) only 15 began while the patient was still drinking, and 3 of these were reducing their intake substantially at the time. In the remainder the hallucinations began after drinking had stopped entirely, usually setting in 12–48 hours later. The factors which determine the occasional prolongation of the hallucinosis or transition to a schizophrenia-like state remain unknown, but there is some indication that repeated attacks may make the patient ultimately more vulnerable to the type which leads on to schizophrenic deterioration.

Phenothiazine drugs are usually effective in treatment. Electroconvulsive therapy may terminate the attack abruptly in those cases which persist beyond a few weeks.

Alcoholic Convulsions ('Rum Fits')

The consumption of alcohol can precipitate fits in a person suffering from epilepsy, and sometimes this happens after a 'normal' evening's drinking. Commonly the fit then occurs next morning during sobering up. Quite distinct from this are the withdrawal fits which may occur in persons without special epileptic predisposition. These occur only after heavy consumption, and usually within 12–48 hours of the termination of a long-continued bout. They are usually seen only after several years of established alcohol addiction. Very occasionally they are seen while consumption continues, presumably as a result of transient falls in the blood alcohol level.

Mostly the fits occur in bouts of two to six at a time, and very occasionally status epilepticus may be precipitated. The fits are usually grand mal in type. If a focal component exists this is likely to be the result of trauma in addition to alcoholism. In almost 30% of cases the fits are followed by delirium tremens. Conversely 30% of cases of delirium tremens and 10% of cases of auditory hallucinosis are preceded by fits (Victor and Adams, 1953).

The electroencephalogram is abnormal at the time of the fits, but reverts to normal thereafter. It remains normal in the intervals between, thus discrediting the wide belief that they represent a latent epileptic process which has been brought to light (Victor, 1966).

DELIRIUM TREMENS

Delirium tremens represents by far the most serious of the alcohol withdrawal phenomena with a mortality of up to 5%. Some large series of cases have been reported to show a lower mortality, but have probably included many partial and incomplete forms (Victor, 1966).

Definition

The fully developed syndrome consists of vivid hallucinations, delusions, profound confusion, tremor, agitation, sleeplessness and autonomic overactivity. Defined in this way delirium tremens is relatively uncommon, and was found to represent only 5% of a consecutive series of 266 patients admitted to Boston City Hospital with an obvious complication of alcoholism (Victor and Adams, 1953). By contrast in the same series acute tremulousness occurred in 34%, transient hallucinosis with tremor in 11%, auditory hallucinosis in 2%, fits in 12%, and the Wernicke-Korsakoff syndrome in 3%.

Before diagnosing delirium tremens McNichol (1970) requires the presence of hallucinations along with at least two of the following: confusion and disorientation, tremulousness, increased psychomotor activity, fearfulness, and signs of autonomic disturbance. He recognises three grades in the development of the complete syndrome: first mental sluggishness with tremor and evidence of residual intoxication; later emotional lability, agitation, fearfulness, increased psychomotor activity, autonomic disturbance, nightmares and disorientation; and finally the onset of definitive delirium tremens with the appearance of hallucinations. The presence of autonomic hyperactivity (tachycardia, sweating, fever) can be of considerable diagnostic importance in pointing towards the condition when the cause of a delirious state is not immediately obvious.

Clinical Features

Delirium tremens frequently presents in a dramatic manner and appears to have had an explosive onset. But when opportunities arise for observation during the evolution of the illness a prodromal phase is commonly seen. The onset is usually at night, with restlessness, insomnia and fear. The patient startles at the least sound, has vivid nightmares and wakes repeatedly in panic. Transient illusions and hallucinations may occur even at this stage, and typically arouse intense anxiety even though insight may still be largely retained.

As the illness becomes more fully declared the face is anxious or terror stricken. The patient is tremulous, and if out of bed is seen to be markedly ataxic. There is evidence of dehydration with dry lips, a coated tongue and scanty urine. Restlessness is extreme, with ceaseless agitated activity by day and night, preventing sleep and leading ultimately to a dangerous state of physical exhaustion. Autonomic disturbance shows in perspiration, flushing or pallor, a weak rapid pulse and mild pyrexia.

Illusions and hallucinations occur in great profusion, principally in the visual modality but also auditory and haptic. Spots on the counterpane may be mistaken for insects, and cracks on the ceiling for snakes. Visual hallucinations typically consist of fleeting, recurrent and changeable images which compulsively hold the patient's attention. Rats, snakes and other small animals are said to be typical, and can appear in colourful and vivid forms. They are frequently Lilliputian in size, and invested with rapid ceaseless activity. The author has observed a patient who followed intently, and with excited comments, a game of football performed for half an hour on end by two teams of normal-coloured miniature elephants in a corner of his room. Other hallucinations may be normal in size, such as threatening faces or fantastic scenes depicting terrifying situations. Other hallucinations may be amusing or playful in nature, and recapture some of the bonhomie of the patient and his companions during drinking spells. The patient's occupation and experience is sometimes involved in the perceptual disorders, the station master seeing trains rapidly approaching him, or the factory worker seeing his bench before him and going excitedly through his work activities.

Auditory hallucinations are commonly of a threatening or persecutory nature. Vestibular disturbances are frequent, and felt by the patient as rotation of the room or movement of the floor. Insects may be felt to be crawling over the skin, perhaps as an elaboration of paraesthesiae.

A marked feature is the intense reality with which the hallucinatory experiences are imbued, and the strong emotional reactions which they produce. Apprehension and fear are typical, but amusement and even jocularity may be seen. Sometimes apprehension and amusement are mixed together in a highly characteristic and paradoxical manner. As with the hallucinations themselves the affective state is often changeable from one moment to another, though fear or even terror is usually uppermost.

The degree of impairment of consciousness varies widely from case to case and in the same patient from one moment to another. It is rarely profound except in the terminal stages, though the true level may be very hard to judge. Diminished awareness of the environment is coupled with overarousal in a characteristic fashion. The patient appears to be alert and over-responsive, but his responsiveness usually proves to be closely tied to his own internal stimuli; he may startle easily but is otherwise largely unaware and indifferent to what proceeds in the real world around him. Disorientation and confusion are very obvious, but the degree of inattention and distractibility may give the impression that consciousness is more severely impaired than is actually the case. When attention can be held fleetingly it is sometimes possible to show that memory and other intellectual functions are surprisingly intact.

Speech is usually slurred and with paraphasic errors. In severe examples it may be incoherent and fragmented. Delusions are secondarily elaborated on the faulty perceptual experiences, but are usually fragmented, transitory, and as changeable as the hallucinations. Suggestibility is marked and adds to the frequency with which illusions occur; pressing on the eyeballs may cause the patient to see whatever one tells him he sees, and when presented with a blank piece of paper he may proceed to 'read' it on instruction.

Outcome

The disorder is usually short lived, lasting less than three days in the majority of cases. Very rarely recurrent phases may be seen over a longer period of time. Typically it terminates in a prolonged sleep after which the patient feels fully recovered apart from residual weakness and exhaustion. In rare cases a prolonged attack of delirium tremens may clear to reveal an amnesic syndrome, when Wernicke's encephalopathy had been present and unnoticed during the acute stage.

Death when it occurs is usually due to cardio-vascular collapse, infection, hyperthermia, or self-injury during the phase of intense restlessness. Any infective process, and particularly pneumonia, markedly increases the mortality.

Aetiology

The precise pathophysiology is unknown. Cerebral oedema was formerly thought to be responsible but has not been adequately confirmed. A primary disorder of the reticular formation is strongly suggested by the clinical components of profound inattention coupled with alertness, overactivity and insomnia. The remarkable association with disturbance of REM sleep has already been described (p. 512).

A low serum magnesium has been found in delirium tremens (Flink *et al.*, 1954) but is not accepted as causal. Adrenal insufficiency has also been blamed, but steroids cannot be shown to be markedly effective in treatment. Low levels of thiamine and nicotinic acid have been found in proportion to the severity of the symptoms (Kershaw, 1967), though this probably reflects the severity of the underlying alcoholism rather than a directly causal relationship. Thus the condition is known to be capable of recovering on water alone, and in the experimental studies of Isbell *et al.* (1955) high vitamin supplements given intramuscularly did not prevent its appearance.

Withdrawal of alcohol is the factor most clearly incriminated in the aetiology of the condition, and in the majority of cases can be detected in the antecedent history. Premonitory symptoms often set in within a day or two of cessation of drinking, but the full-blown syndrome usually appears only after three or four days of abstinence. Refeeding with alcohol has been shown to ameliorate the condition. Nevertheless some cases undoubtedly begin during a bout of heavy consumption, and reduction of intake below some critical value must then be postulated.

However all authorities do not agree about the essential role of alcohol withdrawal. Lundquist (1961) could find evidence of abstinence antedating the onset in only a quarter of cases, and in half of these there was some other complicating factor such as trauma or infection. Those who question the role of withdrawal suggest that the patient has commonly stopped drinking because of nausea or distaste for alcohol, these symptoms being the first sign of the developing illness. Certainly it can be shown that trauma or infection are present from the outset in up to half of the cases, and it is unlikely that this always acts merely by bringing a halt to the drinking. Lundquist (1961) found biochemical evidence of acute liver damage in up to 90% of patients with delirium tremens, and much more commonly than in non-delirious alcoholics.

A multifactorial aetiology will probably prove ultimately to be the complete explanation. Alcohol withdrawal may well be the principal factor in the majority of cases, but this would appear to act by way of complex metabolic and neurophysiological pathways. Hence in some patients equivalent disturbances may sometimes come about by other means.

Treatment

Treatment of minor withdrawal symptoms can often be undertaken on an out-patient basis with the help of sedation from chlordiazepoxide or chlormethiazole. However, patients with a history of withdrawal seizures, and those with any indication of impending delirium tremens, should be admitted to hospital immediately. Management will in essence consist of close nursing observation at regular intervals, so that the dosage of sedative drugs can be titrated against the symptoms displayed. Edwards (1982) recommends chlordiazepoxide up to 40 mg three or four times per day, starting if necessary with an intramuscular dose of 50–100 mg. Treatment with chlormethiazole is an alternative. The drugs are then gradually tailed off over several days at a rate which prevents significant recrudescence of withdrawal symptoms.

With established delirium tremens treatment must always be in hospital, preferably in a setting where the medical and nursing staff are fully experienced with the procedures involved. The necessary steps are described by Rix (1978) and Edwards (1982). Fluid replacement and adequate sedation are the first essentials, with careful examination to detect complicating pathologies which aggravate the delirium and greatly worsen prognosis.

Head injury and infection must always be borne in mind. Skull and chest X-ray will be required. Coincident intoxication with barbiturates or other sedative drugs may lead to particularly severe withdrawal manifestations. Hypoglycaemia, hepatic failure, uraemia and electrolyte imbalance will need to be excluded. Wernicke's encephalopathy must be detected early and treated vigorously. Cardiac failure, gastroduodenal bleeding or bleeding from oesophageal varices may be present. A close watch must be kept at all stages for seizures or circulatory collapse.

The intensity of treatment required will obviously depend on the severity of delirium which has become established. When the syndrome is well developed half-hourly recordings of temperature, pulse and blood pressure should be made, along with a record of fluid intake and output. At least 6 litres of fluid per day will be required, of which 1.5 litres should be given as normal saline. If adequate oral intake cannot be ensured intravenous administration must be started with 5% glucose solution or glucose in saline. Hypokalaemia is a special risk. Hypomagnesaemia may occur.

Adequate sedation is essential, and dosage should be monitored closely against the patient's clinical state and level of consciousness. Chlordiazepoxide or chlormethiazole are now regarded as the drugs of choice in this situation. Chlordiazepoxide may be required in dosage of up to 400 mg daily or even more in divided doses. Initially it may be given by intramuscular injection—100 mg every 6 hours over the first 24 hours. Dosage reduction should then proceed smoothly over the next 5 days if possible. In patients who are very disturbed, a slow intravenous injection of diazepam may be employed in a dosage of 10–15 mg given at not more than 5 mg per minute. Chlormethiazole is preferred in several centres, with a starting dose of up to 2 g orally four times per day. Slow infusion of a 0.8% solution can be given by intravenous drip (Glatt *et al.*, 1966; Glatt and Frisch, 1969). Other sedatives such as phenothiazines, butyrophenones or paraldehyde should where possible be avoided.

Other treatment must always include high potency vitamin preparations as a prophylactic against Wernicke's encephalopathy or nicotinic acid deficiency encephalopathy. Phenytoin or carbamazepine should be given routinely when there is a past history of withdrawal seizures. Cardiovascular collapse, vomiting or hyperthermia will require appropriate management. The use of steroids is controversial but has been advocated when the delirium is severe (McNichol, 1970).

'ALCOHOLIC DEMENTIA' AND CEREBRAL ATROPHY IN ALCOHOLICS

The conception of alcoholic dementia has had a chequered history, figuring prominently in early textbooks of psychiatry but later yielding pride of place to Korsakoff's psychosis (Lishman, 1981). Nowadays the idea of a true dementia caused by alcohol is quite commonly viewed with caution. Many patients labelled as alcoholic dements are indeed suffering from Korsakoff's psychosis; and others are merely displaying profound social disorganisation in the context of chronic continuing inebriation. When opportunities arise to assess the latter after a period of total abstinence, intellectual functions may turn out to be substantially intact. Other alcoholics who dement are suffering essentially from a coincident vascular dementia or a dementia of the Alzheimer type.

Nevertheless clinical experience suggests that the long-continued abuse of alcohol may sometimes contribute directly to an end-state of dementia; the data in Table 14 (p. 415) show that alcohol is suspected of being at least a contributory cause in a substantial number of demented patients seen by hospital services. It features at approximately the same frequency as 'arteriosclerotic dementia' in many of the series shown. One must appreciate, moreover, that for every patient who has reached the stage of being investigated for a frank dementing picture, many others may be suffering the milder, and perhaps protracted, earlier stages of such disorder.

Adequate epidemiological studies are not available to clarify the size of the problem directly. It is only a proportion of alcoholics who come before treatment services, and a comprehensive follow-up of even those who do can present formidable problems. It is possible, moreover, that those who suffer marked impairment are particularly liable to be lost to view as time goes by.

Edwards (1982) estimates that among alcoholics attending any ordinary type of treatment facility upwards of 50% of patients aged over 45, and with a lengthy drinking history, will be found on careful assessment to show some degree of cognitive impairment. At one end of the spectrum one will merely find minor impairments of memory, concentration and judgement, and at the other extreme the fully developed picture of dementia. Among patients coming forward for treatment in Australia, some 8–9% were considered to warrant the label of dementia on the basis of progressive failure of memory, loss of intellect and deterioration of personality (Wilkinson *et al.*, 1971; Horvath, 1975).

Psychological Evidence

Clinical psychologists have presented a now substantial body of evidence to show that severe alcoholics, even after thorough 'drying out', are compromised on a wide range of psychological tests when compared with carefully matched controls. Fitzhugh *et al.* (1960, 1965), for example, compared a group of brain-damaged abstinent alcoholics with non-brain-damaged controls after matching for age and education. On the Wechsler Adult Intelligence Scale (WAIS) the alcoholics scored like the non-brain-damaged group, but on certain tests more specifically related to brain damage (the Trail Making Test and tests from the Halstead battery) they differed from the normals and resembled the brain-damaged population. Similar psychometric evidence, suggesting varying degrees of brain damage in alcoholics despite preserved IQ, was reported by Goldstein and Chotlos (1965), Jones and Parsons (1971) and Long and McLachlan (1974). It has emerged in alcoholics from middle and upper socio-economic classes with higher than average IQ (Smith *et al.*, 1973). Thus formal intelligence tests such as the WAIS may sometimes give a misleading impression of the capabilities of the alcoholic patient.

The more recent and often complex psychological literature has been reviewed by Parsons (1977), Tarter (1980), Acker (1982) and Goldman (1983). Numerous variables among the populations under survey must be taken into account, not least the duration of abstinence prior to testing. Psychological assessments during the first few weeks of abstinence show substantial recovery of intellectual and memory functions, so that accurate assessment of the stable cognitive state must be deferred until a considerable period of sobriety has occurred. Continuing restitution of function may indeed proceed for a period of several months. Nevertheless it seems very likely that deficits still persist on tests of psychomotor speed, perceptual-motor functioning, visuo-spatial competence, and measures of abstracting ability and complex reasoning, even after a year of total abstinence. Careful tests of memory function can likewise remain impaired, to the extent that a continuum of memory impairment has been postulated, ranging from normality at one extreme to the fully-fledged picture of the fixed Korsakoff amnesic defect at the other (Ryback 1971; Ryan and Butters, 1980). New learning capacity, as assessed by a test of forming new associations between ostensibly unrelated material (the Symbol-Digit Paired-Associate Learning Test), has even been found to remain impaired after a minimum of five years' abstinence, likewise capacity for complex figure-ground analysis as measured by the Embedded Figures Test (Brandt *et al.*, 1983).

The vulnerability of tests related to frontal lobe function, such as the Category subtest of the Halstead Reitan Battery or the Wisconsin Card Sorting Test, are particularly noteworthy, in that frontal lobe dysfunction can co-exist with adequate performance on standard intelligence tests. Frontal lobe dysfunction could be relevant to aspects of the personality change encountered in alcoholics—the circumstantiality, plausibility and weakness of volition — which may contribute significantly to relapse. Thus Gregson and Taylor (1977) found that an alcoholic's cognitive status on admission to hospital was the best single predictor of his response to treatment. A vicious circle may often come to be established, with worsening cognitive status contributing to the potentiation of the addiction.

The psychological impairments established in the majority of surveys to date have usually been no more than mild or moderate in degree. This, along with their tendency to ameliorate with abstinence, has probably led to the conception of alcoholic dementia becoming unfashionable. It is no longer unusual, however, to accept a dementia that is capable of improvement. The alternative term, *'reversible alcoholic cognitive deterioration'*, has perhaps something to commend it, though with the proviso that the reversibility may not always be complete. Moreover, with a high incidence of such deterioration among the alcoholic population it is not unlikely that this will sometimes come to be severely developed, perhaps on the basis of special vulnerability in certain individuals. The stage will certainly be set, as the alcoholic gets older, for the brain damage occasioned by alcoholism to couple readily with other pathologies—those of ageing, trauma, vascular changes and hepatic dysfunction—to lead to more serious and irreversible change.

Neuropathology

Direct appraisal of cerebral pathology in alcoholics, over and above that concerned with the classical Wernicke lesion, has met with conflicting findings. Cerebral atrophy, mild or moderate in degree, was reported in a high proportion of Courville's (1955) chronic alcoholics at autopsy, in half of Neuberger's (1957) and all of Lynch's (1960). Other reports, however, do not find it or do not comment on it. Courville (1955) was led to conclude that alcoholism was probably the commonest cause of noteworthy cortical atrophy in patients under 50 years of age; the dorso-lateral aspects of the frontal lobes were especially affected, with enlargement particularly of the frontal horns of the lateral ventricles. Microscopy showed arachnoidal thickening and cell degeneration and loss affecting mainly the smaller pyramidal cells of the superficial and intermediate laminae. Disintegration of nerve fibres was observed, with dissolution of the myelin sheaths. Lynch (1960) described a similar histological picture in 11 chronic alcoholics with adequate nutritional status, when compared with a group of non-alcoholic subjects of the same age and sex. Commenting on the negative reports in the literature, Lynch attributed this to a waning of neuropathological interest in the cortex of alcoholics, with the accent of pathological enquiry centering increasingly on the Wernicke lesion at the base of the brain and on changes in the cerebellum. He stressed also how inherently difficult it is to chart changes, degenerations and loss in such a complex and crowded area as the cortex.

More recent quantitative studies on brains obtained at autopsy are now beginning to indicate that atrophy or 'shrinkage' is indeed often detectable. These investigations from Perth, Australia, have followed in the wake of the CT studies described below and serve to confirm some of their principal findings. Thus Harper and Blumbergs (1982) have found that brain weights tend to be lower, to a small but significant extent, when alcoholics are compared with controls of equivalent age. Measurements of the 'pericerebral space', obtained by subtracting brain volume from intracranial volume, have shown a mean increase of some 50% in alcoholics (Harper and Kril, 1985). Approximately one-third of the alcoholic brains showed pericerebral volumes in excess of the control range, those with Wernicke's encephalopathy or histological evidence of liver disease being particularly affected. More detailed measurements reported by Harper et al. (1985) have revealed significant reductions in white matter volume (by 14%) and significant increases in ventricular volume (by 36%).

Air Encephalography

Several earlier reports suggested that cerebral 'atrophy' might be commoner than expected on air encephalography. These have been summarised by Ron (1977). Pluvinage (1954), for example, demonstrated ventricular dilatation in 17 alcoholic patients who presented with psychological deficits despite a period of abstinence and full vitamin therapy. Tumarkin et al. (1955) found moderate diffuse atrophy in 7 young soldiers between 25 and 38 years of age who had shown declining efficiency at work and impairment of recent memory. The electro-encephalograms were abnormal in every case.

Lereboullet et al. (1956) were able to assemble 77 alcoholics with 'indubitable atrophy' on air encephalography after rigorously excluding those with head injuries or other known causes which might have accounted for it. The frontal lobes were once more particularly affected. Twelve of the patients went on to autopsy and a close correspondence was observed between the radiological and post-mortem findings.

Air encephalography was of course difficult to justify except on specially selected subjects, and adequate control comparisons were hard to achieve. The significance and the generality of the findings thus remained in doubt. Certain studies were nevertheless impressive, such as those of Haug (1968) and Brewer and Perrett (1971), with between half and three-quarters of subjects showing cortical changes or ventricular enlargement, and often when unexpected on clinical grounds. Haug found that the changes were most marked when personality deterioration was severe in addition to intellectual impairment. High correlations were observed in Brewer and Perrett's patients between the degree of atrophy over the cortex and measures of cognitive defect. The electroencephalogram, by contrast, was relatively unhelpful in identifying the presence of impairment. Brewer and Perrett concluded that brain damage due to alcoholism might be considerably more common than is generally recognised; functions such as judgement and logic, and ability to modify and control behaviour might be impaired in consequence, with obvious implications for the perpetuation of drinking.

CT Scanning

CT scanning has now allowed a more thorough-going appraisal of the situation, and several surveys have been conducted on large populations of alcoholics (Bergman et al., 1980a, 1980b; Cala et al., 1980; Carlen et al., 1981; Ron et al., 1982; Ron 1983). They have upheld the main air encephalographic findings. The non-invasive nature of the procedure has, moreover, allowed representative samples to be investigated, and dilation of the sulci, fissures and ventricles has been found to be common even in patients who would otherwise have been rated on clinical grounds as unimpaired. Fine gradings of the degree of morphological change have been possible in relation to controls chosen from healthy non-alcoholic volunteers.

The conclusions to be drawn from these more recent studies are as follows. Some 50–70% of severe chronic alcoholics show indubitable evidence of cortical shrinkage or ventricular dilation or both. Involvement of the frontal lobes of the brain has sometimes been particularly evident. The changes can be found in quite young alcoholics, appearing well within the first decade of alcohol abuse, though they become more marked in the older age groups studied. Planimetric measures of lateral ventricular size show on average some 50% enlargement compared to age-matched controls. This has emerged even in identical twins discordant for a history of alcoholism (Gurling *et al.*, 1984). Atrophy of the cerebellar vermis can also be seen in a high proportion of subjects. However, personal susceptibility to such developments appears to vary widely, in that approximately a third of subjects continue to show normal scans despite long-continued and severe drinking histories.

These cerebral changes clearly antedate clinical evidence of mental impairment, being demonstrable after excluding patients with obvious cognitive deficits. They often appear to set in early during the alcoholic career, and after developing to a certain degree it is possible that they fail to progress further. In seeking for clinical associations of the CT scan findings few have emerged other than age and duration of abstinence. The duration and severity of alcohol abuse appear to bear little relation to the severity of the cerebral changes once age has been taken into account, though there is some indirect evidence that episodic drinking may be less harmful in this respect than steady continuous drinking. The most decisive influence, where the drinking history is concerned, lies with the duration of abstinence prior to scanning. Ron and her colleagues (Ron *et al.*, 1982; Ron, 1983) have shown that with increasing abstinence over a period of several months the cerebral changes become less pronounced, though failing to recede completely. Follow-up with rescanning over an interval of 1–3 years has indeed confirmed that abstinence in the interim is the factor most closely associated with whether or not the scans will show improvement. This partial reversibility with abstinence is, of course, strong evidence against the possibility that the cerebral changes revealed on the scan may have antedated, and predisposed to, the onset of the alcoholism.

Psychometric testing carried out in conjunction with scanning has indicated, as expected, that a considerable proportion of the alcoholics score poorly on many tests. The concordance between measures of functional and structural change has, however, usually proved to be low. Bergman *et al.*

(1980a, 1980b) found some evidence that impairment of memory and general intelligence was associated with the degree of ventricular enlargement, and that the Halstead Impairment Index was associated with cortical status. All such correlations were, however, low. Acker *et al.* (1984) found remarkably few associations on an extensive battery of tests once care had been taken to control for age and estimates of premorbid intellectual competence. It would seem, therefore, that the structural changes revealed by CT scanning are largely independent of functional deficits, at least in the carefully recruited samples examined to date. Where more deteriorated patients have been examined (Carlen *et al.*, 1981), impaired patients have shown greater CT changes than the unimpaired, though age differences in the groups may have been mainly responsible for this. The scan parameters examined to date are thus an inadequate reflection of functional competence and cannot be relied upon alone in the clinical evaluation of the individual patient.

Other Evidence

Further evidence of cerebral disorder in alcoholism has come from the study of event-related potentials, the P_3 component being less well developed in alcoholics than controls, and smaller in alcoholics with demonstrable atrophy than in those without (Begleiter *et al.*, 1980). Neurochemical investigations have revealed impaired cholinergic function in brain samples obtained at autopsy (Antuono *et al.*, 1980; Nordberg *et al.*, 1980), of a nature similar to that encountered in Alzheimer's disease (p. 382). Deficits have likewise been discovered where several brain biogenic amines are concerned (Carlsson *et al.*, 1980). Recent morphometric evidence indicative of changes in brain weight, pericerebral space and white matter volume is described on p. 519.

Possible Causes

These various findings are all pointers to the vulnerability of the alcoholic brain, a vulnerability that is clearly more of a risk for some individuals than others. The determinants of why occasional alcoholics escape brain changes and functional deficits despite severe dependence, while others develop them from an early stage, remain at present unknown. Genetic factors may play a considerable role. In susceptible individuals, however, the brain malfunction may contribute not only to decreased tolerance but also to loss of control; and if some alcoholics have impaired control on an organic basis from early in their drinking careers this could be an important factor in perpetuating the addiction. When susceptibility to the cerebral disorder is marked, this can be seen as paving the way to a later alcoholic dementia.

Several factors may be operative in contributing to such functional and structural deficits—dietary neglect, repeated episodes of head trauma, liver disorder, alcoholic comas with anoxia or hypoglycaemia, or the direct toxic action of alcohol on the central nervous system. Their relative contributions have been hard to determine. In the principal CT scan studies outlined above care has usually been taken to exclude patients with known cerebral trauma, episodes of drug overdosage or other possible reasons for the development of cerebral atrophy. Even so, accumulating minor insults may have made a contribution. A role for dietary neglect in contributing to psychological impairments has sometimes been highlighted (Guthrie and Elliott, 1980) but would seem unlikely as the whole explanation. The brain weights in Harper and Blumbergs' (1982) study were as low in those without histological evidence of nutritional brain damage as in those with changes indicative of a Wernicke's encephalopathy; by contrast Harper and Kril (1985) found that the 'pericerebral space' was more greatly increased in the presence of Wernicke's encephalopathy or liver disease (p. 519). Severity of liver damage, as assessed by biopsy, has shown some association with the degree of cortical shrinkage on the CT scan (Acker *et al.*, 1982), but the relationship was weak and has not emerged in other investigations (Lee *et al.*, 1979; Carlen *et al.*, 1981).

Laboratory evidence lends a good deal of support to the possibility that a direct toxic action of alcohol on the brain may be largely responsible. Studies in mice and rats have shown that brain changes can be induced after a period of several months on a diet supplemented with alcohol (Riley and Walker, 1978; Walker *et al.*, 1980a, 1980b). Marked alterations in dendritic morphology are found in the hippocampal pyramidal neurones, dentate granular layers and cerebellar vermis, proceeding to cell degeneration and loss. These effects are produced despite the maintenance of good nutrition in all other respects. West *et al.* (1982) have shown, moreover, that alcohol inhibits the reactive sprouting of dendrites in the rat hippocampus which constitutes the normal response to injury. Such observations could be relevant to the pervasive CT scan changes encountered in alcoholics, and might help to explain the slow reversal of cortical shrinkage that has been observed with abstinence. As discussed on p. 382 the plasticity inherent in the adult brain with regard to dendritic growth and sprouting has come to be appreciated (Buell and Coleman, 1979), continuing growth of the dendritic domains appearing to compensate for an age-related decline in neuronal numbers. Dendritic growth may stand to be compromised in the alcoholic subject, with a return to normal levels when prolonged abstinence has been assured. Other factors may also be involved, such as changes in protein or lipid synthesis.

Barbiturates

Acute barbiturate intoxication is frequently the result of a suicide attempt, or of self-medication to gain relief from severe tension and anxiety. Chronic intoxication is seen mostly in barbiturate addicts, who appear to be much more numerous than hospital statistics would suggest. Addiction is associated with increasing tolerance so that ultimately enormous amounts may be consumed. A high proportion of addicts have severely abnormal personalities and the barbiturate abuse may be accompanied by alcoholism or addiction to other drugs. The barbiturates may sometimes be taken by intravenous administration. In others the addiction has developed as a result of therapeutic attempts to relieve long-standing symptoms of insomnia, anxiety or depression, though this is now much less common than it used to be on account of more judicious prescribing practices. The recognition of chronic intoxication is of great importance since the patient will usually seek to conceal his addiction and many other conditions may be simulated as described below.

ACUTE INTOXICATION

The clinical picture is well known since barbiturates have commonly been used in suicide attempts. A short period of confusion and drowsiness gives way to deepening coma. The pulse and respiration are slowed, the blood pressure lowered, and the body temperature often sub-normal. The tendon reflexes are diminished, or absent in deep coma. The plantar responses may be up-going. Nystagmus is a prominent feature in the earlier stages together with tremors of the tongue and lips. Death may result from respiratory failure or peripheral circulatory collapse.

During recovery signs of cerebellar disturbance are marked, with nystagmus, ataxia, asynergia, dysarthria and hypotonia. A muddled euphoria is often seen while consciousness is returning, and a period of hypomania may persist after all neurological features have cleared.

Estimation of the blood barbiturate level serves to confirm the cause of the acute intoxication or coma. The electroencephalogram may also be useful in showing generalised fast beta activity during the first 24 hours after overdose, unlike most other severe intoxications which produce slowing of the electroencephalogram in parallel with reduction of the level of consciousness (Kugler, 1964).

CHRONIC BARBITURATE INTOXICATION

Chronic barbiturate intoxication produces a state of drowsiness, fluctuating confusion, dysarthria and ataxia which may closely resemble drunkenness due to alcohol. Withdrawal effects are also similar with epileptic fits and delirium. It is essential to consider covert addiction in patients who present with intermittent confusion of obscure origin, or who develop fits or delirium of uncertain aetiology on admission to hospital. An important clue may lie in the patient's unwillingness for investigations and his strenuous objection to hospitalisation.

The clinical picture was described by Curran (1938, 1944) and has been clarified by the experiments of Isbell and associates on volunteer subjects serving narcotic sentences (Isbell *et al.*, 1950; Fraser *et al.*, 1958). While intoxicated the patient is somnolent and muddled, with difficulty in concentration and periods of disorientation. The usual mood change is towards euphoria with periods of excitement and irritability. Garrulous uninhibited behaviour is common and restlessness may be marked. Prolonged intoxication leads to severe deterioration of habits and self care. Neurological features include nystagmus, dysarthria, tremulousness, and ataxia of gait and stance. The abdominal reflexes are typically depressed or absent.

A prominent feature is the variability from day to day and even from one time of day to the next. This was observed by Isbell *et al.* (1950) among volunteers even though the daily intake was constant. The degree of sonmolence was variable and periods of severe confusion could alternate with periods of lucidity. Behaviour could be facetious, petulant or hostile, changing from one moment to the next. Different subjects also varied in their response; some showed swings between elation and maudlin depression, some became seclusive and withdrawn, and others were combative, abusive or markedly paranoid.

The withdrawal syndrome has also been clarified by Isbell *et al.* Prior to their studies there had been reports of withdrawal fits and delirium in barbiturate addicts but there had often been coincident addiction to other drugs and alcohol. Isbell *et al.* (1950) and Fraser *et al.* (1958) were able to observe the effects of abrupt withdrawal after keeping subjects intoxicated with barbiturates alone for long periods of time.

On withdrawal the signs of intoxication subsided and there was seeming improvement during the first 8–12 hours. Minor withdrawal manifestations then appeared in the form of anxiety, twitching, tremor and distortions of visual perception. These were accompanied by progressive weakness, dizziness, nausea, vomiting and profound insomnia. The pulse and respiration rates were raised, orthostatic hypotension developed, and weight loss was rapid. Pyrexia was often seen.

More severe manifestations usually appeared on the second or third day with one or more grand mal convulsions, sometimes followed by acute delirium. This closely resembled delirium tremens with confusion, disorientation, intense anxiety, agitation, marked insomnia, delusions, and auditory and visual hallucinations. In most cases it terminated spontaneously after several days with a critical sleep, though occasionally the delirium was protracted and dangerously exhausting. It was then necessary to reintoxicate the subject with barbiturates and tail-off the dose in a gradual manner. Complete recovery was usually attained within one to two weeks.

The degree of physical dependence was found to depend on the dose employed during the period of intoxication. A daily intake of less than 400 mg (of quinalbarbitone or pentobarbitone) failed to create significant dependence, and withdrawal symptoms were not observed when the drug was discontinued. After 600 mg per day approximately half of the subjects had minor withdrawal symptoms, and after 800 mg per day all were affected, occasionally with fits or hallucinations but still not to the extent of delirium. With higher dosage the withdrawal manifestations were much more severe. Eighteen patients were kept continuously intoxicated on doses of 900 mg to 2·2 g per day for periods of 32–144 days before withdrawal: all had the minor withdrawal symptoms with sufficient severity to require therapeutic intervention, 14 had fits and 12 developed frank delirium. There was insufficient evidence to determine the minimal length of time required to develop such severe dependence, but it appeared to be in excess of 90 days.

There is little information regarding *possible long-term effects* of barbiturate abuse on the central nervous system. By analogy with alcohol (p. 517, *et seq.*) one might expect that such powerful sedative agents, taken in large dosage and over prolonged periods, could impair cerebral function in the long-term view. It appears that the question has rarely been addressed directly, no doubt because of difficulties in amassing patients for systematic follow-up study. Equivalent difficulties surround the investigation of patients who abuse narcotic or stimulant drugs (Grant and Mohns, 1975). Moreover polydrug abuse has become the common pattern, with a large number of sedative, narcotic and stimulant drugs often featuring in the histories; the effects attributable to any one can then be hard to discern.

Grant and co-workers (Grant and Judd, 1976; Grant *et al.*, 1976) have attempted to investigate the problem in subjects abusing multiple drugs, predominantly those of the sedative-hypnotic class. As judged by neuropsychological testing and electroencephalography almost half showed evidence of mild to moderate generalised cerebral impairment during the early weeks of treatment, perhaps accounting for the inattention, distractibility and lack of motivation encountered in therapy. Abstracting ability and perceptuo-motor control were principally affected, with relative preservation of general intelligence, memory and verbal abilities. The psychological deficits were often evident after many weeks of abstinence, sometimes appearing to persist even beyond 5 months. It was difficult, however, to exonerate the effects of further drug abuse during the follow-up period.

Rumbaugh *et al.* (1971) have drawn attention to cerebral angiographic findings which could also be relevant. Among patients abusing drugs by intravenous injection, many of the intermediate sized cerebral arteries showed irregular segmental areas of constriction. Small arteries could show complete obstructions, perhaps due to emboli or thrombosis secondary to vasculitis. Polydrug abuse had again been the pattern, so specific agents could not be incriminated. Impurities in the injected material, or sepsis, could have been chiefly responsible.

Electroencephalographic Changes

The electroencephalogram during chronic intoxication shows augmented amplitude and an increased percentage of fast frequencies. After withdrawal dramatic changes occur, with high voltage paroxysmal discharges or bursts of high amplitude waves at 4–6 Hz during the first 12–48 hours (Isbell *et al.*, 1950). Records during and after fits are similar to records obtained with the grand mal fits of idiopathic epilepsy. Within 30 days of withdrawal the pattern has usually returned to normal.

Oswald and Priest (1965) have investigated more closely the electroencephalographic changes which can occur with relatively low doses of barbiturates over short periods of time. Two volunteer subjects were given 400 mg of amylobarbitone nightly for nine nights then 600 mg for a further nine nights. REM sleep, which normally makes up a little less than a quarter of the total night's sleep showed an initial fall, but returned to normal at the end of the first week as tolerance developed. The increased dose on the tenth night caused a transient reduction again. On withdrawal at the end of the experiment both subjects complained of insomnia and nightmares, and the electroencephalogram showed a rebound with a high proportion of REM sleep which persisted for several weeks after the last dose had been given.

Differential Diagnosis

Patients with chronic barbiturate intoxication may be suspected of neurological disease when the neurological features are severe. The nystagmus, incoordination and ataxia are of cerebellar type, and may suggest cerebellar disease or multiple sclerosis. When somnolence is profound a diencephalic tumour or encephalitis may be simulated. Presenile dementia is sometimes suspected when the patient is markedly forgetful and unkempt in appearance. It is usually the marked fluctuations in behaviour and the patient's surreptitious attitude which then raise the possibility of drug abuse. Alternatively he may be diagnosed as suffering from severe neurosis or personality disorder when the principal abnormalities are persistent insomnia, irritability and tension.

The differentiation from other intoxications can be difficult until the blood is examined for barbiturate content. Uraemia and other metabolic disorders may first have to be excluded. Alcoholism can present similarly and some patients abuse alcohol and barbiturates together. Addiction to other drugs such as glutethimide (doriden) or chloral hydrate may produce a similar picture. The differentiation from chronic bromide intoxication was formerly important and must still be considered occasionally.

Important distinguishing features listed by Curran (1944) include nystagmus which is usually seen in barbiturate intoxication but rarely with bromides; gag and corneal reflexes are present in barbiturate intoxication but usually lost in severe bromism; an accompanying rash is usually urticarial or scarlatiniform with barbiturates, covering the limbs and trunk, whereas the bromide rash is acneiform and on the face. Moreover bromide intoxication frequently takes the form of delirium, whereas this is rare with barbiturates until withdrawal has occurred.

Withdrawal fits raise the possibility of epilepsy due to other causes when the barbiturate addiction is concealed. Gardner (1967) has described such patients presenting in a general hospital. James (1963) has similarly suggested that drug withdrawal delirium is commoner in hospital practice than is realised. The symptoms resulting from chronic intoxication raise the possibility of physical or psychiatric illness and the patient is duly hospitalised for investigation; 2 or 3 days later the withdrawal delirium develops, sometimes with pyrexia, and is regarded as toxic or infective in origin.

Treatment

The treatment of an acute overdose of barbiturates requires immediate admission to hospital, with facilities at hand for mechanical respiration and dialysis if required. Induced vomiting or gastric lavage must be carried out urgently, and measures may be needed to control peripheral circulatory failure. Deepening or prolonged coma may necessitate artificial respiration and the use of the artificial kidney.

In chronic addicts the drug should under no circumstances be withdrawn abruptly. Status epilepticus can be a grave complication, and Fraser et al. (1953) have reported a patient who died of acute cardiac failure during sudden withdrawal. Gradual reduction of dosage is therefore undertaken after establishing the level of barbiturates which is sufficient to elminate tremor, insomnia and postural hypotension (Slater and Roth, 1969). Pentobarbitone is usually used, either four or six-hourly. Some subjects may require as much as 2–2·5 g in the first 24 hours. Thereafter the dose is reduced by not more than 100 mg per day, with readiness to increase again temporarily if symptoms return. If fits occur phenytoin 100 mg three times daily should be given in addition. The total withdrawal period may need to take 2 or 3 weeks or longer. Chlorpromazine can be a useful adjunct to allay minor symptoms during the

withdrawal phase, but is usually unecessary. Careful attention to the broader aspects of the addiction must then be instituted, with proper psychosocial investigation and every effort at comprehensive follow-up care.

Cannabis
(Indian Hemp, Hashish, Marihuana)

The relationship between cannabis and psychiatric disorder is controversial and has unfortunately tended to become an emotive topic. In spite of considerable attention to the subject there is still uncertainty about the prevalence of seriously adverse psychological reactions to the drug, and case reporting has tended perhaps to highlight the rare and exceptional. It is certain however that some individuals can present with marked mental disturbance occasioned by cannabis, and this must nowadays be increasingly considered in psychiatric differential diagnosis. Both acute and chronic forms of adverse reaction have been described. The main point of contention is how far these represent special vulnerability to breakdown in the patient rather than the direct toxic properties of cannabis on the functioning of the nervous system.

Cannabis Intoxication

The effects of mild intoxication after smoking marihuana are reasonably distinctive and were described in detail by Bromberg (1934) and Allentuck and Bowman (1942). The principal features include a euphoric dream-like state, mild impairment of consciousness and distortion of time sense. More severe intoxication is accompanied by fragmentation of thought processes and often by hallucinations.

Almost immediately after inhalation the subject feels light-headed and dizzy, with ringing in the ears and a sensation of floating on air. Sometimes there is transitory anxiety or panic, but this characteristically gives way to feelings of ease and mild elation. The conjunctivae redden and photophobia and lachrymation may develop. Some subjects show tremors, twitching and ataxia. The pulse and blood pressure are usually increased.

The further development of the mental effects no doubt depends on features in the individual and the circumstances in which the drug is taken. Exhilaration is common, with a vivid sense of happiness, buoyancy and lightness of the limbs. An aphrodisiac effect has been claimed but is not well substantiated.

A phase of psychomotor overactivity often ensues with voluble rapid speech which the subject considers to be brilliant and witty. Answers to questions seem to him to appear ready formed and surprising in their clarity, but to the external observer his performance is usually dull, banal and often confused. By contrast some subjects react to cannabis by becoming markedly apprehensive, querulous or suspicious. Others become lethargic and slip directly into a state of 'delicious and confused lassitude' which sometimes borders on stupor.

Cognitive functions are affected in many subtle ways. The stream of talk tends to be circumstantial and fragmented. There may be difficulty in linking parts to the whole, or sudden interruptions in the stream of thought resembling the blocking of schizophrenia. Time sense is characteristically distorted, often with remarkable lengthening of subjective appreciation of time spans. Sometimes there is unawareness of the passage of time, or a curious disturbance in which the present does not seem to arise out of the past. Attention, concentration and comprehension are only slightly impaired in the milder stages of intoxication, but memory functions can usually be shown to be faulty (Tinklenberg et al., 1970).

With more severe intoxication there are more dramatic symptoms. Waves of ecstasy, perplexity or terror may be experienced, along with marked feelings of depersonalisation or derealisation. Body image disturbances are often alarming. The subjective evaluation of sensations in all modalities is changed. Visual disturbances are the most intrusive, with distortion of shapes and intensification of colours. Hallucinatory experiences consist of flashes of light, amorphous forms of vivid colour, geometrical figures, human faces or pictures of great complexity.

As the acute intoxication subsides the subject usually drifts into a dreamless sleep. After-effects are uncommon, though after excessive doses the subject may wake with some degree of fatigue or generalised aches and pains. Quite commonly a clear memory is retained of the principal phenomena experienced during the acute intoxication.

Keeler et al. (1968) have described spontaneous recurrences of marihuana effects after discontinuation of the drug, and consider this to be relatively frequent. In some of their examples the recurrences served to precipitate severe anxiety and necessitated emergency psychiatric treatment. Whether or not such features are due to persistent biochemical effects of the drug is unknown. They appear to be analogous to the 'flashbacks' of LSD experience discussed on p. 531.

One patient was confused under the drug, with disorientation, panic, inability to talk, and hallucinations of coloured spots and designs. For 3 weeks thereafter he experienced intermittent confusion, disorientation and similar hallucinations most often when attempting to sleep.

Another patient found that under marihuana the limbs of trees would appear to undulate and objects would be covered with sparkling points of light. This would return markedly during the day after drug use and the patient looked forward to such spontaneous recurrences.

(Keeler et al., 1968)

It seems that tetrahydrocannabinols are responsible for most of the psychological effects of cannabis. Different preparations vary in their potency and probably in their content of other toxic constituents, accounting for the somewhat different pictures reported from one investigation to another. Isbell et al. (1967) were able to reproduce the essential manifestations of hashish or marihuana intoxication by giving chemically pure delta-9-trans-tetra-hydro-cannabinol to human volunteers either orally or by smoking.

It was formerly held that tolerance did not appear to develop and that there was no need to increase subsequent doses for an equivalent effect. Evidence of physical dependence was scanty, and abrupt cessation after prolonged use was not found to produce withdrawal symptoms. These assertions have come under closer scrutiny, however, and may be erroneous (World Health Organisation Report, 1971; Nahas, 1973). Some evidence of tolerance in heavy smokers has been reported, likewise possible abstinence phenomena on abrupt discontinuation in the form of anxiety, depression, weakness, sleep disturbances, sweating and fine tremors. Psychological dependence certainly seems to occur in many regular users.

Acute Psychiatric Disorder with Cannabis

It is probable that individuals are affected by cannabis on a continuum, ranging from the relatively benign effects of intoxication described above to episodes of severe psychiatric disturbance. Only the latter are liable to come before medical attention and they may occur in only a small percentage of users. The more florid disturbances are seen usually in markedly unstable individuals.

The pictures which have been described include acute organic reactions and neurotic and psychotic disturbances of variable duration. It is generally agreed that there is no specific 'cannabis psychosis', but rather that the content is determined by individual predisposition, coupled with potent contributions from the circumstances in which the drug is taken and the expectations adopted towards its effect. The evidence incriminating the drug is most obvious in those short-lived episodes which subside as the toxic effects wear off, or in disturbances which clearly grow out of symptoms characteristic of acute intoxication. In many of the longer lasting psychotic manifestations it can be hard to decide how far the drug is responsible, especially when use has been habitual over a long period of time. Indeed severe abuse may sometimes itself be secondary to the development of a manic-depressive or schizophrenic illness.

'*Reactive emotional states*' were among the short-lived disturbances described by Bromberg (1934) and are probably the commonest form of adverse reaction. These emerge in response to features of the acute intoxication. Acute anxiety culminates in episodes of panic, or hysterical dissociation may lead to fugue-like wandering with subsequent amnesia. A period of mania may grow out of the emotional excitement occasioned by the drug, or suicidal ideas may emerge while the patient is confused. Such reactions are self-limiting, lasting from several minutes to several hours, and are said to occur most frequently in novice users, ambivalent users, and users in a strange or threatening situation (Halikas, 1974). The frequency of their occurrence, as with all other adverse reactions, is unknown.

Acute paranoid or schizophrenic reactions probably occur mainly in subjects who are specially predisposed. Delusions and hallucinations take on a markedly paranoid colouring, or schizophreniform features may emerge with negativism, posturing or flexibilitas cerea. Such disturbances gradually subside as the drug is cleared from the body, though some may progress to longer lasting psychotic illnesses.

These usually take the form of manic-depressive or schizophrenia-like psychoses and may last for many weeks or months. Here the toxic effects of cannabis may have served to precipitate the illness which then follows its own independent course, though in many cases the illness may already have been present before the drug was taken. Spencer (1970) has reported several examples with certain features in common, and without a family or previous history of psychotic illness, and concludes that these at least were directly due to the repeated use of cannabis:

The illnesses began abruptly and coincidentally with the acute intoxication. The patients developed severe psychomotor overactivity, pressure of thought and flight of ideas. Many were markedly aggressive. Elation was coupled with incongruity and lability of mood. Bizarre grandiose delusions were common, also passivity phenomena and ideas of reference and influence, but hallucinations were conspicuous by their absence. Consciousness was clouded in the first few days but then cleared rapidly so that the major part of the illness occurred in clear consciousness. All patients showed dense amnesia extending from prior to the onset of the illness until admission to hospital or apprehension by the police, and this amnesic gap remained as a permanent sequel. The acute phase required hospitalisation for one to two months, gradually giving way to flattening of affect and residual thought fragmentation which sometimes appeared to persist indefinitely. Insight was gained into the florid delusional beliefs, but many of the patients remained odd and somewhat suspicious in demeanour after all other features had cleared.

Acute organic reactions with a paranoid colouring were reported by Talbott and Teague (1969) among soldiers in Vietnam. Ten of their twelve examples occurred in soldiers of previously stable personality, and in all of them the disturbance followed the first admitted exposure to the drug. All showed disorientation, impairment of memory, confusion, reduced attention span and tangential or disjointed thinking. Affect was labile with marked anxiety and fearfulness. Delusions, hallucinations and paranoid symptoms figured prominently, though the latter may have been partly determined by the environmental stress to which the men were exposed. The disorders were self-limiting and all subjects returned to duty within a week. Talbott and Teague consider that cannabis should be considered as a possibility whenever a young person presents with an acute toxic psychosis accompanied by paranoid features.

A 26-year-old soldier became aware of a burning choking sensation in his throat immediately after smoking marihuana. Shortly thereafter he felt apprehensive and suspicious. This rapidly increased in intensity and he became fearful that 'Nationals' were out to harm him. He fled in terror to his quarters where a doctor was called to see him. On examination he was anxious, disoriented for time, and showed wave-like fluctuations in the intensity of his paranoid fears. At its worst his fear of the 'Nationals' reached delusional intensity. Affect was appropriate but labile. Thinking was rapid and disjointed, as if he were experiencing a multitude of changing thoughts of dissimilar nature but with a common apprehensive quality. There were no hallucinations. Coordination was impaired on the finger-nose and heel-knee test and Romberg's sign was positive. Tendon reflexes were symmetrical and hyperactive. The conjunctivae were injected. He improved rapidly and was returned to duty within 48 hours. There was no recurrence during the next three months.

(Talbott and Teague, 1969)

Chronic Psychiatric Disorder with Cannabis

The excessive use of cannabis over long periods of time has been reported to lead to insidious personality change ('amotivational syndrome'), chronic psychotic illness resembling schizophrenia, or intellectual and social deterioration akin to organic dementia. The general tendency was to view early reports of such associations with reserve, and to discount a directly causal relationship with cannabis abuse (Slater and Roth, 1969). Decisive evidence is hard to obtain in view of the widespread use of the drug and the relative rarity of examples of chronic mental disorder; where social decompensation is concerned much may be due to social or subcultural influences rather than any direct toxic effects of the drug, and where chronic psychotic illness has developed there may have been crucially important predisposing factors, or even pre-existing illness, in the individuals affected. The problems encountered in attempting to evaluate the literature on the subject are excellently reviewed by Halikas (1974).

One study, for example, showed clearly that it could be erroneous to attribute causal significance to the drug (Halikas *et al.*, 1972). One hundred regular cannabis users were interviewed along with fifty non-user friends of the group. A high incidence of psychopathology was found in both samples, approximately half of each fulfilling criteria for some psychiatric diagnosis. Moreover almost every diagnosed psychiatric illness among the users had begun before first exposure to cannabis. Some users, therefore, come from a population at high risk for psychiatric problems. Nevertheless several reports have brought forward evidence that warrants close consideration, suggesting as it does that cannabis may yet make its own contribution to mental disorder.

Thacore (1973) has presented detailed clinical histories of four Indian patients in whom long-term ingestion of a mild cannabis preparation ('bhang') seemed to be responsible for chronic schizophrenialike psychoses. The illnesses were characterised by disturbance of thinking, fearfulness, hostile perception of the environment, delusions of persecution and auditory and visual hallucinations, but occurred in clear consciousness and with little or no distur-

bance of memory. The data strongly suggested a causal relationship between excessive consumption of bhang and the development of the psychoses; the latter continued and fluctuated with continuing and fluctuating cannabis ingestion, but remitted whenever cannabis was stopped or greatly curtailed.

Kolansky and Moore (1971, 1972) claimed that chronic mental disorder may result from biochemical or structural changes in the central nervous system in chronic marihuana users. Their initial report concerned 38 adolescents and young adults:

Several who had smoked marihuana four or five times per week over several months showed definite neurological impairment—slurred speech, staggering gait, hand tremor and disturbances of perception, Most of the others showed cognitive and emotional changes. Attention and concentration appeared impaired. A frequent complaint was of difficulty in converting thoughts into words, with the result that speech tended to be discursive. In the emotional sphere most subjects showed anxiety, depression, apathy, passivity and general indifference. Some showed hyperactivity, aggression and agitated behaviour. Paranoid developments, social withdrawal and infantile tendencies were common.

Social and ethical standards had often fallen so that promiscuity and venereal disease were frequent and the incidence of unwanted pregnancies was high. Personal cleanliness had deteriorated along with work and study habits. Eight patients showed frank psychotic developments with paranoid ideation, delusional systems, hallucinations, inappropriate affect and outbursts of aggression. The more florid features slowly disappeared on cessation of smoking, but some individuals were left with mild intellectual blunting or residual memory defects which seemed destined to be permanent. Unfortunately there was no attempt at objective psychometric assessment of such persisting cognitive impairments.

Kolansky and Moore stressed that none of the patients had shown evidence of psychiatric disturbance or personality deviation prior to starting use of the drug. Those who showed no more than aggravation of previous neurotic difficulties were excluded from the report, similarly those in whom a predisposition to psychotic illness could be discerned in retrospect. Such judgements, however, are notoriously hard to make with confidence, and the report was criticised on this and other grounds (Benson, 1971).

In a subsequent study Kolansky and Moore (1972) described a further series of adults who had smoked cannabis for periods of 16 months to 6 years. Here the organic impairments were stressed again:

A distinctive clustering of symptoms was described, including chronic headache, reversal of sleep rhythm and 'mental and physical sluggishness'. Confusion appeared to be attributable to difficulty with recent memory, coupled with slowed time sense and incapacity for sustained thought processes. Apathy was associated with poor reality testing, loss of interest in life goals and disturbed awareness of the self. The intensity of the symptoms and the presence of delusions seemed to be directly related to the frequency and length of time of cannabis use. Flattening of affective response was often marked; this was interpreted by the patient as representing a new philosophical calm, but in fact was liable to give way readily to anger or spite under duress.

Again the symptoms were said to have begun only after starting cannabis, and to tend to fade out three months to two years after discontinuation. The stereotyped nature of the symptoms, regardless of psychological predisposition, was cited again as evidence that they were caused by the direct effects of the drug on the central nervous system. Intensity of symptomatology was said to be related to duration and frequency of cannabis use. Kolansky and Moore postulated a specific organic response of the brain to cannabis products which might occur in any prolonged user. In addition to reversible toxicity on a biochemical basis they suggested that structural cerebral changes might occur in some instances.

The lack of controls, and of objective measures of impairment, have led Kolansky and Moore's conclusions to be viewed with considerable reserve. Altman and Evenson (1973) showed that, without controls, variables other than marihuana use could as easily be blamed for the symptoms. Grant et al. (1973) and Culver and King (1974) found no evidence of impairment on neuropsychological testing among students taking marihuana when compared with their fellows, though here it is likely that dosage was relatively mild. These reports indicate, nonetheless, that recreational use at moderate levels is unlikely to have adverse effects.

A more recent investigation among heavy users, however, gives renewed cause for concern. Mendhiratta et al. (1978) compared the psychological performance of 50 'charas' smokers and 'bhang' drinkers with controls of similar age and occupational status, at a minimum of twelve hours since last exposure to the drug. The cannabis users were significantly impaired on a wide range of functions —speed of reaction, concentration, time estimation and perceptuo-motor ability. Moreover, those using charas, which contains a higher concentration of cannabis than bhang, were the more severely

impaired and their deficits covered a wider range of functions.

The possibility of structural brain change appeared at first to find some support from neuroradiological evidence, again controversial, presented by Campbell et al. (1971). Ten patients with an average age of 22 and histories of regular cannabis smoking were reported to show cerebral atrophy on air encephalography. Linear measurements of ventricular size were consistently and significantly increased in comparison to a control group, and three patients showed dilated sulci over the convexity of the hemispheres. Presenting complaints included generalised headache, impairment of recent memory, episodes of amnesia, poor concentration and loss of efficiency at work. Some were depressed and some showed behavioural changes such as increased aggressiveness. On examination most were restless, anxious, suspicious or irritable, and some were morose and withdrawn. Some showed poor memory, difficulty with thinking and obvious lack of insight. Other causes of cerebral atrophy in so young a group of patients could not be discerned.

These findings, however, have come under criticism on several grounds—the nature of the controls, the adequacy of the radiological evidence, and the lack of objective assessments to substantiate the impression of organic mental deficits (Lancet, 1971; Bull, 1971; Brewer, 1972). The authors have argued further to uphold the significance of their findings (Campbell et al., 1972); nevertheless subsequent CT scan studies have been essentially negative (Co et al., 1976; Kuehnle et al., 1977).

Lysergic Acid Diethylamide
(LSD-25, lysergide)

LSD is an indole derivative of ergot and can be manufactured synthetically. It is the most powerful hallucinogen known, doses as small as 30 μg usually having a demonstrable effect on man. In other species its range of effects is extraordinary—it makes cats afraid of mice, reduces spiders' ability to build webs, causes fish to maintain a vertical nose-up position and swim backwards, and induces catatonia in pigeons (Louria, 1968). Chromosomal changes have also been reported, with increased chromosomal breaks and rearrangements of chromosomal material, though studies of patients receiving LSD for therapeutic purposes have failed to confirm such findings (Robinson et al., 1974). The mode of action on the brain is unknown; a competitive action with 5-hydroxytryptamine has been demonstrated in smooth muscle preparations, and this may possibly account in part for its cerebral effects.

Soon after its discovery it enjoyed a vogue in experimental psychiatry for the study of 'model psychoses' which could be induced in normal subjects. Thereafter it was employed as an adjunct in psychotherapy, for abreaction and to assist in the recall of long-forgotten experiences. As a result the acute effects of its administration were closely studied and formed the basis of a good deal of theoretical speculation. Nowadays administration under medical supervision is rare, but the drug continues to be widely taken on an illicit basis. The benefits claimed by users include augmented aesthetic sensitivity, enhanced creativity, the occurrence of transcendental experiences, the acquisition of new insights, and aphrodisiac effects. None of these has been properly substantiated. It is widely abused by unstable individuals in search of dramatic experiences, and often by those who abuse other drugs as well. As a drug of abuse LSD carries the special hazard that it can easily be administered surreptitiously without the subject's knowledge, resulting in profoundly disturbing effects which may sometimes lead to psychiatric referral.

When taken at intervals of more than a week the reaction is just as intense with the same repeated dose; however when taken daily tolerance develops rapidly, but is lost just as quickly when discontinued for a few days (Isbell *et al.*, 1956). There is no evidence that LSD is a drug of addiction in the sense of creating physical dependence, and there are no withdrawal effects on discontinuation. The danger lies rather in psychological dependence on the effects which are produced. Regular users sometimes come to view LSD experiences as central to their existence. They may adhere to a quasi-mystical interpretation of the meaning of the 'psychedelic experience', and sometimes develop a proselytizing zeal to persuade others of its value.

Acute Effects of Ingestion

The acute effects are well described by Isbell *et al.* (1956) and by Freedman (1968). There is some variation in individual susceptibility, but striking psychological changes usually follow doses in the range of 20–120 μg. The predominant effects with small doses are autonomic changes and alterations of mood, while larger doses produce perceptual distortions, vivid hallucinations, and striking subjective changes in the body image. These remarkably intense phenomena are usually not accompanied by clouding of consciousness or demonstrable impairment of intellectual processes; indeed a heightened state of awareness is maintained, and thought processes characteristically remain clear. The subject becomes preoccupied with the phenomena which he is witnessing and experiencing, but usually retains insight into the fact that they are due to the drug. In these respects the 'toxic' state resulting from LSD and related hallucinogens is very different from the acute organic reactions induced by most other agents.

The autonomic effects are the first to appear. They include dilation of the pupils, piloerection and some rise in body temperature. The tendon reflexes are often increased, and muscular tremors and twitching develop in severe reactions. Weakness, somnolence and giddiness may be marked. The earliest mood changes are of euphoria or anxiety. Euphoria is usually the predominant change and may extend to feelings of ecstasy, but this can be followed later by sudden swings to depression, panic or a profound sense of desolation. Some subjects become active and excited, while others become quiet, passive and withdrawn. Some are overwhelmed with a sense of mystical experience. Others become paranoid and hostile to their surroundings. Much probably depends on the premorbid personality of the subject, his expectations, and the setting in which the drug is taken.

Perceptual distortions, illusions and hallucinations are mainly in the visual sphere but can affect all modalities. Vision may be blurred or astonishingly enhanced and vivid. The perception of depth and distance is changed, size and shape distorted, and colour greatly intensified. Hearing may be dulled or hyperacute, the clothing may feel like sand paper, or the body feel extremely light or heavy. Synaesthesia is often marked and is fascinating to the subject—sensory data are transformed from one modality to another so that sounds or tactile stimuli appear as bursts of light or scintillating moving spectra. Hallucinations are again mainly visual and occur in both unformed and formed varieties—kaleidoscopic patterns of light in intense and changeable colour, or complex visions of animals and people. Tactile paraesthesiae, metallic tastes and strange smells are not uncommon, but auditory hallucinations are rare.

Distortions of the body image usually figure prominently and take bizarre forms. Customary boundaries become fluid, so that the patient feels he is one with the chair upon which he is sitting or merged with the body of another. His own hands and feet may appear to be transformed into claws or the extremities of a dead person. Sometimes intense somatic discomfort is experienced with feelings of being twisted, crushed or stretched. Depersonalisation and feelings of unreality may also be marked. These may extend to the impression of being outside of one's own body, difficulty in recognising the self in a mirror, or difficulty in deciding whether a thought refers to a real event or is merely a spontaneous thought.

Despite these experiences the subject is able to respond to questions, and conceptual and abstract thinking can usually be shown to be substantially intact. Except in the most severe reactions a large measure of critical self judgement is preserved. Frank delusions may occasionally be expressed but an organised delusional system rarely develops. However as the effects of the drug increase, external reality becomes progressively less intrusive and self-control may be lessened, occasionally with dangerous results as described below.

Formal intelligence tests may show some decrease, mainly where verbal subtests are concerned (Isbell et al., 1956). The Minnesota Multiphasic Personality Inventory shows a large increase in scores on the psychasthenia, schizophrenia and paranoia scales. Anxiety questionnaires similarly show a marked rise in scores. The effect of LSD on the electroencephalogram is not to slow it, as with agents which produce impairment of consciousness, but to change it towards a pattern associated with increased arousal and vigilance, namely diminution or abolition of alpha activity and an increase in low voltage fast frequencies.

The effects of the drug are usually apparent within 30 minutes of ingestion, rising to a maximum 1–4 hours thereafter. The reaction subsides gradually over the next 8–16 hours and there is usually no residuum on waking next morning. After the vivid effects of the drug experience, however, the real world often appears to be drab and dull, and natural events lack the urgent and compelling quality of what has gone before. Some degree of depression and disillusionment may thus be an understandable aftermath.

Acute Adverse Reactions

Among habitual users the great majority of LSD experiences are apparently without adverse effect. Occasionally, however, profoundly disturbing results may accompany the acute effects of the drug, and lead to emergency medical referral or trouble with the police. Adverse effects appear to be commoner in unstable subjects. Certainly a large proportion of those coming before psychiatrists have a history of previous psychiatric care (Ungerleider et al., 1966). It has been estimated that only 0·08% of normal subjects experience seriously adverse reactions when LSD is taken under medical supervision; among patients under psychotherapy the incidence rises to 0·2–1·0%, and among psychotic subjects to 1–3% (Louria, 1968). The frequency among illicit users is unknown but is probably higher still. Much may also depend on the circumstances in which the drug is taken, on impurities in the preparations used, and on injudicious doses.

The pictures which result have been described by Frosch et al. (1965), Ungerleider et al. (1966), Bewley (1967) and Freedman (1968). They may be divided into acute emotional disturbances, the acting out of impulses, and acute psychotic reactions.

Acute emotional disturbances are the most common, especially an acute panic reaction in which the subject feels overwhelmed by experiences beyond his control. Sometimes he feels he is going insane or he may react in terror to homicidal impulses. He may present himself at hospital seeking relief, or be brought by friends who fear he will come to harm. There is no impairment of consciousness though recollection of the details of the LSD experience may be hazy. Rapid recovery occurs as the drug effects wear off, usually within 8–12 hours, though sometimes one or two days are required to regain stability.

Other acute emotional disturbances include depression, paranoia and outbursts of explosive anger. Profound depression very occasionally leads to attempted or successful suicide. Acute paranoia may cause the subject to flee about the streets in terror, or upsurges of paranoid jealousy may lead to episodes of explosive anger.

The acting out of impulses is facilitated as self-control becomes diminished. The subject may become unmanageable, run amok, attempt to disrobe or make overt homosexual advances. Sociopathic individuals are more prone to commit acts of violence, and attempted homicide has been reported. Feelings of invulnerability may lead the patient to take unwarranted risks with danger of bodily harm. Patients who have fallen from windows or roofs have sometimes apparently acted on the belief that they would float down unharmed.

Acute psychotic reactions are commonly longer lasting, and the majority of Ungerleider et al.'s (1966) patients remained in hospital for more than a month. Most are schizophrenia-like illnesses with hallucinations, delusions and overactive behaviour. Less commonly they take the form of acute organic reactions with confusion, disorientation and marked emotional lability. The latter however may often be the product of multiple drug abuse. Muller (1971) has described the dramatic response which may occur to treatment with ECT when such psychotic reactions are prolonged.

Hatrick and Dewhurst (1970) have reported two interesting examples in which psychotic illnesses followed a lucid interval, well after the effects of acute intoxication had subsided. The illnesses were nevertheless coloured by phenomena reminiscent of the acute phase of intoxication. Both patients were said to have been previously stable and well-adjusted, and the illnesses followed a single exposure to LSD:

A student of 19 had a pleasant 'trip' lasting 8–9 hours and was her usual self next day. Two weeks later she developed a severe psychotic depressive illness requiring admission to hospital. This was accompanied by confusion about the time sequence of recent events. As the depression cleared schizophrenic features were revealed, with tangential thought disorder, depersonalisation, feelings of unreality and disturbed ego boundaries. She experienced uncertainty about objects in her perceptual field, and had difficulty in realising she had a body. Heightened visual perception was associated with these disturbances and everything was described as wonderful and beautiful. She improved rapidly after ECT and had no recurrence during $2\frac{1}{2}$ years follow-up.

A secretary of 21 had been given LSD surreptitiously in her drink, producing various perceptual disturbances and a vivid dream. She remained well for 2 weeks thereafter, then began to have nightmares in which she saw stabbing scenes in gory detail. These represented a sequence from a film which she had attended while still under the effects of LSD. She also experienced hypnagogic hallucinations of a horrifying nature. Thereafter she developed a severe agitated depression with persecutory auditory hallucinations. ECT produced rapid benefit and she remained well when seen four months later.

Features which may be of diagnostic significance in LSD-induced psychoses are discussed by Dewhurst and Hatrick (1972). A particularly striking clinical feature may be the wide variety of schizophreniform, affective and neurotic symptoms present in the same patient. Suggestive symptoms include regression to childhood, loss of time sense, grandiose delusions of a pseudo-philosophical nature, and a wealth of visual hallucinations and perceptual disturbances. Visual hallucinations are said to be more intense than in other acute organic reactions and may be specific, transient and recurring. Auditory hallucinations tend to have a more startling, personal and realistic quality than in schizophrenia. The emotional response is usually constantly shifting with apprehension, panic, elation or depression in rapidly alternating sequence. When an LSD-induced psychosis presents as hypomania, euphoria may alternate with panic effects which is an unusual combination in primary affective illness. Many patients with suicidal ruminations have irrational compulsive urges to self-destruction, arising suddenly and sometimes unbacked by other depressive symptoms.

Recurrences of LSD Effect ('Flashbacks')

Occasionally there may be a simple prolongation of the LSD state lasting several days, with undulating anxiety and persisting visual aberrations, but Frosch et al. (1965) have described more remarkable phenomena in which the LSD experiences recur for many weeks or months after discontinuation of the drug. Sometimes it is merely bewilderment or fear which recur in milder form, but quite commonly sensory phenomena are involved as well. Two of Frosch et al.'s patients experienced depersonalisation and perceptual distortions two months later. Another had many transient episodes of catatonia and visual hallucinations over the course of a year, similar to those which had been induced by LSD.

Horowitz (1969) suggests that perhaps as many as 5% of users experience mild recurrences from time to time. Sensory recurrences have been reported in all modalities, but the visual system is most often involved. Horowitz (1969) describes three main varieties. The commonest consists of the repeated intrusion into awareness of some image derived from the LSD experience. This arrives unbidden and is outside voluntary control. It may be accompanied by distortion of time sense or reality sense. It is usually the same image which recurs, often of a frightening nature, and considerable psychiatric disturbance can occasionally be provoked. The second variety consists of the spontaneous return of perceptual distortions—halo effects, blurring, shimmering, reduplication, distortion of planes, changes of colour, micropsia or macropsia. Thirdly, there may be an increased sensitivity to spontaneous imagery for some time after taking LSD. Such imagery is more vivid than usual, less readily suppressed, and occupies a greater proportion of the subject's thought and time than formerly.

Several explanations have been put forward to account for recurrences but none has been substantiated. Brain damage has been blamed, or the release of some stored metabolite, or neurophysiological changes in the mechanisms underlying imagery formation and suppression. Abraham (1982) has obtained evidence that LSD users are impaired on tests of colour discrimination when examined on average two years after their last exposure, and that those experiencing flashbacks are particularly affected. The tendency for recurrences to accompany periods of stress and anxiety has suggested that they may represent a form of conditioned response or learned reaction to anxiety. Psychodynamic theorists have viewed the recurrent imagery as symbolic of affect states or situational crises, as representing screen images to conceal emotional conflict, or as symbolising the breakthrough of repressed ideas.

Late Adverse Reactions

The use of LSD as an adjunct to psychotherapy was known to lead, very occasionally, to long lasting psychiatric complications. Prolonged states of anxiety and bewilderment could last for several weeks or months, or prolonged depression could follow when considerable feelings of guilt or shame had been mobilised. More serious psychotic developments were attributed to the release of overwhelming conflict-laden material. Cohen and Ditman (1962, 1963) documented similar prolonged adverse reactions after illicit use of the drug, lasting often for several months and sometimes for up to two years.

The psychoses which follow are usually of schizophrenic type. Catatonic and paranoid forms have been reported, often with elements similar to those seen during acute LSD intoxication. Visual hallucinations may be prominent, highly coloured and mobile, and euphoria and grandiosity are often much in evidence. Such reactions can follow a single dose of the drug. Many of the reported examples have been in long-standing schizophrenic subjects, and in them the drug has presumably served merely to precipitate a recurrence. The majority of the remainder have been in obviously unstable personalities. The important question of whether prolonged psychoses can occasionally be provoked in persons without special predisposition remains unanswered.

Rosenthal (1964) drew attention to a further type of prolonged reaction, consisting of visual hallucinosis in clear consciousness. This is rare, and Rosenthal considered it to be specifically related to multiple exposures to LSD over a considerable period of time. The condition is often heralded by a change in the experience produced by the drug, typically a change to unpleasant reactions which may lead to its discontinuation. Spontaneous visual hallucinations then commence, and continue for many months even though LSD is no longer taken. In form and content the hallucinations are similar to those experienced under the drug—droplets of colour, shimmering panels, and brightly coloured shape distortions. Cats, crabs, insects and corpses may also be seen, or the skulls of familiar people. Pleasant hallucinations were often under semivoluntary control, in the sense that the patient could make them more or less intense by his own efforts of concentration, but the unpleasant phenomena were intrusive and liable to provoke severe anxiety. The patients continued to recognise the unreality of the hallucinations, and there was no evidence of thought disorder or other schizophrenic phenomena. Sometimes however, a secondary delusional system was elaborated to explain the hallucinations.

Toxic Effects of Other Drugs

Many other drugs can produce toxic effects on the central nervous system and lead to psychiatric disturbance. The number involved is legion, and the variety of their effects too great to be discussed in detail here. An excellent series of reviews on drug toxicity has been edited by Meyler and Herxheimer (1968), and aspects of particular relevance to psychiatric practice are dealt with by Granville-Grossman (1971) and Shader (1971, 1972). These cover the adverse reactions seen with steroids, insulin, narcotics, analgesics, hypnotics, anticonvulsants, tranquillisers, anticholinergic agents, antiparkinsonian drugs, rauwolfia alkaloids, antihypertensive drugs, digoxin, diuretics, antituberculous drugs, other antibacterial agents, androgens, oestrogens and oral contraceptives. Only some of these will be considered below.

Sometimes the toxic reaction is an idiosyncratic response to the drug given in normal therapeutic dosage, or to several drugs being prescribed in combination. For this reason it is essential to review the patient's current medication when dealing with psychiatric illnesses of obscure origin, and particularly when these take the form of acute organic reactions. Sometimes the cause is excessive self-medication, either in error or when the patient is addicted. The range of drugs which are surreptitiously abused tends to increase steadily.

The commonest form of disturbance is an acute organic reaction of variable duration, usually with features typical of delirium and often with prominent hallucinations. Neurological and other systemic signs specific for the drug in question may be in evidence. Some drugs, however, are associated primarily with mood changes or psychotic reactions in clear consciousness as described below.

The elderly are especially at risk of adverse drug reactions. Concomitant physical illness or incipient dementia will reduce the margins by which delirium is provoked. Common offending drugs are digoxin, barbiturates, minor and major tranquillisers, antihypertensives and diuretics. Hypnotics such as nitrazepam readily accumulate, leading to day-time confusion. Anticholinergic agents—antispasmodics, tricyclic antidepressants, phenothiazines and antiparkinsonian drugs—are particularly liable to induce confusion or memory impairment in the elderly (Potamianos and Kellett, 1982). Anticholinergics have also been clearly incriminated as a major factor leading to post-operative delirium (Tune *et al.*, 1981).

Of special relevance to psychiatry are the toxic reactions to common psychotropic drugs. The severe effects which may occasionally be seen with *antidepressant medication* or combinations of antidepressant drugs are reviewed by Connell (1968). Minor degrees of disturbance are probably quite frequent; Davies *et al.* (1971) have reported episodes of impaired memory and orientation in 13% of patients taking antidepressant drugs, rising to 35% in those over 40 years of age.

Lithium can have serious effects on central nervous system functioning. A fine tremor, representing an exaggeration of normal physiological tremor, must often be accepted, likewise some minor forgetfulness, lethargy and occasionally mild dysarthria. More marked symptoms call for abrupt cessation of treatment—muscle fasciculation, coarse tremor, ataxia, incoordination or extrapyramidal signs. The development of confusion or impairment of consciousness constitutes a medical emergency; the severe encephalopathic reactions which can then ensue sometimes prove to be irreversible or to result in permanent brain damage. Increasing confusion is accompanied by seizures, cerebellar signs, marked generalised tremor or decerebrate rigidity. States of stupor or coma may be prolonged. For reasons that are unclear such reactions may sometimes set in despite normal serum concentrations of lithium (Spiers and Hirsch, 1978; Newman and Saunders, 1979). Upon recovery there may be long-lasting cerebellar and extrapyramidal deficits (Sellers *et al.*, 1982).

The combination of lithium and haloperidol was specially incriminated by Cohen and Cohen (1974) in leading to such severe reactions. Two of their patients were left with permanent parkinsonian-cerebellar deficits and dementia, and two with persistent dyskinesias. Loudon and Waring (1976) reported similar though milder reactions of this nature, and Spring (1979) described severe neurotoxic developments from the combination of lithium with thioridazine. Sometimes the same combination of drugs has been given previously without ill effect as in the following example:

A patient reported by Thomas (1979) had been maintained on lithium within the normal therapeutic range for many years. Haloperidol was then added on account of a hypomanic swing, in a dosage of $1\frac{1}{2}$ mg three times per day. Two days later she developed gross extrapyramidal signs with marked rigidity and oro-facial dyskinesia. She became severely confused and disoriented, and the EEG showed diffuse slow waves. Both drugs were stopped, with gradual resolution of the extrapyramidal disturbance over the course of the next three months. She was left, however, with persistent evidence of brain damage by way of disorientation and memory impairment. This patient had experienced the combination of lithium and haloperidol three years previously without adverse effect.

Such reports must be viewed in the context of the many patients treated safely on the same combinations of drugs. Nevertheless close monitoring of the clinical situation and of serum lithium levels would seem essential whenever lithium is coupled with other neuroleptic agents. Episodes of sleep-walking have also been reported after adding neuroleptics to patients established on lithium; Charney *et al.* (1979) report ten examples, involving haloperidol, thioridazine, chlorpromazine and other neuroleptics, usually occurring within a few days of starting the second drug.

The extrapyramidal disorders associated with the phenothiazines and butyrophenones are described in Chapter 14 (p. 545 *et seq.*). The *'neuroleptic malignant syndrome'* is a more recently recognised complication of such drugs, seemingly rare but of great importance in that it is not infrequently fatal. Reviews of the condition are provided by Caroff (1980), Smego and Durack (1982) and Cope and Gregg (1983). It has been described sporadically since the 1960s, but the syndrome still lacks clear definition and little is known of its pathogenesis. Most examples have been described in patients below the age of 40, and males appear to be affected more commonly than females.

The patient develops severe extrapyramidal rigidity and akinesia, usually setting in abruptly or over the course of several days. Pyrexia is a characteristic accompaniment, along with autonomic disturbances by way of sweating, sialorrhea, tachycardia, hyperventilation and labile blood pressure. Muscular rigidity is the cardinal feature, but may be accompanied by tremor, oro-bucco-lingual dyskinesias and sometimes dysphagia and dysarthria. Fluctuating impairment of consciousness can lead to stupor or coma. Dehydration and prostration may become extreme. Common laboratory findings include a leucocytosis, raised creatinine phosphokinase activity and abnormal liver function tests, but these are not invariable. The electroencephalogram sometimes shows diffuse slowing but is usually normal. The CT scan is uniformative. The picture may be mistaken for encephalitis or meningitis, but cerebrospinal fluid examination is negative. Catatonia may be diagnosed on account of the stupor, posturing or waxy flexibility. Death is estimated to occur in up to 20% of cases, usually from cardiorespiratory or renal failure.

The syndrome has been reported in association with butyrophenones, phenothiazines and thioxanthines, though perhaps most commonly with haloperidol and depot fluphenazines. It may set in shortly after the first dose, though a puzzling feature is its occasional development after many months on the drugs. Earlier courses of the identical drugs may have been given without adverse effect.

Treatment must consist of withdrawal of all neuroleptic medication immediately the condition is suspected, along with intensive supportive measures to maintain respiratory, renal and cardiovascular function. Benefit has been reported from treatment with dantrolene sodium, a peripheral muscle relaxant, and from the dopamine agonist, bromocriptine (Granato et al., 1983; Lancet, 1984). The disorder usually lasts for 5—10 days after stopping the drugs, or rather longer with depot preparations. Resolution is typically complete in those who recover.

Dopamine receptor blockade in the basal ganglia or hypothalamus has been postulated as the cause, though without direct supportive evidence. At autopsy no specific abnormalities have yet been discovered. Attention has been drawn to certain similarities between the condition and the 'fatal catatonia' (p. 473) of the pre-neuroleptic era (Caroff, 1980). Some examples of adverse reactions to the combination of lithium and haloperidol (p. 533) may also represent variants of the syndrome, particularly the cases reported by Cohen and Cohen (1974) where extrapyramidal dysfunction was accompanied by fever, leucocytosis and elevated serum enzymes. On present evidence the condition would seem to represent an idiosyncratic reaction to the neuroleptic medication, though it remains possible that this may merely have served as a trigger to some largely independent pathogenic process.

Withdrawal effects must be considered where drugs with a depressant action on the central nervous system are concerned. Drugs other than alcohol or barbiturates can lead to severe withdrawal phenomena including epileptic fits, hallucinations, and periods of delirium. Such pictures have been reported for glutethimide (Doriden) and etchlorvynol (Placidyl) in patients admitted to hospital for investigation of long-standing intermittent confusion (Lloyd and Clark, 1959; Hudson and Walker, 1961). Similar results may follow withdrawal from paraldehyde, meprobamate, methaqualone (Mandrax) and carbromal (Granville-Grossman, 1971).

Chronic analgesic abuse may readily cause diagnostic confusion. Bizarre behaviour and hyperventilation may lead to a mistaken diagnosis of hysteria. When consciousness is severely impaired diabetic coma may be suspected. Greer et al. (1965) report examples of chronic salicylate intoxication producing pictures of confusion, amnesia, agitation, stupor and coma. Some patients were hallucinated, paranoid and combative. Hyperventilation and tinnitus were important signs, also coarse irregular tremors of the hands and ataxia of gait.

Murray et al. (1971) have drawn attention to another possible hazard of chronic analgesic abuse. Of 8 patients who had consumed very large doses of compound analgesics containing phenacetin, 4 showed definite evidence and 2 possible evidence of dementia. Neuropathological studies of the brains of 9 other analgesic abusers showed a surprisingly high incidence of histological changes typical of Alzheimer's disease even though cerebral atrophy was absent. These interesting findings merit further investigation.

An important group of drugs are those which produce mood changes or psychotic reactions without evidence of confusion or impairment of consciousness. With reactions of this type it is less likely that the essentially 'toxic' nature of the disturbance will be appreciated. Rauwolfia alkaloids were an early example, leading to severe depressive mood changes unaccompanied by organic mental symptoms. The rauwolfia reaction may develop only after several weeks or months on the drug, and has been attributed to a fall in cerebral monoamines (p. 342).

Mood changes accompanying *steroid therapy* more often consist of mild elation than depression, and are likewise much commoner than confusion or delirium (Granville-Grossman, 1971). The elation and social activation seen while on steroids may be replaced by depression when the drugs are withdrawn (Carpenter and Bunney, 1971). More florid reactions have been reported in up to 10% of patients given steroids in large dosage—excited elated behaviour, severe depression, or transient psychoses with perceptual abnormalities, hallucinations, derealisation and paranoia. Such reactions are often deeply alarming to the patient, but generally subside within a few weeks when the drugs can be withdrawn. Their determinants will often be complex when the steroids are given for conditions which implicate the central nervous system. Hall *et al.* (1979), however, restricted attention to the psychoses seen in patients in whom there was no reason to suspect a cerebral lesion. They found that the clinical pictures defied formal classification, often representing a complex admixture of affective, schizophreniform and organic features. Moreover a single episode in a given patient could show a great variety of symptoms from one moment to another, and little was characteristic except this changeability. A common constellation of symptoms was emotional lability, anxiety, distractibility, pressured speech, sensory flooding, insomnia, perplexity, agitation, hypomania, auditory and visual hallucinations, delusions, intermittent memory impairment, mutism and body image disturbance. The onset was usually within three weeks of the start of treatment, mostly within five days, and response to phenothiazines was excellent. Electroencephalographic changes of a non-specific type commonly accompanied the disturbances, reverting to normal on recovery. There was no evidence that a history of previous psychiatric illness was a predisposing factor.

Amphetamine abuse may lead to acute psychiatric disturbance which at first sight has none of the hallmarks of an organic toxic reaction. The classical picture is of an acute paranoid illness virtually indistinguishable from paranoid schizophrenia (Connell, 1958). Disorientation and other organic mental symptoms may occur fleetingly after very large doses, but in the addict are usually conspicuous by their absence. Certainly in the fully developed paranoid reaction it is very rare indeed to find evidence of cerebral impairment. The rapidity of onset, the dream-like quality of the experiences, and the brisk emotional reaction with an emphasis on fear are aspects of the condition which tend to differentiate it from endogenous schizophrenia. Bell (1965) stresses that visual hallucinations predominate to an extent that is unusual for schizophrenia, and formal thought disorder is rarely seen, but none of these are features which allow a truly confident differential diagnosis. It is therefore essential to search for amphetamines in the urine when the condition is suspected. Persistence of the paranoid illness for more than a week after urinary tests have confirmed complete clearance of the drug from the body makes the causal connection unlikely. Similar psychotic reactions have been reported with related drugs such as the appetite suppressant phenmetrazine (Preludin), though disorientation, inattention and difficulty in concentration are more usually in evidence (Bartholomew and Marley, 1959). Amphetamine-like drugs have been shown to produce a disturbance of REM sleep, with rebound effects upon withdrawal (Oswald and Thacore, 1963; Lewis *et al.*, 1971). The possible relationship of these neurophysiological effects to the psychotic reactions remains to be determined.

Solvent Abuse

The abuse of commercially available solvents by inhalation is a relatively recent development, at least on a large scale. In the UK it is mainly confined to adolescent males, usually in the form of 'glue-sniffing' which is carried out sporadically as a small-group activity. At this level serious complications are rare, but the solitary abuser who indulges regularly and over long periods can develop markedly adverse consequences.

A variety of agents may be employed from one subculture to another, differing in their toxicity. Glues contain toluene as the main volatile constituent, also acetone, xylene and *n*-hexane. Polystyrene cements are similar. Paints, varnishes and lacquers contain trichloroethylene and methyl chloride in addition to toluene. Cleaning fluids may contain carbon tetrachloride, trichloroethylene and trichloroethane. Butane may be inhaled from lighter refills, or acetone and amyl acetate from nail polish remover. Aerosols contain fluorinated hydrocarbons ('freons'). Petrol contains hydrocarbons and tetraethyl lead.

Acute Effects

Glue is commonly inhaled from a plastic bag, the 'sniffing' being adjusted for maximal euphoriant effect. Cleaning fluids or petrol may be sniffed from a rag or directly from the tin. Aerosols may be sprayed directly into the mouth, a particularly hazardous procedure.

The result is a period of euphoria and exhilaration, setting in rapidly and accompanied by giddiness and disorientation. This phase may be prolonged for several hours by judicious adjustment of sniffing. Hallucinations may occur, chiefly in the visual modality and often frightening in nature. Spatial distortions, macropsia, micropsia and body image disturbances are commonly experienced. At a deeper level of intoxication there is blurring of vision, ataxia, marked confusion, and drowsiness progressing to coma. Disinhibition during the phase of intoxication may lead to risk-taking, accidents, and aggressive antisocial behaviour. Amnesia for the events of the episode is common upon recovery.

The habitual abuser may be detected by nasal and lachrymal secretions and a perioral rash, glue stains on clothing, or a change to listlessness, moodiness and sullen withdrawn behaviour. Anorexia is sometimes marked. Blood toluene estimations can be useful in confirming suspicion of the practice, remaining positive for several days after the last exposure (King et al., 1981).

Adverse Consequences

The great majority of glue-sniffers do not come before medical attention, and at the level of mild sporadic use appear to escape long-term physical damage. A considerable number of deaths have been reported, however, often due to inhalation of vomit or suffocation from the plastic bag. Inhalation of trichloroethane or aerosol propellants may lead to sudden death from ventricular fibrillation. Physical dependence appears to be uncommon, though Watson (1979a, 1979b) has described a withdrawal syndrome after some months of intensive sniffing.

The danger lies chiefly in those vulnerable individuals for whom inhalation becomes a regular and entrenched habit. The motivation to continue can then be extremely strong. A number of complications, some serious, have now been reported, both with glue-sniffing itself and with abuse of other solvents. Much may depend on individual susceptibility to the chemicals involved.

'*Toluene encephalopathy*' has been described from several centres. It may present acutely with ataxia, hallucinations, convulsions and coma, or as a chronically evolving cerebellar disorder with evidence of diffuse brain damage. Psychotic features may be much in evidence. An early example was reported by Grabski (1961) and followed up by Knox and Nelson (1966):

After some years of regular toluene inhalation a 21-year-old man presented with confusion, inappropriate laughter and long periods of staring into space. He showed the classical titubating gait and intention tremors of cerebellar dysfunction. Over the years he became increasingly slowed and forgetful. On occasions when he stopped inhaling for several days the ataxia would remit considerably. Eight years later he was still abusing toluene and was ataxic, tremulous and emotionally labile. Air encephalography showed diffuse cerebral atrophy.

A similar example was described by Lewis et al. (1981):

A man of 28 had abused toluene for 14 years. After 6 years his hands began shaking, followed gradually by difficulty in walking, blurred vision and considerable loss of weight. He showed scanning speech, nystagmus, labile affect and tangential thinking. Psychotic features were absent but there had been an episode of paranoia some years before. There were coarse tremors of the extremities, head and neck, poor finger–nose coordination and a wide-based gait. Psychometric testing showed an IQ of 62 with slowness, perseveration, and poverty of reasoning, judgement and logic. Immediate memory was severely impaired along with evidence of expressive and receptive dysphasia. The EEG showed slow wave abnormalities in the temporal areas. The CT scan showed symmetrically enlarged ventricles, prominent cortical sulci, and enlargement of the cisterns around the brain stem and cerebellum.

King et al. (1981) have drawn attention to acute encephalopathy in children occasioned by glue sniffing. Of 19 examples 4 presented with coma, 3 with convulsions, 3 with ataxia, 7 with euphoria and hallucinations, and 2 with behaviour disturbance and diplopia. Thirteen recovered completely, 5 still showed personality changes and psychological impairment on discharge, and one showed persisting evidence of cerebellar damage:

A child of 11 presented with a one week history of headache, vomiting, abnormal behaviour, slurred speech and unsteadiness of gait. He was thin, apyrexial, and with superficial ulceration of the lips and nostrils. Examination showed euphoria, dysarthria, coarse rotatory nystagmus, moderate intention tremor and severe ataxia of gait. He denied glue-sniffing but blood toluene assay was positive, and it was later confirmed that he had been sniffing for several months. CT scan and lumbar puncture showed no abnormalities. The EEG showed diffuse slow waves. His condition remained unchanged over 72 hours then improved slightly over the course of 3 weeks. The EEG became normal. On follow-up one year later cerebellar signs persisted despite confirmatory evidence that he had abstained from further sniffing (King *et al.*, 1981).

Fornazzari *et al.* (1983) attempted a comprehensive survey of 24 adolescent and adult toluene abusers admitted to hospital. Eleven showed intention tremor, 11 ataxia, and 5 had obvious memory impairment. Psychological testing revealed deficits in those patients with neurological dysfunction but not in the remainder. CT scans during the second week showed abnormalities in 7 of the 14 examined—widened cortical sulci, enlarged ventricles and marked prominence of the cerebellar sulci. Half of the patients remained in hospital for a two week period, but with little evidence of reversibility of their neurological abnormalities or psychological deficits. Many of the more mildly affected patients discharged themselves prematurely, however, and these may have subsequently improved. Interestingly none of the patients showed withdrawal symptoms or distress while in hospital, despite a clear history of daily toluene abuse for many years and continuing up to the day of admission.

Among adult paint sniffers in the USA, Streicher *et al.* (1981) reported muscle weakness and peripheral neuropathy in addition to mental changes. Memory difficulties, alteration of personality, depression, irritability, lethargy and paranoia have also been described (Wyse, 1973). Korman *et al.* (1980) compared a large group of solvent abusers seen in emergency room practice with polydrug (non-solvent) abusers, and found them to be significantly worse with regard to memory, abstracting ability and capacity for insight and judgement.

Escobar and Aruffo (1980) have reported a patient who came to autopsy after 12 years of inhaling glue and paint thinner. Diffuse cerebral and cerebellar atrophy were obvious, with thinning of the corpus callosum and shrinkage of the basal ganglia. Cell loss and reactive gliosis were accompanied by diffuse demyelination in the subcortical white matter. The cerebellum showed severe Purkinje cell loss.

Anaemia may complicate solvent abuse, likewise gastrointestinal disturbances including haematemesis. Impairment of renal and hepatic function may be found (Will and McLaren, 1981). The chlorinated hydrocarbons—trichloroethylene, trichloroethane and carbon tetrachloride—are particularly hazardous in this regard.

Petrol sniffing carries additional hazards as reviewed by Poklis and Burkett (1977). Intoxication is liable to continue for some hours after exposure, and prolonged or rapid inhalation may lead to a phase of violent excitement followed by coma. Chronic inhalation leads ultimately to loss of appetite and weight, neurasthenic symptoms, and muscular weakness and cramps. EEG abnormalities and other evidence of brain damage have been described, perhaps largely caused by minor constituents such as benzene and xylene rather than by the hydrocarbons themselves.

A special complication is encephalopathy due to the tetra-ethyl lead added to the petrol (pp. 542–3). Law and Nelson (1968) described an example in a woman of 41, presenting as a chronic paranoid psychosis along with memory impairment. Robinson (1978) reported a girl of 15 who presented with hypomania and combative behaviour after some months of deterioration in school work. Both patients responded to treatment with chelating agents.

Heavy Metals and Other Chemicals

LEAD

It has been suggested that lead poisoning may have contributed to the decline of the Roman Empire after the introduction of lead pipes for the supply of drinking water (Gillfillan, 1965). There was a high incidence of mental retardation, sterility and infant mortality among influential Romans, and the bones of wealthy Romans have been found to have a high lead content.

Domestic water supplies remain at risk in areas where the water is soft, and some outbreaks have been traced to beer or cider which has stayed overnight in lead pipes. In children lead poisoning may result from chewing lead-containing paint on toys or furniture. Industrial causes have been greatly reduced as a result of stringent precautions, but a risk exists in the following occupations—painting, plumbing, ship building, lead smelting and refining, brass founding, pottery glazing, vitreous enamelling, the manufacture of storage batteries, white lead, red lead, rubber, glass and pigments, and among compositors who handle type metal. The list is important because a history of exposure is often the crucial factor in arousing suspicion of the disorder.

Overt lead poisoning is now a great deal rarer than earlier in the century. However, a new focus of interest has come to centre on possibilities of 'subclinical' lead poisoning, more specifically on the relationship between quite low lead levels in the body and effects on intelligence in children. This is discussed on p. 539.

Clinical Manifestations

The principal manifestations include abdominal colic, 'lead neuropathy' and 'lead encephalopathy'. Children are more seriously affected than adults, particularly where the cerebral effects are concerned. Useful reviews are provided by Rodgers *et al.* (1934), Byers (1959) and Lee (1981).

Lassitude is almost invariably the earliest symptom. Aching in joints and limbs is also common. Gastrointestinal disturbances then appear, with anorexia, constipation and attacks of severe intestinal colic. The child is pale and often irritable. Acute phases of disturbance tend to be precipitated by intercurrent infection or other sources of acidosis which mobilise lead from the bones.

'Peripheral neuropathy' was formerly common in adults but has always been rare in children. It is now very rare in both. It is unique in being a purely motor disturbance, perhaps with the primary effect on the muscles themselves, though ultimately the nerves are involved as well. The muscles mainly affected are those most used, resulting in the classical picture of wrist drop and paralysis of the long extensors of the fingers. Less commonly there is weakness and wasting of the shoulder girdle muscles or of the dorsiflexors of the foot.

Lead encephalopathy is the most serious manifestation. In adults it may present with episodes of delirium, often in association with fits. During crises the blood pressure is elevated. In severe chronic encephalopathy the patient is dull, with poor memory, impaired concentration, headache, trembling, deafness, or transitory episodes of aphasia and hemianopia (Hunter, 1959). Korolenko *et al.* (1969) describe a picture of acute delirium developing against a background of chronic headache, depression, lowered capacity for work, physical weakness, vertigo, and hyperaesthesia for visual and auditory stimuli. During the delirious phase hypnagogic visual hallucinations appeared in profusion in Korolenko *et al.*'s patients, also isolated visual and auditory hallucinations while awake. Disorientation persisted for several days after the hallucinations had ceased, then cleared to leave a worsened form of the chronic asthenic syndrome.

The most pronounced manifestations, however, are seen in children, and cerebral involvement is reported in about half of those affected. The enceph-

alopathy may sometimes set in very rapidly. The intracranial pressure rises abruptly with headache, projectile vomiting, visual disturbances, and severe impairment of consciousness. Convulsions and muscular twitching are common, and acute delirium may lead on to coma. Ocular and limb pareses may develop. Papilloedema is often seen, and meningeal irritation may cause neck stiffness and head retraction. The cerebrospinal fluid is under increased pressure, the protein is raised, and a moderate pleocytosis may be found. Death can result from medullary compression.

Diagnosis

In the diagnosis of lead poisoning there is no one sign which is pathognomonic. A lead line on the gums may be produced by sub-epithelial deposits of lead sulphide, especially when the teeth are carious. This is rare, however, in children. Anaemia is always present and usually accompanied by basophilic stippling of the erythrocytes. In young children X-ray of the long bones shows a dense band of condensation in the lines of provisional calcification. Repeated examinations of the blood and urine may reveal an elevated lead content, but single readings can be misleading with falsely high or low results. Coproporphyrins are increased in the urine.

Lead encephalopathy should be considered in children who develop fits of obscure origin, and when headache and papilloedema are discovered without obvious cause. Anaemia in association with colic or peripheral neuropathy should similarly raise suspicion. Diseases which may be simulated include encephalitis, cerebral tumour, tuberculous meningitis, uraemia and hypertensive encephalopathy.

Treatment

Most of the lead is held in storage in the bones, and as a temporary measure storage can be promoted by giving calcium lactate and extra milk in the diet. Chelating agents can be used to promote the urinary excretion of lead and have proved to be a great advance in treatment (Sidbury, 1955; Byers, 1959). Disodium calcium ethylenediamine-tetra-acetate ('calcium versenate', 'EDTA') is given parenterally. In severe cases, dimercaprol ('British Antilewisite', 'BAL') may be given as well, since the dose of each drug that can be tolerated is limited. Lead replaces the calcium in the compound and the circulating unionized chelate is excreted by the kidneys. Symptoms are rapidly relieved since the chelate is much less toxic than the ionized metal in the body fluids. In consequence chelating agents have been regarded as life saving in the management of acute lead encephalopathy.

Outcome

The risk of permanent intellectual disablement is considerable among the survivors of lead encephalopathy. Children may be left with mental retardation, cerebral palsy, fits, or blindness due to optic atrophy. Of 40 children seen by McKann (1932) encephalopathy developed in 24, with death in 9 and permanent cerebral damage in 5 of the survivors. Of 20 cases of mild lead poisoning in infancy, Byers and Lord (1943) found that only one child progressed satisfactorily at school thereafter. Byers' (1959) follow-up of 45 children treated with modern chelating agents showed that 4 had died, 8 were feeble-minded, and 7 showed other persistent psychiatric abnormalities. Perlstein and Attala (1966) reviewed a large group of 425 children who had suffered lead poisoning, finding permanent sequelae in 39%. This rose to 82% among those who had presented with encephalopathy.

Cerebral Pathology

The cerebral manifestations have been attributed to a combination of intense cerebral oedema and vascular changes. There is proliferation of the endothelium of small blood vessels, sometimes with occlusion of the lumen, and the development of perivascular nodules of hypertrophied glial cells. Cerebral ischaemia may result from the acute rise of intracranial pressure and lead on to cerebral atrophy. In chronic cases the meninges become fibrosed and hyperplastic, and arachnoiditis obstructs the flow of cerebrospinal fluid (Akelatis, 1941). Internal hydrocephalus is often marked in patients who show residual cerebral impairment.

'Subclinical' Lead Poisoning

The conventional estimate of what may constitute a 'safe' blood lead level in children has gradually been lowered downwards during the past two decades. Once set at 50 or 60 μg/100 ml, some now urge that it should be 30 μg/100 ml. And even below this level there is concern that intellectual development may still be hampered. The debate has been hard to resolve, not least because the correlation is known to be poor between blood lead levels as measured

and the presence or absence of overt toxic symptoms. Furthermore, blood lead levels cannot be taken as a reliable index of past absorption.

Nevertheless public conern has been raised by the finding from screening programmes of higher than expected blood lead levels in many children, principally those from inner city areas. High levels of lead have been found in dust, dirt and soil, which perhaps constitute the principal sources. Moreover, the majority of air-borne lead appears to derive from additives to petrol; hence the campaign, recently successful in the UK, to secure legislation that will ultimately ensure the use of lead-free petrol.

The evidence that body lead levels may be causally related to impaired intelligence or behaviour in children is suggestive, but the case is by no means tightly proven. Methodological difficulties in resolving the issue have proved considerable, and the evidence is far from unanimous. Rutter (1980) and Needleman (1982) have provided recent reviews.

Thus while Lansdown et al. (1974) were able to show that blood lead levels in a large population of children were related to the proximity of their homes to a lead works, no relationship could be demonstrated to measures of mental functioning. Estimates of intelligence and of behavioural disorder were much more closely related to social factors in the homes of the children concerned.

More reliable evidence came from Needleman et al.'s (1979) survey in the USA. Acknowledging the vagaries of blood lead estimations, lead levels were measured in the dentine of shed teeth. Over 2000 children were examined in all. When those in the top tenth percentile for dentine lead were compared with those in the lowest tenth percentile, small but significant differences emerged in intelligence, particularly verbal intelligence, on measures of auditory and speech processing, in reaction times, and on most items of teachers' ratings of classroom behaviour. The latter, measuring distractibility, impulsivity, and capacity for concentration and organisation, varied in a dose-related manner with the dentine lead levels across the whole sample of children. Thus lead exposure, at doses below those which would produce symptoms allowing clinical detection, appeared to be associated with minor psychological deficits and impaired classroom performance. After controlling for the influence of various social factors these associations remained significant.

Yule et al. (1981) have provided further evidence from a preliminary UK study. One hundred and sixty-six children living near a lead works in outer

London had previously been shown to have blood lead levels ranging from 7 to 33 $\mu g/100$ ml. On tests of intelligence, reading and spelling carried out during the following year, significant associations emerged with the blood lead levels. These largely persisted after controlling for social class. Children with lead levels of 13 and above, when compared with those of 12 and below, showed an average difference of 7 points on the WISC full-scale IQ.

These findings, while important, must still be viewed with caution. A large number of studies have shown a close correlation between blood lead levels and social factors, since poverty increases exposure. It is therefore hard to prove a causal relationship between lead levels and intelligence in children, as opposed to a common association of each with a host of intervening social and genetic factors. Rutter (1980), in his detailed review, came to the provisional conclusion that it is very likely that psychological impairment occurs in some asymptomatic children who show repeated blood lead levels of 40–80 $\mu g/100$ ml, and possible, though much less certain, that impairment sometimes occurs with levels below 40 $\mu g/100$ ml.

MERCURY

Chronic mercury poisoning can occur in many settings. It is a hazard among workers involved in recovering the metal from the ore, in chemical workers, thermometer makers and photo-engravers. Groups of cases have been reported among finger-print experts employing a mercury and chalk mixture (Agate and Buckell, 1949), and among repairers of direct current electric meters (Bidstrup et al., 1951). Mercury was also extensively employed in the felt hat industry, where the toxic effects no doubt contributed to the epithet 'mad as a hatter' and to Lewis Carroll's choice of the hatter in 'Alice in Wonderland'. Warkany and Hubbard (1951) made a signal contribution by discovering that the mercury contained in teething powders was the common cause of acrodynia ('pink disease') in infants and young children.

Clinical Manifestations

Physical symptoms include stomatitis, spongy bleeding gums and excessive salivation. A coarse tremor may develop in the hands, face and tongue, characteristically interrupted by coarse jerking movements ('Hatters' shakes').

Psychological symptoms are often an early manifestation. In particular a constellation of symptoms known as 'erythism' has been repeatedly noted. In this the sufferer becomes nervous, timid and shy, blushes readily and gets embarrassed in social situations. He objects to being watched and seeks to avoid people. He becomes irritable and quarrelsome, sometimes to such an extent that he is obliged to give up work because of inability to take orders without losing temper. Such symptoms are usually accompanied by lassitude, tremulousness, ataxia and some degree of impairment of intellectual capacity. Of 32 men involved with finger printing in the Lancashire Constabulary, Agate and Buckell (1949) found 7 with tremor and 4 who showed evidence of past or present erythism:

A detective-sergeant of 45 was trained in fingerprint work and sent to a division where he investigated up to 300 crimes per year. During this time he became a 'nervous wreck', could not hold a cup without spilling it, and found court appearances acutely distressing because he couldn't stand still or answer questions without embarrassment. During the early war years the crime rate declined and his symptoms improved, but they worsened again immediately the crime rate rose in the post-war years. On examination he showed a marked tremor and several teeth were loose.

Bidstrup et al. (1951) found definite evidence of erythism in 10 and probable evidence in 8 of 161 men engaged in mending direct current electric meters:

One employee had noticed tremor of his hands for a year and had become irritable, short tempered and easily embarrassed. He had developed a stammer for the first time in his life. A few months later he became unsteady on his feet and his whole body developed a tremor. His writing became almost illegible. He was ultimately diagnosed as suffering from multiple sclerosis. At this point he read in the daily paper about the above findings in the Lancashire Constabulary and told his general practitioner that he too handled mercury. Six months after transfer to another job he had recovered completely.

Kark et al. (1971) report another example with prominent neurological symptoms:

A man who had worked for two years extracting mercury from batteries showed a gradual decline in memory and loss of interest, becoming less talkative and active. He developed gingivitis, decreased visual acuity and insomnia. Tremor ultimately made eating and drinking impossible, and he was virtually unable to stand on account of titubation and truncal ataxia. On examination he showed dysar-thria, constricted visual fields and diminished acuity of both hearing and vision. There were constant choreiform movements of the face and fingers. The electroencepha-logram showed diffuse theta activity and the air encephal-ogram revealed cerebral atrophy. He recovered slowly on treatment with chelating agents.

Acrodynia is a serious disease of infants and young children. The hands and feet are reddened with desquamation of the skin, itching, burning and evanescent rashes. In severe cases the hair and even the nails may be lost. The child is restless and miser-able, showing periods of apathy alternating with extreme irritability. Anorexia, insomnia and photo-phobia are prominent. On examination there is hypotonia with diminished tendon reflexes and peripheral sensory loss. There is a tachycardia and the blood pressure is raised. The cause was unknown, though a toxic agent had long been suspected. Warkany and Hubbard in 1951 found mercury in the urine in a large number of cases, and proposed that exposure to mercury in hypersensitive infants was the essential factor causing the disease. This has since been well established (Dathan, 1954), the source being mainly from teething powders, worming pills, ointments or nappy powders. Fortu-nately the condition is now very rare indeed.

MANGANESE

Manganese poisoning is essentially an occupational disease. It occurs in manganese ore workers and in those involved in steel manufacture, dry battery manufacture, bleaching and electro-welding. Despite the large number of people at risk manganese poisoning is relatively rare, and it is probable that a large quantity must be absorbed over a long period of time before harmful effects are produced. Individual sensitivity also appears to be important in that some subjects exposed for an equally long period show no ill-effects. The chief route of entry is by inhalation of the dust, fumes or vapour.

Clinical Manifestations

The early manifestations usually develop insidiously with headache, asthenia, torpor and hypersomnia. Impotence is extremely common. Psychological abnormalities then become pronounced and may first draw attention to the disorder. There have been reports of marked emotional disturbances in up to 70 per cent of cases, especially episodes of persistent and uncontrollable laughter and crying (Fairhall and Neal, 1943). There may be strong impulsions to run, dance, sing or talk which the patient finds difficult to resist. Impulsive acts and stupid crimes are a special risk in the early phases (Penalver, 1955). Other abnormalities include forgetfulness, mental dullness, marked irritability and outbursts of aggres-sion. Very occasionally an acute psychotic picture is seen with severe excitement, agitation, hallucina-tions and delusions (Abd El Naby and Hassanein, 1965).

Parkinsonism develops later with typical mask-like facies, slow monotonous speech, and slowing of voluntary movement. Nocturnal leg cramps are a prominent feature. Fine tremor or gross rhythmical movements develop in the hands, limbs and trunk. The gait becomes typically parkinsonian with retro-pulsion and propulsion. A characteristic 'cock-step' gait has been described—a peculiar broad-based slapping walk, with the legs held stiffly on tip-toe and wide apart. On examination muscular rigidity is found, with increased reflexes and ankle clonus. Cerebellar deficits may also be present. Sensory disturbances are rare. Chronic headache and severe insomnia may accompany the neurological develop-ments.

Fully developed examples have been mis-diagnosed as paralysis agitans, Wilson's disease, post-encephalitic parkinsonism or multiple sclerosis. Wilson's disease may be closely simulated since liver damage may also be present.

Removal from exposure at an early stage usually allows considerable recovery to occur. The psycho-logical symptoms resolve quickly but disturbance of speech and gait may persist. In well established cases the neurological disabilities may prove to be irrever-sible and the patients are left permanently disabled. A considerable number have been observed to worsen neurologically even after removal from exposure (Abd El Naby and Hassanein, 1965).

At autopsy the basal ganglia are found to be principally affected, with cell loss, gliosis and shrink-age. This is most marked in the globus pallidus. The thalamus may also be affected. Diffuse changes are found elsewhere including the cerebral cortex and brain stem, and slight generalised cortical atrophy may be seen (Canavan *et al.*, 1934). In advanced cases the peripheral nerves and muscles may also show degenerative changes (Penalver, 1955).

ARSENIC

Arsenic poisoning is encountered in the ore refining industry, the fur industry, and in the manufacture of glass, insecticides and weed killers. Medicinal poisoning was formerly seen when Fowler's solution was prescribed over long periods of time. Acute poisoning may follow the accidental ingestion of insecticides, disinfectants and rat poisons.

Acute poisoning produces vomiting, diarrhoea and violent abdominal cramps. Headache, delirium and fits develop, and coma and death may follow within two or three days.

In chronic arsenic poisoning the picture is different. Early signs include dermatitis, conjunctivitis, lachrymation and coryza. Keratosis and skin pigmentation may be extensive. Anorexia and weight loss are common, but the abdominal cramps and diarrhoea of acute poisoning are often entirely absent. Headache and vertigo develop with apathy, drowsiness and impairment of mental activity. At this stage the mental changes can be the leading clinical manifestations and sometimes closely simulate neurotic disorder (Ecker and Kernohan, 1941). Later restlessness, excitability and confusion become marked. Severe memory disturbance can occasionally produce the picture of Korsakoff's psychosis. Peripheral neuritis is common, with paraesthesiae, burning pain in the limbs, and conspicuous sensory signs.

THALLIUM

Thallium has been widely used as a rodent poison and pesticide. Ginsburg and Nixon (1932) described an outbreak of poisoning in the USA caused by eating barley bread made from contaminated grain. Reed et al. (1963) reported 72 cases in children in Texas who had ingested pesticides.

Tingling in the hands and feet develops within 24 hours of ingestion, followed by severe paroxysmal abdominal pain and vomiting. Headache, tachycardia, stomatitis, salivation and offensive breath are other early features.

Involvement of the nervous system follows within a few days. After small doses ataxia and paraesthesiae develop and may progress to frank peripheral neuropathy. Retrobulbar neuritis is often seen. Tremor, chorea, athetosis and myoclonic jerking are also common. Mental abnormalities may be pronounced, with impairment of consciousness, paranoia and depression (Grinker and Sahs, 1966). After large doses cerebral involvement is severe, with cranial nerve palsies, delirium, hallucinations, fits and coma.

Death often follows from respiratory paralysis.

Alopecia develops some 10 days after ingestion and dystrophic changes appear in the nails. Toxic damage occurs in the kidneys and hypertension is common.

Follow up by Reed et al. (1963) showed that sequelae were limited to the nervous system, both peripherally and centrally, and occurred in half of the survivors. The enduring deficits consisted of features derived from the acute stage—ataxia, tremor, abnormal motor movements, fits and visual disturbance.

BISMUTH

An encephalopathy induced by bismuth salts has recently been described. Most reports have come from Australia, Belgium and particularly France, but it may be expected that cases will arise elsewhere. The cause is excessive ingestion of bismuth preparations taken for gastrointestinal and skin disorders. Most patients have been between the ages of 40 and 70, with more women affected than men.

Collignon et al. (1979) have analysed reports of 99 cases in the literature and describe 7 patients of their own. Neurological abnormalities are prominent during the prodromal phase—disturbances of gait and balance, tremors, myoclonic jerks and other disorders of movement. Headache, insomnia and apathy may be accompanied by difficulties with thinking and memory. Some patients show marked oscillations between depression and euphoria.

The acute encephalopathy then presents with confusion and clouding of consciousness, often accompanied by considerable excitement and agitation. Disturbances of memory and praxis sometimes dominate the picture. Motor neurological abnormalities are marked while the blood bismuth levels are high.

As the acute organic reaction subsides the patient may recover completely, or be left with short-term memory difficulties or more global defects of intellectual function. These can persist for more than a year in certain cases. Collignon et al. stress apraxic and agnosic deficits which may remain along with the memory disorder. The picture may mimic the presenile or senile dementias, chronic subdural haematoma, or suggest the presence of a frontal lobe lesion.

TETRA-ETHYL LEAD

Tetra-ethyl lead is added to petrol as an anti-detonant and may be absorbed through the skin and respiratory tract. Symptoms of poisoning have been reported among those involved in its manufacture or in the cleaning of large petrol storage tanks.

The clinical picture has been described by Machle (1935) and Boyd *et al.* (1957) and differs from other forms of lead poisoning. After severe exposures acute symptoms may begin within hours, but in less severe cases there is often a delay of several days. Prodromata consist of anorexia, nausea, marked weight loss and a metallic taste in the mouth. Other prominent complaints include headache, vertigo, muscular pains and generalised weakness. The patient is anxious and excitable, and has marked insomnia with terrifying dreams. At this stage the condition may easily be mistaken for an anxiety state. In the fully developed reaction the mental manifestations increase and come to dominate the picture. Severe delirium is accompanied by acute terror, misidentifications and hallucinations. Episodes of mania may be seen with flight of ideas. Coarse jerky tremors involve the limbs, lips and tongue, and brief epileptic fits may occur. The precise pattern of the acute psychosis is remarkably variable from one person to another. In the most severe examples coma supervenes. Otherwise, the condition subsides after several weeks with complete recovery, though convalescence is sometimes protracted and an anxiety state may persist for a considerable time.

ORGANIC MERCURY COMPOUNDS

Organic mercury compounds are associated with marked neurological and psychiatric disturbances, especially the ethyl and methyl derivatives which are used in the manufacture of fungicides. From time to time certain accidents have resulted in large outbreaks of poisoning with a heavy mortality. In the Minamata Bay epidemic in Japan, 83 persons were affected, most patients dying or suffering permanent severe disability (Kurland *et al.*, 1960). Inorganic mercury derived from industrial processes had been discharged into rivers, methylated by aquatic microorganisms, and eaten by fish which then became poisonous. In Iraq several outbreaks have resulted from the distribution of grain treated with fungicides, intended for planting but made into bread by mistake. In the 1972 epidemic 6,500 persons were admitted to hospital and there were 459 deaths (Bakir *et al.*, 1973).

Sensory disturbances are in the foreground with numbness of the hands, deafness, blurred vision, and narrowing of the visual fields progressing to blindness (Hunter, 1978). Ataxia and dysarthria may be severe, often in association with sore gums and salivation. Involuntary movements and convulsions are common. Mental dullness is accompanied by restlessness, progressing over the course of weeks or months to coma. Many cases are fatal. At autopsy there is severe atrophy of the medial surface of both occipital lobes and of the cerebellum (Turner, 1955). Selective cortical damage is seen in numerous areas, with neurone loss, porosity of the underlying white matter and swelling of oligodendrocytes (Hay *et al.*, 1963). The corpus callosum is usually severely affected.

METHYL BROMIDE

Methyl bromide is a colourless, odourless gas which is sold as a liquid in pressurised containers. It is used as a fire extinguisher, refrigerant, fumigant and insecticide, and occasional cases of poisoning have been described. It appears to be the methyl element and not the bromide which is responsible. Severe exposures are fatal with acute pulmonary oedema, renal failure and convulsions (De Jong, 1944). Brief exposures are followed by headache, nausea and vertigo, then a characteristic interval occurs of hours or even days during which the patient is symptom free. This is followed by the explosive onset of headache, muscular twitching, convulsions, delirium, visual disturbances, and somnolence progressing to coma (Baker and Tichy, 1953).

CARBON DISULPHIDE

Carbon disulphide is used in industry, mainly as a rubber solvent and in the manufacture of rayon. Many cases of poisoning were reported in France after its introduction in the nineteenth century. Braceland (1942) reported examples from the USA and found that a high proportion of rayon workers were affected by the fumes.

The commonest toxic effect is polyneuritis affecting both motor and sensory nerves and producing aching cramp-like pains in the limbs (Hunter, 1978). Visual changes also occur, with central scotomata and concentric narrowing of the visual fields. Auditory symptoms include dizziness, tinnitus and deafness. Mental changes may be profound and can be the presenting feature. Braceland (1942) described both insidious changes of personality and acute toxic psychoses.

Personality changes consist of mood swings, irritability, and outbursts of inexplicable rage. The worker may be exhilarated when breathing the fumes in the factory but depressed when at home. Constant fatigue may progress to a state of profound apathy. Headache, anorexia and insomnia are usually marked, and loss of libido is common. Later there may be difficulties with memory, and auditory and visual hallucinations may develop.

In Braceland's survey one worker was found to be confused and disoriented with obvious memory difficulties. He had been nervous and irritable for several months and complained of feeling in a fog. He was subject to rapid mood changes and had overwhelming impulses to anger from time to time. He could sleep for only 2 hours at a time and had recurrent dreams of a violent and anxious nature. There was complete loss of libido. Another worker was similarly affected and had experienced auditory and visual hallucinations. Another was extremely agitated and was subject to intermittent visual hallucinations.

The more acute psychoses are usually sudden in onset and sometimes closely resemble episodes of mania. Severe confusion is accompanied by noisy aggressive behaviour, delusions and hallucinations. Most clear rapidly on admission to hospital, but some last for many weeks or months. Residual memory defects occasionally persist. Examples of acute functional psychoses have also been reported, probably in those who are specially predisposed.

Chapter 14. Movement Disorders

The movement disorders form a substantial part of neurological practice and have gradually attracted increasing psychiatric interest. This is partly on account of their psychiatric concomitants, for example a high incidence of depression in Parkinson's disease and of behavioural disturbance in the opening stages of hepatolenticular degeneration. Over and above this, however, biochemical research, particularly in relation to dopamine metabolism, has revealed tantalising analogies between the changes thought to underlie certain movement disorders and those postulated to occur in major psychiatric illnesses. Basic research on such issues has been stimulated to a very considerable extent. We are, in effect, learning to value the lessons for psychiatry that can be gained from the study of extrapyramidal disease, and to appreciate the importance of subcortical activity in contributing to many aspects of mental life.

An additional spur to interest is the need to be conversant, in day-to-day clinical practice, with the wide range of movement disorders induced by neuroleptic medication. The management of the syndromes that result, and the unravelling of underlying mechanisms, have led neurologists and psychiatrists to areas of common endeavour.

Other movement disorders, such as spasmodic torticollis, writer's cramp, blepharospasm and Gilles de la Tourette's syndrome, reflect the striking influence that mental factors may bring to bear on motor dysfunction. So close is this interaction that psychogenic factors may appear to be solely responsible for causing such conditions, yet other evidence suggests that cerebral malfunction may be primarily to blame. Marked psychosensitivity need carry no implications for psychogenesis *per se*, yet attempts to discern the true situation can prove exceptionally difficult. In the discussion of such disorders below the arguments advanced in both directions will be presented.

Drug-Induced Disorders

Soon after the introduction of phenothiazines to psychiatric practice it became apparent that extra-pyramidal movement disorders ranked high among the unwanted effects of treatment. The successive development of new neuroleptics has signally failed to solve the problem, in that all major tranquillisers appear to share these side-effects in some degree. Their propensity to disturb extrapyramidal function has proved, indeed, to be roughly proportional to their antipsychotic effect, though earlier ideas that the two were necessarily and essentially linked to one another are now less firmly held.

Among the phenothiazines, those with a piperazine side chain (e.g. trifluoperazine) show more marked extrapyramidal effects than those with aliphatic or piperidine side chains (e.g. chlorpromazine, thioridazine). The butyrophenones (haloperidol, benperidol, droperidol) are particularly potent in this regard. The thioxanthenes (e.g. flupenthixol) may induce the whole range of disorders considered below, whereas reserpine's effects are usually limited to parkinsonism. Disturbance of dopaminergic mechanisms within the brain has been clearly incriminated as the major factor in leading to these effects, and clarification of the detailed mechanisms involved has had important consequences for the management of some of the more serious disorders.

CLINICAL PICTURES

Four main syndromes have been delineated, namely parkinsonism, akathisia, acute dystonic reactions, and the group of disorders at present subsumed under the term 'tardive dyskinesia'. Precise estimates of their incidence have been hard to obtain, on account of variations in prescribing practice and differences in the populations surveyed. It is now firmly established, however, that the drugs are to be blamed rather than inherent aspects of the psychiatric disorders themselves. Exactly analogous movement disorders are induced whether the neuroleptics are given for schizophrenia, affective disorder, neurotic disability or for the control of chronic pain. It must be granted, however, that the stereotypies and mannerisms of chronic schizophrenia can at times lead to diagnostic difficulty and even obscure for a while the development of the extrapyramidal symptoms.

The clinical pictures encountered are fully described in Marsden *et al.*'s (1975) comprehensive review, and may be summarised as follows:

Parkinsonism

Parkinsonian features usually develop insidiously, often within a week and almost always within the first month of treatment. The development of parkinsonism is broadly dose dependent, increasing as higher levels of neuroleptics are achieved. It emerges, however, in only some 20–40% of persons, individual susceptibility being important. The incidence increases with age, much as with idiopathic Parkinson's disease.

All of the features of paralysis agitans (p. 550) may be induced. Bradykinesia is the earliest and commonest sign, with muscular rigidity and disturbance of posture and gait developing later. Tremor is a good deal less common than with the idiopathic disease, the exception being the occasional appearance late in the course of treatment of fine perioral tremor ('rabbit syndrome'). The latter generally sets in after months or years of therapy as with tardive dyskinesia.

With continuation of the drugs the parkinsonian features may gradually subside as tolerance develops. Short of this they will usually resolve over the course of several weeks when the drugs are stopped. Marsden and Jenner (1980) stress, however, that occasional patients continue to show parkinsonism for as long as eighteen months after cessation of therapy. In the rare examples that fail to recover thereafter one may usually presume that idiopathic Parkinson's disease had already been present.

With the more severe extrapyramidal reactions provoked by potent neuroleptics, the clinical picture may occasionally come to resemble 'catatonia'. Gelenberg and Mandel (1977) describe a group of patients showing negativism, withdrawal, posturing and waxy flexibility, of gradual onset usually in the first few weeks of treatment. Incontinence of urine was sometimes observed. Behrman (1972) has described mutism, sometimes progressing to the full syndrome of akinetic mutism. Such developments may easily be confused with worsening of schizophrenic symptomatology, leading to increase in dosage of the offending medication. Stopping the drugs, by contrast, can lead to slow resolution.

Akathisia

Akathisia consists of motor restlessness accompanied by a subjective feeling of tension in the limbs. It often coexists with parkinsonian features but is possibly even more common. The patient complains of being driven to move, of pulling sensations in the legs and inability to keep them still. The disorder usually appears within the first few days of treatment but may only develop as higher dosage is achieved.

Braude *et al.* (1983) have investigated motor restlessness in detail by repeated ratings of subjective sensations and objective manifestations in a large group of patients on antipsychotic medication. A principal components analysis served to delineate the akathisia syndrome more precisely. Mild examples presented mainly subjectively; inner restlessness was a common and non-specific symptom, but complaints clearly referrable to the legs characterised the akathisia group. Moderate akathisia showed in addition a tendency to rock from foot to foot or to walk on the spot, along with coarse tremor or myoclonic jerks in the feet. The severe akathisia group showed difficulty in maintaining their position, for example rising when seated or walking or pacing when attempting to stand still.

Continuation of the drugs may allow the symptoms to subside, but this is not invariable. An extrapyramidal origin is postulated, but the evidence for this is mainly inferential.

Acute Dystonia

Acute dystonic reactions are considerably rarer than the above, affecting perhaps some 2% of patients. They develop abruptly and early in the course of treatment, within a few days of oral treatment or within hours of intramuscular injection. The more potent piperazine phenothiazines and the butyrophenones are chiefly responsible. Young adults and children appear to be particularly susceptible.

The patient is seized with strong sustained or intermittent muscular spasms which are frequently painful and deeply alarming. Deviation of the eyes, blepharospasm, trismus and grimacing are common. Severe examples show tongue protrusion, dysphagia and respiratory stridor. Extension to the neck and trunk can lead to torticollis, retrocollis, writhing and opisthotonous. Continuous slow writhing may affect the limbs, with dystonic postures of hyperpronation and adduction.

Marked examples may be mistaken for status

epilepticus or tetanus by the inexperienced observer. Hysteria may be diagnosed when muscular spasms are remittant. The disorder is self-limiting and usually of no more than several hours duration, though therapeutic intervention will often be indicated for the relief of acute distress.

Tardive Dyskinesia

As experience was gained of long-term neuroleptic medication it became apparent that a range of movement disorders could make their first appearance only late in the course of treatment. These have attracted considerable attention, on account of their sometimes seriously disabling nature and because in a proportion of patients they can prove to be irreversible. The term 'tardive dyskinesia' is used to refer to such late developments rather than to any phenomenologically distinct dyskinetic picture.

The commonest site of the abnormal movements is around the mouth and tongue, which become involved in a more or less continuous flow of choreiform activity ('orofacial dyskinesia', 'bucco-linguo-masticatory dyskinesia'). The tongue protrudes, twists and curls, along with incessant chewing, pouting and sucking movements of the lips, jaw and cheeks. In severe examples talking and eating can be hampered. The upper face tends typically to be spared, but may show tic-like blinking or blepharospasm. The neck may be affected with twisting dystonic movements.

Involvement of the trunk, arms, hands and legs may also be observed, possibly representing a relatively distinct subgroup (Kidger et al., 1980). The distal extremities show choreiform and athetotic movements, with finger twisting and spreading, tapping of the feet and dorsiflexion of the toes. Abnormalities of gait and posture show as lordosis, rocking and shoulder shrugging. Grunting and disturbance of the respiratory rhythm may be in evidence. The picture may come to involve a complex admixture of tics, chorea, athetosis, dystonia and myoclonic jerks. Rhythmic tremor is not, however, seen. It may worsen dramatically with emotional stress and it decreases with drowsiness. Choreiform movements appear to be commoner in the elderly, and dystonic pictures in the young. Age also influences the topography, oro-lingual movements being especially common in the elderly.

A similar disorder is known to occur spontaneously in the elderly, as the relatively rare 'senile chorea'. In patients on long-term neuroleptics, however, tardive dyskinesia is far from uncommon.

Variable estimates have resulted from different surveys, depending among other factors on readiness to include very minor degrees of movement disorder. The working party appointed by the American Psychiatric Association (Task Force on Late Neurological Effects of Antipsychotic Drugs, 1980) concluded that between 10 and 20% of people given anti-psychotic drugs for a year or more could be expected to develop a clinically appreciable tardive dyskinesia, the rate probably being higher in the elderly. Disabling degrees are, however, rare. In the great majority of cases the patient will have been on neuroleptics for at least 2 years when the disorder makes its first appearance and often for considerably longer. A minimum period of exposure appears to be 3–6 months.

Among predisposing factors highlighted in certain surveys are advanced age, brain damage, or a history of exposure to electro-convulsive therapy or leucotomy, though all of these have been questioned. There is some evidence that prolonged exposure or exposure to high dosage may increase the risk, but this also is disputed. It is clear, however, that most patients will have received large total quantities before tardive dyskinesia supervenes. A female preponderance has sometimes but not invariably been found. A noteworthy feature is that the first signs very often make their appearance when the drugs are discontinued or the dosage is lowered.

A disturbing aspect of the condition is its liability to persist despite stopping the medication. A majority of patients will improve substantially, usually within months but sometimes taking one or two years for complete resolution. Between a quarter and a half of patients may be expected to improve markedly within a year (Task Force, 1980). In children complete recovery can be predicted, but in some 30% of adults the condition seems destined to be permanent.

Important aspects of differential diagnosis include schizophrenic stereotypies and mannerisms, senile chorea, Huntington's chorea, Wilson's disease, and rheumatic chorea.

Tardive Dystonia: Burke et al. (1982) have recently described a rare syndrome of 'tardive dystonia' which appears to be attributable to antipsychotic medication. As with tardive dyskinesia it typically follows several years of treatment with the drugs, and once established it tends to be persistent. The nature of the movement disorder is, however, quite different. The dystonia consists of sustained slow twisting movements affecting the limbs, trunk, neck or face. Among younger patients generalised dystonia is the usual picture, whereas in older patients the movements are often confined to the face, neck or arms. Among Burke et al.'s 42 examples the age of onset varied from 13 to 60, after an average duration of exposure to drugs of 3–7 years. The onset was usually insidious, progressing over some months or years then becoming persistent and static. One patient was sufficiently disabled to be chronically confined to bed. All classes of antipsychotic medication could be incriminated—phenothiazines, butyrophenones and thioxanthenes.

The picture in generalised cases was indistinguishable from idiopathic torsion dystonia (p. 569), though all lacked a family history of such a condition. The possibility that they simply represented a chance association of this disorder appearing while on antipsychotic medication was considered to be remote. Focal cases could present pictures identical to torticollis, blepharospasm or oromandibular dystonia. Wilson's disease always needed to be excluded by appropriate diagnostic studies.

Five of the 42 patients had shown acute dystonic reactions early in their treatment, and 8 showed oral chorea along with the masticatory movements typical of tardive dyskinesia. In other respects, however, the syndrome appeared distinct. Pharmacological differences were shown in that anti-cholinergic agents, which often exacerbate tardive dyskinesia, could sometimes be observed to improve the dystonic movements. Treatment was, however, mostly disappointing. An increase in the offending medication could lead in some cases to temporary amelioration but this was short-lived. Tetrabenazine appeared to be the most effective treatment after withdrawing all other medication, occasionally producing considerable benefit though complete success was rare. Follow-up showed remission in 5 patients and persistence of the disorder in the remainder.

PATHOPHYSIOLOGY

The pathophysiology of the neuroleptic-induced movement disorders appears to lie with various aspects of the dopamine–acetylcholine balance within the brain, more particularly within the corpus striatum. Earlier views have, however, become progressively more complex, with the discovery of both inhibitory and excitatory dopamine receptors in the striatum, and the demonstration of feed-back striatonigral pathways which may be mediated in part by cholinergic or GABA-ergic mechanisms. The maintenance of correct dopamine and acetylcholine levels in the striatum is clearly under highly complex control and stands to be disturbed in a multitude of ways. Hence, no doubt, the variety of movement disorders encountered when this balance is altered by drugs. Important reviews of theories in this area are provided by Klawans (1973), Marsden and Jenner (1980) and Baldessarini and Tarsy (1980).

Among their many pharmacological actions, all neuroleptics have powerful effects on cerebral dopamine mechanisms. These correlate highly with their antipsychotic potency. It is clear, however, that the induction of extrapyramidal motor disorder is not a necessary prerequisite for benefit to psychosis, the latter conceivably hinging on effects within the mesolimbic dopamine projections (arising in the tegmentum of the midbrain and terminating in limbic forebrain structures) rather than on actions within the nigrostriatal system. The phenothiazines, butyrophenones and thioxanthenes act specifically to block cerebral dopamine receptors. Reserpine and tetrabenazine operate differently, interfering with the intraneuronal granular uptake and storage of dopamine.

Drug-induced parkinsonism appears to be chemically closely analogous to naturally occuring Parkinson's disease. The blockade of dopamine receptors within the striatum amounts to 'chemical denervation', resulting in relative dopamine deficiency. Anticholinergic drugs can accordingly be of benefit by helping to restore the correct dopamine-acetylcholine balance.

The genesis of akathisia is little understood, but may possibly rest on dopamine receptor blockade in brain areas other than the striatum. The mechanisms underlying acute dystonic reactions have also until recently been obscure. Marsden and Jenner (1980) discuss evidence that the latter may result from interference with pre-synaptic dopamine mechanisms; or the increased dopamine synthesis seen in the early stages of therapy may have an effect on dopamine receptors of a type not blocked by the drugs.

There is probably not a unitary pathophysiology for tardive dyskinesia; various patterns of movement emerge after varying lengths of treatment and differ in their persistence. It has been especially difficult to explain why drugs which block striatal dopamine receptors should eventually produce forms of dyskinesia known to be associated with dopamine overactivity in the striatum. Thus the choreiform movements of tardive dyskinesia resemble those seen as a complication of levodopa therapy in Parkinson's disease, and the administration of levodopa or of anticholinergic drugs exacerbates the condition. The prolonged blockade may have led to this end result by virtue of increased dopamine turnover, increased dopamine receptor density, or through the ultimate development of denervation hypersensitivity which causes the receptors to respond abnormally to the dopamine reaching them (Baldessarini and Tarsy,

1976, 1980). Hypersensitivity of striatal dopamine mechanisms probably accounts for the worsening of the condition on withdrawal of neuroleptics and the success of their reintroduction in ameliorating the disorder. The co-existence of two types of dopamine receptor, facilitatory and inhibitory, may also be relevant, explaining in particular why drug-induced parkinsonism does not always feature in the histories of patients who develop tardive dyskinesia.

Animal studies have indicated that over the course of prolonged neuroleptic administration, dopamine receptor blockade may actually slowly disappear, giving way to supersensitivity in its place. The latter, moreover, can be shown to persist for many months after withdrawal, providing a convincing analogy to the possible situation in tardive dyskinesia in man (Clow et al., 1979a,b).

No convincing pathology has been described in the brain to account for those tardive dyskinesias which become irreversible. Structural or neurotoxic changes in the neurones, affecting their membranes or the cell respiratory mechanisms, must nevertheless be postulated in such cases.

MANAGEMENT

Anticholinergic drugs are of value in controlling drug-induced parkinsonism. It often transpires, however, that once parkinsonian features have come under control, the anti-parkinsonian medication can then be withdrawn without recrudescence of the motor disorder. Certainly if the risk of tardive dyskinesia is to be minimised it would seem important to give anticholinergic medication as sparingly as possible, and only when the parkinsonism causes definite disability. Long-continued anticholinergic administration as an adjunct to neuroleptic treatment is now considered to be contraindicated. Levodopa should theoretically help drug-induced parkinsonism, but has been little used to date, perhaps because of adverse effects on the psychosis.

When akathisia is a persisting and disabling complaint the most decisive remedy is reduction of drug dosage (Braude et al., 1983). Benzodiazepines may help in some degree, also anticholinergic agents when drug-induced parkinsonism is present as well.

For acute dystonic reactions anticholinergic drugs are best given parenterally. Benztropine (Cogentin), diphenhydramine (Benadryl) and procyclidine (Kemadrin) can be administered intravenously and are often dramatically effective. For milder reactions it is important to remember the efficacy of non-specific calming of the patient, or simple sedation

with diazepam. The previous occurrence of dystonic reactions constitutes one of the few indications for the prophylactic prescription of anticholinergic drugs from the start of a course of neuroleptic medication.

The management of tardive dyskinesia must take into account every effort at prevention. There is no firm evidence that any particular phenothiazine, butyrophenone or thiothanxene is less hazardous than others in this regard, though some think the risk is less with thioridazine, oxypertine or sulpiride. Dosage and duration of neuroleptics should be kept to a minimum, and long-term maintenance therapy strictly reserved for patients in whom definite benefit can be expected. In practice this usually means patients with chronic schizophrenia of a type liable to manifest on-going positive symptoms in the absence of medication. The Task Force (1980) of the American Psychiatric Association recommended that all patients on long-term treatment should be reviewed at 6 or 12 month intervals. Whenever considered safe and feasible at these reviews the drugs should be gradually reduced until stopped completely for a two week period. Such 'drug holidays' have not been shown to be helpful in themselves in preventing tardive dyskinesia, but allow assessment of continuing responsiveness to the drug and facilitate detection of the earlier stages of the disorder. Mild and early examples are perhaps most likely to subside, but even if not the patient will be left with less severe disability. Anticholinergic drugs as an adjunct to treatment should be avoided whenever possible.

Once tardive dyskinesia is detected all neuroleptic medication should be withdrawn if the patient's mental state allows it. Anticholinergic drugs should certainly be discontinued immediately. If the mental state should worsen on withdrawal it will be necessary to balance the risks of aggravating the psychosis against the risks of dyskinesia in the individual case. Reduction to the minimum compatible with the patient's management should always be attempted, perhaps with transfer to thioridazine, oxypertine or sulpiride. Tardive dyskinesia is not uniformly and relentlessly progressive, so the continuation of treatment, at least in the short term, is usually justifiable if the psychosis is active (Task Force, 1980).

Many therapies have been evaluated, sometimes showing a degree of short-term benefit in control comparisons, but the consensus view is that treatment is likely to be disappointing. Tetrabenazine and reserpine have shown occasional success (Sato et al., 1971), acting to deplete striatal dopamine without further adverse effects on dopamine receptor sites. Cholinergic agents such as deanol, choline or lecithin may sometimes help (Growdon *et al.*, 1977; Growdon, 1979). The GABA-ergic agents, sodium valproate (Epilim) and baclofen (Lioresal), have appeared to be more effective than placebo (Linnoila *et al.*, 1976; Korsgaard, 1976). Benzodiazepines may be useful by virtue of their sedating effect. Very often, however, it will be found that no currently available therapy ameliorates the condition and one must merely hope for spontaneous resolution. The temptation to control the dyskinesia by re-introducing neuroleptics at increased dosage is now firmly condemned. It may be highly efficacious in producing short-term relief, but merely postpones the problem by reinstating the original pathogenesis and can be expected to worsen the ultimate disability.

Parkinson's Disease and the Parkinsonian Syndrome

The cardinal neurological deficits which make up the syndrome of parkinsonism are tremor, muscular rigidity, hypokinesis and postural abnormality. A large number of other associated features are also characteristic as described below.

By far the commonest form is 'idiopathic parkinsonism' or paralysis agitans, as described by James Parkinson in 1817. This is now thought to owe its origin to a specific degeneration of pigmented cells in the brain stem, particularly those of the substantia nigra. Some hereditary tendency exists, the pattern seeming usually to be dominant inheritance with clinical manifestations in perhaps 25% of gene carriers (Pratt, 1967). 'Idiopathic parkinsonism' is usually diagnosed when no evidence can be found from the history or examination for the presence of other diseases which could be aetiologically relevant.

The same clinical picture may be induced by certain medications such as reserpine, phenothiazines, butyrophenones and methyldopa ('drug-induced parkinsonism'). This remits slowly over several weeks or months when the offending drug is withdrawn. A similar syndrome, 'post-encephalitic parkinsonism', was a common aftermath of the pandemic of encephalitis lethargica which occurred fifty years ago (p. 292). Cases could appear up to twenty years after the original infection which was sometimes very mild. An early age of onset suggested the post-encephalitic variety, also oculogyric crises, abnormal pupil reactions or continuing marked sleep disturbance.

Many other conditions that affect the basal ganglia

may cause akinetic rigid syndromes along with other features resulting from diffuse brain damage, for example repeated head injuries in boxing, cerebral syphilis, anoxia due to cardiac arrest, or poisoning with carbon monoxide or manganese. Such a syndrome may appear as part of other degenerative disorders such as Alzheimer's disease, Wilson's disease, or cerebral arteriosclerosis. The latter, however, is no longer recognised as a cause of Parkinson's disease *per se*, and the category of 'arteriosclerotic parkinsonism' has fallen into disrepute (Eadie and Sutherland, 1964; Pallis, 1971). Certainly the clinical features which are used to delineate this form of the syndrome are variable from one observer to another. An arteriosclerotic origin tends to be blamed when the onset has been acute or progression has occured in a step-like manner, when progressive dementia has coincided with or preceded the parkinsonism, or when pseudobulbar palsy or pyramidal deficits are present. Some hold that 'marche à petit pas' is also characteristic of the variety. It is hard, however, to establish a causal relationship to cerebral arterial disease when this exists, and the two disorders probably simply occur together by coincidence. In Eadie and Sutherland's (1964) study no more clinical evidence of arterial disease could be found in a large group of parkinsonian patients than among equivalent age-matched controls.

Hoehn and Yahr (1967) reviewed 802 patients from a neurological clinic and considered 84% to be idiopathic, 15% secondary (mostly postencephalitic but also 'arteriosclerotic', toxic and metabolic in origin), and 1% to show uncertain evidence whether primary or secondary.

Clinical Features

The idiopathic disease is slightly commoner among men than women. The mean age of onset is 55 with two-thirds of cases beginning between 50 and 59 (Hoehn and Yahr, 1967). Excellent accounts of the clinical features and natural history are given by Calne (1970) and Pallis (1971).

Tremor is the presenting feature in about three-quarters of the idiopathic cases, consisting of four to eight per second alternating contractions of opposing muscle groups. It is present at rest but ceases during sleep, and may become less marked when the limb is engaged in voluntary movement. It is worsened by excitement, anxiety and fatigue. Most typically it appears in the hands as flexion-extension movements affecting the metacarpophalangeal joints of the fingers and thumb. It is common also in the jaw and tongue and may come to affect the head or the lower limbs. In some cases it is predominantly or entirely unilateral.

Rigidity affects the large and small muscles of the limbs, trunk and neck, involving agonists and antagonists equally and through the whole range of passive movement. In these respects it is quite unlike the spasticity that results from corticospinal tract damage, and feels to the examining hand to have a 'lead pipe' or 'plastic' quality. When tremor is also present, the rigidity is broken up ('cogwheel rigidity'). Rigidity, like tremor, can be predominantly unilateral. It persists during sleep and is unaffected by emotional factors.

Hypokinesia consists of poverty and slowness of movement. This is not due solely to rigidity since stereotactic surgery can relieve rigidity without improving hypokinesia. Hypokinesia is not always sufficiently emphasised in descriptions of the disorder yet can be the most disabling aspect to the patient. Sometimes it dominates the entire picture. It shows in slowness in the initiation and execution of motor acts, and poverty of automatic and associated movements such as the normal swinging of the arms when walking. Hypokinesia probably accounts for many of the classical features of parkinsonism— the mask-like face, infrequent blinking, clumsiness of fine finger movement, crabbed writing and monotonous speech. The gait is affected in many characteristic ways with slowness, shuffling, difficulty in starting and turning and impaired equilibrium. It may show an episodic quality, causing periodic freezing of action or episodes of complete immobility.

More than any other feature hypokinesia can be profoundly affected by the patient's mental state. There are numerous reports of severely disabled patients achieving surprising feats of motor behaviour in response to fear, excitement, or other environmental stimulation.

Postural changes show as a characteristic flexion of the trunk and neck bringing the chin to the chest, with arms adducted at the shoulders and flexed at elbows, wrists and knuckles. The typical 'festinant' gait appears to be a product of the abnormal posture along with difficulty in controlling the centre of gravity. Postural instability leads to frequent falls.

Other features include oculomotor abnormalities, excessive salivation, seborrhoea, constipation, urinary disturbance, subjective sensory discomfort and marked fatigue. Infrequent blinking is common in all forms of parkinsonism, and paresis of convergence may occur. The latter is particularly common

in postencephalitic parkinsonism which may also show oculogyric crises (p. 295). Sialorrhoea is mainly the result of difficulties in coping with normal quantities of saliva on account of dysphagia. Constipation is a major symptom of the disease and a cause of great distress. Urinary frequency and incontinence are frequent complaints. Sensory discomforts include feelings of tightness, pain and cramp in the limbs and back. The fatigue associated with the disorder is often particularly distressing and disabling.

Clinical tests for the detection of early cases are discussed by Jewesbury (1970). The patient shows difficulty when asked to maintain a steady rhythmic movement, as in tapping or making polishing movements. The handwriting often reveals changes at an early stage, or attempts to draw parallel lines close together. The 'glabellar tap reflex' is elicited by tapping over the root of the nose between the eyebrows; parkinsonian patients are said to blink in response to each tap no matter how often or at what frequency, and fail to habituate as normal subjects do. Observation of the gait can also be revealing in early cases when attention is directed at the lack of arm swinging, difficulty in turning sharply, or the exacerbation of tremor in the hands.

Course and Outcome

Idiopathic parkinsonism is usually a progressive disease. Hoehn and Yahr (1967) found that a quarter of patients were severely disabled or dead within 5 years of onset and two-thirds within 10 years. A small number, however, show very slow progression and remain without severe disablement after 20 years or more. The mortality is estimated to be three times that of the general population of the same age and sex. Older treatments did not influence prognosis but it is possible that levodopa therapy has prolonged life expectancy. Common causes of death are cardiac and cerebral vascular disease, bronchopneumonia and neoplasia. The prognosis in terms of rate of progression and mortality is better for postencephalitic cases and worse for those labelled as arteriosclerotic.

Pathology and Pathophysiology

Parkinsonism is associated with lesions in component parts of the extrapyramidal motor system, especially the pigmented nuclei of the brain stem. For many years it proved hard to decide which aspects of the pathology were primarily responsible for the symptoms, but it is now widely accepted that the substantia nigra of the mid-brain is an essential site of origin of the disorder.

Cellular degeneration affects the globus pallidus, putamen, caudate and associated nuclei and is constantly seen in the zona compacta of the substantia nigra (Greenfield, 1963). The melanin-bearing cells of the substantia nigra are particularly affected, to a degree that may be visible to the naked eye. Lewy's hyaline inclusion bodies are often visible in the cytoplasm of cells which remain, also in the pigmented cells of the locus caeruleus, dorsal vagal nucleus and reticular formation. Neuroglial scarring is seen in the islands from which neurones have disappeared. In contrast to the cellular changes tract lesions are slight. Scattered changes may be seen elsewhere in the diencephalon, brain stem, cord and cerebral cortex, but lack specificity. Diffuse cortical atrophy has been reported to be common, and possibly greater than would be expected for healthy individuals of equivalent age (p. 557).

In post-encephalitic parkinsonism the pigmented cells of the substantia nigra and locus caeruleus are similarly lost, but neurofibrillary changes rather than Lewy bodies are seen in those that remain.

A development of the utmost importance has been the growing understanding in recent years of the biochemical basis for parkinsonism, and the realisation that neurotransmitter systems are fundamentally disturbed in the disease. In the idiopathic disease the outstanding defect is degeneration of the melanin-pigmented neurones of the brain stem which manufacture the catecholamine neurotransmitters dopamine and noradrenaline. Dopamine is normally found in high concentration in the pigmented cells of the substantia nigra, the nigrostriatal tract, and its terminals in the caudate and putamen. It is now established that dopamine is much diminished in the brains of most parkinsonian patients, both idiopathic and post-encephalitic, sometimes being reduced to 10% of the normal level in the striatum. This appears to be due to loss of 'dopaminergic' fibres passing from the substantia nigra to the striatum (the 'dopaminergic nigrostriatal tract'). The detailed evidence is discussed by Vogt (1970) and Hornykiewicz (1971) . It emerges that dopamine and acetylcholine are antagonistic in their effects in the striatum, any cause which alters the dopamine–acetylcholine balance in the direction of marked cholinergic dominance leading to parkinsonism.

While the cardinal biochemical feature of parkinsonism is striatal dopamine deficiency, other neuro-transmitters are possibly implicated as well. Cerebral concentrations of noradrenaline and 5-hydroxytryptamine are also reduced. And in some cases at least there is a loss of striatal dopamine receptors as well as a loss of nigrostriatal fibres. In addition to the nigrostriatal pathway, other dopaminergic neurones in the tegmental area project to the cortex and limbic structures. There is evidence that this 'mesolimbic' pathway is also impaired in Parkinson's disease, which may be relevant to some of the psychiatric complications discussed below.

Homovanillic acid is the end-product of dopamine metabolism and has been found usually to be in low concentration in the cerebrospinal fluid in untreated patients with parkinsonism. A low cerebrospinal fluid homovanillic acid can therefore be a useful confirmatory finding if a clinical diagnosis of idiopathic parkinsonism is difficult, as for example in a demented patient with two diseases (Parkes and Marsden, 1973).

Differential Diagnosis

The diagnosis is rarely in doubt once the disease is reasonably well advanced but mistakes can occur in the early stages, particularly if tremor is absent. In elderly patients the signs may be overlooked and complaints of back or limb pain may lead to a diagnosis of arthritis or osteoporosis. Alternatively the presentation may be with unexpected falls which are attributed to vertebrobasilar insufficiency. Strictly unilateral rigidity in the absence of tremor can raise suspicion of a cerebral tumour. Marked hypokinesia may at first raise the question of myxoedema or depressive illness. In patients with evidence of intellectual deterioration the parkinsonian features may be overlooked in favour of a diagnosis of pre-senile or senile dementia. Marked parkinsonian features are indeed not uncommon in Alzheimer's disease (p. 378).

Rapid fluctuations in the early stages can suggest a psychiatric diagnosis by way of neurosis, hysteria or even malingering. Such suspicion will be increased if the family report that the patient can function entirely normally in the face of a stressful situation. In the presence of known psychiatric disorder under treatment with neuroleptic drugs, considerable difficulty may be encountered in distinguishing side effects of therapy from the ingravescent development of idiopathic Parkinson's disease. Here it can be important to remember that the parkinsonian side effects of neuroleptic drugs usually make their appearance early in the course of therapy, then often tend to subside (p. 546). In cases of doubt withdrawal may be necessary for very long periods, sometimes for a year or more, before the true situation is clarified.

Benign essential tremor (juvenile, adult or senile) may lead to difficulties with diagnosis ('Minor's disease'). This can begin at any age, a positive family history is often forthcoming, and improvement with alcohol is characteristic. The hands are principally affected, the tremor disappears when the limbs are inactive, and titubation of the head is commoner than in Parkinson's disease. There is no akinesia or rigidity and the condition is static or perhaps very slowly progressive over several decades.

Other neurological diseases which must sometimes be considered include Huntington's chorea and Wilson's disease. The rigid and akinetic forms of Huntington's chorea may at first resemble Parkinson's disease. Wilson's disease must be carefully excluded when parkinsonian symptoms begin in adolescence or early adult life. The rigidity of Wilson's disease is similar to that of parkinsonism, but the involuntary movements are more varied including choreic jerking, athetoid and dystonic movements, or flapping tremor of the outstretched hands. In progressive supranuclear palsy (p. 567) disordered eye movement is characteristic.

Treatment

The treatment of Parkinson's disease has undergone dramatic changes. Anticholinergic drugs have continued in use but a vogue for stereotactic operations has now largely given way to successful treatment with levodopa. Useful reviews of current management are provided by Jewesbury (1970), Calne (1970), Yahr and Duvoisin (1972) and Marsden (1983). Treatment will be considered only briefly here, but certain aspects of drug treatment and stereotactic operation will be dealt with in more detail in the sections on psychiatric aspects of the disease which follow.

There is no clear evidence that modern therapy alters the underlying pathology of the disease as opposed to suppressing the clinical manifestations. Nevertheless a large proportion of patients can obtain a gratifying degree of relief from their more disabling symptoms, certainly during the earlier stages of the disorder. Some severely crippled patients are now enabled to lead relatively independent lives. Specific therapies must be accompanied by general measures to keep the patient active for as long as possible, with physiotherapy or the use of simple mechanical aids. Psychosocial aspects often need attention, especially since the degree of physical disability may be considerably worsened by stress or concurrent depression.

Anticholinergic drugs are still used alone in mild cases and are usually continued thereafter when further measures need to be instituted. The best known are benzhexol (Artane, Pipanol), benztropine (Cogentin), orphenadrine (Disipal), procyclidine (Kemadrin) and biperiden (Akineton). Their effect is variable. Mobility is usually improved, with some decrease in rigidity and occasionally in tremor. Hypokinesia is usually little affected. Atropine-like side effects limit the dose which can be employed.

Oculogyric crises in post-encephalitic parkinsonism are sometimes reported to diminish with anticholinergic drugs. *Amphetamine* and *chlordiazepoxide* have also been found to help in this regard. Prolonged crises can often be terminated by intramuscular *ethopropazine* (Lysivane).

Amantadine hydrochloride (Symmetrel) is indicated if anticholinergic drugs fail and the patient is only mildly disabled. Among the severely disabled it finds application in patients who cannot tolerate levodopa. Amantadine helps with hypokinesia and postural instability in addition to improving rigidity. Mobility may thereby be considerably improved.

Levodopa (L-dopa) is now well established as a highly effective drug with a wide range of activity on different parkinsonian symptoms. It is a logical form of treatment, being the immediate precursor of dopamine which is known to be deficient in the brain. Approximately one-third of patients can be expected to obtain marked relief, one-third moderate benefit, and the remainder show a modest or disappointing response. Perhaps some 15 per cent do not respond at all. Levodopa is therefore widely regarded as the treatment of choice in patients who can tolerate it. A synergistic action is seen when given in conjunction with anticholinergic drugs and perhaps with amantadine as well. It may take several months before maximal benefit is obtained, and it cannot be said to have failed until it has been tried for 6 months or preferably a year. The variability of response seen from one individual to another cannot yet be accurately predicted.

Rigidity is helped and tremor also improves but less consistently. Propanolol or some other beta blocker may further help the latter. Outstanding benefit is seen where hypokinesia and postural instability are concerned, both of which are rarely responsive to anticholinergic drugs. Thus facial mobility is improved, salivation lessened and the voice strengthened. Gait, handwriting and ability to do fine manipulative tasks all improve. The overall result can be dramatic with the patient able to do such things as shaving, knitting or getting out of bed unaided when these have not been possible for some considerable time.

Unfortunately as time goes by the efficacy of levodopa may diminish. In general over a 5 year period a third of those who responded initially retain their benefit, a third lose some and a third lose all their gains becoming worse than they were before (Marsden and Parkes, 1977). This is most probably due to progression of the underlying disease. Gross variations in benefit may emerge for hours or days at a time, or the effects of each dose may become shorter-lasting. In extreme form this shows as the 'on-off' effect with swings from complete relief to total immobility, often occurring with startling rapidity and sometimes many times a day (Marsden and Parkes, 1976). Considerable improvement may then be obtained by giving the drug in small divided doses, even 2 or 3 hourly through the day. In post-encephalitic patients oculogyric crises may similarly recur later, or even make a first appearance after long-continued treatment.

Adverse effects commonly include anorexia, nausea, vomiting and hypotension. These can usually be overcome by starting with low dosage and increasing very gradually. The gastrointestinal effects can be largely avoided by the use of combined preparations of levodopa with a selective extracerebral decarboxylase inhibitor (Sinemet or Madopar). Tremors, tachypnoea, flushing and cardiac arrhythmias may also be troublesome, but the commonest dose-limiting factor is the appearance of dyskinetic movements. Such dyskinesias can take any form, including orofacial dyskinesia, chorea, dystonia or athetosis of the limbs, analogous in form, and probably in pathophysiology, to the movements seen in tardive dyskinesia (p. 547). A compromise quite often has to be sought between the severity of such adventitious movements and the degree of relief of parkinsonian disability. The psychiatric effects of levodopa are considered on p. 559.

Bromocriptine ('Parlodel') acts as a direct stimulant of dopaminergic receptors. It has been more recently introduced as an adjuvant to levodopa in patients who have lost benefit from the latter and for the non-responders. It must be used with caution owing to a range of side effects similar to those seen with levodopa. Among psychiatric complications there may be intense visual hallucinations. *Pergolide* and *lisuride* are other dopamine agonists in use in clinical trials, both apparently leading to a high incidence of psychiatric complications.

Psychotropic drugs often have an important part to play in management. The relief of depression and anxiety can itself lead to a considerable improvement in physical disability, but over and above this the tricyclic antidepressants may have a more direct effect on parkinsonism symptomatology. Imipramine or amitriptyline are usually employed along with anticholinergic drugs or levodopa, but in mild cases may prove to be effective on their own. The antidepressant nomifensine was regarded as particularly appropriate by virtue of its dopaminergic activity, but has now been withdrawn on account of toxic effects. Diazepam is used when anxiety is the predominant manifestation. Monoamine oxidase inhibitors must never be given in association with levodopa.

Stereotactic surgery has declined abruptly in popularity since the introduction of levodopa, but still finds an occasional place in patients with tremor or rigidity which is predominantly unilateral and when hypokinesia is minimal. The optimal site for stereotactic destruction has been extensively debated. Common targets included the globus pallidus, the ventrolateral nucleus of the thalamus and the pallidofugal fibres in the ansa and fasciculus lenticularis. Sometimes it seemed that results were best when the lesions also encroached on the internal capsule. Pallido-capsular lesions were perhaps most effective in relieving rigidity, and thalamo-capsular lesions in relieving tremor (Gillingham *et al.*, 1964).

The relief of tremor and rigidity could be impressive but the gains in terms of functional ability were often disappointing. This was probably because the hypokinesia of the disorder was unaffected. Thus the festinant gait, postural imbalance and mask-like face persisted unaltered. Side effects of the operations further limited their usefulness—occasional patients suffered speech disturbance, impairment of balance, or some degree of paresis or mental deterioration.

PSYCHIATRIC ASPECTS OF PARKINSONISM

Interest in the psychiatric aspects of parkinsonism has increased as a result of advances in knowledge of the disease. The advent of stereotactic surgery focused renewed attention on the problem of intellectual impairment in the disorder, and the demonstration of disturbance of amine metabolism has brought new interest to its association with depression.

There is a good deal of disagreement in different reports regarding the incidence of mental symptoms, depending no doubt upon the particular population under scrutiny. Thus behavioural disturbance is likely to be more common when a substantial number of post-encephalitic cases are examined, and intellectual impairment will be more frequent when patients with 'arteriosclerotic parkinsonism' are included in the sample. The difficulties of achieving anything like a reliable estimate are increased by the problems inherent in distinguishing these different varieties one from another.

Mjönes (1949) reviewed the earlier work in detail. Three main groups of mental disturbance gradually came to be recognised and were sometimes regarded as an integral part of the pathological picture—a change of personality towards suspicion, irritability and egocentricity, an impairment of memory and intellect, and psychotic developments with depression, paranoia and sometimes visual hallucinations. Some felt that there was a typical paralysis agitans psychopathy, others a characteristic psychosis. Some found a great excess of dementia, others of depression. Mjönes' own investigation of 262 cases of paralysis agitans revealed mental symptoms in approximately 40% of cases. 'Organic' changes predominated over 'reactive' changes, the former consisting of impaired memory and intellect, the latter of depression with irritability, egocentricity and hypochondriasis. Transitional forms were also encountered in which the relative contributions of organic or reactive elements were uncertain.

More recent studies have tended to underline the association with depression, but still to leave somewhat uncertain the question of cognitive decline. Intellectual impairment, when obtrusive, appears to be associated mainly with 'arteriosclerotic parkinsonism', and as described above this may merely represent the fortuitous association of cerebral arteriosclerosis and Parkinson's disease. However cognitive changes may also be detected in a proportion of patients with the idiopathic disease. A typical personality change, or a characteristic form of psychotic reaction, is no longer recognised. These matters are dealt with in more detail in the sections that follow.

Cognitive Impairments

There is no doubt that some parkinsonian patients show impairment of intellect, occasionally severe enough to amount to an easily recognisable progressive dementia. Others by contrast remain intellec-

tually intact despite gross physical disablement. The question which remains unsolved is how far cognitive abnormalities should be regarded as an integral part of the disease process and a reflection of the essential pathology within the extrapyramidal system.

Two major difficulties stand in the way of resolving the issue. The first is the uncertain nosological status of arteriosclerotic parkinsonism and the difficulty of establishing acceptable criteria for separating such a category from the idiopathic disease (p. 550). If some examples of parkinsonism merely reflect an accent on the basal ganglia of diffuse cerebral arteriosclerosis, then the cognitive impairments encountered in certain cases may be due entirely to the diffuse cerebral changes in this group. When, on the other hand, evidence of dementia is used as a criterion for separating arteriosclerotic from idiopathic parkinsonism, the idiopathic cases will tend to be reported as intact. A second difficulty involves the evaluation of cognitive status in parkinsonian patients. Motivational or emotional factors may appear to account for failure to perform in a given situation, rather than restriction of intellectual capacity. Motor slowness must also be taken into account, since the appearance of mental sluggishness may be due to slowness of response rather than diminution of grasp or impairment of reasoning ability. In addition parkinsonian patients are usually elderly so that defects on psychometric testing must be carefully distinguished from what is to be expected in any ageing population. Drugs taken for the treatment of Parkinson's disease may further complicate the issue.

Not surprisingly, therefore, observers have differed in their accounts of the incidence and nature of cognitive impairments in the disorder. Detailed psychometric testing has given conflicting results, but has usually been restricted to rather small samples of patients. Talland (1962) was unable to identify definite signs of impairment in 45 parkinsonian patients when compared with carefully matched controls. Tests were used which did not depend for success on normal motor control. No marked defects were found in attention, concentration or immediate memory. Some deficits were displayed in longer-term memory and problem solving ability, but here it seemed possible that medication was responsible. Asso (1969) tested 61 patients referred for stereotactic surgery using the Wechsler Adult Intelligence Scale, comparing the results with age adjusted scores from the normal standardisation sample. Again no evidence of specific intellectual impairment was obtained. Loranger *et al.* (1972b) found lower performance than verbal intelligence in patients with idiopathic parkinsonism and felt unable to attribute this entirely to motor difficulties. Some subtests which required no motor activity were badly performed, and observation often indicated trouble with cognitive function rather than manual dexterity. The greatest difficulty appeared to lie in the comprehension and analysis of unfamiliar stimuli, also in immediate memory span. By contrast, verbal fluency, general information and practical social judgement were well preserved. Comparison with controls served to discount the role of ageing or depression, and the impairments appeared to be an integral part of the parkinsonian disease process.

Riklan *et al.*'s (1959) extensive study attempted to explore the relationship between particular psychological impairments and specific components of the parkinsonian syndrome. Two hundred and twenty consecutive patients referred for stereotactic surgery were examined clinically and tested with a battery of measures for assessing intellectual and personality functioning. The results were examined in relation to duration of illness, age, degree of muscular rigidity, voluntary movement impairment, and autonomic dysfunction as reflected in hypersalivation and tachycardia. Duration of illness was unrelated to scores on any test. Age was merely related to the type of deficits normally associated with age. Muscular rigidity and autonomic dysfunction were related to decreased intellectual productivity, perceptual difficulties and impoverishment of emotional resources. But the most striking relationships were between the degree of impairment of voluntary movement and a wide range of psychological deficits—loss of drive and energy, impairment of intellectual and perceptual functions, and pervasive personality and emotional disorders. The lack of any relationship to duration of disease suggested that the initial onslaught may have had the most serious psychological consequences. The close relationship between voluntary movement impairment and pervasive psychological changes was thought to reflect not only central factors but also the psychosocial consequences of the disease. Thus voluntary movement impairment was probably the most direct measure of overall parkinsonian disability and of the social isolation this engendered.

An especially useful recent study has tackled the problem by restricting attention to 30 mildly disabled parkinsonian patients, all under the age of 65 and with normal CT scans (Lees and Smith, 1983). Patients with depression or evidence of cerebral ischaemia were excluded. Comparisons with age-matched controls showed no impairment in general intellectual functions (Wechsler Adult Intelligence Scale) or on memory tests, but revealed significant deficits on the Wisconsin Card Sorting Test. The patients showed difficulty in shifting their conceptual sets and produced an excess of perseverative responses. The latter were also revealed on a verbal fluency test. Subtle cognitive deficits of this nature could well underlie the mental inflexibility and rigidity often regarded as present in Parkinson's disease.

In contrast to the psychometric evidence, surveys based on broad clinical assessment of the presence or absence of cognitive impairment have given reasonably consistent results. These have pointed increasingly to cognitive failure, extending even to frank dementia, as a good deal more common than chance expectation in Parkinson's disease. Pollock and Hornabrook (1966) found that 20 per cent of a large unselected series showed significant mental deterioration, the majority being in the group labelled as arteriosclerotic but some being examples of idiopathic parkinsonism. They stressed that intellectual impairment could exist alongside mild parkinsonism, many of the patients being a burden to relatives on account of dementia rather than because of their motor disabilities. Mindham (1970) found that one-third of parkinsonian patients admitted to a psychiatric hospital showed cognitive impairments, this being equally frequent among idiopathic and arteriosclerotic cases. Celesia and Wanamaker (1972) claimed the highest incidence of all, with 40 per cent of 153 patients with idiopathic parkinsonism showing some evidence of cognitive impairment. This correlated in frequency and severity with the duration of the disease.

Marttila and Rinne's (1976) survey was unusually thorough, involving all traceable patients with Parkinson's disease in a defined area of Finland. Of 144 patients, 29% were thought to be demented, 50% of these being mildly, 30% moderately, and 20% severely affected. Patients with evidence of arteriosclerosis were more often demented than those without (56% and 18% of cases respectively). There was a clear rise with age, from 20% among the under 70s to 65% among the over 80s. The severely physically disabled showed dementia more often than the mildly affected, increasing severity of rigidity and hypokinesia showing a positive correlation with the degree of intellectual decline. This association strongly suggested a role of the subcortical structures in the pathophysiology of the dementia. On the other hand, the demented patients were significantly older at onset of the Parkinson's disease and at time of examination than the remainder, so factors associated with the ageing process may have played an additional part.

Lieberman *et al.* (1979) similarly found a later age of onset in those patients who demented, but by using spouses as controls were able to discount a simple age effect. Among 520 parkinsonian patients, 32% showed a moderate to marked dementia, this being ten times the incidence found in similarly aged controls. The demented patients, in addition to a later onset, had become more physically disabled in a shorter time and had responded less well to levodopa; two distinct forms of Parkinson's disease, with and without dementia, thus seemed a possibility.

Clinical surveys have therefore upheld quite strongly an association between parkinsonism and dementia; this, however, perhaps characterises a subgroup alone. Air encephalography has sometimes shown a high incidence of cerebral atrophy in parkinsonian patients (Selby, 1968), and CT scanning has tended towards the same conclusion (Schneider *et al.*, 1977). Sroka *et al.* (1981), in a careful CT study with age-matched controls, found significant enlargement of ventricles and widening of sulci in 93 patients with Parkinson's disease, particularly in those who showed cognitive impairment. Ventricular enlargement appeared to be better correlated with cognitive defects than the cortical atrophy.

Histological studies have concentrated on the prevalence of Alzheimer-type change in the brains of parkinsonian patients, often finding this to be much commoner than in age-matched controls (Alvord *et al.*, 1974; Hakim and Mathieson, 1978, 1979). In Boller *et al.*'s (1980) series the prevalence of plaques and tangles was six times that to be expected, rising moreover as the severity of dementia increased. A cortical pathology of Alzheimer type thus appears to be accelerated in the presence of Parkinson's disease, for reasons that are unknown.

Lenzi *et al.* (1979) have produced further evidence of cortical malfunction, using a radioactive oxygen inhalation technique to demonstrate focal reductions in oxidative metabolism, most markedly in the parietal areas. This was evident even in patients without clinical signs of dementia. In patients with hemiparkinsonism, only the affected hemisphere showed such changes. A reduction in cortical cholinergic activity has also been found, similar to that encountered in Alzheimer's disease (p. 382). Among the small group of Parkinson patients reported by Perry *et al.* (1983), cholinergic deficits were present only in those who showed cognitive impairment, and appeared to be associated with neuronal loss in the subcortical nucleus of Meynert (p. 383) rather than with the presence or absence of plaques and tangles in the cortex.

Altogether, therefore, there are reasons to suspect both cortical and subcortical contributions to cognitive failure in the disorder, the relative roles of each doubtless differing from case to case. The effects of levodopa on cognitive function, which could be relevant to the distinction, are discussed on p. 560. It is conceivable that relatively minor cognitive dysfunction owes most to a subcortical pathology, whereas severe and pervasive dementia rests on coexistent, but accelerated Alzheimer cortical change.

Affective Disorder

An association between parkinsonism and depression is now well established. The depression is often clearly reactive in nature, setting in immediately the patient is informed of the nature of the disease, or developing later as an understandable response to the limitations and discomforts imposed by the disablement. Mindham (1974), for example, was able to show a significant correlation between the severity of the leading signs of parkinsonism and the severity of depression in a group of patients attending a neurological clinic. This relationship persisted during treatment with levodopa, those improving physically showing a fall in the severity of affective symptoms.

In addition, however, there are indications that depression may sometimes bear a more integral relationship to the disease process itself. The high incidence of depression has impressed many observers and it has seemed to be commoner than in other equivalently disabling diseases. In several investigations it has failed to show a proportionate relationship to the degree of disability, and quite often it has been found to respond to antidepressive treatment (including electroconvulsive therapy) while the disability persists unchanged.

Warburton (1967) examined 140 parkinsonian patients referred for thalamotomy and compared them with matched controls suffering from a variety of surgical and medical conditions. Depression was significantly commoner among the parkinsonian patients, particularly among the females. Fifty-six per cent of the males and 71% of the females showed some degree of depression. This was severe enough to have led the patient to contemplate suicide and to warrant psychiatric treatment in 6% of the males and 18% of the females. No relationship could be observed to age, duration of illness or degree of physical handicap.

Mindham (1970), in a retrospective survey of 89 parkinsonian patients admitted to a psychiatric hospital, found that in almost two-thirds the psychiatric diagnosis had been of an affective disorder. Ninety per cent had displayed depressive affect irrespective of other psychiatric features, and this was equally common in post-encephalitic, arterio-sclerotic and idiopathic cases. Several patients improved in mood with appropriate psychiatric treatment even though their physical condition remained unaltered.

Celesia and Wanamaker (1972) found some degree of depression in one third of 153 patients with idiopathic parkinsonism, the severity again being independent of the degree of motor disability or duration of disease. Horn (1974) has confirmed a significant relationship between parkinsonism and depression using an objective rating scale for mood disorder. This relationship was independent of age, duration, or measures of severity of handicap, suggesting an integral association with the disease process itself.

Robins (1976), in a particularly carefully controlled study, supported such an interpretation. Forty-five patients with Parkinson's disease were matched for age and sex with chronically disabled people drawn from the same institutions (patients with hemiplegia, paraplegia and arthritis). The groups resembled each other with regard to the incidence of a pre-illness history of depression or of neurotic symptoms. The duration of disablement was similar in both but the degree of handicap greater in the non-parkinsonian group. Nevertheless the patients with Parkinson's disease were very significantly more depressed than the controls as measured by the Hamilton rating scale. In neither group did the severity of disability affect the presence or absence of depression, suggesting that the latter was not solely reactive in nature. Mayeux *et al.* (1981) examined 55 patients using their spouses as controls. Forty-seven per cent of the patients were deemed depressed, compared with 13 per cent of controls, the depression being mild in two-thirds and moderate to severe in the remainder. The patients as a group showed significantly higher Beck depression scores than did their spouses.

With regard to treatment antidepressant medica-tion can be highly effective in relieving both physical and mental symptoms (p. 554). Electroconvulsive treatment is not contra-indicated, and may result in pronounced motor benefit while alleviating the affective disorder (Lebensohn and Jenkins, 1975). Sometimes, indeed, improvement in parkinsonian features has been observed to antedate the improvement in depression during a course of electroconvulsive therapy (Asnis, 1977).

In the great majority of cases depression follows the onset of the disease, but patients are occasionally encountered where it is the presenting feature. Kearney (1964) reported two examples in whom the first symptom was depression combined with anxiety and agitation. In the first the depressive illness responded well to electroconvulsive therapy, then returned one year later when it was apparent that parkinsonism was developing. The second patient became increasingly depressed over several months with complaints about his legs which he could not describe accurately; he thought he had Parkinson's disease and sought many consultations with negative result until 6 months later when the definitive signs appeared.

To the degree that depression appears to be closely tied to the parkinsonian disease process it is tempting to suppose that common biochemical factors may be operative. In depressive illness, as well as in Parkinson's disease, functional deficiencies of noradrenaline, dopamine and 5-hydroxytryptamine have been postulated to play a part.

Personality Changes

Increasing disability may understandably lead to irritability, as in any disease which results in restriction of activities and dependence upon others. Egocentricity, querulousness, and an exacting attitude towards those around have often been stressed, likewise a change towards suspiciousness or even frank paranoia. However the incidence of such changes is hard to assess. Obsessional traits in the premorbid personality may become exaggerated, and hypochondriasis may be marked. Euphoria by contrast appears to be distinctly rare, and when present is probably closely tied to intellectual deterioration.

There does not appear to be any form of personality change specific for parkinsonism. The majority of the features outlined above are generally held to be accountable in terms of individual vulnerability and the psychological and social stresses which operate upon the disabled person.

Psychoses

The commonest psychotic disorder in parkinsonism is affective in nature. This is almost always depressive, Mindham (1970) finding no examples of mania in a retrospective survey of 89 patients admitted to a psychiatric hospital. Only 2 had schizophrenic illnesses, one with post-encephalitic and one with arteriosclerotic parkinsonism. Davison and Bagley (1969) note that reports of schizophrenia-like psychoses in association with idiopathic Parkinson's disease are rare and review the occasional examples in the literature. Crow *et al.* (1976) report 4 further cases, 2 with post-encephalitic and 2 with idiopathic parkinsonism.

Mjönes (1949) could find no support for the idea of a special paralysis agitans psychosis. Many of the earlier examples, with florid delusions and auditory and visual hallucinations, were no doubt the product of over-medication with hyoscine, atropine or other solanaceous drugs. Even nowadays acute organic reactions in parkinsonian patients are most often due to medication as discussed below. Celesia and Wanamaker (1972) observed acute psychotic episodes in 12% of 153 patients, the majority being attributable to drugs and most occurring in patients who showed impairment of cognitive function.

Psychiatric Complications of Anticholinergic Drugs

Anticholinergic drugs may produce an acute organic reaction which sometimes leads to diagnostic difficulty. Porteous and Ross (1956) reported mental disturbance in 20% of patients treated with benzhexol (Artane), sometimes in response to small doses. Symptoms included excitement, agitation, confusion, paranoid delusions, hallucinations and suicidal intentions, all rapidly disappearing when the drug was withdrawn. The disorder was usually evident within a few days of starting treatment but could sometimes be more gradual in evolution. There was then some risk that the relationship to treatment would be overlooked. Stephens (1967) reviewed other examples, and described the misuse of benzhexol in high dosage by adolescents for its hallucinogenic properties, sometimes with disorientation, outbursts of severe pathological excitement and distortion of time sense. Crawshaw and Mullen (1984) have reported further examples of abuse. Among parkinsonian patients adverse reactions are mostly seen in patients over 60, and especially when cerebral arteriosclerosis is evident.

Duvoisin and Katz (1968) recommend treating such reactions with physostigmine, a parenteral anticholinesterase which gains access to the central nervous system. Symptoms such as confusion, agitation, hallucinations, stupor, ataxia and dysarthria were promptly reversed by the drug in patients who had developed toxic reactions to scopolamine, atropine and other antiparkinsonian medications.

Amantadine in high dosage may likewise provoke acute organic reactions and sometimes epileptic fits.

Psychiatric Aspects of Levodopa Treatment

A great deal of interest has centred on the psychiatric consequences of treatment with levodopa. Adverse reactions range from acute organic reactions to severe affective disorders. Beneficial effects include a feeling of increased well-being and improvements on tests of cognitive function.

Goodwin (1971) reviews the numerous reports of adverse psychiatric reactions, varying in incidence from 10–50% of patients treated. Mental complications appear to be next only to gastrointestinal disturbances and movement disorders as side effects. He summarizes the reported disturbances as confusion and delirium in 4·4%, depression in 4·2%, restlessness and agitation 3·6%, delusions and paranoia 3·6%, hypomania 1·5% and hypersexuality 0·9%. A further 1·5% have other reactions including impulsivity, lethargy, anxiety, insomnia and vivid dreaming. It is not uncommon to find brief episodes of subjective tension, nervousness and restlessness in relation to the ingestion of each dose in the early phases of treatment (Yahr and Duvoisin, 1972). The more severe reactions, however, may set in only after many months on the drug. Jenkins and Groh (1970) emphasise the abrupt appearance, often with little warning, of the mental complications, and the rapid worsening which may occur.

The affective response has proved to be the most variable of all mental side effects. Most patients appear to experience an improvement in mood on levodopa, but severe depression and even suicide have been reported, sometimes in patients who failed to obtain benefit and sometimes in those who have responded well. A depressive state prior to starting levodopa has emerged as the most important predisposing factor.

Acute psychotic symptoms have included paranoid delusions and visual or sometimes olfactory hallucinations. Most occur in the context of acute organic reactions. Celesia and Barr (1970) found that 8 out of 45 patients developed psychotic complications, 6 in the form of acute organic reactions and

2 experiencing visual and auditory hallucinations in clear consciousness. Several showed episodes of aggressive assaultive behaviour.

As experience of long-term treatment has accrued it has become apparent that the prevalence of abnormal mental reactions increases as time goes by. Barbeau (1971) noted quite subtle changes of intellect and behaviour in a fifth of patients maintained on the drug for over 2 years. Attention span and recent memory gradually became impaired, sometimes with decrease of judgement, particularly in the sexual sphere. An 'insouciance' reminiscent of frontal lobe disturbance sometimes accompanied these changes, all of which were reversible with reduction of dosage. Sweet *et al.* (1976) reported that agitation, hallucinations and delusions all increased with the years, rising from 10% of patients initially to 60% after 6 years of treatment. Visual hallucinations were sometimes benign, consisting of images of people, often old friends, and recognised as being unreal. Progressive mental changes could take the form of a steady decline in mental ability which ultimately became as incapacitating as the motor symptoms, or of periods of agitation and confusion against a background of mild dementia. A trial of withdrawal of levodopa commonly diminished the agitated behaviour but rarely helped the cognitive impairments.

It is unclear whether long-term treatment conspires towards the development of fixed intellectual decline, or merely enables patients to survive long enough for this to be revealed. Sometimes resolution of the parkinsonian state may unmask a dementia not previously apparent. Sweet *et al.* (1976) followed a large group of patients for several years; the prevalence of dementia, judged clinically, fell after starting levodopa, but with continuation over the years new cases appeared and established cases could be observed to worsen. Patients with already-established dementia seem usually to show little change on instituting treatment (Yahr *et al.*, 1969; Markham *et al.*, 1974). Some, however, deteriorate abruptly, with changes that may be transient or permanent. Sacks *et al.* (1970, 1972) describe the alarming adverse reactions which may occasionally emerge in such a situation, with the abrupt appearance of agitated hallucinatory delirium accompanied by chorea, akathisia and motor unrest. Some patients proceeded to stupor or coma, with or without the preceding phase of excitement. The disturbances could persist for a week or more after withdrawal of levodopa. Those who had had severe confusional episodes showed worsened intellectual

deficits for many months afterwards.

The adverse effects are clearly variable from one individual to another and no uniform set of mental changes has emerged. The factors reponsible are likely to include genetic variability among the patients, the pre-treatment psychiatric state, the extent of neurological involvement, and perhaps the presence of diffuse brain damage. A previous history of psychiatric illness appears to constitute a special hazard. Damasio *et al.* (1971) suggest that most patients with a previous psychiatric history become worse on levodopa even if neurological improvement is satisfactory. Yahr and Duvoisin (1972) consider that levodopa is contraindicated in patients with prior mental illness, particularly affective disorders or major psychoses. In practice, however, a cautious trial of the drug will frequently be undertaken in patients with such a history.

Beneficial effects have chiefly involved the affective response, many patients experiencing increased well-being on levodopa. Yahr *et al.* (1969) observed renewal of interest in family life and the environment in most of their patients, replacing earlier feelings of depression and apathy. Marsh *et al.* (1971) were unable to confirm such changes using objective scores for mood, but their period of follow-up lasted a few months only.

Intellectual changes have also been reported. Patients who had been dulled from previous medication may show abrupt improvement. Others, irrespective of previous medication, may appear to think more quickly and clearly. The effect has been construed as part of the overall alerting and activating effect of the drug.

Marsh *et al.* (1971) investigated the situation in 29 patients, monitoring changes after treatment with a battery of psychological tests. Significant improvements were found in auditory perception and verbal learning but not in other aspects of cognitive functioning. The improvements were unrelated to changes in anticholinergic medication, improved motor ability, lessening of depression or increase in alertness. Thus a fairly specific cognitive effect emerged, rather than evidence of generalised alerting and activation. Loranger *et al.* (1972a, 1972b) have also reported objective improvements in patients reexamined after a period on the drug. Half of 40 patients rose 10 points or more on the Wechsler Adult Intelligence Scale, the greatest improvement occurring on those subtests originally most impaired. Again there was little or no relationship between the cognitive improvements and physical or affective changes. Fisher and Findley (1981) examined 20 patients 6 months and 2 years after starting on optimal régimes of treatment with levodopa. Significant gains in many aspects of intellectual function were revealed on the WAIS, including aspects independent of motor function. These persisted at the 2 year assessment.

Restoration of sexual interest has been reported, usually in the context of dramatic improvement in motor ability (Goodwin, 1971). In a few cases hypersexuality has emerged, possibly as part of a more general hypomanic reaction. Bowers *et al.* (1971) assessed the effect on sexual behaviour in twelve men and seven women. Six of the men and one woman reported an activation of sexual behaviour at some point during therapy though this was not striking in degree. In the majority the response seemed to be part of a general improvement in strength, mobility and overall functional capacity, though occasionally there appeared to be a transient specific stimulation of the sexual drive. In one patient increased sexual behaviour resulted from the disinhibition associated with an acute toxic reaction to the drug.

Finally mention must be made of the astonishing effects of levodopa observed among long-term survivors of encephalitis lethargica (Sacks, 1973). Institutionalised patients who had spent twenty years or more in states of 'trance' or immobility due to advanced parkinsonism were often dramatically liberated, experiencing virtually a total return to physical and mental health for a time. Sooner or later, however, the majority encountered a variety of difficulties, with the reactivation of symptoms and behaviour patterns from an earlier stage of the disease. Profound motor blocking set in, or a great excess of tics and urges. States of mounting excitement and ecstasy gave way eventually to exhaustion, depression and a recrudescence of the parkinsonism. Sacks' vivid case studies illustrate the profound and far-reaching effects which levodopa had on the mental life of his patients, in addition to its remarkable effects on the motor system.

Psychiatric Consequences of Stereotactic Surgery

The vogue for stereotactic surgery in Parkinson's disease provided an unusual opportunity for examining large numbers of patients before and after circumscribed lesions of the basal ganglia. Extensive psychological studies were pursued, usually with a view to exploring the functions of such regions in relation to intellect, mood or personality. The results have unfortunately often been conflicting, though some interesting general findings emerge. These are reviewed by Crown (1971).

Transient deficits in certain cognitive functions are a common sequel, usually with a return to preoperative status in the months that follow. The side of the lesion has sometimes been found to affect the nature of the immediate post-operative deficits. Riklan and Levita (1970), for example, found verbal impairments after left-sided ventrolateral thalamic lesions, and spatial-perceptual impairments after right-sided lesions. Asso *et al.* (1969) showed transient impairments in auditory verbal learning but found no convincing relationship to the laterality of the lesion. Samara *et al.* (1969) were able to examine the exact site of the lesion at autopsy in the brains of 27 patients and correlate the results with the language deficits which had resulted. They demonstrated convincingly that a lesion strictly confined to the ventrolateral thalamic nucleus could be followed by language deficits. When these occurred the lesion had almost always been in the left dominant hemisphere. Dysarthria could result from a lesion on either side but was usually associated with bilateral operations.

Riklan *et al.* (1962) showed changes in figure drawing, compared to preoperative performance, in a group of patients having operations on the globus pallidus and thalamus. For several months postoperatively there was a significant decrease in the 'humanisation' apparent in the drawings, involving such factors as facial expression, shape and body details. This was interpreted as reflecting the level of self or ego development, in turn related to conceptions of the body image. It seemed possible that the basal ganglia might play a role in the integration of the body image, perhaps through their interactions with the parietal lobes.

Discrepant findings have emerged where emotional reactions are concerned. Hays *et al.* (1966) found that depression commonly improved after operations on the ventrolateral thalamic nucleus, with an elevation of mood that was largely maintained during the following year. This could not be attributed solely to improvement of motor function and appeared to be a specific consequence of the operation. By contrast Asso *et al.* (1969) found a high incidence of anxiety and depression in the first nine months after operation and elevation of mood was rare. These differing results doubtless owe much to the preoperative or premorbid psychiatric status of the patients concerned, and perhaps also to the exact sites of the lesions involved.

Premorbid Personality and Psychological Precipitation of Parkinsonism

As with certain other neurological diseases there have occasionally been suggestions that the premorbid personality of parkinsonian patients has characteristic features. Closely associated is the proposition that psychological influences may be important in the development of the disorder. None of the observations in this area can be regarded as well-founded, but neither can it be said that they have been decisively disproved.

Gowers, in 1893, noted the similarity between the parkinsonian tremor and fright, and stated that the most frequent antecedents were prolonged anxiety and severe emotional shock. Physical injury, when a precipitant, probably operated through its emotional aftermaths. Gowers thus set the stage for the psychological theorizing that followed.

From the turn of the century onwards observers commented on certain striking qualities in parkinsonian patients—their industriousness, rigid moralistic attitudes, and habitual suppression of aggression prior to the appearance of the disease. Sands (1942) and Booth (1948) came to champion the view that persons of a particular psychological make-up were at special risk of developing the disorder. Sands (1942) described what he called the 'masked personality', finding a marked discrepancy between the outward appearance of coping and the turmoil within. Premorbid histories showed the patients to have been exemplary citizens, successful in their undertakings and externally calm, undemonstrative and stable. Close acquaintance, however, revealed a near constant subjective state of tension which was firmly suppressed and concealed from outsiders. With the development of parkinsonism a decompensation could often be observed, exposing the inner turmoil in the form of endless complaints, demands and self-centred behaviour. Sands suggested that the habitual suppression of emotion, doubtless involving intense physiological activity in many parts of the brain, may have led in some way to the degenerative changes responsible for the disease. If recognised early, it might be possible to prevent the parkinsonism by encouraging free expression of worries, fears and anxieties.

Booth (1948) developed such concepts further in a clinical study of 66 patients supplemented with Rorschach protocols. Some were post-encephalitic and some 'senile degenerative' in origin. He concluded that the personality structure had been more decisive for the development of parkinsonism than the immediately obvious pathogenic mechanism; the latter had merely served to precipitate or actualise the disorder. Features stressed by Booth included a marked habitual impulse to action and a striving for success, independence and authority. Tension was prone to arise between this and the equally strong drive towards social conformity. But such tensions, like other emotions and impulses, were very firmly suppressed. Regarding their success in life he found this to be usually the result neither of great intelligence nor of unusual vitality, but attributable to aggressive perseverance and instinctive social conformity. Thus an externally virtuous and docile disposition concealed hostile and sadistic impulses of unusual strength.

Such a character structure would be vulnerable to frustration in a number of ways. In many examples the first clinical symptoms of parkinsonism were preceded by a situation which had imposed a serious handicap to the execution of self-willed strivings and activities—arthritis, exhaustion, other illness, economic losses or professional disappointments. In other patients psychological conflicts engendered by the personality could be identified as precipitants. Booth saw the major symptoms of parkinsonism as reflecting the original personality and its conflicts—rigidity, for example, being the product of a peculiar balance between overcoming obstacles and submission to restrictive influences, the mask-like face eliminating the need for expression of emotion, and the parkinsonian posture being related to unconscious hostility. Psychotherapy, in conjunction with antiparkinsonian medication, was claimed to meet with success in alleviating symptoms.

There has been little support for these ideas from more recent studies. Diller and Riklan (1956) attempted an objective assessment of personality and background in a large number of patients referred for stereotactic surgery, but found a great variety of personality patterns and nothing that could be regarded as characteristic for parkinsonism. Smythies (1967) compared 40 consecutive patients referred for surgery with control groups on a questionnaire relating to childhood disturbance, premorbid neurotic symptoms and life adjustment. No excess of premorbid emotional disability could be discerned, and no unusual difficulties in life adjustment antedating the illness. It is perhaps worth noting, however, that Pollock and Hornabrook (1966) were impressed with the high proportion of teetotallers among their large unselected series of parkinsonian patients, and found that many lacked hobbies and showed narrow intellectual horizons.

Interesting preliminary findings have also been reported from a comparison of 12 pairs of monozygotic twins, one of whom had Parkinson's disease while the other did not (Duvoisin *et al.*, 1981). The affected members tended to describe themselves as more nervous, quiet, serious and introspective, whereas their co-twins were more out-going, self-confident and light-hearted. These tendencies had dated well back into adolescence and early adult life. The affected twins had smoked less often and less heavily than their co-twins. Further discriminating and controlled studies of this nature could obviously be of value.

Hepatolenticular Degeneration
(Wilson's Disease)

Hepatolenticular degeneration is a rare inherited disorder affecting both the liver and the central nervous system. Since its description by Wilson in 1912 understanding of the condition has advanced very considerably, and it is now known to be linked to abnormalities of copper metabolism. This has led to treatment with penicillamine which meets with considerable success in the amelioration of symptoms. Familial concentrations of the disorder have always been recognised. A high consanguinity rate is found among the parents, who are themselves unaffected, and there is now little doubt that the fundamental biochemical abnormality leading to the illness is inherited as an autosomal recessive.

Clinical Features

The onset is usually in childhood or adolescence, but may be delayed as late as the fifth decade of life. The presentation may be with hepatic disorder, neurological disorder or both together. In addition, as discussed below, a considerable proportion present initially with psychiatric disturbance. Bearn (1972) estimates that 40% of cases first show hepatic dysfunction, 40% neurological symptoms, and perhaps 20% psychiatric illness or behavioural disorder. There is a marked tendency for the liver disorder to be the first to appear when the onset is in childhood.

Hepatic involvement is almost invariable but may sometimes be found only on liver biopsy or at autopsy. Jaundice or hepatosplenomegaly can be the presenting features, or later there may be ascites, ankle swelling or haematemesis from rupture of oesophageal varices.

The neurological disorder is confined to the motor system and takes the form of extrapyramidal disturbance with rigidity, tremor, athetoid writhing movements and abnormal dystonic postures of the limbs. In the early stages the disabilities may be transient and sensitive to emotional influences, leading to an erroneous impression of conversion hysteria. A flapping tremor may be seen at the wrists, or characteristic 'wing beating' at the shoulders when the arms are abducted and the elbows flexed. The facial expression is stiff and motionless, often with open mouth and a rigid silent smile. Bulbar symptoms are common in the form of spastic dysarthria and dysphagia.

Occasional patients develop epileptic seizures, usually of Jacksonian type. Hemiplegia is not uncommon. Periods of coma or semicoma may develop, persisting for several weeks but not necessarily heralding a fatal outcome.

Variations in the clinical picture depend to some extent on the age at presentation (Bearn, 1957; Denny-Brown, 1964). In young subjects dystonia or spastic rigidity tend to dominate the picture and tremor may be slight. The course is then liable to be acute and rapidly progressive. In adults tremor predominates and rigidity may be unobtrusive, with a milder course and slower progression. A good deal of overlap occurs, however, and mixed pictures are common. In the earlier literature the term 'lenticular degeneration' was used for cases showing spasticity, rigidity and dystonia, and 'pseudosclerosis' for cases with marked tremor and dysarthria.

The Kayser–Fleischer ring is a diagnostic sign of great importance. It is brown or greyish-green in colour, situated at the margin of the cornea and often evident to the naked eye. It is readily detected on slit-lamp examination. Bearn (1957) suggests that absence of a Kayser–Fleischer ring after such examination makes the diagnosis of Wilson's disease improbable.

The *CT scan* has been found to show a characteristic picture (Williams and Walshe, 1981). Ventricular dilatation, cortical atrophy and enlargement of the cisterns around the brain stem are common, and may be accompanied by characteristic hypodense areas in the basal ganglia. This combination is considered to be specific for Wilson's disease. The hypodense areas are most frequent in patients with neurological disability, but can also be seen in those presenting with hepatic disorder or even in presymptomatic cases. Re-scanning after treatment with chelating agents (p. 565) may show resolution of the changes.

Other features include abnormalities of renal function, with aminoaciduria in a high proportion of cases. The urine may also contain sugar or protein, or unusual quantities of uric acid, calcium or phosphate. Degenerative changes around joints are commonly seen on X-ray examination, even in young persons, and fractures and fragmentations of the bones of the hands and wrists may be detected. Episodes of haemolytic anaemia may occur, presumably due to sudden release of copper from the tissues.

Course and Outcome

Remissions may be seen in the earlier stages, and even thereafter marked fluctuations in severity can occur. Ultimately, however, severe crippling results from spasticity and dystonic contractions. Dysphagia is often profound, and intellectual deterioration is common in the later stages. The prognosis is worse the younger the age of onset. Formerly children rarely survived for more than 4 years, whereas adults might survive without severe disablement for 12 years or more. Death usually occurs from liver failure, rupture of oesophageal varices, inhalation or intercurrent infection.

With treatment this gloomy outlook has been decisively altered as described below.

Pathology

Smith (1976) describes the pathological findings as follows. The brain is usually normal externally, but on section the corpus striatum is found to be shrunken and brownish or brick red in colour. The putamen often shows cavitation. Microscopically neuronal loss is seen in the caudate and putamen, and the latter contains large numbers of astrocytic nuclei, many having a characteristic enlarged and vesicular appearance ('Alzheimer nuclei'). By contrast the globus pallidus often shows relatively little change. Pericapillary concretions which stain for copper may also be detected. Other abnormal elements include large phagocytic 'Opalski' cells, possibly derived from histiocytes.

The thalamus, the subthalamic nuclei and the brain stem nuclei may also show Alzheimer nuclei and Opalski cells. Phagocytes containing iron pigment are commonly found in the substantia nigra. Degeneration of the dentate nuclei and superior cerebellar peduncles has occasionally been observed.

Foci of degeneration are not uncommon in the cerebral cortex, especially in the frontal lobes. Diffuse loss of neurones and fibres may occur, or

status spongiosus involving both the cortex and the white centres of the convolutions. Astrocytic and oligodendrocytic proliferation may be seen.

The liver may be enlarged in the early stages but is usually smaller than normal at autopsy. It is coarsely cirrhotic, varying in colour from yellow to brown or brick red depending on the relative amounts of copper storage, fatty degeneration and bile staining. Microscopically the picture is of multilobular cirrhosis. The spleen is usually enlarged.

Biochemical Abnormalities

Abnormalities of copper metabolism appear to be fundamental to the development both of the hepatic and cerebral lesions. Cumings (1948) showed that the liver and brain contained a marked excess of copper and that this was particularly true of some brain regions including the basal ganglia. The Kayser–Fleischer ring in the cornea is also due to deposition of copper there, and the level may be raised in the kidneys and other tissues. The serum copper is usually low and the excretion of copper in the urine high.

Scheinberg and Gitlin (1952) showed that the caeruloplasmin content of the serum was low or even absent in the disease. This is a globulin fraction of the serum proteins to which 95% of the serum copper is normally bound. The small amount of unbound copper is loosely attached to serum albumin and probably represents the part in transport to various parts of the body.

The exact pathogenesis of the disorder remains uncertain. The favoured theory is that the basic defect lies in diminished synthesis of caeruloplasmin, as a result of which unbound copper persists at a high level, emerging in excessive quantities in the urine and being deposited in organs such as the liver and brain which have a higher affinity for copper than does serum albumin. Against this theory, however, is the lack of a close relationship between the severity of the disease and the extent to which the caeruloplasmin is lowered. Moreover it fails to explain the finding that there is an increased uptake of copper from the gut.

An alternative suggestion is that the basic defect is an abnormal affinity of certain tissues for copper, the low caeruloplasmin being secondary to the diversion of copper to sites in the brain, liver and elsewhere. Increased absorption from the gut may in this theory be due to an increased copper binding capacity of the intestinal mucosa. A further suggestion is that abnormal steroid metabolism may be fundamental to the genesis of the observed metabolic abnormalities (Walker, 1969). None of these theories explains why in some patients the accent of the disorder should fall on the central nervous system and in others on the liver.

Whatever the precise dynamics of the metabolic aberrations, the finding of a low serum caeruloplasmin is of great diagnostic importance. In equivocal cases liver biopsy may be necessary to confirm the diagnosis, revealing increased hepatic copper and the typical cirrhotic changes.

With the advent of an effective treatment special attention has been directed towards the detection of asymptomatic but vulnerable individuals in the families of patients so that prophylactic treatment can be commenced. Once the disease has been diagnosed, all siblings of the patient must be examined: 25% will be at risk and 50% will be heterozygote carriers. A low caeruloplasmin coupled with increased urinary copper or aminoaciduria will strongly suggest that the person is at risk. Liver biopsy will be decisive, revealing increased copper or early cirrhotic changes.

Attempts have also been made to identify heterozygotes who, though not at risk themselves, may pass on the disorder to their offspring. Neale and Fischer-Williams (1958) showed abnormally low caeruloplasmin levels in a high proportion of clinically unaffected relatives, including parents of patients with the disease, but this alone is not a sufficiently constant finding. Sternlieb et al. (1961) proposed a method for identifying heterozygotes by measuring the rate of incorporation of radioactive copper into the serum caeruloplasmin after oral ingestion, but this too is open to some degree of error. Bearn (1972) suggests that the finding of a low caeruloplasmin in the face of a normal level of hepatic copper is strongly indicative of the heterozygous state.

Treatment

The aim of treatment is to eliminate excessive copper from the body and prevent its reaccumulation. Dimercaprol (BAL) was the first chelating agent to be tried (Denny-Brown and Porter, 1951). Results were encouraging but the injections were painful and liable to lead to toxic reactions. Penicillamine is now the treatment of choice, D-penicillamine being preferable to D,L-penicillamine which sometimes leads to renal complications. Sodium diethyldithiocarbamate (DDC) has been found to be successful in the very occasional patient who cannot tolerate penicillamine (Boudin and Pepin, 1968).

Long-term follow-ups of large groups of patients have been reported by Walshe (1968) and Goldstein et al. (1971). All patients have apparently benefited in some degree once a negative copper balance has been established and maintained over time. Transient deterioration may occasionally be observed at the start of treatment, and sometimes real improvement may not be obvious for several weeks or months. The maximal improvement is to be expected in the first year or two, but further progressive gains may continue over many years. Walshe stresses the importance of giving adequate doses of penicillamine, most patients requiring between 900 and 1800 mg per day. When deterioration was observed this had always followed reduction of the dose, and response was again obtained on restoring it to adequate levels. Goldstein et al. recommend a low copper diet to help the penicillamine in its function, but Walshe regards strict dietary measures as unnecessary providing the patient avoids such items as shellfish, liver, nuts, cocoa, chocolate, mushrooms, dried fruits and whisky.

Neurological improvement is often more rewarding than hepatic improvement, but all aspects of the picture can respond. Tremor, rigidity, dystonia, dysarthria and dysphagia may all gradually resolve and some patients become entirely symptom free. In general improvement is more complete the earlier treatment has been commenced. Dramatic results have been reported from states of hopeless incapacity to relative independence, though such cannot always be achieved.

Psychiatric symptoms have been found to improve as well, but less regularly than the neurological manifestations. This is discussed below.

Treatment is indicated in asymptomatic siblings who show a consistently low serum caeruloplasmin and an increased hepatic copper. The manifestations of the disease can then apparently be prevented. Sternlieb and Scheinberg (1968) report that of 8 asymptomatic patients who were left untreated 7 developed the disease, whereas 40 who were treated remained symptom free during an average followup of three years.

Psychiatric Manifestations of Wilson's Disease

Psychiatric abnormalities can form a prominent part of the clinical picture along with the neurological defects. A change of personality frequently occurs soon after the onset or even antedating other manifestations. Marked behavioural disturbance is not uncommon and psychotic developments may arise. Cognitive impairment may become apparent during the course of the illness, and progressive dementia quite often marks the terminal stages.

Psychiatric symptoms were prominent in 8 of Wilson's (1912) 12 original patients. He noted silliness, euphoria, preoccupation with sexual matters, hebephrenia, catatonia and occasional hallucinations. 'Hysterical' behaviour was often much in evidence. Reviewing the psychiatric aspects later he concluded that 'facility, docility, childishness and emotional overaction form the chief features of the more chronic cases' (Wilson, 1940). 'Narrowing of the mental horizons' was also characteristic, but impairment of mental function was sometimes more apparent than real, being to a large extent suggested by the patient's appearance and the difficulty of communication resulting from dysarthria.

The frequency of psychiatric presentations has been emphasised in the more recent literature. Sternlieb and Scheinberg (1964) noted that 5 out of 33 patients developed psychiatric symptoms as the first manifestation of the disease, and in another 8 emotional disturbances appeared simultaneously with the neurological or hepatic disorder. Scheinberg et al. (1968) found that more than a quarter of 49 patients had significant psychiatric disturbance as the first clinical indication that anything was amiss. All 12 of Walker's (1969) patients developed psychiatric symptoms before the first neurological signs, and every one had had psychiatric treatment with drugs, psychotherapy or electroconvulsive therapy. Two had presented with school phobia, one as a behaviour problem, 2 with personality disorder, 2 with depression, 2 with hysteria, 2 with acute schizophrenia and one with mental retardation. Early clues to the presence of organic disease lay in minor difficulties with speech, distractibility or some degree of cognitive impairment.

Personality and emotional disturbances may feature at the start or appear later in the disease. They include severe depression, anxiety, apathy, 'hysterical' behaviour, irritability and excitability. Loss of impulse control can lead to outbursts of rage or destructive behaviour. Antisocial conduct may take the form of lying or stealing. In Scheinberg et al.'s (1968) series almost two-thirds had significant psychiatric disturbance at some time, the great majority being disturbances of this nature. Loss of impulse control was considered to be related to the motor disturbances—in their efforts to control abnormal movements the patients appeared to develop an overall inhibition of drives, resulting in a build-up of tension with periodic sudden release and discharge.

Intellectual decline may occasionally be evident from the outset, but gross and obvious dementia is usually restricted to the terminal phases. Inattentiveness at school may be an early sign in children. In adults there may be inefficiency at work or episodes of forgetfulness. Later a slow deterioration of personality and intellect quite commonly accompanies the progressive neurological disabilities—the patient becomes childish, apathetic and generally slowed in his responses. Emotional lability with forced laughter and crying may result from bulbar involvement.

Knehr and Bearn (1956) demonstrated intellectual impairment on psychological testing in all seven patients examined. Language functions were well preserved but other tests showed evidence of substantial losses, especially where capacity for conceptual thinking was concerned. Those with the longest duration of disease were the most impaired. Among 19 patients tested psychometrically Scheinberg et al. (1968) found that the IQs ranged from 57 to 135 with an average of 94. Most patients showed evidence both of cognitive impairment and of emotional and personality disturbances, but in general the latter predominated.

The psychoses seen in Wilson's disease have been much discussed. Depressive, hypomanic and schizophrenic pictures are reported, sometimes as transient episodes and sometimes as enduring concomitants of the neurological deterioration. Inose (1968) has also drawn attention to fluctuating disturbance of consciousness with episodes of delirium, especially in the later stages.

Particular attention has been given to schizophrenic symptomatology, usually paranoid in form in adults and hebephrenic or catatonic in children. Beard (1959) reviewed the literature on the topic and concluded that in the great majority of cases the diagnosis of schizophrenia had been incorrect. Most were more properly viewed as examples of acute organic reactions or dementia. In his own patient, however, a typical schizophrenic illness developed with olfactory and auditory hallucinations and paranoid delusions. This set in at the time of the first neurological manifestations and persisted over the next 5 years with increasing flattening of affect. Davison and Bagley (1969) considered that there were 11 acceptable and 11 doubtful cases in the literature showing an association between Wilson's disease and schizophrenia, and this was felt to be considerably more frequent than chance expectation. There was reason to suspect, moreover, that there might be an organic basis for some of these schizophrenia-like illnesses—in most cases the psychosis and the neurological abnormalities had appeared at about the same time, a family history of schizophrenia was distinctly uncommon, and the psychoses tended to progress towards dementia.

Cartwright (1978) has emphasised the importance of prompt recognition of Wilson's disease in psychiatric practice if irreversible brain or liver damage are to be avoided. Most patients with psychiatric presentations will already have neurological signs and Kayser–Fleischer rings, and the biochemical signs will be present. The diagnosis should therefore be readily apparent once the question has been raised. The difficulty, of course, lies with the rareness of the disorder and its many forms of presentation. Moreover, when phenothiazines are given the problems are compounded, since abnormal liver function and various forms of motor disorder will often be interpreted as side effects of the drugs. The following case illustrates the scope of the diagnostic difficulties that can arise:

A 17-year-old girl developed emotional lability, nervousness, difficulty with handwriting and deterioration in school performance. She was at first thought to be suffering from adolescent adjustment problems. Chlorpromazine was prescribed, leading to increasing tremor, and she became withdrawn. Abnormal liver function tests were noted, likewise mild extrapyramidal dysfunction, but both were ascribed to the drug. She was later hospitalised with a diagnosis of schizo-affective disorder. Finally she was noted to show excessive drooling, a mask-like face, dysphagia, choreoathetoid movements, dystonia, spasticity, splenomegaly and Kayser–Fleischer rings. A diagnosis of Wilson's disease was confirmed 22 months after the first manifestations. Two years of treatment with penicillamine left her still dysphonic and with severe motor disability.
(Cartwright, 1978)

The different psychiatric manifestations are likely to have a number of determinants. Much of the emotional disorder is probably the result of the patient's reaction to his disability. Hepatic dysfunction may make a contribution particularly with phasic emotional disturbances or episodes of confusion. The prominence of early personality change and other psychiatric disturbance probably owes much to the widespread brain damage, apparent on the CT scan from the early stages, and clearly involving the cortex (Williams and Walshe, 1981). Intellectual impairment will be related directly to

pathological changes in the brain; here it is interesting to note that deposition of copper can occur in the cortex, and improvements in intellectual function can follow removal of copper during treatment. The possible role of pathology in the basal ganglia in the genesis of psychiatric symptoms remains uncertain, but it may be significant, as Slater and Cowie (1971) point out, that Wilson's disease and Huntington's chorea both show a high incidence of behavioural disturbance early in their course and are frequently complicated by schizophrenia-like psychoses.

With regard to response to chelating agents, Sternlieb and Scheinberg (1964) noted definite emotional improvement in 8 of 20 patients who had shown pronounced psychiatric disorder. In one patient, however, a psychosis was revealed as she recovered from a state of anarthria and severe paralysis. Scheinberg et al. (1968) followed 30 patients with both neurological and psychiatric disorder; 25 showed marked resolution of neurological defects and 14 also showed lessened psychiatric disturbance, though in general the latter was less impressive in degree. Goldstein et al. (1968) demonstrated gains on serial psychometric testing in a group of patients, often continuing for several years. All improved to some extent, in a manner which generally paralleled their improvement in neurological status but was less dramatic in degree.

Progressive Supranuclear Palsy
('Steele-Richardson Syndrome')

Steele et al. (1964) described a group of patients with an unusual progressive neurological disorder showing ocular, motor and mental features. Outstanding signs include supranuclear paralysis of external ocular movements, particularly in the vertical plane, dysarthria, pseudobulbar palsy, dystonic rigidity of the neck and trunk, and dementia. Signs of cerebellar and pyramidal tract dysfunction are sometimes seen. In the later stages the eyes are fixed centrally, and widespread rigidity of the limbs reduces the patient to a helpless bedridden state. The onset is usually in the sixth decade, with death a few years later. Subsequent reports have confirmed the main features of the syndrome (David et al., 1968; Blumenthal and Miller, 1969; Steele, 1972). Treatment with levodopa may sometimes ameliorate the rigidity and ophthalmoplegia.

The pathology shows cell loss, neurofibrillary tangles, gliosis and demyelination, particularly affecting the basal ganglia, brain stem and cerebellar nuclei. The distribution of changes is remarkably constant and usually there is a surprising lack of cortical involvement. Steele *et al.* (1964) commented on the resemblance of the histological features to those of post-encephalitic parkinsonism or the parkinsonism-dementia complex of Guam, though the distribution of the changes is different. The aetiology is unknown. Degenerative or viral processes are suspected, but attempts at transmission to primates have been unsuccessful.

Subcortical Dementia

While the disease itself is rare, certain observations made on the mental state of such patients by Albert *et al.* (1974) are of considerable interest. The pattern of dementia seen in progressive supranuclear palsy appears to have distinctive features which may reflect the relative confinement of pathology to subcortical structures. Albert *et al.* term this picture 'subcortical dementia'. In this they have made a valuable contribution, by underlining the fact that cognitive failure does not always imply cortical disease. The cortex depends for its functioning on inputs from the reticular activating systems and other subcortical structures, and when these fail the cortex, though intact, may cease to display its potential.

Albert *et al.* contrasted the behaviour pattern in patients with progressive supranuclear palsy with that seen in patients with cortical disease processes. Among 5 cases seen personally and 42 adequately described in the literature, several key features were evident in the mental state. Though described as 'forgetful' it could frequently be shown that the patient could produce the correct answer if given encouragement and an abnormal amount of time in which to respond. Memory as such appeared not to be truly impaired, but rather the timing mechanism which enables the memory system to function at normal speed. Slowness of thought was similarly prominent; tasks requiring verbal manipulation or perceptual-motor skills were performed incorrectly under normal pressures, but adequately when time was extended. Thus, when the patient was given enough time to proceed, or when provided with structured situations to elicit responses that did not occur spontaneously, his intellect could prove to be surprisingly intact. Defects of higher cortical function such as dysphasia, agnosia or apraxia were strikingly absent, though calculation or ability to deal with abstract material were sometimes defective. Personality and mood changes fell into two categories—the larger group was indifferent, apathetic and depressed, while the smaller showed progressive irritability and/or euphoria. Brief outbursts of rage were common, and inappropriate forced laughing and crying were often in evidence.

A woman of 65 with the disease showed extrapyramidal rigidity, slowed speech and marked limitation of upward and downward gaze. Her cognitive state was described as follows:

'She was alert, attentive, and socially appropriate. Immediate recall of digits was seven forward and five backwards. Recent memory was deficient in an unusual way: her first answer to almost every question was "I don't know". However, if the examiner encouraged her by saying "Sure you know; just take your time", she would correctly respond to 95% of the questions. The latency between question and response was often inordinately long—in some cases as long as $4\frac{1}{2}$ minutes (often taxing the patience of the examiner). Remote memory was intact.

Language functions were as follows. . . . No paraphasias were heard. Naming was excellent on confrontation for high and very low frequency words. Although she complained of having difficulty with words, she had no naming defect. She did, however, have a time-related word-finding defect: in one minute she was able to find only three words beginning with the letter B. At five minutes she had listed 12; at 10 minutes 23; at 15 minutes 33. Tests of repetition, comprehension of spoken and written language, and reading aloud were normal, except for the slow reading rate.

For simple mental calculations her responses were quick and accurate. With more complex arithmetic problems, she was slow but correct. Her proverb interpretations were concrete and she had difficulty finding similarities in two similar objects.'

A 58-year-old woman had dysarthria, a broad-based ataxic gait and striking impairment of upward and downward gaze. 'Evaluation of mental status revealed an awake, generally placid or apathetic woman who reacted in a seemingly angry manner to the examiner's attempts to question her. Despite her apparent anger, she could nonetheless be coaxed to cooperate. Digit span was 6 forward. Questions designed to test recent and remote memory led to the following situation: either she refused to answer, or she answered incorrectly. However, when the examiner waited, either silently or with attempts to encourage her, for longer than normal waiting periods (even as long as four to five minutes for a single question) she then gave the correct answer to 70–80% of the questions. This indicated that her stock of knowledge was not impaired as one might otherwise have concluded. Rather, she was delayed in reaching into the stock for the correct answer. Tests of language and gestures revealed no aphasia or apraxia. No inattention or primary perceptual problems were seen. Proverb interpretations tended to be concrete. Her ability to find the categorical similarities between similar items was impaired. Her calculating ability was poor'.

(Albert *et al.*, 1974)

Attention was drawn to rather similar pictures in other diseases with subcortical pathology, and the authors tentatively proposed that the common mechanisms underlying them were those of impaired timing and activation. Impaired functioning of the reticular formation, or a disconnection of the reticular activating systems from thalamic and subthalamic nuclei, might be the cause of slowing down of intellectual processes, even though the cortical systems for perceiving, storing and manipulating knowledge remained intact.

The situation in progressive supranuclear palsy, in which the cortex is known to be largely spared, is likely to exist in some other dementing processes also. Parkinson's disease with intellectual impairment (p. 555) is an obvious example. Huntington's chorea is another (p. 393). Normal pressure hydrocephalus, Wilson's disease and the dementia associated with deep lacunar infarcts (p. 327) have also been viewed in this way (Benson, 1982b; Cummings, 1982). It could conceivably be the case that some variants of the dementias of old age may have a subcortical rather than a cortical origin to the cognitive difficulties, or at least a prominent subcortical component in the aetiology of the clinical picture. An interesting possibility is that the 'normal' effects of old age upon cognitive functioning may reflect subcortical rather than cortical ageing processes (Albert, 1978).

These suggestions have attracted a good deal of interest, since it is possible that pharmacological means may one day be available to help patients with subcortical dementia perform at an improved level. To the extent that subcortical dementias are due to disturbances of activating, alerting, or timing mechanisms, then drugs which have an effect on the anatomical or biochemical systems dealing with these mechanisms could prove to have therapeutic value.

Dystonia Musculorum Deformans
('Generalised Torsion Dystonia')

The torsion dystonias comprise a group of disease processes in which sustained muscle contractions distort the body and limbs into characteristic postures. The abnormal movements differ from tics or choreiform movements in being slow sustained spasms, and in mainly involving the proximal or axial musculature. Eldridge (1970), Marsden and Parkes (1973) and Marsden *et al.* (1976) review the classification and current state of knowledge about these diseases.

Dystonia musculorum deformans is the term commonly used for a generalised torsion dystonia of unknown aetiology which leads to severe and progressive crippling. A genetic basis is apparent in many cases. It must be distinguished from the 'symptomatic' torsion dystonias in which known cerebral pathology is responsible for the symptoms. A symptomatic torsion dystonia may, for example, follow anoxia or kernicterus at birth ('bilateral athetoid cerebral palsy'), or occur in association with tumours and infarctions of the basal ganglia. A similar picture may be the presenting feature in Wilson's disease and was occasionally encountered after encephalitis lethargica. In contrast to dystonia musculorum deformans the symptomatic torsion dystonias tend to be asymmetrical or unilateral, and to show other evidence of brain damage by way of fits, dementia or pyramidal tract disturbance. An acute dystonic reaction may also occur as a transient complication of medication with phenothiazine or butyrophenone drugs (p. 546).

The idiopathic generalised disease is rare. It occurs both sporadically and familially and particularly among persons with Jewish ancestry. Eldridge (1970) suggests that at least two hereditary forms exist—an autosomal recessive and an autosomal dominant The former is the likely mode of inheritance among cases with seeming sporadic occurrence and is found especially among Ashkenasic Jews. Dominant inheritance appears to account for the non-Jewish cases and here both parent and child may be affected. Apart from these genetic allegiances little is known about the aetiology. Pathological studies have occasionally reported lesions in the basal ganglia, substantia nigra and elsewhere (Davison and Goodhart, 1938), but in a careful review Zeman (1970) has discounted such findings as non-specific or artefactual. The evidence points firmly to involvement of the basal ganglia, however, both by analogy with examples which are symptomatic of known brain lesions and the response which may sometimes be observed to stereotactic surgery. The essential abnormality in the idiopathic cases is likely to be a biochemical disturbance, probably related to dopaminergic neuronal systems.

In addition to torsion dystonias affecting the whole body partial and incomplete forms exist. Thus within families who inherit the major disease other members may show formes frustes of the disorder—

abnormalities of gait, abnormal arm postures, minor speech defects, or static postural abnormalities such as pes equinovarus or kyphoscoliosis (Zeman *et al.*, 1960). It has been argued that spasmodic torticollis may sometimes represent a similar process confined to the muscles of the neck. Indeed some cases of dystonia musculorum deformans present initially with torticollis which later spreads to other body parts.

Marsden *et al.* (1976) recognise 'general', 'segmental' and 'focal' dystonias, the first representing the disorder under present consideration. Segmental dystonias begin more commonly in adults than children, with onset usually in an arm, then restricted spread to the neck or other arm. Focal dystonias are also of adult onset, presenting in the arm or axial musculature and remaining largely confined to their point of onset. In addition to torticollis, mentioned above, dystonic writer's cramp, blepharospasm and some orofacial dyskinesias may be viewed as focal or segmental dystonias, as will be discussed when these conditions are considered below.

Clinical Features

The symptoms usually commence in childhood or early adolescence. The recessive form in Jews has a restricted age of onset, the majority of cases beginning between 6 and 14, while in the dominant variety the onset can be at any age from 1 to 40. The first symptom is usually a disturbance of gait, with plantar flexion, inversion and adduction of the foot when walking. At first the picture is sometimes bizarre, for example with ability to walk backwards or to dance when at the same time the patient is unable to walk forwards in a normal manner. More rarely the initial disturbance may appear in the upper limbs with abnormal postures or actions. A characteristic dystonic posture consists of extension and hyperpronation of the arms, with flexion of the wrist and extension of the fingers. An onset with involvement of the trunk or torticollis of the neck is commoner in the dominant than the recessive variety.

In the early stages the motor abnormalities may become apparent only when activity is attempted and nothing unusual can be found on examination at rest. Remissions lasting for several months at a time may occur, all adding to the impression that the disorder is psychogenic in origin. Indeed an hysterical disturbance is not infrequently diagnosed initially, particularly when there are co-existent emotional problems or adverse psychological factors which can be clearly discerned. Thus patients are occasionally encountered who have undergone years of psychotherapy for 'hysterical spasms' before progression of the disorder reveals the true state of affairs. The mistake is easily made in view of the rarity of the disorder and the bizarre nature of the symptoms. Other objective signs of a cerebral lesion are absent, with normal tendon reflexes and unimpaired intelligence. Moreover the dystonic postures which can occur in conversion hysteria are sometimes indistinguishable from the transient early disturbances of dystonia musculorum deformans.

Later the muscle spasms occur even when the body is relaxed, producing irregular spontaneous movements or fixed dystonic postures. The movements cease during sleep but plague the patient continually while awake. Other parts of the body come to be affected, usually with symmetrical involvement of all four limbs, the trunk and the neck. The proximal muscles tend to be affected more than the distal, and a rotatory element in the axial musculature is typical. The trunk is forced into marked lordosis or scoliosis, and fixed contractures of the limbs lead eventually to severe crippling and permanent deformity. Speech, swallowing and breathing may ultimately be affected. The tendon reflexes become difficult to obtain or may be exaggerated, but the plantar responses remain downgoing. There are no abnormalities of sensation.

Rapid progress and widespread involvement is usual when the onset is in childhood or adolescence. Maximum disability is usually reached within 5–10 years, after which the disease tends to arrest or sometimes may even improve very slightly. Adult-onset dystonias are by contrast usually restricted in their spread, often remaining segmental or focal at the region of onset and normally sparing the legs.

Intelligence in Dystonia Musculorum Deformans

In the symptomatic torsion dystonias the responsible cerebral pathology may lead to intellectual impairment or progressive dementia. In the idiopathic disease, however, this is not so. Eldridge (1970) reports that mental retardation is occasionally found in the dominant variety, both in patients and their families, but by contrast it is usual to find exceptionally good intelligence in the recessive form in Jews. Precocious mental development may have been noted before the appearance of the symptoms, and academic performance may be unusually good thereafter despite the gravity of the physical handicap. Unaffected siblings of patients have also been found to have significantly higher intelligence quotients than carefully matched controls (Eldridge, 1970).

Treatment

Treatment of dystonia musculorum deformans is disappointing in the present stage of knowledge. Drugs may help to control the severity of muscular spasms, perhaps mainly by promoting relaxation and relieving anxiety but also by causing mild drug-induced parkinsonism. Drugs chiefly used include diazepam, benzhexol, phenothiazines, butyrophenones and tetrabenazine. More recently levodopa has been reported to help considerably in some cases. Stereotactic surgery has been claimed to produce beneficial results in several patients, particularly those with unilateral dystonia. Cooper (1962, 1970, 1976) has reported long-standing reversal of symptoms in from half to three-quarters of patients, the target of choice being the posterior half of the ventrolateral nucleus of the thalamus and extending into neighbouring thalamic nuclei. Multiple lesions are quite often required to produce optimal relief.

Treatment should also be directed towards helping the patient and his family adjust to the profound emotional problems generated by the distressing and long drawn-out illness. Psychotherapy can sometimes be of considerable assistance, especially in view of the good intelligence of many of the patients. Some bring astonishing powers of adaptation to bear in learning to cope with their severe disablement.

Spasmodic Torticollis

Spasmodic torticollis is a rare condition characterised by involuntary spasms of the musculature which lead to repeated dystonic movements of the head and neck, or sustained abnormal postures, or both. The element of sustained spasm in the picture serves in the differentiation from a tic. The aetiology remains unknown, and arguments have been advanced both for psychogenic and organic causation as discussed below.

Clinical Features

Males and females are equally affected with an onset predominantly between the ages of 30 and 50. A family history of the disorder is rare but has emerged in occasional cases (Patterson and Little, 1943; Tibbetts, 1971). The onset is usually insidious though in some cases it can be related to an acute shock or an episode of emotional disturbance. Sometimes a pulling or drawing sensation is felt in the neck for several weeks before the actual movements appear.

The movements are typically irregular, forcible and writhing in character, involving several of the neck muscles along with the upper parts of the trapezii. The sternomastoid is usually prominently involved, drawing the head laterally and rotating the chin in a characteristic manner. Less commonly there may be simple lateral flexion, or the head may be pulled directly forwards ('antecollis') or backwards ('retrocollis'). In time the spasms come to be almost continuous and the affected muscle groups may show considerable hypertrophy. Aching may be prominent, and cervical spondylosis may develop from the continual abnormal postures of the neck. Other abnormal movements are occasionally detected—facial twitches and grimaces, blinking, shrugging of the shoulders, or twisting athetoid movements of the upper limbs.

Once the condition is well developed the patient finds himself powerless to relax the offending muscle groups or to resist the abnormal movements except for short periods of time. The movements are noticeably affected by emotional influences, becoming more powerful and frequent under tension, excitement or distress. Any sudden startle or shock is likely to be followed immediately by a spasm. Self-consciousness usually aggravates the condition, likewise walking or engaging in strenuous activity.

The movements subside during sleep, and may temporarily come under a greater measure of control when the patient is engaged in activities such as eating or drinking. An unexplained but striking feature is the ability of some patients to control the spasms by resting a hand or finger lightly against the chin, and not infrequently on the side away from which the turning movements are made ('geste antagoniste').

The course is usually slow progression over very many years but the outcome is extremely variable. Some patients are only mildly affected and can continue with their usual occupations, while others become permanently and severely incapacitated. A few show arrest or resolution of the disorder, others show spontaneous remissions varying from a few days to several years. This uncertain natural history adds greatly to the difficulties of gauging the effects of treatment. The picture may also modify as to detail over time, quick movements changing to slower spasms, or spasms giving way to sustained postures. Different muscle groups may come to be implicated, subsequent relapses even involving turning to the opposite side.

Among 103 cases Patterson and Little (1943) found that 13% pursued a static course, 42% were progressive, 40% were recurrent or intermittent, and 2 patients had complete remissions without treatment. On follow-up 25% were worse, 12% unchanged, 12% slightly improved, 42% much improved and 7% 'cured'. Ten per cent were unable to work, 49% were partially incapacitated for work and 29% were able to work as well as ever.

Meares (1971a) found that unoperated cases tended in general to deteriorate in the first five years and then become static. After the first ten years slight improvement might be seen, those who had had the disability for this length of time often showing considerable adaptation to its effects. Remissions had occurred in a quarter of cases but almost exclusively in the first five years. Certain factors could be identified which appeared to be associated with an improved prognosis (Meares, 1971b). Patients who remitted tended to be younger at onset, with a mean age of 30 compared to 40 for the remainder. They had significantly higher scores on questionnaires measuring neuroticism and anxiety, and rather more evidence of conflict by way of premorbid marital or sexual disturbance. The type of onset also showed some predictive value: the insidious development of a slow turning movement generally signalled a poor outcome, whereas a tic-like jerking onset or a prodromal period of aching in the neck muscles was characteristic of those who remitted.

Aetiology

The disorder has sometimes been ascribed to psychogenic factors and sometimes to organic factors, but definitive evidence either way is lacking. In favour of a non-organic basis one may note the usual absence of other physical signs, the frequent reports of abnormal personalities in the sufferers, the identification of emotional precipitants in certain cases, and the response which has sometimes been observed to psychotherapy or behaviour therapy. In favour of an organic aetiology is the occasional emergence of torticollis in relation to diseases of the extrapyramidal system such as encephalitis lethargica or torsion dystonia, the presence in certain cases of minor associated neurological defects, and the complexity of the movements which appears to transcend what could be expected of a purely psychogenic disorder. To these may be added the

experimental production of a rather similar movement disorder after midbrain lesions in animals, and the results which have been claimed for relief after stereotactic operations on the basal ganglia.

In most large series it has seemed necessary to recognise a spectrum of causation, ranging from cases which have appeared to be purely psychogenic in origin to examples where organic influences have clearly been responsible. Uncertainty arises, however, over the position to be adopted in relation to the 'average' case where associated evidence in one direction or the other is lacking. Thus some authorities have regarded the great majority of their cases as psychogenic in origin and some virtually all their cases as organically based. Much may depend on the nature of the sample observed and also on the bias of the psychiatrist or neurologist concerned.

Attempts have been made to subdivide the syndrome into different varieties and to define the characteristics of each:

Paterson (1945) reviews early attempts in this field. Brissaud (1895) differentiated a 'mental torticollis' which developed from a coordinated purposive act, which, by frequent repetition in predisposed persons led ultimately to its involuntary reproduction. Signs of mental instability were common in such cases. By contrast 'torticollis spasm' was due to irritation in the peripheral reflex arc, was uncoordinated, painful, and sometimes persisted during sleep. Gowers (1888) differentiated an hysterical from a true form. The condition was considered always to be hysterical in patients under 30 and especially in females. The true form was ascribed to abnormal neuronal function in the lower brain centres. Foerster (1928) thought that torticollis was due to a lesion of the corpus striatum, but conceded that in some cases the striatum might be congenitally weak or diseased causing a predisposition to the disorder. It might then be precipitated by emotional distress. Wilson (1940) proposed a purely psychogenic type, sometimes occupational in origin and similar to writer's cramp; a 'torticollis tic' in the nature of a mannerism; an hysterical variety corresponding to Brissaud's 'mental torticollis'; and organic varieties which could follow encephalitis lethargica or local infections irritating nerves.

Hyslop (1949) suggested a division into torticollis of peripheral and of central origin. Peripheral varieties arose from inflammatory conditions affecting muscles or peripheral nerves, from vestibular disorders, or by way of compensation for paresis of external ocular movement. In such examples there was usually fixed involuntary spasm. Central torticollis could be either organic or psychological in origin, extending on a spectrum between these two extremes.

Tibbetts (1971) divided his 72 cases into 'typical' and

'atypical' varieties according to the character of the movements involved. The former showed tonic and clonic movements, or sustained severe spasm if tonic alone; the latter showed much preoccupation over little spasm or else movements which were chaotic and inconsistent. He found strong inferential evidence for regarding the typical cases as linked to an organic aetiology and the atypical cases as largely psychogenic in origin. Thus the typical cases contained a higher proportion with neurological abnormalities—facial dyskinesia, other abnormal movements, or changes of tone or reflexes (40% compared to 13%), a higher proportion with pain as the initial complaint, or with associated disease such as hypertension. The atypical cases contained a higher proportion with abnormal mental states at onset (74% compared to 43%), a heavier loading for neurosis, and more often an onset at an early age. The atypical cases had a higher incidence of remissions and improvements (86% compared to 35%), and there was a strong impression that psychological management had brought about the benefit. Though not considered absolute the distinction between typical and atypical cases was considered useful for the planning of treatment and prognosis.

It is possible, therefore, that different varieties of torticollis may owe their origins to very dissimilar mechanisms, though even this cannot be regarded as well proven. In the present state of knowledge it may be useful merely to examine in some detail the evidence usually quoted in favour of psychogenesis and then the evidence favouring an organic aetiology:

Evidence Regarding Psychogenesis

Instability of premorbid personality has emerged as an impressive finding in several series. Eighty per cent of Paterson's (1945) cases were regarded as having abnormal personalities, the majority showing shy, anxious and immature dispositions. Sixty-three per cent of Herz and Glaser's (1949) patients were said to be emotionally unstable or with maladjustments in work or marriage. Forty-nine per cent of Tibbetts' (1971) 'typical' group and 96% of his 'atypical' group showed neurotic traits. Thus many of the populations studied have appeared to contain a large number of particularly vulnerable individuals.

Cockburn (1971), however, has reported one of the few controlled studies of psychological features in the disorder, with results which suggest that premorbid adjustment differs little from that of the general population. Forty-six patients with spasmodic torticollis were obtained from general hospitals, neurologists and general practitioners in

order to avoid special psychiatric bias. Seventy-eight per cent had been seen by a neurologist and 54% had been to a psychiatrist. They were compared with carefully matched controls admitted to hospital for minor surgery. The two groups were strikingly similar with regard to most of the measures employed—incidence of neurotic symptoms in childhood, job stability, marital stability, previous psychiatric treatment, neuroticism and extraversion scores, alcohol abuse and depressive personality traits. Excessive anxiety was somewhat commoner among the torticollis patients, and obsessional features were commoner among the controls. On such data it would seem most unlikely that the torticollis patients had been drawn from a population specially predisposed to the development of neurotic reactions or hysterical conversion symptoms.

Precipitation by emotional factors has been striking in certain cases, particularly among series reported by psychiatrists. Whiles (1940) described several patients who suffered an initial period of generalised anxiety which subsided when the torticollis became established. Paterson (1945) reported cases which began suddenly and dramatically in connection with a psychological trauma. One, for example, heard a shout, looked up turning his head sideways and saw a load about to fall on him. The torticollis commenced from that moment. In such examples the torticollis has appeared to be a true conversion hysteria, or a manifestation of an anxiety state.

Herz and Glaser (1949), however, could identify no psychogenic factors whatever in most of their cases, or where psychological problems had existed at onset these were rarely prominent enough to be regarded as causative. No correlation could be observed between the severity and progression of the torticollis and the presence or absence of potential psychogenic factors in individual examples. Cockburn's (1971) controlled study showed that 13 of 46 torticollis patients had had a major psychological trauma in the year before the symptoms began, but so did 10 of the controls.

The symbolic meaning of the turning movements has been explored, sometimes appearing to suggest a close relation between the movements and the patients' mental conflicts. Whiles (1940), for example, described cases in which some factor could be identified which the patient could not face and from which he felt compelled to turn away. One patient appeared to be turning away from people because of guilt in connection with her father, another from her sexual role as a woman. Cleveland

(1959) obtained some evidence from projective tests that torticollis patients paid unusual and significant attention to the act of looking, providing some support for the idea that the symbolism of looking away might play a role in the disorder. Beyond this, however, it is extremely hard to know what significance to attach to such scattered observations.

Alternatively torticollis has been regarded as conditioned by movements at work ('occupational torticollis') in the manner of an overlearned and maladaptive response. In five of Paterson's (1945) patients the onset could be traced to some voluntary purposive act which in certain emotional settings had become involuntarily repeated—for example in a telephonist who had to turn her head to one side during work, or in two men whose torticollis set in during army training.

The efficacy of psychotherapy and behaviour therapy in certain cases is discussed below. It seems that complete resolution of the disorder has sometimes been achieved, but improvement has also been noted in cases strongly suspected of resting upon an organic basis (Paterson, 1945). Relief with psychotherapy therefore cannot be accepted unequivocally as favouring a purely psychogenic aetiology.

Evidence Regarding an Organic Basis

In the great majority of cases there is no clear evidence of pathology either peripherally or centrally in the nervous system, but small numbers are found to have other diseases which could be aetiologically relevant. Meares (1971b) refers to examples with histories of rheumatic fever, multiple sclerosis, syphilis or cerebral malaria. Gilbert (1972) reported two patients in whom hyperthyroidism was a possible precipitant. Particularly striking has been the association of spasmodic torticollis with diseases known to affect the extrapyramidal system—it has sometimes emerged along with parkinsonian features after encephalitis lethargica, or proved to be the initial feature of a progressive torsion dystonia (Foerster, 1933; Eldridge, 1970). These associations, though occurring in only a small proportion of patients, have been sufficiently impressive to suggest that torticollis should perhaps be regarded as a partial dystonic manifestation, resulting from extrapyramidal dysfunction that may not be otherwise overt. Marsden (1976a, b) groups torticollis with blepharospasm, oromandibular dystonia and dystonic writer's cramp as representing 'focal' examples of idiopathic torsion dystonia; in their

nature, force, duration and timing the spasms are very similar to those seen in the generalised disease. The induction of short-lived torticollis as a dystonic side-effect of treatment with neuroleptic drugs or levodopa has tended further to support this view.

In most cases, however, the evidence for any extrapyramidal pathology is at best indirect. Paterson and Little (1943) found a history of encephalitis lethargica in only 5 of 103 cases, although they observed partial parkinsonian features in several more. Altogether almost half of their cases showed some form of minor neurological abnormality. Poppen and Martinez-Niochet (1951) reported that half of their cases showed additional abnormal movements by way of grimaces, blepharospasm, tremors of the limbs or choreoathetoid movements. Eldridge (1970) found a similar proportion with other movement disorders. Tibbetts (1971) found that 10 of his 49 'typical' cases developed new patterns of movement disorder on follow-up, including facial dyskinesia and dysarthria. The most impressive evidence, however, comes from Couch (1976) who was able to discern dystonic muscular activity extending to other body parts in 80% of patients with spasmodic torticollis of long standing. This was commonest in the shoulders but could involve the arms, trunk and legs as well. In 10 of the 30 patients some degree of bradykinesia, rigidity and facial masking was also present, sufficiently marked to warrant a diagnosis of parkinsonism in 3 cases.

Detailed analysis of the nature of the torticollis movements has also been interpreted as supporting an organic aetiology. Physiological recording has shown that the patterns of movement are usually more complex than the clinical appearance would suggest (Herz and Hoefer, 1949; Herz and Glaser, 1949). Sustained dystonic activity usually predominated, but quick jerking movements at irregular intervals were also seen, sometimes with superimposed rhythmic activity. In some cases the muscles of the back, shoulder girdles and pectorals were also involved. Altogether the complexity of the movements, and the participation of many muscle groups, suggested more than a learned pattern of behaviour, and appeared quite different from the symbolic patterns of an hysterical disorder.

Autopsy studies have been relatively few and do not answer the problem decisively one way or the other. Scattered reports have described individual patients coming to autopsy, sometimes showing pathological changes largely restricted to the basal ganglia, but the significance of such changes is open to doubt. Foerster (1933) described a case with perivascular lymphocytic infiltration throughout the basal ganglia and symmetrical cavitations in the putamen and substantia innominata. Alpers and Drayer's (1937) case showed atrophy of the caudate, putamen and globus pallidus with marked degeneration of the large ganglion cells. Grinker and Walker (1933) reported a particularly interesting example with diffuse changes indicative of chronic encephalitis even though torticollis had been the only symptom during life. In a careful review, however, Tarlov (1970) throws doubt on the significance of all such findings to date. Other examples in the literature have usually dealt with cases of spasmodic torticollis which were part of a generalised torsion dystonia, and thus cannot clarify the pathology of torticollis alone.

Foltz et al. (1959) have shown that certain focal brain lesions may produce abnormal neck postures in monkeys, including involuntary spasmodic movements accentuated by emotional stress. The common factor was destruction of parts of the medial reticular formation in the vicinity of the red nucleus, the brachium conjunctivum and the medial longitudinal fasciculus. Following this lead Tarlov (1970) examined such regions particularly carefully in a patient coming to autopsy, but with entirely negative results. A structural pathological basis for the syndrome therefore remains elusive, but the possibility of some cerebral biochemical defect remains to be explored.

The evidence relating to relief after operative interventions on the brain is discussed below (p. 576).

In conclusion one must recognise that close study of the syndrome has conspicuously failed to resolve the debate concerning the fundamental nature of spasmodic torticollis. The balance maintained over so long a period of time, between psychogenic and organic viewpoints, should perhaps be taken as significant in itself. It seems inherently unlikely that so striking a syndrome should sometimes owe its development to one set of mechanisms and sometimes to others which are so very different. A possible solution to the dilemma is to regard the abnormal movements as mediated by some functional, possibly biochemical, disturbance in the brain, and to which certain individuals may be predisposed. In some cases the hypothetical disturbance will be sufficiently severe to become overt without superadded pathology, either physical or psychological in nature; in others structural pathology will have served to actualise the disorder; whereas in others emotional influences, well known to aggravate established torticollis, may have served to precipitate the first overt manifestations, and these may then resolve with psychological treatment. Such a model, it must be admitted, remains entirely conjectural.

Treatment

The great range of treatments used in the disorder further shows how little we understand its cause. Unfortunately no form of therapy can be regarded as entirely satisfactory.

Physical measures have been tried extensively by way of heat and massage, halter traction, or immobilization in collars, braces and casts, but almost always with disappointing results. Attempts at immobilization usually lead to extensive bruising and chafing in advanced examples, and any benefit is promptly lost on removal of the restraint.

Drug therapy has included quinine, hyoscine and other sedatives. Myerson and Loman (1942) reported remarkable benefit from amphetamine in two cases but these appear to have been atypical in many ways. Diazepam, phenothiazines, or antiparkinsonian drugs help a small proportion of patients, particularly in the early stages, but the improvements are usually transient. More recently Gilbert (1972) has reported encouraging results with haloperidol and amantadine, sometimes alone and sometimes in combination with each other. Levodopa has apparently not been successful (Barrett et al., 1970; Marsden and Parkes, 1973).

Muscle retraining exercises and systematic relaxation have usually been disappointing except in very mild and early cases. However a more intensive behaviour therapy approach has occasionally been rewarding. Agras and Marshall (1965) found that one patient was greatly helped by a 'negative practice' technique. He was encouraged to repeat the habitual movement as exactly as possible some 200 to 400 times in each daily session, causing muscle fatigue and building up reactive inhibition to the point where he was ultimately obliged to stop. Brierley (1967) reported sustained improvement in two patients using an aversion technique. A head band was worn incorporating a mercury tube switch which closed to produce a shock at the wrist unless the head was maintained in a nearly normal position. Both of these patients, however, had shown steady deviation of the head rather than mobile torticollis. Systematic desensitization to the anxiety induced by head movements in the direction of the torticollis has also been attempted with some success (Meares, 1973).

Biofeedback methods have apparently met with substantial success in certain patients. The numerous reports now available are described by Fischer-Williams *et al.* (1981). Biofeedback may be used as an aid to simple relaxation, or more directly by EMG feedback from the offending sternocleidomastoid muscle. The muscle potentials are amplified and presented to the patient auditorily or by visual display during a number of sessions. Contingent electric shock may be added to the biofeedback programme. Korein and Brudny (1976) reported sustained improvement in 40% of a large series of patients after treatment of this nature.

Psychotherapy has had considerable success in certain patients. Whiles (1940) reported cures in three out of four patients by relatively superficial exploration of the patients' conflicts, and refers to other examples in the literature where patients have responded to psychotherapy even after nerve section had failed. Paterson (1945) obtained 5 cures and 5 substantial improvements in a total of 21 patients, using psychotherapy supplemented with suggestion and sometimes mild hypnosis. The psychotherapy involved detailed analysis of the settings in which the movements had first appeared, with investigation of the patient's drives, attitudes and emotional reactions at that time. Patients referred for such treatment are, of course, a specially selected group, usually in showing an abundance of emotional conflict and an absence of features indicative of organic disease. Paterson considered that psychotherapy was of greatest value where the personality was of the anxious immature type. Even when the torticollis was only slightly improved the patient's attitude to his illness and surroundings was often so much better that he was able to return again to his usual occupation. Thus psychotherapy was regarded by Paterson as the treatment of choice, and indicated for a trial period in all cases unless gross signs of organic disease were present.

Surgical approaches have had a considerable vogue, including transection of the spinal accessory nerve, division of the upper cervical sensory or motor roots, sternomastoid resection, or various combinations of these operations. Olivecrona (1938) reported excellent results in two-thirds of cases, Poppen and Martinez-Niochet (1951) satisfactory results in 60%. However, no patient in the latter series was restored entirely to normal. Sorenson and Hamby (1965) recommended operation as the primary treatment for torticollis after analysing the

results in 70 cases followed up for periods of 1–10 years. More than half had obtained excellent improvement, with almost total relief and little by way of side effects from surgery. Another third had obtained moderate improvement. However, complications of surgery were frequent, including atrophy of the trapezius and sternomastoids in a third of the patients, drooping of the shoulder, sensory loss or persistent dysphagia. Almost half were left with complaints of neck weakness, and almost three-quarters noted some limitation of neck movements. Three patients required neck braces and eight more required some minor form of head support.

Stereotactic surgery has sometimes produced beneficial results without these undesirable effects. Cooper (1964) reported operations on 64 patients with torticollis or retrocollis, either appearing as solitary syndromes or as part of a more generalised dystonia. Targets included the ventrolateral, ventroposterolateral, ventroposteromedial or centrum medianum nuclei of the thalamus. Bilateral lesions led to more profound and lasting improvement than unilateral operations. Other scattered reports of successful outcomes from thalamotomy are to be found (Meares, 1971a; Tibbetts, 1971), but nevertheless the initial enthusiasm for the operation appears to have waned.

Other Dystonic Movement Disorders

Certain other movement disorders occupy an equally uncertain position where aetiology is concerned, and like torticollis are sometimes referred to psychiatrists and sometimes to neurologists. It may be no coincidence that they are also dystonic in nature. Writer's cramp, blepharospasm and oromandibular dystonia are typical examples. The first two have been widely regarded as neurotic in origin, but it is possible that all are based in some degree in extrapyramidal dysfunction.

The impression of psychogenesis is reinforced by the bizarre nature of such movement disorders, their tendency to appear in connection with only a restricted number of actions, and the relief that patients may discover from certain inexplicable tricks or manoeuvres. Their extreme sensitivity to social or mental stress further invites explanation in psychological terms, likewise the readiness with which psychopathological interpretations may be made of their symbolic significance. Marsden (1976a), however, marshals reasons for viewing such disorders as essentially variants of idiopathic torsion dystonia and thus related to one another. In the course of this disease all may come to be displayed. All can be seen with Wilson's disease and could follow in the wake of encephalitis lethargica. Moreover, all can be provoked by neuroleptics or levodopa. A basis in cerebral pathology must therefore remain an open question even in spontaneously occurring examples. The difficulties encountered in the treatment of all these conditions undoubtedly contributes to the widely divergent views about their causation.

Writer's Cramp

Writer's cramp is one of the numerous 'occupational cramps' or 'craft palsies' in which there develops a specific impairment of some educated motor skill, usually due to spasm in the muscles employed. Other examples include pianist's, telegraphist's and typist's cramps, or analogous conditions which may develop in tailors, cigar makers or painters. All affect a particular manual skill which has achieved dexterity through frequent practice, and spare other movements whether skilled or unskilled. The type of error occasioned by the spasm is reminiscent in many respects of the distinction between an unpractised movement and one which has been brought to deftness through constant repetitions (Critchley, 1954).

The condition affects both sexes but males more often than females. The onset is usually in the 3rd or 4th decades. The fingers and hand develop spasm when attempting to write, causing the writing to sprawl in a jerky manner or pushing the point of the pen into the paper. At first the disorder appears only when fatigued or after writing for some time, but later it is evident immediately attempts at writing commence. Both agonists and antagonists can often be seen to be involved, sometimes with the spasm extending well along the upper limb. The finger movements are jerky and incoordinated and tremor may be prominent. Outside the act of writing the symptoms generally disappear.

The precise picture varies considerably from one patient to another but the outcome in terms of disability is broadly similar. Certain tricks or strategies are often tried to circumvent the problem, with unusual postures and ways of holding the pen. These may bring new faulty habits and divorce the patient still further from the original skill.

It is rare for the spasms to spread beyond the upper limb. There is no muscular wasting, weakness, or incoordination in other acts, and the reflexes are normal. Sensory functions remain intact, but pain, aching and feelings of stiffness often develop in the muscles as a result of the spasm.

It is necessary to distinguish the picture from those seen with other diseases which affect fine coordinated movements, such as arthritis, carpal tunnel syndrome, Parkinson's disease or early torsion dystonia. Writer's cramp, *sui generis,* should only be diagnosed when there is no other physical or neurological abnormality to explain it, and when, at least at the outset, actions other than writing are performed with normal facility. The distinction from 'dystonic' writer's cramp is considered on p. 578.

The course may fluctuate but is chronically progressive in the majority of patients. In general the prognosis is bad with lifelong disability though arrest can occur at any stage. Sometimes the left hand becomes similarly involved after the patient has laboriously trained himself to write with this. Very occasionally the disability spreads to other related functions, as described below.

The aetiology remains a considerable puzzle. Attempts have been made to explain it in terms of psychodynamic, organic and learning theory models, but none can be regarded as entirely satisfactory. With regard to psychogenesis the cramps have been viewed as hysterical conversion symptoms arising out of unresolved conflict, particularly ambivalent feelings towards the occupation. Thus spasm involves both prime movers and their antagonists in a manner resembling hysterical motor abnormalities, and other hysterical conversion symptoms are occasionally in evidence. The disability may be influenced by external factors in a manner which is hard to explain on any other basis—for example in a patient who could not write when sitting but could do so when standing (Walton, 1977). It is only very rarely, however, that patients have seemed to gain or take advantage of the symptoms in any degree. Some re-train themselves successfully to write with the left hand and immediately return to work, while those who are cured by re-training or desensitisation rarely appear to develop other substitute symptoms.

Others have pointed to certain personality configurations in the patients which are thought to be aetiologically relevant. Obsessional features are said to be prominent, with striving conscientious attitudes at work and habitual over-control of emotions. Crisp and Moldofsky (1965) found that all 7 patients whom they studied were of this type. In addition they had special difficulties in expressing aggression. The emotional conflict associated with the onset of the disability frequently centred around the need to write under frustrating but unavoidable circumstances, and angry preoccupation with the work situation had usually well antedated the development of symptoms. All such features were supported in Bindman and Tibbetts' (1977) survey. It was suggested that an excessive predisposition to react with muscle tension in the arm when experiencing anger may have contributed in an important fashion to the genesis of the disorder. After improvement through psychotherapy and re-training it was often noted that writing difficulties would re-emerge to some extent under stresses which again evoked conflict over anger.

Some observers, however, have found their patients to be mostly stable and well-adjusted, and with a great diversity of personality patterns. After experience of a particularly large material Sylvester and Liversedge concluded that there was little to indicate special psychological vulnerability (Sylvester and Liversedge, 1960; Liversedge, 1969). Only 20 of 56 cases showed abnormal psychological traits or neurotic features, and personality was so varied that it was felt they could have been selected from the general population. Many showed no evidence whatever of psychological disorder, apart from high levels of anxiety which disappeared immediately the cramps improved. Thus while granting that psychological factors may aggravate the established condition, particularly apprehension over anticipated failure at writing, there seemed little indication that the basic cause could be of a psychiatric nature.

Psychogenic theories have clearly been varied and have not found uniform support. Many who argue for psychogenesis have felt the need to propose some special physiological disposition which determines the character of the 'neurosis'. The firmest evidence in favour of emotional causation is negative in character, namely that it is hard to conceive of an organic disorder in which movements are impaired when they take part in one set of coordinated acts but remain unaffected in others.

Organic theories are just as inferential. The cramp is regarded as akin to extrapyramidal disorders such as parkinsonism, or to represent an extremely localised form of dystonia. Thus the abnormal motor pattern is very consistent, and in a minority of patients the development of writer's cramp may preface the appearance of dystonia elsewhere. Patients carrying the gene for generalised torsion dystonia have sometimes experienced an episode of writer's cramp lasting months or years in childhood or adolescence (Zeman and Dyken, 1968).

Here, however, it is necessary to make a distinction between 'simple' and 'dystonic' writer's cramp.

In the latter, spasms occur in the hand and arm on writing, but also with other actions such as knitting, sewing, shaving or using a knife. The forearm tends to pronate and the fingers extend as attempts at writing continue (Marsden, 1976a). A typical dystonic posture may be seen in the outstretched arm. This is almost certainly the variety sometimes noted in association with torsion dystonia, sometimes also with torticollis (Meares, 1971c; Marsden, 1976a). Sheehy and Marsden (1982) report that of 60 patients with generalised torsion dystonia, 13 had writer's cramp as the initial feature. Of 49 with segmental dystonias, 21 had begun in this fashion. Where dystonic writer's cramp is concerned, therefore, strong arguments can be marshalled for viewing it as an essentially physical illness, namely a focal or fragmentary dystonia.

The relationship of dystonic writer's cramp to the more familiar and restricted simple form remains uncertain, particularly since examples of the latter are more likely to come before the psychiatrist than the neurologist. Nevertheless, Sheehy and Marsden (1982) have been able to report examples which bridge the two conditions. Of 29 patients seen in a neurological clinic, 8 presented from the outset as dystonic writer's cramp and 21 as simple writer's cramp. Eight of the latter eventually progressed to the dystonic variety, 5 within 6 months of onset and 3 after many years. Moreover, even among the patients with simple writer's cramp, subtle physical signs suggestive of basal ganglia dysfunction could sometimes be observed — unilateral tremor, increased tone or decreased arm swinging. It is possible, therefore, that some examples of simple writer's cramp may represent a minor expression of the overtly dystonic form.

These leads certainly combine to suggest that there may be some special susceptibility to extrapyramidal dysfunction in patients with ordinary writer's cramp, though more direct proof has not yet been forthcoming. Any such predisposition may, moreover, need to combine with other factors of a psychological nature before the disorder becomes overt.

The learning theory model proposes that writer's cramp is the outcome of faulty learning processes; or that whatever its origin its persistence may be explained on the basis of the establishment of maladaptive conditioned responses. Close observation often shows that the cramps tend to arise as soon as the pen or the hand touch the paper, and become intensified by further movements of the fingers and thumb as writing proceeds. The remarkably good outcome which can be achieved by deconditioning and desensitising techniques lends considerable support to such views, and again suggests that some special form of pathophysiology may have underlain the development of the cramps.

Treatment has traditionally involved a prolonged period of rest away from writing, followed by the teaching of relaxation and graded re-educative exercises. Return to work must then be gradual with strict avoidance of fatigue. Unfortunately such measures are likely to meet with incomplete and temporary results. In particular the gains obtained during treatment sessions often fail to generalise adequately to other situations.

Detailed psychotherapy has rarely led to striking benefit. Nevertheless sources of current conflict warrant careful evaluation, especially conflicts in relation to work, and counselling on such matters may bring a measure of relief. Diazepam is sometimes of considerable value in relieving spasm and abating secondary anxiety. Propanolol may help with tremor. Antiparkinsonian drugs have been tried with occasional partial benefit.

One of the most promising approaches has come from behavioural treatment as described by Liversedge and Sylvester (1955). Deconditioning procedures were employed to treat both the spasm and tremor evoked by attempts at writing. Simple apparatus allowed shocks to be delivered to the left hand whenever the pen was gripped too tightly or when it deviated from a prescribed course of line drawn patterns. Of 39 cases so treated satisfactory results were obtained in 29, with 50–100% improvement after 3–6 weeks of treatment (Sylvester and Liversedge, 1960). Follow-up showed satisfactory maintenance of response up to $4\frac{1}{2}$ years later in 24 patients; the 5 who relapsed had shown greater psychological disturbance than those who did well, and in particular a higher level of anxiety. Beech (1960) found the technique to fail in certain cases, or even to worsen the situation when anxiety was high. Reciprocal inhibition may then be the treatment of choice, proceeding slowly along a carefully constructed hierarchy of situations which only gradually approach the act of writing, and accompanied by relaxation at every stage. 'Habit reversal', in which patients are taught to practice tightening the muscles that oppose the cramp, has also shown promising results in a small group of patients (Greenberg and Marks, 1982). The use of biofeedback techniques to bring the increased tension in the muscles to the patients' attention at an early stage

has achieved success in certain cases (Reavley, 1975; Bindman and Tibbetts, 1977).

Blepharospasm

Blepharospasm is a rare disorder consisting of an uncontrollable tendency to spontaneous and forcible eye closure. It may begin unilaterally but both eyes are usually soon affected. Repeated contractions of the orbicularis oculi can progress to almost constant involuntary spasm, sometimes rendering the patient virtually unable to see. Spasms are provoked by bright light, embarrassment or attempts at reading. Facial grimacing may be extensive in the efforts to keep the eyes open. Some patients find tricks that help—yawning, neck extension or forced jaw opening. All spasms disappear during sleep.

It is most common in middle-aged or elderly women, with onset particularly in the sixth decade. For some considerable time, even years, it may be intermittent, and the aggravation by emotional influences may give a strong impression of psychogenesis. A considerable proportion of patients show depression around the time of onset (Marsden, 1976c). The affected patients are typically stable, however, and without precipitants that could explain the disorder (Bender, 1969).

The blepharospasm may start and continue as an isolated symptom, though a strong tendency exists for it to be coupled with oromandibular dystonia (p. 580). Marsden's (1976c) composite material showed blepharospasm alone in 13 cases, oromandibular dystonia alone in 9, and both together in 17. When both are present they usually begin contemporaneously, though sometimes the blepharospasm antedates the oromandibular dystonia by several years. The composite picture has been labelled 'Brueghel's syndrome' since both aspects are well depicted in the famous painting.

The association with oromandibular dystonia supports the view that blepharospasm is likely in most instances to represent some subtle form of extrapyramidal disturbance. Direct evidence for this is lacking, but other observations point in the same direction. It may occasionally be seen in Parkinson's disease or emerge as a side-effect of treatment with neuroleptics or levodopa; it may follow encephalitis lethargica, or occur in association with torsion dystonia. The nature of the spasms—prolonged, repetitive and irregular in timing—makes them typical in all respects to other organic dystonias. Continuous chronic blepharospasm can also follow head injury or subarachnoid haemorrhage, or appear with cerebral tumours, degenerative conditions or cerebral arteriosclerosis. In such settings it can also sometimes closely resemble a psychogenic disorder but for the history and abnormal findings on examination (Bender, 1969).

The course is usually chronic and protracted, but it can be intermittent over many years. In Marsden's series blepharospasm as an isolated symptom never progressed to dystonia elsewhere, but when coupled with oromandibular dystonia such progression was ultimately seen in half of the cases—to torticollis, dystonic posturing of the arms, respiratory spasms or flexion spasms of the trunk.

Treatment is difficult and no regularly effective therapy has been discovered. Anticholinergic drugs and benzodiazepines may give some relief, and response is occasionally seen to phenothiazines, haloperidol or tetrabenazine. In many cases, however, these are without effect. Behaviour therapy has been reported to help with one case (Sharpe, 1974) but will often be found to be defeating. Fischer-Williams *et al.* (1981) describe occasional reports of success from biofeedback treatment.

Whether or not a purely psychogenic form of chronic blepharospasm should be recognised is still uncertain. As an acute disorder blepharospasm may accompany severe depression or anxiety, and forcible eye closure with resistance to eye opening is well recognised in conversion hysteria. Such cases, however, are usually transient, and accompanied by much overt emotional disturbance or other conversion phenomena. Psychogenic tics may also be restricted to the eyelids bilaterally, and severe examples can sometimes be hard to distinguish from the blepharospasm associated with extrapyramidal disorders. It would seem most unlikely, however, that the chronic continuing syndrome described above owes much to psychogenesis, sensitive though it may be to psychological influences once it has become established.

Oromandibular Dystonia

As described above, oromandibular dystonia is frequently associated with blepharospasm but it can also occur alone. It likewise affects women more than men, and the peak age of onset is in the sixth decade. The same arguments have surrounded possible psychogenesis, though in marked examples an organic basis cannot be long in doubt. As with blepharospasm it was sometimes seen as an aftermath of encephalitis lethargica and it may be provoked by neuroleptics or levodopa. It may emerge in the course of Wilson's disease or idiopathic torsion dystonia. In many cases, however, oromandibular dystonia presents alone as an 'idiopathic' disorder.

Prolonged spasms affect the muscles of the mouth, jaw and sometimes the tongue. They last for up to a minute and are repetitive but irregular in timing. The lower perioral muscles and the platysma may also be involved. The jaw may be forced open or abruptly closed, the lips purse or retract, and the tongue protrudes or curls within the mouth. Severe grimacing takes place and talking and eating may be rendered difficult.

The picture can at first sight resemble the orofacial dyskinesias seen as a late effect of neuroleptic medication (p. 547) but in essence the movements are different (Marsden, 1976a, 1976c). Orofacial dystonia consists of repetitive prolonged spasms, rather than the incessant flow of choreiform lip smacking, chewing and tongue rolling movements seen in tardive dyskinesia.

The spasms are typically provoked by embarrassment, fatigue, or attempts at speaking, chewing or swallowing. Certain tricks may be learned to abort them, such as grasping the lower jaw firmly, or shaking the head. In the early stages the capricious nature of the spasms may produce bizarre results, for example in one of Marsden's (1976c) patients who could not speak without provoking spasms but could sing normally, and in another where the reverse obtained.

As with blepharospasm no cause has been discovered and no treatment can help decisively. Benzodiazepines may reduce the force and frequency of spasms. Phenothiazines and butyrophenones are perhaps somewhat more effective than with blepharospasm, though often at the expense of induced parkinsonism.

Gilles de la Tourette's Syndrome

Gilles de la Tourette's syndrome, though relatively rare, has attracted a good deal of attention, chiefly on account of the striking nature of the clinical picture. Multiple tics are accompanied by forced vocalisations which often take the form of obscene words or phrases ('coprolalia'). One of the chief interests of the condition is the way in which a verbal component to the picture may give some clue to underlying psychopathological mechanisms; but whether psychopathological factors are sufficient in themselves to cause the disorder or merely shape its manifestations has been much debated. It now seems increasingly probable that there may be an organic component, or perhaps some form of developmental defect, which is at least partly responsible for the genesis of the disorder.

Clinical Features

Valuable reviews of the clinical picture are presented by Kelman (1965), Enoch *et al.* (1967), Fernando (1967) and Shapiro *et al.* (1978). Fernando's criteria for the diagnosis are useful—an onset in childhood below the age of 16, multiple motor tics, and unprovoked loud utterances which may progress to the forced shouting of obscenities. Shapiro *et al.* (1978) have described 145 cases studied personally.

The condition is a good deal commoner among boys than girls, in a ratio of approximately 3 to 1. Onset is rare after 11 and the great majority begin between the ages of 5 and 8. In these respects the syndrome resembles the generality of tics in childhood. A family history of simple tics is not uncommon, occurring in 30% of Shapiro *et al.*'s patients, but it has been considered rare to find other family members with the fully developed syndrome. Occasional examples were reported by Friel (1973), Sanders (1973) and Shapiro *et al.* (1978). The survey by Nee *et al.* (1980) is exceptional in finding a family history of the disorder in no less than 16 of 50 cases gathered from a wide geographical area in the USA.

Simple tics are usually the first manifestation. Tics may be defined as 'sudden, quick, involuntary, and frequently repeated movements of circumscribed groups of muscles, serving no apparent purpose' (Kanner, 1957). They are distinct from chorea and other abnormal motor movements in their stereotyped pattern, the same event occurring time and again, and in the ability of the subject to hold the movements in check for a short while at the expense of mounting inner tension. They commence usually in the face, head and neck, spreading later to the limbs and trunk. Before long there are usually multiple tics, often of great force and severity—blinking, grimacing, jerking of the head, shrugging of the shoulders or jerks of the arms and legs. Whole body movements may be involved, leading to jumping, slipping and hopping. Complex coordinated movements occasionally appear, such as brief slapping of the face or thighs, or wringing of the hands. The picture may at times be highly bizarre, and the detailed pattern tends to change over time.

Vocalisations can occur from the outset but are usually added later. Most begin within five years of onset. At first they are often inarticulate sounds— explosive grunts, barks or coughing noises which accompany the motor movements. These may then progress to the enunciation of words, sometimes muttered and barely discernible but sometimes loudly and clearly articulated. Common oaths and expletives are frequently involved, or brief obscene phrases of aggressive or sexual content. The utterance of obscenities quite commonly sets in at about the time of puberty, but may start as early as ten or be delayed until well into adult life. It appears in perhaps half of the cases ultimately. 'Mental coprolalia' in the form of a compulsion to think obscenities is probably commoner than overt coprolalia, and transition from the former to the latter may be observed.

Both the tics and the utterances are affected by emotional stress, becoming more severe with anxiety, anger or self-consciousness. The patient may struggle greatly to conceal the coprolalia, disguising or distorting obscene words so that their true nature is not at first detected. Intense efforts at control may succeed for a while, but at the expense of mounting inner tension and ultimately an explosive recrudescence. The coprolalia tends to cease when the patient is alone but the tics do not. Both are often markedly relieved by alcohol. They cease during sleep and are also said to disappear during sexual arousal (Shapiro *et al.*, 1973c). They usually diminish during periods of intense concentration or when the patient is firmly preoccupied with matters which do not arouse anxiety.

'Echo-phenomena' have often been stressed in the literature but occur in less than one-third of cases. There may be compulsive repetition of words spoken by others ('echolalia'), or compulsive imitation of actions ('echopraxia') or movements ('echokinesis').

The intelligence of affected persons varies widely but in some series a surprising number have shown superior ability. Childhood neurotic symptoms and a disturbed family background have seemed to be common, but proper controlled comparisons are not available. Fernando (1967) found that at least a third of reported cases had an absent parent or one with abnormal attitudes, and almost a quarter had had an obviously disturbed childhood environment. Childhood hyperkinesis, antedating the tics, has been found in some 10 per cent of cases. Personality disturbance is said to be common, but it is hard to know whether this is primary or secondary to the socially disruptive effects of the illness. Obsessional features have often been stressed, amounting to a definite obsessive-compulsive illness in a high proportion of patients in some series (Nee *et al.*, 1980, 1982; Montgomery *et al.*, 1982). Antisocial and self-destructive behaviour were also prominent in these patients. Restlessness is usually a marked feature, and episodes of severe depression are not uncommon.

The social impact of the illness is often disastrous. Some patients withdraw to a considerable extent, while others appear to maintain surprisingly good work records and social relationships despite their disability.

Course and Outcome

Firm information about the long-term outcome is hard to obtain. Many reports have painted a gloomy picture of apparently life-long disability. Sometimes, however, it seems that the disorder subsides in early adult life, or at least that remissions occur for considerable periods of time. Fernando (1967) found that almost two-thirds of patients in whom the outcome was reported had improved, but less than a quarter could be said to have recovered. However few of the patients were followed beyond the age of 30 and later relapses may yet have occurred. Enoch *et al.* (1967) state that spontaneous arrest can occur at any stage, though the course is usually progressive with remissions alternating with paroxysmal exacerbations.

It is sometimes stated that the disorder may lead on to severe personality disintegration or to a psychosis resembling schizophrenia (Singer, 1963; Polites *et al.*, 1965). This appears, however, to be rare. Only two cases could be identified in the literature by Kelman (1965) or Fernando (1967) who needed permanent committal to hospital for any reason.

Nosology and Aetiology

Different views have been put forward about the nosological status of the condition. Some regard it as a rare and distinct disease entity, while others view it as merely the most severe and persistent presentation of the tic syndrome in childhood.

Giles de la Tourette (1855) himself allied the condition with certain other rare motor and speech disorders reported from various parts of the world— the 'latah' reaction among Malays, the 'myriachit' of Siberia, and the 'jumping Frenchmen of Maine'. It is now realised, however, that this was erroneous. Latah is manifest as echopraxia, echolalia and coprolalia but tic-like phenomena do not occur. Automatic

obedience is a prominent feature. It is essentially a severe startle reaction and does not occur without a provoking stimulus. Yap (1952) regards it as a culturally determined fear response found only in primitive cultures where persons have limited powers of control over the environment. Myriachit is similar. The Jumpers of Maine displayed analogous features as part of a religious ritual.

Corbett and co-workers present data which suggest that the fundamentals of Gilles de la Tourette's syndrome differ little from those of childhood tics generally (Corbett *et al.*, 1969; Corbett, 1971):

Among patients with tics attending child guidance clinics or adolescent departments it was shown that the tics usually began with facial movements, which in severe examples might come to involve progressively more caudal and peripheral parts of the body. The degree of spread could be used in assessing the severity of the tic, those with peripheral involvement tending to be the more persistent. Thus Gilles de la Tourette syndrome is not unique in its progressive spread.

Almost a quarter of Corbett *et al.*'s patients showed vocal tics along with tics of other parts of the body, thereby satisfying the essential criteria for Gilles de la Tourette syndrome. These were compared with further patients selected on the basis of coprolalia in conjunction with multiple body tics. The tics associated with vocalisations tended to affect several parts of the body concurrently, and were particularly widely distributed and severe when coprolalia was present. In terms of intelligence and frequency of clinical evidence of brain damage, there was little to distinguish Gilles de la Tourette patients from other tiquers, but they showed a higher incidence of psychiatric symptoms by way of antisocial behaviour and neurotic disturbances. Sociopathic factors in the family were several times that in the general patient population attending the hospital, likewise a history of parental mental illness. Both factors were particularly pronounced in those with coprodalia.

On follow-up, patients with vocal tics did less well than those without, and patients with coprolalia did particularly badly in terms of symptom resolution.

Thus on Corbett's data Gilles de la Tourette patients appear simply to represent the more disturbed, severely affected and recalcitrant of childhood tiquers, with coprolalia representing the extreme of the distribution.

The main theories advanced to account for tics are the psychogenic, the organic, those based on learning theory models and those which view the disorder in terms of developmental defect. Each may accordingly be applied to Gilles de la Tourette's syndrome.

Psychogenic theories regard emotional traumas and conflicts as fundamental to the genesis of tics. Emotional precipitants can often be discerned at the time of onset, and a high incidence of psychiatric disturbance is commonly found in the patients and their families. The tics are seen as the direct or symbolic expression of emotional disturbance— aggression, anxiety or the handling of sexual conflicts.

Psychoanalysts such as Fenichel (1945) conceive of tics as the involuntary motor equivalents of emotional activity, allowing previously repressed impulses to make their appearance in disguised form. In effect the musculature is used for the immediate discharge of infantile wishes of a sexual or sadistic nature. Such impulses have become 'independent of the organised ego', that is to say they lack the normal integration with the totality of the personality. Other obsessive-compulsive features are said to reveal the 'anal' character structure which is commonly associated with such developments. In a similar vein Mahler and Rangell (1943) regarded the symptoms of Gilles de la Tourette's syndrome as expressing the conflict between erotic and aggressive drives on the one hand and internalised censoring controls on the other. They point out that the latency period, which is the common time of onset, is a time when repressive forces against infantile wishes are at a maximum.

These psychoanalytic conceptions may not seem particularly convincing when applied to tics generally, but it is interesting that in Gilles de la Tourette's syndrome one may meet with vocal and verbal manifestations which lend some support to such views. The noises can often be construed as aggressive or erotic in character, while coprolalia displays such themes in unmistakable form. Sometimes the setting in which coprolalia occurs gives added significance to its role in exposing the patient's conflicts:

Creak and Guttmann (1935) described a boy who uttered words compulsively along with his tic in a low and barely audible voice, but in his home and when teased at school obscenities could be heard. A girl showed only grunts and sniffs, but after delivery of an illegitimate pregnancy these were accompanied for the first time by coprolalic utterances bearing unmistakable sexual connotations. Kurland (1965) described two adolescent girls with Gilles de la Tourette's syndrome who showed as a cardinal feature overwhelming ambivalence and inability to express their hostility towards their mothers. Here coprolalic language appeared to be used overtly and in an uncontrolled way to punish the mothers who they felt to be perfectionistic and pure. At the same time it appeared to gratify their own unacceptable sexual wishes in a verbal manner.

Morphew and Sim (1969) argue strongly for a psychogenic aetiology for Gilles de la Tourette's syndrome, noting a marked preponderance of obsessional personalities in reported cases, precipitating factors which are largely psychological in nature, and the improvements which have been reported after psychotherapy, leaving home, or admission to hospital. They add the suggestion that the psychodynamic matrix from which the disorder stems may share much in common with stammering.

Altogether, however, the evidence is insubstantial for concluding that psychological mechanisms alone are responsible for the condition. Susceptibility to psychological influences need not imply that these are causative. It would seem wiser merely to conclude that Gilles de la Tourette's syndrome may reveal psychodynamic factors at work in an unusually clear fashion, rather than to grant them a primary role in the genesis of the disorder.

Organic theories presuppose that some form of subclinical brain damage contributes directly to the development of tics. This gained support when tics emerged as a sequel of encephalitis lethargica, sometimes in association with parkinsonian deficits but sometimes in relative isolation. Sydenham's chorea has also been claimed as a not infrequent precursor (Creak and Guttmann, 1935), but here there are obvious possibilities that the early manifestations may have been this diagnosed as chorea.

The question arises whether the generality of childhood tiquers may have suffered some form of covert brain damage which has rendered them vulnerable to the disorder, even while showing little or nothing by way of abnormal neurological signs. Pasamanick and Kawi (1956) explored the possibility of brain damage resulting from prenatal or perinatal factors, by identifying 83 childhood tiquers and tracing the birth records of each. When compared to the next born child, matched for sex, race, maternal age and place of birth, the incidence of complications of pregnancy and parturition was found to have been significantly higher among the children with tics. These results were interpreted in terms of Pasamanick's theory of a 'continuum of reproductive casualty', namely that complications of pregnancy and delivery may lead to brain damage extending in degree from that which is gross and obvious to that which normally evades detection. Depending on the nature and severity of the damage the child may later develop a number of neuropsychiatric disorders, ranging from epilepsy and mental defect to behaviour disorders or reading retardation. Tics appeared to take their place as part of this spectrum. Others, however, have argued that the normal or even superior distribution of IQ scores among children with tics, and the absence of other motor abnormalities, make it unlikely that brain damage can play a substantial role.

With regard to Gilles de la Tourette's syndrome Shapiro, Sweet and co-workers have been the most persistent advocates of an organic aetiology (Shapiro *et al.*, 1973b, 1973c; Sweet *et al.*, 1973). They obtained evidence of some degree of central nervous system abnormality in a high proportion of a group of 34 patients with the disorder. Though lacking controls the sum total of their data is impressive. First, clinical ratings of 'organicity', based on a history of hyperactivity, clumsiness or perceptual problems in childhood, or clinical observation of perseveration, confabulation or disturbed cognition, showed that half of the cases had 'mild or moderate' evidence of brain disorder. More than a third had been hyperactive in childhood and a similar proportion were left-handed or ambidextrous. Secondly, psychometry revealed verbal-performance discrepancies exceeding 17 points in more than a third of cases, and ratings derived from the Wechsler, Rorschach and Bender-Gestalt tests showed evidence of organic deficits in three quarters. Electroencephalography showed mild to moderate non-specific abnormalities in half of the patients. Finally, neurological examination revealed minor asymmetries of motor function in half, such as unilateral impairment of rapid alternating movements, drifting of the outstretched arm, or abnormalities of tone or reflexes. Of 29 patients examined in all four respects two-thirds showed abnormalities on at least three of the parameters and only two showed no deficits on any of them. These observations have since been extended to 70 patients (Shapiro *et al.*, 1978) with essentially similar results.

From this Shapiro *et al.* conclude that some form of cerebral disorder underlies the syndrome, of a nature yet to be clarified. Not all reports, however, are consistent with Shapiro's findings. A recent study from The National Hospital, Queen Square, for example, of 53 patients referred chiefly from the UK Gilles de la Tourette Association, found little evidence of structural abnormality in the central nervous system (Lees *et al.*, 1984). Occasional patients showed choreiform movements or focal dystonic symptoms, but in the great majority neurological examination was negative. Electro-encephalographic abnormalities were present in only 13%,

neuropsychological testing showed essentially normal results, and no definite CT scan abnormalities could be detected. Such discrepancies between one survey and another remain at present unexplained.

Short of structural brain disorder there may yet be some biochemical abnormality of the central nervous system which is responsible for the syndrome. Snyder *et al.* (1970) suggested that dopaminergic hyperactivity in the corpus striatum might be a factor, since treatment with haloperidol meets with conspicuous success and the drug is a potent blocker of dopamine receptors. Some support for this has been obtained by Van Woert *et al.* (1976), who found elevated levels of homovanillic acid, the major metabolite of dopamine, in the cerebrospinal fluid of five patients when compared with controls. Moreover, there have been occasional reports of a picture resembling Gilles de la Tourette's syndrome emerging with tardive dyskinesia in patients maintained on long-term neuroleptic medication, again pointing to dopaminergic hypersensitivity as a possible mechanism (Klawans *et al.*, 1978; De Veaugh-Geiss, 1980; Mueller and Aminoff, 1982).

Pressing their claim for an organic causation further, Shapiro *et al.* (1972) discount the role of psychodynamic factors in the aetiology of the illness, and suggest that the observed psychopathology may be an offshoot of the basic organic impairment or arise secondarily to the burden of the illness. Disturbances in parent-child relationships may, for example, be a product of the disorder rather than causative in any sense. They could find no evidence in their own patients to support ideas of inhibition of hostility, obsessive-compulsive character disorder, hysteria or underlying psychosis.

Post-mortem evidence has understandably been sparse and does not clarify the situation in one direction or the other. Only one report has suggested a cerebral abnormality, by way of immature cell structure of the corpus striatum in a single case (Balthasar, 1956). The significance to be attached to this is very doubtful.

The learning theory model views tics as conditioned avoidance responses which have originally been evoked in a traumatic situation, then reinforced by the reduction of anxiety that follows (Yates, 1958). Because of stimulus generalisation the anxiety which the tic reduces will eventually be provoked by many more situations so that the tic becomes an increasingly stronger habit. In essence the tic is a simple learned response which has attained maximal habit strength.

Corbett (1971) points out that there is a striking

similarity between tic movements and the movements seen in the startle response. This applies both to the nature of the movements and their distribution. Thus tics most frequently involve blinking, the face head and neck, and the limbs, in that order, which parallels the distribution of motor activity during startle. Startle responses, moreover, are sometimes associated with vocalisation, and are easily conditioned to neutral stimuli.

Even if such a model is felt inadequate to explain the origin of the tic, it is easy to see how secondary reinforcing properties may come to attach to it later and help to perpetuate the habit. To the extent that problems of aggression and hostility are prominent in patients with Gilles de la Tourette's syndrome the effects of their behaviour on those around must often powerfully gratify the habit. Behavioural treatment based on the learning theory model has sometimes met with a good deal of success, though apparently less so with Gilles de la Tourette's syndrome than with simple motor tics.

A developmental defect has been proposed as the basis of tics and derives support from certain indirect evidence. Such a conception presupposes no necessary special nexus of psychological conflict in the patient, nor some covert form of acquired brain damage, but merely that the normal maturational processes of control over motor movements have not been fully achieved. The patient is accordingly vulnerable to faulty conditioning procedures as set out above, or if he is destined for emotional disturbance his neurosis will be liable to choose the form of a tic on account of his motor lability.

Much of the data presented by Corbett *et al.* (1969) in tiquers fits with a conception of developmental defect. The preponderance in boys is in accordance with their proneness to other developmental disorders. The restricted age of onset between 6 and 8 suggests a developmental defect, similarly the marked tendency to remission at adolescence. Corbett *et al.*'s tiquers showed an excess of other developmental disorders, such as encopresis and speech defects, when compared to the clinic population generally, again suggesting that the tics might be the consequence of developmental failure. The increased incidence of parental mental illness and of adverse social circumstances may have provided the anxiety-provoking environment necessary to bring the predisposition for the development of tics to light.

The question is whether developmental failure could account for the genesis of the more florid manifestations of Gilles de la Tourette's syndrome.

The frequency of a family history of simple tics (Shapiro *et al.*, 1978) argues in favour of some form of constitutional motor lability. But there are not sufficient data on a large enough number of cases to test all of the associations described above, and to see whether they apply with especial force in Gilles de la Tourette's syndrome. Corbett (1971) presents data which suggest that the sex differential in favour of boys is especially great when tics are associated with coprolalia, and that the incidence of parental mental illness and sociopathic family backgrounds is similarly increased. However the tendency for the syndrome to persist through adolescence and indeed well on in adult life would suggest that more than developmental immaturity is involved.

In conclusion one may note that none of these approaches to aetiology is entirely satisfactory in itself. The study of Gilles de la Tourette's syndrome illustrates the difficulty inherent in clarifying aetiology when there is no striking collateral evidence pointing firmly to psychogenic factors or to cerebral disorder, and when at the same time it is difficult to amass large numbers of unselected cases for detailed appraisal and proper control comparisons. It is necessary to remember that Gilles de la Tourette's syndrome is relatively rare, whereas emotional conflict and subclinical brain damage are both likely to be common. If psychological conflict of the type described were alone responsible, one might expect the patients to be very severely crippled in the handling of their sexuality or aggression before so disruptive a disorder should emerge. Yet many patients with Gilles de la Tourette's syndrome appear to be not so very abnormal in overall adjustment. If some form of perinatal brain damage or developmental immaturity were alone responsible one would similarly expect more impressive evidence in other spheres to confirm it. And faulty conditioning processes would be most unlikely to result in so bizarre a syndrome when acting on an otherwise normal person.

The true situation may therefore be represented by some form of compromise or combination between the various points of view outlined above. A child who is vulnerable by virtue of perinatal brain damage or developmental defect (and the former may have led to the latter) may, when passing through an onerous phase of his emotional development, fall prey to this particular form of expression of inner conflicts. To the extent that his conflicts are severe, or instability of motor control is great, his tics may assume the severity and complexity of Gilles de la Tourette's syndrome. Adverse conditioning by way of feed-back from the environment may be important in the elaboration of the picture in the early stages, or in helping to perpetuate it over time. Both emotional and organic factors may have served to render the subject particularly sensitive to such conditioning.

The coexistence in Gilles de la Tourette's patients of multiple motor tics and verbal utterances is at first sight puzzling, but perhaps can be accommodated in what we know of the use of words and body gestures. Both are vehicles of emotional expression and of communication, and must share at some level in their internal representation. Mahler and Rangell (1943) suggest that the cardinal features of Gilles de la Tourette's syndrome can all be regarded as different expressions of dysfunction of the 'system of expressional motility'. Certainly where aggression is concerned the normal processes of development lead from coarse motor expressions of hostile impulses to the more highly differentiated use of language, and the employment of obscenities in connection with aggression is firmly rooted in the culture towards which development proceeds.

Treatment

A great variety of treatments have been employed as reviewed by Shapiro *et al.* (1978). The natural history of the disorder, with spontaneous remissions and exacerbations, has made it difficult to evaluate any therapeutic régime based on small numbers of cases, but a general air of pessimism has surrounded most reports. Rather unexpectedly it is drug treatment, with haloperidol, which has recently come to find wide acceptance as the most effective form of management.

Psychotherapy has often met with failure but improvements have sometimes been reported, very occasionally with seeming total recovery (Mahler and Luke, 1946; Eisenberg *et al.*, 1959; Kurland, 1965). Hypnosis has been tried but apparently without lasting benefit. Abreaction has been attempted with a wide range of drugs, and Michael (1957) reported a patient who underwent a striking remission after a series of carbon dioxide inhalations when intensive psychotherapy had met with no response.

A behaviour therapy approach has sometimes been effective with simple tics but has produced less impressive results with Gilles de la Tourette's syndrome. Yates (1958) used 'massed practice' to extinguish four simple tics in a patient, based on the theory that voluntary practice of the tics for long periods of time would build up reactive inhibition and thus the negative habit of not performing them. With continuing massed practice the number of voluntary evocations of the tic per minute declined and there was coincident improvement in the frequency of spontaneous tics. Very prolonged periods of practice followed by long rest pauses proved most effective. Raft (1962) also reported partial success with the method in simple tics.

Clark (1966) employed massed practice with cases of Gilles de la Tourette's syndrome, reporting remarkably good results in two out of three cases. Coprolalia was eliminated by asking the patient to repeat his most frequently used obscenity as often as possible until he could no longer succeed in saying it even once per minute. Two half-hour treatment sessions were given daily for many days. Twenty-five sessions were required in one patient and forty-nine in the other. Difficulties were encountered in that other words were often interposed, and the patients tended to take voluntary rest pauses. The former was checked by administering electric shocks, and the latter by getting the patient to perform to a metronome. Clark did not comment directly on changes in facial or bodily tics, but states that both cases remained 'symptom free' during 4 years follow-up. Others, however, have had less success with massed practice, finding that it may aggravate the tics by generating increased anxiety, and sometimes finding that new tics appear during therapy (Sand and Carlson, 1973). 'Habit reversal', in which the patient is taught to practise movements incompatible with the tic by tightening the opposing muscle groups, has proved highly effective with simple tics (Azrin *et al.*, 1980) and might be expected to help with the motor components of Gilles de la Tourette's syndrome.

MacDonald's (1963) successful treatment programme for a girl with Gilles de la Tourette's syndrome also incorporated a behavioural approach. It was decided that the patient's control of aggression was central to her disorder, in that she was terrified of what might result if she expressed her anger to the full. A series of abreactive interviews was given with the aim of arousing fear of loss of control, but in the presence of a reassuring and accepting therapist so that such anxieties might be inhibited. She became symptom free in the course of treatment, and four years later was still completely well. It is hard, however, to decide how directly the supposed mechanism of treatment contributed to its success. Cohen and Marks (1977) have described the value of an operant conditioning programme, involving simple rewards for tic-free periods of increasing length, which can be implemented in the patient's home.

Of the drugs which were earlier employed phenothiazines, antiparkinsonian agents and chlordiazepoxide sometimes met with partial success but none achieved wide acclaim. Shapiro et al. (1978) review the scattered reports of successes and failures. Haloperidol, however, has now emerged as the treatment of choice, producing a marked amelioration of symptoms in those who can tolerate it in sufficient dosage.

Connell et al. (1967) convincingly showed the effectiveness of haloperidol in simple tics in a double-blind comparison with diazepam. In Gilles de la Tourette's syndrome Chapel et al. (1964) were among the first to report excellent responses and this has since been amply confirmed (Shapiro and Shapiro, 1968; Shapiro et al., 1973a). Both the tics and the vocalisations may be greatly ameliorated from the first day of treatment. Unfortunately large doses may be required in some patients, and not all can tolerate this without disabling side-effects. Shapiro et al. (1973a) initially advocated a régime in which the dose was rapidly increased to the maximum tolerated or until symptom relief was obtained, then gradually lowered to maintenance levels. They have subsequently altered their procedure (Shapiro et al., 1978), starting with minimal dosage and building up slowly to an end-point of maximal improvement with the minimum of side-effects. This may vary from 2 mg to 40 mg per day in different patients. In some cases the dose can later be reduced over several months or years, often ultimately to very low levels. Follow-up of their patients after an average of three years on the drug showed that the great majority continued to benefit, with a mean decrease in symptoms of 80%.

Phenothiazines appear to be a good deal less effective, but other butyrophenones or pimozide may be used if tolerance develops to haloperidol (Fernando, 1976). Clonidine, a centrally active α-adrenergic agonist, has also proved to be effective (Cohen et al., 1980). Anticholinergic drugs may be indicated in the early stages of haloperidol therapy to counteract acute dystonic side-effects, but should not be prescribed for long on account of the risks of tardive dyskinesia (p. 547). This complication has indeed supervened occasionally in such patients (Caine and Polinsky, 1981).

Finally operative intervention has occasionally been reported in Gilles de la Tourette's syndrome, sometimes with dramatically successful results. Fernando (1967) refers to occasional cases in the literature where frontal leucotomy has been performed. Nadvornik et al. (1972) report a successful result after bilateral stereotactic operation on the dentate nucleus of the cerebellum, normally performed by these workers for the relief of spasticity or myoclonic movements. Hassler and Dieckmann (1970, 1973) apparently obtained considerable success in nine patients after stereotactic coagulation of the rostral intralaminar and medial nuclei of the thalamus. This is the operation they have used in obsessional neurosis, and it seems that most of their patients with Gilles de la Tourette's syndrome had other marked obsessional symptoms by way of hand washing or counting rituals.

Chapter 15. Other Disorders Affecting the Nervous System

Several affections of the nervous system not falling within the province of the foregoing chapters remain to be considered. Attention will be restricted to those which have attracted some degree of psychiatric interest, either on account of the mental symptoms that accompany them or because they can raise problems of differential diagnosis in the overlapping field between neurology and psychiatry.

Patients with neurological disease can first come before the psychiatrist, usually at an early stage and before there is unequivocal evidence of central nervous system pathology. The incidence of erroneous diagnoses is hard to assess but the findings of Tissenbaum et al. (1951) may not be unrepresentative. On reviewing approximately 400 neurological patients attending a Veterans Administration clinic they found that 53 (13%) had been considered to suffer from a psychiatric disorder before the neurological diagnosis was established, the commonest psychiatric diagnoses being conversion hysteria, neurosis or affective disorder. The situation was particularly common among patients with Parkinson's disease or multiple sclerosis. In some instances organic disease had been suspected for some time, though the label of functional psychiatric disorder persisted until the underlying disease had progressed much further.

In some neurological disorders psychiatric symptoms are an integral part of the disease process, representing the direct effects of central nervous system involvement on mental functioning. This is most clearly discerned in the numerous disorders which can lead to cognitive impairment, but cerebral pathology may also play a part in determining more subtle changes of personality, disorder of affect or even psychotic developments. Where there is evidence on such matters this will be discussed. Other psychiatric disturbances in neurological disease have little to do directly with brain pathology, but reflect the reaction of the patient to his disablement. Neurological disability often poses severe threats to independence and security, or provides obstacles to free communication. Not unnaturally these may tax the individual's capacity for psychological adjustment over time. Emotional symptoms and even frank mental illness may then result, and owe their origin predominantly to the patient's individual conflicts and aspects of his social situation. Sometimes, of course, both organic and psychogenic factors will be operative together. The correct appreciation of such matters is an essential prelude to planned intervention and help.

Some of the disorders considered below are not uncommon. Others are very rare, but can nonetheless be important in the present context if they are liable to have marked psychiatric sequelae.

Multiple Sclerosis

Multiple sclerosis is by far the most frequent of the demyelinating diseases, and indeed is one of the commonest diseases of the nervous system in temperate climates. It is particularly common in the Northern hemisphere but rare in tropical and subtropical regions. Although the actual incidence is low the chronicity of the disorder leads it to rank as a major cause of disability.

The aetiology remains unknown despite a large amount of research and a number of tantalising clues. A familial tendency is noted in some five per cent of cases but no clear genetic pattern has emerged. This and the known geographical variation in incidence has directed attention to the possibility that some environmental factor is operative. The various theories which have been put forward are reviewed by Hallpike (1973) and Matthews (1978, 1983). They include allergic, vascular, infective, dietary and metabolic theories but none can be considered well established.

Clinical Features

The onset is chiefly in young adults between 20 and 40 years of age. In England females are affected more often than males. The disorder is protean in its neurological manifestations, traditional diagnostic criteria laying emphasis on both the multi-focal and relapsing nature of the symptoms and signs.

Typically there is evidence, over time if not at a single examination, of disseminated lesions in the neuraxis, which at least in the early stages show a tendency to remission and relapse.

Early manifestations frequently include retrobulbar neuritis, disorders of oculomotor function leading to diplopia or nystagmus, or lesions of the long ascending or descending tracts of the cord producing paraesthesiae or spastic paraparesis. Precipitancy of micturition may be an early symptom, likewise ataxia or intention tremor due to cerebellar involvement. Retrobulbar neuritis is particularly common and can occur as a transient disturbance antedating other manifestations by many years.

The initial symptoms tend to settle within weeks or months, sometimes disappearing completely but sometimes leaving residual disability. Further attacks bring new symptoms or an intensification of those already present. The interval between attacks is extremely variable but in exceptional cases remissions may last for 25 years or more. The majority of cases pursue a relapsing remitting course of this nature, but some show steady progression of disability from the outset. Ultimately almost all show downward progression with an accumulation of multiple handicaps.

On examination typical early stigmata include pallor of the temporal halves of the optic discs, nystagmus, mild intention tremor, exaggerated tendon reflexes, absent abdominal reflexes, extensor plantar responses, and impaired vibration and joint position sense. During early remissions of the disease, however, there may be little or nothing to detect by way of abnormal signs. Later there is evidence of multiple lesions particularly affecting the optic nerves, cerebellum, brain stem and long tracts of the cord. Eventually the patient is likely to show some combination of ataxia, intention tremor, dysarthria, dissociation of conjugate lateral eye movements, paraparesis, sensory loss in the limbs, and urinary incontinence. The psychological manifestations described below will emerge in a large proportion of cases, some being attributable to lesions in the cerebral hemispheres. Epileptic seizures are a rare manifestation, occurring in about two per cent of cases.

Various problems of neurological diagnosis can arise, at least in the early stages, but will not be detailed here. From the psychiatric point of view the principal differentiation which must be made is between hysteria and certain early manifestations of multiple sclerosis as discussed on p. 596.

There are no laboratory findings which are pathognomonic for the disease but abnormalities occur in the cerebrospinal fluid in a high proportion of cases. About half show a slight increase of mononuclear cells in the acute stages or a moderate elevation of protein. A common finding is an abnormal Lange curve, either paretic or luetic in form. The gamma globulins are typically abnormally high, with the relative proportion of immunogloblin G (IgG) selectively raised in some 90% of cases (Hershey and Trotter, 1979). Cerebrospinal fluid electrophoresis commonly shows the striking appearance of oligoclonal bands within the immunoglobulin fraction. False positives may, however, occur with both of these tests.

The EEG pattern is non-specific and the only clear correlation is with the acuteness or chronicity of the disorder (Jasper et al., 1950). Approximately 90% of cases show abnormalities in the acute stage, chiefly in the form of slow waves, diffusely or focally. During subacute phases two-thirds show changes, mostly slight, and during remissions only one-third show significant abnormalities. Residual EEG abnormalities may occasionally be attributable to cortical damage, but for the most part may be ascribed to changes in cortical activity produced by lesions in the projection pathways or by abnormal discharges arising subcortically.

Halliday et al. (1973) have made an important contribution by demonstrating the diagnostic value of studying visual evoked responses in patients suspected of multiple sclerosis. Delayed forms of response from one or both eyes on the presentation of visual patterned stimuli have been shown to correlate highly with the diagnosis, even in patients without a history of optic neuritis and with normal optic discs on ophthalmoscopy. Clearly subclinical lesions of the visual pathways are very common in multiple sclerosis and can readily be detected with such a test. Somatosensory evoked responses, recorded over the cervical spine while stimulating the median nerve at the wrist, can similarly detect subclinical abnormalities in the somatosensory pathways. The two techniques can have complementary value in helping with diagnosis (Mastaglia et al., 1976).

Pathology

The pathological changes within the nervous system consist of scattered sharply circumscribed areas of demyelination, followed later by secondary degeneration of long axonal tracts. Macroscopically the plaques show as greyish translucent areas which may be found in all parts of the neuraxis, chiefly in the white matter but sometimes also in the grey matter of the cortex and spinal cord. Typically the number of lesions greatly exceeds what would have been expected from the clinical findings. The cerebellum and the periventricular areas of the hemispheres are sites of special predilection.

Microscopically the acute lesions show degeneration of the myelin sheaths while the axis cylinders remain intact. The perivascular spaces contain lymphocytes and macrophages laden with neutral fats. Later the damaged myelin disappears and astrocytes proliferate to form a glial scar. At this stage axonal destruction is observed within the plaque.

Treatment

There is very little which can be offered by way of specific treatment. Vitamin B_{12} is often given as hydroxocobalamin injections but this appears to be mainly for placebo effect. Corticotrophin has been shown to benefit acute retrobulbar neuritis and may help acute exacerbations of the disease generally. Propantheline bromide (probanthine) may control precipitancy of micturition, and diazepam or baclofen reduce painful flexor spasms in paraplegia. Intrathecal phenol injections or tendon transplantation may be indicated when the latter are severe. Physiotherapy can help greatly with spastic weakness, and re-educative exercises with mild degrees of ataxia.

Beyond these symptomatic measures, however, there is very little that can be done to improve prognosis. Hallpike (1980) reviews the treatments currently being evaluated, including diets supplemented with linoleate, diets enriched in polyunsaturated fatty acids, and various means of attempting to alter the immune system in the disease—all so far without proven benefit. Avoidance of fatigue is usually recommended, and the patient should be counselled that pregnancy may carry special hazards. The psychological management of the patient demands tact and great understanding. As discussed on p. 598 psychotherapy may be indicated in certain patients, not only for support but also in the hope that the ventilation and avoidance of emotional difficulties will help to delay fresh relapses of the disorder.

PSYCHIATRIC ASPECTS OF MULTIPLE SCLEROSIS

It is well recognised that mental changes are common in multiple sclerosis and there is a large literature dealing with the subject. Some authorities have emphasised intellectual deterioration, others emotional changes. It is sometimes claimed that the mental picture is characteristic for the disease, euphoria being stressed particularly in this regard. But considerable discrepancies have arisen between one investigation and another and matters of special selection have clearly been operative in many large series.

Attention has also been directed to the possibility that psychological factors may be important in precipitating fresh relapses of the disease. The premorbid personality of sufferers has been said to show certain characteristic features, and arguing from slender foundations attempts have been made to suggest a psychogenic aetiology in certain examples. These matters will be considered in detail below (pp. 597–8).

The historical development of psychiatric interest in multiple sclerosis is traced by Surridge (1969). Early investigators regarded intellectual deficits as the main disturbance, and towards the end of the 19th century there were numerous reports of acute psychoses occurring in the disease. Many of these studies, however, were made before multiple sclerosis could be adequately distinguished from cerebrovascular syphilis. Cottrell and Wilson's study (1926) then had an influential effect. In a consecutive series of 100 outpatients they found that emotional changes were strikingly common, usually taking the form of increased cheerfulness and optimism. A sense of physical well-being was extraordinarily frequent among the patients despite their crippled state. In contrast to these affective changes intellectual disorders were minimal or negligible. The triad of change of mood, a feeling of bodily well-being, and impairment of emotional control was considered to be of greater diagnostic value than any neurological symptom complex. Brain (1930) added hysterical conversion symptoms as further characteristic of the disease, suggesting that multiple sclerosis might predispose in some way to the mental dissociation responsible for hysteria. From then onwards euphoria and hysteria continued to be emphasised in the English literature as typical of mutiple sclerosis.

Meanwhile Ombredane (1929) re-emphasised the occurrence of intellectual deficits in the disorder, finding abnormalities of intellect and memory in 72% of his patients on careful investigation. Disturbances of affect were common in the intellectually deteriorated cases, but consisted chiefly of rapid unstable variations in mood rather than constant shifts towards euphoria or depression. Runge (1928) maintained that depression occurred in the early stage but gave way to euphoria as the disease progressed further. Euphoria was seen simply as a concomitant of intellectual deterioration. This view, in sharp contrast to Cottrell and Wilson's findings, became prominent on the European continent thereafter.

More recent investigators have sought to resolve the dilemma by careful surveys of the psychiatric changes in large series of patients. Surridge's (1969) investigation is exceptional for its thoroughness, and in providing a control group suffering from a different progressive paralysing disease, namely muscular dystrophy. One hundred and eight patients suffering from multiple sclerosis were visited in their normal places of residence, and separate accounts were obtained from informants to aid in the assessments of mood, intellectual deficits and personality changes. The sample was considered to be representative of patients with multiple sclerosis, except for some possible bias towards more severely disabled cases. The duration of illness had varied from 3 to 25 years with more than half lasting 6 to 10 years.

Seventy-five per cent of the multiple sclerosis patients were found to suffer some psychiatric abnormality, compared to less than half of the controls. Intellectual deterioration was present in 61%, varying in degree from mild memory loss to profound global dementia, but of at least moderate severity in 20%. None of the controls showed intellectual impairment. Abnormalities of mood were found in 53% of the subjects compared to 13% of controls. Twenty-seven per cent were depressed, 26% euphoric, and 10% showed exaggeration of emotional expression. Euphoria was almost exclusively seen in patients who were intellectually impaired, and a highly significant correlation emerged between increasing euphoria and increasing intellectual deterioration. Euphoria was also significantly associated with denial of disability which was observed in 11% of the patients. Impaired awareness of disability short of complete denial was found in 31%.

Forty per cent of the multiple sclerosis patients showed personality change compared to 33% of the controls. This was predominantly a change towards irritability in multiple sclerosis patients, whereas the muscular dystrophy controls often showed increased patience and tolerance. Functional psychoses were rare. A schizophreniform psychosis occurred in one patient and manic-depressive mood swings in three.

These findings will be considered in further detail in the sections that follow.

Intellectual Impairment

Surridge's (1969) finding of intellectual deterioration in almost two-thirds of cases is in agreement with Ombredane's (1929) earlier finding. In the majority of cases, however, the deterioration, though detectable on clinical examination, was slight in degree. No doubt the high frequency of intellectual troubles in these series reflects the inclusion of patients with long-standing disease and the care that was taken to examine each patient thoroughly.

The predominant changes found by Surridge were loss of memory for recent events and impairment of conceptual thinking. When marked these deficits were often accompanied by confabulation, perseveration, excessive fatiguability and dysphasic speech disturbances. Profound global dementia was encountered in 7% of patients. Not unexpectedly there was a strong association between increasing intellectual deterioration and increasing physical disability. Psychometric testing on the same population confirmed the presence of both general and specific intellectual impairments (Jambor, 1969). The most marked impairments concerned general intellectual efficiency, non-verbal reasoning and memory functions. Circumstantiality and concrete thinking were often revealed.

Psychometric testing in multiple sclerosis has produced widely discrepant findings, some investigations revealing marked impairments, others virtually none. This is perhaps not surprising when small groups are selected, since the accent of the disease can fall on different parts of the neuraxis. Much will also depend on the stage at which patients are examined. The considerable literature on the topic is reviewed by Marsh (1980). Those finding impairments have repeatedly noted especially poor performance on tests involving motor behaviour, though conceptual ability and memory can also be clearly affected. On timed motor tasks and perceptual tasks, multiple sclerosis patients may perform even worse than brain damaged groups. In general deficits have emerged as commoner in patients with illnesses of long duration, and have sometimes been found to correlate with the degree of physical disability. The latter, however, is not inevitable. In Marsh's (1980) own series there was little correlation between disability ratings and IQ scores. Peyser et al. (1980a) were able to show from cluster analysis that cognitive impairment could be present or absent in groups with varying levels of disablement.

Canter's (1951) study was important in revealing significant impairments even early in the disease. Forty-seven army veterans with multiple sclerosis showed losses on most subtests of the Wechsler Bellevue Battery when retested after a six month period, in contrast to gains among normal controls. The deficits increased with neurological ratings of the degree of disability. In 23 patients comparisons could be made with the scores they had obtained on the Army General Classification Test at entry to the army 4 years earlier; highly significant losses were again revealed despite the fact that all patients were in the early stages of the disease. Ivnik's (1978) longitudinal study has reinforced these results. Repeat testing of a small group of patients, on average 3 years later, showed significant deterioration in a wide range of cognitive functions.

Peyser et al. (1980b) have shown the importance of formal psychometric evaluation if cognitive difficulties are not to be missed. Among patients judged on neurological evaluation to be cognitively intact, half were found to be impaired on Halstead's category test. This test, which has no motor speed component, was poorly performed despite normal verbal subtest scores on the WAIS. Impairment could be seen whether neurological involvement was mild or severe, suggesting that cognitive difficulties were sometimes present from early in the disease. Peyser et al. stress that cognitive impairments in multiple sclerosis can be subtle, need not be apparent to the patient, and are liable to be missed in the routine neurological evaluation.

From the above it seems clear that patients with the disease have not only to adapt to progressive physical disability, but must often do this against a background of progressively diminishing intellect and impaired adaptive capacity. The implications for retraining are obviously important. As Surridge (1969) points out the presence and severity of intellectual deterioration may well be crucial in determining the outcome of efforts at rehabilitation.

The frequency of intellectual impairment is hardly surprising in view of the finding that plaque formation is often widespread within the cerebral hemispheres. Brownell and Hughes (1962) showed that cerebral plaques were visible macroscopically in every one of 22 consecutive cases coming to autopsy. They varied in number from 3 to 225, with an average of 72 plaques per case. All parts of the white matter tended to be equally involved but large plaques showed a predilection for the periventricular areas. Air encephalography (Freeman, 1944) and CT

scanning (Hershey et al., 1979) have shown ventricular dilation in a considerable proportion of patients, and the scan may reveal discrete areas of reduced white matter density indicative of plaques. Hershey et al. found that white matter lucencies and ventricular dilatation correlated with the incidence of mental impairment in their series of 66 patients. Three of the four patients with diffuse cortical atrophy had clinical evidence of dementia. The recent introduction of nuclear magnetic resonance (NMR) has proved even more effective in displaying cerebral components to the disease (Young et al., 1981). In 10 patients examined both by CT scanning and NMR, 5 had shown a total of 19 plaques in the periventricular region on the CT scan; all 10, however, showed lesions with NMR, a further 112 plaques being revealed.

Presentation with dementia is occasionally encountered and can raise important problems of differential diagnosis. Koenig (1968) described 7 patients in whom dementia was the sole or predominant manifestation of the disease, the multiple sclerosis being of a relatively silent variety neurologically. The mental symptoms were indistinguishable from organic dementia due to other causes, though the onset was usually fairly acute with memory loss, confusion, disorientation, or personality change. Some showed slight fluctuations in the level of mental functioning from day to day. Three showed progressive deterioration and only one had a partial remission. Neurological symptoms of brain stem or cord dysfunction had preceded the dementia or accompanied its onset in four cases, but all showed evidence of disseminated central nervous system disease on careful examination. Koenig suggested that 'silent' or unrecognised multiple sclerosis may be a commoner cause of organic dementia than is generally recognised. Young et al. (1976) have reported further examples with intellectual impairment as the presenting symptom or forming a prominent part of the picture from the earliest stages.

Sometimes the rate of progression of dementia is astonishingly rapid as in the case described by Bergin (1957):

A woman of 30 developed brief retrobulbar neuritis followed one year later by diplopia, ataxia and precipitate micturition. Over 3 months she became severely incapacitated, apathetic, retarded and vague. Examination showed a pale left optic disc, fine lateral nystagmus, slight right facial and arm weakness, incoordination of the legs and upgoing plantar responses. The cerebrospinal fluid showed 18 lymphocytes and a paretic Lange curve. One week after admission she became confused, uncooperative and disoriented, doubly incontinent and with gross evidence of intellectual impairment. Two weeks later she could not understand even simple sentences. The EEG showed random irregular slow waves in all areas and the AEG showed moderate ventricular enlargement. Six weeks after admission she was bedfast, making noises but no recognisable words. The only active limb was her left arm which was used to strike out at people and tug at her hair. Within ten weeks she died and post mortem examination showed well-defined plaques throughout the brain, cerebellum, brain stem and cord.

Abnormalities of Mood

A variety of affective changes are common in multiple sclerosis. Euphoria—a bland elevation of mood out of keeping with the patient's physical condition—is widely thought to be the usual picture, but it is now clear that depression is at least as common. Much probably depends on the stage at which the patient is examined and whether some degree of intellectual deterioration has occurred. Depression is mostly the logical and understandable response to the patient's predicament in the earlier stages, whereas euphoria is more typical as the disease progresses. The transition over time from depression to euphoria can sometimes be clearly observed in the individual patient.

Braceland and Giffin (1950) found depression in 20% and euphoria in 10% of cases; Surridge (1969) found depression in 27% and euphoria in 26%. Kahana et al. (1971) in a nation-wide survey of cases in Israel found depression in 6% and euphoria in 5%. Cottrell and Wilson's (1926) earlier discordant finding of depression in 10% but euphoria in 63% remains unexplained; this, however, is the view which has tended to persist in clinical teaching. It is possible that an active coping mechanism of denial may quite often be mistaken for euphoria if enquiry is not made into the patient's subjective state.

Depression appears to be reactive in origin in the majority of cases. Thus in Surridge's material the depressed patients showed no special tendency to intellectual deterioration or denial of disability, in sharp contrast to patients with euphoria. In general, therefore, the psychological impact of the disability and the patient's awareness of his situation appear to be the main determining factors. Examples of marked reactive depression may be encountered immediately the patient learns the nature of the diagnosis and prognosis (Gallineck and Kalinowsky, 1958). Sphincter disturbances are an especially severe psychological trauma, increasing dependency and often meaning the end of sexual relationships.

Impotence, ataxia and visual disturbances were also among the most distressing of the disabilities experienced by Surridge's patients.

Sometimes, however, the depression may at least in part be physiologically determined. Goodstein and Ferrell (1977) observed 3 patients in whom episodes of depression predominated from the outset of the disease and before the diagnosis had been established. No precipitants were apparent, and the response to treatment was poor. Because of this, an organic basis was suspected and multiple sclerosis finally declared itself. Whitlock and Siskind (1980) similarly concluded that depression may sometimes be founded in cerebral pathology. They compared 30 multiple sclerosis patients with equivalently disabled controls suffering from other neurological diseases. The patients with multiple sclerosis were not only more depressed at the time of examination, but had experienced significantly more affective disorder in the year preceding the first signs of the disorder. Many had previously been stable people, and the episodes of depression often had endogenous qualities.

Irrespective of its derivation the degree of depression in multiple sclerosis can be severe, and suicide has been reported in a considerable number of cases. Kahana et al. (1971) estimated that in their material suicide was fourteen times commoner than in the general population of Israel.

Euphoria was defined by Surridge (1969) as a mood of cheerful complacency out of context with the patient's total situation. It differed from the elation of hypomania in being unaccompanied by motor restlessness, increased energy or speeding up of thought processes. All but two of the euphoric patients in his series showed intellectual deterioration, and the group as a whole was significantly more disabled than the depressed or normal groups. Braceland and Giffin (1950) had earlier reported that all patients who showed euphoria gave evidence of widespread cerebral disturbance. In contrast to depression, therefore, euphoria appears to depend essentially on damage to the central nervous system.

Quite often the initial impression of euphoria proves to be misleading, and the evidence of cheerfulness or complacency subsides as the interview progresses. Indeed Surridge found that 8 out of 28 euphoric patients confessed to feeling miserable and depressed despite the strong outward impression that they were unreasonably cheerful. No doubt an element of emotional lability is often associated with euphoria and adds to the difficulty of assessing the patient's true subjective feelings.

Closely related to euphoria is a feeling of increased bodily well-being ('eutonia'). Cottrell and Wilson (1926) reported this in 84% of patients, Pratt (1951) in only 6%. The phenomenon is possibly related not only to changes of mood but also to denial or impaired awareness of disability. Surridge (1969) observed that 11% of his patients overtly denied some aspect of their disability, and another 31% showed impaired awareness to the extent of persistently overlooking some striking symptom in their account. The extent to which such denial depends on intellectual deterioration or on psychological factors has not been clarified.

Disorders of emotional control include true exaggeration of emotional feeling ('lability of affect'), or an exaggeration of expression which is unbacked by an equivalent degree of feeling ('disorder of affective expression'). The latter may indeed be incongruous with the underlying mood and is essentially similar to the disorder of emotional expression seen in pseudobulbar palsy. It can be difficult in reports to differentiate clearly between true lability and disorders of expression. Cottrell and Wilson (1926) found that 95% of cases showed 'facility and amplification of emotional expression' and 13% rapid changes of mood. Braceland and Giffin (1950) reported emotional lability in 18%. Pratt (1951) found that 6% admitted to laughing and 29% to crying more easily than usual, while 16% were noted to laugh unduly readily but were not aware of this themselves. Surridge (1969) found exaggeration of emotional expression but without concomitant lability in 10 per cent of patients. Intellectual deterioration is the usual accompaniment of all such pictures.

Personality Changes

Many of the personality changes reported in multiple sclerosis consist essentially of the mood changes described above, with or without an element of blunting or indifference attributable to intellectual deterioration. Over and above this there is little firm evidence that multiple sclerosis makes a specific imprint on the personality. Braceland and Giffin (1950) found that it was rather the reverse—in the early stages the patient's reaction was shaped by factors in his own premorbid personality and reflected his habitual modes of response to incapacity or stress. Much could also depend on the particular functions impaired and their significance in personal, marital, economic and environmental terms.

In consequence a great variety of reactions may be seen. Some patients become anxious and depressed from the outset, others irritable and others withdrawn. Some seek to belittle their disability and continue to strive in the face of hardship, while others readily accept a dependent role and retreat from all responsibility. Later in the chronic phase, however, the classical signs of organic brain disease may come to overshadow the imprint of the patient's particular personality.

Pratt (1951) could discern no special form of personality change which distinguished multiple sclerosis patients from controls with other organic diseases of the nervous system. Surridge (1969) found that irritability, and to some extent apathy, occurred very much more frequently than in muscular dystrophy controls, both tending to co-exist with intellectual deterioration and probably reflecting damage to the central nervous system. In his material deleterious personality changes resulted in great distress to the relatives and were not infrequently the reason why the families could no longer bear the burden of the patient's care.

Harrower (1950, 1954) has produced one of the few pieces of evidence which suggest that multiple sclerosis patients may come to manifest certain personality traits with unusual frequency. The results were largely derived from a battery of psychological tests including the Rorschach. One hundred and forty-five multiple sclerosis patients were investigated and compared with independent control groups—normals, emotionally disturbed patients, parkinsonian patients and patients with poliomyelitis. In every test there were certain items which served to differentiate the multiple sclerosis patients from the controls. As a group they appeared to be unusually willing to abandon themselves to the dependent role, and to show a remarkable absence of anxiety or preoccupation with bodily functions. They showed a minimum of inner conflict, an excessive cordiality to those around, and an unrealistic tendency to view the world through rose-coloured spectacles. Though emerging clearly in group comparisons these traits did not appear in every patient. It is uncertain whether they are to be regarded as reflections of the premorbid personality or as traits conferred by the disease. But on comparing early and advanced cases Harrower found that the amount of anxiety related to the disease was inversely correlated with the extent of physical handicap. The foregoing observations therefore possibly owe much to the presence of brain damage, which doubtless leaves its mark in these respects to a greater or lesser extent according to the individual's premorbid character structure.

Psychoses in Multiple Sclerosis

The rarity with which multiple sclerosis patients are admitted to mental hospitals has often been commented upon (Malone, 1937; Pratt, 1951). This, however, may be largely attributable to their physical disability preventing the seriously disturbed behaviour which would warrant hospitalisation. Moreover a marked feature of the florid mental symptoms in multiple sclerosis is their tendency to be fleeting and to regress, so that the psychotic disorders which do occur may subside over several months as deterioration advances (Brown and Davis, 1922). Nevertheless psychotic illnesses have been described in the disease, sometimes late in the course but occasionally as a presenting feature.

Malone (1937) reported 10 cases of multiple sclerosis complicated by psychosis—4 with dementia associated with outbursts of rage and paranoid beliefs, 3 with recurrent episodes of psychotic depression, 2 with hypomania and one with paranoid schizophrenia. Gallineck and Kalinowsky (1958) reported 3 patients, one with severe depression, one with catatonia and one with paranoid schizophrenia, all responding successfully to electroconvulsive therapy and appearing to be essentially unrelated to the neurological disorder. They also commented on short-lived organic psychotic reactions developing in the course of the disease. Patients showing alternating mania and depression in association with multiple sclerosis have been described by Crémieux et al. (1959) and Whitlock and Siskind (1980). Langworthy et al. (1941) in a follow-up of 199 cases found that 16 ultimately presented serious behaviour problems which required transfer to a psychiatric hospital, and another 21 had obvious behaviour disturbances which were managed at home.

With regard to schizophrenia Davison and Bagley (1969) have identified 39 acceptable cases in the literature, 27 with paranoid-hallucinatory and 12 with hebephrenic-catatonic illnesses. The symptomatology did not differ appreciably from that of other schizophrenia-like psychoses, except that expansive delusional states seemed to be particularly common, and neurological symptoms such as paraesthesiae were sometimes incorporated into paranoid delusional systems. The psychoses often appeared early in the disease, tending to cluster around the time of the first appearance of neurological abnormalities. This, along with the rarity of a family history of schizophrenia, suggested that the central nervous system disease and the psychosis might not be entirely independent. There was no indication, however, that the overall incidence of schizophrenia in multiple sclerosis exceeded chance expectation.

Presentation with psychosis is rare, but sometimes the early neurological abnormalities are so overshadowed by the mental picture that the true diagnosis is missed. Such cases are obviously important Parker (1956) reported a patient who became apathetic and withdrawn in his early twenties and was diagnosed as suffering from schizophrenia. He showed a slight hesitancy of speech and slight irregular nystagmus but this was ignored at the time. Attempts at treatment and rehabilitation met with no success. A few years later he was fatuous and childish, and by then showed impairment of memory, gross spasticity and pronounced incoordination. He died suddenly and the pathological changes of multiple sclerosis were revealed.

Geocaris (1957) has reported 4 instructive examples of patients admitted with an initial diagnosis of psychosis, 3 with schizophrenia and one with the appearance of severe melancholia, who showed evidence of multiple sclerosis a few weeks or months later. A careful review of the past history in each case showed that symptoms referable to the central nervous system had in fact occurred months or years before the onset of the psychiatric disorder, emphasising the need for careful neurological examination of psychotic patients and a comprehensive review of the past medical history.

Mur et al. (1966) have reported 3 unusual examples in patients over 50 in whom psychotic features dominated the course. One had a paranoid psychosis for 5 years before neurological symptoms appeared in the form of a spastic paresis with dementia; another had a relapsing paranoid syndrome for 11 years accompanied by ataxia of gait and intellectual impairment; and the third had a temporary gait and speech disturbance at the onset of a depressive syndrome which dominated the picture until death. In all three cases the plaques were found to be predominantly in the cerebral hemispheres.

Finally, two patients reported by Matthews (1979) are important in drawing attention to the possibility that acute mental disturbance, remitting completely, may sometimes be the initial manifestation of multiple sclerosis:

In the first, a girl of 19, the presentation was with intermittent confusion and episodes of markedly bizarre behaviour, leading to a diagnosis of probable schizophrenia. No neurological abnormalities were apparent on examination. Epileptic fits developed during a course of ECT, leading to lumbar puncture which revealed mild pleocytosis in the cerebrospinal fluid. The EEG was diffusely abnormal, and she was treated with phenytoin. Over the course of the next few weeks she recovered completely, the EEG also reverting towards normality. Thereafter she remained well for 3 years. Symptoms typical of multiple sclerosis then made an appearance, the disease following a relapsing and remitting course over the next few years.

The second patient developed depression of acute onset at the age of 24. She became increasingly withdrawn, self-neglectful and intermittently incontinent of urine and faeces. The tendon reflexes were noted to be increased in the lower limbs and the plantar responses were extensor. Examination of the cerebrospinal fluid showed abnormalities compatible with multiple sclerosis and the EEG showed a marked excess of slow activity bilaterally. Her mental state varied greatly. At times she was almost normally communicative; at others she gave bizarre replies to questions and had outbursts of shouting and kicking. Treatment with prednisolone led to gradual neurological and mental improvement, the patient becoming entirely normal some 3 months from the date of onset. Several months after recovery she developed unilateral optic neuritis and bilateral abnormalities of the visual evoked responses, clearly indicative of multiple sclerosis.

Hysteria and Multiple Sclerosis

The relationship between hysteria and multiple sclerosis has absorbed a good deal of attention. In the early stages considerable difficulty can sometimes arise in making a firm diagnostic differentiation. Later in the established disease hysterical conversion reactions have been claimed to be especially common. It has furthermore been argued that there may be some fundamental relationship between the two disorders, with common antecedents and perhaps even shared pathophysiological mechanisms.

Brain (1930) suggested that hysterical conversion symptoms, in the form of paresis and ataxia, seemed to occur more often in multiple sclerosis than with any other organic disease of the nervous system. In two of his cases he noted that hysterical fugues had occurred early in the course of the illness. Pratt (1951) however could find no evidence that hysteria was a characteristic feature of the disease. In fact conversion hysteria was observed only twice in his series of 100 patients, compared to 3 examples in controls suffering from other disorders of the nervous system.

Wilson (1940) discounted any special relationship between multiple sclerosis and hysteria and suggested that when conversion symptoms were present this was mere coincidence. But he recognised a 'subjective' or 'predisseminated' type of multiple sclerosis in which the symptoms were solely subjective, and where a diagnosis of hysteria was apt to be made. Typical complaints included paraesthesiae, difficulty in using a limb, giddiness, fatiguability or general shakiness, all unbacked by unequivocal signs of organic nervous disease. Suspicion might nonetheless be aroused by minimal signs such as a defective abdominal reflex, nystagmoid jerking, or transient ankle clonus. Aring (1965), however, suggests that there is no need in practical terms to separate Wilson's predisseminated type of multiple sclerosis from conversion hysteria, and indeed while symptoms are confined to the subjective sphere there can be no unequivocal way of making the distinction.

Herman and Sandok (1967) report a patient who illustrates the diagnostic difficulties which can arise, and the impossibility of separating psychogenic from organic symptoms at a certain stage in the disorder. In retrospect conversion symptoms clearly co-existed along with active multiple sclerosis, both aspects relapsing when the patient was subjected to emotional stress:

A 20-year-old enlisted man became homesick and reported to the army doctor with complaints of staggering gait, weakness, numbness and paraesthesiae. On examination he showed astasia abasia, poor coordination easily corrected by reinforcement, decreased sensation in all modalities, 'giving way' on testing muscle strength, and entirely normal reflexes. Nine lymphocytes per ml. were present in the cerebrospinal fluid but otherwise laboratory studies showed no abnormalities. The disorder was considered to be non-organic and he was transferred to a psychiatrist who found emotional immaturity and belle indifference. He improved suddenly and dramatically, though many minor complaints persisted.

A few months later he was again admitted with a diagnosis of a conversion reaction, complaining of shocks down his body on neck flexion ('Lhermitte's sign'). He became asymptomatic when told that he would not be returning to the Far East. Next year after an emotional upset with his father he developed numbness of the left cheek, recurrence of Lhermitte's sign and dragging of the left foot. Examination showed left hypalgesia of non-anatomical distribution, motor weakness of a non-organic type, a bizarre shuffling gait and classical belle indifference. Over the next week, however, severe neurological deterioration occurred with abundant organic signs characteristic of multiple sclerosis. Even thereafter he had an episode in which vibration sense was split over the sternum, skull and spine, in association with a hemisensory deficit with transition at the midline.

Langworthy, rather than establishing a dichotomy, proposed a relationship between hysteria and multiple sclerosis (Langworthy *et al.*, 1941; Langworthy, 1948, 1950). He stressed that the difficulty in making the distinction in early cases was not only due to the inconsistency of the neurological findings but also because the patients often showed a personality structure consonant with the diagnosis of hysteria. The mood was often inappropriate to the situation, and the *belle indifference* of hysteria shared much in common with the denial and complacency of patients with multiple sclerosis. In a detailed study of four women he emphasised their emotional immaturity, particularly in sexual adjustment, and the resentment and hostility which underlay their seemingly passive relationships. Organic symptoms had often first appeared or become accentuated during upheavals in their interpersonal relationships, and especially at times when their husbands had become more self-assertive and dominating.

Pursuing the argument further, Langworthy suggested that in certain multiple sclerosis patients conflicts and anxieties might be converted into physical symptoms in much the same manner as in conversion hysteria. The florid symptoms of conversion hysteria were not unlike those of multiple sclerosis and might sometimes, in some manner, 'gel' into the organic changes characteristic of the disease. He noted that patients with multiple sclerosis often showed great vasomotor instability during stress and at times when new symptoms appeared, and tentatively proposed that vascular changes in the brain, related to the patient's neurotic difficulties, might ultimately predispose to the organic changes of the plaque. Support for these suggestions has not, however, been forthcoming. It would seem, moreover, that the personality constellation described by Langworthy applies to only a small proportion of patients.

Premorbid Personality in Multiple Sclerosis

The premorbid personality of multiple sclerosis patients has usually been found to be unremarkable, though certain authors have suggested that there may be a characteristic dynamic profile. Langworthy's description of an 'hysterical' character structure, outlined just above, was further extended by Grinker *et al.* (1950). From a study of 26 patients it emerged that the majority had shown considerable emotional immaturity throughout their adult lives. An excessive need for love and affection was coupled with a paramount desire to please and be approved. Frustrations and negative feelings were accordingly repressed. To the external view the person had been happy-go-lucky and easy natured, but this was associated with deeply concealed inner tensions. It is hard, of course, to gauge how typical such a personality constellation may be of multiple sclerosis patients generally. It may be largely the product of observations on a selected group who have undergone detailed psychotherapy.

Control studies have attempted to assess the situation more thoroughly, but have produced divergent results. Pratt (1951) compared 100 multiple sclerosis patients with 100 controls, matched for age and sex and suffering from other organic diseases of the nervous system. He could find no clear evidence that the premorbid personality was in any way remarkable. Dynamic formulations were not attempted, and comparisons were restricted to certain personality categories and traits. No clear differences emerged between patients and controls in relation to Sheldon's personality types, the incidence of neurotic traits, or the amount of aggression as measured by the Thematic Apperception Test. No differences were found in the incidence of good or bad childhood environments or of periods of separation from the parents.

Philippopoulos *et al.* (1958), however, have produced very different results which are more in line with Grinker *et al.*'s observations. Forty multiple sclerosis patients were compared with 40 controls, matched for age, sex and social background (17 healthy controls and 23 suffering from cervical spondylosis and other cord disease). Striking differences were noted—70% of multiple sclerotics had had unhappy childhood backgrounds compared to 20% of the controls, and only 55% were socially well adjusted premorbidly compared to 85% of controls. Detailed observations suggested that the majority of the multiple sclerosis patients had previously been emotionally and sexually immature, and deficient in long-term goals and perseverance. They had usually grown up in an atmosphere of emotional deprivation and had erected psychological defences against feelings of being rejected. Almost all showed conflicts over aggression and an inordinate need for affection. Forty-five per cent showed hysterical, anxiety or obsessive-compulsive symptoms, 30% showed personality disorders, 10% had been psychotic or borderline psychotic, and only 15% could be regarded as emotionally well adjusted. Thus although no specific personality type emerged, multiple sclerosis appeared to be a disease which occurred predominantly in chronically anxious persons who had shown evidence of emotional and psychosexual immaturity. The precise implication of these findings, if confirmed, remains uncertain, but the dynamic constellation described would certainly lead the subjects to be unusually vulnerable to emotionally traumatic experiences, and as described below it is possible that these may influence the course of the disease.

Influence of Emotions on the Disease

Physical and emotional traumata have often been regarded as precipitants of multiple sclerosis, or as provocative factors which help to determine relapses. Braceland and Giffin (1950) noted that all types of emotional situations tended to be blamed in this way by patients, but judged that most of the psychic traumas described were unlikely to be significant.

Pratt's (1951) study set out to examine the situation in detail. Thirty-eight per cent of multiple sclerosis patients had had some emotional stress in the months antedating the onset, compared to 26% of controls suffering from other nervous system disease. The difference fell just short of statistical significance, but in most cases the stresses had not been unduly severe. With regard to later relapses 25% were preceded by emotional stress, a figure virtually identical with the proportion of controls who had stress antedating their illness. Thus in the group as a whole there was no clear evidence to incriminate emotional factors in causing relapses. Nevertheless in individual cases a highly suggestive relationship was sometimes observed. In one patient a relapse occurred within an hour of receiving bad news by letter. In another numbness developed in the legs immediately after a narrow escape from a motor cycle accident, and in another the right arm became useless the morning after breaking off an engagement. On the other hand many cases could be identified where emotional upheavals had not been followed by relapse.

Short of major relapses some patients found that emotional disturbances, often of a specific kind, led to transient exacerbation of the symptoms of a pre-existing lesion. This was significantly commoner than among the controls and the examples were often clear-cut and impressive. Altogether 18% of multiple sclerosis patients noted exacerbation invariably, and within one minute of the emotional upheaval. In different patients, for example, worry led invariably to increased unsteadiness, anger to weakness of a leg, fear or quarrelling to weakness of the legs

lasting several hours, self-consciousness to blurring of vision or exacerbation of diplopia. Such observations raise the possibility that short-lived disturbances of function, occasioned by emotional stress, may sometimes lead on to more lasting structural changes. Pratt suggested that they are possibly mediated by vascular mechanisms.

Philippopoulos et al. (1958), in the study already outlined, obtained more definite evidence of emotional precipitation, both of the initial manifestations and of subsequent relapses. Eighty-eight per cent of multiple sclerosis patients had had traumatic life experiences preceding the onset, compared to only 17% of the controls with neurological disease. Ten per cent had had an acute emotional trauma, the other 78% prolonged emotional stress. Examples included prolonged sickness in a family member, the imposition of extra responsibilities or the accumulation of debts, the common feature being the arousal of anxiety.

Relapses often appeared to be precipitated by similar emotional problems, sometimes with an interval so short that the connection could scarcely be doubted. In others relapses coincided with flare-ups of chronic emotional disturbance. Philippopoulos et al. tentatively proposed that exacerbations of multiple sclerosis might be occasioned by emotionally conditioned vasomotor responses or other physical or chemical changes in the central nervous system.

If these findings are accepted, careful on-going social and psychological support will clearly have an important part to play in the management of patients with multiple sclerosis, and may sometimes serve to avert or delay relapses. The case for supportive psychotherapy and the principles to be followed are fully discussed by Langworthy (1950) and Langworthy and LeGrand (1952).

Schilder's Disease
('Diffuse Cerebral Sclerosis', 'Encephalitis Periaxialis Diffusa')

The generic term 'diffuse cerebral sclerosis' has been applied to a variety of conditions in which widespread demyelination and gliosis occurs in the white matter of the hemispheres. Histological examination allows a more precise classification, and it seems that reported cases have included examples of familial leucodystrophy and subacute sclerosing leucoencephalitis in addition to cases pathologically related to multiple sclerosis (Greenfield and Norman, 1963). Greenfield and Norman suggest that the latter is the most appropriate restricted use for the term Schilder's disease.

Most cases have been reported in children but adults may also be affected. Both sporadic and familial examples are encountered. The varied neurological manifestations include spastic paraparesis, sensory changes, and often progressive cerebral blindness. Central deafness may also occur. Mental functions are affected early and severely, dullness and apathy progressing to dementia and stupor. The disease usually runs a rapid course with death within a few months, though some patients survive for two or three years. The cerebrospinal fluid pressure may be raised; often with slight elevation of protein and occasionally a moderate pleocytosis. The CT scan usually shows a characteristic picture, with symmetrical, sharply defined, low density lesions in the occipital or frontal regions.

Pathologically the brain shows large areas of brownish or greyish softening in the white matter, usually maximally involving the occipital lobes and spreading forwards through the hemispheres symmetrically (Greenfield and Norman, 1963). Affected areas are irregularly rounded and do not encroach on the cortex. Similar focal areas may be found in the brain stem. Microscopically they show complete demyelination, and in the older lesions axonal destruction as well. Astrocytic proliferation is marked. Shrinkage in chronic lesions may lead to local dilatations of the ventricles. In the smaller lesions the picture is indistinguishable from that of multiple sclerosis.

Psychiatric Aspects

A point of unusual psychiatric interest has been the occurrence of pictures indistinguishable from schizophrenia in patients who have later shown Schilder's disease at autopsy. Several such reports have now accumulated, mostly in patients who had displayed little or nothing by way of neurological disturbance during life. The cerebral pathological findings were in consequence usually unexpected.

Ferraro (1934, 1943) reported two examples in adolescent boys who had been clinically diagnosed as cases of hebephrenic schizophrenia. In the first the disorder progressed over 2 or 3 years with features only of a functional psychosis—there were no neurological abnormalities and no mental features of an organic psychosis at any stage. The second showed fleeting and inconstant neurological abnormalities early in the illness, and obvious intellectual

deterioration during the months immediately preceding death $3\frac{1}{2}$ years later.

Holt and Tedeschi's (1943) patient showed a classical catatonic picture and died within a week. There were no abnormal neurological signs. He had had a previous episode of acute catatonic schizophrenia 18 years previously, suggesting that the disease process had merely served to re-activate a tendency towards the psychosis. Roizin et al.'s (1945) patient similarly showed the picture of catatonic schizophrenia, with auditory hallucinations and periods of stupor alternating with outbursts of impulsive destructive behaviour. There were again no neurological abnormalities and the patient died within a few weeks. Jankowski (1963) described a chronic example in a man of 28 with repeated hospitalisations over four years prior to death. Severe affective changes of hebephrenic type developed gradually and without discernible intellectual deterioration. Late in the illness the pupillary reactions to light were lost and he complained of impaired vision, but the cerebrospinal fluid remained normal.

Ramani (1981) has reported yet another example, this time diagnosed by CT scan during life and subsequently confirmed by biopsy:

A man of 34 had suffered from chronic schizophrenia, refractory to treatment, for 5 years. It had started with mood swings, leading on to progressive withdrawal, disorganisation of thinking, and paranoid delusions and hallucinations. He showed bizarre posturing at times, and echolalia. There was no family history of schizophrenia. On examination the only neurological abnormalities were bilateral extensor plantar responses and a suggestion of a snout reflex. The CT scan showed large symmetrically situated low density areas in the frontal regions.

In most of these examples the accent of the pathological process was on the frontal lobes of the brain, in contrast to the usual predominant involvement of the occipital lobes. This may have accounted for the atypical presentation and development of the disease.

Tuberous Sclerosis
('Tuberose Sclerosis', 'Epiloia')

The classical picture of tuberous sclerosis includes the triad of mental defect, epilepsy and adenoma sebaceum. Associated abnormalities may include benign visceral tumours of the heart, kidney or intestine, also retinal tumours ('phakomas') which appear on ophthalmoscopy as flat oval or circular patches of a greyish-white colour. Other congenital defects may be present such as hare lip or spina bifida. Bodily growth is often considerably retarded.

The disorder appears to represent a combination of developmental abnormalities of some tissues and overgrowth of others commencing early in foetal life. Ectodermal, endodermal and mesodermal structures can all be involved. It occurs familially, though sporadic cases due to new mutation are not uncommon. The responsible gene is thought to be dominant, though with modifying genes of favourable effect which account for the variability in the clinical picture (Gunther and Penrose, 1935).

Clinical Manifestations

The first clinical manifestations are usually in infancy or childhood. Epilepsy or mental defect are the common presenting features. All varieties of epilepsy may be seen—grand mal, petit mal, Jacksonian seizures or temporal lobe seizures. However patients are increasingly reported who first come to attention much later in life, sometimes on account of late onset epilepsy or sometimes when characteristic skin lesions or X-ray signs have been discovered. Thus it is now recognised that abortive and incomplete cases are perhaps almost as common as the fully developed major disease; epilepsy and adenoma sebaceum may occur without mental defect, or cerebral forms without skin manifestations, or monosymptomatic forms showing adenoma sebaceum alone or visceral tumours alone.

The adenoma sebaceum consists of yellowish-red or brown papules and nodules, chiefly in the naso-labial folds and sometimes extending in a butterfly distribution over the cheeks and bridge of the nose. The name given to the rash is a misnomer since the papules consist largely of hypoplastic connective and vascular tissue. More critical to the diagnosis are 'hypomelanotic macules', seen typically as leaf-shaped dull white patches, particularly over the trunk and buttocks (Rogers, 1979). These may be detected even from infancy by screening with a Wood's lamp which emits light of the appropriate wavelength. Other skin changes may include small pedunculated dermal tags, café au lait patches similar to those of von Recklinghausen's disease, and 'shagreen patches' consisting of irregular areas of raised roughened skin several inches in diameter.

In general the earlier the disorder becomes apparent the more rapid is the course. When the disease is declared in childhood it is usually progressive, often with death in the second or third decade. Death is likely to result from status epilepticus, cerebral tumour or renal disease. Exceptions are seen, however, and even the fully developed disease may undergo long periods of apparent arrest. Patients with partial forms may survive with little disability into old age.

The cerebral changes may be detectable radiologically. Skull X-ray may show numerous discrete irregular intracranial calcifications ('brain stones'). Air encephalography can show nodular protrusions into the ventricles as a characteristic 'candle guttering' effect. CT scanning is now the investigation of choice for early confirmation of the diagnosis (Houser and McLeod, 1979). Calcified subependymal nodules encroaching on the ventricles are the most valuable sign; ventricular dilatation, hamartomatus foci, cortical tubers or astrocytomas may also be seen.

The electroencephalogram is usually abnormal in patients with mental deficiency or currently active epilepsy, but can be quite normal in others. No specific pattern is diagnostic. In general it provides a good indication of the severity of cerebral dysfunction. Dickerson and Hellman (1952) surveyed institutionalised patients and found that two-thirds showed EEG features indicative of one or more focal lesions. Westmoreland (1979) reported abnormalities in 85% of 138 patients. Epileptiform features were most common but a great variety of other changes occurred. The abnormalities were related to the age of onset of seizures and to the severity of mental deficiency.

Pathology

The striking pathological change in the brain consists of pearly white nodules, 0.5–3 cm in diameter, situated along the ventricular surfaces and sometimes over the cortical surface as well. The nodules are hard, like rubber or potato (hence 'tuberous') and may contain minute calcareous fragments. Histologically they contain dense glial material and curious large cells which are thought to derive from undifferentiated spongioblasts. Frank neoplastic changes may be apparent in the form of glioblastoma multiforme or spongioblastoma. Short of this the nodular protrusions are occasionally sufficiently large to obstruct the flow of cerebrospinal fluid within the ventricles. The intervening brain tissue is often markedly disorganised with abnormal cytoarchitecture, reduction of neurones and increased gliosis. The cerebellum and cord may be similarly affected.

Psychiatric Manifestations

In addition to the disabilities which result from epilepsy the principal psychiatric manifestations are intellectual impairment, sometimes progressive, and psychotic disorders.

Mental retardation usually dates from the earliest years of life, but some patients are normal in the early years and then deterioration sets in. The degree of impairment varies from severe subnormality to mild retardation. Many of the lower-grade patients show stigmata such as simian hands, misshapen ears, or prominent epicanthic folds (Critchley and Earl, 1932).

However examples of the condition are now recognised in which there is no intellectual impairment at all. Kofman and Hyland (1959) reported a man of 62 who showed adenoma sebaceum, a phakoma in the left retina, intracranial calcification and focal epilepsy, but whose intelligence was normal. The adenoma sebaceum had first been noticed at 26 and the fits at 31. There had been no clinical progression over the years that followed. Duvoisin and Vinson (1961) reported three cases, one with an excellent scholastic record and the others with intelligence quotients within the average range. Two had presented with unrelated disorders and were diagnosed on account of adenoma sebaceum and intracranial calcification; the third had epilepsy and the air encephalogram showed characteristic intraventricular masses. Other patients dying suddenly with epilepsy have been found to show the characteristic brain changes when these were not at all suspected during life. Among 160 patients reported from the Mayo Clinic approximately one-third have proved to be of normal intelligence (Gomez, 1979).

Intellectual defect or deterioration may be complicated by marked emotional instability or behaviour disorder. Psychotic pictures are quite commonly seen. Thus Critchley and Earl (1932), reporting institutionalised patients, described the essential psychological feature as a combination of intellectual defect with a 'primitive form of catatonic schizophrenia'. The intensity of the psychosis was independent of the degree of intellectual impairment, though the two were so inextricably intertwined that the relative parts played by each were difficult to determine. Similarly, Brain *et al.* (1951) stated that most epiloic patients finally reached a mental condition comparable to an advanced stage of schizophrenia. It is now clear that psychotic developments, like the mental defect, are by no means as invariable as these writers believed. Never-

theless the following case reported by Zlotlow and Kleiner (1965) illustrates the type of schizophrenia-like picture that may be encountered:

The patient had fits from the age of 4 to 7 but thereafter excelled at school. Pimples developed on the nose and cheeks from 15 onwards. In adolescence he became shy, solitary and withdrawn, and at 20 a severe mental change occurred—he became nervous and easily upset, with frequent tantrums and childish unreasonable behaviour. Seizures became frequent and he appeared slightly dull mentally. Adenoma sebaceum was by this time well developed, the EEG showed abnormalities over the left hemisphere and the air encephalogram showed slight ventricular dilatation.

The mental condition worsened, with fear of leaving the house, feelings that he was losing control of his limbs, and beliefs that people were laughing and talking about him. In hospital at 23 he was retarded, emotionally dull, and spoke slowly in whispers. He denied auditory hallucinations but saw 'moving pictures' before his eyes. The IQ was low (70) with evidence of deterioration. He remained seclusive and withdrawn, with frequent mood swings, irritability and overactivity.

At 34 he was regarded as a chronic schizophrenic, often incontinent, speaking incoherently, and with long episodes of mutism. Periods of irritable excitement alternated with catatonic stupor. He remained essentially unchanged over the following years. Skull X-ray now showed small calcifications in the pineal region and a number of globular vacuoles in the frontal and temporal bones. The EEG showed much disorganised slow activity. He was untestable psychometrically.

Friedreich's Ataxia

Friedreich's ataxia is the commonest of the spinocerebellar ataxias and one of the commonest of the hereditary diseases of the nervous system. It occurs both sporadically and familially, several siblings often being affected together. Among unaffected family members abortive forms may be found, sometimes showing little more than pes cavus or kyphoscoliosis. The mode of inheritance is usually recessive (Pratt, 1967).

Clinical Features

The onset is typically in the first or second decades of life. Unsteadiness of gait may at first be mistaken for the clumsiness of adolescence. With progression the gait becomes broad based and lurching, action tremor appears in the arms and titubation may develop in the head. The trunk may eventually be implicated rendering even sitting difficult.

Coarse nystagmus is common, and the speech dysarthric. Cerebellar dysfunction shows also in generalised hypotonia and asynergia of movement. Weakness and wasting sometimes develop distally in the limbs and the tendon reflexes are eventually lost. The plantar responses are upgoing, however, indicating pyramidal tract involvement. Sphincter control is usually unaffected until late in the disease. Posterior column changes are manifest in defective vibration and position sense though other sensory modalities are usually intact.

Characteristic deformities with kyphoscoliosis or pes cavus are found in almost all cases, the latter sometimes long antedating other manifestations. Optic atrophy occurs occasionally and myocardial involvement is common.

The disease pursues a slowly progressive course though in occasional cases long stationary periods are encountered. Incomplete and abortive cases also occur in which the condition is static or progresses very slowly indeed. In the typical case severe incapacity with inability to walk is reached within five years of onset, and few patients live more than twenty years after the disease is declared.

Pathology

The brunt of the pathology falls on the long ascending and descending tracts of the cord. Degeneration is most marked in the posterior columns, spinocerebellar tracts and pyramidal tracts. Fibrous gliosis replaces the atrophied fibres. Atrophy may also be seen in the dorsal roots of the cord and the tracts and nuclei of the lower brain stem. Purkinje cell loss has been reported in the cerebellum, also atrophy of the dentate nuclei and superior cerebellar peduncles (Oppenheimer, 1976). The myocardium may show hypertrophy of muscle fibres and fibrosis.

Psychiatric Aspects

Psychiatric interest in the disorder has centred chiefly on the intellectual impairment noted in some patients, and on the severe mental disturbances which occasionally arise.

Intellectual impairment has been reported in some series of patients but not in others. The conflicting evidence, reviewed by Davies (1949a), is probably attributable to the differing criteria used for the diagnosis of Friedreich's ataxia and for distinguishing it from other forms of heredo-cerebellar ataxia.

Friedreich himself noted an absence of mental defect in his cases, but later workers suggested that a considerable proportion showed mental deterioration, possibly associated with an extension of the pathological process to the cerebral cortex. Bell and Carmichael (1939) collected 242 families with the disease from the literature and noted that mental deficiency had been present in almost a quarter. This varied in degree from idiocy to mild dullness and childishness, the grade of defect tending to be similar in different retarded members of a given family. Severe retardation appeared in the main to be confined to family members afflicted with the neurological disorder, and had usually been conspicuous from the early stages. Sjögren (1943) concluded that 15% of 84 cases showed oligophrenia and 58% progressive dementia.

Davies (1949a), in a careful study of 20 patients, found no case with mental defect of severe degree. The range of intelligence test scores suggested that mental deficiency was no commoner than in the general population, the mean IQ of the group being 101. But in some cases there were minor indications of a dementing process—impairments were sometimes demonstrable in recent memory, attention and concentration, and progressive matrices scores were consistently low in comparison to vocabulary scores. Similar findings did not emerge in a control group of chronic invalids suffering from rheumatic and cardiac disorders. Thus Davies concluded that Friedreich's ataxia patients are initially no different intellectually from the general population, but that as a group they tend to show mild but significant cognitive decline. This appeared to set in early and to be non-progressive, in that it showed no correlation with age or length of illness.

Personality abnormalities are sometimes marked and an association with juvenile delinquency has occasionally been noted. Some of Davies' patients were extremely irritable with episodes of mute, resentful behaviour, while others showed a surprising contentment and serenity (Davies, 1949b, 1949c). A tendency to deny or belittle their disability was sometimes evident. One patient, for example, showed a lofty superiority in the face of severe handicap and affected great disdain for a similarly affected sister. Occasionally there was excessive preoccupation with religion or a turning towards mystical modes of expression.

In a disease which appears so early in life it is hard to assign a precise aetiology to personality abnormalities. Davies felt that the predominant traits were often clearly related to the effect of a disabling disease upon a particular personality, rather than being in any way specific to the illness. Environmental factors were seen to be important, especially in patients confined to the home and exposed to the dominance of parents or siblings. But a high incidence of theta rhythms in the electroencephalograms suggested that the disease process may also have interfered in some way with normal cerebral maturation and thus contributed to the personality disturbances shown.

Psychotic developments have long been recognised in patients with Friedreich's ataxia. Many different forms of abnormal mental state are described but mostly in isolated cases so that the overall incidence is hard to assess.

The form of disturbance which has attracted most attention is a schizophrenia-like illness characterised by paranoid delusions and outbursts of excitement. Davies (1949b) describes a case which illustrates many of the features stressed in the literature— aggressive impulsive behaviour, paranoid beliefs, nocturnal hallucinations and episodes of clouding of consciousness:

A boy of 15 came from a family in which two members showed pes·cavus and two others were subject to attacks of depression. He developed scoliosis, ataxia and titubation of the head at 13. At 15 he became stubborn and irritable, started housebreaking and absconded from home. Four months later he tried to poison his father and bought a rope with which to hang his step-mother. Later that month he was found wandering in a state of confusion.

He had been observed to behave strangely at school where, following a retrosternal 'feeling of excitement', he would bang desks and shout for several minutes, subsequently having no recollection of this behaviour. In bed he had seen visions before falling asleep, often of a diminutive man in ruffles and buckled shoes who would utter the word 'Transformation'.

On admission to hospital he showed advanced features of Friedreich's ataxia, was unhappy and tearful, and claimed that his father and step-mother were plotting against him. Attention, concentration and memory were unimpaired. During four months in hospital he remained paranoid and subject to sudden outbursts of rage. The electroencephalogram was grossly abnormal with theta waves predominantly in the right temporo-occipital region. Towards the end of his stay he suddenly became euphoric, denied his hatred of his family and was discharged.

He worked well as a laboratory technician for 6 months then again had a fugue-like episode. One month later he attacked his family, threw vitriol over a neighbour, and was commited to a psychiatric hospital.

Such severe psychotic pictures have sometimes been labelled 'Freidreich's psychosis'. It seems unlikely, however, that they are in any way specific for the disease. Some appear to be schizophrenic illnesses, occurring in families already tainted with schizophrenia, whereas others may represent the paranoid hallucinatory states of temporal lobe epilepsy. Davies (1949b) and Davison and Bagley (1969) review the evidence available, which proves insufficient to decide whether or not any fundamental relationship with organic cerebral disease can be upheld.

Other disturbances which may be encountered include depressive episodes, often reactive in nature and responsive to treatment, and episodes of clouding of consciousness intimately related to epileptic disturbances (Davies, 1949b).

Motor Neurone Disease
(Amyotrophic Lateral Sclerosis)

Motor neurone disease (or amyotrophic lateral sclerosis) is a disorder of unknown aetiology, commoner in males than females and beginning usually between the ages of 50 and 70. It consists of a combination of muscular atrophy of lower motor neurone type together with spasticity due to corticospinal tract damage. The precise clinical picture depends on the relative prominence of symptoms of upper and lower motor neurone lesions.

The onset is insidious, usually with atrophy of the small hand muscles. The thenar and hypothenar eminences are often the first to be affected. Slow progression comes to involve the arms and legs symmetrically, atrophy being accompanied by prominent fascicular twitching. Spasticity is usually most marked in the legs, with hyperactive reflexes and upgoing plantar responses. The combination of upper and lower motor neurone signs is highly characteristic, exaggerated tendon reflexes being found along with considerable muscular atrophy. There are no sensory changes and the sphincters are rarely affected.

Sometimes atrophy is seen alone without spasticity ('progressive muscular atrophy'). Sometimes the accent is on the bulbar nuclei from the outset ('progressive bulbar palsy'), with atrophy and fasciculation of the tongue, paralysis of the vocal cords and difficulty with deglutition and articulation. Lesions of the corticospinal tracts above the medulla frequently produce an added element of 'pseudobulbar palsy' with loss of emotional control, a hyperactive jaw-jerk, and spastic dysarthria and dysphagia.

The course is invariably progressive, but the rate varies from case to case. Most patients survive for two or three years but rarely longer, death resulting from bulbar involvement or weakness of the muscles of respiration.

The pathological changes consist of degeneration of the anterior horn cells and lateral tracts of the cord with secondary gliosis. The pyramids in the medulla also show progressive degeneration. Affected muscles show denervation atrophy. In the brain there may be loss of Betz cells and degeneration of the pyramidal layers of the precentral cortex. It would appear that in a considerable proportion of patients abnormal gliosis can be detected in the cortex and subcortical nuclear masses, with atrophy sometimes particularly affecting the frontal lobes (Brownell et al., 1970; Hudson, 1981).

Information about aetiology is scanty. Toxic, nutritional and metabolic factors have been considered but no firm evidence has been forthcoming. A past history of poliomyelitis in childhood has been reported as unduly common, but the significance of this is uncertain (Mulder et al., 1972). A family history is found in a very small proportion of cases but genetic factors do not appear to be influential in the disease generally. An exception lies in the island of Guam, and neighbouring islands in the Western Pacific, where there is an astonishingly high incidence of the disease, sometimes with marked familial occurrence. Even so some exogenous factor is thought to be likely in addition to genetic susceptibility. The disorder in Guam bears a close relationship to the 'parkinsonism-dementia complex' as discussed further below (p. 605).

Psychiatric Aspects

Precipitation of the disease by physical or emotional trauma has occasionally been suggested but without good evidence (Grinker and Sahs, 1966). The majority of patients appear to show little by way of psychiatric disturbance, except perhaps for understandable depression due to their progressive incapacitation, or emotional lability resulting from pseudobulbar palsy. Scattered examples of dementia in association with the disease have been reported, also occasional patients with paranoid or schizophrenia-like psychoses. As discussed below, however, there is little reason to view such disturbances as an integral part of the disease.

Emotional lability and loss of emotional control may be extreme when an element of pseudobulbar palsy is part of the picture. Out of 101 cases Ziegler (1930) reported explosive laughing or crying in 19, all except one of whom had signs of brain stem involvement. Several patients described clearly that their subjective emotional state was at variance with such reactions. One patient, besides weeping spasmodically, had violent and uncontrollable outbursts of rage.

Depression in the course of the disease is reported to be common by some observers but surprisingly rare by others. Brown and Mueller (1970) studied ten patients intensively, and found that though all knew about the prognosis none of them spontaneously expressed despair or hopelessness. The lack of depressive affect was sometimes bizarre when patients were discussing their progressive deterioration. Others sought to deny the implications of the disease and went to great lengths to ignore their disability. In premorbid personality and life style Brown and Mueller found evidence of an habitual pattern of active mastery over the environment, and a lifelong tendency to exclude unpleasant affects from conscious awareness. The reactions to the disease appeared to represent continued attempts at denial of depressive and anxious feelings. In support of their findings they produced evidence from a Multiple Affect Adjective Check List that unpleasant items were avoided to a significantly greater extent than by other dying or severely ill patients.

Brown and Mueller also discuss the evidence that patients with amyotrophic lateral sclerosis may show insulin resistance and decreased glucose utilization in a manner similar to patients with severe depressive illnesses. These metabolic abnormalities are said to be reversed by amitriptyline in patients with amyotrophic lateral sclerosis and in those depressives who achieve resolution of affective disorder. Amitriptyline has also been reported to reduce the fasciculations and motor weakness in amyotrophic lateral sclerosis. The implications of these findings are unclear. Brown and Mueller tentatively propose that unresolved or denied depression may play a role in the aetiology or maintenance of symptoms in the disease, but at best the evidence must be regarded as slender. The beneficial effect of amtriptyline, if confirmed, could equally well rest on metabolic actions of the drug which have nothing to do with its antidepressant effect.

The scattered examples of dementia and psychotic illness in association with amyotrophic lateral sclerosis are reviewed by van Bogaert (1925), Wechsler and Davison (1932) and Davison and Bagley (1969). Dementia is clearly rare, the great majority of patients appearing to retain unimpaired intellect throughout. A recent study, however, has raised the possibility that with careful testing certain deficits in memory and frontal lobe function may be revealed (David and Gillham, 1986). Hudson (1981) reviews the literature on patients who develop overt dementia and/or parkinsonism along with the disease, autopsy evidence then pointing to more substantial cortical and subcortical degenerative changes than in the classical disorder. Spongiform changes may sometimes be detected, and many examples may represent the amyotrophic form of Creutzfeldt–Jakob disease (p. 403). The conjunction between amyotrophic lateral sclerosis and parkinsonism-dementia in the island of Guam (see below) appears to be different, with its familial tendency and the histopathological features of neurofibrillary tangles.

Paranoid and schizophrenia-like syndromes are likewise rare and probably usually reflect a chance association. Some may represent acute organic reactions to drugs or to coincident metabolic disturbances and infections. Others may have been precipitated in predisposed persons by the non-specific stresses of coping with the disability.

AMYOTROPHIC LATERAL SCLEROSIS AND THE PARKINSONISM-DEMENTIA COMPLEX OF GUAM

Amyotrophic lateral sclerosis has been found to occur with extraordinary frequency among the indigenous Chamorro population of the island of Guam in the Western Pacific (Kurland and Mulder, 1954). Here the incidence is 100 times greater than in the USA. Cases tend to occur familially but no clear pattern of inheritance has emerged. In the same population a syndrome characterised by parkinsonism and progressive dementia is also found (Lessell et al., 1962), and it is now recognised that the two essentially represent different facets of the same disease process. Both also occur in the neighbouring islands of the Mariana group and in the Kii peninsula of Japan.

The amyotrophic lateral sclerosis is indistinguishable from the classical disease apart from its occasional association with dementia and extrapyramidal changes. The onset also tends to be at a younger age and the course more protracted. The 'parkinsonism-dementia complex' presents with memory deficits and a slowing of mental and motor activity, and progresses to generalised dementia with extrapyramidal rigidity. Some patients develop psychotic disorders in the later stages with delusions, hallucinations and hostile destructive behaviour.

A re-evaluation of 176 patients from Guam has confirmed the close interrelationships between the two disorders (Elizan et al., 1966). Of the 104 who presented intially with amyotrophic lateral sclerosis 5 developed parkinsonism dementia on average five years later, 5 developed parkinsonism alone and 2 an organic mental syndrome without parkinsonism. Of the 72 who presented with parkinsonism-dementia 27 developed amyotrophic lateral sclerosis on follow-up. In the families concerned, amyotrophic lateral sclerosis and parkinsonism-dementia often occurred indiscriminately and in various combinations, giving further evidence of a close relationship between the two syndromes.

The histological pictures similarly show a good deal of overlap. The parkinsonism-dementia complex shows diffuse cerebral atrophy with widespread neurofibrillary changes in the cortex and subcortical nuclei. Atrophy of the globus pallidus is characteristic, also loss of pigment from the substantia nigra (Hirano et al., 1961). The cases with amyotrophic lateral sclerosis show similar neurofibrillary changes throughout the brain in addition to the classical cord pathology (Hirano et al., 1966). Patients who have shown clinical features of only one syndrome are commonly found to show the pathological changes of both.

The interest in these disorders lies in the clues which they might offer to aetiology. An exogenous cause is considered likely in addition to genetic predisposition, and a high concentration of manganese in soil and water has been reported from the areas where they occur (Yase, 1972). A relatively high concentration of manganese has also been found in the Japanese cases with amyotrophic lateral sclerosis from the Kii pensinsula, more especially in the cord than in other parts of the central nervous system. Calcium and aluminium accumulation have also been noted (Yase, 1978).

Yase et al. (1972) have reported a patient with amyotrophic lateral sclerosis and the pathological changes typical of the combined syndrome who had shown schizophrenia for 5 years before the neurological symptoms were declared. The schizophrenia had fluctuated with periods of stupor and mutism, and was regarded by the authors as symptomatic of the organic cerebral changes.

Myasthenia Gravis

Myasthenia gravis is a disorder of the voluntary

musculature characterised by abnormal muscle weakness after activity and a marked tendency for recovery of power after a period of rest. Some defect of neuromuscular transmission is clearly implicated. It is commoner than chance among patients who have had hyperthyroidism or Hashimoto's thyroiditis (Becker *et al.*, 1964), and thymic abnormalities are often present in the form of a persistent thymus, thymus hyperplasia or thymic tumour ('thymoma'). More than two-thirds of cases show characteristic thymic changes with large germinal centres in the medulla, histologically identical with those seen in lymph nodes after antigenic stimulation (Marshall and White, 1961). There is now evidence, indeed, that the disease is essentially an autoimmune disorder in which circulating antibodies interfere with motor end-plate function (see below).

Clinical Features

The disorder can begin at any age but usually appears in the second or third decades. It is more frequent in females than males until late middle age when the sex ratio is reversed. The first complaint is usually of ready fatiguability of certain muscle groups, or some symptom of cranial nerve involvement such as diplopia, difficulty with chewing or difficulty with swallowing. The onset is sometimes insidious, sometimes sudden, and precipitation by emotional upset or a febrile illness is not uncommon.

Ocular muscles are usually involved early leading to ptosis or diplopia. Bulbar symptoms are also common, with difficulty in chewing or swallowing which worsens as the meal progresses, or a characteristic fading and slurring of speech after speaking for several minutes. Facial weakness may produce flattening and loss of wrinkles and the smile may have a characteristic 'snarling' quality. The muscles of the neck are often involved, also the shoulder girdles and flexors of the hip. In general proximal muscle groups are more severely affected than distal groups, and the arms more than the legs, but the distribution is variable. The respiratory muscles may fatigue easily on laughing or crying, and in crises of the disorder respiration can be dangerously embarrassed.

The muscular weakness is typically variable from day to day and sometimes from hour to hour. It tends to be worse towards the end of the day, but is sometimes paradoxically most marked on waking in the morning. Ultimately weakness of certain muscle groups may persist even when these have not been exercised for some time. Wasting is occasionally observed. The tendon reflexes are usually preserved and often brisk, but may decrease or disappear on repeated elicitation. Objective sensory changes are absent but the patient may experience pain in the muscles of the neck and around the eyes, or complain of a feeling of stiffness or paraesthesiae in affected areas.

The course is extremely variable. It is usually slowly progressive but a number of cases prove to be relatively static. Spontaneous remissions and sudden relapses may occur. Simpson (1964) suggests that the 'active' stage is usually limited to the first four to seven years, and the subsequent course then depends on the extent of disability reached during that period.

The diagnosis is confirmed by observing the response to anticholinesterase drugs. Neostigmine methyl sulphate ('Prostigmin injection') intramuscularly produces an increase in strength within thirty minutes. Edrophonium chloride ('Tensilon') intravenously has a briefer but prompter effect beginning within half to one minute. Other pharmacological tests which may be employed are described by Simpson (1964).

Pathophysiology

Myasthenia gravis appears to be largely an autoimmune disorder. The biochemical defect at the neuromuscular junction consists of competitive blocking by circulating antibodies which impair the effects of acetylcholine at the motor end-plate. These antibodies, through binding to acetylcholine receptor sites on the post-synaptic membrane, seem to be largely responsible for the clinical symptomatology (Walton, 1983). There may in addition be some abnormality of the motor end-plate itself; electron microscopy has shown widening of the primary synaptic clefts and simplification of the secondary synaptic clefts and folds (Santa *et al.*, 1972). Lymphocytic infiltrations of muscles have also been described in occasional cases. The significance of such histological features is, however, in doubt.

Treatment

Anticholinesterase drugs are the mainstay of treatment. Neostigmine bromide (Prostogmin) given orally has a continuing effect for 2–6 hours after each dose. Pyridostigmine bromide (Mestinon) has a long duration and wanes more gradually. Subcutaneous injections of neostigmine methylsulphate may be necessary if absorption is erratic. Edrophonium chloride (Tensilon) has too brief an action for use as maintenance therapy.

Thymectomy is widely practised but the results have been hard to evaluate because of the known liability to spontaneous remissions. The response of the individual patient remains unpredictable. Simpson's (1964) survey suggested that after the operation there was a lowered mortality and a greater chance of improvement or remission when compared to medically treated cases. Results were best in patients without a thymoma and when the duration had been less than five years. Herrmann et al. (1963) found that young females benefited more than other groups. The cautious introduction of steroids can be effective in inducing and maintaining remission in patients insufficiently improved by thymectomy or unfit for the operation.

Psychiatric supervision can have an important part to play in patients who develop marked psychological reactions to the disorder. As discussed below the emotional state of the patient may have a considerable influence on clinical progress. Meyer (1966) found evidence that in selected cases psychotherapy might facilitate remissions by allowing the ventilation of frustrations, grief and anxiety. MacKenzie et al. (1969) recommend that in myasthenics who are pursuing a deteriorating course every attempt should be made to investigate and treat possible sources of emotional stress.

Psychiatric Aspects of Myasthenia Gravis

Myasthenia gravis has attracted psychiatric attention on several grounds. Emotional factors have been thought to precipitate the onset in some cases and to play a significant role in aggravating the established disease in others. The psychological make-up of myasthenic patients and their responses to the illness have accordingly been studied in some detail. Finally, important problems of differential diagnosis not infrequently arise, and can involve psychiatric as well as neurological disorders.

The psychological responses seen in the illness are discussed by Brolley and Hollender (1955), MacKenzie et al. (1969) and Sneddon (1980). The patient is faced with the task of adapting to a disease which produces neither physical deformity nor pain and which has ephemeral manifestations. Interpersonal difficulties may be aggravated by the anxiety and uncertainty which the symptoms evoke, and by the tendency for those around to become suspicious of the genuineness of the disorder when there is so little to observe objectively. Patients may be suspected of faking their weakness or of being drunk when the speech is slurred. Meeting strangers can be a source of social embarrassment when facial weakness prevents a smile, likewise eating in public when the jaw must be supported towards the end of a meal.

The individual's reaction to the disease appears to be closely related to his premorbid personality and shows the usual range of responses to physical incapacity. Anxiety can be very marked and the patient's life may come to centre around the schedules of medication. An increase in the dose is regarded as ominous while a decrease leads him to be fearful of symptoms returning. Other patients seek to deny their disability, reducing medication heedlessly and embarking on too much activity. The dependency induced by the disease often sets in train further psychological reactions. Some patients regress to a needless extent and develop increasing dependence on relatives and doctors. An obsessional attendance on every detail of treatment may result. Others become severely depressed, or hostile and frustrated. The expression of anger is often blunted due to motor weakness so that effective relief from psychic tension may be debarred (Hayman, 1941).

Major mental illnesses may occasionally arise. Oosterhuis and Wilde (1964) found that 3 of 150 myasthenics suffered psychotic episodes of a depressive or schizophrenia-like nature. Dorrell (1973) reports a patient with recurrent episodes of schizophrenia, apparently in response to the stress of the myasthenia in a person already predisposed to such a psychosis. Gittleson and Richardson (1973) describe a typical paraphrenic illness in a man of 67, but comment on the surprising rarity of schizophrenia-like reactions in the literature in view of the close medical supervision which myasthenic patients receive. They suggest, indeed, that there may be a mutual antagonism between myasthenia gravis and schizophrenia, biochemically based or otherwise.

The premorbid personality of myasthenics has been described as often unstable but there are no controlled studies on the issue. A high proportion have been observed to come from markedly abnormal backgrounds, or to have had prominent neurotic symptoms before the onset of the illness (Oosterhuis and Wilde, 1964; MacKenzie et al., 1969). Oosterhuis and Wilde stressed a 'psychasthenic' character structure—overmeticulous, pessimistic in outlook, anxious and phobic—and found scores reflecting a high degree of neurotic instability on a personality questionnaire.

Precipitation by emotional impact finds wider acceptance by physicians of experience (Chafetz, 1966; Simpson, 1964, 1968). Specific emotional factors can often be discerned in close relation to the first appearance of symptoms, probably as a result of their aggravating the latent disorder and bringing it to attention. Oosterhuis and Wilde's (1964) study of 150 cases showed that eight per cent had had some acute emotional disturbance directly preceding the onset. A further third had had a fairly long-lasting period of emotional stress co-existent with the onset, such as difficulties at work or marital infidelity. Again control studies will be necessary before the full significance to be attached to these findings is known.

Aggravation by emotional influences has been widely reported once the disease is established. Simpson (1964) noted that double vision could be provoked by embarrassment, or ptosis by emotional disturbance. In Oosterhuis and Wilde's (1964) series 100 patients reported that emotional disturbances worsened their symptoms, 25 denied this and 25 were uncertain. In some of their cases an increase of ptosis could be observed in immediate response to an emotionally provoking question in the course of taking the history. Several patients had had acute respiratory paralysis in association with severe emotional upsets.

Meyer (1966) reported similar observations, including sudden cataplectic-like intensification of weakness in response to severe rage or fright, or sustained aggravation over one to two days in patients prone to episodes of anxiety or depression. Those who were particularly 'action minded' were vulnerable to repeated cycles of aggravation, with weakness provoking anxiety and resentment which in turn further aggravated the disability. MacKenzie *et al.* (1969) added further striking examples from the Mayo Clinic. Half of their 25 patients showed significant exacerbation of weakness following emotional upheavals, anger being the usual provoking factor. The worsening could last from a few minutes to several hours and often required a temporary increase in medication. Three patients showed a major increase in weakness persisting over a prolonged period of emotional tension—one for a week after her son's marriage against her will, another for a week after finalisation of a divorce, and another for 2 weeks after the death of a parent. Conversely improvement could follow when sustained emotional tension was resolved. One patient had had a difficult life with her parents and lost both of them within 2 years; 4 months later the

required dose of neostigmine had dropped from forty to twenty-five tablets per day despite a full working schedule, and 5 years later, when happily married, she was needing very small doses indeed. Sneddon's (1980) patients had often needed to learn techniques for handling anger-provoking situations in order to remain well. Half, for example, left the room and lay down if they felt themselves becoming angry; others found that crying and swearing relieved the tension and caused less weakness.

The course of the illness can accordingly be seriously affected by severe emotional disturbance. In a case described by Collins (1939) a man of 24 with known myasthenia gravis became psychotic with marked overactivity, elation and paranoid delusions. He died from respiratory crisis 6 days later and the psychosis was regarded as contributing directly to his death.

Meyer (1966) proposed that the emotional reaction of an individual to his disease was an important factor in determining prognosis, and supported this with an impressive analysis of data. Of 99 myasthenics from the Johns Hopkins Clinic, 48 were judged to have had some significant emotional or psychiatric condition following the onset of the disease and 51 were without such problems. Follow-up 1–10 years later showed that 46% of the former had died compared to 26% of the latter. Fifty-eight of the survivors were then available for prospective study, 23 with psychiatric problems and 35 without. Over the next 14 years 39% of the former group died compared to 17% of the latter. Anxiety attacks appeared to be of particularly grave significance, increasing the mortality to almost 50%.

The degree of incapacity had been similar in the two groups at the start of the prospective period. Age group analysis showed that the excess mortality among emotionally disturbed patients was evident in each decade and maximal in the 20s and 30s. Further indication of the importance of emotional disturbance in contributing to mortality was obtained from the death certifications of those who had died. Myasthenia gravis had been assigned as the cause of death in 5 out of 9 cases with emotional problems, compared to only 1 of 6 cases without.

Psychiatric Aspects of Differential Diagnosis

Myasthenia gravis must be distinguished from other neurological disorders including ocular and peripheral neuropathies, brain stem lesions, parkinsonism, motor neurone disease and carcinomatous myopathy. These aspects are discussed by Simpson (1964) and Schwab and Perlo (1966). From the psychiatric point of view mistakes may occur in both directions: patients with weakness and fatigue of essentially neurotic origin may be suspected of the disease, or conversely patients with myasthenia gravis may initially be diagnosed as suffering from neurosis, conversion hysteria or personality disorder.

Complaints of weakness and excessive fatigue are commonly encountered in routine medical practice and many such patients are mistakenly suspected of myasthenia gravis. Grob (1958) estimated that 20% of patients referred to him as possible myasthenics were in fact suffering from emotional disorders. Schwab and Perlo (1966), in an analysis of 130 patients wrongly diagnosed as myasthenia gravis, found that by far the greatest proportion (38%) were suffering from a 'chronic fatigue syndrome' attributable to some form of neurosis. Such a mistake is particularly likely to arise when an injection of neostigmine or edrophonium has produced a marked placebo response, and especially if the patient's report of subjective improvement has not been backed by attempts to monitor muscle strength objectively. Sometimes improvement on oral medication alone is accepted as evidence of myasthenia and this can be seriously misleading. Once given the false diagnosis the patient may cling to it and resist attempts at discontinuing medication (Chafetz, 1966).

It has been shown that occasional patients not suffering from myasthenia gravis will tolerate enormous quantities of anticholinesterase drugs without ill effect, in a manner previously considered possible in myasthenics only (McQuillen and Johns, 1963; Johns and McQuillen, 1966). Several such patients were reported, all complaining of weakness and ready fatigue but without objective signs to confirm it. Bulbar symptoms were common in the form of difficulty with chewing, swallowing or phonating, but objective evidence of bulbar deficits was uniformly absent. Most in fact had multiple complaints affecting several systems. The psychiatric diagnoses ranged from depression with hysterical features to psychotic illness. Studies of neuromuscular transmission showed no abnormalities, and no withdrawal symptoms followed stopping the drugs.

Examples of the diagnostic difficulties which can arise in this area are as follows:

A 21-year-old girl was diagnosed as suffering from myasthenia gravis. She had a history of fatiguability from the age of 5, and had noted dysphagia and difficulty with chewing since 20. Generalised weakness then forced her to take to bed. On examination ptosis was observed, varying in severity and improving with neostigmine or edrophonium injections. However photographs showed that the ptosis had been present from the age of 12 months, and placebo injections were found to produce improved strength of grip. Repeat tests with parenteral neostigmine and edrophonium were without effect, and there was no increased sensitivity to quinine or curare which would be expected in myasthenia gravis. The patient was ultimately diagnosed as suffering from hysteria and schizophrenia.

(Rowland, 1955)

A nurse of 31 had been well until eighteen months previously. She then suffered a respiratory infection, followed for three months by complaints of generalised weakness, diplopia and slurred speech. She then returned to work but continued to be readily fatigued. One year before presentation the generalised weakness became progressively worse so that she was obliged to spend most of the day in bed. She improved and again returned to work but complained of difficulty in opening her eyes, diplopia, slurred speech, and unsteady gait. An intramuscular injection of neostigmine produced marked improvement lasting 2 hours, but oral neostigmine had little effect. She was then demonstrated to improve markedly with saline taken from a box labelled 'Tensilon'. The issue was squarely faced, but the patient continued to insist that she had myasthenia gravis.

(Schwab and Perlo, 1966)

Conversely the diagnosis of myasthenia gravis can easily be missed in the early stages or in mild examples, especially if there is a previous history or current evidence of neurotic instability. The influence of emotions on the weakness can suggest a psychogenic disorder, similarly the spontaneous fluctuations which tend to occur. Sometimes the emotional component in patients with true myasthenia gravis is so obtrusive that a clear response is obtained to a placebo. Oosterhuis and Wilde (1964) found that it was common for several months to elapse between the declaration of symptoms and the correct diagnosis, with an interval of more than 2 years in almost a fifth of patients. Mild and atypical cases had sometimes been regarded as hysterical or neurasthenic for ten or twenty years.

Neurotic disorder may be suggested by the multiplicity of complaints or by certain characteristics of the early symptoms. An occupational 'cramp' or 'spasm' may be simulated when the initial complaint involves a muscle group which is particularly fatigued in the course of the patient's work

(Simpson, 1964). Or the first complaint may not be of fatiguability but of other perplexing symptoms. Minimal paresis of ocular muscles may result in 'mistiness' of vision rather than diplopia, slight facial paresis may lead to strange facial sensations, or slight bulbar paresis may produce a feeling of stiffness of the tongue or of something sticking in the throat (Oosterhuis and Wilde, 1964). Conversion hysteria may be suspected in patients who develop sudden paralysis of the legs after exertion or sudden episodes of dyspnoea. Moreover patients may occasionally present with a combination of myasthenia gravis and functional disorder as in the following example:

A woman of 36 complained of fatigue, difficulty with deglutition and double vision. She gave the following history. At 18 she had developed a right hemiplegia on waking the day after a violent quarrel with her stepmother. This had resolved over several months. At 20 she had developed difficulty with swallowing after a row with her stepmother, and this recurred thereafter whenever she was nervous. At 24 the right arm became weak after the birth of her child, progressing to total paralysis over one week then gradually improving over three months. This recurred temporarily after the birth of two subsequent children. At 35 she again noticed weakness of the right arm and leg, this time fluctuating in relation to rest and exertion, and later accompanied by diplopia and difficulty with swallowing.

When examined at the age of 36 she made a theatrical impression. She showed paresis of the left internal rectus, a right hemiparesis with normal reflexes, and a right hemihypalgesia. Neostigmine given by injection in the out-patient clinic caused the diplopia to disappear and enabled her to swallow more easily, but this failed to help when she was studied more closely as an in-patient.

Over the next few years her complaints of weakness, dysphagia and diplopia fluctuated in severity, but increased markedly at 40. She then showed multiple pareses of external ocular movements and a diffuse flaccid paresis of the limbs, right more than left. Placebos did not help but neostigmine produced a good response and thereafter she remained well on medication.

(Oosterhuis and Wilde, 1964)

A further instructive example in which a mistaken diagnosis of functional disorder was made is reported by Bail and Lloyd (1971):

A girl of 16 was sent to stay with an aunt because of increasing difficulties in her relationship with her mother. She complained of feeling tired and lacking in energy, and suddenly lost her voice during an emotional religious meeting. This happened several times thereafter. A few months later she developed difficulty in swallowing when her aunt and uncle were about to go on holiday. She

required hospitalisation because of aspiration pneumonia and tube feeding became necessary on account of her refusal to eat. Nevertheless otolaryngological and neurological assessments revealed no abnormality and she was referred for psychiatric treatment. A diagnosis of hysteria with severe disturbance of personality and schizoid features was made. Her home background was noted to be disturbed and her mother schizophrenic. She had broken off relations with her boy friend just before the aphonia began.

She gradually improved but anergia and feelings of weakness persisted. She was hospitalised for a second psychiatric opinion where she complained of seeing double and often treble. There was only a suspicion of general muscle weakness. However close observation soon showed abnormal fatiguability, and two episodes of unequal ptosis occurred. Myasthenia gravis was eventually diagnosed and the response to neostigmine was excellent. Thymectomy was carried out five months later. On follow-up over the next two years she proved to be an attractive and out-going girl with a stable job and a satisfactory relationship with her boy friend.

(Bail and Lloyd, 1971)

Rowland (1955) usefully summarizes the approach to be adopted in the diagnosis of equivocal cases. The disease must be considered likely in any syndrome of muscular weakness unaccompanied by alteration of reflexes or sensation and in which strength improves significantly in response to anticholinesterase drugs, except when strong evidence of psychogenesis is forthcoming. The diagnosis of myasthenia becomes more certain if there have been remissions in the past, if weakness is aggravated by fatigue and improved by rest, and if symptoms referable to the cranial nerves are prominent. Cautious provocative tests with quinine or curare may be valuable when manifestations are mild, when emotional factors appear to be obtrusive, or when the effects of anticholinesterase drugs are difficult to evaluate. Such tests are dangerous however in severe cases. Placebo injections are valuable prior to all therapeutic tests in equivocal cases, and a voluntary ergogram is best performed in association with the therapeutic tests (Schwab and Perlo, 1966).

The Progressive Muscular Dystrophies

The progressive muscular dystrophies, or myopathies, comprise a group of genetically determined degenerative diseases primarily affecting the voluntary musculature. Different forms vary in age of onset, distribution of muscles affected and rate of progression. The principal varieties appear to be clinically and genetically distinct, namely the pseudohypertrophic dystrophy of Duchenne, the limb girdle dystrophies, and the facioscapulo-humeral dystrophy of Landouzy and Dejerine. Rarer forms include the distal myopathy of Gowers and primary ocular myopathy. In addition to the familial varieties sporadic cases may occasionally be seen in older patients. Atrophy may then remain confined to smaller groups of muscles and progress very slowly with little disablement. The myotonic dystrophies represent a separate group including dystrophia myotonica, myotonia congenita and paramyotonia congenita. For convenience these are considered separately on p. 613 *et seq.*

Walton and Nattrass (1954) attempted to ascertain all cases of myopathy in Northumberland and Durham and reported 105 patients examined personally. Forty-eight had pseudohypertrophic dystrophy, 18 limb girdle, 15 facioscapulohumeral, 2 distal, 1 ocular, 15 dystrophia myotonica and 6 myotonia congenita.

Beyond their genetic allegiances little is known about causation. A metabolic basis is probable but has not yet been clarified. Serum enzyme abnormalities can be detected in preclinical cases of the pseudohypertrophic form and can be used for the identification of female carriers of the gene (Walton, 1964a), but no specific therapy is available for arresting or reversing the progress of the disease.

Clinical Features

The pseudohypertrophic form is by far the most common and occurs predominantly in males. Transmission is by an X-linked recessive gene or very occasionally by an autosomal recessive. The onset is usually in the first three years of life but may sometimes be seen as late as the twenties. The legs are predominantly affected with hypertrophy of the calves and atrophy of the thighs. The pelvic girdles and later the shoulder girdles also become involved. Progressive skeletal deformity tends to occur as a result of atrophy and contractures. Steady progression typically leads to inability to walk within ten years of onset, and death often cccurs in the second or third decades. Myocardial involvement is common in this variety, with electrocardiographic changes in a high proportion of cases. Death sometimes results from abrupt myocardial failure.

The limb girdle form affects both males and females and is usually transmitted as an autosomal recessive. Onset is in middle childhood or early adult life. Either the shoulder or the pelvic girdles may be affected initially, sometimes with later spread from one to the other. Hypertrophy of affected muscles is rare and simple atrophy is the rule. The rate of progression is variable but slower than in the pseudohypertrophic form. Severe disability is usually present 20 to 30 years after onset, and death is common in middle age.

The facioscapulohumeral form also affects both males and females. It is transmitted usually as an autosomal dominant but sometimes as a recessive. Onset can be at any time from childhood to late adult life. The facial and scapulohumeral muscles are first affected, typically with marked facial weakness and winging of the scapulae. Spread may occur to the pelvic girdles many years later. Pseudohypertrophy is very uncommon. Severe disability rarely results and most affected individuals survive to active old age.

In all varieties the tendon reflexes are diminished or lost in relation to affected muscle groups. All forms of sensation are intact. Histologically the affected muscles show great variation in the size of individual fibres and a large amount of connective and adipose tissue. In long-standing cases degeneration of anterior horn cells and thinning of fibre tracts in the cord have occasionally been described, but in such cases the diagnosis is often questionable.

Psychiatric Aspects

From the psychiatric point of view the issue which has attracted most attention concerns the level of intelligence of patients with muscular dystrophy, and the possibility that in some varieties intellectual retardation may be an integral part of the picture. There are obvious difficulties in attempting to assess the intellectual potential of children with severe physical handicaps, and in deciding whether educational backwardness should be attributed to innate deficiencies or to the psychosocial consequences of physical disablement. Nevertheless evidence increasingly favours the view that a substantial proportion of patients, at least with the pseudohypertrophic form of dystrophy, are of low intelligence. There are also indications that this may sometimes reflect cerebral involvement as part of the disease.

Earlier findings were divergent. Walton and Nattrass (1954) concluded that none of their 48 pseudohypertrophic patients were mentally defective and only 4 could be considered backward. Mental dullness was often suggested by their general appearance, but psychometric testing showed some of the patients who looked particularly dull to be of normal intelligence. Truitt (1955) formed the impression that the mental ability of his patients was commensurate with their socioeconomic background and equivalent to that of their siblings, and did not deteriorate with age or progression of the disorder. Morrow and Cohen (1954) found that the mean IQ of their group was 10 points lower than for New York City children generally, but concluded that this was attributable to the social and educational consequences of the disease. Half of the patients were one or more grades behind other children in schooling, and of those over 8 years old many were retarded in reading and number skills. Other studies of groups of physically handicapped children had shown equivalent degrees of under-achievement.

Others, however, have felt that more was involved than environmental deprivation and the emotional consequences of disablement. Allen and Rodgin (1960) found that half of their patients had IQs over 95 and half below; but in the latter group intellectual impairment was often severe and the mean IQ was only 61. No correlation could be found between the degree of intellectual retardation and the severity of physical handicap. Worden and Vignos (1962) found that more than two-thirds of cases of pseudohypertrophic dystrophy had IQs below 90, with the total range extending from 134 to 46. The mean for the group was 83 compared to 100 for unaffected siblings. In a group of patients with myotonia congenita, who showed equivalent or even more severe physical handicap, the mean IQ was 118. Again no correlation could be found between level of intelligence and severity of disability, and performance had often been poor from the outset of schooling. Repeat testing on a group of children 2–3 years later showed no significant decrement in intellect as the disease advanced further.

Dubowitz (1965) has reported a particularly careful study of 65 patients with pseudohypertrophic dystrophy, aged between 3 and 19, involving assessments of reading, writing, arithmetic and general knowledge. On such a basis 46% were estimated to be of average intelligence or above, 22% possibly retarded and 32% definitely retarded. Formal psychometric testing on a group of 27 long-term inpatients showed 3 with IQs above 100, 7 more above 70, 14 between 50 and 70, and 3 below 50. Thus both scholastic and psychometric indices showed that more than half of the patients had intelligence well below the normal range. Three patients who had been diagnosed very early were followed by repeat testing at frequent intervals together with comparative studies of unaffected siblings. All three were found to have intellectual impairment out of proportion to their physical handicaps. In 2 cases younger siblings had already overtaken the patients in intellectual development. At least one patient, and possibly another, showed some evidence of intellectual deterioration over time, in that previously acquired skills were later lost.

Two possibilities have been considered to account for the intellectual dullness in such patients—a genetic component determining low intelligence and inherited along with the dystrophic tendency, or some biochemical disturbance which has affected cerebral development. Dubowitz (1965) noted that a positive family history for dystrophy was much less common in patients with reasonably normal intelligence than in those who were retarded. Thus different genetically determined disease patterns may have been present within the group, or alternatively different genes may have contributed to the dystrophy and the intellectual impairment. Under the latter circumstances, however, one might have expected to find impairment without dystrophy in some of the siblings of patients and this was not so.

A biochemical explanation would have the advantage of perhaps one day allowing preventive measures to be undertaken. Worden and Vignos (1962) suggested that the cerebrum might be damaged at some vulnerable stage of its development, possibly by a by-product of degenerating muscle such as aldolase. Dubowitz (1965) suggested that there may be some biochemical abnormality which affects the metabolism of both brain and muscle. The usual lack of progression of intellectual impairment may be due to maximal involvement of the brain in early life when it is most vulnerable. In patients who preserve a normal intelligence the initial onset may have been less acute and severe. In such a view the skeletal muscle abnormalities are only the most evident reflection of a disease process which can sometimes implicate the central nervous system as well.

Electroencephalographic evidence of cerebral involvement has been conflicting. A high incidence of EEG abnormalities has sometimes been reported, especially in pseudohypertrophic dystrophy (Wayne and Browne-Mayers, 1959; Perlstein et al., 1960; Niedermeyer et al., 1965), and abnormalities have seemed to be commoner when symptoms began in infancy or early childhood. However Barwick et al. (1965) were unable to confirm any excess of abnormal records when patients with pseudohypertrophic, limb girdle or facioscapulohumeral dystrophy were compared with controls matched for age and sex.

Direct pathological studies of the brain have rarely been reported, but Rosman and Kakulas (1966) have undertaken detailed studies on 7 patients with pseudohypertrophic dystrophy. Three of these had documented evidence of mental deficiency during life. One showed grossly visible malformations of cerebral development, 2 showed areas of thickened cortex with disordered cortical architecture (pachygyria), and all 3 showed microscopic 'heterotopias'. These are groups of nerve cells which lie misplaced in the subcortical white matter and probably reflect arrest of the cortical migration of neurones during early development. No such changes were apparent in dystrophic patients with normal intelligence. Rosman and Kakulas concluded that a disorder of cortical development occurring during foetal life was likely to be responsible for the abnormalities in the mentally deficient patients. They favoured a genetic causation. It seemed unlikely that the maldevelopments could have been secondary to biochemical abnormalities arising from the myopathic process, since by their nature they must have been present before such effects could have occurred.

Other psychiatric disturbances in myopathic patients appear to be surprisingly rare, perhaps because of the gradual processes of adaptation which must take place from childhood onwards. Where children are educated together in special schools there is usually said to be little by way of serious behaviour disturbance or neurotic developments. Truitt (1955) found a remarkable absence of depression among 72 boys with pseudohypertrophic dystrophy, but noted a lack of personal identification with their own crippling. Morrow and Cohen (1954), however, found that half of their cases showed emotional immaturity, overdependence and intolerance of frustration, also a tendency to withdraw from people and the environment. Many led an active imaginative life with a good deal of energy spent in unshared fantasy living.

As adulthood approaches the psychosocial consequences of the disorder intrude increasingly, and the patient's psychological adjustment will often be decisively shaped by the milieu in which he is obliged to live. The strain thrown on the families of affected individuals may then be very considerable.

There does not appear to be any special association between non-myotonic forms of muscular dystrophy and psychosis, though occasional families have been reported in which schizophrenia and muscular dystrophy appear to coincide. Davison and Bagley

(1969) summarize the scattered examples in the literature.

The Myotonic Dystrophies

In the myotonic dystrophies a variable degree of muscular wasting and weakness is combined with the phenomenon of 'myotonia', namely delayed relaxation of skeletal muscles after voluntary contraction. The commonest is dystrophia myotonica (Steinert's disease), in which the myotonia is accompanied by progressive wasting and weakness of selected muscle groups together with other characteristic features such as cataract, hypogonadism and frontal baldness. Myotonia congenita (Thomsen's disease) is a more generalised muscle affection with myotonia and hypertrophy, setting in very early in life but rarely progressing to serious disablement. Paramyotonia congenita is similar but with the myotonia and weakness appearing only on exposure to cold. Other myotonic disorders include a variant of myotonia congenita with onset later in childhood, and various forms of potassium provoked periodic paralysis which also show myotonic features. The position regarding the classification and interrelationships between these conditions is reviewed by Zellweger and Ionasescu (1973).

DYSTROPHIA MYOTONICA

Dystrophia myotonica is one of the commoner myopathies and certainly the most frequent of the myotonias. It is of particular psychiatric interest because of the high incidence of mental disorder reported in sufferers from the disease. Transmission is by autosomal dominant inheritance. Penetrance is high but many incomplete and abortive forms occur.

Clinical Features

Males and females are equally affected. It usually begins in late childhood or early adult life but a wide range of onset is recognised from infancy to early old age. The disease has often been reported to show anticipation, i.e. earlier appearance in the filial than the parental generation. This may be largely an artefact of observation, since cases in the filial generation who develop the disease late in life will often have escaped detection. The muscular symptoms consist of a combination of myotonia, weakness, atrophy, and rarely hypertrophy.

The myotonia is usually the first symptom to be declared but is rarely sufficient in itself to lead to medical attention. It chiefly affects the hands, forearms and orbicularis oculi though the legs may be implicated as well. It is best demonstrated by observing the slowed relaxation of hand grip, or the difficulty in opening the eyes after screwing them up tightly. Delayed relaxation may be noted in the tendon reflexes, or a groove may persist in the tongue after depressing it with a spatula. The smile is sometimes characteristically slow and lingering.

The myotonia is rarely a grave handicap. Involvement of the tongue can cause difficulties with articulation, or sudden falls may result from difficulty in adjusting balance after a trip or stumble. Aggravating factors include exposure to cold or prolonged inactivity. It is characteristically worse on waking and improves as the patient begins to move about. Caughey and Myrianthopoulos (1963) also stress that it is often aggravated by emotional factors such as fright or surprise. One of their patients first noticed the myotonia when his legs seemed to freeze while caught in a burning building, and another when his legs became stiff on the signal 'go' in a race. Fear, anger or sudden joy may temporarily increase the symptoms so that a wave of stiffness is felt to run through the muscles of the body. Another patient was liable to fall rigidly to the ground whenever she was suddenly excited or surprised. Several had become housebound because of fear of falls in the street.

The atrophy and weakness is selective, symmetrically affecting the facial muscles, masticatory muscles, sternomastoids and distal parts of the arms and legs. Hypertrophy can occur in the early stages but atrophy usually prevails. The facial appearance is characteristic with hollow temples, a sad lugubrious expression and a tendency for the mouth to hang partially open. Finger grip is weak and foot drop may occur. The tendon reflexes are normal initially, though diminished or absent as the disease progresses. Sensory changes are rare, but slight sensory disturbances and subjective complaints of pain are occasionally encountered.

The progression of the disability is variable but usually slow. Rare cases may be completely disabled within a year or two, though most patients remain ambulant for 15 to 20 years or even longer. In the later stages respiration and swallowing may become embarrassed.

On pathological examination the affected muscles show variation of fibre size, fibrosis and fibre degeneration as in other dystrophic processes. A characteristic finding is multiplication of sarcolemmal nuclei which tend to form long central chains, also sarcolemmal aggregates of mitochondria. Studies of muscle in the early stages show atrophy predominating over such 'dystrophic' changes, suggesting that the disease may represent a neuropathy rather than a primary myopathy. But curare-like substances which affect the neuromuscular junction do not alter the myotonia, suggesting that the basic defect is probably still within the muscle.

Associated defects may involve a number of organs and systems of the body. Cataract is one of the commonest—in some series slit lamp examination has revealed lens opacities in almost every case. Other ocular abnormalities may include sluggishly reacting pupils, limitation of eye movements, or partial constriction of the visual fields. Frontal baldness may be seen in adults, more often in men than women. Endocrine abnormalities include testicular atrophy and hypogonadism in the male, and menstrual abnormalities and infertility in the female. Pituitary-adrenal and thyroid abnormalities have occasionally been reported, also abnormalities of glucose metabolism.

Electrocardiographic abnormalities are found in more than half of the cases. Cardiac failure or sudden death due to cardiac arrest may occur. Smooth muscle dysfunction can involve dilatation of the lower oesophagus, peristaltic incompetence of the small intestine, dilatation of the colon, or a flaccid bladder with urinary retention. Anaesthetics present a special risk, particularly of prolonged respiratory arrest following thiopentone. The serum immunoglobulins are often abnormally low. Skull X-ray may show general thickening of the vault, localised thickening of the frontal bones (hyperostosis frontalis interna), enlarged sinuses or a small sella turcica. Other congenital physical defects include a high narrow palate, hare lip, or talipes equinovarus.

The associated abnormalities may sometimes be found as the sole manifestation of the disease among relatives. Such individuals must be regarded as heterozygotes, but whether or not they will develop the disease is unpredictable. Bundey *et al.* (1970) discuss the question of genetic counselling in some detail, and show that if offspring are still totally symptom free by the age of thirty the risk of developing the disease is reduced from the usual 50% to 25%. They suggest that any first degree relative of a patient who asks for genetic counselling should receive a careful neurological examination, supplemented by slit lamp examination for early cataract, electromyography for the detection of myotonic discharges, and estimation of the serum immunoglobulins. Electrocardiographic abnormalities and changes on skull X-ray proved less useful for the detection of the early heterozygote.

Differential Diagnosis and Treatment

Differentiation from other forms of muscular dystrophy is important on account of the differing prognosis. It can usually be made on the basis of the characteristic distribution of weakness, wasting and myotonia, together with associated abnormalities in other systems as outlined above. The facial appearance may resemble that of facioscapulohumeral dystrophy, though there the limbs are affected proximally rather than distally. Myasthenia gravis may be suspected when ptosis and muscular fatigue are marked. Differentiation from myotonia congenita (see below) can be more difficult when onset is early in life, and indeed the two have sometimes been reported from the same family. Polyneuropathy may be suspected in view of the distal and symmetrical weakness. Peroneal muscular atrophy can usually be distinguished by the associated loss of vibration sense at the ankles. Walton (1964b) discusses the use of electromyography, serum enzyme estimations and muscle biopsy to assist the diagnosis further.

Nothing can be done to prevent the weakness and atrophy progressing. The myotonia can be helped by several drugs—quinine, procaine amide, steroids and phenytoin—but this is rarely sufficiently marked and disabling to require treatment. Quinine and procaine amide should not be given if electrocardiographic abnormalities are present. A great deal of social help is often required for the patients and their families, and this is where the most useful emphasis in treatment is usually placed.

Psychiatric Abnormalities in Dystrophia Myotonica

Psychiatric abnormalities occur in a high proportion of patients and complete the picture of the disease. Klein's (1959) survey from Switzerland showed psychological disorder in over a third of cases, chiefly mental retardation and personality disorder. Others have put the incidence much higher and have stressed the social decline which marks families affected by the disease.

Impairment of intellect is common and sometimes severe. Thomasen (1948) found that one-third of 101 patients with dystrophia myotonica had a 'considerable degree' of mental defect and only one quarter could be considered of normal intelligence. In adults retardation was more advanced when the disease had begun in childhood. In children retardation was sometimes so severe that they were institutionalised as mental defectives, often without the true diagnosis being recognised. Calderon (1966) found that almost 80% of children with the disease were mentally retarded to some degree. Retardation was sometimes found to precede the onset of physical disorder, and also appeared in other family members who had no evidence of the disease. An association between severity of intellectual deficit and severity of physical handicap has often been observed but this is by no means invariable—severe mental defect may sometimes co-exist with mild muscular involvement and vice versa (Zellweger and Ionasescu, 1973).

There are indications not only of poor initial endowment but also of deterioration from previous levels of functioning. Maas and Paterson (1937) found that 17 of 29 adult cases were of low intelligence, 11 having been mentally retarded from birth and 6 having deteriorated after normal performance at school. Walton and Nattrass (1954) found that 2 of their 15 cases were mentally subnormal, 3 showed 'early evidence of dementia' and another 3 were themselves aware of slow deterioration of memory and intellect.

The cause of the intellectual difficulties is uncertain. The effects of co-existent hypothyroidism and other endocrine disorders have not been fully assessed but would seem unlikely to play a major role. Genetic influences are probably mainly responsible, occurring as an integral part of the inherited disease process. Assortative mating may contribute further, since patients with dystrophia myotonica are often in the lower socioeconomic strata and choice of marriage partner is likely to be limited.

There is abundant evidence of cerebral involvement in the disease. Electroencephalographic abnormalities have been reported much more commonly than in other forms of muscular dystrophy. Barwick et al. (1965) found abnormal records in 61% of cases compared to 20% of controls, with theta and delta waves and sometimes focal sharp wave discharges. Lundervold et al. (1969) reported similar abnormalities in almost 50% of patients. Rosman and Kakulas (1966) found pathological changes in the brain at autopsy in 3 out of 4 patients examined, representing all 3 in whom mental deficiency had been noted during life. Two showed grossly visible malformations of cerebral development, 2 had areas of disordered cortical architecture, and all 3 showed microscopic heterotopias indicative of arrest of cortical migration of neurones during early development. As in their patients with mental deficiency and pseudohypertrophic muscular dystrophy (p. 613) they favoured the view that genetic influences operative during foetal life were responsible for the pictures observed.

With regard to progressive decline in intellectual function, Refsum *et al.* (1959, 1967) have demonstrated ventricular enlargement on air encephalography, particularly in patients severely affected by the disease. They concluded that this developed gradually during life, pari passu with the progress of the disease. Patients who had repeat air encephalograms several years later showed increased ventricular width, in a manner which correlated with clinical deterioration. The dilatation could not be ascribed to ageing *per se* since the average age was rather lower in those with progression than those without.

Personality abnormalities and social deterioration are perhaps even commoner than defective intelligence. Thomasen (1948) and Caughey and Myrianthopoulos (1963) laid particular emphasis on reduced initiative and a 'carefree temperament', both of which could contribute directly to social decline. Occasional patients showed concern about their condition and became moody and hostile, but these reactions were exceptional. The great majority showed a surprising equanimity about their physical or social situation. Thomasen found that most were cheerful and rarely got angry despite miserable living conditions. Some were even prone to exaggerated self-esteem, and considered they were managing excellently though physically disabled and leading a vegetative existence.

Reduced initiative was sometimes already obvious in childhood. The affected individual had typically been lazy and uninterested at school, and thereafter failed to complete training and accepted a lowly occupation. This could be noted in retrospect in patients who developed overt signs of the disease only later in life. Women became slovenly and negligent. Men were often content to sit idly at home when only mildly physically incapacitated.

Somnolence may be a marked feature in the disease, adding to the impression of apathy and perhaps related to diencephalic dysfunction or alveolar hypoventilation. True fatigue is also prominent in many cases. But some of Thomasen's patients were unable to perform even very light work, and complained of fatigue far exceeding what would be expected from the degree of muscular involvement.

The social decline which results is usually severe and could be traced in 70% of Thomasen's patients. Caughey and Myrianthopoulos (1963) encountered several families of distinction where the disease,

within two or three generations, had led to marked deterioration in family fortunes and social status.

Psychotic developments have rarely been reported and when they occur are probably coincidental. Maas and Paterson (1937) described one patient with a schizophrenia-like reaction, and one who became paranoid about his wife when impotent. In two others mild grandiosity became exaggerated into a state resembling chronic hypomania. Thomasen (1948) found no examples of psychosis among 101 patients.

MYOTONIA CONGENITA

Thomsen (1876) gave a clear account of the disease which bears his name in four generations of his own family. Thomasen (1948) subsequently collected all cases in the literature and described three further families, resulting in a total of 157 families with 470 affected persons. It is nevertheless a rare disease. The pattern of inheritance is usually as an autosomal dominant though an autosomal recessive form has also been described. Males and females are affected equally.

Onset is usually from shortly after birth and few cases appear after the age of twelve. Myotonia is typically the presenting feature and the sole cause of disability for many years. It presents as a painful stiffness or cramp on attempting voluntary movement, most marked after rest and especially troublesome first thing in the morning. The myotonia is widespread throughout the body muscles, unlike its regional distribution in dystrophia myotonica. Clumsiness on initial movement may lead to frequent falls. Exposure to cold aggravates it, also excitement, tension or emotional disturbance. Most patients find that with repeated movements the stiffness passes off and learn such manoeuvres as limbering up to run.

Generalised muscular hypertrophy is common and atrophy rare. However the strength is not proportional to the size of the muscles and patients fatigue easily. The tendon reflexes are usually normal. The associated features seen in dystrophia myotonica are rarely encountered, and when present tend to be minimal. Occasional cases are reported with cataract, minor lens opacities or endocrine disturbance, but it is hard to be sure that these are not cases of early dystrophia myotonica without atrophy.

The course tends to remain static over the years and progression of myotonia or muscular weakness is rarely observed. The disorder is quite compatible with survival to old age. The myotonia is often severe, however, and can require treatment with procaine amide or steroids.

Maas and Paterson (1950) disputed the clinical distinctions between myotonia congenita and dystrophia myotonica. They considered the former to be merely the early stage of the latter, accounting for the frequent finding of mixed and incomplete cases. This viewpoint has not been upheld by further studies, however, and in particular the psychiatric features of the two disorders have proved to differ considerably.

Psychiatric Aspects of Myotonia Congenita

Patients with myotonia congenita are usually normal in intelligence and personality. In sharp contrast to dystrophia myotonica social deterioration was not observed in Thomasen's (1948) large material. Mental changes were conspicuous by their absence. Thomsen (1876) himself drew attention to an hereditary psychosis in several members of his own family, describing it as a '. . . kind of imbecility, confusion of ideas combined with a tendency for the mind to wander and vacant brooding; it has most in common with a certain kind of mental weakness which occurs in old age'. Since then, however, most investigators have dismissed any association with psychosis as fortuitous, and in fact there are strong indications that the myotonia and the mental disorder were transmitted independently in different branches of Thomsen's family (Caughey and Myrianthopoulos, 1963; Johnson, 1967). Johnson (1967) has reported a patient with myotonia congenita who developed two acute psychotic episodes of mixed affective and schizophrenic type. Two of the siblings had myotonia congenita, and the father and several other family members had had acute psychoses; but here again the muscular disorder and the psychotic propensity appeared to be transmitted independently in the family, and no direct relationship could be established between the two disorders.

PARAMYOTONIA CONGENITA

Paramyotonia congenita resembles myotonia congenita except that the myotonia and weakness only appear on exposure to cold. It is similarly transmitted as an autosomal dominant. Typically the disorder develops early in life, worsens at puberty, then tends to improve or vanish in later decades (Caughey and Myrianthopoulos, 1963). It often principally affects the muscles of the face, tongue and hands. Involvement of the legs may cause 'cramps' or inability to rise from a sitting position in the cold. Severe weakness is sometimes induced by cold, with or without myotonia, and lasts on rare occasions for several hours at a time. In severe attacks the patient may be bedridden and unable to turn, leading to a suspicion of hysterical paralysis. There is no hypertrophy of muscles, and power and reflexes are normal between attacks.

Psychiatric and social complications appear to be as rare as in myotonia congenita. Associated dystrophic features such as cataracts, testicular atrophy and changes on skull X-ray do not occur.

FAMILIAL PERIODIC PARALYSIS

A number of forms of familial periodic paralysis have been described. Some are associated with a low serum potassium and respond to its administration, while others show a high serum potassium and are aggravated by its administration. Among the potassium-provoked varieties there are two myotonic forms; potassium produces weakness in both but cold produces weakness in only one of them. Both are transmitted as autosomal dominants. McArdle (1964) has described the typical clinical pictures and Zellweger and Ionasescu (1973) discuss the complex interrelationships between these disorders. Clinical overlap occurs to a considerable extent and may in part be due to the variable expressivity of the respective mutant genes.

Narcolepsy

The chief symptom in narcolepsy consists of attacks of daytime somnolence, usually irresistible in intensity and leading to several short episodes of sleep per day ('narcoleptic attacks'). Commonly associated are attacks of cataplexy, in which the patient abruptly loses muscle tone and may fall briefly to the ground, usually in response to some emotionally provoking stimulus. Hypnagogic hallucinations and episodes of sleep paralysis are also characteristic of the syndrome in its most complete expression, and considerable disturbance of nocturnal sleep commonly occurs.

Gelineau gave the first definite description of the disorder in 1880. Thereafter the term came to be applied rather indiscriminately to many varieties of morbid somnolence, some due to structural brain lesions and others associated with psychiatric disorders, resulting in a good deal of nosological confusion and faulty discussion about aetiology. Gradually the condition has been separated from these other sleep disorders and established as a distinct disease entity. The great majority if not all cases are without structural brain pathology and appear to represent a functional disturbance of the sleep mechanisms of the brain. Hereditary associations have been demonstrated. Fresh interest has been brought to the syndrome as a result of present day discoveries concerning the physiological mechanisms involved in sleep as discussed below.

Clinical Features

Detailed accounts of the disorder are to be found in Yoss and Daly (1957), Sours (1963), Zarcone (1973) and Guilleminault et al. (1976). The onset is usually between the ages of 10 and 20 and is rare after 40. The precise time of onset may be hard to determine, relatives often becoming aware of the problem before the patient himself. Males are reported considerably more frequently than females, but this is possibly because they are more likely to come to medical attention on account of disablement produced at work. Affected relatives may be found in up to a third of cases when a full family history can be obtained (Yoss and Daly, 1960a).

Approximately three-quarters of cases have at least one of the accessory symptoms in addition to narcoleptic attacks—cataplexy occurs in some 70%, hypnagogic hallucinations in perhaps 30% and sleep paralysis in 25%. The full tetrad occurs in only about 10%. Some authorities have restricted the term to cases with cataplexy in addition to narcoleptic attacks, but this provides difficulties since narcolepsy alone characteristically antedates the development of accessory symptoms. In a large series of patients with cataplexy, Yoss and Daly (1960b) found that this had set in at the same time as the narcoleptic attacks in 55%, 1–5 years later in 25% and more than 10 years later in 15%. One may therefore encounter patients in whom daytime sleep attacks constitute the sole manifestation for some considerable time. Cataplexy antedating narcolepsy is distinctly uncommon. Episodes of sleep paralysis as the sole complaint are also rare. Hypnagogic hallucinations, by contrast, are quite frequently encountered in the general population.

Once it has commenced the disorder appears to persist unchanged throughout life, though perhaps with some diminution in severity after middle age. Very occasionally remissions and exacerbations have been described, but in most large series this has not been the case. Reports of seeming improvement in the pretreatment era (Daniels, 1934) were probably attributable to the patient learning to reconcile his symptoms to the demands of everyday life. Strategies are certainly often adopted to avoid situations in which cataplectic attacks are likely to be provoked.

Narcoleptic attacks consist of an overwhelming sense of drowsiness, usually leading to a brief period of actual sleep. They are commonly of daily occurrence and with several attacks per day. The period of sleep usually lasts some 10–15 minutes though may be much longer according to circumstances. If the majority of attacks exceed 30 minutes, Roth (1980) classifies the disorder as idiopathic hypersomnia (p. 626). The disorder is said to set in quite often during a period of sleep disruption as in military training, or during a period of emotional upheaval (Zarcone, 1973).

The episodes are commoner in situations normally conducive to drowsiness—after meals, in monotonous surroundings, and as the day progresses. Usually there is a period of a minute or two during which the patient struggles against actual sleep. But in severe examples attacks can occur in any situation—while talking, eating, working or when engaged in other activities. Attacks while swimming or driving may very occasionally endanger life, though the prodromal drowsiness will almost always serve as a warning. Some patients are extremely irritable when prevented from falling asleep or when suddenly awakened. Typically the patient awakes refreshed, perhaps more so than after nocturnal sleep, and there is then a refractory period of several hours before the next attack can occur.

The patient may himself complain either of episodic sleep attacks with reasonable alertness between, or more rarely of fighting a constant battle against drowsiness during the day. Yoss and Daly (1957) divided the syndrome into type I and type II varieties on this basis. The second variety can be a diagnostic problem if there are no accessory symptoms. In fact patients with circumscribed sleep attacks will often be found to have episodes of quite profound drowsiness between, though they may not themselves be fully aware of this. Brief 'microsleeps' lasting 10–20 seconds are also not uncommon, as shown by EEG recordings, yet may not be apparent to the patient or observers.

Cataplectic attacks consist of sudden immobility or decrease of muscle tone, which may be generalised or limited to certain muscle groups. In severe attacks the patient collapses in a flaccid heap and is totally unable to move or speak. Serious falls and injuries may occasionally result. Tendon reflexes are abolished for a while and extensor plantar reflexes have been observed. The patient typically remains fully alert, however, and is aware of what is proceeding around him. Mild episodes may show only as drooping of the jaw, head nodding, or a sense of weakness obliging the patient to sit down or lean against a wall. Objects may be dropped or the knees buckle. Dysarthria, aphonia or ptosis may accompany attacks, and double vision or momentary difficulty with focusing may be the sole manifestation. Pallor and change of pulse rate are sometimes observed. Very occasionally, consciousness may be briefly clouded during attacks but this should be regarded as exceptional (Roth, 1980).

The attacks are always of short duration, usually lasting several seconds and rarely more than a minute. They are much less frequent than sleep attacks, rarely occurring more than once per day.

Precipitation by emotional stimuli is usually strikingly evident in the history, in particular precipitation by laughter. But any strong emotion may bring on an attack—surprise, fear, outbursts of anger or feelings of exaltation. Levin (1953) and Sours (1963) suggest that aggression with guilt is a frequent theme in the emotional situations which precipitate attacks. Cataplexy may render participation in sports impossible—the excitement inspired by a good tennis shot may bring on an attack, likewise the element of surprise in hunting or fishing (Yoss and Daly, 1960b). Many patients learn to avoid provoking situations, and to check any inclination to laugh in order to avoid attacks. Sometimes, however, they can occur without any discernible affective stimulus.

Gélardi and Brown (1967) have reported a rare example of a family in which typical laughter-induced cataplexy appeared to be transmitted as an autosomal dominant trait. Eleven members were affected from childhood onwards, with no hint of narcoleptic attacks in eight and questionable narcolepsy in three. Sleep paralysis was an occasional accompaniment.

Hypnagogic hallucinations usually occur in the auditory modality but can be visual or tactile as well. Two or more modalities may be associated in the experience, seeing and hearing quite commonly occurring together. They are experienced during the transition from wakefulness to sleep, or rather less commonly during the phase of recovery from sleep ('hypnopompic hallucinations'). Not uncommonly they occur simultaneously with episodes of sleep paralysis. They may be experienced in the middle of the night when the patient has roused for a while,

and they sometimes accompany daytime narcoleptic attacks.

Typically the hallucinations are intensely vivid and seem to be real at the time. The patient may react momentarily in accordance with what he is experiencing. Later, however, when fully awake, he almost always recognises their alien character. Lively accompanying affects, especially of terror, are widely reported as characteristic. Yoss and Daly (1957), however, found the content to be usually banal, and Bowling and Richards (1961) found them to be pleasant as often as unpleasant. Roth and Bruhova (1969) have stressed the kaleidoscopic nature and bizarre character of the visions. Zarcone (1973) suggests that the hypnagogic hallucinations of narcoleptics differ from those of normals in their complex dream-like quality and the intensity of the accompanying emotion, whereas in non-narcoleptics the hallucination is usually of a mere word or image with little affective meaning. In many examples it is probably difficult to distinguish the hallucinatory phenomena from the content of disturbing dreams which have awoken the patient.

Sleep paralysis consists of attacks of transient inability to move which emerge in the stage between arousal and sleep. They can occur while falling asleep or while awakening, and with nocturnal sleep or with daytime sleep attacks. Usually they are very infrequent.

The onset is abrupt, with the patient suddenly aware that he can neither speak nor move. The paralysis is flaccid and usually complete, though some patients can open the eyes or even cry out briefly. As with cataplectic attacks the episodes are of brief duration, lasting several seconds and rarely more than a minute. One of Bowling and Richards (1961) cases, however, had paralysis for more than an hour. The episode is usually dispelled abruptly if the patient's name is called or if he is touched or shaken. Otherwise it resolves spontaneously. Intense alarm is usually provoked. Hallucinatory voices or sounds sometimes accompany the attack and may lead the patient to fear that he is to be harmed or attacked.

Sleep paralysis as the sole symptom is very rare, but ten such examples were studied by Roth and Bruhova (1969), all occurring in members of two families. The paralysis was always accompanied by terrifying dreams, usually preceding the episodes. In one patient the feeling of despair characteristically carried over from the dreams and persisted next morning in the form of severe depression.

Disturbed nocturnal sleep is also characteristic of narcoleptics. They fall asleep promptly but thereafter are restless, wake again often, and may speak, shout, or even walk about the room. Polygraph recordings confirm frequent periods of wakefulness. Vivid and terrifying dreams are common, occurring in some 60% of patients with narcolepsy and cataplexy and some 20% of patients with narcolepsy alone (Roth and Bruhova, 1969). Themes of murder or of being pursued are said to be common. By contrast dreams are rare during daytime sleep attacks.

A variety of *other symptoms* are reported from time to time. Somnambulism is occasionally a pronounced feature. A rapid weight gain at onset may be observed, and libido or potency may become impaired (p. 625). Hypogenitality, a feminine hair distribution, polyuria and polydipsia are very occasionally present (Smith, 1958a). Bouts of amnesia were mentioned by Daniels (1934) as an occasional complication; the patient suddenly realises he has no knowledge of the past few minutes and has to check what has been done, usually discovering that he has continued to function normally during most of the time. Roth (1980) also reports that automatic behaviour may feature in narcolepsy. The patient tries to overcome his sleepiness and carry on activities but loses awareness of what transpires; he may continue talking without making sense, his handwriting may suddenly change to meaningless scribble, or he may continue walking and wake in fresh surroundings. Such episodes had occurred in over a third of his patients.

Differential Diagnosis

The correct diagnosis is of crucial importance if appropriate treatment is to be given. Sometimes the patient's symptoms have long been attributed by relatives or employers to laziness, irresponsibility or emotional instability. There are no abnormalities on physical examination or routine laboratory tests, and the diagnosis rests essentially on a careful history. Polygraphic recordings may clarify the situation in uncertain examples, by revealing REM episodes at sleep onset as discussed below.

In mild examples a distinction must be drawn from *normal drowsiness*. The classical accessory symptoms will be present in some three-quarters of narcoleptics, and in most of the remainder the sleepiness will be so excessive that there is little real doubt about the distinction. In borderline examples, however, it can be important to note that attacks of drowsiness are irresistible despite the absence of fatigue, or that attacks occur in inappropriate circumstances in addition to those normally conducive to somnolence.

Neurotic fatigue based on anxiety or depression is a common misdiagnosis, especially if the patient presents his complaint as feeling tired instead of describing periods of excessive sleepiness. Neurosis is also liable to be suspected when emotional complications have arisen from disrupted social or economic circumstances. However narcoleptics rarely complain of muscular and physical exhaustion as do patients with neurotic fatigue, and they awake from naps refreshed whereas the neurotic does not. The depressed and anxious patient will rarely complain of drowsiness as such, nor of recurring periods of uncontrollable sleep.

Hysteria may also be suggested. Hysterical dissociation may take the form of sleep in persons of unstable temperament, but this typically follows well defined precipitants. The hysterical 'sleep' represents an active withdrawal, is usually prolonged, and the patient resists being woken. The question of hysteria or of *schizophrenia* may be raised when hypnagogic phenomena are particularly vivid or fantastic. Daniels (1934) described such a patient who saw forms appearing at the windows and entering the room, and felt as if snakes, birds and other creatures were moving about in her abdomen and emerging from her mouth. All such symptoms disappeared with ephedrine.

Hypothyroidism may be the initial diagnosis when the patient complains of dullness and fatigue, or *hypoglycaemia* when he describes dizziness or lightheadedness as part of the attacks. *Epilepsy* will be suspected when the episodes are described as 'blackouts', but a careful history will reveal drowsiness before the loss of consciousness and full alertness on recovery. Witnesses will describe normal sleep from which the patient can be woken and the absence of convulsions. Cataplectic attacks may be mistaken for petit mal akinetic seizures. Precipitation by emotion and the preservation of full alertness are important distinguishing features.

Some patients first seek help on account of diplopia due to latent ocular imbalance brought about by episodes of drowsiness: *multiple sclerosis* or *myasthenia gravis* may then be suspected. Attacks of diplopia or ptosis may also be the principal manifestations of the patient's cataplexy. In older patients cataplexy may be mistaken for drop attacks due to vertebrobasilar insufficiency.

The history will usually readily distinguish narcolepsy from other hypersomnias, such as 'idiopathic hypersomnia' (p. 626), the Kleine–Levin syndrome

(p. 628) or the Pickwickian syndrome (p. 627). The presence of obesity may cause confusion with the latter. Hypersomnia due to structural brain lesions (p. 629) is likely to be long-lasting and with other ancillary evidence by way of neurological abnormalities.

Aetiology

Psychodynamic, Pavlovian and structural theories have all been advanced to account for narcolepsy and will be briefly outlined. It now seems clear, however, that neither psychodynamic factors nor structural brain pathology is responsible in the majority of cases, and that the syndrome rests on a functional disturbance of the sleep mechanisms of the brain. Work on the physiological basis of sleep, and the pathophysiology of its disturbances, will accordingly be described. Genetic factors appear to be operative in leading to the disorder, and in the last analysis a biochemical basis is probable.

Psychogenic theories have had strong adherents, partly because of failure to differentiate between narcolepsy and emotionally-induced hypersomnias, and partly because the sensitivity of narcolepsy to emotional influences has been interpreted as implying a directly causal role. Smith (1958a) reviews the arguments advanced in favour of primary psychogenesis—an onset at adolescence which is a stressful time of life, the great variation in frequency of attacks, the lack of abnormalities on examination, and the favourable response sometimes claimed for psychotherapy.

The formulation presented by Langworthy and Betz (1944) is typical. They viewed the narcoleptic symptoms as having a defensive function, serving to protect the patient from unacceptable feelings and impulses in relation to other people. Both narcoleptic attacks and cataplectic attacks were seen as neurotic reactions with symbolic significance, and closely allied to hysterical phenomena. Narcoleptics were found to have in common a characteristic background of emotional conflict—they felt caught in a life pattern to which they were expected to conform yet deeply resented, and were frustrated in attempts to achieve autonomy. The symptoms served to avert confrontation with the realistic difficulties and provided a more acceptable substitute cause for concern. Barker (1948) argued similarly, and attempted to show how narcoleptic symptoms could interrupt activity in situations which evoked the life problems of the patient. Drake (1949)

presented the case of a boy whose attacks set in one week after his father's remarriage, and two more in whom attacks appeared to be used to ward off unpleasant emotional conflicts.

However there are difficulties in marshalling satisfactory evidence in favour of psychogenesis. Most claims have been made on the basis of small numbers of cases, usually specially referred for psychiatric treatment. Some of the most striking examples, with marked psychopathology and relief from psychotherapy, have occurred in patients who appear to have been suffering from something other than narcolepsy, for example in the case reported by Spiegel and Oberndorf (1946) and described on p. 630. Thus most observers now consider that psychogenic factors are unlikely to bring the syndrome into being, even though secondary emotional difficulties can arise and emotional influences can affect the timing and frequency of attacks (p. 624). It is also noteworthy that symptom substitution has not emerged when attacks are controlled by analeptic drugs.

Pavlovian theories were elaborated by Adie (1926), Levin (1933, 1935) and Fabing (1946). The narcoleptic's brain was regarded as being unusually susceptible to 'cortical inhibition' in Pavlov's sense. In cataplexy, inhibition induced by emotion was confined to the motor and postural centres, while in sleep attacks it spread widely to all parts of the cortex. Sleep paralysis resulted when inhibition failed to disappear from all parts of the brain simultaneously during waking, or when it failed to irradiate uniformly in the process of going to sleep. Thus cataplexy and sleep paralysis were thought to represent special instances of 'localised sleep' in the motor centres while the substrata of consciousness remained active. These conceptions have, of course, given way to a more precise understanding of cerebral physiology.

Structural theories have presupposed that the syndrome is symptomatic of a diencephalic or midbrain lesion. Occasional examples have been reported with tumours, inflammations or degenerative conditions involving the hypothalamus, after head injury or encephalitis lethargica, and in association with general paresis, multiple sclerosis and cerebral arteriosclerosis. In Roth's (1980) large personal series of 360 cases, 20% were considered symptomatic of other cerebral conditions, chiefly encephalitic processes and head injuries. Most observers, however, have found the proportion much smaller. In the 'idiopathic' cases covert hypothalamic pathology has sometimes been suggested by weight gain at onset, hypogenitality, polyuria or polydipsia.

Most of the cases with cerebral pathology, however, are more properly regarded as hypersomnias than narcolepsy, with sleeps of long duration or sustained severe drowsiness. Cataplexy has been extremely rare in such examples. The exception appears to be encephalitis lethargica which has occasionally been followed by cataplexy as well as narcolepsy (Adie, 1926; Sours, 1963). These post-encephalitic cases tended to recover, however, whereas idiopathic narcolepsy persists throughout life. Sours also noted that post-encephalitic narcoleptic attacks tended to be paroxysmal and of longer duration, and were usually accompanied by other evidence of hypothalamic damage, pupillary abnormalities and personality changes.

Altogether when narcolepsy and cataplexy are found together it has proved exceptional to find any evidence of organic brain disease; Yoss and Daly (1957) found no evidence of a cerebral lesion in 59 cases seen personally and 241 records drawn from the Mayo Clinic.

Neurophysiological theories seek to illuminate narcolepsy through what is known of the physiological basis of normal sleep, and in particular through EEG and polygraph observations. It has been established that the routine EEG shows no abnormalities in narcolepsy, beyond the expected changes when the subject is drowsy and the normal sleep changes while asleep (Daly and Yoss, 1957). During cataplectic attacks and episodes of sleep paralysis the EEG tracing remains unchanged. But more discriminating assessment of the stages of sleep shows interesting differences from normals:

Polygraph recordings have established that normal sleep consists of two distinct varieties, REM (rapid eye movement) and non-REM sleep. The EEG in non-REM sleep is synchronous and shows sleep spindles, K-complexes and generalised slowing with delta waves. Four stages are recognised within it, stages 3 and 4 being characterised particularly as slow wave sleep. REM sleep, by contrast, shows an asynchronous mixed frequency EEG accompanied by bursts of rapid conjugate eye movements. Autonomic changes are prominent, with elevation of heart rate, pulse and blood pressure and penile tumescence. There is a marked decrease in general muscle tone, and extensor plantar responses may occur. Thus REM sleep has been characterised as 'an awake brain in a paralysed body' (Zarcone, 1973). It is during this phase that dreaming is liable to occur (Hartmann, 1965).

In normal sleep drowsiness first gives way to non-REM sleep of gradually increasing depth. The first REM period occurs after some 50–90 minutes and lasts some 5–10 minutes, then the whole cycle is repeated at approximately 90 minute intervals. Four to six REM periods occur each night, each tending to be longer as the night progresses. Altogether REM sleep occupies some 20–25% of the total night's sleep.

Evidence has accumulated to suggest that non-REM sleep is related to serotonergic mechanisms which bring about inhibition of the brain stem reticular activity. REM sleep appears to be related to catecholaminergic mechanisms, and to be initiated and regulated by areas in the pontine reticular formation, including the locus caeruleus which is responsible for the muscle inhibition and areflexia.

Rechtschaffen *et al.* (1963) discovered a distinctive feature in the nocturnal sleep of narcoleptics, namely that a REM period occurred at the onset, or very shortly after the onset, instead of after the usual period of 90 minutes or so. Daytime sleep attacks have also been shown to consist of REM-type sleep, almost invariably so when the patient suffers from cataplexy as well as narcolepsy (Dement *et al.,* 1964, 1966; Hishikawa and Kaneko, 1965; Hishikawa *et al.,* 1968). In patients with narcoleptic attacks alone, however, the early REM phase is rarely seen, and daytime attacks are accompanied by non-REM slow wave sleep. Episodes of hallucinations or sleep paralysis have proved to occur exclusively in the sleep onset REM periods, and where recordings could be obtained during cataplectic attacks the REM picture was again obtained. Night time sleep is also generally deranged. In addition to direct or early onset into REM there are often marked phasic REM bursts, poorly regulated sleep cycles, many shifts of phase and frequent awakenings.

Thus it seems that the pathogenesis of the narcolepsy syndrome may lie in an abnormality of the triggering mechanism which produces REM sleep in normal individuals. In essence the principal phenomena represent attacks of REM sleep occurring out of proper context. Cataplectic attacks and episodes of sleep paralysis appear to represent a dissociated manifestation of the descending motor inhibitory component of REM sleep, without triggering of the ascending (sleep) component. Hypnagogic hallucinations may be a variant of the vivid dreaming normally associated with REM sleep.

Many puzzling questions remain, however, particularly regarding the status of patients with narcoleptic attacks alone. In these there is usually no disturbance of REM sleep, suggesting that they may represent a distinct category of the disorder. Roth and Bruhova (1969) suggest that narcolepsy alone may occupy an intermediate place, between narcolepsy with cataplexy on the one hand and hypersomnia on the other. Clearly longitudinal studies will be necessary to indicate what happens in such patients when the accessory symptoms ultimately develop. Moreover the external character of daytime sleep attacks seems identical, whether or not accessory symptoms are present.

The precise pathological mechanisms underlying the abnormalities still remain unknown, even though the polygraphic correlates are gradually being established. It remains unclear whether there is an exceptional reactivity of structures responsible for REM sleep, or a deficiency of the mechanisms producing non-REM sleep, or both. It is likely that the non-REM system is abnormal as well, as witnessed by the frequent periods of drowsiness which occur apart from actual attacks of sleep, also the frequent failure of nocturnal non-REM sleep to reach the normal depth (Roth and Bruhova, 1969). It is even possible that disordered and disrupted nocturnal sleep is the primary phenomenon, with daytime sleep attacks and cataplectic attacks arising in a compensatory manner (Mitchell and Dement, 1968).

Genetic factors have emerged as significant in narcolepsy. Among 400 consecutive patients Yoss and Daly (1960a) found a positive family history in approximately a third. Occasional families were found where the disorder appeared to be transmitted as an autosomal dominant. However, Yoss (1970) suggested that the narcoleptic tendency may be polygenically determined, and emerge in a graded manner similarly to traits such as stature or intelligence. Measurement of pupil size under infra-red light allows the monitoring of ability to remain alert in darkness, and it has been found that unaffected relatives of narcoleptics often show greater drowsiness than normal under such circumstances. The clinically overt disorder may therefore represent one pole of a spectrum which blends into the norm, the opposite being represented by persons who remain alert despite unusually little sleep at night. An inborn error of metabolism may be the link whereby the genetic tendency is realised as abnormalities of the REM and non-REM phases of sleep (Parkes, 1973). Most recently, strong linkage has been found between narcolepsy and certain HLA subtypes, as described by Parkes (1985).

Treatment

Analeptic drugs have proved to be the mainstay of treatment for daytime sleep attacks, though their use is often rather unsatisfactory. Dextroamphetamine sulphate (Dexedrine), racemic amphetamine sulphate (Benzedrine) and methylphenidate (Ritalin) have been most widely employed. The latter was regarded as the drug of choice by Yoss and Daly (1959), with fewer side effects and possibly some improvement in cataplectic attacks as well. Levoamphetamine has been regarded as superior to the dextro-isomer (Schwab and Passouant, 1964), but Parkes and Fenton (1973) were unable to confirm this in a controlled trial. Neither drug had any effect on cataplectic symptoms. In actual practice it is always wise to try the effects of one of the less potent stimulant drugs, such as mazindol or fencamphamin, before proceeding to dextroamphetamine or methylphenidate (Parkes, 1985).

The use of amphetamines has many problems. High dosage may be required to control attacks, resulting in side effects of insomnia, anorexia, irritability, tremor, hypertension, and on rare occasions acute paranoid psychoses. Moreover when pushed to high dosage nocturnal insomnia may lead to an increase in daytime drowsiness and sleep attacks. Addiction is an additional risk, though in fact this appears to be rare among narcoleptics.

Such drugs are known to suppress the REM stage of sleep, which may possibly be the mechanism of their action in narcolepsy rather than a direct stimulant effect. Cataplexy and other accessory symptoms are nevertheless little benefited.

Tricyclic antidepressants such as imipramine have been found to reduce cataplectic attacks, also episodes of sleep paralysis and hypnagogic hallucinations. Clomipramine (Anafranil) is more powerful still, and can work when imipramine fails (Parkes, 1973; Guilleminault *et al.*, 1974). Tricyclic antidepressants have no direct effect on narcoleptic sleep attacks, but when employed along with amphetamines they may allow the dose of the latter to be reduced. In theory it could be dangerous to use tricyclics and amphetamines together, with risk of hypertensive crises, but Zarcone (1973) has employed imipramine with methylphenidate in 45 cases with no apparent harm.

Diazepam can be useful in controlling disturbed nocturnal sleep, since unlike other sedatives this does not deprive the subject of REM sleep.

Monoamine oxidase inhibitors such as phenelzine have been reported to help all components of the syndrome—narcoleptic attacks, cataplexy, sleep paralysis and hypnagogic hallucinations (Wyatt *et al.*, 1971). Side effects are liable to be troublesome, but a trial may nevertheless be warranted in very disabled patients. Levodopa showed reasonably encouraging effects in a preliminary trial (Gunne *et al.*, 1971), but the high incidence of gastrointestinal disturbance suggested that it would be unsuitable for long-term therapy.

Counselling has an important part to play, with advice about acquiring a regular pattern of sleep and daytime activities, and perhaps establishing schedules for daytime naps to ward off spontaneous attacks. Shift work must be avoided, or work where drowsiness or falls could be a hazard. Psychotherapy will stand to help in certain cases where the narcolepsy is aggravated by neurotic or interpersonal conflicts, or where secondary social and personal adjustments must be made to the disability.

PSYCHIATRIC ASPECTS OF NARCOLEPSY

In addition to the problems of differential diagnosis, already discussed, the features which have attracted most psychiatric attention are the role of sudden emotions in precipitating cataplexy and the role of emotional conflicts in exacerbating daytime sleep attacks. Interest has also centred on the possibilities that personality change may follow the onset of the disorder, and that schizophrenia-like psychoses may sometimes develop as an extension of the hypnagogic hallucinations.

Susceptibility to Psychological Factors

Cataplectic attacks usually show such a striking relationship to immediately antecedent emotional stimuli that the causal connection cannot be doubted (p. 619). Laughter is classically regarded as the most common precipitant, but Levin (1953) has stressed that aggression is frequently involved, also that laughter may sometimes be based on hostility. Some patients become immediately weak when attempting to discipline their children or when engaging in other angry interchanges. Levin suggests that it is the guilt associated with anger, and the conflict between impulses to express or restrain the feeling, which is often the true precipitant. When aggression was justified, and not provocative of guilt, cataplexy seemed less likely to occur.

Smith and Hamilton (1959) suggest that emotional factors play an important part in precipitating other component parts of the syndrome as well. They review the scattered evidence that narcoleptic attacks and even episodes of sleep paralysis could be related to conflict situations. Among seven cases of their own they found a close relationship between the intensity of symptoms and current psychological stresses. Situations evoking resentment which could

not be expressed seemed particularly likely to bring on attacks both of narcolepsy and cataplexy. In four of the seven there appeared to be a definite relationship between sleep attacks and strong feelings of suppressed anger. Less surprisingly the content of sleep hallucinations was sometimes related to underlying conflicts or preceding traumatic events. In three patients the illness had set in at a time of considerable emotional stress, but it did not remit thereafter when the life situation improved. Improvements in life circumstances did not alter the course of the illness, whereas analeptics did.

Thus while rejecting a psychogenic aetiology for the condition, Smith and Hamilton stress that psychological factors can often greatly aggravate or ameliorate the manifestations. The relationships which obtain between psychological events, in the context of the individual experiencing them, and the physiological changes which have issue in narcoleptic manifestations, would appear to be a fruitful area for further investigation.

Impact on Personality

There is little consensus of opinion concerning the personality in narcoleptics. Some have regarded the majority of patients as stable and well adjusted, whereas others have reported a high incidence of personality abnormalities. In Daniels' (1934) large material most patients were sensitive about their infirmity, sometimes looking upon it as personal weakness and becoming depressed and socially withdrawn. An air of reserve or gravity was often adopted to avoid precipitation of cataplectic attacks. Severe disturbance of personality was not, however, seen. Only 10 of 147 patients showed clear-cut neurotic or psychopathic tendencies and these were not severe in degree. Very occasionally there was a suspicion of impaired memory or diminished mental acuity.

Pond (1952b) studied eight cases in detail and found all to be of above average intelligence. An emotional flatness and passivity was noted, however, and few had reached social or employment positions commensurate with their intelligence. None showed overt neurotic traits or behaviour disorders, but sexual maladjustment was common. All four married men suffered premature ejaculation and the one married woman was frigid.

Smith and Hamilton's (1959) seven patients appeared to have reacted severely to the illness. Withdrawal, loss of confidence and insecurity were often marked. Several were anxious, lonely and depressed. The embarrassing and humiliating nature of the symptoms appeared to account for such developments, also the disturbing nature of the sleep hallucinations.

Sours (1963) has given a particularly grave account of the psychopathology in 75 cases. The personality configuration was described as predominantly 'passive-aggressive'. Affect was in general flat, though this was hard to evaluate since many were sleepy during interview. Contrary to other accounts based on large numbers of cases there was a high incidence of anxiety and depression, and several showed hysterical symptoms. Eight showed schizoid personality disturbances and ten more developed frank schizophrenic illnesses which required prolonged hospitalisation. Five of the 45 men were impotent.

In a series of 20 patients, 18 from a neurological clinic and 2 from a psychiatric clinic, Roy (1976) has obtained further evidence that psychiatric disability is common. Eight had current evidence of psychiatric disorder and 4 more a history of such, chiefly in the form of depressive neuroses and personality disorders. Five further patients had had difficulties at work, in marriage and in social life. A striking finding was that 9 of the 10 females had been frigid for many years, with failure to achieve orgasm over long periods of time and often throughout their married lives. Of the 10 men one was impotent and another had premature ejaculation.

The impact of the disorder on patient's lives was illustrated in a questionnaire study by Broughton and Ghanem (1976). Many reported recurrent depression, often severe, and almost half described subjective worsening of memory since the onset of the disease. Employment difficulties were common, both on account of sleep attacks and personality difficulties. A surprising number of patients had suffered accidents, either while driving or while engaged in household activities. Recreational pursuits were commonly hampered to a distressing degree.

Roth (1980) reviews evidence of a special association between narcolepsy and depression, which appears to be commoner than in the general population. A parallelism may sometimes be detected, the sleep attacks becoming more pronounced during phases when the patient is depressed.

Psychoses with Narcolepsy

Schizophrenia-like psychoses appear to develop in narcoleptic patients more frequently than chance expectation, and often without clear evidence of genetic predisposition. Davison and Bagley (1969) identified 18 acceptable examples in the literature, only one with a family history of schizophrenia. Such psychoses, when short-lived, may sometimes be attributable to the ingestion of amphetamines, but only 5 of the 18 cases under consideration were taking such medication. Davison and Bagley inclined to the hypothesis that both the narcoleptic syndrome and the psychosis were manifestations of diencephalic dysfunction.

The nosological status of these psychoses, and their relationship to other narcoleptic manifestations, has attracted a good deal of attention. The predominance of visual hallucinations has been noted, often with an emphasis on reptiles and other animals, and sometimes with the patient a spectator of movie-like experiences (Eilenberg and Woods, 1962). Though compatible with schizophrenia such features tend to suggest an organically based psychosis. In many examples the psychosis appears to have developed as a direct extension of vivid dreams or hypnagogic experiences, which then come to determine the content of persisting delusions and hallucinations. Sleep hallucinosis is, however, by no means an invariable precursor. Sours (1963) found no greater degree of sleep hallucinosis in the patients who developed schizophrenic reactions than in those who did not, and Davison and Bagley found a history of sleep hallucinations in only 10 of their 18 examples.

Coren and Strain (1965) suggest that two distinct types of psychosis should be recognised. The first is typical of schizophrenia generally, with the classical features of loosening of associations, formal thought disorder, inappropriate affect, disturbance of volition, and lack of insight into hallucinations and delusional beliefs. These psychoses seem to appear in conjunction with narcolepsy by pure coincidence. The second type is essentially a paranoid-hallucinatory state and is atypical of schizophrenia in many ways. Affect remains appropriate to thought content, there is no formal thought disorder, and rapport and insight are retained to a marked degree. It is in this category that pre-existing dreams and hypnagogic experiences often become strikingly interwoven into the content of the psychosis. Coren and Strain suggest that in such cases the patient has had sufficiently tenuous reality-testing for the hypnagogic hallucinations to bring about a failure of psychological defence mechanisms. Typical examples of this latter group would appear to be as follows:

A girl of 15 had narcoleptic attacks and terrifying nocturnal dreams. The dreams and hallucinatory experiences began to occur by day as well as by night and she came to believe in their reality. After control of the narcolepsy with ephedrine she gained considerable insight though this was not complete.

(Daniels, 1934)

A 34-year-old woman suffering from narcolepsy and cataplexy had vivid dreams at night and also during daytime attacks. Hypnagogic hallucinations occurred in auditory, visual and tactile modalities. She ultimately developed recurrent psychotic episodes in the course of which she would believe in the reality of the dreams and hallucinatory experiences. After hallucinating the presence of her husband with another woman she became convinced that he was having affairs for several weeks. She dreamt about having intercourse with partly human partly animal forms, and developed extensive delusions about persecution by the hospital staff. She always recognised to some extent that she was ill, and would frequently question the reality of her hallucinations. The delusions appeared always to be derived from these, rather than to have arisen independently. But with each recurrence of the psychosis the distinction between hallucinations and reality gradually became more difficult until she believed the events depicted therein had actually occurred. There was no evidence at any stage of loosening of associations, inappropriate affect, or other symptoms fundamental to a diagnosis of schizophrenia.

(Coren and Strain, 1965)

Forms which are intermediate between circumscribed nocturnal hallucinations and frank psychosis also appear to occur:

A narcoleptic patient heard doors banging during episodes of sleep paralysis, and people talking who he believed were trying to poison him. He could hear people walking across the room and feel hands trying to force pills into his mouth. Usually these ideas disappeared the moment he managed to open his eyes but on occasion they persisted for an hour or up to 24 hours. He took to sleeping with a pistol and had grilles put on the windows because he was so afraid at night. Even in recounting his story it seemed that he did not have full insight, and kept reassuring himself that his wife could not be responsible.

(Thigpen and Moss, 1955)

Other Sleep Disorders

Other syndromes of sleep disturbance have come to be recognised, including 'idiopathic hypersomnia', hypersomnia with 'sleep drunkenness', hypersomnias with sleep apnoea (including the Pickwickian syndrome), and the Kleine–Levin syndrome. In addition there are hypersomnias based on identifi-

able cerebral disease and metabolic dysfunction, and others which appear to be based on psychological factors alone. Brief mention will also be made of somnambulism and 'night-terrors' which very occasionally present for medical attention in adult patients.

Idiopathic Hypersomnia

Under this title Roth (1980) delineates a sizeable group of patients, rarely mentioned in the literature but considered by him to represent an independent nosological entity. Among patients referred to Roth's clinic in Prague this group came second only to narcolepsy in frequency.

The chief difference from narcolepsy lies in the longer duration of the day-time sleeps which typically last from half an hour to several hours at a time. Cataplexy and the other classical accessory symptoms of narcolepsy are absent. The periods of day-time somnolence lack the irresistible quality of narcolepsy but the patient is nevertheless obliged to fight against sleepiness for a large part of the day. At night he falls asleep quickly and sleeps deeply, often with difficulty in waking in the morning. 'Sleep drunkenness' (see below) may be a feature on rising. Prolongation of nocturnal sleep may be present, as well as day-time somnolence. At weekends some patients sleep more or less continuously while undisturbed.

The condition sets in usually between the ages of 10 and 20, developing over the course of several months then tending to remain stable as a source of life-long disability. Occasionally the onset may be later, even well into middle age. Males are affected slightly more commonly than females. In some 30% of cases it occurs familially. In all these respects the resemblance to narcolepsy is obvious.

Among Roth's 167 cases, almost half showed psychological difficulties—neurotic problems, personality disturbances and depression. During phases of depression the periods of sleepiness were usually increased. Sixteen per cent had sexual problems, with lack of libido or potency in the men and menstrual disturbances in the women. As with narcolepsy, troubles with education, jobs and recreation were frequent, and often even more severe on account of the long duration of day-time sleeps.

The cause is unknown but presumably rests on biochemical disturbances of the neural mechanisms underlying sleeping and waking. Roth discounts psychogenic factors, likewise any known brain pathology by his criteria for accumulating the sample. EEG and polygraphic records showed non-REM patterns to be prominent during diurnal sleeps, often proceeding to stages 3 and 4. All night records revealed normal sleep organisation except for its long duration. Treatment consists of the administration of central stimulant drugs, as in narcolepsy.

Hypersomnia with 'Sleep Drunkenness'

Roth *et al*. (1972) initially reported this as an independent clinical syndrome, representing 30% of the patients in Prague who were referred for investigation of sleep disturbances. Now, however, it is viewed essentially as a variant or complication of idiopathic hypersomnia (Roth, 1980).

'Sleep drunkenness' consists of difficulty in achieving complete wakefulness, accompanied by confusion, disorientation, poor motor coordination, slowness and repeated returns to sleep. A large group of patients showed this as a chronic symptom, occurring with almost every awakening and typically persisting as a lifelong tendency (Roth *et al*., 1972). In the great majority daytime hypersomnia was present as well. The patients were rarely capable of waking spontaneously but needed vigorous and persistent stimulation. Even when so awakened they were confused, disoriented and ataxic in a manner resembling drunkenness for between 15 minutes and 1 hour or longer. Many showed impaired efficiency for up to 4 hours.

The majority reported extremely deep and prolonged nocturnal sleep, often failing to wake spontaneously for 16–17 hours. At night they fell asleep rapidly within seconds of retiring. Associated symptoms consisted of headache, recurrent depression, difficulty with concentration or emotional lability. Eight patients had severe personality disorders or showed psychotic features. However, there was no characteristic personality type or psychopathology, and psychiatric symptoms were not inevitable accompaniments.

The course appeared to be stationary in the absence of treatment—once declared the disability could last until advanced age. Most patients responded well to analeptic drugs taken by day and immediately before retiring. Alternatively they could be administered immediately after the initial awakening, the patient being allowed thereafter to sleep for half an hour more, after which he would either wake spontaneously or could be easily roused.

In 52 of the 58 examples there was no apparent cause. Six were possibly symptomatic of organic brain disorder, setting in shortly after severe head injury, encephalitis or a cerebrovascular accident. In the idiopathic cases the pathophysiology remained obscure. Essentially the disorder appeared to represent an extension and intensification of the normal processes of sleep.

Apart from the chronic syndrome described above, sleep drunkenness can also occur as an occasional symptom in healthy persons if, for example, they are suddenly awakened after too little sleep. It is facilitated by fatigue, or the consumption of alcohol or hypnotics before retiring. It has also been described in persons of irritable disposition and in people subject to frequent terrifying dreams. Roth *et al*. (1972) refer to such examples in the older psychiatric and criminological literature, including persons who have become aggressive or even homicidal while in a state of sleep drunkenness.

Hypersomnia with Sleep Apnoea

A great deal of interest has come to centre on certain hypersomnias accompanied by alveolar hypoventilation. Best known is the Pickwickian syndrome, so-called by Burwell *et al*. (1956) after the fat boy of *Pickwick Papers*. However, several variants exist. The topic is comprehensively reviewed by Lugaresi *et al*. (1978) and Cummisky (1982).

Most cases develop between the ages of 40 and 60, but children can also be affected. The phases of day-time sleepiness are usually profound and very compelling, sometimes affecting the patient when standing, talking or eating. They are usually of brief duration and frequent throughout the day. Obesity, cyanosis, right heart failure and polycythaemia are common associated features. During sleep, by day and by night, respiratory disturbances give the characteristic stamp to the picture. The breathing becomes periodic, with apnoeic intervals lasting 10–20 seconds, during which the level of sleep steadily deepens. Resumption of breathing is accompanied by deep sighing and gutteral snoring. While apnoeic the blood oxygen falls considerably and the blood carbon dioxide rises. Muscular twitching may be marked. Nocturnal sleep is similarly affected with restlessness, frequent awakenings and myoclonic jerks. While awake, respiratory function studies may show normal results, or persistent alveolar hypoventilation with consequent blood gas changes.

In marked examples mental symptoms can figure prominently. Sackner *et al*. (1975) found a high incidence of personality disturbance with paranoia, hostility and sometimes agitated depression. Guilleminault and Anders (1976) reported that a third of children with the syndrome showed borderline mental retardation when first seen. Repetitive cerebral hypoxia may play a role in the genesis of such disturbances.

The detailed pathophysiology of the situation is often complex, as reviewed by Cummisky (1982). Schwartz *et al.* (1967) proposed that the day-time somnolence and the periodic respiration were both constitutionally determined, and brought to the fore when obesity aggravated the respiratory insufficiency. However, cases may be seen without obesity. Several variants are now recognised, some with primary obstruction to the airways and some with central disturbances of the respiratory regulatory mechanisms. The respiratory centres may be relatively insensitive to carbon-dioxide, with obesity as a secondary complication (Passouant *et al.*, 1967); or there may be an abnormality of the centres manifest as loss of automaticity of breathing while asleep ('Ondine's curse syndrome', Severinghaus and Mitchell, 1962).

The course can be protracted and serious if untreated. Cor pulmonale, heart failure and acute respiratory insufficiency may develop. A high incidence of unexpected deaths has been reported (MacGregor *et al.*, 1970). Treatment must aim at relieving airway obstruction when this exists, and there must be strenuous attempts at reduction of obesity. The day-time somnolence can then improve markedly. Tracheostomy has been widely employed in patients not otherwise responsive and with severely disabling examples of the syndrome.

Kleine–Levin Syndrome

Levin (1936) drew attention to a rare syndrome of periodic somnolence, often lasting for days or weeks at a time and associated with intense hunger. Mental symptoms by way of irritability, excitement and motor unrest also characterised the somnolent phases. Kleine (1925) had earlier reported several examples. Critchley (1962) carried out a detailed analysis of the 15 cases in the literature at that time and added 11 of his own. In contrast to the other sleep disorders considered above this is a 'long-cycle hypersomnia', the episodes being separated by months or even years of normal health.

The great majority of cases have been in young men and with onset in early adolescence. The very occasional cases in women (Gilbert, 1964) or with onset in middle life (Gallinek, 1954), have shown other atypical features. The onset usually appears to be quite spontaneous, though sometimes a 'flu-like illness or a period of physical stress has antedated the first attack. The duration of attacks may range from several days to several weeks. Their frequency varies from one to twelve per year with an average of two per year.

Somnolence is the most conspicuous symptom. It may set in abruptly or follow gradually after several days of mounting malaise and tiredness. The patient sleeps excessively by day and night, rousing only to eat or empty bladder and bowels. Incontinence does not occur. He is always rousable, as from natural sleep, but is then liable to be intensely irritable and truculent. When awake he eats voraciously, typically consuming any food in sight. Critchley (1962) prefers the term 'megaphagia' to 'morbid hunger'; compulsive eating in a wolfish and greedy manner is a conspicuous feature, but the patient does not complain of hunger itself and rarely demands food when this is not in sight.

Throughout the attack there are few if any abnormal physical signs. The temperature and pulse are usually normal, the pupils may be unequal, and a plantar reflex may be upgoing. The cerebrospinal fluid is normal and the electroencephalogram shows the usual changes of drowsiness or sleep. Each attack ends spontaneously, usually in a gradual manner but sometimes abruptly.

Mental abnormalities during attacks have attracted much attention. They may be in evidence when the sleeper is roused or wakes spontaneously. Sometimes they also antedate and follow each attack for a short period of time.

Irritability is typically marked, extending at times to severe aggression when disturbed. Uninhibited insolent behaviour may emerge, or motor unrest with fidgety behaviour, agitation and tearing at the sheets. Confusion of thought is usually evident too, with disorientation, forgetfulness, depersonalisation and muddled speech. Vivid imagery may be prominent, with waking fantasies which are difficult to disentangle from vivid dreams. Visual and auditory hallucinations may occur. Occasionally the picture has a distinctly schizophrenic colouring: one of Critchley's patients felt responsible for all the events of which he was aware, and believed he could stop a clock with his thoughts and control his own hearing and vision.

Usually the mental abnormalities subside as the period of somnolence ends, but sometimes they persist for days or weeks thereafter. Depression with insomnia is not uncommon for several days. In 2 of Gallinek's (1954) patients severe depression persisted for several weeks after every attack, with suicidal tendencies, retardation and pathological guilt. A period of elation lasting several weeks has occasionally been reported (Gilbert, 1964), also a phase of sexual hyperactivity when the sleep is over (Passouant *et al.*, 1967). Quite often anorexia, headache and malaise follow the attack before the patient feels fully refreshed and regains normal clarity of thought. Thereafter, however, the patient returns to his normal personality, usually with a partial or total amnesia for what has occurred.

The rarity of the syndrome can lead to diagnostic difficulties. It is probably rarely recognised until several attacks have occurred, especially since the overeating may be overlooked and is often unapparent to the patient himself. Other causes of morbid somnolence are likely to be diagnosed and hysteria may easily be suspected. Disturbed behaviour may dominate the picture, suggesting that the essential problem is a personality disorder or even schizophrenia. When circumstances prevent the patient from taking to his bed he may become slovenly, unkempt and very erratic in conduct as in the following case reported by Robinson and McQuillan (1951):

An army officer cadet of 19 came to the notice of the army doctors in an abnormal mental state. He was unkempt, offhand, casual and disinterested, answering vaguely and smiling fatuously. Affect was shallow and inappropriate and he experienced auditory hallucinations. He was clearly confused and it was almost impossible to maintain contact with him. Cerebration was slow and there was evidence of thought blocking. In hospital he was hostile and insolent. Behaviour was often bizarre and he masturbated openly, grinning broadly. He slept a great deal and his appetite could not be satisfied. After 4 days in hospital the disturbance cleared abruptly, and he again became smart, respectful and well mannered. He was amnesic for the events of the previous days though he realised that he had behaved badly and had been unable to control himself.

A history was then obtained of previous attacks, 2 years and 3 years earlier, each lasting several days and accompanied by sonmolence and excessive hunger. In the first he had become strange and distant, avoiding company and seeming unaware of what was said to him. On two successive nights he had micturated into a pair of gumboots and was apathetic and unashamed when his family protested. He had sold a bicycle for 25 shillings and spent the money on preserved fruits which he consumed at one sitting. In the second attack he again became drowsy and with an insatiable appetite, and created much disturbance with laughing and shouting. After each attack he had returned abruptly to his normal personality.

Follow-up suggests that the disorder is essentially benign. Attacks appear gradually to lessen in duration, frequency and severity over several years, and ultimately cease. Amphetamines have been claimed to reduce the frequency and severity of the attacks (Gallinek, 1962). Lithium proved remarkably effective in preventing attacks in a typical example of the syndrome, with recurrence immediately the drug was withdrawn (Ogura *et al.*, 1976). Similar success with lithium has also been reported in periodic hypersomnia unaccompanied by appetite changes (Abe, 1977).

Little can be adduced by way of explanation for the disorder. Physical and mental health are usually normal between attacks, and few patients have shown evidence of significant maladjustment. No discernible precipitants can be discovered for individual attacks. Pai (1950) attempted to include the syndrome amongst hypersomnias due to neurosis or hysteria, but most observers have been at pains to reject such an explanation. The similarity between one case and another, and the uniform course pursued, have combined to suggest an organic basis. Diencephalic dysfunction is suggested by the combination of sleep and appetite disturbance.

Hypersomnias Due to Identifiable Organic Disease

The hypersomnias seen with overt cerebral or metabolic disease differ from the syndromes described above in many respects. They are rarely episodic and lack the transient and overwhelming nature of the narcoleptic attack. Sustained drowsiness is characteristic, or periods of sleep greatly in excess of normal requirements. Sometimes sleep inversion is seen with agitated delirium at night. In contrast to narcolepsy the sleep of such hypersomnias does not refresh. Depending on the responsible pathology the patient may be roused with ease or difficulty, and to varying levels of alertness. The sleep is usually undisturbed and vivid dreams are rare.

Lesions involving the midbrain tegmentum or posterior hypothalamus are a common cause. The responsible pathology may be a tumour, vascular lesion or degenerative process. Prolonged hypersomnia may follow head injury, encephalitis lethargica, general paresis, or cerebral oedema from any cause. Infective processes such as encephalitis, typhoid, trypanosomiasis or tuberculous meningitis are regularly accompanied by somnolence. Excessive hunger and weight gain may be seen with the somnolence of hypothalamic lesions, likewise polyuria and polydipsia. Pupillary abnormalities may be seen after encephalitis lethargica or head injury.

Metabolic disorders such as uraemia occasionally present with somnolence, similarly the encephalopathies associated with anoxia, chronic respiratory insufficiency or hepatic disorder. Endocrine causes include myxoedema, Cushing's and Addison's disease, diabetes and hyperinsulinism. Rarer causes are industrial toxins and lead encephalopathy.

Sometimes organic hypersomnias are accompanied by psychiatric symptomatology, chiefly neurasthenic or depressive pictures. A patient described by Roth (1980) showed periodic hypersomnia and manic depressive psychosis following a head injury, the hypersomnia phases accompanying the depression; while depressed he slept for 20 hours per day, while hypomanic for 3 or 4.

The electroencephalogram in such conditions generally shows the picture of sleep together with various anomalies in the form of diffuse slow components or bursts of bifrontal or generalised slow waves. The cyclic organisation of REM and non-REM sleep is often modified or disrupted.

Insomnia following cerebral lesions has very occasionally been described. Bricolo (1967) reported a patient who developed total insomnia for 96 hours following bilateral stereotactic thalamotomy for Parkinson's disease. Thereafter he showed inversion of the sleep-wakefulness rhythm which very gradually became more regular.

A remarkable post-traumatic example was described by Webb and Kirker (1981). A 33-year-old woman still showed severe insomnia $2\frac{1}{2}$ years after a relatively mild head injury. On some nights she claimed she did not sleep at all, while on others she slept for about an hour. In the evenings she felt exhausted but not somnolent. EEG and polygraph recordings on four consecutive nights supported her story, showing brief light sleep for less than an hour and no REM sleep. Hypnotics and sedatives were ineffective in doses that left her alert the following day. Nevertheless, four consecutive nightly doses of L-5-hydroxytryptophan, the precursor of serotonin, were dramatically effective, restoring normal sleep which persisted during several months follow-up. In the absence of further examples it is hard to interpret such a response, though it remains possible that the drug served to trigger normal sleep mechanisms in the presence of some highly discrete brain stem lesion.

Hypersomnias Associated with Psychiatric Disorder

Most studies of patients with hypersomnia reveal cases in which psychological factors are clearly of aetiological importance. The proportion varies, however, according to the orientation of the observer. Roth (1980) points out that during the last century most hypersomnias were thought to be emotional in origin, then organic causes and clear-cut syndromes such as narcolepsy came gradually to be delineated. It still remains uncertain how many cases have a definite psychological causation, as opposed to prominent psychological accompaniments to some other definable cause. Mixed patterns can present especial difficulties, since many of the recognised syndromes described above are strongly influenced by prevailing mood states and environmental factors.

The nosology as well as the incidence of psychogenic hypersomnias remains unclear. In the course of accumulating 88 narcoleptics, Sours (1963) found 7 patients with hypersomnia that was symptomatic of organic conditions and 20 with hypersomnia attributable to psychiatric disorder; of the latter 9 were regarded as neurotic in origin, 2 as depressive reactions, 2 as hysterical and 7 as schizophrenic. Smith (1958b) suggested that most reported cases of psychogenic hypersomnia would more accurately be labelled as hysterical trances or psychotic stupors.

All agree that hysterical dissociation and depression are the major factors in well-marked examples, with a frequent theme of withdrawal from conflict-laden situations. The somnolence may set in abruptly after traumatic events or emotional upheavals, persisting thereafter for hours or days, or the condition may present recurrently over many months or years.

The following examples almost certainly reflect hysterical mechanisms at work:

One remarkable report concerned a patient who slept for 32 years, but during that time she cried when hearing bad news, would allow only certain persons to attend her and was heard occasionally to speak (*The sleeper of Oknö*, Fröderström, 1912).

A woman of 49 had a history of sleeping attacks for a year, sometimes lasting 36 hours at a time. Hysterical conversion features were present and became intensified during somnolent phases. When confronted with painful topics from her past life, drowsy attacks could be precipitated, but if caught in time and persuaded to expose the conflict-laden material she would return to normal alertness within minutes. She had had an incestuous relationship with her father and had also had a lover throughout her married life. 'Confessional catharsis' led to a great lessening of attacks in the years that followed.

(Spiegel and Oberndorf, 1946)

Depressive rather than hysterical mechanisms may have been operative in the following patient:

A 31-year-old teacher had had meningoencephalitis at 3 and was widowed at 22. From the age of 30 she frequently felt ill and suffered from headaches and giddiness whenever upset. After a 10 year relationship she broke off her engagement saying that her fiancé was not sufficiently well educated. After this she claimed to have slept for a whole week. Since then she had often fallen asleep, sometimes against her will and usually for a whole day. This always occurred after an emotionally upsetting experience. She ultimately improved with psychotherapy and light sedation.

(Roth, 1980)

Hysterical states of somnolence will usually differ in several respects from true sleep. The patient may be unrousable even to painful stimuli, or show gross hysterical stigmata. The prolonged maintenance of certain postures, eyelid tremor, increased muscle tension or contraction of the masseters may be in evidence. Electroencephalogram recordings made during such states may show wakefulness, perhaps even greater desynchronisation than usual, with a preponderance of fast activity and a good deal of muscle artefact.

Depressive hypersomnias, by contrast, may consist of long periods of genuine sleep; hence the difficulties that may be encountered in reaching a firm diagnosis. It is well recognised that brief hypersomnia may accompany depression or be the presenting feature (Detre et al., 1972; Kupfer et al., 1972; O'Regan, 1974). In depressive hypersomnias attacks will rarely extend beyond 24 hours at a time, the posture during sleep will be normal, and rousing will usually be possible. Many so-called depressive hypersomnias may, however, represent examples of Roth's 'idiopathic hypersomnia' accompanied by neurasthenic features.

Patients who display negativism, flexibilitas cerea or other catatonic phenomena in the absence of extrapyramidal disease will be suspected of psychotic illness, either affective or schizophrenic in nature.

Unfortunately few modern laboratory studies appear to have been made in relation to reported cases of psychogenic hypersomnia. These would seem essential in working towards adequate differentiation between cases which rest on organic or pathophysiological factors, and those which are primarily due to psychological causes. In the meantime it is necessary to evaluate each patient as fully as possible for neurological and psychiatric disorder. It can be helpful to consider the following aspects individually (Roth, 1980): determination from clinical observation of whether or not the attacks represent genuine sleep; evaluation of the course, whether static over years or intermittent, and

the effect of external factors upon it; the exclusion of any possible organic cause; assessment of the personality for evidence of pre-existent neurotic features; and the mounting of combined EEG and polygraphic studies, wherever possible during attacks. Where psychiatric factors appear to be causative their alleviation may be decisive in clarifying the diagnosis. Treatment with stimulant drugs carries obvious hazards in any patient whose hypersomnia is due to psychological disturbance.

Somnambulism

Sleep walking occurs predominantly in males. There is frequently a family history of the disorder and an association with enuresis. The great majority of cases occur in children, and the rare examples coming to attention in adult life are often among sevicemen or men under indictment for an offence carried out during an alleged sleep-walking spell.

Behaviour during the somnambulistic episode may consist of walking about aimlessly, or more rarely intense activity such as running, jumping or searching for something. Usually the behaviour is banal and stereotyped. Movements tend to be repetitive and purposeless, though there is disagreement about the level of motor performance and dexterity which can be observed. Investigatory eye movements may be seen but awareness of the environment is low. Nevertheless dangerous obstacles are usually avoided and self-injury is rare. If spoken to the subject may answer monosyllabically. Some are suggestible during the episode and will carry out simple commands.

Most attacks last several minutes though some may last for half an hour or more. Spontaneous awakening sometimes occurs, but usually the subject returns to bed and continues normal sleep. Attempts at arousal result in gradual return to full awareness, often with marked disorientation and 'sleep drunkenness'. Dream recall is not reported, and there is usually complete amnesia for what has transpired.

In children sleep-walking is usually a benign condition, outgrown in later childhood, suggesting that it rests on delayed cerebral maturation. However, the cases which come to attention in adult life appear to be frequently associated with severe psychopathology. Sours et al. (1963) studied 14 patients aged between 17 and 27 referred from US Air Force Bases. In most the disorder had begun at the time of puberty, and persisted thereafter with attacks every 1–4 months. Traumatic psychological events had seemed to precipitate the onset in many cases—parental death or divorce, a change of school, or the birth of a sibling. In some patients each episode was precipitated by interpersonal tensions or other emotional problems. There was strong evidence of disturbed family backgrounds and difficult relationships with the parents. The majority had a past history of acting out behaviour, delinquency and thefts, and many showed evidence of anxiety, depression or depersonalisation. Hysterical conversion symptoms were common. Five of the 14 patients were diagnosed as schizophrenic and 4 others were markedly schizoid in personality. The remainder were regarded as having character disorders.

The cause of somnambulism remains unclear. An explanation in psychodynamic terms has often been favoured, especially where episodes have an apparent purpose and the content is explicable in terms of current conflicts. The sleep-walking is then viewed as a dissociative state, similar to the hysterical fugue. The marked disturbance of personality reported in adult somnambulists lends some support to such views. It is probable, however, that sleep-walking rests on an abnormality of the sleep mechanisms of the brain and represents partial arousal out of the deep non-REM stages of sleep. It occurs most often during the first third of the night when stages 3 and 4 predominate—stages during which dreaming is least likely to occur. Kales and Kales (1974) review laboratory studies which confirm this in children, and run counter to the popular notion that sleep-walking represents the acting out of a dream. Episodes could sometimes be induced by lifting somnambulists to their feet during non-REM sleep, whereas this did not provoke attacks in children who were not subject to the disorder.

Special attention has been drawn to the liability of certain drugs, taken at bed-time, to induce somnambulism in susceptible individuals (Huapaya, 1979; Nadel, 1981). Hypnotics, neuroleptics, antidepressants, tranquillisers, stimulants and antihistamines have been incriminated, often in combinations and sometimes when taken with alcohol. Luchins et al. (1978) reported an example, apparently induced by thioridazine and a derivative of chloral hydrate, during which a 44-year-old psychotic woman stabbed her daughter to death. Sleep laboratory studies confirmed the liability of thioridazine to lead to sleep-walking in this patient, which occurred repeatedly out of stage 4 non-REM sleep. The tendency for sleep-walking to be induced by the combination of lithium with other neuroleptics is described on p. 533.

With regard to treatment the most important factor is protection from injury. Doors and windows should be locked and dangerous objects removed. Psychiatric treatment is rarely indicated in children, since most outgrow the disorder and in any case are not markedly disturbed. In adults, however, full psychiatric evaluation and treatment may be required. In persistent cases drugs such as diazepam, which suppresses stages 3 and 4 of non-REM sleep, may warrant a trial, and certainly in children may substantially reduce attacks (Guilleminault and Anders, 1976).

Night Terrors

'Night terrors' also arise out of stages 3 and 4 of non-REM sleep, differing sharply in this respect from nightmares which occur during phases of REM sleep (Fisher et al., 1973; Kales and Kales, 1974). Night terrors and sleep-walking often occur in the same individual. The common time of occurrence is within an hour or so of going to sleep. The episode is accompanied by intense anxiety, autonomic discharge, vocalisations by way of screams, moans and gasps, a racing heart and panting respiration. It lasts a minute or two only and the patient is usually amnesic for the event thereafter. If any content is recalled this is usually limited to a single frightening image.

Follow-up studies show that most children outgrow the disorder in later childhood. As with somnambulism psychological disturbance is common in affected adults but not in children. Daytime anxiety is also high in adults with the disorder. It has been claimed that diazepam is effective in diminishing night terrors, both in children and in adults.

Neuropsychiatric Manifestations of Carcinoma

The last few decades have seen the recognition of several neuropsychiatric syndromes which may accompany neoplasia in various parts of the body even when there is no spread of tumour cells to the brain. Thus patients with carcinoma may develop marked nervous system pathology while the tumour remains confined to its original site or at most metastasises to the regional lymph nodes. Mental symptoms figure prominently in such syndromes as well as neurological defects.

The mechanisms underlying such remote effects remain uncertain. Especially puzzling has been the observation that neuropsychiatric manifestations may precede clinical evidence of the primary tumour by a considerable interval of time, sometimes by several years. Moreover the disorders may continue to progress after apparently successful eradication of the neoplasm. Occasionally they make a first appearance some time after removal of the tumour and without evidence of recurrence of the neoplasm itself.

Before considering these remote effects in detail certain aspects of the orthodox involvement of the nervous system by secondary metastatic deposits will be briefly considered.

METASTATIC INVOLVEMENT OF THE CENTRAL NERVOUS SYSTEM

Tumours which commonly metastasise to the brain include those of the lung, breast, alimentary tract, prostate and pancreas. Carcinoma of the lung is undoubtedly the most frequent variety today. Melanomas may similarly metastasise to the central nervous system.

Secondary cerebral deposits are usually multiple and fast growing, but occasionally a solitary cerebral metastasis may warrant surgical intervention along with treatment of the primary growth. Not infrequently an intracranial metastasis gives rise to symptoms before the primary lesion, especially when this is in the lung, and sometimes the primary lesion is not discovered until autopsy. The clinical features are those of cerebral tumours generally as discussed in Chapter 6.

An 'encephalitic' form of metastatic carcinoma may very occasionally be encountered, as described by Madow and Alpers (1951). Here there is no tumour formation as such within the brain, but diffuse infiltration of carcinomatous cells throughout the central nervous system—within the brain parenchyma and along the perivascular spaces as well as in the meninges. There is no true inflammatory reaction but the presentation may at first closely simulate an encephalitic process. Of the four cases presented by Madow and Alpers three showed organic mental syndromes, three developed hemiparesis, all had fits and all showed signs of meningeal irritation. The cerebrospinal fluid sometimes contained an excess of cells and protein or could be normal. The lung was usually the site of the primary growth.

Carcinomatosis of the meninges may also produce a misleading picture. Secondary deposits invade the leptomeninges diffusely, particularly at the base of the brain, giving rise to an illness which at first resembles meningitis. Pyrexia and neck stiffness may be prominent features. Headache is usually marked and accompanied by cranial nerve palsies and often visual failure. A period of vague ill health has usually preceded more definite manifestations. Fischer-Williams et al. (1955) stress that severe mental disorder may accompany the neurological defects or even be the presenting feature. Some cases have presented with dementia and others have shown maniacal outbursts or mutism. The cerebrospinal fluid pressure is usually raised, with a moderate pleocytosis and elevation of protein. The detection of carcinomatous cells in the cerebrospinal fluid provides the definitive diagnosis.

NON-METASTATIC MANIFESTATIONS OF NEOPLASIA

The number of non-metastatic syndromes known to be causally related to cancer is now considerable. The sensory neuropathies were first described (Denny-Brown, 1948), then the peripheral neuropathies (Lennox and Pritchard, 1950) and shortly) afterwards the subacute cerebellar degenerations (Brain et al., 1951). Myelopathies and myopathies have since been recognised. For some time it was thought that pathological changes were restricted to levels caudal to the basal ganglia, but cerebral involvement is now recognised as well. The most recent syndrome to emerge consists of severe involvement of the limbic areas on the inferomedial surfaces of the temporal lobes, producing an illness with prominent memory disturbances and often some degree of dementia.

Obviously the clinical pictures which characterise these non-metastatic complications are many and various. Table 16 represents an attempt at classification modified from Brain and Adams (1965). Strict classification is impossible since the various affections may appear singly or in combination. With the encephalopathies, particularly, the pathological evidence suggests that a number of syndromes merge into one another as parts of a spectrum. Of the syndromes in the table only those which are likely to be of importance to the psychiatrist will be considered in detail. It should be noted, however, that mental symptoms, including dementia, may feature in all varieties, including cases where neuropathy or myopathy is the predominant part of the clinical picture (Brain and Henson, 1958).

From the pathological point of view the accent may be on widely disparate parts of the nervous

TABLE 16. Neuropsychiatric disorders associated with neoplasms (after Brain and Adams, 1965)

1. Encephalopathies
    Progressive multifocal leucoencephalopathy (see p. 645)
    Encephalopathy with subacute cerebellar degeneration
    Encephalopathy with brain stem lesions
    Diffuse encephalopathies with mental symptoms
    Encephalopathies presumed due to metabolic disturbance
    Limbic encephalopathy
2. Myelopathies (including cases resembling motor neurone disease)
3. Neuropathies
    Sensory neuropathy (with degeneration of posterior root ganglia and dorsal
        columns of cord)
    Peripheral sensorimotor neuropathies
    Metabolic, endocrine and nutritional neuropathies
4. Muscular Disorders
    Polymyopathy (mainly proximal, of limb girdles and trunk)
    Myasthenic myopathy
    Myasthenia gravis
    Polymyositis
    Metabolic myopathies

system. Several of the syndromes show a curious mixture of degenerative and quasi-inflammatory changes within the nervous system, which itself is puzzling from the point of view of aetiology. This is discussed further below.

With regard to incidence the non-metastatic complications are relatively uncommon and some varieties exceptionally so. Nevertheless they constitute an important part of general hospital neurological practice. Among 1476 cases of carcinoma, Croft and Wilkinson (1965) obtained an overall incidence of 7% with non-metastatic complications. Carcinoma of the lung produced by far the highest incidence at 16%. Other common sites of the primary growth were the ovary and stomach.

Subacute Cerebellar Degeneration

This was one of the earlier syndromes to gain recognition (Brain *et al.*, 1951). The presenting symptom is usually ataxia of gait, spreading later to all four limbs and often to the trunk. Dysarthria is severe but nystagmus often slight or absent. Muscle weakness, dysphagia, diplopia and sensory symptoms may also occur. The cerebrospinal fluid is often abnormal with a pleocytosis, raised protein and paretic Lange curve.

Mental symptoms figure prominently in the majority of cases. All but one of Brain and Henson's (1958) 8 examples eventually showed some degree of dementia, and in 2 the initial picture was of agitation and depression. Brain and Wilkinson (1965) found mental changes in two-thirds of 17 cases, usually in the form of dementia but also states of agitation and anxiety.

The onset may antedate the appearance of the carcinoma by several months or up to 3 years, or follow it by a similar interval. In one of Brain and Wilkinson's patients the neurological symptoms first appeared several months after removal of the neoplasm, and recurrence was judged unlikely since the patient survived 6 years without further evidence of the growth. Once started the disorder may progress so rapidly that the patient is bedridden within weeks, while in other cases it may take a year to develop fully. Sometimes arrest may be seen after many months of progression, but remission does not occur. The dementia can continue to progress after the cerebellar affliction has stabilised. Treatment of the neoplasm has no demonstrable effect on the progress of the disorder.

The striking pathological change is disappearance of the Purkinje cells from the cerebellum. Diffuse degeneration is seen in other cerebellar neurones, and patchy microglial proliferation in the white matter of the cerebral and cerebellar hemispheres. By contrast the dentate nuclei are often little affected. Degeneration may occur in the long tracts of the cord, especially the spinocerebellar tracts and posterior columns, and in the oculomotor and lower cranial nerve nuclei. Meningeal and perivascular lymphocytic infiltration is seen in some cases, and inflammatory changes have been observed in the brain stem and subthalamic region.

Encephalopathy with Brain Stem Involvement

This, the so-called 'mixed form of encephalomyelitis' of Brain and Henson (1958) presents with varied neurological signs including cerebellar disorder, bulbar palsy, disordered external ocular movements, wasting and weakness of the limbs, extensor plantar responses, involuntary movements and posterior column sensory disturbance. Mental changes are again prominent in many examples, including dementia.

The disorder can follow a prolonged course over two years or more. In one case the neurological manifestations had been evident for two years before serial X-rays revealed the carcinoma of the lung.

The pathological changes involve degeneration in the dentate nucleus, the superior cerebellar peduncles, the brain stem nuclei, the motor cells of the cord, and the pyramidal tracts and posterior columns. Inflammatory changes may be conspicuous with perivascular cuffing and cellular infiltrations of the meninges.

Diffuse Encephalopathies with Mental Symptoms

Brain and Adams (1965) have given separate emphasis to a group of patients who present, not with neurological dysfunction, but with psychiatric disorders leading sometimes to mental hospital admission. The mental changes may or may not be associated with evidence of focal cerebral lesions later in their course. A wide range of disturbances can occur. The picture may be of a simple dementia which is usually fairly rapidly progressive, or a disorder of memory with or without confusional episodes. Sometimes mood disorder is the predominant feature with depression, anxiety or agitation and much less evidence of cognitive disturbance.

The cerebrospinal fluid is often normal but the electroencephalogram may reveal diffuse changes. A close investigation must always be made into the metabolic, endocrine and nutritional status of the patient since the encephalopathy may be due to disturbance in such factors occasioned by the neoplasm (p. 637). It may also be necessary to search diligently for the primary growth which may so far have escaped detection.

The pathology in this group is described by Brain and Adams as patchy degeneration of the ganglion cells of the grey matter, with gliosis and a variable degree of lymphocytic infiltration. Where memory disorder has been the predominant feature the changes of limbic encephalopathy, described below, may be found. Sometimes, however, remarkably little may be observed in the brain at autopsy.

Encephalopathies Presumed Due to Metabolic Disturbance

An important but apparently rare group of cases has been described in which marked mental disorder is associated with carcinoma of the lung yet cerebral changes prove to be minimal or absent on detailed pathological examination (Charatan and Brierley, 1956; McGovern et al., 1959). The common feature in such cases was a fluctuating disturbance of consciousness with periods of lucidity, extending over several months prior to death and unaccompanied by neurological abnormalities. Affective disturbances were often prominent in the earlier stages. In all cases the mental disturbance had either preceded or overshadowed the presence of the neoplasm. Here it would seem very likely that metabolic disturbances were fundamental to the development of the mental changes:

The first of Charatan and Brierley's cases was a man of 53 who became depressed and quarrelsome over several months. He later developed paranoid religious delusions and episodes of grossly muddled and odd behaviour. There were no organic features in the mental state and a diagnosis of paranoid schizophrenia was made. After recovering briefly for a week or two he abruptly relapsed, and at this stage carcinoma of the lung was detected. A quick decline led to coma and death.

The second was a man of 43 admitted after wandering from home in a depressed and apathetic state. He had lost his memory but this returned four days after admission. The only abnormal sign was some lability of mood. Soon, however, he developed periods of confusion with lucid intervals and deteriorated to death over four months. There had been suspicious shadowing of the lung for some months before presentation.

The third was a man of 63 who for one year had been slow, lethargic and complaining of feeling tired. Six months before presentation there had been an episode of confused nocturnal rambling, and since then his memory had been failing from time to time. Major epileptic fits had commenced at this time and chest X-ray had shown shadowing of the lung. Gradual decline was accompanied by lucid intervals lasting for a few days at a time. The mental state continued to show marked fluctuation in hospital until he died $2\frac{1}{2}$ months later.

The electroencephalograms had shown little abnormality in the first two cases, and the cerebro-spinal fluid was normal except in the first. In all three the brain was free from metastases and only a marginal gliosis of the white matter could be detected. The livers were full of metastases, however, and it was thought possible that liver failure may have contributed to the picture, either with or without other metabolic disturbances occasioned by the neoplasms.

McGovern *et al.* (1959) added two further examples, both in women:

The first presented with restlessness, apprehension, paranoid ideas and confusion about dates and time of some months duration. She was profoundly disturbed, averting her face because of shame at things she imagined she had done, and imbuing every sound with fatal significance. She was disoriented, with poor attention and marked diffi-culties with memory and calculation. The state of severe fear and agitation progressed over three weeks to depres-sive stupor, at which time the chest neoplasm was revealed. She died 2 weeks later after periods of stupor alternating with periods of lucidity.

The second patient had a 6 month history of feeling unwell together with a constant sense of fear, inability to concentrate and occasions when she could not grasp the gist of things properly. There had been two attacks of generalised trembling accompanied by acute terror. In hospital she showed florid depressive thought content and evidence of intellectual impairment. Episodes of delirium gave way to a sustained delirious state for several days, at which point inflammatory changes were discovered in the left lung. Bronchoscopy showed carcinoma of the bronchus. Liver function tests were normal. She improved later to become alert and emotionally composed for several weeks, then episodes of delirium increased until she died some months later.

Again there were no neurological symptoms in either of McGovern *et al.*'s cases. The brains were entirely normal at autopsy, and metastases were minimal or absent from the livers also. The possible metabolic basis for the mental disturbance remained unclarified. A raised blood ammonia was discovered in the second case, but its significance in relation to the clinical picture was uncertain.

Limbic Encephalopathy

One of the more recent developments has been the recognition of cases presenting with mental disturb-ance in association with pathological changes largely limited to the limbic grey matter of the brain. The carcinoma has almost always been of bronchial origin, often with metastases in the hilar lymph nodes but without direct spread to the brain. In several examples the neoplasm has become evident only at post mortem examination. Strangely the primary growth has not always been discovered even then, the only evidence of cancer sometimes being secondary deposits in the mediastinal lymph nodes.

This form of encephalopathy has been compre-hensively described by Corsellis *et al.* (1968). The outstanding clinical feature is a marked disturbance of memory for recent events, though some degree of generalised intellectual impairment often develops later. Affective disturbance has frequently been prominent early in the evolution of the disorder, usually in the form of severe anxiety or depression. Some patients have been hallucinated and some have had epileptic attacks, but otherwise impairment of consciousness has not been observed. Several have shown a coincident carcinomatous neuropathy. The cerebrospinal fluid is usually abnormal with a raised lymphocyte count and raised protein. Electro-encephalographic abnormalities have been most marked over the temporal lobes.

The pathological picture shows a combination of degenerative and inflammatory changes which are concentrated on the medial temporal lobe struc-tures—the hippocampus, uncus, amygdaloid nucleus, dentate gyrus, hippocampal gyrus, cingu-late gyrus, insular and posterior orbital cortex. The changes can sometimes extend throughout the length of the fornices and involve the mamillary bodies. The rest of the hemisphere and the hind brain are only slightly affected. The changes consist of exten-sive neuronal loss, marked astrocytic proliferation and fibrous gliosis, and perivascular infiltration with small round cells and the formation of glial nodules. In no cases have tumour cells been identified within the central nervous system. The severity of the inflammatory component has varied from case to case, but at times has been severe enough to be virtually indistinguishable from viral encephalitis. No inclusion bodies have been seen.

The first report of such a picture in association with carcinoma was included among cases reported by Brierley *et al.* (1960), though the connection was not appreciated at the time. One of their patients with 'subacute encephalitis of later adult life' was a man of 58 who demented over the course of three months and died, revealing an intense inflammatory reaction in the brain, most severe in the medial temporal lobe structures. The mediastinal lymph nodes were extensively infiltrated with oat-celled carcinoma though neoplasia had not been suspected during life.

Soon afterwards several similar examples were reported. Yahr *et al.* (1965) described a woman of 61 who developed impairment of memory and difficulty with her secretarial work together with numbness of the limbs. She became depressed, suspicious, confused and severely disoriented. A non-metastatic complication of carcinoma was suspected and at exploratory operation mediastinal lymph nodes were found to contain oat-celled deposits. She deteriorated gradually and died the following year. A small carcinoma of the lung was discovered and the brain showed the typical changes described above in the medial temporal lobe structures.

Corsellis *et al.* (1968) presented three further examples:

The first, a man of 59, suffered several epileptic fits followed a few weeks later by impairment of recent memory. No cause could be found. He continued to show a gross defect of memorising, but without other intellectual deterioration, until his death two years later. At autopsy oat-celled carcinoma was discovered in a mediastinal lymph node, and the medial temporal lobe areas showed degenerative and inflammatory changes.

The second was a man of 50 with known carcinoma of the lung who became mildly demented with some disorientation and impairment of recent memory. The carcinoma was resected but his mental state showed little change. He gradually developed dysarthria and progressive wasting of the small muscles of the hands and feet. At autopsy two years later there was no evidence of recurrence of the growth but the brain showed extensive changes in the medial temporal lobe structures, basal ganglia and diencephalon.

The third was a woman of 81 who died after a psychiatric illness of some years duration, presenting initially as depression and marked in its later stages by dementia and a prominent defect of recent memory. Carcinoma had not been suspected during life but oat-celled carcinoma of the lung was discovered at autopsy. The medial temporal lobe structures were severely damaged along with some involvement of the midbrain and brain stem.

How commonly mental disturbance in patients with carcinoma may be due to limbic system involvement is hard to assess. As already described some examples are clearly due to more diffuse cerebral pathology or to metabolic disturbances, but where memory failure is a predominant feature the possibility of limbic encephalopathy should be borne in mind.

Mechanisms of Non-metastatic Complications

The mechanisms underlying the neuropsychiatric complications of carcinoma remain elusive. As Brain (1963) pointed out the rarity of such complications suggests some exceptional factor, either in relation to the tumour or in the subject's reaction to it. The principal theories are that the complications are the consequence of some substance secreted by the tumour; or that they reflect a disturbance in the patient's immunological state which has led to invasion by a virus.

The idea of a specific neurotoxin secreted by the tumour has so far obtained no direct support. Very occasionally removal of the neoplasm has produced improvement in the nervous or muscular symptoms, though this is the exception rather than the rule. Special attention has been concentrated on the hormone-like substances which some tumours, including those of the bronchus, are known to secrete (Lebowitz, 1965). Thus hypercalcaemia may be caused by elaboration of an agent with parathormone-like activity and be ameliorated by removal of the primary growth. Cushing's syndrome may result from secretion of an ACTH-like substance, hypoglycaemia from secretion of an insulin-like substance, or hyponatraemia from inappropriate antidiuretic hormone secretion. It is uncertain whether the tumours secrete such hormonally active materials themselves, or produce other substances which serve as releasers for the natural hormones.

In either event this has served as a starting point for exploring the remote effects of tumours on the nervous system. In cases with fluctuating acute organic reactions, as in the encephalopathies described on p. 635, it can be important to investigate the hormonal and metabolic status of the patient as completely as possible. Sethurajan *et al.* (1967), for example, described a woman with carcinoma of the lung who developed a fluctuating confusional state along with Cushing's syndrome. The mental abnormalities appeared to be directly related to the metabolic derangements produced by adrenal overactivity, and radiotherapy to the lung produced a temporary dramatic improvement in both the mental and endocrine symptoms. There is no evidence to date, however, to link such hormonal or metabolic abnormalities with the production of fixed pathological changes within the nervous system.

The suggestion that a viral infection may be responsible has arisen from direct observation of the pathological changes in the brain. The idea has also obtained support from the finding of polyoma virus in the brain in progressive multifocal leucoencephalopathy which is also associated with malignancy (p. 646).

Thus in several of the syndromes discussed above the pathological picture shows inflammatory as well as degenerative changes. The inflammatory component may merely represent a secondary reaction to local products of degeneration, but against such a view is the rarity of such a reaction in other cerebral degenerative processes and the fact that inflammatory changes can be found remote from any area of degeneration. No virus has yet been isolated, however, and the possibility remains hypothetical.

Invasion by a virus would help to explain the lack of any constant relationship between the course of the neuropsychiatric complications and the course of the cancer. Cases in which the complications have first arisen after successful removal of the neoplasm suggest an incubation process of some sort, which once initiated proceeds independently of the tumour. The neoplasm may have disturbed the body's immunological state so as to render it unusually vulnerable to an infective agent, at the same time modifying the pathological reaction to the infection to account for the unusual pictures observed (Adams, 1965). Whether the search should be for a latent virus within the brain which has become activated by the tumour, or for some common infective agent which has provoked an abnormal response, remains uncertain. Corsellis *et al.* (1968) point out that the site of cerebral damage in limbic encephalopathy is similar to that caused by herpes simplex infection; disturbed immunological mechanisms may account for the chronic instead of acute progression of such an infection, likewise the unusual features in the pathological picture.

The diverse remote effects of cancer on the central nervous system need not of course all share a common mechanism. Some of the encephalopathies may be the result of a virus infection, and others the result of metabolic derangements.

Depression and Carcinoma

Finally separate attention must be given to reports of affective disorder as a prodromal feature in patients who develop carcinoma. Fras *et al.* (1967) studied 46 consecutive patients with carcinoma of the pancreas, and found that psychiatric symptoms were closely related to the development of the neoplasm in three quarters. In patients with cancer of the colon, who served as controls, the figure was only 17%. Symptoms of depression, anxiety, and premonitions of serious illness were especially common. Nearly half of the 46 patients had developed psychiatric symptoms before any physical complaint, depression being the most frequent and lasting on average six months before the neoplasm was declared.

Kerr *et al.* (1969) explored the situation with regard to cancers generally. They traced a group of patients who had been admitted to hospital with affective disorders, and investigated the deaths which occurred during the following four years. Of 28 males who had had a depressive illness, 7 had died from physical causes and in 5 the cause was cancer. This was very significantly above the number to be expected on the basis of national statistics. No particular site could be incriminated—deaths had occurred from cancer of the bronchus, prostate, stomach, colon and rectum. By contrast none of the 28 females with a depressive illness had died from cancer.

The five males who died of cancer had not had a previous history of affective disorder, and the depression had evolved without apparent cause. Its course had been unremitting prior to hospitalisation, but electroconvulsive therapy or antidepressants had produced a complete remission. There had been no evidence of organic mental impairment, and examination had failed to reveal physical disease at the time except for a raised ESR in two patients. The mean interval between the onset of depression and death was only 2·4 years, strongly suggesting that latent or undiagnosed cancer may have been present during the evolution of the affective illness.

Others have sought by different survey methods to explore the relationship between depression and cancer, but have so far failed to confirm Kerr *et al.*'s findings (Judelsohn, 1970; Evans *et al.*, 1974). Nevertheless the evidence already at hand underlines the importance of attempting rigorously to exclude physical disease in patients who develop depressive illnesses in middle age, particularly those who do so for the first time and when there is no obvious precipitating factor.

Further evidence of a special association between depressive illness and cancer has come from studies of suicide. Whitlock (1978) reviews the occasional reports of an unusually high incidence of malignancies in patients committing suicide when compared with community norms. His own survey of 273 suicides in Brisbane revealed 17 malignancies, compared with only 2 in controls dying from other violent causes (mostly road traffic accidents). The difference was statistically significant. No special site was involved, and intracranial spread had not occurred. In 7 of the suicides and one of the controls the disease had not been diagnosed prior to death.

Normal Pressure Hydrocephalus
('Occult Hydrocephalus', 'Communicating Hydrocephalus', 'Hydrocephalic Dementia')

The term 'hydrocephalus' refers to diffuse enlargement of the ventricular system within the brain. According to conventional terminology it may be divided into obstructive and non-obstructive forms, or communicating and non-communicating forms. In obstructive hydrocephalus there is a block to the free circulation of the cerebrospinal fluid which has led to ventricular enlargement; in non-obstructive forms the enlargement is secondary to atrophy of the brain substance as in Alzheimer's disease (also termed 'hydrocephalus ex-vacuo'). Most forms of obstructive hydrocephalus are 'non-communicating' in the sense that the ventricles do not communicate freely with the cerebral subarachnoid space, whereas in hydrocephalus ex-vacuo such communication is free.

An important variety however is at the same time obstructive yet communicating. Here the block is not within the ventricular system but in the subarachnoid space, allowing free egress of the cerebrospinal fluid from the ventricles but preventing its subsequent upward flow over the surface of the hemispheres for absorption at the superior saggital sinus. The block in such cases is commonly situated in the basal cisterns of the brain. This variety must be very carefully distinguished from hydrocephalus ex-vacuo since it can present with symptoms closely simulating the primary dementing illnesses. It is not infrequently associated with normal pressure within the ventricular system and headache is usually absent.

Such a syndrome has been variously termed normal pressure hydrocephalus, occult hydrocephalus, communicating hydrocephalus or hydrocephalic dementia.* It owes its delineation to a group of

* None of these terms is entirely satisfactory. The pressure is not always normal, 'occult' hydrocephalus is also used for any hydrocephalus in which the head is not enlarged, 'communicating' hydrocephalus also comprises hydrocephalus ex-vacuo, and dementia is not an inevitable part of the picture.

workers who demonstrated cases in whom marked hydrocephalus was associated with a normal or even low intraventricular pressure, sometimes after head injury or subarachnoid haemorrhage but sometimes in patients suspected of a primary dementing illness (Hakim, 1964; Hakim and Adams, 1965; Adams *et al.*, 1965, Adams, 1966). Air encephalography showed the absence of any block within the ventricular system, but the air failed to ascend over the surface of the hemispheres betokening obstruction within the basal cisterns or cerebral subarachnoid space. Paradoxically, despite the normal intraventricular pressure, the neurological and mental impairments proved to be reversible by shunting procedures which reduced the pressure still further.

The discovery of the syndrome is of great clinical importance. It has led to a greater awareness of the caution which must be exercised in diagnosing primary cerebral atrophy, and has delineated a cause of dementia which is amenable to effective treatment. Well-marked examples are rare, but it remains possible that partial forms may be commoner than is realised.

Clinical Features

The clinical features stressed in the early publications have since been amply confirmed (Ojemann *et al.*, 1969; Ojemann, 1971). Ojemann (1971) has reported clinical experience of 50 such patients. The typical picture is of the development over many weeks or months of memory impairment, physical and mental slowness, unsteadiness of gait and urinary incontinence. However the precise symptomatology varies rather widely between one patient and another. The syndrome predominantly affects patients in their 60s or 70s though examples have occurred in middle or even young adult life.

The mental changes usually appear first and remain a prominent part of the picture throughout. They range from mild memory disturbance or apathy to severe psychomotor retardation and profound intellectual impairment. Forgetfulness is usually a prominent early feature, combined with slowing of mental and physical activity, difficulty with thinking and reduced spontaneity—a combination which may lead to a diagnosis of early presenile dementia or depression. The emotional reactions are less vivid and psychic life seems generally impoverished. Insight is limited or absent from an early stage but social comportment is usually well preserved.

With progression of the disorder the patient becomes increasingly disoriented, calculation is impaired, and dysphasia and disturbances of writing and drawing may develop. Memory impairment may ultimately be as severe as that seen in Korsakoff's psychosis, or the global dementia virtually indistinguishable from that of Alzheimer's disease or senile dementia. Uninhibited or aberrant behaviour is not usually seen, however, and psychotic developments in the form of delusions, hallucinations or paranoia are rare. In very occasional patients, outbursts of aggressive, hostile behaviour may be observed (Crowell et al., 1973). Advanced cases sometimes show long periods of mutism, intermittent interruptions of on-going behaviour, or episodes of severe hypokinesia amounting to catatonia-like immobility.

Disturbance of gait may be the presenting feature in itself. In mild examples the patient walks slowly on a broad base with a stiff-legged shuffling gait. There is difficulty with turning and often difficulty with initiating movements similar to that seen in parkinsonism. Falls are frequent. The precise nature of the disturbance is hard to characterise but is often described as an uncertainty, unsteadiness or carelessness in walking. The ill-defined term 'gait apraxia' has been applied. When coupled with the mental symptoms this abnormality of gait is often the feature which leads one to suspect the presence of normal pressure hydrocephalus. The disturbance may progress eventually to severe difficulty in walking, standing, or arising from a seated position, sometimes even to difficulty in turning over in bed. Signs of spastic paraparesis may be evident with hyperactive tendon reflexes and extensor plantar responses. But even when the disability is pronounced it is rare to find frank ataxia of the limbs, dyssynergia or intention tremor of cerebellar type.

Urinary incontinence usually appears only when other symptoms are well in evidence, but may set in surprisingly early in relation to the degree of mental impairment. Again this may have diagnostic importance in bringing the condition to mind. Rectal incontinence is rare and develops only in the most severe examples.

Other features may include slowness of movement in the upper limbs or occasionally some degree of arm tremor or ataxia. Unexplained nystagmus is occasionally present. Late in the course sucking and grasping reflexes may appear. Headache is rare and when present is usually minimal. Papilloedema does not develop. A history of falling spells with brief impairment of consciousness is common, but frank epileptic seizures have not been reported.

The course without treatment is of slow downward progression with increasing neurological and mental disability. Fluctuations from day to day or from week to week are very characteristic. In some of the more prolonged examples a plateau appears to be reached after many months with a relatively fixed pattern of impairments thereafter. Others progress eventually to coma and death.

The findings on investigation are characteristic and necessary to confirm the diagnosis. At lumbar puncture the cerebrospinal fluid is usually under normal pressure and with normal constituents, though this depends on the condition giving rise to the hydrocephalus. The electroencephalogram is frequently abnormal, showing non-specific random theta or delta activity.

Before the advent of CT scanning, air encephalography usually provided the decisive evidence by way of symmetrically enlarged ventricles, often reaching huge proportions, but with little or no air in the cerebral subarachnoid space above the basal cisterns. Following the procedure, however, there was a risk of rapid deterioration, sometimes requiring urgent neurosurgical intervention. Risa cisternography was widely used as an alternative or confirmatory investigation as discussed on p. 117. Angiography could provide the clue in advanced cases by demonstrating the increased circumferential sweep of the anterior cerebral artery occasioned by the distension of the ventricles.

The favoured diagnostic procedure now is CT scanning followed if necessary by a period of continuous intracranial pressure monitoring. The CT scan demonstrates the marked ventricular enlargement, usually with no more than minimal sulcal widening. Periventricular lucency may be seen around the ventricles, particularly at the angles (Moseley and Radü, 1979). In occasional patients, however, widened sulci may co-exist with normal pressure hydrocephalus, so their presence cannot be taken as excluding the condition.

Intracranial pressure monitoring has gained increasing acceptance as the most reliable way of separating normal pressure hydrocephalus from the atrophy seen with primary dementing illnesses. The methods employed are described by Symon and Dorsch (1975), Crockard et al. (1977) and Pickard (1982). Continuous recording over 2 days or more reveals that the pressure is not, in fact, uniformly within normal limits but shows periods of raised intracranial pressure with characteristic pressure wave patterns (B waves). The identification of such a picture is perhaps the most useful present technique for predicting which patients will show a useful response to operative intervention.

Antecedent Causes

In many examples no antecedent cause can be discovered. In others there is a history of subarachnoid haemorrhage, head injury or meningitis which has presumably led to the organisation of adhesions in the basal cisterns of the brain. After subarachnoid haemorrhage organisation of exudate within the arachnoid villi at the superior saggital sinus may contribute further by obstructing the reabsorption of cerebrospinal fluid (Ellington and Margolis, 1969). Very occasionally the typical clinical syndrome may be due to a partially non-communicating hydrocephalus occasioned, for example, by a third ventricular tumour or aqueduct stenosis. A rare cause has been described by Brieg *et al.* (1967) and Ekbom *et al.* (1969): in hypertensive individuals an elongated 'ectatic' basilar artery may indent the floor of the third ventricle and distort the ventricular system upwards and anteriorly, leading to normal pressure hydrocephalus as described on p. 643.

In Ojemann's (1971) material of 50 cases no cause could be found in 18. These 'idiopathic' cases were all in their 60s or 70s. Eleven showed complete obstruction of the cerebral subarachnoid spaces on air encephalography and 7 showed partial obstruction. Of the 32 with known causes, 12 followed subarachnoid haemorrhage, 11 head injury, and 3 meningitis. Five were due to tumours or the after-effects of posterior fossa surgery and one was due to aqueduct stenosis. The age range in this group was wider, from 26 to 69.

In the idiopathic cases the symptoms had set in insidiously and no precipitants could be discerned. The essential cause remained obscure, but in three such patients who came to autopsy the basal cisterns were found to be obstructed with fibrous tissue, perhaps due to a forgotten episode of head injury or unrecognised subarachnoid haemorrhage. Those following subarachnoid haemorrhage sometimes evolved from almost immediately after the bleeding or could first present several months later. Similarly after head injury signs of brain dysfunction had sometimes been present from the time of injury but occasionally developed only several months later.

Differential Diagnosis

The most important differential diagnosis is from the primary senile and presenile dementias. Thus a substantial proportion of cases have no demonstrable antecedent cause and these tend to occur in patients in their 60s and 70s. McHugh (1966) suggests that the syndrome should be considered in any individual who is declining mentally, particularly if the illness has taken a subacute course over months rather than years or has shown pronounced remissions or exacerbations. It should be strongly suspected if early in the decline there appears a disorder of gait together with marked inertia, apathy and psychomotor retardation. Urinary incontinence developing before the mental impairments have proceeded very far should also raise suspicion.

A depressive illness may be simulated early in the course, when physical and mental slowness are prominent and intellectual impairment minimal. Rice and Gendelman (1973) have drawn attention to other ways in which the patient may first present to a psychiatrist. In 5 patients behavioural abnormalities were in the forefront of the picture, sometimes tending to obscure the organic features in the mental state. Examples included personality change with paranoid trends or increasing belligerence, acute agitation and paranoia accompanied by visual hallucinations, and marked anxiety and depression accompanying progressive dementia. In each case the hydrocephalus appeared to have aggravated pre-existing emotional difficulties in the patient in addition to producing intellectual impairment.

When the gait disturbance is the presenting feature differentiation is required from other causes of mild spasticity and ataxia such as cervical spondylosis. Parkinsonism may be diagnosed initially on account of the pronounced motor slowing. Indeed, the typical parkinsonian syndrome, accompanied by dementia, has sometimes been seen (Sypert *et al.*, 1973). The differential diagnosis must, of course, also include other varieties of obstructive and communicating hydrocephalus and other forms of dementia.

Some of the problems encountered in diagnosis are illustrated in the following cases:

A woman of 66 had had a radical mastectomy for cancer of the breast followed one month later by progressive unsteadiness of gait, forgetfulness and intermittent confusion. Within 6 months the memory disorder was pronounced and psychometry showed widespread impairments. There was no evidence of secondary deposits. The cerebrospinal fluid was normal but air encephalography showed gross dilatation of the ventricles with no air over the cortical surface. She worsened precipitately after air encephalography and became drowsy, confused and almost mute. She could no longer walk and nystagmus was present in all directions of gaze. The cerebrospinal fluid now showed what were thought to be neoplastic cells and a diagnosis of carcinomatous meningeal infiltration was made.

Over the next 15 months she did not deteriorate as expected. She gradually became more alert, though she continued to speak little and took little notice of what went on around her. She lay or sat immobile, idle or watching television. On readmission she was grossly disoriented and with marked memory impairments, and showed no initiative whatsoever. She was incontinent of urine and faeces and could not sit or stand unsupported. The ankle jerks were brisk and the plantars upgoing but there were no cerebellar signs. The syndrome of normal pressure hydrocephalus was recognised and a shunt operation performed. Improvement was evident within 3 days and after 7 weeks her mental state had returned to normal. Control of bowel and bladder was regained, and when seen 9 months later she was walking by herself though still with an uncertain gait.

(Adams *et al.*, 1965)

A man of 49 complained of lethargy, easy fatiguability and vague weakness of the legs. For 6 months his family had noted him to be dull and forgetful. He was found to be slow in motor and verbal responses and with a mild impairment of recent memory. The plantar responses were extensor but there were no other abnormal neurological signs. The cerebrospinal fluid pressure was mildly elevated with a protein of 100 mg/100 ml. Air encephalography showed symmetrical dilatation of the ventricles with a small amount of air over the surface. A tentative diagnosis of Alzheimer's disease was made. In hospital there was considerable improvement in his apathy and inertia but he relapsed after a few weeks at home. Walking became seriously impaired with a stiff-legged gait and several falls. On readmission he was now severely amnesic for recent events and disoriented in time and place. He improved again in hospital but the diagnosis of Alzheimer's disease remained.

Over the next 2 months he gradually declined into severe confusion and was readmitted pending transfer to a long-stay mental hospital. He was now unkempt, apathetic and unconcerned, with great slowness on mental tasks. He walked with a wide based stiff-legged gait and stumbled on turning. Bilateral grasp reflexes were observed, and a prehensile sucking reflex when the lips were touched. The WAIS IQ was 64, where it had been 101 four months earlier. After lumbar puncture he changed remarkably, becoming alert and quick of mind, fully oriented and able to learn new facts, and the WAIS IQ rose to 105. Gait returned to normal but the plantars remained extensor. A shunt operation was performed with excellent results, and a small mass situated on the floor of the third ventricle encroaching on the entrance to the aqueduct was irradiated. Six months later he was back at his usual clerical job.

(McHugh, 1966)

Treatment and Response

Treatment involves a shunt operation to lower cerebrospinal fluid pressure within the ventricles and maintain it at this low level. An indwelling catheter is inserted into a lateral ventricle, incorporating a low pressure one-way valve and opening into the superior vena cava through the jugular venous system ('ventriculo-caval shunt'). The result, though somewhat unpredictable, is gratifyingly successful in certain cases. Those patients who on intracranial pressure monitoring have shown elevated mean pressures or marked spontaneous pressure waves tend to show the best response (Jeffreys and Wood, 1978; Crockard *et al.*, 1980).

Shunt operations, even when dramatically successful initially, are not without their long-term complications (Illingworth 1970; Illingworth *et al.*, 1971). The catheter may become blocked or shift its position, or the valve may cease to function. The development of a subdural haematoma is not infrequent.

Among cases with no known cause Ojemann (1971) found satisfactory improvement after shunting in all patients where a complete block had been demonstrated. The patients with only partial obstruction showed disappointing results, perhaps because some had a primary dementing illness in addition to their normal pressure hydrocephalus. The improvement is often manifest immediately on recovery from the anaesthetic, with further gains in the days that follow. Sometimes, however, there is little change during the first post-operative week and thereafter gradual improvement takes place over the course of several weeks. The mental symptoms are usually the first to resolve. Intellectual impairments, aspontaneity and apathy can ultimately clear completely. Incontinence also clears fairly promptly, but gait disturbance may improve only very gradually and some residual motor disability may persist. Follow-up with repeat evaluation of cognitive function has shown gains more obvious at one year than at 6 months, and well maintained thereafter (Crockard *et al.*, 1980).

In cases following subarachnoid haemorrhage improvement is likely within a few days of shunting, but focal neurological deficits related to the local effects of the haemorrhage will persist unaltered. The response in cases following head injury is governed by the degree and severity of the underlying brain damage. Salmon (1971) has reported 9 post-traumatic cases, operated at intervals of 6 months to 8 years after injury. Two were 'much improved' and 3 'improved', including 2 patients who showed some evidence of cortical atrophy as well. The improvements often took place slowly over several weeks post-operatively.

Shunting has also been tried in presumed cases of Alzheimer's disease, with evidence of cortical atrophy in addition to enlargement of the ventricles. Ojemann *et al.* (1969) found no response in five such cases, but others have reported apparent improvement in cases of Alzheimer's disease, Huntington's chorea and other degenerative conditions (Appenzeller and Salmon, 1967; Salmon and Armitage, 1968; Salmon *et al.*, 1971). The situation remains uncertain in the primary dementing illnesses, and most observers consider that on present evidence shunting is not indicated.

Pathophysiology

The precise mechanisms behind the development of normal pressure hydrocephalus are uncertain. It is difficult to explain how the ventricles come to be so greatly enlarged when the pressure within them is normal, or to account for the production of severe neurological and mental deficits which prove to be reversible when the pressure is reduced still further. Several theories have been put forward but none can be considered entirely satisfactory.

With regard to the ventricular enlargement it has been suggested that the pressure may have been elevated at an earlier stage of the disorder but has subsided by the time the patient is under investigation. This may be so in cases where a definable cause such as subarachnoid haemorrhage has preceded the hydrocephalus, but would seem unlikely in the cases without any antecedent history of acute disturbance. In the latter the evolution of symptoms has often been insidious from the outset, and sometimes it has seemed indubitable that symptoms have progressed during the time that the pressure has appeared to be normal. The discovery of periodic rises of pressure in many cases on continuous intracranial pressure monitoring (p. 640) may go much of the way towards resolving such paradoxes.

Some cases may represent arrested hydrocephalus dating back to earlier life. Intellectual failure would then occur more rapidly than in the normal brain in the presence of the minor degenerative processes of later life. This could perhaps apply to cases who show little response to shunting, but would be unlikely to explain those who derive marked and lasting benefit, including a return towards normal in ventricular size.

An alternative suggestion is that the ventricular walls or surrounding supporting tissues may have become altered in some way, allowing progressive enlargement in the face of normal pressure. Geschwind (1968) suggests that pulsatile forces due to intermittent peaks of high pressure may lead to rapid loss of proteins and lipids from the surrounding white matter, altering its ability to withstand the pressure normally exerted upon it. Or changes in the direction of cerebrospinal fluid flow may have had similar consequences. When prevented from rising up to the parasaggital area for reabsorption in the normal way, an excessive amount of CSF may come to be absorbed through the ventricular walls; this may lead to a change in the properties of the surrounding tissues and allow expansion under normal pressure (Ojemann, 1971). More simply the atrophic changes consequent upon ageing may have diminished the tensile strength in the cerebral tissues surrounding the ventricles with a similar result. Thus the great majority of cases in whom no antecedent cause can be found are patients in their 60s and 70s.

A further interesting mechanism appears to be operative in a rare group of cases reported by Brieg *et al.* (1967) and Ekbom *et al.* (1969). These patients with hypertension and normal pressure hydrocephalus were shown to have elongation of the basilar artery, indenting the floor of the third ventricle and producing a characteristic deformity there on the air encephalogram. A water-hammer effect from the pulsations of the artery may have impaired outflow from the lateral ventricles via the foramina of Monro, thus initiating ventricular distension. This in turn would displace the cortex towards the calvarium and compress the subarachnoid space overlying the hemispheres, thereby hindering resorption of CSF and bringing about a vicious circle in the further development of the hydrocephalus.

With regard to the production of symptoms and alleviation by shunting, several mechanisms have again been postulated. Hakim and Adams (1965) argued in terms of force-pressure relationships and put forward a theory of 'hydraulic-press effect'. They suggested that a normal pressure, when exerted against the greatly increased surface area of the ventricles, would result in a larger than normal total force being expended upon the surrounding cerebral tissues. Symptoms would result from the increased total thrust against important long fibre tracts and nuclei in proximity to the ventricles. The prominence of frontal lobe deficits—apathy, inertia and early incontinence—might thus be due to the especial enlargement of the frontal horns.

Yakovlev's (1947) explanation for the accent of spasticity on the legs in hydrocephalus would also apply—the neurones innervating the legs must sweep round the surface of the ventricles before entering the internal capsule, whereas those destined for the arms and face are laterally placed in the cortex and pursue a more direct route. The hydraulic press hypothesis is supported by the fact that reduction of pressure by as little as 20–33 mm can permit restoration of nervous function and also partially relieve the ventricular distension.

Changes in cerebral blood flow have also been incriminated in the production of symptoms (Greitz, 1969). Cerebral blood flow has been shown to be reduced in the disorder to an extent which correlates with the degree of ventricular dilatation, and improvement in cerebral blood flow follows shunting procedures. The decreased blood flow may be the direct result of compression of capillaries and veins, or the consequence of changes in vasomotor centres.

Others have suggested that the relative stasis in the enlarged ventricles may lead to an accumulation of metabolites capable of interfering with cerebral function. Or perhaps distortion of cerebral tissues, consequent upon the enlargement and displacement of the ventricular bodies, may embarrass cerebral function particularly in diencephalic structures.

These various possibilities await clarification. It is possible that in some cases several factors operate in conjunction with one another.

OTHER FORMS OF HYDROCEPHALUS

The best known form of hydrocephalus is that which declares itself in infancy, resulting from obstruction along the course of the cerebrospinal fluid pathways. This is usually due to developmental defects of the brain, haemorrhage following birth trauma, or an attack of meningitis. When the disturbance is manifest before the cranial sutures have closed there is progressive enlargement of the head. Usual accompaniments are varying degrees of spasticity, mental retardation and sometimes blindness, depending on the severity of the obstruction and the presence or absence of associated developmental brain defects. In some patients the hydrocephalus becomes arrested and intellect may occasionally be surprisingly well preserved. In cases due to developmental defects there are often other congenital abnormalities, particularly spina bifida and meningomyelocoele.

In adults obstructive hydrocephalus is mainly the result of new pathology, such as a tumour strategically situated to impede the cerebrospinal fluid circulation. It commonly presents with symptoms of raised intracranial pressure but sometimes the initial picture can be misleading. Riddoch (1936) described two patients with tumours of the third ventricle who presented as dementia without headache or papilloedema. Akinetic mutism may occur (Messert et al., 1966), or there may be a disturbance of gait as the initial manifestation (Messert and Baker, 1966).

Occasionally, moreover, adult obstructive hydrocephalus is attributable to congenital defects or pathology acquired much earlier in life; a partial balance is then achieved between the production and absorption of cerebrospinal fluid. Developmental defects such as aqueduct stenosis or partial obliteration of the foramina of the fourth ventricle can remain latent in this way. McHugh (1964) has drawn attention to examples of such 'occult' hydrocephalus in adults, occasionally remaining unsuspected until autopsy, sometimes decompensating suddenly with an abrupt rise in intracranial pressure, or sometimes progressing insidiously with the development of spastic paraparesis or mental changes. Headache is usual but not inevitable, and a spectrum is likely to exist between the cases considered here and those already described under the heading of normal pressure hydrocephalus. A common feature is a history of attacks of abrupt loss of consciousness, lasting a few minutes during which the patient lies motionless and flaccid. Such attacks are often preceded or followed by headache and are presumably due to sudden rises of intracranial pressure. The mental changes, which may or may not accompany the neurological developments, can take the form of listlessness, apathy and inattentiveness, progressing to a picture of dementia and inertia resembling frontal lobe disorder.

Aqueduct stenosis, in particular, may fail to declare itself until adolescence or mid-adulthood. Asymptomatic cases have also been found at autopsy. The stenosis is usually the result of congenital defect, though some can be traced to an episode of meningitis in childhood and others show gliosis of unknown cause. Nag and Falconer (1966) and Wilkinson et al. (1966) discuss the pictures which may present in adult life. Symptoms of raised intracranial pressure may occur, sometimes following an intermittent crescendo pattern succeeded by periods of unconsciousness, but in others such evidence is completely lacking. Some present with unsteadiness of gait or with epilepsy, usually of psychomotor type. Others show hypothalamic symptoms such as impotence, amenorrhoea or obesity, due to pressure of the distended third ventricle on the pituitary and hypothalamus. Mental symptoms may be the presenting feature, with impairment of memory or generalised dementia. Of the ten cases reported by Nag and Falconer only five presented with symptoms indicative of raised intracranial pressure, while memory disorder was the initial manifestation in four. Harrison *et al.* (1974) obtained a history of deterioration of memory and concentration in a third of their cases. This was usually mild, but in 2 cases was sufficiently marked to be the feature that brought the patient to medical attention.

A man of 52 showed slow progression of gait disturbance and impotence following the death of his mother to whom he was closely attached. Six years later he was hospitalised and the disorder was ascribed to 'nerves'. Thereafter he developed emotional lability, mild memory impairment and occasional urinary incontinence. One year later mental testing was within normal limits except for moderate slowing of response, but his gait was strikingly abnormal with tiny shuffling steps and difficulty in initiating movement. The cerebrospinal fluid was normal and under normal pressure. Air encephalography showed aqueduct stenosis. Ventriculography showed dilatation of the lateral and third ventricles, and also of the upper 1 cm of the aqueduct. A shunt operation led to excellent resolution of his symptoms. He had had meningitis at the age of 5 and had complained frequently of headache throughout adult life.

(Wilkinson *et al.*, 1966)

An example reported by Ojemann *et al.* (1969) is also instructive:

A woman of 54 had an 18 month history of progressive change of personality and failure of mental functions. She became disinterested in people and activities, and showed inattentiveness and difficulty with calculation. Some months later her gait became unsteady and her left hand tremulous, leading to a diagnosis of parkinsonism. Deterioration progressed relentlessly with marked apathy and incontinence of urine. On examination she showed impairment of memory and other intellectual functions, a slight left hemiparesis and spasticity in the legs. On sitting down she took thirty seconds to go the last four inches, and on approaching a step she raised her foot too early and too high. The cerebrospinal fluid pressure was normal, and air encephalography showed air in the fourth ventricle but none in the aqueduct. Ventriculography displayed large

lateral and third ventricles, with gross dilatation of the rostral part of the aqueduct and a nodular mass projecting from the region of the quadrigeminal plate. A shunt operation produced striking improvement and she was entirely normal one year after operation.

An interesting association of aqueduct stenosis has recently been reported by Reveley and Reveley (1983). In the course of examining the CT scans of schizophrenic patients they found 3 with aqueduct stenosis. Two were known to be hydrocephalic from shortly after birth, while in the third the condition was entirely unsuspected. The significance of this association remains at present unclear.

The diagnosis rests ultimately on X-ray studies, including CT scanning with or without air encephalography and ventriculography. Erosion of the dorsum sellae is shown on plain X-rays in the majority, and the lateral and third ventricles are seen to be symmetrically enlarged. The aqueduct is either not displayed or is seen to be very narrow. Intraventricular pressure may be elevated or normal.

Shunt operations can be dramatically successful in relieving the symptoms whether or not the pressure has been raised. A considerable failure rate is seen, however, mainly due to obstruction within the subarachnoid space (McMillan and Williams, 1977).

Other Disorders Producing Dementia

Kuru

Kuru is a subacute degenerative disease of the brain leading to dementia. It is restricted to members of the Fore tribe who inhabit the eastern highlands of New Guinea, but has special claims to interest since a transmissible agent appears to be involved. Moreover it holds a certain fascination in that spread has possibly been facilitated by cannibalism. It was the experimental observations on this rare disease that led ultimately to the discovery of transmissibility in Creutzfeldt–Jakob disease discussed on p. 400.

The disease was first described by Gajdusek and Zigas (1957) and is reviewed by Alpers (1969). Prodromal symptoms of headache, malaise and limb pains lead on to florid symptoms of cerebellar ataxia and tremor. These soon render walking and speech impossible. Strabismus, marked clonus and emotional lability are characteristic features. Progressive intellectual deterioration leads to death usually within twelve months.

The brain shows a variety of neuronal degenerative changes with status spongiosus and marked astrocytosis. These are found diffusely, but the cerebellum is markedly affected and the cerebral cortex may be relatively spared. There is minimal demyelination and inflammatory changes are absent.

Three factors appear to account for the illness: a genetic predisposition in the Fore people, a transmissible agent, and formerly a possible spread by means of cannibalism. Inoculates of brain tissue from affected persons have been shown to reproduce the disease in chimpanzees, and thence by serial passage from one chimpanzee to another (Gajdusek et al., 1966, 1967). Both the clinical picture and the pathological changes closely resemble the human disease, differing only in increased status spongiosus in the animal brain (Beck et al., 1966). The responsible agent passes a 100 nm filter, and can be transmitted by inoculation directly into the brain or by a peripheral route. It has not, however, been identified under the electron microscope. In all these respects it resembles the transmissible agent of 'scrapie', a much studied degenerative brain disease of sheep, and also the agent discovered in Creutzfeldt–Jakob disease. It is customary to refer to these transmissible agents as 'unconventional' or 'slow' viruses though they differ in several respects from ordinary viruses as described on p. 400. The neuropathological pictures in all three diseases share important interrelationships, as discussed in detail by Beck, Daniel et al. (1969a).

In the case of kuru, spread may have been greatly helped, until recent years at least, by the practice of cannibalism of dead relatives. With the transmissible agent present in the tissues of affected persons cannibalism would provide an especially hazardous means of increasing the incidence of the disease above that to be expected from genetic sources alone. Until recently kuru claimed the lives of more than 50% of the women of the tribe. It affected women principally, but surprisingly children of both sexes as well. Adult males escaped except in very rare instances. This distribution of cases could be related to the cannibalistic practices of the tribe, in which the women and children ate the viscera and brain but the adult males ate muscle only. Recently the disease appears to have died out as the practice of cannibalism has ceased (Gajdusek et al., 1977). It should be emphasised, however, that the cannibalism hypothesis was never firmly proven. Kuru has not been transmitted to chimpanzees by ingestion, only by injection. There may, of course, have been opportunities for 'self-inoculation' through cuts and abrasions when infected tissues were handled during the ritual ceremonies of the tribe.

Progressive Multifocal Leucoencephalopathy

This rare disorder is an occasional complication of chronic diseases affecting the reticuloendothelial system such as lymphoma, Hodgkin's disease, leukaemia or sarcoidosis. Richardson (1961, 1968) describes the typical clinical picture. Most affected patients have been between 30 and 60 years of age. Progressive dementia is accompanied by neurological manifestations indicative of focal involvement of the central nervous system—pareses, ataxia, dysphasia and visual field defects. Rapid mental and neurological deterioration typically leads to death within a few weeks or months, but very occasional cases have shown slow progression over several years. The CT scan shows low density lesions in the central and convolutional white matter, often with a distinctive 'scalloped' appearance to their lateral borders (Carroll et al., 1977). The cerebrospinal fluid is usually normal.

At autopsy scattered crumbling foci of softening are seen as small round greyish areas throughout the brain. They occur in both grey and white matter, affecting the cerebral hemispheres principally and showing a special predilection for the junction of cortex and subcortex. Within such areas there is marked demyelination along with relative preservation of the axis cylinders. Perivascular lymphocytic cuffing is usually well developed. A unique stamp is given by the changes observed in the glial cells. Astrocytes are enormously enlarged, with bizarre distorted nuclei which often show abnormal mitoses. The oligodendroglial nuclei often contain inclusion bodies.

Electronmicroscopy suggests the presence of virus-like particles in the abnormal glial nuclei (Lancet, 1966b; Dayan, 1969). Abundant spherical particles can be detected, sometimes in crystalline arrays, together with cylindrical structures resembling those seen in cells infected with polyoma virus. Recently there have been several reports of the isolation of viral material from the brains of affected individuals, as reviewed by Davies et al. (1974), but the responsible agent has usually not been clearly identified. The disorder is possibly occasioned by a normally harmless virus which gains access to the brain when immune defences have been impaired by the primary reticuloendothelial disease. Bauer et al. (1973) and Marriott et al. (1975) have reported patients who responded to treatment with cytosine arabinoside (cytarabine) after the diagnosis had been confirmed by biopsy. In the latter case a polyoma virus was isolated from the biopsy sample.

Kraepelin's Disease

Kraepelin described the disease which bears his name in 1910, though there is now considerable doubt whether it should be regarded as a clinical or pathological entity. McMenemey (1963b) refers to 17 reported cases in the literature. The onset is usually in the fourth decade but some cases have begun in adolescence. Rapidly progressive mental deterioration is accompanied by restlessness, anxiety, depression and speech defects, and leads to death within one or two years. Catatonia-like features have accompanied the dementia in many examples and some have begun with an acute catatonic psychosis.

The essential feature at autopsy appears to be destruction of Nissl substance and consequent dissolution of ganglion cells. The changes are patchy in distribution but particularly affect the frontal and central areas and Ammon's horns. Glial proliferation is remarkably slight, and tangles and plaques are not seen.

Schaumberg and Suzuki (1968) report six members of a family affected by early presenile dementia in whom the pathological changes at autopsy accorded with those described by Kraepelin. Again the picture was of diffuse cortical atrophy and loss of neurones but without more specific features. Nevertheless they agree that in most reported examples of Kraepelin's disease there have been other plausible explanations for the pathological picture, such as cerebral anoxia or metabolic defects.

Dementia with Thalamic Degeneration

From time to time patients are reported in whom a progressive dementing illness proves to be associated with unusual and unexpected pathological changes in the brain. One such example is the case described by Stern (1939) where thalamic degeneration was the conspicuous finding at autopsy. The case was regarded as unique. It is interesting that a thalamic location has also been reported for tumours and cerebrovascular lesions leading to dementia (pp. 198 and 328).

Severe generalised dementia proceeded to death within three months. Gross memory disturbance was associated with confabulation, perseveration, receptive language disturbance, somnolence, and marked changes in personality by way of inertia and lack of initiative. The only neurological signs were loss of the pupillary reflexes to light and accommodation, forced grasping and prominent sucking reflexes.

At autopsy there was no cerebral atrophy. The cortex showed diffuse non-specific degeneration of neurones and some glial overgrowth. But the striking finding was severe degeneration in the thalamus, with complete disappearance of nerve cells in some regions and dense gliosis. The affected areas were bilaterally symmetrical. There were no inflammatory changes and arteriosclerosis was minimal. The symmetry of the process and its circumscribed nature suggested a 'system degeneration' of the thalamus, affecting the phylogenetically most recent parts.

Dementia with Basal Ganglia Calcification

Dementia appears to be a common late manifestation in patients suffering from 'idiopathic calcification of the basal ganglia'. This rare syndrome tends to occur familially with a pattern suggestive of autosomal dominant inheritance (Moscowitz et al., 1971). The cause remains unknown.

Many affected persons are asymptomatic for long periods of time, though it seems likely that most ultimately show some form of extrapyramidal dysfunction. Parkinsonism or choreoathetosis usually develop in late middle age, or more rarely cerebellar ataxia or pyramidal deficits. Progressive impairment of memory and intellect frequently accompany the motor manifestations, with slowing of cognitive processes typical of subcortical dementia (p. 568). Dysphasia and other focal cortical deficits are not observed. In several cases a psychosis indistinguishable from schizophrenia has been reported, often antedating the motor and cognitive manifestations by many years. Francis (1979) has reported 9 patients in four generations of a family in whom a schizophrenia-like psychosis appeared to be the principal accompaniment of the disorder.

Cummings et al. (1983) review the literature on the condition, finding indications of two relatively distinct patterns of presentation. Those who present with psychotic episodes tend to do so in their early 30s, those with dementia and motor disorder some 20 years later. Both share the characteristic finding of dense calcification symmetrically involving the basal ganglia and particularly the putamen. The dentate nuclei of the cerebellum and the pulvinar of the thalamus may also be heavily affected.

Other conditions leading to calcification within the basal ganglia must be excluded, the commonest being hypoparathyroidism and pseudo-hypoparathyroidism. Hyperparathyroidism may occasionally produce a not dissimilar radiological appearance. Investigation of the serum calcium and phosphate serves to make the distinction since these have uniformly proved to be normal. Other causes of calcification such as toxoplasmosis, tuberous sclerosis or the sequelae of encephalitis or anoxia will also need consideration when the familial nature of the condition is not apparent.

Hallervorden–Spatz Syndrome

Dementia is prominent in the majority of patients with this rare extrapyramidal syndrome and can very occasionally be the presenting feature. Late infantile and juvenile forms make up the majority of cases, though a rare adult variant exists. The nosology of the syndrome has become confused as further examples have been reported.

More than one family member tends to be affected though sporadic cases occur. Dooling *et al.* (1974) describe the typical features as onset at a young age, a motor disorder mainly of extrapyramidal type, the mental changes of dementia, and a relentlessly progressive course leading to death on average 11 years later. Of their 42 examples from the literature mental changes had been the first manifestations in 4. One had begun at the age of 30 and 2 others at 57 and 64. The late onset cases were non-familial and died after 5–6 years.

Motor abnormalities consist mainly of rigidity, dystonia and choreoathetoid movements, though spasticity and pyramidal signs may appear. Dysarthria is almost always present and facial grimacing may occur. Myoclonus and tremor are not uncommon. Abnormalities of posture or movement are the usual presenting symptoms, often interfering with walking.

A change of personality sometimes sets in early, with moodiness, depression and outbursts of aggressive behaviour (Sacks *et al.*, 1966; Rodzilsky *et al.*, 1968). Intellectual deterioration then gradually develops along with the motor manifestations, often progressing to mutism in the terminal stages.

There are no abnormal findings in the blood or cerebrospinal fluid. The electroencephalogram shows slowing as the disease advances, sometimes with spikes and sharp waves. The CT scan may resemble that seen in Huntington's chorea, with prominent atrophy of the basal ganglia (Dooling *et*

al., 1980). Generalised atrophy of the cortex, brain stem and cerebellum may also be apparent.

At autopsy the distinctive finding is reddish-brown discolouration of the globus pallidus and pars reticulata of the substantia nigra, due to the accumulation of iron-containing pigment. Microscopy shows loss of neurones in the affected areas with demyelination and gliosis, and numerous oval or rounded structures ('spheroids') which are identifiable as axonal swellings. The latter are frequently widely disseminated in the cortex, though this may otherwise show little by way of neurone loss or gliosis. The Purkinje cells of the cerebellum may be depleted.

Treatment with iron chelating agents has been tried without success. Levodopa may, however, improve the motor abnormalities for a time.

Metachromatic Leucodystrophy

This rare cause of dementia and motor disorder is inherited as an autosomal recessive. It represents an abnormality of neural lipid metabolism, with the accumulation of galactosyl sulphatide in affected tissues. Deposits of the material stain metachromatically. The diagnosis may be confirmed during life by biopsies of peripheral nerve or rectal wall.

Dulaney and Moser (1978) describe infantile, juvenile and adult forms which appear to be genetically distinct. The infantile form represents the classical disease, setting in before the age of three and progressing to severe motor and mental retardation, sometimes with blindness. The juvenile form is less common, presenting with motor and mental dysfunction and sometimes resembling a spinocerebellar disorder.

The adult form is rarest of all. Onset in recorded cases has varied from 19 to 46 years, presenting sometimes with dementia and sometimes with psychotic disorder. Motor dysfunction is less prominent and may only develop later in the disease. In adults the course can be extremely protracted over several decades. Mistakes in diagnosis are common, and unless a sibling has already been affected the condition is not often suspected during life. Common diagnostic labels are of presenile dementia, schizophrenia or multiple sclerosis. Cummings and Benson (1983) refer to reports of the condition first diagnosed as schizophrenia or presenting with expansive delusions suggestive of mania. When motor abnormalities eventually appear they take the form of pyramidal and extrapyramidal dysfunction with paresis, dystonic movements and a parkinsonian expression. Ataxia, nystagmus and intention tremor are common. Seizures often occur, and peripheral neuropathy is usually present.

The specific diagnosis depends on showing diminished arylsulphatase activity in the white blood cells, serum and urine, and demonstration of sulphatide in the urine. Metachromatic deposits within Schwann cells may be detected in biopsy specimens from the sural nerve or rectal wall. Peripheral nerve conduction velocity is reduced. The heterozygote state may also be detected by measurement of arylsulphatase in the white blood cells.

At autopsy severe white matter destruction is seen in the brain, often with cavitation, along with loss of normal myelin sheaths. Accumulations of strikingly metachromatic material appear as spherical granular masses. Similar changes are found in the peripheral nerves and certain visceral organs.

Kufs' Disease

Kufs' disease, or cerebral ceroid lipofuscinosis, represents a form of cerebral lipidosis in which the abnormal lipopigment deposits consist of a ceroid-like material akin to lipofuscin. The precise nature of the accumulated material remains uncertain, likewise the pathogenesis of the disorder.

Onset in infancy or childhood has attracted various eponyms ('Batten–Bielschowsky', 'Spielmeyer–Vogt') and is usually accompanied by visual symptoms and retinal abnormalities ('cerebromacular degeneration'). These are rare, however, in the adult form which is known as Kufs' disease. Symptoms then begin in adolescence or adulthood, with an insidious dementia accompanied by motor manifestations. Extrapyramidal disturbances and cerebellar disorder appear to be commoner than spasticity in adults. Myoclonic and other forms of seizure are often encountered.

Siakotos (1981) distinguishes autosomal recessive and dominant forms (Kufs type and Parry type respectively), both with motor symptoms and mental deterioration as the main presenting features. Progress tends to be slow, with onset in the 20s or 30s and death some 8–9 years later. Dementia or behavioural change can be the initial manifestation (Greenfield and Nelson, 1978).

The wide variety of motor and mental manifestations makes diagnosis difficult during life when a family history is absent. Rectal biopsy is useful, however, in revealing the abnormal storage material in neurones and smooth muscle from the rectal wall (Brett and Lake, 1975). Skin and skeletal muscle

biopsies can also yield a reliable diagnosis when examined by electron microscopy (Carpenter et al., 1977).

The characteristic finding at autopsy is a striking distension of nerve cells with autofluorescent lipopigment, along with neuronal degeneration and reactive gliosis. Electron microscopy shows the accumulated material to be granular in structure. Cells in the basal ganglia, brain stem and cerebellum tend to be more heavily involved than those of the cortex (Dekaban and Herman, 1974). A variable degree of generalised brain atrophy may accompany such changes.

Whipple's Disease

Whipple's disease is a rare multisystem disorder, known to be infective in origin though the responsible bacilli have not been cultured or characterised. An immunological defect in the host is likely to play an important part in causation. It is very much more common in men than women, setting in usually in the sixth decade. The classical presentation is with weight loss, lassitude, chronic diarrhoea and malabsorption, often pursuing a chronic course to extreme emaciation. Multiple arthralgias, serous effusions, uveitis, lymphadenopathy and low-grade pyrexia are other common manifestations.

Involvement of the nervous system has come increasingly to be recognised, sometimes after the systemic disorder is well advanced but occasionally as the dominant feature. Neurological involvement has been reported several times when gastrointestinal and other symptoms are minimal (Bayless and Knox, 1979). In very rare examples it has represented the sole clinical or pathological manifestation of the disorder (Romanul et al., 1977).

The symptoms tend to be non-specific so that diagnosis may be missed or greatly delayed. Pallis and Lewis (1980) describe the common pictures as dementia progessing over months or years, external ophthalmoplegias, or myoclonic movements of the head trunk or limbs. Other patients have presented with focal neurological signs indicative of a space occupying lesion, or hypothalamic involvement with somnolence, hyperphagia and polydipsia.

A slowly progressive dementia has been reported in several patients. It may be accompanied by motor disorder, particularly supranuclear gaze palsies or myoclonus though such are not always in evidence (Finelli et al., 1977; Feurle et al., 1979). Lampert et al.'s (1962) patient had a 7 year history of progressive mental deterioration leading to an impression of Alzheimer's disease; there was no history of gastrointestinal disturbance though an attack of arthritis had occurred at the onset.

Evidence of malabsorption or anaemia will often be present. The cerebrospinal fluid may be normal or show pleocytosis and elevation of protein. The CT scan can be negative, though some examples have shown intracranial granulomatous lesions in the form of low density contrast-enhancing areas (Halperin et al., 1982). Definitive diagnosis depends on the demonstration of PAS-positive material in macrophages which, in the absence of prior treatment, can almost always be revealed by jejunal biopsy. This must be undertaken whenever the disease is suspected. Lymph node biopsy can be informative too, or the characteristic inclusions may be detected in cells from the cerebrospinal fluid. Brain biopsy will sometimes be performed, but will stand to be negative in patients with hypothalamic involvement alone.

The findings at autopsy are distinctive. Tissues involved by the disease show PAS-positive granules within macrophages, representing membrane-like structures derived from bacterial walls ('sickle-particle-containing cells'). The bacilli themselves can sometimes be seen by electron microscopy. Central nervous system involvement shows as collections of PAS-positive cells in the brain and cord, often with widespread perivascular nodules and indolent inflammatory changes. In Romanul et al.'s (1977) patient the entire cortical ribbon was studded with minute ring-shaped lesions containing PAS-positive material and surrounded by astrocytes. The bacilli could be identified within macrophages in the brain.

Treatment with antibiotics usually meets with a good response where gastrointestinal and other systemic manifestations are concerned. Régimes have included parenteral chloramphenicol and oral tetracycline or penicillin or ampicillin. These must often be continued for many months and relapse can tend to occur. In the treatment of neurological complications less success has been reported, though a vigorous attempt should always be pursued. Feurle et al.'s (1979) patient showed a good response where confusional states, myoclonus and nystagmus were concerned, though paralysis of upward gaze persisted.

Other Disorders affecting the Central Nervous System

Behçet's Syndrome

Behçet's syndrome is a rare disorder of unknown aetiology predominantly affecting young males. The classical triple symptom complex consists of oral ulceration, genital ulceration and ocular lesions (uveitis, iridocyclitis), usually occurring in several attacks per year and pursuing a chronic course over many years. Lassitude, malaise and slight pyrexia may accompany attacks but the degree of constitutional disturbance varies. Common additional manifestations include thrombophlebitis, erythema nodosum and non-specific skin sensitivity. The overall course is unpredictable, but the illness often abates after one or two decades. Blindness may remain as a permanent sequel.

Central nervous system involvement is recognised as a serious additional complication, important not for its frequency but on account of its grave prognosis. No part of the nervous system appears to be immune. A great variety of clinical pictures may result, as described in the comprehensive reviews by Wolf et al. (1965) and Alema (1978).

The onset is usually abrupt, coinciding with a relapse of orogenital ulceration or uveitis. Failing this there is almost always a well-established history of the syndrome before nervous system involvement sets in. The patient develops headaches, fever, slight neck stiffness and a variety of neurological signs. Brain stem involvement is particularly common with giddiness, ataxia, diplopia, cranial nerve palsies or long tract signs. A typical feature is the episodic nature of such defects, the picture seeming to stabilise after several weeks then relapsing with fresh developments. Recurrent attacks of hemiplegia or paraplegia may lead on to pseudobulbar palsy. Periods of remission may result in temporary improvement, or in rare cases complete recovery. In general, however, serious neurological defects persist. The course has been likened to that of severe forms of multiple sclerosis and differentiation may occasionally present difficulties (Whitty, 1958). The cerebrospinal fluid usually shows a slight lymphocytic pleocytosis and rise of protein. When neck stiffness is severe there may be a marked polymorphonuclear response.

Pallis and Fudge (1956) attempted to demarcate three main forms of nervous system involvement— a brain stem form, a meningomyelitic form, and a variety with mental symptoms predominating. The last could present either as transient episodes of confusion or in the form of dementia. The patients with dementia usually showed an insidious onset and steady slow progression, sometimes accompanied by features of parkinsonism and sometimes by pseudobulbar palsy. Alema (1978) stresses that both organic and non-organic psychiatric pictures may arise, the former sometimes being accompanied by meningeal signs and cerebrospinal fluid changes. Depression is common among the non-organic disturbances.

Involvement of the central nervous system is always a serious development. The patient's general condition is often poor, and adverse developments can set in rapidly. The course of each episode is, however, unique and unpredictable. Some patients deteriorate after repeated relapses, some remain quiescent for long periods, and others decline steadily and die. Wolf et al. (1965) estimated the mortality at 40%, more than half of the deaths occurring within a year of the first neurological signs.

The responsible pathology is little understood, and the autopsies reported to date have not clarified the mechanisms of symptom production. Changes include foci of perivascular infiltration, small areas of haemorrhage and necrosis, scattered areas of demyelination, and diffuse neuronal degeneration with a marked glial reaction.

The syndrome has been ascribed to viral, vascular and allergic mechanisms. Steroids have been claimed to help markedly in some patients, including those with involvement of the central nervous system, though others have reported no benefit. Wadia and Williams (1957) recommend that steroids should be given promptly if ocular or neurological symptoms develop at any point in the disease, and Alema (1978) concludes that they may have reduced the mortality from neurological complications. Immunosuppressive drugs (cyclophosphamide, azathioprine, chlorambucil) may also be of benefit, though side-effects limit their usefulness.

Sarcoidosis: Benign Lymphogranulomatosis; Boeck's Sarcoid

Sarcoidosis is characterised by the development of chronic granulomatous lesions in various parts of the body. The aetiology is unknown, though an immunologically determined alteration in tissue reactivity appears to be fundamental to the disease. It may represent some form of collagen disorder or be caused by some unidentified organism. An atypical response to the tubercle bacillus has been suspected but never confirmed.

The characteristic lesion is the epithelioid cell granuloma or follicle, consisting of a well-demarcated collection of epithelioid cells with occasional giant cells. The centres may show necrosis but the caseation seen with tubercular infection is lacking.

The lesions tend to heal spontaneously but provoke surrounding fibrosis. The commonest site is the respiratory system, presenting with hilar lymphadenopathy or reticular shadowing in the lungs. The mildness of symptoms often contrasts with the extent of the lesions, cases sometimes being discovered on routine chest X-ray. Erythema nodosum is another characteristic presentation. Ocular manifestations include iridocyclitis and uveitis. The latter may be accompanied by parotitis ('uveo-parotid fever'). Other parts of the body commonly involved are the superficial lymph nodes, spleen, liver, and phalanges of the hands and feet. Overt myopathy is rare but muscle infiltration is often apparent on biopsy.

The onset is usually between the ages of 20 and 40. In general sarcoid runs an indolent course with relapses and remissions, showing a tendency to subside spontaneously after several years. Individual lesions gradually resolve while others make an appearance, the cycle sometimes being narrowly confined and sometimes widespread in different organs. Complete recovery may be expected in some 80% of cases (Batten, 1978). Others are left disabled by pulmonary fibrosis or ocular complications. Death, when it occurs, may be due to renal failure or cardiac involvement. Affection of the central nervous system (see below) can also carry serious hazards. Treatment with ACTH or steroids is often effective in inducing remission and promoting the healing of lesions, though maintenance therapy must sometimes continue for many years.

A low grade pyrexia is an inconstant accompaniment. During active phases of the disease there may be a normochromic anaemia, raised ESR, and eosinophilia. Mild leucopaenia and thrombocytopaenia are sometimes seen. The serum globulins may be elevated and hypercalcaemia of moderate degree is not infrequent. In uncertain cases and with unusual presentations chest X-ray may reveal the characteristic picture, likewise X-ray of the phalanges. Biopsy of skin lesions, lymph nodes or muscle can give confirmatory evidence. The Kveim test is an intradermal test of fair reliability which yields a nodule with the histological features of sarcoid.

Involvement of the nervous system is estimated to occur in 5% of patients (Sharma, 1975). Neurological dysfunction may be the presenting feature or indeed the sole clinical manifestation, though cases with lesions entirely confined to the nervous system are very rare. Among the 23 patients with neurological involvement reported by Delaney (1977), this had been the first sign in 15. Other series have been described by Hook (1954), Jefferson (1957), Wiederholt and Siekert (1965), Silverstein *et al.* (1965) and Matthews (1965).

There are no clear demarcations between the various forms of nervous system involvement but certain broad categories can be discerned. The parts most frequently involved are the cranial nerves, meninges, hypothalamus and pituitary.

Lesions of the cranial and peripheral nerves are the commonest neurological feature. The seventh cranial nerve is particularly vulnerable, leading to unilateral or bilateral facial palsies. Involvement of the optic nerves results in blurring of vision, papilloedema, optic atrophy or field defects. The peripheral nerves may be affected singly or in combination. Basal meningitis or brain stem involvement can produce a multitude of fluctuating cranial nerve palsies.

Granulomatous meningitis or meningoencephalitis affects mainly the basal brain regions. The meninges become thickened and infiltrated with granulomas and lymphocytes. Lumbar puncture shows an elevated protein and pleocytosis. Chronic headache is accompanied by focal signs as the adjacent chiasm and hypothalamus become infiltrated. An adhesive arachnoiditis can lead to raised intracranial pressure and hydrocephalus. In some cases the meningeal involvement remains entirely sub-clinical; it was evident in all 14 of Delaney's (1977) autopsied cases, yet had been suspected during life in only 9.

The brain parenchyma may become involved by contiguous spread or by the formation of tumour-like masses of granulomatous material. Involvement of the hypothalamus and third ventricular region leads to somnolence, obesity, hyperthermia, and memory difficulties or change of personality. Pituitary dysfunction may show as diabetes insipidus, menstrual irregularities and other endocrine dysfunction (Winnacker *et al.*, 1968). Lesions situated within the cerebral hemispheres may be single or multiple. The cerebellum, brain stem or cord may be similarly affected. Solitary deposits have sometimes been mistaken for neoplasms until biopsy is performed (Jefferson, 1957). Focal signs may make an abrupt appearance, and seizures can be hard to control.

Mental disturbance will often be prominent when sarcoid affects the central nervous system. Hook (1954) reported patients with a variety of pictures—apathy, lack of judgement and personal neglect progressing over a year to semi-coma; acute agitation and hallucinosis leading to residual dementia; profound memory impairment and irritability. Cordingley *et al.*'s (1981) patient presented with progressive dementia, the only abnormal signs being a wide-based gait and incomplete abduction together with nystagmus on lateral gaze. Others have described marked changes of character, fluctuating confusion, and a variety of psychotic pictures. In some the disturbance will be occasioned by hydrocephalus consequent upon basal meningitis or obstruction of cerebrospinal fluid flow by granulomatous masses. In others direct brain infiltration will be responsible. Camp and Frierson (1962) reported a patient who presented with headache and progressive failure of memory and intellect who at autopsy showed extensive nodular infiltration throughout the cortex and basal brain regions. In patients with circumscribed failure of memory, as in the following example, localised involvement of the hypothalamus and limbic structures is probably responsible:

A woman developed sarcoidosis at 24, presenting with bilateral hilar lymphadenopathy. Two years later she had a minor seizure and shortly thereafter developed headache, weakness and incoordination. Examination revealed a sensory level at T4 and a myelogram showed obstruction from T4 to T7. The CT scan demonstrated a right frontal granuloma and basal meningeal sarcoid with mild ventricular dilatation. Dexamethasone produced marked neurological improvement over the following year which was well maintained.

At 28 she became aware of increasing memory impairment over 3 to 4 weeks, then abruptly became agitated, deluded and doubly incontinent. She was disoriented in time and place and heard hallucinatory voices at night. The acute organic reaction settled over 6 to 8 weeks on haloperidol and increased dexamethasone, but her memory remained mildly impaired. Psychometric testing at that time showed a WAIS full scale IQ of 78, with scores of 55% on the Wechsler logical memory test and 45% on the Rey–Osterrieth test.

Some months later her memory deteriorated further and she developed compulsive eating, weight gain and insomnia. At 30 she was obese, mildly ataxic, and with hyper-reflexia in the legs and bilateral extensor plantars. There were no psychotic features but she was disoriented in time and showed a severe defect of short-term memory. She could recall nothing of a name and address or of simple geometrical figures. The WAIS IQ was 82, but the logical memory test now gave a score of only 20% and the Rey–Osterrieth test 30%. The CT scan was unchanged but pulmonary and hepatic involvement were demonstrated. Steroids were increased to high dosage, with improvement 3 weeks later in orientation and on simple tests of recall.

She was discharged to a semi-independent life in her own home which she managed to run with the help of memory aids.

(Thompson and Checkley, 1981)

In some cases a combination of structural and metabolic disturbances are likely to shape the psychiatric picture, particularly in the presence of hypercalcaemia or a degree of renal failure. Steroid therapy may make its own contribution to mental features (p. 535).

It can obviously be important, in patients with organic psychosyndromes and neurological defects of obscure aetiology, to bear the possibility of sarcoidosis in mind. Full investigation along the lines described above will almost certainly produce confirmatory evidence of the disorder, even when nervous system involvement has been the presenting manifestation. The CT scan may show the intra-cranial lesions, and lumbar puncture may reveal the evidence of chronic meningitis. Cordingley et al. (1981) suggest that a consistently normal cerebro-spinal fluid probably excludes the diagnosis.

The prognosis for patients with neuropsychiatric complications is extremely variable, but in general intracranial involvement should be viewed as a grave development. Some show a remittant picture, others slow and incomplete recovery, while others show progressive disability. A few will die of the neuro-logical manifestations. Facial nerve palsy is usually transient and shows a good response to steroids. Basal meningitis may slowly ameliorate and subside. In favourable cases intracerebral granulomas can improve or even resolve with steroid therapy; surgical removal has occasionally been successful.

Hyperostosis Frontalis Interna
(hyperostosis cranii, metabolic craniopathy, endocraniosis, Morgagni's syndrome)

Hyperostosis of the frontal region of the skull was once considered an important clinical sign, indicative of a syndrome with various endocrine and mental manifestations. However, most authorities now consider it to be of no pathological significance, and indeed several major neurological and medical texts make no reference to it. Nevertheless, the condition continues to attract sporadic interest, and there are some indications that it may be commoner than chance expectation in patients with organic psycho-syndromes.

The radiological picture is of thickening of the inner tables of the frontal bones, with smooth rounded exostoses projecting into the cranial cavity. Part of the problem in discerning any putative clini-cal associations lies with the frequency of the condi-tion and with the occurrence of minor variations. It may be found at any age from adolescence upwards, increasing markedly from the third or fourth decades onwards. Females are affected very much more often than males, with an incidence of perhaps 5–6% overall. Higher estimates at almost 50% for women and 6% for men (Silinkova-Malkova and Malek, 1965/66) are probably attributable to the inclusion of sub-categories with diffuse thickening of the calvarium, also patients with normal overall skull thickness but reduction and sclerosis of the diploë. It may sometimes appear familially, and has been described in association with dystrophia myotonica (p. 613).

The pathogenesis is quite unknown. Those who argue for a special association with endocrine dysfunction have claimed an aetiological role via hypothalamic or pituitary dysfunction (e.g. Solomon, 1954) though there is no direct evidence of this. Two 'syndromes' have been proposed, 'Morgagni's syndrome' with hyperostosis, obesity and hirsuitism, and the 'Stewart–Morel syndrome' in which neuropsychiatric features predominate. Neither however, has won wide acceptance.

In most reviews the main features have been headache, obesity, hirsuitism and menstrual disor-ders. Headache was found in 89% of Silinkova and Malek's series compared with 37% of controls; hirsuitism was present in 37% compared with 14% of controls. Thirst, water retention, sleep disturb-ances and a variety of rather minor endocrine changes are also described. Among mental features neurotic complaints figure prominently, also disturbances of personality, memory impairment and occasionally dementia. A number of forms of psychosis have been reported. All agree, however, that the condition is very often entirely asympto-matic.

In part the old claims of a special relationship to mental disease may have resulted from the skull being more closely examined in the course of mental hospital autopsies. Nevertheless, there is some evidence pointing to a higher incidence of the condi-tion in the mentally ill. Hawkins and Martin (1965) compared skull X-rays from patients seen in a general hospital with those from patients currently resident in a psychiatric hospital. Among the females 5·9% of the former and 10·7% of the latter showed hyperostosis, a statistically significant difference which persisted on controlling for age. Among males there were too few cases for comparison. In neither hospital could the patients with hyperostosis be shown to belong to particular diagnostic categories when matched with unaffected controls.

More recently Walinder (1977) has surveyed a large group of women admitted to a psychiatric hospital, finding hyperostosis in 26%. When matched with patients of equivalent age but without the skull changes, dementia emerged as significantly more common in the hyperostosis group. Among the sibs of Walinder's affected patients mental illness also appeared to be significantly more frequent.

Putnam (1974) points to a possibly interesting association, describing a patient with hyperostosis, hirsuitism, diabetes mellitus and borderline hypothyroidism, who was found to have normal pressure hydrocephalus as a basis for her memory failure and incontinence. A shunt operation improved the mental state. Putnam's review of 11 other cases with normal pressure hydrocephalus showed hyperostosis in 8.

Agenesis of the Corpus Callosum

Absence of the corpus callosum, in whole or in part, occurs as a rare developmental abnormality. Other associated defects are usually present—hydrocephalus, microgyria, heterotopias, arachnoid cysts, spina bifida or meningomyelcoele (Merritt, 1979). The anterior and hippocampal commissures may be intact even when the corpus callosum is entirely missing.

Most cases have been reported in children, though the condition can come to light at any age. It usually presents by virtue of symptoms attributable to other cerebral malformations—seizures, mental retardation or hydrocephalus. Occasionally, however, it is discovered only at autopsy or in the course of neuroradiological investigations carried out for some other purpose. The discovery of asymptomatic cases is likely to increase now that CT scanning is so frequently performed.

Ettlinger (1977) has summarised the anatomical findings and theories about causation. Detailed reviews are found in Unterhanscheidt et al. (1968), Loeser and Alvord (1968) and Probst (1973). All have tended to agree that clinical findings, when present, owe little to the absence of the corpus callosum *per se* and much to the associated anomalies. Epilepsy, spasticity and other motor defects are common, likewise varying grades of mental subnormality. When patients with other malformations are excluded, however, intelligence is not infrequently in the normal range (Lehmann and Lampe, 1970).

There has been a renewal of interest in the psychological status of such patients in view of the abnormal functioning known to follow surgical section of the commissures (pp. 38–9). Equivalent evidence of functional disconnection of the cerebral hemispheres has rarely, however, been forthcoming. Some deficits have been demonstrated on tests of bimanual coordination and in crossed-responding to visual stimuli (Jeeves, 1965, 1969), in the transfer of maze-learning from one hand to the other (Lehmann and Lampe, 1970), in cross-location of touch and in the matching of visual patterns between left and right visual fields (Ettlinger et al., 1972, 1974). However, all such deficits are variable, and other tests of interhemispheric transfer appear often to be well performed. Compensatory mechanisms must clearly be at work, by way of bilateral speech representation, increased use of ipsilateral inflow pathways, or utilisation of such other commissural pathways as are intact. Kretschmer's (1968) report of two patients who were unable to read in the left half field of vision, one also being apraxic with the left hand, is exceptional, suggesting that these deficits may have been due to other associated lesions. Milner (1983) provides a valuable recent review of neuropsychological studies in such patients, concluding that while it is likely that both cognitive and skilled performances can suffer, there are clearly great individual differences from one case to another. In particular, there is no good evidence that acallosal brains are less laterally specialised than normal brains, despite conflicting findings on the issue.

The radiological diagnosis, based on the air-encephalogram, has been described by Bull (1967). Marked separation is seen between the lateral ventricles; they show angular dorsal margins, concave medial borders, and dilatation of the caudal portions. The third ventricle is widened with a large dorsal extension. Equivalent features can be detected on the CT scan. Characteristic findings are seen in relation to the pericallosal arteries and other vessels on angiography.

References

The figures in square brackets and italics after each reference show
the page(s) of text on which the item is mentioned.

ABD EL NABY S. & HASSANEIN M. (1965) Neuropsychiatric manifestations of chronic manganese poisoning. *Journal of Neurology,
Neurosurgery and Psychiatry* 28, 282–288 *[541]*.

ABE K. (1977) Lithium prophylaxis of periodic hypersomnia. *British
Journal of Psychiatry* 130, 312–313 *[629]*.

ABENSON M.H. (1970) EEG's in chronic schizophrenia. *British
Journal of Psychiatry* 116, 421–425 *[110]*.

ABRAHAM H.D. (1982) A chronic impairment of colour vision in
users of LSD. *British Journal of Psychiatry* 140, 518–520 *[532]*.

ABRAMS R. & TAYLOR M.A. (1976) Catatonia: a prospective clinical
study. *Archives of General Psychiatry* 33, 579–581 *[299]*.

ABRAMS R. & TAYLOR M.A. (1979) Differential EEG patterns in
affective disorder and schizophrenia. *Archives of General
Psychiatry* 36, 1355–1358 *[76]*.

ABRAMS R. & TAYLOR M.A. (1980) Psychopathology and the electroencephalogram. *Biological Psychiatry* 15, 871–878 *[76]*.

ACHESON J. & HUTCHINSON E.C. (1971) The natural history of focal
cerebral vascular disease. *Quarterly Journal of Medicine* 40, 15–23
[325].

ACHTÉ K.A. & ANTTINEN E.E. (1963) Suizide bei Hirngeschädigten
des Krieges in Finland. *Fortschritte der Neurologie, Psychiatrie*
31, 645–667 *[165]*.

ACHTÉ K.A., HILLBOM E. & AALBERG V. (1967) *Post-traumatic Psychoses Following War Brain Injuries.* Reports from The Rehabilitation Institute for Brain-injured Veterans in Finland, vol. 1:
Helsinki *[164, 165, 166]*.

ACHTÉ K.A., HILLBOM E. & AALBERG V. (1969) Psychoses following
war brain injuries. *Acta Psychiatrica Scandinavica* 45, 1–18 *[164]*.

ACK M., MILLER I. & WEIL W.B. (1961) Intelligence of children
with diabetes mellitus. *Pediatrics* 28, 764–770 *[456]*.

ACKER W. (1982) Objective psychological changes in alcoholics after
the withdrawal of alcohol. *British Medical Bulletin* 38, 95–98 *[518]*.

ACKER W., APS E.J., MAJUMDAR S.K., SHAW G.K. & THOMSON
A.D. (1982) The relationship between brain and liver damage in
chronic alcoholic patients. *Journal of Neurology, Neurosurgery
and Psychiatry* 45, 984–987 *[521]*.

ACKER W., RON M.A., LISHMAN W.A. & SHAW G.K. (1984) A
multi-variate analysis of psychological, clinical and CT scanning
measures in detoxified chronic alcoholics. *British Journal of Addiction* 79, 293–301 *[520]*.

ACKNER B., COOPER J.E., GRAY C.H. & KELLY M. (1962) Acute
porphyria: a neuropsychiatric and biochemical study. *Journal of
Psychosomatic Research* 6, 1–24 *[483, 484]*.

ACKNER B., COOPER J.E., GRAY C.H., KELLY M. & NICHOLSON
D.C. (1961) Excretion of porphobilinogen and d-aminolaevulinic
acid in acute porphyria. *Lancet* 1, 1256–1260 *[484]*.

ADAMS G.F. (1967) Problems in the treatment of hemiplegia. *Gerontologia Clinica* 9, 285–294 *[325, 327, 333]*.

ADAMS G.F. & HURWITZ L.J. (1963) Mental barriers to recovery
from strokes. *Lancet* 2, 533–537 *[325, 326]*.

ADAMS G.F. & HURWITZ L.J. (1974) *Cerebrovascular Disability and
the Ageing Brain,* Churchill Livingstone: Edinburgh & London
[322, 324, 325, 326, 332].

ADAMS J.H. (1976) Parasitic and fungal infections of the nervous
system. Ch. 7 in *Greenfield's Neuropathology,* 3rd Edition, eds.
Blackwood W. & Corsellis J.A.N. Edward Arnold: London *[272]*.

ADAMS J.H. & JENNETT W.B. (1967) Acute necrotizing encephalitis:
a problem in diagnosis, *Journal of Neurology, Neurosurgery and
Psychiatry* 30, 248–260 *[300]*.

ADAMS J.H., MITCHELL D.E., GRAHAM D.I & DOYLE D. (1977)
Diffuse brain damage of immediate impact type. Its relationship
to 'primary brain-stem damage' in head injury. *Brain* 100, 489–
502 *[139]*.

ADAMS K.M. (1976) Behavioral treatment of reflex or sensory-evoked
seizures. *Journal of Behavior Therapy and Experimental Psychiatry*
7, 123–127 *[303]*.

ADAMS P.W., WYNN V., ROSE D.P., SEED M., FOLKARD J. &
STRONG R. (1973) Effect of pyridoxine hydrochloride (Vitamin
B₆) upon depression associated with oral contraception. *Lancet*
1, 897–904 *[487]*.

ADAMS R.D. (1965) Discussion of Part IV. Ch. 20 in *The Remote
Effects of Cancer on the Nervous System,* eds. Brain W.R. &
Norris F.H., Contemporary Neurology Symposia, vol. 1. Grune
& Stratton: New York *[638]*.

ADAMS R.D. (1966) Further observations on normal pressure hydrocephalus. *Proceedings of the Royal Society of Medicine* 59, 1135–1140
[639].

ADAMS R.D., FISHER C.M., HAKIM S., OJEMANN R.G. & SWEET
W.H. (1965) Symptomatic occult hydrocephalus with 'normal'
cerebrospinal fluid pressure: a treatable syndrome. *New England
Journal of Medicine* 273, 117–126 *[639, 642]*.

ADAMS R.D. & KUBIK C.S. (1944) Subacute degeneration of the
brain in pernicious anaemia. *New England Journal of Medicine*
231, 1–9 *[503]*.

ADIE W.J. (1926) Idiopathic narcolepsy: a disease sui generis; with
remarks on the mechanism of sleep. *Brain* 49, 257–306 *[621, 622]*.

ADLER A. (1945) Mental symptoms following head injury. *Archives
of Neurology and Psychiatry* 53, 34–43 *[147, 148, 149, 152]*.

ADLER R., MACRITCHIE K. & ENGEL G.L. (1971) Psychologic processes and ischaemic stroke (occlusive cerebrovascular disease) 1.
Observations on 32 men with 35 strokes. *Psychosomatic Medicine*
33, 1–29 *[339]*.

ADOLFSSON R., GOTTFRIES C.G., ROOS B.E. & WINBLAD B. (1979)
Changes in the brain catecholamines in patients with dementia
of Alzheimer type. *British Journal of Psychiatry* 135, 216–223 *[383]*.

ADVISORY GROUP on the Management of Patients with Spongiform
Encephalopathy (Creutzfeldt-Jakob Disease (CJD)) (1981) *Report
to the Chief Medical Officers of the DHSS, the Scottish Home and
Health Department and the Welsh Office.* HMSO: London *[401]*.

AGATE J.N. & BUCKELL M. (1949) Mercury poisoning from finger-print photography. *Lancet* 2, 451–454 *[540]*.

AGRAS S. & MARSHALL C. (1965) The application of negative practice to spasmodic torticollis. *American Journal of Psychiatry* 122, 579–582 *[575]*.

AITA J.A. (1948) Follow-up study of men with penetrating injury to the brain. *Archives of Neurology and Psychiatry* 59, 511–516 *[150, 152]*.

AITA J.A. (1972) Neurologic manifestations of periarteritis nodosa. *Nebraska Medical Journal* 57, 362–366 *[366, 367]*.

AJURIAGUERRA J.DE & HÉCAEN H. (1960) *Le Cortex Cerebral: Étude Neuro-psycho-pathologique*. 2nd Edition. Masson: Paris *[155]*.

AJURIAGUERRA J.DE & ROUAULT DE LA VIGNE A. (1946) Troubles mentaux de l'intoxication oxycarbonée. *Semaine des Hôpitaux de Paris* 22, 1950–1954 *[469, 470]*.

AJURIAGUERRA J.DE & TISSOT R. (1969) The apraxias. Ch. 3 in *Handbook of Clinical Neurology*, vol. 4, eds. Vinken P.J. & Bruyn G.W. North-Holland Publishing Co.: Amsterdam *[50]*.

AKELATIS A.J. (1941) Lead encephalopathy in children and adults: a clinico-pathological study. *Journal of Nervous and Mental Disease* 93, 313–332 *[539]*.

ALAJOUANINE T. & LHERMITTE F. (1965) Acquired aphasia in children. *Brain* 88, 653–662 *[172]*.

ALBERT M.L. (1978) Subcortical dementia. In *Alzheimer's Disease: Senile Dementia and Related Disorders Aging*, Vol 7, eds. Katzman R., Terry R.D. & Bick K.L., pp. 173–180. Raven Press: New York *[569]*.

ALBERT M.L., FELDMAN R.G. & WILLIS A.L. (1974) The 'subcortical dementia' of progressive supranuclear palsy. *Journal of Neurology, Neurosurgery and Psychiatry* 37, 121–130 *[568, 569]*.

ALBERT M.S., BUTTERS N. & BRANDT J. (1981) Patterns of remote memory in amnesic and demented patients. *Archives of Neurology* 38, 495–500 *[35]*.

ALBERT M.S., BUTTERS N. & LEVIN J. (1979) Temporal gradients in the retrograde amnesia of patients with alcoholic Korsakoff's disease. *Archives of Neurology* 36, 211–216 *[34]*.

ALEMA G. (1978) Behçet's disease. Ch. 24 in *Handbook of Clinical Neurology*, Vol. 34. *Infections of the nervous system. Pt. II*, eds. Vinken P.J. & Bruyn G.W. North Holland Publishing Co: Amsterdam *[650, 651]*.

ALEX M., BARON E.K., GOLDENBERG S. & BLUMENTHAL H.T. (1962) An autopsy study of cerebrovascular accidents in diabetes mellitus. *Circulation* 25, 663–673 *[456]*.

ALEXANDER F. (1939) Emotional factors in essential hypertension. Presentation of a tentative hypothesis. *Psychosomatic Medicine* 1, 173–179 *[341]*.

ALEXANDER L. (1940) Wernicke's disease; identity of lesions produced experimentally by B₁ avitaminosis in pigeons with haemorrhagic polioencephalitis occurring in chronic alcoholism in man. *American Journal of Pathology* 16, 61–70 *[491]*.

ALEXANDER M.P. (1982a) Traumatic brain injury. Ch. 11 in *Psychiatric Aspects of Neurologic Disease* Vol. 2 eds. Benson D.F. & Blumer D. Grune & Stratton: New York & London *[160]*.

ALEXANDER M.P. (1982b) Episodic behaviours due to neurologic disorders other than epilepsy. Ch. 5 in *Pseudoseizures*, eds. Riley T.L. & Roy A. Williams & Wilkins: Baltimore & London *[258]*.

ALEXANDER P.E. & JACKSON A.H. (1981) Calcium and magnesium: relationship to schizophrenia and neuroleptic-induced extrapyramidal symptoms. Ch. 9 in *Electrolytes and Neuropsychiatric Disorders*, ed. Alexander P.E MTP Press: Lancaster *[478]*.

ALFREY A.C., LE GENDRE G.R. & KAEHNY W.D. (1976) The dialysis encephalopathy syndrome. *The New England Journal of Medicine* 294, 184–188 *[475]*.

ALLEN J.E. & RODGIN D.W. (1960) Mental retardation in association with progressive muscular dystrophy. *American Journal of Diseases of Children* 100, 208–211 *[612]*.

ALLEN I.M. (1930) A clinical study of tumours involving the occipital lobe. *Brain* 53, 194–243 *[196]*.

ALLENTUCK S. & BOWMAN K.M. (1942) The psychiatric aspects of marihuana intoxication. *American Journal of Psychiatry* 99, 248–250 *[524]*.

ALLISON R.S. (1961) Chronic amnesic syndromes in the elderly. *Proceedings of the Royal Society of Medicine* 54, 961–965 *[469]*.

ALLISON R.S. (1962) *The Senile Brain: A Clinical Study*. Edward Arnold: London *[15, 80]*.

ALPERS B.J. (1936) A note on the mental syndrome of corpus callosum tumours. *Journal of Nervous and Mental Disease* 84, 621–627 *[193]*.

ALPERS B.J. (1937) Relation of the hypothalamus to disorders of personality. *Archives of Neurology and Psychiatry* 38, 291–303 *[199]*.

ALPERS B.J. (1940) Personality and emotional disorders associated with hypothalamic lesions. Ch. 28 in *The Hypothalamus and Central Levels of Autonomic Function*. Research Publications of the Association for Research in Nervous and Mental Disease, vol. 20. Williams & Wilkins: Baltimore *[199]*.

ALPERS B.J. & DRAYER C.S. (1937) The organic background of some cases of spasmodic torticollis; report of case with autopsy. *American Journal of the Medical Sciences* 193, 378–384 *[575]*.

ALPERS M. (1969) Kuru: clinical and aetiological aspects. In *Virus Diseases and the Nervous System*, eds. Whitty C.W.M., Hughes J.T. & MacCallum F.O. Blackwell Scientific Publications: Oxford *[645]*.

ALSTROM C.H. (1950) A study of epilepsy in its clinical, social and genetic aspects. *Acta Psychiatrica et Neurologica Scandinavica*, supplement 63, 5–284 *[212, 215, 232, 241]*.

ALTER M., MASLAND R.L., KURTZKE J.F. & REED D.M. (1972) Proposed definitions and classifications of epilepsy for epidemiological purposes. Ch. 27 in *The Epidemiology of Epilepsy: A Workshop*, eds. Alter M. & Hauser W.A. National Institute of Neurological Diseases and Stroke Monograph No. 14, U.S. Department of Health, Education and Welfare *[207]*.

ALTER M., NEUGUT R. & KAHANA E. (1978) Familial aggregates of Creutzfeldt-Jakob disease (Abstract). *Neurology* 28, 353 *[401]*.

ALTMAN H. & EVENSON R.C. (1973) Marijuana use and subsequent psychiatric symptoms: a replication. *Comprehensive Psychiatry* 14, 415–420 *[528]*.

ALVAREZ W.C. (1947) The migrainous personality and constitution. The essential features of the disease. A study of 500 cases. *American Journal of the Medical Sciences* 213, 1–8 *[347]*.

ALVAREZ W.C. (1966) *Little Strokes*. Lippincott: Philadelphia & Toronto *[324, 417]*.

ALVORD E.C. JNR., FORNO L.S., KUSSKE J.A., KAUFFMAN R.J., RHODES J.S. & GOETOWSKI C.R. (1974) The pathology of Parkinsonism: a comparison of degenerations in cerebral cortex and brain stem. *Advances in Neurology* 5, 175–193 *[557]*.

ALZHEIMER A. (1907) Über eine eigenartige Erkrankung der Hirnrinde. *Allgemeine Zeitschrift für Psychiatrie* 64, 146–148 *[377]*.

ALZHEIMER A. (1911) Über eigenartige Krankheitsfälle des späteren Alters. *Zeitschrift für die gesamte Neurologie und Psychiatrie* 4, 356–385 *[377]*.

AMBROSE J. (1973) Computerized transverse axial scanning (tomography). Part 2. Clinical application. *British Journal of Radiology* 46, 1023–1047 *[119]*.

AMBROSE J. (1974) Computerized X-ray scanning of the brain. *Journal of Neurosurgery* 40, 679–695 *[119]*.

AMERICAN PSYCHIATRIC ASSOCIATION (1980) *Diagnostic and Statistical Manual of Mental Disorders*, 3rd Edition. American Psychiatric Association: Washington, DC *[5, 8]*.

AMINOFF M.J. & MARSHALL J. (1974) Treatment of Huntington's chorea with lithium carbonate: a double-blind trial. *Lancet* 1, 107–109 *[426]*.

AMINOFF M.J., MARSHALL J., SMITH E.M. & WYKE M.A. (1975) Pattern of intellectual impairment in Huntington's chorea. *Psychological Medicine* 5, 169–172 *[397]*.

ANAND M.P. (1964) Iatrogenic megaloblastic anaemia with neurological complications. *Scottish Medical Journal* 9, 388–390 *[505]*.

ANASTASI A. (1968) *Psychological Testing*, 3rd Edition. Macmillan: New York *[96, 97, 98, 106]*.

ANDERMANN F., KEENE D.L., ANDERMANN E. & QUESNEY L.F. (1980) Startle disease on hyperekplexia. Further delineation of the syndrome. *Brain* 103, 985–997 *[259]*.

ANDERSON C. (1942) Chronic head cases. *Lancet* 2, 1–4 *[168]*.

ANDERSON E.W. & MALLINSON W.P. (1941) Psychogenic episodes in the course of major psychoses. *Journal of Mental Science* 87, 383–396 *[405, 406, 407]*.

ANDERSON E.W., TRETHOWAN W.H. & KENNA J.C. (1959) An experimental investigation of simulation and pseudo-dementia. *Acta Psychiatrica et Neurologica Scandinavica*, supplement 132, 1–42 *[409]*.

ANDERSON J. (1968) Psychiatric aspects of primary hyperparathyroidism. *Proceedings of the Royal Society of Medicine* 61, 1123–1124 *[448]*.

ANDERSON M. (1982) Nuclear magnetic resonance imaging and neurology. *British Medical Journal* 284, 1359–1360 *[122]*.

ANDERSSON P.G. (1970) Intracranial tumours in a psychiatric autopsy material. *Acta Psychiatrica Scandinavica* 46, 213–224 *[203]*.

ANDREASEN N.C., SMITH M.R., JACOBY C.G., DENNERT J.W. & OLSEN S.A. (1982) Ventricular enlargement in schizophrenia: definition and prevalence. *American Journal of Psychiatry* 139, 292–296 *[121]*.

ANDREW J. & NATHAN P.W. (1964) Lesions of the anterior frontal lobes and disturbances of micturition and defaecation. *Brain* 87, 233–262 *[193]*.

ANNETT M. (1970) A classification of hand preferences by association analysis. *British Journal of Psychology* 61, 303–321 *[38]*.

ANTHONY J.C., LE RESCHE L., NIAZ U., VON KORF M.R. & FOLSTEIN M.F. (1982) Limits of the 'Mini-Mental State' as a screening test for dementia and delirium among hospital patients. *Psychological Medicine* 12, 397–408 *[106]*.

ANTUONO P., SORBI S., BRACCO L., FUSCO T. & AMADUCCI L. (1980) A discrete sampling technique in senile dementia of the Alzheimer type and alcoholic dementia: study of cholinergic system. In *Aging of the Brain and Dementia, Aging*, Vol. 13, eds. Amaducci L., Davison A.N. & Antuono P. Raven Press: New York *[520]*.

APPENZELLER O. & SALMON J.H. (1967) Treatment of parenchymatous degeneration of the brain by ventriculo-atrial shunting of the cerebrospinal fluid. *Journal of Neurosurgery* 26, 478–482 *[426, 643]*.

ARING C.D. (1965) Observations on multiple sclerosis and conversion hysteria. *Brain* 88, 663–674 *[596]*.

ARKY R.A., VEVERBRANTS E. & ABRAMSON E.A. (1968) Irreversible hypoglycemia. A complication of alcohol and insulin. *Journal of the American Medical Association* 206, 575–578 *[463, 464]*.

ARNOLD O.H. (1949) Untersuchungen zur Frage der akuten tödlichen Katatonien. *Wiener Zeitschrift für Nervenheilkunde und deren Grenzgebiete* 2, 386–401 *[473]*.

ASHER R. (1949) Myxoedematous madness. *British Medical Journal* 2, 555–562 *[433, 435]*.

ASNIS G. (1977) Parkinson's disease, depression and ECT. A review and case study. *American Journal of Psychiatry* 134, 191–195 *[558]*.

ASSO D. (1969) WAIS scores in a group of Parkinson patients. *British Journal of Psychiatry* 115, 555–556 *[555]*.

ASSO D., CROWN S., RUSSELL J.A. & LOGUE V. (1969) Psychological aspects of the stereo-tactic treatment of parkinsonism. *British Journal of Psychiatry* 115, 541–553 *[561]*.

ASTRUP P. (1972) Some physiological and pathological effects of moderate carbon monoxide exposure. *British Medical Journal* 4, 447–452 *[472]*.

ATKINS C.J., KONDON J.J., QUISMORIO F.P. & FRIOU G.J. (1972) The choroid plexus in systemic lupus erythematosus *Annals of Internal Medicine* 76, 65–72 *[365]*.

AVERY T.L. (1971) Seven cases of frontal tumour with psychiatric presentation. *British Journal of Psychiatry* 119, 19–23 *[193]*.

AVERY T.L. (1973) A case of acromegaly and gigantism with depression. *British Journal of Psychiatry* 122, 599–600 *[442]*.

AZRIN N.H., NUNN R.G. & FRANTZ S.E. (1980) Habit reversal vs. negative practice treatment of nervous tics. *Behavior Therapy* 11, 169–178 *[586]*.

BABCOCK H. (1930) An experiment in the measurement of mental deterioration. *Archives of Psychology* 117, 5–105 *[83]*.

BACH-Y-RITA G., LION J.R. CLIMENT C.E. & ERVIN F.R. (1971) Episodic dyscontrol: a study of 130 violent patients. *American Journal of Psychiatry* 127, 1473–1478 *[74, 264]*.

BACH-Y-RITA G., LION J.R. & ERVIN F.R. (1970) Pathological intoxication: clinical and electroencephalographic studies. *American Journal of Psychiatry* 127, 698–703 *[509]*.

BADDELEY A.D. (1976) *The Psychology of Memory*. Harper & Row: New York *[28]*.

BADDELEY A. (1984) The fractionation of human memory. Editorial in *Psychological Medicine* 14, 259–264 *[28]*.

BAIL J.R.B. & LLOYD J.H. (1971) Myasthenia gravis as hysteria: or sounds of silence. *Medical Journal of Australia* 1, 1018–1020 *[610]*.

BAILES D.R., YOUNG I.R., THOMAS D.J., STRAUGHAN K., BYDDER G.M. & STEINER R.E. (1982) NMR imaging of the brain using spinecho sequences. *Clinical Radiology* 33, 395–414 *[123]*.

BAKER A.B. & KNUTSON J. (1946) Psychiatric aspects of uraemia. *American Journal of Psychiatry* 102, 683–687 *[473]*.

BAKER A.B. & TICHY F.Y. (1953) The effects of the organic solvents and industrial poisonings on the central nervous system. Ch. 26 in *Metabolic and Toxic Diseases of the Nervous System*, Research Publications of the Association for Research in Nervous and Mental Disease, vol. 32. Williams & Wilkins: Baltimore *[543]*.

BAKER L. & BARCAI A. (1970) Psychosomatic aspects of diabetes mellitus. Ch. 7 in *Modern Trends in Psychosomatic Medicine*, Vol. 2, ed. Hill O.W. Butterworths: London *[454]*.

BAKER M. (1973) Psychopathology in systemic lupus erythematosus: 1. psychiatric observations. *Seminars in Arthritis and Rheumatism* 3, 95–110 *[365]*.

BAKIR F., DAMLUJI S.F., AMIN-ZAKI L., MURTADHA M., KHALIDI A., AL-RAWI N.Y., TIKRITI S., DHAHIR H.I., CLARKSON T.W., SMITH J.C. & DOHERTY R.A. (1973) Methylmercury poisoning in Iraq. An Inter-University Report. *Science* 181, 230–240 *[543]*.

BALDESSARINI R.J. & TARSY D. (1976) Mechanisms underlying tardive dyskinesia. In *The Basal Ganglia. Association for Research in Nervous and Mental Disease* 55, ed. Yahr M.D., pp. 433–446. Raven Press: New York *[549]*.

BALDESSARINI R.J. & TARSY (1980) The pathophysiologic basis of tardive dyskinesia. In *Tardive Dyskinesia: Research and Treat-*

ment, eds. Fann W.E., Smith R.C., Davis J.M. & Domino E.F. MTP Press, Lancaster *[548, 549]*.

BALE R.N. (1973) Brain damage in diabetes mellitus. *British Journal of Psychiatry* 122, 337–341 *[456]*.

BALL M.J. (1976) Neurofibrillary tangles and the pathogenesis of dementia: A quantitative study. *Neuropathology and Applied Neurobiology* 2, 395–410 *[376]*.

BALL M.J. & NUTTALL K. (1980) Neurofibrillary tangles, granulovacuolar degeneration and neurone loss in Down's syndrome: quantitative comparison with Alzheimer dementia. *Annals of Neurology* 7, 462–465 *[378]*.

BALLENGER J.C. & POST R.M. (1978) Kindling as a model for alcoholic withdrawal syndromes. *British Journal of Psychiatry* 133, 1–14 *[512]*.

BALTHASAR K. (1956) Über das anatomische Substrat der generalisierten Tic-krankheit (maladie des tics, Gilles de la Tourette): Entwicklungshemmung des Corpus Striatum. *Archiv für Psychiatrie und Nervenkrankheiten* 195, 531–549 *[584]*.

BANAY R.S. (1944) Pathologic reaction to alcohol. Review of the literature and original case reports. *Quarterly Journal of Studies on Alcohol* 4, 580–605 *[509]*.

BANEN D. (1972) An ergot preparation (hydergine) for relief of symptoms of cerebro-vascular insufficiency. *Journal of the American Geriatrics Society* 20, 22–24 *[425]*.

BANNISTER R. (1970) The place of isotope encephalography by the lumbar route in neurological diagnosis. *Proceedings of the Royal Society of Medicine* 63, 921–925 *[117]*.

BANNISTER R., GILFORD E. & KOCEN R. (1967) Isotope encephalography in the diagnosis of dementia due to communicating hydrocephalus. *Lancet* 2, 1014–1017 *[117]*.

BARAITSER M. (1981) Huntington's chorea. *Hospital Update* 7, 71–74 *[394]*.

BARBEAU A. (1971) Long-term side-effects of levodopa. *Lancet* 1, 395 *[560]*.

BARBIZET J. (1963) Defect of memorizing of hippocampal-mammillary origin: a review. *Journal of Neurology, Neurosurgery and Psychiatry* 26, 127–135 *[29]*.

BARCROFT J. (1920) Anoxemia. *Lancet* 2, 485–489 *[465]*.

BARCROFT J. (1925) *The Respiratory Function of the Blood. Part 1: Lessons from high altitudes*. Cambridge University Press *[468]*.

BARD P. (1928) A diencephalic mechanism for the expression of rage with special reference to the sympathetic nervous system. *American Journal of Physiology* 84, 490–515 *[71]*.

BARETTE J. & MARSDEN C.D. (1979) Attitudes of families to some aspects of Huntington's chorea. *Psychological Medicine* 9, 327–336 *[394]*.

BARKER M.G. & LAWSON J.S. (1968) Nominal aphasia in dementia. *British Journal of Psychiatry* 114, 1351–1356 *[15]*.

BARKER W. (1948) Studies in epilepsy: personality pattern, situational stress, and the symptoms of narcolepsy. *Psychosomatic Medicine* 10, 193–202 *[621]*.

BARKER W. & WOLF S. (1947) Studies in epilepsy. *American Journal of the Medical Sciences* 214, 600–604 *[216]*.

BARLOW E.D. & DE WARDENER H.E. (1959) Compulsive water drinking. *Quarterly Journal of Medicine* 28, 235–258 *[445]*.

BARNES L. & KRASNOFF A. (1973) Medical and psychological factors pertinent to the rehabilitation of the epileptic. Ch. 12 in *Medical and Psychological Aspects of Disability*, ed. Cobb A.B. Thomas: Springfield, Illinois *[271]*.

BARRACLOUGH B. (1981) Suicide and epilepsy. Ch. 7 in *Epilepsy and Psychiatry*, eds. Reynolds E.H. & Trimble M.R. Churchill Livingstone: Edinburgh & London *[254]*.

BARRETT R.E., YAHR M.D. & DUVOISIN R.C. (1970) Torsion dystonia and spasmodic torticollis—results of treatment with L-dopa. *Neurology* 20 (part 2), 107–113 *[575]*.

BARRON S.A., JACOBS L. & KINKEL W.R. (1976) Changes in size of normal lateral ventricles during aging determined by computerised tomography. *Neurology* 26, 1011–1013 *[120]*.

BARTHOLOMEW A.A. & MARLEY E. (1959) Toxic response to 2-phenyl-3-methyl tetrahydro-1,4-oxazine hydrochloride (Preludin) in humans. *Psychopharmacologia* 1, 124–139 *[535]*.

BARTLETT F.C. (1932) *Remembering: A Study in Experimental and Social Psychology*. Cambridge University Press *[25]*.

BARTUS R.T., DEAN R.L., BEER B. & LIPPA A.S. (1982) The cholinergic hypothesis of geriatric memory dysfunction. *Science* 217, 408–417 *[426]*.

BARWICK D.D., OSSELTON J.W. & WALTON J.N. (1965) Electroencephalographic studies in hereditary myopathy. *Journal of Neurology, Neurosurgery and Psychiatry* 28, 109–114 *[612, 615]*.

BATTEN, J. (1978) Sarcoidosis. In *Prices Textbook of the Practice of Medicine*, 12th Edition, ed. Bodley Scott, Sir R., pp. 915–919. Oxford University Press: Oxford *[651]*.

BAUER G., MAYR U. & PALLUA A. (1980) Computerised axial tomography in chronic partial epilepsies. *Epilepsia* 21, 227–233 *[256]*.

BAUER W.R., TURREL A.P. & JOHNSON K.P. (1973) Progressive multifocal leukoencephalopathy and cytarabine: remission with treatment. *Journal of the American Medical Association* 226, 174–176 *[646]*.

BAY E. (1953) Disturbances of visual perception and their examination. *Brain* 76, 515–550 *[53]*.

BAY E. (1965) The concepts of agnosia, apraxia and aphasia after a history of a hundred years. *Journal of the Mount Sinai Hospital* 32, 637–650 *[53]*.

BAYLESS T.M. & KNOX D.L. (1979) Whipple's disease: a multisystem infection. *New England Journal of Medicine* 300, 920–921 *[649]*.

BEAR D.M. (1979) Temporal lobe epilepsy—a syndrome of sensory-limbic hyperconnection. *Cortex* 15, 357–384 *[236]*.

BEAR D.M. & FEDIO P. (1977) Quantitative analysis of interictal behaviour in temporal lobe epilepsy. *Archives of Neurology* 34, 454–467 *[234, 236]*.

BEARD A.W. (1959) The association of hepatolenticular degeneration with schizophrenia. *Acta Psychiatrica et Neurologica Scandinavica* 34, 411–428 *[566]*.

BEARN A.G. (1957) Wilson's disease: an inborn error of metabolism with multiple manifestations. *American Journal of Medicine* 22, 747–757 *[563]*.

BEARN A.G. (1972) Wilson's disease. Ch. 43 in *The Metabolic Basis of Inherited Disease*, eds. Stanbury J.B., Wyngaarden J.B. & Fredrickson D.S. Third edition. McGraw-Hill: New York *[563, 565]*.

BECK E., DANIEL P.M., ALPERS M., GAJDUSEK D.C. & GIBBS C.J. (1966) Experimental 'kuru' in chimpanzees. A pathological report. *Lancet* 2, 1056–1059 *[646]*.

BECK E., DANIEL P.M., GAJDUSEK D.C. & GIBBS C.J. (1969a) Similarities and differences in the pattern of the pathological changes in scrapie, kuru, experimental kuru and subacute presenile polioencephalopathy. In *Virus Diseases and the Nervous System*, eds. Whitty C.W.M., Hughes J.T. & MacCallum F.O. Blackwell Scientific Publications: Oxford *[400, 646]*.

BECK E., DANIEL P.M., MATTHEWS W.B., STEVENS D.L., ALPERS M.P., ASHER D.M., GAJDUSEK D.C. & GIBBS C.J. (1969b) Creutzfeldt-Jakob disease: the neuropathology of a transmission experiment. *Brain* 92, 699–716 *[400]*.

BECK H.G. (1936) Slow carbon monoxide asphyxiation. *Journal of the American Medical Association* 107(i), 1025–1029 *[471]*.

BECKER K.L., TITUS J.L., McCONAHEY W.M. & WOOLNER L.B. (1964) Morphologic evidence of thyroiditis in myasthenia gravis. *Journal of the American Medical Association* 187, 994–996 *[606]*.

BEDFORD P.D. (1955) Adverse cerebral effects of anaesthesia on old people. *Lancet* 2, 259–263 *[465]*.

BEDFORD P.D. (1958) Discussion: intracranial haemorrhage—diagnosis and treatment. *Proceedings of the Royal Society of Medicine* 51, 209–213 *[355]*.

BEECH H.R. (1960) The symptomatic treatment of writer's cramp. In *Behaviour Therapy and the Neuroses*, ed. Eysenck H.J. Pergamon Press: Oxford *[579]*.

BEGLEITER H., PORJESZ B. & TENNER M. (1980) Neuroradiological and neurophysiological evidence of brain deficits in chronic alcoholics. *Acta Psychiatrica Scandinavica* 62, Suppl. 286, 3–13, *[520]*.

BEHAN P.O. & BEHAN W.M.H. (1979) Possible immunological factors in Alzheimer's disease. Ch. 6 in *Alzheimer's Disease. Early recognition of potentially reversible effects*, eds. Glen A.I.M. & Whalley L.J. Churchill Livingstone: Edinburgh *[384, 385]*.

BEHAN P.O. & BONE I. (1977) Hereditary chorea without dementia. *Journal of Neurology, Neurosurgery and Psychiatry* 40, 687–691 *[399]*.

BEHAN P.O. & FELDMAN R.G. (1970) Serum proteins, amyloid and Alzheimer's disease. *Journal of the American Geriatrics Society* 18, 792–797 *[385]*.

BEHRMAN S. (1972) Mutism induced by phenothiazines. *British Journal of Psychiatry* 121, 599–604 *[546]*.

BELL D.S. (1965) Comparison of amphetamine psychosis and schizophrenia. *British Journal of Psychiatry* 111, 701–707 *[535]*.

BELL J. & CARMICHAEL E.A. (1939) On hereditary ataxia and spastic paraplegia. *The Treasury of Human Inheritance* 4, 141–281 *[602]*.

BENDER L. (1938) *A Visual Motor Gestalt Test and its Clinical Uses*. American Orthopsychiatric Association: New York *[97]*.

BENDER L. (1942) Post-encephalitic behaviour disorders in childhood. Ch. 8 in *Encephalitis: A Clinical Study*, ed. Neal J.B. Grune & Stratton: New York *[317]*.

BENDER L. (1946) *Instructions for the Use of Visual Motor Gestalt Test*. American Orthopsychiatric Association: New York *[97]*.

BENDER M.B. (1956) Syndrome of isolated episode of confusion with amnesia. *Journal of Hillside Hospital* 5, 212–215. Quoted by Bender M.B. (1960), Bulletin of the New York Academy of Medicine 36, 197–207 *[357]*.

BENDER M.B. (1960) Single episode of confusion with amnesia. *Bulletin of the New York Academy of Medicine* 36, 197–207 *[357]*.

BENDER M.B. (1969) Disorders of eye movements. Ch. 18 in *Handbook of Clinical Neurology*, vol. 1, eds. Vinken P.J. & Bruyn G.W. North-Holland Publishing Co.: Amsterdam *[579, 580]*.

BENEDETTI G. (1952) *Die Alkoholhalluzinosen*. Thieme: Stuttgart *[513]*.

BENNETT R., HUGHES G.R.V., BYWATERS E.G.L. & HOLT P.J.L. (1972) Neuropsychiatric problems in systemic lupus erythematosus. *British Medical Journal* 4, 342–345 *[363, 364, 366]*.

BENSON D.F. (1973) Psychiatric aspects of dysphasia. *British Journal of Psychiatry* 123, 555–566 *[48]*.

BENSON D.F. (1976) Psychiatric care for the aphasic patient. *McLean Hospital Journal* 1, 130–140 *[42, 48]*.

BENSON D.F. (1979) *Aphasia, Alexia and Agraphia*. Churchill Livingstone: New York *[42, 43, 47]*.

BENSON D.F. (1982a) The use of positron emission scanning techniques in the diagnosis of Alzheimer's disease. In *Alzheimer's Disease: A report of Progress in Research. Aging*, Vol. 19, eds. Corkin S., Davis K.L., Growden J.H., Usdin E. & Wurtman R.J., pp. 79–82. Raven Press: New York *[124]*.

BENSON D.F. (1982b) The treatable dementias. Ch. 6 in *Psychiatric Aspects of Neurologic Disease*, eds. Benson D.F. & Blumer D. Grune & Stratton, New York & London *[569]*.

BENSON D.F. & GESCHWIND N. (1971) Aphasia and related cortical disturbances. In *Clinical Neurology*, eds. Baker A.B. & Baker L.H. Harper & Row: New York *[44, 48, 87, 90]*.

BENSON D.F. & GREENBERG J.P. (1969) Visual form agnosia. A specific defect in visual discrimination. *Archives of Neurology* 20, 82–89 *[52]*.

BENSON D.F., KUHL D.E., HAWKINS R.A., PHELPS M.E., CUMMINGS J.L. & TSAI S.Y. (1983) The fluorodeoxyglucose ^{18}F scan in Alzheimer's disease and multi-infarct dementia. *Archives of Neurology* 40, 711–714 *[124]*.

BENSON D.F., KUHL D.E., PHELPS M.E., CUMMINGS J.L. & TSAI S.Y. (1982) Positron emission computed tomography in the diagnosis of dementia. *Transactions of the American Neurological Association*, 1981, 106, 68–71 *[124]*.

BENSON D.F., LeMAY M., PATTEN D.H. & RUBENS A.B. (1970) Diagnosis of normal pressure hydrocephalus. *New England Journal of Medicine* 283, 609–615 *[117]*.

BENSON D.F., MARSDEN C.D. & MEADOWS J.C. (1974) The amnesic syndrome of posterior cerebral artery occlusion. *Acta Neurologica Scandinavica* 50, 133–145 *[323, 361]*.

BENSON V.M. (1971) Marihuana 'study' critique. *Journal of the American Medical Association* 217, 1391 *[527]*.

BENTAL E. (1958) Acute psychoses due to encephalitis following Asian influenza. *Lancet* 2, 18–20 *[303]*.

BENTON A.L. (1955) *The Revised Visual Retention Test: Clinical and Experimental Applications*. The Psychological Corporation: New York *[98]*.

BENTON A.L. (1959) *Right-Left Discrimination and Finger Localization*. Hoeber: New York *[58]*.

BENTON A.L. (1961) The fiction of the 'Gerstmann Syndrome'. *Journal of Neurology, Neurosurgery and Psychiatry* 24, 176–181 *[57]*.

BENTON A.L. (1963) *The Revised Visual Retention Test: Clinical and Experimental Applications*. The Psychological Corporation: New York *[98]*.

BENTON A.L. (1967) Problems of test construction in the field of aphasia. *Cortex* 3, 32–58 *[105]*.

BENTON A.L. (1968) Differential behavioral effects in frontal lobe disease. *Neuropsychologia* 6, 53–60 *[88]*.

BENTON A.L., ELITHORN A., FOGEL M.L. & KERR M. (1963) A perceptual maze test sensitive to brain damage. *Journal of Neurology, Neurosurgery and Psychiatry* 26, 540–544 *[99]*.

BENTON A.L., JENTSCH R.C. & WAHLER H.J. (1959) Simple and choice reaction times in schizophrenia. *Archives of Neurology and Psychiatry* 81, 373–376 *[104]*.

BENTON A.L. & JOYNT J. (1959) Reaction time in unilateral cerebral disease. *Confinia Neurologica* 19, 247–256 *[104]*.

BENTON A.L. & SPREEN O. (1961) Visual memory test: the simulation of mental incompetence. *Archives of General Psychiatry* 4, 79–83 *[409]*.

BENTSON J., REZA M., WINTER J. & WILSON G. (1978) Steroids and apparent cerebral atrophy on computed tomography scans. *Journal of Computer Assisted Tomography* 2, 16–23 *[122]*.

BERG J.M. (1962) Meningitis as a cause of severe mental defect. In *Proceedings of the London Conference on the Scientific Study of Mental Deficiency*, vol. 1, ed. Richards B.W. May & Baker: Dagenham, England *[309]*.

BERGIN J.D. (1957) Rapidly progressing dementia in disseminated sclerosis. *Journal of Neurology, Neurosurgery and Psychiatry* 20, 285–292 *[592]*.

BERLYNE N. (1972) Confabulation. *British Journal of Psychiatry* 120, 31–39 *[15, 29]*.

BERGMAN H., BORG S., HINDMARSH T., IDESTRÖM C.-M. & MÜTZELL
S. (1980a) Computed tomography of the brain and neuropsychological assessment of male alcoholic patients and a random
sample from the general male population. *Acta Psychiatrica
Scandinavica* 62, Suppl. 286, 77–88 *[519, 520]*.

BERGMAN H., BORG S., HINDMARSH T., IDESTRÖM C.-M. & MÜTZELL
S. (1980b) Computed tomography of the brain and neuro-
psychological assessment of male alcoholic patients. Ch. 10 in
Addiction and Brain Damage, ed. Richter D. Croom Helm:
London *[519, 520]*.

BERGMANN K. (1977) Prognosis in chronic brain failure. *Age & Ageing*
6, Supplement, 61–66 *[373]*.

BERNOULLI C., SEIGFRIED J., BAUMGARTNER G., REGLI F.,
RABINOWICZ T., GAJDUSEK D.C. & GIBBS C.J. JNR. (1977) Danger
of accidental person-to-person transmission of Creutzfeldt-Jakob
disease by surgery. *Lancet* 1, 478–479 *[401]*.

BERRIOS G.E. & BROOK P. (1982) The Charles Bonnet syndrome
and the problem of visual perceptual disorders in the elderly.
Age and Ageing 11, 17–23 *[262]*.

BERSOFF D.N. (1970) The revised deterioration formula for the
Wechsler Adult Intelligence Scale: a test of validity. *Journal of
Clinical Psychology* 26, 71–73 *[96]*.

BETTS T.A. (1974) A follow-up study of a cohort of patients with
epilepsy admitted to psychiatric care in an English city. Ch. 56
in *Epilepsy: Proceedings of the Hans Berger Centenary Symposium*,
eds. Harris P. & Mawdsley C. Churchill Livingstone: Edinburgh
[252].

BETTS T.A. (1981) Depression, anxiety and epilepsy. Ch. 6 in *Epilepsy
and Psychiatry*, eds. Reynolds E.H. & Trimble M.R. Churchill
Livingstone: Edinburgh *[243, 252]*.

BETTS T.A. (1982) Psychiatry and epilepsy. In *A Textbook of Epilepsy*,
2nd Edition, eds. Laidlaw J. & Richens A., pp. 227–270.
Churchill Livingstone: Edinburgh *[231]*.

BEUMONT P.J.V., BANCROFT J.H.J., BEARDWOOD C.J. & RUSSELL
G.F.M. (1972) Behavioural changes after treatment with testosterone: case report. *Psychological Medicine* 2, 70–72 *[446]*.

BEWLEY T.H. (1967) Adverse reactions from the illicit use of lysergide. *British Medical Journal* 3, 28–30 *[530]*.

BEWSHER P.D., GARDINER A.Q., HEDLEY A.J. & MACLEAN H.C.S.
(1971) Psychosis after acute alteration of thyroid status. *Psychological Medicine* 1, 260–262 *[432]*.

BICKERSTAFF E.R. (1961a) Basilar artery migraine. *Lancet* 1, 15–17
[344].

BICKERSTAFF E.R. (1961b) Impairment of consciousness in migraine.
Lancet 2, 1057–1059 *[344, 349]*.

BICKERSTAFF E.R. & HOLMES J.M. (1967) Cerebral arterial insufficiency and oral contraceptives. *British Medical Journal* 1, 726–729
[345].

BICKFORD J.A.R. & ELLISON R.M. (1953) The high incidence of
Huntington's chorea in the Duchy of Cornwall. *Journal of Mental
Science* 99, 291–294 *[399]*.

BICKFORD R.G. & KLASS D.W. (1966) Acute and chronic EEG
findings after head injury. Ch. 6 in *Head Injury: Conference
Proceedings*, eds. Caveness W.F. & Walker A.E. Lippincott:
Philadelphia *[140]*.

BICKFORD R.G., WHELAN J.L., KLASS D.W. & CORBIN K.B. (1956)
Reading epilepsy: clinical and electroencephalographic studies
of a new syndrome. *Transactions of the American Neurological
Association* 81, 100–102 *[211]*.

BIDSTRUP P.L., BONNELL J.A., HARVEY D.G. & LOCKET S. (1951)
Chronic mercury poisoning in men repairing direct-current
meters. *Lancet* 2, 856–861 *[540]*.

BINDMAN E. & TIBBETTS R.W. (1977) Writer's cramp—a rational

approach to treatment? *British Journal of Psychiatry* 131, 143–148
[578, 579].

BINGLEY T. (1958) Mental symptoms in temporal lobe epilepsy and
temporal lobe gliomas. *Acta Psychiatrica et Neurologica Scandinavica*, supplement 120, 1–151 *[194, 196]*.

BINNIE C.D., ROWAN A.J., OVERWEG J., MEINARDI H., WISMAN
T., KAMP A. & LOPES DA SILVA F. (1981) Telemetric EEG and
video monitoring in epilepsy. *Neurology* 31, 298–303 *[256]*.

BINSWANGER O. (1894) Die Abgrenzung der allgemeinen progres-
siven Paralyse. *Berliner klinische Wochenshrift* 31, 1137–1139 *[390]*.

BIRD E.D. & IVERSON L.L. (1974) Huntington's chorea—post-
mortem measurement of glutamic acid decarboxylase, choline
acetyl-transferase and dopamine in basal ganglia. *Brain* 97, 457–
472 *[395]*.

BIRD E.D., MACKAY A.V.P., RAYNER C.N. & IVERSEN L.L. (1973)
Reduced glutamic-acid-decarboxylase activity of post-mortem
brain in Huntington's chorea. *Lancet* 1, 1090–1092 *[395]*.

BIRKETT D.P. (1972) The psychiatric differentiation of senility and
arteriosclerosis. *British Journal of Psychiatry* 120, 321–325 *[387]*.

BIRLEY J.L. (1920) The principles of medical science as applied to
military aviation. II War flying at high altitude. *Lancet* 1, 1205–
1211 *[468]*.

BLACK P., JEFFRIES J.J., BLUMER D., WELLNER A. & WALKER A.E.
(1969) The post-traumatic syndrome in children. Ch. 14 in *The
Late Effects of Head Injury*, eds. Walker A.E., Caveness W.F.
& Critchley M. Thomas: Springfield, Illinois *[171, 172, 173]*.

BLACKBURN H.L. & BENTON A.L. (1955) Simple and choice reaction
times in cerebral disease. *Confinia Neurologica* 15, 327–338 *[104]*.

BLACKSTOCK E.E., GATH D.H., GRAY B.C. & HIGGINS G. (1972)
The role of thiamine deficiency in the aetiology of the hallucinatory states complicating alcoholism. *British Journal of Psychiatry*
121, 357–364 *[513]*.

BLACKWOOD W., HALLPIKE J.F., KOCEN R.S. & MAIR W.G. (1969)
Atheromatous disease of the carotid arterial system and embolism
from the heart in cerebral infarction: a morbid anatomical study.
Brain 92, 897–910 *[320]*.

BLAKEMORE C.B. (1969) Psychological effects of temporal lobe
lesions in man. Ch. 10 in *Current Problems in Neuropsychiatry*,
ed. Herrington R.N. British Journal of Psychiatry Special Publication No. 4. Headley Brothers: Ashford, Kent *[275]*.

BLAKEMORE C.B. & FALCONER M.A. (1967) Long-term effects of
anterior temporal lobectomy on certain cognitive functions. *Journal of Neurology, Neurosurgery and Psychiatry* 30, 364–367 *[275]*.

BLASS J.P. & GIBSON G.E. (1977) Abnormality of a thiamine-requir-
ing enzyme in patients with Wernicke-Korsakoff syndrome. *New
England Journal of Medicine* 297, 1367–1370 *[492]*.

BLAU A. (1936) Mental changes following head trauma in children.
Archives of Neurology and Psychiatry 35, 723–769 *[173]*.

BLAU J.N. & DAVIS E. (1970) Small blood vessels in migraine. *Lancet*
2, 740–742 *[346]*.

BLAU J.N. & HINTON J.M. (1960) Hypopituitary coma and
psychosis. *Lancet* 1, 408–409 *[443]*.

BLESSED G. (1980) Clinical aspects of the senile dementias. Ch. 1 in
Biochemistry of Dementia, ed. Roberts P.J. John Wiley:
Chichester *[372, 374]*.

BLESSED G., TOMLINSON B.E. & ROTH M. (1968) The association
between quantitative measures of dementia and of senile change
in the cerebral grey matter of elderly subjects. *British Journal of
Psychiatry* 114, 797–811 *[106, 376]*.

BLESSED G. & WILSON I.D. (1982) The contemporary natural history
of mental disorder in old age. *British Journal of Psychiatry* 141,
59–67 *[375]*.

BLEULER E.P. (1924) *Textbook of Psychiatry* (Translated by A.A.

Brill). Macmillan: New York. Reissued by Dover Publications, 1951 *[413]*.

BLEULER M. (1951) Psychiatry of cerebral diseases. *British Medical Journal* 2, 1233–1238 *[190]*.

BLEULER M. (1967) Endocrinological psychiatry and psychology. *Henry Ford Hospital Medical Journal* 15, 309–317 *[428, 450]*.

BLOOMQUIST E.R. & COURVILLE C.B. (1947) The nature and incidence of traumatic lesions of the brain: a survey of 350 cases with autopsy. *Bulletin of the Los Angeles Neurological Society* 12, 174–183 *[139]*.

BLUESTIEN H.G. & ZVAIFLEV N.J. (1976) Brain-reactive lymphocytotoxic antibodies in the serum of patients with systemic lupus erythematosus. *Journal of Clinical Investigation* 57, 509–516 *[365]*.

BLUGLASS R. (1976) Malingering. In *Encyclopaedic Handbook of Medical Psychology*, ed. Krauss S., pp. 280–281. Butterworths: London *[409]*.

BLUMENTHAL H. & MILLER C. (1969) Motor nuclear involvement in progressive supra-nuclear palsy. *Archives of Neurology* 20, 362–367 *[567]*.

BLUMER D. (1970) Hypersexual episodes in temporal lobe epilepsy. *American Journal of Psychiatry* 126, 1099–1106 *[238, 239]*.

BLUMER D. & BENSON D.F. (1975) Personality changes with frontal and temporal lobe lesions. Ch. 9 in *Psychiatric Aspects of Neurologic Disease*, eds. Benson D.F. & Blumer D. Grune & Stratton: New York *[68]*.

BOBOWICK A.R., BRODY J.A., MATTHEWS M.R., ROOS R. & GAJDUSEK D.C. (1973) Creutzfeldt-Jakob disease: a case-control study. *American Journal of Epidemiology* 98, 381–394 *[401]*.

BOCKMAN J.M., KINGSBURY D.T., McKINLEY M.P., BENDHEIM P.E. & PRUSINER S.B. (1985) Creutzfeldt-Jakob disease prion proteins in human brains. *New England Journal of Medicine* 312, 73–78 *[400]*.

BOGEN J.E. (1969) The other side of the brain. I Dysgraphia and dyscopia following cerebral commissurotomy. II An appositional mind. III The corpus callosum and creativity. *Bulletin of the Los Angeles Neurological Society* 34, 73–105, 135–162 and 191–220 *[57, 276]*.

BOGEN J.E. & GAZZANIGA M.S. (1965) Cerebral commissurotomy in man: minor hemisphere dominance for certain visuospatial functions. *Journal of Neurosurgery* 23, 394–399 *[55]*.

BOGEN J.E. & VOGEL P.J. (1962) Cerebral commissurotomy in man. *Bulletin of the Los Angeles Neurological Society* 27, 169–172 *[276]*.

BOLLER F., MIZUTANI T., ROESSMANN U. & GAMBETTI P. (1980) Parkinson disease, dementia and Alzheimer disease: clinicopathological correlations. *Annals of Neurology* 7, 329–335 *[557]*.

BOLLER F. & VIGNOLO L.A. (1966) Latent sensory aphasia in hemisphere damaged patients: an experimental study with the Token Test. *Brain* 89, 815–830 *[105]*.

BOLT J.M.W. (1970) Huntington's chorea in the West of Scotland. *British Journal of Psychiatry* 116, 259–270 *[393, 394, 399]*.

BOLTON N., BRITTON P.G. & SAVAGE R.D. (1966) Some normative data on the WAIS and its indices in an aged population. *Journal of Clinical Psychology* 22, 184–188 *[96]*.

BOLTON N., SAVAGE R.D. & ROTH M. (1967) The modified word learning test and the aged psychiatric patient. *British Journal of Psychiatry* 113, 1139–1140 *[100, 102]*.

BOLWIG T.G. (1968) Transient global amnesia. *Acta Neurologica Scandinavica* 44, 101–106 *[358, 359]*.

BOND M.R. (1975) Assessment of the psychosocial outcome after severe head injury. In *Outcome of Severe Damage to the Central Nervous System*. Ciba Foundation Symposium No. 34 (New Series), pp. 141–157. Elsevier-Excerpta Medica: Amsterdam *[185]*.

BOND M.R. (1976) Assessment of the psychosocial outcome of severe head injury. *Acta Neurochirurgica* 34, 57–70 *[146, 185]*.

BOND M.R. & BROOKS D.N. (1976) Understanding the process of recovery as a basis for the investigation of rehabilitation for the brain injured. *Scandinavian Journal of Rehabilitation Medicine* 8, 127–133 *[158]*.

BONDAREFF W., BALDY R. & LEVY R. (1981a) Quantitative computed tomography in senile dementia. *Archives of General Psychiatry* 38, 1365–1368 *[121]*.

BONDAREFF W., MOUNTJOY C.Q. & ROTH M. (1981b) Selective loss of neurones of origin of adrenergic projection to cerebral cortex (nucleus locus coeruleus) in senile dementia. *Lancet* 1, 783–784 *[383]*.

BONDAREFF W., MOUNTJOY C.Q. & ROTH M. (1982) Loss of neurons of origin of the adrenergic projection to cerebral cortex (nucleus locus ceruleus) in senile dementia. *Neurology* 32, 164–168 *[383]*.

BONHOEFFER K. (1909) Exogenous psychoses. *Zentralblatt für Nervenheilkunde* 32, 499–505. Translated by H. Marshall in *Themes and Variations in European Psychiatry*, eds. Hirsch S.R. & Shepherd M. John Wright: Bristol, 1974 *[3]*.

BONHOEFFER K. (1910) *Die symptomatischen Psychosen im Gefolge von akuten Infectionen und inneren Erkrankungen*. Deuticke: Leipzig *[3]*.

BOOTH G. (1948) Psychodynamics in parkinsonism. *Psychosomatic Medicine* 10, 1–14 *[562]*.

BOSHES B. (1947) Neuropsychiatric manifestations during the course of malaria: experiences in the Mediterranean theater in World War II. *Archives of Neurology and Psychiatry* 58, 14–27 *[313]*.

BOTEZ M.I., FONTAINE F., BOTEZ T. & BACHEVALIER J. (1977) Folate-responsive neurological and mental disorders: report of 16 cases. Neuropsychological correlates of computerised trans-axial tomography and radionuclide cisternography in folic acid deficiencies. *European Neurology* 16, 230–246 *[505]*.

BOTTOMLEY T.A., HART H.R., EDELSTEIN W.A., SCHENCK J.F., SMITH L.S., LEUE W.M., MUELLER O.M. & REDINGTON R.W. (1983) NMR imaging/spectroscopy system to study both anatomy and metabolism. *Lancet* 2, 273–274 *[123]*.

BOTWINICK J. & BIRREN J.E. (1951) Differential decline in the Wechsler-Bellevue subtests in the senile psychoses. *Journal of Gerontology* 6, 365–368 *[377]*.

DE BOUCAUD P., VITAL C.I. & DE BOUCAUD D. (1968) Thalamic dementia of vascular origin. *Revue Neurologique* 119, 461–468 *[328]*.

BOUDIN M.D. & PEPIN B. (1968) Our experience in the treatment of Wilson's disease with penicillamine and sodium diethyl-dithiocarbamate. In *Wilson's Disease*, ed. Bergsma D. Birth Defects Original Article Series, vol. 4, No. 2. The National Foundation: New York *[565]*.

BOUGHTON C.R. (1970) Neurological complications of glandular fever. *Medical Journal of Australia* 2, 573–575 *[302]*.

BOUR H., TUTIN N. & PASQUIER P. (1967) The central nervous system and carbon monoxide poisoning. I: Clinical data with reference to 20 fatal cases. In *Carbon Monoxide Poisoning*, eds. Bour H. & Ledingham I.McA. Progress in Brain Research, vol. 24. Elsevier: Amsterdam *[469, 470]*.

BOURNE H.R., BUNNEY W.E., COLBURN R.W., DAVIS J.M., DAVIS J.N., SHAW D.M. & COPPEN A.J. (1968) Noradrenaline, 5-hydroxytryptamine, and 5-hydroxyindoleacetic acid in hind-brains of suicidal patients. *Lancet* 2, 805–808 *[24]*.

BOURGEOIS M., HÉBERT A. & MAISONDIEU J. (1970) Depressive senile pseudo-dementia curable by electric shock. *Annales Médico Psychologique* 128, 751–759 *[411]*.

BOVILL D. (1973) A case of functional hypoglycaemia—a medico-legal problem. *British Journal of Psychiatry* 123, 353–358 *[462]*.

BOWEN D.M., SMITH C.B. & DAVISON A.N. (1973) Molecular changes in senile dementia. *Brain* 96, 849–856 *[382]*.

BOWEN D.M. (1981) Alzheimer's Disease. Ch. 24 in *The Molecular Basis of Neuropathology*, eds. Davison A.N. & Thompson R.H.S. Edward Arnold: London *[382]*.

BOWEN D.M., SPILLANE J.A., CURZON G., MEIER-RUGE W., WHITE P., GOODHART M.J., IWANGOFF D. & DAVISON A.N. (1979) Accelerated ageing or selective neuronal loss as an important cause of dementia? *Lancet* 1, 11–14 *[382]*.

BOWER B. (1978) The treatment of epilepsy in children. *British Journal of Hospital Medicine* 19, 8–19 *[267]*.

BOWER H.M. (1967) Sensory stimulation in the treatment of senile dementia. *Medical Journal of Australia* 1, 1113–1119 *[423]*.

BOWERS M.B., WOERT M.V. & DAVIS L. (1971) Sexual behaviour during L-dopa treatment for parkinsonism. *American Journal of Psychiatry* 127, 1691–1693 *[561]*.

BOWLING G. & RICHARDS N.G. (1961) Diagnosis and treatment of the narcolepsy syndrome. *Cleveland Clinic Quarterly* 28, 38–45 *[619]*.

BOWMAN K.M., GOODHART R. & JOLLIFFE N. (1939) Observations on the role of vitamin B_1 in the etiology and treatment of Korsakoff psychosis. *Journal of Nervous and Mental Disease* 90, 569–575 *[493]*.

BOWMAN M. & LEWIS M.S. (1980) Sites of subcortical damage in diseases which resemble schizophrenia. *Neuropsychologia* 18, 597–601 *[76]*.

BOYD P.R., WALKER G. & HENDERSON I.N. (1957) The treatment of tetraethyl lead poisoning. *Lancet* 1, 181–185 *[543]*.

BRACELAND F.J. (1942) Mental symptoms following carbon disulphide absorption and intoxication. *Annals of Internal Medicine* 16, 246–261 *[543]*.

BRACELAND F.J. & GIFFIN M.E. (1950) The mental changes associated with multiple sclerosis (an interim report). Ch. 30 in *Multiple Sclerosis and the Demyelinating Diseases*, Research Publications of the Association for Research in Nervous and Mental Disease, vol. 28. Williams & Wilkins: Baltimore *[593, 594, 598]*.

BRADLEY C. (1979) Life events and the control of diabetes mellitus. *Journal of Psychosomatic Research* 23, 159–162 *[454]*.

BRADSHAW P. & PARSONS M. (1965) Hemiplegic migraine: a clinical study. *Quarterly Journal of Medicine* 34, 65–85 *[345, 351]*.

BRADY J.P. (1964) Epilepsy and disturbed behaviour. *Journal of Nervous and Mental Disease* 138, 468–473 *[236]*.

BRAHAM J. (1971) Jakob-Creutzfeldt disease: treatment by amantadine. *British Medical Journal* 4, 212–213 *[426]*.

BRAIN W.R. (1930) Critical review: disseminated sclerosis. *Quarterly Journal of Medicine* 23, 343–391 *[590, 596]*.

BRAIN W.R. (1955) *Diseases of the Nervous System*, 5th Edition. Oxford University Press *[207]*.

BRAIN W.R. (1963) The neurological complications of neoplasms. *Lancet* 1, 179–184 *[637]*.

BRAIN W.R. (1965) *Speech Disorders: Aphasia, Apraxia and Agnosia*, 2nd Edition. Butterworths: London *[40, 44, 45, 49, 52, 54]*.

BRAIN W.R. & ADAMS R.D. (1965) Epilogue: a guide to the classification and investigation of neurological disorders associated with neoplasms. Ch. 21 in *The Remote Effects of Cancer on the Nervous System*, eds. Brain W.R. & Norris F.H. Contemporary Neurology Symposia, vol. 1. Grune & Stratton: New York *[633, 634, 635]*.

BRAIN W.R., DANIEL P.M. & GREENFIELD J.G. (1951) Subacute cortical cerebellar degeneration and its relation to carcinoma. *Journal of Neurology, Neurosurgery and Psychiatry* 14, 59–75 *[601, 633, 634]*.

BRAIN W.R., GREENFIELD J.G. & RUSSELL D.S. (1943) Discussion on recent experiences of acute encephalomyelitis and allied conditions. *Proceedings of the Royal Society of Medicine* 36, 319–322 *[305]*.

BRAIN W.R., GREENFIELD J.G. & RUSSELL D.S. (1948) Subacute inclusion encephalitis (Dawson type). *Brain* 71, 365–385 *[305]*.

BRAIN W.R., GREENFIELD J.G. & SUTTON D. (1951) Epiloia. In *British Encyclopaedia of Medical Practice*, 2nd Edition, ed. Lord Horder, vol. 5, pp. 266–276. Butterworth: London *[634]*.

BRAIN W.R. & HENSON R.A. (1958) Neurological syndromes associated with carcinoma. *Lancet* 2, 971–975 *[633, 634, 635]*.

BRAIN W.R. & WILKINSON M. (1965) Subacute cerebellar degeneration in patients with carcinoma. Ch. 3 in *The Remote Effects of Cancer on the Nervous System*, eds. Brain W.R. & Norris F.H. Contemporary Neurology Symposia, vol. 1. Grune & Stratton: New York *[634]*.

BRANDT J., BUTTERS N., RYAN C. & BAYOG R. (1983) Cognitive loss and recovery in long-term alcohol abusers. *Archives of General Psychiatry* 40, 435–442 *[518]*.

BRAUDE W.M., BARNES T.R.E. & GORE S.M. (1983) Clinical characteristics of akathisia: a systematic investigation of acute psychiatric in-patient admissions. *British Journal of Psychiatry* 143, 139–150 *[546, 549]*.

BREITNER J.C.S. & FOLSTEIN M.F. (1984) Familial Alzheimer dementia: a prevalent disorder with specific clinical features. *Psychological Medicine* 14, 63–80 *[373]*.

BRENNER C., FRIEDMAN A.P., MERRITT H.H. & DENNY-BROWN D.E. (1944) Post-traumatic headache. *Journal of Neurosurgery* 1, 379–391 *[149]*.

BRESNIHAN B. (1979) Systemic lupus erythematosus. *British Journal of Hospital Medicine* 22, 16–25 *[362]*.

BRESNIHAN B., HOHMEISTER R., CUTTING J., TRAVERS R.I., WALDBURGER M., BLACK C., JONES T. & HUGHES G.R. (1979) The neuropsychiatric disorder in systemic lupus erythematosus: evidence for both vascular and immune mechanisms. *Annals of the Rheumatic Diseases* 38, 301–306 *[365]*.

BRETT E.M. & LAKE B.D. (1975) Reassessment of rectal approach to neuropathology in childhood. *Archives of Disease in Childhood* 50, 753–762 *[649]*.

BREWER C. (1969) Psychosis due to acute hypothyroidism during the administration of carbimazole. *British Journal of Psychiatry* 115, 1181–1183 *[432]*.

BREWER C. (1972) Cerebral atrophy in young cannabis smokers. *Lancet* 1, 143 *[528]*.

BREWER C. & PERRETT L. (1971) Brain damage due to alcohol consumption: an air-encephalographic, psychometric and electroencephalographic study. *British Journal of Addiction* 66, 170–182 *[519]*.

BRICOLO A. (1967) Insomnia after bilateral sterotactic thalamotomy in man. *Journal of Neurology, Neurosurgery and Psychiatry* 30, 154–158 *[630]*.

BRIEG A., EKBOM K., GREITZ T. & KUGELBERG E. (1967) Hydrocephalus due to elongated basilar artery: a new clinicoradiological syndrome. *Lancet* 1, 874–875 *[641, 643]*.

BRIERLEY H. (1967) Treatment of hysterical spasmodic torticollis by behaviour therapy. *Behaviour Research and Therapy* 5, 139–142 *[575]*.

BRIERLEY J.B. (1961) Clinico-pathological correlations in amnesia. *Gerontologia Clinica* 3, 97–109 *[31]*.

BRIERLEY J.B. (1966) The neuropathology of amnesic states. Ch. 7 in *Amnesia*, eds. Whitty C.W.M. & Zangwill O.L. Butterworths: London *[25]*.

BRIERLEY J.B. (1970) Systemic hypotension—neurological and neuropathological aspects, Ch. 9 in *Modern Trends in Neurology*, vol. 5, ed. Williams D. Butterworths: London *[466, 467]*.

BRIERLEY J.B. (1976) Cerebral hypoxia. Ch. 2 in *Greenfield's Neuropathy*, 3rd Edition, eds. Marks W. & Corsellis J.A.N. Edward Arnold: London *[467]*.

BRIERLEY J.B. (1981) Brain damage due to hypoglycaemia. Ch. 22 in *Hypoglycaemia*, 2nd Edition, eds. Marks V. & Rose F.C. Blackwell Scientific Publications: Oxford *[465]*.

BRIERLEY J.B., CORSELLIS J.A.N., HIERONS R. & NEVIN S. (1960) Subacute encephalitis of later adult life: mainly affecting the limbic areas. *Brain* 83, 357–368 *[26, 306, 308, 636]*.

BRILLIANT P.J. & GYNTHER M.D. (1963) Relationships between performances on three tests for organicity and selected patient variables. *Journal of Consulting Psychology* 27, 474–479 *[98]*.

BRISSAUD E. (1895) *Leçons sur les Maladies Nerveuses*. Masson: Paris *[572]*.

BRITISH MEDICAL JOURNAL (1968a) Leading article: Severe head injuries. *British Medical Journal* 2, 637–638 *[133]*.

BRITISH MEDICAL JOURNAL (1968b) Leading article: Nutritional folate deficiency. *British Medical Journal* 2, 377–378 *[503]*.

BRITISH MEDICAL JOURNAL (1970a) Leading article: Epidemic malaise. *British Medical Journal* 1, 1–2 *[314]*.

BRITISH MEDICAL JOURNAL (1970b) Correspondence concerning Royal Free Disease. *British Medical Journal* 1, 170–171 *[315]*.

BRITISH MEDICAL JOURNAL (1971) Leading article: Influenza and the nervous system. *British Medical Journal* 1, 357–358 *[303, 304]*.

BRITISH MEDICAL JOURNAL (1972) Presymptomatic detection of Huntington's chorea. *British Medical Journal* 3, 540 *[395]*.

BRITISH MEDICAL JOURNAL (1975) Leading article: Non-invasive investigations of the brain. *British Medical Journal* 3, 295–296 *[119]*.

BRITISH MEDICAL JOURNAL (1978) Modified neurosyphilis. *British Medical Journal* 2, 647–648 *[284]*.

BRITISH NATIONAL FORMULARY (1985) *British National Formulary* No. 9, p. 150. British Medical Association and The Pharmaceutical Society of Great Britain *[343]*.

BROCA P. (1861) Nouvelle observation d'aphémie produite par une lésion de la moitié postérieure des deuxième et troisième circonvolutions frontales. *Bulletins de la Société Anatomique de Paris* 6, 398–407 *[22]*.

BROCK M. (1971) Cerebral blood flow and intracranial pressure changes associated with brain hypoxia. Ch. 2 in *Brain Hypoxia*, eds. Brierley J.B. & Meldrum B.S. Clinics in Developmental Medicine, No. 39/40. Heinemann: London *[467]*.

BRODY H. (1955) Organisation of the cerebral cortex. III. A study of aging in the human cerebral cortex. *Journal of Comparative Neurology* 102, 511–556 *[381]*.

BRODY H. (1978) Cell counts in cerebral cortex and brainstem. In *Alzheimer's Disease: Senile Dementia and Related Disorders. Aging*, Vol. 7, eds. Katzman R., Terry R.D. & Bick K.L., pp. 345–351. Raven Press: New York *[382]*.

BROLLEY M. & HOLLENDER M.H. (1955) Psychological problems of patients with myasthenia gravis. *Journal of Nervous and Mental Disease* 122, 178–184 *[607]*.

BROMBERG W. (1934) Marihuana intoxication. *American Journal of Psychiatry* 91, 303–330 *[524, 526]*.

BROOK C.G.D. & EVANS P.R. (1969) Psychosis in systemic lupus erythematosus and the response to cyclophosphamide. *Proceedings of the Royal Society of Medicine* 62, 912 *[366]*.

BROOK P., DEGUN G. & MATHER M. (1975) Reality orientation, a therapy for psychogeriatric patients. A controlled study. *British Journal of Psychiatry* 127, 42–45 *[423]*.

BROOKS D.N. (1976) Wechsler Memory Scale performance and its relationship to brain damage after severe closed head injury. *Journal of Neurology, Neurosurgery and Psychiatry* 39, 593–601 *[159]*.

BROOKS N. (1984a) Cognitive deficits after head injury. Ch. 4 in *Closed Head Injury. Psychological, Social and Family Consequences*, ed. Brooks N. Oxford University Press *[158]*.

BROOKS N (1984b) Head injury and the family. Ch. 7 in *Closed Head Injury. Psychological, Social, and Family Consequences*, ed. Brooks N. Oxford University Press *[185]*.

BROUGHTON R. & GHANEM Q. (1976) The impact of compound narcolepsy on the life of the patient. Ch. 13 in *Narcolepsy, Advances in Sleep Research*, Vol. III, eds. Guilleminault C., Dement W.C. & Passouant P. Spectrum Publications Inc: New York *[625]*.

BROWN G., CHADWICK D., SHAFFER D., RUTTER M. & TRAUB M. (1981) A prospective study of children with head injuries: III Psychiatric sequelae. *Psychological Medicine* 11, 63–78 *[172, 173]*.

BROWN J.R. & SIMONSON J. (1957) A clinical study of 100 aphasic patients: Observations on lateralisation and localization of lesions. *Neurology* 7, 777–783 *[43]*.

BROWN S. & DAVIS T.K. (1922) The mental symptoms of multiple sclerosis. *Archives of Neurology and Psychiatry* 7, 629–634 *[595]*.

BROWN W.A. & MUELLER P.S. (1970) Psychological function in individuals with amyotrophic lateral sclerosis. *Psychosomatic Medicine* 32, 141–152 *[604]*.

BROWNELL B. & HUGHES J.T. (1962) The distribution of plaques in the cerebrum in multiple sclerosis. *Journal of Neurology, Neurosurgery and Psychiatry* 25, 315–320 *[592]*.

BROWNELL B. & OPPENHEIMER D.R. (1965) An ataxic form of subacute presenile polioencephalopathy (Creutzfeldt-Jakob disease). *Journal of Neurology, Neurosurgery and Psychiatry* 28, 350–361 *[403]*.

BROWNELL B., OPPENHEIMER D.R. & HUGHES J.T. (1970) The central nervous system in motor neurone disease. *Journal of Neurology, Neurosurgery and Psychiatry* 33, 338–357 *[604]*.

BROZEK J. & CASTER W.O. (1957) Psychologic effects of thiamine restriction and deprivation in normal young men. *American Journal of Clinical Nutrition* 5, 109–120 *[488]*.

BRUCHER J.M. (1967) Neuropathological problems posed by carbon monoxide poisoning and anoxia. In *Carbon Monoxide Poisoning*, eds. Bour H. & Ledingham I.McA. Progress in Brain Research, vol. 24. Elsevier: Amsterdam *[471]*.

BRUETSCH W.L. (1940) Chronic rheumatic brain disease as a possible factor in the causation of some cases of dementia praecox. *American Journal of Psychiatry* 97, 276–296 *[316, 318]*.

BRUN A. & ENGLUND E. (1981) Regional pattern of degeneration in Alzheimer's disease: neuronal loss and histopathological grading. *Histopathology* 5, 549–564 *[382]*.

BRUYN G.W. (1968a) Complicated migraine. Ch. 6 in *Handbook of Clinical Neurology*, vol. 5, eds. Vinkin P.J. & Bruyn G.W. North-Holland Publishing Co.: Amsterdam *[351]*.

BRUYN G.W. (1968b) Huntington's chorea—historical, clinical and laboratory synopsis. Ch. 13 in *Handbook of Clinical Neurology*, vol. 6, eds. Vinken P.J. & Bruyn G.W. North-Holland Publishing Co.: Amsterdam *[397]*.

BUCHSBAUM M.S., CARPENTER W.T., FEDIO P., GOODWIN F.K., MURPHY D.L. & POST R.M. (1979) Hemispheric differences in evoked potential enhancement by selective attention to hemiretinally presented stimuli in schizophrenic, affective and posttemporal lobectomy patients. In *Hemispheric Asymmetries of Function in Psychopathology*, eds. Gruzelier J. & Flor-Henry P., pp. 317–328. Elsevier/North-Holland Biochemical Press: Amsterdam *[76]*.

BUCHSBAUM M.S., INGVAR D.H., KESSLER R., WATERS R.N., CAPPELLETTI J., VAN KAMMEN D.P., KING A.C., JOHNSON J.L., MANNING R.G., FLYNN R.W., MANN L.S., BUNNEY W.E. &

SOKOLOFF L. (1982) Cerebral glucography with positron tomography. *Archives of General Psychiatry* **39**, 251–259 *[76, 125]*.

BUDINGER T.F. (1981) Nuclear magnetic resonance (NMR) in vivo studies: known thresholds for health effects. *Journal of Computer Assisted Tomography* **5**, 800–811 *[124]*.

BUELL S.J. & COLEMAN P.D. (1979) Dendritic growth in the aged human brain and failure of growth in senile dementia. *Science* **206**, 854–856 *[377, 382, 521]*.

BULL J. (1967) The corpus callosum. *Clinical Radiology* **18**, 2–18 *[654]*.

BULL J. (1969) Massive aneurysms at the base of the brain. *Brain* **92**, 535–570 *[357]*.

BULL J. (1971) Cerebral atrophy in young cannabis smokers. *Lancet* **2**, 1420 *[528]*.

BULL J.W.D. & ZILKHA K.J. (1968) Rationalizing requests for X-ray films in neurology. *British Medical Journal* **2**, 569–570 *[116]*.

BULPITT C.J. & DOLLERY C.T. (1973) Side effects of hypotensive agents evaluated by a self-administered questionnaire. *British Medical Journal* **3**, 485–490 *[343]*.

BUNDEY S., CARTER C.O. & SOOTHILL J.F. (1970) Early recognition of heterozygotes for the gene for dystrophia myotonica. *Journal of Neurology, Neurosurgery and Psychiatry* **33**, 279–293 *[614]*.

BURDEN G. (1969) Attitudes towards epilepsy in the U.K. In *Exploring World Attitudes Towards Epilepsy*, Social Studies in Epilepsy No. 7, International Bureau for Epilepsy, London *[236]*.

BURGER P.C. & VOGEL F.S. (1973) The development of the pathologic changes of Alzheimer's disease and senile dementia in patients with Down's syndrome. *American Journal of Pathology* **73**, 457–476 *[378]*.

BURKE C.W. (1983) Adrenocortical diseases. In *Oxford Textbook of Medicine*, vol. 1, eds. Weatherall D.J., Ledingham J.G.G. & Warrell D.A., pp. 10.58–10.69. Oxford University Press *[436]*.

BURKE R., FAHN S., JANKOVIC J., MARSDEN C.D., LANG A.E., GOLLOMP S. & ILSON J. (1982) Tardive dystonia: late-onset and persistent dystonia caused by antipsychotic drugs. *Neurology* **32**, 1335–1346 *[547]*.

BURKLE F.M. & LIPOWSKI Z.J. (1978) Colloid cyst of the third ventricle presenting as psychiatric disorder. *American Journal of Psychiatry* **135**, 373–374 *[198]*.

BURKLUND C.W. & SMITH A. (1977) Language and the cerebral hemispheres. Observations of verbal and non-verbal responses during 18 months following left ("dominant") hemispherectomy. *Neurology* **27**, 627–633 *[39]*.

BURKS J.S., ALFREY A.C., HUDDLESTONE J., NOVENBERG M.D. & LEWIN E. (1976) A fatal encephalopathy in chronic haemodialysis patients. *Lancet* **1**, 764–768 *[474]*.

BURNS B.D. (1959) In discussion following 'The memory defect in bilateral hippocampal lesions' by B. Milner. *Psychiatric Research Reports* **11**, 53–54 *[468]*.

BURSTEN B. (1961) Psychoses associated with thyrotoxicosis. *Archives of General Psychiatry* **4**, 267–273 *[430, 432]*.

BURTON R.C., McDUFFIE F.C. & MULDER D.W. (1971) Lupus erythematosus: an autoimmune disease of the nervous system. Ch. 12 in *Immunological Disorders of the Nervous System*, Research Publications of the Association for Research in Nervous and Mental Disease, vol. 49. Williams & Wilkins: Baltimore *[363, 364]*.

BURWELL C.S., ROBIN E.D., WHALEY R.D. & BICKELMANN A.G. (1956) Extreme obesity associated with alveolar hypoventilation—a Pickwickian syndrome. *American Journal of Medicine* **21**, 811–818 *[627]*.

BUSCH E. (1940) Psychical symptoms in neurosurgical disease. *Acta Psychiatrica et Neurologica Scandinavica* **15**, 257–290 *[189]*.

BUSSE E.W. (1962) Findings from the Duke Geriatric Research Project: the effects of aging upon the nervous system. In *Medical and Clinical Aspects of Aging*, ed. Blumenthal H.T. pp. 115–123. Columbia University Press: New York *[31]*.

BUTFIELD E. & ZANGWILL O.L. (1946) Re-education in aphasia: a review of 70 cases. *Journal of Neurology, Neurosurgery and Psychiatry* **9**, 75–79 *[333]*.

BUTTERS N. (1984) Alcoholic Korsakoff's syndrome: an update. *Seminars in Neurology* **4**, 229–247 *[497]*.

BUTTERS N. & ALBERT M.S. (1982) Processes underlying failures to recall remote events. In *Human Memory & Amnesia*, ed. Cermak L.S. Lawrence Erlbaum Associates: Hillsdale, New Jersey *[34]*.

BUTTERS N. & CERMAK L.S. (1980) *Alcoholic Korsakoff's Syndrome: An Information—Processing Approach to Amnesia.* Academic Press: New York *[30, 32, 33, 35, 498]*.

BUTTERS N., SAX D., MONTGOMERY K. & TARLOW S. (1978) Comparison of the neuropsychological deficits associated with early and advanced Huntington's disease. *Archives of Neurology* **35**, 585–589 *[397]*.

BYDDER G.M. & STEINER R.E. (1982) NMR imaging of the brain. *Neuroradiology* **23**, 231–240 *[122]*.

BYERS R.K. (1959) Lead poisoning. Review of the literature and report on 45 cases. *Pediatrics* **23**, 585–603 *[538, 539]*.

BYERS R.K. & LORD E.E. (1943) Late effects of lead poisoning on mental development. *American Journal of Diseases of Children* **66**, 471–494 *[539]*.

BYROM F.B. (1954) The pathogenesis of hypertensive encephalopathy and its relation to the malignant phase of hypertension. Experimental evidence from the hypertensive rat. *Lancet* **2**, 201–211 *[343]*.

BYRON M.A. & HUGHES G.R.V. (1983) The connective tissue diseases. In *Oxford Textbook of Medicine*, Vol. 2, eds. Weatherall D.J., Ledingham J.G.G. & Warrell D.A., pp. 16.28–16.40. Oxford University Press *[362, 363]*.

CAINE E.D. (1981) Pseudodementia: current concepts and future directions. *Archives of General Psychiatry* **38**, 1359–1364 *[411]*.

CAINE E.D. & POLINSKY R.J. (1981) Tardive dyskinesia in persons with Gilles de la Tourette's disease. *Archives of Neurology* **38**, 471–472 *[587]*.

CAIRNS H. (1950) Mental disorders with tumours of the pons. *Folia Psychiatrica, Neurologica et Neurochirurgica Neerlandica* **53**, 193–203 *[201]*.

CAIRNS H. & MOSBERG W.H. (1951) Colloid cysts of the third ventricle. *Surgery, Gynaecology and Obstetrics* **92**, 545–570 *[26]*.

CAIRNS H., OLDFIELD R.C., PENNYBACKER J.B. & WHITTERIDGE D. (1941) Akinetic mutism with an epidermoid cyst of the 3rd ventricle. *Brain* **64**, 273–290 *[199]*.

CALA L.A., JONES B., WILEY B. & MASTAGLIA F.L. (1980) A computerised axial tomographic (CAT) study of alcohol induced cerebral atrophy—in conjunction with other correlates. *Acta Psychiatrica Scandinavica* **62**, Suppl. 286, 31–40 *[519]*.

CALA L.A. & MASTAGLIA F.L. (1980) Computerised axial tomography in the detection of brain damage. 1. Alcohol, nutritional deficiency and drugs of addiction. *Medical Journal of Australia* **2**, 193–198 *[497]*.

CALDERON R. (1966) Myotonic dystrophy: a neglected cause of mental retardation. *Journal of Pediatrics* **68**, 423–431 *[615]*.

CALNE D.B. (1970) *Parkinsonism: Physiology, Pharmacology and Treatment.* Edward Arnold: London *[550, 553]*.

CALNE D.B. (1973) The drug treatment of epilepsy. *British Journal of Hospital Medicine* 9, 171–175 *[265]*.

CAMERON D.E. (1963) The process of remembering. *British Journal of Psychiatry* 109, 325–340 *[424]*.

CAMERON D.E. (1967) Magnesium pemoline and human performance. *Science* 157, 958–959 *[424]*.

CAMERON D.E. & SOLYOM L. (1961) Effects of ribonucleic acid on memory. *Geriatrics* 16, 74–81 *[424]*.

CAMERON D.E., SVED S., SOLYOM L., WAINRIB B. & BARIK H. (1963) Effects of ribonucleic acid on memory defect in the aged. *American Journal of Psychiatry* 120, 320–325 *[424]*.

CAMP W.A. & FRIERSON J.G. (1962) Sarcoidosis of the central nervous system. *Archives of Neurology* 7, 432–441 *[652]*.

CAMPBELL A.C.P. & RUSSELL W.R. (1941) Wernicke's encephalopathy: the clinical features and their probable relationship to vitamin B deficiency. *Quarterly Journal of Medicine* 34, 41–64 *[492]*.

CAMPBELL A.M.G., EVANS M., THOMSON J.L.G. & WILLIAMS M.J. (1971) Cerebral atrophy in young cannabis smokers. *Lancet* 2, 1219–1224 *[528]*.

CAMPBELL A.M.G., THOMSON J.L.G., EVANS M. & WILLIAMS M.J. (1972) Cerebral atrophy in young cannabis smokers. *Lancet* 1, 202–203 *[528]*.

CANAVAN M.M., COBB S. & DRINKER C.K. (1934) Chronic manganese poisoning. *Archives of Neurology and Psychiatry* 32, 501–512 *[541]*.

CANDY J.M., OAKLEY A.E., KLINOWSKI J., CARPENTER T.A., PERRY R.H., ATACK J.R., PERRY E.K., BLESSED G., FAIRBAIRN A. & EDWARDSON J.A. (1986) Aluminosilicates and senile plaque formation in Alzheimer's disease. *Lancet* 1, 354–357 *[384]*.

CANTER A.H. (1951) Direct and indirect measures of psychological deficit in multiple sclerosis. *Journal of General Psychology* 44, 3–35 and 27–50 *[592]*.

CAPLAN L.R. (1980) 'Top of the basilar' syndrome. *Neurology* 30, 72–79 *[322, 323]*.

CAPLAN F., CHEDRU F., LHERMITTE F. & MAYMAN C. (1981) Transient global amnesia and migraine. *Neurology* 31, 1167–1170 *[350]*.

CAPLAN L.R. & SCHOENE W.C. (1978) Clinical features of subcortical arteriosclerotic encephalopathy (Binswanger disease). *Neurology* 28, 1206–1215 *[390, 391]*.

CARLEN P.L., WILKINSON D.A., WORTZMAN G., HOLGATE R., CORDINGLEY J., LEE M.A., HUZZAR L., MODDEL G., SINGH R., KIRALY L. & RANKIN J.G. (1981) Cerebral atrophy and functional deficits in alcoholics without clinically apparent liver disease. *Neurology* 31, 377–385 *[497, 519, 520, 521]*.

CARLSSON A., ADOLFSSON R., AQUILONIUS S.-M., GOTTFRIES C.-G., ORELAND L., SVENNERHOLM L. & WINBLAD B. (1980) Biogenic amines in human brain in normal aging, senile dementia, and chronic alcoholism. In *Ergot Compounds and Brain Function: Neuroendocrine and neuropsychiatric aspects*, eds. Goldstein M., Calne D.B., Lieberman A. & Thorner M.O., pp. 295–304. Raven Press: New York *[520]*.

CARNEY M. (1983) Pseudodementia. *British Journal of Hospital Medicine* 29, 312–318 *[413]*.

CARNEY M.W.P. (1967) Serum folate values in 423 psychiatric patients. *British Medical Journal* 4, 512–516 *[504]*.

CARNEY M.W.P., RAVINDRAU A., RINSLER M.G. & WILLIAMS D.G. (1982) Thiamine, riboflavin and pyridoxine deficiency in psychiatric in-patients. *British Journal of Psychiatry* 141, 271–272 *[487]*.

CARNEY M.W.P. & SHEFFIELD B.F. (1970) Associations of subnormal serum folate and vitamin B_{12} values and effects of replacement therapy. *Journal of Nervous and Mental Disease* 150, 404–412 *[501, 504]*.

CARNEY M.W.P., WIENBREN I., JACKSON F. & PURNELL G.V. (1971) Multiple adenomatosis presenting with psychiatric manifestations. *Postgraduate Medical Journal* 47, 242–243 *[460]*.

CARNEY M.W.P., WILLIAMS D.G. & SHEFFIELD B.F. (1979) Thiamine-pyridoxine lack in newly-admitted psychiatric patients. *British Journal of Psychiatry* 135, 249–254 *[487]*.

CAROFF S.N. (1980) The neuroleptic malignant syndrome. *Journal of Clinical Psychiatry* 41, 79–83 *[533, 534]*.

CARPENTER S., KARPATI G., ANDERMANN F., JACOB J.C. & ANDERMANN E. (1977) The ultrastructural characteristics of the abnormal cytosomes in Batten-Kufs' disease. *Brain* 100, 137–156 *[649]*.

CARPENTER W.T. & BUNNEY W.E. JR. (1971) Behavioral effects of cortisol in man. *Seminars in Psychiatry* 3, 421–434 *[535]*.

CARR S.A. (1980) Interhemispheric transfer of stereognostic information in chronic schizophrenics. *British Journal of Psychiatry* 136, 53–58 *[77]*.

CARROLL B.A., LANE B., NORMAN D. & ENZMANN D. (1977) Diagnosis of progressive multifocal leukoencephalopathy by computed tomography. *Radiology* 122, 137–141 *[646]*.

CARROLL B.J. (1976a) Limbic system-adrenal cortex regulation in depression and schizophrenia. *Psychosomatic Medicine* 38, 106–121 *[428]*.

CARROLL B.J. (1976b) Psychoendocrine relationships in affective disorders. Ch. 7. In *Modern Trends in Psychosomatic Medicine*, Vol. 3, ed. Hill O.W. Butterworths: London *[438]*.

CARROLL B.J., FINEBERG M., GREDEN J.F., TARIKA J., ALBALA A.A., HASKETT R.F., JAMES N.M., KRONFOL Z., LOHR N., STEINER M., DE VIGNE J.P. & YOUNG E. (1981) A specific laboratory test for the diagnosis of melancholia: standardisation, validation, and clinical utility. *Archives of General Psychiatry* 38, 15–22 *[428]*.

CARTER A.B. (1970) Hypotensive therapy in stroke survivors. *Lancet* 1, 485–489 *[331]*.

CARTER A.B. (1972) Clinical aspects of cerebral infarction. Ch. 12 in *Handbook of Clinical Neurology*, vol. 11, eds. Vinken P.J. & Bruyn G.W. North-Holland Publishing Co.: Amsterdam *[356]*.

CARTWRIGHT G.E. (1978) Diagnosis of treatable Wilson's disease. *New England Journal of Medicine* 298, 1347–1350 *[567]*.

CASALS J. (1958) Viral encephalitis. In *Viral Encephalitis*, eds. Fields W.S. & Blattner R.J. Thomas: Springfield, Illinois *[291]*.

CASSON I.R., SHAM R., CAMPBELL E.A., TARLAU M. & DI DOMENICO A. (1982) Neurological and CT evaluation of knocked-out boxers. *Journal of Neurology, Neurosurgery and Psychiatry* 45, 170–174 *[175]*.

CASSON I.R., SIEGEL O., SHAM R., CAMPBELL E.A., TARLAU M. & DI DOMENICO A. (1984) Brain damage in modern boxers. *Journal of the American Medical Association* 251, 2663–2667 *[175]*.

CATTERALL R.D. (1977) Neurosyphilis. *British Journal of Hospital Medicine* 17, 585–604 *[286]*.

CAUGHEY J.E. & MYRIANTHOPOULOS N.C. (1963) *Dystrophia Myotonica and Related Disorders*. Thomas: Springfield, Illinois *[614, 616, 617]*.

CAVENESS W.F., MEIROWSKY A.M., RISH B.L., MOHR J.P., KISTLER J.P., DILLON J.D. & WEISS G.H. (1979) The nature of post-traumatic epilepsy. *Journal of Neurosurgery* 50, 545–553 *[213]*.

CAVENESS W.F., MERRITT H.H. & GALLUP G.H. (1969) Trend in public attitudes towards epilepsy over the past twenty years in the United States. In *Exploring World Attitudes Towards Epilepsy*, Social Studies in Epilepsy No. 7. International Bureau for Epilepsy, London *[235]*.

CAVENESS W.F. & WALKER A.E. (1966) Appendix: Head Injury Glossary. In *Head Injury: Conference Proceedings*, eds. Caveness W.F. & Walker A.E. Lippincott: Philadelphia *[141]*.

CAWLEY R.H., POST F. & WHITEHEAD A. (1973) Barbiturate tolerance and psychological functioning in elderly depressed patients. *Psychological Medicine* 3, 39–52 [411].

CELESIA G.G. & BARR A.N. (1970) Psychosis and other psychiatric manifestations of levodopa therapy. *Archives of Neurology* 23, 193–200 [559].

CELESIA G.G. & WANAMAKER W.M. (1972) Psychiatric disturbances in Parkinson's disease. *Diseases of the Nervous System* 33, 577–583 [556, 558, 559].

CENTERWALL B.S. & CRIQUI M.H. (1978) Prevention of the Wernicke-Korsakoff syndrome: a cost-benefit analysis. *New England Journal of Medicine* 299, 285–289 [496].

CERMAK L.S. (1982) The long and short of it in amnesia. Ch. 3 in *Human Memory and Amnesia*, ed. Cermak L.S. Lawrence Erlbaum Associates: Hillsdale, New Jersey [28].

CERMAK L.S. & BUTTERS N. (1972) The role of interference and encoding in the short-term memory deficits of Korsakoff patients. *Neuropsychologia* 10, 89–96 [32].

CHADWICK O., RUTTER M., BROWN G., SHAFFER D. & TRAUB M. (1981) A prospective study of children with head injuries: II Cognitive sequelae. *Psychological Medicine* 11, 49–61 [171].

CHAFETZ M.E. (1966) Psychological disturbances in myasthenia gravis. *Annals of the New York Academy of Sciences* 135, 424–427 [608, 609].

CHAMBERS W.R. (1955) Neurosurgical conditions masquerading as psychiatric diseases. *American Journal of Psychiatry* 112, 387–389 [205, 356].

CHANDLER J.H. (1966) EEG in prediction of Huntington's chorea. An eighteen year follow-up. *Electroencephalography and Clinical Neurophysiology* 21, 79–80 [394].

CHAPEL J.L., BROWN N. & JENKINS R.L. (1964) Tourette's disease: symptomatic relief with haloperidol. *American Journal of Psychiatry* 120, 608–610 [587].

CHAPMAN L.F. & WOLFF H.G. (1959) The cerebral hemispheres and the highest integrative functions of man. *Archives of Neurology* 1, 357–424 [23, 26].

CHARATAN F.B. & BRIERLEY J.B. (1956) Mental disorder associated with primary lung carcinoma. *British Medical Journal* 1, 765–768 [635].

CHARNEY D.S., KALES A., SOLDATOS C.R. & NELSON J.C. (1979) Somnambulistic-like episodes secondary to combined lithium-neuroleptic treatment. *British Journal of Psychiatry* 135, 418–424 [533].

CHAUDHRY M.R. & POND D.A. (1961) Mental deterioration in epileptic children. *Journal of Neurology, Neurosurgery and Psychiatry* 24, 213–219 [230].

CHECKLEY S.A. (1978) Thyrotoxicosis and the course of manic-depressive illness. *British Journal of Psychiatry* 133, 219–223 [430].

CHECKLEY S.A., GLASS I.B., THOMPSON C., CORN T. & ROBINSON P. (1984) The GH response to clonidine in endogenous as compared with reactive depression. *Psychological Medicine* 14, 773–777 [428].

CHECKLEY S.A., SLADE A.P. & SHUR E. (1981) Growth hormone and other responses to clonidine in patients with endogenous depression. *British Journal of Psychiatry* 138, 51–55 [428].

CHRISTIANSEN C., BAASTRUP P.C. & TRANSBØL I. (1976) Lithium, hypercalcaemia, hypermagnesaemia, and hyperparathyroidism. *Lancet* 2, 969 [477].

CHRISTIANSEN P., DEIGAARD J. & LUND M. (1975) Poteus, fertilitet og kønshormonudskillelse hos yugre mandlige epilepsilidende. *Ugeskrift for Laeger* 137, 2402–2405 (English abstract) [239].

CHRISTIE BROWN J. (1975) Late recovery from head injury: case report and review. *Psychological Medicine* 5, 239–248 [159].

CHRISTODORESCU D., COLLINO S., ZELLINGHER R. & TAUTU C. (1970) Psychiatric disturbances in Turner's syndrome. Report of three cases. *Psychiatria Clinica* 3, 114–124 [447].

CHYNOWETH R. & FOLEY J. (1969) Pre-senile dementia responding to steroid therapy. *British Journal of Psychiatry* 115, 703–708 [368, 426].

CIRIGNOTTA F., TODESCO C.V. & LUGARESI E. (1980) Temporal lobe epilepsy with ecstatic seizures (so-called Dostoevsky epilepsy). *Epilepsia* 21, 705–710 [219].

CLARK D.F. (1966) Behaviour therapy of Gilles de la Tourette's syndrome. *British Journal of Psychiatry* 112, 771–778 [586].

CLARK E.C. & BAILEY A.A. (1956) Neurological and psychiatric signs associated with systemic lupus erythematosus. *Journal of the American Medical Association* 160, 455–457 [364].

CLARK E.C. & YOSS R.E. (1956) Nervous system findings associated with systemic lupus erythematosus. *Minnesota Medicine* 39, 517–520 [364].

CLARKE E. & HARRISON C.V. (1956) Bilateral carotid artery obstruction. *Neurology* 6, 705–715 [328].

CLAUDE H., BARUK H. & LAMACHE A. (1927) Obsessions-impulsions consécutives à l'encéphalite épidémique. *Encéphale* 22, 716–720 [295].

CLAVIERA L.E., du BOULAY G.H. & MOSELEY I.F. (1976) Intracranial infections: investigation by computerised axial tomography. *Neuroradiology* 12, 59–71 [300].

CLAYER J.R. & DUMBRILL M.N. (1967) Diabetes mellitus and mental illness. *Medical Journal of Australia* 1, 901–904 [456].

CLECKLEY H.M., SYDENSTRICKER V.P. & GEESLIN L.E. (1939) Nicotinic acid in the treatment of atypical psychotic states associated with malnutrition. *Journal of the American Medical Association* 112(ii), 2107–2110 [490].

CLEGHORN R.A. (1951) Adrenal cortical insufficiency: psychological and neurological observations. *Canadian Medical Association Journal* 65, 449–454 [440].

CLEGHORN R.A. (1965) Hormones and humors. In *Hormonal Steroids. Biochemistry, Pharmacology, and Therapeutics*, Vol. 2, eds. Martini L. & Pecile A. Academic Press: New York [439, 440].

CLEOBURY J.F., SKINNER G.R.B., THOULESS M.E. & WILDY P. (1971) Association between psychopathic disorder and serum antibody to herpes simplex virus (type 1). *British Medical Journal* 1, 438–439 [301].

CLEVELAND S.E. (1959) Personality dynamics in torticollis. *Journal of Nervous and Mental Disease* 129, 150–161 [574].

CLOAKE P.C.P. (1951) Certain vascular diseases of the nervous system. Ch. 14 in *Modern Trends in Neurology*, ed. Feiling A. Butterworths: London [368, 369].

CLOW A., JENNER P. & MARSDEN C.D. (1979a) Changes in dopamine-mediated behaviour during one year's neuroleptic administration. *European Journal of Pharmacology* 57, 365–375 [549].

CLOW A., JENNER P., THEODOROU A. & MARSDEN C.D. (1979b) Striatal dopamine receptors become supersensitive while rats are given trifluoperazine for six months. *Nature* 278, 59–61 [549].

CO B.T., GOODWIN D.W., GADO M., MIKHAEL M. & HILL S.Y. (1976) Absence of cerebral atrophy in chronic cannabis users. *Journal of the American Medical Association* 237, 1229–1230 [528].

COBB S. & ROSE R.M. (1973) Hypertension, peptic ulcer, and diabetes in air traffic controllers. *Journal of the American Medical Association* 224, 489–492 [340].

COBB W.A. (1963) The EEG of specific lesions. Ch. 11 in *Electroencephalography*, eds. Hill D. & Parr G., 2nd Edition. Macdonald: London [202].

COBB W.A. & MORGAN-HUGHES J.A. (1968) Non-fatal subacute sclerosing leucoencephalitis. *Journal of Neurology, Neurosurgery and Psychiatry* 31, 115–123 [306].

COCHRANE R. (1969) Neuroticism and the discovery of high blood pressure. *Journal of Psychosomatic Research* 13, 21–25 *[341]*.

COCKBURN J.J. (1971) Spasmodic torticollis: a psychogenic condition? *Journal of Psychosomatic Research* 15, 471–477 *[573]*.

COHEN D. & EISDORFER C. (1980) Serum immunoglobulins and cognitive status in the elderly: 1. A population study. *British Journal of Psychiatry* 136, 33–39 *[385]*.

COHEN D. & MARKS F.M. (1977) Gilles de la Tourette's syndrome treated by operant conditioning. *British Journal of Psychiatry* 130, 315 *[586]*.

COHEN D.J., DETLOR R.N., YOUNG G. & SHAYWITZ B.A. (1980) Clonidine ameliorates Gilles de la Tourette syndrome. *Archives of General Psychiatry* 37, 1350–1357 *[587]*.

COHEN N.J. & SQUIRE L.R. (1980) Preserved learning and retention of pattern analysing skill in amnesia: dissociation of knowing how and knowing that. *Science* 210, 207–209 *[32]*.

COHEN N.J. & SQUIRE L.R. (1981) Retrograde amnesia and remote memory impairment. *Neuropsychologia* 19, 337–356 *[34]*.

COHEN S. & DITMAN K.S. (1962) Complications associated with lysergic acid diethylamide (LSD-25). *Journal of the American Medical Association* 181, 161–162 *[532]*.

COHEN S. & DITMAN K.S. (1963) Prolonged adverse reactions to lysergic acid diethylamide. *Archives of General Psychiatry* 8, 475–480 *[532]*.

COHEN S.I. (1980) Cushing's syndrome: a psychiatric study of 29 patients. *British Journal of Psychiatry* 136, 120–124 *[437, 438]*.

COHEN W. & COHEN N.H. (1974) Lithium carbonate, haloperidol, and irreversible brain damage. *Journal of the American Medical Association* 230, 1283–1287 *[533, 534]*.

COHN R. (1960) *The Person Symbol in Clinical Medicine*. Thomas: Springfield, Illinois *[91]*.

COID J. (1979) Mania à potu: a critical review of pathological intoxication. *Psychological Medicine* 9, 709–719 *[509]*.

COLBOURN C.J. & LISHMAN W.A. (1979) Lateralisation of function and psychotic illness: a left hemisphere deficit? In *Hemisphere Asymmetries of Function in Psychopathology*, eds. Gruzelier J. & Flor-Henry P. pp. 539–559. Elsevier/North Holland, Amsterdam. *[76]*.

COLE E.S. (1970) Psychiatric aspects of compensable injury. *Medical Journal of Australia* 1, 93–100 *[150]*.

COLE G. (1978) Intracranial space-occupying masses in mental hospital patients: necropsy study. *Journal of Neurology, Neurosurgery and Psychiatry* 41, 730–736 *[356]*.

COLE M., RICHARDSON E.P. & SEGARRA J.N. (1964) Central pontine myelinosis: further evidence relating the lesion to malnutrition. *Neurology* 14, 165–170 *[500]*.

COLLEGE OF GENERAL PRACTITIONERS' REPORT (1960) A survey of the epilepsies in general practice. A report by the research committee of the College of General Practitioners. *British Medical Journal* 2, 416–422 *[212, 227]*.

COLLIGNON R., BRAYER R., RECTEM D., INDEKEU P. & LATERRE E.C. (1979) Analyse sémiologique de l'encéphalopathie bismuthique. Confrontation avec sept cas personnels. *Acta Neurologica Belgica* 79, 73–91 *[542]*.

COLLINS P. (1961) The almoner's role. In *Stroke Rehabilitation*. The Chest and Heart Association, Tavistock Square, London *[334]*.

COLLINS R.T. (1939) Psychiatric syndromes in myasthenia gravis. *British Medical Journal* 1, 975–977 *[608]*.

COLON E.J. (1973) The cerebral cortex in presenile dementia. A quantitative analysis. *Acta Neuropathologica (Berlin)* 23, 281–290 *[382]*.

COMMITTEE OF NATIONAL INSTITUTE OF NEUROLOGICAL DISEASES AND BLINDNESS (1958) A classification and outline of cerebrovascular diseases. *Neurology* 8, 395–434 *[319]*.

CONNELL P.H. (1958) *Amphetamine Psychosis*. Maudsley Monograph No. 5. Chapman & Hall: London *[535]*.

CONNELL P.H. (1968) Central nervous system stimulant and anti-depressant drugs. Ch. 1 in *Side Effects of Drugs*, eds. Meyler L. & Herxheimer A. Exerpta Medica: Amsterdam *[533]*.

CONNELL P.H., CORBETT J.A., MATHEWS A.M. & HORNE D.J. (1967) Drug treatment of adolescent ticquers. A double blind trial of diazepam and haloperidol. *British Journal of Psychiatry* 113, 375–381 *[587]*.

CONNOLLY J.H., ALLEN I.V., HURWITZ L.J. & MILLER J.H.D. (1967) Measles-virus antibody and antigen in subacute sclerosing panencephalitis. *Lancet* 1, 542–544 *[305]*.

CONNOLLY J.F., GRUZELIER J.H. & MANCHANDA R. (1983) Electrocortical and perceptual asymmetries in schizophrenia. In *Laterality and Psychopathology*, eds. Flor-Henry P. & Gruzelier J.J., pp. 363–378. Elsevier: Amsterdam *[76]*.

CONSTANTINIDIS J., RICHARD J. & TISSOT R. (1974) Pick's disease: histological and clinical correlations. *European Neurology* 11, 208–217 *[393]*.

CONSTANTINIDIS J., RICHARD J. & TISSOT R. (1977) Maladie de Pick et métabolism du zinc. *Revue Neurologique* 133, 685–696 *[391]*.

CONSTANTINIDIS J., GARRONE G. & AJURIAGUERRA J.de (1962) L'hérédité des démences de l'âge avancé. *Encéphale* 51, 301–344 *[373]*.

COOK R.H., WARD B.E. & AUSTIN J.H. (1979) Studies in aging of the brain: IV. Familial Alzheimer's disease: relation to transmissible dementia, aneuploidy, and microtubular defects. *Neurology* 29, 1402–1412 *[378]*.

COOPER A.F. & SCHAPIRA K. (1973) Case report: depression, catatonic stupor, and EEG changes in hyperparathyroidism. *Psychological Medicine* 3, 509–515 *[448, 449]*.

COOPER I.S. (1962) Dystonia reversal by operation on basal ganglia. *Archives of Neurology* 7, 132–145 *[571]*.

COOPER I.S. (1964) Effect of thalamic lesions upon torticollis. *New England Journal of Medicine* 270, 967–972 *[576]*.

COOPER I.S. (1970) Neurosurgical treatment of dystonia. *Neurology* 20 (part 2), 133–148 *[571]*.

COOPER I.S. (1973) Effect of chronic stimulation of anterior cerebellum on neurological disease. *Lancet* 1, 206 *[276]*.

COOPER I.S. (1976) 20-year follow up study of the neurosurgical treatment of dystonia musculorum deformans. In *Advances in Neurology: Dystonia, 14*, eds. Eldridge R. & Fahn S., pp. 423–447. Raven Press: New York *[571]*.

COPE R.V. & GREGG E.M. (1983) Neuroleptic malignant syndrome. *British Medical Journal* 286, 1938 *[533]*.

COPELAND J.R.M., KELLEHER M.J., KELLETT J.M., GOURLAY A.J., GURLAND B.J., FLEISS J.L. & SHARPE L. (1976) A semi-structured clinical interview for the assessment of diagnosis and mental state in the elderly: the Geriatric Mental State Schedule. *Psychological Medicine* 6, 439–449 *[107]*.

COPPEN A. & ABOU-SALEH M.T. (1982) Plasma folate and affective morbidity during long-term lithium therapy. *British Journal of Psychiatry* 141, 87–89 *[504]*.

CORBETT J.A. (1971) The nature of tics and Gilles de la Tourette's syndrome. *Journal of Psychosomatic Research* 15, 403–409 *[582, 584, 585]*.

CORBETT J.A., MATHEWS A.M., CONNELL P.H. & SHAPIRO D.A. (1969) Tics and Gilles de la Tourette's syndrome: a follow-up study and critical review. *British Journal of Psychiatry* 115, 1229–1241 *[582, 585]*.

CORDINGLEY G., NAVARRO C., BRUST J.C.M. & HEALTON E. (1981) Sarcoidosis presenting as senile dementia. *Neurology* 31, 1148–1151 *[652, 653]*.

COREN H.Z. & STRAIN J.J. (1965) A case of narcolepsy with psychosis (paranoid state of narcolepsy). *Comprehensive Psychiatry* 6, 191–199 *[625, 626]*.

CORKIN S. (1968) Acquisition of motor skill after bilateral medial temporal lobe excision. *Neuropsychologia* 6, 255–265 *[32]*.

CORKIN S. (1982) Some relationships between global amnesias and the memory impairments in Alzheimer's disease. In *Alzheimer's Disease: A Report of Progress in Research, Aging*, 19, eds. Corkin S., Davis K.L., Growdon J.H., Usdin E. & Wurtman R.J., pp. 149–164. Raven Press: New York *[31]*.

CORKIN S., DAVIS K.L., GROWDON J.H., USDIN E. & WURTMAN R.J. (Eds) (1982) *Alzheimer's Disease: A Report of Progress in Research, Aging*, Vol. 19. Raven Press: New York *[425]*.

CORKIN S., GROWDON J.H., NISSEN M.J., HUFF F.J., FREED D.M. & SAGAR H.J. (1984) Recent advances in the neuropsychological study of Alzheimer's disease. In *Alzheimer's Disease: Advances in Basic Research and Therapies. Proceedings of the Third Meeting of the International Study Group on the treatment of memory disorders associated with ageing*, eds. Wurtman R.J., Corkin S. & Growdon J.H., pp. 75–94. Centre for Brain Sciences and Metabolism Trust *[31]*.

CORSELLIS J.A.N. (1962) *Mental Illness and the Ageing Brain.* Maudsley Monograph No. 9. Oxford University Press *[376, 389]*.

CORSELLIS J.A.N. (1969a) Subacute encephalitis and malignancy. In *Virus Diseases of the Nervous System*, eds. Whitty C.W.M., Hughes J.T. & MacCallum F.O. Blackwell Scientific Publications: Oxford *[308]*.

CORSELLIS J.A.N. (1969b) The pathology of dementia. *British Journal of Hospital Medicine* 2, 695–702 *[375, 385, 386, 388]*.

CORSELLIS J.A.N. (1970) The limbic areas in Alzheimer's disease and in other conditions associated with dementia. In *Alzheimer's Disease and Related Conditions*, CIBA Foundation Symposium, eds. Wolstenholme G.E.W. & O'Connor M. Churchill: London *[31, 380]*.

CORSELLIS J.A.N. (1979) On the transmission of dementia: a personal view of the slow virus problem. *British Journal of Psychiatry* 134, 553–559 *[401]*.

CORSELLIS J.A.N. & BRIERLEY J.B. (1954) An unusual type of presenile dementia (atypical Alzheimer's disease with amyloid vascular change). *Brain* 77, 571–587 *[380]*.

CORSELLIS J.A.N. & BRIERLEY J.B. (1959) Observations on the pathology of insidious dementia following head injury. *Journal of Mental Science* 105, 714–720 *[160]*.

CORSELLIS J.A.N., BRUTON C.J. & FREEMAN-BROWNE D. (1973) The aftermath of boxing. *Psychological Medicine* 3, 270–303 *[176]*.

CORSELLIS J.A.N. & EVANS P.H. (1965) The relation of stenosis of the extracranial cerebral arteries to mental disorder and cerebral degeneration in old age. In *Proceedings of the Fifth International Congress of Neuropathology*. Exerpta Medica: Amsterdam *[328]*.

CORSELLIS J.A.N., GOLDBERG G.J. & NORTON A.R. (1968) 'Limbic encephalitis' and its associations with carcinoma. *Brain* 91, 481–496 *[636, 637, 638]*.

CORSTON R.N. & GODWIN-AUSTEN R.B. (1982) Transient global amnesia in four brothers. *Journal of Neurology, Neurosurgery, and Psychiatry* 45, 375–377 *[361]*.

COSIN L.Z., MORT M., POST F., WESTROPP C. & WILLIAMS M. (1958) Experimental treatment of persistent senile confusion. *International Journal of Social Psychiatry* 4, 24–42 *[423]*.

COSTA L.D. & VAUGHAN H.G. (1962) Performance of patients with lateralised cerebral lesions, 1: Verbal and perceptual tests. *Journal of Nervous and Mental Disease* 134, 162–168 *[97]*.

COTTRELL S.S. & WILSON S.A.K. (1926) The affective symptomatology of disseminated sclerosis: a study of 100 cases. *Journal of Neurology and Psychopathology* 7, 1–30 *[590, 593, 594]*.

COUCH J.R. (1976) Dystonia and tremor in spasmodic torticollis. *Advances in Neurology*, vol. 14, eds. Eldridge R. & Fahn S. Raven Press: New York *[574]*.

COURVILLE C.B. (1955) *The Effects of Alcohol on the Nervous System of Man.* San Lucas Press: Los Angeles *[518]*.

COWIE V. & SEAKINS J.W.T. (1962) Urinary alanine excretor in a Huntington's chorea family. *Journal of Mental Science* 108, 427–431 *[395]*.

CRAMMER J. & GILLIES C. (1981) Psychiatric aspects of diabetes mellitus: diabetes and depression. *British Journal of Psychiatry* 139, 171–172 *[456]*.

CRAPPER D.R., KARLIK S. & DE BONI U. (1978) Aluminium and other metals in senile (Alzheimer) dementia. In *Alzheimer's Disease: Senile Dementia and Related Conditions, Aging*, vol. 7, eds. Katzman R., Terry R.D. & Bick K.L., pp. 471–485. Raven Press: New York *[383]*.

CRAPPER D.R., KRISHNAN S.S. & QUITTKAT S. (1976) Aluminium, neurofibrillary degeneration and Alzheimer's disease. *Brain* 99, 67–80 *[384]*.

CRAPPER-MCLACHLAN D.R. & DE BONI U. (1980) Etiologic factors in senile dementia of the Alzheimer type. In *Aging of the Brain and Dementia, Aging*, vol. 13, eds. Amaducci L. & Davidson A.N., pp. 173–181. Raven Press: New York *[384]*.

CRAVIOTO H., KOREIN J. & SILBERMAN J. (1961) Wernicke's encephalopathy: a clinical and pathological study of 28 autopsied cases. *Archives of Neurology* 4, 510–519 *[493, 496]*.

CRAWSHAW J.A. & MULLEN P.E. (1984) A study of benzhexol abuse. *British Journal of Psychiatry* 145, 300–303 *[559]*.

CREAK M. & GUTTMANN E. (1935) Chorea, tics and compulsive utterances. *Journal of Mental Sciences* 81, 834–839 *[583]*.

CRÉMIEUX A., ALLIEZ J., TOGA M. & PACHE R. (1959) Sclérose en plaques à début par troubles mentaux. Etude anatomo-clinique. *Revue Neurologique* 101, 45–51 *[595]*.

CREUTZFELDT H.G. (1920) Über eine eigenartige herdförmige Erkrankung des Zentralnervensystems. *Zeitschrift für die gesamte Neurologie und Psychiatrie* 57, 1–18 *[400]*.

CRISP A.H. & MOLDOFSKY H. (1965) A psychosomatic study of writer's cramp. *British Journal of Psychiatry* 111, 841–858 *[577]*.

CRITCHLEY M. (1931) The neurology of old age. *Lancet* 1, 1221–1230 *[80]*.

CRITCHLEY M. (1937) Musicogenic epilepsy. *Brain* 60, 13–27 *[211]*.

CRITCHLEY M. (1953) *The Parietal Lobes.* Edward Arnold: London *[60, 89]*.

CRITCHLEY M. (1954) Discussion on volitional movement. *Proceedings of the Royal Society of Medicine* 47, 593–599 *[577]*.

CRITCHLEY M. (1957) Medical aspects of boxing, particularly from a neurological standpoint. *British Medical Journal* 1, 357–362 *[174]*.

CRITCHLEY M. (1962) Periodic hypersomnia and megaphagia in adolescent males. *Brain* 85, 627–656 *[628]*.

CRITCHLEY M. (1964) Psychiatric symptoms and parietal disease: differential diagnosis. *Proceedings of the Royal Society of Medicine* 57, 422–428 *[60, 196]*.

CRITCHLEY M. (1969) Definition of migraine. Ch. 18 in *Background to Migraine*. Third Migraine Symposium, ed. Cochrane A.L. Heinemann: London *[344]*.

CRITCHLEY M., COBB W. & SEARS T.A. (1959) On reading epilepsy. *Epilepsia* 1, 403–417 *[211]*.

CRITCHLEY M. & EARL C.J.C. (1932) Tuberose sclerosis and allied conditions. *Brain* 55, 311–346 *[601]*.

CROCKARD H.A., HANLON K., DUDA E.E. & MULLAN J.F. (1977) Hydrocephalus as a cause of dementia: evaluation by computerised tomography and intracranial pressure monitoring. *Journal of Neurology, Neurosurgery, and Psychiatry* 40, 736–740 *[640]*.

CROCKARD A., MCKEE H., JOSHI K. & ALLEN I. (1980) ICP, CAT scans and psychometric assessment in dementia: a prospective analysis. In *Intracranial Pressure, IV*, eds. Shulman K., Marmarou A., Miller J.D., Becker D.P., Hochwald G.M. & Brock M., pp. 501–504. Springer-Verlag: Berlin *[642]*.

CROFT P.B., HEATHFIELD K.W.G. & SWASH M. (1973) Differential diagnosis of transient amnesia. *British Medical Journal* 4, 593–596 *[360]*.

CROFT P.B. & WILKINSON M. (1965) The incidence of carcinomatous neuromyopathy with special reference to carcinoma of the lung and breast. Ch. 6 in *The Remote Effects of Cancer on the Nervous System*, eds. Brain W.R. & Norris F.H. Contemporary Neurology Symposia, vol. 1. Grune & Stratton: New York *[634]*.

CROSS A.J., CROW T.J., PERRY E.K., PERRY R.H., BLESSED G. & TOMLINSON B.E. (1981) Radical dopamine-beta-hydroxylase activity in Alzheimer's disease. *British Medical Journal* 282, 93–94 *[383]*.

CROW T.J. (1978) Viral causes of psychiatric disease. *Post-graduate Medical Journal* 54, 763–767 *[290, 302]*.

CROW T.J. (1983a) Discussion: schizophrenic deterioration. *British Journal of Psychiatry* 143, 80–81 *[318]*.

CROW T.J. (1983b) Is schizophrenia an infectious disease? *Lancet* 1, 173–175 *[318]*.

CROW T.J. (1984) A re-evaluation of the viral hypothesis: is psychosis the result of retroviral integration at a site close to the cerebral dominance gene? *British Journal of Psychiatry* 145, 243–253 *[318]*.

CROW T.J., JOHNSTONE E.C. & MCCLELLAND H.A. (1976) The coincidence of schizophrenia and parkinsonism: some neurochemical implications. *Psychological Medicine* 6, 227–233 *[559]*.

CROW T.J., JOHNSTONE E.C., OWENS D.G.C., FERRIER I.N., MAC-MILLAN J.F., PARRY R.P. & TYRRELL D.A.J. (1979) Characteristics of patients with schizophrenia or neurological disorder and virus-like agent in cerebrospinal fluid. *Lancet* 1, 842–844 *[318]*.

CROWELL R.M., TEW J.M. & MARK V.H. (1973) Aggressive dementia associated with normal pressure hydrocephalus. *Neurology* 23, 461–464 *[640]*.

CROWN S. (1971) Psychosomatic aspects of parkinsonism. *Journal of Psychosomatic Research* 15, 451–459 *[561]*.

CRUICKSHANK E.K. (1961) Neuropsychiatric disorders in prisoners-of-war. In *Psychiatrie der Gegenwart*, vol. 3, eds. Gruhle H.W., Jung R., Mayer-Gross W. & Müller M., pp. 807–836. Springer: Berlin *[492]*.

CRUZ-COKE R. (1960) Environmental influences and arterial blood-pressure. *Lancet* 2, 885–886 *[340]*.

CULL R., GILLIATT R.W., WILLISON R.G. & QUY R. (1982) Prolonged observation and EEG monitoring of epileptic patients. In *A Textbook of Epilepsy*, eds. Laidlaw J. & Richens A., 2nd Edition, pp. 211–226. Churchill Livingstone: Edinburgh & London *[256]*.

CULVER C.M. & KING F.W. (1974) Neuropsychological assessment of undergraduate marihuana and LSD users. *Archives of General Psychiatry* 31, 707–711 *[528]*.

CUMINGS J.N. (1948) The copper and iron content of brain and liver in the normal and in hepatolenticular degeneration. *Brain* 71, 410–415 *[564]*.

CUMMINGS J.L. (1982) Cortical dementias. Ch. 5 in *Psychiatric Aspects of Neurologic Disease*, vol. 2, eds. Benson D.F. & Blumer D. Grune & Stratton: York *[569]*.

CUMMINGS J.L. & BENSON D.F. (1983) *Dementia: A Clinical Approach*. Butterworths: London *[648]*.

CUMMINGS J.L. & DUCHEN L.W. (1981) Klüver-Bucy syndrome in Pick disease: clinical and pathologic correlations. *Neurology* 31, 1415–1422 *[392, 393]*.

CUMMINGS J.L., GOSENFELD L.F., HOULIHAN J.P. & MCCAFFREY T. (1983) Neuropsychiatric disturbances associated with idiopathic calcification of the basal ganglia. *Biological Psychiatry* 18, 591–601 *[647]*.

CUMMISKY J.M. (1982) Sleep apnea syndromes: a review. *Irish Medical Journal* 75, 228–233 *[627, 628]*.

CUNNINGHAM J.A.K. (1968) Transient global amnesia. *New Zealand Medical Journal* 67, 531–532 *[359]*.

CURRAN F.J. (1938) The symptoms and treatments of barbiturate intoxication and psychosis. *American Journal of Psychiatry* 95, 73–85 *[522]*.

CURRAN F.J. (1944) Current views on neuropsychiatric effects of barbiturates and bromides. *Journal of Nervous and Mental Disease* 100, 142–169 *[522, 524]*.

CURRENT PROBLEMS (1983) Sodium valproate (Epilim) and congenital abnormalities. *Current Problems* No. 9. Committee of Safety of Medicines: HMSO *[266]*.

CURRIE S., HEATHFIELD K.W.G., HENSON R.A. & SCOTT D.F. (1971) Clinical course and prognosis of temporal lobe epilepsy—a survey of 666 patients. *Brain* 92, 173–190 *[243]*.

CURRIER R.D., LITTLE S.C., SUESS J.F. & ANDY O.J. (1971) Sexual seizures. *Archives of Neurology* 25, 260–264 *[240]*.

CUTTING J. (1978a) Study of anosognosia. *Journal of Neurology, Neurosurgery, and Psychiatry* 41, 548–555 *[63]*.

CUTTING J. (1978b) The relationship between Korsakov's syndrome and 'alcoholic dementia'. *British Journal of Psychiatry* 132, 240–251 *[498, 499]*.

CUTTING J. (1979) Memory in functional psychosis. *Journal of Neurology, Neurosurgery and Psychiatry* 42, 1031–1037 *[32]*.

CUTTING J. (1985) Memory. Ch. 12 in *The Psychology of Schizophrenia*. Churchill Livingstone: London & Edinburgh *[32]*.

DALBY M.A. (1971) Antiepileptic and psychotropic effect of carbamazepine (tegretol) in the treatment of psychomotor epilepsy. *Epilepsia* 12, 325–334 *[267]*.

DALSGAARD-NIELSEN T. (1965) Migraine and heredity. *Acta Neurologica Scandinavica* 41, 287–300 *[345, 347, 348]*.

DALY D. (1958) Ictal affect. *American Journal of Psychiatry* 115, 97–108 *[219]*.

DALY D.D. & BARRY M.J. (1957) Musicogenic epilepsy. *Psychosomatic Medicine* 19, 399–408 *[211]*.

DALY D.D. & YOSS R.E. (1957) Electroencephalogram in narcolepsy. *Electroencephalography and Clinical Neurophysiology* 9, 109–120 *[622]*.

DAMAS-MORA J., SKELTON-ROBINSON M. & JENNER F.A. (1982) The Charles Bonnet Syndrome in perspective. *Psychological Medicine* 12, 251–261 *[262]*.

DAMASIO A.R., DAMASIO H. & CHUI H.C. (1980) Neglect following damage to frontal lobe or basal ganglia. *Neuropsychologia* 18, 123–132 *[60]*.

DAMASIO A.R., DAMASIO H., RIZZO M., VARNEY N. & GERSH F. (1982a) Aphasia with nonhemorrhagic lesions in the basal ganglia and internal capsule. *Archives of Neurology* 39, 15–20 *[42]*.

DAMASIO A.R., DAMASIO H. & VAN HOESEN G.W. (1982b) Prosopagnosia: anatomic basis and behavioral mechanisms. *Neurology* 32, 331–341 *[53]*.

DAMASIO A.R., LOBO-ANTUNES J. & MACEDO C. (1971) Psychiatric aspects in parkinsonism treated with L-dopa. *Journal of Neurology, Neurosurgery and Psychiatry* 34, 502–507 *[560]*.

DANA-HAERI J., TRIMBLE M.R. & OXLEY J. (1983) Prolactin and gonadotrophin changes following generalised and partial seizures. *Journal of Neurology, Neurosurgery, and Psychiatry* 46, 331–335 *[257]*.

DANDONA P., JAMES I.M., NEWBURY P.A., WOOLLARD M.I. & BECKETT A.G. (1978) Cerebral blood flow in diabetes mellitus: evidence of abnormal cerebrovascular reactivity. *British Medical Journal* 2, 325–326 *[457]*.

DANIELS L.W. (1934) Narcolepsy. *Medicine* 13, 1–122 *[618, 620, 624, 626]*.

DARLEY F.L. (1970) Language rehabilitation. In *Behavioral Change in Cerebrovascular Disease*, ed. Benton A.L. Harper & Row: New York *[333]*.

DATHAN J.G. (1954) Acrodynia associated with excessive intake of mercury. *British Medical Journal* 1, 247–249 *[541]*.

DAUBE J. (1965) Sensory precipitated seizures: a review. *Journal of Nervous and Mental Disease* 141, 524–539 *[211, 216]*.

DAVID A.S. & GILLHAM R.A. (1986) Neuropsychological study of motor neurone disease. *Psychosomatics* 27, 441–445 *[605]*.

DAVID M. & ASKENASY H. (1937) Les troubles mentaux dans les meningiomes de la petite aile du sphénoïde. *Encéphale* 32(I), 169–208 *[193]*.

DAVID N.J., MACKEY E.A. & SMITH J.L. (1968) Further observations in progressive supranuclear palsy. *Neurology* 18, 349–356 *[567]*.

DAVIES B.M. & MORGANSTERN F.S. (1960) A case of cysticercosis, temporal lobe epilepsy, and transvestism. *Journal of Neurology, Neurosurgery and Psychiatry* 23, 247–249 *[239, 240]*.

DAVIES D.L. (1949a) The intelligence of patients with Friedreich's ataxia. *Journal of Neurology, Neurosurgery and Psychiatry* 12, 34–38 *[602]*.

DAVIES D.L. (1949b) Psychiatric changes associated with Friedreich's ataxia. *Journal of Neurology, Neurosurgery and Psychiatry* 12, 246–250 *[602, 603]*.

DAVIES D.L. (1949c) *Psychiatric Changes in Friedreich's Ataxia*. Thesis for D.M., University of Oxford *[602]*.

DAVIES G., HAMILTON S., HENDRICKSON E., LEVY R. & POST F. (1977) The effect of cyclandelate in depressed and demented patients: a controlled study in psychogeriatric patients. *Age and Ageing* 6, 156–162 *[425]*.

DAVIES J.A., HUGHES J.T. & OPPENHEIMER D.R. (1974) Richardson's disease (progressive multifocal leukoencephalopathy): a study of four cases. *Quarterly Journal of Medicine* 42, 481–501 *[646]*.

DAVIES P. (1977) Cholinergic mechanisms in Alzheimer's disease. *British Journal of Psychiatry* 131, 318–319 *[382]*.

DAVIES R.K., TUCKER G.J., HARROW M. & DETRE T.P. (1971) Confusional episodes and antidepressant medication. *American Journal of psychiatry* 128, 95–99 *[533]*.

DAVIS K.L. & MOHS R.C. (1982) Enhancement of memory processes in Alzheimer's disease with multiple-dose intravenous physostigmine. *American Journal of Psychiatry* 139, 1421–1424 *[426]*.

DAVIS L. & PERRET G. (1947) Cerebral thrombo-angiitis obliterans. *British Journal of Surgery* 34, 307–313 *[369]*.

DAVIS P.J., RAPPEPORT J.R., LUTZ H. & GREGERMAN R.I. (1971) Three thyrotoxic criminals. *Annals of Internal Medicine* 74, 743–745 *[432]*.

DAVIS-JONES A., GREGORY M.C. & WHITTY C.W.M. (1973) Permanent sequelae in the migraine attack. Ch. 3 in *Background to Migraine*, 5th Migraine Symposium, ed. Cumings J.N. Heinemann: London *[345]*.

DAVISON C. & GOODHART S.P. (1938) Dystonia musculorum deformans: a clinicopathologic study. *Archives of Neurology and Psychiatry* 39, 939–972 *[569]*.

DAVISON K. & BAGLEY C.R. (1969) Schizophrenia-like psychoses associated with organic disorders of the central nervous system: a review of the literature. In *Current Problems in Neuropsychiatry*, ed. Herrington R.N. British Journal of Psychiatry Special Publication No. 4. Headley Brothers: Ashford, Kent *[75, 76, 164, 194, 200, 205, 246, 249, 251, 297, 330, 559, 566, 595, 603, 605, 613, 625]*.

DAVISON K. (1983) Schizophrenia-like psychoses associated with organic cerebral disorders: a review. *Psychiatric Developments* 1, 1–34 *[75]*.

DAWSON J.R. (1933) Cellular inclusions in cerebral lesions of lethargic encephalitis. *American Journal of Pathology* 9, 7–15 *[305]*.

DAX M. (1836) Lésions de la moitié gauche de l'encéphale coincidait avec l'oubli des signes de la pensée (Lu à Montpellier en 1836). *Gazette Hebdomadaire de Médecine et de Chirurgie* 33, 259–262 *[22]*.

DAYAN A.D. (1969) Progressive multifocal leukoencephalopathy. In *Virus Diseases of the Nervous System*, eds. Whitty C.W.M., Hughes J.T. & MacCallum F.O. Blackwell Scientific Publications: Oxford *[646]*.

DE BONI U. & CRAPPER D.R. (1978) Paired helical filaments of the Alzheimer type in cultured neurones. *Nature* 271, 566–568 *[384]*.

DE JONG R.N. (1944) Methyl bromide poisoning. *Journal of the American Medical Association* 125(ii), 702–703 *[543]*.

DEKABAN R.S. & HERMAN M.M. (1974) Childhood, juvenile, and adult cerebral lipidoses. *Archives of Pathology* 97, 65–73 *[649]*.

DELANEY P. (1977) Neurologic manifestations in sarcoidosis. *Annals of Internal Medicine* 87, 336–345 *[651, 652]*.

DELAY J., BRION S. & DEROUESNÉ C. (1964) Syndrome de Korsakoff et étiologie tumorale. *Revue Neurologique* 111, 97–133 *[197]*.

DELAY J., DENIKER P. & BARANDE R. (1957) Le suicide des épileptiques. *Encéphale* 46, 401–436 *[254]*.

DE LEON M.J., FERRIS S.H., BLAU I., GEORGE A.E., REISBERG B., KRICHEFF I.I. & GERSHON S. (1979) Correlations between CT changes and behavioural deficits in senile dementia. *Lancet* 2, 859–860 *[120]*.

DELGADO J.M.R. (1969) Offensive-defensive behaviour in free monkeys and chimpanzees induced by radio stimulation of the brain. In *Aggressive Behaviour*. Proceedings of International Symposium on the Biology of Aggressive Behaviour, eds. Garattini S. & Sigg E.B. Exerpta Medica: Amsterdam *[72]*.

DELGADO J.M.R., MARK V., SWEET W., ERVIN F., WEISS G., BACHY-RITA G. & HAGIWARA R. (1968) Intracerebral radio stimulation and recording in completely free patients. *Journal of Nervous and Mental Disease* 147, 329–340 *[73, 233]*.

DELLAPORTAS C.I., WILSON A. & ROSE F.C. (1984) Clobazam as adjunctive treatment in chronic epilepsy. In *Advances in Epileptology: XVth Epilepsy International Symposium*, eds. Porter R.J., Mattson R.H., Ward A.A. & Dam M., pp. 363–367. Raven Press: New York *[268]*.

DELMAS-MARSALET P., VITAL C., JULIEN J., BÉRAUD C., BOURGEOIS M. & BARGUES M. (1967) La maladie de Marchiafava et Bignami. *Journal de Médicine de Bordeaux* 144, 1627–1646 *[500]*.

DEMENT W.C., RECHTSCHAFFEN A.R. & GULEVICH G.D. (1964) A polygraphic study of the narcoleptic sleep attack. *Electroencephalography and Clinical Neurophysiology* 17, 608–609 *[622]*.

DEMENT W.C., RECHTSCHAFFEN A. & GULEVICH G.D. (1966) The nature of the narcoleptic sleep attack. *Neurology* 16, 18–33 *[622]*.

DENCKER S.J. (1958) A follow-up study of 128 closed head injuries in twins using co-twins as controls. *Acta Psychiatrica et Neurologica Scandinavica*, supplement 123, 1–125 *[148, 170]*.

DENCKER S.J. (1960) Closed head injury in twins. *Archives of General Psychiatry* 2, 569–575 *[148, 170]*.

DENCKER S.J. & LÖFVING B. (1958) A psychometric study of identical twins discordant for closed head injury. *Acta Psychiatrica et Neurologica Scandinavica*, supplement 122, 1–50 *[157]*.

DENKO J.D. & KAELBLING R. (1962) The psychiatric aspects of hypoparathyroidism. *Acta Psychiatrica Scandinavica*, supplement 164, 1–70 *[450, 451, 452, 453]*.

DENNERLL R.D. (1964) Cognitive deficits and lateral brain dysfunction in temporal lobe epilepsy. *Epilepsia* 5, 177–191 *[229]*.

DENNERLL R.D. (1970) Problems of rehabilitation and employability in epilepsy. In *Epilepsy: Recent Views on Theory, Diagnosis and Therapy of Epilepsy*, ed. Niedermeyer E. Karger: Basel *[271]*.

DENNY-BROWN D. (1945) Disability arising from closed head injury. *Journal of the American Medical Association* 127, 429–436 *[149]*.

DENNY-BROWN D. (1948) Primary sensory neuropathy with muscular changes associated with carcinoma. *Journal of Neurology, Neurosurgery and Psychiatry* 11, 73–87 *[633]*.

DENNY-BROWN D. (1964) Hepatolenticular degeneration (Wilson's disease): two components. *New England Journal of Medicine* 270, 1149–1156 *[563]*.

DENNY-BROWN D. & PORTER H. (1951) The effect of BAL (2, 3-dimercaptopropanol) on hepatolenticular degeneration (Wilson's disease) *New England Journal of Medicine* 245, 917–925 *[565]*.

DENNY-BROWN D. & RUSSELL W.R. (1941) Experimental cerebral concussion. *Brain* 64, 93–164 *[138]*.

DEPARTMENT OF HEALTH & SOCIAL SECURITY (1985) *Acquired Immune Deficiency Syndrome (AIDS): General Information for Doctors*. DHSS: London *[315, 316]*.

DE RENZI E. (1982) *Disorders of Space Exploration and Cognition*. John Wiley & Sons: Chichester *[55]*.

DE RENZI E. & FAGLIONI P. (1965) The comparative efficiency of intelligence and vigilance tests in detecting hemispheric cerebral damage. *Cortex* 1, 410–433 *[94, 97, 104]*.

DE RENZI E. & FAGLIONI P. (1967) The relationship between visuospatial impairment and constructional apraxia. *Cortex* 3, 327–342 *[54]*.

DE RENZI E., FAGLIONI P. & SCOTTI G. (1971) Judgement of spatial orientation in patients with focal brain damage. *Journal of Neurology, Neurosurgery and Psychiatry* 34, 489–495 *[55]*.

DE RENZI E. & SCOTTI G. (1970) Autotopagnosia: fiction or reality? *Archives of Neurology* 23, 221–227 *[63]*.

DE RENZI E. & VIGNOLO L.A. (1962) The token test: a sensitive test to detect receptive disturbances in aphasics. *Brain* 85, 665–678 *[105]*.

DETRE T., HIMMELHOCH J., SWATZBURG M., ANDERSON C.M., BYCK R. & KUPFER D.J. (1972) Hypersomnia and manic depressive disease. *American Journal of Psychiatry* 128, 1303–1305 *[631]*.

DEUCHAR N. (1984) AIDS in New York City with particular reference to the psycho-social aspects. *British Journal of Psychiatry* 145, 612–619 *[315]*.

DE VEAUGH-GEISS J. (1980) Tardive Tourette syndrome. *Neurology* 30, 562–563 *[584]*.

DEWAN M.J., PANDURANGI A.K., LEE S.H., RAMACHANDRAN T., LEVY B., BOUCHER M., YOZAWITZ A. & MAJOR L.F. (1983) Central brain morphology in chronic schizophrenic patients: a controlled CT study. *Biological Psychiatry* 18, 1133–1140 *[76]*.

DEWHURST K. (1969) The neurosyphilitic psychoses today: a survey of 91 cases. *British Journal of Psychiatry* 115, 31–38 *[281, 282, 285, 287]*.

DEWHURST K. & BEARD A.W. (1970) Sudden religious conversions in temporal lobe epilepsy. *British Journal of Psychiatry* 117, 497–507 *[234]*.

DEWHURST K. & HATRICK J.A. (1972) Differential diagnosis and treatment of lysergic acid diethylamide induced psychosis. *Practitioner* 209 327–332 *[531]*.

DEWHURST K., OLIVER J.E. & McKNIGHT A.L. (1970) Sociopsychiatric consequences of Huntington's disease. *British Journal of Psychiatry* 116, 255–258 *[399]*.

DE WIED D., BOHUS B., GISPEN W.H., URBAN I. & VAN WIMERSMA GREIDANUS Tj.B. (1976) Hormonal influences on motivational, learning and memory processes. In *Hormones, Behavior, and Psychopathology*, ed. Sachar E.J., pp. 1–14. Raven Press: New York *[428]*.

DICKERSON W.W. & HELLMAN C.D. (1952) Electroencephalographic study of patients with tuberose sclerosis. *Neurology* 2, 248–254 *[600]*.

DILLER L. & RIKLAN M. (1956) Psychosocial factors in Parkinson's disease. *Journal of the American Geriatrics Society* 4, 1291–1300 *[562]*.

DILLON H. & LEOPOLD R.L. (1961) Children and the post-concussion syndrome. *Journal of the American Medical Association* 175, 86–92 *[172]*.

DIMOND S.J., SCAMMELL R., PRYCE I.J., HUWS D. & GRAY C. (1980) Some failures of intermanual and cross-latency transfer in chronic schizophrenia. *Journal of Abnormal Psychology* 89, 505–509 *[77]*.

DINNICK O.O. (1964) Deaths associated with anaesthesia: observations on 600 cases. *Anaesthesia* 19, 536–556 *[465]*.

DIREKZE M., BAYLISS S.G. & CUTTING J.C. (1971) Primary tumours of the frontal lobe. *British Journal of Clinical Practice* 25, 207–213 *[192]*.

DITCH M., KELLY F.J. & RESNICK O. (1971) An ergot preparation (hydergine) in the treatment of cerebrovascular disorders in the geriatric patient: double-blind study. *Journal of the American Geriatrics Society* 19, 208–217 *[425]*.

DIVRY P. (1927) Étude histo-chimique des plaques séniles. *Journal de Neurologie et de Psychiatrie* 27, 643–657 *[380]*.

DIXON K.C. (1962) The amnesia of cerebral concussion. *Lancet* 2, 1359–1360 *[138]*.

DOBROKHOTOVA T.A. & FALLER T.O. (1969) Concerning the psychopathological symptomatology in tumours of the posterior brain cavity. *Zhurnal Neuropatologi i Psikhiatrii* 8, 1225–1230 *[200]*.

DODRILL C.B. & TROUPIN A.S. (1977) Psychotropic effects of carbamazepine in epilepsy: a double-blind comparison with phenytoin. *Neurology* 27, 1023–1028 *[267]*.

DOLL E.A. (1947) *Vineland Social Maturity Scale. Manual of Directions*. Educational Test Bureau, Division of American Guidance Service: Minneapolis *[108]*.

DONGIER S. (1959) Statistical study of clinical and electroencephalographic manifestations of 536 psychotic episodes occurring in 516 epileptics between clinical seizures. *Epilepsia* 1, 117–142 *[226, 245, 251]*.

DOOLING E.C., RICHARDSON E.P. & DAVIS K.R. (1980) Computed tomography in Hallervorden-Spatz disease. *Neurology* 30, 1128–1130 *[648]*.

DOOLING E.C., SCHOENE W.C. & RICHARDSON E.P. (1974) Hallervorden-Spatz syndrome. *Archives of Neurology* 30, 70–83 *[648]*.

DORFMAN L.J., MARSHALL W.H. & ENZMANN D.R. (1979) Cerebral infarction and migraine: clinical and radiologic correlations. *Neurology* 29, 317–322 *[345]*.

DORKEN H. (1958) Normal senescent decline and senile dementia: their differentiation by psychological tests. *Medical Services Journal, Canada, Ottawa* 14, 18–23 *[377]*.

DORRELL W. (1973) Myasthenia gravis and schizophrenia. *British Journal of Psychiatry* 123, 249 *[607]*.

DOTT N.M. (1938) Surgical aspects of the hypothalamus. In *The Hypothalamus*, eds. Clark W.E.LeG., Beattie J., Riddoch G. & Dott N.M. Oliver & Boyd: Edinburgh *[26]*.

DOUST B.C. (1958) Anxiety as a manifestation of phaeochromocytoma. *Archives of Internal Medicine* 102, 811–855 *[441]*.

DOWNER J.L. DE C. (1962) Interhemispheric integration in the visual system. Ch. 6 in *Interhemispheric Relations and Cerebral Dominance*, ed. Mountcastle V.B. Johns Hopkins Press: Baltimore *[23, 71]*.

DOYLE F.H., PENNOCK J.M., ORR J.S., GORE J.C., BYDDER G.M.,

STEINER R.E., YOUNG I.R., CLOW H., BAILES D.R., BURL M., GILDERDALE D.J. & WALTERS P.E. (1981) Imaging of the brain by nuclear magnetic resonance. *Lancet* 2, 53–57 *[122]*.

DRACHMAN D.A. & ADAMS R.D. (1962) Herpes simplex and acute inclusion-body encephalitis. *Archives of Neurology* 7, 45–63 *[291, 299, 300]*.

DRACHMAN D.A. & ARBIT J. (1966) Memory and the hippocampal complex. *Archives of Neurology* 15, 52–61 *[28, 88]*.

DRACHMAN D.A. & LEAVITT J. (1974) Human memory and the cholinergic system. *Archives of Neurology* 30, 113–121 *[425]*.

DRAKE F.R. (1949) Narcolepsy. Brief review and report of cases. *American Journal of the Medical Sciences* 218, 101–114 *[621]*.

DRESSER A.C., MEIROWSKY A.M., WEISS G.H., McNEEL M.L., SIMON G.A. & CAVENESS W.F. (1973) Gainful employment following head injury. *Archives of Neurology* 29, 111–116 *[185]*.

DREWE E.A. (1974) The effect of type and area of brain lesion on Wisconsin Card Sorting test performance. *Cortex* 10, 159–170 *[104]*.

DRUG AND THERAPEUTICS BULLETIN (1972) Praxilene (naftidrofuryl), vol. 10, 93–94 and 104 *[425]*.

DRUG AND THERAPEUTICS BULLETIN (1975) Treating depression in patients with hypertension, vol. 13, No. 7, 25–26 *[343]*.

DRUG AND THERAPEUTICS BULLETIN (1981) Management of migraine. *Drug and Therapeutics Bulletin* 19, 69–71 *[354]*.

DUBOIS E.L. (1966) *Lupus Erythematosus: Review of the Current Status of Discoid and Systemic Lupus Erythematosus and Their Variants*, ed. Dubois E.L. McGraw Hill: New York *[362, 363, 364, 365, 366]*.

DUBOWITZ V. (1958) Influenzal encephalitis. *Lancet* 1, 140–141 *[303]*.

DUBOWITZ V. (1965) Intellectual impairment in muscular dystrophy. *Archives of Disease in Childhood* 40, 296–301 *[612]*.

DUCHEN L.W. (1972) Personal communication *[449]*.

DUFFY P., WOLF J., COLLINS G., DE VOE A.G., STREETEN B. & COWEN D. (1974) Possible person-to-person transmission of Creutzfeldt-Jakob disease. *New England Journal of Medicine* 290, 692–693 *[401]*.

DULANEY J.T. & MOSER H.W. (1978) Sulfatide lipidosis: metachromatic leukodystrophy. Ch. 38 in *The Metabolic Basis of Inherited Disease*, 4th Edition, eds. Stanbury J.B., Wyngaarden J.B. & Frederickson D.S. McGraw-Hill: New York *[648]*.

DUMAS-DUPORT C. (1970) *Tumeurs Cerebrales chez les Malades Mentaux*. Thesis for Doctorate of Medicine, Faculté de Médicine de Paris *[203, 205]*.

DUNBAR G.C. & LISHMAN W.A. (1984) Depression, recognition-memory and hedonic tone: a signal detection analysis. *British Journal of Psychiatry* 144, 376–382 *[32]*.

DUNBAR J.M., JAMIESON W.M., LANGLANDS J.H.H. & SMITH G.H. (1958) Encephalitis and influenza. *British Medical Journal* 1, 913–915 *[303]*.

DUNLAP H.F. & MOERSCH F.P. (1935) Psychic manifestations associated with hyperthyroidism. *American Journal of Psychiatry* 91, 1215–1238 *[430]*.

DUVOISIN R.C., ELDRIDGE R., WILLIAMS A., NUTT J. & CALNE D. (1981) Twin study of Parkinson disease. *Neurology* 31, 77–80 *[563]*.

DUVOISIN R.C. & KATZ R. (1968) Reversal of central anticholinergic syndrome in man by physostigmine. *Journal of the American Medical Association* 206, 1963–1965 *[559]*.

DUVOISIN R.C. & VINSON W.M. (1961) Tuberose sclerosis: report of three cases without mental defect. *Journal of the American Medical Association* 175, 869–873 *[601]*.

EADIE M.J. & SUTHERLAND J.M. (1964) Arteriosclerosis in parkinsonism. *Journal of Neurology, Neurosurgery and Psychiatry* 27, 237–240 *[550]*.

EAYRS J.T. (1968) Developmental relationships between brain and thyroid. Ch. 14 in *Endocrinology and Human Behaviour*, ed. Michael R.P. Oxford University Press *[428]*.

EBELS E.J. (1978) How common is Wernicke-Korsakoff syndrome? *Lancet* 2, 781–782 *[492]*.

ECKER A. (1954) Emotional stress before strokes: a preliminary report of 20 cases. *Annals of Internal Medicine* 40, 49–56 *[338]*.

ECKER A.D. & KERNOHAN J.W. (1941) Arsenic as a possible cause of subacute encephalomyelitis. *Archives of Neurology and Psychiatry* 45, 24–43 *[542]*.

VON ECONOMO C. (1929) *Encephalitis Lethargica: Its Sequelae and Treatment*. First published 1929. Translated by Newman K.O., 1931, Oxford University Press *[292, 294, 297]*.

EDWARDS A.E. & HART G.M. (1974) Hyperbaric oxygenation and the cognitive functioning of the aged. *Journal of the American Geriatrics Society* 22, 376–379 *[424]*.

EDWARDS A.L. (1942) The retention of affective experiences—a criticism and restatement of the problem. *Psychological Review* 49, 43–53 *[25]*

EDWARDS G. (1974) Drugs, drugs dependence and the concept of plasticity. *Quarterly Journal of Studies on Alcohol* 35, 176–195 *[508]*.

EDWARDS G. (1982) *The Treatment of Drinking Problems*. Grant McIntyre: London *[516, 517]*.

EDWIN E., HOLTEN K., NORUM K.R., SCHRUMPF A. & SKAUG O.E. (1965) Vitamin B_{12} hypovitaminosis in mental diseases. *Acta Medica Scandinavica* 177, 689–699 *[501, 502]*.

EFRON R. (1957) Conditioned inhibition of uncinate fits. *Brain* 80, 251–262 *[272]*.

EHYAI A. & FENICHEL G.M. (1978) The natural history of acute confusional migraine. *Archives of Neurology* 35, 368–370 *[350]*.

EILENBERG M.D. & WOODS L.W. (1962) Narcolepsy with psychosis: report of two cases. *Proceedings of the Staff Meetings of the Mayo Clinic* 37, 561–566 *[625]*.

EISDORFER C. & COHEN D. (1980) Serum immunoglobulins and cognitive status in the elderly: 2. An immunological-behavioral relationship? *British Journal of Psychiatry* 136, 40–45 *[385]*.

EISDORFER C., COHEN D. & BUCKLEY C.E. (1978) Serum immunoglobulins and cognition in the impaired elderly. In *Alzheimer's Disease, Senile Dementia and Related Disorders*, eds. Katzman R., Terry R.D. & Bick K.L., pp. 401–407. Raven Press: New York *[385]*.

EISENBERG L., ASCHER E. & KANNER L. (1959) A clinical study of Gilles de la Tourette's disease (maladie des tics) in children. *American Journal of Psychiatry* 115, 715–723 *[586]*.

EITINGER L. (1959) The importance of atrophy of the brain in psychiatric disease pictures. *Nordisk Medicin* 61, 301–303 *[122]*.

EKBOM K., GREITZ T. & KUGELBERG E. (1969) Hydrocephalus due to ectasia of the basilar artery. *Journal of the Neurological Sciences* 8, 465–477 *[641, 643]*.

ELDRIDGE R. (1970) The torsion dystonias: literature review and genetic and clinical studies. *Neurology* 20 (part 2), 1–78 *[569, 570, 571, 574]*.

ELITHORN A. (1955) A preliminary report on a perceptual maze test sensitive to brain damage. *Journal of Neurology, Neurosurgery and Psychiatry* 18, 287–292 *[99]*.

ELIZAN T.S., HIRANO A., ABRAMS B.M., NEED R.L., VAN NUIS C. & KURLAND L.T. (1966) Amyotrophic lateral sclerosis and parkinsonism-dementia complex of Guam. Neurological re-evaluation. *Archives of Neurology* 14, 356–368 *[605]*.

ELLINGSON R.J. (1954) The incidence of EEG abnormality among patients with mental disorders of apparently non-organic origin: a critical review. *American Journal of Psychiatry* 111, 263–275 [110].

ELLINGTON E. & MARGOLIS G. (1969) Block of arachnoid villus by subarachnoid haemorrhage. *Journal of Neurosurgery* 30, 651–657 [641].

ELLIOT F.A. (1969) The corpus callosum, cingulate gyrus, septum pellucidum, septal area and fornix. Ch. 24 in *Handbook of Clinical Neurology*, Vol. 2., eds. Vinken P.J. & Bruyn G.W. North-Holland Publishing Co.: Amsterdam [193].

ELLIOTT F., GARDNER-THORPE C., BARWICK D.D. & FOSTER J.B. (1974) Jakob-Creutzfeldt disease—modification of clinical and electroencephalographic activity with methylphenidate and diazepam. *Journal of Neurology, Neurosurgery and Psychiatry* 37, 879–887 [402].

ELSOM K.O., LEWY F.H. & HEUBLEIN G.W. (1940) Clinical studies of experimental human vitamin B complex deficiency. *American Journal of the Medical Sciences* 200, 757–764 [488].

EMERSON T.R., MILNE J.R. & GARDNER A.J. (1981) Cardiogenic dementia—a myth? *Lancet* 2, 743–744 [373].

EMSON P.C. & LINDVALL O. (1979) Distribution of putative neurotransmitters in the neocortex. *Neuroscience* 4, 1–30 [383].

ENGEL G.L. (1972) Discussion following paper by Dr. P.B. Storey. In *Physiology, Emotion and Psychosomatic Illness*, Ciba Foundation Symposium 8 (new series). Associated Scientific Publishers: Amsterdam [339].

ENGEL G.L. & ROMANO J. (1959) Delirium, a syndrome of cerebral insufficiency. *Journal of Chronic Diseases* 9, 260–277 [113].

ENGEL G.L., WEBB J.P. & FERRIS E.B. (1945) Quantitative electro-encephalographic studies of anoxia in humans; comparison with acute alcoholic intoxication and hypoglycaemia. *Journal of Clinical Investigation* 24, 691–697 [113].

ENGLISH A., SAVAGE R.D., BRITTON P.G., WARD M.K. & KERR D.N.S. (1978) Intellectual impairment in chronic renal failure. *British Medical Journal* 1, 888–890 [475].

ENOCH M.D., TRETHOWAN W.H. & BARKER J.C. (1967) *Some Uncommon Psychiatric Syndromes*. John Wright: Bristol [404, 581, 582].

ENZMANN D.R. & LANE B. (1977) Cranial computed tomography findings in anorexia nervosa. *Journal of Computer Assisted Tomography* 1, 410–414 [122].

EPSTEIN A.W. (1961) Relationship of fetishism and transvestism to brain and particularly to temporal lobe dysfunction. *Journal of Nervous and Mental Disease* 133, 247–253 [240].

EPSTEIN M.T., HOCKADAY J.M. & HOCKADAY T.D.R. (1975) Migraine and reproductive hormones throughout the menstrual cycle. *Lancet* 1, 543–548 [346].

ERAUT D. (1974) Idiopathic hypoparathyroidism presenting as dementia. *British Medical Journal* 1, 429–430 [451].

ERICKSON T.C. (1945) Erotomania (nymphomania) as an expression of cortical epileptiform discharge. *Archives of Neurology and Psychiatry* 53, 226–231 [218].

ERVIN F.R., DELGADO J., MARK V.H. & SWEET W.H. (1969) Rage: a paraepileptic phenomenon? *Epilepsia* 10, 417 [237].

ESCOBAR A. & ARUFFO C. (1980) Chronic thinner intoxication: clinico-pathologic report of a human case. *Journal of Neurology, Neurosurgery, and Psychiatry* 43, 986–994 [537].

ESPIR M.L.E. & SPALDING J.M.K. (1956) Three recent cases of encephalitis lethargica. *British Medical Journal* 1, 1141–1144 [297].

ESTES D. & CHRISTIAN C.L. (1971) The natural history of systemic lupus erythematosus by prospective analysis. *Medicine* 50, 85–95 [362, 363].

ETTLINGER G. (1956) Sensory deficits in visual agnosia. *Journal of Neurology, Neurosurgery and Psychiatry* 19, 297–307 [53].

ETTLINGER G. (1960) The description and interpretation of pictures in cases of brain lesion. *Journal of Mental Science* 106, 1337–1346 [56].

ETTLINGER G. (1977) Agenesis of the corpus callosum. Ch. 12 in *Handbook of Clinical Neurology*, Vol. 30, eds. Vinken P.J. & Bruyn G.W. North-Holland Publishing Co.: Amsterdam [654].

ETTLINGER G., BLAKEMORE C.B., MILNER A.D. & WILSON J. (1972) Agenesis of the corpus callosum: a behavioural investigation. *Brain* 95, 327–346 [654].

ETTLINGER G., BLAKEMORE C.B., MILNER A.D. & WILSON J. (1974) Agenesis of the corpus callosum: a further behavioural investigation. *Brain* 97, 225–234 [654].

EVANS J.A., RUBITSKY H.J., BARTELS C.C. & BARTELS E.C. (1951) Re-evaluation of the reliability of pharmacologic and cold pressor studies in hypertension and phaeochromocytoma. *American Journal of Medicine* 11, 448–460 [441].

EVANS J.H. (1966) Transient loss of memory: an organic mental syndrome. *Brain* 89, 539–548 [361].

EVANS N.J.R., BALDWIN J.A. & GATH D. (1974) The incidence of cancer among in-patients with affective disorders. *British Journal of Psychiatry* 124, 518–525 [638].

FABING H.D. (1946) Narcolepsy: II. Theory of pathogenesis of the narcolepsy-cataplexy syndrome. *Archives of Neurology and Psychiatry* 55, 353–363 [621].

FABRYKANT M. (1960) Neuropsychiatric manifestations of somatic disease: a review of nutritional, metabolic and endocrine aspects. *Metabolism* 9, 413–426 [487].

FAHY T.J., IRVING M.H. & MILLAC P. (1967) Severe head injuries: a six-year follow-up. *Lancet* 2, 475–479 [137, 158].

FAIRBURN C.G., WU F.C.W., McCULLOCH D.K., BORSEY D.Q., EWING D.J., CLARKE B.F. & BANCROFT J.H.J. (1982) The clinical features of diabetic impotence: a preliminary study. *British Journal of Psychiatry* 140, 447–452 [455].

FAIRHALL L.T. & NEAL P.A. (1943) *Industrial Manganese Poisoning*, National Institute of Health Bulletin No. 182. United States Government Printing Office: Washington [541].

FAIRWEATHER D.S. (1947) Psychiatric aspects of the post-encephalitic syndrome. *Journal of Mental Science* 93, 201–254 [296, 297].

FALCONER M.A. (1969) The surgical treatment of temporal lobe epilepsy. Ch. 16 in *Current Problems in Neuropsychiatry*, ed. Herrington R.N. British Journal of Psychiatry Special Publication No. 4. Headley Brothers: Ashford, Kent [274, 275].

FALCONER M.A. (1973) Reversibility by temporal lobe resection of the behavioural abnormalities of temporal lobe epilepsy. *New England Journal of Medicine* 289, 451–455 [237, 249, 275].

FALCONER M.A. (1974) Mesial temporal (Ammon's horn) sclerosis as a common cause of epilepsy: aetiology, treatment, and prevention. *Lancet* 2, 767–770 [215].

FALCONER M.A. & DAVIDSON S. (1973) Coarse features in epilepsy as a consequence of anticonvulsant therapy. *Lancet* 2, 1112–1114 [267].

FALCONER M.A. & TAYLOR D.C. (1968) Surgical treatment of drug-resistant epilepsy due to mesial temporal sclerosis. Etiology and significance. *Archives of Neurology* 19, 353–361 [215].

FALCONER M.A. & TAYLOR D.C. (1970) Temporal lobe epilepsy: clinical features, pathology, diagnosis, and treatment. Ch. 14 in *Modern Trends in Psychological Medicine*, vol. 2, ed. Price J.H. Butterworths: London [218, 222, 233, 255, 261, 275].

FALK B. & SILFVERSKIÖLD B.P. (1954) Pneumoencephalographic changes in the chronic post-concussion syndrome and non-traumatic cephalgia. *Acta Psychiatrica et Neurologica Scandinavica* 29, 161–171 [152].

FARRELL M.J. & KAUFMAN M.R. (1943) A compendium on neuropsychiatry in the army. *Army Medical Bulletin* 66, 1–112 *[410]*.

FAUST C. (1955) Zur Symptomatik frischer und alter Stirnhirnverletzungen. *Archiv für Psychiatrie und Nervenkrankheiten* 193, 78–97 *[154]*.

FAUST C. (1960) Die psychischen Störungen nach Hirntraumen: Akute traumatische Psychosen und psychische Spätfolgen nach Hirnverletzungen. In *Psychiatrie Der Gegenwart: Forschung Und Praxis*, vol. 2, eds. Gruhle H.W., Jung R., Mayer-Gross W. & Müller M., pp. 552–645. Springer: Berlin *[154]*.

FEEMSTER R.F. (1957) Equine encephalitis in Massachusetts. *New England Journal of Medicine* 257, 701–704 *[291]*.

FEIDO P. & MIRSKY A.F. (1969) Selective intellectual deficits in children with temporal lobe or centrencephalic epilepsy. *Neuropsychologia* 7, 287–300 *[229, 230]*.

FEINDEL W. & PENFIELD W. (1954) Localization of discharge in temporal lobe automatism. *Archives of Neurology and Psychiatry* 72, 605–630 *[221, 222]*.

FELDMAN M.H. (1971) Physiological observations in a chronic case of 'locked-in' syndrome. *Neurology* 21, 459–478 *[323]*.

FENICHEL O. (1945) *The Psychoanalytic Theory of Neurosis*. Norton & Co.: New York *[583]*.

FENNELLY J.J., FRANK O., BAKER H. & LEEVY C.M. (1964) Peripheral neuropathy of the alcoholic. 1: Aetiological role of aneurine and other B-complex vitamins. *British Medical Journal* 2, 1290–1292 *[499]*.

FENTON G. (1974) The straightforward EEG in psychiatric practice. *Proceedings of the Royal Society of Medicine* 67, 911–919 *[110, 111]*.

FENTON G.W. (1972) Epilepsy and automatism. *British Journal of Hospital Medicine* 7, 57–64 *[221, 222, 242, 262]*.

FENTON G.W. (1978) Epilepsy and psychosis. *Journal of the Irish Medical Association* 71, 315–324 *[223]*.

FENTON G.W. (1981) Personality and behavioural disorders in adults with epilepsy. Ch. 8 in *Epilepsy and Psychiatry*, eds. Reynolds E.H. & Trimble M.R. Churchill Livingstone: London and Edinburgh *[233]*.

FENTON G. (1983) Epilepsy. Ch. 13 in *Handbook of Psychiatry*, Vol. 2, *Mental Disorders and Somatic Illness*, ed. Lader M.H. Cambridge University Press *[256, 265, 266]*.

FENWICK P. (1981a) Precipitation and inhibition of seizures. Ch. 22 in *Epilepsy and Psychiatry*, eds. Reynolds E.H. & Trimble M.R. Churchill Livingstone: London and Edinburgh *[211, 216, 272]*.

FENWICK P. (1981b) EEG studies. Ch. 18 in *Epilepsy and Psychiatry*, eds. Reynolds E.H. & Trimble M.R. Churchill Livingstone: London & Edinburgh *[256]*.

FERENCZI S., ABRAHAM K., SIMMEL E. & JONES E. (1921) *Psychoanalysis and the War Neuroses*. International Psychoanalytical Press: London *[149]*.

FERGUSON S.M. & RAYPORT M. (1965) The adjustment to living without epilepsy. *Journal of Nervous and Mental Diseases* 140, 26–37 *[237]*.

FERNANDO S.J.M. (1967) Gilles de la Tourette's syndrome: a report of four cases and a review of published case reports. *British Journal of Psychiatry* 113, 607–617 *[581, 582, 587]*.

FERNANDO S.J.M. (1976) Six cases of Gilles de la Tourette's syndrome. *British Journal of Psychiatry* 128, 436–441 *[587]*.

FERRARO A. (1934) Histopathological findings in two cases clinically diagnosed dementia praecox. *American Journal of Psychiatry* 90 (part 2), 883–903 *[599]*.

FERRARO A. (1943) Pathological changes in the brain of a case clinically diagnosed dementia praecox. *Journal of Neuropathology and Experimental Neurology* 2, 84–94 *[599]*.

FERRIS S.H., REISBERG B., CROOK T., FRIEDMAN E., SCHNECK M.K., MIR P., SHERMAN K.A., CORWIN J., GERSHON S. & BARTUS R.T. (1982) Pharmacologic treatment of senile dementia: choline, l-dopa, piracetam, and choline plus piracetam. In *Alzheimer's Disease: A Report of Progress in Research, Aging*, Vol. 19, eds. Corkin S., Davis K.L., Growdon J.H. & Wurtman R.J., pp. 475–481. Raven Press: New York *[426]*.

FESSEL W.J. & SOLOMON G.F. (1960) Psychosis and systemic lupus erythematosus: a review of the literature and case reports. *California Medicine* 92, 266–270 *[318, 363]*.

FEUCHTWANGER E. (1923) *Die Funktionen des Stirnhirns: ihre Pathologie und Psychologie*. Springer: Berlin *[154]*.

FEUCHTWANGER E. & MAYER-GROSS W. (1938) Hirnverletzung und Schizophrenie. *Schweizer Archiv für Neurologie und Psychiatrie* 41, 17–99 *[164]*.

FEURLE G.E., VOLK B. & WALDHERR R. (1979) Cerebral Whipple's disease with negative jejunal histology. *New England Journal of Medicine* 300, 907–908 *[649, 650]*.

FIELD J.H. (1976) *Epidemiology of Head Injuries in England and Wales*. HMSO *[137, 146]*.

FIELDS W.S. & BLATTNER R.J. (1958) *Viral Encephalitis* (Fifth Symposium, Houston Neurological Society). Thomas: Springfield, Illinois *[26]*.

FINE B.D. (1969) Psychoanalytical aspects of head pain. In *Research and Clinical Studies in Headache*, vol. 2, ed. Friedman A.P., pp. 169–194. Karger: Basel *[347]*.

FINE E.W., LEWIS D., VILLA-LANDA I. & BLAKEMORE C.B. (1970) The effect of cyclandelate on mental function in patients with arteriosclerotic brain disease. *British Journal of Psychiatry* 117, 157–161 *[425]*.

FINELLI P.F., McENTEE W.J., LESSELL S., MORGAN T.F. & COPETTO J. (1977) Whipple's disease with predominantly neuroophthalmic manifestations. *Annals of Neurology* 1, 247–252 *[649]*.

FINK M., GREEN M. & BENDER M.B. (1952) The face-hand test as a diagnostic sign of organic mental syndrome. *Neurology* 2, 46–58 *[100]*.

FINLAY-JONES R. (1986) Should thiamine be added to beer? *Australian and New Zealand Journal of Psychiatry* 20, 3–6 *[496]*.

FINLEY K.H. (1958) Postencephalitis manifestations of viral encephalitides. In *Viral Encephalitis*, eds. Fields W.S. & Blattner R.J. Thomas: Springfield, Illinois *[291]*.

FISCHER M., KORSKJAER G. & PEDERSEN E. (1965) Psychotic episodes in Zarondan treatment. *Epilepsia* 6, 325–334 *[269]*.

FISCHER-WILLIAMS M., BOSANQUET F.D. & DANIEL P.M. (1955) Carcinomatosis of the meninges. *Brain* 78, 42–58 *[633]*.

FISCHER-WILLIAMS M., NIGL A.J. & SOVINE D.L. (1981) *A Textbook of Biological Feedback*. Human Sciences Press: New York and London *[272, 355, 576, 580]*.

FISH F.J. (1962) *Schizophrenia*. John Wright: Bristol *[407]*.

FISHER C., KAHN E., EDWARDS A. & DAVIS D.M. (1973) A psychophysiological study of nightmares and night terrors. 1: Physiological aspects of the stage 4 night terror. *Journal of Nervous and Mental Disease* 157, 75–98 *[632]*.

FISHER M. (1951) Senile dementia—a new explanation of its causation. *Canadian Medical Association Journal* 65, 1–7 *[328]*.

FISHER M. (1954) Occlusion of the carotid arteries: further experiences. *Archives of Neurology and Psychiatry* 72, 187–204 *[328]*.

FISHER C.M. (1965) Lacunes: small deep cerebral infarcts. *Neurology* 15, 774–784 *[321, 327]*.

FISHER C.M. (1966) Concussion amnesia. *Neurology* 16, 826–830 *[361]*.

FISHER C.M. (1968) Dementia in cerebral vascular disease. In *Transactions of the Sixth Conference on Cerebral Vascular Diseases*, American Neurological Association. Grune & Stratton: New York *[321, 322, 323, 327, 328]*.

FISHER C.M. (1971) Cerebral ischaemia—less familiar types. Ch. 15 in *Clinical Neurosurgery*, vol. 18. Proceedings of the Congress of Neurological Surgeons. Williams & Wilkins: Baltimore *[321, 323]*.

FISHER C.M. & ADAMS R.D. (1958) Transient global amnesia. *Transactions of the American Neurological Association*, pp. 143–146 *[357]*.

FISHER C.M. & ADAMS R.D. (1964) Transient global amnesia. *Acta Neurologica Scandinavica*, supplement 9, 7–83 *[357, 358, 359]*.

FISHER K. & FINDLEY L. (1981) Intellectual changes in optimally treated patients with Parkinson's disease. Ch. 8 in *Research in Progress in Parkinson's Disease*, eds. Rose F.C. & Capildeo R. Pitman Medical: Tunbridge Wells *[560]*.

FISMAN M. (1975) The brain stem in psychosis. *British Journal of Psychiatry* 126, 414–422 *[76]*.

FITZHUGH L.C., FITZHUGH K.B. & REITAN R.M. (1960) Adaptive abilities and intellectual functioning in hospitalised alcoholics. *Quarterly Journal of Studies on Alcohol* 21, 414–423 *[518]*.

FITZHUGH L.C., FITZHUGH K.B. & REITAN R.M. (1965) Adaptive abilities and intellectual functioning of hospitalised alcoholics: further considerations. *Quarterly Journal of Studies on Alcohol* 26, 402–411 *[518]*.

FLATAU E. (1912) Die Migräne. In *Monographien aus dem Gesamtgebiet der Neurologie und Psychiatrie*, eds. Alzheimer A. & Levandowsky L. Berlin. Quoted by Klee A. (1968), *A Clinical Study of Migraine with Particular Reference to the Most Severe Cases*. Munksgaard: Copenhagen *[352]*.

FLEWETT T.H. & HOULT J.G. (1958) Influenzal encephalopathy and postinfluenzal encephalitis. *Lancet* 2, 11–15 *[303]*.

FLINK E.B. (1956) Magnesium deficiency syndrome in man. *Journal of the American Medical Association* 160, 1406–1409 *[478]*.

FLINK E.B., STUTZMAN F.L., ANDERSON A.R., KONIG T. & FRASER F. (1954) Magnesium deficiency after prolonged parenteral fluid administration and after chronic alcoholism complicated by delirium tremens. *Journal of Laboratory and Clinical Medicine* 43, 169–183 *[516]*.

FLOR-HENRY P. (1969) Psychosis and temporal lobe epilepsy: a controlled investigation. *Epilepsia* 10, 363–395 *[76, 246, 249, 253]*.

FLOR-HENRY P. (1983) *Cerebral Basis of Psychopathology*. John Wright: Bristol *[76]*.

FLOR-HENRY P., FROMM-AUCH D. & SCHOPFLOCHER D. (1983) Neuropsychological dimensions in psychopathology. In *Laterality and Psychopathology*, eds. Flor-Henry P. & Gruzelier J. pp. 59–82. Elsevier: Amsterdam *[76]*.

FLOR-HENRY P. & GRUZELIER J. (eds) (1983) *Laterality and Psychopathology* Elsevier: Amsterdam *[76]*.

FLOR-HENRY P. & YEUDALL L.T. (1979) Neuropsychological investigation of schizophrenia and manic-depressive psychoses. In *Hemisphere Asymmetries of Function in Psychopathology*, eds. Gruzelier J. & Flor-Henry P., pp. 341–362. Elsevier/North-Holland Biomedical Press: Amsterdam *[76]*.

FLOURENS J.P.M. (1824) *Recherches Experimentales sur les Propriétés et les Fonctions du Système Nerveux, dans les Animaux Vertébrés*. Crevot: Paris *[21]*.

FOERSTER O. (1928) *Verhandlungen der Deutschen Orthopädischen Gesellschaft* 23, 144. Quoted by Paterson M.T., *Lancet* 1945, 2, 556–559 *[572]*.

FOERSTER O. (1933) Mobile spasms of neck muscles and its pathological basis. *Journal of Comparative Neurology* 58, 725–735 *[574, 575]*.

FOLKS D.G. & PETRIE W.M. (1982) Thyrotoxicosis presenting as depression. *British Journal of Psychiatry* 140, 432 *[431]*.

FOLSTEIN M.F., FOLSTEIN S.E. & McHUGH P.R. (1975) 'Mini-mental state'. A practical method for grading the cognitive state of patients for the clinician. *Journal of Psychiatric Research* 12, 189–198 *[106]*.

FOLSTEIN M.F., MAIBERGER R. & McHUGH P.R. (1977) Mood disorder as a specific complication of stroke. *Journal of Neurology, Neurosurgery, and Psychiatry* 40, 1018–1020 *[329]*.

FOLSTEIN S.E., ABBOTT M.H., CHASE G.A., JENSEN B.A. & FOLSTEIN M.F. (1983) The association of affective disorder with Huntington's disease in a case series and in families. *Psychological Medicine* 13, 537–542 *[397]*.

FOLTZ E.L., KNOPP L.M. & WARD A.A. (1959) Experimental spasmodic torticollis. *Journal of Neurosurgery* 16, 55–67 *[575]*.

FONCIN J.F., GACHES J., CATHALA F., EL SHERIF E. & LE BEAU J. (1980) Transmission iatrogène interhumaine possible de maladie de Creutzfeldt-Jakob avec atteinte des grains du cervelet. *Revue Neurologique* 136, 280 *[401]*.

FORD C.V., BRAY G.A. & SWERDLOFF R.S. (1976) A psychiatric study of patients referred with a diagnosis of hypoglycemia. *American Journal of Psychiatry* 133, 290–294 *[462]*.

FORD R.G. & SIEKERT R.G. (1965) Central nervous system manifestations of periarteritis nodosa. *Neurology* 15, 114–122 *[367]*.

FORNAZZARI L., WILKINSON D.A., KAPUR B.M. & CARLEN P.L. (1983) Cerebellar, cortical and functional impairment in toluene abusers. *Acta Neurologica Scandinavica* 63, 319–329 *[537]*.

FORSSMAN H. (1970) The mental implications of sex chromosome aberrations. The Blake Marsh Lecture for 1970. *British Journal of Psychiatry* 117, 353–363 *[446, 447]*.

FORSTER E. (1919) Die psychischen Storungen der Hirnverletzen. *Monatsschrift für Psychiatrie und Neurologie* 46, 61. Quoted by Tow M.P. (1955) *Personality Changes Following Frontal Leucotomy*. Oxford University Press: London *[154]*.

FORSTER F.M. (1969) Clinical therapeutic conditioning in epilepsy. *Wisconsin Medical Journal* 68, 289–291 *[272]*.

FORSTER F.M., KLOVE H., PETERSON W.G. & BENGZON A.R.A. (1965) Modification of musicogenic epilepsy by extinction technique. *Transactions of the American Neurological Association* 90, 179–182 *[272]*.

FORSTER F.M. & LISKE E. (1963) Role of environmental clues in temporal lobe epilepsy. *Neurology* 13, 301–305 *[222]*.

FOURMAN P., DAVIS R.H., JONES K.H., MORGAN D.B. & SMITH J.W.G. (1963) Parathyroid insufficiency after thyroidectomy: review of 46 patients with a study of the effects of hypocalcaemia on the electro-encephalogram. *British Journal of Surgery* 50, 608–619 *[452]*.

FOURMAN P., RAWNSLEY K., DAVIS R.H., JONES K.H. & MORGAN D.B. (1967) Effect of calcium on mental symptoms in partial parathyroid insufficiency. *Lancet* 2, 914–915 *[452]*.

FOWLER R.C., KRONFOL Z.A. & PERRY P.J. (1977) Water intoxication, psychosis, and inappropriate secretion of antidiuretic hormone. *Archives of General Psychiatry* 34, 1097–1099 *[448]*.

FOX J.H., TOPEL J.L. & HUCKMAN M.S. (1975) Use of computerized tomography in senile dementia. *Journal of Neurology, Neurosurgery and Psychiatry* 38, 948–953 *[119]*.

FOX R.H., WILKINS D.C., BELL J.A., BRADLEY R.D., BROWSE N.L., CRANSTON W.I., FOLEY T.H., GILBY E.D., HEBDEN A., JENKINS B.S. & RAWLINS M.D. (1973) Spontaneous periodic hypothermia: diencephalic epilepsy. *British Medical Journal* 2, 693–695 *[211]*.

FRACKOWIAK R.S.J., LENZI G.L., JONES T. & HEATHER J.D. (1980) Quantitative measurement of regional cerebral blood flow and oxygen metabolism in man using ^{15}O and positron emission tomography: theory, procedure and normal values. *Journal of Computer Assisted Tomography* 4, 727–736 *[122, 376]*.

FRACKOWIAK R.S.J., POZZILLI C., LEGG N.J., DU BOULAY G.H., MARSHALL J., LENZI G.L. & JONES T. (1981) Regional cerebral oxygen supply and utilisation in dementia. A clinical and physiological study with oxygen-15 and positron tomography. *Brain* 104, 753–778 *[124, 390]*.

FRANCIS A.F. (1979) Familial basal ganglia calcification and schizophreniform psychosis. *British Journal of Psychiatry* 135, 360–362 *[647]*.

FRAS I., LITIN E.M. & PEARSON J.S. (1967) Comparison of psychiatric symptoms in carcinoma of the pancreas with those in some other intra-abdominal neoplasms. *American Journal of Psychiatry* 123, 1553–1562 *[638]*.

FRASER H.F., SHAVER M.R., MAXWELL E.S. & ISBELL H. (1953) Death due to withdrawal of barbiturates. *Annals of Internal Medicine* 38, 1319–1325 *[524]*.

FRASER H.F., WIKLER A., ESSIG C.F. & ISBELL H. (1958) Degree of physical dependence induced by secobarbital or pentobarbital. *Journal of the American Medical Association* 166(i), 126–129 *[522]*.

FREDERICKS E.J. & LAZOR M.Z. (1963) Recurrent hypoglycaemia associated with acute alcoholism. *Annals of Internal Medicine* 59, 90–94 *[463]*.

FREDERIKS J.A.M. (1969) Disorders of the body schema. Ch. 11 in *Handbook of Clinical Neurology*, vol. 4, eds. Vinken P.J. & Bruyn G.W. North-Holland Publishing Co.: Amsterdam *[52, 58, 59, 61, 65]*.

FREEDMAN D.X. (1968) On the use and abuse of LSD. *Archives of General Psychiatry* 18, 330–347 *[529, 530]*.

FREEMAN W. (1944) Frontiers of multiple sclerosis: 1, Pneumoencephalography, electroencephalography, morbid anatomy and pathogenesis. *Medical Annals of the District of Columbia* 13, 1–10 *[592]*.

FREEMON F.R. (1976) Evaluation of patients with progressive intellectual deterioration. *Archives of Neurology* 33, 658–659 *[414, 415]*.

FREEMON F.R. & NEVIS A.H. (1969) Temporal lobe sexual seizures. *Neurology* 19, 87–90 *[240]*.

FREUD S. (1891) *On Aphasia: A Critical Study*. Translated by Stengel E., 1953 (p. 78). Imago Publishing Co.: London *[52]*.

FREUND G. (1973) Chronic central nervous system toxicity of alcohol. *Annual Review of Pharmacology* 13, 217–227 *[497]*.

FRIEDE R.L. (1961) Experimental concussion acceleration: pathology and mechanics. *Archives of Neurology* 4, 449–462 *[138]*.

FRIEDE R.L. (1965) Enzyme histochemical studies of senile plaques. *Journal of Neuropathology and Experimental Neurology* 24, 477–491 *[381]*.

FRIEDMAN A.P. (1969) The so-called post traumatic headache. Ch. 5 in *The Late Effects of Head Injury*, eds. Walker A.E., Caveness W.F. & Critchley M. Thomas: Springfield, Illinois *[169, 184]*.

FRIEDMAN A.P., BRAZIL P. & VON STORCH T.J.C. (1955) Ergotamine tolerance in patients with migraine. *Journal of the American Medical Association* 157, 881–884 *[354]*.

FRIEDMAN A.P., VON STORCH T.J.C. & MERRITT H.M. (1954) Migraine and tension headaches. A clinical study of two thousand cases. *Neurology* 4, 773–788 *[353]*.

FRIEDMAN E.D. (1932) Head injuries: effects and their appraisal. III, Encephalographic observations. *Archives of Neurology and Psychiatry* 27, 791–810 *[152]*.

FRIEDMAN E., SHERMAN K.A., FERRIS S.H., REISBERG B., BARTUS R.T. & SCHNECK M.K. (1981) Clinical response to choline plus piracetam in senile dementia: relation to red-cell choline levels. *New England Journal of Medicine* 304, 1490–1491 *[426]*.

FRIEL P.B. (1973) Familial incidence of Gilles de la Tourette's disease, with observations on aetiology and treatment. *British Journal of Psychiatry* 122, 655–658 *[581]*.

FRITSCH G. & HITZIG E. (1870) Über dei elektrische Erregbarkeit des Grosshirns. *Archiv für Anatomie, Physiologie und wissenschaftliche Medicin*, pp. 300–332 *[22]*.

FRÖDERSTRÖM H. (1912) La dormeuse d'Oknö: 32 ans de stupeur: guérison complète. *Nouvelle Iconographie de la Salpêtrière* 25, 267–279 *[630]*.

FROMM-REICHMANN F. (1937) Contribution to the psychogenesis of migraine. *Psychoanalytic Review* 24, 26–33 *[347, 355]*.

FROSCH W.A., ROBBINS E.S. & STERN M. (1965) Untoward reactions to lysergic acid diethylamide (LSD) resulting in hospitalisation. *New England Journal of Medicine* 273, 1235–1239 *[530, 531]*.

FRÖSHAUG H. & YTREHUS A. (1956) A study of general paresis with special reference to the reasons for the admission of these patients to hospital. *Acta Psychiatrica et Neurologica Scandinavica* 31, 35–60 *[282, 283, 285]*.

FRY A.H. (1972) *Herpes Simplex Virus Titres and Immunoglobulin Levels in Subjects Showing Antisocial Behaviour Disorder*. Dissertation for M.Phil (Psychiatry), University of London *[301]*.

FULLER G.B. (1967) *Revised Minnesota Percepto-Diagnostic Test*. The Psychological Corporation: New York *[98]*.

FULLER G.B. & LAIRD J.T. (1963) The Minnesota Percepto-Diagnostic Test. *Journal of Clinical Psychology* 19, 3–34 *[98]*.

FULTON J.F. & BAILEY P. (1929) Tumours in the region of the third ventricle: their diagnosis and relation to pathological sleep. *Journal of Nervous and Mental Disease* 29, 1–25, 145–164 and 261–277 *[198]*.

GADE A. (1982) Amnesia after operations on aneurysms of the anterior communicating artery. *Surgical Neurology* 18, 46–49 *[337]*.

GADO M., HUGHES C.P., DANZIGER W., CHI D., JOST G. & BERG L. (1982) Volumetric measurements of the cerebrospinal fluid spaces in demented subjects and controls. *Radiology* 144, 535–538 *[120]*.

GAJDUSEK D.C. (1977) Unconventional viruses and the origin and disappearance of Kuru. *Science* 197, 943–960 *[400]*.

GAJDUSEK D.C., GIBBS C.J. & ALPERS M. (1966) Experimental transmission of a kuru-like syndrome to chimpanzees. *Nature* 209, 794–796 *[645]*.

GAJDUSEK D.C., GIBBS C.J. & ALPERS M. (1967) Transmission and passage of experimental 'kuru' to chimpanzees. *Science* 155, 212–214 *[645]*.

GAJDUSEK D.C., GIBBS C.J., ASHER D.M., BROWN P., DIWAN A., HOFFMAN P., NEMO G., ROHWER R. & WHITE L. (1977) Precautions in medical care of, and in handling materials from, patients with transmissible virus dementia (Creutzfeldt-Jakob disease). *New England Journal of Medicine* 297, 1253–1258 *[401, 646]*.

GAJDUSEK D.C. & ZIGAS V. (1957) Degenerative disease of the central nervous system in New Guinea. The endemic occurrence of 'kuru' in the native population. *New England Journal of Medicine* 257, 974–978 *[645]*.

GALABURDA A.M., LE MAY M., KEMPER T.L. & GESCHWIND N. (1978) Right-left asymmetries in the brain. *Science* 199, 852–856 *[38]*.

GALE E.A.M. & TATTERSALL R.B. (1979) Unrecognised nocturnal hypoglycaemia in insulin-treated diabetics. *Lancet* 1, 1049–1052 *[455]*.

GALLINECK A. & KALINOWSKY L.B. (1958) Psychiatric aspects of multiple sclerosis. *Diseases of the Nervous System* 19, 77–80 *[593, 595]*.

GALLINEK A. (1954) Syndrome of episodes of hypersomnia, bulimia and abnormal mental states. *Journal of the American Medical Association* 154, 1081–1083 *[628]*.

GALLINEK A. (1962) The Kleine-Levin syndrome: hypersomnia, bulimia, and abnormal mental states. *World Neurology* 3, 235–243 *[629]*.

GALVEZ S. & CARTIER L. (1984) Computed tomography findings in 15 cases of Creutzfeldt-Jakob disease with histological verification. *Journal of Neurology, Neurosurgery, and Psychiatry* 47, 1244–1246 *[402]*.

GALVEZ S., MASTERS C. & GAJDUSEK C. (1980) Descriptive epidemiology of Creutzfeldt-Jakob disease in Chile. *Archives of Neurology* 37, 11–14 *[401]*.

GANSER S.J.M. (1898) Ueber einen eigenartigen hysterischen Daemmerzustand. *Archiv für Psychiatrie und Nervenkrankheiten* 30, 633–640. Translated by Schorer C.E. in *British Journal of Criminology* (1965) 5, 120–126 *[404]*.

GANZ V.H., GURLAND B.J., DEMING W.E. & FISHER B. (1972) The study of the psychiatric symptoms of systemic lupus erythematosus: a biometric study. *Psychosomatic Medicine* 34, 207–220 *[364]*.

GARDNER A.J. (1967) Withdrawal fits in barbiturate addicts. *Lancet* 2, 337–338 *[524]*.

GARRON D.C. & VANDER STOEP L.R. (1969) Personality and intelligence in Turner's syndrome. A critical review. *Archives of General Psychiatry* 21, 339–346 *[447]*.

GASCON G. & BARLOW C. (1970) Juvenile migraine, presenting as an acute confusional state. *Pediatrics* 45, 628–635 *[350]*.

GASH D.M. & THOMAS G.J. (1983) What is the importance of vasopressin in memory processes? *Trends in Neurosciences* 6, 197–198 *[499]*.

GASTAUT H. (1970) Clinical and electroencephalographical classification of epileptic seizures. *Epilepsia* 11, 102–113 *[207]*.

GASTAUT H. (1976) Conclusions: computerised transverse axial tomography in epilepsy. *Epilepsia* 17, 337–338 *[256]*.

GASTAUT H. & COLLOMB H. (1954) Étude du comportement sexuel chez les epileptiques psychomoteurs. *Annales Medicopsychologiques* 112(ii), 657–696 *[238]*.

GASTAUT H., COURJON J., POIRÉ R. & WEBER M. (1971) Treatment of status epilepticus with a new benzodiazepine more active than diazepam. *Epilepsia* 12, 197–214 *[270]*.

GASTAUT H. & FISCHER-WILLIAMS M. (1957) Electroencephalographic study of syncope: its differentiation from epilepsy. *Lancet* 2, 1018–1025 *[258]*.

GASTAUT H. & GASTAUT J.L. (1976) Computerised transverse axial tomography in epilepsy. *Epilepsia* 17, 325–336 *[256]*.

GATES E.M., KERNOHAN J.W. & CRAIG W.M. (1950) Metastatic brain abscess. *Medicine* 29, 71–98 *[312]*.

GATEWOOD J.W., ORGAN C.H. & MEAD B.T. (1975) Mental changes associated with hyperparathyroidism. *American Journal of Psychiatry* 132, 129–132 *[448]*.

GATH A., SMITH M.A. & BAUM J.D. (1980) Emotional, behavioural, and educational disorders in diabetic children. *Archives of Disease in Childhood* 55, 371–375 *[455]*.

GAUTIER-SMITH P.C. (1965) Neurological complications of glandular fever (infectious mononucleosis). *Brain* 88, 323–334 *[302]*.

GAWLER J., BULL J.W.D., DU BOULAY G.H. & MARSHALL J. (1975) Computerized axial tomography: the normal EMI scan. *Journal of Neurology, Neurosurgery and Psychiatry* 38, 935–947 *[119]*.

GAWLER J., DU BOULAY G.H., BULL J.W.D. & MARSHALL J. (1974) Computer-assisted tomography (EMI scanner): its place in investigation of suspected cerebral tumours. *Lancet* 2, 419–423 *[119]*.

GAWLER J., DU BOULAY G.H., BULL J.W.D. & MARSHALL J. (1976) Computerized tomography (the EMI scanner): a comparison with pneumoencephalography and ventriculography. *Journal of Neurology, Neurosurgery and Psychiatry* 39, 203–211 *[175]*.

GAZZANIGA M.S., BOGEN J.E. & SPERRY R.W. (1965) Observations on visual perception after disconnection of the cerebral hemispheres in man. *Brain* 88, 221–236 *[276]*.

GAZZANIGA M.S. & SPERRY R.W. (1967) Language after section of the cerebral commissures. *Brain* 90, 131–148 *[38]*.

GEDYE J.L. (1968) Automated instructional techniques in the rehabilitation of patients with head injury. *Proceedings of The Royal Society of Medicine* 61, 858–860 *[183]*.

GEDYE J.L., EXTON-SMITH A.N. & WEDGWOOD J. (1972) A method for measuring mental performance in the elderly and its use in a pilot clinical trial of meclofenoxate in organic dementia (preliminary communication). *Age and Ageing* 1, 74–80 *[425]*.

GELARDI J.A.M. & BROWN J.W. (1967) Hereditary cataplexy. *Journal of Neurology, Neurosurgery and Psychiatry* 30, 455–457 *[619]*.

GELENBERG A.J. (1976) The catatonic syndrome. *Lancet* 1, 1339–1341 *[299]*.

GELENBERG A.J. & MANDEL M.R. (1977) Catatonic reactions to high potency neuroleptic drugs. *Archives of General Psychiatry* 34, 947–950 *[546]*.

GELINEAU (1880) De la narcolepsie. *Gazette des Hôpitaux* 53, 626–628 and 635–637 *[617]*.

GELLERSTEDT N. (1933) Zur Kenntnis der Hirnveränderungen bei der normaler Altersinvolution. *Upsala läkareförenings förhandlinger* 38, 193–404, quoted by Brierley (1966), The neuropathology of amnesic states, Ch. 7 in *Amnesia*, eds. Whitty C.W.M. & Zangwill O.L. Butterworths: London *[31]*.

GEOCARIS K. (1957) Psychotic episodes heralding the diagnosis of multiple sclerosis. *Bulletin of the Menninger Clinic* 21, 107–116 *[595]*.

GERIN J. (1969) Symptomatic treatment of cerebrovascular insufficiency with Hydergine. *Current Therapeutic Research* 11, 539–546 *[425]*.

GERIN J. (1974) Double-blind trial of naftidrofuryl in the treatment of cerebral arteriosclerosis. *British Journal of Clinical Practice* 28, 177–178 *[425]*.

GERSON S.N., BENSON F. & FRAZIER S.H. (1977) Diagnosis: schizophrenia versus posterior aphasia. *American Journal of Psychiatry* 134, 966–969 *[48]*.

GERSTENBRAND F. (1969) Rehabilitation of the head-injured. Ch. 31 in *The Late Effects of Head Injury*, eds. Walker A.E., Caveness W.F. & Critchley M. Thomas: Springfield, Illinois *[182]*.

GERSTMANN J. (1958) Psychological and phenomenological aspects of disorders of the body image. *Journal of Nervous and Mental Disease* 126, 499–512 *[58, 63]*.

GESCHWIND N. (1962) The anatomy of acquired disorders of reading. Ch. 8 in *Reading Disabilities, Progress and Research Needs in Dyslexia*, ed. Money J. Johns Hopkins Press: Baltimore *[19]*.

GESCHWIND N. (1965) Disconnexion syndromes in animals and man. *Brain* 88, 237–294 and 585–644 *[49, 52]*.

GESCHWIND N. (1967) Neurological foundations of language. In *Progress in Learning Disabilities*, ed. Myklebust H.R., pp. 182–198. Grune & Stratton: New York *[40]*.

GESCHWIND N. (1968) The mechanism of normal pressure hydrocephalus. *Journal of the Neurological Sciences* 7, 481–493 *[643]*.

GESCHWIND N. (1979) Behavioural changes in temporal lobe epilepsy. *Psychological Medicine* 9, 217–219 *[236]*.

GESCHWIND N. & KAPLAN E. (1962) A human cerebral deconnection syndrome: a preliminary report. *Neurology* 12, 675–686 *[19]*.

GESCHWIND N. & LEVITSKY W. (1968) Human brain: left-right asymmetries in temporal speech region. *Science* 161, 186–187 *[38]*.

GESCHWIND N., QUADFASEL F.A. & SEGARRA J.M. (1968) Isolation of the speech area. *Neuropsychologia* 6, 327–340 *[47]*.

GIBBENS T.C.N. (1969) The delinquent and his brain. *Proceedings of the Royal Society of Medicine* 62, 57–60 *[70]*.

GIBBERD F.B. (1973) The diagnosis and investigation of epilepsy. *British Journal of Hospital Medicine* 9, 152–158 *[256, 258]*.

GIBBS C.J., GAJDUSEK D.C., ASHER D.M., ALPERS M.P., BECK E., DANIEL P.M. & MATTHEWS W.B. (1968) Creutzfeldt-Jakob disease (spongiform encephalopathy): transmission to the chimpanzee. *Science* 161, 388–389 *[400]*.

GIBBS C.T., AMYX H.L., BACOTE A., MASTERS C.L. & GAJDUSEK D.C. (1980) Oral transmission of Kuru, Creutzfeldt-Jakob disease, and scrapie to non-human primates. *Journal of Infectious Diseases* 142, 205–208 *[400, 401]*.

GIBBS F.A. (1951) Ictal and non-ictal psychiatric disorders in temporal lobe epilepsy. *Journal of Nervous and Mental Disease* 113, 522–528 *[233]*.

GIBBS F.A. & GIBBS E.L. (1964) *Atlas of Electroencephalography Volume 3: Neurological and Psychiatric Disorders.* Addison-Wesley Publishing Company: Reading, Massachusetts *[233]*.

GILBERT G.J. (1964) Periodic hypersomnia and bulimia: the Kleine-Levin syndrome. *Neurology* 14, 844–850 *[628, 629]*.

GILBERT G.J. (1972) The medical treatment of spasmodic torticollis. *Archives of Neurology* 27, 503–506 *[574, 575]*.

GILBERT J.J. & BENSON D.F. (1972) Transient global amnesia: report of two cases with definite aetiologies. *Journal of Nervous and Mental Disease* 154, 461–463 *[361]*.

GILLEARD C.J. & PATTIE A.H. (1977) The Stockton Geriatric Rating Scale: a shortened version with British normative data. *British Journal of Psychiatry* 131, 90–94 *[107]*.

GILLES DE LA TOURETTE (1855) Étude sur une affection nerveuse charactérisée par de l'incoordination motrice accampagnée d'écholalie et de coprolalie (jumping, latah, myriachit). *Archives de Neurologie* 9, 19–42 and 158–200 *[582]*.

GILLFILLAN S.C. (1965) Lead poisoning and the fall of Rome. *Journal of Occupational Medicine* 7, 53–60 *[537]*.

GILLINGHAM F.J., KALYANARAMAN S. & DONALDSON A.A. (1964) Bilateral stereotaxic lesions in the management of parkinsonism and the dyskinesias. *British Medical Journal* 2, 656–659 *[554]*.

GILLMER R.E. (1972) Phaeochromocytoma—an interesting psychiatric presentation. *South African Medical Journal* 46, 174–176 *[441]*.

GILROY J. & MEYER J.S. (1969) *Medical Neurology.* Macmillan: London *[287]*.

GINSBURG H.M. & NIXON C.E. (1932) Thallium poisoning. *Journal of the American Medical Association* 98, 1076–1077 *[542]*.

GITTLESON N.L. & RICHARDSON T.D.E. (1973) Myasthenia gravis and schizophrenia—a rare combination. *British Journal of Psychiatry* 122, 343–344 *[607]*.

GLASER G.H., NEWMAN R.J. & SCHAFER R. (1963) Interictal psychosis in psychomotor-temporal lobe epilepsy: an EEG psychological study. Ch. 14 in *EEG and Behavior*, ed. Glaser G.H. Basic Books: New York *[252]*.

GLASGOW R.E., ZEISS R.A., BARRERA M. & LEWINSOHN P.M. (1977) Case studies on remediating memory deficits in brain damaged individuals. *Journal of Clinical Psychology* 33, 1049–1054 *[182]*.

GLATT M.M. & FRISCH P. (1969) Chlormethiazole in alcoholism. *Current Psychiatric Therapies*, vol. 9, 132–135, ed. Masserman J.H. Grune & Stratton: New York *[517]*.

GLATT M.M., GEORGE H.R. & FRISCH E.P. (1966) Evaluation of chlormethiazole in treatment for alcohol withdrawal syndrome. *Acta Psychiatrica Scandinavica*, supplement 192, 121–137 *[517]*.

GLEES P., COLE J., WHITTY C.W.M. & CAIRNS H. (1950) The effects of lesions in the cingular gyrus and adjacent areas in monkeys. *Journal of Neurology, Neurosurgery and Psychiatry* 13, 178–190 *[23]*.

GLEES P. & GRIFFITH H.B. (1952) Bilateral destruction of hippocampus (cornu Ammonis) in case of dementia. *Monatsschrift für Psychiatrie und Neurologie* 123, 193–204 *[26]*.

GLEN A.I.M. & CHRISTIE J.E. (1979) Early diagnosis of Alzheimer's disease: working definitions for clinical and laboratory criteria. Ch. 26 in *Alzheimer's Disease: Early Recognition of Potentially Reversible Deficits*, eds. Glen A.I.M. & Whalley L.J. Churchill Livingstone: Edinburgh & London *[391]*.

GODDARD G.V., McINTYRE D.C. & LEECH C.K. (1969) A permanent change in brain function resulting from daily electrical stimulation. *Experimental Neurology* 25, 295–330 *[512]*.

GODDARD P. & LOKARE V.G. (1970) Diazepam in the management of epilepsy. *British Journal of Psychiatry* 117, 213–214 *[268]*.

GOLDBERG A. (1959) Acute intermittent porphyria: a study of 50 cases. *Quarterly Journal of Medicine* 28, 183–209 *[483]*.

GOLDBERG A., MOORE M.R., McCOLL K.E.L. & BRODIE M.J. (1983) Porphyrin metabolism and the porphyrias. In *Oxford Textbook of Medicine*, vol. 1, eds. Weatherall D.J., Ledingham J.G.G. & Warrell D.A., pp. 9.81–9.89. Oxford University Press *[482, 483, 484]*.

GOLDFARB A.I. (1972) Multidimensional treatment approaches. In *Aging and the Brain*, ed. Gaitz C.M., pp. 179–191. Plenum Press: New York *[422]*.

GOLDMAN M.S. (1983) Cognitive impairment in chronic alcoholics. Some cause for optimism. *American Psychologist* 38, 1045–1054 *[518]*.

GOLDSMITH J.R. & LANDAW S.A. (1968) Carbon monoxide and human health. *Science* 162, 1352–1359 *[472]*.

GOLDSTEIN G. & CHOTLOS J.W. (1965) Dependency and brain damage in alcoholics. *Perceptual and Motor Skills* 21, 135–150 *[518]*.

GOLDSTEIN K. (1936) The modifications of behavior consequent to cerebral lesions. *Psychiatric Quarterly* 10, 586–610 *[42]*.

GOLDSTEIN K. (1939) *The Organism: A Holistic Approach to Biology Derived from Pathological Data in Man.* American Book Company: New York *[14, 22]*.

GOLDSTEIN K. (1942) *After Effects of Brain Injuries in War.* Grune & Stratton: New York *[14, 81, 151]*.

GOLDSTEIN K. (1948) *Language and Language Disturbances.* Grune & Stratton: New York *[47]*.

GOLDSTEIN K. (1952) The effect of brain damage on the personality. *Psychiatry* 15, 245–260 *[151]*.

GOLDSTEIN K. & SHEERER M. (1941) Abstract and concrete behaviour. An experimental study with special tests. *Psychological Monographs* 53, No, 2, 1–151 *[97]*.

GOLDSTEIN N.P., EWERT J.C., RANDALL R.V. & GROSS J.B. (1968) psychiatric aspects of Wilson's disease: results of psychometric tests during long-term therapy. In *Wilson's Disease*, ed. Bergsma D. Birth Defects Original Article Series, vol. 4, No. 2. The National Foundation: New York *[567]*.

GOLDSTEIN N.P., TAUXE W.N., McCALL J.T., RANDALL R.V. & GROSS J.B. (1971) Wilson's disease (hepatolenticular degeneration): treatment with penicillamine and changes in hepatic trapping of radioactive copper. *Archives of Neurology* 24, 391–400 *[565]*.

GOMERSALL J.D. & STUART A. (1973) Amitriptyline in migraine prophylaxis. *Journal of Neurology, Neurosurgery and Psychiatry* 36, 684–690 *[354]*.

GOMEZ M.R. (1979) Neurologic and psychiatric symptoms. Ch. 6 in *Tuberous Sclerosis*, ed. Gomez M.R. Raven Press: New York *[601]*.

GONEN J.Y. (1970) The use of Wechsler's deterioration quotient in cases of diffuse and symmetrical cerebral atrophy. *Journal of Clinical Psychology* 26, 174–177 *[96]*.

GOODE D.J., PENRY J.K. & DREIFUSS F.E. (1970) Effects of paroxysmal spike-wave on continuous visual-motor performance. *Epilepsia* 11, 241–254 *[230]*.

GOODIN D.S., SQUIRES K.C. & STARR A. (1978) Long-latency event-related components of the auditory evoked potential in dementia. *Brain* 101, 635–648 *[412]*.

GOODSTEIN R. & FERRELL R.B. (1977) Multiple sclerosis—presenting as depressive illness. *Diseases of the Nervous System* 38, 127–131 *[593]*.

GOODWIN D.W., CRANE J.B. & GUZE S.B. (1969a) Alcoholic blackouts: a review and clinical study of 100 alcoholics. *American Journal of Psychiatry* 126, 191–198 *[510]*.

GOODWIN D.W., CRANE J.B. & GUZE S.B. (1969b) Phenomenological aspects of the alcoholic 'blackout'. *British Journal of Psychiatry* 115, 1033–1038 *[510]*.

GOODWIN D.W., POWELL B., BREMER D., HOINE H. & STERN J. (1969c) Alcohol and recall: state-dependent effects in man. *Science* 163, 1358–1360 *[510]*.

GOODWIN F.K. (1971) Behavioural effects of L-dopa in man. *Seminars in Psychiatry* 3, 477–492 *[559, 561]*.

GORDON B. & MARIN O.S.M. (1979) Transient global amnesia: an extensive case report. *Journal of Neurology, Neurosurgery and Psychiatry* 42, 572–575 *[358]*.

GORDON E.B. (1968) Serial EEG studies in presenile dementia. *British Journal of Psychiatry* 114, 779–780 *[379]*.

GORDON E.B. & SIM M. (1967) The EEG in presenile dementia. *Journal of Neurology, Neurosurgery and Psychiatry* 30, 285–291 *[379, 392]*.

GORDON H.W. & BOGEN J.E. (1974) Hemispheric lateralization of singing after intracarotid sodium amylobarbitone. *Journal of Neurology, Neurosurgery and Psychiatry* 37, 727–738 *[57]*.

GORDON N. & RUSSELL S. (1958) The problem of unemployment among epileptics. *Journal of Mental Science* 104, 103–114 *[232]*.

GOSLING R.H. (1955) The association of dementia with radiologically demonstrated cerebral atrophy. *Journal of Neurology, Neurosurgery and Psychiatry* 18, 129–133 *[120]*.

GOSTLING J.V.T. (1967) Herpetic encephalitis. *Proceedings of the Royal Society of Medicine* 60, 693–696 *[300]*.

GOTTLIEB B. (1944) Acute nicotinic acid deficiency (aniacinosis). *British Medical Journal* 1, 392–393 *[490]*.

GOUDSMIT J., MORROW C.H., ASHER D.M., YANAGIHARA R.T., MASTERS C.L., GIBBS C.J. & GAJDUSEK D.C. (1980) Evidence for and against the transmissibility of Alzheimer's disease. *Neurology* 30, 945–950 *[384]*.

GOWERS W.R. (1888) *A Manual of Diseases of the Nervous System*, vol. 2. Churchill: London *[351, 572]*.

GOWERS W.R. (1893) *A Manual of Diseases of the Nervous System*, vol. 2, 2nd Edition. Churchill: London *[562]*.

GRABSKI D.A. (1961) Toluene sniffing producing cerebellar degeneration. *American Journal of Psychiatry* 118, 461–462 *[537]*.

GRAHAM D.I. & ADAMS J.H. (1971) Ischaemic brain damage in fatal head injury. *Lancet* 1, 265–266 *[139]*.

GRAHAM E., HOLLAND A., AVERY A. & ROSS RUSSELL R.W. (1981) Prognosis in giant-cell arteritis. *British Medical Journal* 282, 269–271 *[368]*.

GRAHAM F.K. & KENDALL B.S. (1960) Memory-for-designs test: revised general manual. *Perceptual and Motor Skills* 11, 147–188 *[98]*.

GRAHAM J.D.P. (1945) High blood pressure after battle. *Lancet* 1, 239–240 *[340]*.

GRAHAM P. & RUTTER M. (1968) Organic brain dysfunction and child psychiatric disorder. *British Medical Journal* 3, 695–700 *[227, 228, 235]*.

GRANATO J.E., STERN B.J., RINGEL A., KARIM A.H., KRUMHOLZ A., COYLE J. & ADLER S. (1983) Neuroleptic malignant syndrome: successful treatment with dantrolene and bromocriptine. *Annals of Neurology* 14, 89–90 *[534]*.

GRANT I. & JUDD L.L. (1976) Neuropsychological and EEG disturbances in polydrug users. *American Journal of Psychiatry* 133, 1039–1042 *[523]*.

GRANT I., KYLE G.C., TEICHMAN A. & MENDELS J. (1974) Recent life events and diabetes in adults. *Psychosomatic Medicine* 36, 121–128 *[454]*.

GRANT I. & MOHNS L. (1975) Chronic cerebral effects of alcohol and drug abuse. *International Journal of the Addictions* 10, 883–920 *[523]*.

GRANT I., MOHNS L., MILLER M. & REITAN R.M. (1976) A neuropsychological study of polydrug users. *Archives of General Psychiatry* 33, 973–978 *[523]*.

GRANT I., ROCHFORD J., FLEMING T. & STUNKARD A. (1973) A neuropsychological assessment of the effects of moderate marihuana use. *Journal of Nervous and Mental Disease* 156, 278–280 *[528]*.

GRANT R.H.E. & STORES O.P.R. (1970) Folic acid in folate-deficient patients with epilepsy. *British Medical Journal* 4, 644–648 *[506]*.

GRANVILLE-GROSSMAN K. (1971) *Recent Advances in Clinical Psychiatry*. Churchill: London *[532, 534, 535]*.

GREEN M.A. & FINK M. (1954) Standardisation of the face hand test. *Neurology* 4, 211–217 *[100]*.

GREEN P. (1978) Defective interhemispheric transfer in schizophrenia. *Journal of Abnormal Psychology* 87, 472–480 *[77]*.

GREEN P., HALLETT S. & HUNTER M. (1983) Abnormal interhemispheric integration and hemisphere specialisation in schizophrenics and high-risk children. In *Laterality and Psychopathology*, eds. Flor-Henry P. & Gruzelier J., pp. 443–469. Elsevier: Amsterdam *[77]*.

GREEN P. & KOTENKO V. (1980) Superior speech comprehension in schizophrenics under monaural versus binaural listening conditions. *Journal of Abnormal Psychology* 89, 399–408 *[77]*.

GREENBAUM J.V. & LURIE L.A. (1948) Encephalitis as a causative factor in behavior disorders of children. *Journal of the American Medical Association* 136, 923–930 *[290]*.

GREENBERG D. & MARKS I. (1982) Behavioural psychotherapy of uncommon referrals. *British Journal of Psychiatry* 141, 148–153 *[579]*.

GREENBERG R. & PEARLMAN C. (1967) Delirium tremens and dreaming. *American Journal of Psychiatry* 124, 133–142 *[512]*.

GREENBLATT M. & SOLOMON H.C. (1958) Studies of lobotomy. Ch. 11 in *The Brain and Human Behaviour*. Research Publications of the Association for Research in Nervous and Mental Disease, vol. 36. Williams & Wilkins: Baltimore *[69]*.

GREENFIELD J.G. (1963) In *Greenfield's Neuropathology*, 2nd edition, eds. Blackwood W., McMenemey W.H., Meyer A., Norman R.M. & Russell D.S. Edward Arnold: London *[552]*.

GREENFIELD J.G. & NORMAN R.M. (1963) Demyelinating diseases. Ch. 8 in *Greenfield's Neuropathology*, 2nd edition, eds. Blackwood W., McMenemey W.H., Meyer A., Norman R.M. & Russell D.S. Edward Arnold: London *[598, 599]*.

GREENFIELD R.S. & NELSON J.S. (1978) Atypical neuronal ceroid-lipofuscinosis. *Neurology* 28, 710–717 *[649]*.

GREER H.D., WARD H.P. & CORBIN K.B. (1965) Chronic salicylate intoxication in adults. *Journal of the American Medical Association* 193, 555–558 *[534]*.

GREER S. & PARSONS V. (1968) Schizophrenia-like psychosis in thyroid crisis. *British Journal of Psychiatry* 114, 1357–1362 *[430]*.

GREGORIADIS A., FRAGOS E., KAPSLAKIS Z. & MANDOUVALOS B. (1971) A correlation between mental disorders and EEG and AEG findings in temporal lobe epilepsy. Abstracts from *5th World Congress of Psychiatry, 1971, Mexico*, p. 325. La Prensa Médica Mexicana: Mexico *[249, 253]*.

GREGSON R.A.M. & TAYLOR G.M. (1977) Prediction of relapse in men alcoholics. *Journal of Studies on Alcohol* 38, 1749–1760 *[518]*.

GREITZ T. (1969) Effect of brain distension on cerebral circulation. *Lancet* 1, 863–865 *[644]*.

GRESHAM G.E., FITZPATRICK T.E., WOLF P.A., McNAMARA P.M., KANNELL W.B. & DAWBER T.R. (1975) Residual disability in survivors of stroke. *New England Journal of Medicine* 293, 954–956 *[326]*.

GREWEL F. (1969) The acalculias. Ch 9 in *Handbook of Clinical Neurology*, vol. 4, eds. Vinken P.J. & Bruyn G.W. North-Holland Publishing Co.: Amsterdam *[58]*.

GRINKER R.R., HAM G.C. & ROBBINS F.P. (1950) Some psychodynamic factors in multiple sclerosis. Ch. 31 in *Multiple Sclerosis and the Demyelinating Diseases*. Research Publications of The Association for Research in Nervous and Mental Disease, vol. 28. Williams & Wilkins: Baltimore *[597]*.

GRINKER R.R. & SAHS A.L. (1966) *Neurology*, 6th edition. Thomas: Springfield, Illinois *[309, 316, 542, 604]*.

GRINKER R.R. & WALKER A.E. (1933) The pathology of spasmodic torticollis with a note on respiratory failure from anaesthesia in chronic encephalitis. *Journal of Nervous and Mental Disease* 78, 630–637 *[575]*.

GRIST N.R. (1967) Acute viral infections of the nervous system. *Proceedings of the Royal Society of Medicine* 60, 696–698 *[299, 309]*.

GROAT R.A. & SIMMONS J.Q. (1950) Loss of nerve cells in experimental cerebral concussion. *Journal of Neuropathology and Experimental Neurology* 9, 150–163 *[138]*.

GROB D. (1958) Myasthenia gravis: current status of psychogenesis, clinical manifestations and management. *Journal of Chronic Diseases* 8, 536–566 *[609]*.

GROEN J.J. & ENDTZ L.J. (1982) Hereditary Pick's disease. Second re-examination of a large family and discussion of other hereditary cases, with particular reference to electroencephalography and computerised tomography. *Brain* 105, 443–459 *[391, 392]*.

GRONWALL D. & WRIGHTSON P. (1974) Delayed recovery of intellectual function after minor head injury. *Lancet* 2, 605–609 *[170]*.

GRONWALL D. & WRIGHTSON P. (1975) Cumulative effect of concussion. *Lancet* 2, 995–997 *[174]*.

GROSS M.M. & GOODENOUGH D.R. (1968) Sleep disturbances in the acute alcoholic psychoses. *Psychiatric Research Reports of the American Psychiatric Association* 24, 132–147 *[512]*.

GROWDON J.H. (1979) Choline, lecithin, and tardive dyskinesia. *Advances in Neurology*, 24, 387–394 *[550]*.

GROWDON J.H., HIRSCH M.J., WURTMAN R.J. & WIENER W. (1977) Oral choline administration to patients with tardive dyskinesia. *New England Journal of Medicine* 297, 524–527 *[550]*.

GRUNBERG F. & POND D.A. (1957) Conduct disorders in epileptic children. *Journal of Neurology, Neurosurgery and Psychiatry* 20, 65–68 *[235]*.

GRUNDKE-IQBAL I., JOHNSON A.B., WISNIEWSKI H.M., TERRY R.D. & IQBAL K. (1979) Evidence that Alzheimer neurofibrillary tangles originate from neurotubules. *Lancet* 1, 578–580 *[381]*.

GRUNNET M. (1963) Cerebrovascular disease: diabetes and cerebral arteriosclerosis. *Neurology* 13, 486–491 *[456]*.

GRUNNET M.L. (1969) Changing incidence, distribution, and histopathology of Wernicke's polioencephalopathy. *Neurology* 19, 1135–1139 *[496]*.

GRUT A. (1949) *Chronic Carbon Monoxide Poisoning*. Munksgaard: Copenhagen *[471]*.

GRUVSTAD M., KEBBON L. & GRUVSTAD S. (1958) Social and psychiatric aspects of pre-traumatic personality and post-traumatic insufficiency reactions in traumatic head injuries. *Acta Societatis Medicorum Upsaliensis* 63, 101–113 *[149]*.

GRUZELIER J. (1979) Synthesis and critical review of the evidence for hemisphere asymmetries of function in psychopathology. In *Hemisphere Asymmetries of Function in Psychopathology*, eds. Gruzelier J. & Flor-Henry P., pp. 647–672. Elsevier/North Holland, Biomedical Press, Amsterdam *[76]*.

GRUZELIER J.H. (1973) Bilateral asymmetry of skin conductance orienting activity and levels in schizophrenics. *Biological Psychology* 1, 21–41 *[76]*.

GRUZELIER J.H. & VENABLES P. (1974) Bimodality and lateral asymmetry of skin conductance orienting activity in schizophrenics: replication and evidence of lateral asymmetry in patients with depression and disorders of personality. *Biological Psychiatry* 8, 55–73 *[76]*.

GRUZELIER J.H. (1981) Cerebral laterality and psychopathology: fact and fiction. *Psychological Medicine* 11, 219–227 *[76]*.

GRUZELIER J. & FLOR-HENRY P. (eds.) (1976) *Hemisphere Asymmetries of Function in Psychopathology*. Developments in Psychiatry, Vol. 3. Elsevier/North-Holland, Biomedical Press: Amsterdam *[76]*.

GUDMUNDSSON G. (1966) Epilepsy in Iceland. A clinical and epidemiological investigation. *Acta Neurologica Scandinavica*, supplement 25, 7–124 *[212, 214, 232, 241]*.

GUERRANT J., ANDERSON W.W., FISCHER A., WEINSTEIN M.R., JAROS R.M. & DESKINS A. (1962) *Personality in Epilepsy*. Thomas: Springfield, Illinois *[229, 231, 233]*.

GUEY J., CHARLES C., COQUERY C., ROGER J. & SOULAYROL (1967) Study of psychological effects of ethosuximide (zarontin) on 25 children suffering from petit mal epilepsy. *Epilepsia* 8, 129–141 *[230]*.

GUILLEMINAULT C. & ANDERS T.F. (1976) Sleep disorders in children. *Advances in Paediatrics* 22, 151–174 *[618, 628, 632]*.

GUILLEMINAULT C., CARSKADON M. & DEMENT W.C. (1974) On the treatment of rapid eye movement narcolepsy. *Archives of Neurology* 30, 90–93 *[623]*.

GUILLEMINAULT C., DEMENT W.C. & PASSOUANT P. (eds) (1976) *Narcolepsy: Proceedings of the First International Symposium on Narcolepsy*. Advances in Sleep Research, Vol. III. Spectrum Publications Inc: New York *[618]*.

GUNN J.C. (1969) The prevalence of epilepsy among prisoners. *Proceedings of the Royal Society of Medicine* 62, 60–63 *[241]*.

GUNN J. (1973) Affective and suicidal symptoms in epileptic prisoners. *Psychological Medicine* 3, 108–114 *[254]*.

GUNN J. (1978) Epileptic homicide: a case report. *British Journal of Psychiatry* 132, 510–513 *[242]*.

GUNN J. & BONN J. (1971) Criminality and violence in epileptic prisoners. *British Journal of Psychiatry* 118, 337–343 *[241]*.

GUNN J. & FENTON G.W. (1971) Epilepsy, automatism and crime. *Lancet* 1, 1173–1176 *[241, 242]*.

GUNNE L.M., LIDVALL H.F. & WIDEN L. (1971) Preliminary clinical trial with L-dopa in narcolepsy. *Psychopharmacologia* 19, 204–206 *[623]*.

GUNTHER M. & PENROSE L.S. (1935) The genetics of epiloia. *Journal of Genetics* 31, 413–430 *[600]*.

GURLAND B.J., FLEISS J.L., GOLDBERG K., SHARPE L., COPELAND J.R.M., KELLEHER M.J. & KELLETT J.M. (1976) A semi-structured clinical interview for the assessment of diagnosis and mental state in the elderly: the Geriatric Mental State Schedule. II A factor analysis. *Psychological Medicine* 6, 451–459 *[107]*.

GURLAND B.J., GANZ V.F., FLEISS J.L. & ZUBIN J. (1972) The study of the psychiatric symptoms of systemic lupus erythematosus: a critical review. *Psychosomatic Medicine* 34, 199–206 *[363, 365]*.

GURLAND B., KURIANSKY J., SHARPE L., SIMON R., STILLER P. & BIRKETT P. (1977) The Comprehensive Assessment and Referral Evaluation (CARE)—rationale, development and reliability.

International Journal of Aging and Human Development **8**, 9–42 [107].

GURLING H.M.D., REVELEY M.A. & MURRAY R.M. (1984) Increased cerebral ventricular volume in monozygotic twins discordant for alcoholism. *Lancet* **1**, 986–988 [520].

GURNEY C., HALL R., HARPER M., OWEN S., ROTH M. & SMART G.A. (1967) A study of the physical and psychiatric characteristics of women attending an out-patient clinic for investigation for thyrotoxicosis. Communication to the Scottish Society for Experimental Medicine. Glasgow 1967. Quoted Slater E. & Roth M., *Clinical Psychiatry*, 3rd edition, 1969. Baillière, Tindall & Cassell: London [429, 431].

GUSELLA J.F., WEXLER N.S., CONNEALLY P.M., NAYLOR S.L., ANDERSON M.A., TANZI R.E., WATKINS P.C., OTTINA K., WALLACE M.R., SAKAGUCHI A.Y., YOUNG A.B., SHOULSON I., BONILLA E. & MARTIN J.B. (1983) A polymorphic DNA marker genetically linked to Huntington's disease. *Nature* **306**, 234–239 [395].

GUSTAFSON L. & NILSSON L. (1982) Differential diagnosis of presenile dementia on clinical grounds. *Acta Psychiatrica Scandinavica* **65**, 194–209 [379, 390].

GUSTAFSON L., RISBERG J., JOHANSON M., FRANSSON M. & MAXIMILIAN V.A. (1978) Effects of Piracetam on regional cerebral blood flow and mental functions in patients with organic dementia. *Psychopharmacology* **56**, 115–117 [425].

GUTHRIE A. & ELLIOTT W.A. (1980) The nature and reversibility of cerebral impairment in alcoholism. Treatment implications. *Journal of Studies on Alcohol* **41**, 147–155 [521].

GUTTMANN E. (1936) On some constitutional aspects of chorea and on its sequelae. *Journal of Neurology and Psychopathology* **17**, 16–26 [316, 317].

GUTTMANN E. (1946) Late effects of closed head injuries: psychiatric observations. *Journal of Mental Science* **92**, 1–18 [148, 149, 152].

GUTTMANN E. & HORDER H. (1943) Head injuries in children and their after-effects. *Archives of Disease in Childhood* **18**, 139–145 [171, 173].

GUZE S.B. (1967) The occurrence of psychiatric illness in systemic lupus erythematosus. *American Journal of Psychiatry* **123**, 1562–1570 [364, 365].

GYLDENSTED C. (1977) Measurements of the normal ventricular system and hemispheric sulci of 100 adults with computed tomography. *Neuroradiology* **14**, 183–192 [120].

HABERLAND C. (1965) Psychiatric manifestations in brain tumours. *Bibliotheca Psychiatrica et Neurologica* **127**, 65–86 [195].

HACHINSKI V.C., LASSEN N.A. & MARSHALL J. (1974) Multi-infarct dementia: a cause of mental deterioration in the elderly. *Lancet* **2**, 207–210 [386].

HACHINSKI V.C., ILIFF L.D., ZILHKA E., DU BOULAY G.H., MCALLISTER V.L., MARSHALL J., ROSS RUSSELL R.W. & SYMON L. (1975) Cerebral blood flow in dementia. *Archives of Neurology* **32**, 632–637 [389, 390].

HAGEN A.C. (1969) Communication disorders of the stroke patient. *Clinical Orthopaedics and Related Research* **63**, 102–112 [332].

HAHN R.D. & CLARK E.G. (1946a) Asymptomatic neurosyphilis: a review of the literature. *American Journal of Syphilis, Gonorrhoea and Venereal Diseases* **30**, 305–316 [278].

HAHN R.D. & CLARK E.G. (1946b) Asymptomatic neurosyphilis: prognosis. *American Journal of Syphilis, Gonorrhoea and Venereal Diseases* **30**, 513–548 [278].

HAHN R.D., WEBSTER B., WEICKHARDT G., THOMAS E., TIMBERLAKE W., SOLOMON H., STOKES J.H., MOORE J.E., HEYMAN A., GAMMON G., GLEESON G.A., CURTIS A.C. & CUTLER J.C. (1959) Penicillin treatment of general paresis (dementia paralytica). *Archives of Neurology and Psychiatry* **81**, 557–590 [282, 286, 287, 288].

HAKIM A.M. & MATHIESON G. (1978) Basis of dementia in Parkinson's disease. *Lancet* **2**, 729 [557].

HAKIM A.M. & MATHIESON G. (1979) Dementia in Parkinson's disease: a neuropathologic study. *Neurology* **29**, 1209–1214 [557].

HAKIM S. (1964) *Algunas observaciones sobra la pression del L.C.R. sindrome hidrocefalico en al adulto con 'pression normal' del L.C.R.* Tesis de grado, Universidad Javeriana. Bogota, Columbia, 1964. Quoted by Ojemann *et al.*, 1969, *Journal of Neurosurgery* **31**, 279–294 [639].

HAKIM S. & ADAMS R.D. (1965) The special clinical problem of symptomatic hydrocephalus with normal cerebrospinal fluid pressure: observations on cerebrospinal fluid hydrodynamics. *Journal of the Neurological Sciences* **2**, 307–327 [639, 643].

HALDANE J.S., KELLAS A.M. & KENNAWAY E.L. (1919) Experiments on acclimatisation to reduced atmospheric pressure. *Journal of Physiology* **53**, 181–206 [467].

HALIKAS J.A. (1974) Marijuana use and psychiatric illness. Ch. 11 in *Marijuana: Effects on Human Behaviour*, ed. Miller L.L. Academic Press: New York [526, 527].

HALIKAS J.A., GOODWIN D.W. & GUZE S.B. (1972) Marihuana use and psychiatric illness. *Archives of General Psychiatry* **27**, 162–165 [527].

HALL P. (1963) Korsakov's syndrome following herpes-zoster encephalitis. *Lancet* **1**, 752 [303].

HALL C.W., POPKIN M.K., STICKNEY S.K. & GARDNER E.R. (1979) Presentation of the steroid psychoses. *Journal of Nervous and Mental Disease* **167**, 229–236 [535].

HALL R. (1983) Pituitary and hypothalamic disorders. In *Oxford Textbook of Medicine* Vol. 1. eds. Weatherall D.J., Ledingham J.G.G. & Warrell D.A., pp. 10.7–10.24. Oxford University Press [445].

HALL S.B. (1929) Mental aspect of epidemic encephalitis. *British Medical Journal* **1**, 444–446 [296].

HALL T.C., MILLER A.K.H. & CORSELLIS J.A.N. (1975) Variations in the human Purkinje cell population according to age and sex. *Neuropathology and Applied Neurobiology* **1**, 267–292 [382].

HALLIDAY A.M., MCDONALD W.I. & MUSHIN J. (1973) Visual evoked response in diagnosis of multiple sclerosis. *British Medical Journal* **4**, 661–664 [589].

HALLPIKE J.F. (1973) Multiple sclerosis: problems of aetiology and pathogenesis. *British Journal of Hospital Medicine* **9**, 635–642 [588].

HALLPIKE J.F. (1980) New treatments for multiple sclerosis. *British Journal of Hospital Medicine* **23**, 63–68 [590].

HALONEN P.E., RIMON R., AROHONKA K. & JÄNTTI V. (1974) Antibody levels to herpes simplex type 1, measles and rubella viruses in psychiatric patients. *British Journal of Psychiatry* **125**, 461–465 [301].

HALPERIN J.J., LANDIS D.M.D. & KLEINMAN G.M. (1982) Whipple disease of the nervous system. *Neurology* **32**, 612–617 [650].

HAMBERT G. & FREY T.S. (1964) The electroencephalogram in the Klinefelter syndrome. *Acta Psychiatrica Scandinavica* **40**, 28–36 [446].

HAMBLIN T.J., HUSSAIN J., AKBAR A.N., TANG Y.C., SMITH J.L. & JONES D.B. (1983) Immunological reason for chronic ill health after infectious mononucleosis. *British Medical Journal* **287**, 85–88 [302].

HAMMARSTEN J.F. & SMITH W.O. (1957) Symptomatic magnesium deficiency in man. *New England Journal of Medicine* **256**, 897–899 [478].

HANDLER C.E. & PERKIN G.D. (1982) Anorexia nervosa and Wernicke's encephalopathy: an underdiagnosed association. *Lancet* 2, 771–772 *[492]*.

HANKOFF L.D. & PERESS N.S. (1981) Neuropathology of the brain stem in psychiatric disorders. *Biological Psychiatry* 16, 945–952 *[76]*.

HANNA S., HARRISON M., MACINTYRE I. & FRASER R. (1960) The syndrome of magnesium deficiency in man. *Lancet* 2, 172–176 *[478]*.

HARE E.H. (1959) The origin and spread of Dementia Paralytica. *Journal of Mental Science* 105, 594–626 *[280, 282]*.

HARE E.H. (1973) The duration of the fortification spectrum in migraine. Ch. 12 in *Background to Migraine*, 5th Migraine Symposium, ed. Cumings J.N. Heinemann: London *[344]*.

HARE M. (1978) Clinical check list for diagnosis of dementia. *British Medical Journal* 2, 266–267 *[374]*.

HARGREAVES M.M., RICHMOND H. & MORTON R. (1948) Presentation of two bone marrow elements: the 'tart' cell and the 'L.E.' cell. *Proceedings of the Staff Meetings of the Mayo Clinic* 23, 25–28 *[362]*.

HARPER C. (1979) Wernicke's encephalopathy: a more common disease than realised. A neuropathological study of 51 cases. *Journal of Neurology, Neurosurgery and Psychiatry* 42, 226–231 *[496]*.

HARPER C. (1983) The incidence of Wernicke's encephalopathy in Australia—a neuropathological study of 131 cases. *Journal of Neurology, Neurosurgery and Psychiatry* 46, 593–598 *[496, 497]*.

HARPER C.G. & BLUMBERGS P.C. (1982) Brain weights in alcoholics. *Journal of Neurology, Neurosurgery and Psychiatry* 45, 838–840 *[519, 521]*.

HARPER C. & KRIL J. (1985) Brain atrophy in chronic alcoholic patients—a quantitative pathological study. *Journal of Neurology, Neurosurgery and Psychiatry* 48, 211–217 *[519, 521]*.

HARPER C.G., KRIL J.J. & HOLLOWAY R.L. (1985) Brain shrinkage in chronic alcoholics: a pathological study. *British Medical Journal* 290, 501–504 *[519]*.

HARPER M. & ROTH M. (1962) Temporal lobe epilepsy and the phobic anxiety-depersonalization syndrome. *Comprehensive Psychiatry* 3, 129–151 and 215–226 *[261]*.

HARPER P.S. (1986) The prevention of Huntington's chorea. *Journal of the Royal College of Physicians of London* 20, 7–14 *[395]*.

HARPER P.S., TYLER A., SMITH S. & JONES P. (1981) Decline in the predicted incidence of Huntington's chorea associated with systematic genetic counselling and family support. *Lancet* 2, 411–413 *[394]*.

HARRINGTON J.A. & LETEMENDIA F.J.J. (1958) Persistent psychiatric disorders after head injuries in children. *Journal of Mental Science* 104, 1205–1218 *[173]*.

HARRIS A.I., COX E. & SMITH C.R.W. (1971) *Handicapped and Impaired in Great Britain, Part 1*. Office of Population Censuses and Surveys, H.M.S.O.: London *[319]*.

HARRIS R. (1982) Genetics of Alzheimer's disease. *British Medical Journal* 284, 1065–1066 *[385]*.

HARRISON M.J.G. (1980) Surgery for ischaemic stroke. *British Journal of Hospital Medicine* 24, 108–112 *[331]*.

HARRISON M.J.G., ROBERT C.M. & UTTLEY D. (1974) Benign aqueduct stenosis in adults. *Journal of Neurology, Neurosurgery and Psychiatry* 37, 1322–1328 *[645]*.

HARRISON M.J.G., THOMAS D.J., DU BOULAY G.H. & MARSHALL J. (1979) Multi-infarct dementia. *Journal of the Neurological Sciences* 40, 97–103 *[387, 388, 389, 390]*.

HARRISON M.S. (1956) Notes on the clinical features and pathology of post-concussional vertigo, with especial reference to positional nystagmus. *Brain* 79, 474–486 *[169]*.

HARROWER M.R. (1950) The results of psychometric and personality tests in multiple sclerosis. Ch. 32 in *Multiple Sclerosis and the Demyelinating Diseases*. Research Publications of the Association for Research in Nervous and Mental Disease, vol. 28. Williams & Wilkins: Baltimore *[594]*.

HARROWER M. (1954) Psychological factors in multiple sclerosis. *Annals of the New York Academy of Sciences* 58, 715–719 *[594]*.

HARTMANN E.L. (1965) The D-state. A review and discussion of studies on the physiologic state concomitant with dreaming. *New England Journal of Medicine* 273, 30–35 and 87–92 *[622]*.

HASLAM M.T. (1967) Cellular magnesium levels and the use of penicillamine in the treatment of Huntington's chorea. *Journal of Neurology, Neurosurgery and Psychiatry* 30, 185–188 *[426]*.

HASSLER R. & DIECKMANN G. (1970) Traitement stéréotaxique des tics et cris inarticulés ou coprolaliques considérés comme phénomène d'obsession motrice au cours de la maladie de Gilles de la Tourette. *Revue Neurologique* 123, 89–100 *[587]*.

HASSLER R. & DIECKMANN G. (1973) Relief of obsessive-compulsive disorders, phobias and tics by stereotactic coagulation of the rostral intralaminar and medial-thalamic nuclei. Ch. 19 in *Surgical Approaches in Psychiatry*, eds. Laitinen L.V. & Livingston K.E. Medical and Technical Publishing Co.: Lancaster *[587]*.

HATRICK J.A. & DEWHURST K. (1970) Delayed psychosis due to LSD. *Lancet* 2, 742–744 *[531]*.

HAUG G. (1977) Age and sex dependence of the size of normal ventricles on computed tomography. *Neuroradiology* 14, 201–204 *[120]*.

HAUG J.O. (1962) Pneumoencephalographic studies in mental disease. *Acta Psychiatrica Scandinavica*, supplement 165, 1–104 *[121]*.

HAUG J.O. (1968) Pneumoencephalographic evidence of brain damage in chronic alcoholics. *Acta Psychiatrica Scandinavica*, supplement 203, 135–143 *[519]*.

HAWKINS T.D. & MARTIN L. (1965) Incidence of hyperostosis frontalis interna in patients at a general hospital and at a mental hospital. *Journal of Neurology, Neurosurgery and Psychiatry* 28, 171–174 *[653]*.

HAWTON K., FAGG J. & MARSACK P. (1980) Association between epilepsy and attempted suicide. *Journal of Neurology, Neurosurgery and Psychiatry* 43, 168–170 *[254]*.

HAY W.J., RICKARDS A.G., McMENEMY W.H. & CUMINGS J.N. (1963) Organic mercurial encephalopathy. *Journal of Neurology, Neurosurgery and Psychiatry* 26, 199–202 *[543]*.

HAYMAN M. (1941) Myasthenia gravis and psychosis: report of a case with observations on its psychosomatic implications. *Psychosomatic Medicine* 3, 120–137 *[607]*.

HAYS P., KRIKLER B., WALSH L.S. & WOOLFSON G. (1966) Psychological changes following surgical treatment of parkinsonism. *American Journal of Psychiatry* 123, 657–663 *[561]*.

HEAD H. (1920) *Studies in Neurology*, vol. 2. Oxford University Press *[59]*.

HEATH R.G., MONROE R.R. & MICKLE W.A. (1955) Stimulation of the amygdaloid nucleus in a schizophrenic patient. *American Journal of Psychiatry* 111, 862–863 *[72, 233]*.

HEATHFIELD K.W.G. (1967) Huntington's chorea. *Brain* 90, 203–232 *[394, 396, 426]*.

HEATHFIELD K.W.G., CROFT P.B. & SWASH M. (1973) The syndrome of transient global amnesia. *Brain* 96, 729–736 *[359, 360, 361]*.

HEBB D.O. & MORTON N.W. (1943) The McGill adult comprehension examination: 'verbal situation' and 'picture anomaly' series. *Journal of Educational Psychology* 34, 16–25 *[105]*.

HÉCAEN H. (1962) Clinical symptomatology in right and left hemisphere lesions. Ch. 10 in *Interhemispheric Relations and Cerebral Dominance*, ed. Mountcastle V.B. Johns Hopkins Press: Baltimore *[55, 63]*.

HÉCAEN H. (1969) Aphasic, apraxic and agnosic syndromes in right and left hemisphere lesions. Ch. 15 in *Handbook of Clinical Neurology*, vol. 4, eds. Vinken P.J. and Bruyn G.W. North-Holland Publishing Co.: Amsterdam *[59]*.

HÉCAEN H. & AJURIAGUERRA J. DE (1956a) *Troubles Mentaux au cours des Tumeurs Intracraniennes*. Masson: Paris *[27, 187, 189, 190, 191, 194, 196, 197, 201, 205]*.

HÉCAEN H. & AJURIAGUERRA J. DE (1956b) Agnosie visuelle pour les objets inanimés par lésion unilatéral gauche. *Revue Neurologique* **94**, 222–233 *[53]*.

HÉCAEN H. & ALBERT M.L. (1975) Disorders of mental functioning related to frontal lobe pathology. Ch. 8 in *Psychiatric Aspects of Neurologic Disease*, eds. Benson D.F. & Blumer D. Grune & Stratton: New York *[68]*.

HÉCAEN H. & ANGELERGUES R. (1962) Agnosia for faces (prosopagnosia). *Archives of Neurology* **7**, 24–32 *[53]*.

HECK L.L., HOFFER P.B. & GOTTSHALK A. (1971) Brain-scanning—successes, limitations, and future developments. Ch. 17 in *Clinical Neurosurgery*, Proceedings of the Congress of Neurological Surgeons, vol. 18. Williams & Wilkins: Baltimore *[116]*.

HEIMBURGER R.F., DEMYER W. & REITAN R.M. (1964) Implications of Gerstmann's syndrome. *Journal of Neurology, Neurosurgery and Psychiatry* **27**, 52–57 *[57]*.

HEINE B.E. (1969) Psychiatric aspects of systemic lupus erythematosus. *Acta Psychiatrica Scandinavica* **45**, 307–326 *[363, 364]*.

HEINE B.E., SAINSBURY P. & CHYNOWETH R.C. (1969) Hypertension and emotional disturbance. *Journal of Psychiatric Research* **7**, 119–130 *[340]*.

HEINZ E.R., MARTINEZ J. & HAENGGELI A. (1977) Reversibility of cerebral atrophy in anorexia nervosa and Cushing's syndrome. *Journal of Computer Assisted Tomography* **1**, 415–418 *[122, 438]*.

HEISKANEN O. & SIPPONEN P. (1970) Prognosis of severe brain injury. *Acta Neurologica Scandinavica* **46**, 343–348 *[148]*.

HELWEG-LARSEN P., HOFFMEYER H., KIELER J., THAYSEN E.H., THAYSEN J.H., THYGESEN P. & WULFF M.H. (1952) Famine disease in German concentration camps: complications and sequels. *Acta Psychiatrica et Neurologica Scandinavica*, supplement **83**, 1–460 *[486]*.

HEMPHILL R.E. & STENGEL E. (1940) A study on pure word-deafness. *Journal of Neurology, Neurosurgery and Psychiatry* **3**, 251–262 *[43]*.

HEMSI L.K., WHITEHEAD A. & POST F. (1968) Cognitive functioning and cerebral arousal in elderly depressives and dements. *Journal of Psychosomatic Research* **12**, 145–156 *[101, 411]*.

HENDERSON A.S., DUNCAN-JONES P. & FINLAY-JONES R.A. (1983) The reliability of the Geriatric Mental State Examination. Community survey version. *Acta Psychiatrica Scandinavica* **67**, 281–289 *[107]*.

HENDERSON G., TOMLINSON B.E. & GIBSON P.H. (1980) Cell counts in human cerebral cortex in normal adults throughout life using an image analysing computer. *Journal of the Neurological Sciences* **46**, 113–136 *[381]*.

HENDERSON J.G., STRACHAN R.W., BECK J.S., DAWSON A.A. & DANIEL M. (1966) The antigastric-antibody test as a screening procedure for vitamin B$_{12}$ deficiency in psychiatric practice. *Lancet* **2**, 809–813 *[501, 502, 503]*.

HENDERSON R.G. (1983) Nuclear magnetic resonance imaging: a review. *Journal of the Royal Society of Medicine* **76**, 206–212 *[122]*.

HENDRICK I. (1928) Encephalitis lethargica and the interpretation of mental disease. *American Journal of Psychiatry* **7**, 989–1014 *[292]*.

HENDRICKSON E., LEVY R. & POST F. (1979) Average evoked responses in relation to cognitive and affective state of elderly

psychiatric patients. *British Journal of Psychiatry* **134**, 494–501 *[411]*.

HENKIN R.I., PATTEN B.M., RE P.K. & BRONZERT D.A. (1975) A syndrome of acute zinc loss. Cerebellar dysfunction, mental changes, anorexia and taste and smell dysfunction. *Archives of Neurology* **32**, 745–751 *[478]*.

HENKIN R.I., SCHECHTER P.J., HOYLE R. & MATTERN C.F.T. (1971) Idiopathic hypogeusia with dysgeusia, hyposmia, and dysosmia. A new syndrome. *Journal of the American Medical Association* **217**, 434–440 *[478]*.

HENRIKSEN B., JUUL-JENSEN P. & LUND M. (1970) The mortality of epileptics. In *Life Assurance Medicine: Proceedings of the 10th International Conference of Life Assurance Medicine*, ed. Brackenridge R.D.C. Pitman: London *[253]*.

HENRY G.W. (1932) Mental phenomena observed in cases of brain tumour. *American Journal of Psychiatry* **89**, 415–473 *[188]*.

HENRY J.A. & WOODRUFF G.H.A. (1978) A diagnostic sign in states of apparent unconsciousness. *Lancet* **2**, 920–921 *[260]*.

HENRYK-GUTT R. & REES W.L. (1973) Psychological aspects of migraine. *Journal of Psychosomatic Research* **17**, 141–153 *[347, 348]*.

HENSON R.A. (1966) The neurological aspects of hypercalcaemia: with special reference to primary hyperparathyroidism. *Journal of the Royal College of Physicians, London* **1**, 41–50 *[449]*.

HERBERT M. (1964) The concept and testing of brain-damage in children: a review. *Journal of Child Psychology and Psychiatry* **5**, 197–216 *[93]*.

HERMAN M.N. & SANDOK B.A. (1967) Conversion symptoms in a case of multiple sclerosis. *Military Medicine* **132**, 816–818 *[596]*.

HERMANN B.P. & RIEL P. (1981) Interictal personality and behavioral traits in temporal lobe and generalised epilepsy. *Cortex* **17**, 125–128 *[234]*.

HERRIDGE C.F. & ABEY-WICKRAMA I. (1969) Acute iatrogenic hypothyroid psychosis. *British Medical Journal* **3**, 154 *[432]*.

HERRINGTON R.N. (1969) The personality in temporal lobe epilepsy. Ch. 11 in *Current Problems in Neuropsychiatry*, ed. Herrington R.N. British Journal of Psychiatry Special Publication No. 4. Headley Brothers: Ashford, Kent *[233]*.

HERRMANN C., MULDER D.G. & FONKALSRUD E.W. (1963) Thymectomy for myasthenia gravis. *Annals of Surgery* **158**, 85–92 *[607]*.

HERSHEY L.A., GADO M.H. & TROTTER J.L. (1979) Computerised tomography in the diagnostic evaluation of multiple sclerosis. *Annals of Neurology* **5**, 32–39 *[592]*.

HERSHEY L.A. & TROTTER J.L. (1979) The use and abuse of the cerebrospinal fluid IgG profile in the adult: A practical evaluation. *Annals of Neurology* **8**, 426–434 *[589]*.

HERSOV L.A. & RODNIGHT R. (1960) Hartnup disease in psychiatric practice: clinical and biochemical features of three cases. *Journal of Neurology, Neurosurgery and Psychiatry* **23**, 40–45 *[489]*.

HERTZ P.E., NADAS E. & WOJTKOWSKI H. (1955) Cushing's syndrome and its management. *American Journal of Psychiatry* **112**, 144–145 *[439]*.

HERZ E. & GLASER G.H. (1949) Spasmodic torticollis: II Clinical evaluation. *Archives of Neurology and Psychiatry* **61**, 227–239 *[573, 574]*.

HERZ E. & HOEFER P.F.A. (1949) Spasmodic torticollis: 1 Physiologic analysis of involuntary motor activity. *Archives of Neurology and Psychiatry* **61**, 129–136 *[574]*.

HESTON L.L. (1978) The clinical genetics of Pick's disease. *Acta Psychiatrica Scandinavica* **57**, 202–206 *[391]*.

HESTON L.L., MASTRI A.R., ANDERSON E. & WHITE J. (1981) Dementia of the Alzheimer type. Clinical genetics, natural history and associated conditions. *Archives of General Psychiatry* **38**, 1085–1090 *[373, 375, 377, 380, 385]*.

HEYGSTER H. (1949) Über doppelseitige Stirnhirnverletzungen. *Psychiatrie, Neurologie und Medizinische Psychologie* 1, 114–123 [154].

HEYMAN A., WILKINSON W.E., HURWITZ B.J., SCHMECHEL D., SIGMON A.H., WEINBERG T., HELMS M.J. & SWIFT M. (1983) Alzheimer's disease: Genetic aspects and associated clinical disorders. *Annals of Neurology* 14, 507–515 [377, 385].

HICKMAN J.W., ATKINSON R.P., FLINT L.D. & HURXTHAL L.M. (1961) Transient schizophrenic reaction as a major symptom of Cushing's syndrome. *New England Journal of Medicine* 264, 797–800 [439].

HIERONS R., JANOTA I. & CORSELLIS J.A.N. (1978) The late effects of necrotising encephalitis of the temporal lobes and limbic areas: a clinico-pathological study of 10 cases. *Psychological Medicine* 8, 21–42 [301].

HIERONS R. & SAUNDERS M. (1966) Impotence in patients with temporal lobe lesions. *Lancet* 2, 761–764 [238].

HILL D. (1944) Cerebral dysrhythmia; its significance in aggressive behaviour. *Proceedings of the Royal Society of Medicine* 37, 317–328 [74].

HILL D. (1948) The relationship between epilepsy and schizophrenia: EEG studies. *Folia Psychiatrica, Neurologica et Neurochirurgica Neerlandica*, Congresnummer, 3–19 [246].

HILL D. (1952) EEG in episodic psychotic and psychopathic behaviour. *Electroencephalography and Clinical Neurophysiology* 4, 419–442 [111].

HILL D. (1953) Psychiatric disorders of epilepsy. *Medical Press* 229, 473–475 [233, 246].

HILL D. (1957a) Electroencephalogram in schizophrenia. In *Schizophrenia: Somatic Aspects*, ed. Richter D. Pergamon: London [111, 246].

HILL D. (1957b) Epilepsy. *British Encyclopaedia of Medical Practice* 86–99 [246].

HILL D. (1958) Indications and contra-indications to temporal lobectomy. *Proceedings of the Royal Society of Medicine* 51, 610–613 [275].

HILL D. (1963a) The EEG in psychiatry. Ch. 12 in *Electroencephalography*, eds. Hill D. & Parr G., 2nd edition. Macdonald: London [110].

HILL D. (1963b) Epilepsy: clinical aspects. Ch. 9 in *Electroencephalography*, eds. Hill D. & Parr G., 2nd edition. Macdonald: London [216].

HILL D. & MITCHELL W. (1953) Epileptic anamnesis. *Folia Psychiatrica, Neurologica et Neurochirurgica Neerlandica* 56, 718–725 [220].

HILL D. & POND D.A. (1952) Reflections on one hundred capital cases submitted to electroencephalography. *Journal of Mental Science* 98, 23–43 [241, 242].

HILL D., POND D.A., MITCHELL W. & FALCONER M.A. (1957) Personality changes following temporal lobectomy for epilepsy. *Journal of Mental Science* 103, 18–27 [237].

HILL D. & WATTERSON D. (1942) Electroencephalographic studies of psychopathic personalities. *Journal of Neurology, Neurosurgery and Psychiatry* 5, 47–65 [111].

HILLBOM E. (1951) Schizophrenia-like psychoses after brain trauma. *Acta Psychiatrica et Neurologica Scandinavica*, supplement 60, 36–47 [155, 164].

HILLBOM E. (1960) After-effects of brain-injuries. *Acta Psychiatrica et Neurologica Scandinavica*, supplement 142, 1–195 [147, 151, 155, 156, 166, 168].

HIMMELHOCH J., PINCUS J., TUCKER G. & DETRE T. (1970) Sub-acute encephalitis: behavioural and neurological aspects. *British Journal of Psychiatry* 116, 531–538 [306, 307, 308].

HINKLE L.E. & WOLF S. (1952a) Importance of life stress in course

and management of diabetes mellitus. *Journal of the American Medical Association* 148, 513–520 [453, 454].

HINKLE L.E. & WOLF S. (1952b) A summary of experimental evidence relating life stress to diabetes mellitus. *Journal of the Mount Sinai Hospital* 19, 537–570 [453, 454].

HINTON J. & WITHERS E. (1971) The usefulness of the clinical tests of the sensorium. *British Journal of Psychiatry* 119, 9–18 [82, 84].

HIRANO A., MALAMUD N., ELIZAN T.S. & KURLAND L.T. (1966) Amyotrophic lateral sclerosis and parkinsonism-dementia complex on Guam: further pathologic studies. *Archives of Neurology* 15, 35–51 [605].

HIRANO A., MALAMUD N. & KURLAND L.T. (1961) Parkinsonism-dementia complex, an endemic disease on the island of Guam. II: Pathological features. *Brain* 84, 662–679 [605].

HISHIKAWA Y. & KANEKO Z. (1965) Electroencephalographic study on narcolepsy. *Electroencephalography and Clinical Neurophysiology* 18, 249–259 [622].

HISHIKAWA Y., NANNO H., TACHIBANA M., FURUYA E., KOIDA H. & KANEKO Z. (1968) The nature of sleep attack and other symptoms of narcolepsy. *Electroencephalography and Clinical Neurophysiology* 24, 1–10 [622].

HITCH G.J. (1984) Working memory. Editorial in *Psychological Medicine* 14, 265–271 [28].

HITCHCOCK E., ASHCROFT G.W., CAIRNS V.M. & MURRAY L.G. (1972) Preoperative and postoperative assessment and management of psychosurgical patients. Ch. 14 in *Psychosurgery*, eds. Hitchcock E., Laitinen L. & Vaernet K. Proceedings of the Second International Conference on Psychosurgery. Thomas: Springfield, Illinois [73].

HJERN B. & NYLANDER I. (1962) Late prognosis of severe head injuries in childhood. *Archives of Disease in Childhood* 37, 113–116 [171].

HOCKADAY J. & WHITTY C.W.M. (1969) Factors determining the electroencephalogram in migraine: a study of 560 patients, according to clinical type of migraine. *Brain* 92, 769–788 [349].

HOCKADAY J.M., WILLIAMSON D.H. & ALBERTI K.G.M.M. (1973) Effects of intravenous glucose on some blood metabolites and hormones in migraine subjects. Ch. 13 in *Background to Migraine*, Fifth Migraine Symposium, ed. Cumings J.N. Heinemann: London [346].

HOCKADAY J., WILLIAMSON D.H. & WHITTY C.W.M. (1971) Blood-glucose levels and fatty-acid metabolism in migraine related to fasting. *Lancet* 1, 1153–1156 [346].

HOCKADAY T.D.R., KEYNES W.M. & MCKENZIE J.K. (1966) Catatonic stupor in elderly woman with hyperparathyroidism. *British Medical Journal* 1, 85–87 [448].

HOEHN M.M. & YAHR M.D. (1967) Parkinsonism: onset, progression and mortality. *Neurology* 17, 427–442 [550, 551].

HOFF E.C., GRENELL R.G. & FULTON J.F. (1945) Histopathology of the central nervous system after exposure to high altitudes, hypoglycaemia and other conditions associated with central anoxia. *Medicine* 24, 161–217 [467].

HOFFENBERG R. (1983) Thyroid disorders. In *Oxford Textbook of Medicine*, Vol. 1, eds. Weatherall D.J., Ledingham J.G.G. & Warrell D.A., pp. 10.24–10.41. Oxford University Press [431, 434].

HOHEISEL H.P. & WALCH R. (1952) Über manisch-depressive und verwandte Verstimmungszustände nach Hirnverletzung. *Archiv für Psychiatrie und Nervenkrankheiten* 188, 1–25 [154, 165].

HOLBOURN A.H.S. (1943) Mechanics of head injuries. *Lancet* 2, 438–441 [138].

HOLBROOK M. (1982) Stroke: social and emotional outcome. *Journal of the Royal College of Physicians, London* 16, 100–104 [334].

HOLLANDER D. & STRICH S.J. (1970) Atypical Alzheimer's disease with congophilic angiopathy, presenting with dementia of acute onset. In *Alzheimer's Disease and Related Conditions*, eds. Wolstenholme G.E.W. & O'Connor M. Ciba Foundation Symposium. Churchill: London [378].

HOLLON T.H. (1973) Behaviour modification in a community hospital rehabilitation unit. *Archives of Physical Medicine and Rehabilitation* 54, 65–68 [183].

HOLMES J.M. (1956) Cerebral manifestations of vitamin B_{12} deficiency. *British Medical Journal* 2, 1394–1398 [501, 503].

HOLT E.K. & TEDESCHI C. (1943) Cerebral patchy demyelination. *Journal of Neuropathology and Experimental Neurology* 2, 306–314 [599].

HOOK O. (1954) Sarcoidosis with involvement of the nervous system. Report of nine cases. *Archives of Neurology and Psychiatry* 71, 554–575 [652].

HOOPER R.S., McGREGOR J.M. & NATHAN P.W. (1945) Explosive rage following head injury. *Journal of Mental Science* 91, 458–471 [162].

HOOSHMAND H. & BRAWLEY B.W. (1969) Temporal lobe seizures and exhibitionism. *Neurology* 19, 1119–1124 [241].

HOOSHMAND H., ESCOBAR M.R. & KOPF S.W. (1972) Neurosyphilis. A study of 241 patients. *Journal of the American Medical Association* 219, 726–729 [284, 286].

HORN S. (1974) Some psychological factors in parkinsonism. *Journal of Neurology, Neurosurgery and Psychiatry* 37, 27–31 [558].

HORNYKIEWICZ O. (1971) Neurochemical pathology and pharmacology of brain dopamine and acetylcholine: rational basis for the current drug treatment of parkinsonism. Ch. 2 in *Recent Advances in Parkinson's Disease*, eds. McDowell F.H. & Markham C.H. Blackwell Scientific Publications: Oxford [552].

HOROWITZ M.J. (1969) Flashbacks: recurrent intrusive images after the use of LSD. *American Journal of Psychiatry* 126, 565–569 [531].

HOROWITZ M.J., COHEN F.M., SAUNDERS F.A. & SKOLNIKOFF A.Z. (1970) *Psychosocial Function in Epilepsy*. Thomas: Springfield, Illinois [237].

HORTA-BARBOSA L., FUCCILLO D.A., LONDON W.T., JABBOUR J.T., ZEMAN W. & SEVER J.L. (1969) Isolation of measles virus from brain cell cultures of two patients with subacute sclerosing panencephalitis. *Proceedings of the Society for Experimental Biology and Medicine* 132, 272–277 [305].

HORVATH T.B. (1975) Clinical spectrum and epidemiological features of alcoholic dementia. In *Alcohol, Drugs and Brain Damage*, ed. Rankin J.G. Addiction Research Foundation of Ontario: Toronto [517].

HOUNSFIELD G.N. (1973) Computerized transverse axial scanning (tomography) Part I. Description of system. *British Journal of Radiology* 46, 1016–1022 [119].

HOUSER O.W. & McLEOD R.A. (1979) Roentgenographic experience at the Mayo Clinic. Ch. 3 in *Tuberous Sclerosis*, ed. Gomez M.R. Raven Press: New York [600].

HUAPAYA L. (1979) Seven cases of somnambulism induced by drugs. *American Journal of Psychiatry* 136, 985–986 [632].

HUBBARD B.M. & ANDERSON J.M. (1981) Age, senile dementia, and ventricular enlargement. *Journal of Neurology, Neurosurgery, and Psychiatry* 44, 631–635 [120].

HUBER G. (1957) *Pneumoencephalographische und Psychopathologische Bilder bei Endogenen Psychosen*. Monographien aus dem Gesamtgebiete der Neurologie und Psychiatrie. Springer: Berlin [121].

HUBER G., GROSS G. & SCHÜTTLER R. (1975) A long-term follow-up study of schizophrenia: psychiatric course of illness and prognosis. *Acta Psychiatrica Scandinavica* 52, 49–57 [121].

HUDSON A.J. (1981) Amyotrophic lateral sclerosis and its association with dementia, parkinsonism and neurological disorders: a review. *Brain* 104, 217–247 [604, 605].

HUDSON H.S. & WALKER H.I. (1961) Withdrawal symptoms following ethchlorvynol (placidyl) dependence. *American Journal of Psychiatry* 118, 361 [534].

HUGHES G.V. (1974) Systemic lupus erythematosus. *British Journal of Hospital Medicine* 12, 309–319 [363].

HUNGERFORD G.D., DU BOULAY G.H. & ZILKHA K.J. (1976) Computerised axial tomography in patients with severe migraine: a preliminary report. *Journal of Neurology, Neurosurgery and Psychiatry* 39, 990–994 [345].

HUNT H.F. (1973) The differentiation of malingering, dissimulation, and pathology. Ch. 24 in *Psychopathology: Contributions from the Social, Behavioral and Biological Sciences*, eds. Hammer M., Salzinger K. & Sutton S. John Wiley & Sons: New York [409].

HUNTER D. (1959) *Health in Industry*. Penguin Books Ltd. [538].

HUNTER D. (1978) *The Diseases of Occupations*, 6th Edition. Hodder & Stoughton: London [472, 543].

HUNTER R., BLACKWOOD W. & BULL J. (1968a) Three cases of frontal meningiomas presenting psychiatrically. *British Medical Journal* 3, 9–16 [192, 193, 204, 205].

HUNTER R. & JONES M. (1966) Acute lethargica-type encephalitis. *Lancet* 2, 1023–1024 [298].

HUNTER R., JONES M. & COOPER F. (1968b) Modified lumbar air encephalography in the investigation of long-stay psychiatric patients. *Journal of the Neurological Sciences* 6, 593–596 [121].

HUNTER R., JONES M., JONES T.G. & MATTHEWS D.M. (1967a) Serum B_{12} and folate concentrations in mental patients. *British Journal of Psychiatry* 113, 1291–1295 [502, 504].

HUNTER R., JONES M. & MALLESON A. (1969) Abnormal cerebrospinal fluid total protein and gamma-globulin levels in 256 patients admitted to a psychiatric unit. *Journal of the Neurological Sciences* 9, 11–38 [299, 318].

HUNTER R., JONES M. & MATTHEWS D.M. (1967b) Post-gastrectomy vitamin-B_{12} deficiency in psychiatric practice. *Lancet* 1, 47 [503].

HUNTER R., LOGUE V. & McMENEMY W.H. (1963) Temporal lobe epilepsy supervening on longstanding transvestism and fetishism. A case report. *Epilepsia* 4, 60–65 [239, 240, 241].

HUNTINGTON G. (1872) On chorea. *Medical and Surgical Reporter (Philadelphia)* 26, 317–321 [393].

HUNTINGTON G. (1910) Recollections of Huntington's chorea as I saw it at East Hampton, Long Island, during my boyhood. *Journal of Nervous and Mental Disease* 37, 255–257 [399].

HUPPERT F.A. & PIERCY M. (1978) Dissociation between learning and remembering in organic amnesia. *Nature* 275, 317–318 [35].

HUPPERT F.A. & PIERCY M. (1979) Normal and abnormal forgetting in organic amnesia: effect of locus of lesion. *Cortex* 15, 385–390 [35].

HURDLE A.D.F. & PICTON-WILLIAMS T.C. (1966) Folic acid deficiency in elderly patients admitted to hospital. *British Medical Journal* 2, 202–205 [504].

HURWITZ L.J. & ADAMS G.F. (1972) Rehabilitation of hemiplegia: indices of assessment and prognosis. *British Medical Journal* 1, 94–98 [319, 325, 326, 331].

HUTCHISON G.B., EVANS J.A. & DAVIDSON D.C. (1958) Pitfalls in the diagnosis of phaeochromocytoma. *Annals of Internal Medicine* 48, 300–309 [440, 441].

HUTT S.J., JACKSON P.M., BELSHAM A. & HIGGINS G. (1968) Perceptual-motor behaviour in relation to blood phenobarbitone level: a preliminary report. *Developmental Medicine and Child Neurology* 10, 626–632 [231].

HUTT S.J., NEWTON J. & FAIRWEATHER H. (1977) Choice reaction time and EEG activity in children with epilepsy. *Neuropsychologia* 15, 257–267 *[230]*.

HYSLOP G.H. (1949) Torticollis of central origin. *Medical Clinics of North America* 25, 747–754 *[572]*.

ILLINGWORTH R.D. (1970) Subdural haematomas after the treatment of chronic hydrocephalus by ventriculocaval shunts. *Journal of Neurology, Neurosurgery and Psychiatry* 33, 95–99 *[642]*.

ILLINGWORTH R.D., LOGUE V., SYMON L. & UEMURA K. (1971) The ventriculocaval shunt in the treatment of adult hydrocephalus. Results and complications in 101 patients. *Journal of Neurosurgery* 35, 681–685 *[642]*.

ILLIS L.S. & MERRY R.T. (1972) Treatment of herpes simplex encephalitis. *Journal of the Royal College of Physicians of London* 7, 34–44 *[301]*.

INGLIS J. (1959) A paired-associate learning test for use with elderly psychiatric patients. *Journal of Mental Science* 105, 440–443 *[101]*.

INGVAR D.H. (1970) Cerebral blood flow in organic dementia. In *Research on the Cerebral Circulation*, eds. Meyer J.S., Reivich M., Lechner H. & Eichhorn O. Thomas: Springfield, Illinois *[376]*.

INGVAR D.H. & FRANZEN G. (1974) Abnormalities of cerebral blood flow distribution in patients with chronic schizophrenia. *Acta Psychiatrica Scandinavica* 50, 425–462 *[75]*.

INOSE T. (1968) Neuropsychiatric manifestations in Wilson's disease: attacks of disturbance of consciousness. In *Wilson's Disease*, ed. Bergsma D., Birth Defects Original Article Series, vol. 4, No. 2. The National Foundation: New York *[566]*.

IQBAL K., GRUNDKE-IQBAL I., WISNIEWSKI H.K. & TERRY R.D. (1978) Neurofibers in Alzheimer's disease and other conditions. In *Alzheimer's Disease: Senile Dementia and Related Diseases, Aging* Vol. 7., eds. Katzman R., Terry R.D. & Bick K.L., pp. 409–420. Raven Press: New York *[381]*.

IQBAL K., WISNIEWSKI H.M., SHELANSKI M.L., BROSTOFF S., LIWNICZ B.H. & TERRY R.D. (1974) Protein changes in senile dementia. *Brain Research* 77, 337–343 *[382]*.

IRVING G., ROBINSON R.A. & McADAM W. (1970) The validity of some cognitive tests in the diagnosis of dementia. *British Journal of Psychiatry* 117, 149–156 *[83, 84, 97, 100, 102]*.

IRVING J.G. (1969) Impact of insurance coverage on convalescence and rehabilitation of head-injured patients. Ch. 48 in *The Late Effects of Head Injury*, eds. Walker A.E., Caveness W.F. & Critchley M. Thomas: Springfield, Illinois *[137]*.

ISAACS B. (1971) Identification of disability in the stroke patient. *Modern Geriatrics* 1, 390–402 *[331]*.

ISAACS B. (1973) Stroke. In *Textbook of Geriatric Medicine and Gerontology*, ed. Brocklehurst J.C. Churchill Livingstone: Edinburgh *[331]*.

ISAACS B. & WALKEY F.A. (1964) A simplified paired-associate test for elderly hospital patients. *British Journal of Psychiatry* 110, 80–83 *[88, 102]*.

ISBELL H., ALTSCHUL S., KORNETSKY C.H., EISENMAN A.J., FLANARY H.G. & FRASER H.F. (1950) Chronic barbiturate intoxication. *Archives of Neurology and Psychiatry* 64, 1–28 *[522, 523]*.

ISBELL H., BELLEVILLE R.E., FRASER H.F., WIKLER A. & LOGAN C.R. (1956) Studies on lysergic acid diethylamide (LSD-25): 1. Effects in former morphine addicts and development of tolerance during chronic intoxication. *Archives of Neurology and Psychiatry* 76, 468–478 *[529, 530]*.

ISBELL H., FRASER H.F., WICKLER A., BELLEVILLE R.E. & EISENMAN A.J. (1955) An experimental study of aetiology of 'rum fits' and delirium tremens. *Quarterly Journal of Studies on Alcohol* 16, 1–33 *[509, 511, 516]*.

ISBELL H., GORODETZKY C.W., JASINSKI D., CLAUSSEN U., SPULAK F. VON & KORTE F. (1967) Effects of (—) Δ 9-trans-tetrahydro-cannabinol in man. *Psychopharmacologia* 11, 184–188 *[525]*.

ISHERWOOD I. (1983) Principles of neuroradiology. In *Oxford Textbook of Medicine*. Vol. 2, eds. Weatherall D.J., Ledingham J.G.G. & Warrell D.A., pp. 21.4–21.9. Oxford University Press *[117]*.

ISHII N. & NISHIHARA Y. (1981) Pellagra among chronic alcoholics: clinical and pathological study of 20 necropsy cases. *Journal of Neurology, Neurosurgery and Psychiatry* 44, 209–215 *[491]*.

ISHII S. (1966) Brain swelling: studies of structural, physiologic and biochemical alterations. Ch. 24 in *Head Injury: Conference Proceedings*, eds. Caveness W.F. & Walker A.E. Lippincott: Philadelphia *[140]*.

ISHII T. & HAGA S. (1976) Immuno-electron microscopic localisation of immunoglobulins in amyloid fibrils of senile plaques. *Acta Neuropathologica* 36, 243–249 *[384]*.

IVES E.R. (1963) Mental aberrations in diabetic patients. *Bulletin of the Los Angeles Neurological Society* 28, 279–285 *[456]*.

IVERSEN S.D. (1977) Temporal lobe amnesia. Ch. 6 in *Amnesia: Clinical, Psychological and Medicolegal Aspects*, 2nd Edition, eds. Whitty C.W.M. & Zangwill O.L. Butterworths: London *[27]*.

IVNIK R.J. (1978) Neuropsychological stability in multiple sclerosis. *Journal of Consulting & Clinical Psychology* 46, 913–923 *[592]*.

JABLENSKY A., JANOTA I. & SHEPHERD M. (1970) Neuropsychiatric illness and neuropathological findings in a case of Klinefelter's syndrome. *Psychological Medicine* 1, 18–29 *[447]*.

JACKSON J.H. (1869) Certain points in the study and classification of diseases of the nervous system (Goulstonian Lectures) *Lancet* 1, 307, 344, 379. Reprinted in *Selected Writings of John Hughlings Jackson, vol. 2*, ed. Taylor J., 1932, Hodder & Stoughton: London, p. 246 *[22]*.

JACKSON J.H. (1889) On a particular variety of epilepsy ('intellectual aura'): one case with symptoms of organic brain disease. *Brain* 11, 179–207 *[222]*.

JACOBS E.A., WINTER P.M., ALVIS H.J. & SMALL S.M. (1969) Hyperoxygenation effect on cognitive functioning in the aged. *New England Journal of Medicine* 281, 753–757 *[424]*.

JACOBS L., KINKEL W.R., PAINTER F., MURAWSKI J. & HEFFNER R.R. (1978) Computerised tomography in dementia with special reference to changes in size of normal ventricles during aging and normal pressure hydrocephalus. In *Alzheimer's Disease: Senile Dementia and Related Disorders Aging* Vol. 7, eds. Katzman R., Terry R.D. & Bick K.L., pp. 241–260. Raven Press: New York *[120]*.

JACOBSEN C.F. (1935) Functions of frontal association area in primates. *Archives of Neurology and Psychiatry* 33, 558–569 *[69]*.

JACOBY R.J., DOLAN R.J., LEVY R. & BALDY R. (1983) Quantitative computed tomography in elderly depressed patients. *British Journal of Psychiatry* 143, 124–127 *[411]*.

JACOBY R.J. & LEVY R. (1980a) Computed tomography in the elderly. 2. Senile dementia: diagnosis and functional impairment. *British Journal of Psychiatry* 136, 256–269 *[120]*.

JACOBY R.J. & LEVY R. (1980b) Computed tomography in the elderly. 3. Affective disorder. *British Journal of Psychiatry* 136, 270–275 *[122, 411]*.

JACOBY R.J., LEVY R. & BIRD J.M. (1981) Computed tomography and the outcome of affective disorder: a follow-up study of elderly patients. *British Journal of Psychiatry* 139, 288–292 *[122]*.

JAKOB A. (1921) Über eigenartige Erkrankungen des Zentralnervensystems mit bemerkenswertem anatomischen Befunde. *Zeitschrift für die gesampte Neurologie und Psychiatrie* 64, 147–228 *[400]*.

JAMBOR K.L. (1969) Cognitive functioning in multiple sclerosis. *British Journal of Psychiatry* 115, 765–775 *[591]*.

JAMES I.P. (1960) Temporal lobectomy for psychomotor epilepsy. *Journal of Mental Science* 106, 543–558 *[237, 253]*.

JAMES P. (1963) Drug-withdrawal psychoses. *American Journal of Psychiatry* 119, 880–881 *[524]*.

JANA D.K. & ROMANO-JANA L. (1973) Hypernatremic psychosis in the elderly: case reports. *Journal of the American Geriatrics Society* 21, 473–477 *[475]*.

JANKOWSKI K. (1963) A case of Schilder's diffuse sclerosis diagnosed clinically as schizophrenia. *Acta Neuropathologica* 2, 302–305 *[599]*.

JANOTA I. (1981) Dementia, deep white matter damage and hypertension: 'Binswanger's disease'. *Psychological Medicine* 11, 39–48 *[391]*.

JARVIE H. (1954) Frontal lobe wounds causing disinhibition: a study of six cases. *Journal of Neurology, Neurosurgery and Psychiatry* 17, 14–32 *[149]*.

JARVIK L.F., YEN F-S & GOLDSTEIN F. (1974a) Chromosomes and mental status. *Archives of General Psychiatry* 30, 186–190 *[373]*.

JARVIK L.F., YEN F-S. & MORALISHVILI E. (1974b) Chromosome examinations in ageing institutionalized women. *Journal of Gerontology* 29, 269–276 *[373]*.

JASPER H.H. (1964) Some physiological mechanisms involved in epileptic automatisms. *Epilepsia* 5, 1–20 *[222]*.

JASPER H., BICKFORD R. & MAGNUS O. (1950) The electroencephalogram in multiple sclerosis. Ch. 27 in *Multiple Sclerosis and the Demyelinating Diseases*, Research Publications of the Association for Research in Nervous and Mental Disease, vol. 28. Williams & Wilkins: Baltimore *[589]*.

JASPERS K. (1963) *General Psychopathology*. Translated from the German 7th Edition by Hoenig J. & Hamilton M.W. Manchester University Press *[5]*.

JEAVONS P.M. & HARDING G.F.A. (1970) Television epilepsy. *Lancet* 2, 926 *[211]*.

JEEVES M.A. (1965) Psychological studies of three cases of congenital agenesis of the corpus callosum. In *Functions of the Corpus Callosum*, Ciba Foundation Study Group No. 20, eds. Ettlinger E.G., de Reuck A.V.S. & Porter R., pp. 73–94. J. & A. Churchill: London *[654]*.

JEEVES M.A. (1969) A comparison of interhemispheric transmission times in acallosals and normals. *Psychonomic Science* 16, 245–246 *[654]*.

JEFFCOATE W.J., SILVERSTONE J.T., EDWARDS C.R.W. & BESSER G.M. (1979) Psychiatric manifestations of Cushing's syndrome: response to lowering of plasma cortisol. *Quarterly Journal of Medicine* 191, 465–472 *[437, 438]*.

JEFFERISS F.J.G. (1962) The return of the venereal diseases. *British Medical Journal* 1, 1751–1753 *[277, 287]*.

JEFFERSON G. (1955) *The Invasive Adenomas of the Anterior Pituitary*. The Sherrington Lectures, No. 3, University Press of Liverpool *[200]*.

JEFFERSON M. (1957) Sarcoidosis of the nervous system. *Brain* 80, 540–556 *[652]*.

JEFFREYS R.V. & WOOD M.M. (1978) Adult non-tumourous dementia and hydrocephalus. *Acta Neurochirurgica* 45, 103–114 *[642]*.

JELLINEK E.H. (1962) Fits, faints, coma and dementia in myxoedema. *Lancet* 2, 1010–1012 *[434, 436]*.

JELLINEK E.H. & KELLY R.E. (1960) Cerebellar syndrome in myxoedema. *Lancet* 2, 225–227 *[434]*.

JELLINEK E.M. (1952) Phases of alcohol addiction. *Quarterly Journal of Studies on Alcohol* 13, 673–684 *[510]*.

JELLINGER K. & SEITELBERGER F. (1969) Protracted post-traumatic encephalopathy: pathology and clinical implications. Ch. 18 in

The Late Effects of Head Injury, eds. Walker A.E., Caveness W.F. & Critchley M. Thomas: Springfield, Illinois *[140]*.

JENKINS R.B. & GROH R.H. (1970) Mental symptoms in parkinsonian patients treated with L-dopa. *Lancet* 2, 177–180 *[559]*.

JENNETT B. (1975) *Epilepsy After Non-missile Head Injuries*, 2nd Edition. Heinemann: London *[141, 213]*.

JENNETT B. & BOND M. (1975) Assessment of outcome after severe brain damage: a practical scale. *Lancet* 1, 480–484 *[157]*.

JENNETT B. & PLUM F. (1972) Persistent vegetative state after brain damage. A syndrome in search of a name. *Lancet* 1, 734–737 *[157]*.

JENNETT B., SNOEK J., BOND M.R. & BROOKS N. (1981) Disability after severe head injury: observations on the use of the Glasgow Coma Scale. *Journal of Neurology, Neurosurgery, and Psychiatry* 44, 285–293 *[158, 185]*.

JENNETT B., TEASDALE G., GALBRAITH S., PICKARD J., GRANT H., BRAAKMAN R., AVEZAAT C., MAAS A., MINDERHOUD J., VECHT C.J., HEIDEN J., SMALL R., CATON W. & KURZE T. (1977) Severe head injuries in three countries. *Journal of Neurology, Neurosurgery, and Psychiatry* 40, 291–298 *[142, 158]*.

JENNETT B., TEASDALE G.M. & KNILL-JONES R.P. (1975) Predicting outcome after head injury. *Journal of the Royal College of Physicians* 9, 231–237 *[142]*.

JENNETT W.B. (1962) *Epilepsy After Blunt Head Injuries*. Heinemann: London *[152]*.

JENNETT W.B. (1969) Early traumatic epilepsy. *Lancet* 1, 1023–1025 *[213]*.

JENNINGS W.G. (1972) An ergot alkaloid preparation (hydergine) versus placebo for treatment of symptoms of cerebrovascular insufficiency: double-blind study. *Journal of the American Geriatrics Society* 20, 407–412 *[425]*.

JENSEN I. (1976) Temporal lobe epilepsy. Types of seizures, age, and surgical results. *Acta Neurologica Scandinavica* 53, 335–357 *[275]*.

JENSEN I. & LARSEN J.K. (1979a) Mental aspects of temporal lobe epilepsy: follow-up of 74 patients after resection of a temporal lobe. *Journal of Neurology, Neurosurgery, and Psychiatry* 42, 256–265 *[237, 275]*.

JENSEN I. & LARSEN J.K. (1979b) Psychoses in drug-resistant temporal lobe epilepsy. *Journal of Neurology, Neurosurgery, and Psychiatry* 42, 948–954 *[249, 275]*.

JERVIS G.A. (1948) Early senile dementia in mongoloid idiocy. *American Journal of Psychiatry* 105, 102–106 *[378]*.

JEWESBURY E.C.O. (1970) Parkinsonism. *British Journal of Hospital Medicine* 4, 825–840 *[551, 553]*.

JOFFE R., BLACK M.M. & FLOYD M. (1968) Changing clinical picture of neurosyphilis: report of seven unusual cases. *British Medical Journal* 1, 211–212 *[285]*.

JOHANNESSON G., HAGBERG B., GUSTAFSON L. & INGVAR D.H. (1979) EEG and cognitive impairment in presenile dementia. *Acta Neurologica Scandinavica* 59, 225–240 *[392]*.

JOHNS R.J. & MCQILLEN M.P. (1966) Syndromes simulating myasthenia gravis: asthenia with anticholinesterase tolerance. *Annals of the New York Academy of Sciences* 135, 385–397 *[609]*.

JOHNSON D.A.W. (1968) The evaluation of routine physical examination in psychiatric cases. *Practitioner* 200, 686–691 *[79]*.

JOHNSON J. (1967) Myotonia congenita (Thomsen's disease) and hereditary psychosis. *British Journal of Psychiatry* 113, 1025–1030 *[617]*.

JOHNSON J. (1969) Organic psychosyndromes due to boxing. *British Journal of Psychiatry* 115, 45–53 *[175, 176]*.

JOHNSON J. (1975) Schizophrenia and Cushing's syndrome cured by adrenalectomy. *Psychological Medicine* 5, 165–168 *[437]*.

JOHNSON J. (1982) Stupor: its diagnosis and management. *British Journal of Hospital Medicine* 27, 530–532 *[132]*.

JOHNSON R.T. & RICHARDSON E.P. (1968) The neurological manifestations of systemic lupus erythematosus: a clinical-pathological study of 24 cases and review of the literature. *Medicine* 47, 337–369 *[363, 364, 365]*.

JOHNSON W.O. (1928) Psychosis and hyperthyroidism. *Journal of Nervous and Mental Disease* 67, 558–566 *[430]*.

JOHNSTONE E.C., CROW T.J., FRITH C.D., HUSBAND J. & KREEL L. (1976) Cerebral ventricular size and cognitive impairment in chronic schizophrenia. *Lancet* 2, 924–926 *[121]*.

JOHNSTONE E.C., CROW T.D., FRITH C.D., STEVENS M., KREEL L. & HUSBAND J. (1978) The dementia of dementia praecox. *Acta Psychiatrica Scandinavica* 57, 305–324 *[121]*.

JOHNSTONE J.A., ROSS C.A.C. & DUNN M. (1972) Meningitis and encephalitis associated with mumps infection. A 10 year survey. *Archives of Disease in Childhood* 47, 647–651 *[302]*.

JOLLIFFE N., BOWMAN K.M., ROSENBLUM L.A. & FEIN H.D. (1940) Nicotinic acid deficiency encephalopathy. *Journal of the American Medical Association* 114, 307–312 *[490]*.

JOLLIFFE N., GOODHART R., GENNIS J. & CLINE J.K. (1939) Experimental production of vitamin B_1 deficiency in normal subjects; dependence of urinary excretion of thiamin on dietary intake of vitamin B_1. *American Journal of the Medical Sciences* 198, 198–211 *[488]*.

JOLLIFFE N., WORTIS H. & FEIN H.D. (1941) The Wernicke Syndrome. *Archives of Neurology and Psychiatry* 46 569–597 *[491]*.

JONES B. & PARSONS O.A. (1971) Impaired abstracting ability in chronic alcoholics. *Archives of General Psychiatry* 24, 71–75 *[518]*.

JONES D.P. & NEVIN S. (1954) Rapidly progressive cerebral degeneration (subacute vascular encephalopathy) with mental disorder, focal disturbances and myoclonic epilepsy. *Journal of Neurology, Neurosurgery and Psychiatry* 17, 148–159 *[403]*.

JONES R.K. (1974) Assessment of minimal head injuries: indications for in-hospital care. *Surgical Neurology* 2, 101–104 *[169]*.

JONES-GOTMAN M. & MILNER B. (1977) Design fluency: the invention of nonsense drawings after focal cortical lesions. *Neuropsychologia* 15, 653–654 *[88]*.

JORDAN R.M., KAMMER H. & RIDDLE M.R. (1977) Sulfonylurea-induced factitious hypoglycaemia: a growing problem. *Archives of Internal Medicine* 137, 390–393 *[463]*.

JOUSSE A.T., GEISLER W.O. & WYNNE-JONES M. (1969) Motivation in rehabilitation. Ch. 30 in *The Late Effects of Head Injury*, eds. Walker A.E., Caveness W.F. & Critchley M. Thomas: Springfield, Illinois *[182]*.

JOYCE-CLARK N. & MOLTENO A.C.B. (1978) Modified neurosyphilis in the Cape peninsula. *South African Medical Journal* 53, 10–16 *[284]*.

JOYSTON-BECHAL M.P. (1966) The clinical features and outcome of stupor. *British Journal of Psychiatry* 112, 967–981 *[132, 133]*.

JUDELSOHN F.A. (1970) Depression and carcinoma. *British Journal of Psychiatry* 117, 119–121 *[638]*.

JUDGE T.G. (1968) Quoted by Ferguson Anderson W., in The interrelationship between physical and mental disease in the elderly. Ch. 11 in *Recent Developments in Psychogeriatrics*, eds. Kay D.W.K. & Walk A., British Journal of Psychiatry Special Publication No. 6. Headley Brothers: Ashford, Kent 1971 *[476]*.

JUDGE T.G. & URQUHART A. (1972) Naftidrofuryl—a double blind cross-over study in the elderly. *Current Medical Research and Opinion* 1, 166–172 *[425]*.

JUEL-JENSEN B.E. (1973) The chemotherapy of viral disease. *British Journal of Hospital Medicine* 10, 402–409 *[301]*.

JUS A. & JUS K. (1962) Retrograde amnesia in petit mal. *Archives of General Psychiatry* 6, 163–167 *[229]*.

JUUL-JENSEN P. (1964) Epilepsy: a clinical and social analysis of 1020 adult patients with epileptic seizures. *Acta Neurologica Scandinavica*, supplement 5, 1–148 *[212, 214, 241]*.

KAHANA E., ALTER M., BRAHAM J. & SOFER D. (1974) Creutzfeldt-Jakob disease: focus among Libyan Jews in Israel. *Science* 183, 90–91 *[401]*.

KAHANA E., LEIBOWITZ U. & ALTER M. (1971) Cerebral multiple sclerosis. *Neurology* 21, 1179–1185 *[593]*.

KAHN R.L., GOLDFARB A.I., POLLACK M. & PECK A. (1960) Brief objective measures for the determination of mental status in the aged. *American Journal of Psychiatry* 117, 326–328 *[100]*.

KALES A. & KALES J.D. (1974) Sleep disorders: recent findings in the diagnosis and treatment of disturbed sleep. *New England Journal of Medicine* 290, 487–499 *[632]*.

KALINOWSKY L.B. & KENNEDY F. (1943) Observations in electric shock therapy applied to problems in epilepsy. *Journal of Nervous and Mental Disease* 98, 56–67 *[274]*.

KALLMANN F.J. (1956) Genetic aspects of mental disorders in later life. Ch 3 in *Mental Disorders in Later Life*, ed. Kaplan O.J. Stanford University Press *[372]*.

KANNER L. (1957) *Child Psychiatry*. 3rd Edition. Blackwell Scientific Publications: Oxford *[581]*.

KAPILA C.C., KAUL S., KAPUR S.C., KALAYANAM T.S. & BANERJEE D. (1958) Neurological and hepatic disorders associated with influenza. *British Medical Journal* 2, 1311–1314 *[303]*.

KAPUR N. & COUGHLAN A.K. (1980) Confabulation and frontal lobe dysfunction. *Journal of Neurology, Neurosurgery and Psychiatry* 43, 461–463 *[30]*.

KARAGULLA S. & ROBERTSON E.E. (1955) Psychical phenomena in temporal lobe epilepsy and the psychoses. *British Medical Journal* 1, 748–752 *[261]*.

KARK R.A.P., POSKANZER D.C., BULLOCK J.D. & BOYLEN G. (1971) Mercury poisoning and its treatment with n-acetyl-d, l-penicillamine. *New England Journal of Medicine* 285, 10–16 *[540]*.

KARPATI G. & FRAME B. (1964) Neuropsychiatric disorders in primary hyperparathyroidism: clinical analysis with review of the literature. *Archives of Neurology* 10, 387–397 *[448, 450]*.

KASTE M., VILLKE J., SAINIO K., KUURNE T., KATEVUO K. & MEURALA H. (1982) Is chronic brain damage in boxing a hazard of the past? *Lancet* 2, 1186–1188 *[174, 175]*.

KASZNIAK A.W., GARRON D.C. & FOX J. (1979) Differential effects of age and cerebral atrophy upon span of immediate recall and paired associated learning in older patients suspected of dementia. *Cortex* 15, 285–295 *[31]*.

KATZMAN R. (1976) The prevalence and malignancy of Alzheimer's disease. *Archives of Neurology* 33, 217–218 *[371]*.

KAUFMAN D.M., ZIMMERMAN R.D. & LEEDS N.E. (1979) Computed tomography in herpes simplex encephalitis. *Neurology* 29, 1392–1396 *[300]*.

KAY D.W.K., BEAMISH P. & ROTH M. (1964) Old age mental disorders in Newcastle upon Tyne. Part 1: a study of prevalence. *British Journal of Psychiatry* 110, 146–158 *[372]*.

KAY D.W., BERGMANN K., FOSTER E.M., MCKECHNIE A.A. & ROTH M. (1970) Mental illness and hospital usage in the elderly: a random sample followed up. *Comprehensive Psychiatry* 11, 26–35 *[371]*.

KAY D.W.K., KERR T.A. & LASSMAN L.P. (1971) Brain trauma and the postconcussional syndrome. *Lancet* 2, 1052–1055 *[170]*.

KAYATEKIN M.S. (1981) Personal communication *[491]*.

KAZNER E., LANKSCH W., STEINHOFF H. & WILSKE J. (1975) Die

axiale Computer-Tomographie des Gehirnschädels—Anwendungsmöglichkeiten und klinische Ergebnisse. *Fortschritte der Neurologie-Psychiatrie* 75, 487–574 *[119]*.

KEARNEY T.R. (1964) Parkinson's disease presenting as a depressive illness. *Journal of the Irish Medical Association* 54, 117–119 *[558]*.

KEDDIE K.M.G. (1965) Toxic psychosis following mumps. *British Journal of Psychiatry,* 111, 691–696 *[302]*.

KEELER M.H., REIFLER C.B. & LIPTZIN M.B. (1968) Spontaneous recurrence of marihuana effect. *American Journal of Psychiatry* 125, 384–386 *[525]*.

KELLY M., MYRSTEN A-L. & GOLDBERG L. (1971) Intravenous vitamins in acute alcoholic intoxication: effects on physiological and psychological functions. *British Journal of Addiction* 66, 19–30 *[511]*.

KELLY R. & SMITH B.N. (1981) Post-traumatic syndrome: another myth discredited. *Journal of the Royal Society of Medicine* 74, 275–277 *[151]*.

KELLY W.F., CHECKLEY S.A., BENDER D.A. & MASHITER K. (1983) Cushing's syndrome and depression—a prospective study of 26 patients. *British Journal of Psychiatry* 142, 16–19 *[438]*.

KELMAN D.H. (1965) Gilles de la Tourette's disease in children: a review of the literature. *Journal of Child Psychology and Psychiatry* 6, 219–226 *[581, 582]*.

KENDALL B.E. (1980) The detection of intracranial tumours. *British Journal of Hospital Medicine* 23, 116–133 *[119, 201, 202]*.

KENDALL B.E. (1982) Neuroradiology. Ch. 9 in *A Textbook of Epilepsy,* 2nd Edition, eds. Laidlaw J. & Richens A. Churchill Livingstone: Edinburgh and London *[257]*.

KENDELL R.E. (1967) Psychiatric sequelae of benign myalgic encephalomyelitis. *British Journal of Psychiatry* 113, 833–840 *[314]*.

KENDELL R.E. (1974) The stability of psychiatric diagnoses. *British Journal of Psychiatry* 124, 352–356 *[410]*.

KENDRICK D.C. (1967) A cross-validation study of the use of the SLT and DCT in screening for diffuse brain pathology in elderly subjects. *British Journal of Medical Psychology* 40, 173–178 *[101]*.

KENDRICK D.C., GIBSON A.J. & MOYES I.C.A. (1979) The revised Kendrick battery: clinical studies. *British Journal of Social and Clinical Psychology* 18, 329–340 *[101]*.

KENDRICK D.C., PARBOOSINGH R-C. & POST F. (1965) A synonym learning test for use with elderly psychiatric subjects: a validation study. *British Journal of Social and Clinical Psychology* 4, 63–71 *[101, 102]*.

KENDRICK D.C. & POST F. (1967) Differences in cognitive status between healthy, psychiatrically ill, and diffusely brain-damaged elderly subjects. *British Journal of Psychiatry* 113, 75–81 *[97, 101]*.

KENNARD C. & SWASH M. (1981) Acute viral encephalitis: its diagnosis and outcome. *Brain* 104, 129–148 *[289, 304]*.

KENNEDY A. (1959) Psychological factors in confusional states in the elderly. *Gerontologia Clinica* 1, 71–82 *[422]*.

KENNEDY A. & NEVILLE J. (1957) Sudden loss of memory. *British Medical Journal* 2, 428–433 *[408, 410]*.

KENNEDY A.C., LINTON A.L. & EATON J.C. (1962) Urea levels in cerebrospinal fluid after haemodialysis. *Lancet* 1, 410–411 *[474]*.

KENNEDY A.C., LINTON A.L., LUKE R.G. & RENFREW S. (1963) Electroencephalographic changes during haemodialysis. *Lancet* 1, 408–411 *[474]*.

KENNEDY C. (1968) A ten-year experience with subacute sclerosing panencephalitis. *Neurology* 18 (supplements), 58–59 *[305, 306]*.

KENNEDY J., PARBHOO S.P., MACGILLIVRAY B. & SHERLOCK S. (1973) Effect of extracorporeal liver perfusion on the electroencephalogram of patients in coma due to acute liver failure. *Quarterly Journal of Medicine* 42, 549–561 *[481]*.

KENNEDY W.A. (1959) Clinical and electroencephalographic aspects of epileptogenic lesions of the medial surface and superior border of the cerebral hemisphere. *Brain* 82, 147–161 *[216, 421]*.

KENNEDY W. & SECCOMBE B. (1959) Quoted by James I.P. (1960) *Journal of Mental Science* 106, 543–558 *[232]*.

KERR T.A., KAY D.W.K. & LASSMAN L.P. (1971) Characteristics of patients, type of accident, and mortality in a consecutive series of head injuries admitted to a neurosurgical unit. *British Journal of Preventive and Social Medicine* 25, 179–185 *[148]*.

KERR T.A., SCHAPIRA K. & ROTH M. (1969) The relationship between premature death and affective disorders. *British Journal of Psychiatry* 115, 1277–1282 *[638]*.

KERSHAW P.W. (1967) Blood thiamine and nicotinic acid levels in alcoholism and confusional states. *British Journal of Psychiatry* 113, 387–393 *[516]*.

KERTESZ A. (1967) Paroxysmal kinesigenic choreoathetosis. *Neurology* 17, 680–690 *[258]*.

KERTESZ A. & BENSON D.F. (1970) Neologistic jargon: a clinicopathological study. *Cortex* 6, 362–386 *[48]*.

KESCHNER M., BENDER M.B. & STRAUSS I. (1936) Mental symptoms in cases of tumour of the temporal lobe. *Archives of Neurology and Psychiatry* 35, 572–596 *[193, 194, 195]*.

KESCHNER M., BENDER M.B. & STRAUSS I. (1937) Mental symptoms in cases of subtentorial tumour. *Archives of Neurology and Psychiatry* 37, 1–15 *[188, 200]*.

KESCHNER M., BENDER M.B. & STRAUSS I. (1938) Mental symptoms associated with brain tumour: a study of 530 verified cases. *Journal of the American Medical Association* 110, 714–718 *[187, 189, 190, 197]*.

KESHAVAN M.S., CHANNABASAVANNA S.M. & REDDY G.M. (1981) Post-traumatic psychiatric disturbances: patterns and predictors of outcome. *British Journal of Psychiatry* 138, 157–160 *[170]*.

KESHAVAN M.S., KUMAR Y.V. & CHANNABASAVANNA S.M. (1979) A critical evaluation of infantile reflexes in neuropsychiatric diagnosis. *Indian Journal of Psychiatry* 21, 267–270 *[80]*.

KHAMNEI A.K. (1984) Psychosis, inappropriate antidiuretic hormone secretion, and water intoxication. *Lancet* 1, 963 *[445]*.

KIBRICK S. & GOODING G.W. (1965) Pathogenesis of infection with herpes simplex virus with special reference to nervous tissue. In *Slow, Latent and Temperate Virus Infections,* eds. Gajdusek D.C., Gibbs C.J. & Alpers M. National Institute of Neurological Diseases and Blindness Monograph No. 2, Washington, pp. 143–154 *[299]*.

KIDGER T., BARNES R.E., TRAUER T. & TAYLOR P.J. (1980) Subsyndromes of tardive dyskinesia. *Psychological Medicine* 10, 513–520 *[547]*.

KIDSON M.A. (1973) Personality and hypertension. *Journal of Psychosomatic Research* 17, 35–41 *[341]*.

KIEV A., CHAPMAN L.F., GUTHRIE T.C. & WOLFF H.G. (1962) The highest integrative functions and diffuse cerebral atrophy. *Neurology* 12, 385–393 *[120]*.

KIHLBOM M. (1969) Psychopathology of Turner's syndrome. *Acta Paedopsychiatrica* 36, 75–81 *[447]*.

KILOH L.G. (1961) Pseudo-dementia. *Acta Psychiatrica Scandinavica* 37, 336–351 *[404, 410, 413]*.

KILOH L.G., McCOMAS A.J., OSSLETON J.W. & UPTON A.R.M. (1981) *Clinical Electroencephalography,* 4th Edition. Butterworths: London *[110, 111, 113, 114, 202, 209, 356, 375]*.

KIMURA D. (1961) Some effects of temporal lobe damage on auditory perception. *Canadian Journal of Psychology* 15, 156–165 *[56]*.

KIMURA D. (1963) Right temporal lobe damage: perception of unfamiliar stimuli after damage. *Archives of Neurology* 8, 264–271 *[56]*.

KIMURA D. (1964) Left-right differences in the perception of melodies. *Quarterly Journal of Experimental Psychology* 16, 355–358 [56].

KIND H. (1958) Die Psychiatrie der Hypophyseninsuffienz speziell der Simmondsschen Krankheit. *Fortschritte der Neurologie-Psychiatrie* 26, 501–563 [443].

KING M.D., DAY R.E., OLIVER J.S., LUSH M. & WATSON J.M. (1981) Solvent encephalopathy. *British Medical Journal* 283, 663–665 [536, 537].

KINSBOURNE M. & WARRINGTON E.K. (1962a) A disorder of simultaneous form perception. *Brain* 85, 461–486 [54].

KINSBOURNE M. & WARRINGTON E.K. (1962b) A study of finger agnosia. *Brain* 85, 47–66 [58, 91].

KINSBOURNE M. & WARRINGTON E.K. (1963) The localizing significance of limited simultaneous visual form perception. *Brain* 86, 697–702 [54].

KINSBOURNE M. & WARRINGTON E.K. (1964) Disorders of spelling. *Journal of Neurology, Neurosurgery and Psychiatry* 27, 224–228 [58].

KLABER M. & LACEY J. (1968) Epidemic of glandular fever. *British Medical Journal* 3, 124 [302].

KLAWANS H.L. (1973) The pharmacology of tardive dyskinesia. *American Journal of Psychiatry* 130, 82–86 [548].

KLAWANS H.L., FALK D.K., NAUSIEDA P.A. & WEINER W.J. (1978) Gilles de la Tourette syndrome after long-term chlorpromazine therapy. *Neurology* 28, 1064–1066 [584].

KLAWANS H.L., GOETZ C.G., PAULSON G.W. & BARBEAU A. (1980) Levodopa and pre-symptomatic detection of Huntington's disease—eight-year follow-up. *New England Journal of Medicine* 302, 1090 [395].

KLAWANS H.L., PAULSON G.W., RINGEL S.P. & BARBEAU A. (1973) The use of L-dopa in the presymptomatic detection of Huntington's chorea. In *Advances in Neurology, vol. 1, Huntington's Chorea, 1872–1972*, eds. Barbeau A., Chase T.N. & Paulson G.W. Raven Press: New York [395].

KLEE A. (1968) *A Clinical Study of Migraine with Particular Reference to the Most Severe Cases.* Munksgaard: Copenhagen [348, 349, 351].

KLEE A. & WILLANGER R. (1966) Disturbances of visual perception in migraine. *Acta Neurologica Scandinavica* 42, 400–414 [352].

KLEIN D. (1959) Ten years' inquiries about myotonic dystrophy in Switzerland (1945–1956). In *First International Congress of Neurological Sciences*, vol. 1, eds. van Bogaert L. & Radermecker J. Pergamon: London, pp. 318–319 [615].

KLEIN R. (1952) Immediate effects of leucotomy on cerebral functions and their significance. *Journal of Mental Science* 98, 60–65 [26].

KLEIN R. & MAYER-GROSS W. (1957) *The Clinical Examination of Patients with Organic Cerebral Disease.* Cassell: London [84].

KLEINE W. (1925) Periodische Schlafsucht. *Monatsschrift für Psychiatrie und Neurologie* 57, 285–320 [628].

KLEIST K. (1934) *Kriegverletzungen des Gehirns in ihrer Bedeutung für Hirnlokalisation und Hirnpathologie.* Barth: Leipzig. Quoted by Tow P.M. (1955), *Personality Changes Following Frontal Leucotomy*, Oxford University Press [154].

KLEIST K. (1937) Bericht über die Gehirnpathologie in ihrer Bedeutung für Neurologie und Psychiatrie. *Zeitschrift für die gesampte Neurologie und Psychiatrie* 158, 159–192 [22].

KLIGMAN D. & GOLDBERG D.A. (1975) Temporal lobe epilepsy and aggression. *Journal of Nervous and Mental Disease* 160, 324–341 [233].

KLONOFF H., LOW M.D. & CLARK C. (1977) Head injuries in children: a prospective five year follow-up. *Journal of Neurology, Neurosurgery, and Psychiatry* 40, 1211–1219 [172].

KLOTZ M. (1957) Incidence of brain tumours in patients hospitalised for chronic mental disorders. *Psychiatric Quarterly* 31, 669–680 [203].

KLÜVER H. & BUCY P.C. (1939) Preliminary analysis of functions of the temporal lobes in monkeys. *Archives of Neurology and Psychiatry* 42, 979–1000 [23, 71].

KNEHR C.A. & BEARN A.G. (1956) Psychological impairment in Wilson's disease. *Journal of Nervous and Mental Disease* 124, 251–255 [566].

KNOX J.W. & NELSON J.R. (1966) Permanent encephalopathy from toluene inhalation. *New England Journal of Medicine* 275, 1494–1496 [537].

KNOX S.J. (1968) Epileptic automatism and violence. *Medicine, Science and the Law* 8, 96–104 [221, 242].

KOEHLER K. & JAKUMEIT U. (1976) Subacute sclerosing panencephalitis presenting as Leonhard's speech-prompt catatonia. *British Journal of Psychiatry* 129, 29–31 [306].

KOENIG H. (1968) Dementia associated with the benign form of multiple sclerosis. *Transactions of the American Neurological Association* 93, 227–231 [592].

KOFMAN O. & HYLAND H.H. (1959) Tuberose sclerosis in adults with normal intelligence. *Archives of Neurology and Psychiatry* 81, 43–48 [601].

KOGEORGOS J., FONAGY P. & SCOTT D.F. (1982) Psychiatric symptom patterns of chronic epileptics attending a neurological clinic: a controlled investigation. *British Journal of Psychiatry* 140, 236–243 [243].

KOGEORGOS J. & SCOTT D.F. (1981) Biofeedback and its clinical applications. *British Journal of Hospital Medicine* 25, 601–603 [273, 355].

KOLARSKY A., FREUND K., MACHEK J. & POLAK O. (1967) Male sexual deviation. Association with early temporal lobe damage. *Archives of General Psychiatry* 17, 735–743 [239].

KOLANSKY H. & MOORE W.T. (1971) Effects of marihuana on adolescents and young adults. *Journal of the American Medical Association* 216, 486–492 [527].

KOLANSKY H. & MOORE W.T. (1972) Toxic effects of chronic marihuana use. *Journal of the American Medical Association* 222, 35–41 [527].

KOLODNY R.C. (1971) Sexual dysfunction in diabetic females. *Diabetes* 20, 557–559 [455].

KOLODNY R.C., KAHN C.B., GOLDSTEIN H.H. & BARNETT D.M. (1974) Sexual dysfunction in diabetic men. *Diabetes* 23, 306–309 [455].

KOPELMAN M.D. (1985a) Rates of forgetting in Alzheimer-type dementia and Korsakoff's syndrome. *Neuropsychologia* 23, 623–638 [31].

KOPELMAN M.D. (1985b) Multiple memory deficits in Alzheimer-type dementia: implications for pharmacotherapy. *Psychological Medicine* 15, 527–541 [31, 36].

KOREIN J. & BRUDNY J. (1976) Integrated EMG feedback in the management of spasmodic torticollis and focal dystonia: a prospective study of 80 patients. In *The Basal Ganglia*. Association for Research in Nervous and Mental Disease 55, ed. Yahr M.D., pp. 385–424. Raven Press: New York [576].

KORMAN M., TRIMBOLI F. & SEMLER I. (1980) A comparative evaluation of 162 inhalant users. *Addictive Behaviors* 5, 143–152 [537].

KOROLENKO C.P., YEVSEYEVA T.A. & VOLKOV P.P. (1969) Data for a comparative account of toxic psychoses of various aetiologies. *British Journal of Psychiatry* 115, 273–279 [538].

KORSAKOFF S.S. (1887) Disturbance of psychic function in alcoholic paralysis and its relation to the disturbance of the psychic sphere in multiple neuritis of non-alcoholic origin. *Vestnik Psichiatrii,*

Vol. IV, fasicle 2. Quoted by Victor M., Adams R.D. & Collins G.H. (1971) *The Wernicke-Korsakoff Syndrome*. Blackwell Scientific Publications: Oxford *[492]*.

KORSGAARD S. (1976) Baclofen (Lioresal) in the treatment of neuroleptic-induced tardive dyskinesia. *Acta Psychiatrica Scandinavica* 54, 17–24 *[550]*.

KOSSMANN C.E. (1947) Severe anoxic anoxia: follow-up report of a case with recovery. *Journal of Aviation Medicine* 18, 465–470 *[468]*.

KOVANEN J., HALTIA M. & CANTELL K. (1980) Failure of interferon to modify Creutzfeldt-Jakob disease. *British Medical Journal* 280, 902 *[427]*.

KOZOL H.L. (1945) Pretraumatic personality and sequelae of head injury. *Archives of Neurology and Psychiatry* 53, 358–364 *[147, 149]*.

KOZOL H.L. (1946) Pretraumatic personality and psychiatric sequelae of head injury. *Archives of Neurology and Psychiatry* 56, 245–275 *[149]*.

KRAEPELIN A. (1896) *Psychiatrie*, 5th edn. Barth: Leipzig *[428]*.

KRAEPELIN E. (1910) *Psychaitrie, vol. 2: Klinische Psychiatrie*. Barth: Leipzig *[647]*.

KRAFT E., FINBY N. & SCHILLINGER A. (1963) Routine skull roentgenography of psychiatric hospital admissions. *American Journal of Roentgenography* 89, 1212–1219 *[115, 293]*.

KRAFT E., SCHILLINGER A., FINBY N. & HALPERIN M. (1965) Routine skull radiography in a neuropsychiatric hospital. *American Journal of Psychiatry* 121, 1011–1012 *[115, 203]*.

KRAL V.A. (1959) Amnesia and the amnestic syndrome. *Canadian Psychiatric Association Journal* 4, 61–68 *[36]*.

KRAL V.A. (1962) Senescent forgetfulness: benign and malignant. *Canadian Medical Association Journal* 86, 257–260 *[374]*.

KRAL V.A. (1978) Benign senescent forgetfulness. In *Alzheimer's Disease: Senile Dementia and Related Disorders, Aging* Vol 7, eds. Katzman R., Terry R.D. & Bick K.L., pp. 47–51. Raven Press: New York *[374]*.

KRAL V.A. & DUROST H.B. (1953) A comparative study of the amnesic syndrome in various organic conditions. *American Journal of Psychiatry* 110, 41–47 *[26]*.

KRAPF E.E. (1957) On the pathogenesis of epileptic and hysterical seizures. *Bulletin of the World Health Organisation* 16, 749–762 *[220, 259]*.

KRÄUPL-TAYLOR F. (1966) *Psychopathology: Its Causes and Symptoms*. Butterworths: London *[409, 410]*.

KRAUSS S. (1946) Post-choreic personality and neurosis. *Journal of Mental Sciences* 92, 75–95 *[316, 317]*.

KRAUSS S. (1957) Schizophreniform psychoses in the later lives of encephalopathic persons. *Report of Second International Congress of Psychiatry, Zurich*, vol. 2, 100–103 *[317]*.

KRAWIECKI J.A., COUPER L. & WALTON D. (1957) The efficacy of parentrovite in the treatment of a group of senile psychotics. *Journal of Mental Science* 103, 601–605 *[424]*.

KREISLER O., LIBERT E. & HORWITT M.K. (1948) Psychiatric observations on induced vitamin B complex deficiency in psychotic patients. *American Journal of Psychiatry* 105, 107–110 *[488]*.

KREMER M. (1943) Discussion on disorders of personality after head injury. *Proceedings of the Royal Society of Medicine* 37, 564–566 *[152]*.

KRETSCHMER E. (1949) Die Orbitalhirn- und Zwischenhirnsyndrome nach Schädelbasisfrakturen. *Allgemeine Zeitschrift für Psychatrie* 124, 358–360 *[154]*.

KRETSCHMER E. (1956) Lokalisation und Beurteilung psychophysischer Syndrome bei Hirnverletzten. In *Das Hirntrauma*, ed. Rehwald E., pp. 155–158. Thieme: Stuttgart *[154]*.

KRETSCHMER H. (1968) Zur Klinik des Balkensyndroms. *Archiv für Psychiatrie und Nervenkrankeiten* 211, 250–265 *[654]*.

KRISTENSEN O. & SINDRUP E.H. (1978a) Psychomotor epilepsy and psychosis. I. Physical aspects. *Acta Neurologica Scandinavica* 57, 361–369 *[248, 250, 251, 252]*.

KRISTENSEN O. & SINDRUP E.H. (1978b) Psychomotor epilepsy and psychosis. II. Electroencephalographic findings (sphenoidal electrode recordings). *Acta Neurologica Scandinavica* 57, 370–379 *[249, 251]*.

KRONFOL Z., GREDEN J. & CARROLL B. (1981) Psychiatric aspects of diabetes mellitus: diabetes and depression. *British Journal of Psychiatry* 139, 172–173 *[456]*.

KRONFOL Z., HAMSHER K. DE S., DIGRE K. & WAZIRI R. (1978) Depression and hemispheric functions: changes associated with unilateral ECT. *British Journal of Psychiatry* 132, 560–567 *[76]*.

KRUSE R. & BLANKENHORN V. (1973) Zusammenfassender Erfahrungsbericht über die klinische Anwendung und Wirksamkeit von Ro 5–4023 (Clonezepam) auf verschiedene Formen epileptischer Anfälle. *Acta Neurologica Scandinavica*, supplement 53, 60–71 *[270]*.

KRYNICKI V.E. (1978) Cerebral dysfunction in repetitively assaultive adolescents. *Journal of Nervous and Mental Disease* 166, 59–67 *[74]*.

KUEHNLE J., MENDELSON J.H., DAVIS K.R. & NEW P.F.J. (1977) Computed tomographic examination of heavy marijuana smokers. *Journal of the American Medical Association* 237, 1231–1232 *[528]*.

KUHL D.E., PHELPS M.E., MARKHAM C.H., METTER J., RIEGE W.H. & WINTER J. (1982) Cerebral metabolism and atrophy in Huntington's disease determined by ^{18}FDG and computed tomographic scan. *Annals of Neurology* 12, 425–434 *[124]*.

KUGLER J. (1964) *Electroencephalography in Hospital and General Consulting Practice: An Introduction*. Elsevier: Amsterdam *[111, 112, 300, 375, 522]*.

KUPFER D.J., HIMMELHOCH J.M., SWARTZBURG M., ANDERSON C., BUICK R. & DETRE T.P. (1972) Hypersomnia in manic-depressive disease (a preliminary report). *Diseases of the Nervous System* 33, 720–724 *[631]*.

KURIANSKY J.B., GURLAND B.J. & FLEISS J.L. (1976) The assessment of self-care capacity in geriatric psychiatric patients by objective and subjective methods. *Journal of Clinical Psychology* 32, 95–102 *[108]*.

KURLAND G.S., HAMOLSKY M.W. & FREEDBERG A.S. (1955) Studies in non-myxoedematous hypometabolism. 1: The clinical syndrome and the effect of triiodothyronine, alone or combined with thyroxine. *Journal of Clinical Endocrinology and Metabolism* 15, 1354–1366 *[435]*.

KURLAND L.T., FARO S.N. & SIEDLER H. (1960) The outbreak of a neurologic disorder in Minamata, Japan, and its relationship to the ingestion of seafood contaminated by mercuric compounds. *World Neurology* 1, 370–395 *[543]*.

KURLAND L.T. & MULDER D.W. (1954) Epidemiologic investigations of amyotrophic lateral sclerosis. *Neurology* 4, 355–378 and 438–448 *[605]*.

KURLAND M.L. (1965) Gilles de la Tourette's syndrome: the psychotherapy of two cases. *Comprehensive Psychiatry* 6, 298–305 *[583, 586]*.

KURZE T., TRANQUADA R.E. & BENEDICT K. (1966) Spinal fluid lactic acid levels in acute cerebral injury. Ch. 22 in *Head Injury: Conference Proceedings*, eds. Caveness W.F. & Walker A.E. Lippincott: Philadelphia *[140]*.

LAGENSTEIN I., WILLIG R.P. & KÜHNE D. (1979) Reversible cerebral atrophy caused by corticotrophin. *Lancet* i, 1246–1247 *[122]*.

LAHEY F.H. (1931) Non-activated (apathetic) type of hyperthyroidism. *New England Journal of Medicine* 204, 747–748 *[429, 431]*.

LAIRD S.M. (1962) Incidence of general paralysis of the insane. *British Medical Journal* 1, 524–526 *[277]*.

LAMBERT H. (1972) Virus infections of the central nervous system. *Medicine (monthly add-on series, 1972–3)* 5, 400–405. Medical Eduction (International) Ltd *[310]*.

LAMPERT P., TOM M.I. & CUMINGS J.N. (1962) Encephalopathy in Whipple's disease. A histochemical study. *Neurology* 12, 65–71 *[649]*.

LANCE J.W. (1982) *Mechanisms and Management of Headache*, 4th Edition. Butterworths: London *[344, 346, 353]*.

LANCET (1950) Death of a mind: a study of disintegration by an anonymous author. *Lancet* 1, 1012–1015 *[422]*.

LANCET (1966a) Leading article: Encephalitis of lethargica type in a mental hospital. *Lancet* 2, 1014–1015 *[294]*.

LANCET (1966b) Leading article: Polyoma virus and leuco-encephalopathy. *Lancet* 1, 353–354 *[646]*.

LANCET (1970) Annotation: A new line on age pigment? *Lancet* 2, 451–452 *[425]*.

LANCET (1971) Annotation: Cannabis encephalopathy. *Lancet* 2, 1240–1241 *[528]*.

LANCET (1973) Zinc deficiency in man. *Lancet* 1, 299–300 *[478]*.

LANCET (1977) Cardiogenic dementia. *Lancet* 1, 27–28 *[373]*.

LANCET (1978) Factitious hypoglycaemia. *Lancet* 1, 1293 *[463]*.

LANCET (1981) Carotid stenosis. *Lancet* 1, 535–536 *[331]*.

LANCET (1984) Neuroleptic malignant syndrome. *Lancet* 1, 545–546 *[534]*.

LANDOLT H. (1958) Serial electroencephalographic investigations during psychotic episodes in epileptic patients and during schizophrenic attacks. Ch. 3 in *Lectures on Epilepsy*, ed. Lorentz de Haas A.M. Elsevier: Amsterdam *[223, 225, 245, 251]*.

LANGWORTHY O.R. (1948) Relation of personality problems to onset and progress of multiple sclerosis. *Archives of Neurology and Psychiatry* 59, 13–28 *[597]*.

LANGWORTHY O.R. (1950) A survey of the maladjustment problems in multiple sclerosis and the possibilities of psychotherapy. Ch. 40 in *Multiple Sclerosis and the Demyelinating Diseases*, Research Publications of the Association for Research in Nervous and Mental Disease, vol. 28. Williams & Wilkins: Baltimore *[597, 598]*.

LANGWORTHY O.R. & BETZ B.J. (1944) Narcolepsy as a type of response to emotional conflicts. *Psychosomatic Medicine* 6, 211–226 *[621]*.

LANGWORTHY O.R., KOLB L.C. & ANDROP S. (1941) Disturbances of behaviour in patients with disseminated sclerosis. *American Journal of Psychiatry* 98, 243–249 *[595, 597]*.

LANGWORTHY O.R. & LE GRAND D. (1952) Personality structure and psychotherapy in multiple sclerosis. *American Journal of Medicine* 12, 586–592 *[598]*.

LANSDELL H. & MIRSKY A.F. (1964) Attention in focal and centrencephalic epilepsy. *Experimental Neurology* 9, 463–469 *[230]*.

LANSDOWN R.G., SHEPHERD J., CLAYTON B.E., DELVES H.T., GRAHAM P.J. & TURNER W.C. (1974) Blood-lead levels, behaviour and intelligence. A population study. *Lancet* 1, 538–541 *[539]*.

LAPRESLE J. & FARDEAU M. (1967) The central nervous system and carbon monoxide poisoning, II: Anatomical study of brain lesions following intoxication with carbon monoxide (22 cases). In *Carbon Monoxide Poisoning*, eds. Bour H. & Ledingham I.McA. Progress in Brain Research, vol. 24. Elsevier: Amsterdam *[471]*.

LARSBY H. & LINDGREN E. (1940) Encephalographic examinations of 125 institutionalised epileptics. *Acta Psychiatrica et Neurologica* 15, 337–352 *[121]*.

LARSSON T., SJÖGREN T. & JACOBSON G. (1963) Senile dementia: a clinical, sociomedical and genetic study. *Acta Psychiatrica Scandinavica*, supplement 167, 1–259 *[372, 373, 389]*.

LASHLEY K.S. (1929) *Brain Mechanisms and Intelligence*. University of Chicago Press. Reissued 1963, Dover Publications: New York *[21]*.

LAURENT J., DEBRY G. & FLOQUET J. (1971) *Hypoglycaemic Tumours*. Excerpta Medica: Amsterdam *[465]*.

LAUTER H. & MEYER J.E. (1968) Clinical and nosological concepts of senile dementia. In *Senile Dementia: Clinical and Therapeutic Aspects*, eds. Müller C.H. & Ciompi L. Huber: Bern *[373, 374, 379, 385]*.

LAVENDER A. (1981) A behavioural approach to the treatment of epilepsy. *Behavioural Psychotherapy* 9, 231–243 *[272]*.

LAW W.R. & NELSON E.R. (1968) Gasoline-sniffing by an adult: report of a case with the unusual complication of lead encephalopathy. *Journal of the American Medical Association* 204, 1002–1004 *[537]*.

LAWSON I.R. & MACLEOD R.D.M. (1969) The use of imipramine ('Tofranil') and other psychotrophic drugs in organic emotionalism. *British Journal of Psychiatry* 115, 281–285 *[334]*.

LEBENSOHN Z.M. & JENKINS R.B. (1975) Improvement in parkinsonism in depressed patients treated with ECT. *American Journal of Psychiatry* 132, 283–285 *[558]*.

LE BOEUF A., LODGE J. & EAMES P.G. (1978) Vasopressin and memory in Korsakoff syndrome. *Lancet* 2, 1370 *[499]*.

LEBOWITZ H.E. (1965) Endocrine-metabolic syndromes associated with neoplasms. Ch. 11 in *The Remote Effects of Cancer on the Nervous System*, eds. Brain W.R. & Norris F.H. Contemporary Neurology Symposia, vol. 1. Grune & Stratton: New York *[637]*.

LECHE P. (1972) Speech therapy and the treatment of cerebrovascular diseases. *Proceedings of the Royal Society of Medicine* 65, 85–88 *[333]*.

LECKMAN J., ANANTH J.V., BAN T.A. & LEHMANN H.E. (1971) Pentylenetetrazol in the treatment of geriatric patients with disturbed memory function. *Journal of Clinical Pharmacology* 11, 301–303 *[424]*.

LEDINGHAM J.G.G. (1983) Water and sodium homeostasis. In *Oxford Textbook of Medicine* Vol. 2. eds. Weatherall D.J., Ledingham J.G.G. & Warrell D.A., pp. 18.19–18.28. Oxford University Press *[444]*.

LEE K., MOLLER L., HARDT F., HAUBER A. & JENSEN E. (1979) Alcohol-induced brain damage and liver damage in young males. *Lancet* 2, 759–761 *[521]*.

LEE W.R. (1981) What happens in lead poisoning? *Journal of the Royal College of Physicians of London* 15, 48–54 *[538]*.

LEES A.J., ROBERTSON M., TRIMBLE M.R. & MURRAY N.M.F. (1984) A clinical study of Gilles de la Tourette syndrome in the United Kingdom. *Journal of Neurology, Neurosurgery, and Psychiatry* 47, 1–8 *[584]*.

LEES A.J. & SMITH E. (1983) Cognitive deficits in the early stages of Parkinson's disease. *Brain* 106, 257–270 *[556]*.

LEES F. (1970) *The Diagnosis and Treatment of Diseases Affecting the Nervous System*, vols. 1 and 2. Staples Press: London *[302, 304, 316]*.

LEGG N.J. (1967) Virus antibodies in subacute sclerosing panencephalitis: a study of 22 patients. *British Medical Journal* 3, 350–352 *[305]*.

LEGG N.J. (1979) Intracerebral abscess. *British Journal of Hospital Medicine* 22, 608–614 *[313]*.

LEGROS J.J., GILOT P., SERON X., CLAESSENS J., ADAM A., MOEGLEN J.M., AUDIBERT A. & BERCHIER P. (1978) Influence of vasopressin on learning and memory. *Lancet* 1, 41–42 *[499]*.

LEHMANN H.E. & BAN T.A. (1968) Studies with new drugs in the treatment of convulsive disorders. *International Journal of*

Clinical Pharmacology, Therapy and Toxicology 1, 230–234 [268].

LEHMANN H.J. & LAMPE H. (1970) Observations on the inter-hemispheric transmission of information in 9 patients with corpus callosum defect. *European Neurology* 4, 129–147 [654].

LEIDER W., MAGOFFIN R.L., LENNETTE E.H. & LEONARDS L.N.R. (1965) Herpes-simplex-virus encephalitis: its possible association with reactivated latent infection. *New England Journal of Medicine* 273, 341–347 [300].

LEIGH A.D. (1946) Infections of the nervous system occurring during an epidemic of influenza B. *British Medical Journal* 2, 936–938 [297].

LEIGH D. (1951) Subacute necrotizing encephalomyelopathy in an infant. *Journal of Neurology, Neurosurgery, and Psychiatry* 14, 216–221 [500].

LEIGH D. (1952) Pellagra and the nutritional neuropathies: a neuropathological review. *Journal of Mental Science* 98, 130–142 [489].

LE MAY M. (1976) Morphological cerebral asymmetries and modern man, fossil man, and non-human primate. *Annals of the New York Academy of Sciences* 280, 349–366 [38].

LE MAY M. (1977) Asymmetries of the skull and handedness. *Journal of the Neurological Sciences* 32, 243–253 [38].

LE MAY M. & GESCHWIND N. (1978) Asymmetries of the human cerebral hemispheres. Ch. 15 in *Language Acquisition and Language Breakdown: Parallels and Divergencies*, eds. Caramazza A. & Zurif E.B. Johns Hopkins University Press: Baltimore and London [38].

LENNOX B. & PRITCHARD S. (1950) The association of bronchial carcinoma and peripheral neuritis. *Quarterly Journal of Medicine* 19, 97–109 [633].

LENNOX W.G. (1960) *Epilepsy and Related Disorders*, vols. 1 and 2. Churchill: London [208, 211, 221, 223, 228].

LENZI G.L., JONES T., REID J.L. & MOSS S. (1979) Regional impairment of cerebral oxidative metabolism in Parkinson's disease. *Journal of Neurology, Neurosurgery, and Psychiatry* 42, 59–62 [557].

LEREBOULLET J., PLUVINAGE R. & AMSTUTZ A. (1956) Aspects cliniques et électroencephalographiques des atrophies cerebrales alcooliques. *Revue Neurologique* 94, 674–682 [519].

LESSELL S., HIRANO A., TORRES J. & KURLAND L.T. (1962) Parkinsonism-dementia complex. *Archives of Neurology* 7, 377–385 [605].

LESSER R. & REICH S. (1982) Language disorders. Ch. 5 in *The Pathology and Psychology of Cognition*. ed. Burton A. Methuen: London [40].

LETEMENDIA F. & PAMPIGLIONE G. (1958) Clinical and electro-encephalographic observations in Alzheimer's disease. *Journal of Neurology, Neurosurgery and Psychiatry* 21, 167–172 [379].

LETEMENDIA F.J.J., PROWSE A. & SOUTHMAYD S. (1981) Diagnostic use of sleep deprivation. *British Journal of Psychiatry* 138, 352 [412].

LEVIN M. (1933) The pathogenesis of narcolepsy: with a consideration of sleep-paralysis and localized sleep. *Journal of Neurology and Psychopathology* 14, 1–14 [621].

LEVIN M. (1935) The pathogenesis of cataplexy on anger. *Journal of Neurology and Psychopathology* 16, 140–143 [621].

LEVIN M. (1936) Periodic somnolence and morbid hunger: a new syndrome. *Brain* 59, 494–504 [628].

LEVIN M. (1953) Aggression, guilt and cataplexy. *Archives of Neurology and Psychiatry* 69, 224–235 [619, 624].

LEVIN M.E. (1960) 'Metabolic insufficiency': a double-blind study using triiodothyronine, thyroxine and a placebo: psychometric evaluation of the hypometabolic patient. *Journal of Clinical Endocrinology and Metabolism* 20, 106–115 [435].

LEVINE D.N. & FINKLESTEIN S. (1982) Delayed psychosis after right temporoparietal stroke or trauma: relation to epilepsy. *Neurology* 32, 267–273 [330].

LEVY R., ISAACS A. & BEHRMAN J. (1971) Neurophysiological correlates of senile dementia: II. The somatosensory evoked response. *Psychological Medicine* 1, 159–165 [373].

LEVY R., ISAACS A. & HAWKS G. (1970) Neurophysiological correlates of senile dementia: 1. Motor and sensory nerve conduction velocity. *Psychological Medicine* 1, 40–47 [373].

LEVY R.M., BREDESEN D.E. & ROSENBLUM M.L. (1985) Neurological manifestations of the acquired immunodeficiency syndrome (AIDS): experience at UCSF and review of the literature. *Journal of Neurosurgery* 62, 475–495 [316].

LEWIN W. (1959) The management of prolonged unconsciousness after head injury. *Proceedings of the Royal Society of Medicine* 52, 880–884 [142].

LEWIN W. (1966) *The Management of Head Injuries*. Baillière, Tindall & Cassell: London [137, 181].

LEWIN W. (1968) Rehabilitation after head injury. *British Medical Journal* 1, 465–470 [137, 181].

LEWIN W. (1970) Rehabilitation needs of the brain-injured patient. *Proceedings of the Royal Society of Medicine* 63, 28–32 [183, 213].

LEWINSOHN P.M., DANAHER B.G. & KIKEL S. (1977) Visual imagery as a mnemonic aid for brain-injured persons. *Journal of Consulting & Clinical Psychology* 45, 717–723 [182].

LEWIS A.J. (1938) Some recent aspects of dementia. In *Festskrift tillägnad Olof Kinberg*, pp. 238–244. Asbrink: Stockholm [180].

LEWIS A.J. (1942) Discussion on differential diagnosis and treatment of post-contusional states. *Proceedings of the Royal Society of Medicine* 35, 607–614 [147, 168].

LEWIS A.J. (1956) Psychological medicine. Section 19 in *Price's Textbook of the Practice of Medicine*, ed. Hunter D., Ninth Edition. Oxford University Press [316].

LEWIS A.J. & MINSKI L. (1935) Chorea and psychosis. *Lancet* 1, 536–538 [317].

LEWIS J.D., MORITZ D. & MELLIS L.P. (1981) Long-term toluene abuse. *American Journal of Psychiatry* 138, 368–370 [537].

LEWIS S.A., OSWALD I. & DUNLEAVY D.L.F. (1971) Chronic fenfluramine administration: some cerebral effects. *British Medical Journal* 3, 67–70 [535].

LEZAK M.D. (1976) *Neuropsychological Assessment*. Oxford University Press: New York [88].

LHERMITTE F. (1983) 'Utilization behaviour' and its relation to lesions of the frontal lobes. *Brain* 106, 237–255 [91].

LHERMITTE F. & SIGNORET J.L. (1972) Analyse neuropsychologique et différenciation des symptomes amnesiques. *Revue Neurologique* 126, 161–178 [35].

LIDDELL D.W. (1953) Observations on epileptic automatism in a mental hospital population. *Journal of Mental Science* 99, 732–748 [232].

LIDDELL D.W. (1958) Investigations of EEG findings in presenile dementia. *Journal of Neurology, Neurosurgery and Psychiatry* 21, 173–176 [379].

LIDVALL H.F., LINDEROTH B. & NORLIN B. (1974) Causes of the post-concussional syndrome. *Acta Neurologica Scandinavica*, Suppl. 56, 1–144 [170].

LIEBERMAN A., DZIATOLOWSKI M., KUPERRSMITH M., SERBY M., GOODGOLD A., KOREIN J. & GOLDSTEIN M. (1979) Dementia in Parkinson disease. *Annals of Neurology* 6, 355–359 [557].

LIEPMANN H. (1908) Über die agnostischen Störungen. *Neurologisches Centralblatt* 27, 609–617 and 664–675 [52].

LILLY R., CUMMINGS J.L., BENSON F. & FRANKEL M. (1983) The human Klüver-Bucy syndrome. *Neurology* 33, 1141–1145 [23].

LINDENBERG W. (1951) Hirnverletzung, organische Wesensänderung, Neurose. *Nervenarzt* 22, 254–260 [154].

LINDGREN S.A. (1961) A study of the effect of protracted occupational exposure to carbon monoxide. *Acta Medica Scandinavica*, supplement 356, 1–135 *[472]*.

LINDQVIST G. & NORLÉN G. (1966) Korsakoff's syndrome after operation on ruptured aneurysm of the anterior communicating artery. *Acta Psychiatrica Scandinavica* 42, 24–34 *[337]*.

LINDSAY J., OUNSTED C. & RICHARDS P. (1979a) Long-term outcome in children with temporal lobe seizures: I. Social outcome and childhood factors. *Developmental Medicine and Child Neurology* 21, 285–298 *[233]*.

LINDSAY J., OUNSTED C. & RICHARDS P. (1979b) Long-term outcome in children with temporal lobe seizures. II. Marriage, parenthood and sexual indifference. *Developmental Medicine and Child Neurology* 21, 433–440 *[239]*.

LINDSAY J., OUNSTED C. & RICHARDS P. (1979c) Long-term outcome in children with temporal lobe epilepsy. III. Psychiatric aspects in childhood and adult life. *Developmental Medicine and Child Neurology* 21, 630–636 *[249]*.

LINNOILA M., VIUKARI M. & HIETALA O. (1976) Effects of sodium valproate on tardive dyskinesia. *British Journal of Psychiatry* 129, 114–119 *[550]*.

LIPOWSKI Z.J. (1967) Delirium, clouding of consciousness and confusion. *Journal of Nervous and Mental Disease* 145, 227–255 *[4]*.

LIPOWSKI Z.J. (1980a) *Delirium: Acute Brain Failure in Man*. Charles C. Thomas: Springfield, Illinois *[5, 7, 10]*.

LIPOWSKI Z.J. (1980b) A new look at organic brain syndromes. *American Journal of Psychiatry* 137, 674–678 *[8]*.

LIPPMAN C.W. (1952) Certain hallucinations peculiar to migraine. *Journal of Nervous and Mental Disease* 116, 346–351 *[350]*.

LIPPMAN C.W. (1953) Hallucinations of physical duality in migraine. *Journal of Nervous and Mental Disease* 117, 345–350 *[350, 351]*.

LIPPMANN S., MANSHADI M., BALDWIN H., DRASIN G., RICE J. & ALRAJEH S. (1982) Cerebellar vermis dimensions on computerised tomographic scans of schizophrenic and bipolar patients. *American Journal of Psychiatry* 139, 667–668 *[121, 122]*.

LIPSEY J.R., ROBINSON R.G., PEARLSON G.D., RAO K. & PRICE T.R. (1983) Mood change following bilateral hemisphere brain injury. *British Journal of Psychiatry* 143, 266–273 *[329]*.

LIPSEY J.R., ROBINSON R.G., PEARLSON G.D., RAO K. & PRICE T.R. (1984) Nortriptyline treatment of post-stroke depression: a double-blind study. *Lancet* 1, 297–300 *[334]*.

LISHMAN W.A. (1968) Brain damage in relation to psychiatric disability after head injury. *British Journal of Psychiatry* 114, 373–410 *[146, 152, 153, 155, 156, 168, 170]*.

LISHMAN W.A. (1969) Split minds: a review of the results of brain bisection in man. *British Journal of Hospital Medicine* 2, 477–484 *[276]*.

LISHMAN W.A. (1971) Emotion, consciousness and will after brain bisection in man. *Cortex* 7, 181–192 *[276]*.

LISHMAN W.A. (1972) Selective factors in memory. Part 1: age, sex and personality attributes. *Psychological Medicine* 2, 121–138 *[25]*.

LISHMAN W.A. (1973) The psychiatric sequelae of head injury: a review. *Psychological Medicine* 3, 304–318 *[150, 161, 166]*.

LISHMAN W.A. (1974) The speed of recall of pleasant and unpleasant experiences. *Psychological Medicine* 4, 212–218 *[25]*.

LISHMAN W.A. (1978) Psychiatric sequelae of head injuries: problems in diagnosis. *Journal of the Irish Medical Association* 71, 306–314 *[162, 167]*.

LISHMAN W.A. (1981) Cerebral disorder in alcoholism: syndromes of impairment. *Brain* 104, 1–20 *[491, 496, 497, 517]*.

LISHMAN W.A. (1983a) The apparatus of mind: brain structure and function in mental disorder. *Psychosomatics* 24, 699–720 *[76, 122]*.

LISHMAN W.A. (1983b) *Brain Damage and Psychiatric Disability*. Royal Hospital and Home for Incurables, Booklet 1/83, Putney, London *[185]*.

LISHMAN W.A. & MCMEEKAN E.R.L. (1977) Handedness in relation to direction and degree of cerebral dominance for language. *Cortex* 13, 30–43 *[37]*.

LISHMAN W.A., SYMONDS C.P., WHITTY C.W.M. & WILLISON R.G. (1962) Seizures induced by movement. *Brain* 85, 93–108 *[211, 258]*.

LISHMAN W.A. & WHITTY C.W.M. (1965) Seizures induced by movement. *Rivista di Patologia nervosa e mentale* 86, 237–243 *[258]*.

LISSAUER H. (1890) Ein Fall von Seelenblindheit nebst einem Beitrage zur Theorie derselben. *Archiv für Psychiatrie und Nervenkrankheiten* 21, 222–270 *[52]*.

LISTON E.H. & LA RUE A. (1983) Clinical differentiation of primary degenerative and multi-infarct dementia: a critical review of the evidence. Part II: pathological studies. *Biological Psychiatry* 18, 1467–1484 *[386]*.

LIU M.C. (1960) General paralysis of the insane in Peking between 1933 and 1943. *Journal of Mental Science* 106, 1082–1092 *[282]*.

LIU M.C. (1966) Clinical experience with sulthiame (ospolot). *British Journal of Psychiatry* 112, 621–628 *[268]*.

LIVERSEDGE L.A. (1969) Involuntary movements. Ch. 10 in *Handbook of Clinical Neurology*, vol. 1, eds. Vinken P.J. & Bruyn G.W. North Holland Publishing Company: Amsterdam *[578]*.

LIVERSEDGE L.A. & SYLVESTER J.D. (1955) Conditioning techniques in the treatment of writer's cramp. *Lancet* 1, 1147–1149 *[579]*.

LIVINGSTON K.E. (1977) Limbic system dysfunction induced by 'kindling': its significance for psychiatry. In *Neurosurgical Treatment in Psychiatry, Pain, and Epilepsy*, eds. Sweet W.H., Obrador S. & Martin-Rodriguez J.G., pp. 63–75. University Park Press: Baltimore *[251]*.

LLOYD E.A. & CLARK L.D. (1959) Convulsions and delirium incident to glutethimide (doriden) withdrawal. *Diseases of the Nervous System* 20, 524–526 *[534]*.

LLOYD G.G. & LISHMAN W.A. (1975) Effect of depression on the speed of recall of pleasant and unpleasant experiences. *Psychological Medicine* 5, 173–180 *[32]*.

LLOYD-STILL R.M. (1958) Psychosis following Asian influenza in Barbados. *Lancet* 2, 20–21 *[303]*.

LOESER J.D. & ALVORD E.C. (1968) Clinicopathological correlations in agenesis of the corpus callosum. *Neurology* 18, 745–756 *[654]*.

LOGUE V., DURWARD M., PRATT R.T.C., PIERCY M. & NIXON W.L.B. (1968) The quality of survival after rupture of an anterior cerebral aneurysm. *British Journal of Psychiatry* 114, 137–160 *[336, 337, 338]*.

LOIZOU L.A., KENDALL B.E. & MARSHALL J. (1981) Subacute arteriosclerotic encephalopathy: a clinical and radiological investigation. *Journal of Neurology, Neurosurgery, and Psychiatry* 44, 294–304 *[390, 391]*.

LÖKEN A.C. (1959) The pathologic-anatomical basis for late symptoms after brain injuries in adults. *Acta Psychiatrica et Neurologica Scandinavica*, supplement 137, 30–42 *[139, 140]*.

LOMBROSO C. (1911) *Crime: Its Causes and Remedies*. Translated by Horton H.P., 1918. Little, Brown & Co.: Boston *[241]*.

LONDON P.S. (1967) Some observations on the course of events after severe injury of the head. *Annals of the Royal College of Surgeons of England* 41, 460–479 *[137]*.

LONG J.A. & MCLACHLAN J.F.C. (1974) Abstract reasoning and perceptual-motor efficiency in alcoholics: impairment and reversibility. *Quarterly Journal of Studies on Alcohol* 35, 1220–1229 *[518]*.

LORANGER A.W., GOODELL H., LEE J.E. & MCDOWELL F. (1972a) Levodopa treatment of Parkinson's syndrome: improved intellectual functioning. *Archives of General Psychiatry* 26, 163–168 *[560]*.

LORANGER A.W., GOODELL H., MCDOWELL F.H., LEE J.E. &

SWEET R.D. (1972b) Intellectual impairment in Parkinson's syndrome. *Brain* 95, 405–412 *[556, 560]*.

LORBER J. (1961) Long-term follow-up of 100 children who recovered from tuberculous meningitis. *Pediatrics* 28, 778–791 *[311]*.

LORENTZ DE HAAS A.M. & MAGNUS O. (1958) Clinical and electroencephalographic findings in epileptic patients with episodic mental disorders. Ch. 4 in *Lectures on Epilepsy*, ed. Lorentz de Haas A.M. Elsevier: Amsterdam *[245, 252]*.

LOU H.O.C.L. (1968) Repeated episodes of transient global amnesia. *Acta Neurologica Scandinavica* 44, 612–618 *[359]*.

LOUDON J.B. & WARING H. (1976) Toxic reactions to lithium and haloperidol. *Lancet* 2, 1088 *[533]*.

LOURIA D.B. (1968) Lysergic acid diethylamide. *New England Journal of Medicine* 278, 435–438 *[528, 530]*.

LOVELAND N., SMITH B. & FORSTER F.M. (1957) Mental and emotional changes in epileptic patients on continuous anticonvulsant medication. *Neurology* 7, 856–865 *[230]*.

LUCAS R.N. & FALKOWSKI W. (1973) Ergotamine and methysergide abuse in patients with migraine. *British Journal of Psychiatry* 122, 199–203 *[354]*.

LUCHINS D.J., SHERWOOD P.M., GILLIN J.C., MENDELSON W.B. & WYATT R.J. (1978) Filicide during psychotropic-induced somnambulism: a case report. *American Journal of Psychiatry* 135, 1404–1405 *[632]*.

LUGARESI E., COCCAGNA G. & MANTOVANI M. (1978) *Hypersomnia with Periodic Apnea*. Advances in Sleep Research, Vol. IV. S.P. Medical and Scientific Books: London *[627]*.

VAN DER LUGT P.J.M. & DE VISSER A.P. (1967) Two patients with a vital expansive syndrome following a cerebrovascular accident. *Psychiatria, Neurologia, Neurochirurgia* 70, 349–359 *[330]*.

LUKIANOWICZ N. (1958) Autoscopic phenomena. *Archives of Neurology and Psychiatry* 80, 199–220 *[65]*.

LUKIANOWICZ N. (1967) 'Body image' disturbances in psychiatric disorders. *British Journal of Psychiatry* 113, 31–47 *[64, 65, 66]*.

LUND M. & TROLLE E. (1973) Clonazepam in the treatment of epilepsy. *Acta Neurologica Scandinavica*, supplement 53, 82–90 *[269]*.

LUNDERVOLD A., REFSUM S. & JACOBSEN W. (1969) The EEG in dystrophia myotonica. *European Neurology* 2, 279–284 *[615]*.

LUNDQUIST G. (1961) Delirium tremens: a comparative study of pathogenesis, course, and prognosis with delirium tremens. *Acta Psychiatrica Scandinavica* 36, 443–466 *[516]*.

LURIA A.R. (1964) Neuropsychology in the local diagnosis of brain damage. *Cortex* 1, 3–18 *[22]*.

LURIA A.R. (1966) *Higher Cortical Functions in Man*. Tavistock Publications: London *[70, 90]*.

LURIA A.R. & HOMSKAYA E.D. (1964) Disturbance in the regulative role of speech with frontal lobe lesions. Ch. 17 in *The Frontal Granular Cortex and Behaviour*, eds. Warren J.M. & Akert K. McGraw-Hill: New York *[70, 105]*.

LURIA A.R., KARPOV B.A. & YARBUSS A.L. (1966) Disturbances of active visual perception with lesions of the frontal lobes. *Cortex* 2, 202–212 *[70, 71]*.

LURIA A.R., PRAVDINA-VINARSKAYA E.N. & YARBUSS A.L. (1963) Disorders of ocular movement in a case of simultanagnosia. *Brain* 86, 219–228 *[54]*.

LYCKE E., NORRBY R. & ROOS B. (1974) A serological study on mentally ill patients: with particular reference to the prevalence of herpes virus infections. *British Journal of Psychiatry* 124, 273–279 *[301]*.

LYLE O.E. & GOTTESMAN I.I. (1977) Premorbid psychometric indicators of the gene for Huntington's disease. *Journal of Consulting and Clinical Psychology* 45, 1011–1022 *[394]*.

LYLE O. & QUAST W. (1976) The Bender Gestalt: use of clinical judgement versus recall scores in prediction of Huntington's disease. *Journal of Consulting & Clinical Psychology* 44, 229–232 *[394]*.

LYNCH M.J.G. (1960) Brain lesions in chronic alcoholism. *Archives of Pathology* 69, 342–353 *[518, 519]*.

LYON R.L. (1962) Huntington's chorea in the Moray Firth area. *British Medical Journal* 1, 1301–1306 *[393, 396]*.

MAAS O. & PATERSON A.S. (1937) Mental changes in families affected by dystrophia myotonica. *Lancet* 1, 21–23 *[615, 616]*.

MAAS O. & PATERSON A.S. (1950) Myotonia congenita, dystrophia myotonica and paramyotonia: reaffirmation of their identity. *Brain* 73, 318–336 *[617]*.

MABILLE H. & PITRES A. (1913) Sur un cas d'amnésie de fixation post-apoplectique ayant persisté pendant vingt-trois ans. *Revue de Médicine* 33, 257–279 *[27]*.

MACALPINE I. & HUNTER R. (1966) The 'insanity' of King George III: a classic case of porphyria. *British Medical Journal* 1, 65–71 *[482]*.

MACALPINE I., HUNTER R. & RIMINGTON C. (1968) Porphyria in the royal houses of Stuart, Hanover, and Prussia: a follow-up study of George III's illness. *British Medical Journal* 1, 7–18 *[482]*.

MCARDLE B. (1964) Metabolic and endocrine myopathies. Ch. 15 in *Disorders of Voluntary Muscle*, ed. Walton J.N. Churchill: London *[617]*.

MCCABE R.E., GIBBONS D., BROOKS R.G., LUFT B.J. & REMINGTON J.S. (1983) Agglutination test for diagnosis of toxoplasmosis in AIDS. *Lancet* 2, 680 *[316]*.

MCCONKEY B. & DAWS R.A. (1958) Neurological disorders associated with Asian influenza. *Lancet* 2, 15–17 *[303]*.

MCCORMICK H.M. & NEUBERGER K.T. (1958) Giant-cell arteritis involving small meningeal and intracerebral vessels. *Journal of Neuropathology and Experimental Neurology* 17, 471–478 *[368]*.

MCDERMOTT J.R., FRASER H. & DICKINSON A.G. (1978a) Reduced choline-acetyltransferase activity in scrapie mouse brain. *Lancet* 2, 318–319 *[384]*.

MCDERMOTT J.R., SMITH A.I., WARD M.K., PARKINSON I.S. & KERR D.N.S. (1978b) Brain-aluminium concentration in dialysis encephalopathy. *Lancet* 1, 901–904 *[475]*.

MCDERMOTT J.R., SMITH I.A., IQBAL K. & WISNIEWSKI H.M. (1979) Brain aluminium in aging and Alzheimer disease. *Neurology* 29, 809–814 *[384]*.

MCDONALD C. (1969) Clinical heterogeneity in senile dementia. *British Journal of Psychiatry* 115, 267–271 *[374]*.

MACDONALD I.J. (1963) A case of Gilles de la Tourette's syndrome, with some aetiological observations. *British Journal of Psychiatry* 109, 206–210 *[586]*.

MACDONALD J.M. (1969) *Psychiatry and the Criminal*, 2nd edn. Thomas: Springfield, Illinois *[242]*.

MCDONALD R.D. & BURNS S.B. (1964) Visual vigilance and brain damage: an empirical study. *Journal of Neurology, Neurosurgery and Psychiatry* 27, 206–209 *[104]*.

MCDONALD W.I. (1967) Recurrent cholesterol embolism as a cause of fluctuating cerebral symptoms. *Journal of Neurology, Neurosurgery and Psychiatry* 30, 489–496 *[321]*.

MCENTEE W.J. & MAIR R.G. (1978) Memory impairment in Korsakoff's psychosis: a correlation with brain noradrenergic activity. *Science* 202, 905–907 *[499]*.

MCENTEE W.J. & MAIR R.G. (1980) Memory enhancement in Korsakoff's psychosis by clonidine: further evidence for a noradrenergic defect. *Annals of Neurology* 7, 466–470 *[499]*.

MCENTEE W.J., MAIR R.G. & LANGLAIS J. (1984) Neurochemical

pathology in Korsakoff's psychosis: implications for other cognitive disorders. *Neurology* 34, 648–652 *[499]*.

McEVEDY C.P. & BEARD A.W. (1970a) Royal Free epidemic of 1955: a reconsideration. *British Medical Journal* 1, 7–11 *[315]*.

McEVEDY C.P. & BEARD A.W. (1970b) Concept of benign myalgic encephalomyelitis. *British Medical Journal* 1, 11–15 *[315]*.

McEVEDY C.P. & BEARD A.W. (1973) A controlled follow-up of cases involved in an epidemic of 'benign myalgic encephalomyelitis'. *British Journal of Psychiatry* 122, 141–150 *[315]*.

McFARLAND H.R. (1963) Addison's disease and related psychoses. *Comprehensive Psychiatry* 4, 90–95 *[440]*.

McFARLAND R.A. (1932) The psychological effects of oxygen deprivation (anoxaemia) on human behaviour. *Archives of Psychology*, No. 145 *[467]*.

McFARLAND R.A. (1937) Psycho-physiological studies at high altitudes in the Andes; mental and psychosomatic responses during gradual adaptation. *Journal of Comparative Psychology* 24, 147–188 *[467]*.

MACFIE A.M.C. (1972) *A Study of Ancillary Investigations in Clinical Psychiatric Practice*. Dissertation for M.Phil. (Psychiatry), University of London *[108, 109]*.

McFIE J. (1960) Psychological testing in clinical neurology. *Journal of Nervous and Mental Disease* 131, 383–393 *[56, 94, 96]*.

McFIE J. & PIERCY F.M. (1952) The relation of laterality of lesion to performance on Weigl's sorting test. *Journal of Mental Science* 98, 299–305 *[26]*.

McGEACHIE R.E., FLEMING J.O., SHARER L.R. & HYMAN R.A. (1979) Diagnosis of Pick's disease by computed tomography. *Journal of Computer Assisted Tomography* 3, 113–115 *[392]*.

McGINN N.F., HARBURG E., JULIUS S. & McLEOD J.M. (1964) Psychological correlates of blood pressure. *Psychological Bulletin* 61, 209–219 *[340]*.

McGOVERN G.P., MILLER D.H. & ROBERTSON E.E. (1959) A mental syndrome associated with lung carcinoma. *Archives of Neurology and Psychiatry* 81, 341–347 *[635, 636]*.

McGRATH S.D. & McKENNA J. (1961) The Ganser syndrome: a critical review. *Proceedings of the Third World Congress of Psychiatry*, vol. 1, pp. 156–161. Montreal *[406]*.

MacGREGOR M.I., BLOCK A.J. & BALL W.C. (1970) Serious complications and sudden death in the Pickwickian syndrome. *Johns Hopkins Medical Journal* 126, 279–295 *[628]*.

McHUGH P.R. (1964) Occult hydrocephalus. *Quarterly Journal of Medicine* 33, 297–308 *[644]*.

McHUGH P.R. (1966) Hydrocephalic dementia. *Bulletin of the New York Academy of Medicine* 42, 907–917 *[641, 642]*.

McHUGH P.R. & FOLSTEIN M.F. (1975) Psychiatric syndromes of Huntington's chorea. Ch. 13 in *Psychiatric Aspects of Neurologic Disease*, eds. Benson D.F. & Blumer D. Grune & Stratton: New York *[397, 398]*.

McINTYRE H.D. & McINTYRE A.P. (1942) The problem of brain tumour in psychiatric diagnosis. *American Journal of Psychiatry* 98, 720–726 *[205]*.

McKANN C.F. (1932) Lead poisoning in children: the cerebral manifestations. *Archives of Neurology and Psychiatry* 27, 294–304 *[539]*.

MACKAY A. (1979) Self-poisoning—a complication of epilepsy. *British Journal of Psychiatry* 134, 277–282 *[254]*.

MacKAY M.E., McLARDY T. & HARRIS C. (1950) A case of periarteritis nodosa of the central nervous system. *Journal of Mental Science* 96, 470–475 *[367]*.

MacKENZIE K.R., MARTIN M.J. & HOWARD F.M. (1969) Myasthenia gravis: psychiatric concomitants. *Canadian Medical Association Journal* 100, 988–991 *[607, 608]*.

McKEON J., McGUFFIN P. & ROBINSON P. (1984) Obsessive-compulsive neurosis following head injury. A report of four cases. *British Journal of Psychiatry* 144, 190–192 *[168]*.

McKINLAY W.W., BROOKS D.N., BOND M.R., MARTINAGE D.P. & MARSHALL M.M. (1981) The short-term outcome of severe blunt head injury as reported by relatives of the injured persons. *Journal of Neurology, Neurosurgery, and Psychiatry*, 44, 527–533 *[146, 186]*.

McLARTY D.G., RATCLIFFE W.A., RATCLIFFE J.G., SHIMMINS J.G. & GOLDBERG A. (1978) A study of thyroid function in psychiatric in-patients. *British Journal of Psychiatry* 133, 211–218 *[429]*.

MACLEAN P.D. (1955) The limbic system ('visceral brain') and emotional behavior. *Archives of Neurology* 73, 130–134 *[23]*.

McLESTER J.S. (1943) *Nutrition and Diet in Health and Disease*, 4th edn. Saunders: Philadelphia *[489]*.

McMENEMY W.H. (1941) A critical review: dementia in middle age. *Journal of Neurology, Neurosurgery and Psychiatry* 4, 48–79 *[204]*.

McMENEMEY W.H. (1963a) Alzheimer's disease: problems concerning its concept and nature. *Acta Neurologica Scandinavica* 39, 369–380 *[378]*.

McMENEMEY W.H. (1963b) The dementias and progressive diseases of the basal ganglia. Ch. 9 in *Greenfield's Neuropathology*, eds. Blackwood W., McMenemey W.H., Meyer A., Norman R.M. & Russell D.S. 2nd edn. Edward Arnold: London *[647]*.

MACMILLAN D. (1960) Preventive geriatrics: opportunities of a community mental health service. *Lancet* 2, 1439–1441 *[421]*.

McMILLAN J.J. & WILLIAMS B. (1977) Aqueduct stenosis. *Journal of Neurology, Neurosurgery and Psychiatry* 40, 521–532 *[645]*.

McNICHOL R.W. (1970) *The Treatment of Delirium Tremens and Related States*. Thomas: Springfield, Illinois *[514, 517]*.

McQUILLEN M.P. & JOHNS R.J. (1963) Asthenic syndrome: anticholinesterase tolerance in nonmyasthenic patients. *Archives of Neurology* 8, 382–387 *[609]*.

McRAE D.L., BRANCH C.L. & MILNER B. (1968) The occipital horns and cerebral dominance. *Neurology* 18, 95–98 *[38]*.

MACE N.L. & RABINS P.V. (1981) *The 36-hour Day: A Family Guide to Caring for Persons with Alzheimer's Disease, Related Dementing Illnesses, and Memory Loss in Later Life*. John Hopkins University Press: Baltimore and London *[421]*.

MACHLE W.F. (1935) Tetra-ethyl lead intoxication and poisoning by related compounds of lead. *Journal of the American Medical Association* 105, 578–585 *[544]*.

MADOW L. & ALPERS B.J. (1951) Encephalitic form of metastatic carcinoma. *Archives of Neurology and Psychiatry* 65, 161–173 *[633]*.

MAHENDRA B. (1981) Where have all the catatonics gone? *Psychological Medicine* 11, 669–671 *[299]*.

MAHLER M.S. & LUKE J.A. (1946) Outcome of the tic syndrome. *Journal of Nervous and Mental Disease* 103, 433–445 *[586]*.

MAHLER M. & RANGELL L. (1943) A psychosomatic study of maladie des tics (Gilles de la Tourette's disease). *Psychiatric Quarterly* 17, 579–603 *[583, 586]*.

MAIR W.G.P., WARRINGTON E.K. & WEISKRANTZ L. (1979) Memory disorder in Korsakoff's psychosis: a neuropathological and neuropsychological investigation of two cases. *Brain* 102, 749–783 *[25]*.

MALAMUD N. (1964) Neuropathology. In *Mental Retardation: A Review of Research*, eds. Stevens H.A. & Heber R. University of Chicago Press *[378]*.

MALAMUD N. (1967) Psychiatric disorder with intracranial tumours of limbic system. *Archives of Neurology* 17, 113–123 *[204]*.

MALAMUD N. (1972) Neuropathology of organic brain syndromes associated with aging. In *Aging and the Brain*, ed. Gaitz C.M. Plenum Press: New York *[378]*.

MALAMUD N. & SKILLICORN S.A. (1956) Relationship between the

Wernicke and the Korsakoff syndrome. *Archives of Neurology and Psychiatry* **76**, 585–596 *[493]*.

MALETZKY B.M. (1973) The episodic dyscontrol syndrome. *Diseases of the Nervous System* **34**, 178–185 *[74, 264]*.

MALETZKY B.M. (1976) The diagnosis of pathological intoxication. *Journal of Studies on Alcohol* **37**, 1215–1228 *[509]*.

MALONE W.H. (1937) Psychosis with multiple sclerosis. *Medical Bulletin of the Veterans' Administration* **14**, 113–117 *[595]*.

MANDELBROTE B.M. & WITTKOWER E.D. (1955) Emotional factors in Grave's disease. *Psychosomatic Medicine* **17**, 109–123 *[429]*.

MANDLEBERG I.A. & BROOKS D.N. (1975) Cognitive recovery after severe head injury. I. Serial testing on the Wechsler Adult Intelligence Scale. *Journal of Neurology, Neurosurgery and Psychiatry* **38**, 1121–1126 *[159]*.

MANN A.H. (1972) *A Follow-up Study of Psychiatric Patients Shown to Have Cortical Atrophy by Air Encephalography.* Dissertation for M.Phil. (Psychiatry), University of London *[122]*.

MANN A.H. (1973) Cortical atrophy and air encephalography: a clinical and radiological study. *Psychological Medicine* **3**, 374–378 *[122]*.

MANN A.H. (1977) Psychiatric morbidity and hostility in hypertension. *Psychological Medicine* **7**, 653–659 *[341]*.

MANN A.H. (1981) Factors affecting psychological state during one year on a hypertension trial. *Clinical and Investigative Medicine* **4**, 197–200 *[341]*.

MANN A.H. (1984) Hypertension: Psychological aspects and diagnostic impact in a clinical trial. *Psychological Medicine Monograph Supplement No. 5*, Cambridge University Press *[341]*.

MANN D.M.A., LINCOLN J., YATES P.O., STAMP J.E. & TOPER S. (1980) Changes in the monoamine containing neurones of the human CNS in senile dementia. *British Journal of Psychiatry* **136**, 533–541 *[383]*.

MANUELIDIS E.E., GORGACZ E.J. & MANUELIDIS L. (1978) Viraemia in experimental Creutzfeldt-Jakob disease. *Science* **200**, 1069–1071 *[401]*.

MAPOTHER E. (1937) Mental symptoms associated with head injury: the psychiatric aspect. *British Medical Journal* **2**, 1055–1061 *[152]*.

MARCHAND M.L. (1953) A propos des azotémies dites extra-rénales au cours des affections neuro-mentales aiguës. *Annales Médico-psychologiques* **111**(ii), 203–207 *[473]*.

MARGERISON J.H. & LIDDELL D.W. (1961) The incidence of temporal lobe epilepsy among a hospital population of long-stay female epileptics. *Journal of Mental Science* **107**, 909–920 *[232]*.

MARGO A. (1981) Acromegaly and depression. *British Journal of Psychiatry* **139**, 467–468 *[442]*.

MARIN R.S. & TUCKER G.J. (1981) Psychopathology and hemispheric dysfunction. A review. *Journal of Nervous and Mental Disease* **169**, 546–557 *[76]*.

MARK V.H. & ERVIN F.R. (1970) *Violence and the Brain.* Harper and Row: New York *[74, 264]*.

MARK V.H., SWEET W.H. & ERVIN F.R. (1972) The effect of amygdalotomy on violent behavior in patients with temporal lobe epilepsy. Ch. 12 in *Psychosurgery*, eds. Hitchcock E., Laitinen L. & Vaernet K. Proceedings of the Second International Conference on Psychosurgery. Thomas: Springfield, Illinois *[73]*.

MARKAND O.N., WHEELER G.L. & POLLACK S.L. (1978) Complex partial status epilepticus (psychomotor status). *Neurology* **28**, 189–196 *[223]*.

MARKHAM C.H., TRECIOKAS L.J. & DIAMOND S.G. (1974) Parkinson's disease and levodopa: a five-year follow-up and review. *Western Journal of Medicine* **121**, 188–206 *[560]*.

MARKOWITZ A.M., SLANETZ C.A. & FRANTZ V.K. (1961) Functioning islet cell tumours of the pancreas: twenty-five year follow up. *Annals of Surgery* **154**, 877–844 *[464]*.

MARKS I.M. (1969) *Fears and Phobias.* Heinemann: London *[244]*.

MARKS V. (1981a) Symptomatology. Ch. 5 in *Hypoglycaemia*, 2nd Edition, Marks V. & Rose F.C. Blackwell Scientific Publications: Oxford *[458, 463]*.

MARKS V. (1981b) Pancreatic hypoglycaemia (hyperinsulinism). Ch. 7 in *Hypoglycaemia*, 2nd Edition, Marks V. & Rose F.C. Blackwell Scientific Publications: Oxford *[459]*.

MARKS V. (1981c) The investigation of hypoglycaemia. Ch. 19 in *Hypoglycaemia*, 2nd Edition, Marks V. & Rose F.C. Blackwell Scientific Publications: Oxford *[460]*.

MARLOWE W.B., MANCALL E.L. & THOMAS J.J. (1975) Complete Kluver-Bucy syndrome in man. *Cortex* **11**, 53–59 *[23]*.

MARQUARDSEN J. (1969) The natural history of acute cerebrovascular disease. A retrospective study of 769 patients. *Acta Neurologica Scandinavica*, supplement 38, 1–192 *[325]*.

MARRIOTT P.J., O'BRIEN M.D., MACKENZIE I.C.K. & JANOTA I. (1975) Progressive multifocal leucoencephalopathy: remission with cytarabine. *Journal of Neurology, Neurosurgery and Psychiatry* **38**, 205–209 *[646]*.

MARSAN C.A. & ZIVIN L.S. (1970) Factors related to the occurrence of typical paroxysmal abnormalities in the EEG records of epileptic patients. *Epilepsia* **11**, 361–381 *[256]*.

MARSDEN C.D. (1976a) The problem of adult-onset idiopathic torsion dystonia and other isolated dyskinesias in adult life (including blepharospasm, oromandibular dystonia, dystonic writer's cramp, and torticollis, or axial dystonia). In *Dystonia*, eds. Eldridge R. & Fahn S. *Advances in Neurology, 14*, pp. 259–276. Raven Press: New York *[574, 576, 578, 580]*.

MARSDEN C.D. (1976b) Dystonia: the spectrum of the disease. In *The Basal Ganglia*, ed. Yahr M.D., *Association for Research in Nervous and Mental Disease* **55**, pp. 351–367. Raven Press: New York *[574]*.

MARSDEN C.D. (1976c) Blepharospasm-oromandibular dystonia syndrome (Brueghel's syndrome). A variant of adult-onset torsion dystonia? *Journal of Neurology, Neurosurgery and Psychiatry* **39**, 1204–1209 *[579, 580]*.

MARSDEN C.D. (1982) Basal ganglia and disease. *Lancet* **2**, 1141–1146 *[395]*.

MARSDEN C.D. (1983) Movement disorders. In *Oxford Textbook of Medicine, Vol. 2*, eds. Weatherall D.J., Ledingham J.G.G. & Warrell D.A., pp. 21.100–21.121. Oxford University Press *[553]*.

MARSDEN C.D. & HARRISON M.J.G. (1972) Outcome of investigation of patients with presenile dementia. *British Medical Journal* **2**, 249–252 *[414, 415]*.

MARSDEN C.D., HARRISON M.J.G. & BUNDEY S. (1976) Natural history of idiopathic torsion dystonia. In *Dystonia*, eds. Eldridge R. & Fahn S. *Advances in Neurology* **14**, pp. 177–186. Raven Press: New York *[569, 570]*.

MARSDEN C.D. & JENNER P. (1980) The pathophysiology of extra-pyramidal side-effects of neuroleptic drugs. *Psychological Medicine* **10**, 55–72 *[546, 548]*.

MARSDEN C.D. & PARKES J.D. (1973) Abnormal movement disorders. *British Journal of Hospital Medicine* **10**, 428–450 *[569, 575]*.

MARSDEN C.D. & PARKES J.D. (1976) 'On-off' effects in patients with Parkinson's disease on chronic levodopa therapy. *Lancet* **1**, 292–296 *[554]*.

MARSDEN C.D. & PARKES J.D. (1977) Success and problems of long-term levodopa therapy in Parkinson's disease. *Lancet* **1**, 345–349 *[554]*.

MARSDEN C.D. & REYNOLDS E.H. (1982) Neurology. Ch. 4 Part 1, in *A Textbook of Epilepsy*, Second Edition, eds. Laidlaw J. & Richens A. Churchill Livingstone: Edinburgh and London *[208]*.

MARSDEN C.D., TARSY D. & BALDESSARINI R.J. (1975) Spontaneous and drug-induced movement disorders in psychotic patients. Ch. 12 in *Psychiatric Aspects of Neurologic Disease*, eds. Benson D.F. & Blumer D. Grune & Stratton: New York *[546]*.

MARSH G. (1980) Disability and intellectual function in multiple sclerosis patients. *Journal of Nervous and Mental Disease* 168, 758–762 *[591]*.

MARSH G.G., MARKHAM C.M. & ANSEL R. (1971) Levodopa's awakening effect on patients with parkinsonism. *Journal of Neurology, Neurosurgery and Psychiatry* 34, 209–218 *[560]*.

MARSHALL A.H.E. & WHITE R.G. (1961) Experimental thymic lesions resembling those of myasthenia gravis. *Lancet* 1, 1030–1031 *[606]*.

MARSHALL J. (1964) The natural history of transient ischaemic cerebrovascular attacks. *Quarterly Journal of Medicine* 33, 309–324 *[325]*.

MARSHALL J. (1971) Angiography in the investigation of ischaemic episodes in the territory of the internal carotid artery. *Lancet* 1, 719–721 *[325]*.

MARSHALL J. (1973) Transient ischaemic cerebral attacks. *British Journal of Hospital Medicine* 10, 240–243 *[324]*.

MARSHALL J. (1976) *The Management of Cerebrovascular Disease*, 3rd edn. Blackwell Scientific Publications: Oxford *[331, 343]*.

MARTIN E.A. (1970) Transient global amnesia. *Irish Journal of Medical Science* 3, 331–335 *[359]*.

MARTIN J.M. (1982) Chromosome loss and senescence. *Psychological Medicine* 12, 231–233 *[373]*.

MARTIN J.M., KELLETT J.M. & KHAN J. (1981) Aneuploidy in cultured human lymphocytes: II a comparison between senescence and dementia. *Age and Ageing* 10, 24–28 *[373]*.

MARTIN M.J. (1966) Tension headache: a psychiatric study. *Headache* 6, 47–54 *[353]*.

MARTIN P.R., WEINGARTNER H., GORDON E.K., BURNS R.S., LINNOILA M., KOPIN I.J. & EBERT M.H. (1984) Central nervous system catecholamine metabolism in Korsakoff's psychosis. *Annals of Neurology* 15, 184–187 *[499]*.

MARTLAND H.S. (1928) Punch drunk. *Journal of the American Medical Association* 91, 1103–1107 *[174]*.

MARTTILA R.J. & RINNE U.K. (1976) Dementia in Parkinson's disease. *Acta Neurologica Scandinavica* 54, 431–441 *[556]*.

MASTAGLIA F.L., BLACK J.L. & COLLINS D.W.K. (1976) Visual and spinal evoked potentials in diagnosis of multiple sclerosis. *British Medical Journal* 2, 732 *[589]*.

MASTER D.R. & LISHMAN W.A. (1984) Seizures, dyslexia, and dysgraphia of psychogenic origin. *Archives of Neurology* 41, 889–890 *[49]*.

MASTER D., LISHMAN W.A. & SMITH A. (1983) Speed of recall in relation to affective tone and intensity of experience. *Psychological Medicine* 13, 325–331 *[25]*.

MASTER D.R., TOONE B.K. & SCOTT D.F. (1984) Interictal behaviour in temporal lobe epilepsy. In *Advances in Epileptology: XVth Epilepsy International Symposium*, eds. Porter R.J., Mattson R.H., Ward A.A. & Dam M. *[234]*.

MASTERS C.L., HARRIS J.O., GAJDUSEK D.C., GIBBS C.J., BERNOULLI C. & ASHER D.M. (1979) Creutzfeldt-Jakob disease: patterns of worldwide occurrence and the significance of familial and sporadic clustering. *Annals of Neurology* 5, 177–188 *[400, 401, 403]*.

DE LA MATA C., GINGRAS G. & WITTKOWER E.D. (1960) Impact of sudden severe disablement of the father upon the family. *Canadian Medical Association Journal* 82, 1015–1020 *[334]*.

MATHEW N.T. & MEYER J.S. (1974) Pathogenesis and natural history of transient global amnesia. *Stroke* 5, 303–311 *[359, 361]*.

MATTHES A. (1969) Genetic studies in epilepsy. Ch. 2 in *The Physiopathogenesis of the Epilepsies*, eds. Gastaut H., Jasper H., Bancaud J. & Waltregny A. Thomas: Springfield Illinois *[216]*.

MATTHEWS W.B. (1965) Sarcoidosis of the nervous system. *Journal of Neurology, Neurosurgery, and Psychiatry* 28, 23–29 *[652]*.

MATTHEWS W.B. (1975) Epidemiology of Creutzfeldt-Jakob disease in England and Wales. *Journal of Neurology, Neurosurgery, and Psychiatry* 38, 210–213 *[401]*.

MATTHEWS W.B. (1978) *Multiple Sclerosis*. Oxford University Press *[588]*.

MATTHEWS W.B. (1979) Multiple sclerosis presenting with acute remitting psychiatric symptoms. *Journal of Neurology, Neurosurgery, and Psychiatry* 42, 859–863 *[595]*.

MATTHEWS W.B. (1981) Slow virus infections. *Journal of the Royal College of Physicians of London* 15, 109–112 *[401, 404]*.

MATTHEWS W.B. (1982) Spongiform virus encephalopathy. In *Recent Advances in Clinical Neurology* 3, eds. Matthews W.B. & Glaser G.H. Churchill Livingstone: Edinburgh *[404]*.

MATTHEWS W.B. (1983) Demelinating disease. In *Oxford Textbook of Medicine*. Vol. 2. eds. Weatherall D.J., Ledingham J.G.G. & Warrell D.A., pp. 21.95–21.100. Oxford University Press *[588]*.

MATTHEWS W.B., CAMPBELL M., HUGHES J.J. & TOMLINSON A.H. (1979) Creutzfeldt-Jakob disease and ferrets. *Lancet* 1, 828 *[401]*.

MAUDSLEY H. (1873) *Body and Mind*. Macmillan & Co.: London *[241]*.

MAUDSLEY H. (1906) *Responsibility in Mental Disease*. Kegan Paul, Trench, Trübner & Co.: London *[241]*.

MAWDSLEY C. (1961) Epilepsy and television. *Lancet* 1, 190–191 *[211]*.

MAWDSLEY C. (1972) Neurological complications of haemodialysis. *Proceedings of the Royal Society of Medicine* 65, 871–873 *[473, 474]*.

MAWDSLEY C. & FERGUSON F.R. (1963) Neurological disease in boxers. *Lancet* 2, 795–801 *[174]*.

MAY P.R.A. & EBAUGH F.G. (1953) Pathological intoxication, alcoholic hallucinosis, and other reactions to alcohol: a clinical study. *Quarterly Journal of Studies on Alcohol* 14, 200–227 *[509]*.

MAY R.H., VOEGELE G.E. & PAOLINO A.F. (1960) The Ganser syndrome: a report of 3 cases. *Journal of Nervous and Mental Disease* 130, 331–339 *[405, 406]*.

MAY W.W. (1968) Creutzfeldt-Jakob disease. *Acta Neurologica Scandinavica* 44, 1–32 *[402]*.

MAYER V., OROLIN D. & MITROVA E. (1977) Cluster of Creutzfeldt-Jakob disease and presenile dementia. *Lancet* 2, 256 *[401]*.

MAYEUX R., STERN Y., ROSEN J. & LEVENTHAL J. (1981) Depression, intellectual impairment, and Parkinson's disease. *Neurology* 31, 645–650 *[558]*.

MAZZUCCHI A., MORETTI G., CAFFARA P. & PARMA M. (1980) Neuropsychological functions in the follow-up of transient global amnesia. *Brain* 103, 161–178 *[359]*.

MEADOWS J.C. (1974) The anatomical basis of prosopagnosia. *Journal of Neurology, Neurosurgery and Psychiatry* 37, 489–501 *[53]*.

MEARES R. (1971a) Natural history of spasmodic torticollis, and effect of surgery. *Lancet* 2, 149–150 *[572, 576]*.

MEARES R. (1971b) Features which distinguish groups of spasmodic torticollis. *Journal of Psychosomatic Research* 15, 1–11 *[572, 574]*.

MEARES R. (1971c) An association of spasmodic torticollis and writer's cramp. *British Journal of Psychiatry* 119, 441–442 *[578]*.

MEARES R. (1973) Spasmodic torticollis. *British Journal of Hospital Medicine* 9, 235–241 *[576]*.

MEDICAL RESEARCH COUNCIL (1977) *Senile and Presenile Dementias*. A report of the MRC Subcommittee, compiled by W.A. Lishman. Medical Research Council: London *[381]*.

THE MEDICAL STAFF OF THE ROYAL FREE HOSPITAL (1957) An outbreak of encephalomyelitis in the Royal Free Hospital Group, London, in 1955. *British Medical Journal* 2, 895–904 *[314]*.

MEDUNA L.J. (1937) *Die Konvulsiontherapie der Schizophrenie.* Marhold: Halle *[246]*.

MEER B. & BAKER J.A. (1966) The Stockton Geriatric Rating Scale. *Journal of Gerontology* 21, 393–403 *[107]*.

MEHTA T. (1965) Subdural haematoma. *Journal of the Indian Medical Association* 44, 635–641 *[357]*.

MEIER M.J. (1972) The perceptual maze test. *Seventh Mental Measurements Year Book*, ed. Buros O.K., vol. 1, 285–287. Gryphon Press: Highland Park, New Jersey *[99]*.

MELAMED E. (1979) Neurological disorders related to folate deficiency. Ch. 38 in *Folic Acid in Neurology, Psychiatry, and Internal Medicine*, eds. Botez M.I. & Reynolds E.H. Raven Press: New York *[505]*.

MELDRUM B.S., HORTON R.W. & BRIERLEY J.B. (1974) Epileptic brain damage in adolescent baboons following seizures induced by allylglycine. *Brain* 97, 407–418 *[215]*.

MELDRUM B.S., VIGOUROUX R.A. & BRIERLEY J.B. (1973) Systemic factors and epileptic brain damage: prolonged seizures in paralyzed artificially ventilated baboons. *Archives of Neurology* 29, 82–87 *[215]*.

MENDHIRATTA S.S., WIG N.N. & VERMA S.K. (1978) Some psychological correlates of long-term heavy cannabis users. *British Journal of Psychiatry* 132, 482–486 *[528]*.

MENNINGER K.A. (1924) Paranoid psychosis with uraemia. *Journal of Nervous and Mental Disease* 60, 26–34 *[473]*.

MERLIS J.K. (1970) Proposal for an international classification of the epilepsies. *Epilepsia* 11, 114–119 *[207]*.

MERLIS J.K. (1974) Reflex epilepsy. Ch. 25 in *Handbook of Clinical Neurology, Vol. 15: The Epilepsies*, eds. Vinken P.J. & Bruyn G.W. North-Holland Publishing Co.: Amsterdam *[211]*.

MERRIN E.L. (1981) Schizophrenia and brain asymmetry. An evaluation of evidence for dominant lobe dysfunction. *Journal of Nervous and Mental Disease* 169, 405–416 *[76]*.

MERRITT H.H. (1979) *A Textbook of Neurology*, 6th Edition. Lea and Febiger: Philadelphia *[654]*.

MERSKEY H. & WOODFORDE J.M. (1972) Psychiatric sequelae of minor head injury. *Brain* 95, 521–528 *[151]*.

MESSERT B. & BAKER N.H. (1966) Syndrome of progressive spastic ataxia and apraxia associated with occult hydrocephalus. *Neurology* 16, 440–452 *[644]*.

MESSERT B., HENKE T.K. & LANGHEIM W. (1966) Syndrome of akinetic mutism associated with obstructive hydrocephalus. *Neurology* 16, 635–649 *[644]*.

MESULAM M.-M., WAXMAN S.G., GESCHWIND N. & SABIN T.D. (1976) Acute confusional states with right middle cerebral artery infarctions. *Journal of Neurology, Neurosurgery, and Psychiatry* 39, 84–89 *[322]*.

METRAKOS J.D. & METRAKOS K. (1960) Genetics of convulsive disorders. 1: Introduction, problems, methods, base lines. *Neurology* 10, 228–240 *[215, 228]*.

METRAKOS J.D. & METRAKOS K. (1961) Genetics of convulsive disorders. II: Genetic and electroencephalographic studies in centrencephalic epilepsy. *Neurology* 11, 474–483 *[215]*.

MEUDELL P.R., NORTHERN B., SNOWDEN J.S. & NEARY D. (1980) Long-term memory for famous voices in amnesic and normal subjects. *Neuropsychologia* 18, 133–139 *[34]*.

MEYER E. (1966) Psychological disturbances in myasthenia gravis: a predictive study. *Annals of the New York Academy of Sciences* 135, 417–423 *[607, 608]*.

MEYER J.S. & GOTOH F. (1960) Metabolic and electroencephalographic effects of hyperventilation. *Archives of Neurology* 3, 539–552 *[110]*.

MEYLER L. & HERXHEIMER A. (1968) *Side Effects of Drugs: A Survey of Unwanted Effects of Drugs Reported in 1965–1967*, vol. 6. Excerpta Medica: Amsterdam *[532]*.

MICHAEL R.P. (1957) Treatment of a case of compulsive swearing. *British Medical Journal* 1, 1506–1508 *[586]*.

MICHAEL R.P. & GIBBONS J.L. (1963) Interrelationships between the endocrine system and neuropsychiatry. *International Review of Neurobiology*, vol. 5, 243–302 *[429, 435, 437, 439]*.

MIKKELSEN B. & BIRKET-SMITH E. (1973) A clinical study of the benzodiazepine Ro 5–4023 (clonazepam) in the treatment of epilepsy. *Acta Neurologica Scandinavica*, supplement 53, 91–96 *[269]*.

MILLER D., GREEN J., FARMER R. & CARROLL G. (1985) A 'pseudo-AIDS' syndrome following from fear of AIDS. *British Journal of Psychiatry* 146, 550–551 *[315]*.

MILLER E. (1973) Short- and long-term memory in patients with presenile dementia. *Psychological Medicine* 3, 221–224 *[31]*.

MILLER E. (1974) Dementia as accelerated ageing of the nervous system: some psychological and methodological considerations. *Age and Ageing* 3, 197–202 *[377]*.

MILLER E. (1977) *Abnormal Ageing: The Psychology of Senile and Presenile Dementia.* John Wiley: London *[377, 423]*.

MILLER H. (1961) Accident neurosis. *British Medical Journal* 1, 919–925 and 992–998 *[149, 151, 170]*.

MILLER H. (1966a) Mental after-effects of head injury. *Proceedings of the Royal Society of Medicine* 59, 257–261 *[151]*.

MILLER H. (1966b) Neurological manifestations of collagen-vascular disease. *Journal of the Royal College of Physicians of London* 1, 15–19 *[368]*.

MILLER H. (1969) Problems of medicolegal practice. Ch. 42 in *The Late Effects of Head Injury*, eds. Walker A.E., Caveness W.F. & Critchley M. Thomas: Springfield, Illinois *[151, 178]*.

MILLER H. & CARTLIDGE N. (1972) Simulation and malingering after injuries to the brain and spinal cord. *Lancet* 1, 580–585 *[177]*.

MILLER H. & STERN G. (1965) The long-term prognosis of severe head injury. *Lancet* 1, 225–229 *[159]*.

MILNER B. (1958) Psychological defects produced by temporal lobe excision. Ch. 8 in *The Brain and Human Behavior*, Research Publications of the Association for Research in Nervous and Mental Disease. vol. 36. Williams & Wilkins: Baltimore *[56, 105, 229]*.

MILNER B. (1962) Laterality effects in audition. Ch. 9 in *Interhemispheric Relations and Cerebral Dominance*, ed. Mountcastle V. Johns Hopkins Press: Baltimore *[56, 229]*.

MILNER B. (1963) Effects of different brain lesions on card sorting. *Archives of Neurology* 9, 90–100 *[69, 104]*.

MILNER B. (1964) Some effects of frontal lobectomy in man. Ch. 15 in *The Frontal Granular Cortex and Behaviour*, eds. Warren J.M. & Akert K. McGraw-Hill: New York *[69, 70, 104]*.

MILNER B. (1966) Amnesia following operation on the temporal lobes. Ch. 5 in *Amnesia*, eds. Whitty C.W.M. & Zangwill O. Butterworths: London *[26, 27, 28, 32, 85, 275]*.

MILNER B. (1969) Residual intellectual and memory deficits after head injury. Ch. 7 in *The Late Effects of Head Injury*, eds. Walker A.E., Caveness W.F. & Critchley M. Thomas: Springfield, Illinois *[102, 104]*.

MILNER B., BRANCH C. & RASMUSSEN T. (1964) Observations on cerebral dominance. In *Disorders of Language*, eds. De Reuck A.V.S. & O'Connor M. Ciba Foundation Symposium. Churchill: London *[37, 38]*.

MILNER D. (1983) Neuropsychological studies of callosal agenesis. *Psychological Medicine* 13, 721–725 *[654]*.

MINDHAM R.H.S. (1970) Psychiatric symptoms in parkinsonism. *Journal of Neurology, Neurosurgery and Psychiatry* 33, 188–191 *[556, 558, 559]*.

MINDHAM R.H.S. (1974) Psychiatric aspects of Parkinson's disease. *British Journal of Hospital Medicine* 11, 411–414 *[557]*.

MINSKI L. (1933) The mental symptoms associated with 58 cases of cerebral tumour. *Journal of Neurology and Psychopathology* 13, 330–343 *[189, 205]*.

MINSKI L. & GUTTMANN E. (1938) Huntington's chorea: a study of thirty-four families. *Journal of Mental Science* 84, 21–96 *[399]*.

MISRA P.C. & HAY G.G. (1971) Encephalitis presenting as acute schizophrenia. *British Medical Journal* 1, 532–533 *[290]*.

MITCHELL J.R.A., SURRIDGE D.H.C. & WILLISON R.G. (1959) Hypothermia after chlorpromazine in myxoedematous psychosis. *British Medical Journal* 2, 932–933 *[436]*.

MITCHELL K.R. (1971) A psychological approach to the treatment of migraine. *British Journal of Psychiatry* 119, 533–534 *[355]*.

MITCHELL S.A. & DEMENT W.C. (1968) Narcolepsy syndromes: antecedent, contiguous, and concomitant nocturnal sleep disordering and deprivation. *Psychophysiology* 4, 398 *[623]*.

MITCHELL W., FALCONER M.A. & HILL D. (1954) Epilepsy with fetishism relieved by temporal lobectomy. *Lancet* 2, 626–630 *[240]*.

MITCHELL W. & FELDMAN F. (1968) Neuropsychiatric aspects of hypokalaemia. *Canadian Medical Association Journal* 98, 49–51 *[477]*.

MJÖNES H. (1949) Paralysis agitans: a clinical and genetic study. *Acta Psychiatrica et Neurologica*, supplement 54, 1–195 *[555, 559]*.

MOELI C. (1888) Ueber ihre Verbrecher. Quoted by Enoch M.D., Trethowan W.H. & Barker J.C. In *Some Uncommon Psychiatric Syndromes*, 1967. John Wright: Bristol *[405]*.

MOERSCH F.P. (1924) Psychic manifestations in migraine. *American Journal of Psychiatry* 80, 697–716 *[258, 348, 351]*.

MOFFATT W.R., SIDDIQUI A.R. & MACKAY D.N. (1970) The use of sulthiame with disturbed mentally subnormal patients. *British Journal of Psychiatry* 117, 673–678 *[268]*.

MOHR J.A., GRIFFITHS W., JACKSON R., SAADAH H., BIRD P. & RIDDLE J. (1976) Neurosyphilis and penicillin levels in cerebrospinal fluid. *Journal of the American Medical Association* 236, 2208–2209 *[286]*.

MOHS R.C., DAVIS K.L., TINKLENBERG J.R., PFEFFERBAUM A., HOLLISTER L.E. & KOPELL B.S. (1979) Cognitive effects of physostigmine and choline chloride in normal subjects. In *Brain Acetylcholine and Neuropsychiatric Disease*, eds. Davis K.L. & Berger P.A. Plenum Press: New York *[425]*.

MOMOSE K.J., KJELLBERG R.N. & KLIMAN B. (1971) High incidence of cortical atrophy of the cerebral and cerebellar hemispheres in Cushing's disease. *Radiology* 99, 341–348 *[438]*.

MONEY J. (1963) Cytogenetic and psychosexual incongruities with a note on space-form blindness. *American Journal of Psychiatry* 119, 820–827 *[447]*.

MONEY J. (1964) Two cytogenetic syndromes: psychologic comparisons. 1. Intelligence and specific-factor quotients. *Journal of Psychiatric Research* 2, 223–231 *[447]*.

MONEY J. & EHRHARDT A.A. (1968) Prenatal hormonal exposures: possible effects on behaviour in man. Ch. 3 in *Endocrinology and Human Behaviour*, ed. Michael R.P. Oxford University Press: London *[428]*.

MONPETIT V.J.A., ANDERMANN F., CARPENTER S., FAWCETT J.S., ZBOROWSKA-SLUIS D. & GIBERSON H.R. (1971) Subacute necrotizing encephalomyelopathy. A review and a study of two families. *Brain* 94, 1–30 *[500]*.

MONTGOMERY A., FENTON G.W. & McCLELLAND R.J. (1984) Delayed brainstem conduction time in post-concussional syndrome. *Lancet* 1, 1011 *[170]*.

MONTGOMERY M.A., CLAYTON P.J. & FRIEDHOFF A.J. (1982) Psychiatric illness in Tourette syndrome patients and first-degree relatives. In *Gilles de la Tourette Syndrome*, eds. Friedhoff A.J. & Chase T.N. *Advances in Neurology, Vol. 35*, pp. 335–339. Raven Press: New York *[582]*.

MOORE B.E. & RUESCH J. (1944) Prolonged disturbances of consciousness following head injury. *New England Journal of Medicine* 230, 445–452 *[142]*.

MOORE W.S. & HOLLAND G.N. (1980) Nuclear magnetic resonance imaging. *British Medical Bulletin* 36, 297–299 *[122]*.

MORGAN H.G. (1968) Acute neuropsychiatric complications of chronic alcoholism. *British Journal of Psychiatry* 114, 85–92 *[513]*.

MORGAN M.Y. (1982) Alcohol and the endocrine system. In *Alcohol and Disease* ed. Sherlock, S. *British Medical Bulletin* 38, 35–42 *[436]*.

MORGANSTERN F.S. (1964) The effects of sensory input and concentration on post-amputation phantom limb pain. *Journal of Neurology, Neurosurgery and Psychiatry* 27, 58–65 *[66]*.

MORLEY J.B. (1967) Unruptured vertebro-basilar aneurysms. *Medical Journal of Australia* 2, 1024–1027 *[357]*.

MOROZOV G.V., KACHAEV A.K. & LUKACHER C.I. (1973) The pathogenesis of pathological inebriation. *Zhurnal Neuropatologii i Psikhiatrii Korsakova* 73, 1196–1199 *[509]*.

MORPHEW J.A. & SIM M. (1969) Gilles de la Tourette's syndrome: a clinical and psychopathological study. *British Journal of Medical Psychology* 42, 293–301 *[583]*.

MORRELL F., ROBERTS L. & JASPER H.H. (1956) Effect of focal epileptogenic lesions and their ablation upon conditioned electrical responses of the brain in the monkey. *Electroencephalography and Clinical Neurophysiology* 8, 217–236 *[229]*.

MORRIS G.O. & SINGER M.T. (1966) Sleep deprivation: the content of consciousness. *Journal of Nervous and Mental Disease* 143, 291–304 *[126]*.

MORROW R.S. & COHEN J. (1954) The psycho-social factors in muscular dystrophy. *Journal of Child Psychiatry* 3, 70–80 *[612, 613]*.

MOSCOWITZ M.A., WINICKOFF R.N. & HEINZ E.R. (1971) Familial calcification of the basal ganglions. A metabolic and genetic study. *New England Journal of Medicine* 285, 72–77 *[647]*.

MOSELEY I. (1981) Aneurysms of the cerebral arteries. *British Journal of Hospital Medicine* 26, 613–618 *[335]*.

MOSELEY I.F. & RADÜ E.W. (1979) Factors influencing the development of periventricular lucencies in patients with raised intracranial pressure. *Neuroradiology* 17, 65–69 *[640]*.

MOUNTJOY C.Q., ROTH M., EVANS N.J.R. & EVANS H.M. (1983) Cortical neuronal counts in normal elderly controls and demented patients. *Neurobiology of Aging* 4, 1–11 *[382]*.

DE MOURA M.C., CORREIA J.P. & MADEIRA F. (1967) Clinical alcohol hypoglycaemia. *Annals of Internal Medicine* 66, 893–905 *[463]*.

MOURE J.M.B. (1967) The electroencephalogram in hypercalcemia. *Archives of Neurology* 17, 34–51 *[449]*.

MUELLER J. & AMINOFF M.J. (1982) Tourette-like syndrome after long-term neuroleptic drug treatment. *British Journal of Psychiatry* 141, 191–193 *[584]*.

MULDER D.W., ROSENBAUM R.A. & LAYTON D.D. (1972) Late progression of poliomyelitis or forme fruste amyotrophic lateral sclerosis? *Mayo Clinic Proceedings* 47, 756 *[604]*.

MULLAN S. & PENFIELD W. (1959) Illusions of comparative interpretation and emotion. *Archives of Neurology and Psychiatry* 81, 269–284 *[219]*.

MULLER D.J. (1971) ECT in LSD psychosis: a report of three cases. *American Journal of Psychiatry* 128, 351–352 *[531]*.

MULLER R., NYLANDER I., LARSSON L-E, WIDEN L. & FRANKENHAEUSER M. (1958) Sequelae of primary aseptic meningoencephalitis. *Acta Psychiatrica et Neurologica Scandinavica*, supplement 126, 1–115 *[310]*.

MUNGAS D. (1982) Interictal behavior abnormality in temporal lobe epilepsy. *Archives of General Psychiatry* 39, 108–111 *[234]*.

MUR J., KÜMPEL G. & DOSTAL S. (1966) An anergic phase of disseminated sclerosis with psychotic course. *Confinia Neurologica* 28, 37–49 *[595]*.

MURPHY T.L., CHALMERS T.C., ECKHARDT R.D. & DAVIDSON C.S. (1948) Hepatic coma: clinical and laboratory observations on forty patients. *New England Journal of Medicine* 239, 605–612 *[480]*.

MURRAY R.M., GREENE J.G. & ADAMS J.H. (1971) Analgesic abuse and dementia. *Lancet* 2, 242–245 *[534]*.

MUTSCHLER D. (1956) Neurosebildende Faktoren bei Hirnverletzten. In *Das Hirntrauma,* ed. Rehwald E. Thieme: Stuttgart *[154]*.

MYERS R.H., GROWDON J.H., BIRD E.D., FELDMAN R.G. & MARTIN J.B. (1982) False-negative results with levodopa for early detection of Huntington's disease. *New England Journal of Medicine* 307, 561–562 *[395]*.

MYERSON A. & LOMAN J. (1942) Amphetamine sulfate in treatment of spasmodic torticollis. *Archives of Neurology and Psychiatry* 48, 823–828 *[575]*.

MYRIANTHOPOULOS N.C. (1966) Huntington's chorea. *Journal of Medical Genetics* 3, 298–314 *[393, 394, 395, 397]*.

NADEEM A.A. & YOUNIS Y.O. (1977) Physical illness and psychiatric disorders in Tigani El-Mahi Psychiatric Hospital (Sudan). *East African Medical Journal* 54, 207–210 *[313]*.

NADEL C. (1981) Somnambulism, bed-time medication and over-eating. *British Journal of Psychiatry* 139, 79 *[632]*.

NADVORNIK P., SRAMKA M., LISY L. & SVICKA I. (1972) Experiences with dentatotomy. *Confinia Neurologica* 34, 320–324 *[587]*.

NAESER M.A., ALEXANDER M.P., HELM-ESTABROOKS N., LEVINE H.L., LAUGHLIN S.A. & GESCHWIND N. (1982) Aphasia with predominantly subcortical lesion sites. Description of three capsular putaminal aphasia syndromes. *Archives of Neurology* 39, 2–14 *[42]*.

NAESER M.A., GEBHARDT C. & LEVINE H.L. (1980) Decreased computerised tomography numbers in patients with presenile dementia. Detection in patients with otherwise normal scans. *Archives of Neurology* 37, 401–409 *[121]*.

NAESER M.A. & HAYWARD R.W. (1978) Lesion localisation in aphasia with cranial computed tomography and the Boston Diagnostic Aphasia Exam. *Neurology* 28, 545–551 *[43]*.

NAG T.K. & FALCONER M.A. (1966) Non-tumoral stenosis of the aqueduct in adults. *British Medical Journal* 2, 1168–1170 *[644]*.

NAGUIB M. & LEVY R. (1982a) Prediction of outcome in senile dementia—a computed tomography study. *British Journal of Psychiatry* 140, 263–267 *[374]*.

NAGUIB M. & LEVY R. (1982b) CT scanning in senile dementia. A follow-up of survivors. *British Journal of Psychiatry* 141, 618–620 *[120]*.

NAHAS G.G. (1973) Clinical pharmacology of cannabis sativa with special reference to delta-9-THC. In *Bulletin on Narcotics,* vol. 25, No. 1, 9–39. United Nations: Geneva *[525]*.

NANDY K. (1968) Further studies on the effects of centrophenoxine on the lipofuscin pigment in the neurones of senile guinea pigs. *Journal of Gerontology* 23, 82–92 *[425]*.

NANDY K. (ed.) (1978) *Senile Dementia: A Biomedical Approach.* Developments in Neuroscience, Vol. 3. Elsevier/North-Holland, Biomedical Press: Amsterdam *[384]*.

NANDY K. (1981) Senile dementia: a possible immune hypothesis. Ch. 5 in *The Epidemiology of Dementia,* eds. Mortimer J.A. & Schuman L.M. Oxford University Press *[385]*.

NANDY K. & BOURNE G.H. (1966) Effect of centrophenoxine on the lipofuscin pigments in the neurones of senile guinea-pigs. *Nature* 210, 313–314 *[425]*.

NARABAYASHI H., NAGAO T., SAITO Y., YOSHIDA M. & NAGAHATA M. (1963) Stereotaxic amygdalotomy for behaviour disorders. *Archives of Neurology* 9, 1–16 *[73]*.

NARABAYASHI H. & UNO M. (1966) Long range results of stereotaxic amygdalotomy for behaviour disorders. *Confinia Neurologica* 27, 168–171 *[73]*.

NASRALLAH H.A., JACOBY C.G., McCALLEY-WHITTERS M. & KUPERMAN S. (1982a) Cerebral ventricular enlargement in subtypes of chronic schizophrenia. *Archives of General Psychiatry* 39, 774–777 *[121]*.

NASRALLAH H.A., McCALLEY-WHITTERS M. & JACOBY C.G. (1982b) Cerebral ventricular enlargement in young manic males. A controlled CT study. *Journal of Affective Disorders* 4, 15–19 *[122]*.

NEAL J.B. (1942) The clinical course of epidemic encephalitis. Ch. 4 in *Encephalitis: A Clinical Study* by Neal J.B. Grune & Stratton: New York *[305]*.

NEALE F.C. & FISCHER-WILLIAMS M. (1958) Copper metabolism in normal adults and in clinically normal relatives of patients with Wilson's disease. *Journal of Clinical Pathology* 11, 441–447 *[565]*.

NEARY D. (1976) Neuropsychiatric sequelae of renal failure. *British Journal of Hospital Medicine* 15, 122–130 *[474]*.

NEE L.E., CAINE E.D., POLINSKY R.J., ELDRIDGE R. & EBERT M.H. (1980) Gilles de la Tourette syndrome: clinical and family study of 50 cases. *Annals of Neurology* 7, 41–49 *[581, 582]*.

NEE L.E., POLINSKY R.J. & EBERT M.H. (1982) Tourette syndrome: clinical and family studies. In *Gilles de la Tourette Syndrome,* eds. Friedhoff A.J. & Chase T.N. Raven Press: New York *[582]*.

NEEDLEMAN H.L. (1982) The neuropsychiatric implications of low level exposure to lead. *Psychological Medicine* 12, 461–463 *[539]*.

NEEDLEMAN H.L., GUNNOE C., LEVITON A., REED R., PERESIE H., MAHER C. & BARRETT P. (1979) Deficits in psychologic and classroom performance of children with elevated dentine lead levels. *New England Journal of Medicine* 300, 689–695 *[539]*.

NELSON H.E. (1976) A modified card sorting test sensitive to frontal lobe defects. *Cortex* 12, 313–324 *[104]*.

NELSON H.E. (1982) *The National Adult Reading Test Manual.* NFER-Nelson: Windsor, England *[96]*.

NELSON H.E. & McKENNA P. (1975) The use of current reading ability in the assessment of dementia. *British Journal of Social and Clinical Psychology* 14, 259–267 *[96]*.

NELSON H.E. & O'CONNELL A. (1978) Dementia: the estimation of premorbid intelligence levels using the new adult reading test. *Cortex* 14, 234–244 *[96]*.

NEUBERGER K.T. (1957) The changing neuropathological picture of chronic alcoholism. *Archives of Pathology* 63, 1–6 *[518]*.

NEUGUT R.H., NEUGUT A.I., KAHANA E., STEIN Z. & ALTER M. (1979) Creutzfeldt-Jakob disease: familial clustering among Libyan-born Israelis. *Neurology* 29, 225–231 *[401]*.

NEUMANN M.A. & COHN R. (1967) Progressive subcortical gliosis: a rare form of presenile dementia. *Brain* 90, 405–417 *[393]*.

NEVIN S. (1967) On some aspects of cerebral degeneration in later life. *Proceedings of the Royal Society of Medicine* 60, 517–526 *[387, 403]*.

NEVIN S., McMENEMEY W.H., BEHRAM S. & JONES D.P. (1960) Subacute spongiform encephalopathy—a subacute form of encephalopathy attributable to vascular dysfunction (spongiform cerebral atrophy). *Brain* 83, 519–564 *[401]*.

NEWCOMBE F. (1969) *Missile Wounds of the Brain: A Study of Psychological Deficits.* Oxford University Press *[42, 56, 158]*.

NEWCOMBE F. (1983) The psychological consequences of closed head injury: assessment and rehabilitation. *Injury* 14, 111–136 *[158, 182]*.

NEWCOMBE F., BROOKS N. & BADDELEY A. (1980) Rehabilitation after brain damage: an overview. *International Rehabilitation Medicine* 2, 133–137 *[182]*.

NEWCOMBE F. & MARSHALL J.C. (1981) On psycholinguistic classifications of the acquired dyslexias. *Bulletin of the Orton Society* 31, 29–46 *[40]*.

NEWCOMBE F.B., OLDFIELD R.C. & WINGFIELD A. (1965) Object naming by dysphasic patients. *Nature* 207, 1217–1218 *[87]*.

NEWMAN P.K. & SAUNDERS M. (1979) Lithium neurotoxicity. *Postgraduate Medical Journal* 55, 701–703 *[533]*.

NIEDERMEYER E. & KHALIFEH R. (1965) Petit mal status: an electroclinical approach. *Epilepsia* 6, 250–262 *[223]*.

NIEDERMEYER E., ZELLWEGER H. & ALEXANDER T. (1965) Central nervous system manifestations in myopathies. In *Eighth International Congress of Neurology*, International Congress Series No. 94, pp. 67–68. Exerpta Medica Foundation *[612]*.

NIELSEN J. (1968) Chromosomes in senile dementia. *British Journal of Psychiatry* 114, 303–309 *[373]*.

NIELSEN J. (1969) Klinefelter's syndrome and the XYY syndrome. *Acta Psychiatrica Scandinavica, Suppl.* 209, 1–353 *[446]*.

NIELSEN J. (1970a) Chromosomes in senile, presenile, and arteriosclerotic dementia. *Journal of Gerontology* 25, 312–315 *[373]*.

NIELSEN J. (1970b) Turner's syndrome in medical neurological and psychiatric wards. *Acta Psychiatrica Scandinavica* 46, 286–310 *[447]*.

NIELSEN J.M. (1930) Migraine equivalent. *American Journal of Psychiatry* 9, 637–641 *[350]*.

NIELSEN J.M. (1958) *Memory and Amnesia.* San Lucas Press: Los Angeles *[258, 350, 351]*.

NIELSEN J.M. & BUTT E.M. (1955) Treatment of Huntington's chorea with BAL. *Bulletin of the Los Angeles Neurological Society* 20, 38–39 *[426]*.

NOBLE P. (1974) Depressive illness and hyperparathyroidism. *Proceedings of the Royal Society of Medicine* 67, 1066–1067 *[450]*.

NODINE J.H., SHULKIN M.W., SLAP J.W., LEVINE M. & FREIBERG K. (1967) A double-blind study of the effect of ribonucleic acid in senile brain disease. *American Journal of Psychiatry* 123, 1257–1259 *[424]*.

NOGUCHI H. & MOORE J.W. (1913) A demonstration of treponema pallidum in the brain in cases of general paralysis. *Journal of Experimental Medicine* 17, 232–238 *[280]*.

NORDBERG A., ADOLFSSON R., AQUILONIUS S.-M., MARKLUND S., ORELAND L. & WINBLAD B. (1980) Brain enzymes and acetylcholine receptors in dementia of Alzheimer type and chronic alcohol abuse. In *Aging of the Brain and Dementia, Aging Vol. 13*, eds. Amaducci L., Davison A.N. & Antuono P. Raven Press: New York *[520]*.

NORDENSON I., ADOLFSSON R., BECKMAN G., BUCHT G. & WINBLAD B. (1980) Chromosomal abnormality in dementia of Alzheimer type. *Lancet* i, 481–482 *[378]*.

NORRIS J.W. & PRATT R.F. (1971) A controlled study of folic acid in epilepsy. *Neurology* 21, 659–664 *[506]*.

NORRMAN B. & SVAHN K. (1961) A follow-up study of severe brain injuries. *Acta Psychiatrica Scandinavica* 37, 236–264 *[153, 170]*.

NOSEWORTHY J.H., MILLER J., MURRAY T.J. & REGAN D. (1981) Auditory brainstem responses in post concussion syndrome. *Archives of Neurology* 38, 275–278 *[170]*.

NOTES ON ELICITING AND RECORDING CLINICAL INFORMATION (1973) The Department of Psychiatry Teaching Committee, The Institute of Psychiatry, London. Oxford University Press: London *[78, 83]*.

NOTT P.N. & FLEMINGER J.J. (1975) Presenile dementia: the difficulties of early diagnosis. *Acta Psychiatrica Scandinavica* 51, 210–217 *[410, 414]*.

NUFFIELD E.J.A. (1961) Neuro-physiology and behaviour disorders in epileptic children. *Journal of Mental Science* 107, 438–458 *[232]*.

OAKLEY D.P. (1965) Senile dementia: some aetiological factors. *British Journal of Psychiatry* 111, 414–419 *[375]*.

OATES J.K. (1979) Serological tests for syphilis and their clinical use. *British Journal of Hospital Medicine* 21, 612–617 *[285]*.

OBRADOR S. (1948) Clinical aspects of cerebral cysticercosis. *Archives of Neurology and Psychiatry* 59, 457–468 *[314]*.

OBRECHT R., OKHOMINA F.O.A. & SCOTT D.F. (1979) Value of EEG in acute confusional states. *Journal of Neurology, Neurosurgery and Psychiatry* 42, 75–77 *[113]*.

O'BRIEN M.D. & HARRIS P.W.R. (1968) Cerebral-cortex perfusion-rates in myxoedema. *Lancet* i, 1170–1172 *[435]*.

O'CONNOR J.F. (1959) Psychoses associated with disseminated lupus erythematosus. *Annals of Internal Medicine* 51, 526–536 *[364]*.

O'CONNOR J.F. & MUSHER D.M. (1966) Central nervous system involvement in systemic lupus erythematosus. *Archives of Neurology* 14, 157–164 *[363, 364, 365, 366]*.

O'CONNOR K.P., SHAW J.C. & ONGLEY C.O. (1979) The EEG and differential diagnosis in psychogeriatrics. *British Journal of Psychiatry* 135, 156–162 *[412]*.

ODDY M. (1984) Head injury and social adjustment. Ch. 6 in *Closed Head Injury: Psychological, Social, and Family Consequences*, ed. Brooks N. Oxford University Press *[185]*.

ODDY M. & HUMPHREY M. (1980) Social recovery during the year following severe head injury. *Journal of Neurology, Neurosurgery, and Psychiatry* 43, 798–802 *[186]*.

ODDY M., HUMPHREY M. & UTTLEY D. (1978) Stress upon the relatives of head-injured patients. *British Journal of Psychiatry* 133, 507–513 *[186]*.

OGURA C., OKUMA T., NAKAZAWA K. & KISHIMOTO A. (1976) Treatment of periodic somnolence with lithium carbonate. *Archives of Neurology* 33, 143 *[629]*.

OJEMANN R.G. (1971) Normal pressure hydrocephalus. Ch. 16 in *Clinical Neurosurgery*, Proceedings of the Congress of Neurological Surgeons, vol. 18. Williams & Wilkins: Baltimore *[336, 639, 641, 642, 643]*.

OJEMANN R.G., FISHER C.M., ADAMS R.D., SWEET W.H. & NEW P.J.F. (1969) Further experience with the syndrome of 'normal' pressure hydrocephalus. *Journal of Neurosurgery* 31, 279–294 *[639, 643, 645]*.

OKASHA A., SADEK A. & MONEIM S.A. (1975) Psychosocial and electroencephalographic studies of Egyptian murderers. *British Journal of Psychiatry* 126, 34–40 *[111]*.

OLDENDORF W.H. (1980) *The Quest for an Image of Brain.* Raven Press: New York *[124]*.

OLIN H.S. & WEISMAN A.D. (1964) Psychiatric misdiagnosis in early neurological disease. *Journal of the American Medical Association* 189, 533–538 *[205, 206]*.

OLIVARUS B. DE F. & RÖDER E. (1970) Reversible psychosis and dementia in myxoedema. *Acta Psychiatrica Scandinavica* 46, 1–13 *[433, 434]*.

OLIVECRONA H. (1938) Spasmodic torticollis. *British Medical Journal* 2, 241 *[576]*.

OLIVER J.E. (1970) Huntington's chorea in Northamptonshire. *British Journal of Psychiatry* 116, 241–253 *[393, 399]*.

OLIVER J. & DEWHURST K. (1969) Childhood and adolescent forms of Huntington's disease. *Journal of Neurology, Neurosurgery and Psychiatry* 32, 455–459 *[398]*.

OLSEN S. (1961) The brain in uraemia. *Acta Psychiatrica et Neurologica Scandinavica*, supplement 156, 1–129 *[475]*.

OLSON L.C., BUESCHER E.L., ARTENSTEIN M.S. & PARKMAN P.D. (1967) Herpes virus infections of the human central nervous system. *New England Journal of Medicine* 277, 1271–1277 *[300]*.

OLSON M.I. & SHAW C.-M. (1969) Presenile dementia and Alzheimer's disease in mongolism. *Brain* 92, 147–156 *[378]*.

OLSZEWSKI J. (1962) Subcortical arterosclerotic encephalopathy: review of the literature on the so-called Binswanger's disease and presentation of two cases. *World Neurology* 3, 359–375 *[390]*.

OMBREDANE A. (1929) Sur les troubles mentaux de la sclérose en plaques. Thèse de Paris. Quoted Surridge D., *British Journal of Psychiatry*, 1969, 115, 749–764 *[590, 591]*.

OOSTERHUIS H.J.G.H. & WILDE G.J.S. (1964) Psychiatric aspects of myasthenia gravis. *Psychiatria, Neurologia, Neurochirurgia* 67, 484–496 *[607, 608, 609, 610]*.

OPPENHEIMER D.R. (1976) Diseases of the basal ganglia, cerebellum and motor neurons. Ch. 14 in *Greenfield's Neuropathology*, 3rd Edition, eds. Blackwood W. & Corsellis J.A.N. Edward Arnold: London *[602]*.

ORBAN T. (1957) Experiences with a follow-up of 200 tabetic patients. *Acta Psychiatrica et Neurologica Scandinavica* 32, 89–102 *[279]*.

O'REGAN J.B. (1974) Hypersomnia and MAOI antidepressants. *Canadian Medical Association Journal* 111, 213 *[631]*.

O'RIORDAN J.L.H. (1972) Calcium and the nervous system. *Proceedings of the Royal Society of Medicine* 65, 873–874 *[452]*.

ORME J.E., LEE D. & SMITH M.R. (1964) Psychological assessments of brain damage and intellectual impairment in psychiatric patients. *British Journal of Social and Clinical Psychology* 3, 161–167 *[100]*.

ORWIN A., JAMES S.R.N. & TURNER R.K. (1974) Sex chromosome abnormalities, homosexuality and psychological treatment. *British Journal of Psychiatry* 124, 293–295 *[446]*.

O'SHEA H.E., ELSOM K.O. & HIGBE R.V. (1942) Studies of B-vitamins in the human subject: IV. Mental changes in experimental deficiency. *American Journal of the Medical Sciences* 203, 388–397 *[488]*.

OSTERRIETH P-A. (1944) Le test de copie d'une figure complexe. Contribution à l'étude de la perception et de la mémoire. *Archives de Psychologie* 30, 206–353 *[102]*.

OSTFELD A.M. & LEBOVITS B.Z. (1958) A comparison of the effects of psychological stress in renal and essential hypertension. *Psychosomatic Medicine* 20, 414 *[341]*.

OSTROV F.G., QUENCER R.M., GAYLIS N.B. & ALTMAN R.D. (1982) Cerebral atrophy in Systemic Lupus Erythematosus: Steroid- or disease-induced phenomenon? *American Journal of Euroradiology* 3, 21–23 *[365]*.

OSWALD I. & PRIEST R.G. (1965) Five weeks to escape the sleeping-pill habit. *British Medical Journal* 2, 1093–1095 *[523]*.

OSWALD I. & THACORE V.R. (1963) Amphetamine and phenmetrazine addiction. *British Medical Journal* 2, 427–431 *[535]*.

OTA Y. (1969) Psychiatric studies on civilian head injuries. Ch. 9 in *The Late Effects of Head Injury*, eds. Walker A.E., Caveness W.F. & Critchley M. Thomas: Springfield, Illinois *[156, 166]*.

OTTO R. & MacKAY I.R. (1967) Psychosocial and emotional disturbance in systemic lupus erythematosus. *Medical Journal of Australia* 2, 488–493 *[365]*.

OTTOSON J-O. & RAPP W. (1971) Serum levels of phenylalanine and tyrosine in Huntington's chorea. *Acta Psychiatrica Scandinavica*, supplement 221, 89–102 *[395]*.

OUNSTED C. (1955) The hyperkinetic syndrome in epileptic children. *Lancet* 2, 303–311 *[232, 238]*.

OUNSTED C., HUTT S.J. & LEE D. (1963) The retrograde amnesia of petit mal. *Lancet* 1, 671 *[230]*.

OUNSTED C., LINDSAY J. & NORMAN R. (1966) *Biological Factors in Temporal Lobe Epilepsy*. Heinemann: London *[215, 228]*.

OVERGAARD J. & TWEED W.A. (1974) Cerebral circulation after head injury. Part 1: cerebral blood flow and its regulation after closed head injury with emphasis on clinical correlations. *Journal of Neurosurgery* 41, 531–541 *[140]*.

OVERS R.P. & HEALY J.R. (1973) Stroke patients: their spouses, families and the community. Ch. 5 in *Medical and Psychological Aspects of Disability*, ed. Cobb A.B. Thomas: Springfield, Illinois *[334]*.

OXBURY J.M. & MacCALLUM F.O. (1973) Herpes simplex virus encephalitis: clinical features and residual damage. *Postgraduate Medical Journal* 49, 387–389 *[301]*.

PAI M.N. (1945) Change in personality after cerebrospinal fever. *British Medical Journal* 1, 289–293 *[309]*.

PAI M.N. (1950) Hypersomnia syndromes. *British Medical Journal* 1, 522–524 *[629]*.

PAILLAS J-E. & TAMALET J. (1950) Les tumeurs temporales. *Presse Medicale* 58, 550–554 *[196]*.

PALLIS C.A. (1971) Parkinsonism: natural history and clinical features. *British Medical Journal* 3, 683–690 *[550]*.

PALLIS C.A. & FUDGE B.J. (1956) The neurological complications of Behcet's syndrome. *Archives of Neurology and Psychiatry* 75, 1–14 *[650]*.

PALLIS C. & LEWIS P.D. (1980) Neurology of gastrointestinal disease. Ch. 21 in *Handbook of Clinical Neurology, Vol. 39, Neurological manifestations of systemic diseases, Part II*, eds. Vinken P.J. & Bruyn C.W. North Holland Publishing Co.: Amsterdam *[649]*.

PALLIS C. & LOUIS S. (1961) Television-induced seizures. *Lancet* 1, 188–190 *[211]*.

PAMPIGLIONE G. & FALCONER M.A. (1960) Electrical stimulation of the hippocampus in man. Ch. 57 in *Handbook of Physiology, Section 1: Neurophysiology, vol. 2*, ed. Field J. American Physiological Society *[236]*.

PAPEZ J.W. (1937) A proposed mechanism of emotion. *Archives of Neurology and Psychiatry* 38, 725–743 *[23, 36]*.

PARE C.M.B., YEUNG D.P.H., PRICE K. & STACEY R.S. (1969) 5-hydroxytryptamine, noradrenaline, and dopamine in brain stem, hypothalamus, and caudate nucleus of controls and of patients committing suicide by coal-gas poisoning. *Lancet* 2, 133–135 *[24]*.

PARKER N. (1956) Disseminated sclerosis presenting as schizophrenia. *Medical Journal of Australia* 1, 405–407 *[595]*.

PARKER N. (1957) Manic-depressive psychosis following head injury. *Medical Journal of Australia* 2, 20–22 *[165]*.

PARKER S.A. & SERRATS A.F. (1976) Memory recovery after traumatic coma. *Acta Neurochirurgica* 34, 71–77 *[159]*.

PARKES J.D. (1973) Clomipramine (anafranil) in the treatment of cataplexy. *Journal of International Medical Research* 1, 427–431 *[623, 626]*.

PARKES J.D. (1985) *Sleep and its Disorders*. W.B. Saunders: London *[623]*.

PARKES J.D. & FENTON G.W. (1973) Levo(–)amphetamine and dextro(+)amphetamine in the treatment of narcolepsy. *Journal of Neurology, Neurosurgery and Psychiatry* 36, 1076–1081 *[623]*.

PARKES J.D. & MARSDEN C.D. (1973) The treatment of Parkinson's disease. *British Journal of Hospital Medicine* 10, 284–294 *[552]*.

PARKINSON I.S., WARD M.K., FEEST T.G., FAWCETT R.W.P. & KERR D.N.S. (1979) Fracturing dialysis osteodystrophy and dialysis encephalopathy. An epidemiological survey. *Lancet* 1, 406–409 *[475]*.

PARKINSON J. (1817) *An Essay on the Shaking Palsy.* Sherwood: London *[550]*.

PARRY J. (1968) Contribution à l'étude des manifestations des lesions expansives observées dans un hôpital psychiatrique. Thesis, Faculté de Médicine de Paris *[187, 191]*.

PARSONAGE M. (1973) The differential diagnosis of seizures. *Journal of the Royal College of Physicians of London* 7, 213–233 *[255]*.

PARSONAGE M. (1982) Introduction. In *A Textbook of Epilepsy*, 2nd Edition, eds. Laidlaw J. & Richens A., pp. xiii–xvii. Churchill Livingstone: Edinburgh & London *[210]*.

PARSONAGE M.J. & NORRIS J.W. (1967) User of diazepam in treatment of severe convulsive status epilepticus. *British Medical Journal* 3, 85–88 *[270]*.

PARSONS M. (1979) *Tuberculous Meningitis: A Handbook for Clinicians.* Oxford University Press *[312]*.

PARSONS O.A. (1977) Neuropsychological deficits in alcoholics: facts and fancies. *Alcoholism: Clinical and Experimental Research* 1, 51–56 *[518]*.

PARSONS-SMITH B.G., SUMMERSKILL W.H.J., DAWSON A.M. & SHERLOCK S. (1957) The encephalograph in liver disease. *Lancet* 2, 867–871 *[481]*.

PARTRIDGE M. (1950) *Prefrontal Leucotomy.* Blackwell Scientific Publications: Oxford *[69]*.

PASAMANICK B. & KAWI A. (1956) A study of the association of prenatal and paranatal factors with the development of tics in children. *Journal of Pediatrics* 48, 596–601 *[583]*.

PASQUALINI R.Q., VIDAL G. & BUR G.E. (1957) Psychopathology of Klinefelter's syndrome. Review of thirty-one cases. *Lancet* 2, 164–167 *[446]*.

PASSOUANT P., CADILHAC J. & BALDY-MOULINIER M. (1967) Physiopathologie des hypersomnies. *Revue Neurologique* 116, 585–629 *[628, 629]*.

PATERSON M.T. (1945) Spasmodic torticollis: results of psychotherapy in twenty-one cases. *Lancet* 2, 556–559 *[572, 573, 574, 576]*.

PATTEN B.M. (1972) The ancient art of memory. Usefulness in treatment. *Archives of Neurology* 26, 25–31 *[182]*.

PATTEN D.H. & BENSON D.F. (1968) Diagnosis of normal-pressure hydrocephalus by risa cisternography. *Journal of Nuclear Medicine* 9, 457–461 *[117]*.

PATTERSON A. & ZANGWILL O.L. (1944) Recovery of spatial orientation in the post-traumatic confusional state. *Brain* 67, 54–68 *[11]*.

PATTERSON R.M., BAGGHI B.K. & TEST A. (1948) The prediction of Huntington's chorea. An electroencephalographic and genetic study. *American Journal of Psychiatry* 104, 786–797 *[394]*.

PATTERSON R.M. & LITTLE S.C. (1943) Spasmodic torticollis. *Journal of Nervous and Mental Disease* 98, 571–599 *[571, 572, 574]*.

PATTIE A.H. & GILLEARD C.J. (1975) A brief psychogeriatric assessment schedule. Validation against psychiatric diagnosis and discharge from hospital. *British Journal of Psychiatry* 127, 489–493 *[107]*.

PATTIE A.H. & GILLEARD C.J. (1976) The Clifton Assessment Schedule—further validation of a psychogeriatric assessment schedule. *British Journal of Psychiatry* 129, 68–72 *[107]*.

PATTIE A.H. & GILLEARD C.J. (1978) The two-year predictive validity of the Clifton Assessment Schedule and the Shortened Stockton Geriatric Rating Scale. *British Journal of Psychiatry* 133, 457–460 *[107]*.

PATTON R.B. & SHEPPARD J.A. (1956) Intracranial tumors found at autopsy in mental patients. *American Journal of Psychiatry* 113, 319–324 *[203]*.

PAULSON G.W. (1971) The neurological examination in dementia. Ch. 2 in *Dementia*, ed. Wells C.E. Blackwell Scientific Publications: Oxford *[80]*.

PAXTON R. & AMBROSE J. (1974) The EMI scanner: a brief review of the first 650 patients. *British Journal of Radiology* 47, 530–565 *[119]*.

PEARCE J. (1969) *Migraine: Clinical Features, Mechanisms and Management.* Thomas: Springfield, Illinois *[344, 346, 354]*.

PEARCE J. & MILLER E. (1973) *Clinical Aspects of Dementia.* Baillière Tindall: London *[378, 424]*.

PEARLSON G.D., GARBACZ D.J. & TOMPKINS R.H. (1983) Imaging of the brain: aiding the search for physical correlates of mental illness. *Integrative Psychiatry* 1, 134–138 *[121]*.

PEARLSON G.D. & VEROFF A.E. (1981) Computerised tomographic scan changes in manic-depressive illness. *Lancet* 2, 470 *[122]*.

PEDLEY T.A. & GUILLEMINAULT C. (1977) Episodic nocturnal wanderings responsive to anticonvulsant drug therapy. *Annals of Neurology* 2, 30–35 *[263]*.

PELTONEN L. (1962) Pneumoencephalographic studies on the third ventricle of 644 neuropsychiatric patients. *Acta Psychiatrica Scandinavica* 38, 15–34 *[121]*.

PENALVER R. (1955) Manganese poisoning. *Industrial Medicine and Surgery* 24, 1–7 *[541]*.

PENFIELD W. (1968) Engrams in the human brain. *Proceedings of the Royal Society of Medicine* 61, 831–840 *[24]*.

PENFIELD W. & ERICKSON T.C. (1941) *Epilepsy and Cerebral Localization.* Thomas: Springfield, Illinois *[218]*.

PENFIELD W. & NORCROSS N.C. (1936) Subdural traction and post-traumatic headache. *Archives of Neurology and Psychiatry* 36, 75–95 *[169]*.

PENFIELD W. & PEROT P. (1963) The brain's record of auditory and visual experience. A final summary and discussion. *Brain* 86, 595–696 *[219]*.

PENROSE R.J.J. (1972) Life events before subarachnoid haemorrhage. *Journal of Psychosomatic Research* 16, 329–333 *[339]*.

PENROSE R. & STOREY P.B. (1970) Emotional disturbance and subarachnoid haemorrhage. *Psychotherapy and Psychosomatics* 18, 321–325 *[339]*.

PENTLAND B. & MAWDSLEY C. (1982) Wernicke's encephalopathy following hunger strike. *Postgraduate Medical Journal* 58, 427–428 *[492]*.

PEREZ M.M., TRIMBLE M.R., MURRAY N.N.F. & REIDER I. (1985) Epileptic psychosis: an evaluation of PSE profiles. *British Journal of Psychiatry* 146, 155–163 *[248, 249, 253]*.

PERK D. (1947) Cerebral symptoms in thrombo-angiitis obliterans. *Journal of Mental Science* 93, 748–755 *[369]*.

PERL D.P. & BRODY A.R. (1980) Alzheimer's disease: X-ray spectrometric evidence of aluminium accumulation in neurofibrillary tangle-bearing neurones. *Science* 208, 297–299 *[384]*.

PERLSTEIN M. & ATTALA R. (1966) Neurologic sequelae of plumbism in children. *Clinical Pediatrics* 5, 292–298 *[539]*.

PERLSTEIN M.A., GIBBS F.A., GIBBS E.L. & STEIN M.D. (1960) Electroencephalogram and myopathy. Relation between muscular dystrophy and related diseases. *Journal of the American Medical Association* 173, 1329–1333 *[612]*.

PERRET E. (1974) The left frontal lobe of man and the suppression of habitual responses in verbal categorical behaviour. *Neuropsychologia* 12, 323–330 *[88]*.

PERRY E.K., GIBSON P.H., BLESSED G., PERRY R.H. & TOMLINSON B.E. (1977) Neurotransmitter enzyme abnormalities in senile dementia. Choline acetyltransferase and glutamic acid decarboxylase activities in necropsy brain tissue. *Journal of the Neurological Sciences* 34, 247–265 *[382]*.

PERRY E.K., TOMLINSON B.E., BLESSED G., BERGMANN K., GIBSON

P.H. & PERRY R.H. (1978) Correlation of cholinergic abnormalities with senile plaques and mental test scores in senile dementia. *British Medical Journal* 2, 1457–1459 *[382]*.

PERRY J.C. & JACOBS D. (1982) Overview: clinical applications of the amytal interview in psychiatric emergency settings. *American Journal of Psychiatry* 139, 552–559 *[412]*.

PERRY R.H., TOMLINSON B.E., CANDY J.M., BLESSED G., FOSTER J.F., BLOXHAM C.A. & PERRY E.R. (1983) Cortical cholinergic deficit in mentally impaired parkinsonian patients. *Lancet* 2, 789–790 *[557]*.

PERRY T.L., HANSEN S., DIAMOND S. & STEDMAN D. (1969) Plasma-aminoacid levels in Huntington's chorea. *Lancet* 1, 806–808 *[395]*.

PERRY T.L., HANSEN S. & KLOSTER M. (1973) Huntington's chorea: deficiency of γ-aminobutyric acid in brain. *New England Journal of Medicine* 288, 337–342 *[395]*.

PETERSEN P. (1968) Psychiatric disorders in primary hyperparathyroidism. *Journal of Clinical Endocrinology and Metabolism* 28, 1491–1495 *[448, 449, 450, 477]*.

PETERSON H. DE C. & SWANSON A.G. (1964) Acute encephalopathy occurring during haemodialysis. *Archives of Internal Medicine* 113, 877–880 *[474]*.

PEYSER J.M., EDWARDS K.R. & POSER C.M. (1980a) Psychological profiles in patients with multiple sclerosis. A preliminary investigation. *Archives of Neurology* 37, 437–440 *[591]*.

PEYSER J.M., EDWARDS K.R., POSER C.M. & FILSKOV S.B. (1980b) Cognitive function in patients with multiple sclerosis. *Archives of Neurology* 37, 577–579 *[592]*.

PHELPS C. (1898) *Traumatic Injuries of the Brain and its Membranes.* Kimpton: London *[154]*.

PHELPS M.E., HUANG S.C., HOFFMAN E.J., SELIN C., SOKOLOFF L. & KUHL D.E. (1979) Tomographic measurement of local cerebral glucose metabolic rate in humans with (F-18) 2-Fluoro-2-Deoxy-D-Glucose: validation of method. *Annals of Neurology* 6, 371–388 *[124]*.

PHILIPPOPOULOS G.S., WITTKOWER E.D. & COUSINEAU A. (1958) The etiologic significance of emotional factors in onset and exacerbation of multiple sclerosis. *Psychosomatic Medicine* 20, 458–474 *[597, 598]*.

PICK A. (1892) Ueber die Beziehungen der senilen Hirnatrophie zur Aphasie. *Prager medizinische Wochenschrift* 17, 165–167 *[391]*.

PICKARD J.D. (1982) Adult communicating hydrocephalus. *British Journal of Hospital Medicine* 27, 35–44 *[640]*.

PIERCY M. (1959) Testing for intellectual impairment—some comments on the tests and the testers. *Journal of Mental Science* 105, 489–495 *[93, 94]*.

PIERCY M. (1964) The effects of cerebral lesions on intellectual function: a review of current research trends. *British Journal of Psychiatry* 110, 310–352 *[37, 40, 42, 50, 54, 157]*.

PIERCY M. (1977) Experimental studies of the organic amnesic syndrome. Ch. 1 in *Amnesia: Clinical, Psychological and Medicolegal Aspects*, 2nd Edition, eds. Whitty C.W.M. & Zangwill O.L. Butterworths: London *[28, 33]*.

PIERCY M. & SMYTH V.O.G. (1962) Right hemisphere dominance for certain non-verbal intellectual skills. *Brains* 85, 775–790 *[97]*.

PILLERI G. (1966) The Klüver-Bucy syndrome in man: a clinico-anatomical contribution to the function of the medial temporal lobe structures. *Psychiatria et Neurologia* 152, 65–103 *[23]*.

PINCUS J.H. (1972) Subacute necrotizing encephalomyelopathy (Leigh's disease): a consideration of clinical features and etiology. *Developmental Medicine and Child Neurology* 14, 87–101 *[500]*.

PINCUS J.H., COOPER J.R., ITOKAWA Y. & GUMBINAS M. (1971) Subacute necrotizing encephalomyelopathy: effects of thiamine and thiamine propyl disulfide. *Archives of Neurology* 24, 511–517 *[501]*.

PINTO R. (1972) A case of movement epilepsy with agarophobia treated successfully by flooding. *British Journal of Psychiatry* 121, 287–288 *[243]*.

PLAITAKIS A., WHETSELL W.O., COOPER J.R. & YAHR M.D. (1980) Chronic Leigh disease: a genetic and biochemical study. *Annals of Neurology* 7, 304–310 *[500]*.

PLUM F. & POSNER J.B. (1972) *Diagnosis of Stupor and Coma*, 2nd edn. Davis: Philadelphia *[323]*.

PLUM F., POSNER J.B. & HAIN R.F. (1962) Delayed neurological deterioration after anoxia. *Archives of Internal Medicine* 110, 18–25 *[470]*.

PLUVINAGE R. (1954) Les atrophies cérébrales des alcooliques. *Bulletins et Mémoires de la Société Médicale des Hôpitaux de Paris* 70, 524–526 *[519]*.

POECK K. (1969) Pathophysiology of emotional disorders associated with brain damage. Ch. 20 in *Handbook of Clinical Neurology*, vol 3, eds. Vinken P.J. & Bruyn G.W. North-Holland Publishing Company: Amsterdam *[72]*.

POKLIS A. & BURKETT C.D. (1977) Gasoline sniffing: a review. *Clinical Toxicology* 11, 35–41 *[537]*.

POLITES D.J., KRUGER D. & STEVENSON I. (1965) Sequential treatments in a case of Gilles de la Tourette's syndrome. *British Journal of Medical Psychology* 38, 43–52 *[582]*.

POLKEY C. (1981a) Surgery for epilepsy. *British Journal of Hospital Medicine* 25, 48–57 *[274]*.

POLKEY C. (1981b) Selection of patients with chronic drug-resistant epilepsy for resective surgery: 5 years' experience. *Journal of the Royal Society of Medicine* 74, 574–579 *[274]*.

POLKEY C.E. (1982) Neurosurgery. Ch. 10 Part 1 in *A Textbook of Epilepsy*, 2nd Edition, eds. Laidlaw J. & Richens A. Churchill Livingstone: Edinburgh and London *[257, 274, 275]*.

POLLOCK M. & HORNABROOK R.W. (1966) The prevalence, natural history and dementia of Parkinson's disease. *Brain* 89, 429–448 *[556, 562]*.

POMEROY J.C. (1980) Klinefelter's syndrome and schizophrenia. *British Journal of Psychiatry* 136, 597–599 *[447]*.

POND D.A. (1952a) Psychiatric aspects of epilepsy in children. *Journal of Mental Science* 98, 404–410 *[232]*.

POND D.A. (1952b) Narcolepsy: a brief critical review and study of eight cases. *Journal of Mental Science* 98, 595–604 *[624]*.

POND D.A. (1957) Psychiatric aspects of epilepsy in children. *Journal of the Indian Medical Profession* 3, 1441–1451 *[217, 225, 231, 243, 245, 246, 252, 262]*.

POND D.A. (1961) Psychiatric aspects of epileptic and brain-damaged children. *British Medical Journal* 2, 1377–1382 and 1454–1459 *[228, 229, 238]*.

POND D.A. (1962) Discussion following 'The schizophrenia-like psychoses of epilepsy'. *Proceedings of the Royal Society of Medicine* 55, 316 *[249, 250]*.

POND D.A. & BIDWELL B.H. (1960) A survey of epilepsy in fourteen general practices. II: Social and psychological aspects. *Epilepsia* 1, 285–299 *[227, 232, 233, 243]*.

POND D.A., BIDWELL B.H. & STEIN L. (1960) A survey of epilepsy in fourteen general practices. I: Demographic and medical data. *Psychiatria, Neurologia, Neurochirurgia* 63, 217–236 *[212, 227]*.

POPPEN J.L. & MARTINEZ-NIOCHET A. (1951) Spasmodic torticollis. *Surgical Clinics of North America* 31, 883–890 *[574, 576]*.

PORTEOUS H.B. & ROSS D.N. (1956) Mental symptoms in parkinsonism following benzhexol hydrochloride therapy. *British Medical Journal* 2, 138–140 *[559]*.

POSER C.M., HUNTLEY C.J. & POLAND J.D. (1969) Para-encephalitic parkinsonism. Report of an acute case due to coxsackie virus type B^2 and re-examination of the etiologic concepts of post-encephalitic parkinsonism. *Acta Neurologica Scandinavica* **45**, 199–215 *[292]*.

POSER C.M. & ZIEGLER D.K. (1960) Temporary amnesia as a manifestation of cerebrovascular insufficiency. *Transactions of the American Neurological Association*, 221–223 *[357]*.

POST F. (1944) Some problems arising from a study of mental patients over the age of sixty years. *Journal of Mental Science* **90**, 554–565 *[375]*.

POST F. (1965) *The Clinical Psychiatry of Late Life*. Pergamon: Oxford *[102, 106, 410, 411]*.

POST F. (1968) The development and progress of senile dementia in relationship to the functional psychiatric disorders of later life. In *Senile Dementia: Clinical and Therapeutic Aspects*, eds. Müller Ch. & Ciompi L. Huber: Bern *[374, 375]*.

POTAMIANOS G. & KELLETT J.M. (1982) Anti-cholinergic drugs and memory: the effects of benzhexol on memory in a group of geriatric patients. *British Journal of Psychiatry* **140**, 470–472 *[533]*.

POTTER J.M. (1969) Clinical aspects of herpes simplex encephalitis. In *Virus Diseases and the Nervous System*, eds. Whitty C.W.M., Hughes J.T. & MacCallum F.O. Blackwell Scientific Publications: Oxford *[300]*.

POWELL G.E. (1981) *Brain Function Therapy*. Gower Publishing Co.: Aldershot, Hants *[272]*.

POWELL-PROCTOR L. & MILLER E. (1982) Reality orientation: a critical appraisal. *British Journal of Psychiatry* **140**, 457–463 *[423]*.

PRAKASH C. & STERN G. (1973) Neurological signs in the elderly. *Age and Ageing* **2**, 24–27 *[80]*.

PRATT R.T.C. (1951) An investigation of the psychiatric aspects of disseminated sclerosis. *Journal of Neurology, Neurosurgery and Psychiatry* **14**, 326–335 *[594, 595, 596, 597, 598]*.

PRATT R.T.C. (1967) *The Genetics of Neurological Disorders*. Oxford University Press *[215, 377, 550, 601]*.

PRATT R.T.C. & WARRINGTON E.K. (1972) The assessment of cerebral dominance with unilateral ECT. *British Journal of Psychiatry* **121**, 327–328 *[38]*.

PRIBRAM K.H., AHUMADA A., HARTOG J. & ROOS L. (1964) A progress report on the neurological processes disturbed by frontal lesions in primates. Ch. 3 in *The Frontal Granular Cortex and Behaviour*, eds. Warren J.M. & Akert K. McGraw-Hill: New York *[69]*.

PRIEN R.F. (1973) Chemotherapy in chronic organic brain syndrome—a review of the literature. *Psychopharmacology Bulletin* **9**, 5–20 *[424]*.

PRIEST R.G., TARIGHATI S. & SHARIATMADARI M.E. (1969) A brief test of organic brain disease validation in a mental hospital population. *Acta Psychiatrica Scandinavica* **45**, 347–354 *[102]*.

PRITCHARD B.N.C., JOHNSON A.W., HILL I.D. & ROSENHEIM M.L. (1968) Bethanidine, guanethidine, and methyldopa in the treatment of hypertension: a within-patient comparison. *British Medical Journal* **1**, 135–144 *[342]*.

PROBST F.P. (1973) Congenital defects of the corpus callosum. Morphology and encephalographic appearances. *Acta Radiologica; Diagnosis*, Supplement, 1–152 *[654]*.

PRUDHOMME C. (1941) Epilepsy and suicide. *Journal of Nervous and Mental Disease* **94**, 722–731 *[253]*.

PRUSINER S.B. (1984) Prions. *Scientific American* **251**(4), 48–57 *[400]*.

PUDENZ R.H. & SHELDEN C.H. (1946) The lucite calvarium—a method for direct observation of the brain. *Journal of Neurosurgery* **3**, 487–505 *[138]*.

PUGH L.G.C. & WARD M.P. (1956) Some effects of high altitude on man. *Lancet* **2**, 1115–1121 *[468]*.

PUTNAM C.E. (1974) Morgagni syndrome and hyperostosis frontalis interna. *Lancet* **2**, 1331–1332 *[654]*.

PYKETT I.L. (1982) NMR imaging in medicine. *Scientific American* **246**(5), 54–64 *[123]*.

QUADFASEL A.F. & PRUYSER P.W. (1955) Cognitive deficit in patients with psychomotor epilepsy. *Epilepsia* **4**, 80–90 *[229]*.

RADERMECKER J. & DUMON J. (1969) Genetic epilepsies. Ch. 3 in *The Physiopathogenesis of the Epilepsies*, eds. Gastaut H., Jasper H., Bancaud J. & Waltregny A. Thomas: Springfield, Illinois *[213]*.

RADUE E.W., DU BOULAY G.H., HARRISON M.J.G. & THOMAS D.J. (1978) Comparison of angiographic and CT findings between patients with multi-infarct dementia and those with dementia due to primary neuronal degeneration. *Neuroradiology* **16**, 113–115 *[387, 389]*.

RAFT A.A. (1962) Learning theory and the treatment of tics. *Journal of Psychosomatic Research* **6**, 71–76 *[586]*.

RAIL D., SCHOLTZ C. & SWASH M. (1981) Post-encephalitic parkinsonism: current experience. *Journal of Neurology, Neurosurgery and Psychiatry* **44**, 670–676 *[298]*.

RAMANI S.V. (1981) Psychosis associated with frontal lobe lesions in Schilder's cerebral sclerosis. *Journal of Clinical Psychiatry* **42**, 250–252 *[599]*.

RAMSAY A.M. (1973) Benign myalgic encephalomyelitis. *British Journal of Psychiatry* **122**, 618–619 *[315]*.

RANDALL R.E., ROSSMEISL E.C. & BLEIFER K.H. (1959) Magnesium depletion in man. *Annals of Internal Medicine* **50**, 257–287 *[478]*.

RANSOHOFF J., DERBY B. & KRICHEFF I. (1971) Spontaneous intracerebral haemorrhage. Ch. 14 in *Clinical Neurosurgery*, vol. 18. Proceedings of the Congress of Neurosurgical Surgeons. Williams & Wilkins: Baltimore *[320]*.

RAO D.B. & NORRIS J.R. (1972) A double-blind investigation of hydergine in the treatment of cerebrovascular insufficiency in the elderly. *Johns Hopkins Medical Journal* **130**, 317–324 *[425]*.

RAO N.S. & PEARCE J. (1971) Hypothalamic-pituitary-adrenal axis studies in migraine with special reference to insulin sensitivity. *Brain* **94**, 289–298 *[346]*.

RASKIN N. (1956) Intracranial neoplasms in psychotic patients. *American Journal of Psychiatry* **112**, 481–484 *[203, 204]*.

RASMUSSEN T. (1969) The role of surgery in the treatment of focal epilepsy. *Clinical Neurosurgery* **16**, 288–314 *[274]*.

RATCLIFF G. & NEWCOMBE F. (1973) Spatial orientation in man: effects of left, right, and bilateral posterior cerebral lesions. *Journal of Neurology, Neurosurgery and Psychiatry* **36**, 448–454 *[55]*.

RATCLIFFE J., RITTMAN A., WOLF S. & VERITY M.A. (1975) Creutzfeldt-Jakob disease with focal onset unsuccessfully treated with amantadine. *Bulletin of the Los Angeles Neurological Society* **40**, 18–20 *[427]*.

RAVEN J.C. (1958a) *Guide to the Standard Progressive Matrices*. H.K. Lewis: London *[97]*.

RAVEN J.C. (1958b) *Guide to using the Mill Hill Vocabulary Scale and the Progressive Matrices Scales*. H.K. Lewis: London *[97]*.

RAVEN J.C. (1960) *Guide to Using the Coloured Progressive Matrices*. H.K. Lewis: London *[97]*.

RAYMOND R.W. & WILLIAMS R.L. (1948) Infectious mononucleosis with psychosis; report of case. *New England Journal of Medicine* **239**, 542–544 *[302]*.

READ A.E., GOUGH K.R., PARDOE J.L. & NICHOLAS A. (1965) Nutritional studies on the entrants to an old people's home, with particular reference to folic acid deficiency. *British Medical Journal* **2**, 843–848 *[504, 505]*.

READ A.E., SHERLOCK S., LAIDLAW J. & WALKER J.G. (1967) The neuropsychiatric syndromes associated with chronic liver disease and an extensive portal-systemic collateral circulation. *Quarterly Journal of Medicine* **36**, 135–150 *[480, 481]*.

REAVLEY W. (1975) The use of biofeedback in the treatment of writer's cramp. *Journal of Behaviour Therapy and Experimental Psychiatry* **6**, 335–338 *[579]*.

RECHTSCHAFFEN A.R., WOLPERT E.A., DEMENT W.C., MITCHELL S.A. & FISHER C. (1963) Nocturnal sleep of narcoleptics. *Electroencephalography and Clinical Neurophysiology* **15**, 599–609 *[622]*.

REED D., CRAWLEY J., FARO S.N., PIEPER S.J. & KURLAND L.T. (1963) Thallotoxosis. *Journal of the American Medical Association* **183**(i), 516–522 *[542]*.

REED T.E. & CHANDLER J.H. (1958) Huntington's chorea in Michigan. 1: Demography and genetics. *American Journal of Human Genetics* **10**, 201–225 *[399]*.

REES L.H. (1981) Brain opiates and corticotrophin-related peptides. The Goulstonian Lecture, 1980. *Journal of the Royal College of Physicians of London* **15**, 130–134 *[428]*.

REES W.L. (1961) Fundamentals in the psychological background. In *Stroke Rehabilitation*, pp. 12–15. The Chest and Heart Association, Tavistock Square, London *[330]*.

REES W.L. (1971) Psychiatric and psychological factors in migraine. Ch. 6 in *Background to Migraine*. Fourth Migraine Symposium, ed. Cumings J.N. Heinemann: London *[348]*.

REEVES A.G. & PLUM F. (1969) Hyperphagia, rage and dementia accompanying a ventromedial hypothalamic neoplasm. *Archives of Neurology* **20**, 616–624 *[199]*.

REFSUM S., ENGESET A. & LONNUM A. (1959) Pneumoencephalographic changes in dystrophia myotonica. *Acta Psychiatrica et Neurologica Scandinavica*, supplement 137, 98–99 *[616]*.

REFSUM S., LONNUM A., SJAASTAD O. & ENGESET A. (1967) Dystrophia myotonica: repeated pneumoencephalographic studies in ten patients. *Neurology* **17**, 345–348 *[616]*.

REICHLIN S. (1968) Neuroendocrinology. Ch. 12 in *Textbook of Endocrinology*, ed. Williams R.H., 4th edn. Saunders: Philadelphia *[440]*.

REIO L. & WETTERBERG L. (1969) False porphobilinogen reactions in the urine of mental patients. *Journal of the American Medical Association* **207**, 148–150 *[484]*.

REISBERG B., FERRIS S.H. & GERSHON S. (1981) An overview of pharmacologic treatment of cognitive decline in the aged. *American Journal of Psychiatry* **138**, 593–600 *[425]*.

REISER M.F., ROSENBAUM M. & FERRIS E.B. (1951) Psychologic mechanisms in malignant hypertension. *Psychosomatic Medicine* **13**, 147–159 *[340]*.

REITAN R.M. (1958) Validity of the trail making test as an indicator of organic brain damage. *Perceptual and Motor Skills* **8**, 271–276 *[99]*.

REITAN R.M. (1966) A research program on the psychological effects of brain lesions in human beings. In *International Review of Research in Mental Retardation*, vol. 1, ed. Ellis N.R. Academic Press: New York *[99]*.

REMINGTON F.B. & RUBERT S.L. (1962) Why patients with brain tumours come to a psychiatric hospital. *American Journal of Psychiatry* **119**, 256–257 *[203]*.

RENNIE T.A.C. & HOWARD J.E. (1942) Hypoglycaemia and tension-depression *Psychosomatic Medicine* **4**, 273–282 *[462]*.

REPORT OF THE BOARD OF SCIENCE AND EDUCATION WORKING PARTY (1984) *Boxing*. British Medical Association: London *[175]*.

RESKE-NIELSEN E. & LUNDBAEK K. (1963) Diabetic encephalopathy: diffuse and focal lesions of the brain in long-term diabetes. *Acta Neurologica Scandinavica*, supplement 4, 273–290 *[457]*.

RESNICK J.S., ENGEL W.K. & SEVER J.L. (1968) Subacute sclerosing panencephalitis. *New England Journal of Medicince* **279**, 126–129 *[306]*.

REVELEY A.M. & REVELEY M.A. (1983) Aqueduct stenosis and schizophrenia. *Journal of Neurology, Neurosurgery and Psychiatry* **46**, 18–22 *[645]*.

REVELEY A.M., REVELEY M.A. & MURRAY R.M. (1984) Cerebral ventricular enlargement in non-genetic schizophrenia: a controlled twin study. *British Journal of Psychiatry* **144**, 89–93 *[122]*.

REVELEY M.A. (1985) CT scans in schizophrenia. *British Journal of Psychiatry* **146**, 367–371 *[122]*.

REY A. (1941) L'examen psychologique dans les cas d'encéphalopathie traumatique. *Archives de Psychologie* **28**, 286–340 *[102]*.

REYNOLDS E.H. (1967a) Effects of folic acid on the mental state and fit frequency of drug-treated epileptic patients. *Lancet* **1**, 1086–1088 *[238, 506]*.

REYNOLDS E.H. (1967b) Schizophrenia-like psychoses of epilepsy and disturbances of folate and vitamin B$_{12}$ metabolism induced by anticonvulsant drugs. *British Journal of Psychiatry* **113**, 911–919 *[252, 506]*.

REYNOLDS E.H. (1968) Epilepsy and schizophrenia: relationship and biochemistry. *Lancet* **1**, 398–401 *[252]*.

REYNOLDS E.H. (1973) Anticonvulsants, folic acid, and epilepsy. *Lancet* **1**, 1376–1378 *[506]*.

REYNOLDS E.H. (1975) Chronic antiepileptic toxicity: a review. *Epilepsia* **16**, 319–352 *[267]*.

REYNOLDS E.H. (1978a) Drug treatment of epilepsy. *Lancet* **2**, 721–725 *[265]*.

REYNOLDS E.H. (1978b) How do anticonvulsants work? *British Journal of Hospital Medicine* **19**, 505–512 *[265]*.

REYNOLDS E.H. (1979) Cerebrospinal fluid folate: clinical studies. Ch. 22 in *Folic Acid in Neurology, Psychiatry, and Internal Medicine*, eds. Botez M.I. & Reynolds E.H. Raven Press: New York *[504]*.

REYNOLDS E.H. (1981) The management of seizures associated with psychological disorders. Ch. 3 in *Epilepsy and Psychiatry*, eds. Reynolds E.H. & Trimble M.R. Churchill Livingstone: Edinburgh & London *[265, 267]*.

REYNOLDS E.H. (1982) The pharmacological management of epilepsy associated with psychological disorders. *British Journal of Psychiatry* **141**, 549–557 *[265, 267]*.

REYNOLDS E.H. (1983) Interictal behaviour in temporal lobe epilepsy. *British Medical Journal* **286**, 918–919 *[233]*.

REYNOLDS E.H., CHANARIN I., MILNER G. & MATTHEWS D.M. (1966) Anticonvulsant therapy, folic acid and vitamin B$_{12}$ metabolism and mental symptoms. *Epilepsia* **7**, 261–270 *[506]*.

REYNOLDS E.H., MILNER G., MATTHEWS D.M. & CHANARIN I. (1966) Anticonvulsant therapy, megaloblastic haemopoeisis and folic acid metabolism. *Quarterly Journal of Medicine* **35**, 521–537 *[506]*.

REYNOLDS E.H., PREECE J.M., BAILEY J. & COPPEN A. (1970) Folate deficiency in depressive illness. *British Journal of Psychiatry* **117**, 287–292 *[504]*.

REYNOLDS E.H., PREECE J. & CHANARIN I. (1969) Folic acid and anticonvulsants. *Lancet* **1**, 1264–1265 *[506]*.

REYNOLDS E.H., PREECE J. & JOHNSON A.L. (1971) Folate metabolism in epileptic and psychiatric patients. *Journal of Neurology, Neurosurgery and Psychiatry* **34**, 726–732 *[506]*.

REYNOLDS E.H., ROTHFELD P. & PINCUS J.H. (1973) Neurological disease associated with folate deficiency. *British Medical Journal* **2**, 398–400 *[505]*.

REYNOLDS E.H. & SHORVON S.D. (1982) Monotherapy or polytherapy for epilepsy? *Epilepsia* 22, 1–10 *[265]*.

REYNOLDS E.H. & TRAVERS R.D. (1974) Serum anticonvulsant concentrations in epileptic patients with mental symptoms: a preliminary report. *British Journal of Psychiatry* 124, 440–445 *[230, 238]*.

REYNOLDS E.H., WRIGHTON R.J., JOHNSON A.L., PREECE J. & CHANARIN I. (1971) Interrelations of folic acid and vitamin B_{12} in drug-treated epileptic patients. *Epilepsia* 12, 165–171 *[507]*.

REYNOLDS G.P. (1983) Increased concentrations and lateral asymmetry of amygdala dopamine in schizophrenia. *Nature* 305, 527–529 *[77]*.

RICE E. & GENDELMAN S. (1973) Psychiatric aspects of normal pressure hydrocephalus. *Journal of the American Medical Association* 223, 409–412 *[641]*.

RICHARDSON A. (1969) Subarachnoid haemorrhage. *British Medical Journal* 4, 89–92 *[335]*.

RICHARDSON A. (1973) Surgical management of subarachnoid haemorrhage. *Journal of the Royal College of Physicians of London* 7, 245–250 *[335]*.

RICHARDSON E.P. (1961) Progressive multifocal leucoencephalopathy. *New England Journal of Medicine* 265, 815–823 *[646]*.

RICHARDSON E.P. (1968) Progressive multifocal leucoencephalopathy. Ch. 2 in *The Remote Effects of Cancer on the Nervous System*, eds. Brain W.R. & Norris F.H. Contemporary Neurology Symposia, vol. 1, Grune & Stratton: New York *[646]*.

RICHARDSON J.C., CHAMBERS R.A. & HEYWOOD P.M. (1959) Encephalopathies of anoxia and hypoglycaemia. *Archives of Neurology* 1, 178–190 *[465, 467, 470]*.

RICHENS A. (1982) Clinical pharmacology and medical treatment. Ch. 8, Part 1 in *A Textbook of Epilepsy* 2nd Edition, eds. Laidlaw J. & Richens A. Churchill Livingstone: Edinburgh & London *[265, 270]*.

RICHET G., LOPEZ DE NOVALES E. & VERROUST P. (1970) Drug intoxication and neurological episodes in chronic renal failure. *British Medical Journal* 1, 394–395 *[474]*.

RICHET G. & VACHON F. (1966) Troubles neuro-psychiques de l'urémie chronique. *Présse Medicale* 74, 1177–1182 *[474]*.

RICHTER D. (1966) Biochemical aspects of memory. In *Aspects of Learning and Memory*, ed. Richter D. Heinemann: London *[24]*.

RIDDOCH G. (1936) Progressive dementia, without headache or changes in the optic discs, due to tumours of the third ventricle. *Brain*, 59, 225–233 *[644]*.

RIGG G.A. & BERCU B.A. (1967) Hypoglycaemia—a complication of haemodialysis. *New England Journal of Medicine* 277, 1139–1140 *[474]*.

RIGONI H.C. (1969) Psychologic consideration in evaluating and treating the stroke patient. *Clinical Orthopaedics and Related Research* 63, 94–101 *[332]*.

RIKLAN M. & LEVITA E. (1970) Psychological studies of thalamic lesions in humans. *Journal of Nervous and Mental Disease* 150, 251–265 *[561]*.

RIKLAN M., WEINER H. & DILLER L. (1959) Somato-psychologic studies in Parkinson's disease. 1: An investigation into the relationship of certain disease factors to psychological functions. *Journal of Nervous and Mental Disease* 129, 263–272 *[556]*.

RIKLAN M., ZAHN T.P. & DILLER L. (1962) Human figure drawings before and after chemosurgery of the basal ganglia in parkinsonism. *Journal of Nervous and Mental Disease* 135, 500–506 *[561]*.

[...] & WALKER D.W. (1978) Morphological alterations in [...] after long-term alcohol consumption in mice. [...]–648 *[521]*.

RILEY T.L. (1982) Syncope and hyperventilation. Ch. 3 in *Pseudoseizures*, eds. Riley T.L. & Roy A. Williams & Wilkins: Baltimore & London *[258]*.

RIMALOVSKI A.B. & ARONSON S.M. (1966) Pathogenic observations in Wernicke-Korsakoff encephalopathy. *Transactions of the American Neurological Association* 91, 29–31 *[492]*.

RIMON R. & HALONEN P. (1969) Herpes simplex virus infection and depressive illness. *Diseases of the Nervous System* 30, 338–340 *[301]*.

RISK W.S., HADDAD F.S. & CHEMALI P. (1978) Substantial spontaneous long-term improvement in subacute sclerosing panencephalitis. Six cases from the Middle East and a review of the literature. *Archives of Neurology* 35, 494–502 *[307]*.

RIX K.J.B. (1978) Alcohol withdrawal states. *Hospital Update, July 1978*, 403–407 *[516]*.

ROBBINS F.C. (1958) The clinical and laboratory diagnosis of viral infections of the central nervous system. In *Viral Encephalitis*, eds. Fields W.C. & Blattner R.J. Thomas: Springfield, Illinois *[289, 291, 304]*.

ROBBINS L.R. & VINSON D.B. (1960) Objective psychologic assessment of the thyrotoxic patient and the response to treatment: preliminary report. *Journal of Clinical Endocrinology and Metabolism* 20, 120–129 *[429]*.

ROBERTS A.H. (1969) *Brain Damage in Boxers*. Pitman: London *[174, 176]*.

ROBERTS A.H. (1976) Sequelae of closed head injuries. *Proceedings of the Royal Society of Medicine* 69, 137–141 *[146, 160, 161]*.

ROBERTS A.H. (1979) *Severe Accidental Head Injury: An Assessment of Long-term Prognosis*. Macmillan: London *[160, 161, 167]*.

ROBERTS J.K.A. & LISHMAN W.A. (1984) The use of the CAT head scanner in clinical psychiatry. *British Journal of Psychiatry* 145, 152–158 *[108]*.

ROBERTS J.K.A., ROBERTSON M.M. & TRIMBLE M.R. (1982) The lateralising significance of hypergraphia in temporal lobe epilepsy. *Journal of Neurology, Neurosurgery and Psychiatry* 45, 131–138 *[235]*.

ROBERTS M.A. & CAIRD F.I. (1976) Computerised tomography and intellectual impairment in the elderly. *Journal of Neurology, Neurosurgery and Psychiatry* 39, 986–989 *[120]*.

ROBERTSON E.E., LE ROUX A. & BROWN J.H. (1958) The clinical differentiation of Pick's disease. *Journal of Mental Science* 104, 1000–1024 *[392]*.

ROBERTSON E.G. (1954) Photogenic epilepsy: self-precipitated attacks. *Brain* 77, 232–251 *[211]*.

ROBERTSON M.M. (1983) *Depression in patients with epilepsy*. Thesis for MD Degree, University of Cape Town, South Africa *[252, 253]*.

ROBERTSON M.M. (1985) Depression in patients with epilepsy: an overview and clinical study. Ch. 5 in *The Psychopharmacology of Epilepsy*, ed. Trimble M.R. John Wiley & Sons Ltd: Chichester *[252, 253, 273]*.

ROBERTSON M.M. & TRIMBLE M.R. (1983) Depressive illness in patients with epilepsy: a review. *Epilepsia*, 24 (Suppl. 2) S.109–S116 *[252]*.

ROBINS A.H. (1976) Depression in patients with parkinsonism. *British Journal of Psychiatry* 128, 141–145 *[558]*.

ROBINSON J.O. (1963) A study of neuroticism and casual arterial blood pressure. *British Journal of Social and Clinical Psychology* 2, 56–64 *[341]*.

ROBINSON J.O. (1969) Symptoms and the discovery of high blood pressure. *Journal of Psychosomatic Research* 13, 157–161 *[342]*.

ROBINSON J.T., CHITHAM R.G., GREENWOOD R.M. & TAYLOR J.W. (1974) Chromosome aberrations and LSD: a controlled study in 50 psychiatric patients. *British Journal of Psychiatry* 125, 238–244 *[528]*.

ROBINSON J.T. & McQUILLAN J. (1951) Schizophrenic reaction associated with the Kleine-Levin syndrome. *Journal of the Royal Army Medical Corps* 96, 377–381 *[629]*.

ROBINSON K.C., KALLBERG M.H. & CROWLEY M.F. (1954) Idiopathic hypoparathyroidism presenting as dementia. *British Medical Journal* 2, 1203–1206 *[451]*.

ROBINSON R.A. (1961) Some problems of clinical trials in elderly people. *Gerontologia Clinica* 3, 247–257 *[107]*.

ROBINSON R.A. (1977) Differential diagnosis and assessment in brain failure. *Age and Ageing*, Supplementary Issue 1977, pp. 42–49 *[107]*.

ROBINSON R.G. & BENSON D.F. (1981) Depression in aphasic patients: frequency, severity, and clinico-pathological correlations. *Brain and Language* 14, 282–291 *[329]*.

ROBINSON R.G. & BLOOM F.E. (1977) Pharmacological treatment following experimental cerebral infarction: implications for understanding psychological symptoms of human stroke. *Biological Psychiatry* 12, 669–680 *[329]*.

ROBINSON R.G. & PRICE T.R. (1982) Post-stroke depressive disorders: a follow-up study of 103 patients. *Stroke* 13, 635–641 *[329]*.

ROBINSON R.G., SHOEMAKER W.J. & SCHLUMPF M. (1980) Time course of changes in catecholamines following right hemispheric cerebral infarction in the rat. *Brain Research* 181, 202–208 *[329]*.

ROBINSON R.G. & SZETELA B. (1981) Mood change following left hemisphere brain injury. *Annals of Neurology* 9, 447–453 *[329]*.

ROBINSON R.O. (1978) Tetraethyl lead poisoning from gasoline sniffing. *Journal of American Medical Association* 240, 1373–1374 *[537]*.

ROCHFORD G. & WILLIAMS M. (1962) Studies in the development and breakdown of the use of names. *Journal of Neurology, Neurosurgery and Psychiatry* 25, 222–233 *[46]*.

ROCHFORD G. & WILLIAMS M. (1965) Studies in the development and breakdown of the use of names. *Journal of Neurology, Neurosurgery and Psychiatry* 28, 407–413 *[46]*.

RODGERS T.S., PECK J.R.S. & JUPE M.H. (1934) Lead poisoning in children. *Lancet* 2, 129–133 *[538]*.

RODIN E.A. (1982) Epilepsy and work. Ch. 13 in *A Textbook of Epilepsy*, 2nd Edition. eds. Laidlaw J. & Richens A, Churchill Livingstone: Edinburgh & London *[271]*.

RODZILSKY B., CUMINGS J.N. & HUSTON A.F. (1968) Hallervorden-Spatz disease—late infantile and adult types, report of two cases. *Acta Neuropathologica* 10, 1–16 *[648]*.

ROGERS R.S. (1979) Dermatologic manifestations. Ch. 7 in *Tuberous Sclerosis*, ed. Gomez M.R. Raven Press: New York *[600]*.

ROIZIN L., MORIARTY J.D. & WEIL A.A. (1945) Schizophrenic reaction syndrome in course of acute demyelination of central nervous system: clinicopathological report of a case, with brief review of the literature. *Archives of Neurology and Psychiatry* 54, 202–211 *[599]*.

ROMANO J. & COON G.P. (1942) Physiologic and psychologic studies in spontaneous hypoglycaemia. *Psychosomatic Medicine* 4, 283–300 *[459]*.

ROMANO J. & ENGEL G.L. (1944) Delirium: I, EEG data. *Archives of Neurology and Psychiatry* 51, 356–392 *[113]*.

ROMANUL F.C.A., RADVANY J. & ROSALES R.K. (1977) Whipple's disease confined to the brain: a case studied clinically and pathologically. *Journal of Neurology, Neurosurgery and Psychiatry* 40, 901–909 *[649, 650]*.

RON M.A. (1977) Brain damage in chronic alcoholism: a neuropathological, neuroradiological and psychological review. *Psychological Medicine* 7, 103–112 *[519]*.

RON M.A. (1983) The alcoholic brain: CT scan and psychological findings. *Psychological Medicine, Monograph Suppl.* 3 *[519, 520]*.

RON M.A., ACKER W., SHAW G.K. & LISHMAN W.A. (1982) Computerised tomography of the brain in chronic alcoholism. A survey and follow-up study. *Brain* 105, 497–514 *[519, 520]*.

RON M.A., TOONE B.K., GARRALDA M.E. & LISHMAN W.A. (1979) Diagnostic accuracy in presenile dementia. *British Journal of Psychiatry* 134, 161–168 *[410, 414]*.

ROOS R.P. (1981) Alzheimer's disease and the lessons of transmissible virus dementia. Ch. 4 in *The Epidemiology of Dementia*, eds. Mortimer J.A. & Schuman L.M. Oxford University Press *[400, 401]*.

RÖPER E. (1917) Zur Prognose der Hirnschüsse. *Meunchener Medizinische Wochenschrift* 64(i), 121–125. Quoted by Tow P.M. (1955), *Personality Changes Following Frontal Leucotomy*. Oxford University Press: London *[154]*.

ROSE F.C. (1981) Electroencephalography. Ch. 20 in *Hypoglycaemia*, 2nd Edition. eds. Marks V. & Rose F.C., Blackwell Scientific Publications: Oxford *[460]*.

ROSE F.C. & SYMONDS C.P. (1960) Persistent memory defect following encephalitis. *Brain* 83, 195–212 *[26, 301]*.

ROSEN J.A. (1964) Paroxysmal choreoathetosis: associated with perinatal hypoxic encephalopathy. *Archives of Neurology* 11, 385–387 *[258]*.

ROSEN J.A. (1968) Dilantin dementia. *Transactions of the American Neurological Association* 93, 273 *[231]*.

ROSEN W.G., TERRY R.D., FULD P.A., KATZMAN R. & PECK A. (1980) Pathological verification of ischaemic score in differentiation of dementias. *Annals of Neurology* 7, 486–488 *[390]*.

ROSENBAUM M. & NAJENSON T. (1976) Changes in life patterns and symptoms of low mood as reported by wives of severely brain-injured soldiers. *Journal of Consulting and Clinical Psychology* 44, 881–888 *[186]*.

ROSENTHAL R. & BIGELOW L.B. (1972) Quantitative brain measurements in chronic schizophrenia. *British Journal of Psychiatry* 121, 259–264 *[77]*.

ROSENTHAL S.H. (1964) Persistent hallucinosis following repeated administration of hallucinogenic drugs. *American Journal of Psychiatry* 121, 238–244 *[532]*.

ROSMAN N.P. & KAKULAS B.A. (1966) Mental deficiency associated with muscular dystrophy: a neuropathological study. *Brain* 89, 769–787 *[613, 615]*.

ROSS E.D. (1981) The aprosodias: functional-anatomic organisation of the affective components of language in the right hemisphere. *Archives of Neurology* 38, 561–569 *[39]*.

ROSS E.D. & MESULAM M.-M. (1979) Dominant language functions of the right hemisphere. Prosody and emotional gesturing. *Archives of Neurology* 36, 144–148 *[39]*.

ROSS E.D. & RUSH J. (1981) Diagnosis and neuroanatomical correlates of depression in brain-damaged patients. *Archives of General Psychiatry* 38, 1344–1354 *[334]*.

ROSS E.J. (1972a) Clinical aspects of phaeochromocytoma. *Proceedings of the Royal Society of Medicine* 65, 792–793 *[440]*.

ROSS E.J. (1972b) Diseases of the adrenal medulla. *Medicine (monthly add-on series 1972–3)* 2, 157–160. Medical Education (International) Ltd: London *[440, 441]*.

ROSS R.J., COLE M., THOMPSON J.S. & KIM K.H. (1983) Boxers—computed tomography, EEG and neurological evaluation. *Journal of the American Medical Association* 249, 211–213 *[175]*.

ROSS W.D. & McNAUGHTON F.L. (1945) Objective personality studies in migraine by means of the Rorschach method. *Psychosomatic Medicine* 7, 73–79 *[347]*.

ROSSER R. (1976) Depression during renal dialysis and following transplantation. *Proceedings of the Royal Society of Medicine* 69, 832–834 *[473]*.

Rossor M.N. (1981) Parkinson's disease and Alzheimer's disease as disorders of the isodendritic core. *British Medical Journal* 283, 1588–1590 *[383]*.

Rossor M.N., Garrett N.J., Johnson A.L., Mountjoy C.Q., Roth M. & Iversen L.L. (1982) A post-mortem study of the cholinergic and GABA systems in senile dementia. *Brain* 105, 313–330 *[383]*.

Rossor M.N., Iversen L.L., Johnson A.J., Mountjoy C.Q. & Roth M. (1981) Cholinergic deficit in frontal cerebral cortex in Alzheimer's disease is age dependent. *Lancet* 2, 1422 *[383]*.

Rossor M.N., Iversen L.L., Reynolds G.P., Mountjoy C.Q. & Roth M. (1984) Neurochemical characteristics of early and late onset types of Alzheimer's disease. *British Medical Journal* 288, 961–964 *[383]*.

Rosvold H.E., Mirsky A.F., Sarason I., Bransome E.D. & Beck L.H. (1956) A continuous performance test of brain damage. *Journal of Consulting Psychology* 20, 343–350 *[104]*.

Roth B. (1980) *Narcolepsy and Hypersomnia*. Translated by Schierlova, M. Revised and edited by Broughton R. Basel: Karger *[618, 619, 620, 621, 625, 626, 627, 630, 631]*.

Roth B. & Bruhova S. (1969) Dreams in narcolepsy, hypersomnia and dissociated sleep disorders. *Experimental Medicine and Surgery* 27, 187–209 *[619, 620, 622, 623]*.

Roth B., Nevsimalova S. & Rechtschaffen A. (1972) Hypersomnia with sleep drunkenness. *Archives of General Psychiatry* 26, 456–462 *[627]*.

Roth M. (1955) The natural history of mental disorder in old age. *Journal of Mental Science* 101, 281–301 *[375, 388]*.

Roth M. (1968) Cerebral disease and mental disorders of old age as causes of antisocial behaviour. In *The Mentally Abnormal Offender*, Ciba Foundation Symposium, eds. Rueck A.V.S. & Porter R. Churchill: London *[242]*.

Roth M. (1971) Classification and aetiology in mental disorders of old age: some recent developments. Ch. 1 in *Recent Developments in Psychogeriatrics*, eds. Kay D.W.K. & Walk A. British Journal of Psychiatry Special Publication No. 6. Headley Brothers: Ashford, Kent *[376, 389]*.

Roth M. (1981) The diagnosis of dementia in late and middle life. Ch. 2 in *The Epidemiology of Dementia*, eds. Mortimer J.A. & Schuman L.M. Oxford University Press *[128, 413, 417]*.

Roth M. & Myers D.H. (1969) The diagnosis of dementia. *British Journal of Hospital Medicine* 2, 705–717 *[15, 128, 411]*.

Roth M., Tomlinson B.E. & Blessed G. (1967) The relationship between quantitative measures of dementia and of degenerative changes in the cerebral grey matter of elderly subjects. *Proceedings of the Royal Society of Medicine* 60, 254–259 *[376]*.

Roth N. (1945) The neuropsychiatric aspects of porphyria. *Psychosomatic Medicine* 7, 291–301 *[483]*.

Rothschild D. (1941) The clinical differentiation of senile and arteriosclerotic psychoses. *American Journal of Psychiatry* 98, 324–333 *[387, 417]*.

Rothschild D. (1956) Senile psychoses and psychoses with cerebral arteriosclerosis. In *Mental Disorders in Later Life*, ed. Kaplan O.J. Stanford University Press: Stanford, U.S.A. *[376]*.

Roubicek J. (1946) Laughter in epilepsy, with some general introductory notes. *Journal of Mental Science* 92, 734–755 *[211]*.

Roubicek J., Geiger C. & Abt K. (1972) An ergot alkaloid preparation (hydergine) in geriatric therapy. *Journal of the American Geriatrics Society* 20, 222–229 *[425]*.

Rovira M., Romero F., Torrent O. & Ibarra B. (1980) Study of tuberculous meningitis by CT. *Neuroradiology* 19, 137–141 *[310]*.

Rowe M.J. & Carlson C. (1980) Brainstem auditory evoked potentials in postconcussion dizziness. *Archives of Neurology* 37, 679–683 *[170]*.

Rowland L.P. (1955) Prostigmine-responsiveness and the diagnosis of myasthenia gravis. *Neurology* 5, 612–624 *[609, 610]*.

Roy A. (1976) Psychiatric aspects of narcolepsy. *British Journal of Psychiatry* 128, 562–565 *[625]*.

Roy A. (1979) Hysterical seizures. *Archives of Neurology* 36, 447–448 *[260]*.

Roy A. (1981) Schizophrenia and Klinefelter's syndrome. *Canadian Journal of Psychiatry* 26, 262–264 *[447]*.

Royal College of Physicians (1981) Organic mental impairment in the elderly: implications for research, education and the provision of services. Report of the Royal College of Physicians by the College Committee on Geriatrics. *Journal of the Royal College of Physicians of London* 15, 141–167 *[371, 381]*.

Rubin R.T. & Rubin L.E. (1966) Skull roentgenography in hospitalised psychiatric patients. *American Journal of Psychiatry* 122, 1028–1032 *[115]*.

Ruesch J. & Bowman K.M. (1945) Prolonged post-traumatic syndromes following head injury. *American Journal of Psychiatry* 102, 145–163 *[147, 150, 167]*.

Rumbaugh C.L., Bergeron R.T., Fang H.C. & McCormick R. (1971) Cerebral angiographic changes in the drug abuse patient. *Radiology* 101, 335–344 *[523]*.

Runge W. (1928) Psychische Störungen bei multipler Sklerose. In *Handbuch der Geisteskrankheiten*, vol. 7, special part 3, ed. Bumke O. Springer: Berlin *[591]*.

Rusk H.A., Block J.M. & Lowman E.W. (1969) Rehabilitation of the brain-injured patient: a report of 157 cases with long-term follow-up of 118. Ch. 29 in *The Late Effects of Head Injury*, eds. Walker A.E., Caveness W.F. & Critchley M. Thomas: Springfield, Illinois *[185]*.

Ruskin A., Beard O.W. & Schaffer R.L. (1948) 'Blast hypertension': elevated arterial pressures in victims of the Texas City disaster. *American Journal of Medicine* 4, 228–236 *[340]*.

Russell E.W., Neuringer C. & Goldstein G. (1970) *Assessment of Brain Damage*. Wiley: New York *[99]*.

Russell R.W.R. (1959) Giant cell arteritis. A review of 35 cases. *Quarterly Journal of Medicine* 28, 471–489 *[523]*.

Russell R.W.R. (1963) Observations on intracerebral aneurysms. *Brain* 86, 425–442 *[320]*.

Russell R.W.R. (1970) The origin and effects of cerebral emboli. Ch. 10 in *Modern Trends in Neurology*, vol. 5, ed. Williams D. Butterworths: London *[321, 324]*.

Russell R.W.R. & Harrison M.J.G. (1973) The completed stroke. *British Journal of Hospital Medicine* 10, 244–249 *[331]*.

Russell R.W.R. & Pennybacker J.B. (1961) Craniopharyngioma in the elderly. *Journal of Neurology, Neurosurgery and Psychiatry* 24, 1–13 *[198]*.

Russell W.R. (1932) Cerebral involvement in head injury. *Brain* 55, 549–603 *[145, 148]*.

Russell W.R. (1935) Amnesia following head injuries. *Lancet* 2, 762–763 *[143]*.

Russell W.R. (1951) Disability caused by brain wounds. *Journal of Neurology, Neurosurgery and Psychiatry* 14, 35–39 *[146]*.

Russell W.R. (1959) *Brain: Memory: Learning*. Oxford University Press *[172]*.

Russell W.R. (1968) Nucleic acid metabolism in neurology. Ch. 11 in *Biochemical Aspects of Neurological Disorders*, 3rd series, eds. Cumings J.N. & Kremer M. Blackwell Scientific Publications: Oxford *[24]*.

Russell W.R. & Nathan P.W. (1946) Traumatic amnesia. *Brain* 69, 280–300 *[145]*.

Russell W.R. & Schiller F. (1949) Crushing injuries to the skull. *Journal of Neurology, Neurosurgery and Psychiatry* 12, 52–60 *[138, 146]*.

RUSSELL W.R. & SMITH A. (1961) Post-traumatic amnesia in closed head injury. *Archives of Neurology* 5, 4–17 *[145]*.

RUSSELL W.R. & WHITTY C.W.M. (1952) Studies in traumatic epilepsy. 1: Factors influencing the incidence of epilepsy after brain wounds. *Journal of Neurology, Neurosurgery and Psychiatry* 15, 93–98 *[213]*.

RUTHERFORD W.H., MERRETT J.D. & McDONALD J.R. (1977) Sequelae of concussion caused by minor head injuries. *Lancet* 1, 1–4 *[170]*.

RUTTER M. (1980) Raised lead levels and impaired cognitive/ behavioural functioning: a review of the evidence. *Developmental Medicine and Child Neurology* 22, Suppl. 42, 1–26 *[539, 540]*.

RYAN C. & BUTTERS N. (1980) Further evidence for a continuum-of-impairment encompassing male alcoholic Korsakoff patients and chronic alcoholic men. *Alcoholism: Clinical and Experimental Research* 4, 190–198 *[498, 518]*.

RYBACK R.S. (1971) The continuity and specificity of the effects of alcohol on memory. *Quarterly Journal of Studies on Alcohol* 32, 995–1016 *[498, 518]*.

RYLANDER G. (1939) Personality changes after operations on the frontal lobes: a clinical study of 32 cases. *Acta Psychiatrica et Neurologica Scandinavica*, supplement 20, 1–327 *[69]*.

RYLANDER G. (1943) Mental changes after excision of cerebral tissue. *Acta Psychiatrica et Neurologica Scandinavica*, supplement 25, 1–81 *[69]*.

SABOT L.M., GROSS M.M. & HALPERT E. (1968) A study of acute alcoholic psychoses in women. *British Journal of Addiction* 63, 29–49 *[513]*.

SACHS E. (1950) Meningiomas with dementia as the first and presenting failure. *Journal of Mental Science* 96, 998–1007 *[191, 192]*.

SACKNER M.A., LANDA J., FORREST T. & GREENELTCH D. (1975) Periodic sleep apnea: chronic sleep deprivation related to intermittent upper airway obstruction and central nervous system disturbance. *Chest* 67, 164–171 *[627]*.

SACKS O.W. (1970) *Migraine: The Evolution of a Common Disorder.* Faber: London *[344, 347, 349, 351, 352, 354]*.

SACKS O. (1973) *Awakenings.* Duckworth: London *[296, 561]*.

SACKS O.W., AGUILAR M.J. & BROWN W.J. (1966) Hallervorden Spatz disease. Its pathogenesis and place among the axonal dystrophies. *Acta Neuropathologica* 6, 164–174 *[648]*.

SACKS O.W., KOHL M.S., MESSELOFF C.R. & SCHWARTZ W.F. (1972) Effects of levodopa in parkinsonian patients with dementia. *Neurology* 22, 516–519 *[560]*.

SACKS O.W., MESSELOFF C., SCHWARTZ W., GOLDFARB A. & KOHL M. (1970) Effects of L-dopa in patients with dementia. *Lancet* 1, 1231 *[560]*.

SAINSBURY P. (1964) Neuroticism and hypertension in an outpatient population. *Journal of Psychosomatic Research* 8, 235–238 *[341]*.

SAINSBURY P., COSTAIN W.R. & GRAD J. (1965) The effects of community service on the referral and admission rates of elderly psychiatric patients. In *Psychiatric Disorders of the Aged*, Report on Symposium held by the World Psychiatric Association, pp. 23–37. Geigy (U.K.) Ltd: Manchester *[373]*.

ST. CLAIR D. & WHALLEY L.J. (1983) Hypertension, multi-infarct dementia and Alzheimer's disease. *British Journal of Psychiatry* 143, 274–276 *[386]*.

SAITO I., UEDA Y. & SANO K. (1977) Significance of vasospasm in the treatment of ruptured intracranial aneurysms. *Journal of Neurosurgery* 47, 412–429 *[335]*.

SALMON J.H. (1971) Surgical treatment of severe post-traumatic encephalopathy. *Surgery, Gynaecology and Obstetrics* 133, 634–636 *[642]*.

SALMON J.H. & ARMITAGE J.L. (1968) Surgical treatment of hydrocephalus ex-vacuo: ventriculoatrial shunt for degenerative brain disease. *Neurology* 18, 1223–1226 *[426, 643]*.

SALMON J.H., GONEN J.Y. & BROWN L. (1971) Ventriculoatrial shunt for hydrocephalus ex-vacuo: psychological and clinical evaluation. *Diseases of the Nervous System* 32, 299–307 *[426, 643]*.

SALMONS P.H. (1980) Psychological aspects of chronic renal failure. *British Journal of Hospital Medicine* 23/6, 617–622 *[474]*.

SAMARA K., RIKLAN M., LEVITA E., ZIMMERMAN J., WALTZ J.M., BERGMANN L. & COOPER I.S. (1969) Language and speech correlates of anatomically verified lesions in thalamic surgery for parkinsonism. *Journal of Speech and Hearing Research* 12, 510–540 *[561]*.

SAND P.L. & CARLSON C. (1973) Failure to establish control over tics in the Gilles de la Tourette syndrome with behaviour therapy techniques. *British Journal of Psychiatry* 122, 665–670 *[586]*.

SANDERS D.G. (1973) Familial occurrence of Gilles de la Tourette syndrome. Report of the syndrome occurring in a father and son. *Archives of General Psychiatry* 28, 326–328 *[581]*.

SANDERS H.I. & WARRINGTON E.K. (1971) Memory for remote events in amnesic patients. *Brain* 94, 661–668 *[34]*.

SANDERS W.L. (1979) Creutzfeldt-Jakob disease treated with amantadine. *Journal of Neurology, Neurosurgery and Psychiatry* 42, 960–961 *[427]*.

SANDERS W.L. & DUNN T.L. (1973) Creutzfeldt-Jakob disease treated with amantadine. *Journal of Neurology, Neurosurgery and Psychiatry*, 36, 581–584 *[426]*.

SANDS I.J. (1928) The acute psychiatric type of epidemic encephalitis. *American Journal of Psychiatry* 7, 975–987 *[293]*.

SANDS I.R. (1942) The type of personality susceptible to Parkinson disease. *Journal of the Mount Sinai Hospital* 9, 792–794 *[562]*.

SANO K., SEKINO H. & MAYANAGI Y. (1972) Results of stimulation and destruction of the posterior hypothalamus in cases with violent, aggressive, or restless behaviors. Ch. 5 in *Psychosurgery*, eds. Hitchcock E., Laitinen L. & Vaernet K. Proceedings of the Second International Conference on Psychosurgery. Thomas: Springfield, Illinois *[73]*.

SANO K., YOSHIOKA M., OGASHIWA M., ISHIJIMA B. & OHYE C. (1966) Postero-medial hypothalamotomy in the treatment of aggressive behaviors. *Confinia Neurologica* 27, 164–167 *[73]*.

SANTA T., ENGEL A.G. & LAMBERT E.H. (1972) Histometric study of neuromuscular junction ultrastructure. 1: Myasthenia gravis. *Neurology* 22, 71–82 *[606]*.

SAPHIR W. (1945) Chronic hypochloremia simulating psychoneurosis. *Journal of the American Medical Association* 129, 510–512 *[476]*.

SATO S., DALY R. & PETERS H. (1971) Reserpine therapy of phenothiazine induced dyskinesia. *Diseases of the Nervous System* 32, 680–685 *[549]*.

SATZ P., ACHENBACH K. & FENNELL E. (1967) Correlations between assessed manual laterality and predicted speech laterality in a normal population. *Neuropsychologia* 5, 295–310 *[37]*.

SAUGET J., BÉNTON A.L. & HÉCAEN H. (1971) Disturbances of the body schema in relation to language impairment and hemispheric locus of lesion. *Journal of Neurology, Neurosurgery and Psychiatry* 34, 496–501 *[58]*.

SAUL L. (1939) Hostility in cases of essential hypertension. *Psychosomatic Medicine* 1, 153–161 *[341]*.

SCARLETT J.A., MAKO M.E., RUBENSTEIN A.H., BLIX P.M., GOLDMAN J., HORWITZ D.L., TAGER H., JASPAN J.B., STJERNHOLM M.R. & OLEFSKY J.M. (1977) Factitious hypoglycemia. Diagnosis by measurement of serum C-peptide immunoreactivity and insulin binding antibodies. *New England Journal of Medicine* 297, 1029–1032 *[463]*.

SCHAUMBERG H.H. & SUZUKI K. (1968) Non-specific familial presenile dementia. *Journal of Neurology, Neurosurgery and Psychiatry* 31, 479–486 [647].

SCHEIBEL A.B. (1978) Structural aspects of the aging brain: spine systems and the dendritic arbor. In *Alzheimer's Disease: Senile Dementia and Related Disorders, Aging, Vol. 7*, eds. Katzman R., Terry R.D. & Bick K.L., pp. 353–373. Raven Press: New York [377, 382].

SCHEIBEL A.B. & TOMIYASU U. (1978) Dendritic sprouting in Alzheimer's presenile dementia. *Experimental Neurology* 60, 1–8 [382].

SCHEINBERG I.H. & GITLIN D. (1952) Deficiency of ceruloplasmin in patients with hepatolenticular degeneration (Wilson's disease). *Science* 116, 484–485 [564].

SCHEINBERG I.H., STERNLIEB I. & RICHMAN J. (1968) Psychiatric manifestations in patients with Wilson's disease. In *Wilson's Disease*, ed. Bergsma D., Birth Defects Original Article Series, vol. 4, No. 2. The National Foundation: New York [566, 567].

SCHEINBERG P. (1951) Cerebral blood flow and metabolism in pernicious anaemia. *Blood* 6, 213–227 [503].

SCHEINBERG P., STEAD E.A., BRANNON E.S. & WARREN J.V. (1950) Correlative observations on cerebral metabolism and cardiac output in myxoedema. *Journal of Clinical Investigation* 29, 1139–1146 [435].

SCHILDER P. (1935) *The Image and Appearance of the Human Body: Studies in the Constructive Energies of the Psyche*. Psyche Monographs No. 4. Kegan Paul, Trench, Trubner: London [59].

SCHILDER P. (1938) The organic background of obsessions and compulsions. *American Journal of Psychiatry* 94, 1397–1413 [295].

SCHLESINGER B. (1950) Mental changes in intracranial tumours, and related problems. *Confinia Neurologica* 10, 225–263 and 322–355 [27, 193, 194].

SCHMID B. (1969) Occupational rehabilitation of the brain-injured worker. Ch. 34 in *The Late Effects of Head Injury*, eds. Walker A.E., Caveness W.F. & Critchley M. Thomas: Springfield, Illinois [185].

SCHNEIDER E., FISCHER P.A., BECKER H., HACKER H., PENEZ A. & JACOBI P. (1977) Relationship between arteriosclerosis and cerebral atrophy in Parkinson's disease. *Journal of Neurology* 217, 11–16 [557].

SCHOTT G.D., McLEOD A.A. & JEWITT D.E. (1977) Cardiac arrhythmias that masquerade as epilepsy. *British Medical Journal* 1, 1454–1457 [258].

SCHWAB R.S., FABING H.D. & PRICHARD J.S. (1951) Psychiatric symptoms and syndromes in Parkinson's disease. *American Journal of Psychiatry* 107, 901–907 [296].

SCHWAB R.S. & PASSOUANT P. (1964) Levo-amphetamine in the treatment of the cataplexy-narcolepsy syndrome. *Transactions of the American Neurological Association* 89, 276–277 [623].

SCHWAB R.S. & PERLO V.P. (1966) Syndromes simulating myasthenia gravis. *Annals of the New York Academy of Sciences* 135, 350–366 [609, 610].

SCHWANDT P., RICHTER W. & WILKENING J. (1979) Chronic insulin overtreatment, *Lancet* 2, 261–262 [455].

SCHWARTZ B.A., SEGUY M. & ESCANDE J-P. (1967) Correlations EEG, respiratoires, oculaires et myographiques dans le 'syndrome pickwickien' et autres affections paraissant apparentées: proposition d'une hypothèse. *Revue Neurologique* 117, 145–152 [628].

SCHWARTZ C.J. & MITCHELL J.R.A. (1961) Atheroma of the carotid and vertebral arterial systems. *British Medical Journal* 2, 1057–1063 [328].

SCHWARTZ M.S. & SCOTT D.F. (1971) Isolated petit-mal status presenting de novo in middle age. *Lancet* 2, 1399–1401 [223].

SCOTT D.F. (1982a) Recognition and diagnostic aspects of non-epileptic seizures. Ch. 2 in *Pseudoseizures*, eds. Riley T.L. & Roy A. Williams & Wilkins: Baltimore & London [259, 261].

SCOTT D.F. (1982b) The use of EEG in pseudoseizures. Ch. 6 in *Pseudoseizures*, eds. Riley T.L. & Roy A. Williams & Wilkins: Baltimore & London [261].

SCOTT M. (1970) Transitory psychotic behaviour following operation for tumours of the cerebello-pontine angle. *Psychiatria, Neurologia, Neurochirurgia* 73, 37–48 [201].

SCOTT M.L., GOLDEN C.J., RUEDRICH S.L. & BISHOP R.J. (1983) Ventricular enlargement in major depression. *Psychiatry Research* 8, 91–93 [122].

SCOTT P.D. (1965) The Ganser syndrome. *British Journal of Criminology* 5, 127–131 [405, 406].

SCOVILLE W.B. (1954) The limbic lobe in man. *Journal of Neurosurgery* 11, 64–66 [26].

SCOVILLE W.B. & MILNER B. (1957) Loss of recent memory after bilateral hippocampal lesions. *Journal of Neurology, Neurosurgery and Psychiatry* 20, 11–21 [26].

SEARLEMAN A. (1977) A review of right hemisphere linguistic capabilities. *Psychological Bulletin* 84, 503–528 [39].

SEGARRA J.M. (1970) Cerebral vascular disease and behavior. 1 The syndrome of the mesencephalitic artery (basilar artery bifurcation). *Archives of Neurology* 22, 408–418 [133].

SELBY G. (1968) Cerebral atrophy in Parkinsonism. *Journal of the Neurological Sciences* 6, 517–559 [557].

SELBY G. & LANCE J.W. (1960) Observations on 500 cases of migraine and allied vascular headache. *Journal of Neurology, Neurosurgery and Psychiatry* 23, 23–32 [347, 348].

SELECKI B.R. (1964) Cerebral mid-line tumours involving the corpus callosum among mental hospital patients. *Medical Journal of Australia* 2, 954–960 [193].

SELECKI B.R. (1965) Intracranial space-occupying lesions among patients admitted to mental hospitals. *Medical Journal of Australia* 1, 383–390 [356].

SELLERS J., TYRER P., WHITELEY A., BANKS D.C. & BARER D.H. (1982) Neurotoxic effects of lithium with delayed rise in serum lithium levels. *British Journal of Psychiatry* 140, 623–625 [533].

SELLS C.J., CARPENTER R.L. & RAY C.G. (1975) Sequelae of central-nervous-system enterovirus infections. *New England Journal of Medicine* 293, 1–4 [291].

SELTZER B. & SHERWIN I. (1983) A comparison of clinical features in early- and late-onset primary degenerative dementia. *Archives of Neurology* 40, 143–146 [374, 380, 385].

SEMMES J., WEINSTEIN S., GHENT L. & TEUBER H-L. (1955) Spatial orientation in man after cerebral injury. 1: Analyses by locus of lesion. *Journal of Psychology* 39, 227–244 [55].

SENSENBACH W., MADISON L., EISENBERG S. & OCHS L. (1954) The cerebral circulation and metabolism in hypothyroidism and myxoedema. *Journal of Clinical Investigation* 33, 1434–1440 [435].

SENSKY T., WILSON A., PETTY R., FENWICK P.B.C. & ROSE F.C. (1984) The interictal personality traits of temporal lobe epileptics: religious belief and its association with reported mystical experiences. In *Advances in Epileptology, XVth Epilepsy International Symposium*, eds. Porter R.J., Mattson R.H., Ward A.A. & Dam M. Raven Press: New York [234].

SERAFETINIDES E.A. (1965) Aggressiveness in temporal lobe epileptics and its relation to cerebral dysfunction and environmental factors. *Epilepsia* 6, 33–42 [233].

SERAFETINIDES E.A. & DOMINIAN J. (1963) A follow-up study of late-onset epilepsy. 1: Neurological findings. *British Medical Journal* 1, 428–431 [214].

SERAFETINIDES E.A. & FALCONER M.A. (1962a) Some observations on memory impairment after temporal lobectomy for epilepsy. *Journal of Neurology, Neurosurgery and Psychiatry* 25, 251–255 *[26]*.

SERAFETINIDES E.A. & FALCONER M.A. (1962b) The effects of temporal lobectomy in epileptic patients with psychosis. *Journal of Mental Science* 108, 584–593 *[252, 253, 275]*.

SERAFETINIDES E.A. & FALCONER M.A. (1963) Speech disturbances in temporal lobe seizures: a study in 100 epileptic patients submitted to anterior temporal lobectomy. *Brain* 86, 333–346 *[219]*.

SERGENT J.S., LOCKSHIN M.D., KLEMPNER M.S. & LIPSKY B.A. (1975) Central nervous system disease in systemic lupus erythematosus. Therapy and prognosis. *American Journal of Medicine* 58, 644–654 *[366]*.

SERVIT Z., MACHEK J., STERCOVA A., KRISTOF M., CERVENKOVA V. & DUDAS D. (1963) Reflex influences in the pathogenesis of epilepsy in the light of clinical statistics. In *Reflex Mechanisms in the Genesis of Epilepsy*, ed. Servit Z. Elsevier: Amsterdam *[216]*.

SETHURAJAN C., CROFT P.B. & WILKINSON M. (1967) Bronchial neoplasm with endocrine, metabolic, and neurological manifestations. *Neurology* 17, 1169–1173 *[637]*.

SEVERINGHAUS J.W. & MITCHELL R.A. (1962) Ondine's curse: failure of respiratory centre automaticity while awake. *Clinical Research* 10, 122 *[628]*.

SHADER R.I. (1971) Psychiatric effects of non-psychiatric drugs. *Seminars in Psychiatry* 3, 401–492 *[532]*.

SHADER R.I. (1972) (Ed.) *Psychiatric Complications of Medical Drugs*. Raven Press: New York *[532]*.

SHAGASS C. (1965) The EEG in affective psychosis. In *Applications of Electroencephalography in Psychiatry*, ed. Wilson W.P. Duke University Press: Durham, North Carolina *[111]*.

SHAGASS C., ROEMER R.A. & STRAUMANIS J.J. (1983) Evoked potential studies of topographic correlates of psychopathology. In *Laterality and Psychopathology*, eds. Flor-Henry P. & Gruzelier J., pp. 395–408. Elsevier: Amsterdam *[76]*.

SHAGASS C., ROEMER R.A., STRAUMANIS J.J. & AMADEO M. (1979) Evoked potential evidence of lateralised hemispheric dysfunction in psychoses. In *Hemisphere Asymmetries of Function in Psychopathology*, eds. Gruzelier J. & Flor-Henry P., pp. 293–316. Elsevier/North Holland Biomedical Press, Amsterdam *[76]*.

SHAH K.V., BANKS G.D. & MERSKEY H. (1969) Survival in atherosclerotic and senile dementia. *British Journal of Psychiatry* 115, 1283–1286 *[375, 388]*.

SHANKWEILER D. (1966) Effects of temporal-lobe damage on perception of dichotically presented melodies. *Journal of Comparative and Physiological Psychology* 62, 115–119 *[56, 57]*.

SHAPIRO A.K. & SHAPIRO E. (1968) Treatment of Gilles de la Tourette's syndrome with haloperidol. *British Journal of Psychiatry* 114, 345–350 *[587]*.

SHAPIRO A.K., SHAPIRO E.S., BRUUN R.D. & SWEET R.D. (1978) *Gilles de la Tourette Syndrome*. Raven Press: New York *[581, 584, 585, 586, 587]*.

SHAPIRO A.K., SHAPIRO E. & WAYNE H. (1973a) Treatment of Tourette's syndrome. *Archives of General Psychiatry* 28, 92–97 *[587]*.

SHAPIRO A.K., SHAPIRO E., WAYNE H. & CLARKIN J. (1972) The psychopathology of Gilles de la Tourette's syndrome. *American Journal of Psychiatry* 129, 427–434 *[584]*.

SHAPIRO A.K., SHAPIRO E., WAYNE H. & CLARKIN J. (1973b) Organic factors in Gilles de la Tourette's syndrome. *British Journal of Psychiatry* 122, 659–664 *[584]*.

SHAPIRO A.K., SHAPIRO E., WAYNE H.L., CLARKIN J. & BRUUN R.D. (1973c) Tourette's syndrome: summary of data on 34 patients. *Psychosomatic Medicine* 35, 419–435 *[581, 584]*.

SHAPIRO L.B. (1939) Schizophrenia-like psychosis following head injury. *Illinois Medical Journal* 76, 250–254 *[164]*.

SHAPIRO M.B. POST F., LÖFVING B. & INGLIS J. (1956) 'Memory function' in psychiatric patients over sixty; some methodological and diagnostic implications. *Journal of Mental Science* 102, 233–246 *[82, 84, 98]*.

SHAPIRO S.K. (1959) Psychosis due to bilateral carotid artery occlusion. *Minnesota Medicine* 42, 25–27 *[330]*.

SHARMA O.P. (1975) *Sarcoidosis: A Clinical Approach*. Charles C. Thomas: Springfield, Illinois *[651]*.

SHARMAN M.G., WATT D.C., JANOTA I. & CARRASCO L.H. (1979) Alzheimer's disease in a mother and identical twin sons. *Psychological Medicine* 9, 771–774 *[377]*.

SHARPE R. (1974) Behaviour therapy in a case of blepharospasm. *British Journal of Psychiatry* 124, 603–604 *[580]*.

SHAW D. & HILL D. (1947) A case of musicogenic epilepsy. *Journal of Neurology, Neurosurgery and Psychiatry* 10, 107–117 *[211]*.

SHAW D.M., CAMPS F.E. & ECCLESTON E.G. (1967) 5-hydroxytryptamine in the hind-brain of depressive suicides. *British Journal of Psychiatry* 113, 1407–1411 *[301]*.

SHEARD M.H. (1971) Effect of lithium on human aggression. *Nature* 230, 113–114 *[265]*.

SHEARER M.L. & FINCH S.M. (1964) Periodic organic psychosis associated with recurrent herpes simplex. *New England Journal of Medicine* 271, 494–497 *[300]*.

SHEEHAN H.L. & SUMMERS V.K. (1949) The syndrome of hypopituitarism. *Quarterly Journal of Medicine* 18, 319–378 *[443]*.

SHEEHY M.P. & MARSDEN C.D. (1982) Writers' cramp—a focal dystonia. *Brain* 105, 461–480 *[578]*.

SHEFER V.F. (1973) Absolute number of neurones and thickness of the cerebral cortex during aging, senile and vascular dementia, and Pick's and Alzheimer's diseases. *Neuroscience and Behavioral Physiology* 6, 319–324 *[382]*.

SHEPHERD R.H. & WADIA N.H. (1956) Some observations on atypical features in acoustic neuromas. *Brain* 79, 282–318 *[201]*.

SHERLOCK S. (1981) *Diseases of the Liver and Biliary System*. 6th Edition. Blackwell Scientific Publications: Oxford *[481, 482]*.

SHERWIN I. (1980) Specificity of psychopathology in epilepsy: significance of lesion laterality. In *Limbic Epilepsy and the Dyscontrol Syndrome*, eds. Girgis M. & Kiloh L.G. *Developments in Psychiatry*, Vol. 4. Elsevier/North Holland Biomedical Press: Amsterdam *[233]*.

SHERWIN I. (1981) Psychosis associated with epilepsy: significance of the laterality of the epileptogenic lesion. *Journal of Neurology, Neurosurgery and Psychiatry* 44, 83–85 *[249]*.

SHERWOOD S.L. (1962) Self-induced epilepsy. *Archives of Neurology* 6, 49–65 *[211]*.

SHEVITZ S.A., JAMIESON R.C., PETRIE W.M. & CROOK J.E. (1980) Compulsive water drinking treated with high dose propanolol. *Journal of Nervous and Mental Diseases* 168, 246–248 *[445]*.

SHILLITO F.H., DRINKER C.K. & SHAUGHNESSY T.J. (1936) The problem of nervous and mental sequelae in carbon monoxide poisoning. *Journal of the American Medical Association* 106, 669–674 *[469, 470]*.

SHORVON S.D., CARNEY M.W.P., CHANARIN I. & REYNOLDS E.H. (1980) The neuropsychiatry of megaloblastic anaemia. *British Medical Journal* 281, 1036–1038 *[504, 505]*.

SHORVON S.D. & REYNOLDS E.H. (1979) Reduction of polypharmacy for epilepsy. *British Medical Journal* 2, 1023–1025 *[265]*.

SHOULSON I. & PLASSCHE W. (1980) Huntington disease: the specificity of computed tomography measurements. *Neurology* 30, 382–383 *[398]*.

SHUKLA G.D., SRIVASTAVA O.N. & KATIYAR B.C. (1979) Sexual

disturbances in temporal lobe epilepsy: a controlled study. *British Journal of Psychiatry* **134**, 288–292 *[238, 239]*.

SHULMAN R. (1967a) A survey of vitamin B$_{12}$ deficiency in an elderly psychiatric population. *British Journal of Psychiatry* **113**, 241–251 *[501, 503, 504]*.

SHULMAN R. (1967b) Vitamin B$_{12}$ deficiency and psychiatric illness. *British Journal of Psychiatry* **113**, 252–256 *[502]*.

SHULMAN R. (1967c) Psychiatric aspects of pernicious anaemia: a prospective controlled investigation. *British Medical Journal* **3**, 266–270 *[502]*.

SHULMAN R.G. (1983) NMR spectroscopy of living cells. *Scientific American* **248**(1), 76–83 *[123]*.

SHUTTLEWORTH E.C. & MORRIS C.E. (1966) The transient global amnesia syndrome. *Archives of Neurology* **15**, 515–520 *[359]*.

SIAKOTOS A.N. (1981) Neuronal ceroid lipofuscinosis, adult (Kufs); Neuronal ceroid lipofuscinosis, adult (Parry). In *Handbook of Clinical Neurology, Vol. 42, Part 1. Neurogenetic Directory*, eds. Vinken P.J. & Bruyn G.W., pp. 465–468. North-Holland Publishing Company: Amsterdam *[649]*.

SIDBURY J.B. (1955) Lead poisoning. Treatment with disodium calcium ethylenediamine-tetra-acetate. *American Journal of Medicine* **18**, 932–946 *[538]*.

SIEDLER H. & MALAMUD N. (1963) Creutzfeldt-Jakob's disease: clinicopathologic report of 15 cases and review of the literature. *Journal of Neuropathology and Experimental Neurology* **22**, 381–402 *[400]*.

SIEKERT R.G. & CLARK E.C. (1955) Neurologic signs and symptoms as early manifestations of systemic lupus erythematosus. *Neurology* **5**, 84–88 *[363]*.

SILFVERSKIÖLD B.P. (1952) Vegetative disorders of the post concussion syndrome. *Journal of Nervous and Mental Disease* **116**, 897–901 *[152]*.

SILINKOVA-MALKOVA E. & MALEK J. (1965/66) Endocraniosis. *Neuroendocrinology* **1**, 68–82 *[653]*.

SILLANPÄÄ M. (1981) Carbamazepine. Pharmacology and clinical uses. *Acta Neurologica Scandinavica* **64**, Suppl 88, 1–202 *[267]*.

SILVERMAN M. (1949) Paranoid reaction during the phase of recovery from subarachnoid haemorrhage. *Journal of Mental Science* **95**, 706–708 *[338]*.

SILVERMAN M. (1964) Organic stupor subsequent to a severe head injury treated with E.C.T. *British Journal of Psychiatry* **110**, 648–650 *[184]*.

SILVERSTEIN A., FEVER M.M. & SILTZBACH L.E. (1965) Neurologic sarcoidosis. *Archives of Neurology* **12**, 1–11 *[652]*.

SIM M. (1968) *Guide to Psychiatry*. Livingstone: Edinburgh and London *[287]*.

SIM M., TURNER E. & SMITH W.T. (1966) Cerebral biopsy in the investigation of presenile dementia: 1, clinical aspects. *British Journal of Psychiatry* **112**, 119–125 *[379]*.

SIMARD D. (1971) Regional cerebral blood flow and its regulation in dementia. In *Brain and Blood Flow*, ed. Russell R.W.R. Pitman: London *[376]*.

SIMON A. & CAHAN R.B. (1963) The acute brain syndrome in geriatric patients. *Psychiatric Research Reports* No. 16, 8–21 *[79]*.

SIMPSON F.O. & WAAL-MANNING H.J. (1971) Hypertension and depression: interrelated problems in therapy. *Journal of the Royal College of Physicians of London* **6**, 14–24 *[342, 343]*.

SIMPSON J.A. (1964) Myasthenia gravis and myasthenic syndromes. Ch. 13 in *Disorders of Voluntary Muscle*, ed. Walton J.N. Churchill: London *[606, 607, 608, 609, 610]*.

SIMPSON J.A. (1968) Myasthenia gravis: clinical aspects. *Proceedings of the Royal Society of Medicine* **61**, 757–759 *[608]*.

SIMS N.R., BOWEN D.M., SMITH C.C.T., FLACK R.H.A., DAVISON

A.N., SNOWDEN J.S. & NEARY D. (1980) Glucose metabolism and acetylcholine synthesis in relation to neuronal activity in Alzheimer's disease. *Lancet* **1**, 333–335 *[382]*.

SINGER K. (1963) Gilles de la Tourette's disease. *American Journal of Psychiatry* **120**, 80–81 *[582]*.

SINGH S., PADI M.H., BULLARD H. & FREEMAN H. (1985) Water intoxication in psychiatric patients. *British Journal of Psychiatry* **146**, 127–131 *[445]*.

SITARAM N., WEINGARTNER H. & GILLIN J.C. (1978) Human serial learning enhancement with arecholine and choline. Impairment with scopolamine. *Science* **201**, 274–276 *[425]*.

SJÖGREN T. (1943) Klinische und erbbiologische Untersuchungen über die Heredoataxien. *Acta Psychiatrica et Neurologica Scandinavica*, supplement 27, 1–200. Quoted by Davies D.L. *Journal of Neurology, Neurosurgery and Psychiatry*, 1949, **12**, 34–38 *[602]*.

SJÖGREN T., SJÖGREN H. & LINDGREN A.G.H. (1952) Morbus Alzheimer and morbus Pick. A genetic, clinical and patho-anatomical study. *Acta Psychiatrica et Neurologica Scandinavica*, supplement 82, 1–152 *[377, 378, 391, 393]*.

SKILLICORN S. (1955) Presenile cerebellar ataxia in chronic alcoholics. *Neurology* **5**, 527–534 *[500]*.

SKINHOJ E. & STRANDGAARD S. (1973) Pathogenesis of hypertensive encephalopathy. *Lancet* **1**, 461–462 *[343]*.

SKÖLDENBERG B., FORSGREN M., ALESTIG K., BERGSTRÖM T., BURMAN L., DAHLQVIST E., FORKMAN A., FRYDEN A., LÖVGREN K., NORLIN K., NORRBY R., OLDING-STENKVIST E., STIERNSTEDT G., UHNOO I. & DE VAHL K. (1984) Acyclovir versus vidarabine in herpes simplex encephalitis. Randomised multicentre study in consecutive Swedish patients. *Lancet* **2**, 707–711 *[301]*.

SLADE P.D. & RUSSELL G.F.M. (1971) Developmental dyscalculia: a brief report of four cases. *Psychological Medicine* **1**, 292–298 *[182]*.

SLATER E. (1942) Psychosis associated with vitamin B deficiency. *British Medical Journal* **1**, 257–258 *[491]*.

SLATER E. (1943) The neurotic constitution: a statistical study of 2000 neurotic soldiers. *Journal of Neurology and Psychiatry* **6**, 1–16 *[148, 167]*.

SLATER E.T.O. (1962) Psychological aspects. In *Modern Views on 'Stroke' Illness*. The Chest and Heart Association: Tavistock Square, London *[328]*.

SLATER E., BEARD A.W. & GLITHERO E. (1963) The schizophrenia-like psychoses of epilepsy. *British Journal of Psychiatry* **109**, 95–150 *[246, 247, 248, 249, 250, 251, 252]*.

SLATER E. & COWIE V. (1971) *The Genetics of Mental Disorders*. Oxford University Press *[215, 216, 394, 395, 567]*.

SLATER E. & ROTH M. (1969) *Clinical Psychiatry*, 3rd edn. Baillière,Tindall & Cassell: London *[243, 254, 262, 274, 278, 296, 313, 466, 472, 476, 524, 527]*.

SMALL J.G., MILSTEIN V. & STEVENS J.R. (1962) Are psychomotor epileptics different? *Archives of Neurology* **7**, 187–194 *[233]*.

SMALL J.G., SMALL I.F. & HAYDEN M.P. (1966) Further psychiatric investigations of patients with temporal and non-temporal lobe epilepsy. *American Journal of Psychiatry* **123**, 303–310 *[233, 249]*.

SMALS A.G., KLOPPENBORG P.W., NJO K.T., KNOBEN J.M. & RUTLAND C.M. (1976) Alcohol-induced Cushingoid syndrome. *British Medical Journal* **2**, 1298 *[436]*.

SMEGO R.A. & DURACK D.T. (1982) The neuroleptic malignant syndrome. *Archives of Internal Medicine* **142**, 1183–1185 *[533]*.

SMITH A. (1961) Duration of impaired consciousness as an index of severity in closed head injuries: a review. *Diseases of the Nervous System* **22**, 69–74 *[145]*.

SMITH A. (1962) Ambiguities in concepts and studies of 'brain damage' and 'organicity'. *Journal of Nervous and Mental Disease* 135, 311–326 *[93]*.

SMITH A. (1966a) Speech and other functions after left (dominant) hemispherectomy. *Journal of Neurology, Neurosurgery and Psychiatry* 29, 467–471 *[39]*.

SMITH A. (1966b) Intellectual functions in patients with lateralised frontal tumours. *Journal of Neurology, Neurosurgery and Psychiatry* 29, 52–59 *[192]*.

SMITH A. (1978) Lenneberg, Locke, Zangwill, and the neuropsychology of language and language disorders. Ch. 7 in *Psychology and Biology of Language and Thought*, eds. Lenneberg E., Brown R. & Miller G. Academic Press: New York *[43]*.

SMITH A. (1972) Dominant and non-dominant hemispherectomy. Ch. 3 in *Drugs, Development and Cerebral Function*, ed. Smith W.L. Thomas: Springfield, Illinois *[39]*.

SMITH A.D.M. (1960) Megaloblastic madness. *British Medical Journal* 2, 1840–1845 *[501]*.

SMITH C.M. (1958a) Psychosomatic aspects of narcolepsy. *Journal of Mental Science* 104, 593–607 *[620, 621]*.

SMITH C.M. (1958b) Comments and observations on psychogenic hypersomnia. *Archives of Neurology and Psychiatry* 80, 619–624 *[630]*.

SMITH C. & HAMILTON J. (1959) Psychological factors in the narcolepsy-cataplexy syndrome. *Psychosomatic Medicine* 21, 40–49 *[624]*.

SMITH C.M. & SWASH M. (1980) Effects of cholinergic drugs on memory in Alzheimer's disease. In *Aging of the Brain and Dementia, Aging, Vol. 13*, eds. Amaducci L., Davison A.N. & Antuono P. Raven Press: New York *[426]*.

SMITH D.B. & OBBENS E.A.M.T. (1979) Antifolate-antiepiletpic relationships. Ch. 28 in *Folic Acid in Neurology, Psychiatry, and Internal Medicine*, eds. Botez M.I. & Reynolds E.H. Raven Press: New York *[506]*.

SMITH J.S. & BRANDON S. (1970) Acute carbon monoxide poisoning—3 years experience in a defined population. *Postgraduate Medical Journal* 46, 65–70 *[469, 470]*.

SMITH J.S. & BRANDON S. (1973) Morbidity from acute carbon monoxide poisoning at three-year follow-up. *British Medical Journal* 1, 318–321 *[470, 471]*.

SMITH J.S. & KILOH L.G. (1981) The investigation of dementia: results in 200 consecutive admissions. *Lancet* 1, 824–827 *[414, 415]*.

SMITH J.W., BURT D.W. & CHAPMAN R.F. (1973) Intelligence and brain damage in alcoholics: a study in patients of middle and upper social class. *Quarterly Journal of Studies on Alcohol* 34, 414–422 *[518]*.

SMITH M.G., LENNETTE E.M. & REAMES H.R. (1941) Isolation of the virus of herpes simplex and the demonstration of intranuclear inclusions in a case of acute encephalitis. *American Journal of Pathology* 17, 55–68 *[299]*.

SMITH R. (1982a) The world's best system of compensating injury? *British Medical Journal* 284, 1243–1245 *[176]*.

SMITH R. (1982b) Problems with a no-fault system of accident compensation. *British Medical Journal* 284, 1323–1325 *[176]*.

SMITH W.L., PHILLIPPUS M.J. & GUARD H.L. (1968) Psychometric study of children with learning problems and 14-6 positive spike EEG patterns treated with ethosuximide (zarontin) and placebo. *Archives of Disease in Childhood* 43, 616–619 *[231]*.

SMITH W.T. (1976) Intoxications, poisons and related metabolic disorders. Ch. 4 in *Greenfield's Neuropathology*, 3rd Edition, eds. Blackwood W. & Corsellis J.A.N. Edward Arnold, London *[564]*.

SMYTH G.E. & STERN K. (1938) Tumours of the thalamus—a clinicopathological study. *Brain* 61, 339–374 *[198]*.

SMYTHIES J.R. (1967) The previous personality in parkinsonism. *Journal of Psychosomatic Research* 11, 169–171 *[562]*.

SNAITH R.P. & MCCOURIE M. (1974) Antihypertensive drugs and depression. *Psychological Medicine* 4, 393–398 *[342]*.

SNAITH R.P., MEHTA S. & RABY A.H. (1970) Serum folate and vitamin B_{12} in epileptics with and without mental illness. *British Journal of Psychiatry* 116, 179–183 *[506]*.

SNEATH P., CHANARIN I., HODKINSON H.M., McPHERSON C.K. & REYNOLDS E.H. (1973) Folate status in a geriatric population and its relation to dementia. *Age and Ageing* 2, 177–182 *[505]*.

SNEDDON J. (1980) Myasthenia gravis: a study of social, medical, and emotional problems in 26 patients. *Lancet* 1, 526–528 *[607, 608]*.

SNIDER W.D., SIMPSON D.M., NIELSEN S., GOLD W.M., METROKA C.E. & POSNER J.B. (1983) Neurological complications of acquired immune deficiency syndrome: analysis of 50 patients. *Annals of Neurology* 14, 403–418 *[315]*.

SNYDER S.H., TAYLOR K.M., COYLE J.T. & MEYERHOFF J.L. (1970) The role of brain dopamine in behavioural regulation and the actions of psychotropic drugs. *American Journal of Psychiatry* 127, 199–207 *[584]*.

SOFFER L.J., IANNACCONE A. & GABRILOVE J.L. (1961) Cushing's syndrome. A study of fifty patients. *American Journal of Medicine* 30, 129–146 *[438]*.

SOLOMON S. (1954) A critical review of the Morgagni-Stewart-Morel syndrome. *New York State Journal of Medicine* 54, 629–648 *[653]*.

SORENSON B.F. & HAMBY W.B. (1965) Spasmodic torticollis. Results in 71 surgically treated patients. *Journal of the American Medical Association* 194, 706–708 *[576]*.

SOURANDER P. & SJÖGREN H. (1970) The concept of Alzheimer's disease and its clinical implications. In *Alzheimer's Disease*, Ciba Foundation Symposium, eds. Wolstenholme G.E.W. & O'Connor M. Churchill: London *[374, 375, 379, 385]*.

SOURS J.A. (1963) Narcolepsy and other disturbances in the sleep-waking rhythm: a study of 115 cases with review of the literature. *Journal of Nervous and Mental Disease* 137, 525–542 *[618, 619, 622, 625, 630]*.

SOURS J.A., FRUMKIN P. & INDERMILL R.R. (1963) Somnambulism: its clinical significance and dynamic meaning in late adolescence and adulthood. *Archives of General Psychiatry* 9, 400–413 *[631]*.

SPENCER D.J. (1970) Cannabis induced psychosis. *West Indian Medical Journal* 19, 228–230 *[526]*.

SPERLING M. (1953) Psychodynamics and treatment of petit mal in children. *International Journal of Psychoanalysis* 34, 248–252 *[271]*.

SPERLING M. (1964) A further contribution to the psychoanalytic study of migraine and psychogenic headaches. *International Journal of Psychoanalysis* 45, 549–557 *[347, 355]*.

SPERRY R.W. (1966) Brain bisection and consciousness. Ch. 13 in *Brain and Conscious Experience*, ed. Eccles J.C. Springer: Berlin *[38]*.

SPERRY R.W. & GAZZANIGA M.S. (1967) Language following surgical disconnection of the hemispheres. In *Brain Mechanisms Underlying Speech and Language*, ed. Darley F.L. Grune & Stratton: New York *[38, 276]*.

SPIEGEL L.A. & OBERNDORF C.P. (1946) Narcolepsy as a psychogenic symptom. *Psychosomatic Medicine* 8, 28–35 *[621, 630]*.

SPIELMEYER G. (1969) Causation in German law. Ch. 45 in *The Late Effects of Head Injury*, eds. Walker A.E., Caveness W.F. & Critchley M. Thomas: Springfield, Illinois *[179]*.

SPIERS J. & HIRSCH S.R. (1978) Severe lithium toxicity with 'normal' serum concentrations. *British Medical Journal* 1, 815–816 *[533]*.

SPIES T.D., ARING C.D., GELPERIN J. & BEAN W.B. (1938) The mental symptoms of pellagra: their relief with nicotinic acid. *American Journal of the Medical Sciences* 196, 461–475 *[489]*.

SPILLANE J.A., WHITE P., GOODHARDT M.J., FLACK R.H.A., BOWEN D.M. & DAVISON A.N. (1977) Selective vulnerability of neurones in organic dementia. *Nature* 266, 558–559 *[382]*.

SPILLANE J.D. (1947) *Nutritional Disorders of the Nervous System.* Livingstone: Edinburgh *[489, 492]*.

SPILLANE J.D. (1951) Nervous and mental disorders in Cushing's syndrome. *Brain* 74, 72–94 *[437]*.

SPILLANE J.D. (1962) Five boxers. *British Medical Journal* 2, 1205–1210 *[174]*.

SPITZER R.L., FLEISS J.L., BURDOCK E.I. & HARDESTY A.S. (1964) The mental status schedule: rationale, reliability and validity. *Comprehensive Psychiatry* 5, 384–395 *[107]*.

SPOKES E.G.S. (1980) Neurochemical alterations in Huntington's chorea: a study of post-mortem brain tissue. *Brain* 103, 179–210 *[395]*.

SPRATLING W.P. (1902) Epilepsy in its relation to crime. *Journal of Nervous and Mental Disease* 29, 481–496 *[224]*.

SPRING G.K. (1979) Neurotoxicity with combined use of lithium and thioridazine. *Journal of Clinical Psychiatry* 40, 135–138 *[533]*.

SPROFKIN B.E. & SCIARRA D. (1952) Korsakoff psychosis associated with cerebral tumours. *Neurology* 2, 427–434 *[197]*.

SQUIRE L.R. (1981) Two forms of human amnesia: an analysis of forgetting. *The Journal of Neuroscience* 1, 635–640 *[35]*.

SQUIRE L.R. (1982) The neuropsychology of human memory. *Annual Review of Neuroscience* 5, 241–273 *[35]*.

SQUIRE L.R. & COHEN N.J. (1982) Remote memory, retrograde amnesia, and the neuropsychology of memory. In *Human Memory and Amnesia*, ed. Cermak L.S. Lawrence Erlbaum Associates: Hillsdale, New Jersey *[34, 35]*.

SQUIRE L.R. & MOORE R.Y. (1979) Dorsal thalamic lesion in a noted case of human memory dysfunction. *Annals of Neurology* 6, 503–506 *[25]*.

SQUIRE L.R. & SCHLAPFER W.T. (1981) Memory and memory disorders: a biological and neurologic perspective. Ch. 8 in *Handbook of Biological Psychiatry, Part IV, Brain Mechanisms and Abnormal Behavior—Chemistry*, eds. Van Praag H.M., Lader M.H., Rafaelsen O.J. & Sachar E.J. Marcel Dekker: New York and Basel *[24]*.

SQUIRE L.R. & SLATER P.C. (1975) Forgetting in very long-term memory as assessed by an improved questionnaire technique. *Journal of Experimental Psychology: Human Learning and Memory* 104, 50–54 *[34]*.

SROKA H., ELIZAN T.S., YAHR M.D., BURGER A. & MENDOZA M.R. (1981) Organic mental syndrome and confusional states in Parkinson's disease. Relationship to computerised tomographic signs of cerebral atrophy. *Archives of Neurology* 38, 339–342 *[557]*.

STAFFORD-CLARK D. & TAYLOR F.H. (1949) Clinical and electroencephalographic studies of prisoners charged with murder. *Journal of Neurology, Neurosurgery and Psychiatry* 12, 325–330 *[111, 241]*.

STANDAGE K.F. & FENTON G.W. (1975) Psychiatric symptom profiles of patients with epilepsy: a controlled investigation. *Psychological Medicine* 5, 152–160 *[243]*.

STARR A. & PHILLIPS L. (1970) Verbal and motor memory in the amnestic syndrome. *Neuropsychologia* 8, 75–88 *[32]*.

STATON M.A., DONALD A.G. & GREEN G.B. (1976) Zinc deficiency presenting as schizophrenia. *Current Concepts in Psychiatry* 2, 11–14 *[478]*.

STAUDER K.H. (1934) Die tödliche Katatonie. *Archiv für Psychiatrie und Nervenkrankheiten* 102, 614–634 *[473]*.

STEADMAN J.H. & GRAHAM J.G. (1970) Head injuries: an analysis and follow-up study. *Proceedings of the Royal Society of Medicine* 63, 23–28 *[145, 146, 151, 152, 178]*.

STEEL R. (1960) GPI in an observation ward. *Lancet* 1, 121–123 *[285]*.

STEELE J.C. (1972) Progressive supranuclear palsy. *Brain* 95, 693–704 *[567]*.

STEELE J.C., RICHARDSON J.C. & OLSZEWSKI J. (1964) Progressive supranuclear palsy. *Archives of Neurology* 10, 333–359 *[567, 568]*.

STEIN J.A. & TSCHUDY D.P. (1970) Acute intermittent porphyria. A clinical and biochemical study of 46 patients. *Medicine* 49, 1–16 *[483]*.

STEINBERG D., HIRSCH S.R., MARSTON S.D., REYNOLDS K. & SUTTON R.N.P. (1972) Influenza infection causing manic psychosis. *British Journal of Psychiatry* 120, 531–535 *[304]*.

STEINMETZ E.F. & VROOM F.Q. (1972) Transient global amnesia. *Neurology* 22, 1193–1200 *[359, 360, 361]*.

STENBÄCK A. & HAAPANEN E. (1967) Azotaemia and psychosis. *Acta Psychiatrica Scandinavica*, supplement 197, 1–65 *[472, 473]*.

STENGEL E. (1941) On the aetiology of the fugue states. *Journal of Mental Science* 87, 572–599 *[263]*.

STENGEL E. (1943a) Further studies on pathological wandering (fugues with the impulse to wander). *Journal of Mental Science* 89, 224–241 *[263]*.

STENGEL E. (1943b) A study on the symptomatology and differential diagnosis of Alzheimer's disease and Pick's disease. *Journal of Mental Science* 89, 1–20 *[393]*.

STENGEL E. (1964) Psychopathology of dementia. *Proceedings of the Royal Society of Medicine* 57, 911–914 *[15]*.

STENGEL E. (1965) Pain and the psychiatrist. *British Journal of Psychiatry* 111, 795–802 *[66]*.

STEPHENS D.A. (1967) Psychotoxic effects of benzhexol hydrochloride (artane). *British Journal of Psychiatry* 113, 213–218 *[559]*.

STERKY G. (1963) Diabetic schoolchildren. *Acta Paediatrica Scandinavica, Suppl.* 144, 1–39 *[455]*.

STERN K. (1939) Severe dementia associated with bilateral symmetrical degeneration of the thalamus. *Brain* 62, 157–171 *[647]*.

STERN R. & ELDRIDGE R. (1975) Attitudes of patients and their relatives to Huntington's disease. *Journal of Medical Genetics* 12, 217–223 *[394]*.

STERNER R.T. & PRICE W.R. (1973) Restricted riboflavin: within-subject behavioral effects in humans. *American Journal of Clinical Nutrition* 26, 150–160 *[487]*.

STERNLIEB I., MORELL A.G., BAUER C.D., COMBES B., DE BOBES-STERNBERG S. & SCHEINBERG I.H. (1961) Detection of the heterozygous carrier of the Wilson's disease gene. *Journal of Clinical Investigation* 40, 707–715 *[565]*.

STERNLIEB I. & SCHEINBERG I.H. (1964) Penicillamine therapy for hepatolenticular degeneration. *Journal of the American Medical Association* 189, 748–754 *[566, 567]*.

STERNLIEB I. & SCHEINBERG I.H. (1968) The detection of Wilson's disease and the prevention of the clinical manifestations in apparently healthy subjects. In *Wilson's Disease*, ed. Bergsma D. Birth Defects Original Article Series, vol. 4, No. 2. The National Foundation: New York *[565]*.

STEVENS H. (1966) Paroxysmal choreo-athetosis. *Archives of Neurology* 14, 415–421 *[258]*.

STEVENS J.R. (1959) Emotional activation of the electroencephalogram in patients with convulsive disorders. *Journal of Nervous and Mental Disease* 128, 339–351 *[216]*.

STEVENS J.R. (1966) Psychiatric implications of psychomotor epilepsy. *Archives of General Psychiatry* 14, 461–471 *[221, 233, 249, 258]*.

STEVENS J.R. (1982) Neuropathology of schizophrenia. *Archives of General Psychiatry* 39, 1131–1139 *[76]*.

STEVENSON J.F. (1967) M.Sc Thesis, University of Cambridge. Quoted by Warrington E.K., 1970, in *The Psychological Assessment of Mental and Physical Handicaps*, ed. Mittler P. Methuen: London *[91]*.

STEWART I.McD.G. (1953) Headache and hypertension. *Lancet* 1, 1261–1266 *[342]*.

STORES G. (1978) School-children with epilepsy at risk for learning and behaviour problems. *Developmental Medicine and Child Neurology* 20, 502–508 *[229, 233]*.

STORES G. (1981) Problems of learning and behaviour in children with epilepsy. Ch. 4 in *Epilepsy and Psychiatry*, eds. Reynolds E.H. & Trimble M.R. Churchill Livingstone: Edinburgh and London *[231]*.

STOREY P.B. (1966) Lumbar air encephalography in chronic schizo-. phrenia: a controlled experiment. *British Journal of Psychiatry* 112, 135–144 *[121]*.

STOREY P.B. (1967) Psychiatric sequelae of subarachnoid haemorrhage. *British Medical Journal* 3, 261–266 *[336]*.

STOREY P.B. (1969) The precipitation of subarachnoid haemorrhage. *Journal of Psychosomatic Research* 13, 175–182 *[339]*.

STOREY P.B. (1970) Brain damage and personality change after subarachnoid heamorrhage. *British Journal of Psychiatry* 117, 129–142 *[336, 337]*.

STOREY P.B. (1972) Emotional disturbances before and after subarachnoid haemorrhage. In *Physiology, Emotion and Psychosomatic Illness*, eds. Porter R. and Knight J., Ciba Foundation Symposium No. 8 (new series), pp. 337–343. Associated Scientific Publishers: Amsterdam *[336, 338, 339]*.

STORM VAN LEEUWEN W. *et al.* (1966) Proposal for an EEG terminology by the terminology committee of the international federation for electroencephalography and clinical neurophysiology. *Electroencephalography and Clinical Neurophysiology* 20, 306–310 *[109]*.

STORM-MATHISEN A. (1969) General paresis. A follow up study of 203 patients. *Acta Psychiatrica Scandinavica* 45, 118–132 *[283, 284]*.

STRACHAN R.W. & HENDERSON J.G. (1965) Psychiatric syndromes due to avitaminosis B$_{12}$ with normal blood and marrow. *Quarterly Journal of Medicine* 34, 303–317 *[502, 503]*.

STRACHAN R.W. & HENDERSON J.G. (1967) Dementia and folate deficiency. *Quarterly Journal of Medicine* 36, 189–204 *[505]*.

STRAUSS I. & KESCHNER M. (1935) Mental symptoms in cases of tumour of the frontal lobe. *Archives of Neurology and Psychiatry* 33, 986–1005 *[188, 192]*.

STRECKER E.A. & EBAUGH F.G. (1924) Neuropsychiatric sequelae of cerebral trauma in children. *Archives of Neurology and Psychiatry* 12, 443–453 *[173]*.

STREICHER H.Z., GABOW P.A., MOSS A.H., KONO D. & KAEHNY W.D. (1981) Syndromes of toluene sniffing in adults. *Annals of Internal Medicine* 94, 758–762 *[537]*.

STRICH S.J. (1956) Diffuse degeneration of the cerebral white matter in severe dementia following head injury. *Journal of Neurology, Neurosurgery and Psychiatry* 19, 163–185 *[139]*.

STRICH S.J. (1969) The pathology of brain damage due to blunt head injuries. Ch. 51 in *The Late Effects of Head Injury*, eds. Walker A.E., Caveness W.F. & Critchley M. Thomas: Springfield, Illinois *[139, 160]*.

STROBOS R.R.J. (1953) Tumours of temporal lobe. *Neurology* 3, 752–760 *[194, 196]*.

STUSS D.T., ALEXANDER M.P., LIEBERMAN A. & LEVINE H. (1978) An extraordinary form of confabulation. *Neurology* 28, 1166–1172 *[30]*.

STUTEVILLE P. & WELCH K. (1958) Subdural haematoma in the elderly person. *Journal of the American Medical Association* 168, 1445–1449 *[355, 356]*.

SUBIRANA A. (1969) Handedness and cerebral dominance. Ch. 13 in *Handbook of Clinical Neurology*, vol. 4, eds. Vinken P.J. & Bruyn G.W. North-Holland Publishing Co.: Amsterdam *[38]*.

SUMMERSKILL W.H.J., DAVIDSON E.A., SHERLOCK S. & STEINER R.E. (1956) The neuropsychiatric syndrome associated with hepatic cirrhosis and an extensive portal collateral circulation. *Quarterly Journal of Medicine* 25, 245–266 *[479, 480, 481]*.

SUMNER D. (1969) The diagnosis of intracranial tumours. *British Journal of Hospital Medicine* 2, 489–494 *[201, 203, 204, 214]*.

SURRIDGE D. (1969) An investigation into some psychiatric aspects of multiple sclerosis. *British Journal of Psychiatry* 115, 749–764 *[590, 591, 592, 593, 594]*.

SURRIDGE D.H.C., ERDAHL D.L.W., LAWSON J.S., DONALD M.W., MONGA T.N., BIRD C.E. & LETEMENDIA F.J.J. (1984) Psychiatric aspects of diabetes mellitus. *British Journal of Psychiatry* 145, 269–276 *[455]*.

SUTULA T.P., SACKELLARES J.C., MILLER J.Q. & DREIFUSS F.E. (1981) Intensive monitoring in refractory epilepsy. *Neurology* 31, 243–247 *[256]*.

SWAIN J.M. (1959) Electroencephalographic abnormalities in presenile atrophy. *Neurology* 9, 722–727 *[379, 392]*.

SWANSON D.W. & STIPES A.H. (1969) Psychiatric aspects of Klinefelter's syndrome. *American Journal of Psychiatry* 126, 814–822 *[446]*.

SWEET R.D., McDOWELL F.H., FEIGENSON J.S., LORANGER A.W. & GOOD H. (1976) Mental symptoms in Parkinson's disease during chronic treatment with levodopa. *Neurology* 26, 305–310 *[560]*.

SWEET R.D., SOLOMON G.E., WAYNE H., SHAPIRO E. & SHAPIRO A.K. (1973) Neurological features of Gilles de la Tourette's syndrome. *Journal of Neurology, Neurosurgery and Psychiatry* 36, 1–9 *[584]*.

SWEET W.H., ERVIN F. & MARK V.H. (1969) The relationship of violent behaviour to focal cerebral disease. In *Aggressive Behaviour*, Proceedings of International Symposium on the Biology of Aggressive Behaviour, eds. Garattini S. & Sigg E.B. Exerpta Medica: Amsterdam *[72, 162]*.

SWEET W.H., TALLAND G.A. & BALLANTINE H.T. (1966) A memory and mood disorder associated with ruptured anterior communicating aneurysm. *Transactions of the American Neurological Association* 91, 346–348 *[337]*.

SWEET W.H., TALLAND G.A. & ERVIN F.R. (1959) Loss of recent memory following section of fornix. *Transactions of the American Neurological Association* 84, 76–82 *[26]*.

SWIFT C.R., SEIDMAN F. & STEIN H. (1967) Adjustment problems in juvenile diabetes. *Psychosomatic Medicine* 29, 555–571 *[455]*.

SYDENSTRICKER V.P. (1943) Psychic manifestations of nicotinic acid deficiency. *Proceedings of the Royal Society of Medicine* 36, 169–171 *[490]*.

SYLVESTER J.D. & LIVERSEDGE L.A. (1960) A follow-up study of patients treated for writer's cramp by conditioning techniques. In *Behaviour Therapy and the Neuroses*, ed. Eysenck H.J. Pergamon Press: Oxford *[578, 579]*.

SYMON L. & DORSCH N.W.C. (1975) Use of long-term intracranial pressure measurement to assess hydrocephalic patients prior to shunt surgery. *Journal of Neurosurgery* 42, 258–273 *[640]*.

SYMONDS C.P. (1937) Mental disorder following head injury. *Proceedings of the Royal Society of Medicine* 30, 1081–1092 *[165]*.

SYMONDS C. (1951) Migrainous variants. *Transactions of the Medical Society of London* 67, 237–250 *[351]*.

SYMONDS C. (1959) Excitation and inhibition in epilepsy. *Brain* 82, 133–146 *[217]*.

SYMONDS C. (1962a) Concussion and its sequelae. *Lancet* 1, 1–5 *[145]*.

SYMONDS C.P. (1962b) Discussion following 'The schizophrenia-like psychoses of epilepsy'. *Proceedings of the Royal Society of Medicine* 55, 314–315 *[249, 250]*.

SYMONDS C.P. (1966) Disorders of memory. *Brain* 89, 625–644 *[34]*.

SYMONDS C.P. & RUSSELL W.R. (1943) Accidental head injuries. *Lancet* 1, 7–10 *[145, 147]*.

SYPERT G.W., LEFFMAN H. & OJEMANN G.A. (1973) Occult normal pressure hydrocephalus manifested by Parkinsonism-dementia complex. *Neurology* 23, 234–239 *[641]*.

TAGLIAVINI F. & PILLERI G. (1983) Neuronal counts in basal nucleus of Meynert in Alzheimer's disease and in simple senile dementia. *Lancet* 1, 469–470 *[383]*.

TALBOTT J.A. & TEAGUE J.W. (1969) Marihuana psychosis. *Journal of the American Medical Association* 210, 299–302 *[526, 527]*.

TALLAND G.A. (1962) Cognitive function in Parkinson's disease. *Journal of Nervous and Mental Disease* 135, 196–205 *[555]*.

TALLAND G.A. (1965) *Deranged Memory: A Psychonomic Study of the Amnesic Syndrome*. Academic Press: New York *[29, 30]*.

TALLAND G.A., SWEET W.H. & BALLANTYNE H.T. (1967) Amnesic syndrome with anterior communicating artery aneurysm. *Journal of Nervous and Mental Disease* 145, 179–192 *[337]*.

TAMERIN J.S., WEINER S., POPPEN R., STEINGLASS P. & MENDELSON J.H. (1971) Alcohol and memory: amnesia and short-term memory function during experimentally induced intoxication. *American Journal of Psychiatry* 127, 1659–1664 *[510]*.

TARACHOW S. (1939) The Korsakoff psychosis in spontaneous sub-arachnoid haemorrhage. *American Journal of Psychiatry* 95, 887–899 *[336]*.

TARLOV E. (1970) On the problem of the pathology of spasmodic torticollis in man. *Journal of Neurology, Neurosurgery and Psychiatry* 33, 457–463 *[575]*.

TARTER R.E. (1980) Brain damage in chronic alcoholics: a review of the psychological evidence. Ch. 15 in *Addiction and Brain Damage*, ed. Richter D. Croom Helm: London *[518]*.

TARTER R.E. & SCHNEIDER D.U. (1976) Blackouts: relationship with memory capacity and alcoholism history. *Archives of General Psychiatry* 33, 1492–1496 *[510]*.

TASK FORCE ON LATE NEUROLOGICAL EFFECTS OF ANTIPSYCHOTIC DRUGS (1980) Tardive dyskinesia: summary of a task force report of the American Psychiatric Association. *American Journal of Psychiatry* 137, 1163–1172 *[547, 549]*.

TATTERSALL R.B. (1981) Psychiatric aspects of diabetes—a physician's view. *British Journal of Psychiatry* 139, 485–493 *[453, 454]*.

TAYLOR A.R. & BELL T.K. (1966) Slowing of cerebral circulation after concussional head injury. *Lancet* 2, 178–180 *[170]*.

TAYLOR D.C. (1969a) Aggression and epilepsy. *Journal of Psychosomatic Research* 13, 229–236 *[233]*.

TAYLOR D.C. (1969b) Sexual behaviour and temporal lobe epilepsy. *Archives of Neurology* 21, 510–516 *[237, 238, 239, 240]*.

TAYLOR D.C. (1972) Mental state and temporal lobe epilepsy: a correlative account of 100 patients treated surgically. *Epilepsia* 13, 727–765 *[249]*.

TAYLOR D.C. (1975) Factors influencing the occurrence of schizophrenia-like psychosis in patients with temporal lobe epilepsy. *Psychological Medicine* 5, 249–254 *[249]*.

TAYLOR D.C. & FALCONER M.A. (1968) Clinical, socioeconomic, and psychological changes after temporal lobectomy for epilepsy. *British Journal of Psychiatry* 114, 1247–1261 *[229, 235, 236, 237, 275]*.

TAYLOR J.W. (1975) Depression in thyrotoxicosis. *American Journal of Psychiatry* 132, 552–553 *[431]*.

TAYLOR M.A., REDFIELD J. & ABRAMS R. (1981) Neuropsychological dysfunction in schizophrenia and affective disease. *Biological Psychiatry* 16, 467–478 *[76]*.

TAYLOR P.J., DALTON R. & FLEMINGER J.J. (1980) Handedness in schizophrenia. *British Journal of Psychiatry* 136, 375–383 *[76]*.

TAYLOR P.J. & KOPELMAN M.D. (1984) Amnesia for criminal offences. *Psychological Medicine* 14, 581–588 *[36]*.

TCHICALOFF M. & GAILLARD F. (1970) Quelques effets indésirables des médicaments antiépileptiques sur les rendements intellectuels. *Revue de Neuropsychiatrie Infantile* 18, 599–603 *[230]*.

TEASDALE G. & JENNETT B. (1974) Assessment of coma and impaired consciousness: a practical scale. *Lancet* 2, 81–84 *[142]*.

TEASDALE G. & MENDELOW D. (1984) Pathophysiology of head injuries. Ch. 2 in *Closed Head Injury. Psychological, Social and Family Consequences*, ed. Brooks N. Oxford University Press *[139]*.

TENNENT T. (1937) Discussion on mental disorder following head injury. *Proceedings of the Royal Society of Medicine* 30, 1092–1093 *[164]*.

TERRY R.D. (1979) Morphological changes in Alzheimer's disease—senile dementia: ultrastructural changes and quantitative studies. In *Congenital and Acquired Disorders*, ed. Katzman R. Research Publications: Association for Research in Nervous and Mental Disease, Vol. 57, pp. 99–105. Raven Press: New York *[382]*.

TERRY R.D., FITZGERALD C., PECK A., MILLNER J. & FARMER P. (1977) Cortical cell counts in senile dementia. *Journal of Neuropathology and Experimental Neurology* 36, 633 *[382]*.

TERRY R.D. & KATZMAN R. (1983) Senile dementia of the Alzheimer type. *Annals of Neurology* 14, 497–506 *[371, 377, 382, 385]*.

TERRY R.D., PECK A., DE TERESA R., SCHECHTER R. & HOROUPIAN D.S. (1981) Some morphometric aspects of the brain in senile dementia of the Alzheimer type. *Annals of Neurology* 10, 184–192 *[377, 382]*.

TERRY R.D. & WISNIEWSKI H. (1970) The ultrastructure of the neurofibrillary tangle and the senile plaque. In *Alzheimer's Disease and Related Conditions*, eds. Wolstenholme G.E.W. & O'Connor M. Ciba Foundation Symposium. Churchill: London *[380, 381]*.

TERRY R.D. & WISNIEWSKI H.M. (1972) Ultrastructure of senile dementia and of experimental analogs. In *Aging and the Brain*, ed. Gaitz C.M. Plenum Press: New York and London *[381]*.

TEUBER H-L. (1959) Some alterations in behaviour after cerebral lesions in man. In *Evolution of Nervous Control*, ed. Bass A.D. Publication No. 52 of the American Association for the Advancement of Science: Washington *[154, 157]*.

TEUBER H-L. (1962) Effects of brain wounds implicating right or left hemisphere in man. In *Interhemispheric Relations and Cerebral Dominance*, ed. Mountcastle V.B. Johns Hopkins Press: Baltimore *[154, 157]*.

TEUBER H-L. (1964) The riddle of frontal lobe function in man. Ch. 20 in *The Frontal Granular Cortex and Behaviour*, eds. Warren J.M. & Akert K. McGraw-Hill: New York *[68, 70]*.

TEUBER H-L. & MILNER B. (1968) Alteration of perception and memory in man: reflection on methods. Ch. 11 in *Analysis of Behavioural Change*, ed. Weiskrantz L. Harper & Row: New York *[102]*.

TEUBER H-L., MILNER B. & VAUGHAN H.G. (1968) Persistent anterograde amnesia after stab wound of the basal brain. *Neurophsychologia* 6, 267–282 *[102]*.

TEUBER H-L. & RUDEL R.G. (1962) Behaviour after cerebral lesions in children and adults. *Developmental Medicine and Child Neurology* 4, 3–20 *[171, 172]*.

TEUBER H-L. & WEINSTEIN S. (1956) Ability to discover hidden figures after cerebral lesions. *Archives of Neurology and Psychiatry* 76, 369–379 *[42]*.

THACORE V.R. (1973) Bhang psychosis. *British Journal of Psychiatry* 123, 225–229 *[527]*.

THE CANADIAN COOPERATIVE STUDY GROUP (1978) A randomised trial of aspirin and sulfinpyrazone in threatened stroke. *New England Journal of Medicine* 229, 53–59 *[331]*.

THEANDER S. & GRANHOLM L. (1967) Sequelae after spontaneous

subarachnoid haemorrhage, with special reference to hydro
cephalus and Korsakoff's syndrome. *Acta Neurologica Scandinavica* **43**, 479–488 *[336, 337, 338]*.

THIGPEN C.H. & MOSS B.F. (1955) Unusual paranoid manifestations
in a case of psychomotor epilepsy and narcolepsy. *Journal of
Nervous and Mental Disease* **122**, 381–385 *[626]*.

THOMAS C.J. (1979) Brain damage with lithium/haloperidol. *British
Journal of Psychiatry* **134**, 552 *[533]*.

THOMAS F.B., MAZZAFERI E.L. & SKILLMAN T.G. (1970) Apathetic
thyrotoxicosis: in a distinctive clinical and laboratory entity.
Annals of Internal Medicine **72**, 679–685 *[431]*.

THOMAS S. (1982) Ethics of a predictive test for Huntington's chorea.
British Medical Journal **284**, 1383–1385 *[394]*.

THOMASEN E. (1948) *Myotonia: Thomsen's Disease (Myotonia Congenita), Paramyotonia, and Dystrophia Myotonica.* Universitetsforlaget: Aarhus *[615, 616, 617]*.

THOMPSON C. & CHECKLEY S. (1981) Short term memory deficit in
a patient with cerebral sarcoidosis. *British Journal of Psychiatry*
139, 160–161 *[653]*.

THOMPSON L.W., DAVIS G.C., OBRIST W.D. & HEYMAN A. (1976)
Effects of hyperbaric oxygen on behavioral and physiological
measures in elderly demented patients. *Journal of Gerontology*
31, 23–28 *[424]*.

THOMPSON P.J., HUPPERT F. & TRIMBLE M. (1980) Anticonvulsant
drugs, cognitive function and memory. *Acta Neurologica Scandinavica* **62**, *Suppl. 80*, 75–81 *[267]*.

THOMPSON P.J. & TRIMBLE M.R. (1982) Anticonvulsant drugs and
cognitive functions. *Epilepsia* **23**, 531–544 *[230]*.

THOMPSON P.J. & TRIMBLE M.R. (1983) Anticonvulsant serum levels:
relationship to impairments of cognitive functioning. *Journal of
Neurology, Neurosurgery and Psychiatry* **46**, 227–233 *[230]*.

THOMPSON R.H.S. (1967) The value of blood pyruvate determination
in the diagnosis of thiamine deficiency. In *Thiamine Deficiency*,
Ciba Foundation Study Group No. 28, eds. Wolstenholme
G.E.W. & O'Connor M. Churchill: London *[487]*.

THOMSEN I.V. (1974) The patient with severe head injury and his
family: a follow-up study of 50 patients. *Scandinavian Journal
of Rehabilitation Medicine* **6**, 180–183 *[146, 186]*.

THOMSEN J. (1876) Tonische Krämpfe in willkürlich beweglichen
Muskeln in Folge von ererbter psychischer Disposition. *Arkiv
für Psychiatrie und Nervenkrankheiten* **6**, 702–718. Quoted by
Johnson J., 1967, *British Journal of Psychiatry* **113**, 1025–1030 *[616, 617]*.

THORNDIKE E.L. & LORGE I. (1944) *The Teacher's Word Book of
30,000 Words.* Teachers' College Press; Columbia University: New
York *[87]*.

TIBBETTS R.W. (1971) Spasmodic torticollis. *Journal of the
Psychosomatic Research* **15**, 461–469 *[571, 572, 573, 574, 576]*.

TINKLENBERG J.R., MELGES F.T., HOLLISTER L.E. & GILLESPIE
H.K. (1970) Marihuana and immediate memory. *Nature* **226**,
1171–1172 *[525]*.

TISSENBAUM M.J., HARTER H.M. & FRIEDMAN A.P. (1951) Organic
neurological syndromes diagnosed as functional disorders.
Journal of the American Medical Association **147**, 1519–1521 *[588]*.

TIZARD B. & MARGERISON J.H. (1964) Psychological functions during wave-spike discharge. *British Journal of Social and Clinical
Psychology* **3**, 6–15 *[209, 230]*.

TOGLIA J.U. (1969) Dizziness after whiplash injury of the neck and
closed head injury: electronystagmographic correlations. Ch. 6
in *The Late Effects of Head Injury*, eds. Walker A.E., Caveness
W.F. & Critchley M. Thomas: Springfield, Illinois *[169]*.

TOMLINSON B.E. (1979) The ageing brain. Ch. 6 in *Recent Advances
in Neuropathology*, eds. Smith W.T. & Cavanah J.B. Churchill
Livingstone: Edinburgh & London *[382]*.

TOMLINSON B.E. (1982) Plaques, tangles and Alzheimer's disease.
Psychological Medicine **12**, 449–459 *[376]*.

TOMLINSON B.E., BLESSED G. & ROTH M. (1968) Observations on
the brains of non-demented old people. *Journal of the Neurological
Sciences* **7**, 331–356 *[376]*.

TOMLINSON B.E., BLESSED G. & ROTH M. (1970) Observations on
the brains of demented old people. *Journal of the Neurological
Sciences* **11**, 205–242 *[372, 376, 381, 386, 389]*.

TOMLINSON B.E., IRVING D. & BLESSED D.G. (1981) Cell loss in the
locus coeruleus in senile dementia of Alzheimer type. *Journal of
the Neurological Sciences* **49**, 419–428 *[383]*.

TONKS C.M. (1964) Mental illness in hypothyroid patients. *British
Journal of Psychiatry* **110**, 706–710 *[435, 436]*.

TOONE B.K. (1981) Psychoses of epilepsy. Ch. 10 in *Epilepsy and
Psychiatry*, eds. Reynolds E.H. & Trimble M.R. Churchill
Livingstone: Edinburgh & London *[223, 273]*.

TOONE B.K., DAWSON J. & DRIVER M.V. (1982a) Psychoses of
epilepsy: a radiological evaluation. *British Journal of Psychiatry*
140, 244–248 *[249]*.

TOONE B.K., EDEH J., FENWICK P., GRANT R., NANJEE M., PURCHES
A.C. & WHEELER M. (1984) Hormonal and behavioural changes
in male epileptics. In *Advances in Epileptology: XVth Epilepsy
International Symposium*, eds. Porter R.J., Mattson R.H., Ward
A.A. & Dam M. Raven Press: New York *[239]*.

TOONE B.K. & FENTON G.W. (1977) Epileptic seizures induced by
psychotropic drugs. *Psychological Medicine* **7**, 265–270 *[214]*.

TOONE B.K., GARRALDA M.E. & RON M.A. (1982b) The psychoses
of epilepsy and the functional psychoses: a clinical and
phenomenological comparison. *British Journal of Psychiatry* **141**,
256–261 *[248, 249, 252]*.

TOONE B.K., WHEELER M., NANJEE M., FENWICK P. & GRANT R.
(1983) Sex hormones, sexual activity and plasma anticonvulsant
levels in male epileptics. *Journal of Neurology, Neurosurgery and
Psychiatry* **46**, 824–826 *[239]*.

TORREY E.F. & PETERSON M.R. (1974) Schizophrenia and the limbic
system. *Lancet* **2**, 942–946 *[75]*.

TOW P.M. (1955) *Personality Changes Following Frontal Leucotomy.*
Oxford University Press *[69]*.

TOWER D.B. (1966) Commotio cerebri from a neurochemical
standpoint. Ch. 37 in *Head Injury: Conference Proceedings*, eds.
Caveness W.F. & Walker A.E. Lippincott: Philadelphia *[140]*.

TOWNSEND J.J., BARINGER J.R., WOLINSKY J.S., MALAMUD N.,
MEDNICK J.P., PANITCH H.S., SCOTT R.A.T., OSHIRO L.S. &
CREMER N.E. (1975) Progressive rubella panencephalitis. Late
onset after congenital rubella. *New England Journal of Medicine*
292, 990–993 *[307]*.

TOWNSEND J.J., WOLINSKY J.S. & BARINGER J.R. (1976) The
neuropathology of progressive rubella panencephalitis of late
onset. *Brain* **99**, 81–90 *[307]*.

TRAMONT E.C. (1976) Persistence of Treponema pallidum following
penicillin G therapy. *Journal of American Medical Association*
236, 2206–2207 *[286]*.

TRAUB R., GAJDUSEK D.C. & GIBBS C.J. (1977) Transmissible virus
dementia: the relation of transmissible spongiform encephalopathy to Creutzfeldt-Jakob disease. Ch. 5 in *Aging and
Dementia*, eds. Lynn Smith W. & Kinsbourne M. Spectrum
Publications: New York *[384]*.

TRAVERS R.L. (1979) Polyarteritis nodosa and related disorders.
British Journal of Hospital Medicine **22**, 38–45 *[367]*.

TRAVIESA D.C. (1974) Magnesium deficiency: a possible cause of
thiamine refractoriness in Wernicke-Korsakoff encephalopathy.
Journal of Neurology, Neurosurgery and Psychiatry **37**, 959–962
[497].

TREFFERT D.A. (1963) The psychiatric patient with an EEG temporal lobe focus. *American Journal of Psychiatry* 120, 765–771 [234, 262].

TRETHOWAN W.H. & COBB S. (1952) Neuropsychiatric aspects of Cushing's syndrome. *Archives of Neurology and Psychiatry* 67, 283–309 [437, 438].

TREUTING T.F. (1962) The role of emotional factors in the etiology and course of diabetes mellitus: a review of the recent literature. *American Journal of the Medical Sciences* 244, 93–109 [453, 454].

TRIBOLETTI F. & FERRI H. (1969) Hydergine for treatment of symptoms of cerebrovascular insufficiency. *Current Therapeutic Research* 11, 609–620 [425].

TRIMBLE M.R. (1978) Serum prolactin in epilepsy and hysteria. *British Medical Journal* 2, 1682 [257].

TRIMBLE M.R. (1981a) *Post-Traumatic Neurosis: from Railway Spine to the Whiplash.* John Wiley & Sons: Chichester [179].

TRIMBLE M.R. (1981b) Psychotropic drugs in the management of epilepsy. Ch. 24 in *Epilepsy and Psychiatry*, eds. Reynolds E.H. & Trimble M.R. Churchill Livingstone: Edinburgh & London [273].

TRIMBLE M.R. (1982) Anticonvulsant drugs and hysterical seizures. Ch. 9 in *Pseudoseizures*, eds. Riley T.L. & Roy A. Williams & Wilkins: Baltimore [259].

TRIMBLE M.R. (1983) Pseudoseizures. *British Journal of Hospital Medicine* 29, 326–333 [260].

TRIMBLE M.R., CORBETT J.A. & DONALDSON D. (1980) Folic acid and mental symptoms in children with epilepsy. *Journal of Neurology, Neurosurgery and Psychiatry* 43, 1030–1034 [230].

TRIMBLE M.R. & REYNOLDS E.H. (1976) Anticonvulsant drugs and mental symptoms: a review. *Psychological Medicine* 6, 169–178 [230].

TRIMBLE M.R. & REYNOLDS E.H. (1984) Neuropsychiatric toxicity of anticonvulsant drugs. Ch. 12 in *Recent Advances in Clinical Neurology, No. 4*, eds. Matthews W.B. & Glaser G.H. Churchill Livingstone: Edinburgh & London [230, 238].

TROUSSEAU A. (1868) *Lectures on Clinical Medicine*, vol. 35, p. 453. New Sydenham Society, London. Quoted by Williams M. and Smith H.V. (1954), *Journal of Neurology, Neurosurgery and Psychiatry* 17, 173–182 [310].

TRUITT C.J. (1955) Personal and social adjustments of children with muscular dystrophy. *American Journal of Physical Medicine* 34, 124–128 [612, 613].

TUCCI J.R. (1981) Neuropsychiatric syndromes of electrolyte imbalance. Ch. 1 in *Electrolytes and Neuropsychiatric Disorders*, ed. Alexander P.E. MTP Press, Lancaster [478].

TULVING E. (1972) Episodic and semantic memory. Ch. 10 in *Organisation of Memory*, eds. Tulving E. & Donaldson W. Academic Press: New York [28].

TUMARKIN B., WILSON J.D. & SNYDER G. (1955) Cerebral atrophy due to alcoholism in young adults. *United States Armed Forces Medical Journal* 6, 67–74 [519].

TUNE G.S. (1964) Psychological effects of hypoxia: a review of certain literature from the period 1950 to 1963. *Perceptual and Motor Skills* 19, 551–562 [468].

TUNE L.E., HOLLAND A., FOLSTEIN M.F., DAMLOUJI N.F., GARDENER T.J. & COYLE J.T. (1981) Association of post-operative delirium with raised serum levels of anticholinergic drugs. *Lancet* 2, 651–652 [533].

TUPIN J.P., SMITH D.B., CLANON T.L., KIM L.I., NUGENT A. & GROUPE A. (1973) The long-term use of lithium in aggressive prisoners. *Comprehensive Psychiatry* 14, 311–317 [265].

TUREK I., KURLAND A.A., OTA K.Y. & HANLON T.E. (1969) Effects of pipradol hydrochloride on geriatric patients. *Journal of the American Geriatrics Society* 17, 408–413 [424].

TURLAND D.N. & STEINHARD M. (1969) The efficiency of the Memory-For-Designs Test *British Journal of Social and Clinical Psychology* 8, 44–49 [99].

TURNER E.A. (1969) A surgical approach to the treatment of symptoms in temporal lobe epilepsy. Ch. 17 in *Current Problems in Neuropsychiatry*, ed. Herrington R.N. British Journal of Psychiatry Special Publication No. 4. Headley Brothers: Ashford, Kent [73, 275].

TURNER E.A. (1972) Operations for aggression: bilateral temporal lobotomy and posterior cingulectomy. Ch. 18 in *Psychosurgery*, eds. Hitchcock E., Laitinen L. & Vaernet K. Proceedings of the Second International Conference on Psychosurgery. Thomas: Springfield, Illinois [73].

TURNER J.W.A. (1955) Metallic poisons of the nervous system. *Lancet* 1, 661–663 [543].

TYLER H.R. (1968) Neurologic disorders in renal failure. *American Journal of Medicine* 44, 734–748 [473, 474].

TYRRELL D.A.J., PARRY R.P., CROW T.J., JOHNSTONE E. & FERRIER I.N. (1979) Possible virus in schizophrenia and some neurological disorders. *Lancet* 1, 839–841 [318].

ULLMAN M. (1962) *Behavioural Changes in Patients Following Strokes.* Thomas: Springfield, Illinois [329, 330, 331, 338].

ULLMAN M., ASHENHURST E.M., HURWITZ L.J. & GRUEN A. (1960) Motivational and structural factors in the denial of hemiplegia. *Archives of Neurology* 3, 306–318 [62].

UNGERLEIDER J.T., FISHER D.D. & FULLER M. (1966) The dangers of LSD. *Journal of the American Medical Association* 197, 389–392 [530].

UNTERHANSCHEIDT F., JACHNIK D. & GÖTT H. (1968) Der Balkenmangel *Vol. 128, Monographien aus dem Gesamtgebiete der Neurologie und Psychiatrie (Berlin)*. Quoted by ETTLINGER G. (1977) Agencies of the corpus callosum. Ch. 12 in *Handbook of Clinical Neurology, Vol. 30*, eds. Vinken P.J. & Bruyn G.W. North Holland Publishing Co.: Amsterdam [654].

UPTON A.R.M. (1982) Cerebellar stimulation. Ch. 10, Part 3, in *Textbook of Epilepsy*, 2nd Edition. eds. Laidlaw J. & Richens A., Churchill Livingstone: Edinburgh & London [276].

URSIN H. (1960) The temporal lobe substrate of fear and anger. *Acta Psychiatrica et Neurologica Scandinavica* 35, 378–396 [233].

UYENO E. (1963) Differentiating psychotics from organics on the Minnesota Percepto-Diagnostic Test. *Journal of Consulting Psychology* 27, 462 [98].

VAERNET K. & MADSEN A. (1970) Stereotaxic amygdalotomy and baso-frontal tractotomy in psychotics with aggressive behaviour. *Journal of Neurology, Neurosurgery and Psychiatry* 33, 858–863 [73].

VALENTINE A.R., MOSELEY I.F. & KENDALL B.E. (1980) White matter abnormality in cerebral atrophy: clinico-radiological correlations. *Journal of Neurology, Neurosurgery and Psychiatry* 43, 139–142 [390].

VALLEE B.L., WACKER W.E.C. & ULMER D.D. (1960) The magnesium-deficiency tetany syndrome in man. *New England Journal of Medicine* 262, 155–161 [478].

VAN AMBERG R.J. (1942) Prognosis of carbon monoxide poisoning in 15 patients, previously mentally ill. *Psychiatric Quarterly* 16, 668–680 [470].

VAN BOGAERT L. (1925) Les troubles mentaux dans la sclérose latérale amyotrophique. *Encéphale* 20, 27–47 [604].

VAN BOGAERT L. (1945) Une leuco-encéphalite sclérosante subaigue. *Journal of Neurology, Neurosurgery and Psychiatry* 8, 101–120 *[305]*.

VAN BOGAERT L. (1970) Cerebral amyloid angiopathy and Alzheimer's disease. In *Alzheimer's Disease and Related Conditions*, eds. Wolstenholme G.E.W. & O'Connor M., Ciba Foundation Symposium. Churchill: London *[384]*.

VAN LIERE E.J. & STICKNEY J.C. (1963) *Hypoxia*. University of Chicago Press *[468]*.

VAN WAGENEN W.P. & HERREN R.Y. (1940) Surgical division of commissural pathways in the corpus callosum. Relation to spread of an epileptic attack. *Archives of Neurology and Psychiatry* 44, 740–759 *[276]*.

VAN WOERT M.H., JUTKOWITZ R., ROSENBAUM D. & BOWERS M.B. (1976) Gilles de la Tourette's syndrome: biochemical approaches. In *The Basal Ganglia*, ed. Yahr M.D., pp. 459–465. *Association for Research in Nervous and Mental Disease* 55. Raven Press: New York *[584]*.

VAN ZOMEREN A.H., BROUWER W.H. & DEELMAN B.G. (1984) Attentional deficits: the riddles of selectivity, speed, and alertness. Ch. 5 in *Closed Head Injury. Psychological, Social and Family Consequences*, ed. Brooks N. Oxford University Press *[158]*.

VARMA L.P. (1952) The incidence and clinical features of general paresis. *Indian Journal of Neurology and Psychiatry* 3, 141–163 *[282]*.

VAUHKONEN K. (1959) Suicide among the male disabled with war injuries to the brain. *Acta Psychiatrica et Neurologica Scandinavica*, supplement 137, 90–91 *[165]*.

VEREKER R. (1952) The psychiatric aspects of temporal arteritis. *Journal of Mental Science* 98, 280–286 *[368]*.

VESSIE R.P. (1932) On the transmission of Huntington's chorea for 300 years—the Bures family group. *Journal of Nervous and Mental Disease* 76, 553–573 *[394]*.

VICTOR M. (1964) Observations on the amnestic syndrome in man and its anatomical basis. In *Brain Function, vol. II: RNA and Brain Function, Memory and Learning*, ed. Brazier M.A.B. University of California Press: Berkeley and Los Angeles *[25, 28, 496]*.

VICTOR M. (1966) Treatment of alcoholic intoxication and the withdrawal syndrome. *Psychosomatic Medicine* 28, 636–650 *[514]*.

VICTOR M. & ADAMS R.D. (1953) The effect of alcohol on the nervous system. Ch. 28 in *Metabolic and Toxic Diseases of the Nervous System*. Research Publications of the Association for Research in Nervous and Mental Disease, vol. 32. Williams & Wilkins: Baltimore *[511, 512, 513, 514]*.

VICTOR M. & ADAMS R.D. (1962) The acute confusional states. Ch. 38 in *Principles of Internal Medicine*, eds. Harrison T.R., Adams R.D., Bennett I.L., Resnick W.H., Thorn G.W. & Wintrobe M.M. McGraw-Hill: New York *[4]*.

VICTOR M., ADAMS R.D. & COLE M. (1965) The acquired (non-Wilsonian) type of chronic hepatocerebral degeneration. *Medicine* 44, 345–396 *[482]*.

VICTOR M., ADAMS R.D. & COLLINS G.H. (1971) *The Wernicke-Korsakoff Syndrome*. Blackwell Scientific Publications: Oxford *[29, 30, 491, 492, 493, 494, 495, 496, 497, 499, 500]*.

VICTOR M., ADAMS R.D. & MANCALL E.L. (1959) A restricted form of cerebellar cortical degeneration occurring in alcoholic patients. *Archives of Neurology* 1, 579–688 *[499]*.

VICTOR M., ANGEVINE J.B., MANCALL E.L. & FISHER C.M. (1961) Memory loss with lesions of hippocampal formation. *Archives of Neurology* 5, 244–263 *[25, 323]*.

VICTOR M. & HOPE J.M. (1958) The phenomenon of auditory hallucinations in chronic alcoholism. A critical evaluation of the status of alcoholic hallucinosis. *Journal of Nervous and Mental Disease* 126, 451–481 *[513, 514]*.

VICTORATOS G.C., LENMAN J.A.R. & HERZBERG L. (1977) Neurological investigation of dementia. *British Journal of Psychiatry* 130, 131–133 *[414, 415]*.

VIGNOLO L.A. (1969) Auditory agnosia: a review and report of recent evidence. Ch. 7 in *Contributions to Clinical Neuropsychology*, ed. Benton A.L. Aldine Publishing Company: Chicago *[56]*.

VILLA J.L. & CIOMPI L. (1968) Therapeutic problems of senile dementia. In *Senile Dementia: Clinical and Therapeutic Aspects*, eds. Müller Ch. & Ciompi L. Huber: Bern *[424]*.

VILLIERS J.C. DE (1966) Intracranial haemorrhage in patients treated with monoamine oxidase inhibitors. *British Journal of Psychiatry* 112, 109–118 *[334]*.

VISLIE H. & HENRIKSEN G.F. (1958) Psychic disturbances in epileptics. Ch. 2 in *Lectures on Epilepsy*, ed. Lorentz de Haas A.M. Elsevier: Amsterdam *[228, 231]*.

VOGT M. (1970) Drug-induced changes in brain dopamine and their relation to Parkinsonism. Ch. 16 in *The Scientific Basis of Medicine Annual Reviews, 1970*. Athlone Press: London *[552]*.

VON KNORRING L. (1983) Interhemispheric EEG differences in affective disorders. In *Laterality and Psychopathology*, eds. Flor-Henry P. & Gruzelier J., pp. 315–326. Elsevier: Amsterdam & London *[76]*.

WADA J. & RASMUSSEN T. (1960) Intracarotid injection of sodium amytal for the lateralization of cerebral speech dominance: experimental and clinical observations. *Journal of Neurosurgery* 17, 266–282 *[37]*.

WADIA N. & WILLIAMS E. (1957) Behçet's syndrome with neurological complications. *Brain* 80, 59–71 *[651]*.

WAGGONER R.W. & BAGCHI B.K. (1954) Initial masking of organic brain changes by psychic symptoms: clinical and electroencephalographic studies. *American Journal of Psychiatry* 110, 904–910 *[203]*.

WAITZKIN L. (1966a) A survey for unknown diabetics in a mental hospital. I. Men under age fifty. *Diabetes* 15, 97–104 *[456]*.

WAITZKIN L. (1966b) A survey for unknown diabetics in a mental hospital. II. Men from age fifty. *Diabetes* 15, 164–172 *[456]*.

WAKELING A. (1972) Comparative study of psychiatric patients with Klinefelter's syndrome and hypogonadism. *Psychological Medicine* 2, 139–154 *[446]*.

WALCH R. (1956) Orbitalhirn und Charakter. In *Das Hirntrauma*, ed. Rehwald E., pp. 203–213. Thieme: Stuttgart *[154]*.

WALINDER J. (1977) Hyperostosis frontalis interna and mental morbidity. *British Journal of Psychiatry* 131, 155–159 *[654]*.

WALKER A.E. (1961) Murder or epilepsy? *Journal of Nervous and Mental Disease* 133, 430–437 *[242]*.

WALKER A.E. & ERCULEI F. (1969) *Head Injured Men Fifteen Years Later*. Thomas: Springfield, Illinois *[149, 169]*.

WALKER A.E. & JABLON S. (1959) A follow-up of head-injured men of World War II. *Journal of Neurosurgery* 16, 600–610 *[152]*.

WALKER A.E. & JABLON S. (1961) *A Follow-up Study of Head Wounds in World War II*. Veterans Administration Medical Monograph No. 5: Washington, DC *[213]*.

WALKER D.W., BARNES D.E., RILEY J.N., HUNTER B.E. & ZORNETZER S.F. (1980a) Neurotoxicity of chronic alcohol consumption: an animal model. In *Psychopharmacology of Alcohol*, ed. Sandler, M. Raven Press: New York *[521]*.

WALKER D.W., BARNES D.E., ZORNETZER S.F., HUNTER B.E. & KUBANIS P. (1980b) Neuronal loss in hippocampus induced by prolonged ethanol consumption in rats. *Science* 209, 711–713 *[521]*.

WALKER S. (1969) The psychiatric presentation of Wilson's disease (hepatolenticular degeneration) with an etiologic explanation. *Behavioral Neuropsychiatry* 1, 38–43 *[565, 566]*.

WALSH A.C. (1969a) Arterial insufficiency of the brain: progression prevented by long-term anticoagulant therapy in eleven patients. *Journal of the American Geriatrics Society* 17, 93–104 *[424]*.

WALSH A.C. (1969b) Prevention of senile and presenile dementia by bishydroxycoumarin (dicumarol) therapy. *Journal of the American Geriatrics Society* 17, 477–487 *[424]*.

WALSHE F.M.R. (1958) The role of injury, of the law and of the doctor in the aetiology of the so-called traumatic neurosis. *Medical Press* 239, 493–496 *[170]*.

WALSHE J.M. (1968) Some observations on the treatment of Wilson's disease with penicillamine. In *Wilson's Disease*, ed. Bergsma D. Birth Defects Original Article Series, vol. 4, No. 2. The National Foundation: New York *[565]*.

WALTON D. & BLACK D.A. (1957) The validity of a psychological test of brain damage. *British Journal of Medical Psychology* 30, 270–279 *[100]*.

WALTON D. & BLACK D.A. (1959) The predictive validity of a psychological test of brain damage. *Journal of Mental Science* 105, 807–810 *[100]*.

WALTON D. & MATHER M.D. (1961) A further study of the predictive validity of a psychological test of brain damage. *British Journal of Medical Psychology* 34, 73–75 *[100]*.

WALTON D., WHITE J.G., BLACK D.A. & YOUNG A.J. (1959) The Modified Word-Learning Test: a cross validation study. *British Journal of Medical Psychology* 32, 213–220 *[100]*.

WALTON J.N. (1952) The late prognosis of subarachnoid haemorrhage. *British Medical Journal* 2, 802–808 *[335, 338]*.

WALTON J.N. (1953) The Korsakoff syndrome in spontaneous subarachnoid haemorrhage. *Journal of Mental Science* 99, 521–530 *[336, 338]*.

WALTON J.N. (1956) *Subarachnoid Haemorrhage*. Livingstone: Edinburgh and London *[335]*.

WALTON J.N. (1964a) Muscular dystrophy: some recent advances in knowledge. *British Medical Journal* 1, 1271–1274 and 1344–1348 *[611]*.

WALTON J.N. (1964b) Progressive muscular dystrophy. Ch. 11 in *Disorders of Voluntary Muscle*, ed. Walton J.N. J. & A. Churchill: London *[615]*.

WALTON J.N. (1977) *Brain's Diseases of the Nervous System*, 8th Edition. Oxford University Press *[278, 280, 305, 310, 314, 316, 577]*.

WALTON Sir J. (1982) *Essentials of Neurology*, 5th Edition. Pitman: London *[114, 321, 335, 368, 457]*.

WALTON J.N. (1983) Myasthenia gravis. In *Oxford Textbook of Medicine, Vol. 2*, eds. Weatherall D.J., Ledingham J.G.G. & Warrell D.A., pp. 22.14–22.16. Oxford University Press *[606]*.

WALTON J.N., KILOH L.G., OSSELTON J.W. & FARRALL J. (1954) The electroencephalogram in pernicious anaemia and subacute combined degeneration of the cord. *Electroencephalography and Clinical Neurophysiology* 6, 45–64 *[503]*.

WALTON J.N. & NATTRASS F.J. (1954) On the classification, natural history and treatment of the myopathies. *Brain* 77, 169–231 *[611, 615]*.

WARBURTON J.W. (1967) Depressive symptoms in Parkinson patients referred for thalamotomy. *Journal of Neurology, Neurosurgery and Psychiatry* 30, 368–370 *[557]*.

WARD A.A. (1948) The cingular gyrus: area 24. *Journal of Neurophysiology* 11, 13–22 *[23]*.

WARD A.A. (1966) The physiology of concussion. Ch. 16 in *Head Injury: Conference Proceedings*, eds. Caveness W.F. & Walker A.E. Lippincott: Philadelphia *[140]*.

DE WARDENER H.E. & LENNOX B. (1947) Cerebral beri beri (Wernicke's encephalopathy). *Lancet*, 1, 11–17 *[492, 493, 494, 496]*.

WARKANY J. & HUBBARD D.M. (1951) Adverse mercurial reactions in the form of acrodynia and related conditions. *American Journal of Diseases of Children* 81, 335–373 *[540, 541]*.

WARRINGTON E.K. (1970) Neurological deficits. Ch. 9 in *The Psychological Assessment of Mental and Physical Handicaps*, ed. Mittler P. Methuen: London *[54, 58, 59, 88]*.

WARRINGTON E.K. (1971) Neurological disorders of memory. *British Medical Bulletin* 27, 243–247 *[33]*.

WARRINGTON E.K. (1974) Deficient recognition memory in organic amnesia. *Cortex* 10, 289–291 *[102]*.

WARRINGTON E.K. (1984) *Manual for Recognition Memory Test for Words and Faces*. NFER-Nelson: Windsor *[102]*.

WARRINGTON E.K. & JAMES M. (1967a) An experimental investigation of facial recognition in patients with unilateral cerebral lesions. *Cortex* 3, 317–326 *[53]*.

WARRINGTON E.K. & JAMES M. (1967b) Tachistoscopic number estimation in patients with unilateral cerebral lesions. *Journal of Neurology, Neurosurgery and Psychiatry* 30, 468–474 *[55]*.

WARRINGTON E.K. & JAMES M. (1967c) Disorders of visual perception in patients with localised cerebral lesions. *Neuropsychologia* 5, 253–266 *[56]*.

WARRINGTON E.K., LOGUE V. & PRATT R.T.C. (1971) The anatomical localisation of selective impairment of auditory verbal short-term memory. *Neuropsychologia* 9, 377–387 *[47]*.

WARRINGTON E.K. & PRATT R.T.C. (1973) Language laterality in left handers assessed by unilateral ECT. *Neuropsychologia* 11, 423–428 *[38]*.

WARRINGTON E.K. & PRATT R.T.C. (1981) The significance of laterality effects. *Journal of Neurology, Neurosurgery and Psychiatry* 44, 193–196 *[38]*.

WARRINGTON E.K. & SHALLICE T. (1969) The selective impairment of auditory verbal short-term memory. *Brain* 92, 885–896 *[47]*.

WARRINGTON E.K. & WEISKRANTZ L. (1968) New method of testing long-term retention with special reference to amnesic patients. *Nature* 217, 972–974 *[33]*.

WARRINGTON E.K. & WEISKRANTZ L. (1970) Amnesic syndrome-consolidation or retrieval? *Nature* 228, 628–630 *[33]*.

WARRINGTON E.K. & WEISKRANTZ L. (1978) Further analysis of the prior learning effect in amnesic patients. *Neuropsychologia* 16, 169–177 *[33]*.

WATERS W.E. (1971) Migraine: intelligence, social class and familial prevalence. *British Medical Journal* 2, 77–81 *[345, 348]*.

WATSON C.G. (1965) WAIS profile patterns of hospitalised brain-damaged and schizophrenic patients. *Journal of Clinical Psychology* 21, 294–295 *[96]*.

WATSON J.M. (1979a) Glue sniffing: two case reports. *Practitioner* 222, 845–847 *[537]*.

WATSON J.M. (1979b) Morbidity and mortality statistics on solvent abuse. *Medicine, Science and the Law* 19, 246–252 *[537]*.

WATSON L. (1968) Clinical aspects of hyperparathyroidism. *Proceedings of the Royal Society of Medicine* 61, 1123 *[448]*.

WATSON L. (1972) Diseases of the parathyroid glands. *Medicine (monthly add-on series, 1972–3)* 2, 148–156. Medical Education (International) Ltd.: London *[452]*.

WATSON R.T. & HEILMAN K.M. (1979) Thalamic neglect. *Neurology* 29, 690–694 *[60]*.

WATSON R.T., VALENSTEIN E. & HEILMAN K.M. (1981) Thalamic neglect. Possible role of the medial thalamus and nucleus reticularis in behaviour. *Archives of Neurology* 38, 501–506 *[60]*.

WATTS R.W.E. (1983) Amino acid transport defects. In *Oxford Textbook of Medicine, Vol. 1.*, eds. Weatherall D.J., Ledingham

J.G.G. & Warrell D.A., pp. 9.101–9.105. Oxford University Press *[489]*.

WAXMAN S.G. & GESCHWIND N. (1974) Hypergraphia in temporal lobe epilepsy. *Neurology* 24, 629–636 *[234]*.

WAXMAN S.G. & GESCHWIND N. (1975) The interictal behavior syndrome of temporal lobe epilepsy. *Archives of General Psychiatry* 32, 1580–1586 *[234, 236]*.

WAYNE E.J. (1960) Clinical and metabolic studies in thyroid disease. *British Medical Journal* 1, 1–11 and 78–90 *[431]*.

WAYNE H.L. & BROWNE-MAYERS A.N. (1959) Clinical and EEG observations in patients with progressive muscular dystrophy. *Diseases of the Nervous System* 20, 288–291 *[612]*.

WEBB M. & KIRKER J.G. (1981) Severe post-traumatic insomnia treated with L-5-hydroxytryptophan. *Lancet* 1, 1365–1366 *[630]*.

WEBSTER J.E. & GURDJIAN E.S. (1943) Acute physiological effects of gunshot and other penetrating wounds of the brain. *Journal of Neurophysiology* 6, 255–262 *[138]*.

WECHSLER D. (1945) A standardised memory scale for clinical use. *Journal of Psychology* 19, 87–95 *[102]*.

WECHSLER D. (1958) *The Measurement and Appraisal of Adult Intelligence*, 4th edn. Williams and Wilkins: Baltimore *[96]*.

WECHSLER D. & STONE C.P. (1945) *Wechsler Memory Scale Manual*. The Psychological Corporation: New York *[102]*.

WECHSLER I.S. & DAVISON C. (1932) Amyotrophic lateral sclerosis with mental symptoms. *Archives of Neurology and Psychiatry* 27, 859–880 *[605]*.

WEDDELL R., ODDY M. & JENKINS D. (1980) Social adjustment after rehabilitation: a two year follow-up of patients with severe head injury. *Psychological Medicine* 10, 257–263 *[186]*.

WEIL M.L., ITABASHI H.H., CREMER N.E., OSHIRO L.S., LENNETTE E.H. & CARNAY L. (1975) Chronic progressive panencephalitis due to rubella virus simulating subacute sclerosing panencephalitis. *New England Journal of Medicine* 292, 994–998 *[307]*.

WEINBERGER D.R., DE LISI L.E., PERMAN G.P., TARGUM S. & WYATT R.J. (1982) Computed tomography in schizophreniform disorder and other acute psychiatric disorders. *Archives of General Psychiatry* 39, 778–783 *[122]*.

WEINBERGER D.R., TORREY E.F., NEOPHYTIDES N. & WYATT R.J. (1979a) Lateral cerebral ventricular enlargement to chronic schizophrenia. *Archives of General Psychiatry* 36, 735–739 *[121]*.

WEINBERGER D.R., TORREY E.F., NEOPHYTIDES N. & WYATT R.J. (1979b) Structural abnormalities in the cerebral cortex of chronic schizophrenic patients. *Archives of General Psychiatry* 36, 935–939 *[121]*.

WEINBERGER D.R., TORREY E.F. & WYATT R.J. (1979c) Cerebellar atrophy in chronic schizophrenia. *Lancet* 1, 718 *[121]*.

WEINBERGER D.R., WAGNER R.L. & WYATT R.J. (1983) Neuropathological studies of schizophrenia: a selective review. *Schizophrenia Bulletin* 9, 193–212 *[76, 121]*.

WEINSTEIN E.A. & COLE M. (1963) Concepts of anosognosia. In *Problems of Dynamic Neurology*, ed. Halpern L. Hadassah Medical School: Jerusalem *[62]*.

WEINSTEIN E.A. & KAHN R.L. (1950) The syndrome of anosognosia. *Archives of Neurology and Psychiatry* 64, 772–791 *[62]*.

WEINSTEIN E.A. & KAHN R.L. (1955) *Denial of Illness: Symbolic and Physiological Aspects*. Thomas: Springfield, Illinois *[62]*.

WEINSTEIN E.A., KAHN R.L. MALITZ S. & ROZANSKI J. (1954) Delusional reduplication of parts of the body. *Brain* 77, 45–60 *[65]*.

WEINSTEIN E.A., LYERLY O.G., COLE M. & OZER M.N. (1966) Meaning in jargon aphasia. *Cortex* 2, 165–187 *[48]*.

WEINSTEIN M.C. (1978) Prevention that pays for itself. *New England Journal of Medicine* 299, 307–308 *[496]*.

WEINSTEIN S., TEUBER H-L., GHENT L. & SEMMES J. (1955) Complex visual task performance after penetrating brain injury in man. *American Psychologist* 10, 408 *[42]*.

WEISBERG L.A. (1982) Lacunar infarcts. Clinical and computed tomographic correlations. *Archives of Neurology* 39, 37–40 *[321, 327, 328]*.

WEIZMAN A., ELDAR M., SHOENFELD Y., HIRSHORN M., WIJSENBEEK W. & PINKHAS J. (1979) Hypercalcaemia-induced psychopathology in malignant diseases. *British Journal of Psychiatry* 135, 363–366 *[477]*.

WELLS C.E.C. (1971a) Neurological complications of so-called influenza. A winter study in South-east Wales. *British Medical Journal* 1, 369–373 *[303]*.

WELLS C.E. (1971b) The clinical management of the patient with dementia. Ch. 11 in *Dementia*, ed. Wells C.E. Blackwell Scientific Publications: Oxford *[422]*.

WELLS C.E. (1978) Chronic brain disease; an overview. *American Journal of Psychiatry* 135, 1–12 *[414]*.

WELLS C.E. (1979) Pseudodementia. *American Journal of Psychiatry* 136, 895–900 *[411]*.

WELLS C.E. (1982) Pseudodementia and the recognition of organicity. Ch. 8 in *Psychiatric Aspects of Neurologic Disease*, eds. Benson D.F. & Blumer D., Vol. 2. Grune & Stratton: New York *[411]*.

WELMAN A.J. (1969) Right-sided unilateral visual spatial agnosia, asomatognosia and anosognosia with left hemisphere lesions. *Brain* 92, 571–580 *[327]*.

WERNICKE C. (1874) *Der aphaisische Symptomencomplex. Eine psychologische Studie auf anatomischer Basis*. Cohn & Weigert: Breslau *[22, 42]*.

WERNICKE C. (1881) *Lehrbuch der Gehirnkrankheiten*, part 2, p. 229. Kassel: Berlin *[491]*.

WEST J.R., LIND M.D., DEMUTH R.M., PARKER E.S., ALKANA R.L., CASSELL M. & BLACK A.C. (1982) Lesion-induced sprouting in the rat dentate gyrus is inhibited by repeated ethanol administration. *Science* 218, 808–810 *[521]*.

WESTLAKE E.K., SIMPSON T. & KAYE M. (1955) Carbon dioxide narcosis in emphysema. *Quarterly Journal of Medicine* 24, 155–173 *[479]*.

WESTMORELAND B.F. (1979) Electroencephalographic experience at the Mayo Clinic. Ch. 4 in *Tuberous Sclerosis*, ed. Gomez M.R. Raven Press: New York *[600]*.

WESTON M.J. & WHITLOCK F.A. (1971) The Capgrass syndrome following head injury. *British Journal of Psychiatry* 119, 25–31 *[143]*.

WEXLER B.E. (1980) Cerebral laterality and psychiatry: a review of the literature. *American Journal of Psychiatry* 137, 279–291 *[76]*.

WHEATLEY D., BALTER M., LEVINE J., LIPMAN R., BAUER M.L. & BONATO R. (1975) Psychiatric aspects of hypertension. *British Journal of Psychiatry* 127, 327–336 *[340]*.

WHELAN T.B., SCHTEINGART D.E., STARKMAN M.N. & SMITH A. (1980) Neuropsychological deficits in Cushing's syndrome. *Journal of Nervous and Mental Disease* 168, 753–757 *[438]*.

WHILES W.H. (1940) Treatment of spasmodic torticollis by psychotherapy. *British Medical Journal* 1, 969–971 *[573, 576]*.

WHITE J.C. & COBB S. (1955) Psychological changes associated with giant pituitary neoplasms. *Archives of Neurology and Psychiatry* 74, 383–396 *[200]*.

WHITE J.G., MERRICK M. & HARBISON J.J.M. (1969) Williams' scale for the measurement of memory: test reliability and validity in a psychiatric population. *British Journal of Social and Clinical Psychology* 8, 141–151 *[103]*.

WHITE P., HILEY C.R., GOODHARDT M.J., CARRASCO L.H., KEET

J.P., WILLIAMS I.E.I. & BOWEN D.M. (1977) Neocortical cholinergic neurons in elderly people. *Lancet* 1, 668–670 *[382]*.

WHITE S.J., McLEAN A.E.M. & HOWLAND C. (1979) Anticonvulsant drugs and cancer. A cohort study in patients with severe epilepsy. *Lancet* 2, 458–461 *[253]*.

WHITEHOUSE P.J., PRICE D.L., STRUBLE R.G., CLARK A.W., COYLE J.T. & DELONG M.R. (1982) Alzheimer's disease and senile dementia: loss of neurons in the basal forebrain. *Science* 215, 1237–1239 *[383]*.

WHITLOCK F.A. (1967a) The aetiology of hysteria. *Acta Psychiatrica Scandinavica* 43, 144–162 *[168]*.

WHITLOCK F.A. (1967b) The Ganser syndrome. *British Journal of Psychiatry* 113, 19–29 *[404, 405]*.

WHITLOCK F.A. (1978) Suicide, cancer and depression. *British Journal of Psychiatry* 132, 269–274 *[638]*.

WHITLOCK F.A. & SISKIND M.M. (1980) Depression as a major symptom of multiple sclerosis. *Journal of Neurology, Neurosurgery and Psychiatry* 43, 861–865 *[593, 595]*.

WHITTY C.W.M. (1953) Familial hemiplegic migraine. *Journal of Neurology, Neurosurgery and Psychiatry* 16, 172–177 *[345, 346]*.

WHITTY C.W.M. (1956) Mental changes as a presenting feature in subcortical cerebral lesions. *Journal of Mental Science* 102, 719–725 *[200]*.

WHITTY C.W.M. (1958) Neurologic implications of Behçet's syndrome. *Neurology* 8, 369–373 *[650]*.

WHITTY C.W.M. & HOCKADAY J.M. (1968) Migraine: a follow-up study of 92 patients. *British Medical Journal* 1, 735–736 *[345]*.

WHITTY C.W.M., HOCKADAY J.M. & WHITTY M.M. (1966) The effect of oral contraceptives on migraine. *Lancet* 1, 856–859 *[344, 345]*.

WHITTY C.W.M. & LEWIN W. (1960) A Korsakoff syndrome in the post-cingulectomy confusional state. *Brain* 83, 648–653 *[26]*.

WHITTY C.W.M. & LISHMAN W.A. (1966) Amnesia in cerebral disease. Ch. 2 in *Amnesia*, eds. Whitty C.W.M. & Zangwill O.L. Butterworths: London *[224, 460]*.

WHITTY C.W.M., LISHMAN W.A. & FITZGIBBON J.P. (1964) Seizures induced by movement: a form of reflex epilepsy. *Lancet* 1, 1403–1405 *[211]*.

WHITTY C.W.M. & ZANGWILL O.L. (1966) Traumatic amnesia. Ch. 4 in *Amnesia*, eds. Whitty C.W.M. & Zangwill O.L. Butterworths: London *[144]*.

WHYBROW P.C. & HURWITZ T. (1976) Psychological disturbances associated with endocrine disease and hormone therapy. In *Hormones, Behavior and Psychopathology*, ed. Sachar E.J. Raven Press: New York *[437]*.

WHYBROW P.C., PRANGE A.J. & TREADWAY C.R. (1969) Mental changes accompanying thyroid gland dysfunction. *Archives of General Psychiatry* 20, 48–63 *[429]*.

WIEDERHOLT W.C. & SIEKERT R.G. (1965) Neurological manifestations of sarcoidosis. *Neurology* 15, 1147–1154 *[652]*.

WILCOCK G.K. & ESIRI M.M. (1982) Plaques, tangles, and dementia: a quantitative study. *Journal of the Neurological Sciences* 56, 343–356 *[376, 381]*.

WILCOCK G.K., ESIRI M.M., BOWEN D.M. & SMITH C.C.T. (1982) Alzheimer's disease. Correlations of cortical choline acetyltransferase activity with the severity of dementia and histological abnormalities. *Journal of the Neurological Sciences* 57, 407–417 *[382]*.

WILKINSON A.E. (1972) Problems in the treatment of venereal disease: bacterial resistance: treatment. *Journal of the Royal College of Physicians of London* 6, 175–180 *[277]*.

WILKINSON D.G. (1981) Psychiatric aspects of diabetes mellitus. *British Journal of Psychiatry* 138, 1–9 *[453]*.

WILKINSON H.A., LEMAY M. & DREW J.H. (1966) Adult aqueductal stenosis. *Archives of Neurology* 15, 643–648 *[644, 645]*.

WILKINSON P., KORNACZEWSKI A., RANKIN J.G. & SANTAMARIA J.N. (1971) Physical disease in alcoholism: initial survey of 1000 patients. *Medical Journal of Australia* 1, 1217–1223 *[517]*.

WILL A.M. & McLAREN E.H. (1981) Reversible renal damage due to glue sniffing. *British Medical Journal* 283, 525–526 *[537]*.

WILL R.G. & MATTHEWS W.B. (1982) Evidence for case-to-case transmission of Creutzfeldt-Jakob disease. *Journal of Neurology, Neurosurgery and Psychiatry* 45, 235–238 *[401]*.

WILLANGER R., THYGESEN P., NIELSEN R. & PETERSEN O. (1968) Intellectual impairment and cerebral atrophy: a psychological, neurological and radiological investigation. *Danish Medical Bulletin* 15, 65–93 *[120]*.

WILLIAMS D. (1956) The structure of emotions reflected in epileptic experiences. *Brain* 79, 29–67 *[219]*.

WILLIAMS D. (1963) The psychiatry of the epileptic. *Proceedings of the Royal Society of Medicine* 56, 707–710 *[231, 235]*.

WILLIAMS D. (1966) Temporal lobe epilepsy. *British Medical Journal* 1, 1439–1442 *[220]*.

WILLIAMS D. (1968) The management of epilepsy. *Hospital Medicine* 2, 702–707 *[274]*.

WILLIAMS D. (1969) Neural factors related to habitual aggression: consideration of the differences between those habitual aggressives and others who have committed crimes of violence. *Brain* 92, 503–520 *[74]*.

WILLIAMS D.G. (1976) Methods for the estimation of three vitamin dependent red cell enzymes. *Clinical Biochemistry* 9, 252–255 *[488]*.

WILLIAMS D.T., MEHL R., YUDOFSKY S., ADAMS D. & ROSEMAN B. (1982) The effect of propanolol on uncontrolled rage outbursts in children and adolescents with organic brain dysfunction. *Journal of the American Academy of Child Psychiatry* 21, 129–135 *[265]*.

WILLIAMS F.J.B. & WALSHE J.M. (1981) Wilson's disease. An analysis of the cranial computerised tomographic appearances found in 60 patients and the changes in response to treatment with chelating agents. *Brain* 104, 735–752 *[563, 567]*.

WILLIAMS M. (1956) Studies of perception in senile dementia; cue-selection as a function of intelligence. *British Journal of Medical Psychology* 29, 270–279 *[422]*.

WILLIAMS M. (1968) The measurement of memory in clinical practice. *British Journal of Social and Clinical Psychology* 7, 19–34 *[84, 103]*.

WILLIAMS M. & PENNYBACKER J. (1954) Memory disturbances in third ventricle tumours. *Journal of Neurology, Neurosurgery and Psychiatry* 17, 115–123 *[197]*.

WILLIAMS M. & SMITH H.V. (1954) Mental disturbances in tuberculous meningitis. *Journal of Neurology, Neurosurgery and Psychiatry* 17, 173–182 *[25, 310, 311]*.

WILLIAMS R.D., MASON H.L., POWER M.H. & WILDER R.M. (1943) Induced thiamine (vitamin B₁) deficiency in man. *Archives of Internal Medicine* 71, 38–53 *[488]*.

WILLIAMS R.D., MASON H.L., WILDER R.M. & SMITH B.F. (1940) Observations on induced thiamine (vitamin B₁) deficiency in man. *Archives of Internal Medicine* 66, 785–799 *[488]*.

WILLIAMSON J., STOKOE I.H., GRAY S., FISHER M., SMITH A., McGHEE A. & STEPHENSON E. (1964) Old people at home. Their unreported needs. *Lancet* 1, 1117–1120 *[372]*.

WILSON G. & RUPP C. (1946) Mental symptoms associated with extramedullary posterior fossa tumours. *Transactions of the American Neurological Association*, pp. 104–107 *[200]*.

WILSON L.G. (1976) Viral encephalopathy mimicking functional psychosis. *American Journal of Psychiatry* 133, 165–170 *[290]*.

WILSON P.J.E. (1970) Cerebral hemispherectomy for infantile hemiplegia. *Brain* 93, 147–180 *[237, 276]*.

WILSON P.J.E. (1973) The surgical treatment of epilepsy. *British Journal of Hospital Medicine* 9, 161–168 *[276]*.

WILSON R.S., KASZNIAK A.W. & FOX J.H. (1981) Remote memory in senile dementia. *Cortex* 17, 41–48 *[31, 35]*.

WILSON S.A.K. (1912) Progressive lenticular degeration: a familial nervous disease associated with cirrhosis of the liver. *Brain* 34, 295–509 *[563, 566]*.

WILSON S.A.K. (1940) *Neurology*. Edward Arnold: London *[280, 281, 283, 566, 572, 596]*.

WINDLE W.F., GROAT R.A. & FOX C.A. (1944) Experimental structural alterations in the brain during and after concussion. *Surgery Gynaecology and Obstetrics* 79, 561–572 *[138]*.

WING J.K., BIRLEY J.L.T., COOPER J.E., GRAHAM P. & ISAACS A.D. (1967) Reliability of a procedure for measuring and classifying 'Present Psychiatric State'. *British Journal of Psychiatry* 113, 499–515 *[107]*.

WINICK M. (1976) *Malnutrition and Brain Development*. Oxford University Press *[486]*.

WINICK M. (1979) Malnutrition and mental development. Ch. 2 in *Nutrition: Pre- and Postnatal Development*, ed. Winick M. Plenum Press: New York *[486]*.

WINNACKER J.L., BECKER K.L. & KATZ S. (1968) Endocrine aspects of sarcoidosis. *New England Journal of Medicine* 278, 483–492 *[652]*.

WISNIEWSKI H.M., BRUCE M.E. & FRASER H. (1975) Infectious aetiology of neuritic (senile) plaques in mice. *Science* 190, 1108–1110 *[384]*.

WISNIEWSKI K., HOWE J., WILLIAMS D.G. & WISNIEWSKI H.M. (1978) Precocious aging and dementia in patients with Down's syndrome. *Biological Psychiatry* 13, 619–627 *[378]*.

WITTENBORN J.R. (1981) Pharmacotherapy for age-related behavioural deficiencies. *Journal of Nervous and Mental Disease* 169, 139–156 *[425]*.

WOLF P. (1982) Manic episodes in epilepsy. In *Advances in Epileptology, XIIIth Epilepsy International Symposium*, eds. Akimoto H., Kazamatsuri H., Seino M. & Ward A.A., pp. 237–240. Raven Press: New York *[253]*.

WOLF P. & TRIMBLE M.R. (1985) Biological antagonism and epileptic psychosis. *British Journal of Psychiatry* 146, 272–276 *[246]*.

WOLF S.M., SCHOTLAND D.L. & PHILLIPS L.L. (1965) Involvement of nervous system in Behçet's syndrome. *Archives of Neurology* 12, 315–325 *[650, 651]*.

WOLFF H.G. (1937) Personality features and reactions of subjects with migraine. *Archives of Neurology and Psychiatry* 37, 895–921 *[347]*.

WOLFF H.G. (1963) The relation of life situations, personality features, and reactions to the migraine syndrome. Ch. 11 in *Headache and Other Head Pain*, 2nd edn, by Wolff H.G. Oxford University Press: New York *[347]*.

WOOD R.L. (1984) Behaviour disorders following severe brain injury: their presentation and psychological management. Ch. 10 in *Closed Head Injury. Psychological, Social and Family Consequences*, ed. Brooks N. Oxford University Press *[183]*.

WOOD R. & EAMES P. (1981) Application of behaviour modification in the treatment of traumatically brain-injured adults. Ch. 4 in *Applications of Conditioning Theory*, ed. Davey G. Methuen: London *[183]*.

WOODCOCK S.M. (1967) Mental symptoms in patients with acoustic neuromas. *Journal of Neurology, Neurosurgery and Psychiatry* 30, 587 *[200]*.

WOODS R.T. (1979) Reality orientation and staff attention: a controlled study. *British Journal of Psychiatry* 134, 502–507 *[423]*.

WOODS R.T. & BRITTON P.G. (1977) Psychological approaches to the treatment of the elderly. *Age and Ageing* 6, 104–112 *[423]*.

WOODS R.T. & PIERCY M. (1974) A similarity between amnesic memory and normal forgetting. *Neuropsychologia* 12, 437–445 *[33]*.

WORDEN D.K. & VIGNOS P.J. (1962) Intellectual function in childhood progressive muscular dystrophy. *Pediatrics* 29, 968–977 *[612]*.

WORLD HEALTH ORGANISATION REPORT (1955) Alcohol and alcoholism. *World Health Organisation Technical Report Series*, No. 94. World Health Organisation: Geneva *[510]*.

WORLD HEALTH ORGANISATION REPORT (1971) The use of cannabis: report of a WHO scientific group. *World Health Organisation Technical Report Series*, No. 478. World Health Organisation: Geneva *[525]*.

WORRAL E.P. & DEWHURST D. (1979) Manipulating central cholinergic functions: studies with deanol and physostigmine. Ch. 37 in *Alzheimer's Disease: Early Recognition of Potentially Reversible Deficits*, eds. Glen A.I.M. & Whalley L.J. Churchill Livingstone: Edinburgh & London *[426]*.

WORTIS S.B., HERMAN M. & LONDON J. (1943) Mental changes in patients with subdural haematomas. Ch. 11 in *Trauma of the Central Nervous System*, Research Publications of the Association for Research in Nervous and Mental Disease, vol. 24, Williams & Wilkins: Baltimore *[357]*.

WRIGHT G.D.S., McLELLAN D.L. & BRICE J.G. (1984) A double-blind trial of chronic cerebellar stimulation in twelve patients with severe epilepsy. *Journal of Neurology, Neurosurgery and Psychiatry* 47, 769–774 *[276]*.

WYATT R.J., FRAM D.H., BUCHBINDER R. & SNYDER F. (1971) Treatment of intractable narcolepsy with a monoamine oxidase inhibitor. *New England Journal of Medicine* 285, 987–991 *[623]*.

WYKE B. (1963) *Brain Function and Metabolic Disorders*. Butterworths: London *[479]*.

WYKE M. (1968) The effect of brain lesions in the performance of an arm-hand precision task. *Neuropsychologia* 6, 125–134 *[51]*.

WYKE M. (1971) Dysphasia: a review of recent progress. *British Medical Bulletin* 27, 211–217 *[40]*.

WYKE M.A. (1977) Musical ability: a neuropsychological interpretation. Ch. 10 in *Music and the Brain*, eds. Critchley M. & Henson R.A. Heinemann: London *[57]*.

WYSE D.G. (1973) Deliberate inhalation of volatile hydrocarbons: a review. *Canadian Medical Association Journal* 108, 71–74 *[537]*.

YAHR M.D. & DUVOISIN R.C. (1972) Drug therapy of parkinsonism. *New England Journal of Medicine* 287, 20–24 *[553, 559, 560]*.

YAHR M.D., DUVOISIN R.C. & COWEN D. (1965) Encephalopathy associated with carcinoma. *Transactions of the American Neurological Association* 90, 80–86 *[637]*.

YAHR M.D., DUVOISIN R.C., SCHEAR M.J., BARRETT R.E. & HOEHN M.M. (1969) Treatment of parkinsonism with levodopa. *Archives of Neurology* 21, 343–354 *[560]*.

YAKOVLEV P.I. (1947) Paraplegias of hydrocephalics. *American Journal of Mental Deficiency* 51, 561–576 *[644]*.

YAKOVLEV P.I. & RAKIC P. (1966) Patterns of decussation of bulbar pyramids and distribution of pyramidal tracts on two sides of the spinal cord. *Transactions of the American Neurological Association* 91, 366–367 *[38]*.

YAP P.M. (1952) The Latah reaction: its pathodynamics and nosological position. *Journal of Mental Science* 98, 515–564 *[582]*.

YASE Y. (1972) The pathogenesis of amyotrophic lateral sclerosis. *Lancet* 2, 292–296 *[605]*.

YASE Y. (1978) ALS in the Kii peninsula: one possible etiological hypothesis. In *Amyotrophic Lateral Sclerosis*, eds. Tsubaki T. & Toyokura Y. University Park Press: Baltimore *[605]*.

YASE Y., MATSUMOTO N., AZUMA K., NAKAI Y. & SHIRAKI H. (1972) Amyotrophic lateral sclerosis: association with schizophrenic symptoms and showing Alzheimer's tangles. *Archives of Neurology* 21, 118–128 *[605]*.

YATES A.J. (1954) The validity of some psychological tests of brain damage. *Psychological Bulletin* 51, 359–379 *[93]*.

YATES A. (1958) The application of learning theory to the treatment of tics. *Journal of Abnormal and Social Psychology* 56, 175–182 *[584, 586]*.

YATES A.J. (1966) Psychological deficit. *Annual Review of Psychology* 17, 111–144 *[93, 98]*.

YATES A.J. (1972) The perceptual maze test. In *Seventh Mental Measurements Year Book*, ed. Buros O.K., vol. 1, 287–288. Gryphon Press: Highland Park, New Jersey *[99]*.

YATES C.M., SIMPSON J., MALONEY A.F.J., GORDON A. & REID A.H. (1980a) Alzheimer-like cholinergic deficiency in Down syndrome. *Lancet* 2, 979 *[378]*.

YATES C.M., SIMPSON J., MALONEY A.F.J. & GORDON A. (1980b) Neurochemical observations in a case of Pick's disease. *Journal of the Neurological Sciences* 48, 257–263 *[391]*.

YESAVAGE J.A., TINKLENBERG J.R., HOLLISTER L.E. & BERGER P.A. (1979) Vasodilators in senile dementias. *Archives of General Psychiatry* 36, 220–223 *[425]*.

YOSS R.E. (1970) The inheritance of diurnal sleepiness as measured by pupillography. *Proceedings of the Staff Meetings of the Mayo Clinic* 45, 426–437 *[623]*.

YOSS R.E. & DALY D.D. (1957) Criteria for the diagnosis of the narcoleptic syndrome. *Proceedings of the Staff Meetings of the Mayo Clinic* 32, 320–328 *[618, 619, 622]*.

YOSS R.E. & DALY D.D. (1959) Treatment of narcolepsy with Ritalin. *Neurology* 9, 171–173 *[623]*.

YOSS R.E. & DALY D.D. (1960a) Hereditary aspects of narcolepsy. *Transactions of the American Neurological Association*, pp. 239–240 *[618, 623]*.

YOSS R.E. & DALY D.D. (1960b) Narcolepsy. *Medical Clinics of North America* 44, 953–968 *[618, 619]*.

YOUNG J., HALL P. & BLAKEMORE C. (1974) Treatment of the cerebral manifestions of arteriosclerosis with cyclandelate. *British Journal of Psychiatry* 124, 177–180 *[425]*.

YOUNG A.C., SAUNDERS J. & PONSFORD J.R. (1976) Mental change as an early feature of multiple sclerosis. *Journal of Neurology, Neurosurgery and Psychiatry* 39, 1008–1013 *[592]*.

YOUNG I.R., BAILES D.R., BURE M., COLLINS A.G., SMITH D.T., McDONNELL M.J., ORR J.S., BANKS L.M., BYDDER G.M., GREENSPAN R.H. & STEINER R.E. (1982) Initial clinical evaluation of a whole body nuclear magnetic resonance (NMR) tomograph. *Journal of Computer Assisted Tomography* 6, 1–18 *[122]*.

YOUNG I.R., HALL A.S., PALLIS C.A., BYDDER G.M., LEGG N.J. & STEINER R.E. (1981) Nuclear magnetic resonance imaging of the brain in multiple sclerosis. *Lancet* 2, 1063–1066 *[592]*.

YOZAWITZ A., BRUDER G., SUTTON S., SHARPE L., GURLAND B., FLEISS J. & COSTA L. (1979) Dichotic perception: evidence for right hemisphere dysfunction in affective psychosis. *British Journal of Psychiatry* 135, 224–237 *[76]*.

YULE W., LANSDOWN R., MILLAR I.B. & URBANOWICZ M-A. (1981) The relationship between blood lead concentrations, intelligence and attainment in a school population: a pilot study. *Developmental Medicine and Child Neurology* 23, 567–576 *[539]*.

ZAIDEL E. (1977) Unilateral auditory language comprehension on the token test following cerebral commissurotomy and hemispherectomy. *Neuropsychologia* 15, 1–18 *[39]*.

ZAIDEL E. (1978) Auditory language comprehension in the right hemisphere following cerebral commissurotomy and hemispherectomy: a comparison with child language and aphasia. In *Language Acquisition and Language Breakdown*, eds. Caramazza A. & Zurif E. Johns Hopkins University Press: Baltimore *[39]*.

ZANGWILL O.L. (1946) Some qualitative observations on verbal memory in cases of cerebral lesion. *British Journal of Psychology* 37, 8–19 *[85]*.

ZANGWILL O.L. (1947) Psychological aspects of rehabilitation in cases of brain injury. *British Journal of Psychology* 37, 60–69 *[182]*.

ZANGWILL O.L. (1961) Psychological studies of amnesic states. *Proceedings of the Third World Congress of Psychiatry*, vol. III, p. 219–222. McGill University Press: Montreal *[36]*.

ZANGWILL O.L. (1966) The amnesic syndrome. Ch. 3 in *Amnesia*, eds. Whitty C.W.M. & Zangwill O.L. Butterworths: London *[30]*.

ZANGWILL O.L. (1967) The Grünthal-Störring case of amnesic syndrome. *British Journal of Psychiatry* 113, 113–128 *[31]*.

ZANGWILL O.L. (1969) Intellectual status in aphasia. Ch. 6 in *Handbook of Clinical Neurology, Vol. 4, Disorders of Speech, Perception, and Symbolic Behaviour*, eds. Vinken P.J. & Bruyn G.W. North-Holland Publishing Company: Amsterdam *[42]*.

ZARCONE V. (1973) Narcolepsy. *New England Journal of Medicine* 288, 1156–1166 *[618, 619, 622, 623]*.

ZATZ L.M., JERNIGAN T.L. & AHUMADA A.J. (1982) White matter changes in cerebral computed tomography related to aging. *Journal of Computer Assisted Tomography* 6, 19–23 *[120]*.

ZEIFERT M., PENNELL W.H., FINLEY K.H. & RIGGS N. (1962) The electroencephalogram following Western and St. Louis encephalitis. *Neurology* 12, 311–319 *[291]*.

ZELLWEGER H. & IONASESCU V. (1973) Myotonic dystrophy and its differential diagnosis. *Acta Neurologica Scandinavica*, supplement 55, 5–28 *[613, 615, 617]*.

ZEMAN W. (1970) Pathology of the torsion dystonias (dystonia musculorum deformans). *Neurology* 20 (part 2), 79–88 *[569]*.

ZEMAN W. & DYKEN P. (1968) Dystonia musculorum deformans. Ch. 21 in *Handbook of Clinical Neurology*, vol. 6, eds. Vinken P.J. & Bruyn G.W. North Holland Publishing Co.: Amsterdam *[578]*.

ZEMAN W., KAELBLING R. & PASAMANICK B. (1960) Idiopathic dystonia musculorum deformans. II: The formes frustes. *Neurology* 10, 1068–1075 *[570]*.

ZEUMER H., SCHONSKY B. & STURM K.W. (1980) Predominent white matter involvement in subcortical arteriosclerotic encephalopathy (Binswanger's disease). *Journal of Computer Assisted Tomography* 4, 14–19 *[390]*.

ZIEGLER L.H. (1930) Psychotic and emotional phenomena associated with amyotrophic lateral sclerosis. *Archives of Neurology and Psychiatry* 24, 930–936 *[604]*.

ZLOTLOW M. & KLEINER S. (1965) Catatonic schizophrenia associated with tuberose sclerosis. *Psychiatric Quarterly* 39, 466–475 *[601]*.

ZUCKER D.K., LIVINGSTON R.L., NAKRA R. & CLAYTON P.J. (1981) B_{12} deficiency and psychiatric disorders: case report and literature review. *Biological Psychiatry* 16, 197–205 *[501]*.

ZUCKERMAN M. (1964) Perceptual isolation as a stress situation. *Archives of General Psychiatry* 11, 255–276 *[126]*.

ZÜLCH K-J. (1969) Medical causation. Ch. 46 in *The Late Effects of Head Injury*, eds. Walker A.E., Caveness W.F. & Critchley M. Thomas: Springfield, Illinois *[179]*.

Index